14

12/2010

ert's

Movie Yearbook

2011

Other Books by Roger Ebert

An Illini Century

A Kiss Is Still a Kiss

Two Weeks in the Midday Sun:
A Cannes Notebook

Behind the Phantom's Mask

Roger Ebert's Little Movie Glossary

Roger Ebert's Movie Home Companion
annually 1986–1993

Roger Ebert's Video Companion
annually 1994–1998

Roger Ebert's Movie Yearbook
annually 1999–2007, 2009

Questions for the Movie Answer Man

Roger Ebert's Book of Film: An Anthology

Ebert's Bigger Little Movie Glossary

I Hated, Hated, Hated This Movie

The Great Movies

The Great Movies II

Your Movie Sucks

Roger Ebert's Four-Star Reviews—1967–2007

Awake in the Dark: The Best of Roger Ebert

Scorsese by Ebert

With Daniel Curley
The Perfect London Walk

With Gene Siskel
The Future of the Movies: Interviews with Martin Scorsese,
Steven Spielberg, and George Lucas

DVD Commentary Tracks
Citizen Kane
Dark City
Casablanca
Floating Weeds
Crumb
Beyond the Valley of the Dolls

Roger Ebert's Movie Yearbook 2011

Andrews McMeel Publishing, LLC

Kansas City • Sydney • London

Roger Ebert's Movie Yearbook 2010
copyright © 1999, 2000, 2001, 2002, 2003,
2004, 2005, 2006, 2007, 2008, 2009, 2010, 2011
by Roger Ebert.
All rights reserved.
Printed in the United States of America.
No part of this book may be used or reproduced
in any manner whatsoever except in the case
of reprints in the context of reviews.
For information write
Andrews McMeel Publishing, LLC,
an Andrews McMeel Universal company,
1130 Walnut Street,
Kansas City, Missouri 64106.

ISBN: 978-0-7407-9769-9

10 11 12 13 14 MLT 10 9 8 7 6 5 4 3 2 1

www.andrewsmcmeel.com

All the reviews in this book originally appeared
in the *Chicago Sun-Times*.

This book is dedicated
to Robert Zonka, 1928–1985.
God love ya.

ATTENTION: SCHOOLS AND BUSINESSES

Andrews McMeel books are available at quantity discounts with bulk purchase for educational, business, or sales
promotional use. For information, please write to: Special Sales Department, Andrews McMeel Publishing, LLC,
1130 Walnut Street, Kansas City, Missouri 64106.

Contents

Introduction

In the most basic terms, it will give me pleasure to hold this *Yearbook* in my hands, because it will have the traditional heft of thirty months of reviews and other writings. Last year's edition, you may have noticed, was thinner, and one year was replaced altogether by *Roger Ebert's Four-Star Reviews*. My patient publishers were seeing me through that period of surgery and complications. With this 2011 edition I'm back in full production, and that feels good.

Actually, I'm writing more than ever, partly because I have more time. My troubles have narrowed my focus. I go to the movies, or watch DVDs on demand or Netflix Instant at home, write reviews, and write for my blog. Not being able to speak or eat limits your social life wonderfully. I'm not complaining. I'm happy to be alive.

What I realize now, more than ever, is what a useful social art the movies are. Most people probably go simply for entertainment, and there's nothing wrong with that. In the most basic sense, that's what movies are for. But they are also windows into other lives, and they can make our ideas less narrow. Because of movies, I know more about people in other lands. People in those lands know more about me. Those who limit themselves to special-effects extravaganzas know little about others and learn little about themselves.

Movies can help us look more intensely and notice more carefully. One way they do that is by encouraging us to look at the way the movies are made. A director who is any good is likely to see things in a very particular way, and if we notice that way, it helps us understand how that man or woman sees the world. If we don't notice—if we relate only on a superficial level—we may be wasting our time.

Two movies like that are reviewed in this volume: *The Hurt Locker* and *Knowing*. One took the Academy Award for the year's best film. The other didn't. Both were on my list of the year's best films. I received a great deal of negative feedback for liking both of those movies. There were a lot of people who hated them. For praising *The Hurt Locker* I was accused of being too highbrow, and for praising *Knowing* it was said I was too lowbrow. I don't believe I was either. I believe those who liked either film saw qualities others overlooked.

The strength of *The Hurt Locker* is in its meticulous construction. Without a single computer-generated special effect, it creates suspense other films can only envy. It does that with character and situation, so that we care, and editing, so that we care even more because we are forced into situations with the characters. Then there's the conflict between the bomb-disposal expert and his team, who think he takes crazy chances with his life and their own. Why didn't people admire this? Some cited actual bomb-disposal experts to say it was inaccurate. I'm usually not much moved by that sort of complaint. If a film convinces me of its own premises, that's enough to allow me to accept it on its terms. A bomb-disposal expert is going to be looking at *The Hurt Locker* with eyes that will never be mine. It can be fatal to know too much about a movie's subject. It was Truffaut who said we can never enjoy a film shot in our own childhood home, because that's all we'd be thinking about.

Others were looking for the usual sorts of war-movie action and missed it. I find action essentially boring. Something explodes. So what? Car chases are exercises in several basic kinds of shots edited together with more or less skill. Only when a movie joins action and personality does it involve me. It's not what the protagonist is doing, but why.

Knowing, on the other hand, was an utterly preposterous film involving a prescient child, aliens or angels from somewhere else, and the possibility that all existence is predetermined. Wow, did it have holes and paradoxes in its plot, and I heard about them in great detail. I remained unmoved. *Knowing* was a film I loved for its energy and style, and its confidence to hurtle through a plot that was not merely preposterous but somehow intellectually challenging. It depended on ideas. You don't have to believe in an idea to enjoy thinking about it. I don't believe in predestination. But it creates fascinating possibilities for logical speculation.

And no matter what I may think about routine special effects (planets exploding and boring stuff like that), good ones can astonish. There has never been an airplane crash like the one in *Knowing*. Not in scope, not on realism, not in the way it all seemed to unfold in one shot. Never. I was stunned.

Those who are able to regard a film on its own terms can accept or dislike it. Those who are looking for a different film should have gone to see that one instead. Movie critics have been accused of being jaded because we've seen too many movies. Maybe so. If a film is merely a rearrangement of basic formulas, what's the point? If a director sees things in a new way, I am excited to see with him. With some so-called great directors, I fail, and I realize I must have areas of blindness. But at least I am willing to look.

Now that my mobility and speech are limited, I depend more than ever on movies to open up my life. Like the hero of Walker Percy's *The Moviegoer*, I suspect that some of the most indelible experiences of my life happened at the movies.

* * *

My sincere gratitude to Dorothy O'Brien, who has been the book's valued editor at Andrews McMeel Publishing in recent years. Also to Sue Roush, my editor at Universal Uclick, and to Laura Emerick, Miriam Dinunzio, Darel Jevens, Teresa Budasi, Jeff Johnson, Chris Woldt, Thomas Conner, and all the other heroes at the *Chicago Sun-Times*, and Jim Emerson, John Barry, and the Web staff at rogerebert.com. Many others are thanked in the acknowledgments.

In 2010, the University of Chicago Press published *The Great Movies III*, continuing a series that gives me a lot of pleasure. And Andrews McMeel has published *The Pot and How to Use It: The Romance and Mystery of the Rice Cooker*, a rather unlikely book coming from me, which must mean I was compelled to use it. My Andrews McMeel book *I Hated, Hated, Hated This Movie* inspired a sequel in 2007, *Your Movie Sucks*, and now it appears that there may be yet another, *A Horrible Experience of Unbearable Length*.

ROGER EBERT

Acknowledgments

My editor is Dorothy O'Brien, tireless, cheerful, all-noticing. My friend and longtime editor Donna Martin suggested the yearbook approach to the annual volume. The design is by Cameron Poulter, the typographical genius of Hyde Park.

My thanks to production editor Christi Clemons Hoffman, who renders Cameron's design into reality. John Yuelkenbeck at Coleridge Design is the compositor who has worked diligently on the series for years. I have been blessed with the expert and discriminating editing of Laura Emerick, Miriam DiNunzio, Darel Jevins, Jeff Johnson, and Teresa Budasi at the *Chicago Sun-Times*; Sue Roush at Universal Uclick; and Michelle Daniel and David Shaw at Andrews McMeel Publishing. For much advice and counsel, thanks to Jim Emerson and John Barry of www.rogerebert.com.

Many thanks are also due to Marsha Jordan at WLS-TV. My gratitude goes to Carol Iwata, my expert personal assistant, and to Gregory Isaac, who is a computer whiz and invaluable aide-de-camp. I must also thank those who have given me countless observations and corrections, including Peter Debruge, Jana J. Monji, and Troylene Ladner.

And special thanks and love to my wife, Chaz, who was always at my side during a difficult illness, helped see three books through the press during that time, and was a cheerleader for this one. I am so grateful to her as we once again, relieved, enter a period of good health.

ROGER EBERT

Key to Symbols

★★★★   A great film
★★★   A good film
★★   Fair
★   Poor

          G, PG, PG-13, R, NC-17:
          Ratings of the Motion Picture
          Association of America

G   Indicates that the movie is
          suitable for general audiences

PG   Suitable for general audiences
          but parental guidance is
          suggested

PG-13   Recommended for viewers
          13 years or above; may contain
          material inappropriate for
          younger children

R   Recommended for viewers
          17 or older

NC-17   Intended for adults only

141 m.   Running time

2008   Year of theatrical release

☞   Refers to "Questions for the
          Movie Answer Man"

Reviews

A

Accomplices ★★★

NO MPAA RATING, 93 m., 2010

Gilbert Melki (Herve Cagan), Emmanuelle Devos (Karine Mangin), Cyril Descours (Vincent Bouvier), Nina Meurisse (Rebecca Legendre), Joana Preiss (Esther). Directed by Frederic Mermoud and produced by Damien Couvreur and Tonie Marshall. Screenplay by Mermoud and Pascal Arnold.

Accomplices coils through two stories, cutting between them as they converge, as we know they will, because the film has opened with a corpse floating in the river Seine. This body, as a flashback establishes, belongs to a boy about nineteen, and the film will watch as he meets a cute girl in a cyber café and leads her into his dangerous world. The other story involves two police inspectors, who begin with the corpse.

Sometimes when a movie cuts between parallel stories it's tiresome. Not this one. The director, Frederic Mermoud, does an interesting thing with time: As the cops are working their way back from the dead body, the other story works its way forward to the point that the body became dead. Then the stories join up and conclude in a surprising and particularly satisfying way.

Vincent (Cyril Descours) is a hustler who meets his male clients in hotel rooms. He meets Rebecca (Nina Meurisse), likes her, gets her phone number, and they start seeing each other. He says he works in real estate—unlikely, given his scruffy appearance and the shabby mobile home he lives in. She is bourgeois but ready for the wild side, and they fall truly in love, like Bonnie and Clyde and other couples where crime is in the mix.

Vincent eventually tells Rebecca what he really does, and the way the movie charts her reaction is touchingly realistic. She learns of his world and stirs the jealousy of his pimp— or *friend,* as he considers him. It's thrilling for her to glimpse his outlaw life, and fun when they use prostitution income to pay cash for sneakers.

Herve (Gilbert Melki) and Karine (Emmanuelle Devos) are like a long-established couple, skilled in police work, functioning expertly together, sharing personal feelings. We think it's a possibility they might hook up, but the plot isn't that obvious. The film is a police procedural explaining how they begin with a nameless body and find their way back to Vincent's associates and clients. One interview, with a businesswoman who shared Vincent with her husband, is startling: The woman is forthcoming, matter-of-fact, defiant.

Without making a big deal out of it, *Accomplices* puts several plausible murder suspects on stage, including Rebecca, who disappeared the day of Vincent's murder. It's like an Agatha Christie in which lots of people have the opportunity and the motive. But Mermoud works so close to the characters, sees them in such detail, that only later do we pull back and observe the workings of the plot.

The original English title of the film was *Partners,* and that would have been accurate. It's about two partnerships. The one is the sad, doomed story of Vincent and Rebecca, incapable of dealing with the risks they run. The other is about how Herve and Karine shy away from risks in their lonely personal lives; how police routine creates a way for them to spend most of their waking hours together without having to deal with the sleeping hours.

I appreciate the way French films, in particular, often approach their characters at eye level. There's no artificial heightening. No music pounding out emotional instruction. They're cool, curious, looking for performances with the tone of plausible life. All four of these actors are completely natural in front of the camera.

You may have seen Emmanuelle Devos in films such as *Read My Lips* (2001) or *The Beat That My Heart Skipped* (2005); she's in the wonderful *L'Origin,* still unreleased, about a small-town mayor and a desperate con man. She's always attractive, never distractingly so, and comes equipped with intelligence and hidden motives. I like actors who make me want to figure them out.

Accomplices is technically a murder mystery. But the murder is only what happens. A lot of other things could have happened, and the story plays fair with the fateful role that chance takes. You would even argue that no one is actually murdered in this movie, and that when they die it is simply the result of bad decisions.

Adam ★★ ½

PG-13, 97 m., 2009

Hugh Dancy (Adam Raki), Rose Byrne (Beth Buchwald), Frankie Faison (Harlan), Mark Linn Baker (Mr. Klieber), Amy Irving (Rebecca Buchwald), Peter Gallagher (Marty Buchwald). Directed by Max Mayer and produced by Leslie Urdang, Miranda de Pencier, and Dean Vanech. Screenplay by Mayer.

Adam seems to be a good catch for a young woman. He's good-looking, works as an engineer, has a big, comfy apartment, is fascinated by astronomy, and knows lots and lots of stuff. On the other hand, he has Asperger's syndrome. Beth has never met anyone like him. He behaves in social situations with an honesty that approaches cruelty and doesn't seem much aware of that.

Adam, the story of a romance involving this unlikely couple, would seem even more unlikely if Beth herself weren't self-centered. Perhaps it takes a man even less outgoing to inspire her nurturing side. At first Adam simply offends her with his baffling objectivity. Then he explains, "I have Asperger's," and she understands. If she knows the term, it's surprising she hasn't already arrived at that diagnosis.

Asperger's is sometimes described as high-functioning autism, although some argue the conditions are not related. The syndrome produces people who can be quite intelligent and functioning, but lack ordinary social skills or insights. Adam (Hugh Dancy) does not know, for example, that when a proud young mother shows off her cute new baby, he should ooh and aah. There is not a single ooh or aah in him.

Yet he feels a perplexing attraction to Beth (Rose Byrne). He even—what's this?—experiences sexual feelings for another person for perhaps the first time in his life. Beth is touched. Adam's condition draws her out of her own self-absorption. When he faces a daunting job interview, she coaches him: "Look the other person in the eye. Seem interested. Don't go on autopilot with one of your streams of information. Look like you want the job."

In a way, she could be coaching him about how to behave toward herself. And indeed such coaching is one of the forms of therapy used with Asperger's. He responds slowly, awkwardly, with breaches of behavior that at times infuriate her. The film somehow extracts from their situation a sweet, difficult relationship, although it's a good question how she finds the will to persist.

The film complicates their story with one about Beth's parents, Rebecca and Marty (Amy Irving and Peter Gallagher). They're concerned that she broke up with a suitable young man and now brings Adam home. They're also worried by a court case charging that Marty, an accountant, misrepresented a client's books. There are even courtroom scenes touching on this separate drama that I'm not sure really relate to the central story.

Adam himself seems completely isolated except for Beth and his only other friend, Harlan (Frankie Faison). Harlan gives him lifts, has lunch with him, advises him, instinctively understands him. These two accept each other without question, and Adam needs Harlan, although it's unclear if he realizes just how much.

Hugh Dancy and Rose Byrne, he from England, she from Australia, have seamless American accents, and make a pleasant couple. You may remember her as Diana, the grown-up daughter of the little girl at the beginning of *Knowing*, who wrote down the numbers. As her parents, Irving and Gallagher are always plausible, never over the top, showing that her father, too, has had his difficulties in communicating and her mother knows all about that.

The film has a storybook ending—literally, from a children's book Beth writes. It's unclear how much of a storybook lifetime the two will have together. *Adam* wraps up their story in too tidy a package, insisting on finding the upbeat in the murky, and missing the chance to be more thoughtful about this challenging situation.

Adoration ★ ★ ★
R, 101 m., 2009

Arsinee Khanjian (Sabine), Devon Bostick (Simon), Scott Speedman (Tom), Rachel Blanchard (Rachel), Noam Jenkins (Sami), Kenneth Walsh (Morris). Directed by Atom Egoyan and produced by Egoyan, Simone Urdl, and Jennifer Weis. Screenplay by Egoyan.

Atom Egoyan is fascinated by the way life coils back on itself. He uses coincidences and chance meetings not as plot devices but as illustrations of the ways we are linked across generations and national boundaries. His characters are often not completely connected to where they find themselves, and they bring along personal, sometimes secret, associations. These often reflect much larger realities in the outer world. *Adoration* circles around a central event or nonevent. A report is read about a woman who falls in love with a man from the Middle East. His family is in Israel, he says, although I am not sure that is true. She becomes pregnant. He is unhappy at first but later overjoyed. They seem deeply in love. He wants her to fly to meet his parents in Bethlehem. For business reasons, he must take a later flight.

In an age of terrorism, this triggers alarms, but not for her. What becomes of these people and the flight is not for me to relate now. We see them only in flashbacks. The story presents more than one way they possibly did meet. The film is about other people in their lives—before, and after, they met. It is also about how these other people think about what they did and didn't do.

The buried issues involve nationalism, religion, and prejudice. But this is not a message film. It is about people trying to find their way through emotional labyrinths. We are not always sure what these are, or what really happened, or what these people really feel about it, or their motives. Neither are they. *Adoration* isn't confusion; it's about confused people. Most movies make it easy for us. The central characters know what they want, and we understand.

Here there is the illusion that we are feeling our way along with these people. The most important connection, although we don't realize it for a while, is a Toronto high school drama teacher named Sabine (Arsinee Khanjian, Egoyan's muse). She reads a story about the original air travel incident as an exercise in French class. Why that story? An exercise in comprehending spoken French. And something more . . .

A student named Simon (Devon Bostick) transforms this into a first-person story, with his mother as the pregnant woman and his father as the treacherous fiancé. Simon's parents are dead, and he lives with his Uncle Tom (Scott Speedman). Sabine encourages him to read his story to the class as if it were true—as an acting exercise, she says. The story is picked up in Internet chat rooms involving Simon's high school friends.

I don't want to say too much about what is real or imagined here, and nothing at all about the secret connection the teacher Sabine is hiding. Egoyan contrives meetings between Sabine and Tom with two rather brilliant sequences that keep us guessing even while played out in full view. And there are flashbacks to the couple in Simon's story and to his actual parents, played by the same actors, so that, as it frequently does in Egoyan's films, reality takes on uncertain implications.

Throbbing beneath are ideas about terrorism, about Israeli-Palestinian feelings, about Muslims in Canada, and about the role of the Internet in creating factoids that might as well be real. Statements are made involving these subjects, but they're all suspended in an incomplete resolution; the movie withholds closure. There are areas only suggested: the boy's anger at his father, the use of the original story to him, the circumstances of two deaths, the placing of blame.

Some viewers may find the film confusing; I found it absorbing. One problem with reviewing an Egoyan film is that you find yourself struggling to describe a fractured plot line and what characters (and we) may believe at one point and not later. This can be confusing and unsatisfactory. Yet the film presents emotions that are clear. Why does Egoyan weave a tangled web? Because his characters are caught in it. Our lives consist of stories we tell ourselves about our lives. They may be based on reality, but not necessarily, and maybe they shouldn't always be. If you couldn't do a little rewriting, how could you stand things?

3

Adventureland ★ ★ ★
R, 107 m., 2009

Jesse Eisenberg (James Brennan), Kristen Stewart (Em Lewin), Martin Starr (Joel Schiffman), Bill Hader (Bobby), Kristen Wiig (Paulette), Ryan Reynolds (Mike Connell), Margarita Levieva (Lisa P.). Directed by Greg Mottola and produced by Ted Hope, Anne Carey, and Sidney Kimmel. Screenplay by Mottola.

It is a truth of twenty-somethings that if you have a crappy summer job with other twenty-somethings, the way to take your mind off work is daydreaming of sex with your workmates. You are trapped there together, eight or ten hours a day for three months, right, so what else is there to make you dance to unheard melodies?

Take James. Here he is, all set to move to New York, and his dad loses his job and he's forced to take a job at a shabby Pittsburgh amusement park. All of the rides look second-hand, all of the games are rigged, and all of the prizes look like surplus. Your job is to encourage customers even more luckless than you are to throw baseballs at targets that are glued down, while inflamed with hopes of taking home a Big Ass Panda. That's what Bobby the owner calls them when he instructs you, "Nobody *ever* wins a Big Ass Panda."

Director Greg Mottola, who made the rather wonderful *Superbad*, is back now with a sweeter story, more quietly funny, again about a hero who believes he may be a virgin outstaying his shelf life. Jesse Eisenberg, from *The Squid and the Whale*, plays James, who has a degree in Renaissance studies. (The movie is set in the 1980s, and there may still be a few jobs around.) He's out of his element at Adventureland; Bobby has to coach him to fake enthusiasm when he announces the horse race game, where you advance your horse by rolling balls into holes. His performance reminded me uncannily of my last visit to Dave & Buster's.

Most of the male employees in the park lust for Lisa P. (Margarita Levieva), whose Adventureland T-shirt unfortunately advertises Rides Rides Rides. James is much more interested in Em (Kristen Stewart), who is quieter and deeper (Games Games Games). She's smart, quirky, and seems more grown-up than the others. A quick rapport springs up, despite her edge on James in sexual experience. She thinks he's kinda sweet. They talk about subjects that require more than one sentence.

This romance takes fragile bloom while Mottola, also the screenwriter, rotates through a plot involving James's friends, one of whom expresses his devotion by hitting him in the netherlands every time he sees him. We cut often to the owner, Bobby, and his wife, Paulette (Kristen Wiig), who are lovebirds and have firm ideas about how every job at the park should be performed, which doesn't endear them to the employees because they're usually right. Oh, and then there's Connell (Ryan Reynolds), the good-looking maintenance man, who is married, and why am I telling you that?

As the summer lurches between deadly boredom and sudden emergencies (someone wins a Big Ass Panda), James and Em grow closer. This is absorbing because they reveal themselves as smarter than anyone else realizes. From his earlier work, I expected to like Eisenberg. What surprised me was how much I admired Kristen Stewart, who in *Twilight* was playing below her grade level. Here is an actress ready to do important things. Together, and with the others, they make *Adventureland* more real and more touching than it may sound.

I worked two summers at Crystal Lake Pool in Urbana. I was technically a lifeguard and got free Cokes, but I rarely got to sit in the lifeguard chair. As the junior member of the staff, I was assigned to Poop Patrol, which involved plunging deep into the depths with a flyswatter and a bucket. Not a lot of status when you were applauded while carrying the bucket to the men's room. ("No spilling!" my boss, Oscar Adams, warned me.) But there was another lifeguard named Toni and—oh, never mind. I don't think she ever knew.

After.Life ★ ★ ½
R, 97 m., 2010

Liam Neeson (Eliot Deacon), Christina Ricci (Anna Taylor), Justin Long (Paul Conran), Chandler Canterbury (Jack), Josh Charles (Tom

Peterson), Celia Weston (Beatrice Taylor). Directed by Agnieszka Wojtowicz-Vosloo and produced by Brad Michael Gilbert, Bill Perkins, and Celine Rattray. Screenplay by Wojtowicz-Vosloo, Paul Vosloo, and Jakub Korolczuk.

"You people!" says Eliot Deacon sadly, and with a touch of frustration. He is referring to the dead. They are whiners. They're not ready to die, they've got unfinished business, there are things they still desire, the death certificate is mistaken, and on and on and on. Deacon, as a mortician, has to put up with this.

Take Anna as an example. She drove away from a disastrous dinner with her boyfriend, was speeding on a rainy night, and was killed in a crash. Now here she is on a porcelain slab in his prep room, telling him there's been some mistake. Deacon tries to reason with her. He even shows her the coroner's signature on the death certificate. But no. She's alive, as he can clearly see. Besides, if he's so sure she's dead, why does he carefully lock the door from the outside whenever he leaves the room?

After.Life is a strange movie that never clearly declares whether Anna (Christina Ricci) is dead or alive. Well, not alive in the traditional sense, but alive in a sort of middle state between life and death. Her body is presumably dead. She has no pulse, and we assume her blood has been replaced by embalming fluid. Yet she protests, argues, can sit up and move around. Is Deacon (Liam Neeson) the only one who can see this? Maybe he's fantasizing? No, the little boy Jack (Chandler Canterbury) sees her, too, through a window.

Jack tells her boyfriend, Paul (Justin Long). He believes it. He's had a great deal of difficulty accepting her death. He still has the engagement ring he planned to offer her on that fateful night. He tries to break into the funeral home. He causes a scene at the police station. He sounds like a madman to them.

After.Life is a horror film involving the familiar theme of being alive when the world thinks you're dead. It couples that with a possibility that has chilled me ever since the day when, at far too young an age, I pulled down Poe from my dad's bookshelf, looked at the table of contents, and turned straight to "The Premature Burial." From Anna's point of view, she's still alive when the earth starts thudding on the coffin. From Deacon's point of view? Yes, I think from his POV, too.

From ours? The director, Agnieszka Wojtowicz-Vosloo, says audiences split about half and half. That's how I split. Half of me seizes on evidence that she's still alive, and the other half notices how the film diabolically undercuts all that evidence. I think the correct solution is: Anna is a character in a horror film that leaves her state deliberately ambiguous.

Neeson's performance as Deacon is ambiguous but sincere. He has been working with these people for years. He explains he has the "gift" of speaking with them. And little Jack, the eyewitness? Oh, but Deacon thinks he has the gift, too. So once again, you don't know what to believe. Perhaps the gift is supernatural, or perhaps it's madness or a delusion.

The film has many of the classic scenes of horror movies set in mortuaries. The chilling stainless steel paraphernalia. The work late at night. The moonlit graveyard. The burial. The opened grave. Even her desperate nails shredding the lining inside the coffin—although we see that from Anna's POV and no one else's.

I think, in a way, the film shortchanges itself by not coming down on one side or the other. As it stands, it's a framework for horror situations, but cannot be anything deeper. Yes, we can debate it endlessly—but pointlessly, because there is no solution. We can enjoy the suspense of the opening scenes and some of the drama. The performances are in keeping with the material. But toward the end, when we realize that the entire reality of the film is problematical, there is a certain impatience. It's as if our chain is being yanked.

Ajami ★★★
NO MPAA RATING, 120 m., 2010

Shahir Kabaha (Omar), Ibrahim Frege (Malek), Fouad Habash (Nasri), Youssef Sahwani (Abu Elias), Ranin Karim (Hadir), Eran Naim (Dando), Scandar Copti (Binj). Directed by Scandar Copti and Yaron Shani and produced by Moshe Danon, Thanassis Karathanos, and Talia Kleinhendler. Screenplay by Copti and Shani.

Americans didn't know we had the right idea, but we did. We welcomed those from foreign lands (or, in some cases, forced them to come here). Then we shook them up together and left them to sort things out. We have every race, ethnicity, and religion, and that helps. Unhappy are those who live in a land with only a few.

Consider Israel, where Jews, Arabs, Muslims, and Christians by and large think it is extremely important that they are Jews, Arabs, Muslims, and Christians. There is a growing minority that says, hey, here we all are together, and since nobody is budging, let's get along. Most people apparently think someone should budge and it's not them.

Ajami is the latest and one of the most harrowing films set along the religious divides in Israel. It was cowritten and codirected by an Israeli and a Palestinian, and set in Jaffa, technically a part of Tel-Aviv, which has high crime and unemployment rates. The focus is on mean streets that Scorsese might understand. Gangsters, cops, and drug dealers are tossed in with religious conflicts and the ancient Romeo and Juliet dilemma. God help anyone who marries outside their tribe.

I have never seen a film from either Israeli or Palestinian filmmakers that makes a case for anything other than coexistence. There are probably such films. But the dominant theme is the tragedy of the social divides, the waste, the loss, the violence that often claims innocent victims.

Why, in an area where tension and indeed hatred runs so high, aren't there more partisan or sectarian films? Beginning with the advantage of ignorance, I'll speculate that those Palestinians and Israelis who are inclined to make feature films are drawn from the elites of their societies. They see more widely and clearly. They may be better educated. They are more instinctively liberal. They've grown beyond the group mentality.

Ah, but there is still family. No matter how advanced your views, blood ties run deep, especially when reinforced by religion. A young couple may fall in love outside their tribe, but their fathers and uncles and cousins to remote degrees will feel threatened by their love, and God will be invoked on both sides. It is the same when a relative is murdered. Instincts demand revenge.

Ajami is about an interlocking series of such situations, starting in the first place when a man is shot dead. Then another man is mistakenly killed in revenge. Was he mistaken for the original killer? No, he was mistaken for a member of the original killer's family—which he was, although not the correct member. Now two people are dead, more vengeance is required, nothing has been proven, and everyone involved is convinced they are in the right.

Calm heads try to prevail and stop the killing. The actual original killer (are you following?) is levied with a fine. To pay it, he finds he must sell drugs. That means we are now headed into gang territory. The source of the drugs is a Palestinian in love with a Jewish girl. An Israeli cop becomes involved in the case. I won't describe more. I'm not sure I can. It's clear enough in the film who is who, but I suspect even the characters lose track of the actual origins of their vendetta. What happens is that hatred continues to claim lives in a sort of domino effect.

The film doesn't reduce itself to a series of Mafia-style killings, in which death is a way of doing business. There are situations in which characters kill as a means of self-defense. And the filmmakers, Scandar Copti and Yaron Shani, by and large show characters on all sides who essentially would like simply to be left alone to get on with their lives. Few of them possess the *personal* hatred necessary to fuel murder. But the sectarian divide acts as an artery to carry murder to everyone downstream. Was that a mixed metaphor, or what?

The specifics of the plot in *Ajami* aren't as important as the impact of many sad moments built up one after another. Hatred is like the weather. You don't agree with the rain but still you get wet. What justifies this is the "honor" of your family, your religion, your tribe. The film deplores this. So do we all, when we stand back. The film has no solution. Nor is there one, until people find the strength to place more value upon an individual than upon his group. Sometimes I fear we're all genetically programmed not to do that. One solution is the mixing of gene pools so that groups are differently perceived. I'm not holding my breath.

Alexandra ★ ★ ★ ½
NO MPAA RATING, 91 m., 2008

Galina Vishnevskaya (Alexandra), Vasily Shevtsov (Denis), Raisa Gichaeva (Malika).

Directed by Alexander Sokurov and produced by Andrei Sigle. Screenplay by Sokurov.

It is as simple as this. An old lady is helped on board an armored military train and journeys all night to visit a remote Russian army outpost. The soldiers seem to know about her and her visit, and after a couple of local boys apparently try to "guide" her away from her suitcase, two soldiers in uniform turn up and escort her to the base.

We already know a lot about her. We know she is opinionated, proud, stubborn, and not afraid to express her opinion. She marches through the heat and dust into the base and is guided to her "hotel," a room with two cots in a barracks made of tents. Other information is revealed, slowly. Her name is Alexandra (Galina Vishnevskaya). She is here to visit her grandson, Denis. He is a captain in the army.

The base is located in Chechnya. It is a Muslim republic, occupied by the Russians, who are sullenly disliked. On the base, discipline seems informal, the soldiers lax. When Denis (Vasily Shevtsov) turns up, she is appalled by the state of his uniform and advises him to wash up. She also sniffs disapprovingly at other soldiers, tells helpers "Don't pull my arm" and "Don't push me!" and that she is perfectly capable of taking care of herself.

The next day she wanders the base so early that no one seems to be around, and that was when I remembered a similar scene in Bergman's *Wild Strawberries*, about an old man who dreams of wandering a deserted town. There are other parallels between the two films, but Bergman's is about an old man discovering himself, and *Alexandra* is about an old woman being discovered. She is a transformative presence.

The film was written and directed by Alexander Sokurov, maker of the remarkable *Russian Ark*—remember that one, in which he used only one uninterrupted shot to tour the Hermitage Museum? He follows the woman as she talks her way past a guarded checkpoint and wanders into town to find the market. She is tired and hot. It must be 100 degrees. She meets Malika (Raisa Gichaeva), a woman about her age, who gives her a seat in her booth, is friendly, and gives her cigarettes and

cookies knowing that they will go to Russian soldiers. Then she invites Alexandra home to her flat in a building missing a big chunk because of bombs or shells. The two old women bond, and their conversation is the essence of the film.

If the locals do not like the Russians, the Russians do not like their duty. They can't see the point of it. They are not wanted, they will never be wanted, so why are they forced to stay? These conclusions aren't said in so many words, but they permeate the film. And notice the way some locals look at her with pointed dislike and some soldiers simply stare at her, perhaps because she is the only woman on the base and reminds them of grandmothers, mothers, sisters, girlfriends—the whole world outside their existence.

Alexandra is not a sweet little old lady. The fact that she is played by Vishnevskaya, who once ruled the Russian opera, may supply a hint of where she gets her confidence, her imperious manner. But when she hugs her grandson, when he braids her hair, when she says he "smells like a man" and she loves that smell, we get a window into her youth and her memories. Remarkable, how little Sokurov tells us, while telling us so much.

The color strategy of the movie is part of its effect. It is drab, brown, unsaturated. Reds and greens are pale, sometimes not even visible. Everything is covered with dust. Brighter colors would add vitality to the base, but that would be wrong. The point is that for the soldiers it's a dead zone, life on hold, a cheerless existence. And this plainspoken old woman reminds them of a lifetime they are missing.

Alice in Wonderland ★★★
PG, 108 m., 2010

Johnny Depp (Mad Hatter), Mia Wasikowska (Alice), Anne Hathaway (Mirana, the White Queen), Helena Bonham Carter (Iracebeth, the Red Queen), Crispin Glover (Stayne, the Knave of Hearts), Matt Lucas (Tweedledee/Tweedledum). And the voices of: Stephen Fry (Cheshire Cat), Michael Sheen (White Rabbit), Alan Rickman (Absolem), Timothy Spall (Bayard), Barbara Windsor (Dormouse), Christopher Lee (Jabberwocky). Directed by

Tim Burton and produced by Burton, Joe Roth, Jennifer Todd, Suzanne Todd, and Richard D. Zanuck. Screenplay by Linda Woolverton, based on the books *Alice's Adventures in Wonderland* and *Through the Looking-Glass* by Lewis Carroll.

As a young reader, I found *Alice in Wonderland* creepy and rather distasteful. Alice's adventures played like a series of encounters with characters whose purpose was to tease, puzzle, and torment her. Few children would want to go to Wonderland, and none would want to stay. The problem may be that I encountered the book too young and was put off by the alarming John Tenniel illustrations. Why did Alice have such deep, dark eye sockets? Why couldn't Wonderland be cozy like the world of Pooh? Watching the 1951 film, I feared the Cheshire Cat was about to tell me something I didn't want to know.

Tim Burton's new 3-D version of *Alice in Wonderland* answers my childish questions. This has never been a children's story. There's even a little sadism embedded in Carroll's fantasy. I think of uncles who tickle their nieces until they scream. *Alice* plays better as an adult hallucination, which is how Burton rather brilliantly interprets it until a pointless third act flies off the rails. It was a wise idea by Burton and his screenwriter, Linda Woolverton, to devise a reason why Alice (Mia Wasikowska) is now a grown girl in her late teens, revisiting a Wonderland that remains much the same, as fantasy worlds must always do.

Burton is above all a brilliant visual artist, and his film is a pleasure to regard; I look forward to admiring it in 2-D, where it will look brighter and more colorful. No artist who can create these images is enhancing them in any way by adding the annoying third dimension. But never mind that.

He brings to Carroll's characters an appearance as distinctive and original as Tenniel's classic illustrations. These are not retreads of familiar cartoon images. They're grotesques, as they should be, from the hydrocephalic forehead of the Red Queen (Helena Bonham Carter) to Tweedledee and Tweedledum (Matt Lucas), who seem to have been stepped on. Wonderland itself is not limited to necessary props, such as a tree limb for the Cheshire Cat

and a hookah for the caterpillar, but extends indefinitely as an alarming undergrowth beneath a lowering sky. Why you can see the sky from beneath the Earth is not a fair question. (The landscape was designed by Robert Stromberg of *Avatar*.)

When we meet her again, Alice has decidedly mixed feelings about her original trip down the rabbit hole, but begins to recall Wonderland more favorably as she's threatened with an arranged marriage with Hamish Ascot (Leo Bill), a conceited snot-nose twit. At the moment of truth in the wedding ceremony, she impulsively scampers away to follow another rabbit down another rabbit hole, and finds below that she is actually remembered from her previous visit.

Burton shows us Wonderland as a perturbing place where the inhabitants exist for little apparent reason other than to be peculiar and obnoxious. Do they reproduce? Most species seem to have only one member, as if Nature quit while she was ahead. The ringleader is the Mad Hatter, played by Johnny Depp, that rare actor who can treat the most bizarre characters with perfect gravity. Whomever he plays (Edward Scissorhands, Sweeney Todd, Jack Sparrow, Willy Wonka, Ichabod Crane), he is that character through and through.

This is a Wonderland that holds perils for Alice, played by Mia Wasikowska with beauty and pluck. The Red Queen wishes her ill and the White Queen (Anne Hathaway) wishes her well, perhaps because both are formed according to the rules of Wonderland queens. To be sure, the insecure White Queen doesn't exhaust herself in making Alice welcome. The Queens, the Mad Hatter, Alice, the Knave of Hearts (Crispin Glover), and presumably Tweedledee and Tweedledum are versions of humans; the others are animated, voiced with great zest by such as Stephen Fry (Cheshire), Alan Rickman (Absolem the Caterpillar), Michael Sheen (White Rabbit), and Timothy Spall, Barbara Windsor, and Christopher Lee.

The film is enchanting in its mordant way until, unfortunately, it arrives at its third act. Here I must apologize to faithful readers for repeating myself. Time after time I complain when a film develops an intriguing story and then dissolves it in routine and boring action. We've *seen* every conceivable battle sequence, every duel, all carnage, countless showdowns, and all-too-long fights to the finish.

Why does *Alice in Wonderland* have to end with an action sequence? Characters not rich enough? Story run out? Little minds, jazzed by sugar from the candy counter, might get too worked up without it? Or is it that executives, not trusting their artists and timid in the face of real stories, demand an action climax as insurance? Insurance of what? That the story will have a beginning and a middle but nothing so tedious as an ending?

Alien Trespass ★ ★

PG, 90 m., 2009

Eric McCormack (Ted Lewis/Urp), Jenni Baird (Tammy), Robert Patrick (Vern), Dan Lauria (Chief Dawson), Jody Thompson (Lana Lewis). Directed by R. W. Goodwin and produced by Goodwin and James Swift. Screenplay by Steven P. Fisher.

Alien Trespass is a sincere attempt to make a film that looks like one of those 1950s B movies where a monster from outer space terrorized a small town, which was almost always in the desert. Small, to save on extras and travel. In the desert, because if you headed east from Hollywood that's where you were, and if you headed west you were making a pirate picture.

The movie is in color, which in the 1950s was uncommon, but otherwise it's a knowing replication of the look and feel of those pictures, about things with jaws, tentacles, claws, weapons that shot sparks, and eyes that shot laser beams at people, only they weren't known as laser beams but as Deadly Rays. Facing them are plucky locals, dressed in work clothes from Sears, standing behind their open car doors and looking up to watch awkward special effects that are coming—coming!—this way!

The movie doesn't bend over backward to be "bad." It tries to be the best bad movie that it can be. A lot of its deliberate badness involves effects some viewers might not notice. For example: bad back projection in shots looking back from the dashboard at people in the front seat. In the 1950s, before CGI, the car never left the sound stage, and in the rear window they projected footage of what it was al-

legedly driving past. Since people were presumed not to study the rear window intently, they got away with murder. In *Casablanca*, Rick and Ilsa drove from the Champs-Elysées to the countryside instantly.

The plot: Astronomer Ted Lewis (Eric McCormack) and his sexpot wife, Lana (Jody Thompson), are grilling cow-sized steaks in the backyard when something shoots overhead and crashes in the mountains. The sexpot wife is an accurate touch: The monster genre cast pinups like Mamie Van Doren and Cleo Moore, who were featured on the posters with Deadly Rays shooting down their cleavage.

Ted goes to investigate. When he returns, his body has been usurped by Urp, an alien. Urp means well. He needs help to track down another alien who arrived on the same flying saucer, named the Ghota, which has one eye, enough to qualify it as a BEM, or a Bug-Eyed Monster. The Ghota consumes people in order to grow, divide, and conquer. Sort of like B.O.B. in *Monsters vs. Aliens*, which is *also* a send-up of 1950s BEM movies. So far, Todd Haynes's *Far from Heaven* (2002) is the only movie ever made in tribute to a *great* movie of the 1950s.

The Ghota is battled by Urp and his plucky new buddy Tammy (Jenni Baird), a local waitress who is a lot more game than Lana. As nearly as I can recall, in the 1950s good girls were never named Lana and bad ones were never named Tammy. There are also hapless but earnest local cops (Robert Patrick and Dan Lauria) and an assortment of Threatened Townspeople. Also great shots of the Lewis family home, separated from the desert by a white picket fence, surrounded by the age-old story of the shifting, whispering sands.

Alien Trespass, directed by R. W. Goodwin (*The X Files* on TV) from a screenplay by Steven P. Fisher, is obviously a labor of love. But why? Is there a demand for cheesy 1950s sci-fi movies not met by the existing supply? Will younger audiences consider it to be merely inept, and not inept with an artistic intention? Here is a movie more suited to Comic-Con or the World Science Fiction Convention than to your neighborhood multiplex.

If you must see a science fiction movie about a threat from beyond Earth, there's one right now that I think is great: *Knowing*. If you're looking for a *bad* sci-fi movie about a threat, etc., most of the nation's critics mistakenly believe it qualifies. How can you lose? "From beyond the stars—a mysterious force strikes terror into the hearts of men!"

All About Steve ★ ½
PG-13, 98 m., 2009

Sandra Bullock (Mary Horowitz), Thomas Haden Church (Hartman Hughes), Bradley Cooper (Steve), Ken Jeong (Angus). Directed by Phil Traill and produced by Sandra Bullock and Mary McLaglen. Screenplay by Kim Barker.

It is not much fun to laugh at a crazy person. None, I would say. Sandra Bullock plays a character who is bonkers in *All About Steve*, which is billed as a comedy but more resembles a perplexing public display of irrational behavior. Seeing her run around as a basket case makes you appreciate Lucille Ball, who could play a dizzy dame and make you like her. Overacting is risky even in a screwball comedy. Perhaps especially.

Bullock plays Mary Horowitz, a crossword puzzle constructor who knows a vast number of words and how they're spelled, but not much about how they might enlighten her. Because her apartment has to be fumigated, she moves back home with her parents. The headline here is how she earned enough to move out in the first place. I may be mistaken, but I think of crossword puzzle construction as more of a second job for smart people.

Anyway, Mary is fortyish and still single, perhaps in part because she wears extraordinarily clumpy shiny red disco boots everywhere, all the time—even on a 5K charity hike, I can only assume. Her parents arrange a blind date with Steve (Bradley Cooper of *The Hangover*), a television cameraman for a cable news network. The network must not be as big as CNN because there's only evidence of one crew: Steve and his on-air talent Hartman Hughes (Thomas Haden Church).

Mary lays her eyes on Steve and wants to lay everything else. This isn't love at first sight; it's erotomania. On their first date, she gives his tonsils a tongue massage. Soon he's fleeing from sightings of her, and she's in hot pursuit. Her desperation extends to a scene where she

runs in her disco boots beside the TV news van, breathlessly small-talking to Steve through the window. If Steve had mercy, he would stop or speed up—anything would be better than playing her along.

The crew is assigned to the site of a big breaking story. A group of small deaf children has fallen into a well. Why deaf? Diversity in casting, I guess. It's not like they have to do anything other than be rescued. Mary pursues them to the accident scene, and in a shot destined to go viral on YouTube, she runs across the field behind Steve, waving wildly, and falls into the hole herself.

You see what I mean. The point comes when we're rolling our eyes right along with Mary. But don't get me wrong. I am fond of Sandra Bullock. I've given her some good reviews, as recently as this summer (*The Proposal*). But how does she choose her material? If she does it herself, she needs an agent. If it's done by an agent, she needs to do it herself. The screenplay by Kim Barker requires her to behave in an essentially disturbing way that began to wear on me. It begins as merely peculiar, moves on to miscalculation, and becomes seriously annoying. One of its most unfortunate elements is seeing Bullock so stranded and helpless in a would-be comic frenzy. An actress should never, ever be asked to run beside a van in red disco boots for more than about half a block, and then only if her child is being kidnapped. ☞

Amelia ★★★
PG, 111 m., 2009

Hilary Swank (Amelia Earhart), Richard Gere (George Putnam), Ewan McGregor (Gene Vidal), Christopher Eccleston (Fred Noonan), Joe Anderson (Bill), Cherry Jones (Eleanor Roosevelt), Mia Wasikowska (Elinor Smith). Directed by Mira Nair and produced by Lydia Dean Pilcher, Kevin Hyman, and Ted Waitt. Screenplay by Ronald Bass and Anna Hamilton Phelan.

I am drawn to every news story about the attempts, which still continue, to solve the mystery of Amelia Earhart's disappearance on July 2, 1937. It's pretty clear she ditched at sea, but you just never know. Those clues found on a Pacific atoll are tantalizing. It is not her disappearance but her life that fascinates me.

She was strong, brave, and true, and she looked fabulous in a flight suit. No ladylike decorum for her; before she wed George Putnam she wrote him their marriage would have "dual controls," and said neither one should feel bound to "a medieval code of faithfulness." Maybe she was keeping a loophole for Gene Vidal (Ewan McGregor), the founder of TWA and father of Gore, who told his son he loved her but didn't marry her "because I didn't want to marry a boy."

Hilary Swank uncannily embodies my ideas about Earhart in Mira Nair's *Amelia*. She looks like her, smiles like her, evokes her. Swank is an actress who doesn't fit in many roles, but when she's right, she's right. The tousled hair, the freckles, the slim figure, the fitness, the physical carriage that says: "I know precisely who I am and I like it—and if you don't, bail out." Not only was she the first person after Lindbergh to fly solo across the Atlantic, she even looked like him.

Amelia tells this story with sound performances and impeccable period detail. It deals with her final flight so accurately that many of the radio transmissions between her and the Coast Guard cutter *Itasca*, stationed off Howland Island, are repeated verbatim. (They could hear her but she couldn't hear them.) It ends on exactly the correct note. As Red River Dave sang in the lyrics of the first song ever broadcast on U.S. television:

Half an hour later, her SOS was heard,
Her signal's weak, but still her voice was
*   brave.*
In shark-infested waters, her aeroplane
*   went down that night*
In the blue Pacific to a watery grave.

She was an early feminist role model, an American hero not tainted like Lindbergh by chumminess with the Nazis. A few years after her death, U.S. women would be asked to hang up their aprons, put on overalls, and work on the production lines of the war. She was the real thing. Yes, she signed contracts to endorse chewing gum, soap, and a fashion line, but she needed the money to finance her flights, and she always chewed the gum, used the soap, wore the clothes.

I suppose I vaguely knew she married the famous New York publisher G. P. Putnam (Richard Gere). It never registered. The film reports, correctly, that Putnam was instrumental—promoting her, booking her lectures, publishing her book, raising money for flights. The movie doesn't much deal with how a small-town Kansas tomboy got along with the famous New York socialite who published Lindbergh's *We*. It was love at first sight for George, and forever after for both of them.

That's the trouble with Amelia Earhart's life, seen strictly as movie material. What we already know is what we get. To repeat: She was strong, brave, and true, she gained recognition for women fliers, and she looked fabulous in a flight suit. She flew the Atlantic solo, she disappeared in the Pacific, she died too young, and there was no scandal or even an indiscretion. She didn't even smoke, although Luckies wanted her for an endorsement.

I'm not suggesting that Mira Nair and her writers, Ronald Bass and Anna Hamilton Phelan, should have invented anything. It is right that they resisted any temptation. It's just that there's a certain lack of drama in a generally happy life. At least by treating her big flights as chapters in a longer life, they sidestepped the dilemma that defeated Billy Wilder when he starred Jimmy Stewart in *The Spirit of St. Louis* (1957). Lindbergh's life offered such promising details as a 1930s decoration by the Nazis and the kidnapping of his baby, but Wilder focused on the long flight itself, during which the most exciting event is the appearance of a fly in the cockpit.

Amelia is a perfectly sound biopic, well directed and acted, about an admirable woman. It confirmed for me Earhart's courage—not only in flying, but in insisting on living her life outside the conventions of her time for well-behaved females. The next generation of American women grew up in her slipstream.

There's a beautiful, beautiful field
Far away in a land that is fair.
Happy landings to you, Amelia Earhart
Farewell, first lady of the air.

Note: Listen to "Amelia Earhart's Last Flight" at www.youtube.com/watch?v=xRMu3dEHCaM.

☞

American Teen ★ ★ ★
PG-13, 95 m., 2008

Featuring Hannah Bailey, Colin Clemens, Megan Krizmanich, Geoff Haase, Mitch Reinholt, Jake Tusing, and Ali Wikalinska. A documentary directed by Nanette Burstein and produced by Burstein, Jordan Roberts, Eli Gonda, and Chris Huddleston.

American Teen observes a year in the life of four high school seniors in Warsaw, Indiana. It is presented as a documentary, and indeed these students and their friends and families are all real people, and these are their stories. But many scenes seem suspiciously staged. Why would Megan, the "most popular" girl in school, allow herself to be photographed spreading toilet paper on a lawn and spray-painting "FAG" on the house window of a classmate? Is she really that unaware? She's the subject of disciplinary action in the film; why didn't she tell the school official she only did it for the movie?

Many questions like that occur while you're watching *American Teen*, but once you make allowance for the factor of directorial guidance, the movie works effectively as what it wants to be: a look at these lives, in this town ("mostly middle-class, white, and Christian"), at this time.

The director is Nanette Burstein, whose credits include the considerable documentaries *On the Ropes* and *The Kid Stays in the Picture*. She spent a year in Warsaw, reportedly shot one thousand hours of footage, and focused on four students who represent segments of the high school population.

Megan Krizmanich is pretty, on the school council, a surgeon's daughter, "popular," but sometimes considered a bitch. She dreams of going to Notre Dame, as her father, a brother, and a sister did. She seems supremely self-confident until late in the film, when we learn about a family tragedy that her mother blames for her "buried anger."

Colin Clemens, with a Jay Leno chin, is the basketball star. His dad has a sideline as an Elvis impersonator (pretty good, too). The family doesn't have the money to send him to college, so everything depends on winning an athletic scholarship, a fact he is often re-

minded of. He doesn't have a star personality but is a nice guy, funny.

Hannah Bailey is the girl who wants to get the hell out of Warsaw. She dreams of studying film in San Francisco. Her parents warn her of the hazards of life for a young girl alone in the big city, but she doesn't want to spend her life at a nine-to-five job she hates. "This is my life," she firmly tells her parents. She also goes into a deep depression when a boyfriend breaks up with her and misses so many days of school as a result that she is threatened with not graduating.

And Jake Tusing is the self-described nerd, member of the band, and compulsive video game player, who decorates his room with an astonishing array of stuffed, framed, or mounted animals. He has a bad case of acne, which is a refreshing touch, since so many movie teenagers seem never to be afflicted with that universal problem.

During this year, a guy will break up with his girl by cell phone. A topless photo of a girl will be circulated by Internet and cell phone to everyone in school, and, seemingly, in the world. Megan will make a cruel phone call to the girl. Romances will bloom and crash. Crucial basketball games will be played. And the focus will increasingly be on what comes next: college or work? Warsaw or the world?

Warsaw Community High School, with its sleek modern architecture, seems like a fine school, but we don't see a lot of it. Most of the scenes take place in homes, rec rooms, basements, fast-food restaurants, basketball games, and school dances (curiously, hardly anyone in the film smokes, although one girl says she does). We begin to grow familiar with the principals and their circles, and start to care about them; there's a certain emotion on graduation day.

American Teen isn't as penetrating or obviously realistic as her *On the Ropes,* but Nanette Burstein (who won the best directing award at Sundance 2008) has achieved an engrossing film. No matter what may have been guided by her outside hand, it is all in some way real, and often touching.

American Violet ★ ★ ★
PG-13, 103 m., 2009

Nicole Beharie (Dee Roberts), Tim Blake Nelson (David Cohen), Will Patton (Sam Conroy),

Michael O'Keefe (Calvin Beckett), Xzibit (Darrell Hughes), Charles S. Dutton (Reverend Sanders), Alfre Woodard (Alma Roberts). Directed by Tim Disney and produced by Bill Haney. Screenplay by Haney.

You may recall the story from the news in 2000. The cops in a small Texas town arrested forty black people on drug charges in a sweep of a public housing project. They were working on a tip from a single informant, a former mental patient who had good reason to cooperate with them. Dee, a young mother of four, who was not found with drugs and had no history of drug use, was arrested primarily because she went outside to drag her little girl to safety. She, along with the others, is offered a plea bargain: If she pleads guilty, she gets probation. She refuses to plead guilty.

American Violet is clear about the motivation for such raids with little or no evidence. A guilty plea helps the district attorney build up a record as a crime fighter, even though he is the one who has committed the crime. A defendant who pleads guilty cannot continue to live in public housing and will always have a felony on her record. But if Dee caves in, she goes free and is reunited with her children. Her snaky ex-husband has snatched his kids and moved them in with his new girlfriend, who has a history of child abuse.

This is all based on an actual case (the names have been changed). This stuff happens all the time and is far from rare in Texas, a state with a shameful record of law enforcement practices. The movie occasionally intercuts commercials from the Gore-Bush campaign then under way, to no particular purpose except to remind me that as Texas governor, Bush commuted the sentence of only one of the 131 people put to death under his reign, even though public defenders presented no defense at all for 41 of them and a third of their defense attorneys were later disbarred or sanctioned.

American Violet stars Nicole Beharie, a recent Juilliard graduate in her second role, as Dee Roberts. It is a stunning performance: She is small, vulnerable, fearful for her children, but damned if she will plead guilty to a crime she did not commit. She stands firm even as her mother, Alma (Alfre Woodard),

begs her to take the plea; Alma argues the harsh racial realities of their small town. When Dee vows to stay in jail, she attracts the attention of the ACLU, which sends a lawyer named David Cohen (Tim Blake Nelson) down to defend her. Because he needs a local partner, he persuades the lawyer Sam Conroy (Will Patton), himself a former DA, to join him; Sam refuses at first but agrees out of guilt because he knows full well how the system works.

The DA is Calvin Beckett (Michael O'Keefe), a man of whom it can fairly be said that he has no interest at all in whether the people he has arrested are guilty. How would it look in an election year if he went around dropping drug charges? And now the stage is set for a docudrama that may have an outcome we already know but is a loud lesson about truth, justice, and the Texas Way. I know I'll hear complaints from Texans of a certain stripe. They won't see this film. They know all they want about the ACLU from their favorite broadcasters.

Some critics have found *American Violet* to be too mainstream, too agenda-driven, too much like made-for-TV, not enough "suspense." Say what? Dee is innocent, her lawyers are putting themselves at risk because of their outrage, and the DA is a heartless scofflaw. If the movie tries to have fun concealing that, it's jerking our chain.

What worked for me was the strength of the performances, beginning with Nicole Beharie as the convincing heroine. Alfre Woodard in attack mode is formidable; Tim Blake Nelson underplays as a determined, methodical lawyer, not a showboat, and Will Patton in some ways steals the show as a good man who has done bad in the past, knows it, and is trying to make up. As Beckett, Michael O'Keefe is rock-solid as a man who has more important things on his mind than justice.

American Violet, it's true, is not blazingly original cinema. Tim Disney's direction and the screenplay by Bill Haney are meat and potatoes, making this story clear, direct, and righteous. But consider the story. How would you feel if this happened to you? What if cases like this were to lead to disregard of due process of law at even the highest levels? I wish I could convince . . . hell, never mind. I can't. That district attorney? Still in office.

America the Beautiful ★ ★ ★
R, 106 m., 2008

A documentary written, directed, and narrated by Darryl Roberts and produced by Michele G. Bluthenthal, Roderick Gatlin, and Stela Georgieva.

The documentary *America the Beautiful* is not shrill or alarmist, nor does it strain to shock us. Darryl Roberts, its director and narrator, speaks mostly in a pleasant, low-key voice. But the film is pulsing with barely suppressed rage, and by the end I shared it. It's about a culture "saturated with the perfect," in which women are taught to seek an impossible physical ideal, and men to worship it.

It opens with shots of a pretty girl named Gerren Taylor, who looks terrific in the skimpiest of bikinis and draws admiration at a topless pool party, although she keeps her top on. Gerren is twelve. Her life as a fashion model began when a woman handed her a card for a modeling agency. She is tall, has a good figure and a model's "walk," and an ambitious mother named Michelle.

Roberts will follow her career in a film that's also a general look at the media-driven worship of women whom the average woman may never resemble (or, if they have any sense, feel the need to). To establish the world Gerren enters, he calmly assembles facts and observations: (1) "Three minutes of looking at a fashion magazine makes 90 percent of women of all ages feel depressed, guilty, and shameful"; (2) three years after the introduction of television to the Fiji Islands, the culture's rate of teenage bulimia went from zero to 11 percent; (3) a model who is six feet tall and weighs 130 pounds is told she must lose fifteen pounds; (4) the "average woman" in those crypto-feminist Dove soap ads became "average" only after complex makeup and photo retouching.

Roberts watches as Gerren becomes, for a season, a sensational success. Her appeal is based largely on her age. Celebrity magazines are fascinated by a twelve-year-old who models adult fashions, and she conquers Fashion Week in New York. But a year later her novelty has worn off, she is rejected by the same casting directors who selected her earlier, and after learning her hips are "too wide" for Milan, she and her mother seek success in London and Paris. After becoming a cover girl and overnight success, Gerren and her mom, who seem to live prudently, are essentially broke. Yes, she gets paid in London: She gets to keep the clothes she wears.

Their quest leads to an unsettled personal life for the young girl. During an argument with her mother over wearing a padded bra to school, Gerren sobs that her mom is ruining her high school years, but those years are impacted in ways she doesn't yet understand. Her sensible Los Angeles middle school principal finds she has become a classroom problem and asks her to sign a "behavior contract." Insulted, Michelle moves her daughter to a more "understanding" school in Santa Monica, and finally opts for home schooling.

Talking to models about the profession that drives them to starvation, Roberts is tentative and quiet as he asks things like, "Do you ever think this might have an impact on your . . . health?" The one time his voice lifts in anger is after a photographer fights with an African-American woman who refuses to wear makeup that will lighten her skin by four or five shades. Roberts, black himself, listens incredulously as the photographer berates the model for being ignorant, "unable to listen," and "knowing nothing" about beauty, fashion, and society. The "problem" of the model's dark skin tone is simply one manifestation of the "problems" all women are told they have if they don't match the fashion ideal. Roberts knows women like the model, and the photographer doesn't, but as the man with the camera, the photographer ordains himself with authority.

Roberts has a powerful message here, but he includes too much material not really necessary for his story. We could have done without his own experiences on a Web site named beautifulpeople.net, where applicants are rated on a sliding scale to discover if they're beautiful enough to qualify. We don't need still more standard footage of Paris Hilton, Britney Spears, and other plastic creatures. Even more unnecessary is an interview with celebrity-gossip journalist Ted Casablanca, whose four-letter language earns an R rating for a film that might rescue the lives of some girls age twelve and up.

But *America the Beautiful* carries a persuasive message and is all the more effective because of the level tone Roberts adopts. The cold fact is that no one can look like a supermodel and be physically healthy. And in a film filled with astonishments, one of the most stunning is that designers like their models the skinnier the better because—are you ready for this?—they save money on the expensive fabrics they use.

Amreeka ★★★ ½
PG-13, 96 m., 2009

Nisreen Faour (Muna Farah), Melkar Muallem (Fadi Farah), Hiam Abbass (Raghda Halaby), Alia Shawkat (Salma Halaby), Yussef Abu Warda (Nabeel Halaby), Joseph Ziegler (Mr. Novatski). Directed by Cherien Dabis and produced by Christina Piovesan and Paul Barkin. Screenplay by Dabis.

Muna is a nonreligious Palestinian, which makes her an outsider on both sides of the Israeli checkpoint she has to pass daily on the way to her job as a bank accountant. She dreams of immigrating to America with her teenage son, Fadi, so he can grow up in a less sectarian society. When against all odds she wins the U.S. lottery for green cards, they leave for a new life that is more, and less, than they expected.

So begins Cherien Dabis's heartwarming and funny first feature, with a title using the Arabic word for *America*. Muna and Fadi have the misfortune to arrive soon after the start of the war in Iraq, when Homeland Security is in a lather and anti-Arab sentiment runs high. Her life savings are confiscated by customs at O'Hare airport, along with the cookie tin she kept them in. She arrives in a distant Chicago suburb with no money but high hopes. "Occupation?" asks the immigration official. "Yes, we are occupied," she smiles proudly.

They move in with her sister and her husband, a doctor. Muna (Nisreen Faour, from *The Visitor*) is fully qualified in accounting, but her race causes her to lose a bank job. She finds work at a nearby White Castle, hiding this comedown from her family. She can't understand why anybody would want to eat one of those greasy sliders. If it is any consolation to the good sports at White Castle, who allowed a real restaurant to be used as a location, they looked mighty appetizing to me.

Her son, Fadi (Melkar Muallem), finds an ally in Salma (Alia Shawkat), a cousin about the same age. She masterminds an American teenage wardrobe for him and is a friend at school, where he is bullied as an Arab (i.e., possible teenage terrorist). At home, his uncle the doctor (Yussef Abu Warda) sees his practice decline for the same reason. Does it occur to xenophobic Americans that almost all immigrants, like their own ancestors, come here because they admire America? Explain that to Lou Dobbs. *Amreeka* isn't a story of American prejudice, but of American reality, the good and the bad. When Fadi is bullied, fights back, and is called into the principal's office, his mother sheds her White Castle uniform and hurries to the school, deeply concerned. Here she finds the Jewish principal (Joseph Ziegler) not only sympathetic but responding to her own warmth and charisma. He wonders if she'd like to join him for coffee . . .

Cherien Dabis incorporates some of her own story in her film. A Jordanian raised in Dayton, Ohio, during the years of the Gulf War, she was discriminated against. American anti-Arab prejudice apparently considers all Arabs to be on the wrong side of every problem. To explain that Palestinians had no involvement with Saddam's invasion of Kuwait would be a waste of time with such people, who seem to believe Arabs shouldn't exist at all, or at the very least should stay at home. My Irish-American ancestors faced similar discrimination, my German-American father was bullied during World War I, Japanese-Americans were locked up during World War II, and the ancestors of African-Americans scarcely came here voluntarily. How soon we forget.

Amreeka is a heartwarming film, not a political dirge. Much of this warmth comes from the actress Nisreen Faour. To see her in action is to smile. Some people are blessed with being quickly likable. As for Melkar Muallem, who plays her son, set aside his Arabic origins and he could be the hero of any American high school film. Joseph Ziegler, as the principal, is not demonstrating his open-mindedness by expressing affection for Muna, but is responding as any man in his shoes might naturally feel. When this woman smiles, you want it to be on you.

Angels and Demons ★ ★ ★
PG-13, 138 m., 2009

Tom Hanks (Professor Robert Langdon), Ewan McGregor (Camerlengo Patrick McKenna), Ayelet Zurer (Dr. Vittoria Vetra), Stellan Skarsgård (Commander Richter), Pierfrancesco Favino (Ernesto Olivetti), Nikolaj Lie Kaas (Assassin), Armin Mueller-Stahl (Cardinal Strauss). Directed by Ron Howard and produced by Howard, Brian Grazer, and John Calley. Screenplay by David Koepp and Akiva Goldsman, based on the novel by Dan Brown.

Since *Angels and Demons* depends on a split-second schedule and a ticking time bomb that could destroy the Vatican, it's a little distracting when the Camerlengo, a priest entrusted with the pope's duties between papacies, breaks into the locked enclave of the College of Cardinals and lectures them on centuries of church history.

These men, many of them elderly, may face death in minutes, which the Camerlengo knows. The commander of the Swiss Guard *thinks* he can evacuate the Vatican and the hundreds of thousands of faithful waiting in St. Peter's Square in fifteen minutes before an explosion vaporizes "a big chunk of Rome," but frankly, we in the audience think a lot of monsignors back home are going to receive promotions real soon.

Since very few plot details in the film are remotely plausible, including its desperate chase across Rome, the history lesson is excusable. Having been told about the long war between the Church and the Illuminati, and religion and science, we are grateful for the briefing, even if the cardinals already know most of the history. This kind of film requires us to be very forgiving, and if we are, it promises to entertain. *Angels and Demons* succeeds.

It's based on a novel that came before *The Da Vinci Code* in Dan Brown's oeuvre, but is set afterward. Professor Robert Langdon (Tom Hanks) is back at Harvard when he is summoned from a swimming pool by an emissary from the Vatican and flown to Rome to face a crisis. Earlier, we learned, a rare sealed vial of antimatter was stolen from the CERN Large Hadron Collider in Geneva, and a note taking credit comes from the Illumi-

nati, a secret society that has long hated the Church because of the days when it persecuted Galileo and other scientists.

A "popular and progressive" pope has just died. The cardinals have been summoned to elect his successor. Four of them, the *preferati*, the favorites to be the next pope, have been kidnapped. One will be executed at 8, 9, 10, and 11 p.m., until the battery on the antimatter vial runs out of juice at midnight, and the faithful will see more than a puff of white smoke above the Vatican. I don't recall if the Illuminati had any demands. Maybe it just wants revenge.

In that case, why hide the vial at the end of a trail that can be followed only by clues discovered or intuited by Professor Langdon? Why not just blow up the place? What is the purpose of the scavenger hunt? Has it all been laboriously constructed as a test of professor Langdon's awesome knowledge? Are the Illuminati trying to get even after Langdon foiled Opus Dei, another secret society, in *The Da Vinci Code*?

I don't know, and, reader, there is no time to care. Langdon uses his knowledge of Illuminati symbols to follow the trail through four Rome churches. He has uncanny luck. He spots and correctly identifies every clue, even though they're very well hidden. Just as well because one dungeon overlooked or one statue pointing the wrong way, and he loses. For his companion he has the beautiful and brilliant Vittoria Vetra (Ayelet Zurer) from CERN. Her father was murdered in the antimatter theft. Her purpose is (a) to explain that the battery will indeed run down, (b) request her father's secret journals from Geneva, although they are never read, and (c) run along everywhere with Tom Hanks to provide him with urgent conversation.

Meanwhile, there is intrigue within the Vatican and lots of red herrings among all the red hats. The young Camerlengo (Ewan McGregor) joins the professor's desperate quest, as does the commander of the pope's protectors, the Swiss Guard (Stellan Skarsgård). Inside the conclave, Cardinal Strauss (Armin Mueller-Stahl) is in charge of the election. Because of his sinister mien (I love the phrase "sinister mien"), German accent, and absolutist views on Church tradition, he seems set up to be a suspect, since the progressive pope's death may have been an inside job. (I forgot to mention that there has also been time to exhume the pontiff's remains and discover evidence of poisoning.)

All of this happens at breakneck speed, with little subtlety but with fabulous production values. The interiors of the Sistine Chapel, the Pantheon, churches, tombs, and crypts are rendered dramatically; the College of Cardinals looks both (a) very impressive and (b) like a collection of elderly extras from Cinecittà.

The film by no means tilts the conflict between science and religion one way or the other. The professor is not religious, indeed seems agnostic, but the Church, on the other hand, is not portrayed as antiscience. Galileo would be happy that there is now a Vatican Observatory. If the Illuminati are indeed scientists, they would better employ themselves not avenging ancient deeds, but attacking modern fundamentalist cults.

The professor has a fascinating exchange with the Camerlengo, who asks him if he believes in God. He believes, he says, that the existence of God is beyond his mind to determine. "And your heart?" asks the priest. "My heart is not worthy." Agnostics and believers can both find something to agree with there; director Ron Howard does an even-handed job of balancing the scales.

So good, indeed, that even after Howard accused the Church of refusing him access to Vatican locations, and although the dependable William Donohue of the Catholic League has attacked his film, *Angels and Demons* received a favorable review from the official Vatican newspaper *L'Osservatore Romano*, which wrote it is a "harmless entertainment which hardly affects the genius and mystery of Christianity."

And come on, Ron: Would you *expect* the Church to let you shoot a Dan Brown thriller in the Sistine Chapel? Get real.

Anita O'Day: The Life of a Jazz Singer ★ ★
NO MPAA RATING, 92 m., 2008

A documentary directed by Robbie Cavolina and Ian McCrudden and produced by Cavolina, McCrudden, and Melissa Davis.

Anita O'Day. In the 1940s and '50s, her name was routinely linked with Ella Fitzgerald, Billie Holiday, and Sarah Vaughan. If she is not as famous today, it isn't for a lack of talent. Perhaps it's that she spent most of her time singing and too much of it using heroin, and could not be bothered to focus on fame. She was good. I came home from this film and started downloading tracks into my iPod.

The film record of her career isn't as extensive as many other singers. She just didn't care about publicity. If you've seen her on a screen, it was probably in *Jazz on a Summer's Day*, the legendary doc about the 1958 Newport Jazz Festival. Standing in the sun that day, wearing a big floppy hat, a cocktail dress, and glass slippers—yes, glass slippers—she sang "Sweet Georgia Brown" as few songs have ever been sung; it is considered one of the best performances in jazz history.

She didn't even have all the tools for jazz singing. In a bold, cheeky interview she taped for *Anita O'Day: The Life of a Jazz Singer* not long before her death in 2006 at eighty-seven, she reveals that a bungled tonsillectomy left her minus her uvula, and prevented her from sustaining the vibrato necessary for proper jazz phrasing. Listening to her, I'd say she found a workaround.

Her life, she observes without regret or apology, was a "jazz life." That means she left home young, was hired by Gene Krupa the moment he heard her, toured with Krupa, Woody Herman, and Stan Kenton, was addicted to heroin for fifteen years, did four months for marijuana possession, drank too much, was never without work, was usually broke, had four marriages and several abortions, had her longest relationship with a drummer and fellow addict she never married, recorded many albums with the premiere jazz label Verve, was on the charts, was a big hit touring Japan and Sweden, and— sorry, my vibrato just broke.

As remarkable as her life was, surviving it was her most astonishing accomplishment. It wasn't as tragic as Billie Holiday's, but that wasn't for lack of trying. After an overdose, she was once declared dead in an emergency room. You may think you're not eager to watch a woman in her mid-eighties remembering old times, but that would be before you heard her singing "The Nearness of You." This is one great dame. In her heyday, she had a fresh, perky Doris Dayish face, just the right slight overbite, and she looked smart when she was singing; she didn't smile a whole lot.

She was a serious musician. Listen to her discussing eighth notes and why they work for her. Her alto voice could sound like an instrument, and she fit right in with a sax. She didn't sing over a band; her voice was one of its soloists. In duets, she was a collaborator. Oscar Peterson could play the piano about as fast as it could be played, and she once raced him to the end of a song, never dropped a syllable unless she intended to, and finished first. The film includes footage of her first hit with Krupa. It was a 1941 duet with Roy Eldridge and his trumpet. The pairing of a white singer and a black musician was dangerous in those days. Krupa kept the song in when he toured the South. O'Day doesn't seem particularly impressed by any chances they were taking.

Anita O'Day: The Life of a Jazz Singer chooses from all the existing materials and is invaluable. It is also flawed. Too many performances are interrupted. The talking heads are infringed upon by graphics that hide a third of the screen. Hardly matters. Here was a great artist. She enjoyed her life. She didn't complain at the time, she didn't complain when she went cold turkey, she didn't complain in her eighties. We see an interview where Bryant Gumbel presses her about her disorderly life, which was no secret. She doesn't bite. As if it's the most obvious thing in the world, she tells him, "That's the way it went down, Bryant."

The Answer Man ★★

R, 95 m., 2009

Jeff Daniels (Arlen Faber), Lauren Graham (Elizabeth), Lou Taylor Pucci (Kris Lucas), Kat Dennings (Dahlia), Olivia Thirlby (Anne), Nora Dunn (Terry Fraser), Tony Hale (Mailman). Directed by John Hindman and produced by Kevin Messick. Screenplay by Hindman.

Anyone writing a book titled *Me & God* has a big idea of himself or a small idea of God. Yet Arlen Faber's best-seller has captured 10 percent of the "God market" and held that position for twenty years. During those two decades his idea of himself has grown smaller. He tries to do his daily meditation, he really tries, but when the doorbell interrupts, he instinctively reacts with a string of fairly impressive swear words, strung together as if he's had practice.

Here is a man in deep spiritual doo-doo. One day he throws out his back and is in such pain he must crawl on his hands and knees to the new local chiropractor. She pushes here and probes there and soon he's back on his feet. He was in such pain when he crawled in that he gave his real name, having long been under deep cover and avoiding his fellow man. Elizabeth the doctor (Lauren Graham) has never heard of him, but her receptionist Anne (Olivia Thirlby) certainly has, and this is the start of his gradual recovery as a social being.

Arlen (Jeff Daniels) does an excellent job of portraying a misanthrope with back pain, but not so much as a man on a first-pronoun basis with God. Everything we see of him leads us to suspect that readers whose lives were changed by his book did the heavy lifting themselves. What's amazing is that his book is still read after twenty years and yet no one in the film, no one, repeats a single thing to be learned from it. Inquiring minds need to know: "What did he tell God?"

This is not a movie about spirituality, however, but a romantic comedy, with a clunky subplot involving a book seller (Lou Taylor Pucci) who has just graduated from rehab and needs advice only this shambling, foulmouthed wreck Arlen can give. Arlen is thus reluctantly hauled into the problems of another human being, while meanwhile gradually becoming involved in the life of Elizabeth and her young son, Alex (Max Antisell).

Early sequences in the film seem inspired by outtakes from a manic Jim Carrey comedy. That's not such a bad thing. Later the movie follows the timeworn pathways of countless romcoms before it. How much more interesting is a film like *500 Days of Summer*, which is about the complexities of life, in comparison with this one, which cheerfully cycles through the clichés?

Now about that God business. It is necessary for me to share one of my favorite journalism stories. It's said that Richard Harding

Davis was dispatched by William Randolph Hearst to cover the Johnstown flood. Here was his lead: "God stood on a mountaintop here and looked at what his waters had wrought." Hearst cabled back: "Forget flood. Interview God."

A wonderful story. Checking out the quote online, I found a blog entry by Dennis G. Jerz of Seton Hill University, reporting that I have related this same story four times in print since 1993, sometimes changing it slightly. Good gravy! My only defense for using it once again is that it's more interesting than anything else I could write about *The Answer Man*.

Antichrist ★★★ ½
NO MPAA RATING, 105 m., 2009

Willem Dafoe (He), Charlotte Gainsbourg (She). Directed by Lars von Trier and produced by Meta Louise Foldager. Screenplay by von Trier.

The term "antichrist" is commonly used to mean "the opposite of Christ." It actually translates from the Greek as "opposed to Christ." This is a useful place to begin in considering Lars von Trier's new film. The central character in *Antichrist* is not supernatural, but an ordinary man who loses our common moral values. He lacks all good and embodies evil, but that reflects his nature and not his theological identity.

This man, known only as He, is played by Willem Dafoe as a somber, driven, tortured soul. The film opens with He and his wife, She (Charlotte Gainsbourg), making passionate love. This is a moment of complete good. In the next room, their infant son begins to crawl around to explore and falls to his death. This in itself is a neutral act. It inspires the rest of the film, which labels itself in three stages: Grief, Pain, and Despair.

We must begin by assuming that He and She are already at psychological tipping points. She has been doing research on witchcraft, and it leads her to wonder if women are inherently evil. That may cause her to devalue herself. He is a controlling, dominant personality, who I believe is moved by the traumatic death to punish the woman who delivered his child into the earth.

Their first stage, Grief, is legitimate. Their error is in trying to treat it instead of accepting it and living it through. Of course they blame themselves for having sex when they should have been attentive to the infant. Guilt requires punishment. She mentally punishes herself. For reasons he may not be aware of, he is driven to deal with her guilt as a problem, lecturing her in calm, patient, detached psychobabble. Her grief is her fault, you see, and he will blame her for it. This leads to Pain, most directly when he insists, at this of all times, on them going to their remote cabin in a dark wood that she fears at the best of times. The cabin is named Eden; make of that what you will. They have already eaten of the fruit, and it will never be Eden for them again.

The psychic pain of his counseling and their removal to the forest are now joined by pain inflicted upon them by nature and each other. The woods are inhabited by strange animals that look ordinary—a deer, a fox, a crow—but are possessed and unnatural. He and She don't much seek refuge in their cabin but increasingly find themselves outside in the wilderness. They begin to inflict pain on each other in unspeakable and shockingly intimate ways.

These passages have been referred to as "torture porn." Sadomasochistic they certainly are, but porn is entirely in the mind of the beholder. Will even a single audience member find these scenes erotic? That is hard to imagine. They are extreme in a deliberate way; von Trier, who has always been a provocateur, is driven to confront and shake his audience more than any other serious filmmaker—even Bunuel and Herzog. He will do this with sex, pain, boredom, theology, and bizarre stylistic experiments. And why not? We are at least convinced we're watching a film precisely as he intended it, and not after a watering-down by a fearful studio executive.

That said, I know what's in it for von Trier. What was in it for me? More than anything else, I responded to the performances. Feature films may be fiction, but they are certainly documentaries showing actors in front of a camera. Both Dafoe and Gainsbourg have been risk takers, as anyone working with von Trier must be. The ways they're called upon to act in this film are extraordinary. They respond without hesitation. More important, they convince. Who can say what von Trier intended? His own explanations have been vague. The actors take the words and actions at face value and invest them with all the conviction they can. The result, in a sense, is that He and She get away from von Trier's theoretical control and act on their own, as they are compelled to.

We don't know as much as we think we do about acting. I asked Dafoe what discussions he had with Gainsbourg before their most difficult scenes. He said they discussed very little: "We had great intimacy on the set but the truth is we barely knew each other. We kissed in front of the camera the first time, we got naked for the first time with the camera rolling. This is pure pretending. Since our intimacy only exists before the camera it makes it more potent for us."

So it is a documentary in one way. What does it document? The courage of the actors, for one thing. The realization of von Trier's images, for another. And on the personal level, our fear that evil does exist in the world, that our fellow men are capable of limitless cruelty, and that it might lead, as it does in the film, to the obliteration of human hope. The third stage is Despair.

Anvil! The Story of Anvil ★ ★ ★

NO MPAA RATING, 90 m., 2009

Featuring Steve "Lips" Kudlow, Robb Reiner, G5, Ivan Hurd, Tom Araya, Chris Tsangarides, Tiziana Arrigoni, Cut Loose, Mad Dog, Lars Ulrich, Lemmy, Scott Ian, Slash. A documentary directed by Sacha Gervasi and produced by Rebecca Yeldham.

This is the sound of optimism: "Everything on the tour went drastically wrong. But at least there was a tour for it to go wrong on." The optimist is Steve "Lips" Kudlow, lead guitarist in Anvil, a band you've never heard of. In 1973, he made a friend named Robb Reiner in Toronto, who had a drum set, and they vowed to make rock 'n' roll until they were old. Now they are old, at least for heavy metal rockers.

Anvil! The Story of Anvil is a documentary about the moderate rise and long, long fall of their band, where musicians in the two other slots came and went, but Lips and Robb rocked on. "How many bands stay together for thirty years?" asks Slash of Guns N' Roses, in a backstage interview. "You've got the Stones, the Who, U2—and Anvil." Yeah. And Anvil.

Anvil had one modestly successful album (*Metal on Metal*), is credited as an influence by lots of heavy metal bands, had bad management and lousy record labels, and was Canadian at a time (as now) when that didn't feel synonymous with heavy metal. "I was raised to be polite," says Reiner, after he fails at a job in telephone hard selling.

Reiner is also seen working on a demolition project. Kudlow drives a delivery truck carrying school meals, and explains the menu. One day maybe lamb stew and meat loaf. Then meat loaf and pizza. Then pizza and lamb stew. He burns with the original fire: The band will, will, will win the success it deserves.

There are still loyal fans. One, Tiziana Arrigoni of Sweden, books a European tour for them. This was the tour that went drastically wrong. They missed trains. Couldn't find the club in Prague. Weren't paid. Were invited to the Monsters of Transylvania, a heavy metal concert. Lips shares the news that the venue seats 10,000: "I hear the mayor of Transylvania is going to be there!" The audience numbers 178.

The documentary, directed by Anvil fan (and *The Terminal* screenwriter) Sacha Gervasi, spends time in Toronto with Lips's and Robb's spouses, siblings, children. The wives are loyal but not optimistic. The rockers are good family men. They were apparently spared the heavy metal plague of heavy drugs, although there is a little weed in one shot.

Down and down they fall. They get the veteran producer Chris Tsangarides to cut their thirteenth album ("our best work"—Lips), but have to release it themselves. One CD finds its way to Japan, and they are invited to a Tokyo concert with a venue seating (an ominous omen) 10,000. They play at the unheavy-metal hour of 9:45 a.m. How many people turn up?

I don't know if their music is any good. Their fans think so. The doc doesn't show one song all the way through. But they swore a pledge when they were fourteen, and they're still honoring it, and at fifty-one Lips knows he still has it and that Anvil will be back on the charts. Maybe there is hope for Susan Boyle.

Appaloosa ★ ★ ★
R, 115 m., 2008

Ed Harris (Virgil Cole), Viggo Mortensen (Everett Hitch), Renee Zellweger (Allison French), Jeremy Irons (Randall Bragg), Timothy Spall (Phil Olson), Lance Henriksen (Ring Shelton). Directed by Ed Harris and produced by Harris, Robert Knott, and Ginger Sledge. Screenplay by Knott and Harris, based on the novel by Robert B. Parker.

Appaloosa started out making me feel the same as I did during the opening chapters of Larry McMurtry's *Lonesome Dove* and its TV miniseries. At its center is a friendship of many years between two men who have seen a lot together and wish they had seen less. This has been called a Buddy Movie. Not at all. A buddy is someone you acquire largely through juxtaposition. A friend is someone you make over the years. Some friends know you better than you know yourself.

That would be true of Everett Hitch (Viggo Mortensen), who for years has been teamed up with Virgil Cole (Ed Harris). They make a living cleaning bad guys out of Western towns. Virgil wears a sheriff's badge, and Everett is his deputy, but essentially they're hired killers. They perform this job with understated confidence, hair-trigger instincts, a quick draw, and deadeye aim. They're hired by the town of Appaloosa to end its reign of terror under the evil rancher Randall Bragg (Jeremy Irons).

So already you've got an A-list cast. Harris plays a man of few words, many of them pronounced incorrectly, and steel resolve. Mortensen is smarter than his boss, more observant, and knows to tactfully hold his tongue when he sees the sheriff making mistakes, as long as they're not fatal. Irons plays the rancher as one of those narrow-eyed snakes who is bad because, gosh darn it, he's good at it. Then a lady comes into town on the stage.

This is Allison French (Renee Zellweger), a widow, she says. No, she hasn't come to Appaloosa to find work as a schoolmarm or a big-hearted whore (the two standard female occupations in Westerns). She plays the piano and the organ and dresses like a big-city lady in fancy frocks and cute bonnets. She inquires at the sheriff's office about where she might find respectable lodgings. Her budget is limited. She has one dollar.

Zellweger is powerfully fetching in this role. She wins the sheriff's heart in a split second, and he "explains" to the hotel clerk that Miss French will be staying there and will play the piano. Virgil Cole has practiced for a lifetime at avoiding the snares of females, but he's a goner. Everett looks at him quizzically. But you don't keep a friend if you criticize his women—too quickly, anyway. Is there anything about Allison to criticize? The movie has a ways to go.

Virgil and Everett reminded me immediately of Gus McCrae and Woodrow Call in *Lonesome Dove*, not only in their long-practiced camaraderie, but also in their conversations about women. So smitten is Virgil that he abandons his tumbleweed ways and starts building a house for the widow. Meanwhile, Bragg sends three boys into town, who get themselves killed. A showdown approaches, viewed warily by the town leaders. Phil Olson (Timothy Spall) is their spokesman, and who better than Spall? He is the master of telegraphing subdued misgivings.

No more of the plot. What is seductive about *Appaloosa* is its easygoing rhythm. Yes, we know there will be a shoot-out; it can't be avoided. But there is also time for chicken dinners and hot pies and debates about the new curtains, and for Miss French to twinkle and charm and display canny survival instincts. What makes the movie absorbing is the way it harmonizes all the character strands and traits and weaves them into something more engaging than a mere 1-2-3 plot. I felt like I did in *Lonesome Dove*—that there was a chair for me on the porch.

The film has been directed by Ed Harris and bears absolutely no similarity, as you might have anticipated, to his *Pollock* (2000), the story of an alcoholic abstract expressionist. Harris as a director allows the actors screen time to live. They're not always scurrying around to fulfill the requirements of the plot. They are people before the plot happens to them—and afterward, too, those who survive. He has something to say here about hard men of the Old West and their naive, shy idolatry of "good" women.

Harris comes ready for the gunplay. He just doesn't think it's the whole point. The shootin' scenes are handled with economy. Everett observes that one shoot-out is over

21

lickety-split, and Virgil tells him: "That's because we're good shots." At the end of the day, everything works out as I suppose it had to, and we're not all tied in emotional knots or existential dread. I know I want me another slice of that hot pie.

Araya ★★★ ½
NO MPAA RATING, 90 m., 2010

Featuring the Pereda, Salazar, and Ortiz families. A documentary directed by Margot Benacerraf and produced by Henry Nadler. Screenplay by Benacerraf.

To be born here is to be born into hell. That must have happened for more than three hundred years, because no one would ever want to come to live here. *Araya* tells the story of life on the remote, barren Araya peninsula of Venezuela, where Spanish conquistadors found salt about 1550. Salt was treasure in Europe, to the misfortune of those whose lives were devoted to it.

This astonishing documentary, so beautiful, so horrifying, was filmed in the late 1950s, when an old way of life had not yet ended. It was the belief of the filmmaker, Margot Benacerraf, that the motions of the salt workers became ritualized over the decades, passed down through the generations, and that here we could see the outcome of the endless repeating of arduous tasks that would destroy others.

The salt cake is taken up from the floor of a shallow marsh, loaded into flat-bottomed wooden boats, broken up, carted onto land in wheelbarrows, and loaded into 120-pound baskets to be balanced on the heads of workers who trudge up the side of an ever-growing pyramid to deposit it. At the top, a man with a rake forms each mound into a towering, geometrically perfect shape. Now it is ready to be hauled away in trucks.

The workers, bronzed by the sun, all muscle and sinew, work in a blazing sun in a land where nothing grows. Food comes from the sea and from corn meal that is carted in. They live in small rude shacks. They get their water from a tank truck. Some work all day. Some work all night. Such is their life.

And just such a phrase, *such is their life*, is

used in the doc's narration, which seems to hover in detachment above the sweat on the ground. I imagine Benacerraf's purpose was to make the toilers of Araya seem heroic in a "land where nothing lives." Where the sun is hot and pitiless so often it becomes a mantra. The effect is odd at first, but then we grow accustomed: The idea is to see these not as individuals but almost as a species evolved to take salt from the sea, build it into pyramids, watch it hauled away, and start again.

We learn something about salt along the way. It was so prized that the Spanish built their largest overseas fortress on the peninsula to guard it. The men who died building it were the first of many who paid for salt with their lives. The working conditions of the salt workers were brutal; their feet and legs were ulcerated by the salt, and if they faltered, they had no income. Their existence is agonizing, and we feel no regret that their way of life is ending. They have been reduced to robots. Small wonder the film contains so little dialogue. Yet these people lived and died, and we had salt in our shakers. It would be too sad if they were not remembered.

This black-and-white doc, so realistic in its photography, so formal in its words, played at Cannes in 1959 and shared the critics' prize with Alain Resnais's *Hiroshima, Mon Amour*. Benacerraf, a Venezuelan director born in 1926, it still alive and much honored. Her work was almost lost in the years since it was made. Now it has been restored to pristine beauty by Milestone Films, and is on a national tour of art venues.

The Art of the Steal ★★★ ½
NO MPAA RATING, 101 m., 2010

Featuring John Anderson, Colin B. Bailey, Julian Bond, Carolyn T. Carluccio, David D'Arcy, Richard Feigen, D. Michael Fisher, Tom L. Freudenheim, Jim Gerlach, Richard H. Glanton, Nancy Herman, Walter Herman, Christopher Knight, Meryl Levitz, Bruce H. Mann, Robert Marmon, Toby Marmon, Ross Mitchell, Barry Munitz, Irvin Nahan, Marcelle Pick, David W. Rawson, Jay Raymond, Edward G. Rendell, Mark D. Schwartz, Harry Sefarbi, Richard Segal, Nick Tinari, Robert Zaller. A documentary directed by Don Argott.

Dr. Albert C. Barnes accomplished two things for which we must be grateful: He invented a treatment for VD, and he founded the Barnes Foundation in the Philadelphia suburb of Merion. The first paid for the second, so the wages of sin were invested wisely. In his imposing private structure, far from the power brokers of the city, Barnes created an oasis for serious students, who could learn from his collection without rubbing elbows with crowds of art tourists.

How important was the Barnes Collection? I learn from the press notes of *The Art of the Steal* that it included 181 Renoirs, 69 Cezannes, 59 Matisses, 46 Picassos, 16 Modiglianis, and 7 Van Goghs. Barnes collected these during many trips to Paris at a time when establishment museums, such as the Philadelphia Museum of Art, considered these artists beneath their attention. Some of the paintings are today literally priceless; one estimate of the worth of the collection is $25 billion.

That was a lot of art to be sitting in Merion. Barnes knew it was. He designed every detail of his collection with personal care, grouping paintings to reflect and comment on one another, placing period furniture and wall ornaments near them, and filling walls with a richness of paintings close, but not too close, together. He loved his collection, and he hated the Philadelphia Main Line establishment—most particularly, the Museum of Art, which had scorned his collection in its early days.

Barnes was a rich man. He hired himself some Philadelphia lawyers and drew up an iron-clad will, endowing the foundation with funds enabling it to be maintained indefinitely where it was and how it was. It was his specific requirement that the collection not go anywhere near the Philadelphia Museum of Art. And that is exactly where it is today.

He hated the museum. He hated its benefactors, the Annenberg family, founded by a gangster, enriched by *TV Guide*, chummy with the Nixon administration. The Annenbergs published the *Philadelphia Inquirer*, which consistently and as a matter of policy covered this story with slanted articles and editorials.

Don Argott's *The Art of the Steal* is a documentary that reports the hijacking of the Barnes Collection with outrage, as the Theft of the Century. It was carried out in broad daylight by elected officials and Barnes trustees, all of whom justified it by placing the needs of the vast public above the whims of a dead millionaire.

The film explains in great detail the chain of events that began after the death of Barnes at the wheel of his own car in 1951. It involves Lincoln University, the small African-American college to which he entrusted control of the foundation, no doubt to piss off the establishment. It involves how the president of Lincoln, Richard H. Glanton, sidestepped the wishes of Barnes by taking many of the treasures on tour, bringing honor to himself for such a benefaction. But Glanton is not the final villain. As he perhaps overspent and depleted Barnes's endowment, the vultures from Philadelphia were hovering, ready to pounce and fly off with their masterpieces to their nest in the museum—yes, at the top of the same great stairs Rocky Balboa ran up in *Rocky*. It is not difficult to imagine them at the top, their hands in triumph above their heads.

Well, was this such a bad thing? The Renoirs and Picassos can now be seen by anyone visiting the museum, instead of by a limited number of art students. That is good, I suppose, although I've seen tourists jogging past the *Mona Lisa* in Paris just to check it off their itinerary. The film could do a better job of allowing the public access issue to be defended. But what it does is tell a cautionary tale.

It is perfectly clear exactly what Barnes specified in his will. It was drawn up by the best legal minds. It is clear that what happened to his collection was against his wishes. It is clear that the city fathers acted in obviation of those wishes, and were upheld in a court of appeals. What is finally clear is this: It doesn't matter a damn what your will says if you have $25 billion and politicians and the establishment want it.

Ashes of Time Redux ★ ★

R, 93 m., 2008

Brigitte Lin (Murong Yin/Murong Yang), Leslie Cheung (Ouyang Feng), Maggie Cheung (Brother's Wife), Tony Leung Chiu Wai (Blind

Swordsman), Jacky Cheung (Hung Qi), Tony Leung Ka Fai (Huang Yaoshi), Li Bai (Hung Qi's Wife), Carina Lau (Peach Blossom), Charlie Yeung (Young Girl). Directed by Wong Kar Wai and produced by Wong, Jeffrey Lau, and Jacky Pang Yee Wah. Screenplay by Wong, based on the novel by Louis Cha.

---

redux (adj.): Brought back; revived.

If Wong Kar Wai were a painter, he might sometimes create bold, bright swirls on his canvas, with something figurative swimming into view. That's my impression of *Ashes of Time Redux*, first released in 1994, now re-duxed. I didn't see the first version, which the director considered unfinished, requiring fourteen years of additional thought. So far has Kar Wai's, or Wong's, art grown and deepened in the meantime (especially in the great *In the Mood for Love*) that I am not quite sure why he set himself the task. Apparently he could not forget it, although many of his admirers have.

I watched attentively. I was dazzled by the beauty of the palette and the fluidity of the camera, and it was good to see familiar Hong Kong stars like Brigitte Lin, Leslie Cheung, Maggie Cheung, Tony Leung Chiu Wai, and Tony Leung Ka Fai in younger days. I have had Chinese names explained to me a dozen times, about how the family name goes first and the first name goes last. It's just that I never know how to deal with names that are half-Chinese and half-Western. Surely it's not Lin Brigitte?

IMDb is no help because they use their arcane knowledge of every name on Earth, so if you follow them, your editor is always complaining, That's not how the *New York Times* has it. I decided to eliminate the middleman and go straight to the *Times* review, which alas does not include a cast listing and refers unhelpfully to "both Tony Leungs," although this time it is made easy because Tony Leung Chiu Wai plays the Blind Swordsman and Tony Leung Ka Fai does not.

While I was there I decided to find out how Manohla Dargis handled the plot, which is somewhat confusing. I respect her work. She attends to these things. Here is her plot description: "See, there's this swordsman . . ."

That's it. That's all of it. Oh, wait, she adds that "Mr. Cheung, as a desert dweller called Ouyang, is a broker for itinerant swordsmen and their prospective clients." She doesn't say which Mr. Cheung. Probably not the blind swordsman.

I'm sure wisenheimers on the blogs will write, "Did she really see it?" I'm dead certain she did. I know I've seen it, and that's about as far as I could get. If you attempt to finish her sentence, you will find yourself either (a) lost in a thicket of interlocking flashbacking confusion, or (b) forced to fall back on the old "evocation" strategy, in which you are elusive and poetic ("It is a humble little tavern in Chinese medieval times, but through its doors . . .").

Sometimes a director is too familiar with the material. He has internalized it until it all makes sense to him. I remember when we were collaborating on *Beneath the Valley of the Ultra-Vixens,* and Russ Meyer would start lecturing about what Junkyard Sal could or couldn't do until you'd swear she was a Greek goddess. "Junkyard Sal wouldn't do that!" Russ would thunder. Once I said, "Of course she would. I've got the typewriter." At least in Russ Meyer's cinema, characters could or couldn't do things. That's why he was an artist and never had to make porn movies, in which the characters can do only one thing, or you want your money back.

But I stray. I enjoyed *Ashes of Time Redux,* up to a point. It's great looking, and the characters all know what they would do, although we do not. Wong Kar Wai doesn't supply much of a plot with a narrative engine to pull us through. He adds section headings like Spring, Summer, Autumn, Winter (a direct quote from e.e. cummings), but that only helps you to think, "Oh, now I see! I don't understand it, but it's happening in winter!"

It's perfectly OK in a case like this to relax and enjoy the experience. It is a beautiful film and never boring, not with its swordfights and romantic angst. This is a lush and well-choreographed example of the wuxia genre, which I have just now found out about, although it reaches back centuries and involves stories about swordplay and the martial arts. "Wuxia" means a lot less typing than "swordplay and the martial arts," so I want you to remember it.

Astro Boy ★★★
PG, 94 m., 2009

With the voices of Freddie Highmore (Astro, Toby), Kristen Bell (Cora), Nathan Lane (Hamegg), Eugene Levy (Orrin), Matt Lucas (Sparx), Bill Nighy (Dr. Elefun), Donald Sutherland (President Stone), Charlize Theron (*Our Friends* Narrator), Nicolas Cage (Dr. Tenma). Directed by David Bowers and produced by Maryann Garger. Screenplay by Bowers and Timothy Hyde Harris.

Astro Boy is yet another animated comedy in which the hero, who is about the same age as his target audience, is smarter, braver, and stronger than the adults in his world. Toby is also a quick learner; after he dies in an accident, he's reborn inside a robot that looks just like him and retains all of his memories. His father, in fact, treats him just like the original Toby. But "Toby is dead!" my inner logician insisted. Here's a good question: Does Astro Boy with Toby's memory wonder why he is a robot and can fly?

No time to ask questions. Metro City is in upheaval. Astro Boy (voice by Freddie Highmore) is powered by a Blue energy source discovered by his dad (Nicolas Cage); it's safe and clean, but its opposite is Red energy, which is dirty and dangerous and desired by the warmonger president (Donald Sutherland), who wants to use it to seize complete control. That seems like a shame, because Metro City is in peaceful orbit around the earth, its citizens waited on hand and foot by robots.

Below on Earth, there is devastation as garbage piles high. The precocious Astro Boy does battle with the president and then vamooses to Earth, where he meets some scavenger human kids, led by the Faginesque Hamegg (Nathan Lane), who builds fighting robots out of scrap parts. Apparently Battle-Bots still thrives.

All builds up to Astro Boy, back up in Metro City, leading the Blues against the evil, polluting Reds, in an apocalypse where any thoughts of Blue and Red states would of course be completely inappropriate.

The movie contains less of its interesting story and more action and battle scenes than I would have preferred. Has market research

discovered our children are all laboring with attention deficits, and can only absorb so much story before brightly colored objects distract them with deafening combat? Still, *Astro Boy* is better than most of its recent competitors, such as *Monsters vs. Aliens* and *Kung Fu Panda*.

It may have a building audience because of loyalty to the Astro Boy character, first introduced in a Japanese manga and then adapted into two generations of TV cartoons. Daffy Duck, he ain't; in fact, he's a boy robot of few words and simple ideas, but he has pluck, and cannons built into his chest and butt. You don't see that every day.

Now try this test. *Astro Boy* was filmed in glorious 2-D. Take the kids if they insist on going, and afterward ask them if there was anything missing. I'll bet not a single kid says, "I wish it had been in 3-D." So the kids are happy, plus you've saved $3 a ticket and didn't have to wear those damned glasses.

The A-Team ★ ½
PG-13, 121 m., 2010

Liam Neeson (Hannibal), Jessica Biel (Charisa), Bradley Cooper (Face), Sharlto Copley (Murdock), Quinton "Rampage" Jackson (B.A.), Patrick Wilson (Lynch). Directed by Joe Carnahan and produced by Stephen J. Cannell, Jules Daly, Tony Scott, Spike Seldin, Iain Smith, and Alex Young. Screenplay by Joe Carnahan, Brian Bloom, and Skip Woods, based on the TV series by Cannell and Frank Lupo.

The A-Team is an incomprehensible mess with the 1980s TV show embedded inside. The characters have the same names, they play the same types, they have the same traits, and they're easily as shallow. That was OK for a TV sitcom, which is what the show really was, but at over two hours of queasy-cam anarchy it's punishment.

The movie uses the new style of violent action, which fragments sequences into so many bits and pieces that it's impossible to form any sense of what's happening, or where, or to whom. The actors appear in flash-frames, intercut with shards of CGI and accompanied by loud noises, urgent music, and many explosions. This continues for the required length, and then there's some dialogue. Not a lot. A few words, a sentence, sometimes a statement that crosses the finish line at paragraph length.

The plot: Wrongly framed for counterfeiting, the team members, all Iraq veterans, bust out of various prisons and go after the engraving plates, which would be pretty much worn out while printing enough $100 bills to pay for the millions in property damage they cause in the process.

Bored out of my mind during this spectacle, I found my attention wandering to the subject of physics. The A-Team has an action scene that admirably demonstrates Newton's Third Law, which instructs us that for every action there is always an equal and opposite reaction.

The movie illustrates this as the heroes fall from an exploding airplane while inside an armored tank. As the tank hurtles to the ground (cf. Newton's Law of Gravity), the team leader, Hannibal Smith (Liam Neeson), looks out an opening and barks out commands for the tank's gun. I am paraphrasing: "Turn forty-five degrees to the left! Fire! Twenty-five degrees to the right! Fire!" etc. In this way he is able to direct the fall of the tank and save their lives. This is very funny.

The action scenes also benefit from everyone having had a glance at the choreography beforehand. Consider a scene when a team member is confronted by a Talking Killer. This is, of course, a killer who only has to pull the trigger but pauses to sneer and boast. He and his target are standing in the middle of a jumble of dozens of freight shipping containers that have been spilled onto a dock. He talks just a little too long, and B. A. Baracus ("Rampage" Jackson) comes roaring to the rescue through the air on his motorcycle and wipes him out.

I know there are Harley lovers among my devoted readers. Am I right in assuming that it is difficult to get enough speed for a good aerial jump while biking across a crooked heap of freight containers? I ask because, as I hinted above, no action in this movie necessarily has any relationship to the actions surrounding it.

The characters here have that annoying ability to precisely predict what will happen and coordinate their response to it. An example. A slimy double-dealer is about to kill another team member, never mind who, when suddenly behind him a container is lifted into the air, and behind it are revealed all of the other team members lined up in a row, with choice words and brief phrases to say.

I don't want to be tiresome, but (1) how did they know the two guys were behind precisely that container; (2) how did they line up a crane and hook up the container without being heard or noticed; (3) how were they able to gather the members so quickly after the chaos of the preceding action; and (4) was someone eavesdropping to give the cue at the right moment to lift the container? Ten seconds later, and it might have been too late. Ten seconds earlier, and dialogue would have been stepped on.

Are my objections ridiculous? Why? How is it interesting to watch a movie in which the "action" is essentially colorful abstractions? Isn't it more satisfying if you know where everyone is and what they're doing and how they're doing it in real time? In other words, isn't The Hurt Locker more interesting than The A-Team?

To give it credit, the movie knows it is childish. The PG-13 is appropriate. There's little actual gore, no sex beyond a chaste kiss, no R-rated language, but—ohmigod—there's smoking! Alert to preteens: Try one of those fat cigars Hannibal smokes and you won't feel like dinner.

The Audition ★ ★ ★
NO MPAA RATING, 107 m., 2009

Featuring Jamie Barton, Kiera Duffy, Michael Fabiano, Disella Larusdottir, Ryan McKinny, Angela Meade, Nicholas Pallesen, Matthew Olenk, Alek Shrader, Ryan Smith, Amber Wagner, Conductor Marco Armiliato, General Manager Peter Gelb, and Brian Dickie of the Lyric Opera of Chicago, a judge. A documentary directed by Susan Froemke and produced by the Metropolitan Opera.

Attending the Metropolitan Opera's annual National Council Auditions must be one of the great pleasures of operagoing. From forty-five districts of the nation, hopeful young singers compete to advance to fifteen regionals, from which they advance to semifinals in New

York, and ten become national finalists. Of these, five become grand winners after public performances with the Met's full orchestra. "I sang on the Met stage with their orchestra!" exults Ryan Smith, one of the singers. "That's enough!"

The Audition is a backstage and onstage documentary observing this process as it unfolded two years ago. A sad element in the film is the fact that Ryan Smith, blessed with a sunny presence and a magnificent tenor voice, died at thirty-one, since the film was made. Chosen for the Lyric's Ryan Opera Center ensemble, he was diagnosed with lymphoma soon after. He speaks briefly about himself; he's older than the other finalists and actually stopped singing for three years, he says, before telling his parents he was going to give it two years of his best effort. That was good enough. It doesn't get any better than winning at this level.

I am far from being a music critic, but I am an opera lover; we've had season tickets at Chicago's Lyric for twenty years, and my love of opera began when I was twenty and drove a rental Vespa to the Baths of Caracalla in Rome, where I was delighted to see elephants and camels under the stars and discover that the Italians sold *glace* during the performance.

It goes without saying that any singer making it to the national auditions is gifted. The film is centered on their performances, as we follow them up the final steps of their ascent. The Met has produced the film, allowed access to backstage, rehearsals, costume fittings, and so on, and (most interesting) allows us to listen in on some of the jury's deliberations; the judges include Brian Dickie of Chicago's own Lyric.

However, and this is a big however, what we eavesdrop on is almost entirely complimentary. A gingerly discussion on the sensitive topic of the weights of singers is only fleetingly followed. Visiting dressing rooms and rehearsals, we see only pleasant, smiling, sometimes nervous faces. I suppose we shouldn't expect fiascos, breakdowns, or temper tantrums—and at this level, maybe there were none. The American opera stars I've met, such as Sam Ramey, are absolutely down-to-earth. I doubt if Maria Callas would have been a delight at the National Council.

I suspect the director, Susan Froemke, may have had some inside information. As the winners are being announced, her camera stays focused on one of them as if she knows what's going to happen. Speaking of that camera, I wonder why she chose a wide lens if she was going to do so much panning; the stretching at the sides of shots becomes distracting.

As a documentary, *The Audition* isn't cutting-edge. As an introduction to a new generation of American opera stars and an opportunity to hear them sing, it is splendid.

Australia ★ ★ ★
PG-13, 165 m., 2008

Nicole Kidman (Lady Sarah Ashley), Hugh Jackman (Drover), David Wenham (Neil Fletcher), Bryan Brown (King Carney), Jack Thompson (Kipling Flynn), David Gulpilil (King George), Brandon Walters (Nullah). Directed by Baz Luhrmann and produced by Luhrmann, G. Mac Brown, and Catherine Knapman. Screenplay by Luhrmann, Stuart Beattie, Ronald Harwood, and Richard Flanagan.

Baz Luhrmann dreamed of making the Australian *Gone with the Wind*, and so he has, with much of *GWTW*'s lush epic beauty and some of the same awkwardness with a national legacy of racism. This is the sort of film described as a "sweeping romantic melodrama," a broad family entertainment that would never have been made without the burning obsession of its producers (Luhrmann for *Australia*, David O. Selznick for *GWTW*). Coming from a director known for his punk-rock *Shakespeare's Romeo + Juliet* and the visual pyrotechnics of *Moulin Rouge*, it is exuberantly old-fashioned, and I mean that as a compliment.

The movie is set in 1939. Hitler has invaded Poland. The armies of the free world will need beef. In England, Lady Sarah Ashley (Nicole Kidman) is alarmed by reports that her husband is philandering on his enormous cattle station, Faraway Downs, in northern Australia. She comes to see for herself but arrives to find him murdered. Now the owner of an expanse as large as some countries, she dresses as if for tea. The British long followed the practice of dressing in warm climates as if they were not, and Lady Ashley keeps up the standard.

Here is the situation she finds: Drover

(Hugh Jackman), named for his trade, is a rough-hewn free-standing cowboy who has never seen a woman anything like her. He runs cattle drives. She wants him to become manager of the station, but he's a rolling stone. At Faraway Downs, he drives with experienced Aborigine ranch hands, and has under his special protection the Aboriginal boy Nullah (Brandon Walters), who is eleven or twelve. Nullah's grandfather is King George (David Gulpilil, who played a boy about Nullah's age in *Walkabout* from 1971). He has been accused of the murder of Lady Ashley's husband and has fled to a mountaintop, from which he seemingly sees everything. Nullah is a beautiful boy, biracial, bright, and filled with insight, and he provides the narration for the film.

As *Australia* is essentially a Western, there must be an evil rancher with a posse of stooges, and there is: King Carney (Bryan Brown). He wants to add Faraway Downs to his empire. Much will depend on whether Carney or Faraway can be first to deliver cattle to the port city of Darwin. Lady Ashley, prepared to sell out to Carney, sees things that make her reconsider and determines to join Drover, Nullah, and a ragtag band on a cattle drive that will eventually lead into No Man's Land. Meanwhile, the delicate lady and the rugged Drover begin to fall in love, just like Scarlett O'Hara and Rhett Butler.

She grows to love the boy and emotionally adopts him. Nullah is under constant threat of being swept up by the local police, enforcing a national policy of "capturing" part-white Aboriginal children and taking them to missions where they can "have the black bred out of them" and trained to be servants. Incredibly, this practice was ended by Australia only in 1973. And you think we were slow to change.

All the elements are in place for a cross between *GWTW* and *Red River*, with an infusion of *Rabbit-Proof Fence* (2002) and World War II. Luhrmann, known for his close work with the camera, pulls back here to show the magnificent landscape and the enormity of the cattle drive. The cattle are supplied mostly by CGI, which explains how they can seem to stampede toward a high cliff. No doubt some will find this scene hokey, but it also provides the dramatic high point of the movie, with Nullah channeling the teachings of his grandfather.

It's a great scene, but it also dramatizes the film's uncertainty about race. Luhrmann is rightly contemptuous of Australia's "reeducation" policies; he shows Nullah taking pride in his heritage and paints the white enforcers as the demented racists they were. But *Australia* also accepts Aboriginal mystical powers lock, stock, and barrel, and that I think may be condescending.

Well, what do you believe? Can the Aboriginal people materialize wherever they desire? Become invisible? Are they telepaths? Can they receive direct guidance from the dead? Yes, certainly, in a spiritual or symbolic sense. But in a literal sense? The Australians, having for decades treated their native people as subhuman, now politely endow them with godlike qualities. I am not sure that is a compliment. What they suffered, how they survived, how they prevailed, and what they have accomplished they have done as human beings, just as we all must.

The film is filled with problems caused by its acceptance of mystical powers. If Nullah is prescient at some times, then why does he turn into a scared little boy who needs rescuing? The climactic events in the film require action sequences as thrilling as they are formulaic, as is the love story. Scarlett and Rhett were products of the same society. Lady Sarah and Drover meet across a divide that separates not only social class but lifestyle, education, and geography. Such a gap can be crossed, but not during anything so simple as a moonlit night with "Over the Rainbow" being played on a harmonica.

GWTW, for all its faults and racial stereotyping, at least represented a world its makers believed in. *Australia* envisions a world intended largely as fable, and that robs it of some power. Still, what a gorgeous film, what strong performances, what exhilarating images, and—yes, what sweeping romantic melodrama. The kind of movie that is a *movie*, with all the word promises and implies.

Avatar ★★★★
PG-13, 163 m., 2009

Sam Worthington (Jake Sully), Zoe Saldana (Neytiri), Sigourney Weaver (Grace Augustine), Stephen Lang (Colonel Miles Quaritch),

Michelle Rodriguez (Trudy Chacon), Giovanni Ribisi (Parker Selfridge), Joel David Moore (Norm Spellman), CCH Pounder (Mo'at), Wes Studi (Eytukan), Laz Alonso (Tsu'tey). Directed by James Cameron and produced by Cameron and Jon Landau. Screenplay by Cameron.

Watching *Avatar*, I felt sort of the same as when I saw *Star Wars* in 1977. That was another movie I walked into with uncertain expectations. James Cameron's film has been the subject of relentlessly dubious advance buzz, just as his *Titanic* was. Once again, he has silenced the doubters by simply delivering an extraordinary film. There is still at least one man in Hollywood who knows how to spend $250 million, or was it $300 million, wisely.

Avatar is not simply sensational entertainment, although it is that. It's a technical breakthrough. It has a flat-out Green and antiwar message. It is predestined to launch a cult. It contains such visual detailing that it would reward repeated viewings. It invents a new language, Na'vi, as *The Lord of the Rings* did, although mercifully I doubt this one can be spoken by humans, even teenage humans. It creates new movie stars. It is an Event, one of those films you feel you must see to keep up with the conversation.

The story, set in the year 2154, involves a mission by U.S. armed forces to an Earth-sized moon in orbit around a massive star. This new world, Pandora, is a rich source of a mineral Earth desperately needs. Pandora represents not even a remote threat to Earth, but we nevertheless send in the military to attack and conquer it. Gung-ho Marines employ machine guns and pilot armored hover ships on bombing runs. You are free to find this an allegory about contemporary politics. Cameron obviously does.

Pandora harbors a planetary forest inhabited peacefully by the Na'vi, a blue-skinned, golden-eyed race of slender giants, each one perhaps twelve feet tall. The atmosphere is not breathable by humans, and the landscape makes us pygmies. To venture out of our landing craft, we use avatars—Na'vi look-alikes grown organically and mind-controlled by humans who remain wired up in a trancelike state on the ship. While acting as avatars, they see, fear, taste, and feel like Na'vi, and have all the same physical adeptness.

This last quality is liberating for the hero, Jake Sully (Sam Worthington), who is a paraplegic. He's been recruited because he's a genetic match for a dead identical twin, whom an expensive avatar was created for. In avatar state he can walk again, and as his payment for this duty he will be given a very expensive operation to restore movement to his legs. In theory he's in no danger because if his avatar is destroyed, his human form remains untouched. In theory.

On Pandora, Jake begins as a good soldier and then goes native after his life is saved by the lithe and brave Neytiri (Zoe Saldana). He finds it is indeed true, as the aggressive Colonel Miles Quaritch (Stephen Lang) briefed them, that nearly every species of life here wants him for lunch. (Avatars are not made of Na'vi flesh, but try explaining that to a charging thirty-ton rhino with a snout like a bullet-head shark.)

The Na'vi survive on this planet by knowing it well, living in harmony with nature, and being wise about the creatures they share with. In this and countless other ways they resemble Native Americans. Like them, they tame another species to carry them around—not horses, but graceful, flying dragonlike creatures. The scene involving Jake capturing and taming one of these great beasts is one of the film's greatest sequences.

Like *Star Wars* and *LOTR*, *Avatar* employs a new generation of special effects. Cameron said it would, and many doubted him. It does. Pandora is largely CGI. The Na'vi are embodied through motion-capture techniques, convincingly. They look like specific, persuasive individuals, yet sidestep the eerie Uncanny Valley effect. And Cameron and his artists succeed at the difficult challenge of making Neytiri a green-skinned giantess with golden eyes and a long, supple tail, and yet—I'll be damned—sexy.

At 163 minutes, the film doesn't feel too long. It contains so much. The human stories. The Na'vi stories, for the Na'vi are also developed as individuals. The complexity of the planet, which harbors a global secret. The ultimate warfare, with Jake joining the resistance against his former comrades. Small graceful details like a floating creature that looks like a cross between a blowing dandelion seed and a drifting jellyfish, and embodies goodness. Or astonishing floating cloud-islands.

I've complained that many recent films abandon storytelling in their third acts and go for wall-to-wall action. Cameron essentially does that here but has invested well in establishing his characters so that it *matters* what they do in battle and how they do it. There are issues at stake greater than simply which side wins.

Cameron promised he'd unveil the next generation of 3-D in *Avatar.* I'm a notorious skeptic about this process, a needless distraction from the perfect realism of movies in 2-D. Cameron's iteration is the best I've seen—and more important, one of the most carefully employed. The film never uses 3-D simply because it has it and doesn't promiscuously violate the fourth wall. He also seems quite aware of 3-D's weakness for dimming the picture, and even with a film set largely in interiors and a rain forest, there's sufficient light. I saw the film in 3-D on a good screen and was impressed.

It takes a hell of a lot of nerve for a man to stand up at the Oscarcast and proclaim himself king of the world. James Cameron just got reelected. ☞

Away We Go ★ ★ ★ ½
R, 97 m., 2009

John Krasinski (Burt), Maya Rudolph (Verona), Jeff Daniels (Jerry), Maggie Gyllenhaal (LN), Allison Janney (Lily), Chris Messina (Tom), Catherine O'Hara (Gloria), Paul Schneider (Courtney), Carmen Ejogo (Grace), Jim Gaffigan (Lowell). Directed by Sam Mendes and produced by Edward Saxon, Marc Turtletaub, and Peter Saraf. Screenplay by Dave Eggers and Vendela Vida.

Burt and Verona are two characters rarely seen in the movies: thirty-something, educated, healthy, self-employed, gentle, thoughtful, whimsical, not neurotic, and really truly in love. Their great concern is finding the best place and way to raise their child, who is a bun still in the oven. For every character like this

I've seen in the last twelve months, I've seen twenty, maybe thirty, mass murderers.

Sam Mendes's *Away We Go* is a film for nice people to see. Nice people also go to *Terminator: Salvation,* but it doesn't make them any nicer. The movie opened June 5, 2009, in New York and Los Angeles, and then rolled out after lukewarm reviews accusing Verona and Burt of being smug, superior, and condescending. These are not sins if you have something to be smug about and much reason to condescend. Are the supporting characters all caricatures or simply a cross-section of the kinds of grotesques we usually meet in movies? I use the term "grotesque" as Sherwood Anderson does in *Winesburg, Ohio*: a person who has one characteristic exaggerated beyond all scale with the others.

Burt (John Krasinski) and Verona (Maya Rudolph) live in an underheated shabby home with a cardboard window. "We don't live like grown-ups," Verona observes. It's not that they can't afford a better home, so much that they are stalled in an impoverished student lifestyle. Now that they're about to become parents, they can't keep adult life on hold.

Away We Go is about an unplanned odyssey they take around North America to visit friends and family and essentially do some comparison shopping among lifestyles. Her parents are dead, so they begin with his: Gloria (Catherine O'Hara) and Jerry (Jeff Daniels). The parents truly *are* self-absorbed, and have no wish to wait around to welcome their first grandchild. They're moving to Antwerp.

Verona is of mixed race, and Gloria asks her conversationally, "Will the baby be black?" Is this insensitive? Why? Parents on both sides of an interracial couple would naturally wonder, and the film's ability to ask the question is not racist, but matter-of-fact in an America slowly growing tolerant. In moments like that the married screenwriters, Dave Eggers and Vendela Vida (both novelists and magazine editors), reflect a society in which race is no longer the primary defining characteristic.

After the parents vote for Belgium, Burt and Verona head for Phoenix and a visit with her onetime boss Lily (Allison Janney) and her husband, Lowell (Jim Gaffigan). Lily is a monster, a daytime alcoholic whose speech is grossly offensive and whose husband and children are in shock. Burt and Verona flee to Madison, where Burt's childhood friend Ellen (Maggie Gyllenhaal) has changed her name to "LN" and become one of those rigid campus feminists who have banned human nature from their rule book.

Then to Montreal and friends from college, Tom and Munch (Chris Messina and Melanie Lynskey), who are unhappily convinced they're happy. And next down to Miami and Burt's brother (Paul Schneider), whose wife has abandoned her family. Not a single example of healthy parenting in the lot of them.

The almost perfect relationship of (the unmarried) Verona and Burt seems to survive inside a bubble of their own devising, and since they can blow that bubble anywhere, they, of course, find the perfect home for it, in a scene of uncommon sunniness. They have been described as implausibly ideal, but you know what? So are their authors, Eggers and Vida. Consider: Thirty-somethings. Two children. Novelists and essayists. He publishes *McSweeney's*; she edits *The Believer*.

They are playful and at the same time socially committed. Consider his wonderful project 826 Valencia, a nonprofit storefront operation in San Francisco, Chicago, Los Angeles, New York, Seattle, Boston, and Ann Arbor. It runs free tutoring and writing workshops for young people from six to eighteen. The playful part can be seen in San Francisco, where the front of the ground floor is devoted to a Pirate Store. Yes. With eye patches, parrots' perches, beard dye, peg legs, planks for walking—all your needs.

I submit that Eggers and Vida are admirable people. If their characters find they are superior to many people, well, maybe they are. "This movie does not like you," sniffs Tony Scott of the *New York Times*. Perhaps with good reason.

The Axe in the Attic ★ ★ ★
NO MPAA RATING, 110 m., 2008

A documentary written, produced, and directed by Ed Pincus and Lucia Small.

I had no idea what happened after Hurricane Katrina devastated New Orleans and the Gulf Coast. No idea. I read the papers and watched the news on TV, and I had no idea. I learned the things they like to report: how hard the wind blew, how many inches of rain fell, the early death toll, victims living on a bridge, the people sheltered and/or imprisoned in the Superdome. But then another big story came along, and the news moved on, and I didn't think about Katrina so much.

Ed Pincus and Lucia Small saw the pictures on TV and decided to do something. They took an HD camera and set off on a sixty-day road trip from their home state of Vermont to Louisiana. Along the way they interviewed refugees who had settled for the time being in Philadelphia, Cincinnati, smaller cities, and government-funded trailer parks. *The Axe in the Attic* is their story of that journey.

When they arrived in the disaster zone, the sights were overwhelming. Square miles, whole counties, were destroyed. Families were uprooted. A way of life was torn apart. And the people they met were outraged by the pathetic inadequacy of the response by the federal government. FEMA, the optimistically named Federal Emergency Management Agency, was a target of scorn.

Not only did FEMA set up a bewildering barricade of red tape, in many cases it treated the hurricane victims as if they were homeless by choice. The National Guard was no better; on the bridge, troops leveled weapons at the refugees. The reason was not hard to understand: Many of the refugees were black. It was as if the government was trying to drive them out of the city by bulldozing rebuilding efforts and blocking relief agencies from delivering food and water, which would "only encourage people to stay."

Not only blacks are angry. The film also listens to white victims, who are angry on their own behalf and in many cases on behalf of blacks they have seen targeted for abuse rather than aid. They didn't know, but I have learned from another new documentary, *I.O.U.S.A.*, that federal accountants uncovered massive theft and fraud of FEMA funds, which paid for cars, vacations, champagne, lap dances, and porno films.

The hurricane didn't merely destroy by wind and flood. Its waters were contaminated by chemicals, and even weeks later, returning citizens wear face masks. Any clothes that got wet had to be destroyed; they burned the skin.

One opinion about the victims was that instead of expecting government aid, they should have gotten jobs. This at a time when tens of thousands of jobs disappeared. The film talks with one man who has to walk two and a half hours each way to a low-paying factory job because he can't afford a bus pass. He asks Lucia Small for money to buy a pass. She is conflicted: "Documentary ethics say we shouldn't pay people." I say to hell with documentary ethics, buy the man a pass.

Her moral argument is part of an element of the film I could have done without: Small and Pincus, partners in filmmaking but not in life, devote too much time to themselves. Their arguments quickly lose our interest. The film should have allowed the victims to speak for themselves, instead of going off-topic to become the story of its own making.

All the same, this is a shattering documentary. The witnesses in it mourn the loss of their homes and possessions, but also their loss of a city. "In New Orleans, nobody ever locked a door," one woman says. She saw her friends every day. She is now living in Florida: "I don't know anyone. Saturday at the mall is their family day."

The title? After an earlier hurricane, many residents learned to keep an axe in the attic in case the waters rose so high they had to hack a hole in their roofs. "That's why you saw so many people on roofs." Another says: "They say we got a warning. They got a warning six years ago to strengthen the levees." Strange that a levee separating white and black neighborhoods gave way only on the black side.

B

The Baader Meinhof Complex ★★ ½
R, 149 m., 2009

Martina Gedeck (Ulrike Meinhof), Moritz Bleibtreu (Andreas Baader), Johanna Wokalek (Gudrun Ensslin), Bruno Ganz (Horst Herold), Nadja Uhl (Brigitte Mohnhaupt), Jan Josef Liefers (Peter Homann), Stipe Erceg (Holger Meins). Directed by Uli Edel and produced by Bernd Eichinger. Screenplay by Eichinger and Edel, based on the book by Stefan Aust.

In the 1970s, Germany was transfixed by the outlaw Baader Meinhof Gang, terrorists who robbed banks, set off explosives, kidnapped, assassinated, and otherwise attempted to bring the government to its knees. What were they against? The usual: American imperialism and German capitalist oppression. What were their politics? Marxist, they thought, but actually reflecting the anarchist theory that random acts of violence could destroy the fabric of a society. They resembled the Weathermen, but were longer lived and much more destructive.

The Baader Meinhof Complex is an ambitious attempt to chart the group's rise, fall, and tentative rebirth over the course of a decade, when it called itself the Red Army Faction. The film is historically accurate, I gather—perhaps too accurate, with too many names and places and dates and victims to easily comprehend. No doubt a German who lived through those years would understand it more easily.

As it is, we grasp at a handful of high-profile characters and relate to the others only in general terms. The central figures are Andreas Baader (Moritz Bleibtreu), Gudrun Ensslin (Johanna Wokalek), and Ulrike Meinhof (Martina Gedeck). Baader and Ensslin are lovers and radicals, inflamed by Vietnam, German industrialism, an attempt on the life of a left-wing leader, and a laundry list of other causes that lead them to conclude that violence is the only effective form of opposition.

Entering their world near the beginning is the well-known journalist Meinhof, who comes to share their convictions. She's the most enigmatic figure in the film. At first a confidante and adviser, she becomes a participant, disappears from view, abandons her husband and their two children. This decision is not satisfactorily examined by the film; because it was actually taken, I suppose we're intended to accept it as granted.

The film is an impressive period re-creation, directed by Uli Edel, whose best work involves Jennifer Jason Leigh's astonishing performance in *Last Exit to Brooklyn* (1989). The screenplay is by Edel and Bernd Eichinger, who wrote the great *Downfall* (2004), about Hitler's last days in his Berlin bunker. That film was intensified by its limitations of time and space. *The Baader Meinhof Complex* is diluted by too many events and characters distributed over too much time.

The unifying character, supplying a sort of focus, is Horst Herold (Bruno Ganz), the top law enforcement officer in West Germany, who makes an attempt to understand the thought processes of the terrorists. He patiently tries to argue why some police tactics are futile and counterproductive. He certainly doesn't agree with Baader Meinhof, but he comprehends them. That's the Sherlock Holmes theory: Understand the mind of the criminal.

Ganz effortlessly brings all the weight of his distinguished career to this role. There is a quality in his face that adds authenticity to everything he says. Hard to believe this is the same actor who played the trembling, disintegrating, paranoid Hitler. As event piles on event, he supplies an observer who assists us.

I suspect that Uli Edel finds some sympathy, in abstract principle anyway, with the cause of the gang. Yes, but their tactics are murderous and futile. At the very beginning, after it is agreed that no guns will be used in a bank robbery, one conspirator brings one and kills someone, and after that, murder becomes part of the Baader Meinhof charter. I submit that it is insane to judge an ordinary citizen as directly responsible for the activities of his government. Yes, we all "share some blame" for what our nations do, but to set off a bomb is to execute a random passerby. That is the evil of terrorism in general, although, of course, in the classic theory of anarchism it is theoretically justified. I understand anarchy expressed in art, literature, or film that seeks the downfall of an establishment. But to take a price in blood? You must be very full of yourself.

The film meanders but finds focus again toward the end, after the first members of the gang are rounded up and held in prison. They go on a hunger strike, are forcibly fed, find the means to commit suicide. Exactly how and why—and even if—some of them take this action is left in some doubt. No doubt it was the same in life. The film would have benefited by being less encompassing and focusing on a more limited number of emblematic characters—Meinhof and Herold, for starters.

Babies ★★★

PG, 79 m., 2010

Featuring Ponijao, Bayar, Mari, and Hattie. A documentary directed by Thomas Balmes and produced by Amandine Billot, Alain Chabat, and Christine Rouxel.

Babies is the perfect film for anyone who has never had the opportunity to interact with humans at an early age. You may never have had one, held one, or baby-sat one, yet remained curious about the infants you see in a park, on the beach, or in baby carriers at the mall. Now a French documentarian has traveled to Africa, Asia, and America to bring back charming footage of babies in their natural habitats.

If, however, you've raised children and/or grandchildren, or had little brothers and sisters, the movie may resemble seventy-nine minutes of unpaid baby-sitting. When Baby Mari starts screaming, you're wishing you could turn on the TV and use something bright and noisy as a distraction. But no, you're at a movie. On the other hand, *Babies* may be fascinating viewing for babies, just as many dogs and cats have their favorite programs. At last, programming for the Mommy & Me screenings.

The babies are cute. Well, all babies are cute. That's just as well, because how could filmmakers audition a baby and wait six months to give it a callback? It's not a baby anymore. The director, Thomas Balmes, has found exemplary babies in Namibia, Mongolia, Tokyo, and San Francisco, and observes them lovingly as they nurse, play, doze, poke kittens, and happily hit one another. The movie is really about the babies, not their parents, and in most cases we see only those parts of the parents ranking highest on the infant's interest scale: nipples, hands, arms, and male and female chests. Not all of the nipples are real, but the babies don't discriminate as long as they work.

Two of the babies come from poor parts of the world, and two from rich. They seem equally happy and healthy. The Japanese and American babies are subjected to an awesome array of baby training strategies so they can begin climbing the success ladder as early as possible. I have no argument against baby yoga classes, but I have never known a baby that wasn't naturally able to contort itself into alarming positions and get lost in meditation on the spur of the moment.

The African baby, Ponijao, lives in a forest hut with an earth floor, but this is Home and here is Mother and there are sticks to play with that may not be made of plastic and ornamented with Disney creatures but are excellent sticks nonetheless, and satisfying. Bayar, whose family lives in a yurt in Mongolia, passes time by becoming expert in sibling rivalry. Mari, from Japan, and Hattie, from America, are surrounded by a baffling array of devices to entertain them, serve them, shelter them, protect them, and help them grow up big and strong. Can the epidemic of attention deficit disorder be explained by the First World's lack of opportunities for babies to be bored? How can babies concentrate when things are forever being jingled and dangled at them? Is there too much incoming?

I dunno. What I do know is that babies are miraculous. From a sprawling, bawling start, they learn to walk, talk, plan, scheme, play, and figure stuff out. Generations of scientists have hurled themselves at the question of exactly how babies learn to talk. They must be getting so frustrated by the fact that the babies just go ahead and do it with no training.

Did I like the movie? Aw, yeah, I did. How could I not? Did I feel I needed to see it? Not really. I appreciated the fact that there was no narrator to explain what I was seeing; no voice-overs like "little Bayar learns early to appreciate the mystery of yogurt." No parents asking, "Are you a good little boy?" and answering, "Yes, he's good little boy." Just babies. Wonderful. I was once in that state myself. I remember being flat on my stomach with my eyes an inch away from ants all crawling in a line on the front sidewalk. I've never been so entertained in my life.

The Back-up Plan ★
PG-13, 104 m., 2010

Jennifer Lopez (Zoe), Alex O'Loughlin (Stan). Directed by Alan Poul and produced by Todd Black, Jason Blumenthal, and Steve Tisch. Screenplay by Kate Angelo.

Some movies are no better than second-rate sitcoms. Other movies are no better than third-rate sitcoms. *The Back-up Plan* doesn't deserve comparison with sitcoms. It plays like an unendurable TV commercial about beautiful people with great lifestyles and not a thought in their empty little heads. So timid is this film that when it finally arrives at its inevitable childbirth scene, it bails out after two "pushes"!

Jennifer Lopez has never looked better. That's about all she does here, is look better. She is talented and deserves more than this birdbrained plot about characters who have no relationship to life as it is lived by, you know, actual people. The movie deals with artificial insemination, romance, sex, and organic goat cheese, which are promising areas for investigation, but it's so watered down it approaches homeopathy.

Lopez plays Zoe, a Manhattan pet shop owner who despairs of finding the perfect inseminator and decides to become artificially impregnated. Leaving the doctor's office, she is so happy she finds herself singin' in the rain. Then she hails a cab and a strange man pops into the backseat the same moment she does. As a Meet Cute, this ranks right down there with two characters bending over to pick up the same thing and bumping heads, which is what Tony Randall is always doing whenever I think of Meet Cutes.

This stranger is Stan (Alex O'Loughlin). We know, according to the Law of Conservation of Dramatic Resources, that (a) Zoe will become pregnant, and (b) she and Stan will fall in love. Consider the alternatives: (a1) she doesn't become pregnant, and (b2) they never see each other again. Anyway, fate brings them together, and then again, and soon they're falling for each other.

This Stan is a prime catch. Not only does he personally sell organic goat cheese in a ridiculously upscale farmers' market, but he produces it himself, on his own upstate farm. I am at a loss to explain why the movie squandered an opportunity to show Lopez milking a goat. Or having a goat eat her shoes, or whatever goats usually do in movies of this sort.

Obviously, the only way to make this feature-length is for Zoe and Stan to break up and get back together again, which they do, I think, three times. Their breakups tend toward communications difficulties, as one or the other idiotically misunderstands dialogue that is crystal clear to everyone in the audience. In Little Movie Glossary lore this is Damon Knight's famous Idiot Plot, in which all difficulties could be resolved by the uttering of one or two words.

I don't believe *The Back-up Plan* is intended to be set in the real Manhattan. Take a close look at the farmers' market. It's more of a Farmer's Faire at a church benefit in a rich suburb. Farmer Stan and his goats, indeed. But consider the scene where Zoe is a bridesmaid at a wedding, and her water breaks. What does she do? Rush to the hospital? No, she commandeers the wedding's rented white Bentley and is driven to the market, where the auto shoulders its way right down the middle of the street and halts before the organic goat cheese stall, where Zoe can leap out and make up with Stan right there in public, while onlookers all smile and listen like benevolent insiders, instead of New Yorkers wondering who the hell these jerks are. Does Stan happen to have one of those little boxes with a ring in it handy? What does a goat do in the woods?

I have neglected poor little Nuts, Zoe's Boston terrier. Nuts follows her everywhere, and whenever he gets a close-up, he barks appropriately, as if he understands what is said. When was the last time in a movie where somebody said something, and there was a cut to a dog who barked, and you thought, "That's so funny!" Nuts is paralyzed from the waist down and pulls himself everywhere on his little cart, without the benefit of much loving and cooing from his mistress, who relates to him as exactly what he is, a prop. But the little tyke can really wheel around and is always there when he's needed on camera.

This movie is desperately boring. No one says much of anything interesting. They have extremely limited ranges of interest. There are older characters: Zoe's Nana (Linda Lavin) and grandpa (Tom Bosley) and gynecologist (Robert Klein). They seem human, so the camera cuts away lest they get started on something. At the playground where Stan hangs out (allegedly fascinated by the prospect of fatherhood), there's "Playground Dad" (Anthony Anderson), a proud black father who gives Stan pep talks on the joys of parenting. African-Americans are so wise in movies like this, always playing proud dads and wise advisers and God and so forth, it's a wonder the movies are about anyone else.

Bad Lieutenant:
Port of Call New Orleans ★★★★
R, 122 m., 2009

Nicolas Cage (Terence McDonagh), Eva Mendes (Frankie Donnenfield), Val Kilmer (Stevie Pruit), Alvin "Xzibit" Joiner (Big Fate), Fairuza Balk (Heidi), Shawn Hatosy (Armand Benoit), Jennifer Coolidge (Genevieve), Tom Bower (Pat McDonagh). Directed by Werner Herzog and produced by Stephen Belafonte, Nicolas Cage, Randall Emmett, Alan Polsky, Gabe Polsky, Edward R. Pressman, and John Thompson. Screenplay by William Finkelstein.

Werner Herzog's *Bad Lieutenant: Port of Call New Orleans* creates a dire portrait of a rapist, murderer, drug addict, corrupt cop, and degenerate paranoid, very apprehensive about iguanas. It places him in a devastated New Orleans not long after Hurricane Katrina. It makes no attempt to show that city of legends in a flattering light. And it gradually reveals itself as a sly comedy about a snaky but courageous man.

No one is better at this kind of performance than Nicolas Cage. He's a fearless actor. He doesn't care if you think he goes over the top.

If a film calls for it, he will crawl to the top, hand over hand, with bleeding fingernails. Regard him in films as various as *Wild at Heart* and *Leaving Las Vegas*. He and Herzog were born to work together. They are both made restless by caution.

In the gallery of bad cops, Terence McDonagh belongs in the first room. Everyone will think of Harvey Keitel's lieutenant in Abel Ferrara's 1992 masterpiece *Bad Lieutenant* for the obvious reason. I hope this film inspires you to seek out that one. It deserves to be sought. Ferrara is Shakespearean in his tragedy, Herzog more like Cormac McCarthy. Sometimes on the road to hell, you can't help but laugh.

In a city deserted by many of its citizens and much of its good fortune, McDonagh (Cage) roams the midnight streets without supervision. He serves and protects himself. He is the law, and the law exists for his personal benefit. Lurking in his prowler outside a night club, he sees a young couple emerge and follows them to an empty parking lot. He stops them, searches them, finds negligible drugs on the man, begins the process of arrest. The man pleads. He's afraid his father will find out. He offers a bribe. McDonagh isn't interested in money. He wants the drugs and the girl, whom he rapes, excited that her boyfriend is watching.

The film's only similarities with the Ferrara film are in the title and the presentation of a wholly immoral drug addict. It's not what a movie is about, but how it's about it. Ferrara regards his lieutenant without mercy. Herzog can be as forgiving as God. An addict in need can be capable of about anything. He will betray family, loved ones, duty, himself. He's driven. Because addiction is an illness (although there is debate), we mustn't be too quick to judge. Drugs and alcohol are both terrible, but drugs can drive a victim more urgently to ruin.

Herzog shows McDonagh lopsided from back pain. He begins with prescription Vicodin and moves quickly to cocaine. As a cop, he develops sources. He steals from other addicts and from dealers. In the confusion after Katrina, he steals from a police evidence room. George Carlin said: "What does cocaine feel like? It makes you feel like some more cocaine."

McDonagh has a girlfriend named Frankie (Eva Mendes). She's a hooker. He's okay with this. He gives her drugs; she sometimes has them for him. They share something an addict craves: sympathy and understanding. They stand together against the horrors. He's also close to his sixtyish father, Pat (Tom Bower), not close to Pat's fortyish partner, Genevieve (Jennifer Coolidge). His father has a history with AA. Genevieve is a bosomy all-day beer drinker. They live in a slowly decaying rural manse somewhere in the parish. Pat knows what to look for in his son and sees it.

Colorful characters enrich McDonagh's tunnel-visioned life. There's Alvin "Xzibit" Joiner as Big Fate, a kingpin who holds the key to the execution of five Nigerian drug dealers. Fairuza Balk as a cop and his sometime lover. Brad Dourif as his bookie (he gambles, too). Val Kilmer as his partner, in an uncharacteristically laid-back performance. Maybe we couldn't take Cage and Kilmer both cranked up to eleven. Tom Bower plays his father as a troubled man but one with good instincts. Jennifer Coolidge, with great screen presence as always, changes gears and plays an MI-wouldn't-LF.

The details of the crimes need not concern us. Just admire the feel of the film. Peter Zeitlinger's cinematography creates a New Orleans unleavened by the picturesque. Herzog, as always, pokes around for the odd detail. Everyone is talking about the shots of the iguanas and the alligator, staring with cold, reptilian eyes. Who else but Herzog would *hold* on their gaze? Who else would foreground them, placing the action in the background? Who but Cage could regard an iguana sideways in a look of suspicion and disquiet? You need to keep an eye on an iguana. The bastards are always up to something.

Bad Lieutenant: Port of Call New Orleans is not about plot but about seasoning. Like New Orleans cuisine, it finds that you can put almost anything in a pot if you add the right spices and peppers and simmer it long enough. Yet, surely, *Bad Lieutenant: Port of Call New Orleans* is an odd title, isn't it? Let me give you my fantasy about that.

Herzog agrees with Ed Pressman to do a remake of the 1992 film, which Pressman also produced. Pressman is no fool and knows a Werner Herzog remake will be nothing like the original. Abel Ferrara is outraged, as well he might be. Martin Scorsese picked *Bad Lieutenant* as one of the ten best films of the 1990s.

"Gee, I dunno," Pressman says. "Maybe we *should* change the title. How about taking a line from the screenplay? How about calling it *Port of Call New Orleans*?"

"We will compromise," Herzog says with that precision he uses when explaining something he needs to make clear. "We will call it *Bad Lieutenant: Port of Call New Orleans.*" He's not going to back down from Ferrara. These are proud men.

Baghead ★ ½
R, 84 m., 2008

Ross Partridge (Matt), Steve Zissis (Chad), Greta Gerwig (Michelle), Elise Muller (Catherine). Directed by Mark Duplass and Jay Duplass and produced by John Bryant, Jay Duplass, and Mark Duplass. Screenplay by Mark Duplass and Jay Duplass.

The modestly named "mumblecore" movement in new American indies is not an earthquake like the French New Wave, more of a trembling in the shrubbery. *Baghead,* by the Duplass brothers, Mark and Jay, is an example. Mumblecore movies are very low budget, shot on video, in love with handheld QueasyCam effects, and more often than not shot in the woods, where locations and extras are not a problem. *The Blair Witch Project* was not really a mumblecore movie, according to Peter Debruge, whose *Variety* article was definitive in defining the genre, but it's an early example of a Do It Yourself in the Woods genre that doesn't really cry out for more titles. On the other hand, I am informed by Jim Emerson, editor of rogerebert.com, a mumblecore shot in the woods is a bonus: "Actually, they're more likely to be shot in the filmmakers' apartments."

If you walk out after ten or fifteen minutes, you will have seen the best parts of the film. It opens at an underground film festival, where the director of a $1,000 epic (*We Came Naked*) takes questions after his premiere. Knowledgeable festival veterans will smile at the questions: "What was your budget?" of course, and

"Did you use improvisation?" Why the budget is such a matter of concern puzzles me, but the people who ask that obligatory question always nod gratefully for the answer.

Anyway, our heroes attend the screening and attempt to crash the after-party without invitations. Walking past the security guard while carrying on an animated cell phone conversation seems to work, but not when you lack a cell phone and try to fake it with your wallet. At their own after-after-party, the four protagonists decide, the hell with it—they'll make their own movie.

The heroes are Matt (Ross Partridge), leader of the pack; his longtime on-again, off-again girlfriend Catherine (Elise Muller); his buddy Chad (Steve Zissis); and Chad's date, Michelle (Greta Gerwig), who seems more attracted to Matt than Chad. This generates what can be generously described as sexual tension in the woods, although not by me.

Their location is a cabin eleven miles up a country road (this distance later becomes important). They settle down to write a screenplay about four people in a cabin in the woods (that is, themselves), who are threatened by a guy with a bag over his head. I guess it's a guy. Girls aren't that stupid. During the course of their creativity session, one of them is indeed frightened by a guy with a bag ever his head, and it apparently couldn't be one of the other three. This baghead appears again at such perfectly timed moments that he must have a copy of the (unwritten) screenplay.

Here's where I have my problem. How is an uninformed total outsider going to *happen* to be eleven miles out in the woods with a bag over his head, and just *happen* to stumble upon these four people who *happen* to be writing exactly such a story? I weary, yes, I weary. He is obviously simply a device to make the movie long enough to qualify as a feature, and the denouement will be one of stunning underwhelmingness.

The dialogue contains way too many cries of "Matt!" and "Catherine!" and "Chad!" and "Michelle!" and "Matt! Where are you, Matt?" and so forth. There are better movies to be seen. Thousands. Their budget was low. Yes, I think I sensed they used improvisation. The film had its premiere at Sundance 2008, where I assume they were all invited to their after-party. I hope someone slipped in making a cell phone call on his wallet.

Ballast ★ ★ ★ ★
NO MPAA RATING, 96 m., 2008

Micheal J. Smith (Lawrence), JimMyron Ross (James), Tarra Riggs (Marlee), Johnny McPhail (John). Directed by Lance Hammer and produced by Hammer and Nina Parikh. Screenplay by Hammer.

Ballast is the very life of life. It observes three good, quiet people as they sink into depression, resentment, and rebellion. Then it watches patiently, gently, as they help one another find their futures together. There is a bedrock reality to it that could not be fabricated. It was filmed on locations in the Mississippi Delta and uses actors who had never acted before, but who never step wrong. Few professional actors could convince us so deeply.

But already you are filing this film away to forget. You don't care about the Mississippi Delta. You want to go see real movie stars. You already have too much reality in your life. You are suspicious of words like "quiet," "patiently," "gently." The film's own director does a better sales job in writing his synopsis, where you will find words like "embattled," "act of violence," "emotionally devastated," "the fury of a bitter and longstanding conflict." Be honest. Now it sounds less threatening to you.

The film centers on two households side by side on an open flatland. A man named Lawrence (Micheal J. Smith) lives in the house next to his sister-in-law Marlee (Tarra Riggs) and her twelve-year-old son, James (JimMyron Ross). After the death of Lawrence's brother, they are not on speaking terms. They ran a roadside convenience store and gas station together, but now it stands closed, its gate padlocked, and Lawrence sits at home alone, a cigarette burning itself down in his fingers. James comes to visit him one day.

That's really all I should tell you. The events in this film arrive when they happen, how they happen, in the order that they happen. The plot doesn't have "surprises," just things we didn't expect to happen. *Ballast* doesn't take the point of view of any one character. It regards them all. Because they all know what has happened before the story opens, the film doesn't use artificial dialogue to fill us in. We find out everything in the course of events. You will see how it unfolds the way life does.

Let me talk about the actors. They *are* these characters, with all the abilities and problems of real life. Be honest. When I wrote "Mississippi Delta," you immediately thought of poor black people. You know you did. The race of these characters has no relevance to the story. Lawrence and Marlee are not poor. Hell, they have a gas station and a store. They're having a hard time right now because the store is closed and they are sad and angry, but you can see from the insides of their houses that while they're far from rich, they have what they need and a little more. James has his own motor scooter.

There is not one single shred of "amateur" about these performances. Not the smallest hint. After a long casting process, the writer-director, Lance Hammer, brought them all together and they discussed their characters. Hammer described the general outline. They improvised potential scenes every day for two months. The Mike Leigh approach. They all agreed that they had the final form more or less right. They were never given a finished script. They didn't have to memorize dialogue because they knew it from inside out: who they were, how they would say these things, how they would feel, what they would do.

There is a fourth named character, their neighbor John (Johnny McPhail). He is their friend and will help them if he can. He is not a saintly do-gooder. He is a decent man, has done OK in life, is older, is tactful, doesn't butt in when he isn't needed. He is a good neighbor, not The Good Neighbor. Then there are some kids who are alarming influences on James. Have you ever known a twelve-year-old who didn't know kids who are bad influences? Of course, if your kid is a bad influence, it's those other kids who got him that way.

Life goes on from day to day. We grow more and more intensely absorbed. The film uses no devices to punch up tension, manufacture suspense, underline motives. When there is anger, we see it coming from a long way away, and we watch it take its time to subside. Ordi-

nary life begins to stir because it must. There is an ending that in one sense we probably anticipated, but it's like very few endings. When it comes, we think: "Yes. It would be like that. Exactly like that. We don't even need to see their faces. We feel their hearts."

Especially in its opening scenes, *Ballast* is "slower" and "quieter" than we usually expect. You know what? So is life, most of the time. We don't wake up and immediately start engaging with plot points. But *Ballast* inexorably grows and deepens and gathers power and absorbs us. I always say I hardly ever cry at sad films, but I sometimes do, just a little, at films about good people.

Note: Lance Hammer won the award for Best Director at Sundance 2008.

Bandslam ★★★
PG, 111 m., 2009

Aly Michalka (Charlotte Banks), Vanessa Hudgens (Sa5m), Gaelan Connell (Will Burton), Scott Porter (Ben Wheatly), Lisa Kudrow (Karen Burton), Ryan Donowho (Basher Martin), Charlie Saxton (Bug). Directed by Todd Graff and produced by Elaine Goldsmith-Thomas, Ron Schmidt, and Marisa Yeres. Screenplay by Graff and Josh A. Cagan.

Will Burton lives within himself. A high school kid, new in town, he's too much of a geek to have any hope of dating the girls he notices in school. He lives in a room where he has made a shrine to David Bowie (with whom he has a daily one-way e-mail correspondence) and wishes he had been born soon enough to frequent CBGB, a legendary New York club that was the launching pad for punk rock.

Not that you'd think he was a punk if you saw him. He's just an ordinary kid, always joined with his iPod until one day his life changes when his musical expertise is recruited by the popular Charlotte (Aly Michalka, of Aly & AJ). She has a three-piece group that will compete in an upcoming tristate battle of the bands, and Will thinks (correctly) it doesn't have a chance.

He in turn spots a loner girl named Sa5m ("the five is silent"). She's played by Vanessa Hudgens (*High School Musical*) as withdrawn, usually in black, keeping secrets. One of them is that she has musical talent. Will adds her to the band, along with other side musicians, including a very quiet Asian girl named Kim Lee (Lisa Chung), who is a classical pianist but plays a great pop keyboard even if it looks like it might kill her to smile.

Charlotte's band is called the Glory Dogs. Will renames it "I Can't Go On I'll Go On," which inevitably reflects a situation that comes up in the film. He throws himself into reshaping the group's music, to the concern of his hovering single mom (Lisa Kudrow)—who comes to hear for herself and is converted.

Will knows zip about girls. When Charlotte says she really likes him, he believes it, even though a former head cheerleader is unlikely to choose a nerd like him. Sa5m expresses great disinterest in the subject of romance, and, of course, is obviously the girl for him. Also in the picture is the handsome senior Ben (Scott Porter), whose own group won Bandslam last year, and who used to be Charlotte's b.f. He's the kind of jerk who accidentally bangs against you in the corridor.

The movie leads up to the tristate Bandslam, of course, at which many relationships are settled and problems solved. So the plot conceals no surprises. What makes the film work is its feeling for the characters and the appeal of the leads. Gaelan Connell has been compared to the young John Cusack and Tom Hanks, with reason; he's attractive but a little quirky, not too handsome, good at replacing his down-on-himself attitude with newfound confidence as a band producer. It does wonders for his high school rep that everyone believes Charlotte likes him.

The student body is, of course, oblivious to the qualities of Sa5m, which is often the case. Look around a school for the bright misfits and you will find those destined to make more of themselves than the "popular crowd"; it's not a foolproof indicator, but useful. You will also find someone who, if they say they like you, probably means it.

Both Aly Michalka and Vanessa Hudgens are gifted musicians, which makes the rehearsal and performance segments convincing. They also possess beauty and presence, and yet look plausible, and Lisa Kudrow avoids the pitfalls of the hysterically overpro-

tective mother; we learn some of the reasons for her concern. This isn't a breakthrough movie, but for what it is, it's charming, and not any more innocuous than it has to be.

The Band's Visit ★ ★ ★ ★
PG-13, 86 m., 2008

Sasson Gabai (Tewfiq), Ronit Elkabetz (Dina), Saleh Bakri (Haled), Khalifa Natour (Simon), Imad Jabarin (Camal), Tarak Kopty (Iman). Directed by Eran Kolirin and produced by Eilon Ratzkovsky, Ehud Bleiberg, Yossi Uzrad, Koby Gal-Raday, and Guy Jacoel. Screenplay by Kolirin.

The eight men wear sky-blue uniforms with gold braid on the shoulders. They look like extras in an opera. They dismount from a bus in the middle of nowhere and stand uncertainly on the sidewalk. They are near a highway interchange, leading, no doubt, to where they'd rather be. Across the street is a small café. Regarding them are two bored layabouts and a sadly, darkly beautiful woman.

They are the Alexandria Ceremonial Police Orchestra, a band from Egypt. Their leader, a severe man with a perpetually dour expression, crosses the street and asks the woman for directions to the Arab Cultural Center. She looks at him as if he stepped off a flying saucer. "Here there is no Arab culture," she says. "Also no Israeli culture. Here there is no culture at all."

They are in a dorp in the middle of the Israeli desert, having taken the wrong bus to the wrong destination. Another bus will not come until tomorrow. *The Band's Visit* begins with this premise, which could supply the makings of a light comedy, and turns it into a quiet, sympathetic film about the loneliness that surrounds us all. Oh, and there is some comedy, after all.

The town they have arrived at is lacking in interest even for those who live there. It is seemingly without activity. The bandleader, named Tewfiq (Sasson Gabai), asks if there is a hotel. The woman, Dina (Ronit Elkabetz), is amused. No hotel. They communicate in careful, correct English—she more fluent, he weighing every word. Tewfiq explains their dilemma. They are to play a concert tomorrow at the opening of a new Arab Cultural Center in a place that has almost, but not quite, the same name as the place they are in.

Tewfig starts out to lead a march down the highway in the correct direction. There is some dissent, especially from the tall young troublemaker Haled (Saleh Bakri). He complains that they have not eaten. After some awkward negotiations (they have little Israeli currency), the Egyptians are served soup and bread in Dina's café. It is strange how the static, barren, lifeless nature of the town seeps into the picture even though the writer-director, Eran Kolirin, uses no establishing shots or any effort at all to show us anything beyond the café—and later, Dina's apartment and an almost empty restaurant.

Dina offers to put up Tewfig and Haled at her apartment, and tells the young layabouts (who seem permanently anchored to their chairs outside her café) that they must take the others home to their families. And then begins a long, quiet night of guarded revelations, shared isolation, and tentative tenderness. Dina is tough but not invulnerable. Life has given her little that she hoped for. Tewfig is a man with an invisible psychic weight on his shoulders. Haled, under everything, is an awkward kid. They go for a snack at the restaurant, its barren tables reaching away under bright lights, and Dina points out a man who comes in with his family. A sometime lover of hers, she tells Tewfig. Even adultery seems weary here.

When the three end up back at Dina's apartment, where she offers them wine, the evening settles down into resignation. It is clear that Dina feels tender toward Tewfig, that she can see through his timid reserve to the good soul inside. But there is no movement. Later, when he makes a personal revelation, it is essentially an apology. The movie avoids what we might expect, a meeting of the minds, and gives us instead a sharing of quiet desperation.

As Dina and Tewfig, Ronit Elkabetz and Sasson Gabai bring great fondness and amusement to their characters. She is pushing middle age; he is being pushed by it. It is impossible for this night to lead to anything in their future lives. But it could lead to a night to remember. Gabai plays the bandleader as so repressed, or shy or wounded, that he seems closed inside himself. As we watch Elkabetz putting on a new dress for the evening and inspecting herself in the mirror, we see not vanity but hope. And throughout the evening we note her assertion, her confidence, her easily assumed air of independence. Yet when she gazes into the man's eyes, she sighs with regret that as a girl she loved the Omar Sharif movies that played daily on Israeli TV, but play no more.

There are some amusing interludes. A band member plays the first few notes of a sonata he has not finished (after years). A band mate calls him "Schubert." A local man keeps solitary vigil by a pay phone, waiting for a call from the girl he loves. He has an insistent way of showing his impatience when another uses the phone. In the morning, the band reassembles and leaves. *The Band's Visit* has not provided any of the narrative payoffs we might have expected, but it has provided something more valuable: an interlude involving two "enemies," Arabs and Israelis, that shows them both as only ordinary people with ordinary hopes, lives, and disappointments. It has also shown us two souls with rare beauty.

Battle for Terra ★ ★ ★
PG, 85 m., 2009

With the voices of: Luke Wilson (Jim Stanton), Evan Rachel Wood (Mala), Brian Cox (General Hemmer), James Garner (Doron), Chris Evans (Stewart Stanton), David Cross (Giddy), Justin Long (Senn), Dennis Quaid (Roven). Directed by Aristomenis Tsirbas and produced by Keith Calder, Ryan Colucci, Jessica Wu, and Dane Allan Smith. Screenplay by Evan Spiliotopoulos.

Battle for Terra is a bewitchingly animated story about an invasion from outer space by aliens who threaten to destroy all life on the planet so they can claim it as their own. I know what you're thinking. Here's the surprise: The aliens are the human race. The inhabitants of Terra look like cute tadpoles, combined with features of mermaids and seahorses.

The planet Terra (so named by the Terrans) is one of the stars of the film. A world where nearly everything seems to be organic, it has a unique scale. Although a Terran is of considerable size, about as large as a human child of six of seven, the vegetation grows on a much larger scale, so that a hollow reed can be used for high-rise living. The civilization includes certain mechanical features (helicopter chairs, ultralight aircraft), but seems very much a part of nature.

The thinking that went into this other world is typical of classic science fiction, both in its physical details and its sociological ones. The atmosphere is apparently dense enough that the Terrans can hover with a minimal effort by their tadpole tails. It can also support huge, friendly sky leviathans, who float among the clouds like peaceful whales. The planet is ruled by a well-meaning thought-control autocracy, which enforces strict conformity and discourages independent thought.

When a vast human vessel appears in the sky, the Terrans assume it is God. The bright, rebellious Mala (voice by Evan Rachel Wood) thinks otherwise. When her light aircraft is pursued by a human fighter plane, she lures it into a crash, then rescues its pilot, Jim Stanton (Luke Wilson). Helped by Jim's chirpy robot companion, Giddy (David Cross), she saves his life and builds a dome within which he can breathe oxygen.

Oxygen is the problem. The humans, exhausted after a generations-long voyage through the cosmos, intend to replace Terra's atmosphere with oxygen, thus providing a new Earth for themselves, but alas, killing all life forms on Terra. This gaiacide is directed by the militarist General Hemmer (Brian Cox), who brushes away Jim's arguments that the two races can peacefully coexist.

All leads to war, which was a disappointment to me, because a film that offers invention and originality reduces itself to essentially just another aerial battle with, however, some nice touches. Are kids taught to require combat at the end? Could they perhaps be trusted to accept a character-based resolution?

The movie contains a subtle level of sociopolitical commentary, involving the blind faith encouraged by the leaders on both sides, the questioning of orthodoxy by Mala and her friend Senn (Justin Long), and the nuke-the-enemy strategy of General Hemmer. The assumption that the Earthlings are gods shows the pitfalls of imposing a supernatural solution to a natural problem.

The animation is nicely stylized and the color palette well chosen, although the humans are so square-jawed they make Dick Tracy look like Andy Gump. The voice performances are persuasive. The obvious drawback is that the film is in 3-D. If you can find a theater showing it in 2-D, seek out that one. The 3-D adds nothing and diminishes the light intensity, as if imposing a slightly cloudy window between the viewer and a brightly colored wonderland. Take off the glasses to see how much you're losing.

Battle in Seattle ★ ★ ★
R, 99 m., 2008

Andre Benjamin (Django), Woody Harrelson (Dale), Martin Henderson (Jay), Ray Liotta (Mayor Tobin), Connie Nielsen (Jean), Michelle Rodriguez (Lou), Channing Tatum (Johnson), Jennifer Carpenter (Sam), Charlize Theron (Ella). Directed by Stuart Townsend and produced by Townsend, Kirk Shaw, Maxime Remillard, and Mary Aloe. Screenplay by Townsend.

Battle in Seattle takes the actual 1999 protests against a summit meeting of the World Trade Organization and uses them as a backdrop for a fictional story about characters swept up in the tumult. The result is not quite a documentary and not quite a drama, but interesting all the same. It uses the approach of Haskell Wexler's *Medium Cool,* but without the same urgency; Wexler's actors were plunged into the actual demonstrations at the 1968 Chicago Democratic Convention, and *Battle* is not as convincing.

Much of the story involves an unnecessary romantic attraction between Jay (Martin Henderson), leader of the protesters, and Lou (Michelle Rodriguez), a member of the movement. They have to have disputes about tactics and motivations, etc., while drawing closer together, and in this context, they're just a distraction.

More to the point is Dale, the cop played by Woody Harrelson, whose pregnant wife (Charlize Theron), a bystander, is caught up in the crowd and beaten by police. Dale asks for leave time, but is ordered back on the street by his commanding officer and releases his grief through rage. Harrelson's emotional arc in the film is convincing and effective.

But what to make of Jean, the TV newswoman (Connie Nielsen), who plunges with her cameraman into the thick of the fighting, ignores orders from her station, and becomes sympathetic? Yes, it happens (a lot of reporters during Hurricane Katrina vented their anger at FEMA). That's not the problem. What seems odd is that she always seems to be at the crossroads between the action and the film's subplots, is always there for dramatic moments on video, and most of the time is the only TV news presence in the movie. Street reporters and their cameramen (and women!) tend to congregate at the same hotspots.

Those glitches aside, the movie makes a case for the way the WTO punishes Third World nations, allows the dumping of surpluses that drive workers away from jobs, and is managed for the benefit of the fat-cat nations. Some of the disagreement about the big Wall Street bailout reflects anger about the way money protects itself; should there even be a *question* that the executives who steered their companies into bankruptcy should be stripped of their multimillion-dollar bonuses?

Most people have never quite understood why there are protests all over the world about the WTO. *Battle in Seattle* has a commendable prologue and some dialogue that helps explain, but for a very moving ground-level doc that makes it all crystal clear, you might want to rent *Life and Debt* (2001), which is a close-up portrait of the destruction of small Jamaican farmers and the exploitation of workers. Would you believe the WTO pushes Third World nations into establishing poverty-wage barbed-wire enclaves for multinational corporations, inside of which local laws and protections do not apply?

The Beaches of Agnes ★★★★
NO MPAA RATING, 110 m., 2009

With Agnes Varda, Rosalie Varda, Mathieu Demy, Jim McBride, Zalman King, Jane Birkin, and others. A documentary produced and directed by Agnes Varda. Screenplay by Varda.

Dear Agnes Varda. She is a great director and a beautiful, lovable, and wise woman, through and through. Her face is still framed by a cap of shining hair. Her eyes are still merry and curious. She is still brimming with energy, and in *The Beaches of Agnes* you will see her setting up shots involving mirrors on the beach, or operating her own camera, or sailing a boat single-handedly down the Seine under the Pont Neuf, her favorite bridge.

And she has given us the most poetic shot about the cinema I have ever seen, where two old fishermen, who were young when she first filmed them, watch themselves on a screen. Yes, and the screen and the 16 mm projector itself are both mounted on an old market cart that they push through the nighttime streets of their village.

If you have never seen a single film by Agnes Varda, perhaps it is best to start with *The Beaches of Agnes*. This is not an autobiography, although it is about her lifetime. She closes it by saying, "I am alive, and I remember." The film is her memories, evoked by footage from her films and visits to the places and people she filmed. But that makes it sound too straightforward. The film is a poem, a song, a celebration. Although she's in robust health, she accepts, as she must, that she's approaching the end. She expresses no thoughts about an afterlife, and only one great regret about this one: that Jacques and she could not complete the journey together, as they had planned.

She doubts she had seen ten films by the time she was twenty-five, when she made her first film. She had no theory and never desired any. She filmed as she felt, even in her first work, which boldly brings together two story lines. Its visual compositions are compared to Bergman's in an enormously useful IMDb user comment. It starred the great actor Philippe Noiret in his first role. Coming before the first films of Godard, Truffaut, Chabrol, Demy, Rivette, and Resnais, Varda is sometimes called the grandmother, not the mother, of the New Wave.

For Varda, film has been a family business. Her husband, Jacques Demy, of course, is most famous for *The Umbrellas of Cherbourg*, the all-singing musical that won the Palme d'Or at Cannes. Varda's *Vagabond* won the Golden Lion at Venice. They supported each other when needed, but kept a "respectful" distance from each other's work.

Their great collaboration came at the end, when Demy started to write down memories of his youth in Nantes, and Agnes said, "Jacques, do you want me to make a film of these?" Jacques said he did, and Agnes began immediately, that very day. The story is in *Beaches*. Calling on friends and collaborators, she started to film with Demy at her side and everyone aware he was dying. It was a period piece, with actors playing young Demy and the others. *Jacquot* was finished with a few days to spare. She must have had a personal agenda for beginning work so quickly; right to the end of his life, Demy was needed. There is no use in waiting passively to die.

In *The Beaches of Agnes,* there is a sequence in which all of her children and grandchildren, dressed in white, perform a slow ballet on the beach, and Varda dances behind them, dressed all in black. And that's all I need to say about that. Many times when we see her in the film, she is walking backward, as the film itself walks backward through her life, and as she perhaps sees herself receding from our view. But her films will not recede, and neither will Varda. There is absolutely no hint to suggest this will be her last film.

The film most central to her life in many ways is *The Gleaners and I,* where she ennobles a trade she traces back to the Middle Ages: the trade of moving through the places of Man and rescuing those things that can usefully be used again. When I see men moving down our alley with grocery carts, searching garbage bins for items of value, I do not think of the words "homeless," "mendicants," "vagrants." Having been taught by Varda, I think "gleaners." They have a life to live and a living to make, and are of greater actual use to society than some who make millions a year.

In that way all of Varda's films have been gleanings. Although she is happy when one of them is successful ("*Vagabond* was a big hit," she recalls cheerfully), I don't believe a single one was made because of its commercial prospects. They were made out of love of the art form, and constructed by what fell to hand and seemed good to her. And now at eighty-one she can walk backward with more serenity than most of us, because she will not stumble.

Bedtime Stories ★ ★ ½
PG, 95 m., 2008

Adam Sandler (Skeeter Bronson), Keri Russell (Jill), Guy Pearce (Kendall), Russell Brand (Mickey), Richard Griffiths (Barry Nottingham), Courteney Cox (Wendy), Lucy Lawless (Aspen), Teresa Palmer (Violet Nottingham), Jonathan Morgan Heit (Patrick), Laura Ann Kesling (Bobbi). Directed by Adam Shankman and produced by Jack Giarraputo, Andrew Gunn, and Adam Sandler. Screenplay by Matt Lopez and Tim Herlihy.

Bedtime Stories was not my cup of tea, or even the saucer. Fairness requires me to report, however, that it may appeal to, as they say, "kids of all ages." I am not a kid of any age and do not qualify, but this is a harmless and pleasant Disney comedy and one of only three family movies playing over the holidays. It will therefore win the box-office crown big time, with Adam Sandler crushing Tom Cruise, Brad Pitt, Cate Blanchett, Mickey Rourke, Samuel L. Jackson, Kate Winslet, and others not in harmless Disney comedies. *The Tale of Despereaux* and *Marley and Me* also qualify as family films, although some parents may be frightened by Marley the dog.

Sandler plays a hotel handyman named Skeeter, which is a name even more unwise than Hussein if you want your child to run for president. His dear old dad ran a family motel at the corner of Sunset and La Cienega, an unlikely story, and was bought out by Nottingham the hotel tycoon (Richard Griffiths), who erected a towering heap of rooms on the site and put Skeeter in charge of changing the lightbulbs. Now Skeeter is also in charge of the overnight maintenance work on his niece and nephew while his sister (Courteney Cox) looks for work in Arizona.

The kids (Laura Ann Kesling and Jonathan Morgan Heit) want to be told bedtime stories, and Skeeter spins some terrific ones—so terrific, the movie's budget seems to be the best-kept secret this season. Literally hundreds of special-effects technicians labored to visualize Skeeter's fantasies, which involve a zero-gravity battle in outer space, a cowboy with a bright red horse, a medieval king, a gladiator, and so on. The kids start providing their own output, the stories have a weird way of coming true in real life, Skeeter tries to slant them to affect future events, and, as you know from the poster, gumballs rain from above.

Intercut with this folderol are (a) Skeeter's rivalry with Nottingham's evil hotel manager (Guy Pearce) for the hand of Nottingham's daughter (Teresa Palmer); (b) an attempt to save an eco-friendly school run by his sister's best friend (Keri Russell); and (c) reaction shots by Bugsy, the kids' pet guinea pig, whose hyperthyroid eyes the size of half-dollars are not cute. Sort of sad, really. Almost scary.

There are some nice sight gags. One involves a misunderstanding about fire-retardant spray. Another involves Skeeter being bitten on the tongue by a bee. He cannot utter one intelligible word during a crucial presentation to Nottingham and is funny in his desperate attempts. His scruffy friend Mickey (Russell Brand) leaps to the rescue and translates. Mickey is also an employee at the hotel, although anyone looking like him would be barred from any prudent hotel and might excite the curiosity of city health inspectors.

And that's about it. The first family comedy starring Adam Sandler. Just what you're looking for. Sandler reprises once again his clueless, well-meaning nebbish who wants to be liked. Once again the character relates best to kids, perhaps because there is so much he can learn from them. Once again, the message is that you have to believe. Apparently it doesn't matter so much *what* you believe. Just the act of believing is sufficient. Then you can believe you want to see the sequel.

Note: Our Chicago publicist, a really nice guy, announced that any movie critic attending in pajamas would be presented with free popcorn and a soft drink. How could he have known that the 7:30 p.m. screening would take place during a snowstorm on the coldest night of the winter? One of the critics nevertheless wore his PJs and cashed in. It must be true what they're saying about salaries in hard times.

Before the Rains ★ ★ ½
PG-13, 98 m., 2008

Linus Roache (Henry Moores), Rahul Bose (T.K. Neelan), Nandita Das (Sajani), Jennifer Ehle (Laura Moores), John Standing (Charles Humphries), Leo Benedict (Peter Moores). Directed by Santosh Sivan and produced by Doug Mankoff, Andrew Spaulding, Paul Hardart, Tom Hardart, and Mark Burton. Screenplay by Cathy Rabin, based on the film *Red Roofs* by Danny Verete.

Before the Rains tells the kind of story that would feel right at home in a silent film, and I suppose I mean that as a compliment. It's a melodrama about adultery, set against the backdrop of southern India in 1937. There's something a little creaky about the production, especially in its frequent use of large crowds of torch-bearing men, who can be summoned in an instant at any hour of day or night to blaze a trail, search for a missing woman, or group in front of the house of a possibly guilty man.

The movie comes from the Merchant-Ivory group, long associated with films made in English and filmed in India. It's directed by Santosh Sivan, originally a cinematographer, whose masterpiece *The Terrorist* (1999) involved a young woman committed to being a suicide bomber. That's the most thoughtful and empathetic film I've seen about the mind of a person who arrives at such a decision. It involves an assassination attempt; this one is set against the tide of Indian nationalism.

But it's not really a political film. It's driven by lust, guilt, and shame of a melodramatic sort that was right at home in the silent era. That doesn't mean it's old-fashioned, but that it's broadly melodramatic. It centers on the lives of a British landowner in India, his Indian right-hand man, and his affair with his beautiful young servant woman. Both the man and the woman are married, so there are problems in addition to the taboo against mixing the races and classes.

The man is Henry Moores (Linus Roache), who lives in a big, comfortable house with his wife, Laura (Jennifer Ehle), and young son, Peter (Leo Benedict). Next door lives his assistant, T.K. (Rahul Bose), who has abandoned his roots in the nearby village and cast his lot with the Brits. They run a tea plantation and discover cinnamon higher in the hills. That involves the construction of a road up a steep hillside that must zigzag its way to the top to avoid being washed away in the monsoons.

Laura and Peter are away at the beginning of the film, and Henry and his servant Sajani (Nandita Das) seek honey for their tea in a "sacred grove." They're seen by two talkative young boys and that leads, as it must, to tragedy. Laura and Benjamin return. Sajani is beaten by her husband, who has learned of her secret tryst (but not the identity of her partner). And that sets into motion a series of events involving whom she can trust, whom she can believe, and where she can turn.

SPOILER WARNING: Henry gives T.K. all the money he has on hand and asks him to send Sajani "away." T.K. reports, "I put her in a boat—for the North." But India is a big country, and the North is a distant destination for a woman in a small boat with one oarsman. Sajani, covered in blood, returns in the middle of the night to T.K.'s house, where Henry meets her. He's desperate. The village has reported her "missing," his wife is having suspicions, and when Sajani asks him, "Do you really love me?" he replies, "No." I think he says that for her own good. But she takes a handy pistol and kills herself.

It's in the details that a film reveals its origins. How does that pistol come into her hands? Henry gave it to T.K. in an early scene, and at the midnight meeting T.K. takes it out for no good reason and doesn't even seem to notice as he drops it where her hand can find it. All of this is explained in close-ups. Silent films knew just how to handle such prop deliveries.

Before the Rains is lushly photographed, as we would expect, by Sivan himself. It's told sincerely and with energy. It enjoys its period settings and costumes, and even its conventions. In a movie with plenty of room for it, there isn't a trace of cynicism. I am growing weary (temporarily, I think) of films that are cynical about themselves. Having seen several films recently whose characters have as many realities as shape-shifters, I found it refreshing to see a one-level story told with passion and romanticism.

But I can't quite recommend it. In a plot depending on concealment and secrecy, Henry and T.K. make all the wrong decisions, including a cover-up that almost seems designed to fail. And I didn't even mention the banker who pulls the plug on the financing of the road. That's part of the silent tradition, too: bankers who pull plugs.

Be Kind Rewind ★ ★ ½
PG-13, 101 m., 2008

Jack Black (Jerry), Mos Def (Mike), Danny Glover (Mr. Fletcher), Mia Farrow (Miss Falewicz), Melonie Diaz (Alma). Directed by Michel Gondry and produced by Georges Bermann and Julie Fong. Screenplay by Gondry.

whimsy (n.): Playfully quaint or fanciful behavior or humor.

Michel Gondry's *Be Kind Rewind* is whimsy with a capital W. No, it's WHIMSY in all caps. Make that all-caps italic boldface. Oh, never mind. I'm getting too whimsical. Maybe Gondry does, too. You'll have to decide for yourself. This is a movie that takes place in no possible world, which may be a shame, if not for the movie, then for possible worlds.

The place: Passaic, New Jersey. On a street corner stands a shop so shabby that only an art director could have designed it. This is Be Kind Rewind, a store that rents a skimpy selection of VHS tapes. Not a DVD in sight. It's owned by Mr. Fletcher (Danny Glover), who has convinced himself the store was the birthplace of Fats Waller (identified only as "some old-time jazz musician" on one Web site, which has plainly never heard of him). Behind in his rent, Mr. Fletcher faces eviction, and the store will be pulled down, no doubt to make way for Starbucks or Dunkin' Donuts.

Mr. Fletcher's faithful, long-suffering clerk is Mike (Mos Def), who is entrusted with the store while the owner goes undercover, hoping to scope out the success of the big competitor down the street, West Coast Video. Maybe it's because they rent DVDs? To be in the video rental business and not have heard of DVDs does not speak well for Mr. Fletcher's knowledge of the market, but then we suspect that when we see his store. I was once in a dirt-floored "store and bar" in a poor rural district of Ireland that had a stock of one (1) bottle of Guinness. Same idea.

One of the store's most loyal visitors and nuisances is Jerry (Jack Black), who works nearby in a garage. Paranoid about a power plant next door, he breaks in to sabotage it and is zapped with so much electricity he looks like a lightning strike during one of Victor Frankenstein's experiments. This does not turn him into a cinder, only magnetizes him, after which he visits the store and inadvertently erases all the tapes.

Crisis. What to do before Mr. Fletcher comes back? The tapes can't be replaced, because Mike and Jerry don't have the money and besides, how easy is it to get VHS tapes except on eBay? I take that back. Amazon lists six VHS tapes of *Ghostbusters*, one of the erased movies, for one (1) cent each. At that rate, you could build up a decent VHS library for a dollar. Anyway, the lads have a masterstroke: They will *reenact* the movies and rent them to unsuspecting customers like Miss Falewicz (Mia Farrow), who won't know the difference anyway. Costarring as their female leads in these movies is the fetching Alma (Melonie Diaz), who has the sexiest smile since Rosario Dawson.

The reenactments are not very skillful, to put it mildly, but they have the advantage, as Mike argues, of not taking up all your time because they're as short as twenty minutes. They explain that they import their versions from Sweden, which is why they call them *sweded*. You can see the works of Mike and Jerry on the Web, by the way, which might be about two-thirds as good as seeing the whole movie. One of the perhaps inevitable consequences of reenacting movies is that the exercise brings out all the latent manic excess within Jack Black, who when he is trying that hard reminds me of a dog I know named Mick Q. Broderick, who gets so excited when you come over you have to go to the dry cleaners after every visit.

Whether their scheme works, whether the store is saved, whether Hollywood considers their work homage or piracy, I will leave for you to discover. But you haven't read this far unless you hope to learn whether I would recommend the movie. Not especially. I felt positive and genial while watching it, but I didn't break out in paroxysms of laughter. It's the kind of amusing film you can wait to see on DVD. I wonder if it will come out on VHS?

Big Fan ★★★ ½
R, 88 m., 2009

Patton Oswalt (Paul Aufiero), Kevin Corrigan (Sal), Marcia Jean Kurtz (Theresa Aufiero), Michael Rapaport (Philadelphia Phil), Matt Servitto (Detective Velardi), Gino Cafarelli (Jeff Aufiero), Serafina Fiore (Gina Aufiero), Jonathan Hamm (Quantrell Bishop). Directed by Robert Siegel and produced by Elan Bogarin and Jean Kouremetis. Screenplay by Siegel.

Paul is a short, chubby thirty-five-year-old man who lives with his mother and works the night shift as an attendant at a parking garage. His mother screams at him that he only dates his own right hand. But there is another Paul, "Paul of Staten Island," who is a regular caller to a sports radio station, defending his beloved New York Giants against the hated Eagles fan "Philadelphia Phil." This Paul is proud, articulate, and happy.

He and his best (or only) friend, Sal, never miss a Giants home game. They're tailgaters. They park in the Giants parking lot and watch the game on a TV set that runs off his car battery. Behind them inside the towering stadium walls, the great quarterback Quantrell Bishop leads the Giants toward a championship.

Big Fan, one of the more thought-provoking sports movies I've seen, is the directorial debut of Robert Siegel, who wrote *The Wrestler*. It's a comedy with dark undertones that asks: What kind of a man listens to and calls sports talk radio compulsively, even in the middle of the night? Even out of season? Even on, say, Thanksgiving, or Election Day? He should get a life, do you think? That's what his mother thinks. Paul believes he has a life, a glorious life, as a Fan.

I've known such people. They identify so strongly with their idols that it's a kind of derangement. They *are* their city, their team, their heroes. When their team loses, they bleed. Supporters of a rival team are their enemies. Pro athletes get paid. Pro fans work pro bono. For anyone to describe himself as a team's "number one fan" is kind of pathetic.

One night Paul (Patton Oswalt) and Sal (Kevin Corrigan) are out late eating pizza when they see the great Quantrell Bishop (Jonathan Hamm) at a gas station. They tail him. He is driven to a dicey neighborhood in Staten Island for murky purposes (a cocaine buy, is my guess). Then he drives into Manhattan, and Paul and Sal follow him into a lap-dance emporium. They approach "QB" to praise him, and he's nice enough at first. Then they recklessly tell him they've been following him all the way from the shady neighborhood. Are they implying a shakedown? QB explodes and hammers Paul, who awakens three days later in a hospital after emergency surgery for bleeding in the brain.

QB is suspended. Paul is not eager to testify against him. A detective (Matt Servitto) tries to question him. He says he can't remember. "Can't—or won't?" the cop asks. His hunch is correct. When Paul's shyster brother files a multimillion-dollar lawsuit against QB, Paul refuses to cooperate. He can't think of Quantrell Bishop as the man who nearly killed him. That's because, in a sense, Paul *is* Quantrell Bishop. Without QB, there is no Paul there.

And then the film follows Paul more deeply into the consequences of his obsession. I will leave you to discover for yourself what happens. I've seen films about fanatic sports fans before, in particular frightening films about British football hooligans, who organize into armed gangs and battle with one another. Paul is a more common American type, one who is especially tiresome to sportswriters, whom they zero in on with a combination of fascination and resentment: Who are you to pass judgment on my team?

Patton Oswalt, best known as a stand-up comedian, brings a kind of brilliance to his performance. He plays a man limited in curiosity, confidence, and ambition. He sounds good on the radio because he's listened to thousands of hours of sports radio, which largely comes down to the same verbal formulas repeated time and again. Alone in his toll booth late at night, he scripts words for "Paul from Staten Island" and reads from legal pads, striding back and forth in his bedroom while his mother, next door, shouts for him to shut up so she can get some sleep.

This isn't only, or even, a sports movie. It's about leading a life vicariously. There's a movie called *Surrogate*, about a future time when people recline at home hooked up to brain sensors, and lead their lives through more attractive and younger android versions of themselves. This practice is going on now. Quantrell Bishop is Paul's surrogate. Discon-

nect him, and Paul is a body on a bed, dreaming with his right hand.

Bigger, Stronger, Faster ★ ★ ★ ½
PG-13, 106 m., 2008

A documentary directed by Christopher Bell and produced by Alex Buono, Tasmin Rawady, and Jim Czarnecki. Screenplay by Bell, Buono, and Rawady.

Midway through watching Chris Bell's *Bigger, Stronger, Faster,* I started to think about another film I'd seen recently. The Bell documentary is about the use of steroids in sports and bodybuilding. The other film is Darryl Roberts's *America the Beautiful,* about the guilt some women feel because they don't look like the models in fashion magazines. The steroid users want to be bigger. The weight-obsessed women want to be thinner. The Roberts doc focuses on Gerren Taylor, who at twelve achieved fame as a child who looked like an adult fashion model. A year later, she was dropped by those who cast for runway models, but she tried to make a comeback. At thirteen.

Bell is one of three brothers. They've all used steroids, and two still do. Mike ("Mad Dog") Bell had some success in pro wrestling but never as the star, always as the scripted loser. Wrestling has dropped him, but he's still in training, even though he's now "too old," he's told. "I was born to attain greatness," he tells Chris, "and I'm the only one that's holding myself back."

The third Bell brother, Mark ("Smelly") Bell, has promised his wife he will stop taking steroids after he achieves his dream of powerlifting seven hundred pounds. He attains it, but later tells Chris he will use steroids again. Chris tells him, "I'm afraid you'll lose your job, your wife, and yourself." Smelly replies, "If I lose my job and my wife, what else do I have but myself?" Both of Chris's brothers are remarkably frank in talking to him, as are his parents, who are "opposed to steroids" but are red-faced with cheering after Smelly lifts the weights.

Bell uses a clip from the movie *Patton,* in which the famous general addresses his troops: "Americans love a winner and will not tolerate a loser." That is the bottom line of *Bigger, Stronger, Faster*. We say we're opposed to steroids, but we're more opposed to losing. Steroids are not nearly as dangerous as amphetamines, he points out, but the United States is the only nation that *requires* its fighter pilots to use amphetamines. They may be harmful, but they work.

This movie is remarkable in that it seems to be interested only in facts. I was convinced that Bell was interviewing people who knew a lot about steroids, and the weight of scientific, medical, and psychological opinion seems to be that steroids are not particularly dangerous. Is the movie "pro-steroid"? Yes, but it is even more against the win-win mentality. We demand that our athletes bring home victories, and yet to compete on a level playing field, they feel they have to use the juice.

The movie goes against the drumbeat of anti-steroid publicity, news reports, and congressional hearings to say that steroids are not only generally safe but have been around longer and been used more widely than most people know. Bell and his brothers grew up pudgy in a Poughkeepsie family, were mesmerized by early heroes like Hulk Hogan, Rambo, and Conan the Barbarian, got into weight-lifting, and still have muscular physiques. They all used muscles as a powerful boost to their self-esteem.

But think for a second. *America the Beautiful* quotes this statistic: "Three minutes of looking at a fashion magazine makes 90 percent of women of all ages feel depressed, guilty, and shameful." I don't have similar statistics about bodybuilders, but I assume they study the muscle magazines with similar feelings. Those who cannot be too thin or too muscular are attracted to opposite extremes but use the same reasoning: By pursuing an ideal that is almost unattainable and may be dangerous to their health, they believe they will be admired, successful, the object of envy.

Bell interviews some bodybuilders who are over fifty, maybe sixty, and still "in training." The words "in training" suggest that a competition is approaching, but they're in training against themselves. Against their body's desire to pump less iron, eat different foods, process fewer proteins, and, in general, find moderation. Anorexia represents one extreme of this

reasoning. At another extreme is Gregg Valentino, who has the world's largest biceps; they look like sixteen-inch softballs straining against his skin. He makes fun of himself: He walks into a club and no chick is gonna go for that, "but the dudes come over." There are men who envy him.

What's sad is that success in both fashion and bodybuilding is so limiting. For every Arnold Schwarzenegger, who used the Mr. Universe crown to catapult himself into movie and political stardom, there are hundreds, thousands who spend their lives "in training." When a model gets thin enough (few do, especially in their own minds), they must spend their lives staying that thin.

The question vibrating below the surface of both docs is, has America become maddened by the need for victory? When our team is in the World Series, do we seriously give a damn what the home run kings have injected? We are devout in Congress, but heathens in the grandstands. That is one of Bell's messages, and the other is that steroids have become demonized far beyond their actual danger to society. Which side do you vote on? Chris Bell marks his ballot twice: Steroids are not very harmful, but by using them, we reveal a disturbing value system.

Big Man Japan ★ ★ ★ ½
PG-13, 113 m., 2009

Hitosi Matumoto (Dai Sato), Riki Takeuchi (Jumpy Monster), Ua (Sato's Manager), Ryunosuke Kamiki (Baby Monster), Itsuji Itao (Smelly Monster). Directed by Hitoshi Matsumoto and produced by Akihiko Okamoto. Screenplay by Matsumoto and Mitsuyoshi Takasu.

Well, I guess this is the movie I've been asking for. Whenever I see a superhero epic, I'm always nagged by logical questions—like, when the Incredible Hulk becomes enormous, how do his undershorts also expand? *Big Man Japan* answers that question with admirable clarity. Before Big Man grows, workers winch an enormous pair of undershorts up on two poles, and he straddles the crotch. Then he expands to fill them. Had to be something like that.

The movie, which is very funny in an insidious way, takes the form of a slice-of-life documentary about Dai Sato (Hitosi Matumoto), the latest generation in a Tokyo dynasty of monster killers. He is a quiet, introverted, unhappy man, whose wife has left him and taken away their daughter. He lives alone in cluttered bachelor squalor. Nothing much happens, but he's always on call, and when the Department of Defense needs him, he has to rush to the nearest power plant, be zapped with massive bolts of electricity, and grow into a giant ready to battle the latest monster with his only weapon, a steel club.

These are some monsters. One has expanding cables for arms, embraces skyscrapers, pulls them out of the ground, and throws them over his back. Then he has to flick his comb-over back in place. One consists of a giant body and one foot, with which he jumps on things. One exudes an overpowering stink. One breathes fire and looks like Hellboy. One has a single giant eyeball on a long stem hanging from its crotch, and wields it like a bola.

These monsters come from who knows where, and when they die we see their souls take flight and ascend to heaven. Their battles take place in cities that look gloriously like phony special effects, and unlike most monster movies with terrified mobs, these streets and buildings do not have a single person visible.

In contrast with the action scenes, the movie takes the form of a downbeat doc about the nightmare of being Big Man. Dai Sato never gets time off. He isn't paid much. He raises cash from TV specials about his fights and selling advertising space among his tattoos. People hate him for stepping on things, soiling the environment, and disturbing the peace. His TV ratings are down. He wonders why his agent, a chain-smoking, cell phone–addicted woman, has a new car but he takes the train. His only company comes from professional geishas.

Matumoto plays the role absolutely on the straight and level. So do all of the human characters. He is as concerned about the practical problems of being a superhero as I am. The film takes, or seems to take, his dilemma with utter seriousness. Matumoto is also the writer and director, and it becomes clear that he is satirizing three genres: the personal documentary, monster movies, and reality TV. And he does this slyly, with a scalpel instead of a hatchet. Only the monsters are over the top, and are they ever. The weird thing is that thanks to CGI, some of them have worried, middle-aged human faces on their grotesque bodies.

Note: Something has been nagging you. That name Matumoto doesn't seem quite right. You would be correct. Hitosi Matumoto's real name is Hitoshi Matsumoto, but he misspells both names in the credits. Little joke. Think Ada Sadler. He's a popular Japanese comedian. I hope all his overseas viewers get the joke.

Birdwatchers ★★★
NO MPAA RATING, 102 m., 2010

Claudio Santamaria (Roberto), Alicelia Batista Cabreira (Lia), Chiara Caselli (Beatrice), Abrisio da Silva Pedro (Osvaldo), Ademilson Concianza Verga (Ireneu), Ambrosio Vilhalva (Nadio), Fabiane Pereira da Silva (Maria), Leonardo Medeires (Lucas Moreira). Directed by Marco Bechis and produced by Bechis, Caio Gullane, Fabiano Gullane, and Amedeo Pagani. Screenplay by Bechis and Luiz Bolognesi.

There's an opening overhead shot of the Brazilian rain forest, dense and limitless. As a tourist boat slides along a river, native Indians materialize on the banks to regard it reproachfully. They hold bows and arrows and don't seem fond of these visitors. But hold on; one of the young men has a layered haircut with the top blond.

As recently as the 1970s, when Herzog filmed *Aguirre* in such a forest, these Indians would have been "real." But the time is the present and the forest a preserved facade shielding fields, which have been stripped of trees and devoted to farming. The Indians can, if they want, pile into the back of a truck and hire out as day laborers. But all of their traditions center on the forest and its spirits, and this new life is alienating. Some simply commit suicide.

This is all true, as we have been told time and again, and meanwhile the Brazilian government remains benevolent toward the destruction of the planet's richest home of life forms and its crucial oxygen source. Indians have been stripped of ownership of their ancestral lands and assigned to reservations far from the bones of their parents; it is the same genocide the United States practiced, for those with power have not developed a conscience in the years since.

Marco Bechis's *Birdwatchers* is a ground-level drama involving a group of Indians that packs up one day, leaves "their" federal land, and builds shelters of tree limbs and plastic sheets on farmland that once was their tribe's. This goes down badly with the farmer, who with his family lives in a spacious home with a pool and (Indian) servants.

The film portrays the descendants of colonialists very broadly; its strength is in the directness of the performances by Indians. I assume their performances are informed by actual life experience, because Bechis shot on location with local nonactors. They're cohesive in the group, grow depressed when separated from it, are attuned to spirit omens (or believe they are, which amounts to the same thing). Without conversational preludes, they say bluntly what they mean: "I want to be with you, you're a big dick man, you must leave here and never return."

This doesn't mean they lack subtlety. It means they keep a lot of things to themselves. We follow two adolescent boys, Osvaldo (Abrisio da Silva Pedro) and Ireneu (Ademilson Concianza Verga), the first the son of the leader, the second he of the haircut and a yearning for sneakers. The leader, Nadio (Ambrosio Vilhalva), is strong enough to lead the group onto the farmlands, enforce discipline, and deal with many newcomers. But he's an alcoholic, his booze happily supplied by a merchant who controls them by giving credit. Shades of the company store.

Sex is in the air. The farmer's teenage daughter, in a bikini, and one of the boys, in a loincloth, begin meeting at the river, he to collect water, she to swim, and although they don't get very far, an intriguing tension is there between them. On both sides there is the allure of unfamiliarity.

The group is chronically low on food and funds, and Nadio correctly realizes that day labor is a form of bondage. He begins to call his followers "the movement." Sooner or later there will be a clash and there is, but one that unfolds in a way unique to these people.

Birdwatchers is impressively filmed and never less than interesting. If it has a weakness, it's that this is a familiar sermon: Save the rain forest. Respect its inhabitants. Bechis and his cowriter, Luiz Bolognesi, don't really develop the characters much beyond their functions. But the reality of the Indians and the locations adds its own strength.

Note: I learn from the press notes that the European-sounding sacred music was composed by Domenico Zipoli, an Italian Jesuit who lived with this same Guarani tribe in the 1700s.

The Black Balloon ★ ★ ★

PG-13, 97 m., 2009

Rhys Wakefield (Thomas Mollison), Luke Ford (Charlie Mollison), Gemma Ward (Jackie Masters), Erik Thomson (Simon Mollison), Toni Collette (Maggie Mollison). Directed by Elissa Down and produced by Tristram Miall. Screenplay by Down and Jimmy Jack.

At the center of *The Black Balloon* is Toni Collette's performance as the mother of an autistic son. The way she meets this challenge opens a way to understand all the other characters. Her son, Charlie, can be sweet and lovable. He can also make life for his family all but unbearable. Collette, as his mother, Maggie, has been dealing with him for seventeen years and seems to have long ago made her peace with the fact that Charlie is who he is and is not going to change. As his mother, she loves him.

The film is concerned largely with how her other son, Thomas (Rhys Wakefield), exists with his brother. Tom is a military brat, used to new towns and new schools, affable but shy. He shares the burden of Charlie (Luke Ford), cares for him, loves him, but is ashamed of him. Thomas is at just that point in adolescence when he's acutely conscious of all his defects, and in teenage social terms, Charlie is a defect.

In an acutely embarrassing scene, Thomas is revealed during a swimming class as a sixteen-year-old who cannot swim. This makes him a target for other students, who like many teenagers are quick to mock. One girl is nice to him. This is Jackie (Gemma Ward), a tall blonde who quietly makes it clear that she likes Thomas. Thomas doesn't really know how to deal with this, but his first instinct is to try to hide Charlie from her. And a crisis is building at home; his mom is pregnant again, his dad, Simon (Erik Thomson), insists on bed rest for her, and when Simon is away the burden of running the household falls on Thomas.

The Black Balloon establishes this family with a delicate mixture of tenderness and pain. Charlie is not made into a cute movie creature. He cannot speak, he cannot control his rages, he can have instant, violent mood changes. He runs through the neighborhood in his underpants. He throws a tantrum in a supermarket. He rubs his feces into the carpet. Thomas is supposed to protect Charlie from himself and perform the damage control.

The story elements of *The Black Balloon* could have been manipulated to make the film false and cute. In some circles, that would be interpreted as upbeat. The film tries to be true. The uplift comes in how the family, and Jackie, respond to Charlie. Maggie and Simon are strongly bonded in a marriage that has survived Charlie. They have no time for nobility; they are focused on doing what needs to be done. Charlie is theirs and will not be stored in a "facility." Thomas agrees with this, but he has a breaking point.

It is Jackie who turns out to be special. Although Gemma Ward, who plays her, is a well-known model and this is her first substantial role, there is nothing of the professional model in her performance. She creates a spontaneously warm young woman who cares for Thomas, sympathizes with him, accepts Charlie without question, and helps Charlie accept himself.

Luke Ford's performance as Charlie is a convincing tour de force. You may recall him as Brendan Fraser's heroic son in *The Mummy: Tomb of the Dragon Emperor*. Rhys Wakefield, in his first feature role, is a good casting decision, suggesting inner turmoil without overacting. But it is Toni Collette who explains, without even seeming to try, why this family is still together at all.

Elissa Down, who directed and cowrote the film, reportedly has two autistic brothers. Her experience informs this story, particularly in the way enormous pressure is brought to bear on the family. Perhaps she wrote from experience about how the two parents begin with unconditional love; how rare to see a happy, long-surviving marriage in a movie, where so often the father is flawed. Rare, too, and a tribute to the Australian film industry, to see a film that doesn't allow star power to compromise its vision.

The mainstream cinema would no doubt be eager to employ Gemma Ward in a no-brainer teeny romcom. She made the right choice here and seems poised to follow the example of another onetime model, Nicole Kidman, in treating herself seriously and not getting lost in the soul-deadening life of a professional model.

Black Dynamite ★★★
R, 90 m., 2009

Michael Jai White (Black Dynamite), Kym Whitley (Honey Bee), Tommy Davidson (Cream Corn), Kevin Chapman (O'Leary), Byron Minns (Bullhorn), Salli Richardson (Gloria), Cedric Yarbrough (Giddy Up), Mykelti Williamson (Chicago Wind), Brian McKnight (Sweet Meat), Bokeem Woodbine (Back Hand Jack), Arsenio Hall (Tasty Freeze), John Salley (Kotex), James McManus (Richard M. Nixon), Nicole Sullivan (Patricia Nixon). Directed by Scott Sanders and produced by Jenny Wiener Steingart and Jon Steingart. Screenplay by Sanders, Michael Jai White, and Byron Minns, from a story by White and Minns.

I've seen a *lot* of 1970s blaxploitation films, and I'm here to tell you that *Black Dynamite* gets it mostly right, and when it's wrong, it's wrong on purpose and knows just knows what it's doing. It's one of those loving modern retreads of older genre movies.

It's built around a pitch-perfect leading man, Michael Jai White, who has been kicking around in movies for twenty years and apparently building those muscles in his time. That means he effortlessly evokes real blaxploitation stars such as Fred Williamson, who kicked around in thankless roles before hammering villains to death in urban action movies. White has a *Shaft* moustache and like all of the characters is dressed in 1970s gaucherie: oversize hats, bell bottoms, bling, shades, and unbuttoned or missing shirts in patterns resembling a hippie's ideal of wallpaper.

The women are also dressed in period, and many have big Afros. I am happy to say it brings back an element sadly missing in recent movies, gratuitous nudity. Sexy women would "happen" to be topless in the 1970s movies for no better reason than that everyone agreed, including themselves, that their breasts were a genuine pleasure to regard—the most beautiful naturally occurring shapes in nature, I believe. Now we see breasts only in serious films, for expressing reasons. There's been such a comeback for the strategically positioned bedsheet you'd think we were back in the 1950s.

The plot is deliberately fashioned to seem familiar. Michael Jai White plays Black Dynamite, a one-man street army who wants vengeance for the death of his kid brother (named Jimmy, as so many kid brothers are). Jimmy was killed by drug dealers, protected by The Man, of course. Black Dynamite has lethal chops, socks, fists, kicks, elbows, forearms, and, it goes without saying, a .44 Magnum, which you will recall from Dirty Harry "is the most powerful handgun in the world." He's a formidable fighter and a charming playa, leading to gratifying interludes with such babes as Gloria (Salli Richardson) and Honey Bee (Kym Whitley).

Honey Bee's name reminds us that many 1970s characters had names that were actually more like titles. Nobody was ever "Mike" or "Phil." Here we get Cream Corn (Tommy Davidson as a wildly politically incorrect gay man), and such others as Bullhorn, Giddy Up, Chicago Wind, Sweet Meat, Back Hand Jack, Tasty Freeze, Kotex, and Richard M. Nixon. No, wait, Richard M. Nixon isn't a nickname, as Dynamite discovers during a showdown in the Oval Office. One would like to know more about how these nicknames were earned, especially in the case of Chicago Wind.

The movie looks and sounds so much like 1970s blaxploitation that anyone finding it while cable surfing could be excused for assuming it is one. Technical expertise has been used to meticulously reproduce such details as an oversaturated color scheme, bonus camera moves, smash cuts to close-ups on big lines, and dramatic camera angles. There's also "Mickey Mouse music," so called because whatever the hero does, the music does it too. Black Dynamite even has his own theme—three fearsome chords whenever *Dynamite* needs to underlined.

Why the plot leads us to the White House is actually less interesting than how. There is a pathetic orphanage where the children use drugs, perhaps to train them as users who will be dealers. So you see the kind of evil Black Dynamite is up against. But he's the man to Take Back the Streets.

Blindness ★ ½
R, 120 m., 2008

Julianne Moore (Doctor's Wife), Mark Ruffalo (Doctor), Alice Braga (Woman with Dark Glasses), Danny Glover (Man with Black Eye Patch), Gael Garcia Bernal (Bartender/King of Ward Three). Directed by Fernando Meirelles and produced by Niv Fichman, Andrea Barata Ribeiro, and Sonoko Sakai. Screenplay by Don McKellar, based on the novel by Jose Saramago.

Blindness is one of the most unpleasant, not to say unendurable, films I've ever seen. It is a metaphor about a group of people who survive under great stress, but frankly, I would rather have seen them perish than sit through the final three-quarters of the film. Not only is it despairing and sickening, it's ugly. Denatured, sometimes overexposed, sometimes too shadowy to see, it is an experiment to determine how much you can fool with a print before ending up with mud, intercut with brightly lit milk.

In an unspecified city (Toronto, mostly), an unspecified cause spreads blindness through the population. First a driver goes blind at a traffic light. Then his eye doctor goes blind. And so on, until just about the entire population is blind, except for the doctor's wife. Three wards in a prison are filled with people who are quarantined; armed guards watch them. Then I guess the guards go blind. I am reminded of my Latin teacher, Mrs. Link, making us memorize a phrase every day:

Pone seram, prohibe. Sed quis custodiet ipsos custodes?*

Many of the imprisoned survivors soon descend into desperation and hunger. The big problem is with Ward Three and its savage leader (Gael Garcia Bernal). Finding a gun, he confiscates all the food and sells it to Ward One in return for jewelry and sexual favors. Oddly enough, I don't recall Ward Two, unless Ward Three was Ward Two and I missed Ward Three, and who cares?

Oh, what an ordeal. Clothes falling off. Nude in the cold. People fighting, dying, and raping. Blundering around and tripping over things. Hitting their heads. Being struck by pipes they don't see coming, swung by people who don't know what they're swinging at. In the midst of the hellhole is the doctor's wife (Julianne Moore), who doesn't know why she can still see, but loyally stays with her husband.

Is she a symbol of a person with sight leading the blind against the evildoers? Ouch, I stumbled! Who put that there? Maybe that's what she is. In a film that doesn't even try to explain the blindness (not that it could), there's room for nothing but symbols and metaphors and the well-diversified group we identify with, which includes an Asian couple (Yusuke Iseya and Yoshino Kimura), the doctor and his wife (Mark Ruffalo and Moore), a wise old black man (Danny Glover), a single woman (Alice Braga), a boy (Mitchell Nye), and a dog (uncredited).

And the noise. Lordy! This is a sound track so aggressive I was cringing in my seat. No merciful slumber during this film. Metal clangs, glass shatters, bullets are fired, people scream, and the volume of these sounds seems cranked up compared to the surrounding dialogue, like they do with TV commercials. My eyes, ears, and patience were assaulted. My hands and feet, OK.

What a pedigree this film has. Directed by Fernando Meirelles. Based on the novel by Portugal's Jose Saramago, winner of the 1998 Nobel Prize. I learn he long resisted offers to make his book into a movie. Not long enough. It is my good fortune to be attending a screening tonight of the newly restored print of *The Godfather*. I'm looking forward to the peace and quiet.

54

*Lock her up; put away the key. But who will guard the guards?

—Juvenal

Mrs. Link told me that someday, and that day may never come, I'd call upon that phrase to do a service for me.

Blood Done Sign My Name ★★★

PG-13, 128 m., 2010

Rick Schroder (Vernon Tyson), Nate Parker (Ben Chavis), Nick Searcy (Robert Teel), Lela Rochon (Roseanna Allen), Afemo Omilami (Golden Frinks), Darrin Dewitt Henson (Eddie McCoy), Michael Rooker (Billy Watkins), Gattlin Griffith (Tim Tyson). Directed by Jeb Stuart and produced by Mel Efros, Jeb Stuart, and Mari Stuart. Screenplay by Jeb Stuart, based on the book by Tim Tyson.

In 1970 in Oxford, North Carolina, it was perfectly possible for a young black man to be beaten and clubbed by three whites, and shot dead by one of them. And for an all-white jury to hear from two eyewitnesses, and watch the white defendant's young son break down in tears and confess his testimony had been forced on him by his father's lawyers. And for the jury to vote unanimously that the white man was not guilty.

Blood Done Sign My Name tells the story of that murder, and how it was a catalyst for change in Oxford and in the lives of those who lived there. It's based on a memoir by the son of a liberal white Methodist preacher, and there's a scene in the film that has details I'm pretty sure the son witnessed when he was a boy.

His father said he wanted to show him something. They crept behind a rock and observed a Ku Klux Klan meeting. A cross was being erected. "It's a revival!" young Tim Tyson said. "No, it's not a revival," his father said, and that night they watched the cross being burned. The part I believe he remembers was this: The whole event was treated as a family picnic, with kids playing and mothers unpacking picnic hampers, and the sickness of racism almost *looking* like a revival.

The film tells two parallel stories. One involves a young black man who graduates from college and comes home to Oxford to teach at a black high school (black, although the schools had in theory been integrated). This is Ben Chavis (Nate Parker), who later became the president of the NAACP. The other is Vernon Tyson (Rick Schroder), the minister, who lost his congregation because of his liberal views, but found other churches in North Carolina and retired only recently. His son, Tim, went on to become a scholar of African-American studies and now teaches at Duke.

I go into biographical details because the events in 1970 are clearly remembered by Chavis and the younger Tyson as the turning points in their lives. The civil rights movement sent Golden Frinks (Afemo Omilami), an "outside agitator," to Oxford to organize the black community after the murder. He led a historic march fifty miles from Oxford to Raleigh, the state capital, where the governor refused to meet with the marchers—but the point had been made.

Unlike a more conventional film, *Blood Done Sign My Name* doesn't end with the courtroom verdict. It starts there, as Chavis leads an economic boycott of stores that took black dollars and valued black customers but hired no blacks in a county that was 40 percent African-American.

The movie tells this story in a traditional, straightforward way. No fancy footwork. No chewing the scenery. Meat and potatoes, you could say, but it's thoughtful and moving. The writer and director, Jeb Stuart, focuses on the events and people and lets them speak for themselves. He uses a level, unforgiving gaze.

Apart from the Oxford racists, his only major white characters are the minister and his family. And they're rather remote from the turmoil. Rev. Tyson invites the president of a black college to speak to his congregation, which clears out half the Christians pretty quickly, and then his son recorded these momentous days in his book.

Ben Chavis is energized and angered, but it's clear the prime mover was Golden Frinks, also a real man, whose full-time job, you could say, was outside agitating. The day of the trial, he tells Chavis he's on his way to another town: "It's up to you now." And that's what happened, essentially: The civil rights marchers led the way for the rise of a black middle class in the South.

In the opening scenes of the film, you assume the stories of Chavis and the Tyson family will connect. They don't. Each man undoubtedly knew about the other, but they were on paths that didn't intersect. I guess that's the way it was. By the time Oxford began to change, Rev. Tyson had an African-American congregation elsewhere in the state. One story at a time, things change.

Those born in 1970 will be forty this year. The acquittal of white racists by all-white juries is no longer the Southern routine. It took unpopular and courageous actions by a lot of people to bring about that change, and it is not yet complete. But it happened, and I think Tim Tyson, who isn't fifty yet, wrote his book to say it happened. If you know how to look, history doesn't take place too fast to be seen.

Blood: The Last Vampire ★★★
R, 89 m., 2009

Gianna (Saya), Allison Miller (Alice McKee), Liam Cunningham (Michael), J. J. Field (Luke), Koyuki (Onigen), Yasuaki Kurata (Kato Takatora), Larry Lamb (General McKee). Directed by Chris Nahon and produced by William Kong and Abel Nahmias. Screenplay by Chris Chow, based on the 2001 anime film.

Saya is sixteen and has been sixteen for a very long time. What's interesting about teenage vampires, such as the hero of *Twilight*, is that they're frozen in time while old enough to be sexy, but too young to have developed a complex sensibility. Apparently your maturation is put on hold along with your appearance, since Saya is four hundred years old.

In *Blood: The Last Vampire*, her life has been a thankless slog through the extermination of demons that have plagued Japan down through the centuries. Whether these demons are vampires is a good question. I suppose so; the movie is a little hazy on its definition of vampires. Saya, for example, must be a vampire since she drinks bottled blood supplied to her by a shadowy Council.

Saya (Gianna) doesn't personally sink fangs into anyone, but there must be sad goings-on back at the bottling works. No matter; since the demons/vampires prey on human victims and she eviscerates them with her invincible swordplay, she can fairly be considered the solution and not the problem. They must not be quick studies if they haven't figured out after four hundred years of immortality that Saya never loses. They are witless creatures, and Saya is bright and attractive, perhaps because she's half vampire and half human (never mind the rules say the two don't mix).

The movie is surprisingly entertaining. It's an international hybrid. Filmed in Hong Kong and Argentina, set in Japan, mostly in English, with a French director, a Chinese writer, a beautiful Korean star (Gianna, known in her homeland as Jeon Ji-hyun), a Japanese villainess (Koyuki as the evil Onigen), and an otherwise American cast, it has a plot that conveniently explains why this is: The Council has assigned Saya to an American military base where the vampires have been focusing their attention.

The plot makes sense, I guess, but is inconsequential, serving as a laundry line on which to hang action sequences. These are mostly cut too quickly to emulate the grace of classic martial arts films, which can approach a sort of impossible ballet. That may be because Gianna is never really convincing as a martial artist, although she sure looks great.

What we're seeing is the price we pay for CGI. When computer graphics make anything seem possible, they are overused to the point where they make everything look impossible. In classic kung fu films, we knew the actors were shot from angles to enhance their movements, were suspended from invisible wires, were often stuntmen, but were in some sense really there. Now they're essentially replaced in action scenes by very realistic animation. This devalues actual achievement. I remember praising Ang Lee for the "astonishing realism" of his treetop swordfight in *Crouching Tiger, Hidden Dragon*, only to be told: Those were the actors themselves, suspended by wires from cranes. The rooftop chase was really happening, too.

Blood: The Last Vampire is essentially a CGI fantasy, pleasing to the eye, and indeed based on a well-known 2001 Japanese anime. Gianna holds it together with a sympathetic performance, trying to win acceptance as the only Japanese girl in an otherwise all-American student body in the school on the U.S.

military base. It doesn't help her fit in when she dresses for her first day in a sailor suit; her wardrobe ideas must have become fixed in the *Madame Butterfly* era. Still, you gotta admit she's fetching.

This isn't a great movie. But it's sincere as an entertainment, it looks good, it's atmospheric, and I will perk up the next time I hear Gianna is in a picture. There probably cannot be a sequel, however, since in this film she seems to be putting herself out of a job. Oops, I gave away the title.   ☞

Body of Lies ★ ★ ★
R, 129 m., 2008

Leonardo DiCaprio (Roger Ferris), Russell Crowe (Ed Hoffman), Mark Strong (Hani Salaam), Golshifteh Farahani (Aisha), Oscar Isaac (Bassam), Alon Aboutboul (Al Saleem), Simon McBurney (Garland). Directed by Ridley Scott and produced by Scott and Donald De Line. Screenplay by William Monahan, based on the novel by David Ignatius.

If you take a step back from the realistic locations and terse dialogue, Ridley Scott's *Body of Lies* is a James Bond plot inserted into today's headlines. The film wants to be persuasive in its expertise about modern spy craft, terrorism, the CIA, and Middle East politics. But its hero is a lone ranger who operates in three countries, single-handedly creates a fictitious terrorist organization, and survives explosions, gunfights, and brutal torture. Oh, and he falls in love with a local beauty. And, of course, he speaks Arabic well enough to pass for a local.

This is Roger Ferris (Leonardo DiCaprio), who seems to operate as a self-directed freelancer in the war against a deadly terrorist organization (obviously a double for al-Qaida). His brainstorm is to fabricate a rival terrorist organization out of thin air, fabricate a fictitious leader for it, create a convincing evidence trail, and use it to smoke out Al Saleem, the secretive leader of the real terrorists (a surrogate for bin Laden). Why will Al Saleem risk everything to come out of hiding? Jealousy, I think. Guarding his turf.

I can imagine a similar story as told by John Le Carre, even right down to the local beauty.

Some of the characters seem worthy of Le Carre, especially Hoffman (Russell Crowe), Ferris's CIA handler, and Hani Salaam (Mark Strong), the brilliant and urbane head of Jordanian security. But Le Carre would never be guilty of such preposterous thriller-style action. Here we have a spy who doesn't come in from the cold, crossed with Jason Bourne.

The most intriguing aspect of Ferris's activities is his growing disillusionment with them. He feels one local comrade has been abandoned to death, and after he sets up an innocent architect to unwittingly play the head of the fictitious terrorist agency, he single-handedly tries to save his life from an inevitable attack. That Ferris survives this man's fate is highly unlikely. And it leads to a situation where his own life is saved by the last-second arrival of the cavalry.

The movie depends on two electronic wonderments. One is the ability of Ferris to maintain instant, effortless cell phone contact with Hoffman, back in Washington. Wearing one of those ear-mounted devices, he seems to keep up a running conversation with his boss, even during perilous situations (his boss is often distracted by taking care of his kids).

The other wonderment is aerial surveillance so precise it can see a particular man walking down a street. The surveillance POV is so stable it's hard to believe it originates from a fast-moving high-altitude spy plane. In discussing Ridley Scott's superior *Black Hawk Down* (2002), I questioned the infrared technology that allowed distant commanders to monitor troop movements on the ground. Many readers informed me that was based on fact. Perhaps the astonishing images in *Body of Lies* is accurate; if so, it's only another step to locating Bin Laden with an aerial eyeball scan.

Ferris's romance in Amman involves a pretty nurse named Aisha (Golshifteh Farahani), who cares for him after he nearly dies in a blast. (One nice touch: A surgeon removes something from his arm and explains, "Bone fragment. Not yours.") The movie is realistic in showing a Muslim woman's difficulties in dating a Westerner; spying eyes are everywhere. It is less realistic in establishing why they are willing to take such a risk, since they're allowed no meaningful conversations to create their relationship. Aisha obviously exists as a convenience of the plot and to set up the film's overwhelmingly unlikely conclusion.

The acting is convincing. DiCaprio makes Ferris almost believable in the midst of absurdities; the screenplay by William Monahan, based on the novel by David Ignatius, portrays him as a man who grows to reject the Iraq war and the role of the CIA in it. Crowe, who gained fifty pounds for his role, always dangerous for a beer drinker, is a remorselessly logical CIA operative. And I particularly admired the work of Mark Strong as the suave Jordanian intelligence chief, who likes little cigars, shady nightclubs, and pretty women, but is absolutely in command of his job.

The bottom line: *Body of Lies* contains enough you can believe, or almost believe, that you wish so much of it weren't sensationally implausible. No one man can withstand such physical ordeals as Ferris undergoes in this film, and I didn't even mention the attack by a pack of possibly rabid dogs. Increasing numbers of thrillers seem to center on heroes who are masochists surrounded by sadists, and I'm growing weary of the horror! Oh, the horror!

Boogie Man: The Lee Atwater Story ★ ★ ★ ½

NO MPAA RATING, 86 m., 2008

Featuring Tucker Eskew, Howard Fineman, Ed Rollins, Michael Dukakis, Eric Alterman, Sam Donaldson, Tom Turnipseed, Terry McAuliffe, Robert Novak, Ishmael Reed, and Mary Matalin. A documentary directed by Stefan Forbes and produced by Forbes and Noland Walker.

When he was a little boy, Lee Atwater pulled an electric cord, and a fryer full of hot grease fell on his little brother Joe, killing him. "He said he heard those screams every single day for the rest of his life," a friend remembers. "He grew up in a world without mercy."

A plausible case can be made that Lee Atwater was the greatest single influence on American politics in the past forty years. He was instrumental in the elections of Ronald Reagan and George H. W. Bush. Karl Rove and Bush 43 were his protégés. It is universally acknowledged that he wrote the modern Republican playbook. "If he had lived," a friend believes, "Bill Clinton would never have been elected president." Atwater predicted before anyone else that Clinton would be the greatest threat to Bush 41. He took the Clintons' Whitewater investment, in which they lost their entire $28,000, and made it the target of a $70 million federal investigation, which produced little of interest except a campaign talking point.

The funny thing was, Atwater didn't much care if he was a Republican or a Democrat. It was only about winning. Looking for opportunities in college, he picked the Young Republicans because there were fewer of them and better opportunities for him. Ever since he managed a campaign for class president in high school, he found himself more at home behind the scenes. In the Young Republicans, he managed Karl Rove's campaign to lead the organization. Members of the YRs at the time believe Rove probably lost, but say Atwater stole the election and then placed the decision into the hands of Vice President George H. W. Bush, who decided in favor of Rove.

Soon he was inside the GOP national party. Having helped Reagan survive Iran-Contra, he more or less appointed himself Bush 41's campaign adviser. He created the infamous Willie Horton ads when Bush ran against Dukakis, and floated rumors that Dukakis was against the Pledge of Allegiance. Asked at the time about the labeling of Dukakis as unpatriotic, young Bush 43 said to call him that would be a "mis-adjective."

Even while running Bush 41's campaign, Atwater was never admitted to the Bush inner circle; Barbara Bush distrusted him, and he came close to being fired. Then Bush started winning primaries. Remembering that presidential year, the Republican strategist Mary Matalin says: "Bush was a wimp and a wuss. Atwater was a hick and a hack." Atwater perfected at that time the technique of the "push poll," where the question itself served to spread suspicion ("Do you believe Gov. Dukakis opposes saluting the flag?"). He and George W. Bush became fast friends soon after they met, Rove adopted his tactics, and Atwater's posthumous influence could be seen in the swift-boating of John Kerry.

Boogie Man: The Lee Atwater Story, a

remarkable documentary directed by Stefan Forbes, uses interviews with Atwater's targets and, especially, his old comrades, to paint a remarkable portrait of Atwater, who was charming, funny, smart, and a good enough blues musician to play on David Letterman and cut an album with B. B. King. He was also tortured and driven, and a bipartisan backstabber. Ed Rollins, Atwater's White House boss at the time, says in the doc that Atwater leaked a false story to ABC that "top GOP sources" said Rollins was leading an undercover effort to smear Geraldine Ferraro. Atwater wanted to force Rollins out in a new Bush administration, he says. Rollins hated him. But when Atwater was dying, he begged Rollins to look after him. "They're trying to destroy me," he said.

Atwater was popular with many reporters because he was good for quotes and leaks (or "leaks") and denials that were outrageous but delivered with disarming charm. About Iran-Contra: "We don't discuss how we make sausage." About the Willie Horton ad: "I don't think a lot of Southerners even noticed there was a black man in that ad." He had a genius for creating language that voters would remember. Learning that Tom Turnipseed, a Democratic opponent to his South Carolina congressional candidate, had received shock therapy as a young man, Atwater gleefully translated: "They had to hook him up to jumper cables." This is a fascinating portrait of an almost likable rogue. You'd rather spend time with him than a lot of more upstanding citizens. It makes a companion piece to Oliver Stone's *W.*

Atwater's death by brain tumor at age forty was preceded by deathbed regrets. The film has heartbreaking footage of this boyishly handsome man turned by chemo and radiation into a feeble, bloated caricature of himself. On his deathbed, he called for a Bible and sent telegrams of apology to those he had offended, even Willie Horton. "He said what he had done was bad and wrong," Rollins remembers. "He was scared to death of the afterlife." Mary Matalin, who never trusted or approved of Atwater, says: "After he died they found the Bible still wrapped in its cellophane." She thinks he might have been spinning right to the end.

Unusually for a South Carolina boy, Atwater had absolutely no interest in sports. None, except for professional wrestling. He loved it because it was fake, and everyone knew it was fake, and that was the whole point.

The Book of Eli ★★★
R, 118 m., 2010

Denzel Washington (Eli), Gary Oldman (Carnegie), Mila Kunis (Solara), Ray Stevenson (Redridge), Jennifer Beals (Claudia), Frances de la Tour (Martha), Michael Gambon (George). Directed by the Hughes brothers and produced by Broderick Johnson, Andrew A. Kosove, Joel Silver, and David Valdes. Screenplay by Gary Whitta.

I'm at a loss for words, so let me say these right away: *The Book of Eli* is very watchable. You won't be sorry you went. It grips your attention, and then at the end throws in several WTF! moments, which are a bonus. They make everything in the entire movie impossible and incomprehensible—but, hey, WTF.

Now to the words I am at a loss for. The story involves a lone wanderer (Denzel Washington) who wears a name tag saying, "Hi! My name is Eli." It may not be his name tag, but let's call him Eli anyway. Eli has been walking west across the devastated landscape of America for thirty years, on his way to the sea. I haven't walked it myself, but I'm pretty sure it doesn't take that long.

On the other hand, maybe Eli only thought he was walking west. On his final trek, he walks from right to left across the screen, which in movie shorthand is walking east. "How do you know you're walking the right way?" he's asked. "Faith," he says, a reply that takes on added resonance later in the film.

Eli is a quick hand with knives, pistols, rifles, shotguns, and karate. He needs to be. After a catastrophe has wiped out most of the earth's population and left ruin and desolation behind, the remaining humans are victimized by roaming motorcycle gangs of hijackers and thieves. These gangs are each issued with a perquisite tall bald man, a short hairy scruffy one, and their gofers.

The Hughes brothers, Albert and Allen, film this story in sunburned browns and pale blues, creating a dry and dusty world under a merciless sky. Water is treasure. This wasteland Eli treks at an implacable pace. Set upon in an ambush, he kills all his attackers. He's got one of those knives that makes a "snicker-snack" noise all by itself, and is a one-man army. Why don't the bad guys just shoot at him? Later in the film, they try that.

Denzel and the Hughes brothers do a good job of establishing this man and his world, and at first *The Book of Eli* seems destined to be solemn. But then Eli arrives at a Western town ruled by Carnegie (Gary Oldman), who, like all the local overloads in Westerns and gangster movies, sits behind a big desk flanked by a tall bald guy and of course a short scruffy one. How are these guys recruited? "Wanted: Tall bald guy to stand behind town boss and be willing to sacrifice life. All the water you can drink."

In this town, desperate and starving people live in rusty cars and in the streets. We meet Carnegie's abused wife, Claudia (Jennifer Beals), and her daughter, Solara (Mila Kunis), named for some reason after the cause of all the destruction. She's a prostitute in Carnegie's bar, having made the mistake of coming on Take Your Child to Work Day. Carnegie hurts Claudia to control Solara. How he controls the fearsome bald guy is hard to say.

The third act is recycled, but done well, out of many Westerns in which the hero and the girl hole up and are surrounded. So many other movies are quoted that we almost miss it when their hideout house is perforated by bullets, *L.A. Confidential* style. That allows countless beams of sunlight to shine in and function as a metaphor.

Carnegie needs Eli because Eli has maybe the last remaining copy of a book that Carnegie believes will allow him to expand and rule many more towns. I am forbidden by the Critic's Little Rule Book from naming the volume, but if you've made a guess after seeing numerous billboards stating "Religion Is Power," you may have guessed right.

The Hughes brothers have a vivid way with imagery here, as in their earlier films such as *Menace II Society* and the underrated *From Hell.* The film looks and feels good, and Washington's performance is more uncanny the more we think back over it. The ending is "flawed," as we critics like to say, but it's so magnificently, shamelessly, implausibly flawed that (a) it breaks apart from the movie and has a life of its own, or (b) at least it avoids being predictable.

Now do yourself a favor and don't talk to *anybody* about the film if you plan to see it. ☞

The Boondock Saints II: All Saints Day ★
R, 121 m., 2009

Sean Patrick Flanery (Connor MacManus), Norman Reedus (Murphy MacManus), Billy Connolly (Poppa M), Clifton Collins Jr. (Romeo), Julie Benz (Agent Eunice Bloom), Peter Fonda (The Roman), Judd Nelson (Concezio Yakavetta). Directed by Troy Duffy and produced by Chris Brinker and Don Carmody. Screenplay by Duffy.

The Boondock Saints II: All Saints Day is an idiotic ode to macho horseshite (to employ an ancient Irish word). It is, however, distinguished by superb cinematography. It's the first film in ten years from Troy Duffy, whose original *Boondock Saints* (1999) has become a cult fetish. It's such a legendary cult film, a documentary was even released about it.

No, not one of those "the making of" jobs. One made by two of Duffy's former pals who got pissed off during the filming. They show him as a possibly alcoholic egomaniac. You know you're in trouble when your movie scores 16 percent on the Tomatometer, and the documentary about it scores 79 percent.

To quote from my review of the 2004 doc: "*Overnight* tells a riches-to-rags story, like *Project Greenlight* played in reverse. *Greenlight,* you will recall, is the Miramax contest to choose and produce one screenplay every year by a hopeful first-time filmmaker. In *Overnight,* the director starts out with a contract and money from Miramax, and works his way back to no contract, no film, and no money. Call it *Project Red Light.*"

The documentary validates Gene Siskel's favorite verdict on a film: "I'd rather see a documentary of the same people having lunch." In this case, you see the same people getting drunk. After Duffy signs with the William Morris Agency, he brags to his pals, "I get drunk at night, wake up the next morning

hung over, go into those meetings in my overalls, and they're all wearing suits." Being Hollywood agents, they were probably more familiar with the danger signals of alcoholism than Duffy was.

The Boondock Saints cost $7 million and grossed $25,000 in two weeks in five theaters. Then a miracle occurred. It became a big hit on DVD—so big, this sequel was justified. It's a well-photographed picture with extensive special effects and good actors (Sean Patrick Flanery, Norman Reedus, Billy Connolly, Clifton Collins Jr., Julie Benz, Judd Nelson, and an unrecognizable Peter Fonda).

Flanery and Reedus are back from the original, as Connor and Murphy MacManus, two Irish Catholic brothers who executed countless Boston villains with bullets through the head and pennies on their eyes. Brothers? To me they look like twins. They now lead a quiet life in Ireland, herding sheep and smoking. Brokeback bachelors. After ten years, still unmarried, they live at home with old Poppy MacManus (Billy Connolly) in a cottage perhaps once inhabited by Ryan's Daughter's great-grandmother.

Word comes that a beloved Irish-American priest has been executed back in Boston, with pennies on his eyes. This calls for revenge: Someone is imitating their style! Electrified, the lads rush back to the States on a freight ship and go into action killing, oh, I'd say, hundreds of people, easily. This is done very well, in the way of stunts, f/x, and heavy metal cranked up to twelve.

The lads borrow a page from their old Poppy and don leather vests with built-in holsters for either four or six handguns, I forget. These they typically use while leaping in slo-mo off concealed trampolines while firing two guns each at the camera. If they always jump side by side, does that make it harder for their enemies to miss at least one? Can you fly forward through the air while firing two heavy-duty handguns without your arms jerking back and smacking you in the chin? Would that violate one of Newton's laws? Just askin'.

There's a lot of pious Roman Catholic iconography in the movie, although no one except the beloved executed priest ever goes into a church for purposes other than being murdered. The lads are loyal to the church in the same way fans are loyal to Da Bears. They aren't players themselves, but it's their team and don't mess with it. They do hold a quasi-religious ceremony, however, standing in a circle with a pal and vowing to never, ever stop smoking or drinking or attend an AA meeting. Drinking doesn't bother them anyway. They chug Irish whiskey like Gatorade. The only thing that bothers them, and they're super sensitive about this, is the slightest suggestion that they're gay.

Bottle Shock ★ ★ ★ ½
PG-13, 112 m., 2008

Alan Rickman (Steven Spurrier), Chris Pine (Bo Barrett), Bill Pullman (Jim Barrett), Rachael Taylor (Sam), Freddy Rodriguez (Gustavo Brambilia), Dennis Farina (Maurice), Bradley Whitford (Professor Saunders), Miguel Sandoval (Mr. Garcia), Eliza Dushku (Joe). Directed by Randall Miller and produced by J. Todd Harris. Screenplay by Jody Savin, Miller, and Ross Schwartz.

In 1976, the year of the American bicentennial, the tall ships sailed from Europe to America and back again. But a smaller event was, in its way, no less impressive. In a blind taste-testing held in France, the wines of California's Napa Valley defeated the best the French had to offer—and all the judges were French! A bottle of the winning American vintage, it is said, now rests on exhibit in the Smithsonian Institution.

Bottle Shock is a charming fictionalized version of the victory, "based," as they love to say, "on a true story." Shot in locations near the locale of *Sideways* but set much closer to the earth, it tells the story of a struggling vineyard named Chateau Montelena, deeply in debt with three bank loans. It's run by the hard-driving Jim Barrett (Bill Pullman), who despairs of his layabout, long-haired son Bo (Chris Pine).

Meanwhile, in Paris, we meet a British wine lover named Steven Spurrier (Alan Rickman), whose tiny wine shop is grandly named The Academy of Wine. We never see a single customer in the shop, only the constant visits of a neighboring travel agent, Maurice (Dennis Farina, in full Chicago accent). Maurice encourages Steven by praising his wines, which he samples freely while passing out business advice.

Spurrier (yes, a real man) has been hearing about the wines of California and has an inspiration: His grand-sounding "academy" will sponsor a blind taste test between the wines of the two countries. That he is able to gather a panel of expert judges says much for the confidence of the French, who should have realized it was a dangerous proposition.

In Napa, we meet two other major players: A pretty summer intern named Sam (Rachael Taylor) and an employee of Jim's named Gustavo Brambilia (Freddy Rodriguez—yes, another real character). Gustavo has wine in his bones, if such a thing is possible, and would go on to found a famous vineyard. The two boys raise cash by Gustavo's (partially true) ability to identify any wine and vintage by tasting it, and of course they both fall in love with Sam, who lives for the summer in a shack out of *The Grapes of Wrath*.

The outcome is predictable; anyone who cares even casually knows the Yanks won, but the director milks great entertainment, if not actual suspense, out of the competition. Much of its effect is due to the precise, quietly comic performance by Alan Rickman as Spurrier. "Why do I hate you?" asks Jim Barrett, who resists the competition. "Because you think I'm an asshole," Spurrier replies calmly. "Actually, I'm not an asshole. It's just that I'm British, and, well . . . you're not."

We see him navigating the back roads of Napa in a rented Gremlin, selecting wines for his competition and getting around U.S. customs by convincing twenty-six fellow air travelers to each carry a bottle back for him. That the momentous competition actually took place, that it shook the wine world to its foundations, that it was repeated twenty years later, is a story many people are vaguely familiar with. But *Bottle Shock* is more than the story. It is also about people who love their work, care about it with passion, and talk about it with knowledge. Did you know that a thirsty, struggling vine produces the best wines? It can't just sit there sipping water. It has to struggle—just like Chateau Montelena.

Note: Read the credits to find out how the movie fudges a few names, facts, and vineyards—and what happened to Gustavo.

The Bounty Hunter ★ ½
PG-13, 110 m., 2010

Jennifer Aniston (Nicole Hurly), Gerard Butler (Milo Boyd), Christine Baranski (Kitty Hurley). Directed by Andy Tennant and produced by Neal H. Moritz. Screenplay by Sarah Thorp.

I'm on the brink of declaring a new entry for Ebert's Little Movie Glossary: No comedy not titled *Caddyshack* has ever created a funny joke involving a golf cart. The only thing preventing me is that I can't remember if *Caddyshack* had golf cart jokes. In any event, if there is a golf cart, it will sooner or later drive into a water hazard. The funny angle here is that the filmmakers went to all that trouble because they trusted the audience to laugh.

I stared with glazed eyes at *The Bounty Hunter*. Here is a film with no need to exist. Among its sins is the misuse of Jennifer Aniston, who can be and has been very funny, but not in dreck like this. Lacking any degree of character development, it handcuffs her to a plot of exhausted action comedy clichés—and also to a car door and a bed.

The handcuffer is her former husband, Milo (Gerard Butler), a former cop who is now a bounty hunter and draws the assignment of tracking down his ex-wife, who has skipped bail. Have I lost touch here, or are bounty hunters routinely deployed to track down criminals accused of no more than a nonfatal traffic violation? Never mind.

Let's do a little mental exercise here, the same sort that the screenplay writer, Sarah Thorp, must have done. Remember the ground rules: The movie must contain only clichés. I used to test this exercise on my film class. I'd give them the genre, and begin sentences ending with an ellipsis. They'd compete to be first to shout out the answer.

1. The story involves a formerly married couple. He is a bounty hunter tracking her down for . . .
2. They dislike one another. Therefore by the end of the movie . . .
3. He drives a . . .
4. Because . . .
5. And his beloved . . .
6. He loves to gamble. Their road trip takes them to . . .
7. Where he . . .
8. And gets into trouble with . . .
9. Inspiring . . .
10. In a golf cart, they . . .
11. During the movie, he gets kicked . . .
12. She wears clothes so we can . . .

Well, I already gave you number ten. To the others, clever students would answer: (1) a nonserious crime, since this is a comedy; (2) they will fall back in love; (3) vintage convertible; (4) movies like them because older cars look like real cars, and with a convertible you can more easily light the characters and show the landscape at the same time; (5) gets damaged; (6) you can be excused for guessing Las Vegas, but it's Atlantic City; (7) wins big or loses big, but either way . . . ; (8) gangsters; (9) chase scenes, CGI sequences, impossible action, and lots of shots of her running in high heels; (10) you know; (11) in the crotch; (12) peek down her neckline.

Why, oh why, was this movie necessary? Could it have been redeemed by witty dialogue? Perhaps, but neither character is allowed to speak more than efficient sentences serving to further the plot. Hollywood movies started to simplify the dialogue when half the gross started to roll in from overseas. Has anyone noticed the great majority of nations dub foreign movies, so that subtitles aren't a problem?

Gerard Butler is a handsome hunk who can also act; he's currently starring in Ralph Fiennes's *Coriolanus*. Jennifer Aniston is a gifted comedienne. If you could pay their salaries, wouldn't you try to put them in a better movie than this? I saw the poster and had a sinking feeling the title gave away the whole story.

The Box ★★★
PG-13, 113 m., 2009

Cameron Diaz (Norma Lewis), James Marsden (Arthur Lewis), Frank Langella (Arlington Steward), James Rebhorn (Norm Cahill), Holmes Osborne (Dick Burns). Directed by Richard Kelly and produced by Kelly, Dan Lin, Kelly McKittrick, and Sean McKittrick. Screenplay by Kelly, based on the short story "Button, Button" by Richard Matheson.

I know, I know, *The Box* triumphantly qualifies for one of my favorite adjectives, "preposterous." But if you make a preposterous movie that isn't boring, I count that as some kind of a triumph. This one begins as traditional science fiction and branches out into radio signals from Mars, nosebleeds, Sartre's theories about free will, amputated toes, NASA, the National Security Agency, wind tunnels, murders, black Town Cars, obnoxious waiters, and a mysterious stranger.

His name is Arlington Lewis Steward (Frank Langella). He drops a box on the front porch of Norma and Arthur Lewis and returns with an offer: If they push the button on top of the box, they will be paid $1 million in crisp $100 bills ("nontaxable"), but unfortunately, someone not known to them will die. Well, what would you do? Norma (Cameron Diaz) has just learned their son's tuition is going up, and Arthur (James Marsden) has been dropped from astronaut training. The hell with it: Norma, so sweet and earnest, pushes the button.

This sets into motion a chain of events that I will not describe for you even if I could. The writer-director, Richard Kelly, goes from A to Z using fifty-two letters, but his transitions flow so uncannily it's only when you look back you realize you're off the road. Everything, including some impressive high-tech rocket science, is taken so seriously that you get sucked in. There's also the matter of the 360-degree camera that Arthur Lewis has designed for the Mars Lander. Well, what about it? After you've seen the movie, you tell me. At least the nosebleeds are explained.

The Box is based on the story "Button, Button" by Richard Matheson, published by *Playboy* in 1970. It inspired a simpler adaptation for a *Twilight Zone* episode in 1986, which had a different ending but a very similar box design. Well, what can you do with a box with a button on top? Matheson, who has three films in preproduction at eighty-three, has inspired or written at least twenty-three films (*I Am Legend* has been made three times) and countless TV episodes.

Here he seems motivated by the Milgram Experiment, one of the most famous psychological tests ever conducted. You've heard of it. Professor Stanley Milgram of Yale told volunteers he was testing the limits of human pain endurance. He showed them a dial and said it would administer electrical shocks to test subjects. The high range on the dial was painted red, indicating danger. The volunteers could hear the subjects screaming. They were told by the test supervisor it was *essential* to continue administering shocks (even though the dial indicated they might become fatal). In one round of experiments, 65 percent of the volunteers followed orders even when it meant a fatal shock.

What *would* you do? And what if the victim wasn't a person you had met who was screaming in another room, but someone unknown to you? And the reward wasn't helping out Yale with its research, but a cool million? Norma and Arthur Lewis aren't bad people—pretty nice ones, in fact. They regret her impulsive action immediately. But then the plot grows sinister, coiling around to involve them, which we expect, but also venturing into completely unanticipated directions and inspiring as many unanswered questions as *Knowing*, which I loved.

Many readers hated *Knowing*, and many will hate *The Box*. What can I say? I'm not here to agree with you. This movie kept me involved and intrigued, and for that I'm grateful. I'm beginning to wonder whether, in some situations, absurdity might not be a strength.

Boy A ★ ★ ★½
R, 100 m., 2008

Andrew Garfield (Jack Burridge), Peter Mullan (Terry), Katie Lyons (Michelle), Shaun Evans (Chris). Directed by John Crowley and produced by Lynn Horsford, Nick Marston, and Tally Garner. Screenplay by Mark O'Rowe, based on the novel by Jonathan Trigell.

Eric was a preadolescent with a violent streak and the wrong kind of friend in Philip. Together, they murdered a girl about their age and were put on trial as Boy A and Boy B. They were essentially evil, the prosecutor argued, and deserved the maximum legal sentence. Philip died in prison. Now Eric, at twenty-four, has been paroled and given a new identity: Jack Burridge.

Boy A is based on a novel by Jonathan Trigell, possibly inspired by the real-life British case of two youths seen on a shopping mall's security video as they led away a child who was found dead. Such cases raise the question: Are children who murder indeed essentially evil, or can they heal and change over a period of years? Should society give them a second chance?

That is the fervent belief in this film of Terry (Peter Mullan), the rehabilitation counselor for the renamed Jack (Andrew Garfield). He lectures Jack that he must never, ever reveal his secret. He believes Jack has changed, but society doesn't believe it and will crucify him. So warned, Jack takes a delivery job with a Manchester firm and begins his new life.

Mullan and Garfield anchor the film—Mullan, that splendid Scots actor (*My Name Is Joe*), and Garfield, twenty-four, with his boyish face and friendly grin. When Jack is rebuilding his existence, Terry is his lifeline, who encourages him almost daily. At first the new job goes well. He makes a friend of his job partner, Chris (Shaun Evans). And Michelle (Katie Lyons), the secretary at the office, boldly asks, "Aren't you going to ask me out for a drink, then?"

He does, and they fall sweetly in love. He urgently wants to tell her his secret, but Terry forbids it. One day when Jack and Chris are driving a country road, they come upon a car crash and rescue a young girl from the wreckage. They're hailed as heroes and get their photo on the front page of the *Manchester Evening News*—Jack with his hat brim pulled low over his eyes.

A series of events eventually leads to Jack's exposure by a shameless London tabloid, which runs the photo and breathlessly boasts that they've found Boy A, the embodiment of evil, now free to walk the streets. Jack's life collapses, and he goes on the run. These scenes are the movie's most desperate, ending at Brighton, where he has a fairly improbable chance encounter with Michelle.

By now we have seen, in a pub brawl, that Jack is still capable of violence. In flashbacks, we see boyhood behavior leading up to the tragic murder. And Terry's own son, a layabout, resents his father's clear preference for Boy A. The whole alternative identity falls apart, and Jack/Eric is left homeless and wandering.

Well, should he be forgiven? Judeo-Christian tradition teaches that a boy becomes a

man ("reaches the age of reason," Catholics say) at about twelve. Eric looks nine or ten when he commits his crime. Mistreated at home by a drunken father, raped by his brother, bullied at school, he has much to resent, much cruelty to absorb. When we see him at twenty-four, we are inclined to believe he deserves a new chance.

The film, directed by John Crowley and written by Mark O'Rowe, paints an accurate portrait of working-class life in the north of England, the grimness of the streets contrasting with the beauty of the countryside. It is spoken with accents, Mullan's Scots the hardest to understand. He can speak standard English, but the accent is one of his tools. I've never had a problem with his speech because he is such great actor you can forget the words and listen to the music.

He and Andrew Garfield fit well together—both have faces you like on first sight, both have charm, both have warmth. Garfield, just now emerging as a talent to watch (*The Other Boleyn Girl*), inhabits Jack effortlessly, showing his hope, his fears, his nightmares, his doubt that he deserves his new life. And the movie poses the age-old question of forgiveness. At this moment in Chicago, children with handguns kill people. Can we say, "Father, forgive them, for they know not what they do"?

The Boy in the Striped Pajamas ★ ★ ★ ½
PG-13, 94 m., 2008

Asa Butterfield (Bruno), David Thewlis (Father), Vera Farmiga (Mother), Rupert Friend (Lieutenant Kotler), Jack Scanlon (Shmuel), Amber Beattie (Gretel), Sheila Hancock (Grandma), Richard Johnson (Grandpa), Jim Norton (Herr Liszt). Directed by Mark Herman and produced by David Heyman. Screenplay by Herman, based on the novel by John Boyne.

Mark Herman's *The Boy in the Striped Pajamas* depends for its powerful impact on why, and when, it transfers the film's point of view. For almost all of the way, we see events through the eyes of a bright, plucky eight-year-old. Then we begin to look out through the eyes of his parents. Why and when that transfer takes place gathers all of the film's tightly wound tensions and savagely uncoils them. It is not what happens to the boy, which I will not tell you. It is all that happens. All of it, before and after.

Bruno (Asa Butterfield) is a boy growing up in a comfy household in Berlin, circa 1940. His dad (David Thewlis) goes off to the office every day. He's a Nazi official. Bruno doesn't think about that much, but he's impressed by his ground-level view of his father's stature.

One day Bruno gets the unwelcome news that his dad has a new job, and they will all be moving to the country. It'll be a farm, his parents reassure him. Lots of fun. Bruno doesn't want to leave his playmates and his much-loved home. His grandma (Sheila Hancock) doesn't approve of the move either. There seems to be a lot she doesn't approve of, but children are made uneasy by family tension and try to evade it.

There's a big house in the country, surrounded by high walls. It looks too stark and modern to be a farmhouse. Army officials come and go. They fill rooms with smoke as they debate policy and procedures. Bruno can see the farm fields from his bedroom window. He asks his parents why the farmers are wearing striped pajamas. They give him one of those evasive answers that only drive a smart kid to find out for himself.

At the farm, behind barbed wire, he meets a boy about his age. They make friends. They visit as often as they can. The other boy doesn't understand what's going on any more than Bruno does. Their stories were told in a 2007 young adult's novel of the same name by John Boyne, which became a best-seller. I learn the novel tells more about what the child thinks he hears and knows, but the film is implacable in showing where his curiosity leads him.

Other than what *The Boy in the Striped Pajamas* is about, it almost seems to be an orderly story of those British who always know how to speak and behave. Those British? Yes, the actors speak with crisp British accents, which I think is actually more effective than having them speaking with German accents or in subtitles. It dramatizes the way the German professional class internalized Hitler's rule and treated it as business as usual. Charts, graphs, titles, positions, uniforms, promotions, performance evaluations.

How can ordinary professional people proceed in this orderly routine when their business is evil? Easier than we think. I still obsess about those few Enron executives who knew the entire company was a Ponzi scheme. I can't forget the Oregon railroader who had his pension stolen. The laughter of Enron soldiers who joked about killing grandmothers with their phony California "energy crisis." Whenever loyalty to the enterprise becomes more important than simple morality, you will find evil functioning smoothly.

There has not again been evil on the scale of 1939–45. But there has been smaller-scale genocide. Mass murder. Wars generated by lies and propaganda. The Wall Street crash stripped people of their savings, their pensions, their homes, their jobs, their hopes of providing for their families. It happened because a bureaucracy and its status symbols became more important than what it was allegedly doing.

Have I left my subject? I don't think so. *The Boy in the Striped Pajamas* is not only about Germany during the war, although the story it tells is heartbreaking in more than one way. It is about a value system that survives like a virus. Do I think the people responsible for our economic crisis were Nazis? Certainly not. But instead of collecting hundreds of millions of dollars in rewards for denying to themselves what they were doing, I wish they had been forced to flee to Paraguay in submarines.

The Boys Are Back ★★ ½
PG-13, 103 m., 2009

Clive Owen (Joe Warr), Emma Booth (Laura), Laura Fraser (Katy), George MacKay (Harry), Nicholas McAnulty (Artie). Directed by Scott Hicks and produced by Greg Brenman and Timothy White. Screenplay by Allan Cubitt, based on the memoir *The Boys Are Back in Town* by Simon Carr.

An opening shot in *The Boys Are Back* shows a small boy balanced on the hood of an SUV, which his father is driving on a beach. No, his father isn't drunk; he's simply a man whose idea of giving his son freedom comes recklessly close to endangerment. Surprisingly, the film considers him to be a good dad.

His name is Joe Warr (Clive Owen). He's a British sportswriter who moved to Australia to follow his second wife, Katy (Laura Fraser). After her sudden death, he becomes the single parent of Artie (Nicholas McAnulty), who is six and doesn't quite understand how his mom could die, although he acts out erratically. During Artie's earlier years, his dad, one of Australia's top sportswriters, was away frequently covering events or working on deadline. His mom provided a secure home. Joe is new to the day-after-day responsibility of fatherhood and running a household (how *do* rooms get themselves cleaned and straightened?).

Joe's belief is that kids need to be challenged, trusted, and given as much freedom as possible. That may sound good in theory, but children also require structure and rules. They don't always want their parents screaming at them that they're going to break their necks, but on the other hand, it can be unsettling to have a dad who almost seems OK with neck breaking.

I believe in the benefits of raising "free-range children"—within reason. When I was a kid, we ran around the neighborhood and could be away from home all day without anyone calling the police—just so we were home when the street lights went on. At the same time, we knew all the parents in the neighborhood had an eye on us through a window or from a porch chair, we knew there were rules, we knew we were loved and worried about.

Artie is treated by Joe almost like a college buddy. This suits Joe's personality, but doesn't work so well with the uncertain kid, and also not with Laura (Emma Booth), a woman he eventually starts dating, who is a single mom with more sensible ideas about parenting. The film seems to regard Joe with affection, and Owen certainly portrays him as a nice man. But why are his unformed theories about raising Artie supposed to fill us with affection and sentiment?

There's a problem, too, when Joe's teenage son, Harry (George MacKay), from his first marriage comes out from England for a summer with Dad. Harry and Artie bond quickly, but Harry was raised in a more structured way (too structured, judging from what we see) and has big problems with Joe's child-rearing theories. Some of the film's more successful passages involve the ways Harry becomes the father his poor little brother doesn't have.

There's something a little too absent about Joe. I want to call it selfishness. With Artie, he needs to look and listen more closely. Just because Joe thinks things are fine doesn't mean they are. Clive Owen can be a likable actor, but the character is working against him. *The Boys Are Back* was directed by Scott Hicks, whose *Shine* remains a moving experience, but here he has all the pieces in place (cast, cinematography, music) and doesn't quite have the story he thinks he has. And please, please, give us a break from the scenes where the ghost of the departed turns up and starts talking as if she's not dead.

Brick Lane ★ ★ ★ ½
PG-13, 101 m., 2008

Tannishtha Chatterjee (Nazneen), Satish Kaushik (Chanu), Christopher Simpson (Karim), Naeema Begum (Shahana), Lana Rahman (Bibi), Zafreen (Hasina). Directed by Sarah Gavron and produced by Alison Owen and Christopher Collins. Screenplay by Abi Morgan and Laura Jones, based on the novel by Monica Ali.

Brick Lane tells a story we think we already know, but we're wrong: It has new things to say within an old formula. It begins with a young woman from Bangladesh, whose mother's suicide causes her father to arrange her marriage with a man now living in London, older than her, whom she has never met. Nazneen (Tannishtha Chatterjee) is a stunning beauty, seventeen when she marries Chanu (Satish Kaushik), who is fat, balding, and easily twenty years older. So this will be a story of her servitude to this beast, right?

Not exactly. Chanu is not a hateful man. He is not a fountain of warmth and understanding and has few insights into his wife, but he is an earnest citizen, a hard worker, and there is sometimes a twinkle in his eye. He likes to sing little songs to himself. The two have three children; their first, a son, is a victim of crib death. The next two are daughters, Shahana (Naeema Begum) and Bibi (Lana Rahman). Time passes. Sex for Nazneen is a matter of closing her eyes and dreaming of her village back home and the sister she receives regular letters from.

Her husband is so unwise as to take loans from the usurer who works their council flat in East London; these loans apparently can never quite be repaid and delay their dream of returning "home." Meanwhile, Chanu pursues his dream of becoming a properly educated Brit, which for him means familiarity with Thackeray, Hume, and other authors not much read anymore, alas, by Brits. He dreams such knowledge will win him a promotion at work, but it doesn't; he loses his job and starts working as a minicab driver. And Nazneen does what other women in the public housing estate do—she buys a sewing machine and does piece work, finishing blue jeans.

That's how Karim (Christopher Simpson) comes into her life—young, handsome, charming, the delivery man for the unfinished jeans. Yes, they fall in love, have sex, talk of her divorce and their marriage. Chanu walks into the flat at times when he must be blind not to understand what's happening—but he doesn't, or at least he doesn't say anything; his method is to remain jolly at all times, as if everything's fine. The performance by Kaushik makes him almost impossible to dislike, although he's no doubt an ordeal to live with.

Now comes the part of the story that caused controversy when Monica Ali's best-selling novel was announced for filming. The attacks of 9/11 take place, anti-Muslim sentiment increases in London, community meetings are held, Karim starts growing a beard and becomes more militant, and then Chanu, of all people, turns into a spokesman against extremist militancy and in favor of a faith based not in politics but in the heart.

His sentiment aroused so much opposition among Muslims in London that the novel could not be filmed on Brick Lane (the center of London's Bangladeshi population), but in fact what Chanu says is deeply felt and seems harmless enough. Without getting into the politics, however, let me say that the film's story surprised me by being less about the illicit love affair and more about the marriage, Nazneen's deepest feelings, and the two daughters—the young one docile, the older one scornful of her father.

"Tell him you don't want to go home," says Shahana. "I've never once heard you tell him what you really feel." But what Nazneen really feels is a surprise even to herself, and the final notes of the film are graceful and tender. Watching it, I was reminded of how many shallow, cynical, vulgar movies I've seen in this early summer season, and how few that truly engage in matters of the heart. *Brick Lane* is about characters who have depth and reality, who change and learn, who have genuine feelings. And it keeps on surprising us, right to the end.

Brideshead Revisited ★ ★ ★

PG-13, 135 m., 2008

Matthew Goode (Charles Ryder), Ben Whishaw (Sebastian Flyte), Hayley Atwell (Julia Flyte), Emma Thompson (Lady Marchmain), Michael Gambon (Lord Marchmain), Ed Stoppard (Bridey Flyte), Felicity Jones (Cordelia Flyte), Greta Scacchi (Cara), Jonathan Cake (Rex Mottram). Directed by Julian Jarrold and produced by Kevin Loader, Robert Bernstein, and Douglas Rae. Screenplay by Andrew Davies and Jeremy Brock, based on the novel by Evelyn Waugh.

No love story can be wholly satisfying in which the crucial decisions are made by the mother of the loved woman; still less, when she is the mother of both the loved woman and the loved man, and believes she is defending their immortal souls. That is the dilemma in Evelyn Waugh's masterful novel *Brideshead Revisited*, made into an inspired TV miniseries in 1981 and now adapted into a somewhat less inspired film.

The story is told by Charles Ryder (Matthew Goode), who when we meet him is a famous painter, a guest on a postwar Atlantic crossing. On board he encounters Julia Mottram (Hayley Atwell), who, when she was Julia Flyte in the years between the wars, inflamed Charles with love. That he was previously, less ardently in love with her brother Sebastian (Ben Whishaw) was a complication. That he was a middle-class boy infatuated with the entire family—their inherited Marchmain title, their wealth, their history, their great mansion Brideshead—was in a way at the bottom of everything.

The novel begins during the war, when Charles is posted to Brideshead, requisitioned as a military headquarters. His memories come flooding back, bittersweet, mournful. Time rolls back to the autumn day at Oxford, when Charles has moved into his ground-floor rooms just in time for Sebastian to throw up through the open window. Sebastian is a dazzling youth, witty, beautiful, the center of a gay coterie. Charles is not his type, is apparently not even gay, but that for Sebastian is the whole point, and he takes the boy under his arm.

The friendship between Charles and Sebastian during a summer holiday at Brideshead is enchanted and platonic until a tentative but passionate kiss. Then Lady Julia comes into view, and during a later holiday in Venice, she and Charles fall in love—and Sebastian is shattered when he realizes it. To blame his disintegration on lost love would be too simple, however, because from being an alcoholic he rapidly progresses into self-destruction in the hashish and opium dens of Morocco, his youthful perfection turned into a ghastly caricature.

At the center of all of this is Lady Marchmain (Emma Thompson, in a superb performance). Of her son's proclivities she professes a certain vagueness. Of her daughter's love for Charles, she makes it clear that it is not the matter of his lower caste that is the problem (that could be lived with), but the fact that he is an atheist, and the Marchmains have been Roman Catholic from time immemorial.

This theme must have attracted Waugh because he was a Catholic convert and was fascinated by the division between Catholics and Protestants as a social, as well as a religious, issue. Catholicism was once a practice punishable by death in England, and no doubt hidden somewhere in the stones of Brideshead is an ancient "priest hole," used by aristocratic Catholic families to conceal a priest if royal troops came sniffing. Lady Marchmain (and Julia) are not casually Catholic, but believe firmly in the dogma of the Church, and that any unbaptized children would be forbidden the sight of God. Since Charles will not renounce his atheism, he loses Julia, although not before first going as an ambassador for Lady Marchmain to Sebastian—one of the film's best scenes.

There are two peculiar fathers in the film.

Lord Marchmain (Michael Gambon), still officially married of course, lives in exile in a Venetian palazzo with his mistress, Cora (Greta Scacchi). Charles's father (Patrick Malahide) is a pronounced eccentric who lives embalmed in a London house and apparently prefers playing chess with himself than conversing with his son. He is a character from Dickens.

Charles is Dickensian in a way, too: the impecunious and parentless youth adrift in an unfamiliar social system. Matthew Goode plays him as a little bland, a mirror for the emotions he attracts. Ben Whishaw steals all of his scenes as Sebastian, the carefree ones and the doom-laden ones. Hayley Atwell, as Julia, could have been drawn a little more carefully. The actress does what she can, but why, really, does Julia marry the odious and insufferable Rex Mottram, who is nothing more than a marked-down Jay Gatsby?

The movie, while elegantly mounted and well-acted, is not the equal of the TV production, in part because so much material had to be compressed into such a shorter time. It is also not the equal of the recent film *Atonement*, which in an oblique way touches on similar issues, especially unrequited love and wartime. But it is a good, sound example of the British period drama; midrange Merchant-Ivory, you could say. And I relished it when Charles's father barely noticed that he had gone away to Oxford—or come back, for that matter.

Bride Wars ★ ★

PG, 90 m., 2009

Kate Hudson (Liv), Anne Hathaway (Emma), Kristen Johnston (Deb), Bryan Greenberg (Nate), Candice Bergen (Marion), Steve Howey (Daniel), Chris Pratt (Fletcher). Directed by Gary Winick and produced by Julie Yorn, Alan Riche, and Kate Hudson. Screenplay by Greg DePaul, Casey Wilson, and June Diane Raphael.

Is there anyone old enough to care about weddings and naive enough to believe *Bride Wars*? Here is a sitcom about consumerism, centering on two bubble-brained women and their vacuous fiancés, and providing them with not a single line that is smart or witty. The dialogue is fiercely on-topic, dictated by the needs of the plot, pounding down the home stretch in clichés, obligatory truisms, and shrieks.

Kate Hudson and Anne Hathaway, who play the would-be brides, are good actors and quick-witted women, here playing characters at a level of intelligence approximating HAL 9000 after he has had his chips pulled. No one can be this superficial and survive without professional care. Compare this film with the wonderful *Rachel Getting Married*, for which Hathaway won an Oscar nomination as Rachel's sister, and now see how she plays a prenuptial Stepford Wife.

I am sure there are women who will enjoy *Bride Wars*, as a man might enjoy a film about cars and Hooters girls. It's like a moving, talking version of *Brides* magazine. Hudson and Hathaway play Liv and Emma, girlhood friends who made a vow to realize their dreams of both getting married at the Plaza. They're serious. They've been saving up the money for their big days for more than ten years. No daddies are around to fork over.

Liv is a lawyer and has perhaps made some money. Emma, without parents, is a schoolteacher. They both go to the most famous wedding planner in Manhattan (Candice Bergen) and, with *three months' notice*, are able to nail down dates at the Plaza for a June wedding. This is before Madoff forced the wholesale cancellation of reservations.

Do you have any idea what such weddings would cost, after flowers and table decorations, invitations, gowns, limos, a reception, dinner, music, the sweets table, the planner, the event room at the Plaza, and rooms for the wedding parties to get dressed? Plus tips? For enough room to get the bride and her bridesmaids whipped into shape, I think you could all squeeze into an Edwardian Park suite, 1,000 square feet with a king-size bed, which next June 7 will go for $2,195. Family of the bride? Impecunious out-of-town relatives? Groom and his best men? Have them wait in the hallway.

At least there will be no expenses for a honeymoon, since neither couple ever discusses one. The movie is about the brides and their weddings, and that's that. The grooms are, in fact, remarkably inconsequential, spending a lot of time sitting on couches and watching their brides act out romantic and revenge fantasies. That's because after both weddings are scheduled for the same time, Emma and Liv forget their lifelong bonds of friendship, start feuding, and play practical jokes involving a deep orange suntan, blue-dyed hair, and a projected video from their bachelorette party. They end up in a cat fight in the aisle. Fortunately neither one thinks of introducing E. coli into the punch bowl.

Women and men have different visions of wedding ceremonies. This I know from *Father of the Bride* (1991), with Steve Martin and Diane Keaton as the parents. Martin envisions the swell ceremony he will provide for his daughter: lots of balloons in the backyard and him manning the barbecue grill. Keaton gently corrects him. Even at the time I reviewed the movie, there was a newspaper story about a father who offered his daughter the choice of a nice ceremony or a condo.

Bride Wars is pretty thin soup. The characters have no depth or personality, no quirks or complications, no conversation. The story twist is so obvious from the first shot of two characters talking that they might have well been waving handkerchiefs over their heads and signaling: "Watch this space for further developments." The whole story is narrated by Candice Bergen as the wedding coordinator, who might as well have been instructing us how to carve bars of Ivory Soap into little ducks.

Bright Star ★★★ ½
PG, 119 m., 2009

Abbie Cornish (Fanny Brawne), Ben Whishaw (John Keats), Paul Schneider (Mr. Brown), Kerry Fox (Mrs. Brawne). Directed by Jane Campion and produced by Jan Chapman and Caroline Hewitt. Screenplay by Campion.

John Keats wasn't meekly posing as a Romantic poet. He was the real thing, and the last-born of the group that also included Blake, Wordsworth, Coleridge, Byron, and Shelley. He died at twenty-five and remains forever young.

The great and only love of his life was Fanny Brawne, the daughter of his landlady. He lived with his friend Charles Brown and she with her mother, sister, and brother in the two halves of a Hampstead cottage so small it gives meaning to the phrase "living in each other's pockets." Their love was grand and poetic and—apart from some sweet kisses—platonic, for he had neither the means nor the health to propose marriage, and they were not moved to violate the moral code of what was not yet quite the Victorian era.

Jane Campion's beautiful and wistful new film shows them frozen in courtship, like the young man Keats wrote about in "Ode on a Grecian Urn"—the youth who is immortalized forever in pursuit of a maid he is destined never to catch. He could have been writing about himself and Fanny: "Bold Lover, never, never canst thou kiss, / Though winning near the goal—yet, do not grieve; / She cannot fade, though thou hast not thy bliss, / For ever wilt thou love, and she be fair!"

It is almost as if they were spiritually inflamed by their doomed love. She was not shy but she was proper, and he loved her, but perhaps he had some difficulty in thinking of her as physical. When his younger brother Tom died and his own health began to fail, he immortalized his loss of that which he had never possessed. (From his deathbed in Italy, however, he did indeed write Brown that he wished he had "had her" when he had a chance.) Dr. Johnson observed to Mr. Boswell: "Marriage, sir, is a state with few pleasures. Chastity, with none." Yet Keats and Fanny seemed quite pleased enough.

I have visited the Keats House many times, and I can tell you it is shockingly small. The dividing wall between the two households was knocked out in the mid-1880s, but propriety must have erected a stouter wall. John and Fanny court and flirt as if they live in neighboring counties. It's to Campion's credit that she doesn't heat up the story or go for easy emotional payoffs, and we're spared even the pathetic deathbed scene that another director might have felt necessary.

The key figure is Fanny, played by Abbie Cornish with effervescence. "I confess I do not find your poems easy," she tells Keats (Ben Whishaw). But she studies at them earnestly, with a touching faith that they must contain clues to the stirrings in her heart. He requires her as a muse. For a reader, he has the bearded, gruff Brown (Paul Schneider), possessive, de-

manding, a taskmaster. Brown is hostile to Fanny's appeal to his friend and resents it when she interrupts them "working," which seems to consist of him scowling morosely at a manuscript while Keats idly dreams. Brown is a poet himself, but to his credit he recognizes the better craftsman and behaves like a coach or an agent.

There might be some question whether Brown felt sexual stirrings of his own involving Keats, but I think he is oblivious to such a possibility. He knows the real thing, he wonders if Keats would daydream his career away, as always at his back he hears time's winged chariot hurrying near. When Keats leaves for Italy, it is Brown who accompanies him—not Fanny, of course, who waits forlornly for the postman to approach down the little lane beneath the tree where Keats perhaps heard the nightingale sing. (The tree now growing on the spot is not the same one, but don't tell everyone.)

What Campion does is seek visual beauty to match Keats's verbal beauty. There is a shot here of Fanny in a meadow of blue flowers that is so enthralling it beggars description. Hampstead in those days was a village on the slopes north of London, almost rural, where shepherds could graze their flocks on the public land of Hampstead Heath. Coleridge lived not far way in Highgate, and the two met during their rambles on the heath. To support oneself seems to have been relatively possible, despite Dickens's portraits of poverty at the time. Mrs. Brawne (Kerry Fox) observes to her daughter that he has "no living and no income," the volumes of verse brought in only a few pounds, but when it is time for Keats to live in Italy, he finds the means. It appears that an English gentleman could support himself on air and credit.

It is famously impossible for the act of writing to be made cinematic. How long can we watch someone staring at a blank sheet of paper? It is equally unenlightening to show the writer seeing something and dashing off to scribble down impassioned words while we hear him reading them in his mind. Campion knows all this, and knows, too, that without the poetry John Keats is only a moonstruck young man. How she works in the words is one of the subtle beauties of the film. And over the end credits, Whishaw reads the "Ode" and you will want to stay.

Note: Tom O'Bedlam reads the poem Keats wrote about Fanny Brawne, "Bright Star": www.youtube.com/watch?v=QyymuJqZJtM.

Broken Embraces ★★★★
R, 128 m., 2009

Penelope Cruz (Lena Rivero), Lluis Homar (Harry Caine), Jose Luis Gomez (Ernesto Martel), Blanca Portillo (Judit Garcia), Ruben Ochendiano (Ray X), Tamar Novas (Diego Garcia). Directed by Pedro Almodovar and produced by Esther Garcia. Screenplay by Almodovar.

Pedro Almodovar loves the movies with lust and abandon and the skill of an experienced lover. *Broken Embraces* is a voluptuary of a film, drunk on primary colors, caressing Penelope Cruz, using the devices of a Hitchcock to distract us with surfaces while the sinister uncoils beneath. As it ravished me, I longed for a freeze frame to allow me to savor a shot.

The movie confesses its obsession up front. It is about seeing. A blind man asks a woman to describe herself. Since we can see her perfectly well, one purpose of this scene is to allow us to listen to her. How to describe the body, the hair, the eyes? Movies are really about the human body more than anything else. I was recently faulted for lingering overmuch on Ingrid Bergman's lips in *Casablanca*. Anyone, man or woman, who doesn't want to linger on Ingrid Bergman's lips is telling us something about themselves we'd rather not know.

The blind man is Harry Caine (Lluis Homar). Harry Lime and Citizen Kane, get it? Both played by Orson Welles, the great man of the cinema. Welles's *Magnificent Ambersons* was infamously botched by being re-edited in his absence.

Harry Caine is the name Mateo Blanco took after being blinded in an automobile accident. Perhaps only he knew why. As Blanco, he directed a film named *Girls and Suitcases*. It was produced by a man named Ernesto Martel (Jose Luis Gomez). Harry/Mateo hates Martel for reasons that will be explored. One day he's visited by Ray X (Ruben Ochandiano). X-Ray: Yeah, you got it. X despises the memory of his father and wants to enlist Caine, now a famous writer, to do the screenplay. Perhaps he has hidden reasons for contacting Caine.

Guarding Caine in his blindness is Judit (Blanca Portillo), who was his trusted aide when he could see and has now become indispensable. It is clear, although she has never revealed it to him, that she loves him. We sense her feelings go beneath love, however, into realms he doesn't guess.

Penelope Cruz has been Almodovar's constant muse since *Live Flesh* (1997). When Martel and Blanco/Caine were preparing *Girls and Suitcases*, the producer hired Lena (Cruz) as his assistant. In the time-honored tradition of such arrangements, in particular when the woman has been a prostitute, he arranges for Lena to audition for a role in the new picture. The director falls in love with her during the screen test.

Martel is enraged as only a rich middle-aged man who has purchased love can be. He sics his son on them. Yes, the future Ray X follows them with his camera like a nerdy fanboy. That it's unwholesome to spy on the behavior of your father's mistress goes without saying; can the boy be blamed for growing up to hate Martel? His videos are screened for the father, who combines jealousy with voyeurism, a common enough mixture.

I've really only scratched the surface of where *Broken Embraces* goes and what it discovers. To find that this passion comes to fruition in a blind man's editing room is to demonstrate that all films, and all of us, are blind until the pieces are put together. There are two, or really four, movies within this one: Martel's film in its first and second cuts, and Ray X's video seen one way and then another. The nature of each film changes in transition, and the changes have deep meaning for the characters.

Look at Almodovar's command of framing here. There's one unbroken shot so "illogical" it may even slip past you. There's urgent action on a sofa in the foreground and then a character stands and moves to the right, talking, and dawdles slightly and then moves to the left, and now we see for the first time the

71

next room completely open to this one, and there is a young man seated at a table in there. What? He must have been there all along, yet the foreground action took no notice of him, the camera didn't establish him, and now no acknowledgment is made of his incongruous presence. I *think* this shot may be about the ability of camera placement and film editing to dictate absolutely what is and is not in a scene. I'm sure it also has meaning in terms of the characters, but I don't know what. It shows Almodovar saying he'll do things just for the hell of it and keep a straight face.

Mention must be made of red. Almodovar, who always favors bright primary colors, drenches this film in red: in the clothing, the decor, the lipstick, the artwork, the furnishings—everywhere he can. Red, the color of passion and blood. Never has he made a film more visually pulsating, and Almodovar is not shy. Never has Penelope Cruz been more clearly the brush he uses, the canvas he covers, and the subject of his painting. To see this film once is to experience his deliberate abandon. To see it twice, as I've been able to, is to understand that his style embodies his subject. That subject is this: Film and life rush ahead so heedlessly that the frames are past before we can contemplate them.

Bronson ★★★

R, 92 m., 2009

Tom Hardy (Michael Peterson/Bronson), Matt King (Paul Daniels), Amanda Burton (Mum), James Lance (Phil). Directed by Nicolas Winding Refn and produced by Daniel Hansford and Rupert Preston. Screenplay by Refn and Brock Norman Brock.

Michael Peterson tells us he was born into a normal middle-class family. He doesn't blame his childhood or anything else for the way he turned out, and neither does this film. It regards him as a natural history exhibit. No more would we blame him on his childhood than we would blame a venomous snake's. It is their nature to behave as they do.

At an early age, after seeing *Death Wish*, young Michael took the name of Charles Bronson. And as Bronson, he has become the U.K.'s most famous prisoner and without any

doubt its most violent. With a shaved head and a comic-opera mustache, he likes to strip naked and grease himself before going into action.

His favorite pastime is taking a hostage and then engaging in a bloody battle with the guards who charge to the rescue, swinging clubs and beating him into submission. He has triggered this scenario many times, perhaps because he enjoys it so much. Originally sentenced to seven years ("You'll be out in three," his mother calls to him in the courtroom), he has now served thirty-four uninterrupted years, thirty of them in solitary confinement.

Why? We don't know. The movie doesn't know. If Bronson knows, he's not telling. The movie takes on a fearsome purity, refusing to find reasons, indifferent to motives, not even finding causes and effects. It is ninety-two minutes of rage, acted by Tom Hardy. This is a versatile actor. As you'd expect, he's made a lot of British gangster movies (*RocknRolla, Layer Cake, Sucker Punch*), but he's also played Bill Sikes in *Oliver Twist* and Heathcliff in a TV adaptation of *Wuthering Heights*.

Hardy brings a raw physicality to the role, leaping naked about his cell, jumping from tables, hurtling himself into half a dozen guards, heedless of pain or harm. It must hurt him, because it makes us wince to watch. The word is animalistic.

They say one definition of insanity is when you repeat the same action expecting a different result. Bronson must therefore not be insane. He repeats the same actions expecting the same results. He goes out of his way to avoid different outcomes. During one stretch of comparative passivity, he's allowed to go to the prison art room and work with an instructor. He enjoys this, I think. He isn't a bad artist. When it appears he may be showing progress, what does he do? He takes the instructor hostage, and is beaten senseless by guards.

"I showed magic in there!" he shouts after one brawl, bleeding in triumph. How's that? Magic, like an opening night? Does he expect a standing ovation? I believe most of us, no matter how self-destructive, expect some sort of reward for our behavior. It may not be some people's idea of a reward, but it's ours. Is

Bronson then an extreme masochist, who wants only to be hurt? They say there are masochists like that, but surely there's a limit. What kind of passionate dementia does it require to want to be beaten bloody for thirty-four straight years?

I suppose, after all, Nicolas Winding Refn, the director and cowriter of *Bronson,* was wise to leave out any sort of an explanation. Can you imagine how you'd cringe if the film ended in a flashback of little Mickey undergoing childhood trauma? There is some human behavior beyond our ability to comprehend. I was reading a theory the other day that a few people just happen to be pure evil. I'm afraid I believe it. They lack any conscience, any sense of pity or empathy for their victims. But—Bronson is his own victim. How do you figure that?

Brooklyn's Finest ★★★

R, 140 m., 2010

Richard Gere (Eddie), Don Cheadle (Tango), Ethan Hawke (Sal), Wesley Snipes (Caz), Will Patton (Hobarts), Lili Taylor (Angela), Shannon Kane (Chantel), Ellen Barkin (Smith). Directed by Antoine Fuqua and produced by Elie Cohn, Basil Iwanyk, John Langley, Avi Lerner, and John Thompson. Screenplay by Michael C. Martin.

Three cops, three journeys to what we suspect will be doom. No good can come of the lives they lead. They aren't bad guys, not precisely, but they occupy a world of such unremitting violence and cynicism that they're willing to do what it takes to survive. In the kind of coincidence provided only by fate or screenplays, each one will mean trouble for the other two.

Richard Gere gets top billing as Eddie, a veteran with one week left before retirement. It is a movie convention that anyone who has a week to go before retirement must die before that week is up, but Eddie seems impatient. As the film opens, he wakes up, chugs some whiskey from a bottle, and points a revolver into his mouth, never a good sign.

Don Cheadle is Tango, who is completely embedded undercover in Brooklyn's toughest drug precinct, where he has blended in so well with the bad guys that it's a fine line separating him from crime. His friend is Caz (Wesley Snipes), a dealer trying to go straight after prison; they share one of those inexplicable bonds between two tough guys, causing them to consider each other brothers when they should really be nothing of the kind.

The third cop, Sal (Ethan Hawke), is a narc whose wife (Lili Taylor) provides him with more of a melodramatic emergency than we are perhaps prepared to believe. They have seven kids, live in a house too small for them, and the mold in the walls provokes potentially dangerous asthma attacks. Oh, and she's pregnant. Having twins.

Sal has made an offer on a new place for which he cannot make the first payment. He desperately needs cash, and there's a lot of it around in his work. Tango needs to somehow use Caz and yet spare him. Eddie needs to negotiate an alcoholic haze for seven more days before he can go fishing.

The film and the actors do a good job of establishing these characters in their own lives. Indeed, the best things about *Brooklyn's Finest* are the one-on-one scenes. These are fine actors. The milieu involves a tough, poker-playing, substance-abusing, hard-bitten world where the law meets crime and the two sides have more in common with each other than with civilians. I don't believe it's like this for most cops, but somehow it is for the great majority of movie cops.

Cheadle and Snipes have some very good scenes involving what is left unsaid but not unsuspected. Ethan Hawke has a fierce loyalty to his wife and family, and Lili Taylor does her usual touching job with what's basically a soap opera role. Hawke is especially effective in desperate scenes where he takes crazy risks because he needs to raise cash quickly. Richard Gere's character is not as rich as the other two, is more depressed, is on a more predictable trajectory.

What is rather startling is the level of the violence and killing. Although cops-vs.-drugs movies are traditionally awash in blood, *Brooklyn's Finest* demonstrates a trope I've seen with disturbing frequency: the scene in which one character lifts a firearm and peremptorily blows away another one—almost casually or unemotionally, like cleaning house. I complained for years about the

Talking Killer Syndrome, in which the shooter delays in order to explain himself to a man who will presumably be dead soon. But Instant Killers are not the answer. The fact of taking life is robbed of weight and meaning. The gun becomes the instrument of merciless self-will.

The director of *Brooklyn's Finest*, Antoine Fuqua, made *Training Day* (2001), the film Denzel Washington won an Oscar for. That powerfully costarred Ethan Hawke. This film has the same level of savage violence and the same cops operating outside the same law, but the human stakes are more obvious and less convincing. The lives of the three cops intersect through a series of coincidences and inevitabilities, and I think we become a little too conscious that they're being guided less by chance than by a screenwriter. The film has a basic strength in its performances and craft, but falls short of the high mark Fuqua obviously set for himself.

Brothers ★★★ ½

R, 104 m., 2009

Tobey Maguire (Captain Sam Cahill), Jake Gyllenhaal (Tommy Cahill), Natalie Portman (Grace Cahill), Sam Shepard (Hank Cahill), Bailee Madison (Isabelle Cahill), Taylor Geare (Maggie Cahill). Directed by Jim Sheridan and produced by Michael De Luca, Ryan Kavanaugh, and Sigurjon Sighvatsson. Screenplay by David Benioff, based on the motion picture *Brothers* written by Susanne Bier and Anders Thomas Jensen.

Brothers is the new film by Jim Sheridan, a director who has a sure hand with stories about families (*In America*, *In the Name of the Father*, *The Boxer*). This one is about a family twisted from its natural form when the father leaves for service in Afghanistan just after his brother comes home from prison. The good brother goes into harm's way while the bad brother is shielded by his own misbehavior.

The brothers are played by two leading young actors I hadn't thought of as plausible brothers before, but I do now. Tobey Maguire is Captain Sam Cahill, very warmly married to Grace (Natalie Portman), father of Isabelle and Maggie. Jake Gyllenhaal is his brother,

Tommy, out after a term for armed robbery. Their father, Hank Cahill (Sam Shepard), makes little secret of his pride in Sam and his contempt for Tommy.

But Tommy in his own way is trying to avoid more trouble. Word arrives that Sam has died in a helicopter crash in Afghanistan. Portman handles this blow, and the whole movie, in a touchingly mature way; it redoubles her love for her daughters. Tommy, awkwardly, almost fearfully, tries to help her out with jobs around the house that Sam would have done. She doesn't want this help, but over a time she softens. She knows all about Tommy's history, but she married into it; she didn't grow up with it.

I will try to avoid unnecessary detail. You will have anticipated that with Sam dead, the mother raising the girls and Tommy trying to help, there is the possibility that the two survivors will grow close. Whether they do is not the subject of the picture. That becomes whether Sam suspects they do and what he thinks about it.

It's not a spoiler to observe that Sam didn't die in the crash because from the very first *Brothers* shows him alive in Afghanistan. The film cuts between life at home and the cruel tortures of the Taliban. The prisoner scenes are handled with a ruthless realism, showing Sam placed in the grip of a moral and emotional paradox that makes it, I would say, necessary that he commit acts he will never forgive himself for.

He returns home. He's greeted with love and joy. He feels no joy in return. Sam is so deeply scarred that ordinary emotion is unavailable to him, and he is strange even toward his children. He makes little secret that he suspects Grace and Tommy may have been sleeping together. What can set his mind at ease, especially when, if he had died, that might have been something he desired? And there is always his own unbearable guilt locked within.

Sheridan and his screenplay sources make *Brothers* much more than a drama about war and marriage. It is about what we can forgive ourselves for—and that, too, has been a theme running through Sheridan's films. As an Irish Catholic of sixty, he was raised to feel a great deal about guilt. This becomes Tobey

Maguire's film to dominate, and I've never seen these dark depths in him before. Actors possess a great gift to surprise us, if they find the right material in their hands.

The principal actors, with Shepard's well-timed and not overacted appearances, make this a specific story about particular people, and avoid temptations toward melodrama. It's about guilt and happiness, and how Tommy treats his guilt by righteous action, and Sam sinks into self-destruction. As a mother who seeks to preserve her daughters in the middle, Portman is the emotional heart of the story, as mothers are for so many families.

Brothers is a very close remake of a 2005 Danish film by Susanne Bier, which starred as the mother Connie Nielsen, that remarkable Danish actress equally at home in English (*Gladiator, The Ice Harvest*). Same story, same characters, same moral crisis. I cannot fault the Sheridan remake except in a way that perhaps only an experienced filmgoer would understand.

It is too finished. It is smooth Hollywood craftsmanship, cinematography, editing. The Danish film, loosely associated with the Dogma movement, was rougher, shakier, and more improvised: therefore, more reality, less fiction. You might find it interesting to see the two films together. If it's true that a film is not what it's about but how it's about it, these two will cause you to ask yourself how a film should be about this story.

Brothers at War ★ ★ ★

R, 110 m., 2009

Featuring Jake Rademacher, Captain Isaac Rademacher, Sergeant Joe Rademacher, Jenny Rademacher, Claus Rademacher, Mahmoud Hamid Ali, Edward Allier, Zack Corke, Danelle Fields, Ben Fisher, Kevin Keniston, Frank McCann, Brandon "Mongo" Phillips, and Robert Smallwood. A documentary directed by Jake Rademacher and produced by Rademacher and Norman S. Powell.

I've been waiting for this film since the early days of the war in Iraq. *Brothers at War* is an honest, on-the-ground documentary about the lives of Americans fighting there. It has no spin. It's not left or right. I don't recall if it even mentions President Bush. It's not pro- or antiwar, although obviously the two brothers fighting there support it. It is simply about men and women.

The film is about the men in the Rademacher family from Decatur, Illinois. Jake, the oldest, always planned to go into the military but didn't make it into West Point and found himself as an actor. Isaac, the next, graduated top of his class at West Point and married his classmate Jenny. Joe, next in line, enlisted and was top of his class at Army Ranger school. The brothers were very close growing up, but Jake sensed a distance growing as they came home on leave. He felt he could never know their experience.

What Jake decided to do was visit them in Iraq and film a documentary of them at work—easier because Sergeant Joe was assigned to Captain Isaac's unit. This sounds simple enough, but it involved investment, logistical problems, and danger under fire. The result is a film that benefits from an inside view, as Jake is attached to Isaac's group and follows them for extended periods under fire in the Sunni Triangle and on patrol on the Syrian border. It is clear that the brothers are expert soldiers.

But this is not a war film. It is a life film, and its scenes filmed at home are no less powerful than those filmed in Iraq. Jenny Rademacher served in Kuwait and elsewhere, then has their child. Isaac is deployed to Iraq soon after, and when he returns home it's to a daughter who has never met him. Jake films the homecomings and departures of both brothers, attends family gatherings, and watches Isaac as he trains troops of the Iraqi Army. The filmmakers are often under fire, and a man is killed on one mission by a roadside bomb.

Jake's entree gives him access to many moments of the kind you never see on the news. Nicknamed "Hollywood" and such an accustomed daily sight that soldiers are not self-conscious around his camera, he listens in on small talk, shop talk, and gab sessions. He watches during meals. He walks along on a door-to-door operation. He looks at houses and roadsides in a way that recognizes they may harbor his death. He gives a stark idea of the heat, the dust, the desolate landscape.

I've reviewed many documentaries about

Iraq. All of them have been antiwar. "Why don't you ever review a pro-war documentary?" readers asked me. The answer was simple: There weren't any. There still aren't, because no one in this film argues in favor of the war—or against it, either. What you hear is guarded optimism, pride in the work, loyalty to the service. This is deep patriotism. It involves risking your life for your country out of a sense of duty.

Every time he saw Isaac or Joe deployed, Jake says, he wondered if he would ever see them again. In filming his documentary, he feels he has walked a little way in their shoes. As is often the case among men, the brothers leave these things unspoken. But now Jake sees their war as more of a reality and less of an abstraction. He invites his audience to do the same.

The Brothers Bloom ★ ★ ½
PG-13, 109 m., 2009

Rachel Weisz (Penelope), Adrien Brody (Bloom), Mark Ruffalo (Stephen), Rinko Kikuchi (Bang Bang), Maximilian Schell (Diamond Dog), Robbie Coltrane (The Curator), Ricky Jay (Narrator). Directed by Rian Johnson and produced by Ram Bergman, James D. Stern, and Wendy Japhet. Screenplay by Johnson.

Those con-man movies are best that con the audience. We should think at some point that everything is for real or, even better, that we can see through it when we can't. I offer as examples works by the master of the genre, David Mamet: *House of Games*, *The Spanish Prisoner*, and *Redbelt*.

Rian Johnson's new film *The Brothers Bloom* lets us in on the con and then fools us. It does that in an interesting way. It gives us Stephen (Mark Ruffalo) and Bloom (Adrien Brody), and I might as well get this out of the way: I don't know why they're called the "brothers" Bloom when that's the first name of one, and neither seems to have a family name. Maybe I missed something.

From childhood, Stephen fabricates con scenarios and creates the characters and scripts for his younger brother, Bloom, to join him in. When they're adults, Stephen's girlfriend Bang Bang (Rinko Kikuchi), who speaks extremely rarely, is mostly involved as a

passive bystander, witness, validator, or sometimes more. For Stephen, life is a con and he's living it. For Bloom, the game is getting old.

They meet a promising mark named Penelope (Rachel Weisz) who is rich, beautiful and lonely, even though most women who are rich and beautiful don't have a crushing problem with loneliness. She falls into a scheme fashioned by the brothers, and I will not specify which falls in love with her, but one does, and then . . . I have to watch my step here. The brothers are such perfectionists that they like to involve as many marks as they can. Let's leave it at that.

At a certain point we think we're in on the moves of the con, and then we think we're not, and then we're not sure, and then we're wrong, and then we're right, and then we're wrong again, and we're entertained up to another certain point, and then we vote with Bloom: The game gets old. Or is it Stephen who finds that out? Bloom complains, "I'm tired of living a scripted life." We're tired on his behalf. And on our own.

The problem with the movie is that the cons have too many encores and curtain calls. We tire of being (rhymes with "perked") off. When an exercise seems to continue for its own sake, it should sense it has lost its audience, take a bow, and sit down. And even then, *The Brothers Bloom* has another twist that might actually be moving, if we weren't by this time so paranoid. As George Burns once said, "Sincerity is everything. If you can fake that, you've got it made." A splendid statement, and I know it applies to this movie, but I'm not quite sure how.

This is a period picture but a little hazy as to which period. It's the second feature by the thirty-five-year-old Rian Johnson, who made the acclaimed Sundance "originality" winner *Brick* in 2005. That was a film noir crime story transplanted to a California high school. Now we have *The Sting* visiting eastern Europe. *The Brothers Bloom* was filmed for a reported $20 million, which was chickenfeed if you consider the locations in Montenegro, Serbia, Romania, and the Czech Republic.

The acting is a delight. Rachel Weisz creates a New Jersey heiress who is delightfully ditzy. Ruffalo is sincere at all times, even when he's not. Adrien Brody is so smooth his logical contradictions slide right past: He makes them sound as if they *must* mean something. The enigmatic Bang Bang, who acts as an assistant to the brothers, never says a word but often seems as if she's about to. And Johnson wisely hired Ricky Jay, veteran of so many Mamet films, to provide a narration in that voice that suggests he knows a lot more than he's telling.

Johnson has a fertile imagination, a way with sly comedy, and a yearning for the fantastical. But he needs to tend to his nuts and bolts and meat and potatoes. The film is just too smug and pleased with itself; as a general rule, an exercise in style needs to convince us it cares about more than style. Lesson in point: *The Life Aquatic with Steve Zissou.* The movie is lively at times, it's lovely to look at, and the actors are persuasive in very difficult material. But around and around it goes, and where it stops, nobody by that point much cares.

Bruno ★★★ ½

R, 82 m., 2009

Sacha Baron Cohen (Bruno), Gustaf Hammarsten (Lutz). Cameos, knowingly or not, by Paula Abdul, Harrison Ford, Ron Paul, Bono, Chris Martin, Elton John, Slash, Snoop Dogg, Sting. Directed by Larry Charles and produced by Sacha Baron Cohen, Jay Roach, Dan Mazer, and Monica Levinson. Screenplay by Cohen, Anthony Hines, Mazer, and Jeff Schaffer.

Bruno is a no-holds-barred comedy permitting several holds I had not dreamed of. The needle on my internal Laugh Meter went haywire, bouncing between hilarity, appreciation, shock, admiration, disgust, disbelief, and appalled incredulity. Here is a film that is eighty-two minutes long and doesn't contain thirty boring seconds. There should be a brief segment at the next Spirit Awards with John Waters conferring the Knighthood of Bad Taste to Sacha Baron Cohen. If he decides to tap Cohen on each shoulder with his sword, I want to have my eyes closed.

To describe Cohen's character Bruno as flamboyantly gay would be an understatement. He makes Bruce Vilanch seem like Mike Ditka. Bruno is disgraced in his native Austria when he wears a Velcro suit to Fashion Week

and sticks to backdrops, curtains, and models. It's slapstick worthy of Jerry Lewis. Then he flies to Los Angeles with his loyal worshipper Lutz (Gustaf Hammarsten), vowing to become a celebrity.

As in his 2007 hit *Borat,* Cohen places his character into situations involving targets who may not be in on the joke and have never heard of Bruno or, for that matter, Sacha Baron Cohen. Some of the situations may be set up with actors, but most are manifestly the real thing. I include an interview in which Bruno lures Congressman Ron Paul into a hotel room, his appearance on a Dallas TV morning show, the screening of a TV pilot before a focus group, counseling with two Alabama ministers dedicated to "curing" homosexuals, and a gay wrestling match before a crowd that is dangerously real.

The setups include an interview with Paula Abdul and originally included one with La Toya Jackson, which was cut because of her brother's death. That accounts for the running time being three minutes shorter than at the movie's London opening. I also believe those are real parents at interviews trying to get their babies hired for a proposed film—mothers who say their babies are ready to work with pyrotechnics, dress as Nazis, or be strapped to a cross. These moms want their babies to be stars.

One incredible scene involved a darling little black boy Bruno claims to have adopted in Africa. He appears with this child on the *Richard Bey Morning Show* in Dallas, before a manifestly real, outraged, and all-black studio audience. The host is indeed Richard Bey, but I suspect he was in on the gag. I learn that the audience wasn't. Shows like Jerry Springer and Maury Povich have dredged up such astonishing lowlifes that audiences are prepared to believe almost anything.

Certainly it takes sheer nerve for Cohen to walk into some of these situations, knowing he'll only get one take—if he's lucky. He plays an allegedly gay-hating straight wrestler in a scene promising gay-bashing, and then shows the two men in the cage getting turned on as they grapple. There is also an eerie tension in a scene where Bruno the gay new hunter sits around a campfire with macho hunters who are very, very silent.

It is no doubt unfair of Cohen to victimize an innocent such as Ron Paul. Watching Paul trying to deal with this weirdo made me reflect that as a fringe candidate, he has probably been subjected to a lot of strange questions on strange TV shows, and is prepared to sit through almost anything for TV exposure. On the other hand, he has made a lot of intolerant comments about homosexuals, so by shouting "Queer!" as he stalked out along a hotel corridor, he blew his chance of making amends. Helpful rule: If you find you have been the subject of a TV ambush, the camera is probably still rolling.

The movie is directed by Larry Charles, who in *Borat*, Bill Maher's *Religulous*, and his TV series *Curb Your Enthusiasm* has specialized in public embarrassment. Come to think of it, this may explain his outstandingly awful feature film debut, the Bob Dylan vehicle *Masked and Anonymous* (2003). In that one, stars such as Jeff Bridges, Penelope Cruz, Angela Bassett, John Goodman, Val Kilmer, and Luke Wilson appeared as straight men while Dylan occasionally deigned to utter brief and enigmatic proverbs. Maybe they were told, ha ha, they were going to appear in a real movie.

Note: The R rating is very, very hard. ☞

The Bucket List ★
PG-13, 97 m., 2008

Jack Nicholson (Edward Cole), Morgan Freeman (Carter Chambers), Sean Hayes (Thomas), Rob Morrow (Dr. Hollins), Beverly Todd (Virginia Chambers). Directed by Rob Reiner and produced by Craig Zadan, Neil Meron, and Alan Greisman. Screenplay by Justin Zackham.

The Bucket List is a movie about two old codgers who are nothing like people, both suffering from cancer that is nothing like cancer, and setting off on adventures that are nothing like possible. I urgently advise hospitals: Do not make the DVD available to your patients; there may be an outbreak of bedpans thrown at TV screens.

The film opens with yet another voice-over narration by Morgan Freeman, extolling the saintly virtues of a white person who deserves our reverence. His voice takes on a sort of wonderment as he speaks of the man's greatness; it was a note that worked in *The Shawshank Redemption* and *Million Dollar Baby*, but not here, not when he is talking of a character played by Jack Nicholson, for whom lovability is not a strong suit.

Nicholson plays Edward, an enormously rich man of about seventy, who has been diagnosed with cancer, given a year to live, and is sharing a room with Carter (Freeman), about the same age, same prognosis. Why does a billionaire not have a private room? Why, because Edward owns the hospital, and he has a policy that all patients must double up, so it would look bad if he didn't.

This is only one among countless details the movie gets wrong. Doesn't Edward know that hospitals make lotsa profits by offering private rooms, "concierge service," etc.? The fact is, Edward and Carter must be roommates to set up their Meet Cute, during which they first rub each other the wrong way, and then have an orgy of male bonding. Turns out Carter has a "bucket list" of things he should do before he kicks the bucket. Edward embraces this idea, announces, "Hell, all I have is money," and treats Carter to an around-the-world trip in his private airplane, during which they will, let's see, I have the itinerary right here, visit the pyramids, the Taj Mahal, Hong Kong, the French Riviera, and the Himalayas.

Carter is faithfully married to his loving wife, Virginia (Beverly Todd), who is remarkably restrained about seeing her dying husband off on this madcap folly. She doesn't take it well, but I know wives who would call for the boys with butterfly nets. Edward, after four divorces, has no restraints, plenty of regrets, and uses his generosity to mask egotism, selfishness, and the imposition of his goofy whim on poor Carter. That his behavior is seen as somehow redemptive is perhaps the movie's weirdest fantasy. Meanwhile, the codgers have pseudo-profound conversations about the Meaning of It All, and Carter's superior humanity begins to soak in for the irascible Edward.

The movie, directed by Rob Reiner, is written by Justin Zackham, who must be very optimistic indeed if he doesn't know that there is nothing like a serious illness to bring you to the end of sitcom clichés. I've never had chemo, as Edward and Carter must endure, but I have had cancer, and believe me, during convalescence after surgery the *last* item on your bucket list is climbing a Himalaya. It's more likely to be topped by keeping down a full meal, having a triumphant bowel movement, keeping your energy up in the afternoon, letting your loved ones know you love them, and convincing the doc your reports of pain are real and not merely disguising your desire to become a drug addict. To be sure, the movie includes plenty of details about discomfort in the toilet, but they're put on hold once the trots are replaced by the globe-trotting.

Edward and Carter fly off on their odyssey, during which the only realistic detail is the interior of Edward's private jet. Other locations are created, all too obviously, by special effects; the boys in front of the pyramids look about as convincing as Abbot and Costello wearing pith helmets in front of a painted backdrop. Meanwhile, we wait patiently for Edward to realize his inner humanity, reach out to his estranged daughter, and learn all the other life lessons Carter has to bestow. All Carter gets out of it is months away from his beloved family, and the opportunity to be a moral cheering section for Edward's conversion.

I'm thinking, just once, couldn't a movie open with the voice-over telling us what a great guy the Morgan Freeman character was? Nicholson could say, "I was a rich, unpleasant, selfish jerk, and this wise, nice man taught me to feel hope and love." Yeah, that would be nice. Because what's so great about Edward, anyway? He throws his money around like a pig and makes Carter come along for the ride. So what?

There are movies that find humor, albeit perhaps of a bitter, sardonic nature, in cancer. Some of them show incredible bravery, as in Mike Nichols's *Wit*, with its great performance by Emma Thompson. *The Bucket List* thinks dying of cancer is a laff riot, followed by a dime-store epiphany. The sole redeeming merit of the film is the steady work by Morgan Freeman, who has appeared in more than one embarrassing movie but never embarrassed himself. Maybe it's not Jack Nicholson's fault that his role cries out to be overplayed, but it's his fate, and ours.

Burn After Reading ★ ★ ★
R, 96 m., 2008

George Clooney (Harry Pfarrer), Frances McDormand (Linda Litzke), John Malkovich (Osborne Cox), Tilda Swinton (Katie Cox), Brad Pitt (Chad Feldheimer), Richard Jenkins (Ted Treffon), J. K. Simmons (CIA Boss), David Rasche (CIA Officer). Directed by Ethan Coen and Joel Coen and produced by Tim Bevan, Eric Fellner, Ethan Coen, and Joel Coen. Screenplay by Ethan Coen and Joel Coen.

The Coen brothers' *Burn After Reading* is a screwball comedy that occasionally becomes something more. The characters are zany, the plot coils upon itself with dizzy zeal, and the roles seem like a perfect fit for the actors—yes, even Brad Pitt, as Chad, a gum-chewing, fuzzy-headed physical fitness instructor. I've always thought of him as a fine actor, but here he reveals a dimension that, shall I say, we haven't seen before.

What do I mean by "something more"? There is a poignancy in the roles played by Frances McDormand and George Clooney, both looking for love in all the wrong places. She plays Linda Litzke, one of Chad's fellow instructors, and is looking for her perfect match on the Web. This despite her conviction that she's far from perfect. In a scene of astonishing frankness (using a body double, I think) she submits to a merciless going-over by a plastic surgeon, and decides to have some work done on her thighs, abdomen, breasts, underarms, and eyes. "I've gotten about as far as this body can take me," she decides.

Clooney is a happily married man, if only he knew it, named Harry Pfarrer. (It's one of those Jack Lemmony kind of names that sound like a cough, but I don't remember anyone saying it in the movie.) Harry also looks for dates on the Web, and, in general terms, will happily date anyone. He and Linda meet and seem to like each other, and then Linda and Chad find a computer disc at the gym. They read it and find it belongs to a CIA man named Osborne Cox (John Malkovich), who has just been fired for alcoholism. Cox is married to Katie (Tilda Swinton), who is also having an affair with Harry. You see how it goes.

No need to describe the plot. It goes around

and around and comes out here, there, every-where. All nicely put together, of course, but as an exercise, not an imperative. The movie's success depends on the characters and the dialogue. Linda and Chad, who remind me a little of Rupert and Masha in *The King of Comedy,* try to peddle their disc to the Russian embassy. Anything to raise money for that plastic surgery. The CIA, baffled, gets involved. A gung-ho officer (David Rasche), confused but determined, reports to his CIA boss (J. K. Simmons, *Juno's* dad). The boss doesn't have much dialogue, but every line is a punch line.

The Malkovich character is a right proper SOB, one of those drunks who thinks he's not an alcoholic because he prudently watches the second hand on the clock until it's precisely five o'clock. He's a snarky, shaved-headed, bow-tie-wearing misanthrope who would be utterly amazed if he knew how his files got into the hands of two peons at a gym.

As for Clooney, in one movie he's the im-probably handsome, superintelligent hero, and in the next, he's the forlorn doofus. You wouldn't believe what he's constructing in his basement. The Coens say that this film completes their "idiot trilogy" with Clooney, after *O Brother, Where Art Thou?* (2000) and *Intolerable Cruelty* (2003). Clooney as an idiot? As to the manner born.

Frances McDormand is wonderful. Here she channels a little of the go-getter determination of her police chief in *Fargo.* She's innocent of deep thoughts, but nothing can stop her. From the first time I noticed her, in a great scene with Gene Hackman in *Mississippi Burning,* she has had that rare ability to seem correctly cast in every role.

This is not a great Coen brothers film. Nor is it one of their bewildering excursions off the deep end. It's funny, sometimes delightful, sometimes a little sad, with dialogue that sounds perfectly logical until you listen a little more carefully and realize all of these people are mad.

The movie is only ninety-six minutes long. That's long enough for a movie, but this time, I dunno, I thought the end felt like it arrived a little arbitrarily. I must be wrong, because I can't figure out what could have followed next. Not even the device in the basement would have been around for another chapter.

The Burning Plain ★★ ½
R, 106 m., 2009

Charlize Theron (Sylvia), Kim Basinger (Gina), Jennifer Lawrence (Mariana), John Corbett (John), Joaquim de Almeida (Nick), Danny Pino (Santiago), J. D. Pardo (Young Santiago), Jose Maria Yazpik (Carlos). Directed by Guillermo Arriaga and produced by Laurie MacDonald and Walter F. Parkes. Screenplay by Arriaga.

The Burning Plain involves events perhaps twenty years and one thousand miles apart, with many of the same characters. Told chronologically, it might have accumulated considerable power. Told as a labyrinthine tangle of intercut timelines and locations, it is a frustrating exercise in self-indulgence by the writer-director, Guillermo Arriaga.

He is familiar with intercut story lines. As the favorite writer of Alejandro Gonzalez Inarritu, he wrote *Amores Perros, Babel,* and *21 Grams,* three splendid films that moved among people and places. They were all different characters, and it was clear where everything was happening. That made it easier. And the human drama in each place had continuity and integrity; the story strands might even have been reassembled as self-contained short films.

In *The Burning Plain,* his first film as a director, Arriaga should have asked harder questions of his screenwriter, himself. I don't know if it's a spoiler or just merciful assistance to tell you that many of the characters we see are the same people at different times in their lives, and that some of the men at different ages are hard to tell apart.

Certainly a time comes when you figure that out for yourself—before, I hope, the movie belatedly relents and makes it clear. Given the Law of Economy of Characters, you eventually realize that there would be no need for separate stories apparently destined never to meet. You can see there are two main locations—New Mexico and Oregon—and you decide that years must have passed, although the visual cues (cars, clothes) don't provide clues.

What is Arriaga's purpose in this construction? Search me. He's being too clever for his own good. That's a shame, because his actors provide him with effective performances, even though they must emotionally build up or refer back to the same characters played by different actors.

Having possibly diminished your experience (or maybe enhanced it) by tipping off the two time periods, I will deliberately avoid additional details and simply describe the characters we meet. In New Mexico, Gina (Kim Basinger) is a married woman, passionately in love with Nick (Joaquim de Almeida), a man not her husband. They live in separate towns, and he places a house trailer midway so they can meet. This mobile home is isolated enough that traffic never passes, and close enough that Mariana (Jennifer Lawrence), Gina's teenage daughter, can reach it by bicycle. Coincidentally, Mariana meets Santiago (J. D. Pardo), Nick's son. These coincidences have a way of happening in Arriaga's screenplays.

In Oregon, Sylvia (Charlize Theron) manages a chic seaside restaurant and is deeply unhappy. She has quick, meaningless sex with, seemingly, almost any man, and has a way of leaving her job at key hours and smoking morosely above the waves. A mysterious man named Carlos (Jose Maria Yazpik) follows her and insists they must meet. Perhaps he desires sex? No, it is more complicated.

And that's all I'll say. Basinger and Theron have the key roles and are excellent, although by the nature of the story construction, their characters are denied continuity, and that's something leading characters usually require. Theron is one of the film's producers. She is intelligent and daring in her choice of roles, and must have trusted that the author of those three great screenplays and *The Three Burials of Melquiades Estrada* would know how to negotiate this tangle. Unfortunately, he doesn't.

C

Cadillac Records ★ ★ ★
R, 108 m., 2008

Adrien Brody (Leonard Chess), Jeffrey Wright (Muddy Waters), Gabrielle Union (Geneva Wade), Columbus Short (Little Walter), Cedric the Entertainer (Willie Dixon), Emmanuelle Chriqui (Revetta Chess), Eamonn Walker (Howlin' Wolf), Mos Def (Chuck Berry), Beyonce Knowles (Etta James). Directed by Darnell Martin and produced by Andrew Lack and Sofia Sondervan. Screenplay by Martin.

An argument could be made that modern rock 'n' roll was launched not at Sun Records in Memphis, but at Chicago's Chess Records, 2120 S. Michigan Ave., and its earlier South Side locations since the late 1940s. The Rolling Stones even recorded a song named after the address. The great Chess roster included Muddy Waters, Howlin' Wolf, Etta James, Willie Dixon, Chuck Berry, and Little Walter. They first made Chicago the home of the blues, and then rhythm and blues, which, as they say, had a child and named it rock 'n' roll.

Cadillac Records is an account of the Chess story that depends more on music than history, which is perhaps as it should be. The film is a fascinating record of the evolution of a black musical style and the tangled motives of the white men who had an instinct for it. The Chess brothers, Leonard and Phil, walked into neighborhoods that were dicey for white men after midnight, packed firearms, found or were found by the most gifted musicians of the emerging urban music, and recorded them in a studio so small it forced the sound out into the world.

This movie sidesteps the existence of Phil Chess, now living in Arizona, and focuses on the enigmatic, chain-smoking Leonard (Adrien Brody). Starting with an early liaison with Muddy Waters, who in effect became his creative partner, he visited "race music" radio stations in the South with his artists and payola, found and/or created a demand, and gave his musicians shiny new Cadillacs but never a good look at their royalties. Muddy (Jeffrey Wright) was probably paid only a share of the money he earned, but the more ferocious

Howlin' Wolf (Eamonn Walker), seemingly less sophisticated, held on to his money, made his own deals, and incredibly even paid health benefits for the members of his band.

It is part of the legend that Muddy was nice, Howlin' was scary, and they disliked each other. In the film, they are guarded, but civil and fierce competitors. Walker plays the six-foot-six Wolf as a scowler who somehow from that height looks up at people under hooded eyes and appears willing to slice you just for the convenience. The real Howlin' Wolf must have been more complex; he couldn't read or write until he was past forty, but then he earned his high school equivalency diploma and studied accounting, an excellent subject for an associate of Leonard Chess.

Did Chess love the music? Brody's performance and the screenplay by director Darnell Martin leave that question a little cloudy. Certainly, he had good taste and an aggressive business instinct, and he didn't sit in an office in the Loop, but was behind the bar at the Macomba Lounge on Saturday nights in the 1950s, when some of his more alarming customers must have figured, hey, a white man that crazy, maybe it's not a good idea to mess with him.

Leonard was married but maintained a wall between his business and his family. Martin's movie speculates that later in his career he may have fallen in love with his new discovery Etta James (Beyonce Knowles). If so, romance didn't blind him to her gifts, and in a movie where the actors do most of their own singing, her performances are inspired and persuasive.

The Chess artists had an influence in more than one way on white rock singers. The Beach Boys' "Surfing USA" has the same melody as Chuck Berry's "Sweet Little Sixteen." Frank Zappa borrowed Howlin's favorite exclamation, "Great Googley Moogley!" The Rolling Stones, who acknowledged their Chicago influences, paid a pilgrimage to South Michigan Ave. and arranged a European tour for Chess stars, and Keith Richards talked Chuck Berry into the concert shown in the great doc *Hail! Hail! Rock and Roll* and played backup guitar.

Given the number of characters and the

time covered, Darnell Martin does an effective job of sketching the backgrounds of some of her subjects, and doesn't go out of her way to indict Leonard's business methods. (Did the singers know their Cadillacs were paid for from their own money?) There is a poignant scene where Leonard arranges the first meeting between Etta James and her white father (who was—are you ready for this?—Minnesota Fats), and a close look at the troubled but durable marriage of Muddy Waters and his wife, Geneva Wade (Gabrielle Union).

The casting throughout is successful. Columbus Short suggests the building inner torments of Little Walter, and Cedric the Entertainer plays the singer-songwriter Willie Dixon as a creator and synthesizer. Nobody can really play Chuck Berry, but Mos Def does a great duck walk.

Eamonn Walker, at six-foot-one, is five inches shy of the towering Howlin', but he evokes presence and intimidation. Sometimes I'm amazed at actors. Seeing Howlin' Wolf bring danger into the room in this film, you'd never guess Walker started as a dancer, was a social worker, acts in Shakespeare, and is married to a novelist. Could any of the regulars at 2120 S. Michigan Ave. have guessed they would be instrumental in creating a music that would dominate the entire world for the next fifty years?

The Cake Eaters ★ ★ ★
NO MPAA RATING, 95 m., 2009

Kristen Stewart (Georgia), Aaron Stanford (Beagle), Bruce Dern (Easy), Elizabeth Ashley (Marge), Jayce Bartok (Guy), Melissa Leo (Ceci), Miriam Shor (Stephanie). Directed by Mary Stuart Masterson and produced by Masterson, Allen Bain, Darren Goldberg, Elisa Pugliese, and Jesse Scolaro. Screenplay by Jayce Bartok.

Kristen Stewart has been in feature films since 2003, but this year, still only eighteen, she became a big star as a vampire's girlfriend in *Twilight*. Now comes her remarkable performance in *The Cake Eaters,* made two years ago, showing her as a very different kind of lover in a very different kind of film. It's the directorial debut of Mary Stuart

Masterson, herself a fine actress (*Fried Green Tomatoes*).

Stewart plays Georgia, a high school student who has a degenerative muscular disease. It causes her to walk unsteadily, stand crookedly and, as Beagle tells her, talk like she's had a few beers. Beagle (Aaron Stanford) is the kid she meets at a flea market. She asks him to come over to her house that evening. Beagle says, uh . . . ah . . . yeah, sure. He has no problems with her condition; it's just that he's terrified of girls.

Beagle is going through a rough time emotionally. His mom has recently died after a long ordeal with cancer. His dad, Easy (Bruce Dern), is a good guy and in his corner. His brother, Guy (Jayce Bartok, writer of the screenplay), sat out the entire illness in New York, seeking success as a rock or folk star, and has returned just too late for the funeral. Beagle is enraged at him. Beagle cared for his mom the whole three years.

Georgia, as played by Stewart, is not looking for sympathy. She's looking for sex and is very forthright about that. When a hairdresser asks her if she isn't rushing things, she says simply, "I don't have a lot of time." Why did she choose Beagle? He's OK-looking, he's not bothered by her disability, you can see he's gentle, and perhaps she suspects she can get him to do what she wants.

Masterson and her cast make these characters, and others, into specific people and not elements in a docudrama. Nobody is a "type," certainly not Georgia's grandmother Marge (Elizabeth Ashley), the kind of woman you know once raised some hell and hasn't completely stopped. When Beagle happens to see his dad kissing Marge, so soon after the funeral, he's devastated. This creates enormous tension among all three men in the family and a connection between Beagle and Georgia they're not aware of.

Beagle is three or four years older than Georgia, but behind her in emotional development, I sense. He's very naive. Georgia's mother (Melissa Leo, this year's Oscar nominee) is suspicious of him but has no hint of her daughter's plans for the unsuspecting boy. And Beagle's father is reassuring: "My boy has no game in that area, I promise you."

So there are three simultaneous romances:

Beagle and Georgia, Easy and Marge, and I forgot to mention Guy, who has a local girl named Stephanie (Miriam Shor), furious at him because he proposed marriage and then left for New York without even saying good-bye.

You might think with all of these plot lines and colorful characters, the movie turns into a carnival. Not at all. I won't say why. I'll only say it all leaves us feeling good about most of them. Masterson, like many actors, is an assured director even in her debut; working with her brother Pete as cinematographer, she creates a spell and a tenderness, and pushes exactly as far as this story should go.

Capitalism: A Love Story ★★★ ½
R, 117 m., 2009

A documentary directed by Michael Moore and produced by Michael Moore and Anne Moore. Screenplay by Michael Moore.

The loudest voice in Michael Moore's new film speaks to us from the grave. It belongs to Franklin Delano Roosevelt, less than a year before his death, calling for a Second Bill of Rights for the American people. He says citizens have a right to homes, jobs, education, and health care. In measured, judicious words, he speaks gravely to the camera.

Until a researcher for Moore uncovered this footage, it had never before been seen publicly. Too ill to deliver his State of the Union address to Congress in person, Roosevelt delivered it on the radio, and then invited in Movietone News cameras to film it. It was included in no newsreels of the time. Today, eerily, it still seems relevant, and the improvements he calls for are still unachieved.

In moments like that, Moore's *Capitalism: A Love Story* speaks eloquently. At other times his message is a little unclear. He believes that capitalism is a system that claims to reward free enterprise but in fact rewards greed. He says it is responsible for accumulation of wealth at the top: The richest 1 percent of Americans have more than the bottom 95 percent. At a time when America debates legalized gambling, it has long been practiced on Wall Street.

But what must we do to repair our economy? Moore doesn't recommend socialism.

He has faith in the ballot box, but believes Obama has been too quick to placate the rich and has not brought about substantial reforms. The primary weapon Moore employs is shame. That corporations and financial institutions continue to exploit the majority of Americans, including tea-baggers and Town Hall demonstrators, is a story that hasn't been told.

Here are two shocking revelations Moore makes. The first involves something that is actually called "peasant insurance." Did you know that companies can take out life insurance policies on their workers so that *they* collect the benefits when *we* die? This is one form of employee insurance they don't have a problem with. Companies don't usually inform a surviving spouse of the money they've made from a death.

The second is the reckless, immoral gambling referred to as "derivatives." I've read that derivatives are so complex they're created by computers, and not even the software authors really understand them. Moore asks three experts to explain them to him. All three fail. Essentially, they involve bets placed on the expectation that we will default on our mortgages, for example. If we do, the bets pay off. What if we don't? Investors can hedge their bets, by betting that *they* will fail. They hope to win both ways.

Our mortgages are the collateral for these bets. Moore says they are sliced and diced and rebundled and scattered hither and yon. He has an interview with Congresswoman Marcy Kaptur, D-Ohio, who advises her constituents: If a bank forecloses, don't move, and demand they produce a copy of your mortgage. In many cases, they can't. Your mortgage is no longer a signed document in a safety deposit box. It has been fragmented into scattered bits on the world financial markets.

You may have seen that weirdo screaming on the financial cable show about shiftless homeowners who obtained mortgages they couldn't afford. Moore says that in fact two-thirds of all American personal bankruptcies are caused by the cost of health care. Few people can afford an extended illness in this country. Moore mentions his film *Sicko* (cough).

Capitalism is most effective when it explains or reveals these outrages. It is less effective, but perhaps more entertaining, when it shows Michael being Michael. He likes to grandstand. On Wall Street, he uses a bullhorn to demand our money back. He uses bright yellow police crime scene tape to block off the stock exchange. He's a classic rabble rouser. Love him or hate him, you gotta give him credit. He centers our attention as no other documentarian ever has.

He is also a working-class kid, no college education, still with the baseball cap and saggy pants, who feels sympathy for victims. Watch him speaking with a man who discovered his wife's employer collected "peasant insurance." Listen to him speak with a family that is losing a farm after four generations. Consider that a great deal of wealth in America has been earned from *our* failures. When union-busting companies move jobs overseas, workers lose but the companies don't.

The film's title is never explained. What does Moore mean by *Capitalism: A Love Story?* Maybe he means that capitalism means never having to say you're sorry.

Cassandra's Dream ★ ★
PG-13, 108 m., 2008

Ewan McGregor (Ian Blaine), Colin Farrell (Terry Blaine), Tom Wilkinson (Uncle Howard), Sally Hawkins (Kate), Hayley Atwell (Angela Stark). Directed by Woody Allen and produced by Letty Aronson, Stephen Tenenbaum, and Gareth Wiley. Screenplay by Allen.

Woody Allen's *Cassandra's Dream* is about two brothers, one single and modestly successful, one struggling but in a happy relationship, who are both desperate to raise money and agree to commit a crime together. The identical premise is used in Sidney Lumet's *Before the Devil Knows You're Dead,* which is like a master class in how Allen goes wrong.

The Lumet film uses actors (Ethan Hawke and Philip Seymour Hoffman) who don't look like brothers but feel like brothers. Allen's actors (Ewan McGregor and Colin Farrell) look like brothers but don't really feel related. Lumet's film involves family members in a crime that seems reasonable but goes spectacularly wrong. Allen has a family member propose a crime that seems spectacularly unreasonable and goes

right, with, however, unforeseen consequences. One of the brothers in both movies is consumed with guilt. And so on.

Lumet seems comfortable with his milieu, middle-class affluence in a New York suburb. Allen's milieu is not and perhaps never will be the Cockney working class of London, and his actors seem as much tourists as he is. Nevertheless, they plug away, in a plot that is intrinsically absorbing at times even with so much going against it.

McGregor and Farrell play Ian and Terry Blaine, Ian a partner in his dad's restaurant, Terry a hard-drinking, chain-smoking garage mechanic. Terry at least seems comfortable with his life and his supportive girlfriend (Sally Hawkins), although he dreams of getting rich quick; he gambles unwisely at the dog tracks. Ian also wants cash, and not only for a fishy-sounding opportunity to invest in California hotels. While driving a classic Jaguar borrowed from the garage where his brother works, he meets a high-maintenance sexpot actress (Hayley Atwell) and presents himself as a "property speculator" far richer than he is.

The brothers share a dream to own a boat. Terry wins big at the track, enough to buy a rusty bilge bucket, fix it up, and have a great day sailing with their two girls. But then Terry loses big-time, owes ninety thousand pounds, and discovers that guys are after him to break his legs. That's when rich Uncle Howard (Tom Wilkinson) returns from China (or somewhere) to make a proposition. His business empire is built on fraud, a colleague is about to squeal, and Howard wants the boys to do him a favor and murder the man.

Wilkinson, always a cool persuader, couches this in terms of family loyalty. That convinces the boys not nearly as much as does their own desperation. What happens I will not detail. This stretch of the movie does work and involves us, but then the lads run smack into an ending that was, to me, completely possible but highly unsatisfactory. Its problem is its sheer blundering plausibility. Allen's great *Match Point* (2005), on the other hand, also about crime and social con games, had an ending that was completely implausible and sublimely satisfactory. Remember how that ring falls at the end? What is fiction for, if not to manipulate the possible?

85

Chandni Chowk to China ★ ★

NO MPAA RATING, 168 m., 2009

Akshay Kumar (Sidhu), Deepika Padukone (Sakhi/Meow Meow), Mithun Chakraborty (Dada), Ranvir Shorey (Chopstick), Gordon Liu (Hojo), Roger Yuan (Chiang). Directed by Nikhil Advani and produced by Mukesh Talreja, Rohan Sippy, and Ramesh Sippy. Screenplay by Rajat Aroraa and Shridhar Raghavan.

Chandni Chowk is a historic marketplace in the walled city of old Delhi, so now you understand the title of *Chandni Chowk to China*, and because the plot is simplicity itself there is nothing else to understand but its origins. This is the first Bollywood movie to get a North American release from a major studio, and was chosen, I suspect, because it is a slapstick comedy containing a lot of kung fu. That, and maybe because it stars Akshay Kumar, described in the publicity as "the heartthrob of Indian cinema and current reigning king of Bollywood."

I would need to see Kumar in something other than this to understand his fame. He comes across here as a cross between Jerry Lewis and Adam Sandler, but less manic than Jerry and not as affable as Sandler. What I can understand is that his costar, Deepika Padukone, abandoned a promising start as a badminton champion to become a model and actress. She is breathtaking, which of course is standard in Bollywood, where all the actresses are either breathtaking or playing mothers.

The story plays as though it could be remade as a Sandler comedy with no changes except for length. When you go to a movie in India, you get your money's worth, in what takes the time of a double feature. As my Mumbai friend Uma da Cunha told me, big Bollywood movies give you everything: adventure, thrills, romance, song, dance, stunts, the works. In India, when you go to the movies, you go to *the movies. Chandni Chowk to China* plays at 168 minutes, having been shortened, I learn, for the American release. It would be safe to say few viewers will complain of its brevity.

Kumar stars as Sidhu, a lowly potato and onion chopper in his father's potato pancake stand. He adores his Dada (Mithun Cha-

kraborty), despite the old man's propensity for kicking him so high over Delhi that he's a hazard to low-flying aircraft. As eager to please as a puppy, he has a gift for getting into trouble, but all that changes the day he finds the image of a god on one of his potatoes. This image, to my eye, makes the eBay portraits on grilled cheese sandwiches look like Norman Rockwells.

No matter. He exhibits the potato and collects donations, which are stolen by the nefarious Chopstick (Ranvir Shorey), while meanwhile, in China, a village is menaced by an evil hoodlum named Hojo (Gordon Liu), no relation to the U.S. pancake vendor. Two villagers happen upon Sidhu in Chandni Chowk and are convinced he is the reincarnation of the mighty kung fu warrior who saved them from bandits in times long past. Sidhu is soon lured to their village, being promised wealth and voluptuous pleasures, but is now expected to defeat Hojo, who uses his bowler hat as a flying guillotine and may plausibly be related to Odd Job.

Enter the ravishing Deepika Padukone, in a dual role of Sakhi and Meow Meow, an Indian home shopping network hostess and Chinese tigress. As you see the film, you may reflect that the opportunities of an Indian actress to achieve dramatic greatness are limited by the industry's practice in filming them only as spectacular beauties, preferably with the wind rippling their hair. Kissing in public is severely frowned upon in India, so that the greatest tension in all romances comes as a heroine is maybe, just maybe, *about* to kiss someone. This is always spellbinding and illustrates my maxim that it is less erotic to snoggle for sixty minutes than spend sixty seconds wondering if you are almost about to be snoggled.

I gather that Akshay Kumar usually plays more stalwart heroes, with the obligatory unshaven look, wearing his testosterone on his face. It's unlikely he could have become the heartthrob of Indian cinema playing doofuses like this. He becomes involved with both Sakhi and Meow Meow, whose surprise relationship might have been more surprising had they not been played by the same actress. There are lots of martial arts sequences, and of course several song-and-dance numbers, including an Indian rap performance. It's done with great energy but with a certain detachment, as if nothing really matters *but* the energy.

My guess is that *Chandni Chowk to China* won't attract many fans of kung fu—or Adam Sandler, for that matter. The title and the ads will cause them to think for a second, an unacceptable delay for fanboys. The movie will appeal to the large Indian audiences in North America and to Bollywood fans in general, who will come out wondering why this movie of all movies was chosen as Hollywood's first foray into commercial Indian cinema. I don't know a whole lot about Bollywood, and even I could name some better possibilities.

Changeling ★ ★ ★ ½
R, 140 m., 2008

Angelina Jolie (Christine Collins), John Malkovich (Reverend Gustav Briegleb), Jeffrey Donovan (Captain J. J. Jones), Colm Feore (Chief James E. Davis), Jason Butler Harner (Gordon Northcott), Amy Ryan (Carol Dexter), Michael Kelly (Detective Lester Ybarra), Geoff Pierson (S. S. Hahn). Directed by Clint Eastwood and produced by Eastwood, Brian Grazer, Ron Howard, and Robert Lorenz. Screenplay by J. Michael Straczynski.

Clint Eastwood's *Changeling* made me feel sympathy, and then anger, and then back around again. It is the factual account of a mother whose little boy disappeared, and of a corrupt Los Angeles Police Department running wild. Angelina Jolie stars as Christine Collins, whose nine-year-old son, Walter, went missing in March 1928. Some months later, the LAPD announced her son had been found alive in DeKalb, Illinois.

There was a problem. Collins said the boy was not hers. The police, under fire for lawlessness and corruption, had positioned the case as an example of their good work. They were determined to suppress Collins's protest. Even though the returned boy was three inches shorter than Walter, was not recognized by his teacher and classmates, and had dental records that did not match, Collins was informed she was crazy and locked up in a psychiatric ward on the strength of a captain's signature.

If her "rediscovered son" was a poster boy for the cops, her disappearance became the cause of an early radio preacher named Gustav Briegleb (John Malkovich), who had been thundering against police corruption. Meanwhile, a determined detective named Lester Ybarra (Michael Kelly) was led to the buried bodies of twenty young boys on an isolated chicken ranch outside Winesville, California.

Eastwood's telling of this story isn't structured as a thriller, but as an uncoiling of outrage. It is clear that the leaders of the LAPD serve and protect one thing: its own tarnished reputation. Jolie joins many other female prisoners whose only crime was to annoy a cop. The institution drugs them, performs shock treatment, punishes any protest. Mental illness is treated as a crime. This is all, as the film observes, based on a true story.

Eastwood is one of the finest directors now at work. I often say I'm mad at Fassbinder for dying at thirty-three and denying us decades of his films. In a way, I'm also mad at Eastwood for not directing his first film until he was forty-one. We could not do without his work as an actor. But most of his greatest films as a director have come after *retirement age.* Some directors start young and get tired. Eastwood is only gathering steam.

Changeling is seen with the directness and economy of his mentor, Don Siegel. It has not a single unnecessary stylistic flourish. No contrived dramatics. No shocking stunts. A score (by Eastwood) that doesn't underline but observes. The film simply tells its relentless story and rubs the LAPD's face in it. This is the story of an administration that directed from the top down to lie, cheat, torture, extract false confessions, and serve and protect its image. In a way, it is prophetic.

The Los Angeles Police Department, perhaps in part because it is unlucky enough to exist in Los Angeles, has often had a dark image in recent movies. Consider *L.A. Confidential, Training Day, Lakeview Terrace.* Lots of movies involve corrupt cops, but no city's police department has been as dramatically portrayed. Yes, there are hero cops, but they're mavericks. Dirty Harry, for all his problems, might have admired this movie.

Jolie, Malkovich and Geoff Pierson, as a lawyer who takes Collins's case before the Police Board, are very good at what they do very well. The film's most riveting performance is by Jason Butler Harner as Gordon Northcott, the serial killer. The character could not be adequately described on the page. Harner's mesmerizing performance brings him to sinister life as a self-pitying weasel specializing in smarmy phony charm. He doesn't play a sick killer. He embodies one.

The screenplay by J. Michael Straczynski follows the factual outlines of the story while condensing, dramatizing, and inventing. A man like Northcott can never be explained, but much of his oddness may have emerged from his childhood. That, and his parents, are left out of the film. He didn't discover until a later murder trial that his real parents were his sister and his father. Surely he sensed something was very wrong.

This whole background of Northcott is wisely sidestepped by Eastwood; eerie as it is, it would have been a detour in the story's relentless progress. Northcott comes over in Harner's portrayal as a man like John Gacy, Ted Bundy, and Jeffrey Dahmer: irretrievably evil, inexplicable, unreachable from the sane world. You don't have to gnash your teeth to be evil. Profoundly creepy is more like it.

Jolie plays Christine Collins without unnecessary angles or quirks. She is a supervisor at the telephone company, she loves her son, they live in a nice bungalow, all is well. She reacts to her son's disappearance as any mother would. But as weeks turn into months, and after the phony "son" is produced, her anger and resolution swell up until they bring the whole LAPD fabrication crashing down. Malkovich as the minister is refreshing: not a sanctimonious grandstander who gets instructions directly from God, but a crusading activist. And one more thing: the phony boy's reason for pretending to be Walter. It almost makes you want to hug him. Almost.

The Chaser ★★★ ½

NO MPAA RATING, 124 m., 2010

Kim Yoon-suk (Jung-ho), Ha Jung-woo (Young-min), Seo Young-hee (Mi-jin), Koo Bon-woong (Meathead). Directed by Na Hong-jin and produced by Choi Moon-su. Screenplay by Na Hong-jin, Hong Won-chan, and Lee Shin-ho.

The Chaser is an expert serial killer film from South Korea and a poster child for what a well-made thriller looked like in the classic days. Its principal chase scene involves a foot race through the deserted narrow nighttime streets of Seoul. No exploding cars. The climax is the result of everything that has gone before. Not an extended fight scene. This is drama, and it is interesting. Action for its own sake is boring.

The film is a police procedural with a difference: The hero is an ex-cop named Jung-ho (Kim Yoon-suk), now a pimp, and he is not a nice man. He is angered because a client of his call-girl service has been, he believes, kidnapping his girls and selling them. When another girl disappears, a phone number raises an alarm, and he sets out to track down the client—who didn't give an address but arranged a street rendezvous.

What we know is that the client, Young-min (Ha Jung-woo), is a sadistic murderer. The girl, named Mi-jin (Seo Young-hee), is driven in his car to an obscure address that she is not intended to ever leave alive. It is a characteristic of South Korean films that they display the grisly details of violence without flinching; the rights to this film have been picked up by Warner Bros., and it's dead certain the violence and the shocking outcome itself will be greatly toned down. Let me simply note that Young-min's tools of choice are a hammer and a chisel, for reasons a police psychiatrist has much to say about.

The film's structure is relentless in maintaining suspense. We have reason to suspect the prostitute may still be alive, but dying. Both the pimp and the killer are arrested. A ludicrous attack on the mayor of Seoul becomes a media sensation and puts pressure on the cops to charge someone with something to change the headlines. The killer, a calm psychopath, claims first nine murders, then twelve, but changes his story and says he has no idea what he did with the bodies. He's released on lack of evidence.

The story is an exercise in audience manipulation, especially with the corruption and incompetence of the police. The director, Na Hong-jin, knows exactly what he's doing. Like the master, Hitchcock, he gives the audience precisely enough information to be frustrated. It is obvious to us what the characters should be doing, but there are excellent reasons why it isn't obvious to them. If you can contrive that in a screenplay, you have already surpassed the level of the modern thriller.

Another strength of the film is in its attention to characters. The killer is seen as a mental dead zone, a man without conscience to whom good and evil are equally meaningless. The pimp begins as a merchant of sex, goes looking for Young-min for simple mercenary reasons, and very gradually expands his concerns in response to the presence of the call girl's young daughter. The daughter follows the Glossary Rule, which instructs us that all children in movies, told to stay put, quickly wander away into danger. Well, can we blame the director? How interesting would it be if she obediently stayed put?

What I responded to was the street-level reality of the film. There are no supermen and no sensational stunts. When the actors run, we see that they are running. These shots extend in time and are not constructed of baffling editing. The spatial realities of the chases are respected; we begin to learn our way around the neighborhood. The cops are not stock characters, but just your average officers. No one in *The Chaser* seems on autopilot.

When I see a film like this, it reminds me of what we're missing. So many recent movies are all smoke and mirrors. A thriller is opening soon in which the star cannot be clearly seen to complete any physical act in an action sequence. We might as well be reading a comic strip, where our minds are expected to fill in the movement between the frames. You sit there and *The Chaser* unfolds and the director knows what he wants and how to do it without insulting us. In addition to remaking this movie, Hollywood should study it.

Che ★ ★ ★ ½
R, 258 m., 2009

Benicio Del Toro (Che Guevara), Demian Bichir (Fidel Castro), Santiago Cabrera (Camillo Cienfuegos), Elvira Minguez (Celia Sanchez), Jorge Perugorria (Joaquin), Edgar Ramirez (Ciro Redondo), Victor Rasuk (Rogelio Acevedo), Catalina Sandino Moreno (Aleida Guevara). Directed by Stephen Soderbergh and produced by Benicio Del Toro and Laura Bickford. Screenplay by Peter Buchman and Benjamin A. van der Veen.

Che Guevara is conventionally depicted either as a saint of revolution or a ruthless executioner. Stephen Soderbergh's epic biography *Che* doesn't feel the need to define him. It is not written from the point of view of history, but from Guevara's own POV on a day-to-day basis in the process of overthrowing the Batista regime in Cuba and then failing to repeat his success in Bolivia. Both parts of the film are based on his writings, including a diary in Bolivia written in the field, day to day.

The film plays in two parts, named *The Argentine* and *Guerrilla*. It resists the temptation to pump up the volume, to outline Che (Benicio Del Toro) against the horizon, to touch conventional biographical bases. In Cuba, we join him in midstream. We learn that he is a doctor but not how and why he became one. It is a given that he is a revolutionary. He is a natural leader of men. Fidel Castro is his comrade, but the film does not show them in a detailed relationship; much of the time, they are apart.

There isn't an explanation of why he chose to secretly leave Cuba after the revolution, no reference to his time in the Congo, no explanation about why he chose Bolivia as his next field of operation, no reference to the political decisions he made as a young man motorcycling across South America (as described in the 2004 film *The Motorcycle Diaries*).

Che is all in the present tense. He has made an irrevocable decision to overthrow governments. He explains why in his descriptions of injustice; he identifies with peasants and not with his own ruling class, and although he is nominally a Communist, we do not hear discussion of theory and ideology. He seems completely focused on the task immediately before him. His method is to give voice to popular resentment against a dictator, win the support of the people, and demoralize opposing armies of unenthusiastic soldiers. He needs few men because he has a powerful idea behind him.

That method worked in Cuba and failed in Bolivia. Soderbergh's 258-minute film works

89

as an arc: upward to victory, a pause with his family in Argentina, downward to defeat. The scenes in Argentina show him with his second wife, Aleida (Catalina Sandino Moreno), and children but do not engage in why he left them, how his wife really feels, how he feels about them. A wanted person, he has disguised himself so successfully that his children do not recognize him as he presides over the dinner table. His wife shared his political ideas but must have had deep feelings about a man who would leave his children to lead a revolutionary war in another country; but we don't hear them, and in a way it's a relief to be spared the conventional scenes of recrimination. It is all as it is.

That helps explain another peculiarity of the film. Surprising attention is given to Che meeting the volunteers who join his guerrilla bands. Names, embraces. But little effort is made to single them out as individuals, to develop complex relationships. Che enforces an inviolable rule: He will leave no wounded man behind. But there is no sense that he is *personally* emotionally involved with his men. It is *a man* he will not leave behind, not *this* man. It is the idea.

In Cuba, the rebels are greeted by the people of the villages, given food and cover, cheered on in what becomes a triumphal tour. In Bolivia there seems little sympathy. Villagers betray him. They conceal government troops, not his own. When he lectures on the injustice of the government medical system, his audience seems unresponsive. You cannot lead a people into revolution if they do not want to follow. Soderbergh shows U.S. military advisers working with the Bolivians but doesn't blame the United States for Che's failure. Che chose the wrong war at the wrong time and place.

In showing both wars, Soderbergh does an interesting thing. He doesn't structure his battle scenes as engagements with clear-cut outcomes. Che's men ambush and are ambushed. They trade fire with distant enemies. There is usually a cut to the group in the aftermath of battle, its casualties not lingered over. This is not a war movie. It is about one man's unrealistic compulsion to stay his course.

Soderbergh made the film himself, directing, photographing, editing. There is no fancy camera work; he looks steadily at Che's dogged determination. There are very few subjective shots, but they are effective; Che's POV during his last moments, for example. There is a lot of the countryside, where these men live for weeks at a time. The overwhelming impression is of exhaustion, and Guevara himself has malaria part of the time and suffered from asthma. There is nothing more powerful than an idea whose time has come, and more doomed than one whose time is not now.

Benicio Del Toro, one of the producers, gives a heroic performance, not least because it's self-effacing. He isn't foregrounded like most epic heroes. In Cuba he emerges in victory; in Bolivia he is absorbed in defeat and sometimes almost hard to recognize behind a tangle of beard and hair. He embodies not so much a personality as a will.

You may wonder if the film is too long. I think there's a good reason for its length. Guevara's experience in Cuba and especially Bolivia was not a series of events and anecdotes, but a trial of endurance that might almost be called mad.

Chéri ★ ★ ★ ½
R, 92 m., 2009

Michelle Pfeiffer (Lea de Lonval), Rupert Friend (Chéri), Kathy Bates (Charlotte Peloux), Felicity Jones (Edmee), Iben Hjejle (Marie-Laure). Directed by Stephen Frears and produced by Andras Hamori, Bill Kenwright, Thom Mount, and Tracey Seaward. Screenplay by Christopher Hampton, based on the novels *Chéri* and *The Last of Chéri* by Colette.

Near the beginning of Colette's novel *Chéri*, Lea gives her young lover a necklace with forty-nine pearls. We can imagine there is one pearl for every year of her age. Her lover is twenty-four years younger than she. Therefore, twenty-five. Six years pass. In a way, the movie is about how twenty-five and forty-nine are not the same as thirty-one and fifty-five. Colette tells us their tragedy is that they were destined to be the only perfect love in each other's lives, yet were not born on the same day.

The success of Stephen Frears's film *Chéri* begins with its casting. Michelle Pfeiffer, as

Lea, is still a great beauty, but nearing that age when a woman starts counting her pearls. Rupert Friend, as her lover Chéri, is twenty-seven and looks younger—too young to play James Bond, although he was considered. They are both accomplished actors, which is important, because *Chéri* tells a story of nuance and insinuation, concealed feelings and hidden fears.

Lea is a courtesan, currently without court. She has a lot of money and lives luxuriously. Chéri is the son of a courtesan, Charlotte Peloux (Kathy Bates). She and Lea have been friends for years; courtesans may be rich and famous, but they cannot really talk freely with women not like themselves. Lea was constantly in the life of her friend's son, named Fred but called Chéri ("darling") by one and all. One day Madame Peloux comes to her and asks her to take in the boy. She does not quite say (as Lee Marvin tells a whore in *Paint Your Wagon*), "I give you the boy. Give me back the man," but she might as well have.

Chéri is far from a virgin, but he needs some reining in. It turns out he accepts Lea's saddle quite willingly. What begins as lovemaking quickly becomes love, and they float in a perfumed world of opulent comfort, Lea paying all the bills. The two things a courtesan cannot ever do are really fall in love, and reveal what she is really thinking. Lea fails at the first.

You need not be told what happens in the story, or how thoughtless and cruel Chéri can be when it suits him. Be content to know that Lea knows sooner and Chéri later that what they had was invaluable and irreplaceable. *Chéri* became Colette's most popular book because of its air of describing familiar lives with detached regret, and that is the tone Frears goes for: This is not a tear-jerker, but a record of what can happen when people toy with their hearts.

How well I remember that day in 1983 when I walked across Blackfriars Bridge in London and came upon an obscure little used book shop, and inside discovered a set of the works of Colette, small volumes, bound in matching maroon leatherette with cloth bookmarks. I have been in awe of her writing ever since. When Donald Richie, the great authority on Japanese cinema, was moving to a smaller flat in Tokyo and had to perform triage on his li-

brary, he gave away Shakespeare, because he felt he had internalized him, but could not bring himself to give away Colette.

Colette, who was eighty-one when she died in 1954, is probably best known to you as the author of *Gigi*. After leaving an unfaithful first husband, Colette, already a successful author, supported herself as a music hall performer, knew many courtesans in the era of La Belle Epoque, had affairs with women, shocked *tout le monde* with the first onstage kiss between two women, married the editor of *Le Matin*, and was divorced at fifty-one after she had an affair with her twenty-year-old stepson. So *Chéri* is not entirely a work of the imagination.

Colette's many books are considered difficult to film because much of what happens is based on emotions rather than events. This is a challenge Frears and his screenwriter, the playwright Christopher Hampton, have accepted. The film is about how to behave when you live at a distance from your real feelings. It is fascinating to observe how Pfeiffer controls her face and voice during times of painful hurt. It is bad to feel pain, worse to reveal it; a courtesan has her pride.

The performances seem effective to me, including Bates as Charlotte, who like many an older prostitute plays a parody of her profession. Laugh, and the world laughs with you. The cinematography by Darius Khondji and costumes by Consolata Boyle are meticulous in evoking decadence. The most emotional moments at the end occur off-screen and are related by the narrator (Frears himself). That is as it should be. Some things don't happen to people. They happen about them.

The Children of Huang Shi ★ ★ ½
R, 125 m., 2008

Jonathan Rhys Meyers (George Hogg), Radha Mitchell (Lee Pearson), Chow Yun Fat (Jack Chen), Michelle Yeoh (Madame Wang), David Wenham (Barnes), Guang Li (Shi Kai). Directed by Roger Spottiswoode and produced by Arthur Cohn, Wieland Schulz-Keil, Peter Loehr, Jonathan Shteinman, and Martin Hagemann. Screenplay by James MacManus and Jane Hawksley.

George Hogg is a British journalist sent to China to cover the 1930s war involving Japanese invaders and communist and nationalist Chinese. It's surprising he survived a day. Inexperienced and naive, he journeys into unfamiliar territory and spends way too much time standing in full view and taking photos. Some of the photos have real news value, such as a series involving a Japanese massacre of civilians, but, of course, the Japanese capture him and the photos.

This leads to the first of two moments when Hogg (Jonathan Rhys Meyers) is seconds from death; an executioner's sword seems already slicing down from the sky when he's rescued by a Chinese nationalist named Chen (Chow Yun Fat). Later he's rescued again, by a beautiful British woman named Lee Pearson (Radha Mitchell), a brave heroine who roams the countryside on horseback by herself, bringing food and medical help to the countless displaced people who need it.

She had a civilian occupation before necessity thrust this mission upon her. Soon Hogg finds the same thing happens to him: Lee takes him to an orphanage, puts him in charge of sixty children, and tells him he must feed and educate them, and tend to their health. How can he do that? Hogg has no training, but Lee gives him no choice. He teaches himself.

All of this seems impossible, but Roger Spottiswoode's film is based on fact; there was a real George Hogg. After he stars in an embarrassing public demonstration of the usefulness of flea powder, Hogg travels by mule to a nearby city where Madame Wang (Michelle Yeoh) runs a business dealing in seed, grains, and perhaps other things. He convinces her they are in business together: She gives him the seeds and shares in the harvest.

The scenes of Hogg making the orphanage into a functioning community transform the movie from an unlikely adventure into an absorbing life story. The filmmaking is careful but not original; one kid is a rebel, one kid is a quick learner, and so on, and there is a goat that bleats every time it is on the screen. Hogg and the children miraculously restore a rusty generator, coax crops from the stony soil, and hold English classes ("Table! Table! Chair! Chair!"), although I am not sure why twelve-year-old or-

phans in the middle of China in the late 1930s needed to learn English. Math, maybe?

Thrown out of their orphanage, Hogg and the orphans make an exhausting five-hundred-mile trek across snow-covered mountains to find refuge. When they finally reach their destination, they gaze in silence, and the goat gets one close-up when it doesn't bleat. During this stretch of film, Hogg has fallen in love with Lee, and we learn that Chen and Madame Wang have, as they say, a history. Other secrets are revealed, but they come a little too quickly after the film's leisurely middle passages.

The Children of Huang Shi tells an engrossing story of a remarkable man, but nevertheless it's underwhelming. Dramatic and romantic tensions never coil very tightly, as the film settles into a contented pace. The photography is awesome, especially scenes set in the Gobi desert, which yes, they travel across, although not the whole way, I'm sure. I'm pleased to have seen the film and it has a big heart, but that doesn't make it urgent viewing.

Note: The R rating is earned by some very mild, nonexplicit lovemaking, some violence, some drug content. Nothing so strong it would bother teenagers, who might enjoy this film more than I did.

Chloe ★★★ ½

R, 96 m., 2010

Julianne Moore (Catherine Stewart), Liam Neeson (David Stewart), Amanda Seyfried (Chloe), Max Thieriot (Michael Stewart), R. H. Thomson (Frank), Nina Dobrev (Anna). Directed by Atom Egoyan and produced by Jeffrey Clifford, Joe Medjuck, Ivan Reitman, Simone Urdl, and Jennifer Weiss. Screenplay by Erin Cressida Wilson, based on the motion picture *Nathalie*, directed by Anne Fontaine.

Looking down from her office window, she sees a young woman who has the manner and routine of a high-priced call girl. This she stores in her memory. When her husband says he missed his flight back to Toronto and she finds a disturbing photo on his iPhone, she goes to the hotel where she saw the girl, makes eye contact with her in a bar, contrives a conversation in the powder room. The girl, with perfect calm, explains that single women are not usually her clients. Couples, maybe.

Atom Egoyan finds intrigue at the edges of conventional sex. *Chloe,* like his great film *Exotica* (1994), is about sexual attraction confused by financial arrangements. It centers on a powerfully erotic young woman with personal motives that are hidden. It is not blatant but seductive, depending on the ways that our minds, more than our bodies, can be involved in a sexual relationship. It's not so much what we're doing as what I'm thinking about it— and what you're thinking, which may be more complex than I realize.

Catherine Stewart (Julianne Moore) is a gynecologist, a successful one, judging by the house she inhabits fresh from the cover of *Architectural Digest.* Her husband, David (Liam Neeson), is an expert on opera. The call girl she saw from her window is Chloe (Amanda Seyfried), young, red-lipped, intelligent. Catherine explains to Chloe that she suspects her husband of adultery and wants to test if he would try to pick up another woman. She tells Chloe where her husband always has lunch.

Early in the film, talking with a patient uncertain about her sex life, Catherine explains that an orgasm is a simple muscular contraction, quite natural, nothing to be frightened of or make mysterious. Orgasms for Catherine, however, involve a great deal more than muscles, and a great deal depends on whom they are experienced with, and why. Chloe tells her about entering a café, boldly asking David if she can take the sugar from his table, and returning to her own. David understands that Chloe is not interested in sugar.

Chloe meets with Catherine to relate this encounter. Chloe is good at this. She informs us early in the film that she is skilled at what she does. It's not a matter of renting her body. She uses her intelligence to intuit what a client desires—really desires, no matter what the client might claim. And she knows how to provide this in a way that will provoke curiosity, even fascination. Now she describes details to Catherine that do a great deal more than provoke a wife's jealousy about her husband. They provoke an erotic curiosity about her husband.

Chloe is perhaps twenty-five years younger than Catherine, but in many ways wiser and more experienced. She is certainly more clear about what it is she really wants. She enjoys the psychological control of her clients, and her own skill in achieving that. She looks so young and innocent, but her life has taught her many lessons. Seyfried plays Chloe as a woman in command of her instrument—her body, which is for sale, and her mind, which works for itself. Moore, that consummate actress, undergoes a change she only believes is under her control. Neeson is an enigma to his wife and in a different way to us.

Egoyan follows his material to an ultimate conclusion. Some will find it difficult to accept. Is it arbitrary? Most of life's conclusions are arbitrary. I am not sure this particular story should, or can, be wound up in a conventional manner. It's not the kind of movie that depends on the certainty of an ending. It's more about how things continue. I have deliberately withheld much of the story, which he leaves for you to understand. His central fascination is with Chloe's motives. Does she act only for money? Does she do only what is requested? Does she remain emotionally detached? Does she get anything for herself besides money?

At one point she's asked how she can relate to some of her clients, who might seem unattractive, even repugnant. A call girl has no idea who will open the door after her knock, and the ground rules are that she will gratify the client's desires, if he can pay and she doesn't feel in personal danger. But how can she endure some of them? "I try to find something I can love," she says.

After you see the movie, run through it again in your mind. Who wants what? Who gets what? Who decides what? Whose needs are gratified? Atom Egoyan never makes a story with one level. He never reveals all of the motives, especially to his characters. He invites us to be voyeurs of surfaces that may not conceal what they seem. Fundamental shifts can alter all the relationships. All the same, their sexuality compels his characters to make decisions based on their own assumptions. It is a tangled web he weaves.

Choke ★ ★ ½
R, 89 m., 2008

Sam Rockwell (Victor Mancini), Angelica Huston (Ida Mancini), Brad William Henke

(Denny), Kelly Macdonald (Paige Marshall). Directed by Clark Gregg and produced by Johnathan Dorfman, Temple Fennell, Beau Flynn, and Tripp Vinson. Screenplay by Gregg, based on the novel by Chuck Palahniuk.

All the pieces are here, but you have to glue the kite together to make it fly. *Choke* centers on a character who is content to be skanky and despicable, and who does not reform although the plot seems to be pushing him alarmingly in that direction. His name is Victor, and he is a sex addict.

Yes. So much is without joy in his life that he would live, if he could, in a constant state of orgasm. He probably perks up when the TV ads warn about four-hour tumescence. He's the kind of guy who attends Sex Addicts Anonymous meetings and sneaks out halfway to have dirty sex. His comrade in arms is Denny, who is a compulsive masturbator. I believe he only puts on his pants so he can reach inside.

Victor is played by Sam Rockwell, who seems to have become the latter-day version of Christopher Walken—not all the time, but when you need him, he's your go-to guy for weirdness. Denny is played by Brad William Henke. The fact that he has his sight disproves many warnings.

In addition to sex, Victor's life centers on sadness and fake near-death experiences. He spends a commendable amount of time at a nursing home where his mother, Ida (Anjelica Huston), has absolutely no idea who he is, which makes two of them. She provided him with a corrosive childhood, when as a mother she resembled the criminal character she played in *The Grifters*.

When Victor is not at his mother's side, he works a con game as a sideline. Carefully choosing a new restaurant each time, he pretends to have swallowed a big bite and be choking to death. Inevitably someone will rush over and clutch him in the Heimlich maneuver, and it has been his experience that such Samaritans often insist on giving him money. There is an ancient belief that when you save someone's life, you are responsible for it. I forget whose ancient belief it is, but take my word for it.

His mother is assigned to a hospital bed and tended by Nurse Paige (Kelly Macdonald), whose utility to the mother saves her from Victor's instant ravaging, and who oddly enough has theories on the forefront of medical knowledge that may find a sex addict useful. This is fascinating to Victor, whose days are spent in costume as an eighteenth-century colonialist at a theme park, where I believe Paul Revere rides every hour on the hour. Maybe not.

The movie was written and directed by Clark Gregg, who adapted a novel by Chuck Palahniuk (*Fight Club*). Some stretches are very funny, although the laughter is undermined by the desperation and sadness of the situations. Victor is presented as not so much a zany screwball, more of a case study. The film makes a flywheel kind of progress toward its conclusion, feeling like it has arrived not at a resolution but at a rest stop. Still, one of the problems with sex addicts may be that they cannot get enough rest.

A Christmas Carol ★★★★
PG, 95 m., 2009

Jim Carrey (Scrooge/Ghosts of Christmas), Robin Wright Penn (Belle/Fan), Gary Oldman (Cratchit/Marley/Tiny Tim), Colin Firth (Fred), Cary Elwes (Dick Wilkins/Fiddler/Businessman), Bob Hoskins (Fezziwig/Old Joe), Fionnula Flanagan (Mrs. Dilber). Directed by Robert Zemeckis and produced by Zemeckis, Steve Starkey, and Jack Rapke. Screenplay by Zemeckis, based on the story by Charles Dickens.

A Christmas Carol by Robert Zemeckis (and Charles Dickens, of course) is an exhilarating visual experience and proves for the third time he's one of the few directors who knows what he's doing with 3-D. The story that Dickens wrote in 1838 remains timeless, and if it's supercharged here with Scrooge swooping the London streets as freely as Superman, well, once you let ghosts into a movie there's room for anything.

The story I will not repeat for you. The ghosts of Christmas Past, Present, and Future will not come as news. I'd rather dwell on the look of the picture, which is true to the spirit of Dickens (in some moods) as he cheerfully exaggerates. He usually starts with plucky young heroes or heroines and surrounds them with a gallery of characters and caricatures. Here his protagonist is the caricature: Ebenezer Scrooge, never thinner, never more stooped, never more bitter.

Jim Carrey is in there somewhere beneath the performance-capture animation; you can recognize his expressive mouth, but in general the Zemeckis characters don't resemble their originals overmuch. In his *Polar Express,* you were sure that was Tom Hanks, but here you're not equally sure of Gary Oldman, Robin Wright Penn, and Bob Hoskins.

Zemeckis places these characters in a London that twists and stretches its setting to reflect the macabre mood. Consider Scrooge's living room, so narrow and tall just as he is. The home of his nephew, Fred, by contrast, is as wide and warm as Fred's personality.

Animation provides the freedom to show just about anything, and Zemeckis uses it. Occasionally, he even seems to be evoking the ghost of Salvador Dalí, as in a striking sequence where all the furniture disappears and a towering grandfather clock looms over Scrooge, a floor slanting into distant perspective.

The three starring ghosts are also spectacular grotesques. I like the first, a little elfin figure with a head constantly afire and a hat shaped like a candlesnuffer. Sometimes he playfully shakes his flames like a kid tossing the hair out of his eyes. After another (ahem) ghost flies out through the window, Scrooge runs over to see the whole street filled with floating spectral figures, each one chained to a heavy block, like so many Chicago mobsters sleeping with the fishes.

Can you talk about performances in characters so much assembled by committee? You can discuss the voices, and Carrey works overtime as not only Scrooge but all three of the Christmas ghosts. Gary Oldman voices Bob Cratchit, Marley, and Tiny Tim.

I remain unconvinced that 3-D represents the future of the movies, but it tells you something that Zemeckis's three 3-D features (also including *Beowulf*) have wrestled from me eleven of a possible twelve stars. I like the way he does it. He seems to have a more sure touch than many other directors, *using* 3-D instead of being used by it. If the foreground is occupied by close objects, they're usually looming inward, not out over our heads. Note the foreground wall-mounted bells we look past when Scrooge, far below, enters his home; as one and then another slowly starts to move, it's a nice little touch.

Another one: The score by Alan Silvestri sneaks in some traditional Christmas carols, but you have to listen for such as "God Rest Ye, Merry Gentlemen" when its distinctive cadences turn sinister during a perilous flight through London.

So should you take the kiddies? Hmmm. I'm not so sure. When I was small, this movie would have scared the living ectoplasm out of me. Today's kids have seen more and are tougher. Anyway, *A Christmas Carol* has the one quality parents hope for in a family movie: It's entertaining for adults.

A Christmas Tale ★ ★ ★ ½
NO MPAA RATING, 151 m., 2008

Catherine Deneuve (Junon), Jean-Paul Roussillon (Abel), Anne Consigny (Elizabeth), Mathieu Amalric (Henri), Melvil Poupaud (Ivan), Hippolyte Girardot (Claude), Emmanuelle Devos (Faunia), Chiara Mastroianni (Sylvia), Laurent Capelluto (Simon). Directed by Arnaud Desplechin and produced by Pascal Caucheteux. Screenplay by Desplechin and Emmanuel Bourdieu.

A Christmas Tale skates on thin ice across a crowded lake, arrives safely on the far shore, and shares a cup of hot cocoa and marshmallows with Death. It stars Catherine Deneuve as a woman dying of liver cancer and considering a bone marrow transplant, which could also kill her. Because she is almost weirdly resigned to her fate and doesn't seem to worry much, her serenity prevents the film from being a procession into dirgeland.

What it is, instead, is a strangely encompassing collection of private moments among the members of a large family with a fraught history. Some of the moments are serious, some revealing, some funny, some simply wry in the manner of a *New Yorker* story about small insights into the lives of characters so special as to deserve to be in the story.

The family involves parents, children, grandchildren, spouses, a girlfriend, and

95

others. I will not name all of them and their relationships because what use is that kind of information if you haven't seen them and don't know who I'm talking about? For example, Junon Vuillard (Catherine Deneuve) and her husband, Abel (Jean-Paul Roussillon), have had four children, each one arriving with a different emotional meaning, but even in explaining this the movie grows murky, like a cousin at a family reunion telling you who the great-aunts of the in-laws are.

More to the point is the quietly playful approach of the director, Arnaud Desplechin, who seems to be demonstrating that *A Christmas Tale* is a movie that could have been made in several different tones, and showing us how he would have handled each of them. That leads to a wide range of musical genres, mood swings from solemn to the ribald, and always the peculiarity of the Deneuve character's cheerful detachment from her fate. She's like someone preparing for a familiar journey.

Desplechin doesn't focus on her troubles with a grim intensity. Sometimes he seems to be looking for ways to distract himself. For example, he is obviously familiar with Hitchcock's greatest film, *Vertigo*, which has no themes in common with this one. If you happen to have a video on hand, go to twenty-five minutes and fifty-two seconds into it, and watch what follows in the art gallery, as Jimmy Stewart stealthily approaches Kim Novak from behind. While you're at it, watch the whole film.

When you're watching *A Christmas Tale*, Desplechin's homage to that scene is unmistakable. It's not a shot-by-shot transposition, nor is the score a literal lift from Bernard Herrmann. They're evocations, uncannily familiar. The proof is, you'll see exactly what I saw when I watched the film. Now why does Desplechin do that? For fun, I think. Just showing off, the way I sneaked some e.e. cummings lines into my Answer Man column this week, for no better reason than that I could. Of course, an homage has to work just as well if you don't know its source. In fact, it may work better because you're not distracted by the connection. But nothing like a little value-added, as the British say.

Here's another way Desplechin pleases himself. He begins with the happy fact that

Catherine Deneuve and Marcello Mastroianni were the parents of Chiara Mastroianni. In *A Christmas Tale,* Mastroianni plays Deneuve's daughter-in-law, a little poke in the ribs because when they're in the same movie they are invariably playing mother and daughter. OK, so we know that.

But look where he goes with it. It's obvious that Chiara has a strong facial resemblance to her mother. Desplechin doesn't make any particular effort to make the point, although he can hardly avoid showing her full face sometimes. Here's what he does. He almost makes it a point to demonstrate how much Chiara looks like her father. Luckily, her parents, when they conceived her, were the two most beautiful people in the world.

When he films her in profile and from very slightly below and behind, we're looking at the essence of Mastroianni. The images burned into our memories from *La Dolce Vita* and elsewhere are of a sad, troubled man, resigned to disappointment and all the more handsome because of it. I always feel tender toward Mastroianni. No actor—no actor—was more loved by the camera. So here he is, and the character he is sad about is played by Catherine Deneuve. I imagine Desplechin and his cinematographer, Eric Gautier, discussing these shots sotto voce in a far corner of the sound stage.

The film must be packed with Desplechin's invisible self-indulgences. Those we can see allow us to see the movie smiling to itself. Mastroianni smoked all the time. So does his daughter here, the same moody way. Desplechin has Deneuve smoking long, thin cigarettes, like Virginia Slims. When was the last time you saw anyone smoking those in a movie? Every time you see one, it's a tiny distraction. I'll tell you when. The last time was also Deneuve. They are the cigarettes she really smokes.

For long stretches *A Christmas Tale* seems to be going nowhere in particular and using a lot of dialogue to do so. These are not boring stretches. The movie is 151 minutes long and doesn't feel especially lengthy. The actors are individually good. They work together to feel like a family. Subplots threaten to occupy the foreground. All the while, something is preparing itself beneath the surface. In the film's last scene (in the final two shots, as I recall) all the hidden weight of the film uncoils and pounces. It really was about something, and it knew it all the time.

I recommend you seek other reviews to orient you to the actual plot. These words have been sort of value-added. If you have *Vertigo*, arm yourself before you attend.

Cirque du Freak: The Vampire's Assistant ★ ½
PG-13, 108 m., 2009

John C. Reilly (Larten Crepsley), Ken Watanabe (Mr. Tall), Josh Hutcherson (Steve), Chris Massoglia (Darren), Ray Stevenson (Murlaugh), Patrick Fugit (Evra the Snake Boy), Willem Dafoe (Gavner Purl), Salma Hayek (Madame Truska), Michael Cerveris (Mr. Tiny). Directed by Paul Weitz and produced by Ewan Leslie and Lauren Shuler Donner. Screenplay by Weitz and Brian Helgeland, based on the Cirque du Freak series of books by Darren Shan.

Cirque du Freak: The Vampire's Assistant includes good vampires, evil Vampaneze, a wolf-man, a bearded lady, a monkey girl with a long tail, a snake boy, a dwarf with a four-foot forehead, and a spider the size of your shoe, and they're all boring as hell. The movie has good special effects and suitably gruesome characters, but it's bloodless.

It's also a mess. The movie is shot through with curious disconnects. Often within a single sequence of events, we won't know where we are or how they're related in space or time. Characters like the bearded lady (Salma Hayek) drop in and out at random. Willem Dafoe plays a man who keeps intensely bursting in, but I didn't know who he was or where he went when he wasn't on the job. His name, I learn, is Gavner Purl, which doesn't ring a bell.

There is a mannered giant named Mr. Tiny (Michael Cerveris), who has flaming gay affectations for no purpose, since anyone who can evoke purple gas to shrink humans into living mummies already has, you would think, sufficient interest. Cerveris gives the only really interesting performance in the movie. And there's a paternal vampire named Larten Crepsley (John C. Reilly), who is proud of

having developed a system of feeding off humans without killing them or turning them into vampires (i.e., "blooding them").

All of these characters travel with the Cirque du Freak, which comes to town for a one-night stand in an abandoned and shuttered theater. You slide your money into a slot at the bottom and something tries to bite you. Inexplicably, there is a small audience of normal customers who apparently don't object to this treatment.

Oh, and I almost forgot the two high school kids (Josh Hutcherson and Chris Massoglia) who are allegedly the hero and the antihero. They're equally bland, for my money. Turns out there are warring vampire factions: The followers of Larten Crepsley, who don't kill when they dine, and the evil Vampanese, who don't need to kill but do anyway, apparently because the habits of centuries are hard to break. The lads end up on opposing teams.

All of this gruesome grotesquerie is incredibly wrapped up into a story that grunts and groans and laboriously offers up a moral at the end, which is, and I quote: "It's not about what you are, it's about who you are." I could have told you that.

City Island ★★★
PG-13, 103 m., 2010

Andy Garcia (Vince Rizzo), Julianna Margulies (Joyce Rizzo), Steven Strait (Tony Nardella), Alan Arkin (Michael Malakov), Emily Mortimer (Molly Charlesworth), Ezra Miller (Vinnie Rizzo), Dominik Garcia-Lorido (Vivian Rizzo). Directed by Raymond de Felitta and produced by Felitta, Andy Garcia, Zachary Matz, and Lauren Versel. Screenplay by Felitta.

Vince is a man with a dream. Marlon Brando is his god. He would like to become an actor. This is not likely. He's well into his forties, a prison guard living with his family on City Island, a bucolic outcrop of the Bronx known mostly to its residents. Telling his wife he's going to a poker game, he attends acting classes in Manhattan. In one class, Vince creates a spot-on imitation, not of Marlon Brando, but of bad Brando imitators.

Vince, played by Andy Garcia with brawny blue-collar dialogue, is married to Joyce

(Julianna Margulies), who's convinced the poker games mean a mistress. His children hide secret lives. His daughter, Vivian (Dominik Garcia-Lorido), has dropped out of college and is working as a stripper in hopes of saving money to reapply. His son, Vinnie (Ezra Miller), is hooked not just on any old Internet porn, but on sites featuring fat women who eat on camera. The younger son in so many movie families is somehow weird.

Two life-changing experiences happen to Vince. At work, he gets a new prisoner whose name he has reason to recognize. He pulls the kid's file to confirm it: Tony (Steven Strait) is the son he fathered in a long-ago affair. Meanwhile, in acting class, his teacher (Alan Arkin) assigns the students to pair up and share their biggest secret in order to prepare for a monologue. He draws Molly (Emily Mortimer), who slowly draws this secret from him. They meet often in the city—not to have an affair, but because they become friends and confidants.

Tony is eligible to be released into the community, but has no family member to sign for him. Vince determines to bring him home for a month. This is the catalyst for upheaval in the long-established pattern of his life. *City Island*, written and directed by Raymond de Felitta, has a serious side but is essentially a human comedy, at times almost a gentle farce, as discoveries and revelations drop like explosives. You can imagine this story as the outline for an opera.

Garcia and Margulies, who worked so well together in George Hickenlooper's *The Man from Elysian Fields* (2001), show a sure feel for comedy here, especially after he introduces an unexplained stranger into his home: "You just decided to bring a prisoner home to *live* with us?" Convinced the poker games are a cover-up, she toys with the idea of fooling around with the hunky Tony. Molly, meanwhile, convinces Vince to try his luck at an open audition for a new movie.

There's a jolly subplot involving their next-door neighbor on City Island, a fat woman who Vinnie was following on the Web when—OMG!—he sees her on the way to the grocery store, and she asks if he wants to come along. This cheerful woman, played by an actress not listed on IMDb, defuses any awkwardness or discomfort and invites Vinnie and Tony over for some lasagna. Thus Felitta sidesteps a story hazard.

The last scene of the movie could indeed be used in an opera, with all of the leads on stage. It may strike you as a tad coincidental. So it is. Felitta has the good sense not to make it realistic, which it could not be. In the satisfactory tradition of comic melodrama, he tidies up all the loose ends. But don't get the idea *City Island* is a laff riot. For this story about these people, it finds about the right tone. They're silly and foolish, as are we all, but deserve what happiness they can negotiate.

Note: City Island *won the Audience Award at the Tribeca Film Festival 2009.*

City of Ember ★ ★ ½
PG, 95 m., 2008

Saoirse Ronan (Lina Mayfleet), Harry Treadaway (Doon Harrow), Tim Robbins (Loris Harrow), Bill Murray (Mayor Cole), Martin Landau (Sul), Toby Jones (Barton Snode), Mackenzie Crook (Looper), Marianne Jean-Baptiste (Clary). Directed by Gil Kenan and produced by Tom Hanks and Gary Goetzman. Screenplay by Caroline Thompson, based on the novel by Jeanne Duprau.

City of Ember tells of a city buried deep within the Earth as a shelter for human survivors after something awful happened upstairs—I'm not clear exactly what. Might have involved radiation, since giant mutant bees, moles, and beetles are roaming around down there. The moles have evolved into obese creatures with slimy tentacles surrounding their fangs, the better to eat you with, my dear.

But stop me before I get warmed up. This is a Boys' and Girls' Own Adventure, rousing and action-packed and short, and if the sets are interesting and cheesy at the same time, well, Ember is *supposed* to be a set, constructed by The Builders to resemble a village. The population seems to consist of maybe three hundred people, all of them English-speaking, and apparently only two of them black. I didn't spot any evident Asians or Latinos, but I wasn't able to take a complete head count when Mayor Bill Murray was addressing them all in the square.

The heroes are young Doon Harrow (Harry Treadaway) and Lina Mayfleet (Saoirse Ronan), the son of a single father and the daughter of a single mom. Her dad drowned in an escape attempt with Doon's dad, Loris (Tim Robbins). We learn that The Builders endowed Ember's first mayor with a box displaying our old friend, the Red Digital Readout, which counts down two hundred years, at which point I guess it's safe to return to the surface. Given the advanced state of RDR technology, one that clicks only once a year is risky; ya could start watchin' the dern thing for like eleven months and get to thinkin' its batteries were runnin' a little low there.

It is hopeless to try to understand everything that's thrown at us. Does the magic box *really* contain only a disintegrating list of instructions? After all that fancy clicking when it slides open? Did it really just get shoved on a back shelf after one mayor dropped it? Why did the clock start running again?

The people live on canned foods. The storerooms look about as big as at your average supermarket. Could you really store enough food for more than two hundred years in there? The subterranean world is illuminated by countless regulation light bulbs that dangle high above. How are they changed?

At one point, Doon and Lina get into a boat as small as a bathtub, survive two waterwheels that revolve on principles unclear to me, and hurtle down a water chute that suggests someone must have been watching the underground railway scene in *Indiana Jones and the Temple of Doom* real close there. Although Lina at one point uses a crayon to scribble a blue sky on a drawing, the movie gives no idea how she knows there is a sky and it is blue.

And so on. But to be fair, this movie would probably entertain younger viewers, if they haven't already been hopelessly corrupted by high-powered sci-fi on TV and video. It's innocent and sometimes kind of charming. The sets are entertaining. There are parallels in appearance and theme to a low-rent *Dark City*. And carrying the connection a little further, the uncredited narrator sounds a whole lot to me like Kiefer Sutherland, who did the voiceovers in the non-director's cut of *Dark City*. One strange aspect: There are no computers in this future world. Therefore, no e-mail. They have messengers wearing red vests who run around and tell people things. So you never accidentally copy your boss.

Clash of the Titans ★★★
PG-13, 106 m., 2010

Sam Worthington (Perseus), Gemma Arterton (Io), Mads Mikkelsen (Draco), Alexa Davalos (Andromeda), Jason Flemyng (Calibos/King Acrisius), Ralph Fiennes (Hades), Liam Neeson (Zeus). Directed by Louis Leterrier and produced by Kevin De La Noy and Basil Iwanyk. Screenplay by Travis Beacham, Phil Hay, and Matt Manfredi, based on the 1982 screenplay by Beverley Cross.

There are too many Greek gods for me to keep straight, since as a child I didn't have action figures as a learning tool. I was prepared to take notes during *Clash of the Titans,* but only wrote down a single one: "'Release the Kraken!'—Conan O'Brien." I know I was intended to be terrified by the release of the Kraken, but all I could think of was O'Brien shouting "Release the bear!" and then some guy in a bear suit runs out and sits on the lap of a guest. In this case, the Kraken is the nuclear option for Zeus, who has been persuaded by Hades to put down a revolt by the upstart mortals of Argos.

The mortals are fed up with the whims of the gods. It would be one thing if they stayed on Olympus and killed time leaning on pillars and addressing one another in thundering ultimatums. Now they meddle in the affairs of men. King Acrisius of Argos declares war and enlists the aid of a demigod who has been found at sea. This is Perseus (Sam Worthington), son of Zeus (Liam Neeson) and a human mother. He didn't ask to be a savior, but would be happier as a simple fisherman. You know the type.

Zeus, it should be explained, disguised himself as the husband of Perseus's mother and stole into her bedchamber to father the boy. So he is a rapist. Just sayin.' Perseus so loved his mother and adoptive father that he will never forgive Poseidon for drowning them, and wants nothing to do with gods. Yet such is his destiny.

The outcome is told in *Clash of the Titans* with impressive technical mastery and somewhat lesser dramatic command. For its intended audience I suspect this will play as a great entertainment. I enjoyed myself, particularly after they released the Kraken. There's no particular dramatic conflict in the movie: Perseus has to wrestle with his demigod ambiguity; Hades (Ralph Fiennes) nurses a resentment against Zeus; he demands the sacrifice of King Acrisius's daughter Andromeda (Alexa Davalos) to spare the city, and the citizens seem prepared to get along very nicely without her. That's about it.

It's strange how the sacrifice of one person makes us uneasy. Earlier in the film, the entire fleet of Argos is lost at sea, with the exception of the vessel holding Perseus. The king is philosophical: They were patriots. But the sacrifice of his own daughter—now you're talkin' real death.

Most of the film involves terrifying battles between mortals and special effects. After Calibos has a hand chopped off, his fingers grow into claws. Later, his blood drops start growing, creating a crowd of huge lobster-monsters that come crawling over rocks and snapping at everyone. Later in the film, inexplicably, these lobsters appear to be tame and walk obediently across the desert, bearing little houses on their backs for the mortals. What, did they forget they were the blood of Calibos?

There's worse to come. Perseus and his comrades must invade the lair of Medusa, one of the three Gorgon girls, whose hair is a writhing mass of snakes and body is a long, lethal snake's tail. Look at her, and you'll turn to stone! Maybe this explains the high quality of Greek sculpture. The struggles with Medusa take place on ledges over a flaming lake of lava far below. She must be beheaded, which Perseus does, thoughtfully keeping the head, which he carries around like the head of Alfredo Garcia. Is that a spoiler? The story has been out since 490 B.C.

The climax is classic, with the fair Andromeda hung by her wrists and suspended in a clinging white gown over a flaming pit at the edge of the sea. Meanwhile, Perseus flies to the rescue on the wings of the great flying horse Pegasus. The townspeople clamor for her

death, but lose their enthusiasm after the Kraken rears up from the sea.

I like this kind of stuff. I don't say it's good cinema, although I recognize the craftsmanship that went into it. I don't say it's good acting, when the men have so much facial hair they all look like Liam Neeson. I like the energy, the imagination, the silliness. I even like the one guy who doesn't have a beard. That's Perseus. From the first moment we see him as an adult until his last scene in the movie, he has the Standard Regulation Macho-Length Stubble on his chin. And in a city where all the men go to Jerry Garcia's barber, he has a burr cut on the short clipper setting.

So do I recommend the movie? Yes, if you intuit that this review is affectionate and have the same tolerance for goofy Greek gods as I do. One word of consumer advice, however. Explain to kids that the movie was not filmed in 3-D and is only being shown in 3-D in order to charge you an extra five dollars a ticket. I saw it in 2-D, and let me tell you, it looked terrific. Split the difference: "We see it in 2-D, I save five bucks, and I increase your allowance by $2.50 this week."

The Class ★ ★ ★ ★
PG-13, 128 m., 2009

Francois Begaudeau (Francois), Wei Huang (Wei), Esmeralda Ouertani (Esmeralda), Franck Keita (Souleymane), Carl Nanor (Carl), Arthur Fogel (Arthur). Directed by Laurent Cantet and produced by Carole Scotta, Caroline Benjo, Barbara Letellier, and Simon Arnal. Screenplay by Cantet, Francois Begaudeau, and Robin Campillo, based on the novel *Entre les Murs* by Francois Begaudeau.

The Class might have been set in any classroom in the Western world, and I believe most teachers would recognize it. It is about the power struggle between a teacher who wants to do good and students who disagree about what "good" is. The film is so fair that neither side is seen as right, and both seem trapped by futility.

In a lower-income melting pot neighborhood in Paris, Francois, the teacher, begins a school year with high hopes and a desire to be liked by his students. They are a multiethnic group of fifteen- and sixteen-year-olds, few of them prepared by the educational system to be promising candidates for Francois' hopes. None of them seems stupid, and indeed intelligence may be one of their problems: They can see clearly that the purpose of the class is to make them model citizens in a society that has little use for them.

The movie is bursting with life, energy, fears, frustrations, and the quick laughter of a classroom hungry for relief. It avoids lockstep plotting and plunges into the middle of the fray, helping us become familiar with the students, suggesting more than it tells, allowing us to identify with many points of view. It is uncannily convincing.

The reason for that, I learn, involves the method of the director, Laurent Cantet, one of the most gifted new French directors. He began with a best-selling autobiographical novel by a teacher, Francois Begaudeau. He cast Begaudeau as the teacher. He worked for a year with a group of students, improvising and filming scenes. So convincing is the film that it seems documentary, but all of the students, I learn, are playing roles and not themselves.

There is a resentful Arab girl, who feels she is being undervalued by the teacher. A high-spirited African boy, very intelligent, but prone to anger. An Asian boy, also smart, who has learned (from his family's culture, perhaps) to keep a low profile and not reveal himself. Others who are confederates, pals, coconspirators.

A lot of grief in the classroom has to do with the rote teaching of French. As the students puzzle their way through, I don't know, the passive pluperfect subjunctive or whatever, I must say I sided with them. Despite the best efforts of dedicated and gifted nuns, I never learned to diagram a sentence, something they believed was of paramount importance. Yet I have made my living by writing and speaking. You learn a language by listening and speaking. You learn how to write by reading. It's not an abstraction. Do you think the people who first used the imperfect tense felt the need to name it?

The title of the original novel translates as *Between the Walls,* and indeed the film stays for the most part within the classroom. We know from Jack London that the members of a dog pack intensely observe one another. There can only be one top dog, and there are always candidates for the job. A school year begins with the teacher as top dog. Whether it ends that way is the test of a good teacher. Do you stay on top by strict discipline? With humor? By becoming the students' friend? Through psychology? Will they sense your strategy? Sometimes I think the old British public school system was best: Teachers were eccentric cranks, famous for their idiosyncrasies, who baffled their students.

Cloud Nine ★★★
NO MPAA RATING, 97 m., 2009

Ursula Werner (Inge), Horst Rehberg (Werner), Horst Westphal (Karl), Steffi Kuehnert (Petra). Directed by Andreas Dresen and produced by Peter Rommel. Screenplay by Dresen, Cooky Ziesche, Laila Stieler, and Jorg Hauschild.

When I was much younger, I would experience an "oh, no!" feeling if I realized I was falling in love. It was a mixture of joy in the moment and dread of the usual complications that had, around the age of nineteen, tutored me that there was no such thing as living happily ever after—usually, anyway. I suspect that feeling never entirely leaves us. Consider Inge (Ursula Werner), who is sixty-seven and has been married with reasonable happiness for thirty years to Werner (Horst Rehberg), and finds herself knocking hopefully on the door of a seventy-six-year-old man she hardly knows.

This is Karl (Horst Westphal), who had dropped off his pants to be altered. Inge is a seamstress, working on a sewing machine in the bedroom, living in a nice little apartment with Werner, who in the evenings likes to listen to recordings of steam engines arriving in train stations. His idea of a nice day out for the two of them is taking a train to no particular place while they look out the window.

Werner is not presented as a boring monster, because he isn't. Looking out a train window is often the occasion for dreamy reveries, and as I watched this film I felt the desire, easily suppressed, to go to the Amtrak station and buy a ticket to no particular place. Werner helped Inge raise her family, her daughter Petra (Steffi Kuehnert) considers him her father, and they carry out a soothing ritual of drinking coffee and watching TV.

What came over Inge when she was measuring Karl for his pants? Why did she deliver them herself? Why did he invite her in, and why did they fall into each other's arms a moment later and find themselves losing their underwear so quickly? There's no accounting for such things. The French call it a *coup de foudre*, a lightning bolt to the heart.

Petra advises her not to confess to Werner. "Go ahead, Mother, enjoy yourself—but tell no one!" Sound advice. Inge, however, finds confession necessary. Werner doesn't take the news at all well. "I didn't want to!" she cries out. "I didn't want this to happen to me!" One of those "oh no!" moments.

We shy away from details about elder sex. I had a friend who protested: "Dad, I don't want to know!" Inge and Karl are like a couple of kids, enjoying each other's bodies and presence. She's no beauty, never wears makeup, and apparently goes through the whole film without washing her hair, unless the time she skinny-dips with Karl counts. But when she smiles: Well, everyone has a beautiful face when they look at you with love in their eyes. In this film without deeply complex characters, so much depends on how Karl and Werner look at Inge and how she looks at them.

The director, Andreas Dresen, presents the sex scenes as if they involve two twenty-year-olds, as she should. During sex you have only two ages: immortal or dead. She regards their total nudity with all the detachment we might feel in a steam room. There is a scene where the actress stands naked in front of a mirror and looks at herself. Such a moment of honesty is common enough in the movies, but she does it for so long that our minds begin to supply her thoughts about the inexorable fading of youth.

Paul Cox's great film *Innocence* also considers a late-life romance and is deeper than *Cloud Nine*, I think, because its characters are more sensitive and thoughtful. Inge and Werner in their late sixties don't seem to know much more about such matters than they did when they were teens. About Karl we can't be

sure. Yet these performances are so quietly effective that we watch, absorbed. I'm not sure, however, that where this film comes from quite earns the place it goes to.

Note: Cloud Nine *was the winner of the Un Certain Regard jury prize at Cannes 2008.*

Cloudy with a Chance of Meatballs ★★ ½
PG, 90 m., 2009

With the voices of: Bill Hader (Flint Lockwood), James Caan (Tim Lockwood), Anna Faris (Sam Sparks), Andy Samberg (Brent McHale), Mr. T (Earl Devereaux), Bruce Campbell (Mayor Shelbourne). Directed by Phil Lord and Chris Miller and produced by Pam Marsden. Screenplay by Lord and Miller, based on the book by Judi Barrett and Ron Barrett.

Let me search my memory. I think—no, I'm positive—this is the first movie I've seen where the hero dangles above a chasm lined with razor-sharp peanut brittle, while holding onto a red licorice rope held by his girlfriend, who has a peanut allergy, so that when she gets cut by some brittle and goes into anaphylactic shock and her body swells up, she refuses to let go, and so the hero bites through the licorice to save her. You don't see that every day.

Cloudy with a Chance of Meatballs is a 3-D animated comedy based on a children's book popular in the 1980s, about a kid named Flint who survives on an island in the Atlantic by catching and canning sardines. When the sardine market collapses and the citizens grow tired of eating their own sardines, he decides to save his island by creating a machine that can convert ordinary water into any food on Earth: hamburgers, ice cream, jelly beans, you name it. As the only practicing film critic who has visited an actual sardine cannery on the coast of Namibia, I am here to tell you that a large cannery on a small island would make you yearn for such a machine.

Flint wants to be an inventor, but his dad insists he help out in the family fishing tackle and sardine store. His dad possibly needs help because he has no visible eyes, only one bushy eyebrow growing straight across his face like a hairy hedge. But Flint works late at night in his tree house, which eventually grows into the largest structure in town, and eureka! Kids eat jelly beans all day long. Gummi bears frolic. Hamburgers grow on trees. The machine seems to create only food kids like. Pizza, but no broccoli. There is a problem. Because of an error, the machine runs out of control, deluging the island in a cascade of edibles.

It's a good thing the movie is animated. That makes it easier to create a tornado funnel cloud made of spaghetti and meatballs. Its velocity causes meatballs to spin off and rain down upon the town, looking like—well, never mind what they look like.

There is a giant refuse heap outside town, looking like a slag heap and held back by a dam. In an attempt to stop the food storm, Flint, his girlfriend, and his buddy tunnel into a candy mountain, leading to the peanut brittle crisis. There are other characters, including the town's bombastic mayor, a Herculean mascot for the sardine ad campaigns, a monkey, and so on.

It seemed to me the mountains of fudge, ice cream, and pancakes overshot the mark and looked silly, and the airborne food cast a pall over the city, but by golly those kids are plucky. They look a little odd, however; Flint seems to be all nose, like his dad is all eyebrow.

This is the first outing for the new Sony digital 3-D imaging software. I continue to find 3-D a distracting nuisance, but it must be said that the Sony process produces a sharp, crisp picture, with no visible imprecision between the matches of the images. There is clear definition between closer and farther elements. I've seen a lot of 3-D recently, and in terms of technical quality, this is the best.

Cloverfield ★ ★ ★
PG-13, 80 m., 2008

Michael Stahl-David (Rob Hawkins), Mike Vogel (Jason Hawkins), Odette Yustman (Beth McIntyre), Lizzy Caplan (Marlena Diamond), Jessica Lucas (Lily Ford), T. J. Miller (Hud). Directed by Matt Reeves and produced by J. J. Abrams and Bryan Burk. Screenplay by Drew Goddard.

Godzilla meets the "queasy-cam" in *Cloverfield*, a movie that crosses the Monster-Attacks-Manhattan formula with *The Blair Witch Project*. No, Godzilla doesn't appear in person, but the movie's monster looks like a close relative on the evolutionary tree, especially in one close-up. The close-up ends with what appears to be a POV shot of the guy with the video camera being eaten, but later he's still around. Too bad. If he had been eaten but left the camera's light on, I might have been reminded of the excellent video of my colonoscopy.

The movie, which has been in a vortex of rumors for months, is actually pretty scary at times. It's most frightening right after something very bad begins to happen in lower Manhattan and before we get a good look at the monster, which is scarier as a vaguely glimpsed enormity than as a big reptile. At least I think it's a reptile, although it sheds babies by the dozens, and they look more like spiders crossed with crabs. At birth they are already fully formed and functioning, able to scamper all over town, bite victims, grab them in subway tunnels, etc. I guess that makes the monster a female, although Godzilla, you will recall, had a baby, and the fanboys are still arguing over its gender. (Hold on! I just discovered online that those are not its babies at all, but giant parasitic lice, which drop off and go looking for dinner.)

The film, directed by Matt Reeves, is the baby of producer J. J. Abrams, creator of TV's *Lost*. It begins with home video–type footage and follows the fortunes of six twenty-something yuppies. The lead character is Rob (Michael Stahl-David), who is about to leave town for a job in Japan. At a farewell surprise party, Hud (T. J. Miller) takes over the camera and tapes friends wishing Rob well, including Jason (Mike Vogel) and the beautiful Lily (Jessica Lucas). Hud is especially attentive toward Marlena (Lizzy Caplan), who says she's just on her way to meet some friends. She never gets there. The building is jolted, the lights flicker, and everyone runs up to the roof to see all hell breaking loose.

The initial scenes of destruction are glimpsed at a distance. Then things heat up when the head of the Statue of Liberty rolls down the street. Several shots of billowing smoke clouds are unmistakable evocations of 9/11, and indeed, one of the movie's working titles was *1/18/08*. So the statute has run out on the theory that after 9/11 it would be in bad taste to show Manhattan being destroyed. So explicit are *Cloverfield's* 9/11 references that the monster is seen knocking over skyscrapers, and one high-rise is seen leaning against another.

The leaning high-rise contains Beth (Odette Yustman), whom Rob feels duty-bound to rescue from her forty-ninth-floor apartment near Central Park. The others all come along on this foolhardy mission (not explained: how, after walking all the way to Columbus Circle, they have the energy to climb forty-nine flights of stairs, Lily in her high heels). Part of their uptown journey is by subway, without the benefit of trains. They're informed by a helpful soldier that the last rescue helicopter leaving Central Park will "have wheels up at oh-six-hundred," prompting me to wonder how many helicopters it would take to rescue the population of Manhattan.

The origin of the monster goes unexplained, which is all right with me after the tiresome opening speeches in so many of the thirty or more Godzilla films. The characters speculate that it came from beneath the sea, or maybe from outer space, but incredibly not one of them ever pronounces the word "Godzilla," no doubt for trademark reasons. The other incredible element is that the camcorder's battery apparently lasts, on the evidence of the footage we see, more than seven hours.

The entire film is shot in queasy-cam handheld style, mostly by Hud, who couldn't hold it steady or frame a shot if his life depended on it. After the sneak preview, I heard some fellow audience members complaining that they felt dizzy or had vertigo, but no one barfed, at least within my hearing. Mercifully, the movie is even shorter than its alleged ninety-minute running time; how much visual shakiness can we take? And yet, all in all, it is an effective film, deploying its special effects well and never breaking the illusion that it is all happening as we see it. One question, which you can answer for me after you see the film: Given the nature of the opening government announcement, how did the camera survive?

Coco Before Chanel ★★★ ½
PG-13, 110 m., 2009

Audrey Tautou (Gabrielle "Coco" Chanel), Benoit Poelvoorde (Etienne Balsan), Alessandro Nivola (Arthur "Boy" Capel), Marie Gillain (Adrienne Chanel), Emmanuelle Devos (Emilienne). Directed by Anne Fontaine and produced by Caroline Benjo, Philippe Carcassonne, and Carole Scotta. Screenplay by Anne Fontaine and Camille Fontaine, with Christopher Hampton and Jacques Fieschi, adapted from the book *L'Irreguliere ou Mon Itineraire Chanel* by Edmonde Charles-Roux.

We talk about people "inventing themselves." That assumes they know who they want to invent. *Coco Before Chanel* begins with an abandoned orphan girl, watches her grow into a music hall chanteuse, and then sidestep prostitution by becoming a mistress. All the while from behind the clouds of her cigarettes she regards the world with unforgiving realism and stubborn ambition. She doesn't set out to become the most influential fashion icon of the twentieth century. She begins by designing a hat, making a little money, and striving to better herself. She wants money and independence. One suspects she would have been similarly driven if she had invented a better mousetrap and founded a home appliance empire.

The naturalism of Anne Fontaine's film would be at home in a novel by Dreiser. Her star, Audrey Tautou, who could make lovability into a career, avoids any effort to make Coco Chanel nice, or soft, or particularly sympathetic. Her fashions may have liberated women from the hideous excesses of the late nineteenth century, but she creates them not out of idealism, but because they directly reflect her inalterable personality. She didn't put women in sailor shirts out of conviction. She liked to wear them.

Perhaps because of its unsentimental approach to Chanel's life, *Coco Before Chanel* struck me as less of a biopic, more of a drama. It's not about rags to riches but about survival of the fittest. Is Coco, young and poor, used by the rich playboy Etienne Balsan (Benoit Poelvoorde)? Perhaps he thought so early in their relationship, but she uses him as well.

She likes him, but she signed aboard for money, status, and entrée, not merely sex and romance. She sees theirs as a reasonable transaction. She isn't a brazen temptress but a capitalist, who collects on her investment.

Through Balsan she meets the bold actress Emilienne (Emmanuelle Devos) and Boy Capel, an Englishman. It's clear that to Chanel, love with a man or a woman is pretty much the same, but Boy truly does love her, and this is a unique experience for Coco. Things might have proceeded quite differently in her life if that relationship had survived. Baron Balsan, not blinded by love, sees Boy as exactly what he is—something Coco, for once, hasn't done.

Tautou isn't stereotypically beautiful but more uniquely fetching. It's her spirit as much as her face, and the tilt of her upper lip more than her curves. Coco is above all a disciplinarian of herself; at the end of the film we learn she died in 1971—"on a Sunday," at work, just as she worked every day of her life. She had an original vision of fashion, yes, but we get the feeling she didn't depend on it for her success. She worked hard, dealt with people realistically, drove hard bargains, and saw fashion as a job, not a career or a vocation.

By underlining that, the movie becomes more absorbing. We've seen enough films about heroines carried along by the momentum of their blessed fates. That's not how it works. To the winner belongs the spoils, even if in life you started pretty far back from the starting line. In the case of little Gabrielle Chanel and her sister Adrienne (Marie Gillain), the orphanage probably gave them better chances in life than the parents they missed. They got an education, and it's possible Chanel's fashion sense was influenced by the unadorned, severe lines of the black and white habits of the nuns. Did she start identifying simplicity in dress with women in power?

The young teenage girls break into the lowest rungs of music halls, performing songs in a duet of which it must be said their youth is more appealing than their talent. Music halls attract sugar daddies, and they both size up the situation and make their choices. The film loses some of its fascination, for me, when Coco Chanel is unmistakably launched on her career path. But that's when the story ends; this is titled *Coco Before Chanel* for a reason.

Note: Her story continues in an entirely different film, Coco Chanel & Igor Stravinsky.

Cold Souls ★★★

PG-13, 101 m., 2009

Paul Giamatti (Paul Giamatti), David Strathairn (Dr. Flintstein), Dina Korzun (Nina), Emily Watson (Claire), Katheryn Winnick (Sveta), Lauren Ambrose (Stephanie). Directed by Sophie Barthes and produced by Andrij Parekh, Dan Carey, Elizabeth Giamatti, Paul Mezey, and Jeremy Kipp Walker. Screenplay by Barthes.

Would an actor sell his own soul for a great performance? No, but he might pawn it. Paul Giamatti is struggling through rehearsals for Chekhov's *Uncle Vanya* and finds the role is haunting every aspect of his life. His soul is weighed down, it tortures him, it makes his wife miserable. He sees an article in the *New Yorker* about a new trend: People are having their souls extracted for a time, to lighten the burden.

The man who performs this service is Dr. Flintstein, whose Soul Storage service will remove the soul (or 95 percent of it, anyway) and hold it in cold storage. As played by a droll David Strathairn, whose own soul seems in storage for this character, Flintstein makes his service sound perfectly routine. He's the type of medical professional who focuses on the procedure and not the patient. Giamatti, playing an actor named after himself, has some questions, as would we all, but he signs up.

Cold Souls is a demonstration of the principle that it is always wise to seek a second opinion. The movie is a first feature written and directed by Sophie Barthes, whose previous film was a short about a middle-aged condom tester who considers buying a box labeled "Happiness" at the drugstore. Clearly this is a filmmaker who would enjoy having dinner with Charlie Kaufman. Perhaps inspired by Kaufman's screenplay for *Being John Malkovich,* she also credits *Dead Souls,* the novel by Gogol about a Russian landowner who buys up the souls of his serfs.

Gogol was writing satire, and so is Barthes. We hope that medical intervention can help us do what we cannot do on our own: focus better, look younger, lose weight, cheer up, be smarter. If only it were as simple as taking a pill. Or, in Giamatti's case, lying on his back to be inserted into a machine looking uncannily like a pregnant MRI scanner.

His soul is successfully extracted and kept in an airtight canister. He's allowed to see it. It has the size and appearance of a chickpea. Lightened of the burden, he becomes a different actor: easygoing, confident, upbeat, energetic— and awful. Rehearsals are a disaster, and he returns to Flintstein demanding his old soul back.

This is not easily done, for reasons involving Nina (Dina Korzun), a sexy Russian courier in the black market for souls. A Russian soul is made available to Giamatti, with alarming results. All of this is dealt with in the only way that will possibly work, which is to say, with very straight faces. The material could be approached as a madcap comedy, but it's funnier this way, as a neurotic, self-centered actor goes through even more anguish than Chekhov ordinarily calls for.

I suppose *Cold Souls* is technically science fiction. There's a subset of SF involving a world just like the one we inhabit, with only one element changed. In an era of Frankenscience, *Cold Souls* objectifies all the new age emoting about the soul and inserts it into the medical care system. Certainly if you have enough money to sidestep your insurance company, a great many cutting-edge treatments are available. And soul extraction is not such a stretch when you reflect that personality destruction, in the form of a prefrontal lobotomy, was for many years medically respectable. Insert an ice pick just so, and your worries are over.

I enjoy movies like this, that play with the logical consequences of an idea. Barthes takes her notion and runs with it, and Giamatti and Strathairn follow fearlessly. The movie is rather evocative about the way we govern ourselves from the inside out. One of Nina's problems is that she has picked up little pieces from the souls of all the other people she has carried. Don't we all?

Collapse ★★★★

NO MPAA RATING, 80 m., 2009

A documentary featuring Michael Ruppert.

Directed by Chris Smith and produced by Smith and Kate Noble.

If this man is correct, then you may be reading the most important story in today's paper.

I have no way of assuring you that the bleak version of the future outlined by Michael Ruppert in Chris Smith's *Collapse* is accurate. I can only tell you I have a pretty good built-in BS detector, and its needle never bounced off zero. There is controversy over Michael Ruppert, and he has many critics. But one simple fact at the center of his argument is obviously true, and it terrifies me.

That fact: We have passed the peak of global oil resources. There are only so many known oil reserves. We have used up more than half of them. Remaining reserves are growing smaller, and the demand is growing larger. It took about a century to use up the first half. That usage was much accelerated in the most recent fifty years. Now the oil demands of giant economies such as India and China are exploding. They represent more than half the global population, and until recent decades had small energy consumption.

If the supply is finite and usage is potentially doubling, you do the math. We will face a global oil crisis, not in the distant future, but within the lives of many now alive. They may well see a world without significant oil.

Oh, I grow so impatient with those who prattle on about our untapped resources in Alaska, yada yada yada. There seems to be only enough oil in Alaska to power the United States for a matter of months. The world's great oil reserves have been discovered.

Saudi Arabia sits atop the largest oil reservoir ever found. For years the Saudis have refused to disclose any figures at all about their reserves. If those reserves are vast and easy to tap by drilling straight down through the desert, then ask yourself this question: *Why are the Saudis spending billions of dollars to develop off-shore drilling platforms?*

Michael Ruppert is a man ordinary in appearance, on the downhill slope of middle age, a chain-smoker with a mustache. He is not all worked up. He speaks reasonably and very clearly. *Collapse* involves what he has to say, illustrated with news footage and a few charts, the most striking of which is a bell-shaped curve. It takes a lot of effort to climb a bell-shaped curve, but the descent is steep and dangerous.

He recites facts I knew, vaguely. Many things are made from oil. Everything plastic. Paint. Eight gallons of oil in every auto tire. Oil supplies the energy to convert itself into those by-products. No oil, no plastic, no tires, no gas to run cars, no machines to build them. No coal mines except those operated by men and horses.

Alternative energies and conservation? The problem is the cost of obtaining and using it. Ethanol requires more energy than it produces. Hybrid and battery cars need engines, tires, and batteries. Nuclear power plants need to be built with oil. Electricity from wind power is most useful near its source. It is transmitted by grids built and maintained by oil. Wave power is expensive to collect. Solar power is cheap and limitless, but we need a whole hell of a lot more solar panels and other collecting devices.

Like I say, you do the math. Ruppert has done his math, and he concludes our goose is cooked. He doesn't have any answers. We're passing the point of diminishing returns on the way to our rendezvous with the point of no return. It was nice while it lasted. People lived happily enough in the centuries before oil, electricity, and steam, I guess. Of course, there were fewer than six billion of us. And in this century, Ruppert says, there will be a lot fewer than six billion again. It won't be a pretty sight.

I'm not going to mention his theories about global warming, because that's a subject that inflames too many zealots. About peak oil, his reasoning is clear, simple, and hard to refute.

So you can stop reading now. That's the heart of Ruppert's message, delivered by a calm guy who could be Wilford Brimley's kid brother, lives alone with his dog, and is behind on his rent.

I was fascinated by some of the directions peak oil takes him into. For him, he says, it was the key to understanding many seemingly unconnected geopolitical events. The facts he outlines are known to world leaders. They don't talk a lot about them in alarmist terms, but they explain why Bush/Cheney were happy to have an excuse to invade Iraq. And why our embassy compound in Baghdad is the largest we've ever built, larger than the Vatican City. And why we're so much more worried by Iran than North Korea. They may also explain Obama's perplexing decision to increase troops in Afghanistan. An undeclared world war for oil is already under way.

I don't know when I've seen a thriller more frightening. I couldn't tear my eyes from the screen. *Collapse* is even entertaining, in a macabre sense. I think you owe it to yourself to see it.

Confessions of a Shopaholic ★ ★ ½
PG, 112 m., 2009

Isla Fisher (Rebecca Bloomwood), Hugh Dancy (Luke Brandon), Joan Cusack (Jane Bloomwood), John Goodman (Graham Bloomwood), John Lithgow (Edgar West), Kristin Scott Thomas (Alette Naylor), Leslie Bibb (Alicia Billington), Fred Armisen (Ryan Koenig), Julie Hagerty (Hayley), Krysten Ritter (Suze Cleath-Stewart), Robert Stanton (Derek Smeath). Directed by P. J. Hogan and produced by Jerry Bruckheimer. Screenplay by Tracey Jackson, Tim Firth, and Kayla Alpert, based on the books by Sophie Kinsella.

I liked *Confessions of a Shopaholic* about as much as I disliked *Sex and the City*. Both are about clueless women, but this one knows it. *SATC* is about women searching for love in most of the wrong places, and *Shopaholic* is about a woman searching for happiness in the places that are absolutely right for her: Prada, Gucci, Macy's, Barneys, Saks, and on down the avenue.

The plotting is on automatic pilot. It needs Chesley B. Sullenberger III. There is not a single unanticipated blip in the story arc. But here's what sort of redeems it: It glories in its silliness, and the actors are permitted the sort of goofy acting that distinguished screwball comedy. We get double takes, slow burns, pratfalls, exploding clothes wardrobes, dropped trays, tear-away dresses, missing maids of honor, overnight fame, public disgrace, and not, amazingly, a single obnoxious cat or dog.

At the center of this maelstrom is a genuinely funny comedienne named Isla Fisher.

She reminded me of Lucille Ball, and not only because she's a redhead. She does one of the most difficult things any actress can do, which is physical comedy: walk into doors, drop trays, fall into people, go ass over teakettle. She plays a Perfect Ditz in the sense of the Perfect Storm, carrying all before her. Give her a fan and twenty seconds of tango lessons, and get off the floor.

It is to the credit of the director, P. J. Hogan of *My Best Friend's Wedding*, that he gives Fisher freedom and yet modulates it, so her character's earnest desire to please shines through. It was the same on *I Love Lucy.* Lucy wasn't a klutz because she was trying to look funny. She was a klutz because she was trying not to.

Fisher plays Rebecca Bloomwood, the only child of blue-collar parents (Joan Cusack and John Goodman), who has been reborn as a Most Preferred Customer through the miracle of credit cards. She begins with a narration describing the nearly erotic bliss she feels while shopping, and we follow her through store after store in an endless cycle of accessorizing outfits, and then buying outfits to match the accessories. It's like the dilemma of the ten hot dogs and eight buns: You can never come out even at the end.

She dreams of working for a famous fashion magazine but stumbles, literally, into a money management magazine published by the same company. How does this woman who knows nothing about money or its management get the job? By impressing the editor (Hugh Dancy) with her eccentric brilliance. Everything she does that's wrong turns out right. Also she benefits from a brave roommate, Suze (Krysten Ritter), who plays the Ethel Mertz role: coconspirator and occasional voice of reason.

Meanwhile, the villainous bill collector Derek Smeath (Robert Stanton) is on her trail, hints that breaking her legs is not out of the question, and eventually has one of the funnier scenes in the movie. After she gains (highly improbable) international fame overnight on the basis of her writing, it would destroy her, she fears, to be unmasked. Whether it does or not, I leave it to your experience of cinematic plotting to determine.

Look, *Confessions of a Shopaholic* is no masterpiece. But it's funny, Isla Fisher is a joy, and—of supreme importance—it is more entertaining to a viewer with absolutely no eagerness to see it (like me) than *Sex and the City* was. Also, no movie can be all bad where the heroine attends a Shopaholics Anonymous meeting and meets a former Chicago Bulls star.

Constantine's Sword ★ ★ ★
NO MPAA RATING, 95 m., 2008

A documentary directed by Oren Jacoby and produced by Jacoby, James Carroll, Michael Solomon, and Betsy West. Screenplay by Carroll and Jacoby, based on the book by Carroll.

James Carroll speaks calmly and thoughtfully, and comes across as a reasonable man. He is our companion through *Constantine's Sword,* a film about the misalliance of church and state. In terms of screen presence, he is the opposite of one of his interview subjects, the Reverend Ted Haggard of Colorado Springs. To look upon Haggard's face is to wonder what he is really thinking because his mouth seems locked in an enormous smile ("Fiery-eyed and grinning maniacally, Mr. Haggard suggests a Paul Lynde caricature of a fire-and-brimstone preacher." —Stephen Holden, *New York Times*)

Carroll went to Colorado to interview Haggard and others about the alleged infiltration of the Air Force Academy by evangelical Christians. He also speaks with an academy graduate, Mikey Weinstein, who brought suit against the academy alleging that his cadet son, Casey, was the focus of officially sanctioned anti-Semitism. One academy chaplain, we learn, lectured new cadets on their duty to proselytize those who had not found Jesus.

For Haggard, that is the exercise of free speech. For Weinstein and Carroll, it is another chapter of the long-running history of Christianity's crusade against the Jews. Not long after, Carroll finds himself standing on the bridge in Rome where the Emperor Constantine is said to have had a vision of the cross of Jesus, with the words, "In this sign, you shall conquer." The linking of Christianity with the state began then and there, Carroll believes.

The film is a ninety-five-minute distillation of Carroll's best-seller *Constantine's Sword:*

The Church and the Jews and is concerned with medieval anti-Semitism, the questionable record of Pius XII on Nazism, the Crusades, the wars in Vietnam and Iraq, and his own life as a former Catholic priest, the son of an Air Force general, an antiwar protestor, and still a practicing Catholic. That is too much ground to cover, but *Constantine's Sword* does an engrossing job of giving it a once-over. Perhaps it is the calm in Carroll's voice and the measured visual and editing style of the director, Oren Jacoby, that create an evocative journey out of what is really a hurtle through history.

Carroll has a lot of stories to tell us: Haggard and the explosion of evangelicalism ("a new megachurch of two-thousand-plus members comes into being every other day"); Constantine and the conversion of Rome from paganism; the Middle Ages and the crusaders who warmed up with the massacre of ancient Jewish cities in Germany; Edith Stein, a Jewish woman who became a Catholic nun and saint and a victim of Auschwitz; the Jewish family that has lived for centuries in the same district in Rome and supplied the popes with all their tableware for 150 years; and his own father, who was a strategist during the Cuban Missile Crisis.

Each topic is intrinsically interesting, even if the film sometimes seems short of visuals to illustrate it. There are too many shots of Carroll on the road, going places and looking at things. There isn't a lot new about his revisionist history of Christianity, but there is a lot that is not widely known, including the fact that the present pope has overturned the reforms of Vatican II and returned to the Mass a prayer for the conversion of the Jews. How much do we appreciate the Muslim prayers for *our* conversion? Or do they want us?

I've read over the years about the Air Force Academy controversy but didn't realize how deeply the academy's culture is embedded in evangelical zealotry. A similar controversy developed at the University of Colorado about an evangelical football coach's training sermons. Does religion belong in such contexts? In the academy's dining room, which seats thousands, every place setting for a week included a flyer promoting Mel Gibson's *The Passion of the Christ*. If those in charge of the academy did not understand instinctively why

allowing that is an unacceptable crossing of the boundary between church and state, they should not have been allowed high office.

But I ramble. So does the movie, in an insidiously fascinating way. Perhaps it benefits by lacking a clear agenda and not following a rigid outline. Carroll is a man of limitless curiosity about his subjects, the kind of conversationalist you urge to keep on talking. As for Rev. Haggard, some months after his interview was filmed, he resigned as president of the National Association of Evangelicals, describing himself as a "liar and hypocrite" after his affair with a onetime male prostitute was revealed. I wonder how widely he was smiling then.

Cop Out ★ ½
R, 110 m., 2010

Bruce Willis (Jimmy Monroe), Tracy Morgan (Paul Hodges), Adam Brody (Barry Mangold), Kevin Pollak (Hunsaker), Ana de la Reguera (Gabriela), Guillermo Diaz (Poh Boy), Michelle Trachtenberg (Ava), Seann William Scott (Dave). Directed by Kevin Smith and produced by Polly Cohen Johnsen, Marc Platt, and Michael Tadross. Screenplay by Robb Cullen and Mark Cullen.

Jimmy and Paul are cops hunkered down across the street from a stakeout when they see a mysterious figure run across rooftops and break into a house. Seconds later, he can clearly be seen in an upper window, sitting on a toilet and reading a magazine. "What kindofa guy breaks into a house and takes a crap?" asks Paul, or words to that effect.

Paul explains he always delays this elementary function until he gets home. He's not relaxed until then. But once he's home—ooohhh boy! Then he lets loose. He describes the results in great detail. The walls, the ceilings. All right! I'm thinking, all right, already! I got it! Mudslide! Paul isn't finished. Now he's talking about the reaction of the neighbors.

How do you know this is a scene from a Kevin Smith film? The imitation of a nine-year-old describing bodily functions might be a clue. But the clincher is when that mysterious guy runs across the rooftops. Paul (Tracy Morgan) explains to his partner Jimmy (Bruce Willis): "That's known as 'parkour.' It's a new martial art." Well, thanks, Paul. I didn't know that until yesterday, when it was explained in *District 13: Ultimatum*. What synchronicity. That other movie costars the man who gave "parkour" its name. The movie is filled with it. I suspect its presence as a brief walk-on in *Cop Out* can be explained this way: Kevin found out about it, thought it was cool, and slipped in a little quick "parkour" for fun.

If you combine the enthusiasms of a geek with the toilet humor of a third-grader, you'll be pretty close to defining the art of Kevin Smith. Hey, I'm not complaining. If we lose our inner third-grader, we begin to die. When the muse visits him, Smith gets inspired and makes fun movies like *Zack and Miri Make a Porno*. Alas, *Cop Out* is not one of those movies. Tracy Morgan is forced to go way over the top; Bruce Willis seems eager to have a long, sad talk with his agent; and Kevin Pollak, who gets costar billing, does at least appear for longer than a quark at Fermilab.

Cop Out tells your standard idiotic story about buddy cops who screw up, get suspended by the captain, and redeem themselves by overthrowing a drug operation while searching for the valuable baseball card Jimmy wants to sell to pay for his daughter's wedding. Paul spends an unreasonable amount of time dressed as a cell phone, considering there is nothing to prevent him from taking it off.

A lot of the dialogue is intended to be funny, but man, is it lame. Many of the gags possibly looked good on paper, but watching Willis and Morgan struggle with them is like watching third-graders do Noel Coward, if Noel Coward had been rewritten by Kevin Smith. At St. Joseph's Boys' Camp there was this Chicago kid named Bob Calvano who was naturally hilarious around the campfire every night. Then I'd get up and flop with my memorized bits from Buddy Hackett records. "Ebert," he advised me kindly, "it isn't funny if you act like it's supposed to be funny. Act like you don't know." All I can do is pass along Calvano's advice.

Coraline ★ ★ ★
PG, 101 m., 2009

With the voices of: Dakota Fanning (Coraline Jones), Teri Hatcher (Mother/Other Mother), John Hodgman (Father/Other Father), Ian McShane (Mr. Bobinsky), Jennifer Saunders (Miss Spink), Dawn French (Miss Forcible), Robert Bailey Jr. (Wybie Lovat). Directed by Henry Selick and produced by Claire Jennings and Mary Sandell. Screenplay by Selick, based on the novel by Neil Gaiman.

The director of *Coraline* has suggested it is for brave children of any age. That's putting it mildly. This is nightmare fodder for children, however brave, under a certain age. I know kids are exposed to all sorts of horror films via video, but *Coraline* is disturbing not for gory images but for the story it tells. That's rare in itself: Lots of movies are good at severing limbs but few at telling tales that can grab us down inside where it's dark and scary.

Even more rare is that Coraline Jones (Dakota Fanning) is not a nice little girl. She's unpleasant, complains, has an attitude, and makes friends reluctantly. Nor does she meet sweet and colorful new pals in her adventure, which involves the substitution of her parents by ominous doubles with buttons sewn over their eyes. She is threatened with being trapped in their alternate world, which is reached by an alarming tunnel behind a painted-over doorway in her own house.

Not that Coraline's own parents are all that great. They're busy, distracted, bickering, and always hunched over their computers. They hardly hear her when she talks. That's why she recklessly enters the tunnel and finds her Other Mother and Other Father waiting with roasted chicken and a forced cheerfulness. All she needs to stay there is to have buttons sewn into her own eye sockets.

Coraline is the new film by Henry Selick, who made *The Nightmare Before Christmas* and again combines his mastery of stop-motion and other animation with 3-D. The 3-D creates a gloomier image (take off the glasses and the screen is bright), but then this is a gloomy film with weird characters doing nasty things. I've heard of eating chocolate-covered insects, but not when they're alive.

The ideal audience for this film would be admirers of film art itself, assuming such people exist. Selick creates an entirely original look and feel, uses the freedom of animation to elongate his characters into skeletal specters looming over poor Coraline. Her new friend Wybie (Robert Bailey Jr.) is a young hunchback whose full name is Wyborn, and it doesn't take Coraline long to wonder why his parents named him that.

Other Mother and Other Father (voices by Teri Hatcher and John Hodgman, who are also Mother and Father) essentially want to steal Coraline from her real but distracted parents and turn her into some kind of a Stepford Daughter. Their house, which looks like Coraline's own, has two old ladies (Jennifer Saunders and Dawn French) in the basement, boarders who seem in retirement from subtly hinted careers in the adult entertainment industry. The upstairs boarder is Mr. Bobinsky (Ian McShane), a sometime vaudevillian who has a troupe of trained mice. One of the rooms of the house has insects bigger than Coraline who act as living furniture.

It's more or less impossible, for me anyway, to be scared by 3-D animation. The process always seems to be signaling, "I'm a process!" I think it's harder to get involved in a story when the process doesn't become invisible. I hear from parents who say, "My kids didn't even notice the 3-D!" In that case, why have it in the first place?

Kids who will be scared by the story may not all be happy to attend, 3-D or not. I suspect a lot of lovers of the film will include admirers of Neil Gaiman, whose Hugo Award–winning novel inspired Selick's screenplay. Gaiman is a titan of graphic novels, and there's a nice irony that one of his all-words books has been adapted as animation.

I admire the film mostly because it is good to look at. Selick is as unconventional in his imagery as Gaiman is in his writing, and this is a movie for people who know and care about drawing, caricature, grotesquery, and the far shores of storytelling. In short, you might care little about a fantasy, little indeed about this story, and still admire the artistry of it all, including an insidious score by Bruno Coulais, which doesn't pound at us like many horror scores, but gets under our psychic fingernails.

Credit is due to those who backed this film. I'm tired of wall-to-wall cuteness like *Kung Fu Panda* and wonder if Selick's approach would be suited to films for grown-ups adapted from

material like stories by August Derleth or Stephen King. And perhaps I didn't make it clear that it's fine with me that Coraline is an unpleasant little girl. It would be cruelty to send Pippi Longstocking down that tunnel, but Coraline deserves it. Maybe she'll learn a lesson.

Couples Retreat ★★
PG-13, 107 m., 2009

Vince Vaughn (Dave), Jason Bateman (Jason), Faizon Love (Shane), Jon Favreau (Joey), Malin Akerman (Ronnie), Kristen Bell (Cynthia), Kristin Davis (Lucy), Kali Hawk (Trudy), Tasha Smith (Jennifer), Carlos Ponce (Salvadore), Peter Serafinowicz (Sctanley), Jean Reno (Marcel), Temuera Morrison (Briggs). Directed by Peter Billingsley and produced by Scott Stuber and Vince Vaughn. Screenplay by Vaughn, Jon Favreau, and Dana Fox.

Couples Retreat tells the story of four troubled couples and how they're healed by sitcom formulas. Why are they troubled? Because the screenplay says so. It contains little comedy except for freestanding one-liners, and no suspense except for the timing of the obligatory reconciliation. It doesn't even make you think you'd like to visit its island paradise.

The couples are apparently all from Buffalo Grove, which supplies nothing visual except for a T-shirt. Three of them think they're reasonably happy, but their friends Jason (Jason Bateman) and Cynthia (Kristen Bell) beg them to join them for a week at a resort devoted to healing relationships (if four couples go, it's half price).

Jason and Cynthia are anguished because they haven't had a child. The other couples are Dave (Vince Vaughn) and Ronnie (Malin Akerman); Joey (Jon Favreau) and Lucy (Kristin Davis); and Shane (Faizon Love) and Trudy (Kali Hawk). Their troubles: (1) Parenting duties distract from romance; (2) Joey's wandering eye; (3) Shane has split from his wife and is dating a twenty-year-old bimbo.

They fly to the Eden resort, which uses locations on Bora Bora, a truly enchanted place that's reduced to the beach party level. Eden is run by Monsieur Marcel (Jean Reno), a martial arts mystic, and managed by Sctanley

(Peter Serafinowicz), who explains his name is spelled with a C. Other staff include Salvadore (Carlos Ponce), doubling for a model on the cover of a lesser romance novel.

The formula itself might have supported hilarity, but the story lacks character specifics. Each couple behaves relentlessly as an illustration of their problem. The movie depends for excitement on a shark attack during a scuba-diving exercise, featuring clueless sharks and an enormous pool of blood apparently leaked from a tiny superficial scratch. Salvadore charms the wives somewhat ambiguously with his oiled pecs and bottles of pineapple-rum drinks. The men don't bond so much as stand together on-screen and exchange bonding dialogue.

There is a twin resort named East Eden, which has all swinging singles as opposed to troubled couples. It's a party scene every night; as nearly as I could tell, our four couples are the only clients on West Eden, so no wonder there was a 50 percent off deal, despite Sctanley's talk of the long waiting list.

Among the better things in the movie, I count Vaughn's well-timed and smart dialogue; the eccentricity of Love and Hawk in contrast to the cookie-cutter couples; and Serafinowicz's meticulous affectations, which suggest psychotropic medication.

The concluding scenes are agonizing in the way they march through the stages dictated by an ages-old formula. We know all four couples must arrive at a crisis. We know their situations must appear dire. We expect a transitional event during which they realize the true nature of their feelings. This is a wild party night at East Eden. We expect sincere confessions of deep feelings. And we know there must be a jolly conclusion that wraps everything up.

In the context of the film, the jolly conclusion must be seen to be believed. Were all the transitional events anticipated, even planned, by the all-seeing Monsieur Marcel? Marcel hands each couple an animal representing their true inner animal spirits. These are carved from a dark wood, which I deduced after seeing the second, third, and fourth animals. The first was a rabbit, which looked like nothing else than a chocolate bunny. That would have been strange.   ☞

The Cove ★★★★
PG-13, 94 m., 2009

Featuring Richard O'Barry, Louie Psihoyos, Simon Hutchins, Mandy-Rae Cruickshank, Kirk Krack, David Rastovich, and Scott Baker. A documentary directed by Louie Psihoyos and produced by Fisher Stevens and Paula DuPre Pesman. Screenplay by Mark Monroe.

Flipper was smiling on the outside but crying on the inside. That's what Richard O'Barry thinks. He's the man who trained five dolphins for use on the *Flipper* TV show, and then began to question the way dolphins were used in captivity. In the years since, he has become an activist in the defense of captive dolphins exploited in places such as Sea World.

The dolphins who are captured are luckier than the thousands harpooned to death. In a hidden cove near the Japanese coastal village of Taiji, sonar is used to confuse dolphins and lead them into a cul-de-sac where they're trapped and killed. Since their flesh has such a high concentration of mercury that it's dangerous to eat, why slaughter them? To mislabel them as whale meat, that's why. Having long ignored global attempts to protect whales from being fished to extinction, the Japanese have found dolphins easier to find. But who would eat the meat? Japanese children, whose school lunches incredibly include mislabeled dolphin.

Is it necessary to mention that dolphins are not fish, but mammals? Indeed, they're among the most intelligent of mammals and seem naturally friendly toward man. They're even tool-users, employing sponges to protect their snouts in some situations, and teaching that learned behavior to their offspring.

The Cove, a heartbreaking documentary, describes how Richard O'Barry, director Louie Psihoyos, and a team of adventurers penetrated the tight security around the Taiji cove and obtained forbidden footage of the mass slaughter of dolphins. Divers were used to sneak cameras into the secret area; the cameras, designed by Industrial Light and Magic, were hidden inside fake rocks that blended with the landscape.

The logistics of their operation, captured

by night vision cameras at times, has the danger and ingenuity of a caper film. The stakes are high: perhaps a year in prison. The footage will temper the enjoyment of your next visit to see performing dolphins.

It is an accident of evolution that dolphins seem to be smiling, the film informs us. They just happen to look that way. Their hearing is incredibly more acute than a human's, and the sounds of loudspeakers and recorded music, rebounding off the walls of their enclosures, can cause them anxiety and pain. O'Barry believes one of the dolphins he trained for *Flipper* literally died in his arms of depression.

There are many documentaries angry about the human destruction of the planetary peace. This is one of the very best—a certain Oscar nominee. It includes a great many facts about the craven International Whaling Commission and many insights into the mistreatment of dolphins; Simon Hutchins is especially helpful.

But when all of the facts have been marshaled and the cases made, one element of the film stands out above all, and that is the remorse of Richard O'Barry. He became rich and famous because of the TV series, which popularized and sanitized the image of captive dolphins. He has been trying for twenty-five years to make amends. But why, you may ask, are performing dolphins so willing to perform on cue? Well, you see, because they have to, if they want to eat. ☞

The Crazies ★★ ½
R, 101 m., 2010

Timothy Olyphant (David Dutton), Radha Mitchell (Judy Dutton), Joe Anderson (Russell Clank), Danielle Panabaker (Becca Darling), Christie Lynn Smith (Deardra Farnum), Brett Rickaby (Bill Farnum), Preston Bailey (Nicholas), John Aylward (Mayor Hobbs). Directed by Breck Eisner and produced by Michael Aguilar, Rob Cowan, and Dean Georgaris. Screenplay by Scott Kosar and Ray Wright.

The Crazies is a perfectly competent genre film in a genre that has exhausted its interest for me, the zombie film. It provides such a convenient storytelling device: Large numbers of mindless zombies lurch toward the camera and the hero, wreaking savage destruction, and can be quickly blown away, although not without risk and occasional loss of life. When sufficient zombies have been run through, it's time for a new dawn.

I know there can be good zombie films. I've seen some: *Dawn of the Dead, 28 Days Later, Shaun of the Dead,* and so on. If I saw another one, I'd like it. But all depends on good living characters and a director with something new to say about zombies, who are a subject easily exhausted.

Are the zombies in *The Crazies* real zombies? Maybe, maybe not. Is there an agreed definition of what is a zombie, and how they get that way? Not that I know of. I think zombies are defined by behavior and can be "explained" by many handy shortcuts: the supernatural, radiation, a virus, space visitors, secret weapons, a Harvard education, and so on. I suppose it would be a "spoiler" if I revealed why the Crazies are lurching, but come on, does it matter? What if I revealed they got that way because of, oh, say, eating Pringles? Would that spoil things for you? What difference does it make? All that matters is that they got to be zombies *somehow*. Before that, they were your friends and neighbors. Then they started in on the damn Pringles.

The protagonists, of course, have to be healthy. I cannot imagine a zombie as a leading character. Vampires, now, I grant you. Werewolves. But a zombie doesn't bring much to the party. So we start in sweet little Ogden Marsh, Iowa, described on its Web site as "the friendliest place on Earth," and no wonder. Its sheriff is so good-looking he could be the star of this movie. Must be a quiet place. The sheriff's office is open only from eight to five Monday through Friday.

One day after work Sheriff David Dutton (Timothy Olyphant) and his deputy, Russell Clank (Joe Anderson), are watching a local school baseball game when the town drunk comes lurching into the outfield holding a shotgun. When the autopsy shows he had a 0.0 blood alcohol level, that's the first signal something is wrong in Ogden Marsh. For one thing, their town drunk is a slacker.

The sheriff's wife, Judy (Radha Mitchell), is the local doctor. She starts treating some strange cases. I don't want to spoil anything, so I'll simply say the sheriff and Deputy Russell discover the probable origin of this plague, but of course can't get the mayor to declare an emergency, because he learned the mayoring trade from *Jaws*. Meanwhile, it's up to Dave, Judy, and Russell to defend themselves from zombies and survive after the town is isolated and quarantined and the cure seems worse than the disease.

That requires many scenes involving people and objects that jump out from the sides of the screen with loud noises and alarming musical chords. I'm thinking, so what? The last thing I need is another jump out/loud noise/ alarming chord movie. Even a well-made one—like this one, directed by Breck Eisner. It was inspired by George Romero's 1973 movie of the same name, although I can't tell you if the zombies match because that would be a spoiler.

Here is what I can say to aspiring young screenwriters: Movies like this are fairly simple to write. You need zombies. You need heroes. At first there's a mystery, and then the horror. You describe lots of jump/noise/chord situations. When you figure you're up to around ninety minutes, the sun can rise. You'll get an R rating, so throw in a little nudity. Not too much, because if there's a combination that gives me the creeps, it's zombies and nudity. Especially when—but never mind. That's enough for today.

Crazy Heart ★★★★
R, 112 m., 2009

Jeff Bridges (Bad Blake), Maggie Gyllenhaal (Jean Craddock), Robert Duvall (Wayne Kramer), Ryan Bingham (Tony), Colin Farrell (Tommy Sweet), James Keane (Manager). Directed by Scott Cooper and produced by T-Bone Burnett, Judy Cairo, Rob Carliner, Cooper, and Robert Duvall. Screenplay by Cooper, based on the novel by Thomas Cobb.

Some actors are blessed. Jeff Bridges is one of them. Ever since his first starring role in *The Last Picture Show* in 1971, he has, seemingly without effort, created a series of characters whom we simply believe, even the alien in *Starman*. He doesn't do this with mannerisms but with their exclusion; his acting is as clear as running water. Look at him playing Bad Blake in *Crazy Heart*. The notion of a broke-down, boozy country singer is an archetype in pop culture. We've seen this story before. The difference is, Bad Blake makes us believe it happened to *him*.

That's acting. There's a line of dialogue in the movie that I jotted down at the time, and it's been cited by several critics. Bad Blake is being interviewed in his shabby motel room by Jean Craddock (Maggie Gyllenhaal), a reporter for a newspaper in Santa Fe. She's taking him, gently, to places he doesn't want to go. He's been interviewed about the subject too many times. He doesn't say that. He says, "I want to talk about how bad you make this room look."

It's such a good line I can hardly believe I've never heard it before. Bad Blake perhaps knows it sounds like an old movie. It's also the kind of line written by a singer-songwriter, the masking of emotion by ironic displacement, the indirect apology for seedy circumstances. She blushes. I can't think of a better way for the movie to get to where it has to go next. No shy apologies. No cynicism. Just that he wrote a great line of a country song, and it was for her.

Bridges, Gyllenhaal, and Scott Cooper, the first-time writer-director, find that note all through the movie. It's like a country-and-western cliché happening for the first time. Bridges doesn't play drunk or hung over or newly in love in the ways we're accustomed to. It's like Bad has lived so long and been through so much that he's too worn out to add any spin to exactly the way he feels.

Bad Blake was a star once, years ago. He has lyrics that go, "I used to be somebody, but now I'm somebody else." His loyal manager (James Keane) once booked him in top venues. As *Crazy Heart* opens, Bad is pulling up to a bowling alley. "It's this year's *The Wrestler*," one of my colleagues observed after the screening. Yes. Bad still has a few loyal fans, but you get the feeling they've followed him to the bottom. He has a son he's lost touch with, and he hasn't written a good song in a long time. In the old days he toured with a kid named Tommy Sweet (Colin Farrell). Now Tommy is a big star, but contrary to the conventions of such stories, hasn't forgotten his old teacher and remains loyal.

Maybe, we're thinking, with the love of a good woman he can turn it around. It's not that simple in *Crazy Heart*. Jean is a good woman, but can she afford to love this wreck twenty-five years older than she is? Certainly not if he continues to drink, and maybe not in any case. And it's not easy for Bad to stop drinking; he's descended below his bottom.

How does Bridges do this without making the character some sort of pitiful and self-pitying basket case? The presence of Robert Duvall here, playing his old friend and acting as one of the producers of this movie, is a reminder of Duvall's own *Tender Mercies* (1983), another great film about a has-been country singer and a good woman (Tess Harper). It's a measure of Bridges and Duvall, and Gyllenhaal and Harper, that they create completely different characters.

One of the ways the movie might have gone wrong is if the singing and the songs hadn't sounded right. They do. Bridges has an easy, sandpapery voice that sounds as if it's been through some good songs and good whiskey, and the film's original songs are by T-Bone Burnett and Stephen Bruton (who died of cancer in May 2009 at Burnett's home). Bridges conveys the difficult feelings of a singer keeping his dogged pride while performing in a bowling alley.

The movie knows more about alcoholism than many films do and has more of that wisdom onscreen, not least from the Duvall character. Gyllenhaal's character, too, is not an enabler or an alibi artist, but a woman who feels with her mind as well as her heart. Watch her as she and Bridges find the same level of mutual confidence for their characters. One of the reasons we trust the film is that neither Bad nor Jean is acting out illusions. Colin Farrell, too, is on the same page. We understand why he stays loyal, to the degree that he can. This is a rare story that knows people *don't* always forget those who helped them on the way up.

Jeff Bridges is a virtual certainty to win his first Oscar, after four nominations. The movie was once set for 2010 release (and before that, I hear, for going straight to cable). The more people saw it, the more they were convinced this was a great performance. Fox Searchlight stepped in, bought the rights, and screened it extensively in December for critics' groups, who all but unanimously voted for Bridges as the year's best actor. We're good for something. ☞

Creation ★★★
PG-13, 108 m., 2010

Paul Bettany (Charles Darwin), Jennifer Connelly (Emma Darwin), Jeremy Northam (Rev. Innes), Toby Jones (Thomas Huxley), Benedict Cumberbatch (Joseph Hooker), Martha West (Annie Darwin). Directed by Jon Amiel and produced by Jeremy Thomas. Screenplay by John Collee, based on the book *Annie's Box* by Randal Keynes.

Darwin, it is generally agreed, had the most important idea in the history of science. Thinkers had been feeling their way toward it for decades, but it took Darwin to begin with an evident truth and arrive at its evident conclusion: Over the passage of many years, more successful organisms survive better than less successful. The result is the improvement of future generations. This process he called "natural selection."

It worked for bugs, birds, and bees. It worked for plants, fish, and trees. In 1859, when he published *On the Origin of Species,* it explained a great many things. Later, we would discover it even explained the workings of the cosmos. But—and here was the question even Darwin himself hesitated to ask—did it explain Man?

Emma Darwin didn't think so. Darwin's wife was a committed Christian who believed with her church that God alone was the author of Man. And for her it wasn't God as a general concept, but the specific God of Genesis, and he created Man exactly as the Old Testament said he did. He did it fairly recently, too, no matter that Darwin's fossils seemed to indicate otherwise.

Creation is a film about the way this disagreement played out in Darwin's marriage. Charles and Emma were married from 1830 until his death in 1882. They had ten children, seven of whom survived to beget descendants who even today have reunions. They loved each other greatly. Darwin at first avoided spelling out the implications for Man of the theory of evolution so as not to disturb her. But his readers could draw the obvious conclusion, and so could Emma: If God created Man, he did it in the way Darwin discovered, and not in the way a four-thousand-year-old legend prescribed.

The problems this created in the Darwin marriage were of interest primarily to Emma and Charles, probably their children, and few others except in the movie business, which seldom encounters an idea it can't dramatize in terms of romance. It helps to know that going in. *Creation* will give you an idea of the lives and times of the Darwins, but unless you bring a knowledge of evolution to the movie you may not leave with much of one.

The film stars the real-life couple Paul Bettany and Jennifer Connelly, as Charles and Emma, who a few years before the publication of *Origins* are grieving the death of their ten-year-old, Annie (Martha West). This loss has destroyed Darwin's remaining faith in God and reinforced his wife's. But it is to Charles that Annie reappears throughout the film, in visions, memories, and perhaps hallucinations.

The film suggests that Darwin was forced almost helplessly toward the implications of his theory. He had no particular desire to stir up religious turmoil, especially with himself as its target. He famously delayed publication of his theories as long as he could. Two close friends tell him he owes it to himself to publish, and Thomas Huxley, who called himself "Darwin's bulldog," tells him: "Congratulations, sir! You've killed God!"

Not every believer in evolution, including the pope, would agree. But Huxley's words are precisely those Darwin feared the most. Consider that he had no idea in the 1850s how irrefutably correct his theory was, and how useful it would be in virtually every hard science. Emma and their clergyman, Rev. Innes (Jeremy Northam), try to dissuade him from publishing, but his wife finally tells him to go ahead because he must. If he hadn't, someone would have: The theory of evolution was a fruit hanging ripe from the tree.

The director Jon Amiel tells his story with respect and some restraint, showing how sad and weakened Charles is and yet not ratcheting up his grief into unseemly melodrama.

One beautiful device Amiel uses is a series of digressions into the natural world, in which we observe everyday applications of the survival of the fittest. What's often misunderstood is that Darwin was essentially speaking of the survival of the fittest genes, not the individual members of a species. This process took millions of years, and wasn't a case of humans slugging it out with dinosaurs.

Both Darwins understood and agreed about the role that inheritance (later to be known as genetics) played in health. As first cousins, they wondered if Annie's life expectancy had been compromised. She died of complications from scarlet fever, which wasn't their fault—but did they know and believe that?

I have a feeling that the loss of their child and the state of their marriage were what most interested the backers of this film. They must have wanted to make a film about Darwin the man, not Darwin the scientist. The filmmakers do their best to keep Darwin's theory in the picture, but it sadly isn't fit enough to struggle against the dominant species of Hollywood executives.

Crossing Over ★ ★ ½

R, 114 m., 2009

Harrison Ford (Max Brogan), Ray Liotta (Cole Frankel), Ashley Judd (Denise Frankel), Jim Sturgess (Gavin Kossef), Cliff Curtis (Hamid Baraheri), Alice Braga (Mireya Sanchez), Alice Eve (Claire Sheperd), Justin Chon (Yong Kim), Summer Bishil (Taslima Jahangir), Ogechi Egonu (Alike). Directed by Wayne Kramer and produced by Frank Marshall. Screenplay by Kramer.

We spend a lot of time talking about the American Dream and have too much suspicion about those who want to live it. Feelings against immigrants are so freely expressed even in polite society that you'd think they all came here for the free lunch. *Crossing Over* creates a mosaic, too simplistic to be sure, of recent arrivals who came here for admirable reasons and will be valuable citizens if they get the chance. Most of them will, anyway. Some were damaged goods at home and have not traveled well.

It is hard to immigrate to this country legally and potentially fatal to do it illegally. That's why I speculate we get some of the best and the brightest; it takes determination, ambition, and skill to get into America either way. Many of those who arrive want to improve themselves, and in the process they will improve us.

I've been taking a lot of cabs the last couple of years, and I've noticed something. Most of the drivers are obviously immigrants, from India, Pakistan, Africa, the Philippines, the Middle East, and the Americas. Without a single exception they all have their car radios tuned to the same station, the best station we have, National Public Radio. It tells you something.

Crossing Over borrows the structure of *Crash* to tell interlocking stories about several immigrants, their problems, and their families. All of their lives connect in some way, if only through U.S. immigration officials. *Crash* wove its pattern fairly naturally. *Crossing Over* seems to strain, with too many characters, too many story strands, and too much of an effort to cover the bases. We meet immigrants new and established, legal and illegal, from Mexico, Nigeria, Bangladesh, Iran, England, Korea, and Australia. It feels like a list.

The connecting links are two immigration officers played by Harrison Ford and Cliff Curtis, an adjudicator (Ray Liotta), and an immigration defense attorney (Ashley Judd). The stories involve a Mexican woman separated from her child in a raid; an Iranian family, well established, which is about to be naturalized; a Muslim teenager who attracts an FBI investigation by reading an outspoken (but legitimate) paper about 9/11 in class; a Korean teenager (Justin Chon) who is being pressured to join a Korean gang; an Australian would-be actress; an atheist Jew from the United Kingdom who poses as a teacher whose presence is needed in a Hebrew school; and a little Nigerian orphan who has been stranded in a holding center and will be sent back to Africa and danger.

Some of these stories are fascinating and some are heartbreaking, but together they seem too contrived. It's too neat the way they mingle, like the traffic on freeway interchanges seen in overhead shots that separate the passages. I was especially moved by Ford's

involvement with the Mexican woman (Alice Braga), who is hauled away pleading with him to retrieve her child from the babysitter. He plays a decent man whose conscience won't let him forget, and he ends up uniting the child with grandparents in Mexico. And there's more to it than that. It's hard for him to leave his job at work.

Harrison Ford supplies the strong central strand in the story, but sometimes it grows so implausibly melodramatic we're distracted. Ashley Judd's character provides insights in the way our legal system handles immigration, and the Australian actress (Alice Eve) shows what she is willing to do for the venal official (Liotta) who happens to be Judd's husband. There is a contrast between an Iranian father who thinks of himself as a good Muslim, and a daughter (Summer Bishil) who thinks of herself as a good Muslim and a good American.

Yes, the film is "flawed"—that prissy film critic's complaint. If you're looking for plausibility and resist manipulation, you'll object to it. But sometimes movies are intriguing despite their faults, and you want to keep on watching. This one is like that.

The Curious Case of Benjamin Button ★ ★ ½
PG-13, 167 m., 2008

Brad Pitt (Benjamin Button), Cate Blanchett (Daisy), Taraji P. Henson (Queenie), Julia Ormond (Caroline), Jason Flemyng (Thomas Button), Elias Koteas (Mr. Gateau), Tilda Swinton (Elizabeth Abbott). Directed by David Fincher and produced by Cean Chaffin, Kathleen Kennedy, and Frank Marshall. Screenplay by Eric Roth, based on a short story by F. Scott Fitzgerald.

The Curious Case of Benjamin Button is a splendidly made film based on a profoundly mistaken premise. It tells the story of a man who is old when he is born and an infant when he dies. All those around him, everyone he knows and loves, grow older in the usual way, and he passes them on the way down. As I watched the film, I became consumed by a conviction that this was simply *wrong*.

Let me paraphrase the oldest story I know: In the beginning there was nothing, and *then*

God said, "Let there be light." Everything comes after the beginning, and we all seem to share this awareness of the direction of time's arrow. There is a famous line by e.e. cummings that might seem to apply to Benjamin Button: "and down he forgot as up he grew."

But no, it involves the process of forgetting our youth as we grow older.

We begin a movie or novel and assume it will tell a story in chronological time. Flashbacks and flash-forwards, we understand. If it moves backward through a story (Harold Pinter's *Betrayal*), its scenes reflect a chronology seen out of order. If a day repeats itself (Harold Ramis's *Groundhog Day*), each new day begins with the hero awakening and moving forward. If time is fractured into branching paths (*Synecdoche, New York*), it is about how we attempt to control our lives. Even time-travel stories always depend on the inexorable direction of time.

Yes, you say, but Benjamin Button's story is a fantasy. I realize that. It can invent as much as it pleases. But the film's admirers speak of how deeply they were touched, what meditations it invoked. I felt instead: Life doesn't work this way. We are an observer of our passage and so are others. It has been proposed that one reason people marry is that they desire a witness to their lives. How could we perform that act of love if we were aging in opposite directions?

The movie's premise devalues any relationship, makes futile any friendship or romance, and spits, not into the face of destiny, but backward into the maw of time. It even undermines the charm of compound interest. In the film, Benjamin (Brad Pitt) as an older man is enchanted by a younger girl (Cate Blanchett). Later in the film, when he is younger and she is older, they make love. This is presumably meant to be the emotional high point. I shuddered. NO! NO! What are they *thinking* during sex? What fantasies apply? Does he remember her as a girl? Does she picture the old man she loved?

Pitt will, of course, be nominated for best actor and may deserve it because of his heroic struggle in the performance. Yes, he had to undergo much makeup, create body language, and perform physically to be manipulated by computers. He portrays the Ages of Man with much skill. That goes with the territory. But how did he prepare *emotionally*? What exercises would the Method suggest? You can't go through life waving good-bye. He is born looking like a baby with all the infirmities of old age. He grows younger, until he resembles Brad Pitt, and then a younger Brad Pitt, and then—we do not follow him all the way as he recedes into the temporal distance.

The film was directed by David Fincher, no stranger to labyrinths (*Zodiac, Fight Club*). The screenplay is by Eric Roth, who wrote *Forrest Gump* and reprises the same approach by having his hero's condition determine his life experience. To say, however, that Roth "adapted" the original short story by F. Scott Fitzgerald would be putting it mildly. Fitzgerald wrote a comic farce, which Roth has made a forlorn elegy. Roth's approach makes Benjamin the size of a baby at birth. Fitzgerald sardonically but consistently goes the other way: The child is born as an old man, and grows smaller and shorter until he is finally a bottle-fed baby. Not much is said about Benjamin's mother, which is a pity, because he is five feet eight at birth, and I wonder how much pushing *that* required.

I said the film is well-made, and so it is. The actors are the best: Taraji P. Henson, Julia Ormond, Elias Koteas, Tilda Swinton. Given the resources and talent here, quite a movie might have resulted. But it's so hard to *care* about this story. There is no lesson to be learned. No catharsis is possible. In Fitzgerald's version, even Benjamin himself fails to comprehend his fate. He's born as a man with a waist-length beard who can read the encyclopedia, but in childhood plays with toys and throws temper tantrums, has to be spanked, and then disappears into a wordless reverie. *Benjamin* rejects these logical consequences because, I suspect, an audience wouldn't sit still for them.

According to the odds makers at Movie City News, *The Curious Case of Benjamin Button* is third among the top five favorites for Best Picture. It may very well win. It expends Oscar-worthy talents on an off-putting gimmick. I can't imagine many people wanting to see it twice. There was another film this year that isn't in the "top five," or listed among the front-runners at all, and it's a profound consideration of the process of living and aging.

That's Charlie Kaufman's *Synecdoche, New York*. It will be viewed and valued decades from now. You mark my words.

Cyrus ★★★ ½
R, 91 m., 2010

John C. Reilly (John), Jonah Hill (Cyrus), Marisa Tomei (Molly), Catherine Keener (Jamie), Matt Walsh (Tim). Directed by Mark Duplass and Jay Duplass and produced by Michael Costigan. Screenplay by Mark Duplass and Jay Duplass.

Marisa Tomei plays warm and friendly as well as anyone, and those qualities are essential to *Cyrus,* a film about her grown son and her new boyfriend waging what amounts to war over the possession of her body. There's no incest, but a photo in her bedroom suggests the son was still getting to second base well into his adolescence. The boyfriend is pathetically happy to get on base at all, and this creates a comedy of awkwardness, private thoughts, passive aggression, and veiled hostility. All Molly (Tomei) wants is for everybody to like one another and get along.

Her boyfriend, John (John C. Reilly), is fine with that goal, but her son, Cyrus (Jonah Hill), is jealous and possessive, and very intelligent about how to use his feelings in a sneaky way, so it's not always obvious what he's up to. Not obvious to Molly, anyway, because she doesn't really want to know. More obvious to John, who's on such thin ice he's slow to admit how unpleasant the situation has become.

I can imagine how a sex comedy could spring from this premise, or even an Oedipal drama. What's intriguing about *Cyrus* is the way it sort of sits back and observes an emotional train wreck as it develops. The movie doesn't eagerly jump from one payoff to another, but attunes itself to nuance, body language, and the habitual politeness with which we try to overlook social embarrassment. With only three people, however, it's a problem when one is deliberately creating embarrassment.

Jonah Hill, who is a fairly large man, is able to morph himself somehow into a big baby here; he cleverly uses immature conduct to excuse inappropriate behavior. When he hugs his mommy, for example, there's the not-so-slight suggestion that he does so not as her son but as her smoocher. There's no suggestion that actual sex has ever been involved, but to poor John (and to us), he's over the top. Molly seems oblivious.

Cyrus pretends to welcome and like John. His very welcome outreaches the bounds of propriety. Then little things happen. John's shoes disappear. If Cyrus took them, he could easily throw them away. But *whoever* took them, they're left where they will eventually be found, a ticking time bomb. Little things like that.

Marisa Tomei has the trickiest role here. She's lonely, she's been single too long, and she likes John, the big lug. She befriends him at a party where he's desperately unhappy. She discovers him peeing in the shrubbery and says what, under these circumstances, is a remarkably tactful thing to relieve the embarrassment: "Nice penis." He needs a woman like this. He's apart from his first wife (Catherine Keener), who was maybe too smart for him. Molly isn't dumb, but she's—well, sometimes she's improbably clueless. She is also very sexy, so you can understand that a boy the age of Cyrus (but not her son) would be attracted. That avoids possible Eww Moments.

Cyrus was written and directed by the Duplass brothers, Mark and Jay, who up until now have been identified with "mumblecore," a term I hope I never have to use again. Let's put it this way: If a movie is mumblecore, it probably doesn't much want to be enjoyed, and if it isn't, why call it failed mumblecore? Their previous film, *Baghead* (2008), was not beloved by me. Now here is a film that uses very good actors and gives them a lot of improvisational freedom to talk their way into, around, and out of social discomfort. And it's not snarky. It doesn't mock these characters. It understands they have their difficulties and hopes they find a way to work things out. There's your suspense: How can they?

D

Daddy Longlegs ★★★
NO MPAA RATING, 100 m., 2010

Ronnie Bronstein (Lenny), Sage Ranaldo (Sage), Frey Ranaldo (Frey), Victor Puccio (Principal Puccio), Eleonore Hendricks (Leni), Leah Singer (Paige), Sean Williams (Dale). Directed by Josh Safdie and Benny Safdie and produced by Casey Neistat and Tom Scott. Screenplay by Josh Safdie and Benny Safdie.

Lenny isn't a bad father. He's no father at all. He doesn't understand the concept. I don't believe he ever will. He doesn't understand being an adult. He doesn't understand anything. The question at the heart of *Daddy Longlegs* is, why did his former wife ever think she could trust him with two weeks a year of child custody? Lenny shouldn't even have custody of himself.

He's in constant motion during *Daddy Longlegs*. If he has role models at all, they're provided by his two sons, Sage and Frey. Lenny acts like their playmate, not their father. "Guys," he calls them. "Guys." I heard him call Sage by name once. Frey, I don't remember even once. They are a unit, the Child Unit, to be plunged into his idea of a good time.

Lenny is played by Ronnie Bronstein, who directed *Frownland*, a 2008 film about a man all bottled up inside. Lenny is the opposite. He projects an almost relentless upbeat enthusiasm, until sometimes he loses it and we see the anger. He tries to babysit the kids, who are five and seven, while at the same time working as a movie projectionist and dating, or breaking up, with his current girlfriend (Eleonore Hendricks). With one kid riding his shoulders and another tagging behind, he rushes out on unclear missions.

For parents, this may play like a horror film. At one point he actually gives these two children fifty-five dollars and sends them by themselves to a supermarket some blocks away in New York City to buy supplies for dinner. At another time, he talks a complete stranger into taking the three of them along on a trip with her boyfriend to upstate New York.

He jumps on the bed with the "guys" and wrestles them. He forgets to pick them up after school. He takes them to work and they print out a thousand Xeroxes. And then, in an unbelievable act of criminal irresponsibility, he figures out a way for them to stay out of trouble for two, maybe three days, while his big mouth manages to get himself arrested.

The Safdie brothers, Benny and Josh, have a dedication on the film that may or may not refer to their own father. Their cinematic father is obviously John Cassavetes, whose own manic heroes ran crazy loops around their lives. If *Daddy Longlegs* is influenced by Cassavetes, well, that's not a bad thing. Few filmmakers have the nerve to travel that path.

Bronstein's performance is crucial. It's difficult to make a manic character plausible, but he does. He never goes over the top. His mania seems devoted more to lifting off from the bottom. How he ever convinced his wife (Leah Singer) to marry him is hard to explain, most of all, probably, to herself.

Note: This film is available in some markets via Video on Demand.

The Damned United ★★★ ½
R, 97 m., 2009

Michael Sheen (Brian Clough), Timothy Spall (Peter Taylor), Colm Meaney (Don Revie), Henry Goodman (Manny Cussins), Maurice Roeves (Jimmy Gordon), Jim Broadbent (Sam Longson), Stephen Graham (Billy Bremner), Brian McCardie (Dave Mackay). Directed by Tom Hooper and produced by Andy Harries and Grainne Marmion. Screenplay by Peter Morgan, based on the 2006 novel *The Damned Utd* by David Peace.

Imagine if Al Lopez, not long after leading the White Sox to their pennant, had resigned to take Casey Stengel's job at the Yankees, insulted the players and fans, and plummeted the team into a losing streak. That would parallel the career of Brian Clough, who led the underdog Derby County to British football glory, and then took the manager's job at its hated archrival, Leeds United, and informed the players they were hooligans.

That we haven't heard of Brian Clough in

this country is no reason not to see *The Damned United,* the story of a man and the nature of professional sports. Football, known as soccer on this side of the waves, inflames passions in a way unknown to American football fans. To insult a Brit's team is to defame his mother. It's more democratic than U.S. football, because all it really requires to play is a ball. What must they think of us around the world when they witness pro football with its fearsome protective equipment and brief spurts of activity? "How do you find the *patience* to watch it?" I was asked by a London friend. I countered with cricket, the nearest thing in sports to a timeout.

Clough was the youngest manager in history when he took over Derby County. He was funny and friendly, and once before a match tousled the hair of a young man and told him, "You will never forget this day." That fan grew up to be the novelist David Peace, who wrote *The Damned Utd* about the Shakespearean tragedy of Clough.

Clough was a helpless partisan. He identified with Derby so deeply that when he took over Leeds it became almost an act of revenge. Even as their leader, he hated them. And he was stepping into the shoes of their legendary manager Don Revie, who had been named manager of the English national team. Revie, who once neglected to shake his hand after a match. He hated Leeds, Revie, and the team's management, and it's believed by some that Leeds players deliberately lost matches to sabotage him.

The enigma of Brian Clough has long fascinated British fans. *The Damned United* offers no easy explanation, but plunges into the mysteries of the personality. It stars Michael Sheen, who now in three films has embodied modern British icons so uncannily that he's all but disappeared into them. He was Prime Minister Tony Blair in *The Queen,* David Frost in *Frost/Nixon,* and now Brian Clough. He completes these transformations largely without the disguise of makeup, primarily by seeming so intensely *them. The Damned United* again unites Sheen with screenwriter Peter Morgan and producer Andy Harries of the other two. Tom Hooper directs.

Clough is a nervous man. His passion eats at him. During one match with Leeds, he can-

not force himself onto the field, but remains in the locker room, trying to interpret the cheers of the crowd. His tortured psyche gains a measure of balance from Peter Taylor (Timothy Spall), his loyal assistant, who is quiet, wise, and prudent, and acts as his drag anchor. Tactless to the core, Clough insults this good man, who doesn't follow him to Leeds. That is the start of his undoing.

Spall is one of three first-rank supporting actors who bring the film richness. Colm Meaney plays Revie, a Woody Hayes or Vince Lombardi type who has the confidence of royalty. Jim Broadbent plays Sam Longson, owner of Derby, who is a Jerry Reinsdorf type, if you see what I mean. At some level, professional sports must be considered, after all, as a retail business.

The Damned United avoids all sports movie clichés, even the obligatory ending where the team comes from behind. Is this the first sports movie where the hero comes from ahead and loses? David Peace says before writing his novel he reread the great proletarian Angry Young Men fictions circa 1960, such as *Look Back in Anger, Saturday Night and Sunday Morning,* and *Loneliness of the Long Distance Runner.* He has a hero who is most comfortable as underdog—indeed, almost needs to be.

The film is not primarily concerned with showing the game. It skillfully uses some archival footage, which evokes the pitch of feeling during a match. Soccer crowds are a mass of unanimous emotion and not so much a collection of individuals. Fans lose themselves in the surging collective like Japanese men at an annual festival of a god.

The film focuses squarely on Brian Clough. We sense what wounded love his admirers felt. He was so good, so true, and fell so swiftly after joining the other side; today in Britain, all you have to do is mention "the forty-four days" and everyone will know you mean Clough's brief tenure at the damned Leeds United. *Therefore the flight shall perish from the swift, and the strong shall not strengthen his force, neither shall the mighty deliver himself.*

Note: In educating myself about Brian Clough, I came across an extraordinary passage by William Thomas in Empire *magazine. He writes that soccer is "a sport that defeats a* *cinematic treatment—that swift, Brownian motion transformed into Keystone Cop capering as soon as a camera rolls."* "Brownian motion"? I looked it up on Wikipedia: "the seemingly random movement of particles suspended in a fluid (e.g., a liquid or gas)." Yes! The players on a soccer field are guided at all times by their own free will—unlike American football, with its offensive plays and defensive patterns. The whole field is always in play. The action is too quick on too large a scale to be contained on a screen. Thomas explains something I'd wondered about but never articulated.*

The Dark Knight ★ ★ ★ ★
PG-13, 152 m., 2008

Christian Bale (Bruce Wayne), Michael Caine (Alfred), Heath Ledger (Joker), Gary Oldman (James Gordon), Aaron Eckhart (Harvey Dent), Maggie Gyllenhaal (Rachel Dawes), Morgan Freeman (Lucius Fox). Directed by Christopher Nolan and produced by Nolan, Charles Roven, and Emma Thomas. Screenplay by Christopher Nolan and Jonathan Nolan.

Batman isn't a comic book anymore. Christopher Nolan's *The Dark Knight* is a haunted film that leaps beyond its origins and becomes an engrossing tragedy. It creates characters we come to care about. That's because of the performances, because of the direction, because of the writing, and because of the superlative technical quality of the entire production. This film, and to a lesser degree *Iron Man*, redefine the possibilities of the "comic book movie."

The Dark Knight is not a simplistic tale of good and evil. Batman is good, yes; the Joker is evil, yes. But Batman poses a more complex puzzle than usual: The citizens of Gotham City are in an uproar, calling him a vigilante and blaming him for the deaths of policemen and others. And the Joker is more than a villain. He's a Mephistopheles whose actions are fiendishly designed to pose moral dilemmas for his enemies.

The key performance in the movie is by the late Heath Ledger, as the Joker. Will he become the first posthumous Oscar winner since Peter Finch? His Joker draws power from the actual inspiration of the character in the silent classic *The Man Who Laughs* (1928). His clown's makeup more sloppy than before, his cackle betraying deep wounds, he seeks revenge, he claims, for the horrible punishment his father exacted on him when he was a child. In one diabolical scheme near the end of the film, he invites two ferry-loads of passengers to blow up the other before they are blown up themselves. Throughout the film, he devises ingenious situations that force Batman (Christian Bale), Commissioner Gordon (Gary Oldman), and District Attorney Harvey Dent (Aaron Eckhart) to make impossible ethical decisions. By the end of the film, the whole moral foundation of the Batman legend is threatened.

Because these actors and others are so powerful, and because the movie does not allow its spectacular special effects to upstage the humans, we're surprised how deeply the drama affects us. Eckhart does an especially good job on Harvey Dent, whose character is transformed by a horrible fate into a bitter monster. It is customary in a comic book movie to maintain a certain knowing distance from the action, to view everything through a sophisticated screen. *The Dark Knight* slips around those defenses and engages us.

Yes, the special effects are extraordinary. They focus on the expected explosions and catastrophes, and have some superb, elaborate chase scenes. The movie was shot on location in Chicago, but it avoids such familiar landmarks as Marina City, the Wrigley Building, or the skyline. Chicagoans will recognize many places, notably LaSalle Street and Lower Wacker Drive, but director Nolan is not making a travelogue. He presents the city as a wilderness of skyscrapers, and a key sequence is set in the still-uncompleted Trump Tower. Through these heights the Batman moves at the end of strong wires, or sometimes actually flies, using his cape as a parasail.

The plot involves nothing more or less than the Joker's attempts to humiliate the forces for good and expose Batman's secret identity, showing him to be a poseur and a fraud. He includes Gordon and Dent on his target list, and contrives cruel tricks to play with the fact that Bruce Wayne once loved, and Harvey Dent now loves, Assistant D.A. Rachel Dawes (Maggie Gyllenhaal). The tricks are more cruel than he realizes, because the Joker doesn't know Batman's identity. Heath Ledger has a good deal of dialogue in the movie, and a lot of it isn't the usual jabs and jests we're familiar with: It's psychologically more complex, outlining the dilemmas he has constructed and explaining his reasons for them. The screenplay by Christopher Nolan and his brother Jonathan (who first worked together on *Memento*) has more depth and poetry than we might have expected.

Two of the supporting characters are crucial to the action and are played effortlessly by the great actors Morgan Freeman and Michael Caine. Freeman, as the scientific genius Lucius Fox, is in charge of Bruce Wayne's underground headquarters and makes an ethical objection to a method of eavesdropping on all of the citizens of Gotham City. His stand has current political implications. Caine is the faithful butler Alfred, who understands Wayne better than anybody and makes a decision about a crucial letter.

Nolan also directed the previous, and excellent, *Batman Begins* (2005), which went into greater detail than ever before about Bruce Wayne's origins and the reasons for his compulsions. Now it is the Joker's turn, although his past is handled entirely with dialogue, not flashbacks. There are no references to Batman's childhood, but we certainly remember it, and we realize that this conflict is between two adults who were twisted by childhood cruelty—one compensating by trying to do good, the other by trying to do evil. Perhaps they instinctively understand that themselves.

Something fundamental seems to be happening in the upper realms of the comic book movie. *Spider-Man II* (2004) may have defined the high point of the traditional film based on comic book heroes. A movie like the new *Hellboy II* allows its director free rein for his fantastical visions. But now *Iron Man* and even more *The Dark Knight* move the genre into deeper waters. They realize, as some comic book readers instinctively do, that these stories touch on deep fears, traumas, fantasies, and hopes. And the Batman legend, with its origins in film noir, is the most fruitful one for exploration. In his two Batman movies, Nolan has freed the character to be a canvas for a broader scope of human emotion. For Bruce

Wayne is a deeply troubled man, let there be no doubt, and if ever in exile from his heroic role, it would not surprise me what he finds himself capable of doing. ☞

Dark Streets ★ ★
R, 83 m., 2008

Gabriel Mann (Chaz), Bijou Phillips (Crystal), Izabella Miko (Madelaine), Elias Koteas (Lieutenant), Michael Fairman (Nathaniel). Directed by Rachel Samuels and produced by Andrea Balen, Claus Clausen, and Glenn M. Stewart. Screenplay by Wallace King, based on the play *City Club* by Glenn Stewart.

Dark Streets is the kind of film you can appreciate as an object, but not as a story. It's a lovingly souped-up incarnation of the film noir look, contains well-staged and performed musical numbers, and has a lot of cigarettes, tough tootsies, bad guys, and shadows. What it doesn't have is a story that pulls us along or a hero that seems as compelling as some of the supporting characters.

The hero is Chaz (Gabriel Mann), who has inherited a nightclub from his secretive father, who was a power magnate. Night after night, he sits in the club, smoking and regarding his stage shows. Too many nights after nights. The most noticeable thing about Chaz is his pencil-thin mustache. OK, so it's the 1930s, and actors like William Powell and Clark Gable had mustaches like that and played good guys, but somehow don't you associate the style more with snaky villains and riverboat gamblers? A very young man wearing such a mustache is trying to tell us something we don't want to know.

His club feels more like a set than a business. The whole film feels that way: as if the sets, actors, and dialogue are self-consciously posing as classic film noir instead of sinking into the element. Look at a film like *Dark City*, which is obviously made of sets but feels like noir to its very bones. Here, the moment Bijou Phillips and Izabella Miko appear on the screen, they exude: *I'm the dame in a movie nightclub!*

That's not to say they're not good. In fact, they're surprisingly good, especially in the club's jazz-based production numbers, where they sing and dance and are sultry and entertaining. It's wrong of me, but I'm always a little startled when someone like Bijou or Paris Hilton turns out to be talented, because it's wrong that's not what they're famous for.

It's difficult to imagine how Chaz's smallish club, even though it does good business, can afford to stage those production numbers, which, although not Vegas in scope, are at least comparable to those on a big-time cruise ship. I'm reminded of Broadway musicals where six extras play the audience in *42nd Street*. Other details seem out of scale. If Chaz's dad really was a power tycoon, shouldn't the offices of this vast monopoly be more impressive than some gold stenciling on the glass of an office door? I think the power blackouts that keep shutting down the city may be intended to remind us of Enron's deliberate California blackouts, but that plot thread leads nowhere.

The movie is directed by Rachel Samuels, with a screenplay by Wallace King, based on Glenn Stewart's play *City Club*. Since it plays more like the book for a musical, maybe she should have just gone ahead and made it a musical. That would have forgiven the lapses in logic, explained the sets and production numbers, and shrugged off problems of scale. And it would have built on the movie's strength (not just the performances but a nice sound track presence by Etta James, B. B. King, Natalie Cole, and others). You'd still need to make Chaz more formidable. At least in a musical, he doesn't need to be Robert De Niro.

Date Night ★★★ ½
PG-13, 88 m., 2010

Steve Carell (Phil Foster), Tina Fey (Claire Foster), Mark Wahlberg (Holbrooke), Taraji P. Henson (Detective Arroyo), Common (Collins), James Franco (Taste), Mila Kunis (Whippit), Ray Liotta (Mob Boss). Directed by Shawn Levy and produced by Levy and Tom McNulty. Screenplay by Josh Klausner.

Steve Carell and Tina Fey play a nice, unassuming couple in *Date Night*, and that's one of the reasons the movie works so well. Their Phil and Claire Foster are a normal, overworked, sincere, good-natured New Jersey couple whose lives have become routine. But

they love each other, and all they really want is to hire a babysitter and enjoy a nice night out on the town.

We believe that. We're halfway prepared for a low-key romantic comedy when all hell breaks loose. They pretend to be an absent couple in order to grab a reservation at a trendy restaurant, and two hit men assume they *are* that couple and topple them into a screwball comedy. Yet all the time Phil and Claire seem like the kind of people who don't belong in a screwball comedy. That's why it's funny. They're bewildered.

Date Night supplies them with the *real* Tripplehorns (James Franco and Mila Kunis), two mob-employed cops (Jimmi Simpson and Common), a mob boss (Ray Liotta), and a muscular security expert (Mark Wahlberg) who never wears a shirt. These characters are also somewhat believable. Plots like this have a way of spinning over the top with insane, manic behavior. It's as if the characters are desperately signaling, "Look at us! Aren't we hilarious?" But the audience has to bring hilarity to you. It can't be assumed.

So what we have is a situation set in motion because a couple named the Tripplehorns don't turn up for a restaurant reservation. The Fosters, mistaken for the Tripplehorns, find themselves in way over their heads with the Tripplehorns' potentially fatal problems. The criminal characters aren't simply stupid, but bright enough to perceive this causes a problem for everyone. And the security agent (Wahlberg) is not simply a muscle-bound goon. He's a caricature, all right, but one living in a condo out of *Architectural Digest* and capable of feeling some sympathy for these pathetic New Jerseyites who've lost their way.

Carell and Fey are both natural comic performers who know (as Second City teaches) that a comedian must never seem to know that it's funny. They play Phil and Claire as nearly as possible like plausible people trapped by this nightmare misunderstanding. Yes, things heat up a little, and yes, there is an obligatory chase scene, and yes, it's a little unlikely how they end up appealing to the security expert. That goes with the territory.

But they know, as great comic actors like Cary Grant and Jack Lemmon knew, that their job in a comedy is to behave with as much realism as possible and let the impossibilities whirl around them. To begin with, Carell and Fey *look* like they might be a pleasant married couple. Attractive, but not improbably so. Young, but not that young. Fit, but they don't reveal unexpected skills. And frightened when they need to be. Do you ever wonder why the characters in some movies are never gobsmacked in the face of what seems like certain death?

All of this is a way of saying that *Date Night* is funny because, against all odds, it is involving. Each crazy step in the bizarre plot made a certain sense because it followed from what went before; it's like the Scorsese masterpiece *After Hours*. The director is Shawn Levy, who committed the two *Night at the Museum* movies, and here shows that he is much more successful when he stays far away from CGI. Remember that he also made the entertaining *Cheaper by the Dozen* with Steve Martin and Bonnie Hunt as a hard-pressed married couple.

A movie like *Date Night* encourages Hollywood comedy to occasionally dial down and realize that comedy emerges from characters and situations and can't be manufactured from manic stunts and overkill. If you don't start out liking the Fosters and hoping they have a really nice date night, not much else is going to work.

Daybreakers ★★ ½
R, 98 m., 2010

Ethan Hawke (Edward Dalton), Willem Dafoe (Elvis), Claudia Karvan (Audrey Bennett), Michael Dorman (Frankie Dalton), Vince Colosimo (Christopher Caruso), Isabel Lucas (Alison Bromley), Sam Neill (Charles Bromley). Directed by Peter Spierig and Michael Spierig and produced by Chris Brown, Bryan Furst, and Sean Furst. Screenplay by the Spierig brothers.

Ten years in the future, a global epidemic has infected most of the population with vampirism. The few remaining humans are on the run, hunted down by the militant Vampire Army, which doesn't hate them but mostly is just hungry. This depletion of the planet's food supply might be an opening for a parable about our dwindling resources, but no: Instead of making the humans a breeding stock for blood harvesting as practiced by the giant Bromley Marks Corp., the army members eat them. Al Gore must have a chart showing how that's self-defeating.

Bromley Marks is a major supplier of human blood, but is spending a fortune to develop a synthetic blood substitute. Like so many big companies in agribusiness, it wants to wean us off that healthy organic food and sell us a substitute, no doubt sweetened by corn syrup. The B-M's chief hematologist is Edward (Ethan Hawke), who like some of the atomic scientists at Los Alamos feels guilty about his work. He pushes for a cure for vampirism, not just a handy new product.

That sets the stage for this grave new world where life is designed to be lived at night. Underground moving walkways replace sidewalks, curfew starts before dawn, and so on. Edward has ethics and believes it is wrong to exploit comatose humans for their blood. He's one of those damned lefties who years ago probably was against eating beef. He's a vampire with a conscience.

Edward hooks up with the human underground, notably the cute Audrey (Claudia Karvan), and is introduced to Lionel, code name Elvis (Willem Dafoe), who has a cheap and easy vampirism antidote but is being hunted by Edward's hothead brother Frankie (Michael Dorman), because—I dunno. Because Frankie's not about to give up blood for a healthier lifestyle, I guess.

The movie, directed by Australia's twin Spierig brothers (*Undead*, 2003), looks good in its gray, sunless scenes evoking twilight (cough). The newspapers and TV anchors report on hopes for a vaccine, apparently because the constant demands of vampirism maintenance are a grind. Imagine if the price of blood was beyond the pocketbook of the average family of four, and you had to go out human hunting every day to feed the kids. A homeless person holds up a cardboard sign: "Hungry. Will work for blood."

This intriguing premise, alas, ends as so many movies do these days, with fierce fights and bloodshed. Inevitably, the future of the planet will be settled among the handful of characters we've met and a lot of extras with machine guns. I guess, but can't be sure, that audiences will enjoy the way these vampires die. They don't shrivel up into Mr. and Mrs. Havisham but explode, spraying blood all over everyone. Toward the end, their heads blow off like human champagne corks. Well, not human.

The Day the Earth Stood Still ★ ★
PG-13, 103 m., 2008

Keanu Reeves (Klaatu), Jennifer Connelly (Helen Benson), Kathy Bates (Secretary of Defense), John Cleese (Professor Barnhardt), Jaden Smith (Jacob Benson), Jon Hamm (Michael Granier). Directed by Scott Derrickson and produced by Paul Harris Boardman, Gregory Goodman, and Erwin Stoff. Screenplay by David Scarpa.

SPOILER WARNING: *The Day the Earth Stood Still* need not have taken its title so seriously that the plot stands still along with it. There isn't much here you won't remember from the 1951 classic, even if you haven't seen it. What everyone knows is that a spaceship lands on Earth, a passenger named Klaatu steps out and is shot, and then a big metal man named Gort walks out and has rays shooting from its eyes, and the army opens fire.

That movie is at No. 202 in IMDb's top 250. Its message, timely for the nuclear age, was that mankind would be exterminated if we didn't stop killing one another. The message of the 2008 version is that we should have voted for Al Gore. This didn't require Klaatu and Gort. That's what I'm here for. Actually, Klaatu is nonpartisan and doesn't name names, but his message is clear: Planets that can sustain life are so rare that the aliens cannot allow us to destroy life on this one. So they'll have to kill us.

The aliens are advanced enough to zip through the galaxy yet have never discovered evolution, which should have reassured them life on Earth would survive the death of mankind. Their space spheres have landed all over the planet, and a multitude of species have raced up and thrown themselves inside, and a Department of Defense expert intuits: "They're arks! What comes next?" The defense secretary (Kathy Bates) intones: "A flood." So this is the first sci-fi movie based on intelligent

design, except the aliens plan to save all forms of life *except* the intelligent one.

All this is presented in an expensive, good-looking film that is well-made by Scott Derrickson, but to no avail. As is conventional in such films, the fate of the planet narrows down to a woman, a child, and Klaatu. Jennifer Connelly plays Helen Benson, a Harvard scientist who is summoned by the government to advise it on the glowing sphere in Central Park. She has to leave behind her beloved little Jacob (Jaden Smith), her late husband's son by his first wife (more detail than we require, I think; just "her son" would have been fine). She meets Klaatu (Keanu Reeves), who looks human (and we already know why), but is a representative, or negotiator, or human-looking spokesthing, or something, for the aliens.

She discovers his purpose, takes him with her in her car, flees a federal dragnet, walks in the woods, introduces him to her brilliant scientist friend (John Cleese), lets him listen to a little Bach, tells him we can *change* if we're only given the chance, and expresses such love for Jacob that Klaatu is so moved he looks on dispassionately.

That's no big deal, because Klaatu looks on everything dispassionately. Maybe he has no passions. He becomes the first costar in movie history to elude falling in love with Jennifer Connelly. Keanu Reeves is often low-key in his roles, but in this movie, his piano has no keys at all. He is so solemn, detached, and uninvolved he makes Mr. Spock look like Hunter S. Thompson at closing time. When he arrives at a momentous decision, he announces it as if he has been rehearsing to say: "Yes, one plus one equals two. Always has, always will."

Jennifer Connelly and Kathy Bates essentially keep the human interest afloat. Young Jaden Smith is an appealing actor, but his character Jacob could use a good spanking, what with endangering the human race with a snit fit. Nobody is better than Connelly at looking really soulful, and I am not being sarcastic—I am sincere. There are scenes here requiring both actors to be soulful, and she takes up the extra burden effortlessly.

As for Bates, she's your go-to actress for pluck and plainspoken common sense. She announces at the outset that the president and vice president have been evacuated to an undisclosed location (not spelling out whether undisclosed to her or by her), and they stay there for the rest of the movie, not even calling her, although the president does make an unwise call to a military man. Make of this what you will. I suspect a political undertow.

One more detail. I will not disclose how the aliens plan to exterminate human life, because it's a neat visual. Let me just observe that the destruction of human life involves the annihilation of Shea Stadium, which doesn't even have any humans in it at the time. And that since the destruction begins in the mountains of the Southwest, yet approaches Shea from the East, the task must be pretty well completed by the time Jennifer Connelly needs to look soulful. And that Klaatu is a cockeyed optimist if he thinks they can hide out in an underpass in the park.

Dead Snow ★★ ½
NO MPAA RATING, 91 m., 2009

Vegar Hoel (Martin), Stig Frode Henriksen (Roy), Charlotte Frogner (Hanna), Lasse Valdal (Vegard), Evy Kasseth Rosten (Liv), Jeppe Beck Laursen (Erlend), Orjan Gamst (Colonel Herzog). Directed by Tommy Wirkola and produced by Tomas Evjen and Terje Stromstad. Screenplay by Wirkola and Stig Frode Henriksen.

They've finally assembled a horror film entirely from clichés. They even know they're doing it. As a carload of young medical students drives to a secluded cabin in a snowy forest, they find their cell phones don't work. "That's just like *Friday the 13th*," one says but is corrected: *"They didn't have cell phones then."*

Yes, they are in a cabin so far in the woods, they have to leave their car behind and follow snowmobile tracks, all except for Sara, who decides to trek overland. We suspect Sara will not be getting a lot of dialogue in this movie. The others settle in and break out the beer but are disturbed by a scary, whiskery old-timer who warns them of a vicious Nazi unit that lurked in these mountains during the war, *and probably froze to death*. Not with seventy-five minutes left in the movie, they didn't.

But how would the Nazis survive until the present day? Well, of course they are zombies, which the kids recognize when their cabin is attacked by shambling decaying men in Nazi uniforms. This crisis throws the threatened students into overdrive, clicking off as many items from *Ebert's Little Movie Glossary* as they possibly can.

I will not list all of them because to do so would summarize the plot. I was especially happy to hear "Let's split up," and later, after two girls wander off alone, to hear them discuss splitting up themselves. One bitter student says, "We should have gone to the beach like I said." I do not recall if he is the same one who sets his backpack on fire to cauterize his wound after amputating his own arm with the obligatory chainsaw.

One thing about the director, Tommy Wirkola. He's thrifty. Once his actors have their faces completely spattered with blood, he lets it stay on for hours. Your average medical students, when they get splattered with blood, they clean it off. It's part of their training. Especially with zombie blood.

One girl, wearing bright red, tries to hide from the Nazi zombies by climbing a tree. Remember that in winter there are no leaves. Yet the zombies, who are not the swiftest corpses in the mortuary, miss spotting her red ski jacket until she disturbs the eggs in a crow's nest, the crow screeches at her, and the Nazis hear her shushing it. In my opinion, shushing a crow is a fool's errand.

But practical details should not concern us. Particularly not after one of the guys disembowels a Nazi and then another Nazi grabs him and they both topple off a high cliff, but the guy holds on by grabbing the dead Nazi's large intestine, which is many yards long. If you have a large intestine that will support the weight of two men, you can forget about the colonoscopy. Apparently zombies evolve such intestines, since when a disemboweled human is seen earlier in the film, he is clearly grasping greasy frankfurter links.

Dead Snow, as you may have gathered, is a comedy, but played absolutely seriously by sincere, earnest young actors. At no point, for example, do they notice that the snow is dead. The movie is pretty funny. One of the guys discovers his cell phone is working and calls 911. "We've been attacked by what look like

Germans from the Second World War!" he shouts. "And we set our cabin on fire by accident!" He removes his phone from his ear and stares at it vengefully: "The bitch hung up on me!"

The film comes to us from Norway, which no doubt explains the snow. Nazi ski patrols did once haunt these slopes. It is the second feature by the director-writer team of Tommy Wirkola and Stig Frode Henriksen. Their first film was a satire of Tarantino's *Kill Bill* named *Kill Buljo: The Movie* ("In Kautokeino no one can hear you scream"). If *Mystery Science Theater 3000* had never existed, *Dead Snow* would have had to invent it.

Dear John ★★
PG-13, 105 m., 2010

Channing Tatum (John Tyree), Amanda Seyfried (Savannah Curtis), Henry Thomas (Tim), Scott Porter (Randy), Richard Jenkins (Mr. Tyree). Directed by Lasse Hallstrom and produced by Marty Bowen, Wyck Godfrey, and Ryan Kavanaugh. Screenplay by Jamie Linden, based on a novel by Nicholas Sparks.

Lasse Hallstrom's *Dear John* tells the heartbreaking story of two lovely young people who fail to find happiness together because they're trapped in an adaptation of a Nicholas Sparks novel. Their romance leads to bittersweet loss that's so softened by the sweet characters that it feels like triumph. If a Sparks story ended in happiness, the characters might be disappointed. They seem to have their noble, resigned dialogue already written. Hemingway wrote one line that could substitute for the third act of every Sparks story: "Isn't it pretty to think so?"

Channing Tatum stars as John Tyree, a handsome Army Special Forces specialist home on two weeks' leave at the South Carolina shore. Amanda Seyfried plays Savannah, an ethereal beauty whose purse falls off a pier. John dives in and retrieves it, and we guess it could have been worse. He could have gotten her kitten down from a tree. In the few precious days they share, they fall deeply into PG-13 love.

John was raised by his father (Richard Jenkins), a quiet man who wears white gloves while admiring his coin collection, and cooks chicken every Saturday and lasagna every Sunday. Savannah meets him and casually observes to John that he is autistic—a mild case, she gently suggests. John is angered by this insult. Did he never, by the age of twenty-two, observe that his father was strangely mannered? Did no one else? What was his (now absent) mother's thinking? Did the movie mention any employment history for Mr. Tyree? I could have missed it.

In a Sparks story, as we know from *The Notebook,* problems like autism and Alzheimer's are never seen in their tragic stages, but always allow the good souls of their victims to visibly glow. Diseases don't destroy and kill, but exist primarily to inspire admirable conduct by nexts of kin. John and Savannah get over his unhappiness, and he pledges that he'll be back at the end of twelve months so they can wed.

But then 9/11 happens, and like every man in his group he re-enlists. And continues to re-enlist until the movie's title hints at what he receives in the mail. Because Savannah is a true-blue heroine, her new love is of course a nice and decent man, someone John can accept, so that we can smile sadly and not get all messy and depressed. That's the note Sparks aims for: the sad smile. First love is not to be, but the moon still looks so large when it rises, and people treat each other gently, and if someone should die, that is very sad, but perhaps it will provide an opportunity for someone else to live a little longer before they, too, must travel to that undiscovered country from whose bourne no traveler ever returns.

John and Savannah are awfully nice. She comes from a rich family who have a mansion, and John and his dad live in a humble but cozy frame house that in its South Carolina island location might easily be purchased for less than $500,000. That would leave a portion of Mr. Tyree's unspecified income free to invest in rare coins and amass a collection worth a fortune. I am just enough of a numismatist to know that you need to invest money to collect rare coins. You don't just find them in your spare change.

I know I'm being snarky. I don't get much pleasure from it. *Dear John* exists only to coddle the sentiments of undemanding dreamers, and plunge us into a world where the only evil is the interruption of the good. Of course John is overseas on a series of missions so secret that Savannah cannot be told where, exactly, he is. In the years after 9/11, where, oh where, could he be? Apparently not in Iraq or Afghanistan, because it can hardly be a military secret that the men of Special Forces are deployed there. But somewhere, anyway, and he re-enlists for a good chunk of her early childbearing years, perhaps because, as *The Hurt Locker* informs us, "war is a drug."

It matters not. In this movie, war is a plot device. It loosens its grip on John only long enough to sporadically renew his romance, before claiming him again so that we finally consider Savannah's Dear John letter just good common sense. And now that I've brought that up: Considering that the term "Dear John Letter" has been in constant use since World War II, and that the hero of this movie is inevitably destined to receive such a letter, is it a little precious of Sparks to name him "John"? I was taught in Dan Curley's fiction class that when the title of a story is repeated in the story itself, the story's spell is broken. But then Sparks never took Curley's class.

Death at a Funeral ★★★ ½
R, 92 m., 2010

Chris Rock (Aaron), James Marsden (Oscar), Loretta Devine (Cynthia), Peter Dinklage (Frank), Martin Lawrence (Ryan), Regina Hall (Michelle), Zoe Saldana (Elaine), Kevin Hart (Brian), Danny Glover (Uncle Russell), Keith David (Reverend Davis), Ron Glass (Duncan), Tracy Morgan (Norman), Columbus Short (Jeff), Luke Wilson (Derek), Regine Nehy (Martina). Directed by Neil LaBute and produced by William Horberg, Sidney Kimmel, Laurence Malkin, Chris Rock, and Share Stallings. Screenplay by Dean Craig.

Oh, I know a lot of *Death at a Funeral* is in very bad taste. That's when I laughed the most. I don't laugh at movies where the characters are deliberately being vulgar. But when they desperately don't want to be—now that's funny. Consider the scene when Uncle Russell eats too much nut cake and is seized by diar-

rhea. And Norman wrestles him off his wheelchair and onto the potty, and gets his hand stuck underneath. Reader, I laughed. I'm not saying I'm proud of myself. That's not the way I was raised. But I laughed.

I laughed all the way through, in fact. This is the best comedy since *The Hangover,* and although it's almost a scene-by-scene remake of a 2007 British movie with the same title, it's funnier than the original. For the character of Frank, the mysterious guest who wants to speak privately with the dead man's sons, it even uses the same actor, Peter Dinklage, and he's funnier this time. Maybe that's because when a comedy gets on a roll, everything is funnier.

The funeral is taking place at home, because that's how the deceased wanted it. Also living at home are his oldest son, Aaron (Chris Rock), Aaron's wife, Michelle (Regina Hall), and his mother, Cynthia (Loretta Devine). Both Michelle and Cynthia are on his case for having not yet fathered a child. Aaron dreams of publishing a novel, while his younger brother Ryan (Martin Lawrence) has published several, which sound like porn to me, but hey, they're in print.

The mourners arrive after various adventures of the cadaver, and get into all sorts of bizarre and dire trouble in ways that the screenplay carefully explains. How was Elaine (Zoe Saldana) to know that a bottle labeled "Valium" contained a next-generation hallucinogen when she gave one to her boyfriend, Oscar (James Marsden)? It's an old gag, the guy accidentally freaked out on drugs, but Marsden elevates it to bizarre heights with a rubber face that reflects horror, delight, nausea, and affection more or less simultaneously.

There's no use in my providing a blow-by-blow of the plot, since it's deliriously screwball and it doesn't much matter what happens, as long as something always is. But I can mention what deft timing and high energy this cast has, each actor finding the rhythm for each character instead of all racing about in manic goofiness. Dinklage, for example, is as good at playing dead serious as Tommy Lee Jones, and here he's always on tone for a man who has come for compelling personal reasons. The brothers and Norman don't really wish harm to befall him, but you can see how it does. Then there is a certain logic to how they react. They're only human.

Loretta Devine has a possibly thankless role as the surviving matriarch, but her timing is delicious as she associates the death of a husband with the absence of a grandchild. Both Regina Hall and Zoe Saldana are steadfast in their love in the midst of chaos, and Danny Glover goes over the top as the cantankerous uncle because, well, that's what the role requires.

British actors are rightly known for their skill, and there were some good ones in the 2007 version of the same Dean Craig screenplay. But playing proper upper-crust characters tends to restrain them. The family in *Death at Funeral* is obviously wealthy, but loose—more human. Their emotions are closer to the surface, and these actors work together like a stock company.

Notice, too, the way director Neil LaBute directs traffic. Because the action is screwball doesn't mean it can be confusing. Screwball depends crucially on our knowing where key characters are, and why. LaBute juggles parallel actions in the big family home so we understand who's in the bathroom and who's in the living room and why everybody is out on the lawn. There's a smooth logic to it that works like spatial punch lines.

LaBute is a brilliant playwright and director who is usually the director of very dark comedies (*In the Company of Men, Your Friends and Neighbors*). But a good director is a good director, and LaBute here, like David Gordon Green with *Pineapple Express*, masters the form. And oooh, that's a mean line about R. Kelly.

Death Race ½★
R, 89 m., 2008

Jason Statham (Jensen Ames), Tyrese Gibson (Machine Gun Joe), Ian McShane (Coach), Joan Allen (Hennessey), Natalie Martinez (Case). Directed by Paul W. S. Anderson and produced by Anderson, Paula Wagner, and Jeremy Bolt. Screenplay by Anderson.

Hitchcock said a movie should play the audience like a piano. *Death Race* played me like a drum. It is an assault on all the senses, including common. Walking out, I had the impression I had just seen the video game and was still waiting for the movie.

The time is the near future, not that it matters. Times are bad. Unemployment is growing. A steelworker named Jensen Ames (Jason Statham) loses his job when the mill closes. He comes home to his loving wife and baby daughter, a masked man breaks in, the wife is killed, he is wounded, he is found guilty of his wife's murder and sentenced to the dreaded Terminal Island prison.

Treasure those opening scenes of drama, however brief they may be. The movie will rarely pause again. Prisons, we learn, are now private corporations, and Terminal raises money by pay-for-view Internet races. Its Death Race involves prisoners driving heavily armored cars bearing weapons such as machine guns, rocket launchers, and other inconveniences. If a prisoner wins five races, he gets his freedom.

But why, oh why, must I describe the rules of a Death Race? They hardly matter, nor will I take your time to tell you why Jensen Ames is enlisted to drive as the superstar Frankenstein, who wears a mask, so he could be anybody, which is the point. All of that is simply babble to set up the races.

In a coordinated visual and sound attack, mighty cars roar around the prison grounds, through warehouses, down docks, and so on, while blasting at each other, trying to avoid booby traps, and frequently exploding. Each car is assigned gimmicks like oil slicks and napalm, which can be used only once. Did I say this played like a video game? Jensen's archenemy is Machine Gun Joe (Tyrese Gibson), who is gay, which the plot informs us and thereafter forgets. Jensen's chief mechanic is Coach (Ian McShane), whose oily voice provides one of the film's best qualities. Natalie Martinez plays Case, Jensen's copilot, who screams, "Left turn! Left turn! NOW!"

And the warden of the prison is Hennessey, played by Joan Allen. Yes, that ethereal beauty, that sublime actress, that limitless talent, reduced to standing in an observation post and ordering her underlings to "activate weapons." She has a line of dialogue that employs both the f-word and the s-word and describes a possible activity that utterly baffles me. It is a threat, shall we say, that has never been uttered before and will never be uttered again. She plays her scenes with an icy venom that I imagine she is rehearsing to use in a chat with her agent.

Roger Corman is one of this film's producers, but *Death Race* is not a remake of his *Death Race 2000* (1975). That was a film about a cross-country race in which competitors were scored by how many people they ran over (one hundred points for someone in a wheelchair, seventy points for the aged, fifty points for kids, and so on). Sylvester Stallone played Machine Gun Joe. David Carradine played Frankenstein, but here he only plays the voice of one of the earlier (doomed) Frankensteins. Let us conclude that *Death Race* is not a brand that guarantees quality. That it will no doubt do great at the box office is yet another sign of the decline of the national fanboy mentality.

Defiance ★ ★ ½
R, 136 m., 2009

Daniel Craig (Tuvia Bielski), Liev Schreiber (Zus Bielski), Jamie Bell (Asael Bielski), Alexa Davalos (Lilka Ticktin), Allan Corduner (Shimon Haretz), Mark Feuerstein (Isaac Malbin), Mia Wasikowska (Chaya). Directed by Edward Zwick and produced by Zwick and Pieter Jan Brugge. Screenplay by Zwick and Clayton Frohman, based on the book *Defiance: The Bielski Partisans* by Nechama Tec.

Defiance is based on the true story of a group of Jews in Belarus who successfully defied the Nazis, hid in the forest, and maintained a self-contained society while losing only about 50 of their some 1,200 members. The "Bielski Partisans" represented the war's largest and most successful group of Jewish resisters, although when filmmakers arrived on the actual locations to film the story, they found no local memory of their activities and, for many reasons, hardly any Jews. Edward Zwick's film shows how they survived, governed themselves, and faced ethical questions, and how their stories can be suited to the requirements of melodrama.

This story has all the makings of a deep emotional experience, but I found myself oddly detached. Perhaps that's because most of the action and principal characters are within the group. The Nazis are seen in large part as an ominous threat out there somewhere in the forest, like "Those We Don't Speak Of" in M. Night Shyamalan's *The Village*. Do I require a major Nazi speaking part for the film to work? No, but the drama tends to focus on issues, conflicts, and romances within the group, and in that sense could be a very good reality show but lacks the larger dimension of, say, *Schindler's List*.

What the film comes down to is a forest survival story with a few scenes of Nazis trying to find and destroy them and a few battle scenes, which furnish the trailer and promise more of an action film. The survival story may contain omens for our own time. In the most fearsome of future scenarios, we may all have to survive in the wilderness, and we should be so lucky to have the Bielski brothers to help us. They were farmers, strong, fierce, skilled in survival skills, pragmatic.

The brothers are Tuvia Bielski (Daniel Craig), Zus Bielski (Liev Schreiber), and Asael (Jamie Bell). After they flee from genocide into the forest, others come hoping to join them, and word of their encampment spreads through the refugee underground. Tuvia decides early on that they must take in all Jews, even the helpless ones who cannot contribute; Zus, a firebrand, is less interested in saving Jews than killing Nazis, which he reasons will save more Jews. This conflict—between helping our side or harming theirs—is seen even today in the controversy over the invasion of Gaza, with Israel playing the role of the Bielski settlement.

The refugees sort out into leadership and support roles, feed their growing group largely by stealing food, establish such institutions as a hospital, a court, and even a tannery. Romance blossoms, which is common in life but indispensable in a movie, and there are tender scenes that are awfully warmly lit and softly scored, under the circumstances. Craig and Schreiber bring conviction to their roles, differing so sharply that they even come to blows before the younger brother leaves to join the Russians (who hate Jews every bit as much as the Nazis do).

Early in the film there's a scene where a

feckless middle-aged man named Shimon Haretz (Allan Corduner) hopes to join the group and is asked what he does. He thinks maybe he's an intellectual. This is no use to the partisans, although he is allowed to stay. At the time of the story, the region was largely agrarian and peasant, and many were skilled craftsmen, artisans, and laborers. I thought, I'm also an . . . intellectual. Of what use would I be in the forest? The film works in a way as a cautionary tale. Most of us live in a precarious balance above the bedrock of physical labor. Someday we may all be Shimon Haretz.

The best performance, because it's more nuanced, is by Liev Schreiber. His Zus Bielski is more concerned with the big picture, more ideological, more driven by tactics. Daniel Craig is very effective as Tuvia, the group leader, but his character, perhaps of necessity, is concerned primarily with the organization, discipline, and planning of the group. A farmer, he becomes an administrator, chief authority, and court of last resort.

As a Nazi observes, not without admiration, the Bielskis set up a self-sustaining village in the wilderness. Their situation is more precarious because they are surrounded by anti-Semites not only from Germany but also from Russia and Poland. They cooperate with Soviet forces from necessity but cannot delude themselves. Their efforts prevailed, and today there are thousands who would not have been born if they had not succeeded.

Departures ★ ★ ★
PG-13, 130 m., 2009

Masahiro Motoki (Daigo Kobayashi), Ryoko Hirosue (Mika, his wife), Tsutomu Yamazaki (Ikuei Sasaki), Kazuko Yoshiyuki (Tsuyako Yamashita), Takashi Sasano (Shokichi Hirata), Kimiko Yo (Yuriko Kamimura). Directed by Yojiro Takita and produced by Yasuhiro Mase, Toshiaki Nakasawa, and Toshihisa Watai. Screenplay by Kundo Koyama, based on the novel *Coffinman* by Shinmon Aoki.

"Death is for the living and not for the dead so much." This observation from the mourner of a dead dog in Errol Morris's *Gates of Heaven* strikes me as simple but profound. It is the insight inspiring *Departures*, the lovely Japanese movie that won this year's Oscar for best foreign film.

The story involves a young man who apprentices to the trade of "encoffinment," the preparation of corpses before their cremation. As nearly as I can recall, there is no discussion of an afterlife. It is all about the living. There is an elaborate, tender ceremony carried out before the family and friends of the deceased, with an elegance and care that is rather fascinating.

The hero is a man who feels he is owed a death. The father of Daigo (Masahiro Motoki) walked out on his mother when the boy was six, and ever since Daigo has hated him for that abandonment. Now about thirty, Daigo is a cellist in a small classical orchestra that goes broke. He and his wife, Mika (Ryoko Hirosue), decide to move back to a small town in the north of Japan and live in his childhood home, willed to him by his recently departed mother. He finds no work. He answers a want ad for "departures," which he thinks perhaps is from a travel agency.

The company serves clients making their final trip. Daigo is shocked to discover what the owner (Tsutomu Yamazaki) does; he cleans and prepares bodies, and painstakingly makes them up to look their best. The ritual involves undressing them behind artfully manipulated shrouds in front of the witnesses. The boss is a quiet, kind man, who talks little but exudes genuine respect for the dead.

Daigo doesn't tell his wife what he does. They need the money. His job is so low-caste that an old friend learns of it and snubs him. The clients are generally grateful; one father confesses cheerfully that the process freed him to accept the true nature of his child.

A lot is said about the casting process for a movie. Director Yojiro Takita and his casting director, Takefumi Yoshikawa, have surpassed themselves. In a film with four principal roles, they've found actors whose faces, so very human, embody what *Departures* wants to say about them. The earnest, insecure young man. The wife who loves him but is repulsed by the notion of him working with the dead. The boss, oracular, wise, kind. The office manager, inspirational but with an inner sadness. All of these faces are beautiful in a realistic, human way.

The enterprise of undertaking is deadly serious but has always inspired a certain humor, perhaps to mark our fears. The film is sometimes humorous, but not in a way to break the mood. The plot involves some developments we can see coming, but they seem natural, inevitable. The music is lush and sentimental in a subdued way, the cinematography is perfectly framed and evocative, and the movie is uncommonly absorbing. There is a scene of discovery toward the end with tremendous emotional impact. You can't say it wasn't prepared for, but it comes as a devastating surprise, a poetic resolution.

Some of the visual choices are striking. Observe the way Takita handles it when the couple are given an octopus for their dinner and are surprised to find it still alive. See how vividly Daigo recalls a time on the beach with his dad when he was five or six, but how in his memory his father's face is a blur. And how certain compositions suggest that we are all in waiting to be encoffined.

In this film, Kore-Eda's *After Life*, and, of course, Kurosawa's great *Ikiru*, the Japanese reveal a deep and unsensational acceptance of death. It is not a time for weeping and the gnashing of teeth. It is an observation that a life has been left for the contemplation of the survivors.

Diary of a Wimpy Kid ★★★ ½
PG, 92 m., 2010

Zachary Gordon (Greg Heffley), Robert Capron (Rowley Jefferson), Rachael Harris (Susan Heffley), Steve Zahn (Frank Heffley), Devon Bostick (Rodrick Heffley), Chloe Moretz (Angie Steadman), Grayson Russell (Fregley). Directed by Thor Freudenthal and produced by Nina Jacobson and Bradford Simpson. Screenplay by Jackie Filgo, Jeff Filgo, Gabe Sachs, and Jeff Judah, based on the books by Jeff Kinney.

It is so hard to do a movie like this well. *Diary of a Wimpy Kid* is a PG-rated comedy about the hero's first year of middle school, and it's nimble, bright, and funny. It doesn't dumb down. It doesn't patronize. It knows something about human nature. It isn't as good as *A Christmas Story*, as few movies are, but it deserves a place in the same sentence. Here is a

family movie you don't need a family to enjoy. You must, however, have been a wimpy kid. Most kids are wimpy in their secret hearts. Those who never were grow up to be cage fighters.

Greg Heffley isn't the shortest student in his class. That would be Chirag Gupta. Greg (Zachary Gordon) is only the second shortest. He's at that crucial age when everybody else has started to grow. There's a funny slide show illustrating how his class looked in sixth grade, and how they look now—some with mustaches. The girls, of course, are taller than the boys.

The onset of adolescence is an awkward age, made marginally easier for Greg because he still hasn't developed an interest in girls. Even his best friend, Rowley (Robert Capron), is flattered to be noticed by a girl, and Rowley is so out of it he thinks that at his age kids still *play*, when, as we all know, they *hang*.

The girl who notices Greg and Rowley is Angie (Chloe Moretz), who seems wise beyond her years. We first see her under the bleachers, reading *Howl* by Allen Ginsberg. Keep your eye on her in high school. She looks way older than her two new friends, but I checked, and Moretz was only twelve when she made the movie.

In middle school we find cliques, cruelty, and bullying. The pack is poised to pounce. *Diary* is especially funny about a slice of Swiss cheese that was dropped on a playground sometime in the distant past, and has grown an alarming coating of mold. Some kid poked it once, and all the other kids avoided him like the plague. He had the dreaded Cheese Touch. He only got rid of it by touching another kid. Then that kid had the Touch, until . . . and so on. The cheese nicely symbolizes the hunger kids have for an excuse, any excuse, to make other kids pariahs. Remember what happened to anyone who wore green on a Thursday?

Where do they find these actors? They come up on TV, I guess. Chloe Moretz has been acting since she was seven. Zachary Gordon has the confidence and timing of an old pro; he plays wimpy as if it's a desirable character trait. Robert Capron, as the pudgy Rowley, pulls off the tricky feat of being an inch or two taller than Greg and yet still childish; wait until you see his Halloween costume. Greg's parents (Rachael Harris and Steve Zahn) aren't major characters because what happens in school consumes all of Greg's psychic energy. His older brother, Rodrick (Devon Bostick), is, of course, a sadistic teaser who makes life miserable. But at that age, so it goes.

The movie is inspired by the books of Jeff Kinney, and the titles reproduce his hand-lettering and drawing style. The movie reproduces his charm. The director, Thor Freudenthal, made *Hotel for Dogs* (2009), received affectionately in some circles, but this time his touch is more sure and his humor more sunny.

Did You Hear
About the Morgans? ★ ½
PG-13, 107 m., 2009

Hugh Grant (Paul Morgan), Sarah Jessica Parker (Meryl Morgan), Sam Elliott (Clay Wheeler), Mary Steenburgen (Emma Wheeler), Elisabeth Moss (Jackie), Michael Kelly (Vincent), Wilford Brimley (Earl Granger). Directed by Marc Lawrence and produced by Liz Glotzer and Martin Shafer.

What possible reason was there for anyone to make *Did You Hear About the Morgans?* Or should I say "remake," because this movie has been made over and over again, and oh, so much better. Feuding couple from Manhattan forced to flee town, find themselves Fish Out of Water in Strange New World, meet Colorful Characters, survive Slapstick Adventures, end up Together at the End. The only part of that formula that still works is The End.

I grant you Hugh Grant and Sarah Jessica Parker evoke charm in the right screenplay. This is the wrong screenplay. I concede that Sam Elliott is always welcome, except in that one eerie role he played without his mustache. I agree Mary Steenburgen is a merry and fetching lass. I realize yet once again the durable validity of Siskel's Question: Is this movie more entertaining than a documentary of the same actors having lunch?

Grant and Parker play Paul and Meryl Morgan, a wealthy Manhattan couple, childless, but they hope to adopt. This virtually guarantees a cute little orphan in the final reel. She is Manhattan's number-one "boutique Realtor."

One night they're going together to show one of her multimillion-dollar properties when they witness her client being pushed from its balcony by a mean-looking villain.

He gets a good look at them. It was an important murder. Of course they must be sealed inside the Witness Protection Program and shipped out west, to where the men are men and the women are happy of it. In this strange new world where the men wear cowboy hats and the women wear cowboy hats and bake, will they find themselves in a rodeo? Let's put it this way: The close-up of a local rodeo poster and the matching shot of Hugh Grant squinting at it virtually guarantee that.

Saints preserve us! Not another one of those movies where Hugh Grant and Sarah Jessica Parker end up as the front and back halves of the rodeo clowns' cow suit! What's that you say? This is the first one where they've been inside the cow? Does it feel that way to you? What's that you say? You bet they'll be chased by a bear? Come on, now: Surely only one of them!

Paul and Meryl (unusual name, that; where did they find it?) end up as the houseguests of Clay and Emma Wheeler (Elliott and Steenburgen), the local sheriff and his deputy. Now that's clever thinking! Where better to hide Protected Witnesses than as the guests of the local law enforcement couple. Of course, Clay and Emma are hard to spot as they patrol on their horses with rifles and cowboy hats and mustaches and whatnot.

Paul and Meryl are dudes without a ranch. The small town embraces them. It's in Wyoming, I think someone said, and of course it has all of Wyoming's friendliness: The locals turn out with open arms, as they always do when two East Coast elites hit town and start asking people in the local cafe to refrain from smoking. Why, look! There, at the next table! It's Wilford Brimley! Smoking! It's not every day one movie offers the two most famous mustaches in Hollywood.

Well, you'll never be able to guess what happens then. And whether the villain turns up. And whether anyone is chased by a bear. And whether Paul and Meryl go to the rodeo. And what kind of an animal they wind up playing the front and back halves of. And whether they adopt a cute little orphan. And whether that mean old Wilford Brimley ends up grudgingly liking them after all. And whether he ever stops smoking. But one thing's for sure. You'll feel like you've already heard about the Morgans.

Diminished Capacity ★ ★
NO MPAA RATING, 89 m., 2008

Matthew Broderick (Cooper), Alan Alda (Uncle Rollie), Virginia Madsen (Charlotte), Louis C.K. (Stan), Jimmy Bennett (Dillon), Dylan Baker (Mad Dog McClure), Bobby Cannavale (Lee Vivyan), Jim True-Frost (Donny Prine), Lois Smith (Belle). Directed by Terry Kinney and produced by Celine Rattray, Galt Niederhoffer, and Daniel Taplin Lundberg. Screenplay by Sherwood Kiraly, based on his novel.

Diminished Capacity is a mild pleasure from one end to the other, but not much more. Maybe that's enough, serving as a reminder that movie comedies can still be about ordinary people and do not necessarily have to feature vulgarity as their centerpiece. Yes, I'm still hurting from the *The Love Guru* nightmare.

Dim Cap, as Uncle Rollie shortens the phrase, is about Cooper, a Chicago political columnist (Matthew Broderick), and his Uncle Rollie (Alan Alda), who are both suffering from memory loss. With Cooper, who was banged against a wall in somebody else's bar fight, the impairment is temporary. With Uncle Rollie, it may be progressing; his sister, Belle (Lois Smith), who is Cooper's mother, asks Cooper to come home and help her talk Rollie into a mental health facility. It's easy for Cooper to get away since he's just been fired from his newspaper job (at the *Tribune*, as you can tell from countless hints, although the paper is mysteriously never mentioned).

Cooper drives to his small hometown to find his mother overseeing Rollie, who has a big new project: He has attached fishing lines to an old-fashioned typewriter, so that every time he gets a bite, a letter gets typed. He searches the resulting manuscripts for actual words and combines them into poetry. Well, if monkeys can do it, why not fish?

The plot deepens. Uncle Rollie treasures a baseball card given him by his grandfather.

The card features Frank Schulte, who played right field for the 1908 Chicago Cubs, and I don't need to tell you what the Cubs did in 1908. It may be the only card of its kind in existence, and Cooper and his mom realize that if Rollie sold it, all of his unpaid bills would be behind him. Meanwhile, Cooper has run into his old girlfriend Charlotte (Virginia Madsen), who has split with her husband; they slowly rekindle their romance. And what with one thing and another Charlotte and her son drive with Cooper and Rollie back to Chicago for a big sports memorabilia convention. They're trailed by the fiendish, rifle-toting hometown drunk Donny Prine (Jim True-Frost), who wants to steal the card.

Matthew Broderick has two light comedies in release this summer; the other is *Finding Amanda*, where he goes to Vegas to try to rescue his niece from a life of sin. In both films he reminded me of his amiability and quietly meticulous comic timing. He and Madsen find the right note for two old lovers who are casually renewing their romance.

The convention provides the movie's big set piece, as our heroes meet a nice baseball card dealer named Mad Dog McClure (Dylan Baker) and a crooked one named Lee Vivyan (Bobby Cannavale). It is Mad Dog who levels Lee with a withering curse: "You're bad for the hobby!" Baker and Cannavale more or less walk away with the scenes at the sports convention.

There is, of course, a duel over the invaluable card, and a fight, and a highly improbable showdown on a catwalk far above the convention arena, and a bit part for Ernie Banks, and a big kiss between Cooper and Charlotte, and it's all very nice, but not a whole lot more. The film is a coproduction of Chicago's Steppenwolf Theater, directed by veteran actor Terry Kinney, and inspired by Sherwood Kiraly's novel. Kinney shows himself a capable director, but isn't the material a little lightweight for Steppenwolf?

Disgrace ★★★★
NO MPAA RATING, 118 m., 2009

John Malkovich (David Lurie), Jessica Haines (Lucy), Eriq Ebouaney (Petrus), Fiona Press (Bev), Antoinette Engel (Melanie). Directed by

Steve Jacobs and produced by Jacobs, Anna-Maria Monticelli, and Emile Sherman. Screenplay by Monticelli, based on the novel by J. M. Coetzee.

I awaited the closing scenes of *Disgrace* with a special urgency because the story had gripped me deeply but left me with no idea how it would end. None—and I really cared. This is such a rare movie. Its characters are uncompromisingly themselves, flawed, stubborn, vulnerable. We feel we know them pretty well, but then they face a situation of such pain and moral ambiguity that they're forced to make impossible decisions. It's easy to ask them to do the right thing. But what is the right thing?

David Lurie (John Malkovich) teaches the Romantic poets at the University of Cape Town. He lingers over Wordsworth's word choices before a classroom of distracted students. One seems to care: Melanie (Antoinette Engel). He offers her a ride home in the rain. She accepts. I spent a year in that university on the slopes of Table Mountain. When someone offers you a ride home in the rain, you accept.

This is South Africa in the years soon after the fall of apartheid. Sexual contact between the races is no longer forbidden by law, and indeed the film opens with a liaison between David and a black prostitute. Melanie is Indian. David is white, at least thirty-five years older, very confident, sardonic, determined. They have sex. We don't see exactly how they get to that point, but it is clear afterward that Melanie is very unhappy. It was probably not literal rape, we're thinking, but it was a psychological assault.

David should be content with his conquest, but he's a cocky and deeply selfish man, and Malkovich, in one of his best performances, shows him acting entirely on his desires. There's a scene where he faces a university disciplinary board; the board obviously hopes to avoid scandal and offers him a graceful exit. He cheekily tells them he is guilty, accepts blame, requests punishment.

Now the divorced David goes to visit his daughter Lucy (Jessica Haines), a lesbian who owns a remote farm and supports herself with a market garden and dog breeding. Her farm manager is an African named Petrus (Eriq Ebouaney, who played the lead in *Lumumba*).

This man is more independent than years in South Africa have led David to expect. He doesn't believe Lucy is safe living on the farm with him.

Now events take place I will not describe, except to say that Lucy is indeed not safe, and that David becomes locked in essentially a territorial dispute with Petrus. This dispute has a background in the old and new South Africas, strong racial feelings, and difficult moral choices. The nature of the personalities of David, Lucy, and Petrus are deeply tested.

The film is based on a novel by Nobel laureate J. M. Coetzee, which won the Booker Prize. I read it in 1999, remembered it well, but not the details of the ending. Now I understand why. It isn't so much about what happens, as about the way things are. The final shot by the director Steve Jacobs is in its own way perfect. There cannot be a resolution, apart from the acceptance of reality.

I imagine those seeing *Disgrace* will find themselves in complex discussions about right and wrong. In any sense, what David did with Melanie was wrong, and what happens later to Lucy is wrong. We agree. But whose response is better? David's or Lucy's? To ask that question is the whole purpose of this story. There are two more questions: What does it mean when David decides to put down a dog he feels affection for, and what has happened within him by the time of the final scene? As the last shot begins, you will be asking yourself. The shot will not make it easy for you. I know what I think, but it isn't a comfortable conclusion.

This is one of the year's best films. Before discussing Malkovich, I want to mention four other performances. Fiona Press as Bev, a warm, comfortable middle-aged woman who runs the animal shelter in town, is a necessary center of comfort and calm. Jessica Haines plays Lucy with unbending, clear-eyed conviction. Eriq Ebouaney has a crucial role and plays it wisely, not signaling what we should think of him but simply playing a man who is sure of his ground. Antoinette Engel has a smaller role, also crucial, with perfect pitch: She, too, doesn't parade her feelings. After the film is over, it may occur to you that Melanie and Lucy have undergone similar experiences.

Then there is Malkovich, an actor who is so particular in the details of voice and action.

After you see *Disgrace,* you may conclude no other actor could possibly have been cast for the role. He begins as a cold, arrogant, angry man, accustomed to buying his way with his money and intelligence. He is also accustomed to being a white man in South Africa. In no sense does David think of himself as a racist, and he probably always voted against apartheid. But at least it was always there for him to vote against. Now he undergoes experiences that introduce him to an emerging new South Africa—and no, I don't mean he undergoes conversion and enlightenment. This isn't a feel-good parable. I simply mean he understands that something fundamental has shifted, and that is the way things are.

District 9 ★★★
R, 111 m., 2009

Sharlto Copley (Wikus van der Merwe), Jason Cope (voice of Christopher Johnson), David James (Koobus Venter), Mandla Gaduka (Fundiswa Mhlanga), William Allen Young (Dirk Michaels), Vanessa Haywood (Tania van der Merwe), Kenneth Nkosi (Thomas). Directed by Neill Blomkamp and produced by Peter Jackson and Carolynne Cunningham. Screenplay by Blomkamp and Terri Tatchell.

I suppose there's no reason the first alien race to reach Earth shouldn't look like what the cat threw up. After all, they love to eat cat food. The alien beings in *District 9*, nicknamed "prawns" because they look like a cross between lobsters and grasshoppers, arrive in a spaceship that hovers over Johannesburg. Found inside, huddled together and starving to death, are the aliens, who benefit from a humanitarian impulse to relocate them to a location on the ground.

Here they become not welcomed but feared, and their camp turns into a prison. Fearing alien attacks, humans demand they be resettled far from town, and a clueless bureaucrat named Wikus van der Merwe (Sharlto Copley) is placed in charge of this task. The creatures are not eager to move. A private security force, headed by van der Merwe, moves in with armored vehicles and flamethrowers to encourage them, and van der Merwe cheerfully destroys houses full of their young.

Who are these aliens? Where did they come from? How did their ship apparently run out of power (except what's necessary to levitate its massive tonnage)? No one asks: They're here, we don't like them, get them out of town. There doesn't seem to be a lot to like. In appearance they're loathsome, in behavior disgusting, and evoke so little sympathy that killing one is like—why, like dropping a seven-foot lobster into boiling water.

This science fiction fable, directed by newcomer Neill Blomkamp and produced by Peter (*The Lord of the Rings*) Jackson, takes the form of a mockumentary about van der Merwe's relocation campaign, his infection by an alien virus, his own refuge in District 9, and his partnership with the only alien who behaves intelligently and reveals, dare we say, human emotions. This alien, named Christopher Johnson—yes, Christopher Johnson— has a secret workspace where he prepares to return to the mother ship and help his people.

Much of the plot involves the obsession of the private security firm in learning the secret of the alien weapons, which humans cannot operate. Curiously, none of these weapons seem superior to those of the humans and aren't used to much effect by the aliens in their own defense. Never mind. After van der Merwe grows a lobster claw in place of a hand, he can operate the weapons, and thus becomes the quarry of both the security company and the Nigerian gangsters who exploit the aliens by selling them cat food. All of this is presented very seriously.

The film's South African setting brings up inescapable parallels with its now-defunct apartheid system of racial segregation. Many of them are obvious, such as the action to move a race out of the city and onto a remote location. Others will be more pointed in South Africa. The title *District 9* evokes Cape Town's historic District 6, where Cape Coloureds owned homes and businesses for many years before being bulldozed out and relocated. The hero's name, van der Merwe, is not only a common name for Afrikaners, the white South Africans of Dutch descent, but also the name of the protagonist of van der Merwe jokes, of which the point is that the hero is stupid. Nor would it escape a South African ear that the alien language incorporates clicking sounds,

137

just as Bantu, the language of a large group of African apartheid targets.

Certainly this van der Merwe isn't the brightest bulb on the tree. Wearing a sweater vest over a short-sleeved shirt, he walks up to alien shanties and asks them to sign a relocation consent form. He has little sense of caution, which is why he finds himself in his eventual predicament. What Neill Blomkamp somehow does is make Christopher Johnson and his son, Little CJ, sympathetic in spite of appearance. This is achieved by giving them, but no other aliens, human body language, and little CJ even gets big wet eyes, like E.T.

District 9 does a lot of things right, including giving us aliens to remind us not everyone who comes in a spaceship need be angelic, octopod, or stainless steel. They are certainly alien, all right. It is also a seamless merger of the mockumentary and special effects (the aliens are CGI). And there's a harsh parable here about the alienation and treatment of refugees.

But the third act is disappointing, involving standard shoot-out action. No attempt is made to resolve the situation, and if that's a happy ending, I've seen happier. Despite its creativity, the movie remains space opera and avoids the higher realms of science fiction.

I'll be interested to see if general audiences go for these aliens. I said they're loathsome and disgusting, and I don't think that's just me. The movie mentions Nigerian prostitutes servicing the aliens, but wisely refrains from entertaining us with this spectacle.

District 13: Ultimatum ★★★
R, 100 m., 2010

Cyril Raffaelli (Damien), David Belle (Leito), Philippe Torreton (President), Daniel Duval (Gassman), MC Jean Gab'1 (Molko), La Fouine (Ali-K), James Deano (Karl). Directed by Patrick Alessandrin and produced by Luc Besson. Screenplay by Besson.

There is a limit to how far down you can jump and land on your feet and not break an ankle. Well, isn't there? I ask because these limits don't seem to apply to the cops who are the heroes of *District 13: Ultimatum*. Nor, incredibly, do they apply to the bad cops who

chase them across the rooftops of Paris while burdened with full SWAT team uniforms, including bulletproof vests. There isn't a single character who lands badly, and limps away.

I know, I know. It's all done with special effects. Yes, but . . . well, see the movie. The height of a jump can be exaggerated by oblique camera angles and lenses. Hong Kong experts use wires and trampolines. Hollywood sidesteps the issue by editing so quickly no physical movement is ever quite entirely seen. Yes. But consider that the costar of *District 13* is a thirty-five-year-old Frenchman named David Belle, famed as the man who named "parkour," which is "the art of flight." This is a hot modern martial art. Not only do the shots look convincing, not only are they held long enough to allow us to see an entire action, but Belle in real life does a version of this stuff.

The stuff is what intrigues me. The screenplay is another of the countless works of Luc Besson, who is the most productive person in modern action movies. It's a sequel to his 2004 film in which a walled-off segment of Paris in 2010 was run by black, white, Asian, and Arab warlords, with a fifth one left over I couldn't categorize. There is a plot within a crooked high-level security agency to destroy the district and rebuild it. This massive work will be accomplished by the corporation that has bribed them, named Harriburton, which does not remind you of anything, of course.

The president of the French republic is not in on the plot. He believes in liberty, equality, fraternity, and the constitution, which would make him unpopular with Harriburton. Anyway, after they luckily see a citizen video showing bad cops murdering good cops and blaming it on gangs in District 13, it's up to Damien (Cyril Raffaelli) and Leito (David Belle) to single-handedly stop the evil scheme.

This they do in many ways, but mostly by running away. Parkour is the "art of flight," you recall. So they grab incriminating tapes and computer drives, the bad cops want to catch them, and this leads to the real point of the movie, which is one chase scene after another. These actors are clearly in superb physical shape. I'm not going to believe they actually do all these stunts, but I believe we clearly see them doing parts of them, which all by themselves would be awesome.

They leap, fall, tumble, twist, climb up and down walls and buildings, swing from wires, slide down wires, and have an alarming eagerness to jump out of buildings without knowing what is below. (Luckily, there are nice comfy landing spots like the roofs of cars.) At one point, after Damien comes home to his girlfriend (Sophie Ducasse), he complains he feels "stiff." Ha. This man needs an intensive care unit. Still, the parkour motto is "*etre et duress*," which means "to be and to endure," or in other words, not to get yourself killed or twist an ankle.

If anyone is going to convince fanboys to attend a movie with French subtitles, that man is Luc Besson. They'll catch on that Besson, working without enormous budgets and A-list stars, knows what he's doing. A movie like *District 13: Ultimatum* may be as preposterous as the lame *From Paris with Love*, but it delivers the goods. You want an action movie where you can see that the actors are really there, and not concealed by editing that looks like someone fed the film through an electric fan? Here's your movie. For that matter, although the characters indeed speak French, they don't talk much, and sometimes the SWAT teams use English they learned from cop movies, like "Go! Go! Go!"

Doubt ★ ★ ★ ★
PG-13, 104 m., 2008

Meryl Streep (Sister Aloysius), Philip Seymour Hoffman (Father Flynn), Amy Adams (Sister James), Viola Davis (Mrs. Miller), Joseph Foster II (Donald Miller), Alice Drummond (Sister Veronica), Audrie Neenan (Sister Raymond). Directed by John Patrick Shanley and produced by Scott Rudin. Screenplay by Shanley, based on his play.

A Catholic grade school could seem like a hermetically sealed world in 1964. That's the case with St. Nicholas in the Bronx, ruled by the pathologically severe principal Sister Aloysius, who keeps the students and nuns under her thumb and is engaged in an undeclared war with the new parish priest. Their issues may seem to center on the reforms of Vatican II, then still under way, with Father Flynn (Philip Seymour Hoffman) as the progressive, but for the nun, I believe it's more of a power struggle. The pope's infallibility seems, in her case, to have descended to the parish level.

Some will say the character of Sister Aloysius, played without a hint of humor by Meryl Streep, is a caricature. In my eight years of Catholic school not a one of the Dominican nuns was anything but kind and dedicated, and I was never touched, except by Sister Ambrosetta's thunking forefinger to the skull in first grade. But I clearly remember being frightened by Sister Gilberta, the principal; being sent to her office in second or third grade could loosen your bowels. She never did anything mean. She just seemed to be able to.

Sister Aloysius of *Doubt* hates all inroads of the modern world, including ballpoint pens. This is accurate. We practiced our penmanship with fountain pens, carefully heading every page *JMJ*—for Jesus, Mary, and Joseph, of course. Under Aloysius's command is the sweet young Sister James (Amy Adams, from *Junebug*), whose experience in the world seems limited to what she sees out the convent window. Gradually during the autumn semester, a situation develops.

There is one African-American student in St. Nicholas, Donald Miller (Joseph Foster II), and Father Flynn encourages him in sports and appoints him as an altar boy. This is all proper. Then Sister James notes that the priest summons the boy to the rectory alone. She decides this is improper behavior and informs Aloysius, whose eyes narrow like a beast of prey. Father Flynn's fate is sealed.

But *Doubt* is not intended as a docudrama about possible sexual abuse. Directed by John Patrick Shanley from his Pulitzer- and Tony-winning play, it is about the title word, *doubt*, in a world of certainty. For Aloysius, Flynn is certainly guilty. That the priest seems innocent, that Sister James comes to believe she was mistaken in her suspicions, means nothing. Flynn knows a breath of scandal would destroy his career. And that is the three-way standoff we watch unfolding with precision and tension.

Something else happens. The real world enters this sealed parochial battlefield. Donald's mother (Viola Davis) fears her son will be expelled from the school. He has been accused of drinking the altar wine. Worse, being given it by Father Flynn. She appeals directly to Sister Aloysius, in a scene as good as any I've seen this year. It lasts about ten minutes, but it is the emotional heart and soul of *Doubt*. Viola Davis goes face-to-face with the preeminent film actress of this generation, and it is a confrontation of two equals that generates terrifying power.

Doubt. It is the subject of the sermon Father Flynn opens the film with. Doubt was coming into the church and America in 1964. Would you still go to hell if you ate meat on Friday? After the assassination of Kennedy and the beginnings of Vietnam, doubt had undermined U.S. certainty in general. What could you be sure of? What were the circumstances? The motives? The conflict between Aloysius and Flynn is the conflict between old and new, between status and change, between infallibility and uncertainty. And Shanley leaves us doubting.

I know people who are absolutely certain what conclusion they should draw from this film. They disagree. *Doubt* has exact and merciless writing, powerful performances, and timeless relevance. It causes us to start thinking with the first shot, and we never stop. Think how rare that is in a film.

The Duchess ★ ★ ★ ½
PG-13, 109 m., 2008

Keira Knightley (Georgiana), Ralph Fiennes (William Cavendish), Charlotte Rampling (Lady Spencer), Dominic Cooper (Charles Grey), Hayley Atwell (Bess Foster), Simon McBurney (Charles Fox), Aidan McArdle (Richard Sheridan). Directed by Saul Dibb and produced by Gabrielle Tana and Michael Kuhn. Screenplay by Dibb, Jeffrey Hatcher, and Anders Thomas Jensen, based on a book by Amanda Foreman.

Much is made in Britain of the fact that Georgiana, the Duchess of Devonshire (1757–1806), was the great-great-great-great-aunt of Diana, Princess of Wales. I wouldn't know where to start in counting my own great-great-great-great-aunts, but the Brits have an obsession with genealogy, and then too both women married men who were fabulously wealthy, had several enormous houses, and kept a mistress, and both women had lovers. The difference is, Georgiana was more interesting.

She was married off by her mother at sixteen to William Cavendish, the fifth Duke of Devonshire, a man who loved his dogs more than her. She was treated like chattel, valued only for her breeding ability, raped by the duke at least once, and became the most famous woman in England, save for Queen Charlotte, whose husband was merely mad. Georgiana was an outspoken liberal, a supporter of the American and French revolutions, a campaigner for one Whig prime minister (Charles Fox) and the lover of another (Charles Grey, whose daughter she bore). She was a feminist who dared to speak publicly on politics, although she accepted that women did not have the vote.

The Duchess is a handsome historical film, impeccably mounted, gowned, wigged, and feathered, where a husband and wife spend hours being dressed in order to appear at dinner to argue about whether the mutton is off. With Keira Knightley playing the duchess and Ralph Fiennes playing her husband, such a conversation is a minefield. The man has no conversation, addresses her primarily to issue instructions, and is obsessed with the production of a male heir, who would have much to inherit, including the grandest private house in London, and Chatsworth, in Derbyshire, the favorite of all British country houses. I have visited Chatsworth, and I was in awe. At today's prices, not even Bill Gates could live like the Devonshires.

For a woman to be duchess of such a private kingdom, to be immersed in politics, to be a beauty, a wit, a fashion leader, and a feisty scrapper with an appetite for better sex than the duke provisioned, Georgiana must have been extraordinary. I am not sure *The Duchess* quite does her justice. Yes, her marital views were flexible. She disliked but tacitly accepted the duke's numerous adulteries. She made only one close female friend, Lady Elizabeth Foster (Hayley Atwell), and the duke rogered her, too. Georgiana was enraged not only because of his infidelity but also for being robbed of her friend. Later they made it up, and she accepted Bess and her three sons into their household, referring to William as "our husband."

There was a reason for Bess's betrayal, and it wasn't lust. Her cruel husband had banned her from ever seeing her sons again, and William was powerful enough to reunite her with them. Later, he is quite prepared to prevent Georgiana from ever seeing their four children. Women had no rights even to their offspring. The Whigs, although behind the curve, were clearly the party of the future; the Tories supported the status quo.

The duke, duchess, and even Lady Elizabeth are capable of behaving according to the rules governing their class in even the most inflammatory situations. They often act as if on stage, and they are. When Lady Spencer (Charlotte Rampling), Georgiana's mother, says her affair with Grey is the talk of London, why should she be surprised? Every conversation in this film takes place in the presence of at least two servants.

I deeply enjoyed the film, but then I am an Anglophile. I imagine the behavior of the characters will seem exceedingly odd to some viewers. Well, it is. William is a right proper bastard without normal feelings—a monster. How do you make love with the fifth Duke of Devonshire? You close your eyes and think of the sixth Duke of Devonshire. Georgiana puts up with more than we can imagine. When we see her tender and playful in the company of Earl Grey, it is a refreshing change. We do not see William and Bess bedding each other, and just as well. We hear them.

This is not one of those delightful movies based on a Jane Austen novel. It is about hard realists, constrained in a stifling system and using whatever weapons they can command. It is rather fascinating on that level, although I would have loved to learn more about what the Whigs at that formal dinner *really* thought about Charles Fox's vision of the rights of man and the abolition of the slave trade.

Note: Yes, the famous tea is named after Earl Grey. It is my second favorite, after Lapsang Souchong, which has an aroma stirring nostalgia for fresh tar in autumn.

The Duchess of Langeais ★ ★ ★ ½
NO MPAA RATING, 138 m., 2008

Jeanne Balibar (Antoinette de Langeais), Guillaume Depardieu (Armand de Montriveau), Bulle Ogier (Princesse de Blamont-Chauvry), Michel Piccoli (Vidame de Pamiers), Barbet Schroeder (Duc de Grandlieu), Anne Cantineau (Clara de Serizy). Directed by Jacques Rivette and produced by Martine Marignac and Maurice Tinchant. Screenplay by Pascal Bonitzer and Christine Laurent, based on the novel by Honore de Balzac.

The lovers in *The Duchess of Langeais* never consummate their love, but it consummates them. The film is about two elegant aristocrats whose stubborn compulsions eat them alive. They're bullheaded to the point of madness. Their story is told with a fair amount of passion, but it's interior passion, bottled up, carrying them to a point far beyond what either one expects or desires.

The director is Jacques Rivette, one of the founders of the French New Wave, here giving himself over to a deliberate style that intensifies the impact of his fairly simple story. He begins in the 1820s with Armand, the marquis of Montriveau (Guillaume Depardieu), a general whose battlefield exploits have made him a national hero. At a ball, Armand sees the celebrated Antoinette, the duchess of Langeais (Jeanne Balibar), and approaches her with unmistakable designs. She agrees to be visited by him. At his own door that evening, he exalts to himself: "The duchess of Langeais is my mistress!" That she is married never really figures in the story; her husband exists only as a throwaway line, and when she eventually locks herself up with a cloistered order of nuns, who knows if he was even consulted? (Now there's a conversation-stopper: Q: "How is your wife, Duke?" A: "Still cloistered with those nuns.")

The relationship between Armand and Antoinette takes place mostly at arm's length, on sofas in her rooms, which follow one after another, leading us more deeply into her chamber of secrets. Through these rooms and others, the characters walk on hardwood floors, their sharp footfalls creating a harsh counterpoint to their words of yearning and rejection. The marquis desires to possess the duchess. Such is only natural for a national hero. She does not intend to be touched, but refuses in such an alluring way that he is left with hope. Their conversations take months, during which the marquis gradually loses his temper, starts shouting at her, and one night even has her abducted and taken to his rooms, where he threatens to brand her with a red-hot iron. If he were a rapist, all would be over, but he is not. What's her game, anyway? She invites him back again and again, makes it clear she will always be home to him after eight, and teases him by demanding more stories about his journey across the burning sands of the desert. After the end of each episode, she rises and goes to attend a ball. We see her at one of these affairs, where she could not be more remote and disdainful of the company if she were an automaton.

The story is eventually one of merciless teasing. The duchess has an aged relative, played by the great Michel Piccoli, who warns her: "Avoid, my dear duchess, getting too coquet with such a man." Armand is an eagle, he says, and will lose patience and snatch her away to his aerie. Still she leads Armand on. He asks to kiss the hem of her garment.

"I think so much of you," she says. "I will give you my hand."

He kisses it through the hem and asks, "Will you always think so much of me?"

"Yes, but we will leave it at that."

Adapted from a novel by Balzac, the movie makes much use of intertitles, one of which reads: "If the previous scene is the civil period of this sentimental war, the following is the religious one." I assume these are Balzac's words. The film opens with religion, as Armand recognizes her singing voice in the invisible choir of the cloistered convent on Majorca. It ends there, too, as one of his comrades unforgettably says (and read no further to avoid inescapable conclusions), "She was a woman. Now she is nothing. Let's tie a ball to each foot and throw her into the sea."

Will you like this film? The everyday moviegoer will find it as impenetrable as its heroine. But if you vibrate to nuances of style, if you enjoy tension gathering strength beneath terrible restraint, if you admire great acting, then you will. You might also notice Rivette's subtle design touches, with furniture, costumes, and candles.

Guillaume Depardieu, son of Gerard, plays the marquis as a tall, physically imposing figure who is gradually made the psychological captive of the duchess. And Jeanne Balibar,

as Antoinette, makes the heroine into a real piece of work. Surely she knows she is driving this man mad and destroying herself. Why does she persist? Because she cannot help herself? Or because, sadistically, she knows that she can?

Duplicity ★ ★ ★
PG-13, 125 m., 2009

Julia Roberts (Claire Stenwick), Clive Owen (Ray Koval), Tom Wilkinson (Howard Tully), Paul Giamatti (Richard Garsik). Directed by Tony Gilroy and produced by Jennifer Fox, Kerry Orent, and Laura Bickford. Screenplay by Gilroy.

Julia Roberts and Clive Owen generate fierce electricity in *Duplicity*, but we (and they) don't know if it's romantic or wicked. They're Claire and Ray, government spies (she CIA, he MI6) who meet on assignment in Dubai; she sleeps with him, then steals his secret documents. They both enter the private sector, working for the counterespionage departments of competing shampoo giants. At stake: the formula for a top-secret product that, when revealed, does indeed seem to be worth the high-tech games being played to steal and protect it.

The movie resembles *Mad* magazine's Spy vs. Spy series, elevated to labyrinthine levels of complexity. Nothing is as it seems or even as it seems to seem; triple-crosses are only the warm-up. What's consistent through all of the intrigues is the (certain) lust and (possible) love between them. The theory is, they'll scheme together to steal the formula, sell it in Switzerland, split millions, and spend the rest of their lives spying on each other under the covers.

They're both such incurable operatives that neither one can trust the other. We're not even sure they trust themselves. They play an emotional cat-and-mouse game, cleverly scripted by director Tony Gilroy (*Michael Clayton*) to reflect classic romcoms; both actors seem to be channeling Cary Grant.

Claire and Ray seem to have hollow hearts. Can they, in their trade, sincerely love anyone? Knowing all the tricks, they know the other one knows them, too. This removes some of the romantic risk from the story, replacing it with a plot so ingenious that at the end we know more or less what happened, but mostly less. That's fun but deprives Roberts of her most winning note, which is lovability.

This isn't a two-hander; Gilroy uses his supporting cast for key roles. Tom Wilkinson and Paul Giamatti play the two enemy soap tycoons, both consumed by desperate intensity. Carrie Preston steals a scene from Roberts with her hilarious role as a company travel agent who may have been seduced by Ray but bubbles over about how glad she is that it happened. Roberts is amusingly inscrutable as she listens.

Duplicity is entertaining, but the complexities of its plot keep it from being really involving: When nothing is as it seems, why care? The fun is in watching Roberts and Owen fencing with dialogue, keeping straight faces, trying to read each other's minds. That, and admiring the awesome technology that goes into corporate espionage. I don't understand why Wall Street executives deserve millions, but I can see why these two might. All the money they hope to steal, added together, wouldn't amount to an annual bonus for one of the bankruptcy masterminds.

E

Eagle Eye ★ ★
PG-13, 118 m., 2008

Shia LaBeouf (Jerry Shaw), Michelle Monaghan (Rachel Holloman), Rosario Dawson (Agent Zoe Perez), Michael Chiklis (Secretary Callister), Anthony Mackie (Major Bowman), Billy Bob Thornton (Agent Thomas Morgan). Directed by D. J. Caruso and produced by Alex Kurtzman, Roberto Orci, Patrick Crowley, and Edward L. McDonnell. Screenplay by John Glenn, Travis Wright, Hillary Seitz, and Dan McDermott.

SPOILER WARNING: The word "preposterous" is too moderate to describe *Eagle Eye*. This film contains not a single plausible moment after the opening sequence, and that's borderline. It's not an assault on intelligence. It's an assault on consciousness. I know, I know. I liked *The Mummy: Tomb of the Dragon Emperor*, but that film intended to be absurd. *Eagle Eye* has real cars and buildings and trains and CNN and stuff, and purports to take place in the real world.

You might like it, actually. Lots of people will. It involves relentless action: chases involving planes, trains, automobiles, buses. Hundreds of dead. Enough crashes to stock a junkyard. Lots of stuff being blowed up real good. Two heroes who lack any experience with violence but somehow manage to stick up an armored car at gunpoint, walk on board an unguarded military transport plane, and penetrate the ultrasecret twenty-ninth-floor basement of the Pentagon.

They are Jerry and Rachel (Shia LaBeouf and Michelle Monaghan). Both are ordinary Chicagoans until they start getting commands from a mysterious female voice on their cell phones. Now try to follow this: Whatever force is behind the voice has control of every cell phone and security camera in the nation. "They" can control every elevated train and every stoplight. Can observe the traffic and give precise driving instructions. Can control the movements of cranes in junkyards, the locations of garbage barges, and arrange for a rendezvous on a dirt road in an Indiana country field. Oh, and when a guy

drives down the road to meet them in a van, They can instruct them to warn the guy that if he walks away he will be killed. If They don't want him dead, then why do They kill him—since the situation clearly reflects Their power?

We haven't even arrived at the Pentagon yet, and already the audience is chuckling at the impossibilities. I won't even get started on the air cargo container, the syringes inside, and the on-time recovery of the heroes after they give themselves shots. Turns out the syringes were in a briefcase that the heroes survived incredible death and destruction to pick up, and it isn't even needed after the plane takes off. I won't give it away, but the only thing They really need is an attribute of Jerry's. So here's an idea that would save billions of dollars and hundreds of lives: Why not get a couple of no-neck guys from the West Side to kidnap Jerry, haul him on board a private jet, and transport him to Them?

OK, OK. Enough with the implausibilities. This whole movie is a feature-length deus ex machina, and if you don't know what that is, look it up, because you're going to need it to discuss *Eagle Eye*. And yet, I think I'll use the tricky star-rating system to give it two stars. Now why would I give it two instead of, oh, say, one star? Both *because* of the elements I've complained about, and *in spite* of the elements I've complained about.

Let me explain. If you're looking for a narrative that makes much sense, *Eagle Eye* lacks one. It's essentially a lot of CGI and stunt work, all stuck together in a row. Shia LaBeouf is a good young actor, but you wouldn't discover that here. I barely had time to observe that he resembles an underweight John Cusack when he was off and running, as Jerry and Rachel became elements in effects scenes. The movie obviously intends to resemble and inspire a video game, and at that it is slick. I look forward to professor David Bordwell's students using their clickers to work out the average shot length. I'm predicting less than three seconds. So to summarize, *Eagle Eye* is great at all the things I object to, and I admit it. But I didn't enjoy it.

144

Earth ★ ★ ★
G, 99 m., 2009

A documentary directed by Alastair Fothergill and Mark Linfield and produced by Sophokles Tasioulis and Alix Tidmarsh. Screenplay by Fothergill, Linfield, and Leslie Megahey.

Made between 1948 and 1960, Walt Disney's *True Life Adventures* won three Oscars for best documentary feature, and several others won in the since-discontinued category of two-reel short features. Now the studio has returned to this admirable tradition with *Earth*. It's a film that younger audiences in particular will enjoy.

To be sure, Disney didn't produce the film. It is a feature-length compilation from the splendid BBC and Discovery channel series *Planet Earth*, utilizing the big screen to make full use of its high-def images. The feature's original narrator, Patrick Stewart, has been replaced by James Earl Jones.

What we see is astonishing. Polar bear cubs tumble their way to the sea. Birds of paradise make displays of ethereal beauty. Storks fly above the Himalayas. Elephants trek exhausted across a bone-dry desert. Humpback whales swim three thousand miles to their summer feeding grounds off Antarctica. A predator cat outruns a springbok. Ducklings leap from their nest to fly and plummet to the ground—a learning experience.

The most poignant sequence in the film shows a polar bear, lost at sea and searching for ice floes in a time of global warming, finally crawling ashore exhausted and starving. Desperate for food, he hopelessly attacks a herd of walruses, fails, and slumps dying to the earth; nearby walruses are indifferent.

In the tradition of such favorites of my childhood as Disney's *The Living Desert* and *The Vanishing Prairie*, the narration provides these animals with identities. It opens with a mother polar bear and two cubs. The desperate polar bear is identified as their father, although I will bet a shiny new dime that the authors of the narration have absolutely no evidence of its paternal history. I'm not complaining; in a film like this, that goes with the territory.

The film is filled with unexpected facts. Did

you know the fir trees beginning at the northern tree line circle the globe with an almost unbroken forest, harbor almost no birds and mammals because they are not edible, and supply more of the planet's oxygen than the rain forests? Or that baby whales have to be taught to breathe?

Earth is beautiful and worthwhile. At its pre-opening press screening, cosponsored by the Lincoln Park Zoo in Chicago, we were supplied not with free popcorn but tiny evergreens to take home and plant.

Easy Virtue ★ ★ ★
PG-13, 96 m., 2009

Jessica Biel (Larita), Colin Firth (Mr. Whittaker), Kristin Scott Thomas (Mrs. Whittaker), Ben Barnes (John), Kris Marshall (Furber), Kimberley Nixon (Hilda), Katharine Parkinson (Marion). Directed by Stephan Elliott and produced by Joseph Abrams, James D. Stern, and Barnaby Thompson. Screenplay by Elliott and Sheridan Jobbins, based on the play by Noel Coward.

Unusually for a play by Noel Coward, love has a struggle conquering all in *Easy Virtue*, a subversive view of British country house society between the wars. That era has been described as the most blessed in modern history (assuming you were upstairs and not down), but not here, where the Whittaker family occupies a moldering pile in the countryside. It is said that nothing in a country house should look new. Nothing in this one looks as if it were ever new.

To his ancestral seat, a fresh young man named John (Ben Barnes) brings his great love, Larita (Jessica Biel), to meet his hostile mother (Kristin Scott Thomas), his shambling father (Colin Firth), and his unfortunate sisters Marion (Katharine Parkinson) and Hilda (Kimberley Nixon), one snobbish, the other fawning. Perhaps the innocent John never realized how toxic his mother and elder sister were until Larita arrived to attract their poison.

Larita is an auto racer, the recent winner of the Monaco Grand Prix. It's worth remembering that in the 1920s racing drivers and pilots were admired almost like astronauts (see Shaw's *Man and Superman*), and females were goddesses. Yet Larita, an American un-schooled in the labyrinth of the British upper crust, earnestly hopes to make her alliance with John a success. She does everything an American girl is taught to do, even supervis-ing the preparation of what may be the first edible meal ever served in the stately home (all-purpose 1920s Brit recipe: "Cook until dead").

Scott Thomas and Firth are old hands at their characters, the one brittle and unpleas-ant, the other depressed, disillusioned, and unhappily wed. Ben Barnes is your prototypi-cal fresh young man. Jessica Biel will surprise some with her skill; she takes to Coward as if to the manner (if not manor) born. She has certainly left her work in *The Texas Chainsaw Massacre* (2003) far behind. She makes Larita independent and able, yet capable of a love more sincere than the feckless John can comprehend. She would be the best thing that ever happened to him, and the story is essen-tially about whether he can get that through his head.

Mr. and Mrs. Whittaker are both more nu-anced than the clichés they first seem. She has her urgent reasons for wishing her son to marry elsewhere. He is a member of that gen-eration where most of the best and brightest died in the trenches of France—including, we learn, all of the men under his command. The matriarch clings desperately to the shreds of her fading family. Her husband retreats into dotty distraction and a studied casual evasive-ness that masks despair.

Easy Virtue is being presented, and was no doubt intended by Coward, as a comedy. As we'd expect, the dialogue has an edgy wit, al-though it has no ambitions to be falling-down funny. Here is the *Odd Couple* formula ap-plied in a specific time and place that make them feel very odd indeed.

The Eclipse ★★★
R, 88 m., 2010

Ciaran Hinds (Michael Farr), Aidan Quinn (Nicholas Holden), Iben Hjejle (Lena Morelle), Jim Norton (Malachy McNeill), Eanna Hardwicke (Thomas), Hannah Lynch (Sarah). Directed by Conor McPherson and produced by Robert Walpole. Screenplay by McPherson and Billy Roche, based on Roche's *Tales from Rainwater Pond*.

The supernatural never seems far out of sight in Ireland, and it creeps in here and there dur-ing *The Eclipse*, a dark romance set at a liter-ary festival in the County Cork cathedral town of Cobh. I'm not sure it's required, but it does little harm. The story centers on a quiet, enduring man named Michael Farr (Ciaran Hinds), who has lost his wife to cancer and is raising their two children. He volunteers to drive two visiting authors around town.

The authors have a history that is fondly re-called by only one of them. Nicholas Holden (Aidan Quinn) is a best-selling American nov-elist not a million miles removed from Nicholas Sparks. Lena Morelle (Iben Hjejle) is a British writer of upscale ghost stories. Once, at another festival, they had a brief fling, which only Nicholas thinks was a wise idea. Lena is warm and curious, a good person, and Nicholas, who after all is married, considers himself entitled to her comforts on the basis of her earlier mistake. Nicholas, when he drinks, can become quite unpleasant.

Of the other two key characters, one is dead and the other nearly so. Michael's late wife, Sarah (Hannah Lynch), is alive in his memory, and also occasionally turns up to offer advice or share his problems. She's simply there, seemingly in the flesh. Her father, Thomas (Eanna Hardwicke), his father-in-law, is still alive, but begins manifesting to Michael as a ghostly figure in the still of the night. Michael doesn't deserve this. His steadfast quality throughout the movie is goodness. Is he see-ing a ghost, or is the old man prowling around?

Daytimes, Michael dutifully ferries Nicholas or Lena to their festival events, and shows them something of the town and its idyllic set-ting. He quickly picks up on the tension be-tween them. If he were not so recently widowed, he might warm to Lena himself, but he isn't operating on that frequency. They slowly begin to bond in mutual sympathy.

Nicholas is a bit of an ass. Full of himself, fond of attention, lacking in insight, imperi-ous. Michael, on the other hand, is almost too humble. He sees himself as an attendant, not a celebrant. And Lena? Smart, nice, increasingly worried about Nicholas's urgency, grateful for Michael as a port in the storm. All of this arrives at what I suppose is an inevitable crescendo involving lust, drinking, threats, and confusion, complicated by the increasingly dire supernatural manifestations Michael has experienced.

The Eclipse is needlessly confusing. Is it a ghost story or not? Perhaps this is my problem. Perhaps people who think they perceive the supernatural must simply incorporate that into their ordinary lives. Michael is a steady soul, and essentially does that. On another level, Aidan Quinn is superb at creating a man with the potential to behave as a monster, but with a certain buried decency. What of Lena and Michael? They deserve each other and will probably someday work that out.

Edge of Darkness ★★ ½
R, 117 m., 2010

Mel Gibson (Thomas Craven), Ray Winstone (Darius Jedburgh), Danny Huston (Jack Bennett), Bojana Novakovic (Emma Craven), Shawn Roberts (Burnham). Directed by Martin Campbell and produced by Tim Headington, Graham King, and Michael Wearing. Screenplay by William Monahan and Andrew Bovell.

Can we think of Mel Gibson simply as an action hero? A star whose personal baggage doesn't upstage his performances? I find that I can. He has made deplorable statements in recent years, which may be attributed to a kind of fanatic lunacy that can perhaps be diagnosed as a disease. The fact remains that in *Edge of Darkness* he remains a likable man with a natural screen presence.

Here he plays a Boston cop named Craven (always a dependable movie name). The great love of his life is his daughter, Emma (Bojana Novakovic). She works for a giant secretive corporation named Northmoor. Few corporations with *moor* in their titles are wholly trustworthy; we think too much about bodies being buried there.

Emma comes home for a visit rather unexpectedly. She is having nosebleeds. A bleeding nose can be a symptom of numerous disorders, but in a thriller, as we all know, there's

only one possible diagnosis. Emma has hardly arrived when there's a knock on the door, they answer it together, and a man in a hood screams "Craven!" and shoots her dead.

It is assumed that the detective Thomas Craven was the intended target. Craven's not so sure. His investigation leads him to Northmoor and its silky, sinister chairman, Jack Bennett (Danny Huston, ominously courteous just as his father was in *Chinatown*). Bennett tears himself away from planning Northmoor's campaign contributions long enough to greet Craven in his office, atop a towering aerie overlooking his feudal lands.

Because much of the movie is a cranked-up thriller with chases, fights, conspiracies, and all that stuff, permit me a digression on secretive, shadowy corporations. What kinds of headquarters buildings do they inhabit? I Googled. Blackwater, which supplies our mercenaries in Iraq, has a drab two-story building outside Cleveland with eight cars parked out in front. Halliburton, Dick Cheney's old company, recently moved from Houston to an anonymous skyscraper in Dubai, closer to its place of business.

I mention this because Northmoor, which you will not be surprised to learn traffics in illegal, traitorous, and dangerous activities, occupies a spectacular structure atop a tall riverside hill, visible from miles around: its tower, its modernistic design, and its curious enormous gleaming globe suggesting a planetarium. It is a building worthy of magazine covers, not least *Architectural Digest*.

One purpose of corporate architecture is to impress. Northmoor's desire is to impress us, the moviegoer. Its structure looks left over from a James Bond movie, and indeed, the *Edge of Darkness* director, Martin Campbell, made *Casino Royale* (2006). It's the kind of edifice that inspires such questions as, "What do they *do* in there?" Much of what they do takes place in enormous buried spaces within the hill. This low-profile corporation undertook a construction project on a par with a subway line.

I explain this not merely to avoid discussing the off-the-shelf thriller plot, but to illustrate that *Edge of Darkness*, like so many recent thrillers, has no ambition to be taken seriously. If the corporation were more realistic, the movie would be, too. And then the fate of the world wouldn't depend yet once again on One Cop . . . With Nothing to Lose . . . On a Personal Mission.

Gibson inhabits this gazebo with as much conviction as is probably possible. He's joined in this by the superb British actor Ray Winstone, as an intriguing free agent who turns up in Craven's garden one night with a cigar and an enigmatic line of patter. Whom does he work for? Why does he know so much? Why does he work alone? He reminds me of a man I know, Jean-Jacques de Mesterton, who told me: "If you have a problem, you go to the cops. If they can't help you, you go to the FBI. If they can't help you, you go to the CIA. If they can't help you, you come to me."

Winstone's interaction with Gibson provides the movie with much of its interest. For the rest, it's a skillful exercise in CGI and standard-order thriller supplies. Gibson is a credible, attractive hero, as he has always been, so if you want fast-food action, here's your movie.

It does have a useful subtext. It serves as a reminder that the purpose of a corporation is not to be patriotic, but to maximize profits for its officers and shareholders. This is required by its bylaws. I suppose if we, as shareholders, don't agree with its profit-making strategies, we can always sell our stock, assuming we can find out what those strategies are.

The Edge of Heaven ★ ★ ★ ★
NO MPAA RATING, 122 m., 2008

Baki Davrak (Nejat Aksu), Nursel Kose (Yeter Ozturk), Nurgul Yesilcay (Ayten Ozturk), Patrycia Ziolkowska (Lotte Staub), Hanna Schygulla (Susanne Staub), Tuncel Kurtiz (Ali Aksu). Directed by Fatih Akin and produced by Andreas Thiel, Klaus Maeck, and Akin. Screenplay by Akin.

The best approach is to begin with the characters, because the wonderful, sad, touching movie *The Edge of Heaven* is more about its characters than about its story. There is a reason for that: This is one of those films of interlocking narrative strands, called a hyperlink movie, but the strands never link. True, they link for us because we possess crucial

information about the characters—but they never link for the characters because they lack that information. I liked it that way.

There is an old man named Ali (Tuncel Kurtiz) in Bremen, Germany. He is from Turkey. He has a smile that makes you like him. Think of Walter Matthau. One day (as is his habit, I suspect), he goes to visit a prostitute. This is a middle-aged Turkish woman named Yeter (Nursel Kose), who works from the doorway of a brothel. Yeter is heard speaking by a group of Turkish men, who assume she is Muslim and tell her they will kill her unless she quits the business. Ali makes her an offer: He will pay her to move in with him on a permanent basis. She accepts.

Spoiler warning, I suppose, although this segment of the film is titled "Yeter's Death." Ali gets drunk, he hits her, she falls, she's dead, he's in prison. She was heartbroken in life because her daughter, Ayten (Nurgul Yesilcay), had been long out of touch with her. Yeter's body is shipped back to Istanbul, where we meet Ali's son, Nejat (Baki Davrak). Nejat is a professor at a German university but makes it his business to track down Yeter's daughter and somehow make reparation. In this process he moves back to Istanbul and buys a German-language bookstore from a man who is homesick for Germany.

Back and forth, between Turkey and Germany, the strands tangle. We meet Yeter's daughter, who is a member of a militant group. Deeply in trouble with the authorities, she flees to Germany, where she is befriended and taken home by a young woman named Lotte (Patrycia Ziolkowska). The two fall quickly and passionately in love. For reasons we will leave to them, Ayten ends up in a Turkish prison, Lotte goes to Istanbul to try to help her, and . . . well, nevermind.

You must also meet Lotte's mother, Susanne, who is played by the magnificent Hanna Schygulla, the legendary German actress, best known for her Fassbinder films. She is not pleased with her daughter's romance but in the end goes to Istanbul so that she, too, can try to help Ayten. In Turkey she meets Nejat and ends up living in the same room that her daughter had rented from him.

One of the deepest pleasures of going to the movies for many years is that we can watch actors age and ripen and understand what is happening to ourselves. Hanna Schygulla was once a sexpot in Fassbinder's *The Bitter Tears of Petra von Kant* (1972), and was a commanding star in his great film *The Marriage of Maria Braun* (1979). She was Fassbinder's most important acting talent and his muse, and has appeared in eighty-two films or TV projects. She was a young vixen once, then a sultry romantic lead, and now she is a plumpish woman of sixty-five. My own age, it occurs to me. But *what* a woman of sixty-five! Not a second of plastic surgery. She wears every year as a badge of honor. And here she is so tactful, so warm, so quietly spoken, so glowing, that she all but possesses the film, and we love her for her years and her art.

All this time, while perhaps thinking such thoughts, we are waiting for the penny to drop. Surely some combination of these people will discover how they are connected? But they never do. Maybe that requires a spoiler warning, too, because we are so accustomed to all the stories converging at the end of a hyperlink film. Not this time. The characters are related in theme, but not in plot.

Fatih Akin, who wrote and directed, made the powerful *Head-On* (2004), which in a very different way was about being Turkish and feeling dispossessed or threatened. Here he gives us three parents, a son, and two daughters, all of whose lives are affected, even governed, by the fact that some are Turks, some German. Religion doesn't really enter into it so much, except in inspiring Yeter's retirement. Akin's purpose, I think, is a simple one: He wants us to meet these people, know them, sympathize with them. Even old Ali is not so very evil; he had no intention to murder Yeter, and who among us, drunk or sober, has never unwisely done shameful things? My hand is not raised.

What happened to me during *The Edge of Heaven* was that I did care about the characters. I found them fascinating. They were not overwritten and didn't spend too much time explaining or justifying themselves. They just got on with their lives, and their lives got on with them, all the time swimming in the seas of two different cultures, two different sets of possibilities. Even the authorities are not the villains in the film.

Now if five, or four, of the characters found out how they were connected, what difference would that make? We are all connected, if only we could stand tall enough, see widely enough, and understand adequately. Mere plot points are meaningless. Fatih Akin wants us to realize that, I believe, and he also wants us to understand his creatures, who are for the most part good people, have good intentions, make mistakes, suffer for their errors, and try to soldier on, as do we all.

An Education ★★★★
PG-13, 100 m., 2009

Carey Mulligan (Jenny), Peter Sarsgaard (David), Dominic Cooper (Danny), Rosamund Pike (Helen), Alfred Molina (Jack), Cara Seymour (Marjorie). Directed by Lone Scherfig and produced by Finola Dwyer and Amanda Posey. Screenplay by Nick Hornby, based on a memoir by Lynn Barber.

An Education tells the story of a sixteen-year-old girl who is the target of a sophisticated seduction by a thirty-five-year-old man. This happens in 1961, when sixteen-year-old girls were a great deal less knowing than they are now. Yet the movie isn't shabby or painful, but romantic and wonderfully entertaining.

It depends on a British actress named Carey Mulligan, who in her first major feature role is being compared by everyone with Audrey Hepburn. When you see her you can't think of anyone else to compare her with. She makes the role luminous when it could have been sad or awkward. She has such lightness and grace you're pretty sure this is the birth of a star.

All very well and good, you're thinking, but how is this a romance? Oh, it's not so much a romance between the teenager and the middle-aged man. That only advances to the level of an infatuation. It's a romance between the girl, named Jenny, and the possibilities within her, the future before her, and the joy of being alive. Yes, she sheds a few tears. But she gets better than she gives, and in hindsight this has been a valuable experience for her.

But wait. Doesn't this girl have parents? She certainly does. Jack and Marjorie (Alfred Molina and Cara Seymour) are proper, traditional middle-class parents in the London suburb of Twickenham, and there's nothing but love in the home. They aren't wealthy or worldly, but they wish the best for their girl and are bursting with pride that she's won a scholarship to Oxford. Then she springs David (Peter Sarsgaard) on them.

This is a smooth operator. He sees her standing at a bus stop in the rain holding her cello case. He offers her a lift in his sports car. He engages her in conversation about classical music. He "happens" to run into her again, and they have a nice chat. He wonders if she might enjoy . . .

You see how it goes. He opens a door she eagerly wants to enter, to concerts, plays, restaurants, double dates with his fascinating friends, talk about the great world when the boys at school have nothing to say. At some point it must become clear to her that he intends to sleep with her if he can, but by now she's thinking that he very possibly can.

I forgot to tell you about her parents. They dote and protect, but are very naive. David is good-looking, well dressed, well spoken, and very, very polite. He has *taken an interest* in Jenny because, why? He is impressed by this young woman's mind and enjoys sharing his advantages. He offers implicit guarantees of her safety, and they're so proud of her they believe a wealthy older man would be interested for purely platonic motives. They're innocents. Jenny will be safe with him for a weekend in Paris—because he has an aunt who lives there and will be her chaperone.

Paris! The city embodies Jenny's wildest dreams! And to see it with a worldly dreamboat like David, instead of going there on the boat-train with a grotty, pimply seventeen-year-old! Is she cynically taking advantage of David for her own motives? Well, yes. Now close your eyes and remember your teens, and tell me you don't forgive her at least a little.

Part of the genius of *An Education* is it unfolds this relationship at a deliberate pace. Sarsgaard plays an attractive, intelligent companion. He is careful to keep a distance. Must be a good trout fisherman. To some degree he's truthful: He enormously enjoys this smart, pretty girl. He loves walking along the Seine with her. He knows things about the world that she eagerly welcomes.

Yes, he's also a rotter, a bounder, a cad, a dirty rotten scoundrel. But you can't get far in any of those trades if you're not also a charmer. To some degree, Jenny welcomes being deceived. The screenplay by Nick Hornby (*About a Boy, High Fidelity*) is based on a memoir by a real person, the British journalist Lynn Barber. It became well-known in the United Kingdom that when she was sixteen, she had a two-year affair with a man named Simon in his late thirties.

There are many scene-by-scene parallels between book and movie, and much closely adapted dialogue. We know that Lynn Barber is smart and that she was pretty when she was sixteen. But her affair wasn't such a great experience, at least not in its second year. What transforms it in *An Education* is Carey Mulligan, who has that rare gift of enlisting us on her side and making us like her. She's so lovable that whatever happens must be somehow for Jenny's benefit. She glows.

So, young women, let this movie offer useful advice. When a man seems too good to be true, he probably isn't—good or true. We all make mistakes when we're growing up. Sometimes we learn from them. If we're lucky, we can even learn during them. And you must certainly see Paris. Do *not* count on meeting the aunt.

Lynn Barber writes: "What did I get from Simon? An education—the thing my parents always wanted me to have. . . . I learned about expensive restaurants and luxury hotels and foreign travel. I learned about antiques and Bergman films and classical music. But actually there was a much bigger bonus than that. My experience with Simon entirely cured my craving for sophistication. By the time I got to Oxford, I wanted nothing more than to meet kind, decent, straightforward boys my own age, no matter if they were gauche or virgins. I would marry one eventually and stay married all my life and for that, I suppose, I have Simon to thank."

Note: Lynn Barber's full account: www. guardian.co.uk/culture/2009/jun/07/lynn-barber-virginity-relationships. 🖙

Eight Miles High ★ ★ ½
NO MPAA RATING, 114 m., 2008

Natalia Avelon (Uschi Obermaier), Matthias Schweighofer (Rainer Langhans), David Scheller

(Dieter Bockhorn), Alexander Scheer (Keith Richards), Victor Noren (Mick Jagger). Directed by Achim Bornhak and produced by Eberhard Junkersdorf and Dietmar Guntsche. Screenplay by Bornhak and Olaf Kraemer.

She was Germany's uber-groupie, a small-town Bavarian girl who lucked her way onto a magazine cover, became a famous model, slept with Jimi Hendrix and Mick Jagger, and had something a little more than that with Keith Richards. Along the way she was also involved with a radical commune, was on the cover of *Playboy*, traveled the world with a wealthy playboy in the bus he constructed for her, and gave a face to the word "Eurotrash." Whew.

Uschi Obermaier was a real woman. She slept her way to what looked like the top to her, but she was fiercely independent, rejected all offers of marriage, walked out on contracts to indulge her free spirit, and lived the life all groupies dream about (I guess). Then she told all in her autobiography, *High Times*. The distance "eight miles" has been added to the movie title no doubt in reference to the Byrds' song.

Critics have pretty much hated this film, although some have been kind ("deliciously dumb, reasonably well-made"—Andrew O'Hehir, Salon). It has much to be kind about. Natalia Avelon plays Uschi with a disdain for bras and blouses, her radical boyfriend has more hair than Angela Davis, her playboy boyfriend leaps about with the frenzied excitement of a forty-something hippie, and the impersonators of Jagger and Richards sometimes look a little like the real thing, in the right shadows, at certain angles. Jimi Hendrix is only cited.

The movie presents the surfaces of Obermaier's life, but never really lets us understand who she was. Avelon has a face for the role that is maddeningly unrevealing; sometimes she pouts, sometimes she's happy, sometimes she's pensive, sometimes she's out to lunch. As Rainer Langhans, the real-life leader of a Berlin commune, Matthias Schweighofer reflects a quality I noticed in a few real-life 1960s leftist radicals I knew: He's like a strict, scolding mother, lecturing those in his charge to correct their flawed ideas. That he and Uschi are "in love" is, I think, an ideological

decision for both. He's not comfortable with her celebrity, and she's not happy to be lectured. Although her modeling is accepted by the commune as a source of funds, they don't think she's really sincere in her worship of the cause, nor is she.

David Scheller is more interesting as the real-life Dieter Bockhorn, who ran a nightclub in Hamburg, which he often closed to throw wild parties for his friends. Uschi has seen photos of him cavorting with African dancers, responds to his invitation to see the world, travels by bus with him for, I dunno, several years, it seems like. In those carefree years lots of hippies were drawn to India, and so are they, using a newspaper headline to convince a maharaja they are a prince and princess. She offers to throw them a wedding, and does, with a brass band, horses, elephants, costumed dancers, and all you can eat. Uschi, opposed to marriage, is told by Dieter that the ceremony "isn't really real," and going along with it is like a favor. Later, she pouts, "But I think it was real for him."

Now, what can I say about this biopic? Well, it's deliciously dumb and reasonably well-made, for starters. It has few human insights, and those of the most obvious kind. But it is not boring. That goes for something. If Uschi Obermaier comes across as shallow and heedless, well, maybe she was. This is not a role for an actress who radiates intelligence, like Tilda Swinton. The story of Uschi's life would not easily support depth and thoughtfulness, especially not with the amount of weed around.

There are some nice moments. She breaks up with Keith Richards, but later meets him by accident on a Mexican beach, and they find they're still in love. But he is getting married, and observes, "Seems like we're always meeting at the wrong end of the stick." Nice line. It seems doubtful that Jagger would come sniffing around Berlin without a bodyguard, but if you see Uschi in this movie, you may sympathize. The real Uschi, I learn from Wiki, was thin and slender. Not Avelon. She possesses a matched set of expensive breasts.

By the way, do not confuse this Uschi with my old pal Uschi Digard, the Russ Meyer supervixen from the late 1960s and early 1970s, although like Obermaier she became a diamond merchant and jewelry designer. She was from Sweden, was as famous a model as Obermaier, although not in French *Vogue*, and was all real. "Silicone," Russ believed, "spoils the fun," although he was later forced to relax his vigilance. It's an evocative name, Uschi. Makes me think of mashing ice cream.

El Camino ★ ★ ★
NO MPAA RATING, 87 m., 2009

Leo Fitzpatrick (Elliot), Christopher Denham (Gray), Elisabeth Moss (Lily), Wes Studi (Dave), Richard Gallagher (Matthew), Amy Hargreaves (Sissy). Directed by Erik S. Weigel and produced by Fran Giblin and Jason Noto. Screenplay by Weigel and Salvatore Interlandi.

El Camino is a pure American road movie, freed of the requirements of plot, requiring only a purpose and a destination. It is so pure that it involves two men and a woman, all in their twenties, all in the same station wagon, and there is *not* a romantic triangle. All three have different needs in life, and have joined only for this journey.

They meet for the first time when their friend Matthew (Richard Gallagher) dies. Elliot (Leo Fitzpatrick) and Matthew were in foster care together. Lily (Elisabeth Moss) was his former girlfriend. Gray (Christopher Denham) met him and felt an immediate bond. After the funeral, Gray and Lily decide to steal Matthew's ashes and scatter them in Mexico. Elliot insists on going along, and he will pay. That's the deal maker.

What did Matthew really mean to them? The movie lacks the usual heart-spilling confessions. All three are reticent, revealing themselves in elliptical asides. Nor do they spill the beans about their own lives. They pound on, mile after mile, North Carolina to Mexico, one cheap motel after another, lots of cigarettes, desultory talk, honky-tonk bars, a fight, unhappy telephone calls.

Road movies require colorful people along the way. This one has a couple. Wes Studi plays a self-employed man who repairs their car, invites them to dinner, has strong political opinions (not the ones you might expect), and contempt for Gray's cynicism. Amy Hargreaves plays an older woman in a bar who smiles at Gray and ends up listening to his

introspections. And no, she's not a hooker; she's lonely and nice.

Mystery surrounds Elliot. Flashbacks suggest a confused childhood. We have no idea where he lives now, what he does, where he gets his money. I first saw the gawky Leo Fitzpatrick in the breakthrough movie *Kids* (1995), which also introduced Rosario Dawson, Chloe Sevigny, Justin Pierce, and Jon Abrahams. Fitzpatrick is gawky no more. He only gradually sheds his funeral suit and tie, tends to lean forward thoughtfully, gives the impression of not saying a lot of things that he could.

We begin to wonder what ashes will be scattered: only Matthew's, or perhaps the ashes of the false starts and undirected lives of the living? There are moments of self-discovery along the way, but not underlined with fraught dialogue or painfully intense acting. All three characters seem to be focusing mostly on themselves. In the way this confounds our road movie expectations, it becomes quietly absorbing.

The film is elegantly shot by Till Neumann in rarely seen 2.35:1 widescreen, good for the big boat they're driving in and for the landscape they're driving through. This is the opposite of queasy-cam, and it makes sense that one of those thanked by the filmmakers is the contemplative Terrence Malick (another is Gus Van Sant, himself a master of uncertain journeys). At the end, one of the characters has a next destination in mind. The other two seem prepared to simply move away from, not toward, their lives until now—and that, too, is in keeping with the tone. At a time of life when everything is still tentative, there's insight in a film that doesn't force them into corners.

Elegy ★ ★ ★
R, 108 m., 2008

Penelope Cruz (Consuela), Ben Kingsley (David Kepesh), Dennis Hopper (George O'Hearn), Patricia Clarkson (Carolyn), Peter Sarsgaard (Kenneth Kepesh), Deborah Harry (Amy O'Hearn). Directed by Isabel Coixet and produced by Tom Rosenberg, Gary Lucchesi, and Andre Lamal. Screenplay by Nicholas Meyer, based on a novel by Philip Roth.

Ben Kingsley, who can play just about any role, seems to be especially effective playing slimy intellectuals. *Elegy* is a film that could have been made for him, although by the time it's over, Penelope Cruz has slipped away with it and transformed Kingsley's character in the process. It's nicely done.

Kingsley plays David Kepesh, a professor of literature whose classroom manner seems designed to seduce the young student of his choice from each new class. He narrates the film and is not shy about describing his methods. To stay out of trouble, he waits until the semester is over and the grades have been given, and then throws a party at his book- and art-filled apartment, where he singles out his prey and dazzles her with flattering insights, intellectual bravado, and an invitation to meet sometime—just for coffee or a drink and conversation, you know.

His target this semester is the lithesome Consuela, played by Penelope Cruz as a Cuban-American who is old enough to know better but discerning enough to see that there may really be something to old Kepesh after all. The professor appoints himself her tutor to all the mysteries of life, art, New York, music, and sex. And for a while they mesh and enjoy each other.

But David grows obsessed with jealousy, convinced Consuela is seeing someone else—younger, of course, and more handsome and virile. He even accidentally drops in at a dance he knows she's attending to check up on her. His distrust spoils everything because she cannot abide not being trusted.

And then—the movie takes a dramatic turn, which I will not reveal, even though it contains all the deepest emotions and real feelings of the story. And in these scenes, Cruz is quietly powerful and very true. You understand why the Spanish director, Isabel Coixet, chose Cruz instead of, say, a nineteen-year-old. An actress needs depth and the experience of life to play these scenes, and Cruz has them.

The film is based on a novel by Philip Roth, who has just about exhausted my desire to read his stories about young babes falling for older, wiser intellectuals like, say, Philip Roth. I was reading his Library of America volume about Zuckerman recently and finally just put it down and said to the book: Sorry, Phil, but I cannot read one more speech founded on the f-word. I don't object to the f-word itself, but sorry, I've simply been overserved.

That *Elegy* is not simply a fantasy about the horny old rascal and the comely maid is to its credit. That it sees Manhattan clearly as a setting is also an advantage, since it is a place where we believe things like this are likely to happen. And then there is a wealth of supporting characters, notably Carolyn (Patricia Clarkson), no spring chicken, who has been David's mistress for years. She can't believe there's another woman in his life and launches a barrage of f-words, but she makes the character real and poignant. I also liked Dennis Hopper as George, the old pal he has coffee with, who attempts to bring sanity into David's behavior, but despairs. And Peter Sarsgaard, as David's son, with problems of his own and a father who has become not only an embarrassment but, worse, an irrelevancy.

The movie is not great. I'm not sure why. Maybe the payoff plays too much like a payoff. Consuela asks David to do something I think we might be better off hearing about, instead of seeing. I'm not sure. The movie is obviously going for a big emotional charge at the end and might have been more effective with a quieter one. But you decide.

Elsa & Fred ★ ★ ½
PG, 106 m., 2008

China Zorrilla (Elsa), Manuel Alexandre (Alfredo), Blanca Portillo (Cuca), Roberto Carnaghi (Gabriel), Jose Angel Egido (Paco), Gonzalo Urtizberea (Alejo). Directed by Marcos Carnevale and produced by Jose Antonio Felez. Screenplay by Carnevale, Lily Ann Martin, and Marcela Guerty.

Elsa and I have one big thing in common. We both love the famous scene in Fellini's *La Dolce Vita* when Anita Ekberg and Marcello Mastroianni wade in the waters of the Trevi Fountain in Rome at dawn. That shared love is almost but not quite enough to inspire a recommendation from me for *Elsa & Fred,* which is a sweet but inconsequential romantic comedy.

Alfredo (Manuel Alexandre) has been a

153

widower for seven months. He has been moved into a new apartment in Madrid by his shrill daughter, Cuca (Blanca Portillo). What would make him happier would be if she would stop micromanaging his life. His dog, Bonaparte, is better company. Through a Meet Cute involving a fender bender, he meets Elsa (China Zorrilla), an Argentinean neighbor in the same building.

They are both lonely, both looking for companionship. Alfredo is seventy-eight. Elsa says she is seventy-seven. Can you believe everything she says? On her wall there is a photograph of Ekberg in the great Fellini scene. When she was young, Elsa tells Fred, she was a ringer for Ekberg—often mistaken for her. Now she is no longer young, but she begins to take on beauty in the eyes of her new admirer, and tentatively they begin a romance.

The structure of the film, directed by Marcos Carnevale of Argentina, is foreordained. They will flirt, grow closer, spat, make up, grow even closer, and then time will inexorably exact some sort of toll. All of those things happen right on schedule, although the two actors give them a bittersweet appeal. Subplots involving a business deal and old secrets from the past are fitfully interesting. More entertaining are such stunts as how they deal with the bill in an expensive restaurant.

SPOILER WARNING: But what I really loved was the film's last act, when Alfredo fulfills Elsa's lifelong dream. He flies her to Rome for the first visit of her life, and after seeing all the other sights, they do indeed wade in the Trevi Fountain at dawn, in a scene photographed to remind us vividly of the Fellini original. This scene held me spellbound. It is true that Elsa no longer resembles Ekberg, if she ever did. But in her mind she does, and old Alfredo looks like young Marcello, and none of us look as we wish we did, but all of us can dream.

Encounters at the End of the World ★ ★ ★ ★
G, 99 m., 2008

Directed and narrated by Werner Herzog and produced by Henry Kaiser. Screenplay by Herzog.

Read the title of *Encounters at the End of the*

World carefully, for it has two meanings. As he journeys to the South Pole, which is as far as you can get from everywhere, Werner Herzog also journeys to the prospect of man's oblivion. Far under the eternal ice, he visits a curious tunnel whose walls have been decorated by various mementos, including a frozen fish that is far away from its home waters. What might travelers from another planet think of these souvenirs, he wonders, if they visit long after all other signs of our civilization have vanished?

Herzog has come to live for a while at the McMurdo Research Station, the largest habitation on Antarctica. He was attracted by underwater films taken by his friend Henry Kaiser, which show scientists exploring the ocean floor. They open a hole in the ice with a blasting device, then plunge in, collecting specimens, taking films, nosing around. They investigate an undersea world of horrifying carnage, inhabited by creatures so ferocious we are relieved they are too small to be seen. And also by enormous seals who sing to one another. In order not to limit their range, Herzog observes, the divers do not use a tether line, so they must trust themselves to find the hole in the ice again. I am afraid to even think about that.

Herzog is a romantic wanderer, drawn to the extremes. He makes as many documentaries as fiction films, is prolific in the chronicles of his curiosity, and here moseys about McMurdo chatting with people who have chosen to live here in eternal day or night. They are a strange population. One woman likes to have herself zipped into luggage and performs this feat on the station's talent night. One man was once a banker and now drives an enormous bus. A pipe fitter matches the fingers of his hands together to show that the second and third are the same length—genetic evidence, he says, that he is descended from Aztec kings.

But I make the movie sound like a travelogue or an exhibit of eccentrics, and it is a poem of oddness and beauty. Herzog is like no other filmmaker, and to return to him is to be welcomed into a world vastly larger and more peculiar than the one around us. The underwater photography alone would make a film, but there is so much more.

Consider the men who study the active volcanoes of Antarctica and sometimes descend into volcanic flumes that open to the surface—although they must take care, Herzog observes in his wondering, precise narration, not to be doing so when the volcano erupts. It happens that there is another movie opening now that also has volcanic tubes (*Journey to the Center of the Earth*). Do not confuse the two. These men play with real volcanoes.

They also lead lives revolving around monster movies on video, a treasured ice-cream machine, and a string band concert from the top of a Quonset hut during the eternal day. And they have modern conveniences of which Herzog despairs, like an ATM machine, in a place where the machine, the money inside it, and the people who use it, must all be airlifted in. Herzog loves these people, it is clear, because like himself they have gone to such lengths to escape the mundane and test the limits of the extraordinary. But there is a difference between them and Timothy Treadwell, the hero of *Grizzly Man*, Herzog's documentary about a man who thought he could live with bears and not be eaten, and was mistaken. The difference is that Treadwell was a foolish romantic, and these men and women are in this godforsaken place to extend their knowledge of the planet and of the mysteries of life and death itself.

Herzog's method makes the movie seem like it is happening by chance, although chance has nothing to do with it. He narrates as if we're watching movies of his last vacation—informal, conversational, engaging. He talks about people he met, sights he saw, thoughts he had. And then a larger picture grows inexorably into view. McMurdo is perched on the frontier of the coming suicide of the planet. Mankind has grown too fast, spent too freely, consumed too much, and the ice is melting and we shall all perish. Herzog doesn't use such language, of course; he is too subtle and visionary. He is nudged toward his conclusions by what he sees. In a sense, his film journeys through time as well as space, and we see what little we may end up leaving behind us. Nor is he depressed by this prospect, but only philosophical. We came, we saw, we conquered, and we left behind a frozen fish.

His visit to Antarctica was not intended, he warns us at the outset, to take footage of "fluffy penguins." But there are some penguins in the film, and one of them embarks on a journey that haunts my memory to this moment, long after it must have ended.

Note: Herzog dedicated this film to me. I am deeply moved and honored. The letter I wrote to him from the 2007 Toronto Film Festival is in the Essays chapter.

The End of the Line ★★★
NO MPAA RATING, 90 m., 2009

A documentary directed by Rupert Murray and produced by George Duffield and Claire Lewis. Based on the book by Charles Clover.

It once was said that the cod were so populous off the coast of Nova Scotia that you could walk on the sea on their backs. Now they have virtually disappeared. The cod, the fish in fish 'n' chips, has been overfished to near extinction. Other fish species are following.

There is heartfelt footage in *The End of the Line*, circa 1992, of angry, panicked fishermen besieging a hearing room where a government minister is calling for a moratorium on cod fishing. The Canadian prime minister, Brian Mulroney, declares it a necessity. These fishermen have depended on the cod for a living, and in many cases, so have their fathers back for many generations. The Canadian maritime provinces were largely settled because of the fishing industry.

The moratorium was imposed. But in 1992 it was already too late. The cod did not come back. They are virtually gone from those waters. Many documentaries about ecology issue dire warnings of crises that will strike at some point in the future. Opponents of these films scoff at them. But *The End of the Line* in large part is about what has already, irrefutably, happened.

Factory fishing grew too quickly, unsupervised, and damaged some fish populations so severely that their very sustainability was put into question. Giant trawlers prowled the seas halfway around the world from their ports. They used technology such as sonar to pinpoint schools of fish, and bottom trawling to capture great masses of them, while incidentally wreaking havoc with the seabed.

155

Some nations continue outlaw behavior. Japan continues its whaling in the face of international opprobrium. The role of other nations has been more subtle. International fishery experts were puzzled, for example, by the paradox that regional catches were down everywhere but the global catch remained steady.

How could this be? It appeared that all nations posted losses except China, which had steady gains. Were the Chinese overfishing? Just the contrary: Scientists discovered they were making up their numbers, as regional party officials supplied fake growth statistics to look better in Beijing.

The End of the Line documents what threatens to become an irreversible decline in aquatic populations within forty years. Opportunist species move in to take advantage. Oddly, the disappearance of cod has resulted in an explosion of the lobster population, as they lose their chief rival for food.

There are some bright spots. The state of Alaska, for example, is praised for its fishing policies, which restrict fishing waters, the number of boats, the length of the season, and the size of the catch. These policies contribute to "sustainable populations." Walmart, which sells enormous quantities of fish, is switching to sustainable sources. Ninety percent of the fish in McDonald's fish sandwiches is from sustainable sources.

For every bright spot, there is an omen. Fish farms, for example, seem like progress, but their fish are fed the ground-up bodies of captured free-range fish. It takes five kilos of anchovies to produce one of salmon. Bluefin tuna is an endangered species. A lot of retail tuna is not tuna at all. Some of it is dolphin, itself a threatened species.

The famous sushi restaurant Nobu declines to remove bluefin from its menu but promises to add a consumer advisory for consumers, comparing the situation to the health warnings on cigarettes. Not precisely a parallel: Eating bluefin is dangerous to *their* health, not ours.

The question arises: If fish are threatened, and beef production requires much more land and crop consumption than justified in terms of feeding the Earth's population, what are we to eat? The answer is staring us in the

face: We should eat a more largely vegetarian diet, using animal proteins as humans have traditionally used them, as a supplement, rather than a main course.

The End of the Line, directed by Rupert Murray, based on a book by Charles Clover, is constructed from interviews with many experts, a good deal of historical footage, and much incredible footage from under the sea, including breathtaking vistas of sea preserves, where the diversity of species can be seen to grow annually. We once thought of the sea as limitless bounty. I think I may even have heard that in school. But those fantasies are over.

Enlighten Up! ★ ★ ★
NO MPAA RATING, 82 m., 2009

Featuring Nick Rosen, Norman Allen, B. K. S. Iyengar, Pattabhi Jois, Gurusharananda, Cyndi Lee, Alan Finger, Dharma Mittra, Shyamdas, Sharon Gannon, David Life, Joseph Alter, David Gordon White, Diamond Dallas Page, Madan Kataria. A documentary directed and produced by Kate Churchill. Screenplay by Churchill and Jonathon Hexner.

An unemployed journalist and a documentary filmmaker spend six months traveling far enough to circle the globe, and they discover that the secret of yoga is the same as how to get to Carnegie Hall: practice, practice, practice. Apart from that, apparently, there is no secret at all to yoga. At least, they don't find a yogi who will admit to one.

Kate Churchill and her subject, Nick Rosen, travel from New York to Boulder to California to Hawaii, and then on to India. Nick practices under masters ranging from the legendary Yogacharya B. K. S. Iyengar, ninety-one, named by *Time* as one of the one hundred most influential people in the world, to Diamond Dallas Page, named by *Pro Wrestling Illustrated* as the most hated wrestler of the year (1999).

All of these teachers, young and old, male and female, Eastern and Western, refuse to define or even really name the ultimate state one hopes to reach. When you get there, you will know it. You will find it within yourself. You just have to do it. Practice does not make perfection, but it makes improvement. One must not focus on the destination but on the journey. Live in the moment. Live in eternity. Find God. Let the body flow into a yoga position as light fills a diamond (Iyengar). Your reward will be tits and ass (Diamond Dallas).

This was all fine with me because I wasn't much interested in arriving at ultimate answers, and neither, it must be said, is Nick Rosen. He does, however, log a lot of miles and has a particularly interesting time in India. He practices fervently. His body assumes positions on which, unlike a diamond, the sun don't shine. He begins as a skeptic about the spiritual side of yoga, and ends the same way, and doesn't find any yogis who try to proselytize him.

Instead, they offer variations of "Just do it!" Nick just does it, and at the end of his trial he tells Kate that he feels good, sleeps better, is stronger, has an improved digestive system, and in theory a better sex life (in practice, he tells her, "I haven't been alone with a woman for months—except you").

He also has better breath control, an area of particular interest to me. Once at Rancho La Puerta I was taking a yoga class, and we were all told to close our eyes and emit the sound "ahhhhhhh." I did so. When I opened my eyes, everyone was staring at me. "You sustained that three times as long as anyone else in the room," the yoga instructor told me. "In fact, I've never seen anyone holding out that long." Chaz theorized it had something to do with my ability to keep talking without letting anyone get a word in edgeways.

Enlighten Up! may prove a disappointment to anyone seeking to discover the secrets of yoga, or have their own beliefs confirmed. Apparently it does all come down to practice. Some seem addicted to it, which seems a shame to me, because a discipline should be a path to a fuller life, not an alternative. If you spend the rest of your life practicing yoga, well, that's what you did with the rest of your life. It's healthier than sinning, but that's about the best you can say.

And yet this is an interesting movie, and I'm glad I saw it. I enjoyed all the people I met during Nick's six-month quest. Most seemed cheerful and outgoing, and exuded good health. They smiled a lot. They weren't creepy true believers obsessed with converting every-

one. They seemed happy with where they were, and they assumed Nick wanted to be there, too. And for the most part they seem to live contented lives, although Diamond Dallas advises yoga as a way to meet chicks, and (a sharp shake of the wind chime, please) that man will never find tranquillity who has not divested himself of subterfuge in meeting chicks.

Kate Churchill's role is intriguing. At the outset she tells us she's a yoga practitioner who thought there would be a documentary in recruiting a novice and exposing that person to yoga, then filming what happened. She obviously hopes Nick will take to yoga more than he does, and sounds wistful in her off-camera questions. Is he beginning to find something more in it? Does he have a favorite teacher? Has his appreciation deepened?

Nick is an affable man who goes along with her plan. Recently downsized, he has little better to do than be flown around the world to yoga experiences. But he's not cut out to practice, practice, practice, and he's so laid back that few sparks fly. This is a peaceful kind of film, not terribly eventful, but I suppose we wouldn't want a yoga thriller. Relax. Let it happen. Or not.

Everlasting Moments ★ ★ ★ ★
NO MPAA RATING, 131 m., 2009

Maria Heiskanen (Maria Larsson), Mikael Persbrandt (Sigfrid Larsson), Jesper Christensen (Sebastian Pedersen), Callin Ohrvall (Maja Larsson). Directed by Jan Troell and produced by Thomas Stenderup. Screenplay by Niklas Radstrom, based on a story by Agneta Ulfsater Troell.

Rarely is there a film that evokes our sympathy more deeply than *Everlasting Moments*. It is a great story of love and hope, told tenderly and without any great striving for effect. It begins in Sweden in 1911 and involves a woman, her daughter, her husband, a camera, and the kindness of a stranger. It has been made by Jan Troell, a filmmaker whose care for these characters is instinctive.

The woman is named Maria Larsson. She lives with her husband, Sigfrid, in Malmo, a port city at the southern tip of Sweden. They eventually have seven children. "Sigge" is a laborer on the docks who takes the pledge time and again at the Temperance Society but falls back into alcoholism. He is a loving and jovial man when sober, but violent when he is drunk, and the children await his homecomings with apprehension.

The movie is not really about Sigge. It is about Maria, who is a strong woman, resilient, complex. She raises the children, works as a house cleaner, copes with the family's poverty. Once, when newly married, she won a camera in a lottery. Now she finds it and takes it to a photo shop to pawn it and buy food. There she meets Sebastian Pedersen, and he finds an undeveloped plate still in the camera. He develops it, and something about the photograph or Maria causes him to say he will buy the camera, but she must hold it for him and continue to take pictures.

Maria is not sophisticated and may have little education, but she is a deep and creative woman and an instinctively gifted photographer. She has no theory, but her choices of subjects and compositions are inspired. And perhaps Mr. Pedersen inspires her, too. He is much older and always polite and proper with her, but over a time it becomes clear that they have fallen in love.

No, the film is not about how she leaves her drunken husband and becomes a famous photographer. It is about how her inner life is transformed by discovering that she has an artistic talent. She continues to be committed to Sigge by a bond deeper than marriage or obligation. But she tentatively takes steps toward personal independence that were rare in that time. When Sigge goes to fight in the war, she supports the family by taking marriage photographs.

Maria Heiskanen, who plays Maria, makes her a shy woman who is almost frightened to take a larger view of herself. She is strong when she needs to be but unaccustomed to men like Mr. Pedersen, who treat her as something more than she conceives herself. One of the film's mysteries is how clearly she defines her marriage to Sigge, which endures, even though she fully feels the possibilities that Sebastian never quite offers. Mikael Persbrandt makes Sigge not a bad man but powerless over alcohol. His labor is back-breaking. And look at the tact of Jesper Christensen as Sebastian, who loves Maria from the moment he sees her

but wants to protect her from the problems that could bring. The movie is intensely observant about these gradations of love.

Everlasting Moments reflects the great self-assurance of Jan Troell, whose work includes such masterpieces as *The Emigrants, The New Land,* and *Hamsun.* All of his films are about lives striving toward greater fullness. He respects work, values, and feelings. He stands apart from the frantic hunger for fashionable success. After I saw this film, I looked through a few of the early reviews of it and found critics almost startled by its humanism. Here is Todd McCarthy of *Variety:* "Beholding Troell's exquisite images is like having your eyes washed, the better to behold moving pictures of uncorrupted purity and clarity."

The story comes from the heart. Troell, who showed *Everlasting Moments* at Telluride 2008, adapted it from a novel by his wife, Agneta, who based it on one of her own family members, Maria Larsson. Maria lived this life and took some of the photographs we see. The film is narrated by her daughter, Maja Larsson (Callin Ohrvall), and in my imagination I hear Maja telling the story to Agneta, for Jan was born in Malmo, and the dates work out that they might both have known her well and always thought hers was a story worth telling.

Everybody's Fine ★★ ½
PG-13, 95 m., 2009

Robert De Niro (Frank Goode), Drew Barrymore (Rosie), Kate Beckinsale (Amy), Sam Rockwell (Robert). Directed by Kirk Jones and produced by Vittorio Cecchi Gori, Ted Field, Glynis Murray, and Gianni Nunnari. Screenplay by Jones, based on Giuseppe Tornatore's 1990 film *Stanno tutti bene.*

A man in his sixties after the death of his wife is a leaky ship without a bailer. Frank Goode has everything above deck shipshape, but he's sinking. The garden is his pride and joy. Everything inside is mopped, scrubbed, polished, dusted, arranged, and alphabetized. He buys big steaks and a new electric grill to cook them on. He selects a wine with the advice of a clueless stock boy. He reclines in his lawn chair on his manicured lawn and awaits the arrival of his four children.

At the last minute, none of them can make it. One can't even be bothered to call, but his regrets are passed along. Frank (Robert De Niro) steers a steady course to his doctor, saying he plans to do some traveling. His doctor says this is a bad idea. Frank decides not to drive, and by train, plane, and automobile visits the homes of his family diaspora. He is not greeted with unalloyed joy. He was a distant disciplinarian, often critical, a chilly alternative to the wife who held them together. They don't hate him, but they have their lives to lead.

Everybody's Fine tells the story of his journey and his discoveries along the way. If we have seen a dozen movies in our lifetime, we can feel pretty safe in predicting that each child will reveal, and present, a different kind of problem. That Frank will discover things he didn't know about himself and them. That he will reevaluate his life in the process. That a great deal of the American landscape will pass by on the screen. And, since all story pegs exist to hang things from, his lifetime of manufacturing telephone cables will result in many, many shots of telephone lines stringing along the way, symbolizing lines of communication. What will we do when the need for landlines disappears?

All that could redeem this thoroughly foreseeable unfolding would be colorful characters and good acting. *Everybody's Fine* comes close, but not close enough. The children are David, an artist who seems not to be at home in his marginal New York apartment building, but whose work is on display in the gallery downstairs; Amy (Kate Beckinsale), a Chicago advertising woman with a high-flying lifestyle; Robert (Sam Rockwell), a classical musician in Denver; and Rosie (Drew Barrymore), a successful professional dancer in Las Vegas with a luxurious apartment.

The more the children feed him vague evasions about David, the more Frank realizes how much they have always concealed from him. He isn't stupid, and picks up on stray dialogue and other clues to realize their lives are all deceptive fictions. And so is his own?

Everybody's Fine is based on a 1990 Giuseppe Tornatore film named *Stanno tutti bene,* which starred Marcello Mastroianni as a man in the same situation. Mastroianni and De Niro are not interchangeable. Mastroianni is effortlessly relaxed and embracing, the life source in a body. De Niro is not. There are many things he does better than anyone else alive, but playing nice isn't one of them.

What he does do is play Frank with respect and affection. There are no De Niro trademarks visible. He builds Frank from the ground up as a man who always tried to do the right thing, usually in the wrong way. He's like an actor singing well after much vocal coaching; Mastroianni in these matters was born pitch-perfect. Of modern comparable actors, I think above all of Jack Lemmon.

Of the actors playing the children, everybody's fine. Drew Barrymore has the central role and as always is a magnet for our affection. In twenty-five years she'd be right for a remake of this story about a widow, not a widower. In general, however, my advice would be, not "rent it" (you know how I feel about that), but the more realistic "check it out if you come upon it by accident while channel-surfing."

Every Little Step ★ ★ ★
PG-13, 96 m., 2009

A documentary directed and produced by James D. Stern and Adam Del Deo.

Every Little Step is a documentary about the casting process starting in 2006 for a Broadway revival of *A Chorus Line,* a musical that has been running somewhere in the world since its premiere in 1975 and inspired Richard Attenborough's 1985 film. The musical is about seventeen dancers who audition for their roles. The doc honors countless more who auditioned but were not chosen.

As I watched the film, one thought above all others was inspired: These people must love dancing to the point of abandon to submit themselves to this ordeal. Dancers must be in physical shape as good as most pro athletes and better than many. In fact, they *are* professional athletes, because although what they perform in is art, what they do is demanding physical work.

Often starting as young children, they practice, rehearse, and at some point forgo ordinary lives to submerge themselves in this

159

process. It's the same with Olympians. They train and condition and focus and sacrifice. They turn up by the hundreds for auditions (the shots of the lineup outside the open call in Manhattan would make a doc in themselves). To get a call-back means they are superbly talented. Even then, the odds are they won't be chosen. Then it's back to more painstaking preparation, another job done for the paycheck, more dreams, more lines, more auditions, and usually more disappointments.

What we sense in the film is the camaraderie among these hopeful dancers. They've all been through the process before, all have been disappointed before, all know better than anyone else what it takes, all believe the best candidates don't always win the jobs.

The stakes are so high that to be one of the judges must cause restless dreams. Among them are Bob Avian, Michael Bennett's fellow choreographer in the 1975 production, and a vivacious force of nature named Baayork Lee, a dancer who played Connie, many people's favorite character, in that production. She handles the lineups, leads routines, and is, in her presence and energy, a testimony that it is possible to survive and find joy in this world.

I was reminded of *The Audition*, a film I saw last month, about the Metropolitan Opera's annual National Council Auditions. The art forms are different; the ordeals are the same. Then we buy our tickets and attend, and make dinner plans, and worry about parking, and chat at intermission, and admire what we see, when admiration is not adequate. We should be kneeling on concrete to remind ourselves what dues these artists pay.

Exit Through the Gift Shop ★★★ ½
R, 86 m., 2010

A documentary narrated by Rhys Ifans. Featuring Thierry Guetta, Banksy, Space Invader, Shepard Fairey, Neckface, and Swoon. Directed by Banksy and produced by Holly Cushing, Jaimie D'Cruz, and James Gay-Rees.

The widespread speculation that *Exit Through the Gift Shop* is a hoax only adds to its fascination. An anonymous London graffiti artist named Banksy arrives to paint walls in Los Angeles. He encounters an obscure Frenchman named Thierry Guetta, who has dedicated his life to videotaping graffiti artists.

The Frenchman's hundreds of tapes have been dumped unorganized into boxes. Banksy thinks they might make a film. Guetta makes a very bad one. Banksy takes over the film and advises Guetta to create some art himself. Guetta does, names himself Mr. Brainwash, and organizes an exhibition of his work through which he makes a fortune in sales.

Surely Thierry Guetta cannot be real? With his dashing mustache and Inspector Clouseau accent, his long-suffering wife and his zealous risk taking to film illegal artists by stealth? Surely he didn't rent a former CBS television studio and transform it into an exhibition space? Surely people didn't line up at dawn to get in—and pay tens of thousands of dollars for the works of an artist who had never held a show, sold a work, or received a review? Surely not if his work looked like art school rip-offs of the familiar styles of famous artists?

Even while I sat spellbound during this film, that's what I was asking myself. But Thierry Guetta surely did. His art exhibition was written up in a cover story in *L.A. Weekly* on June 12, 2008. It mentions this film, which Banksy was "threatening to do." Common sense dictates that no one would rent a CBS studio and fill it with hundreds of artworks in order to produce a hoax indie documentary. Nor would they cast Guetta, indubitably a real person, as himself. Right? Right?

The film depends entirely on Guetta, a cross between a TV pitchman, a cartoon Frenchman, and a chatty con man. Its footage really has been edited from a decade of tapes made clandestinely while L.A. graffiti artists risked arrest and death to create their paintings in spectacular places. Guetta fearlessly followed them right out onto ledges and helped them carry supplies to places a human fly might balk at. And all the time he's talking, talking, telling his life story and his hero worship for these artists.

There are all kinds of graffiti. Much of it is ugly defacement, the kind of territorial marking a dog does so much more elegantly. Chicago mayor Richard Daley's Graffiti Busters have my support and admiration. Some graffiti, however, is certainly art, as Norman Mailer was one of the first to argue in his book *The Faith of Graffiti* (1974). Banksy and others at his level, such as Guetta's hero Shepard Fairey, find ways to visually reinvent public spaces and make striking artistic statements.

But what does Guetta do? One of his artworks, inspired by Andy Warhol's Campbell's soup can, shows a can of tomato paint spray. OK, that's witty enough for a nice editorial cartoon. How many thousands would you spend to have it in your house? Or a morph of Joan Crawford and Warhol's Marilyn? Then again, at the time, people said Andy Warhol wasn't creating art either. Surely Warhol's message was that Thierry Guetta has an absolute right to call his work art and sell it for as much as he can.

There are currently more than 3,600 comments on my recent blog headlined "Video Games Can Never Be Art." At least 95 percent of them inform me I am a fool and that "art is in the eye of the beholder." I believe video games are not an art *form*, for reasons I am certainly not going to bring up again. I am quite willing to agree that graffiti is Art, but I don't believe the act of painting them is an art form, if you see what I mean. Or maybe you don't. You may be too old to understand my argument.

Anyway, comment No. 3,307 on my blog was from Kristian, and it said: "The wafting smell of dried mung beans pervades my nostrils." That's kind of . . . poetic, don't you think? But I stray from my thoughts, which are (1) *Exit Through the Gift Shop* is an admirable and entertaining documentary; (2) I believe it is not a hoax; (3) I would not much want a Thierry Guetta original; (4) I like Thierry Guetta; and (5) Banksy, the creator of this film, is a gifted filmmaker whose thoughts, as he regards Guetta, must resemble those of Victor Frankenstein when he regarded his monster: It works, but is it Art?

The Express ★ ★ ★
PG, 129 m., 2008

Dennis Quaid (Ben Schwartzwalder), Rob Brown (Ernie Davis), Omar Benson Miller (Jack Buckley), Clancy Brown (Roy Simmons), Charles S. Dutton (Pops Davis). Directed by Gary Fleder and produced by John Davis. Screenplay by Charles Leavitt, based on a book by Robert Gallagher.

The Express is involving and inspiring in the way a good movie about sports almost always is. The formula is basic and durable, and when you hitch it to a good story, you can hardly fail. Gary Fleder does more than that in telling the story of Ernie Davis (the "Elmira Express"), the running back for Syracuse who in 1961 became the first African-American to win the Heisman Trophy. Davis was drafted by pro football, but then leukemia was discovered; he never played a pro game and died in 1963. He was twenty-three.

Set during Syracuse's undefeated 1959 season (actually two years before the season Davis won the Heisman), the movie shows him as the MVP at the Cotton Bowl in Dallas. He was informed he could be present to receive his trophy but could not attend the banquet in a segregated venue. Most of his teammates boycotted the banquet. Most. I'd like to talk today with the few who didn't.

The film remembers a time when black players were unwelcome in the South. It shows racist fans screaming at him and throwing beer cans at the West Virginia and Texas games. He had to enter the hotels by back doors and sleep in servants' quarters. This all took place well within the lifetimes and memories of many people. Jackie Robinson joined the Brooklyn Dodgers in 1949, but the Dodgers didn't play in the South. Davis was far from the first black star on a college team; Jim Brown preceded him at Syracuse, and how well I remember cheering beside my dad as we watched J. C. Caroline play for the University of Illinois in 1953–54. He was an All-American, but I recall the uproar when a barbershop in Champaign refused to cut his hair.

What makes *The Express* special is that it focuses not only on football but also on the relationship Davis had with his coach, Ben Schwartzwalder (Dennis Quaid). Schwartzwalder, who beat out fifty other schools (including Notre Dame) to recruit Davis, wasn't a racist by the standards of that time, which is to say he was a racist by today's standards. Not overtly, but as Quaid subtly shows in his performance, the coach had a certain mental distance from African-Americans. He promised Davis he would develop his awesome ability, and he did. In the process, getting to know Davis was part of a fundamental development of Schwartzwalder's attitude. They both became better men because of their friendship. The film is about football, but that relationship is its deeper subject.

The heroic athlete achieving his dreams and dying too soon is an enduring movie archetype; remember *Brian's Song* (1971). Because we walk into these films knowing the hero will die, every scene takes on an added significance. Rob Brown plays Davis as a focused young man with a strong family behind him, confident, not intimidated or obsessed by racism, open to everyone (he became the first African-American member of the predominantly Jewish fraternity Sigma Alpha Mu). The movie deals in expected ways with his life off the field and concentrates on his playing.

There is a lot of football in the movie. It's well presented, but there is the usual oddity that it almost entirely shows success. I may have missed it, but I don't remember a single time when Davis is caught behind the line of scrimmage, fumbles, or drops a pass. We see these stars as our surrogates, and we don't enjoy watching ourselves fail.

The key supporting performance is by Omar Benson Miller (*Miracle at St. Anna*) as Buckley, Davis's black friend on the team, who advises him of situations Buckley has already experienced. The resonating Charles S. Dutton plays the grandfather who raised Davis. They reinforce him through some hostility to the team newcomer at first, but mercifully the team lacks a stereotyped racist; the emphasis under Schwartzwalder is so intensely on winning that anything else is unthinkable—if not for reasons of mortality, then for hard reality.

I'm a fall guy for movies like this. Yes, I see the formula grinding away, as it actually must, because Davis's real life corresponds to it. I can't remember a film about an untalented athlete, and not many about losing teams (they always win in the end). In the final analysis, it's not how you play the game that counts, but whether you win or lose.

Extract ★★ ½
R, 91 m., 2009

Jason Bateman (Joel), Mila Kunis (Cindy), Kristen Wiig (Suzie), Ben Affleck (Dean), J. K. Simmons (Brian), David Koechner (Nathan), Clifton Collins Jr. (Step), Dustin Milligan (Brad), Gene Simmons (Joe Adler). Directed by Mike Judge and produced by Michael Rotenberg and John Altschuler. Screenplay by Judge.

Granted that they're now human beings and not cartoons, Mike Judge's characters may never grow much smarter than Beavis and Butthead, who launched him on his career. The people in *Extract* are not as stupid as the ones in *Idiocracy* (2006), his previous film, but then those idiots had the benefit of a few hundred extra years during which to refute Darwin by evolving less intelligence. The *Extract* people work in a bottling plant that's up for sale when everything goes wrong in the life of its owner, Joel (Jason Bateman, of *Juno*).

Joel suffers in an unhappy marriage with Suzie (Kristen Wiig), whose potential sex life closes every evening at the moment when she tugs tight the drawstring on her sweatpants. That works better for her than a chastity belt. He shares his frustrations with the friendly bartender Dean (Ben Affleck), who advises him to cheat. But Joel can't bring himself to do that to Suzie. All right then, Dean says: Hire a gigolo to seduce her. Once Suzie has cheated, Joel's conscience will be clear.

Many of the other problems in Joel's life stem from the bottling plant, whose floor he overlooks from a high window. One involves a potential lawsuit from an employee named Step (Clifton Collins Jr.) who loses a testicle in a most unfortunate accident. Others come from a lazy and racist woman who does as little work as possible but resents the good workers, especially the Mexican-Americans.

Then there's the arrival of Cindy (Mila Kunis), a sexy con woman who is working far below her competence level on the bottling line, but precisely at her morality level. She understands that almost any man will believe it when a desirable woman says she's attracted to him. Hey, some babes have a fetish for schleppers.

Cindy, who is superb at putting two and

two together and putting money in her pocket, convinces Step to sue the company. He hires a lawyer famous for his ads on the benches at bus stops, Joe Adler (Gene Simmons, no more subtle than when he was in Kiss). Meanwhile, Joel recruits a gigolo (Dustin Milligan), who even in this crowd isn't the brightest bulb.

There are some good stretches in the film, Bateman is persuasive as the overwhelmed factory owner, and Mila Kunis brings her role to within shouting distance of credibility. The funniest element for me was supplied by Joel's neighbor Nathan (David Koechner), a pest who lurks in the shrubbery to burst forth with undesired friendliness. He is a case study of a bore, as once defined by John D. MacDonald: "Someone who deprives you of solitude without providing you with companionship." It cannot be easy for an actor to be as inspired as Koechner in the timing and facial language of a man who *cannot* comprehend urgent conversational signals that he get lost immediately.

The movie otherwise is sort of entertaining but lacks the focus and comic energy of Judge's *Office Space* (1999), and to believe that Suzie would be attracted to the gigolo requires not merely the suspension of disbelief but its demolition. A comedy need not be believable. But it needs to seem as if it's believable at least to itself.

Extraordinary Measures ★★

PG, 105 m., 2010

Brendan Fraser (John Crowley), Harrison Ford (Robert Stonehill), Keri Russell (Aileen), Meredith Droeger (Megan), Diego Velazquez (Patrick), Sam Hill (John Jr.). Directed by Tom Vaughn and produced by Carla Santos Shamberg, Michael Shamberg, and Stacey Sher. Screenplay by Robert Nelson Jacobs, based on *The Cure* by Geeta Anand.

Extraordinary Measures is an ordinary film with ordinary characters in a story too big for it. Life has been reduced to a Lifetime movie. The story, based on fact, is compelling: Two sick children have no more than a year to live when their father determines to seek out a maverick scientist who may have a cure. This is *Lorenzo's Oil* with a different disease, Pompe disease, although it fudges the facts to create a better story. The film centers on two dying children, nine and seven. In life, most children with Pompe die before age two, and those in the real story were fifteen months and seven days old when they got sick, and five and three when they were treated.

With children that young, the drama would have focused on the parents. By making Megan Crowley (Meredith Droeger) a wise and cheerful nine-year-old, *Extraordinary Measures* improves her as a story element. Her father is John Crowley (Brendan Fraser), an executive at Bristol-Myers. Her mother is Aileen (Keri Russell). Neither is developed any more deeply than the story requires. Their personal relationship is defined by their desperation as the deadlines for their children grow nearer.

Crowley discovers on the Internet a professor at the University of Nebraska named Dr. Robert Stonehill (Harrison Ford). He's working on a controversial cure for Pompe that the medical establishment rejects, and when he won't return messages, Crowley impulsively flies to Nebraska to confront him.

Dr. Robert Stonehill doesn't exist in life. The Pompe cure was developed by Dr. Yuan-Tsong Chen and his colleagues while he was at Duke University. He is now director of the Institute of Biomedical Science in Taiwan. Harrison Ford, as this film's executive producer, perhaps saw Stonehill as a plum role for himself; a rewrite was necessary because he couldn't very well play Dr. Chen. The real Chen, a Taiwan University graduate, worked his way up at Duke from a residency to professor and chief of medical genetics at the Duke University Medical Center. He has been mentioned as a Nobel candidate.

I suspect Dr. Chen might have inspired a more interesting character than "Dr. Stonehill." The Nebraskan seems inspired more by Harrison Ford's image and range. He plays the doctor using only a few spare parts off the shelf. (1) He likes to crank up rock music while he works. (2) He doesn't return messages. (3) He's so feckless he accidentally hangs up on Crowley by pulling the phone off his desk. (4) He likes to drink beer from longneck bottles in a honky-tonk bar and flirt with the

163

waitress. (5) "I'm a scientist, not a doctor." He's not interested in Pompe patients, only the chemistry of the disease.

This becomes tiresome. Later he becomes invested in the Crowleys, but of course he does. They hope to fund a high-tech startup and deal with venture capitalists whose scenes are more interesting than many of the medical ones. Contrast this with the character of Augusto Odone, played by Nick Nolte in *Lorenzo's Oil*—a self-taught parent who discovers his own cure for a rare nerve disease. Ford is given no lines that suggest depth of character, only gruffness that gradually mellows.

The film also fails to explain that the cost of the medication is $300,000 a year for life, which limits its impact in the United States because many American insurance companies refuse to pay for it. According to Wikipedia: "The vast majority of developed countries are providing access to therapy for all diagnosed Pompe patients."

Make no mistake. The Crowleys were brave and resourceful, and their proactive measures saved the lives of their children—and many more with Pompe. This is a remarkable story. I think the film lets them down. It finds the shortest possible route between beginning and end. And it sidesteps the point that the U.S. health care system makes it unavailable to many dying children; they are being saved in nations with universal health coverage.

F

The Fall ★ ★ ★ ★
R, 117 m., 2008

Catinca Untaru (Alexandria), Lee Pace (Roy Walker), Justine Waddell (Nurse Evelyn), Daniel Caltagirone (Governor Odious), Leo Bill (Charles Darwin), Sean Gilder (Walt Purdy), Julian Bleach (Indian Mystic), Marcus Wesley (Otta Benga), Robin Smith (Luigi). Directed and produced by Tarsem. Screenplay by Dan Gilroy, Nico Soultanakis, and Tarsem, based on the 1981 screenplay for *Yo Ho Ho*, by Valeri Petrov.

Tarsem's *The Fall* is a mad folly, an extravagant visual orgy, a free fall from reality into uncharted realms. Surely it is one of the wildest indulgences a director has ever granted himself. Tarsem, for two decades a leading director of music videos and TV commercials, spent millions of his own money to finance it, filmed it for four years in twenty-eight countries, and has made a movie that you might want to see for no other reason than because it exists. There will never be another like it.

The Fall is so audacious that when *Variety* calls it a "vanity project," you can only admire the man vain enough to make it. It tells a simple story with vast romantic images so stunning I had to check twice, three times, to be sure the film actually claims to have *absolutely no* computer-generated imagery. None? What about the Labyrinth of Despair, with no exit? The intersecting walls of zig-zagging staircases? The man who emerges from the burning tree? Perhaps the trick words are "computer-generated." Perhaps some of the images are created by more traditional kinds of special effects.

The story framework for the imagery is straightforward. In Los Angeles, circa 1915, a silent movie stuntman has his legs paralyzed while performing a reckless stunt. He convalesces in a half-deserted hospital, its corridors of cream and lime stretching from ward to ward of mostly empty beds, their pillows and sheets awaiting the harvest of World War I. The stuntman is Roy (Lee Pace), pleasant in appearance, confiding in speech, happy to make a new friend of a little girl named Alexandria (Catinca Untaru). She has broken her arm falling from a tree while picking oranges in a nearby grove; an elbow brace holds it sticking sideways from her body, and in that hand she carries an old cigar box everywhere, with her treasures.

Roy tells a story to Alexandria, involving adventurers who change appearance as quickly as a child's imagination can do its work. We see the process. He tells her of an "Indian" who has a wigwam and a squaw. She does not know these words and envisions an Indian from a land of palaces, turbans, and swamis. The verbal story is input from Roy; the visual story is output from Alexandria.

The story involves Roy (playing the Black Bandit) and his friends, a bomb-throwing Italian anarchist, an escaped African slave, an Indian (from India), and Charles Darwin and his pet monkey Otis. Their sworn enemy, Governor Odious, has stranded them on a desert island, but they come ashore (riding swimming elephants, of course) and wage war on him. One scene shows the governor's towering private carriage, pulled by hundreds of slaves, while others toil on its wheels like human hamsters. The governor is protected by leather-clad warriors with helmets shaped like coal scuttles.

Roy draws out the story for a personal motive; after Alexandria brings him some communion wafers from the hospital chapel, he persuades her to steal some morphine tablets from the dispensary. Paralyzed and having lost his great love (she is the princess in his story), he hopes to kill himself. There is a wonderful scene of the little girl trying to draw him back to life.

Either you are drawn into the world of this movie or you are not. It is preposterous, of course, but I vote with Werner Herzog, who says if we do not find new images, we will perish. Here a line of bowmen shoots hundreds of arrows into the air. So many of them fall into the back of the escaped slave that he falls backward and the weight of his body is supported by them, as on a bed of nails, dozens of foot-long arrows. There is a scene of the monkey Otis chasing a butterfly through impossible architecture. When the monkey is shot, I was touched by the death of the lovable little simian.

At this point in reviews of movies like *The Fall* (not that there are any), I usually announce that I have accomplished my work. I have described what the movie does, how it looks while it is doing it, and what the director has achieved. Well, what has he achieved? *The Fall* is beautiful for its own sake. And there is a sweet charm from the young Romanian actress Catinca Untaru, who may have been dubbed for all I know, but speaks with the innocence of childhood, working her way through tangles of words. She regards with equal wonder the reality she lives in and the fantasy she pretends to. It is her imagination that creates the images of Roy's story, and they have a purity and power beyond all calculation. Roy is her perfect storyteller, she is his perfect listener, and together they build a world.

Note: The R rating should not dissuade bright teenagers from this celebration of the imagination.

Fame ★★
PG, 107 m., 2009

Naturi Naughton (Denise), Kay Panabaker (Jenny), Anna Maria Perez de Tagle (Joy), Megan Mullally (Fran Rowan), Bebe Neuwirth (Lynn Kraft), Charles S. Dutton (Alvin Dowd), Kherington Payne (Alice), Debbie Allen (Principal Simms), Walter Perez (Victor Taveras), Paul McGill (Kevin), Paul Iacono (Neil Baczynsky), Asher Book (Marco), Collins Pennie (Malik), Kelsey Grammer (Joel Cranston). Directed by Kevin Tancharoen and produced by Mark Canton, Gary Lucchesi, Tom Rosenberg, and Richard S. Wright. Screenplay by Allison Burnett, based on the 1980 film written by Christopher Gore.

Why bother to remake *Fame* if you don't have a clue about why the 1980 movie was special? Why take a touching experience and make it into a shallow exercise? Why begin with an R-rated look at plausible kids with real problems and tame it into a PG-rated after-school special? Why cast actors who are sometimes too old and experienced to play seniors, let alone freshmen?

The new *Fame* is a sad reflection of the new Hollywood, where material is sanitized and dumbed down for a hypothetical teen market that is way too sophisticated for it. It plays like a dinner theater version of the original. That there are some genuinely talented actors in the film doesn't help, because they're given little to build on or work with.

Do we, at this point, need another version of the creaky scene where a boyfriend misunderstands the way his girl smiles at another guy, and gets mad? Do we require parents who want their daughter to be a classical pianist and don't understand the need in her soul to perform hip-hop? Above all, do we need a big finale so elaborate and overproduced it looks like a musical number on the Oscars and could not possibly be staged in any high school?

As an admirer of Alan Parker's 1980 film, I was interested to see what would be done with this one. I suspect its director, Kevin Tancharoen (*Britney Spears Live from Miami*), didn't understand the Parker film. It was not an excuse for a musical. It was a film with great musical performances growing out of tangible dramatic situations.

The new screenplay by Allison Burnett is shallow and facile. No personal or family relationships are dealt with in other but clichés. Some of the student-teacher scenes are expected, but effective, because such adult actors as Charles S. Dutton, Bebe Neuwirth, Megan Mullally, and Debbie Allen (from the original film and TV series) speak from conviction and not plot contrivance.

The film, like the original, is broken into segments: "Freshman Year," and so on. In 1980 we got a sense of time passing and characters changing. In the new film these years relentlessly follow the standard screenplay formula: Introduction, Development, Problems, Resolution, Happy Ending. As "Junior Year" started, I looked at my watch to confirm how little time had passed. The film feels hurried. It is perhaps evidence of postproduction cutting that the fourth-billed Kelsey Grammer, playing a teacher, is on screen so rarely (his first dialogue is nice, however).

I got little sense of who these kids were. Some of them I liked a lot. They don't parallel the original characters or use their names, but I gather that Naturi Naughton, as Denise, is intended to function like Irene Cara, as Coco. Naughton is touching and talented, but the scenes involving her controlling father are written on autopilot. And is it plausible that such a gifted classical pianist would have so little feeling for her art?

Kay Panabaker, as Jenny, makes a sort of Molly Ringwald impression, but her character isn't gifted enough to convince us she'd make it through auditions. Anna Maria Perez de Tagle, as Joy, looks so fetching we wish she had been given more substantial scenes. Collins Pennie, as Malik, has the thankless role of the kid angry about childhood memories; that he is twenty-five makes his adolescent angst less convincing.

The filmmakers have stacked the deck, with several experienced actors in their twenties looking very little like fourteen-year-old freshmen and dancing like Broadway veterans. Their inexperience is acted, not felt. The irony is that Dutton's character in the film provides advice the film should have taken to heart.

Fanboys ★ ½

PG-13, 90 m., 2009

Sam Huntington (Eric), Christopher Marquette (Linus), Dan Fogler (Hutch), Jay Baruchel (Windows), Kristen Bell (Zoe). Directed by Kyle Newman and produced by Evan Astrowsky, Dana Brunetti, Matthew Perniciaro, and Kevin Spacey. Screenplay by Ernest Cline and Adam F. Goldberg.

A lot of fans are basically fans of fandom itself. It's all about them. They have mastered the Star Wars or Star Trek universes or whatever, but their objects of veneration are useful mainly as a backdrop to their own devotion. Anyone who would camp out in a tent on the sidewalk for weeks in order to be first in line for a movie is more into camping on the sidewalk than movies.

Extreme fandom may serve as a security blanket for the socially inept, who use its extreme structure as a substitute for social skills. If you are Luke Skywalker and she is Princess Leia, you already know what to say to each other, which is so much safer than having to ad lib it. Your fannish obsession is your beard. If you know absolutely all the trivia about your cubbyhole of pop culture, it saves you

from having to know anything about anything else. That's why it's excruciatingly boring to talk to such people: They're always asking you questions they know the answer to.

But enough about my opinions; what about Fanboys? Its primary flaw is that it's not critical. It is a celebration of an idiotic lifestyle, and I don't think it knows it. If you want to get in a car and drive to California, fine. So do I. So did Jack Kerouac. But if your first stop involves a rumble at a Star Trek convention in Iowa, dude, beam your ass down to Route 66.

The movie, set in 1999, involves four Star Wars fanatics and, eventually, their gal pal, who have the notion of driving to Marin County, breaking into the Skywalker Ranch, and stealing a copy of a print of Star Wars Episode 1: The Phantom Menace so they can see it before anyone else. This is about as plausible as breaking into the U.S. Mint and stealing some money so you can spend it before anyone else.

Fanboys follows in the footsteps of Sex Drive by allowing one of its heroes to plan a rendezvous with an Internet sex goddess. To avoid revealing any plot secrets in this movie, I will recycle my earlier warning: In a chat room, don't be too hasty to believe Ms. Tasty.

This plot is given gravitas because one of the friends, Linus (Christopher Marquette), is dying of cancer. His buddy Eric (Sam Huntington) is in favor of the trip because, I dunno, it will give Linus something to live for, I guess. The other fanboys are Hutch (Dan Fogler), who lives in his mother's garage/coach house, and Windows (Jay Baruchel), who changed his name from MacOS. Just kidding. Windows, Hutch, and Linus work in a comic book store, where their favorite customer is Zoe (Kristen Bell). She's sexy and a Star Wars fan. How cool is that? She's almost better than the date who turns into a pizza and a six-pack when the deed is done.

The question of Linus's cancer became the subject of a celebrated Internet flame war last summer, with supporters of Fanboys director Kyle Newman running Anti-Harvey Web sites opposing Harvey Weinstein's alleged scheme to cut the subplot out of the movie. The subplot survived, but it's one of those movie diseases that is mentioned occasionally so everyone can look solemn, and then dropped when the ailing Linus dons a matching black camouflage outfit and scales the Skywalker Ranch walls with a grappling hook.

Fanboys is an amiable but disjointed movie that identifies too closely with its heroes. Poking a little more fun at them would have been a great idea. They are tragically hurtling into a cultural dead end, mastering knowledge that has no purpose other than being mastered, and too smart to be wasting their time. When a movie's opening day finally comes and fanboys leave their sidewalk tents for a mad dash into the theater, I wonder who retrieves their tents, sleeping bags, portable heaters, and iPod speakers. Warning: Mom isn't always going to be there to clean up after you.

Fantastic Mr. Fox ★★★ ½
PG, 88 m., 2009

George Clooney (Mr. Fox), Meryl Streep (Mrs. Fox), Jason Schwartzman (Ash), Eric Anderson (Kristofferson), Bill Murray (Badger), Wally Wolodarsky (Kylie), Owen Wilson (Coach Skip), Willem Dafoe (Rat). Directed by Wes Anderson and produced by Anderson, Allison Abbate, Jeremy Dawson, and Scott Rudin. Screenplay by Anderson and Noah Baumbach, based on the book by Roald Dahl.

Some artists have a way of riveting your vision with the certitude of what they do. This has nothing to do with subject or style. It's inexplicable. Andy Warhol and Grandma Moses. The spareness of Bergman and the Fellini circus. Wes Anderson is like that. There's nothing consistent about his recent work but its ability to make me go *zooinng!* What else do *The Darjeeling Limited* and *The Life Aquatic with Steve Zissou* have in common?

Now here's *Fantastic Mr. Fox,* an animated picture with nothing in common with traditional animation, except that it's largely in one of the oldest animation styles of all—stop motion, the one used in *King Kong.* The animals aren't smaller than people, but often larger and more mature.

They live in a sometimes flat dimension; the cameras are happier sliding back and forth than moving in and out. It's sometimes like an old-fashioned slide projector. The landscapes and structures of this world are mannered

and picture-booky. Yet the extraordinary faces of the animals are almost disturbingly human (for animals, of course). We venture into the UnCanny Valley, that no man's land dividing humans from the devised. Above all their fur is so *real.* I've rarely seen such texture in a film.

The story involves a valley somewhere, by which is meant the world, which is ruled by,

Boggis and Bunce and Bean
One fat, one short, one lean
These horrible crooks
So different in looks
Were nonetheless equally mean.

Nor are the animals all saints. Mr. Fox, voiced by George Clooney, was a flourishing chicken thief until times grew risky. Then, like a bootlegger after repeal, he went straight—or, more precisely, into journalism. He's the Walter Winchell of the valley, until he slips back into dining on takeout chicken, taking them out himself. This he keeps a secret from the upright Mrs. Fox (Meryl Streep).

His deception is blown, to everyone's great disappointment, when the fat, short, and lean ones all turn mean ones and declare war. Leading a team of other animals, Mr. Fox starts tunneling like the heroes of *The Great Escape*—but in, rather than out.

These adventures provide the setting for personal drama, as an uncertainty arises between Mr. Fox's callow son, Ash (Jason Schwartzman), and a cousin named Kristofferson (Eric Anderson). Kristofferson is all a fox should be, as with that name how could he not be? He's the family golden child, or fox. Does Mr. Fox admire the cousin more than his son? What kind of pop has he been, anyway?

All of the animals have excellent tailoring, which adds to their stature. They're not forced to wear silly sailor suits or, like Donald Duck, to never put on pants. The art design is a large part of the film's appeal. It stays fresh all the way through. Think back to the color palettes of *Darjeeling* and *Life Aquatic.*

The film's based on the famous children's book by Roald Dahl, which like all of his work has ominous undertones, as if evil can steal in at any moment. These animals aren't catering to anyone in the audience. We get the feeling they're intensely leading their own lives without slowing down for ours.

Like the hero of *Willy Wonka and the Chocolate Factory*, also based on one of his books, the creatures of Dahl's valley seem to know more than they're letting on, perhaps even secrets we don't much want to know. Children, especially, will find things they don't understand and things that scare them. Excellent. A good story for children should suggest a hidden dimension, and that dimension, of course, is the lifetime still ahead them. Six is a little early for a movie to suggest to kids that the case is closed. Oh, what if the kids start crying about words they don't know?— "Mommy, mommy! What's crème brûlée?" Show them, for goodness' sake. They'll thank you for it. Take my word on this.

Fast and Furious ★ ½
PG-13, 107 m., 2009

Vin Diesel (Dominic Toretto), Paul Walker (Brian O'Conner), Michelle Rodriguez (Letty), Jordana Brewster (Mia Toretto), John Ortiz (Campos), Laz Alonso (Fenix). Directed by Justin Lin and produced by Neil Moritz, Michael Fottrell, and Vin Diesel. Screenplay by Chris Morgan.

Fast and Furious is exactly and precisely what you'd expect. Nothing more, unfortunately. You get your cars that are fast and your characters that are furious. You should. They know how to make these movies by now. Producer Neil Moritz is on his fourth, and director Justin Lin on his second in a row. Vin Diesel and other major actors are back from *The Fast and the Furious* (2001). All they left behind were two definite articles.

This is an expertly made action film, by which I mean the special effects are good and the acting is extremely basic. The screenplay rotates these nouns through various assortments of dialogue: Race. Driver(s). Nitro. Meth. Sister. FBI. Border. Dead. Mexico. Murder. Prison. Traffic violations. Tunnel. Muscle car. Import. Plymouth. Funeral. Helicopter(s). Toretto. Ten seconds. Corona. Cocaine.

The plot. Dom Toretto (Vin Diesel) has been in the Dominican Republic for the last six years but now returns to America, where he is a wanted man. Probable charges: vehicular homicide, murder, smuggling, dating an

FBI agent's sister. Reason for return: Letty (Michelle Rodriguez), the girl he loved, has been killed.

After Toretto's arrest all those years ago, he was allowed to escape by FBI agent Brian O'Conner (Paul Walker), for reasons explained in this film. Now Brian is back, on a task force to track down Toretto and the leader of a drug cartel.

This provides a scaffolding on which to hang the body of the movie, which involves a series of chase scenes, fights, explosions, and sexy women who would like to make themselves available to Toretto, to no avail. He is single-minded.

The pre-title chase scene is pretty amazing. Toretto and his group team up in four racing vehicles to pursue a truck hauling not one, not two, not three, but *four* enormous tanks of gasoline. Their method: Toretto drives close behind fourth tank, girl climbs out of sun roof, stands on hood, leaps to ladder on back of tank, climbs on top, runs to front of tank, leaps down, uncouples tank from third one. The reason the girl does this while Toretto drives is, I guess, well, you know what they say about women drivers.

Ever seen a truck hauling four enormous gas containers? I haven't. On a narrow mountain road? With a sudden, steep incline around a curve, when it narrows to one lane? Not me. Why are they going to this trouble? So their buddies can have free gas for a street race that night in L.A. I say let them buy their own damn gas. The race is down city streets with ordinary traffic on them. Then the wrong way on an expressway. Not a cop in sight. Where are the TV news choppers when you want them? This would get huge ratings.

I dunno. I admire the craft involved, but the movie leaves me profoundly indifferent. After three earlier movies in the series, which have been transmuted into video games, why do we need a fourth one? Oh. I just answered my own question.

The Father of My Children ★★★ ½
NO MPAA RATING, 110 m., 2010

Louis-Do de Lencquesaing (Gregoire), Chiara Caselli (Sylvia), Alice de Lencquesaing (Clemence), Alice Gautier (Valentine), Manelle

Driss (Billie), Eric Elmosnino (Serge). Directed by Mia Hansen-Love and produced by Oliver Damian, Philippe Martin, and David Thion. Screenplay by Hansen-Love.

"How much do I owe you?" the producer asks someone on his cell phone. He chuckles. "That much?" He is amused, busy, filled with energy. He handles two phones at a time while threading through Paris traffic and heading for a country weekend with his family. He smokes. He drives. He tells his wife, "I'm almost on the highway." He's stopped by the cops, who ask if he knows why they stopped him. "I have a vague idea," he says.

In the opening sequence, we meet a plausible human being. A French film producer, an honest hustler, a loving father and husband, confident of his powers, enjoying his work. *The Father of My Children* will watch this man come to pieces. It will not be dark melodrama or turgid psychology. It will simply be the story of a good man, well-loved, who runs into a dead end.

The man is named Gregoire (Louis-Do de Lencquesaing). The actor, like many French actors, is good-looking without being improbable. He runs his business in his head. He explains, "I don't work with the kinds of directors who do television." He commits to a filmmaker and goes to the limit for the film not because he has lofty ideas about Art, but because that's the kind of man he is.

In the movie, he is plunging into debt while producing an obscure project of a temperamental auteur not a million miles distant from Lars von Trier. He gets phone reports from the set from his trusted assistant, hears of troublesome actors and bad weather, deals with money and debt, and loves his wife, Sylvia (Chiara Caselli), and three daughters, Clemence (Alice de Lencquesaing), Valentine (Alice Gautier), and Billie (Manelle Driss). Their country house evokes quiet family togetherness, which is the idea, but Gregoire's mind is often elsewhere, trying to find a way out of his troubles.

When very busy men are also essentially good men and working at something worthwhile, they tend to find themselves surrounded by supporters and enablers. Gregoire's office is also a family, in a way, and his employees share

his vision. When calamity strikes, even his wife pitches in to help salvage his dream. The second half of the film is the most touching, because it shows that our lives are not merely our own, but also belong to the events we set in motion.

Louis-Do de Lencquesaing is effective here at *not* going into a manic mode. He runs his business while improvising from moment to moment, he has some plans for getting through, he tries some scenarios, and he doesn't need anyone to tell him when they're not working. I appreciate the ability of the director, Mia Hansen-Love, to allow the situation to develop through observation of her hero, not dialogue explaining everything.

Chiara Caselli, as Gregoire's wife, is, like many wives of workaholic men, better informed on his business than he can imagine. She believes in him, therefore in his hopes, and touchingly relates with the members of his office family as they all try to move things along. And the film gives due attention to the children, particularly Clemence (played by de Lencquesaing's own daughter), who negotiate unfamiliar emotional territory with their mother. The title (in French, *Le pere de mes enfants*) is appropriate.

SPOILER WARNING: The story is said to be inspired by the life of the real-life producer Humbert Balsan, who made Lars von Trier's *Manderlay* (2005). Balsan had considerable success, making nearly seventy films, including three by James Ivory, and even acting for Bresson. He committed suicide when his business imploded.

Note: The film won the special jury prize in the Un Certain Regard section of Cannes 2009.

Fear(s) of the Dark ★ ★ ½
NO MPAA RATING, 85 m., 2008

With the voices of: Aure Atika, Arthur H, Guillaume Depardieu, Nicole Garcia, Christian Hincker, Lino Hincker, Melaura Honnay, Amelie Lerma, Florence Maury, Amaury Smets, Brigitte Sy, Laurent Van Der Rest, Charlotte Vermeil, and Andreas Vuillet. Directed by Blutch, Charles Burns, Marie Caillou, Pierre di Sciullo, Lorenzo Mattotti, and Richard McGuire, and produced by Valerie Schermann and Christophe Jankovic. Screenplay by Blutch,

Burns, di Sciullo, Jerry Kramsky, Michel Pirus, and Romain Slocombe.

Ideally, a film should flow smoothly into the mind, with no elbows sticking out. From the time some months ago when I first heard of *Fear(s) of the Dark,* I was annoyed by the *(s).* This is ridiculous, I know. Such a detail has nothing to do with the quality of a movie. But let me ask you: What does *(s)* do for you? Or *Peur(s) du Noir* in French? Less than nothing? Yes.

Oh, well. The film is an anthology by six animators. It involves untitled shorts, punctuated by segments by the graphic artist Blutch featuring an aristocrat holding savage hounds straining at a leash. Each time a hound breaks free, it leaps upon the next story, and occasionally a victim. Some of the stories are pretty good, especially Charles Burns's tale involving a nasty and vaguely humanoid insect that burrows under the skin. The sight of the creature trapped in a jar is unsettling. The story reminded me of Guillermo del Toro's *Cronos* (1993), and indeed he is cited on the Web site as a champion of this film.

Richard McGuire has an effective haunted house story that reminded me a little of *Ugetsu* in the way it uses spirits who seem to possess the space the hero wanders into. Japanese echoes stir also in a story by Marie Caillou, about a bug-eyed young girl who is a student trapped in a nightmare.

Despite the title and the ads, this is not really a horror movie but more of a demonstration of the skills of the animators. The segments are like calling cards. Younger horror movie fans will not much identify with it. The hateful hounds don't supply a linking device so much as a separation. And although I admired most of the animation, during the film I found myself reminded of the four ghostly episodes of the classic Japanese ghost story anthology *Kwaidan* (1964), so hauntingly beautiful, which combined live action with frankly employed sound stage sets.

Note: Guillaume Depardieu's voice-over work here represents one of the final credits for the son of Gerard and Elisabeth Depardieu, who died October 13, 2008, of pneumonia at thirty-seven. Born into French acting royalty, he had a sad life, including a 2003 suspended sentence for an armed threat, and a leg amputation resulting from a motorcycle accident. His most interesting film was Pola X (1999), an exceedingly strange modern adaptation of Herman Melville's Pierre.

Fifty Dead Men Walking ★★★
R, 118 m., 2009

Ben Kingsley (Fergus), Jim Sturgess (Martin), Rose McGowan (Grace), Kevin Zegers (Sean), Natalie Press (Lara). Directed by Kari Skogland and produced by Skogland, Stephen Hegyes, Peter La Terriere, and Shawn Williamson. Screenplay by Skogland, inspired by the book by Martin McGartland and Nicholas Davies.

Belfast, 1988. The height of the Troubles. British troops occupy the city and are at war with the Irish Republican Army. The British want to retain Northern Ireland as part of the United Kingdom. The IRA considers them invaders. Martin McGartland doesn't much care.

Like many young criminals, he is devoutly nonpolitical. He's a two-bit hustler, stealing and reselling clothing or whatever else he can move. A wise guy, he moves confidently on the mean streets. McGartland (Jim Sturgess) doesn't like the British, but when the IRA breaks his friend's legs with a baseball bat, he likes that even less.

He's recruited by Fergus (Ben Kingsley), an officer in the Special Branch of the British police, to become a double agent, an informer. Fergus has noticed how he moves through Belfast, known to the IRA, unintimidated by the British troops. Both sides already think they know who he is.

Informing on the IRA was, of course, a nearly certain death sentence. It seems incredible that anyone would take such a risk, and very few did. McGartland's information is credited with saving the lives of at least fifty men, and you'd think the IRA might have noticed parallels between their assassination operations and McGartland's participation, but apparently not. Only at the end of the film is there a situation where his role will be betrayed, and by then he already realizes that he will be living for the rest of his life in hiding.

The Troubles were a messy business. The

171

British troops were acting under orders that not all of them necessarily appreciated. They were not fighting in a foreign land, but against those who spoke and lived much as they did. The Protestant/Catholic hatred involved also muddied the water. To step into the middle of this is almost a foolhardy act, and *Fifty Dead Men Walking* never really explains McGartland's decision. Still, it is a fact that he made it, even with the risk to his girlfriend and their child.

The performance of Jim Sturgess as McGartland helps place his decision into the day-by-day process of acting on it. He meets clandestinely with Fergus, rises in the trust of the IRA, is able to use information he gets from Fergus to enhance his position. The two men become not friends, exactly, but mutually dependent, and as the net grows tighter toward the end, their dependence takes on an urgent desperation.

The writer and director is Kari Skogland, a young Canadian whose previous film, *The Stone Angel* (2007), could not be more different. It stars Ellen Burstyn as an old lady who runs away from the children who want to place her in a nursing home. In this film, Skogland, like Kathryn Bigelow does in *The Hurt Locker,* demolishes the notion that women can't direct action.

This movie is based on real events and a book written by McGartland and Nicholas Davies. It presents the usual disclaimers that "some of the events, characters, and scenes in the film have been changed." And McGartland himself has made a statement from hiding that he doesn't endorse the film and it was "inspired by," not "adapted from" the book. Does this reflect his hope that the IRA won't take it personally? Setting entirely aside the accuracy of the film, the IRA still has him marked for death, and indeed there was an attempt on his life in Canada ten years after he fled. He's still out there somewhere.

Fighting ★ ★ ★
PG-13, 105 m., 2009

Channing Tatum (Shawn MacArthur), Terrence Howard (Harvey Boarden), Luis Guzman (Martinez), Zulay Henao (Zulay Valez), Brian White (Evan Hailey), Altagracia Guzman (Lila).

Directed by Dito Montiel and produced by Kevin Misher. Screenplay by Montiel and Robert Munic.

I like the way the personalities are allowed to upstage the plot in *Fighting*, a routine three-act fight story that creates uncommonly interesting characters. Set in the streets of Manhattan, Brooklyn, and the Bronx, involving a naive kid from Alabama and a mild-mannered hustler from Chicago, it takes place in a secret world of street fighting for high cash stakes. Do rich guys really bet hundreds of thousands on a closed-door bare-knuckle brawl? I dunno, but it's cheaper than filming a prize-fight arena.

Channing Tatum plays Shawn, whose dad was a wrestling coach near Birmingham. Terrence Howard plays Harvey, whom everybody seems to know. Shawn is a hot-tempered kid not doing very well at selling shoddy merchandise on the sidewalks. Harvey is soft-spoken, with a gentle voice and an almost passive personal style even though he works as an illegal fight promoter. He sees Shawn in a fight, recruits him, and lines up fights with $5,000, $10,000 and finally $100,000 purses.

He does this with stunning speed, even though at the first fight no one has ever seen Shawn before. The movie offers that and other problems of plausibility and logic, but I don't care about them because the director, Dito Montiel, doesn't. Possibly hired to make a genre picture, he provides the outline and requirements, and then focuses on his characters. Terrence Howard's Harvey is the most intriguing: He's too laid back to be in the profession, so philosophical that he even faces what seems to be his own inevitable murder with calm resignation. He knows his world, is known in it, moves through it, yet seems aloof from it.

Channing Tatum, convincing as a former school athlete (which he was), quickly agrees to the fights, even against terrifying opponents. But *Fighting* invests much more feeling in his tentative relationship with Zulay (Zulay Henao), a single mom who works as a waitress in a private club where the private fight world hangs out. He approaches her like a well-raised southern boy would, politely, respectfully.

This arouses greater interest because of the screen presence of Zulay Henao, who sidesteps countless hazards suggested by her character and makes her sweet, sensuous, and perceptive. And then look at Altagracia Guzman as Lila, playing Zulay's elder relative (grandmother?), who was a great audience favorite as she guarded her beloved from the threat of a male predator. The way her talent is employed in the film is an ideal use of a supporting actress.

Listen also to the dialogue by Robert Munic and Montiel, which is far above formula boilerplate and creates the illusion that the characters might actually be saying it in the moment. An extended flirtation between Zulay and Shawn isn't hurried through for a bedroom payoff, but grows sweeter and more tender the longer it continues. This scene illustrates my theory that it is more exciting to wonder if you are about to be kissed than it is to be kissed.

Fighting is not a cinematic breakthrough, but it is much more involving than I thought it would be. The ads foreground the action, no doubt because that's what sells. The film transcends the worldview that produced the ad campaign and gives audiences a well-crafted, touching experience. Sometimes you can feel it when an audience is a little surprised by how deeply they've become involved.

Filth and Wisdom ★ ★
NO MPAA RATING, 81 m., 2008

Eugene Hutz (A.K.), Holly Weston (Holly), Vicky McClure (Juliette), Richard E. Grant (Professor Flynn), Stephen Graham (Harry Beechman), Inder Manocha (Sardeep). Directed by Madonna and produced by Nicola Doring. Screenplay by Madonna and Dan Cadan.

Aren't we all way beyond being shocked by sexual fetishes simply because they exist? Haven't we all stopped thinking, "Ohmigod! That's a guy in drag!" or "Ohmigod! That's a dominatrix!" or "Ohmigod! She's tattooed!" or having any kind of reaction to body piercing, which no longer even qualifies as a fetish, except when practiced on body areas we are unlikely to see anyway?

We live in a time, a sad time, I think, when some fetishes are even marketed to children. Consider the dominatrix Barbie doll. Of course, films that are *about* sexual fetishes can be fascinating. Remember *Secretary,* about S&M, or *The Crying Game,* about transvestism, or *Kissed,* about necrophilia. All very good films. But in simply observing the fact of a fetish, the old frisson is gone. I mention this because Madonna still gets intrigued, I guess, simply by regarding a stripper sliding down a pole.

Filth and Wisdom, Madonna's directing debut, is a pointless exercise in "shocking" behavior, involving characters in London so shallow that the most sympathetic is the lecherous Indian dentist (Inder Manocha) who is supposed to be a villain, maybe. The central character is A.K. (Eugene Hutz), a rock singer who moonlights as a male dominator and will dress up like a ringmaster and whip you if you pay the big bucks. He is a fountain of wise little axioms, of which one is actually profound: "The problem with treating your body like a cash register is that you always feel empty."

A.K. is the landlord for flatmates Holly (Holly Weston) and Juliette (Vicky McClure), and also their unpaid adviser, who steers Holly into stripping at a lap-dance sleaze pit. Madonna thinks it's funny, or sad, or something, that Holly is not too good at hanging upside-down from the pole and erotically sliding down it.

I saw my first strip show at the old Follies Burlesque on South State Street one day after I moved to Chicago, and I interviewed the immortal Tempest Storm when she appeared here. The strippers at that time performed slowly and seductively, and it was a "tease." Today's strippers leap on stage already almost naked and perform contortions that gotta hurt. Some are so gifted they can get one boob going clockwise and the other counterclockwise.

Ugh. They're erotic only to men who enjoy seeing women humiliate themselves. I was but a callow youth from a small town amid the soy fields, but, reader, I confess I idealized some of them. I haven't attended a strip show in years and years, and for that I am grateful. Oh, there was that time we were in Bangkok and saw the show with the Ping Pong balls. Who could think of sex during such a skillful display?

But I wander. *Filth and Wisdom* also places a blot on the record of Richard E. Grant, who brought snarkiness to perfection in *Withnail and I* and *How to Get Ahead in Advertising*. Here he's made to play an elderly, blind, gay, depressed poet who is smiling on the outside, and you know the rest. For what purpose? To help Madonna fill the endless eighty-one-minute running time with characters we don't care about, who don't care about one another except when dictated to by the screenplay, in a story nobody cares about. This is a very deeply noncaring movie. I liked Hutz when he sang. I imagine Gene Shalit ate his heart out when he saw Hutz's moustache.

Finding Amanda ★ ★ ½
R, 90 m., 2008

Matthew Broderick (Taylor Peters), Brittany Snow (Amanda), Steve Coogan (Jerry), Maura Tierney (Lorraine Mendon), Peter Facinelli (Greg). Directed by Peter Tolan and produced by Richard Heller and Wayne Allan Rice. Screenplay by Tolan.

A quietly perfect scene in *Finding Amanda* involves Taylor, the hero, arriving at a Las Vegas casino. Without overstating the case, the film makes it clear that Taylor is well-known here: The doorman, the bellboy, even the room maid greet him by name. That may be one of the danger signals of a gambling addiction. Another one may be taking a check from out of the middle of your wife's checkbook.

Taylor (Matthew Broderick) is indeed an addicted gambler. He claims to be recovering. Hasn't placed a bet since . . . earlier today. He is also, over a longer span of time, a recovering alcoholic and drug addict. He works as a well-paid writer for a TV sitcom that everybody seems to agree is terrible and lives in a comfortable home with his comely wife, Lorraine (Maura Tierney), who is fed up to here with his gambling and has called an attorney.

That sets the stage for the central drama of the film. Taylor's twenty-year-old niece, Amanda (Brittany Snow) has left home, gone to Vegas and become a "dancer," which, we learn, is a euphemism for "stripper," which is a euphemism for "hooker." The girl's mother is begging him to intervene. Taylor is happy to oblige, since it means a trip to Vegas, where even the room maid, etc.

And so commences a peculiar film that is really two films fighting to occupy the same space. The first film, the one of the "quietly perfect scene," is about Taylor, his addictions, his emotions, and Jerry (Steve Coogan), a host at the casino. The second film, which has no perfect scenes, is about his niece, her life, and her boyfriend, Greg (Peter Facinelli). If there were more of the first story line and less of the second, this would be a better film. If there were none of the second story line, it might really amount to something. But there we are.

Broderick is splendid as the gambler. He knows, as many addicts do, that the addictive personality is very inward, however much acting-out might take place. He plays Taylor as a man constantly taking inventory of himself: How does he feel? Could he feel better? Can he take a chance? Does he feel lucky? Will one little bet, or drink, really hurt? How about two? Taylor evolves as a sympathetic man, one to be pitied (as his wife knows, although she is running low on pity). He is likable, intelligent, decent, really does hope to help his niece, and has several monkeys scrambling for space on his back.

Brittany Snow (Amber Von Tussle in *Hairspray*) does what she can with the role of Amanda as written, but that's just the problem: how it's written. She has it all figured out how she can have a nice car, house, clothes, and boyfriend while hooking, which her old job at the International House of Pancakes did not make possible. Why she felt she had to move to Vegas to work at IHOP remains unexplained. Also unexplained, in my mind, is how she became a hooker (her "explanation" is harrowing and intended as heartbreaking, but sounds more like the story of someone looking for trouble). There is also the matter of the boyfriend, Greg. I know such men exist and someone has to date them, but why Amanda? This guy is such a scummy lowlife, he gives pimps a bad name. Why does she support him and endure his blatant cheating?

You will not find a convincing answer in this film. What you will find is a nicely modulated performance by Steve Coogan (*24-Hour Party People*) as Jerry, the casino's host, who knows Taylor from way back, extends him credit against his better judgment, knows an addictive gambler when he sees one and is looking at one. He makes Jerry not the heavy and not the comic foil, but an associate in a circular process of betting and losing and winning a little and betting and losing a lot, and so on. How Taylor's luck changes, and what happens, is for me entirely believable.

Finding Amanda will be followed closely in theaters by *Diminished Capacity*, a film starring Broderick as a newspaper columnist who goes to his hometown to help his uncle (Alan Alda). Broderick is just right in both films, acting his way under, over, around, and occasionally straight through the material. Now we need him in a better screenplay.

Fired Up ★
PG-13, 89 m., 2009

Nicholas D'Agosto (Shawn Colfax), Eric Christian Olsen (Nick Brady), Sarah Roemer (Carly), Molly Sims (Diora), Danneel Harris (Bianca), David Walton (Dr. Rick), Adhir Kalyan (Brewster), AnnaLynne McCord (Gwyneth), Juliette Goglia (Poppy), Philip Baker Hall (Coach Byrnes), Hayley Marie Norman (Angela). Directed by Will Gluck and produced by Matthew Gross, Peter Jaysen, and Charles Weinstock. Screenplay by Freedom Jones.

After the screening of *Fired Up*, one of my colleagues grimly observed that *Dead Man* was a better cheerleader movie. That was, you will recall, the 1995 Western starring Johnny Depp, Robert Mitchum, Billy Bob Thornton, and Iggy Pop. I would give almost anything to see them on a cheerleading squad. Here is a movie that will do for cheerleading what *Friday the 13th* did for summer camp.

The story involves two callow and witless high school football players, Shawn and Nick, who don't want to attend summer football training camp in the desert. They also want to seduce the school cheerleaders, so they decide to attend cheerleading camp, ha ha. Their high school is in Hinsdale, Illinois, whose taxpayers will be surprised to learn the school team trains in the desert just like the Cubs, but will be even more surprised to learn the entire film was shot in California. And they will be puzzled about why many of the cheers involve

chants of the letters *F!U!*—which stand for *Fired Up*, you see.

Oh, is this movie bad. The characters relentlessly attack one another with the forced jollity of minimum-wage workers pressing you with free cheese samples at the supermarket. Every conversation involves a combination of romantic misunderstandings, double entendres, and flirtation that is just sad. No one in the movie has an idea in their bubbly little brains. No, not even Philip Baker Hall, who plays the football coach in an eruption of obligatory threats.

The plot involves a cheerleading competition along the lines of the one in *Bring It On* (2000), the *Citizen Kane* of cheerleader movies. That movie involved genuinely talented cheerleaders. This one involves ungainly human pyramids and a lot of uncoordinated jumping up and down. Faithful readers will recall that I often ask why the bad guys in movies wear matching black uniforms. They do in this one, too. The villains here are the Panther cheerleading squad. How many teams play in all black?

I could tell you about Carly, Bianca, Gwyneth, Poppy, and the other sexy cheerleaders, but I couldn't stir myself to care. There is an old rule in the theater: If the heroine coughs in the first act, she has to die in the third. In this movie, the cutest member of the squad is Angela (Hayley Marie Norman). She also has the nicest smile and the best personality and is on screen early and often, so I kept expecting her big scene, but no: She seems destined to be the cheerleader's cheerleader, pepping them up, cheering them on, smiling, applauding, holding up the bottom of the pyramid, laughing at funny lines, encouraging, bouncing in sync, and projecting with every atom of her being the attitude *You go, girls!* You've got a problem when you allow the most intriguing member of the cast to appear in that many scenes and never deal with her. That is not the movie's fatal flaw, however. Its flaw is that I was thinking about things like that.

Fish Tank ★★★★
NO MPAA RATING, 123 m., 2010

Katie Jarvis (Mia), Michael Fassbender (Connor), Kierston Wareing (Joanne), Rebecca

Griffiths (Tyler), Harry Treadaway (Billy). Directed by Andrea Arnold and produced by Kees Kasander. Screenplay by Arnold.

Andrea Arnold's piercing *Fish Tank* is the portrait of an angry, isolated fifteen-year-old girl who is hurtling toward a lifetime of misery. She is so hurt and lonely we pity her. Her mother barely even sees her. The film takes place in a bleak British public housing estate and in the streets and fields around it. There is no suggestion of a place this girl can go to find help, care, or encouragement.

The girl is Mia, played by Katie Jarvis in a harrowing display of hostility. She's been thrown out of school, is taunted as a weirdo by boys her age, converses with her mother and sister in screams, and retreats to an empty room to play her music and dance alone. She drinks what little booze she can get her hands on.

And where is her mother? Right there at home, all the time. Joanne (Kierston Wareing) looks so young she may have had Mia at Mia's age. Joanne is shorter, busty, dyed blond, a chain-smoker, a party girl. The party is usually in her living room. One day she brings home Connor (Michael Fassbender), a good-looking guy who seems nice enough. Mia screams at him, too, but it's a way of getting attention.

Joanne seems happiest when Mia isn't at home. The girl wanders the streets and gets in a fight when she tries to free a horse chained in a barren lot near some shabby mobile homes. She has no friends. She surfs in an Internet café, goes to an audition for sexy dancers, breaks into a house at random.

One day differs from the routine. Connor takes Mia, her mom, and her little sister, Tyler (Rebecca Griffiths), on a drive to the country. This isn't an idyllic picnic; they simply park in a field and hike to a river, Joanne staying with the car. Connor takes Mia in wading ("I can't swim"). Walking back barefoot she gets a ride on his back and rests her chin on his shoulder and what was in the air from the first is now manifest.

Some reviews call Connor a pedophile. I think he's more of an immoral opportunist. *Fish Tank* in any event isn't so much about sex as about the helpless spiral Mia is going through. The film has two fraught but ambiguous scenes—one when she goes to Connor's home, another involving a young girl—that we can make fairly obvious assumptions about. But the movie doesn't spell them out; Arnold sees everything through Mia's eyes and never steps outside to explain things from any other point of view. She knows who the young girl is, and we are left to assume. Whatever she thinks after the visit to Connor's house we are not specifically told. The film so firmly identifies with Mia that there may even be a possibility Joanne is better than the slutty monster we see. A slim possibility, to be sure.

In a film so tightly focused, all depends on Katie Jarvis's performance. There is truth in it. She lives on an Essex housing estate like the one in the movie, and she was discovered by Arnold while in a shouting match with her boyfriend at the Tilbury train station, which is seen in the movie. Now eighteen, she gave birth to a daughter conceived when she was sixteen.

We can fear, but we can't say, that she was heading for a life similar to the one Mia seems doomed to. Her casting in this film, however, led to Cannes, the Jury Prize, and contracts with British and American agents. She is a powerful acting presence, flawlessly convincing here. And Arnold, who won an Oscar for her shattering short film *Wasp* (2003), also about a neglectful alcoholic mother, deserves comparison with British director Ken Loach.

500 Days of Summer ★★★★
PG-13, 95 m., 2009

Joseph Gordon-Levitt (Tom Hansen), Zooey Deschanel (Summer Finn), Geoffrey Arend (McKenzie), Matthew Gray Gubler (Paul), Chloe Grace Moretz (Rachel Hansen), Clark Gregg (Vance), Rachel Boston (Alison), Minka Kelly (Girl). Directed by Marc Webb and produced by Jessica Tuchinsky, Mark Waters, Mason Novick, and Steven J. Wolfe. Screenplay by Scott Neustadter and Michael H. Weber.

We never remember in chronological order, especially when we're going back over a failed romance. We start near the end, and then hop around between the times that were good and the times that left pain. People always say "start at the beginning," but we didn't know at the time it was the beginning. *500 Days of Summer* is a movie that works that way.

Some say they're annoyed by the way it begins on Day 488 or whatever and then jumps around, providing utterly unhelpful data labels: "Day 1," "Day 249." Movies are supposed to reassure us that events unfold in an orderly procession. But Tom remembers Summer as a series of joys and bafflements. What kind of woman likes you perfectly sincerely and has no one else in her life but is *not* interested in ever getting married?

Zooey Deschanel is a good choice to play such a woman. I can't imagine her playing a clinging vine. Too ornery. As Summer, she sees Tom with a level gaze and is who she is. It's Tom's bad luck she is sweet and smart and beautiful—it's not an act. She is always scrupulously honest with him. She is her own person, and Tom can't have her. Have you known someone like that? In romance, we believe what we want to believe. That's the reason *500 Days of Summer* is so appealing.

Tom (Joseph Gordon-Levitt) is in love with Summer from the moment he sees her. His thoughts on love may not run as deeply as, say, those of the Romantic poets. He writes greeting cards, and you suspect he may believe his own cards. It's amazing people get paid for a job like that. I could do it: "Love is a rose, and you are its petals." Summer is his new assistant. He needs an assistant in this job? She likes his looks and makes her move one day over the Xerox machine.

Can he accept that she simply likes him for now, not for forever? The movie, which is a delightful comedy, alive with invention, is about Tom wrestling with that reality. The director, Marc Webb, seems to be casting about for templates from other movies to help him tell this story; that's not desperation but playfulness. There's a little black-and-white, a little musical number, a little Fellini, which is always helpful in evoking a man in the act of yearning. Tom spends this movie in the emotional quandary of Mastroianni in *La Dolce Vita*, his hand always outstretched toward his inaccessible fantasies.

Summer remains mysterious all through the film, perhaps because we persist with Tom in expecting her to cave in. When we realize she is not required to in this movie because it's not playing by the Hollywood rules, we perk up; anything could happen. The kaleidoscopic time structure breaks the shackles of the three-act grid and thrashes about with the freedom of romantic confusion.

One thing men love is to instruct women. If a woman wants to enchant a man, she is wise to play his pupil. Men fall for this. Tom set out in life to be an architect, not a poet of greeting cards. He and Summer share the same favorite view of Los Angeles (one you may not have seen before), and he conducts for her an architectural tour. This is fun not because we get to see wonderful buildings, but because so rarely in the movies do we find characters arguing for their aesthetic values. What does your average character played by an A-list star believe about truth and beauty? Has Jason Bourne ever gone to a museum on his day off?

Joseph Gordon-Levitt has acted in a lot of movies, ranging from one of the *Halloween* sequels to the indie gem *Brick*. He comes into focus here playing a believable, likable guy, hopeful, easily disappointed, a little Tom Hanksian. He is strong enough to expect love, weak enough to be hurt. Zooey Deschanel evokes that ability in some women to madden you with admiration while never seeming to give it the slightest thought. She also had that quality in the overlooked *Gigantic* (2008), although the movie's peculiar supporting characters obscured it.

Tom opens the film by announcing it will not be your typical love story. Are you like me, and when you realize a movie is on autopilot you get impatient with it? How long can the characters pretend they don't know how the story will end? Here is a rare movie that begins by telling us how it will end, and is about how the hero has no idea why.

Note: The movie's poster insists the title is (500) Days of Summer. *Led by* Variety, *every single film critic I could find has simply ignored that. Good for them.*

Five Minutes of Heaven ★★★
NO MPAA RATING, 89 m., 2009

Liam Neeson (Alistair), James Nesbitt (Joe), Anamaria Marinca (Vika), Richard Dormer (Michael), Mark Davison (Young Alistair), Kevin O'Neill (Young Joe), Gerard Jordan (Jim).

Directed by Oliver Hirschbiegel and produced by Eoin O'Callaghan and Stephen Wright. Screenplay by Guy Hibbert.

One of the characteristics of films about the Troubles in Northern Ireland, a period when members of the Protestant Ulster Volunteer Force and the Catholic Irish Republican Army were mounting assassinations against one another, is that we never see anyone at church, or in prayer. Their hatred was not theological but tribal. The Protestants were allied with the British, who consider Northern Ireland a part of the United Kingdom, and the IRA called for the unification of all Ireland. Protestants feared Catholic majority rule.

The dispute inflamed passions on both sides. Consider seventeen-year-old Alistair Little, who wants to gain stature within the UVF and agrees to kill a nineteen-year-old Catholic dock worker because of sectarian rivalry over jobs on the docks. He's given a gun, driven to the man's house, shoots him three times through the glass of the front door, and only then notices a small boy standing transfixed on the sidewalk. This is Joe, the victim's little brother. Alistair, wearing a black hood, regards him for many seconds, spares his life, and then hurries away.

Five Seconds of Heaven leads toward an eventual meeting of these two men thirty-three years later. They are being driven in separate cars to a confrontation arranged by a reality TV show, and as they drive and talk with their drivers, we see in flashbacks what led up to this day. Alistair (Liam Neeson) served twelve years in prison, repented of the murder, now works in conflict resolution. Joe (James Nesbitt) spent a tortured youth being blamed by his mother for his brother's death. "Why didn't you save him?" she screams, as if there was any way the little boy could have.

This story is inspired by real events; the filmmakers, director Oliver Hirschbiegel and writer Guy Hibbert, spent much time talking with the actual Alistair and Joe, who in life have never met. Joe has spent years talking of the "five minutes of heaven" it would mean to him to kill Alistair in revenge.

The film looks for a resolution that has not, perhaps could not, taken place in life. It is very well acted, by Neeson as a large, solemn,

reformed man, and by Nesbitt as a sweaty, desperately unhappy one. Because of their acting, the intercut scenes in the two cars are more involving than they might have been. Knowing that Nesbitt is bringing a knife to the meeting staged for television creates considerable tension.

It is the reality show itself that feels wrong. The entire genre is contemptible to some degree. It sidesteps the cathartic function of drama by preying on the lives of real people. We are asked not to identify but to be voyeurs—to be entertained by another's misfortune.

What are the producers of the TV show in *Five Minutes of Heaven* hoping for? If Joe were to murder Alistair on camera, that would certainly be unplanned, but it would make sensational "tragic" footage.

Joe considers the whole project simply a convenience for placing him within striking range. What does Alistair think? If he is indeed the international expert in conflict resolution portrayed in the film, wouldn't he consider the program a cheap stunt? Yes, he deeply regrets the crime he committed against Joe's family. But is there no other way to express this?

The scenes involving the taping of the show nevertheless work on their own terms, not least because of the performance of Anamaria Marinca as an assistant producer assigned to handle *talent*. You may recall her as the best friend in *4 Months, 3 Weeks, and 2 Days*, the Romanian film that won Cannes 2007. Her fraught scenes show an active sympathy at work and draw out the trembling Joe.

It is on the levels of acting and drama that the film works, and also in showing how religious "convictions" can be reduced to completely unspiritual hatred. A final confrontation between the two men is unlikely but well handled. Neeson's ultimate appeal to Joe is effective. But the film seems based on the fabrication of unlikely events. It is true that Alistair and Joe have never met. I learn that if they ever do, Joe would still hope for his five minutes of heaven.

Flame and Citron ★★★
NO MPAA RATING, 132 m., 2009

Thure Lindhardt (Flammen), Mads Mikkelsen (Citronen), Stine Stengade (Ketty Selmer), Peter

Mygind (Aksel Winther), Mille Hoffmeyer Lehfeldt (Bodil), Christian Berkel (Karl Heinz Hoffmann). Directed by Ole Christian Madsen and produced by Lars Bredo Rahbek. Screenplay by Madsen and Lars K. Andersen.

Murder takes an emotional toll, no matter how righteous the motivation. We might all be capable of pulling the trigger on Hitler, but would we reach the point when our willingness to kill others runs out? What if you're a Danish Resistance fighter, executing your fellow countrymen who are Nazi collaborators? I suppose the purpose of war is to provide a reality in which killing is objectified.

Flame and Citron takes place in Copenhagen in 1944, as the approaching Nazi defeat looms ever more clearly. It involves a two-man Resistance hit squad: the red-headed Flame (Thure Lindhardt) and the introverted, nervous, sweaty Citron (Mads Mikkelsen, who played the Bond villain Le Chiffre in the 2006 *Casino Royale*). Flame is empowered by killing, even grows reckless with shadings of omnipotence. For Citron, their lives, lived always on the run and in hiding, gnaw at his soul. The more Flame takes bold chances, the more Citron feels dread.

At first they kill men. Eventually, they become capable of killing women. There comes a point when even Flame is moved to make a small gesture of mercy toward a victim. By now they are in so deep the only way out is ahead.

The SS knows their identities. It has their descriptions. There is a foolhardy scene where they enter a bar filled with Nazis but escape detection. Flame seems almost oblivious to the giveaway of his hair color. They kill a great many collaborators, mostly by simply walking up to them and shooting them dead. The day comes when they kill a German officer. They were already living under a death sentence, but that seems to bring their execution date closer. The Nazi dragnet is under the command of Karl Heinz Hoffmann (Christian Berkel), a complex man with an unsettling way of drawing out the ambiguities of the situation.

It seems a simple matter, in outline: You are a patriot, you are a Dane with hatred of the Nazi occupation, you kill Danes who are collaborating, they have it coming to them.

Flame is born to the task. Citron feels they are in the right, but he is disintegrating. And who can they trust? Who is giving their orders? What if there has been insidious infiltration and their skills are being misused? Is romance an unacceptable danger in this world?

Flame and Citron, based on the lives of two actual Resistance heroes, is a taut, handsome production—the most expensive Danish film to date—and it looks like a film noir, as indeed the costumes, cars, guns, and fugitives force it to. The director, Ole Christian Madsen, has said he was influenced by *Army of Shadows,* Jean-Pierre Melville's film about the French Resistance. Melville was himself a Resistance fighter and knew the life from inside. It is a messy business, killing your civilian countrymen. Better a uniformed man, speaking another language, who hopes to kill you. And in a world of duplicity and disguise, whose motives are pure?

Note: Army of Shadows *is in the Great Movies Collection at rogerebert.com.*

Flash of Genius ★ ★ ★
PG-13, 120 m., 2008

Greg Kinnear (Robert Kearns), Lauren Graham (Phyllis Kearns), Dermot Mulroney (Gil Previck), Alan Alda (Gregory Lawson). Directed by Marc Abraham and produced by Gary Barber, Roger Birnbaum, and Michael Lieber. Screenplay by Philip Railsback, based on the *New Yorker* article by John Seabrook.

Why do corporations tend to be greedy? I suspect it's because their executives are paid millions and millions to maximize profits, minimize salaries, and slash benefits that cut into the bottom line. Sometimes this can be taken to comic-opera extremes, as when the (now) convicted thief David Radler was stealing millions from the *Sun-Times* and actually turned off the escalators to save on electricity. I guess that helps explain why the Ford Motor Co., followed by Chrysler, stole the secret of the intermittent windshield wiper from a little guy named Robert Kearns.

Why bother? Why not just pay the guy royalties? Simple: Because Ford thought it could get away with it. He was only a college professor. They had teams of high-priced lawyers with infinite patience. They risked having the legal fees cost them more than the patent rights, but what the hell. You can't go around encouraging these pipsqueaks.

I am aware that I sound just like a liberal, but at this point in history, I am sick and tired of giant corporations running roughshod over decent people—cutting their wages, polluting their work environment, cutting or denying them health care, forcing them to work unpaid overtime, busting their unions, and other crimes we have never heard George Bush denounce while he was cutting corporate taxes. I'm sure lower taxes help corporations to function more profitably. But why is that considered progress when many workers live in borderline poverty and executives have pissing contests over who has the biggest stock options?

But enough. I have *Flash of Genius* to review. Yes, I am agitated. I am writing during days of economic meltdown, after Wall Street raped Main Street while the Bush ideology held it down. Believe me, I could go on like this all day. But consider the case of Robert Kearns, played here touchingly by Greg Kinnear. He was a professor of engineering, a decent, unremarkable family man, and had a *Eureka!* moment: Why did windshield wipers only go on and off? Why couldn't they reflect existing conditions, as the human eyelid does?

Working in his basement, Kearns put together the first intermittent wiper from off-the-shelf components and tested it in a fish tank. He patented it in 1967. He demonstrated it to Ford but wouldn't tell them how it worked until he had a deal. After Ford ripped it off and reneged on the deal, he sued in 1982. Thirteen years later, he won thirty million dollars in a settlement where the automakers didn't have to admit deliberate theft.

Flash of Genius tells this story in faithful and often moving detail. If it has a handicap, it's that Kearns was not a colorful character—more of a very stubborn man with tunnel vision. He alienates his family, angers his business partner (Dermot Mulroney), and sorely tries the patience of his lawyer (Alan Alda), whom he is not afraid to accuse of incompetence. Was his victory worth it? The movie asks us to decide. For Robert Kearns, as depicted in this movie, it was. If he had not

been obsessively obstinate, Ford would have been counting its stolen dollars.

The movie covers events taking place from 1953 to 1982. The wiper was hard to perfect. There are some gaps along the way, and we don't get to know his wife (Lauren Graham) and his family very well, nor perhaps does he. He calls his kids his "board of directors," but they mostly resign, only to return loyally in the end. Alda gives the film's strongest performance. Kinnear, often a player of light comedy, does a convincing job of making this quiet, resolute man into a giant-slayer.

Todd McCarthy of *Variety* notices an odd fact: Right to the end, Kearns always drove Fords. He remained loyal. I remember those days. You were a Ford, a Dodge, a Cadillac, or a Studebaker family, and that's what you remained. It was nice when sensible wipers were added to the package. Thanks, professor.

Food, Inc. ★ ★ ★ ½
PG, 94 m., 2009

A documentary directed by Robert Kenner and produced by Kenner and Elise Pearlstein.

The next time you tuck into a nice T-bone, reflect that it probably came from a cow that spent much of its life standing in manure reaching above its ankles. That's true even if you're eating it at a pricy steakhouse. Most of the beef in America comes from four suppliers.

The next time you admire a plump chicken breast, consider how it got that way. The egg-to-death life of a chicken is now six weeks. They're grown in cages too small for them to move, in perpetual darkness to make them sleep more and quarrel less. They're fattened so fast they can't stand up or walk. Their entire lives they are trapped in the dark, worrying.

All of this is overseen by a handful of giant corporations that control the growth, processing, and sale of food in this country. Take Monsanto, for example. It has a patent on a custom gene for soybeans. Its customers are *forbidden* to save their own soybean seed for use next year. They have to buy new seed from Monsanto. If you grow soybeans outside their jurisdiction but some of the altered genes sneak into your crop from your neighbor's fields, Monsanto will investigate you for patent infringement. They know who the outsiders are and send out inspectors to snoop in their fields.

Food labels depict an idyllic, pastoral image of American farming. The sun rises and sets behind reassuring red barns and white frame farmhouses, and contented cows graze under the watch of the Marlboro Cowboy. This is a fantasy. The family farm is largely a thing of the past. When farmland comes on the market, the corporations outbid local buyers. Your best hope of finding real food grown by real farmers is at a local farmers' market. It's not entirely a matter of "organic" produce, although usually it is. It's a matter of food grown nearby, within the last week.

Remember how years ago you didn't hear much about E. coli? Now it seems to be in the news once a month. People are even getting E. coli poisoning from spinach and lettuce, for heaven's sake. Why are Americans getting fatter? A lot of it has to do with corn syrup, which is the predominant sweetener. When New Coke failed and Coke Classic returned, it wasn't to the classic recipe; Coke replaced sugar with corn sweeteners.

Cattle have been trained to eat corn instead of grass, their natural food. The Marlboro Cowboys should be riding through cornfields. Corn, in fact, is an ingredient in 80 PERCENT of supermarket products, including batteries and Splenda. Processing concentrates it. You couldn't eat enough corn kernels in a day to equal the calories in a bag of corn chips. Corn syrup can be addictive. Also fat and salt. A fast food meal is a heart attack in a paper bag. Poor families can't afford to buy real food to compete with the cost of $1.00 burgers and $1.98 "meals."

If this offends you, try to do something about it. The Texas beef growers sued Oprah. She won in court because she had the money to fight teams of corporate lawyers. You don't. Consider Carol Morrison, who refused to seal her chicken houses off from the daylight and opened them to the makers of this documentary. Morrison's chickens are not jammed into cages, but we see chickens that are unable to stand up. A giant chicken processor canceled her contract and refused to do any more business with her. She was getting sick of how she treated chickens, anyway.

Good food is not a cause limited to ac-

tresses on talk shows. Average people are getting concerned. Amazingly, Wal-Mart signed up with Stonyfield Farm. Consumer demand. When you hear commentators complaining about how the "government is paying farmers to not grow food," understand that "farmers" are corporations, and that the government is buying their surpluses to undercut local farmers around the world. The farmers who grew Bermuda onions are just about out of business because of the dumping of American onions. "Socialized agriculture" benefits megacorporations, which are committed to the goals of most corporations: maximizing profits and executive salaries.

This doesn't read one thing like a movie review. But most of the stuff I discuss in it, I learned from the new documentary *Food, Inc.,* directed by Robert Kenner and based on the recent book *The Omnivore's Dilemma* by Michael Pollan. I figured it wasn't important for me to go into detail about the photography and the editing. I just wanted to scare the bejesus out of you, which is what *Food, Inc.* did to me.

It's times like these I'm halfway grateful that after surgery I can't eat regular food anymore, and have to live on a liquid diet out of a can. Of course, it contains soy and corn products, too, but in a healthy form. They say your total cholesterol level shouldn't exceed your age plus one hundred. Mine is *way* lower than that. And I don't have to tip. ☞

The Foot Fist Way ★ ★
R, 87 m., 2008

Danny McBride (Fred Simmons), Mary Jane Bostic (Suzie Simmons), Ben Best (Chuck "The Truck" Wallace), Spencer Moreno (Julio Chavez), Carlos Lopez IV (Henry Harrison), Jody Hill (Mike McAlister). Directed by Jody Hill and produced by Erin Gates, Jody Hill, Robbie Hill, and Jennifer Chikes. Screenplay by Jody Hill, Danny McBride, and Ben Best.

The hero of *The Foot Fist Way* is loathsome and reprehensible and isn't a villain in any traditional sense. Five minutes spent in his company, and my jaw was dropping. Ten minutes, and I realized he existed outside any conventional notion of proper behavior. Children should not be allowed within a mile of this film, but it will appeal to *Jackass* fans and other devotees of the joyously ignorant.

The hero is named Fred Simmons. He's played by Danny McBride with a cool confidence in the character's ability to transgress all ordinary rules of behavior. Fred runs a Tae Kwan Do studio. He has the instincts of a fascist. His clients are drilled to obey him without question, to always call him "sir," to respect him above all others. Some of his clients are four years old. He uses profanity around them (and to them) with cheerful oblivion.

To a boy about nine years old, named Julio, he explains, "People are shit. The only person that you can trust is me, your Tae Kwan Do instructor." Julio needs consoling after he's disrespected by little Stevie, who is maybe a year younger. To teach Stevie respect, Fred beats him up. Yes. There are several times in the movie when Fred pounds on kids. He doesn't pull his punches. Most people in the audience will wince and recoil. I did. Others will deal with that material by reasoning that the fight stunts are faked and staged, their purpose is to underline Fred's insectoid personality, and "it's only a movie."

Which side of that fence you come down on will have a lot to do with your reaction. A zero-star rating for this movie could easily (in my case, even rapturously) be justified, and some fanboys will give it four. In all fairness it belongs in the middle. Certainly *The Foot Fist Way* doesn't like Fred; it regards him as a man who has absorbed the lingo of the martial arts but doesn't have a clue about its codes of behavior. He's as close to a martial arts practitioner as Father Guido Sarducci is to a Catholic priest. And the movie is often funny; I laughed in spite of myself.

Fred's offensiveness applies across a wide range of behavior. He is insulting to his wife's dinner guests, tries to kiss and maul students in his office, and asks one young woman who studies yoga: "Have you ever heard of it saving anyone from a gang-rape type of situation?" He has found very few friends. He introduces his students to his buddy from high school, Mike McAllister (Jody Hill, the director), who has a fifth-degree black belt and a penetrating stare that seems rehearsed in front of a mirror. Fred and Mike worship above all others

Chuck "The Truck" Wallace (Ben Best, the cowriter), a movie star whose credits include the intriguingly titled *7 Rings of Pain 2*. When Chuck appears at a nearby martial arts expo, Fred asks him to visit his studio's "testing day," and then invites him home and shows him the master bedroom ("the wife and I will bunk on the couch"). That he assumes a movie star will want to spend the night is surprising, although perhaps less so when The Truck gets a look at Fred's wife, Suzie (Mary Jane Bostic). Fred leaves the two of them together while he teaches a class and is appalled when he returns to find Suzie and The Truck bouncing on the couch. What does he expect? Suzie has photocopies of her boobs and butt in "work papers from the office," and excuses her behavior at a party by saying, "I got really drunk—Myrtle Beach drunk."

McBride's performance is appallingly convincing as Fred. Despite all I've written, Fred comes across as a person who might almost exist in these vulgar times. McBride never tries to put a spin on anything, never strains for laughs. He says outrageous things in a level, middle-American monotone. He seems convinced of his own greatness, has no idea of his effect on others, and seems oblivious to the manifest fact that he is very bad at Tae Kwan Do. He is a real piece of work.

I cannot recommend this movie, but I can describe it, and then it's up to you. If it sounds like a movie you would loathe, you are correct. If it doesn't, what can I tell you? What it does, it does well, even to its disgusting final scene.

Note: The title is a translation of Tae Kwan Do.

Formosa Betrayed ★★ ½
R, 100 m., 2010

James Van Der Beek (Jake Kelly), Will Tiao (Ming), Kenneth Tsang (General Tse), Tzi Ma (Kuo), Wendy Crewson (Susan Kane), John Heard (Tom Braxton), Leslie Hope (Lisa Gilbert). Directed by Adam Kane and produced by Kane, David Allen Cluck, and Will Tiao. Screenplay by Tiao, Charlie Stratton, Yann Samuell, Brian Askew, Nathaniel Goodman, and Katie Swain.

Formosa Betrayed is a political thriller with an agenda. It argues that Formosa, now known as Taiwan, has been the pawn of great powers for centuries. Occupied by Japan in the prewar years, it was claimed by the Nationalists of Chiang Kai-shek after the war, and his army retreated there after its defeat by Red China. Although Americans have long been schooled that Chiang flew the banner of freedom, the film says he seized property, killed thousands of native Formosans, wiped out the leadership class, and established a dictatorship.

This history is related to an FBI agent named Kelly (James Van Der Beek), who has been sent to Taiwan to act as "liaison" in the search for the murderer of a prominent Taiwanese professor in Lake Forest, Illinois. Why Kelly—who speaks no Chinese and scarcely knows that Taiwan was once named Formosa? Perhaps precisely because of his ignorance. In the Cold War years, neither Washington nor Taipei want a scandal. The story takes place in 1983, but that hasn't changed.

Kelly flies in, is greeted by an American official named Susan Kane (Wendy Crewson), and is whisked off to a lavish welcome party while his key witness is being murdered. Secretly contacted by friends of the dead Lake Forest professor, he realizes their lives, and his, are in danger from the police state. At this point, the movie takes hold. Earlier, it seemed to linger overmuch on past history, including even newsreel footage from World War II and Chiang meeting Roosevelt and Churchill.

We realize, somewhat to our surprise, that *Formosa Betrayed* is a thriller that's actually *about* something. Most thrillers are about the good guy trying to outshoot and outrun the bad guys, and their settings are incidental. This one has a bone to chew. One of the screenplay writers is Will Tiao, who also plays Ming, the film's Taiwanese hero, an underground activist committed to regaining control of the island for its original Formosans.

I sense that his desire to make a point about history was equally or more important for the filmmakers than making a taut thriller. That explains the title *Formosa Betrayed*, which is completely accurate in terms of the story, but uses a name for the island that hasn't been current for fifty years. That it works fairly well as a thriller is a tribute to the actors, particularly Tiao, whose emotion can be felt as he relates his homeland's history.

James Van Der Beek's FBI agent might be skilled enough at domestic crime, but Kelly is out of his element in Taiwan. It's when he realizes this that the movie engages. One detail struck me: Van Der Beek insists on the official three-day beard required by all action heroes to signal their pumping testosterone. But in 1983, the FBI required its agents to be clean-shaven. And the action is set in the year before the first season of *Miami Vice*, which popularized the obligatory stubble.

Wendy Crewson's role seems thankless at first: She's limited to advising Kelly to cool it and asking him to keep his nose out of Taiwan's business. Turns out that she and Kelly's boss (John Heard) know many things the agent doesn't. As a result, *Formosa Betrayed* begins as rather clunky, but ends by making a statement that explains a great many things. One question left unasked: Why did we promise to defend Taiwan with nuclear weapons, but refuse to recognize it as a sovereign nation?

Four Christmases ★ ★

PG-13, 82 m., 2008

Vince Vaughn (Brad), Reese Witherspoon (Kate), Robert Duvall (Howard), Jon Favreau (Denver), Mary Steenburgen (Marilyn), Dwight Yoakam (Pastor Phil), Tim McGraw (Dallas), Kristin Chenoweth (Courtney), Jon Voight (Creighton), Sissy Spacek (Paula). Directed by Seth Gordon and produced by Roger Birnbaum, Gary Barber, and Jonathan Glickman. Screenplay by Matt R. Allen, Caleb Wilson, Jon Lucas, and Scott Moore.

So here's the pitch, boss. *Four Christmases.* We star Reese Witherspoon and Vince Vaughn as a happily unmarried couple whose parents are divorced and remarried, and since nobody is talking to one another, they have to visit all four households on Christmas.

Why don't they just invite everybody over to their house or rent a private room at Spago?

No, no. They usually don't go to Christmas with *anyone.* They usually tell their parents they're out of cell phone contact, breast-feeding orphans in Guatemala.

Both of them?
They're really in Fiji. But their flight is canceled because of heavy fog. They're interviewed on TV, and now everybody knows they're still in town, and they have to make the rounds.

How long will this take to establish?
We introduce them, they go to the airport, they're on TV, *ba-bing, ba-bing, ba-bing.*

Cut two ba-bings. *What's next?*
First stop, Vince's dad. We'll get Robert Duvall. Mean old snake. Both of Vince's brothers are like extreme duel-to-the-death cage fighters. They beat the crap out of Vince, while ol' dad sits in his easy chair and verbally humiliates him.

Who are the brothers?
Jon Favreau and Tim McGraw.

Jon Favreau as a cage fighter?
He got a trainer.

Does McGraw sing?
That would slow down the family fight.

What about Reese?
Wait until she gets to her mom. Wait until we get to both moms. Her mom is Mary Steenburgen. She's sex hungry. His mom is Sissy Spacek. She's in love with Vince's best friend.

Those are both good actresses.
Right, but they can handle this. Jon Voight for her dad. He lives on Lake Tahoe. Perfect for Christmas.

What's his problem?
He lends the picture gravitas.

The audience, does it laugh while his brothers beat the crap out of Vince?
That's what we're hoping.

Tell me something else that's funny.
Two babies that urp on everyone.

That's funny?
OK, they projectile vomit.

A little better.
Also, we have Dwight Yoakam as Pastor Phil.

Spare me the religious details. All I want to know is, does Yoakam sing?
Nope.

We got two gold record singers and they don't sing?
So? We got five Oscar-winning actors and they don't need to act much. There *can't* be any singing, boss. If McGraw doesn't sing,

then Yoakam doesn't sing. It's in the contract. A most-favored-nations clause.

Most-favored-nations would not even remotely apply here. That is insane.
There ain't no sanity clause.

45365 ★★★★
NO MPAA RATING, 91 m., 2010

Featuring the townspeople of Sidney, Ohio. A documentary directed by Bill Ross IV and Turner Ross. Produced by Bill Ross IV.

The first shot tells us "45365 is the zip code of this city." In this achingly beautiful film, that zip code belongs to Sidney, Ohio, a handsome town of about twenty thousand residents. The brothers Bill and Turner Ross were born there perhaps thirty years ago. Of course they knew everybody in town, and when they spent seven months of 2007 filming its daily life, their presence must have eventually become commonplace. Their film evokes what *Winesburg, Ohio* might have looked like as a documentary.

Take me for an example. I knew everyone in the film. I grew up there. Well, actually in zip code 61802, which is Urbana, Illinois. My hometown was close to Sidney, Illinois, just as 45365 is not far from Urbana, Ohio. There are also towns named Homer and Philo near both towns named Urbana. East central Illinois was settled by people from Ohio.

In my midwestern town, I knew these people, their homes, their friendliness, the trouble some of them got into, and I knew why after the high school football game some of the kids hung out under the arc lamps and others were in the shade of the bleachers with the hoods pulled up on their sweatshirts. I even recognized, because I once covered the police beat, exactly the tone of voice a policeman will use after stopping a drunk driver he's known for ten years.

The film is privileged. No one is filmed with a hidden camera. The camera must have been right there, in the living room, the riverbank, the barbershop, the backseat, the football practice, the front lawn when a man agrees to put up a sign supporting a judge running for reelection. The Rosses must have filmed so much they became both trusted and invisible.

They know this town without even thinking about it.

There is a beautiful shot during a church service that pans slowly to the right over the congregation and pauses looking into a door to a stairwell. A woman and small girl come up the stairs. The camera follows them back to the left until the girl is deposited back in her pew, having obviously just been taken to the potty. Were those two people cued? Obviously not. I suggest the cameraman, Bill or Turner, observed them getting up, intuited where they were going and why, and composed the camera movement instinctively. A brief shot you may not even consciously notice, but a perfect shot, reading the room as our minds do. All human life is in it.

I've never seen a barbershop like the one in the film. All three barbers are surprisingly young; one seems to be a teenager. Yet there is the order and routine of a small-town barbershop with barbers as old as Moses. Do these kids own the shop? Well, why not? It would cost less than a Supercuts franchise. What do they talk about? What all barbers talk about: the Friday night football game.

Sidney has what can only be described as a great radio station. Local human beings sit before the mikes and run the boards. This station isn't a robot from Los Angeles. They play hits of the '80s and '90s, they make announcements, they have a sports talk show about the Sidney Yellowjackets. The team has a chicken dinner benefit coming up. Adults seven dollars, kids three dollars.

It looks like rain on the day of the parade, but the station's reporter is on the spot. He's hooked up via his cell phone, and interviews a woman on the street with a tiny mike he holds up to his mouth and then to hers. He tells everyone to come on downtown, the skies are clearing. At the carnival, Elvis Junior is onstage. It's pouring rain. A guy uses a broom to push up the canvas roof of the tent and spill out the rainwater. A mobile home has been painted up as an exhibit for "LIVE! The World's Smallest Woman!"

Trains rumble through Sidney on business of their own. The radio station is used for the judicial candidate to record ". . . and I approve of this message." A man goes to court for sentencing. Drunk. We've seen two of his former wives agreeing that he needs to get his act together. They argue over whether he left the one *for* the other, or left the one and *then* married the other. They don't exactly seem to be fighting over him.

Spring, summer, autumn, winter. Summer showers. The first snow falling out at the abandoned drive-in theater. Music on Radio 105.5. Lawns. Good-looking old buildings. Sidney still looks like a town, not a squatter's camp of fast food outlets. One extraordinarily stupid review of the film complains "all of these situations are filmed as if we already know the story of who these people are. We don't even learn anyone's names." This isn't that kind of a documentary. If you need to know everybody's name, you'll never, ever understand this film. Hell, I could go to Sidney, Ohio, tomorrow and feel right at home.

Note: 45365 won the $25,000 Roger and Chaz Ebert Truer Than Fiction Award at the 2010 Independent Spirits. The contest was independently judged.

4 Months, 3 Weeks and 2 Days ★ ★ ★ ★
NO MPAA RATING, 113 m., 2008

Anamaria Marinca (Otilia), Laura Vasiliu (Gabita), Alex Potocean (Adi), Vlad Ivanov (Mr. Bebe). Directed by Cristian Mungiu. Produced by Mungiu and Oleg Mutu. Screenplay by Mungiu.

Gabita is perhaps the most clueless young woman to ever have the lead in a movie about her own pregnancy. Even if you think Juno was way too clever, two hours with Gabita will have you buying a ticket to Bucharest for Diablo Cody. This is a powerful film and a stark visual accomplishment, but no thanks to Gabita (Laura Vasiliu). The driving character is her roommate, Otilia (Anamaria Marinca), who does all the heavy lifting.

The time is the late 1980s. Romania still cringes under the brainless rule of Ceausescu. In Cristian Mungiu's *4 Months, 3 Weeks and 2 Days*, Gabita desires an abortion, which was then illegal, not for moral reasons, but because Ceausescu wanted more subjects to rule. She turns in desperation to her roommate, Otilia, who agrees to help her and does. Helps her so much, indeed, she does everything but have the abortion herself. In a period of twenty-four hours, we follow the two friends in a journey of frustration, stupidity, duplicity, cruelty, and desperation, set against a background of a nation where if it weren't for the black market, there'd be no market at all.

For Gabita, the notion of taking responsibility for her own actions is completely unfamiliar. We wonder how she has survived to her current twentyish age in a society that obviously requires boldness, courage, and improvisation. For starters, she convinces Otilia to raise money for the operation. Then she asks her to go first to meet the abortionist. Then she neglects to make a reservation at the hotel the abortionist specifies. That almost sinks the arrangement: The abortionist has experience suggesting that hotel will be a safe venue and suspects he may be set up for a police trap. His name, by the way, is Mr. Bebe (Vlad Ivanov), and no, *bebe* is apparently not Romanian for "baby," but it looks suspicious to me.

The movie deliberately levels an unblinking gaze at its subjects. There are no fancy shots, no effects, no quick cuts, and Mungiu and his cinematographer, Oleg Mutu, adhere to a rule of one shot per scene. That makes camera placement and movement crucial, and suggests that every shot has been carefully prepared. Even shots where the ostensible subject of the action is half-visible, or not seen at all, serve a purpose, by insisting on the context and the frame. Visual is everything here; the film has no music, only words or silences.

Otilia is heroic in this context; she reminds me a little of the ambulance attendant in the 2005 Romanian film *The Death of Mr. Lazarescu,* who drove a dying man around all night insisting on a hospital for him. Otilia grows exasperated with her selfish and self-obsessed friend, but she keeps on trying to help, even though she has problems of her own.

One of them is her boyfriend, Adi (Alex Potocean), who is himself so self-oriented that we wonder if Otilia is attracted to the type. Even though she tries to explain that she and Gabita have urgent personal business, he insists on Otilia coming to his house to meet his family that night. He turns it into a test of her

love. People who do that are incapable of understanding that to compromise would be a proof of their own love.

The dinner party she arrives at would be a horror show even in a Mike Leigh display of social embarrassment. She's jammed at a table with too many guests, too much smoking, too much drinking, and no one who pays her the slightest attention. As the unmoving camera watches her, we wait for her to put a fork in somebody's eye. When she gets away to make a phone call, Adi follows her and drags her into his room, and then Adi's mother bursts in on them and we see who Adi learned possessiveness from.

When the friends finally find themselves in a hotel room with the abortionist, the result is as unpleasant, heartless, and merciless as it could possibly be. I'll let you discover for yourself. And finally there is a closing scene where Otilia and Gabita agree to never refer to this night again. Some critics have found the scene anticlimactic. I think it is inevitable. If I were Otilia, I would never even see Gabita again. I'd send over Adi to collect my clothes.

Filmmakers in countries of the former Soviet bloc have been using their new freedom to tell at last the stories they couldn't tell then. *The Lives of Others,* for example, was about the East German secret police. And in Romania, the era has inspired a group of powerful films, including the aforementioned *Mr. Lazarescu, 12:08 East of Bucharest* (2006), and *4 Months,* which won the Palme d'Or at Cannes 2007, upsetting a lot of American critics who admired it but liked *No Country for Old Men* more.

The film has inspired many words about how it reflects Romanian society, but obtaining an illegal abortion was much the same in this country until some years ago, and also in Britain, as we saw in Leigh's *Vera Drake.* The fascination of the film comes not so much from the experiences the friends have, however unspeakable, but in who they are, and how they behave and relate. Anamaria Marinca gives a masterful performance as Otilia, but don't let my description of Gabita blind you to the brilliance of Laura Vasiliu's acting. These are two of the more plausible characters I've seen in a while.

The Fourth Kind ★ ½
PG-13, 98 m., 2009

Milla Jovovich (Abigail), Elias Koteas (Psychologist), Will Patton (Sheriff), Corey Johnson (Tommy), Olatunde Osunsanmi (Professor). Directed by Olatunde Osunsanmi and produced by Paul Brooks, Joe Carnahan, and Terry Robbins. Screenplay by Osunsanmi.

Boy, is the Nome, Alaska, chamber of commerce going to be pissed off when they see *The Fourth Kind.* You don't wanna go there. You can't drive there, that's for sure. The only ways in are by sea, air, dogsled, or birth canal. Why the aliens chose this community of 9,261 to abduct so many people is a mystery, as is why owls stare into bedroom windows.

Nome has been the center of an alarming series of strange disappearances, we learn. So many, the FBI has sent agents there ten times more than to big Anchorage. *The Fourth Kind* is based on the testimony of a psychologist who found, circa 2000, that many of her patients reported waking at 3 a.m. with the sense that something was wrong and seeing an owl with its eyes on them.

The film goes to great lengths to be realistic. "I am the actress Milla Jovovich," Jovovich tells us at the outset, explaining that in the film she plays the psychologist Abigail, whose testimony was videotaped. Other fact-based characters are her colleague (Elias Koteas), the local sheriff (Will Patton), and a professor who interviews her (Olatunde Osunsanmi). "Every scene in this movie is supported by archived footage," she says, and to prove it, Osunsanmi, who's also the director, uses split screen to show Jovovich and the *real* Abigail talking almost simultaneously. The real Abigail's name has been changed, but since she's right there on the screen, how much of a mystery can she be in Nome?

It was with crushing disappointment that my research discovered this is all made up out of whole cloth, including the real Abigail. It wasn't even shot in Nome, but mostly in Bulgaria. And Dallas Massie, a retired state trooper who's acting police chief, says he's heard nothing about aliens. I learn all this from the blog of an *Anchorage Daily News* reporter, Kyle Hopkins, who says about twenty people have indeed disappeared in the area since the 1960s, and writes: "The FBI stepped in, reviewing two dozen cases, eventually determining that excessive alcohol consumption and the winter climate were a common link in many of the cases. Some of the dead were killed by exposure or from falling off a jetty into the frigid Snake River."

All right then, *The Fourth Kind* is a pseudo-documentary like *Paranormal Activity* and *The Blair Witch Project.* But unlike those two, which just forge ahead with their home video cameras, this one encumbers the flow of the film with ceaseless reminders that it is a dramatization of real events. When we see Will Patton, for example, there's a subtitle informing us: "Will Patton, actor." Oh! I already know well that Will Patton and Elias Koteas are actors, and Jovovich identifies herself at the start. I wish they'd had a really big-name star. It might have been funny to read "Bruce Willis: Actor."

Now here's a good question. In the film we see the "real" footage of the "actual" client interviews with "Abigail." Why would an actual psychologist release confidential videotapes to a horror film, especially tapes showing the clients having seizures? Who *are* those "actual clients," really? The end credits don't thank them, although the film claims to account for them. Remember, even in a movie "based on a true story" (like *Fargo*), nothing before the actual end credits needs to be true. You want to watch those like a hawk. My theory is, the "actual" clients are played by the actors playing their fictional versions. Of course, I can't be sure of that. Think about it.

Jovovich is good, actually. It's a broad, melodramatic role with lots of screaming, and after two *Resident Evil* movies, she's good at being an endangered heroine and makes a competent psychologist. And a successful one, too. Her log cabin arts and crafts office looks like it was surely subleased from a (Bulgarian) millionaire. We see there's a lot of business in Nome for a specialist in owl staring.

Free for All! ★ ★ ★
NO MPAA RATING, 93 m., 2008

A documentary directed, written, and produced by John Wellington Ennis.

I'm getting tired of being angry about the 2004 presidential election. It is now clear enough that it may have been stolen. The vote totals in Ohio are particularly suspect. Florida in 2000 you know all about. But did you ever seriously focus on Ohio 2004?

You perhaps have vague memories of a controversy about polling machines. And confused voters. And how the chairman of George Bush's Ohio campaign was the secretary of state in charge of overseeing the election. And how the state awarded a $100 million contract for voting machines to Diebold, whose chairman attended a strategy session at Bush's Texas ranch, hosted a $1,000-a-plate dinner for Bush in his mansion, and told the press he would do whatever he could to ensure that Bush won Ohio.

You may have missed some details. Such as that Kenneth Blackwell, the GOP secretary of state/campaign manager, decreed (1) that a vote not cast in your precinct would not be counted; (2) that all precinct lines be redrawn; (3) that the new precincts would be explained on the secretary/chairman's Web site, which unfortunately was six months behind in being updated. Some voters actually found their way to the right place, such as a school gym, but didn't know that as many as four precincts were voting there, so that mathematically three of four were in the wrong lines and voted in the wrong precinct. Of course the Republicans efficiently informed their mailing and e-mail list members of correct voting sites.

These details and others are alleged in a new documentary named *Free for All!* by John Wellington Ennis, who traveled to Ohio in 2006 to see how the gubernatorial election (Blackwell against Democrat Ted Strickland) was going. Turns out it was not going well. In a state newly energized to correct voting irregularities, Blackwell lost to Strickland, winning only 37 percent of the vote. What a turnaround in two years.

The doc is engrossing, even enraging. It's essentially a narration by Ennis, illustrated with video, stills, news footage, photos, and standard talking-head interviews. It doesn't have the visual liveliness of the Michael Moore docs that clearly influenced it. There is too much Ennis, whose I-can't-believe-this tone of voice wears out its welcome. But he has a lot to say. There's no easy way to summarize, so let me quote:

That the world got the official Ohio election results from a Web site made by the same Web designer smearing Bush's opponent (i.e., Mike Connell, a man instrumental in the Swift Boat attacks) wasn't the only suspect thing in election night. The Web servers for the election results in Ohio were suddenly moved in the middle of the night from Ohio to Tennessee. The entire business of reporting these numbers on the Web, where media and the rest of America take them from, was being run by this far-right partisan Web company. The same company hosted Bush's own Web site, and GOP.com, Ohio-GOP.com, Newt.com, and so on.

Would you trust an election supervised by Bush's campaign manager and reported by a site designed by the Swift Boat guy? Strange thing: All the exit polls showed Kerry winning Ohio, but then Bush pulled ahead late in the evening. If Bush had lost Ohio, he would have lost the election.

Free Style ★★
PG, 94 m., 2009

Corbin Bleu (Cale Bryant), Madison Pettis (Bailey Bryant), Sandra Echeverria (Alex Lopez), Penelope Ann Miller (Jeanette Bryant), Jesse Moss (Justin Maynard), Matt Bellefleur (Derek Black), David Reivers (Dell). Directed by William Dear and produced by Corbin Bleu, Rob Cowan, Michael Emanuel, Dean E. Fronk, Donald Paul Pemrick, and David Reivers. Screenplay by Jeffrey Nicholson and Joshua Leibner.

There are some charming actors in this movie, all dressed up but with no place to go. *Free Style* is remorselessly formulaic, with every character and plot point playing its assigned role. That it works is primarily because of the charisma of Corbin Bleu (did his parents meet in a French restaurant?) and Sandra Echeverria, as a boy who likes to ride motorcycles and a girl who likes to ride horses.

Bleu plays Cale, a teenager who delivers pizza and races for a motocross team. His best friend runs off the track and crashes during a race, and he turns his bike around and drives upstream to the rescue. I am not a motocross expert, but doesn't this seem idiotic?

The sponsor of his bike withdraws his support, as indeed he should. One day Cale delivers a pizza to a farm and two things catch his eye: a beaten-up old motorcycle, and Alex (Sandra Echeverria), who is not old nor the least bit beaten-up. He's given the bike and goes to work fixing it up, and Alex becomes his girlfriend—although not without the exhausted scene where she sees him with his former girl and leaps to the wrong conclusion. This scene is so obligatory, I think sometimes they even create an old girlfriend just to make it possible.

Cale and his mom (Penelope Ann Miller) argue about his career track. He dreams of making the professional motocross tour. His mom thinks he should focus on school. I think she's right. But noooo—he has a Dream. When will there be a film about a motocross racer or skateboarder, say, who decides, the hell with it, I could break my neck. I think I'll just go to college.

You may know that Penelope Ann Miller is white, and that Corbin Bleu (star of all the *High School Musical* films) is biracial. Why do I mention this? Because the movie makes a big point of it, even providing an absent black father Cale seeks out, perhaps because then, God help us, the father can turn up at the end of the Big Race and nod approvingly. Why not simply provide the kid with two parents? Because the Single Mom is also a beloved cliché, you say? Two for the price of one.

Anyway, all leads up to the Big Race, etc., and the False Dawn, the Fake Crisis, and the Real Dawn, all following the recipe. My primary enjoyment was entertaining myself by mentally casting Corbin Bleu and Sandra Echeverria in other movies. Well, there's hope. Echeverria has the lead in three upcoming movies from Mexico. Bleu (who is handsome and not merely cute) works constantly. In later years people won't be wearing out their DVDs of a movie like this, but as a career step, it's a good one. Better than pro motocross.

Friday the 13th ★ ★
R, 91 m., 2009

Jared Padalecki (Clay Miller), Amanda Righetti (Whitney Miller), Arlen Escarpeta (Lawrence), Danielle Panabaker (Jenna), Travis Van Winkle (Trent), Aaron Yoo (Chewie), Derek Mears (Jason Voorhees). Directed by Marcus Nispel and produced by Michael Bay, Andrew Form, Brad Fuller, and Sean Cunningham. Screenplay by Damian Shannon and Mark Swift.

Friday the 13th is about the best *Friday the 13th* movie you could hope for. Its technical credits are excellent. It has a lot of scary and gruesome killings. Not a whole lot of acting is required. If that's what you want to find out, you can stop reading now.

OK, it's just us in the room. You're not planning to see *Friday the 13th*, and you wonder why anyone else is. Since the original movie came out in 1980, there were ten more films—sequels, retreads, fresh starts, variations, whatever. Now we get the 2009 *Friday the 13th*, which is billed as a "remake" of the original.

That it is clearly not. Let me test you with a trick question: How many kids did Jason kill in the first movie? The answer is none, since Mrs. Voorhees, his mother, did all of the killings in revenge on the camp counselors who let her beloved son drown in Crystal Lake.

Mrs. Voorhees is decapitated at the end of number one and again in the new version, so the new movie is technically a remake up until that point—but the decapitation, although preceded by several murders, comes *before* this movie's title card, so everything after that point is new.

It will come as little surprise that Jason still lives in the woods around Crystal Lake and is still sore about the decapitation of his mom. Jason must be sore in general.

So far in the series, he has been drowned, sliced by a machete in the shoulder, hit with an ax in the head, supposedly cremated, aped by a copycat killer, buried, resurrected with a lightning bolt, chained to a boulder and thrown in the lake again, resurrected by telekinesis, drowned again, resurrected by an underwater electrical surge, melted by toxic waste, killed by the FBI, resurrected through the possession of another body, returned to his own body, thrown into hell, used for research, frozen cryogenically, thawed, blown into space, freed to continue his murder spree on Earth 2, returned to the present, faced off against Freddy Krueger of *A Nightmare on Elm Street*, drowned again with him, and

189

made to emerge from Crystal Lake with Freddy's head, which winks.

I know what you're thinking. No, I haven't seen them all. Wikipedia saw them so I didn't have to. The question arises: Why does Jason continue his miserable existence, when his memoirs would command a seven-figure advance, easy? There is another question. In the 1980 movie, twenty years had already passed since Jason first went to sleep with the fishes. Assuming he was a camper aged twelve, he would have been thirty-two in 1980, and in 2009 he is sixty-one. That helps explain why one of my fellow critics at the screening was wearing an AARP T-shirt.

SPOILER WARNING: At the end of this film, Jason is whacked with an ax and a board, throttled with a chain, and dragged into a wood chipper, although we fade to black just before the chips start to fly, and we are reminded of Marge Gunderson's immortal words. The next day brings a dawn, as one so often does, and two survivors sit on the old pier with Jason's body wrapped and tied in canvas. Then they throw him into Crystal Lake. Anyone who thinks they can drown Jason Voorhees for the fifth time is a cockeyed optimist.

Note: In my research, I discovered that the scientific name for fear of Friday the 13th is "paraskavedekatriaphobia." I envision a new franchise: Paraskavedekatriaphobia: A New Beginning, Paraskavedekatriaphobia: Jason Lives, Paraskavedekatriaphobia: Freddy's Nightmare, *etc.*

From Paris with Love ★★
R, 92 m., 2010

John Travolta (Charlie Wax), Jonathan Rhys Meyers (James Reece), Kasia Smutniak (Carolina), Richard Durden (Ambassador Bennington). Directed by Pierre Morel and produced by Luc Besson and India Osborne. Screenplay by Adi Hasak, based on a story by Besson.

Pauline Kael has already reviewed this movie in her book *Kiss Kiss Bang Bang,* and it only took her the title. I could go through my usual vaudeville act about chase scenes and queasy-cams and Idiot Plots, but instead I'd like you to join me in the analysis of something that increasingly annoys me.

Imagine we are watching *From Paris with Love* on a DVD with a stop-action button. We look at an action scene all the way through. John Travolta stars as Charlie Wax, an American Mr. Fix-It with a shaved head and goatee, who has been sent to Paris on a mysterious assignment. Not mysterious to him, mysterious to us. It involves Asian drug dealers and/or terrorists from the Middle East. Doesn't matter who they are or what they do, because their only function here is to try to kill Charlie and his fall-guy partner James Reece (Jonathan Rhys Meyers).

OK. We're on the sofa. We look at the scene. We take a second look. We focus on Travolta. This is an athlete. His reflexes are on a hair-trigger. He can deal with several enemies at a time. He can duck, jump, hurdle, spin, and leap. One slight miscalculation, and he's dead. He doesn't miss a beat. He's in superb condition, especially for a guy whose favorite food is Cheese Royales. That's a little joke reminding us of *Pulp Fiction,* and the *last* thing you should do is remind the audience of a movie they'd rather be watching.

Now we go through the scene a frame at a time. We don't miss much in the way of continuity because it's pretty much glued together a frame at a time. We see a dizzying cascade of images, but here's a funny thing: We don't see Travolta completing many extended physical movements, and none involving any danger. The shots of him involve movement, but in bursts of a few frames, intercut with similar bursts of action by his attackers. There is no sense of continuous physical movement taking place within a defined space. No overall sense of the choreography.

I hasten to say this is not criticism of John Travolta. He succeeds in this movie by essentially acting in a movie of his own. The fight construction is the same with most modern action movies. In past decades studios went so far as to run fencing classes for swordfights. Stars like Buster Keaton, Douglas Fairbanks Sr., and Errol Flynn did their own stunts and made sure you could see them doing them. Most of the stunts in classic kung fu movies, starring such as Bruce Lee and Jackie Chan, were really happening. Sure, they used camera angles, trampolines, and wires, but you try it and see how easy it is.

CGI makes that unnecessary. The stunt work is done by computers and the editing process. I fear that classic action sequences would be too slow for today's impatient action fans, who have been schooled on impossibilities. The actual stunt driving done in such chase landmarks as *The French Connection* and *Bullitt*, where you could observe real cars in real space and time, has been replaced by what is essentially animation.

I mention this because last week I saw a good South Korean thriller named *The Chaser*, and its best scene involved a foot chase through the narrow streets of Seoul by two actors who, you could see, were actually running down streets. In modern actioners, the only people who work up a sweat are the editors.

Anyway, that's what I had on my mind. As for *From Paris with Love*, it's mostly bang bang and not kiss kiss, and as an actress once asked Russ Meyer, what's love got to do with it?

Frost/Nixon ★ ★ ★ ★
R, 122 m., 2008

Frank Langella (Richard Nixon), Michael Sheen (David Frost), Oliver Platt (Bob Zelnick), Sam Rockwell (James Reston Jr.), Kevin Bacon (Jack Brennan), Rebecca Hall (Caroline Cushing), Toby Jones (Swifty Lazar), Matthew Macfadyen (John Birt), Patty McCormack (Pat Nixon), Andy Miller (Frank Gannon), Kate Jennings Grant (Diane Sawyer), Eve Curtis (Sue Mengers). Directed by Ron Howard and produced by Howard, Tim Bevan, Eric Fellner, and Brian Grazer. Screenplay by Peter Morgan, based on his play.

Strange, how a man once so reviled has gained stature in the memory. How we cheered when Richard M. Nixon resigned the presidency! How dramatic it was when David Frost cornered him on TV and presided over the humiliating confession he had stonewalled for three years. And yet how much more intelligent, thoughtful, and, well, presidential, he now seems, compared to the occupant of the office from 2001 to 2009.

Nixon was thought to have been destroyed by Watergate and interred by the Frost inter-

views. But wouldn't you trade him in a second for Bush? The confession wrung out of him by Frost acted as a catharsis. He admitted what everyone already knew, and that freed him to get on with things, to end his limbo at San Clemente, to give other interviews, to write books, to be consulted as an elder statesman. Indeed, to show his face in public.

Ron Howard's *Frost/Nixon* is a somewhat fictionalized version of the famous 1977 interviews, all the more effective in taking the point of view of the outsider, the "lightweight" celebrity interviewer, then in his own exile in Australia. Precisely because David Frost (Michael Sheen) was at a low ebb professionally and had gambled all his money on the interviews, his point of view enhances and deepens the shadows around Nixon (Frank Langella). This story could not have been told from Nixon's POV, because we would not have cared about Frost.

The film begins as a fascinating inside look at the TV news business and then tightens into a spellbinding thriller. Early, apparently inconsequential scenes (Frost as a "TV star," Frost picking up a woman on an airplane, Frost partying) are crucial in establishing his starting point. He was scorned at the time for even presuming to interview Nixon. He won the interview for two reasons: He paid the ex-president $600,000 from mostly his own money, and he was viewed by Nixon and his advisers as a lightweight pushover.

And so he seems during the early stages of the interviews (the chronology has been much foreshortened for dramatic purposes). Nixon sidetracks Frost, embarks on endless digressions, evades points, falls back on windy anecdotes. Frost's team grows desperate. Consisting of an experienced TV newsman, Bob Zelnick (Oliver Platt), and a researcher, James Reston Jr. (Sam Rockwell), they implore him to interrupt Nixon, to bear down hard, to keep repeating questions until he gets an answer. Frost was a man accustomed to being nice to Zsa Zsa Gabor. He doesn't have to be nice to Nixon. He has hired Nixon.

I can't be sure how much of the film's relationship between the two men is fictionalized. I accept it as a given in the film, because this is not a documentary. The screenplay, by Peter Morgan, is based on his award-winning

London and Broadway play, which also starred Langella and Sheen. What Morgan suggests is that even while he was out-fencing Frost, two things were going on deep within Nixon's mind: (1) a need to confess, which may have been his buried reason for agreeing to the interviews in the first place, and (2) an identification with Frost and even sympathy for him. Nixon always thought of himself as the underdog, the outsider, the unpopular kid. "You won't have Nixon to kick around anymore," he told the press when his political career apparently ended in his loss of the 1962 California gubernatorial election.

Now look at Frost. Although he had a brilliant early career in England, which Nixon may not have been very familiar with, he is shown in the film as a virtual has-been, exiled to Australia. You can count on Nixon and his agent Swifty Lazar (Toby Jones) to know that Frost had failed to find financial backing, was paying Nixon out of his own pocket, and would be ruined if he didn't get what he clearly needed. Then factor in Nixon's envy of Frost's popularity and genial personality. In one revealing moment, Nixon confides he would do anything to be able to attend a party and just relax around people. Nixon also questions him closely about his "girlfriends." Frost represented Nixon's vulnerabilities, his shortcomings, and even some of his desires.

This all sets the stage for the (fictionalized) scene that is the crucial moment in the story. A drunken Nixon calls Frost late at night. The next day, he doesn't remember the call, but like an alcoholic after a blackout, he has an all too vivid imagination of what he might have said. At that day's interview, he's not only playing their chess game with a hangover but has sacrificed his queen.

Frank Langella and Michael Sheen do not attempt to mimic their characters but to embody them. There's the usual settling-in period, common to all biopics about people we're familiar with, when we're comparing the real with the performance. Then that fades out, and we've been absorbed into the drama. Howard uses authentic locations (Nixon's house at San Clemente, Frost's original hotel suite), and there are period details, but the film really comes down to these two

compelling, intense performances, these two men with such deep needs entirely outside the subjects of the interviews. All we know about the real Frost and the real Nixon is almost beside the point. It all comes down to those two men in that room while the cameras are rolling.

Frownland ★ ★ ★ ½
NO MPAA RATING, 106 m., 2008

Dore Mann (Keith Sontag), Paul Grimstad (Charles), Mary Wall (Laura), David Sandholm (Sandy), Carmine Marino (Carmine), Paul Grant (Exam Man). Directed by Ronald Bronstein and produced by Marc Raybin. Screenplay by Bronstein.

Frownland is a movie like a shriek for help. It centers on an extraordinary performance that plays like an unceasing panic attack. To call it uncompromising is to wish for a better word. It doesn't ask us to like its central character; after all, no one in the film does. I don't think he likes himself.

The character is named Keith (Dore Mann). He is in his late twenties, a chain-smoker, a shabby dresser, a door-to-door salesman for dubious coupon booklets benefiting multiple sclerosis. His girlfriend, Laura (Mary Wall), arrives sobbing at his tiny room, sleeps with her face to the wall, sticks him with a pushpin.

I feel sympathy for Keith, but I wouldn't want to spend time with him. He has a punishing manner of speech that involves starting sentences again and again, blurting out impassioned and inarticulate appeals, overwhelming his listeners. You can see his jaw working as he gathers the courage to speak again. He is constantly wiping his face with his hand. He makes his only friend desperate to get rid of him. His flatmate is jobless and can't pay his share. Keith's room is a single bed on the left and a row of kitchen implements on the right, with a two-foot aisle between.

His flatmate, Charles (Paul Grimstad), agrees to pay the electric bill, but Keith doesn't trust him. This sets up a devastating verbal assault from Charles—who, in fact, never pays the bill. His "friend" Sandy (David Sandholm) doesn't want him to visit and tricks him into leaving. When he fails at his hopeless door-to-door job, his boss, Carmine (Carmine Marino), who drives a crew of salesmen in his van, asks him how he'd like to walk home. His very way of speaking to people invites a "no."

One curiosity is that the film leaves Keith for an extended scene involving Charles taking a test for a job application. I can see how the idea of testing people might apply to Keith, but otherwise this plays as a digression. Then we return to Keith with a harrowing scene where he is mocked by drunks at a disco. Incredibly, even here, Mann's work never goes over the top. We believe at every moment that this suffering creature is really feeling what he seems to feel, really saying what he needs to say. It is easy to imagine the performance going wrong, but it doesn't.

Now, why would you want to see this picture? Most readers of this review probably wouldn't. I'm writing for the rest of us. It is a rebirth of the need for expression that inspired the American independent movement in the first place, fifty years ago. It was written, directed, and edited by Ronald Bronstein, who had a crew of one cameraman, one soundman, and one grip. It has not been picked up for distribution; he is distributing it himself at shrines to outsider cinema (Facets Cinematheque in Chicago, the IFC Center in New York).

Yet the film has gained a foothold. It won a special jury prize at the important SXSW Festival in Austin. It won a Gotham Award from the Independent Feature Project in New York. It has been nominated for an Indie Spirit Award. To give you an idea of the challenge it presents, the *New York Times* praised it, but it was hated by *Film Threat,* "Hollywood's indie voice."

Such reactions are inspired by Dore Mann's performance, which in intensity equals Peter Greene's work in Lodge Kerrigan's *Clean, Shaven* (1993). Indeed, Kerrigan is one of the champions of the film. What Dore Mann does is not caricature, not "performance," not contrived. It is full throttle all the way with insecurity, needfulness, loneliness, mistrust, desperation, self-hate, apology, and despair.

Frownland has been described as a test for audiences. There will be walk-outs. But it doesn't set out to alienate its viewers; its only purpose is to do justice to Keith by showing him as he is. I will not forget him.

Frozen River ★ ★ ★ ★
R, 97 m., 2008

Melissa Leo (Ray Eddy), Misty Upham (Lila Littlewolf), Charlie McDermott (T.J.), Mark Boone Jr. (Jacques Bruno), Michael O'Keefe (Trooper Finnerty), James Reilly (Ricky). Directed by Courtney Hunt and produced by Heather Rae and Chip Hourihan. Screenplay by Hunt.

Sometimes two performances come along that are so perfectly matched that no overt signals are needed to show how the characters feel about each other. That's what happens between Melissa Leo and Misty Upham in *Frozen River,* playing two mothers who live without male support in shabby house trailers on the U.S.-Quebec border: Mohawk territory.

Leo plays Ray Eddy, whose husband left his car at a Mohawk bingo parlor and disappeared, perhaps on the bus to Atlantic City. He is an addicted gambler and has taken all the money they were saving to buy a better trailer. Ray scrapes by on a part-time job at the Yankee One Dollar store, and until payday, her kids, fifteen and five, are dining on popcorn and Tang.

Upham plays Lila Littlewolf, a Mohawk who works at the bingo hall and lives alone; her mother-in-law has "stolen" her one-year-old. The two women meet after Lila finds the keys in the husband's abandoned car and drives it away, and Ray follows her home: "That's my car." Lila says she knows a smuggler who will give her two thousand dollars for it, no questions asked. She knows a lot more than that, which is how Ray finds them both in the business of smuggling aliens across the border into the United States. This involves the two women in making hazardous car trips across the ice of a frozen river, dealing with unsavory types on both sides, and carrying Chinese and Pakistanis in the trunk.

Frozen River, a debut film written and directed by Courtney Hunt, never steps wrong. It resists all temptations to turn this plot into some kind of a thriller and keeps it grounded on the struggle for economic survival. The winner of the Grand Jury Prize at Sundance 2008, it is one of those rare independent films that knows precisely what it intends and what the meaning of the story is.

Ray Eddy is a heroine in her life. She refuses

all offers by her son T.J. (Charlie McDermott) to drop out of school and get a job. She begs for full-time work at the store. She never set out to smuggle humans (she's tricked into it), but once she gets into it, she finds it pays well. She has no particular feelings about the people in the car trunk and throws away the Pakistani's precious duffel bag because it "might contain poison gas, and I don't want to be responsible for that."

T.J. watches solemnly and knows the real story: His dad has run off on them, there is no food, he is responsible for his little brother, the men are coming to collect the TV set. For Lila, life is sad; she perches on a freezing night in a tree outside her mother-in-law's window for glimpses of her baby and shares Pringles with the watchdog. She has Ray count the money in all of their deals because she can't see the bills.

Do these two women bond? This is not a story of bonding. It is a story of need. They hardly have a conversation that isn't practical and immediate, and theory and sentiment are beyond them. Neither actress is afraid to seem cold and detached. That we know their inner feelings is a tribute to the film. I don't know how Courtney Hunt came by her knowledge of this world, but it feels exact and familiar. Even the scenes with a state trooper (Michael O'Keefe) are played quietly and with a certain sympathy. But notice the grim realism of a scene at a topless bar (also in a house trailer).

And there is an awesome, terrifying beauty in their journeys across the ice. "I've seen semis make it," Lila says. The Mohawk reservation on the American side provides a kind of sanctuary for smugglers—although the tribal elders are wise to her and won't let her own a car. Ray's status as a white woman gives them a kind of immunity—for a while. The way the trooper approaches the case is matter-of-fact and humane.

In detail after detail, *Frozen River* is the story of two lives in economic emergency, and two women who are brave and resourceful and ready to do what is necessary. It doesn't play sides. It isn't about illegal aliens or smuggling. It's about replacing popcorn and Tang with a meal at the Chopper and some nice TV dinners. That it climaxes on Christmas Eve doesn't even seem contrived, just sad.

Fugitive Pieces ★ ★ ★ ½
R, 108 m., 2008

Stephen Dillane (Jakob), Rade Sherbedgia (Athos), Rosamund Pike (Alex), Ayelet Zurer (Michaela), Robbie Kay (Young Jakob), Ed Stoppard (Ben), Rachelle Lefevre (Naomi). Directed by Jeremy Podeswa. Produced by Robert Lantos. Screenplay by Podeswa, based on the novel by Anne Michaels.

"To live with ghosts requires solitude."

So says the hero of *Fugitive Pieces,* a Canadian writer who as a child in Poland saw the Nazis murder his parents and drag away his sister. Rescued by a Greek archaeologist who was miraculously working on a dig near his hiding place, the boy is taken to safety on the man's home island in Greece, and eventually fate and a teaching position take them to Toronto. Having been gripped by the big silent eyes of the boy Jakob (Robbie Kay), we now meet him as an adult (Stephen Dillane). Both he and his savior, Athos (Rade Sherbedgia), are committed to recording the past so it will be saved from oblivion.

But it is his own past Jakob is most concerned about losing. He obsessively returns to his memories of his parents and sister, especially the tragic event he glimpsed from his hiding place behind some wallpaper. There are moments when he focuses on his lovely mother and we wonder if they ever happened; has desire augmented his memories? In the present, he is married to Alex (Rosamund Pike). He relentlessly tells her about the importance of not forgetting (one Holocaust survivor, he tells her, kept a photograph hidden under her tongue for three months; its discovery would have brought death). Alex encourages him to live sometimes in the present, but then she finds in his diary that he fears she is stealing that past away. "It makes your brain explode," she says, "his obsession with these details."

She walks out, and that triggers the thoughts about living in solitude. The line and all the poetic narration in the film come from the novel by Anne Michaels that inspired it. Jakob shares the original Toronto apartment he moved into with Athos, who grows older and, if such a thing is possible, kinder; such saints are rare. "You must try to be buried in ground that will remember you," he says, and that leads to Jakob's return to the Greek island, where he divides his year with Toronto. There are neighbors in Toronto, Yiddish-speaking, whose son, Ben (Ed Stoppard), grows up and introduces the adult Jakob to another woman, a museum curator named Michaela (Ayelet Zurer). This woman is too good to be true, but then, for such a morose and fearful person, Jakob is blessed with wonderful people in his life. He takes her to Greece, he feels love, he begins to free himself from his ghosts.

Such a summary barely captures the qualities of *Fugitive Pieces*, written and directed by Jeremy Podeswa (*The Five Senses, Into the West*). He doesn't tell, he evokes, with the nostalgic images of his cinematographer, Gregory Middleton, the understated melancholy of the score by Nikos Kypourgos and the seamless time transitions of his editor, Wiebke von Carolsfeld. The film glides between the past and different periods in Jakob's later life, as it tries to show this man whose love for his family has essentially frozen him at the time he last saw them. He tortures himself: If he hadn't run away, would his sister have returned to their home? After being taken by the Nazis? Not likely.

There are other harrowing scenes, showing the Nazi occupation of the Greek island and the heroism of Athos in protecting Jakob and doing risky favors for neighbors. But the film is not about the Holocaust so much as it is about memory, how we use it, how we must treasure it, how we must not be enslaved by it. The lushly photographed earth tones of the Toronto scenes indeed almost evoke a storehouse for the past, and its shadows are finally burned away by the sunshine of Greece.

Since the film premiered in September 2007 at Toronto, more than one viewer has talked in wonder about its comforting qualities. For a film about the Holocaust, it is gentler than we might expect. A lot of that quality is caused by the face and presence of Rade Sherbedgia, an actor whose name you may not know although you have probably seen him many times. Some people have a quality of just smiling at you and making things heal. He does. And Stephen Dillane's worried, haunted face

gives him the right person to work on, if only Athos, too, were not so absorbed in the past. If *Fugitive Pieces* has a message, it is that life can heal us, if we allow it.

Funny People ★★★ ½
R, 146 m., 2009

Adam Sandler (George Simmons), Seth Rogen (Ira Wright), Leslie Mann (Laura), Eric Bana (Clarke), Jonah Hill (Leo), Jason Schwartzman (Mark), Aubrey Plaza (Daisy), Torsten Voges (Dr. Lars). Directed by Judd Apatow and produced by Apatow, Clayton Townsend, and Barry Mendel. Screenplay by Apatow.

Stand-up comics feel compelled to make you laugh. They're like an obnoxious uncle, with better material. The competition is so fierce these days that most of them are pretty good. I laugh a lot. But unlike my feelings for Catherine Keener, for example, I don't find myself wishing they were my friends. I suspect they're laughing on the outside but gnashing their teeth on the inside.

Judd Apatow would possibly agree with this theory. I e-mailed him a bunch of questions, and that was the only one he ignored. He was writing material for comics when he was a teenager, and his insights into the stand-up world inform *Funny People*, his new film that has a lot of humor and gnashing. It's centered on Adam Sandler's best performance, playing George Simmons, a superstar comic who learns he has a very short time to live.

He is without the resources to handle this news. He doesn't have the "support group" they say you need when you get sick. He's made a dozen hit movies and lives in opulence in a house overlooking Los Angeles but is so isolated he doesn't even seem to have any vices for company. Sandler modulates George's desperation in a perceptive, sympathetic performance; I realized here, as I did during his *Punch Drunk Love*, that he contains an entirely different actor than the one we're familiar with. His fans are perfectly happy with Sandler's usual persona, the passive-aggressive semi-simpleton. This other Sandler plays above and below that guy, and more deeply.

Funny People is not simply about George Simmons's struggle with mortality. It sees that struggle within the hermetically sealed world of the stand-up comic, a secret society that has merciless rules, one of which is that even sincerity is a joke. "No—seriously!"

Here is a man without confidants. When you depend on your agent for emotional support, you're probably only getting 10 percent as much as you need. On the circuit, he meets a hungry, ambitious kid named Ira Wright (Seth Rogen), who has written some good material. George hires him to write for him, and then gives him a chance to open for him, and then finds himself pouring out his worries to him.

There was a girl once in George's past named Laura (Leslie Mann). She was the one who got away. He encounters her again, married to an obnoxious macho Aussie named Clarke (Eric Bana, playing him as a guy who seems to be weighing the possibility of hitting everyone he meets). George apparently was once able to sort of confide in Laura, until success shut him down, and now he finds he still sort of can.

The thing about *Funny People* is that it's a real movie. That means carefully written dialogue and carefully placed supporting performances—and it's *about something*. It could have easily been a formula film, and the trailer shamelessly tries to misrepresent it as one, but George Simmons learns and changes during his ordeal, and we empathize.

This is a new Seth Rogen on the screen. Much thinner, dialed down, with more dimensions. Rogen was showing signs of forever playing the same buddy-movie costar, but here we find that he, too, has another actor inside. So does Jason Schwartzman, who often plays vulnerable but here presents his character as the kind of successful rival you love to hate.

Rogen and Leslie Mann find the right notes as George's impromptu support group. The plot doesn't blindly insist that George and Laura must find love; it simply suggests they could do better in their lives. Eric Bana makes a satisfactory comic villain, there is a rolling-around-on-the-lawn fight scene that's convincingly clumsy, and Mann mocks him with a spot-on Aussie accent (not the standard pleasant one, more of a bray).

Apatow understands that every supporting actor has to pull his weight. The casting director who found him Torsten Voges to play George's doctor earned a day's pay. Voges is in some eerie, bizarre way convincing as a cheerful realist bringing terrible news: miles better than your stereotyped grim movie surgeon.

After an enormously successful career as a producer, this is Apatow's third film as a director, after *The 40-Year-Old Virgin* and *Knocked Up*. Of him it can be said: He is a real director. He's still only forty-one. So here we go.

G

Gentlemen Broncos ★★
PG-13, 89 m., 2009

Michael Angarano (Benjamin Purvis), Jennifer Coolidge (Judith Purvis), Jemaine Clement (Dr. Ronald Chevalier), Hector Jimenez (Lonnie Donaho), Halley Feiffer (Tabitha), Sam Rockwell (Bronco/Brutus). Directed by Jared Hess and produced by John J. Kelly and Mike White. Screenplay by Jared Hess and Jerusha Hess.

As an amateur collector of the titles of fictional novels in movies, I propose that this one has the worst of all time: *Yeast Lords: The Bronco Years.* You say you smiled? Me, too, and there are precious few smiles and laughs in *Gentlemen Broncos,* which is not a very good movie title either, although it might work for an x-rated film. The author of *Yeast Lords* is a teenager named Benjamin who hopefully writes science fiction and idolizes a famous sci-fi novelist named Dr. Ronald Chevalier as much as I once, and still do, admire the good doctor Asimov.

Benjamin Purvis (Michael Angarano) lives in a Buckydome house with his mother, Judith (Jennifer Coolidge), and let's pause right here to observe that Jennifer Coolidge, here and in Werner Herzog's forthcoming *Bad Lieutenant,* possesses what I like to think of as the Walken Factor. That is, her appearance in any scene immediately inspires our particular interest because we sense something unexpected and amusing is about to happen. So it was with her iconic appearance as Stifler's mom in *American Pie* (1999), in which she had the rare honor of inspiring the Internet acronym *MILF.* If you doubt me, look it up in Wiktionary. Hard as it is to believe, *MILF* was not used until Stifler's mom appeared.

Here she is Purvis's mom, and she encourages his budding writing skills by allowing him attend the Cletus Fest, a teenage authors' event that offers the awesome presence of Dr. Ronald Chevalier (Jemaine Clement). He's a science-fiction author with writer's block, and when Benjamin presses a copy of *Yeast Lords: The Bronco Years* into his hands, in a moment of desperation he snatches it up, makes some changes, and submits it as his own work.

That sounds, I suppose, as if *Gentlemen Broncos* might tell a good story. Perhaps the Hollywood gurus who advise, "story, story story" might add: "but don't stop there." The director, Jared Hess, who made *Napoleon Dynamite,* a film I admit I didn't get, has made a film I don't even begin to get. He invents good characters: Purvis, Purvis's mom, Dr. Ronald Chevalier, and Tabitha (Halley Feiffer, daughter of the immortal Jules), who is a wannabe romance novelist, as are we all. Mike White turns up toward the end, providing another Walken Factor moment. But then Hess loses them in a jumbled plot that sometimes seems to mystify the characters. A character-driven plot, if it isn't *The Big Lebowski,* involves people who know what they want and when they want it.

Benjamin sells the film rights to his work to Tabitha and her friend Lonnie (Hector Jimenez), who is the Masha to her Rupert Pupkin. They plan a production that promises to be a mumblecore version of *Star Wars,* and, of course, there are problems with Dr. Ronald Chevalier. This film, Benjamin's novel, and the doctor's rewrite inspire different versions of the fictional hero under various names, and these fantasy sequences are sometimes amusing, but they seem freestanding and a little forlorn. They do suggest that the worst movie title in history would be *Yeast Lords: The Bronco Years: The IMAX Experience.*

Get Him to the Greek ★★★
R, 108 m., 2010

Jonah Hill (Aaron Green), Russell Brand (Aldous Snow), Elisabeth Moss (Daphne Binks), Rose Byrne (Jackie Q), Colm Meaney (Jonathan Snow), Sean Combs (Sergio Roma). Directed by Nicholas Stoller and produced by Judd Apatow, David L. Bushell, and Rodney Rothman. Screenplay by Stoller.

Aldous Snow is the sort of rock star who can seriously propose himself for the role of White African Jesus. What would his duties be? He has no idea. It's just the sort of thing he throws out to keep people on their toes. Aldous was first seen as a rock star, clean and sober, in *Forgetting Sarah Marshall* (2008), and he returns in *Get Him to the Greek* as a wild man deep into a relapse.

It is the task of an earnest and square young man, Aaron Green, to fly to London and in exactly three days get him to New York for a *Today* show appearance and then to Los Angeles for a comeback concert at the Greek Theater. *Get Him to the Greek* is the story of those three days, and nights, which pass in a blur for the innocent Green. They are a blur for Aldous as well, but then, that's his lifestyle.

The movie is funny in the way of *The Hangover* about what trouble lads can get into when their senses are whirling. Unlike some depictions of binges, it doesn't shortchange vomit. The adventures of Aldous and Aaron remind me of a friend I used to meet on Saturday mornings for what we called Drunch. "Sometimes," she said, "it can be really exhausting having a good time." Aaron (Jonah Hill), who has been threatened with flaying if he doesn't deliver Aldous (Russell Brand) on time, panics when he can't get him to Heathrow airport for the right flight, can't get him to the *Today* show on time, can't get him to the sound check at the Greek, and very nearly can't get him to the Greek. Aldous, for the most part, floats benevolently above these small misunderstandings. When it comes to himself, he's a very understanding man.

There are really two movies here. One is a gross-out comedy that grows lyrical in its exuberant offensive language, its drug excesses, its partying, its animal behavior. The other movie, which comes into focus, so to speak, in the last half, is surprisingly sweet, and shows that Aldous and Aaron arrive at a friendship that has been tempered in the forge of their misbehavior. Both movies were produced by Judd Apatow, who does a nice line in gross-out comedies.

The lads share loneliness and a feeling of failure with women. Aaron is in love with Daphne Binks (Elisabeth Moss of *Mad Men*), a hospital intern who works endless shifts and gets a great job offer in Seattle, far from the music biz. Aldous has split from Jackie Q (Rose Byrne) as a consequence of his spectacular fall from sobriety. We learn they earlier collaborated on an album voted the worst of all time, but while Aldous has plunged, Jackie Q has soared. In a movie jammed with celebrity cameos (Paul Krugman?), we see bits of her music videos, which, incredible as they may be, aren't entirely improbable. We are so deep into post-irony that it's hard to be sure if a video is *intended* to be bad.

The reason the friendship works is that Russell Brand and Jonah Hill are good actors. Hill's character is required to be blotto half of the time, but there's the sense that he's desperately trying to do the right thing. Russell Brand is convincing as a rock star, imperious, self-destructive, smarter than he seems, calculating, measuring out wretched excess in survivable portions. When it comes time for him to sing, he does it convincingly, with songs that sound like real rock songs. I was reminded a little of Rod Stewart.

The urgency of Aaron's mission depends entirely on his fear of Sergio Roma (Sean Combs), the owner of Aldous's record label. Combs is convincing in an early scene as an egotistical, hard-driving music executive. Then his character has a comic flowering in later scenes, as he reveals his true rock 'n' roll roots. He can party at top speed *and* send Aldous onstage at the Greek despite a bleeding wound from a jump from a rooftop. That Aldous may collapse onstage doesn't occur to him. And indeed Aldous rises to the occasion, as from many reports a lot of rock stars are able to do. They may not remember their performances, but they were great.

What I'm backing into here is that under the cover of slapstick, cheap laughs, raunchy humor, gross-out physical comedy, and sheer exploitation, *Get Him to the Greek* is also fundamentally a sound movie. The writer-director, Nicholas Stoller, who also directed *Forgetting Sarah Marshall*, carefully places the foundations of the story and restrains himself from making Aldous and Aaron into *completely* unbelievable caricatures. The fundamentals are in place.

Get Smart ★ ★ ★ ½
PG-13, 110 m., 2008

Steve Carell (Maxwell Smart), Anne Hathaway (Agent 99), Dwayne Johnson (Agent 23), Alan Arkin (The Chief), Terence Stamp (Siegfried), James Caan (The President). Directed by Peter Segal and produced by Andrew Lazar, Charles

Roven, Alex Gartner, and Michael Ewing.
Screenplay by Tom J. Astle and Matt Ember.

The closing credits of *Get Smart* mention Mel Brooks and Buck Henry, creators of the original TV series, as "consultants." Their advice must have been: "If it works, don't fix it." There have been countless comic spoofs of the genre founded by James Bond, but *Get Smart* (both on TV and now in a movie) is one of the best. It's funny, exciting, preposterous, great to look at, and made with the same level of technical expertise we'd expect from a new Bond movie itself. And all of that is very nice, but nicer still is the perfect pitch of the casting.

Steve Carell makes an infectious Maxwell Smart, the bumbling but ambitious and unreasonably self-confident agent for CONTROL, a secret U.S. agency in rivalry with the CIA. His job is to decipher overheard conversations involving agents of KAOS, its Russian counterpart. At this he is excellent: What does it mean that KAOS agents discuss muffins? That they have a high level of anxiety, of course, because muffins are a comfort food. Brilliant, but he misses the significance of the bakery they're also discussing—a cookery for high-level uranium.

Smart is amazingly promoted to field agent by The Chief (Alan Arkin, calm and cool) and teamed with the beautiful Agent 99 (Anne Hathaway, who never tries too hard but dominates the screen effortlessly). They go to Russia, joining with Agent 23 (Dwayne Johnson, once known as The Rock). Their archenemy is waiting for them; he's Siegfried (Terence Stamp), a cool, clipped villain.

And that's about it, except for a series of special effects sequences and stunt work that would truly give envy to a James Bond producer. *Get Smart* is an A-level production, not a cheapo rip-off, and some of the chase sequences are among the most elaborate you can imagine—particularly a climactic number involving planes, trains, and automobiles. Maxwell Smart, of course, proves indestructible, often because of the intervention of Agent 99; he spends much of the center portion of the film in free fall without a parachute, and then later is towed behind an airplane.

The plot involves a KAOS scheme to nuke the Walt Disney concert hall in Los Angeles, during a concert being attended by the U.S.

president. The nuclear device in question is concealed beneath the concert grand on the stage, which raises the question, since you're using the Bomb, does its location make much difference, give or take a few miles?

It raises another question, too, and here I will be the gloom-monger at the festivities. Remember right after 9/11, when we wondered if Hollywood would ever again be able to depict terrorist attacks as entertainment? How long ago that must have been, since now we are blowing up presidents and cities as a plot device for Maxwell Smart. I'm not objecting, just observing. Maybe humor has a way of helping us face our demons.

The props in the movie are neat, especially a Swiss Army–style knife that Maxwell never quite masters. The locations, many in Montreal, are awesome; I learned with amazement that Moscow was not one of them but must have been created on a computer. The action and chase sequences do not grow tedious because they are punctuated with humor. I am not given to quoting filmmakers in praise of their own work in press releases, but director Peter Segal does an excellent job of describing his method: "If we plan a fight sequence as a rhythmic series of punches, we would have a 'bump, bump, bam' or a 'bump, bump, smack.' We can slot in a punch line instead of a physical hit. The rhythm accentuates the joke and it becomes 'bump, bump, joke' with the verbal jab as the knockout or a joke, immediately followed by the last physical beat that essentially ends the conversation."

Yes. And the jokes actually have something to do with a developing story line involving Anne Hathaway's love life, the reason for her plastic surgery, and a love triangle that is right there staring us in the face. One of the gifts of Steve Carell is to deliver punch lines in the middle of punches and allow both to seem real enough, at least within the context of the movie. James Bond could do that, too. And in a summer with no new Bond picture, will I be considered a heretic by saying *Get Smart* will do just about as well?

G-Force ★★ ½
PG, 89 m., 2009

Voices of animated characters: Nicolas Cage (Speckles), Sam Rockwell (Darwin), Jon Favreau

(Hurley), Penelope Cruz (Juarez), Steve Buscemi (Bucky), Tracy Morgan (Blaster). Homo sapiens: Bill Nighy (Leonard Saber), Will Arnett (Kip Killian), Zach Galifianakis (Ben Kendall), Kelli Garner (Marcie), Tyler Patrick Jones (Connor), Piper Mackenzie Harris (Penny), Gabriel Casseus (Agent Trigstad), Jack Conley (Agent Carter). Directed by Hoyt Yeatman and produced by Jerry Bruckheimer. Screenplay by Cormac and Marianne Wibberley, Ted Elliott, Terry Rossio, and Tim Firth.

G-Force is a pleasant, inoffensive 3-D animated farce about a team of superspy guinea pigs who do battle with a mad billionaire who wants to conquer the earth by programming all the home appliances made by his corporation to follow his instructions. It will possibly be enjoyed by children of all ages.

The film is nonstop, wall-to-wall madcap action. It's possible to imagine Jerry Bruckheimer, the producer, and his cast and crew side by side with the little creatures on their whirling hamster wheels. But be careful what you say out loud. The guinea pigs resent being mistaken for hamsters, as do we all.

The evil billionaire is named Saber and played by Bill Nighy in what we might describe as a one-of-a-kind performance. The FBI has been on his trail for two years, but in one single night the G-Force is able to save the planet by stealthily introducing a worm, or virus, or something into his diabolical software. All of the cyber work is done by a keyboard whiz with the intensity appropriate for a programmer racing to key in code to outwit the program. You should see that little fella type. Man, oh man.

There are a limited number of other creatures in the film, including the gaseous hamster Hurley (Jon Favreau), who is loudly and frequently flatulent. I thought I heard some of his pals calling him "Farty," but that could be just me. The G-Force also includes Darwin (Sam Rockwell), Juarez (Penelope Cruz), and Bucky (Steve Buscemi). Nicolas Cage plays a mole named Speckles with a wise lack of his usual intensity. You don't want a hyperactive mole. I didn't know they had those twitchy pink feelers on their noses. Must tickle. Juarez (Cruz) provides the animal sex appeal, al-

though, if you ask me, one guinea pig looks about like another.

Now here is the neat part. How will the remote-controlled home appliances conquer the earth? Well, sir, they will all fly together and amalgamate themselves into gigantic robots made of assorted mechanical parts. We see one of these metal monsters, and why, if I didn't know better, I'd have to say it looks like a . . . yes, I think so . . . a . . . Transformer! Except made from Cuisinarts instead of Chevys. How will they all conquer the earth? By stomping on things.

These slave appliances can be dangerous. Hurley becomes entrapped in a microwave oven, which cycles itself through several settings, from Cake to Chicken, yet is unable to cook its captive. I had a microwave like that once. It wouldn't cook doodley-squat.

There is also a human cast, including not only Bill Nighy but Kelli Garner as a veterinarian, Zach Galifianakis as a big, shaggy guy, Will Arnett as a thin, not shaggy guy, and Gabriel Casseus as Agent Trigstad. Anything else you need to know?

Ghosts of Girlfriends Past ★ ★
PG-13, 100 m., 2009

Matthew McConaughey (Connor Mead), Jennifer Garner (Jenny Perotti), Michael Douglas (Uncle Wayne), Breckin Meyer (Paul Mead), Lacey Chabert (Sandra Volkom), Robert Forster (Sergeant Volkom), Anne Archer (Vondra Volkom), Emma Stone (Allison Vandermeersh). Directed by Mark Waters and produced by Jon Shestack and Brad Epstein. Screenplay by Jon Lucas and Scott Moore.

Remember *Harry, the Rat with Women*? This time his name is Connor Mead, but he's still a rat. A modern Scrooge who believes marriage is humbug, he is taught otherwise by the ghosts of girlfriends past, present, and future, and one who spans all of those periods. Just like Scrooge, he's less interesting after he reforms.

Matthew McConaughey plays Connor as a rich and famous *Vanity Fair* photographer whose ambition is to have sex with every woman he meets, as soon as possible. Sometimes this leads to a logjam. Impatient to sleep with his latest quarry, a model who just allowed an apple to be shot off her head with an arrow, Connor actually arranges an online video chat session to break up with three current girlfriends simultaneously, but is big-hearted enough to allow them to chat with one another after he logs off.

Connor appears on the eve of the wedding of his younger brother Paul (Breckin Meyer), who lives in the mansion of their late Uncle Wayne (Michael Douglas), a structure designed roughly along the lines of Versailles. (Actually, it's Castle Hill, in Ipswich, Massachusetts, built by the Crane family of Chicago, whose toilets you may have admired.) Connor is attending the wedding only to warn against it; he has a horror of getting hitched and extols a lifetime of unrestrained promiscuity.

The movie is apparently set in the present. I mention that because every woman Connor meets knows all about his reputation for having countless conquests, and yet is nevertheless eager to service him. These days, I suspect a great many of those women, maybe all of them, would view him primarily as a likely carrier of sexually transmitted diseases. To be fair, in a fantasy scene, his used condoms rain from the heavens, an event not nearly as thought-provoking as the raining frogs in *Magnolia.*

Attending the wedding is Jenny (the lovely Jennifer Garner, from *Juno*), who was his first girlfriend and the one he should have married. The ghost of Uncle Wayne materializes as a spirit guide and takes Connor on a guided tour of his wretched excess, after which he bitterly regrets his loss of Jenny, leading to a development which I do not have enough shiny new dimes to award to everyone who can predict it.

Michael Douglas is widely said to have modeled his hair, glass frames, and general appearance on the noted womanizer Bob Evans, but actually he reminded me more of Kirk Douglas playing Bob Evans. It's an effective performance either way you look at it.

The potential is here for a comedy that could have been hilarious. But the screenplay spaces out some undeniably funny lines in too much plot business, and Matthew McConaughey, while admirably villainous as a

lecher, is not convincing as a charmer. Just this weekend a new Michael Caine movie is opening, which makes me remember his Alfie, a performance that is to lechers as Brando is to godfathers.

Maybe the movie's problem runs a little deeper. It's not particularly funny to hear women described and valued exclusively in terms of their function as disposable sexual partners. A lot of Connor's dialogue is just plain sadistic and qualifies him as that part of an ass it shares with a doughnut.

Ghost Town ★ ★ ★
PG-13, 102 m., 2008

Ricky Gervais (Bertram Pincus), Tea Leoni (Gwen), Greg Kinnear (Frank Herlihy), Billy Campbell (Richard), Kristen Wiig (Surgeon), Dana Ivey (Marjorie Pickthall), Aasif Mandvi (Dr. Prashar). Directed by David Koepp and produced by Gavin Polone. Screenplay by Koepp and John Kamps.

Why do I think Ricky Gervais is so funny in *Ghost Town*? Because he doesn't want to appear funny. He wants to appear aggravated. He plays a character named Bertram Pincus, who does not suffer fools gladly. When you consider everyone to be a fool, that can be a heavy cross to bear. Gervais, a British actor whose work on television is legion, has at last found a leading role in a feature, and it's a good one.

Bertram Pincus is not a happy camper. He is a dentist, a profession in which he finds delight in preventing patients from talking with him. He is unmarried, friendless, a loner, meticulous, obtuse, at times ridiculous. When a birthday cake is laid on for a friendly colleague in his office, he sneaks out. To join in the celebration would make his skin crawl. He is nasty to innocent bystanders.

He does all of this in a British accent, almost between clenched teeth, and reminds me a little of Terry-Thomas at full flood: an unmitigated bounder wrapped in propriety. He is about to have his moat breached. This assault is set in motion when a bus flattens Frank Herlihy (Greg Kinnear). Frank's death turns out to be linked to Bertram's colonoscopy. As you can imagine, Bertram is a man who considers a colonoscopy a grievous viola-tion of privacy.

Bertram is technically dead for seven min-utes during the procedure. (Don't put yours off; this is a microscopically rare phenome-non.) That makes him sort of half-dead, half-alive after he recovers, and as a result he can see both living people and ghosts. This puts him in urgent demand among the ghosts, who yearn to communicate with their loved ones and need him as a medium. The most desper-ate ghost he encounters is Frank, who was having an affair with his yoga instructor but now deeply regrets it and wants to communi-cate with his wife, Gwen (Tea Leoni).

Never mind about the plot details, which spin out in more or less obligatory fashion. Focus instead on Tea Leoni, lovable down to her toenails, and Frank, cursed by having to live (or die, that is) enveloped in guilt and gloom. Bertram recoils when a stranger ap-proaches him. He is even more inconve-nienced by ghosts. And he is the last man on earth who would attract Gwen, or be attracted by her, so of course he and Gwen find them-selves falling in love, causing unspeakable frustration for Frank.

Ghost Town is a lightweight rom-com ele-vated by its performances. It is a reminder that the funniest people are often not comedians but actors playing straight in funny roles. Consider Cary Grant in *Topper* (1937), the ob-vious inspiration for David Koepp, who di-rected and cowrote *Ghost Town* with John Kamps. Because both Gervais and Kinnear seem so urgent in their desires, and because Tea Leoni has a seemingly effortless humor and grace, this material becomes for a while sort of enchanting.

Yes, it is required that the plot have some of its characters living happily ever after, and that requires some dialogue that is, excuse me, corny. I suppose it comes with the territory. There is poignancy in a subplot involving Dana Ivey as a woman who wants to commu-nicate with her daughters, and indeed a whole crowd of ghosts hoping to send messages to the other side. We have this comforting notion of our deceased loved ones smiling down benevolently from heaven. Now that they're getting a good look at us, they're probably tearing out their hair.

The Ghost Writer ★★★★
PG-13, 124 m., 2010

Ewan McGregor (The Ghost), Pierce Brosnan (Adam Lang), Kim Cattrall (Amelia Bly), Olivia Williams (Ruth Lang), Tom Wilkinson (Paul Emmett), Timothy Hutton (Sidney Kroll), Robert Pugh (Richard Rycart), James Belushi (John Maddox), Eli Wallach (Old Man). Directed by Roman Polanski and produced by Polanski, Robert Benmussa, and Alain Sarde. Screenplay by Polanski and Robert Harris, based on a novel by Harris.

In Roman Polanski's movie *The Ghost Writer,* a man without a past rattles around in the life of a man with too much of one. He begins by reading the work of an earlier ghost who mys-teriously drowned, and finds it boring and conventional. Hired to pep it up to justify a $10 million advance, he discovers material to make it exciting, all right, and possibly deadly.

This movie is the work of a man who knows how to direct a thriller. Smooth, calm, confident, it builds suspense instead of de-pending on shock and action. The actors cre-ate characters who suggest intriguing secrets. The atmosphere—a rain-swept Martha's Vineyard in winter—has an ominous, gray chill, and the main interior looks just as cold.

This is the beach house being used by Adam Lang (Pierce Brosnan), a former British prime minister so inspired by Tony Blair that he might as well be wearing a name tag. Lang has one of those households much beloved by British authors of country house mysteries, in which everyone is a potential suspect—of something, anyway. His wife, Ruth (Olivia Williams), smart and bitter, met Lang at Cam-bridge. His assistant, Amelia (Kim Cattrall), smart and devious, is having an affair with him. The wife knows and isn't above referring to it before the Ghost (Ewan McGregor). Se-curity men lurk about, and a serving couple look rather sinister.

Just as his ghost writer starts work, Lang is accused by his former foreign minister of sanctioning the kidnapping and torture of suspects. The World Court prepares an indict-ment. It would be unwise for him to return to Britain, and he flees to Washington for a photo op with the U.S. administration, unnamed, although the secretary of state looks a whole lot like Condi Rice.

The story is based on a best-seller by Robert Harris, who cowrote the screenplay with Polanski. He implies parallels between his story and the Blair and (both) Bush administrations, but uses a light touch and sly footwork so that not every viewer will necessarily connect the dots. There is also a loud, clanging alarm inviting comparison between Lang, an exile sought by a court, and Polanski himself. This is also the fourth thriller in recent months to make a villain of a corporation obviously modeled on Halliburton.

The Ghost is left to his own devices in a house haunted by the unsaid, and Polanski slips into a pure filmmaking mode. I won't describe what the Ghost searches for, but I will tell you that Polanski evokes Hitchcock in a conversation with an elderly local (Eli Wallach) and some forbidding beach scenes. And that he is masterful in the way he shows the dead former ghost providing the new one with directions, so to speak, leading to a possible source.

There is also a Hitchcock touch in visuals where an incriminating note is passed from hand to hand; the scene is so well done that it distracts from the fact that the Ghost didn't need the information in the note to arrive at the same inference.

There are a few other loose ends. The film seems to have a high incidence of black cars designed to be used as murder weapons. It's far from clear what Ruth Lang's emotional state is on one rainy night. The Ghost himself seems too much a lightweight to explain his daring sleuthing. But the performances are so convincing in detail that they distract us from our questions. McGregor's character has no family, little pride, and much insouciance, but is very smart and doesn't enjoy his intelligence being insulted. And Olivia Williams projects the air of a wife who is committed to her husband in more than expected ways.

The Ghost Writer is handsome, smooth, and persuasive. It is a Well Made Film. Polanski at seventy-six provides a reminder of directors of the past who were raised on craft, not gimmicks, and depended on a deliberate rhythm of editing rather than mindless quick cutting. The film immerses you in its experience. It's a reminder that you can lose yourself in a story because all a film really wants to do is tell it.

Gigante ★★★

NO MPAA RATING, 88 m., 2010

Horacio Camandule (Jara), Leonor Svarcas (Julia). Directed by Adrian Biniez and produced by Fernando Epstein. Screenplay by Biniez.

We are all voyeurs, although some people fondly describe themselves as "people watchers." Going to the movies is at some level pure voyeurism—if they involve people, that is. Transformers don't count. I admire films that consist only or in large part of watching. *Vertigo* is the classic example, and *The Lives of Others* was voyeurism by eavesdropping.

Gigante is a film that has little meaningful dialogue; just incidental comments along the stream of a boring life. Jara (Horacio Camandule), is a big, strong, lonely man, who works the night shift in a huge supermarket in Montevideo, watching security monitors. He lives alone, and his social life is restricted to messing around with his young nephew. In the company lunchroom, he doesn't chat. Nor does he drink, smoke, watch TV, or much of anything else. He sometimes works as a nightclub bouncer.

One night on his video monitors, Jara notices Julia (Leonor Svarcas). She's a member of the corps of cleaning women, mopping the aisles. He observes her shoplifting something. He doesn't care. Clicking on his cameras, he's able to follow her around the store. Almost immediately, he starts following her around her life.

Since Julia is heard to say nothing until the very end of the film, all depends on the performance of Camandule. Since he says so little, it depends in turn on his presence, his aura. He is tall, broad, overweight, taciturn. He isn't the "gentle giant" type. On the other hand, because he can (as we see) efficiently wallop anyone, he has no need to act intimidating. He just sits or walks around, absorbed in his thoughts.

Of course he wants to ask Julia out. Of course he lacks the nerve. He follows her everywhere—shopping, home, to the movies, to an Internet café, even on a date with a pudgy nerd. Jara is innovative. Later he manages to strike up a conversation with the nerd and discovers the nerd doesn't think Julia liked him. It was their first date. Their tastes didn't match. For one thing, she likes heavy metal, and the nerd can't stand it.

This news is Tabasco for Jara. He has Metallica posters on his wall, listens to metal on his iPod, keeps rhythm with his hands. Does this give him courage? Not exactly. Is it creepy that he follows her? Technically, yes, but we sense he's no threat; his presence reads more as protective, and sad. We have no idea if they have a future together, but we hope he'll work up the courage to at least speak to her.

Because of the limitations imposed by the nature of *Gigante*, and because of Jara's simple, almost childish shyness, the film doesn't transcend its characters. Like Jara, it waits and watches. I kept watching. I was curious. We were both wondering if he would ever ask her out. I think I wanted him to more than he did.

Gigantic ★ ★ ½
R, 98 m., 2009

Paul Dano (Brian Weathersby), Zooey Deschanel (Harriet Lolly), Ed Asner (Mr. Weathersby), Jane Alexander (Mrs. Weathersby), John Goodman (Al Lolly), Sean Dugan (Gary Wynkoop), Brian Avers (Larry Arbogast). Directed by Matt Aselton and produced by Christine Vachon and Mindy Goldberg. Screenplay by Aselton and Adam Nagata.

On the basis of *Gigantic*, Matt Aselton can make a fine and original film. This isn't quite it, but it has moments so good all you wish for is a second draft. Nor is it ever boring. You can't say that about a lot of debuts. I suspect he was trying too hard to be terrific and not hard enough to get organized.

His hero, Brian Weathersby (the willfully bland Paul Dano), is a young and feckless mattress salesman. He was a late son in a tribe of unconventional brothers. When they all get together with Dad (Ed Asner) in the family's cottage in the woods, Dad bonds with him by consuming hallucinogenic mushrooms. How Brian would know he was hallucinating is a

good question, because much of his life unfolds on the border of reality.

The Swiss mattress showroom occupies a vast upper floor of a warehouse. Into this space one day marches Al Lolly (John Goodman), a big man with a painful back problem. Brian shows him the high-end $14,000 mattress, which uses real horsehair, which is a big deal in the mattress universe. The mattress also inspires an inspection by Al's daughter Harriet (Zooey Deschanel), a beautiful girl with startling blue-green eyes. Although you might expect to find her on magazine covers, she is as inward as Brian; they speak in minimalist murmurs, as when she asks if he feels like having sex with her, and he confides that he does. Later he tells a friend that he doesn't know if he likes her or not. More accurately, probably, he doesn't know if he liked being jolted out of his lifelong dubiousness.

Ever since he was a little boy, Brian has been obsessed with the idea of adopting a Chinese baby. He doesn't understand why; he just is. Harriet might upset that dream in some obscure way. She invites him to her home, and he enters into a strange world ruled by Al Lolly, a rich, opinionated eccentric, who is driven everywhere flat on his back in the rear of a Volvo station wagon. The great open spaces of their apartment have been decorated by spending a great deal of money on a limited selection of furniture.

Brian's life is complicated by a berserk madman who ambushes him with assaults. This man seems imaginary, until Brian receives facial wounds that don't go away. To summarize: A loser mattress salesman with a peculiar father meets a beautiful lost girl with an eccentric millionaire father, and is attacked by a loony while trying to evade love and adopt a Chinese baby. Does this sound like a screenplay or a contest entry? In the UK it would be described as too clever by half, and "clever" is not a compliment over there.

The strange thing is, the characters are interesting. You could make a movie about them. That Brian's very sane mother is played by Jane Alexander is an example of how well the film is cast. The delicate relationship between Harriet and Brian is beautifully played by Deschanel and Dano, but the movie jars us out of it with bizarre sidetracks such as a scene set in a massage parlor; it's intended as funny but is finally a toss-up between odd and sad.

Gigantic is an example of a certain kind of "Sundance movie" made after the ship has sailed. The pendulum is swinging back toward the more classical forms of filmmaking. It's not enough to add, "Oh—and this homeless guy keeps attacking him." If you want a homeless guy, do something meaningful with him, as Mike Leigh did in *Happy-Go-Lucky*. Wackiness for its own sake is not a substitute for humor or much of anything else.

And yet look at the things here that are really good: the conversation between Brian and Harriet in the doctor's waiting room. The way the parents take to the Chinese baby. The way John Goodman modulates his performance to make Al Lolly a character and not a caricature. The way Harriet falls asleep on the $14,000 mattress, and what they say after she wakes up. Matt Aselton's next film might be a marvel.

G.I. Joe: The Rise of Cobra ★ ½
PG-13, 118 m., 2009

Adewale Akinnuoye-Agbaje (Heavy Duty), Christopher Eccleston (McCullen/Destro), Joseph Gordon-Levitt (The Doctor/Rex), Byung-hun Lee (Storm Shadow), Sienna Miller (Ana/Baroness), Rachel Nichols (Scarlett), Ray Park (Snake Eyes), Jonathan Pryce (U.S. President), Said Taghmaoui (Breaker), Channing Tatum (Duke), Marlon Wayans (Ripcord), Dennis Quaid (General Hawk). Directed by Stephen Sommers and produced by Sommers, Lorenzo di Bonaventura, and Bob Ducsay. Screenplay by Stuart Beattie, David Elliot, and Paul Lovett.

G.I. Joe: The Rise of Cobra is a 118-minute animated film with sequences involving the faces and other body parts of human beings. It is sure to be enjoyed by those whose movie appreciation is defined by the ability to discern that moving pictures and sound are being employed to depict violence. Nevertheless, it is better than *Transformers: Revenge of the Fallen*.   ·

The film is inspired by Hasbro's famous line of plastic action figures. The heroes are no longer exclusively Americans, but a multinational elite strike force from many nations, which provides Paramount the opportunity to give top billing to an actor named Adewale Akinnuoye-Agbaje. And to think there was a time when Maurice Micklewhite was not considered a good name for a star. At last Hollywood allows actors to possess their real names.

The Joes, as they are called, are needed to counter "nanomites," a secret weapon that eats up people and buildings and stuff. This weapon has been invented by the evil disfigured scientist named McCullen (Christopher Eccleston), who steals it *back* from the people he sold it to and plans to use it to conquer the world. Why is McCullen so pissed off? His Scottish clan was insulted centuries ago. Those Scots.

His conquest plans are not sophisticated. He launches four nano-missiles at world capitals. Two of them are Moscow and Washington. The third one is destroyed, and if I'm not mistaken the fourth one is forgotten by the plot and is still up there somewhere. But that's the kind of detail I tend to get wrong because that's more fun than getting it right.

How fast are these missiles? They rocket into space and zoom down to Earth. A Joe named Ripcord (Marlon Wayans) commandeers the enemy's rocket airplane, and even though he's never seen it before, flies it so well that he catches up to the Moscow missile and destroys it, and *then* he turns around and flies halfway around the globe to catch up with the missile headed for Washington. He uses verbal commands to fire his air-to-air weapons, after a fellow Joe named Scarlett (Rachel Nichols) intuits that McCullen would have programmed his plane to respond to Celtic, which, luckily, she happens to speak.

These plot details are not developed at great depth, because the movie is preoccupied with providing incomprehensible wall-to-wall computer-generated special effects. I should have been carrying a little clicker to keep count, but I believe that director Stephen Sommers has more explosions in his movie than Michael Bay had in *Transformers 2* only last month. World records don't last long these days.

What is Cobra? What nationality are its leaders, other than Scottish? What will it gain by destroying world capitals? Reader, I do not know. Even the U.S. president (Jonathan Pryce) asks incredulously, "Don't they have any demands?" His role is otherwise limited to being briefed about the Joes.

Cobra has a woman named the Baroness (Sienna Miller) to match Scarlett of the Joes. These women are interesting. They have leather fetishwear and are seductively made up, but are otherwise honorary boys, because us Joe fans don't like to watch a lot of spit swapping. But because us fans liked the two jive-talkin' robots in *Transformers*, *G.I. Joe* gives us Ripcord, who is comic relief, says black stuff, and can't control his high-tech armored suit, so he runs into things. We guess he's a contrast to the calm, macho heroism of Adewale Akinnuoye-Agbaje.

The two teams also each have a skilled Ninja fighter from Japan. Why is this, you might ask? Because Japan is a huge market for CGI animation and video games, that's why. It also has a sequence set in the Egyptian desert, although there are no shots of dead robots or topless pyramids. And Cobra headquarters are buried within the miles-deep ice of the Arctic. You think construction costs are high here. At one point, the ice cap is exploded real good so it will sink and crush the G.I. Joes' submarine. We thought ice floated in water, but no, you can see big falling ice chunks real good here. It must be only in your Coke that it floats.

There is never any clear sense in the action of where anything is in relation to anything else. You get more of a binary action strategy. You see something, it fires. You see something else, it gets hit. Using the power of logic, you deduce that the first thing was aiming at the second thing.

Yet I say this movie is certainly better than *Transformers: Revenge of the Fallen*. How so? Admittedly, it doesn't have as much cleavage. But the high-tech hardware is more fun to look at than the transforming robots, the plot is as preposterous, and although the noise is just as loud, it's more the deep bass rumbles of explosions than the ear-piercing bang of steel robots pounding on each other.

I mentioned the lack of pyramids. We do, however, see the Eiffel Tower as it is eaten up by nano technology and topples over onto the Place de la Concorde. Missiles also strike Mount Rushmore. No, wait! That was during one of the Coming Attractions.

Girl Cut in Two ★ ★ ★ ½
NO MPAA RATING, 114 m., 2008

Ludivine Sagnier (Gabrielle Deneige), Benoit Magimel (Paul Gaudens), Francois Berleand (Charles Saint-Denis), Mathilda May (Capucine Jamet), Caroline Silhol (Genevieve Gaudens), Marie Bunel (Marie Deneige), Valeria Cavalli (Dona Saint-Denis). Directed by Claude Chabrol and produced by Patrick Godeau. Screenplay by Chabrol and Cecile Maistre.

Claude Chabrol's *Girl Cut in Two* plays like a triangular romantic comedy until we discover that all three of the lovers are hurtling headlong to self-destruction. Even then it is comedic, in that macabre, Hitchcockian way that takes a certain delight in the flaws of mankind. It's a crime movie, as most of Chabrol's sixty-nine films have been, and at first the crime seems to be adultery. He doesn't leave it at that.

At the center of everything is Gabrielle Deneige (Ludivine Sagnier), a peppy young blonde who does the weather at the local TV station. Her mother runs a bookstore in Lyon and holds an autographing for the best-selling author Charles Saint-Denis (Francois Berleand). Also at the event is a spoiled local rich kid, Paul Gaudens (Benoit Magimel). These two men are going to bring her to a lot of grief.

But notice how nimbly Chabrol glides through his establishing scenes, and how adroitly he introduces other characters (the lecherous TV boss, the spoiled kid's bitchy mother, Gabrielle's sensible mother, the author's femme fatale agent). The story hums along in efficient although absorbing confidence, seeming to show us Gabrielle trapped between Saint-Denis and Paul, who both vow that they love her. Is this what the title means? Surely we won't really see her cut in two? Well, yes and no.

Hitchcock in *Psycho* made a point in the opening scenes that the film was Janet Leigh's story, that she was a woman with a secret, and that the story would be about that secret. Then she checked into the motel. Gabrielle doesn't disappear from *Girl Cut in Two*, but the film will be about a lot more than her romantic problems. It is important that she seem young, naive, and unguarded, so that we can watch both men trying to seduce her with unwholesome motives.

Chabrol and DePalma are often cited as the directors most influenced by Hitchcock. Consider the scene in this film where Saint-Denis takes Gabrielle to an exclusive private club and asks her to follow him down a corridor. For what purpose? We know it must be sexual, but Chabrol never shows us. This is the Hitchcock technique of building curiosity by deferring action. (Bomb explodes under table equals action. Bomb is under table but it doesn't explode equals suspense.) I was also reminded of the brothel client's little lacquered box in Bunuel's *Belle de Jour*. By never showing us what it contains, he generates enormous erotic curiosity.

The men are odd and interesting. Francois Berleand's Charles is an old rake, hair and beard trimmed to the same length, expertly seductive, a good actor, but devious. Does he really consider his wife a saint? What precisely is his relationship with his agent, who looks like an up-market Vampira? As for Paul, he's such a vain, preening, foppish creature that Gabrielle should see right through him—which she does, in fact. Paul's mother, Genevieve (Caroline Silhol), a rich widow, has a monologue that is hypnotizing, expertly delivered and . . . make up your own mind. The three central characters are in an emotional fencing match, and Gabrielle lacks a mask.

The plot was probably inspired by an actual event, which I will not mention because you may be familiar with it. In any event, Chabrol's insidious style is more absorbing than the plot, as it should be. Chabrol, at seventy-eight, is one of four living members of the French New Wave. The others: Jean-Luc Godard (seventy-seven), Eric Rohmer (eighty-eight), Jacques Rivette (eighty). They've all made films within the last two years and are said to be in preproduction on new projects. And they said it would never last.

The Girlfriend Experience ★ ★ ★ ★

R, 77 m., 2009

Sasha Grey (Chelsea), Chris Santos (Chris), Peter Zizzo (Wealthy Client). Directed by Steven Soderbergh and produced by Mark Cuban, Gregory Jacobs, and Todd Wagner. Screenplay by Brian Koppelman and David Levien.

This film is true about human nature. It clearly sees needs and desires. It is not universal, but within its particular focus it is unrelenting. Steven Soderbergh's *The Girlfriend Experience* is about a prostitute and her clients. In such a relationship, the factor of money makes the motives fairly direct on both sides.

In the language of escort advertising, "GFE" promises a "girlfriend experience." Sometimes sex may not even be involved, although it is implicitly permitted. A man seeking a girlfriend experience offers to pay for companionship, conversation, another human being in his life. The women offering a GFE are acting a role, but in some ways it can be a therapeutic one. We know what sexual surrogates do. A "girlfriend" may be playing a human surrogate.

The film involves a woman named Chelsea and the men in her life. She has been living with one of them for eighteen months, and in a way he may be a boyfriend experience. He doesn't seem much more meaningful to her than a client. The other men are of various ages and backgrounds, but they all have one thing in common: They are wealthy, and Chelsea is not inexpensive. Typically they take her to an expensive restaurant and then a luxury hotel. They may send a limousine for her.

We listen to them talking. We watch them talking. Most of them want to talk about what she does for a living. There is the polite fiction that she is talking about other men, hypothetical men, and not the one she is with. They like to give her advice about how to invest her money and who to vote for (the story takes place during the 2008 campaign). Each one has some reason for thinking he is somehow special. Set during the run-up to the stock market crash, it shows both sides more interested in investing than sex.

These men don't want a girlfriend experience. They want a boyfriend experience. They want to feel as if they're on a date. They will be listened to. Their amazing comments will be smiled at. Their hair will be tousled. They will be kidded. They have told Chelsea about their wives and children, and she remembers their names. They can kiss her. There is no illusion that they are leaving their wives, and none that she wants them to. She simply empowers them to feel younger, more looked up to, more clever than they are.

What draws a powerful man to pay for a woman outside of marriage? It's not the sex. In fact, sex is the beard, if you know what I mean. By paying money for the excuse of sex, they don't have to say: "I am lonely. I am fearful. I am growing older. I am not loved. My wife is bored with me. I can't talk to my children. I'm worried about my job, which means nothing to me." Above all, they are saying: "Pretend you like me."

The film was written by Brian Koppelman and David Levien. Believe it or not, the same two wrote the screenplay for Soderbergh's *Ocean's Thirteen*. I imagine the three of them sitting around on the *Ocean's* set and asking, "What could we be doing instead of this?"

Chelsea is played by Sasha Grey. She is twenty-one. Since 2006, according to IMDb, she's made 161 porn films, of which only the first title can be quoted here: *Sasha Grey Superslut*. No, here's another, which makes me smile: *My First Porn No. 7*. I haven't seen any of them, but now I would like to see one, watching very carefully, to see if she suggests more than one level.

Grey wasn't hired because of her willingness to have sex on the screen; there's no explicit sex in the movie, and only fleeting nudity. I suspect Soderbergh cast her because of her mercenary approach to sex—and her acting talent, which may not be ready for Steppenwolf but is right for this film. She owns her own agency and Web site, manages other actresses, has a disconnect between herself and what she does for a living. So does Chelsea.

The film is intent on her face. It often looks over the shoulder of her clients. She projects precise amounts of interest and curiosity, but conceals real feelings. It is a transaction, and she is holding up her end. Notice the very small nods and shakes of her head. Observe her word choices as she sidesteps questions without refusing to answer them. When her roommate/boyfriend insists on knowing the name of one of her clients, she is adroit in her reply.

Once she allows her mask to slip: a surprising moment when she reveals what she may feel. Sasha Grey perfectly conveys both her hope and her disappointment, keeping both within boundaries. You wonder how a person could look another in the eye and conceal everything about themselves. But the financial traders who are her clients do it every day. Their business is not money, but making their clients feel better about themselves.

The Girl from Monaco ★★★
R, 94 m., 2009

Fabrice Luchini (Bertrand Beauvois), Roschdy Zem (Christophe Abadi), Stephane Audran (Edith Lassalle), Gilles Cohen (Louis Lassalle), Louise Bourgoin (Audrey Varela). Directed by Anne Fontaine and produced by Philippe Carcassonne and Bruno Pesery. Screenplay by Fontaine, Benoit Graffin, and Jacques Fieschi.

Casting can be the reason one movie works and another doesn't. It is the first reason for the success of *The Girl from Monaco*, the kind of romantic thriller with a twist that used to star Jack Lemmon. That kind of role is played this time by Fabrice Luchini, a fifty-seven-year-old veteran French character actor whose first significant role was thirty-nine years ago in *Claire's Knee*.

He plays Bertrand, a smooth, powerful defense attorney, confident, well-known, who is hired for a difficult case. The millionaire widow Edith Lassalle (Stephane Audran) is on trial for murder in Monaco, charged with killing a reputed member of the Russian mafia, and she refuses to utter a single word in her own defense. From the day he arrives in Monaco, Bertrand finds himself shadowed constantly by Christophe (Roschdy Zem), behind sunglasses, a tall, dark young man in a black suit and tie.

This is, he discovers, his bodyguard, hired by Edith's son, Louis (Gilles Cohen), because the Russians may represent a threat. Bertrand believes he is in no danger, doesn't want a bodyguard, finds it absurd how Christophe insists on entering his hotel room first and "checking the perimeter." Christophe is indifferent to his objections. He has to follow "protocol."

This odd couple works because its members are so different. Bertrand is not tall, not handsome, very busy, suave. Christophe is tall, handsome, formal, and distant. No attempt is made to supply them with banter. They are both focused on doing their jobs. Into this mix comes a fiercely ambitious weather girl from Monaco TV named Audrey (Louise Bourgoin). She sees Bertrand as her meal ticket to get a better TV job and wants to do an exclusive feature about the famous man down from Paris.

Audrey, young and sexy, means trouble. Bertrand can see that. Yet when she claims to be in love with him—that they were destined for each other—he goes along, no doubt because her explorations in his bed discover uncharted lands. Audrey is known to Christophe, and indeed perhaps to many of the men in Monaco. He warns his boss away: This woman is a slut, she'll damage him, she's not worth the time of day.

An interesting dynamic takes place. Christophe himself has fallen a little in love with Bertrand, not for sexual reasons, but out of admiration for the older man's work ethic. Since he represents a threat to Audrey's plans, tension grows. Meanwhile, the murder trial marches ahead, and some of the Russians make an appearance.

The director and cowriter, Anne Fontaine, makes no attempt to make this situation cute or sitcommy. As Billy Wilder did with Lemmon, she makes Luchini an everyman, wearied, fearful, not getting any younger, who like all men finds it plausible that a beautiful younger woman would fall for him. Because Luchini's character is so convincingly mundane, the situation grows interesting. And when Christophe's determination to keep her away grows, the plot discovers shadows—even an element of evidence that could be taken two ways, in a Hitchcockian twist.

The Girl from Monaco is no more than an entertainment, but an assured and well-oiled one. It is about its characters, not its stars. It assumes an audience that appreciates complex motivations and an adult situation. Nobody gets shot, and a "chase" down Monaco's lovely mountain roads takes place within the speed limit. We almost don't notice as Christophe becomes the most interesting character, but he surely does.

The Girl on the Train ★★★
NO MPAA RATING, 101 m., 2010

Emilie Dequenne (Jeanne), Catherine Deneuve (Louise), Michel Blanc (Samuel Bleistein), Ronit Elkabetz (Judith Bleistein), Mathieu Demy (Alex Bleistein), Nicolas Duvauchelle (Franck), Jeremy Quaegebeur (Nathan). Directed by Andre Techine and produced by Said Ben Said. Screenplay by Techine, Odile Barski, and Jean-Marie Besset, based on the play *RER* by Besset.

The girl in Andre Techine's *The Girl on the Train* is Jeanne, who has never fully engaged in the society she occupies. She Rollerblades through French suburbs with her iPod blocking out other sounds, as the world glides past unobserved. Was it the job interview with the lawyer Bleistein that put Jews into her mind? One doubts she had given them, or anything else, much thought.

Jeanne (Emilie Dequenne) is sent to Samuel Bleistein by her mother, Louise (Catherine Deneuve). He was once in love with her. One of the nation's most powerful lawyers, he makes time to see the girl because of old memories. His secretary pages through her résumé and observes there isn't much there. Nor does the interview itself go well. Jeanne doesn't know much, hasn't done much, doesn't even realize how little she's done or what there is to be known. She lives in a cocoon of electronic distraction.

She doesn't care. She's having a romance with a young athlete, a wrestler, tattooed and a little strange. They break up. Now she's jobless, alone, and with her mother on her case—Louise, who provides home care for toddlers, works in the garden, and is gentle enough with her—but anything that interrupts Jeanne's reverie is annoying.

For no particular reason, perhaps hoping to win Bleistein's sympathy, perhaps not, perhaps she doesn't know, she makes up a false story of being assaulted on a train by North Africans who taunted her as a Jew, beat her, and carved a swastika on her stomach. She isn't Jewish, not that it's a point. The case becomes a national scandal. The French president can't get on the phone fast enough to express his sympathy and solidarity.

The police are not as sympathetic because there is absolutely no evidence to back up her claims. No witnesses, no evidence on security cameras—and why is the swastika drawn backward? Well, it can be difficult for the inexperienced. I don't know if I could draw one correctly.

These events occupy the first movement of the film, titled "Circumstances." The second is titled "Consequences," and is really the reason for the first. It deals more fully with Bleistein (the shortish, quite bald Michel Blanc) and his family: his son, Alex (Mathieu Demy), and son's wife, Judith (Ronit Elkabetz), and their child, Nathan (Jeremy Quaegebeur), who is preparing for his bar mitzvah.

The movie seems likely to be about anti-Semitism, but that's more the occasion than the subject. Bleistein gets involved in the case, sees there is nothing to do, doesn't consider Jeanne's lie a case of anti-Semitism so much as a case of utter cluelessness. Within his family, tensions uncoil that are typical of all families. What the film is really about is social embarrassment, and Bleistein's clear-headed, calm understanding that his old friend has a stupid daughter who has caused fraudulent trouble for a great many people.

The story, I understand, is based on a real French case not long ago. I can think of two similar cases—Tawana Brawley, the black girl who said she was attacked by whites, and Ashley Todd, who scratched a B on her face and made up a story that a black man robbed her and was angered by her McCain sticker.

Do these stories inspire others? Do dim TV viewers see them and come away with the impression that such stories inspire sympathy? Don't they hear about the later disgrace? Are they hungry for attention? Who knows? The perpetrators don't inspire much interest, but the effects do: How the media handles them, how politicians jump aboard, how false incidents reveal real racism.

Techine is a French master about the same age as Scorsese. His credits include such splendid films as *My Favorite Season* and *Les Voleurs*. He's worked before with Deneuve, who here strikes a nice balance of sweetness and vagueness. Perhaps she simply forgot to raise a girl with an idea in her head.

The Girl with the Dragon Tattoo ★★★★
NO MPAA RATING, 152 m., 2010

Michael Nyqvist (Mikael Blomkvist), Noomi Rapace (Lisbeth Salander), Lena Endre (Erika Berger), Sven-Bertil Taube (Henrik Vanger), Peter Haber (Martin Vanger), Peter Andersson (Nils Bjurman), Marika Lagercrantz (Cecilia Vanger), Ingvar Hirdwall (Dirch Frode). Directed by Niels Arden Oplev and produced by Soren Staermose. Screenplay by Nikolaj Arcel and Rasmus Heisterberg, based on the novel by Stieg Larsson.

The Girl with the Dragon Tattoo is a compelling thriller to begin with, but it adds the rare quality of having a heroine more fascinating than the story. She's a twenty-four-year-old Goth girl named Lisbeth Salander, with body piercings and tattoos: thin, small, fierce, damaged, a genius computer hacker. She smokes to quiet her racing heart.

Lisbeth is as compelling as any movie character in recent memory. Played by Noomi Rapace with an unwavering intensity, she finds her own emotional needs nurtured by the nature of the case she investigates, the disappearance of a young girl forty years earlier. As this case is revealed as part of a long-hidden pattern of bizarre violence against women, her own abused past returns with a vengeance.

Rapace makes the character compulsively interesting. She plays against a passive forty-something hero, Mikael Blomkvist (Michael Nyqvist), an investigative journalist who has six months of freedom before beginning a prison sentence for libel against a Swedish tycoon. Mikael, resourceful and intelligent, is hired by an elderly billionaire named Henrik Vanger (Sven-Bertil Taube), who inhabits a gloomy mansion on a remote island and broods about the loss of his beloved niece, Harriet. She vanished one day when the island was cut off from the mainland. Her body was never found. Because the access bridge was blocked, the killer must have been a member of Vanger's large and greedy family, which he hates. Three brothers were Nazi sympathizers during the war.

The notion of a murder with a limited list

of suspects was conventional even before Agatha Christie. Niels Arden Oplev's *The Girl with the Dragon Tattoo* pays it lip service, with Mikael covering a wall with photos of the suspects. But this is a new age, and in addition to his search of newspaper and legal archives, he uses the Internet. That's how he comes across Lisbeth, who has been investigating *him*. She's described as Sweden's best hacker, a claim we have no reason to doubt, and the intensity of her focus, contrasted to her walled-off emotional life, suggests Asperger's.

They team up on the case, and might become lovers if not for Mikael's diffidence and her secretive hostility. They become efficient partners. Scenes involving newspaper photographs and Internet searches create sequences like a *Blow Up* for the digital age. The film is unique in my memory for displaying screen shots of an actual computer operating system, Mac OS X, and familiar programs like Google, e-mail, and iPhoto. Ever notice how most movie computers work like magic?

The forbidding island setting, the winter chill, the frosty inhabitants, all combine with dread suspicions to create an uncommonly effective thriller. It's longer than average, but not slow, not after we become invested in the depravity of the case. There are scenes involving rape, bondage, and assault that are stronger than most of what serves in the movies for sexual violence, but these scenes are not exploitation. They have a ferocious feminist orientation, and although *The Girl with the Dragon Tattoo* seems a splendid title, the original Swedish title was the stark *Men Who Hate Women.*

The novel, one of a trilogy that Stieg Larsson completed before his untimely death at forty-four, was an international best-seller. It is destined to be remade by Hollywood. That may be a good film, but if I were you, I'd be sure to watch this version. The Hollywood version will almost certainly tone down the sexual violence. I can't think of an American actress who could play Lisbeth. Kristen Stewart, whom I respect, has been mentioned. Dakota Fanning. I dunno. A younger Jodie Foster, maybe. Someone able to play hard as nails and emotionally unavailable. Make her a Swede, and simply cast Noomi Rapace.

This is not a deep, psychological study. But it's a sober, grown-up film. It has action, but not the hyperkinetic activity that passes for action in too many American movies. It has sex, but not eroticism. Its male lead is brave and capable, but not macho. Its female lead is sexy in the abstract, perhaps, but not seductive or alluring. This is a movie about characters who have more important things to do than be characters in an action thriller. ☞

Gomorrah ★ ★ ★ ★
NO MPAA RATING, 136 m., 2009

Marco Macor (Marco), Ciro Petrone (Piselli/Ciro), Salvatore Abruzzese (Toto), Toni Servillo (Franco), Carmine Paternoster (Roberto), Gianfelice Imparato (Don Ciro), Maria Nazionale (Maria), Salvatore Cantalupo (Pasquale). Directed by Matteo Garrone and produced by Domenico Procacci. Screenplay by Garrone, Maurizio Braucci, Ugo Chiti, Gianni Di Gregorio, Massimo Gaudioso, and Roberto Saviano, based on the book by Saviano.

It is all so sordid. *Gomorrah* is a film about Italian criminals killing one another. One death after another. Remorseless. Strictly business. The question arises: How are there enough survivors to carry on the business? Another question: Why do willing recruits submit themselves to this dismal regime?

The film is a curative for the romanticism of *The Godfather* and *Scarface*. The characters are the foot soldiers of the Camorra, the crime syndicate based in Naples that is larger than the Mafia but less known. Its revenues in one year are said to be as much as $250 billion—five times as much as Madoff took years to steal. The final shot in the film suggests the Camorra is invested in the rebuilding of the World Trade Center. The film is based on fact, not fiction.

Gomorrah, which won the grand prize at Cannes 2008 and the European Film Award, is an enormous hit in Europe. It sold five hundred thousand tickets in France, which at ten dollars a pop makes it a blockbuster. There was astonishment that the Academy passed it over for foreign film consideration. I'm not so surprised. The Academy committee more often goes for films that look good and provide people we can care about. *Gomorrah* looks grimy and sullen and has no heroes, only victims.

That is its power. Here is a movie about the day laborers of crime. Somewhere above them are the creatures of the $250 billion, so rich, so grand, so distant, with no apparent connection to crime. No doubt New York and American officials sat down to cordial meals with Camorra members while deciding the World Trade contracts and were none the wiser.

Roberto Saviano, who wrote the best-seller that inspired the movie, went undercover, used informants, even (I learn from John Powers on NPR) worked as a waiter at their weddings. His book named names and explained exactly how the Camorra operates. Now he lives under twenty-four-hour guard, although as the Roman poet Juvenal asked, "Who will guard the guards?"

Matteo Garrone, the director, films in the cheerless housing projects around Naples. "See Naples and die" seems to be the inheritance of children born here. We follow five strands of the many that Saviano unraveled in his book, unread by me. There is an illegal business in the disposal of poisonous waste. A fashion industry that knocks off designer lines and works from sweatshops. Drugs, of course. And then we meet teenagers who think they're tough and dream of taking over locally from the Camorra. And kids who want to be gangsters when they grow up.

None of these characters ever refer to *The Godfather*. The teenagers know De Palma's *Scarface* by heart. Living a life of luxury, surrounded by drugs and women, is perhaps a bargain they are willing to make even if it costs their lives. The problem is that only the death is guaranteed. No one in this movie at any time enjoys any luxury. One of them, who delivers stipends to the families of dead or jailed Camorra members, doesn't even have a car and uses a bicycle. The families moan that they can't make ends meet, just like Social Security beneficiaries.

Garrone uses an unadorned documentary style, lean, efficient, no shots for effect. He establishes characters, shows their plans and problems, shows why they must kill or be killed—often, be killed because of killing. Much is said about trust and respect, but little is seen of either. The murders, for the most part, have no excitement and certainly no glamour—none of the flash of most gangster movies. Sometimes they're enlivened by surprise, but it is the audience that's surprised, not the victims, who often never know what hit them.

The actors are skilled at not being "good actors," if you know what I mean. There is no sizzle. Only the young characters have much life in them. Garrone directs them to reflect the bleak reality of their lives, the need and fear, the knowledge that every conversation could be with their eventual killer or victim. Casual friendship is a luxury. Families hold them hostage to their jobs. The film's flat realism is correct for this material.

You watch the movie with growing dread. This is no life to lead. You have the feeling the men at the top got there laterally, not through climbing the ladder of promotion. The Camorra seems like a form of slavery, with the overlords inheriting their workers. The murder code and its enforcement keep them in line: They enforce their own servitude.

Did the book and the movie change things? Not much, I gather. The film offers no hope. I like gangster movies. *The Godfather* is one of the most popular movies ever made—most beloved, even. I like them as movies, not as history. We can see here they're fantasies. I'm reminded of mob bosses like Frank Costello walking into Toots Shor's restaurant in that fascinating documentary *Toots*. Everyone was happy to see him—Jackie Gleason, Joe DiMaggio, everyone. At least they knew who he was. The men running the Camorra are unknown even to those who die for them.

Gonzo: The Life and Work of Dr. Hunter S. Thompson ★ ★ ★ ½
R, 121 m., 2008

Johnny Depp (Narrator). A documentary directed by Alex Gibney and produced by Gibney, Graydon Carter, Jason Kliot, Joana Vicente, Eva Orner, and Alison Ellwood. Screenplay by Gibney.

In all the memories gathered together in *Gonzo: The Life and Work of Dr. Hunter S. Thompson*, there was one subject I found conspicuously missing: the fact of the man's misery. Did he never have a hangover? The film finds extraordinary access to the people in his life, but not even from his two wives do we get a description I would dearly love to read, on what he was like in the first hour or two after he woke up. He was clearly deeply addicted to drugs and alcohol, and after a stupor-induced sleep he would have awakened in a state of withdrawal. He must have administered therapeutic doses of booze or pills or *something* to quiet the tremors and the dread. What did he say at those times? How did he behave? Are the words "fear and loathing" autobiographical?

Of course, perhaps Thompson was immune. One of the eyewitnesses to his life says in wonderment, "You saw the stuff go in, and there was no discernible effect." I don't think I believe that. If there was no discernible effect, how would you describe his behavior? If he had been sober all his life, would he have hunted wild pigs with a machine gun? Thompson was the most famous (or notorious) inebriate of his generation, but perhaps he really was one of those rare creatures who had no hangovers, despite the debaucheries of the day(s) before. How much did he consume? A daily bottle of bourbon, plus wine, beer, pills of every description.

The bottom line is, he got away with it, right up until his suicide, which he himself scripted and every one of his friends fully expected. As a journalist, he got away with murder. He reported that during a presidential primary Edward Muskie ingested Ibogaine, a psychoactive drug administered by a "mysterious Brazilian doctor," and this information, which was totally fabricated, was actually picked up and passed along as fact. Thompson's joke may have contributed to Muskie's angry tantrums during the 1972 Florida primary. No other reporter could have printed such a lie, but Thompson was shielded by his legend: He could print anything. "Of all the correspondents," says Frank Mankiewicz, George McGovern's 1972 campaign manager, "he was the least factual, but the most accurate."

He was an explosive, almost hypnotic, writer, with a savage glee in his prose. I remember eagerly opening a new issue of *Rolling Stone* in the 1970s and devouring his work. A great deal of it was untrue, but it dealt in a kind of exalted super-truth, as when he spoke of Richard Nixon the vampire roaming the night in Washington. Thompson had never heard of objectivity. In 1972 he backed George McGovern as the Democratic nominee, and no calumny was too vile for him to attribute to McGovern's opponents in both parties. I suppose readers were supposed to know that and factor it into the equation.

This documentary by Alex Gibney (*Taxi to the Dark Side, No End in Sight*) is remarkable, first of all, for reminding us how many pots Hunter dipped a spoon in. He rode with the Hells Angels for a year. Ran for sheriff of Pitkin County, home of Aspen, and lost, but only by 204 to 173. Covered the 1972 and 1976 presidential primaries in a way that made him a cocandidate (in the sense of codependent). Had a baffling dual personality, so that such as McGovern, Jimmy Buffett, Tom Wolfe, and his wives and son remember him fondly but say that he could also be "absolutely vicious."

He taught himself to write by typing Fitzgerald's *The Great Gatsby* again and again, we're told. How many times? we ask ourselves skeptically. Was that part of the fantastical legend? Nobody in the film was around while he was doing it. He became famous for writing about "the edge" in his Hells Angels book—that edge of speed going around a curve that you could approach, but never cross without wiping out and killing yourself. He did a lot of edge riding on his motorcycle and never wiped out. He said again and again that the way he chose to die was by his own hand, with a firearm, while he was still at the top. He died that way, using one of his twenty-two firearms, but "he was nowhere near the top," says Sondi Wright, his first wife.

He started to lose it after Africa, says Jann Wenner, who ran his stuff in *Rolling Stone*. He went to Zaire at great expense to cover the Rumble in the Jungle for the magazine, got hopelessly stoned, missed the fight (while reportedly in the hotel pool), and never filed a story. "After Africa," says Sondi, "he just couldn't write. He couldn't piece it together." He did some more writing, of course, such as a heartfelt piece after 9/11. But he had essentially disappeared into his legend, as the outlaw of Woody Creek, blasting away with his weapons, making outraged phone calls, getting impossibly high. Certainly he made an impression on his time like few other journalists ever do; the comparison would be with H. L. Mencken.

This film gathers interviews from a wide and sometimes surprising variety of people (Pat Buchanan, Jimmy Carter, Hells Angel Sonny Barger). It has home movies, old photos, TV footage, voice recordings, excerpts from files about Thompson. It is narrated by Johnny Depp, mostly through readings from Thompson's work. It is all you could wish for in a doc about the man. But it leaves you wondering, how was it that so many people liked this man who does not seem to have liked himself? And what about the hangovers?

Goodbye Solo ★ ★ ★ ★
NO MPAA RATING, 91 m., 2009

Souleymane Sy Savane (Solo), Red West (William), Carmen Leyva (Quiera), Diana Franco Galindo (Alex), Lane "Roc" Williams (Roc), Mamadou Lam (Mamadou). Directed by Ramin Bahrani and produced by Bahrani and Jason Orans. Screenplay by Bahrani and Bahareh Azimi.

Two actors. One from Africa. The other who was a bodyguard for Elvis. Who but Ramin Bahrani would find these men and pair them in a story of heartbreaking depth and power? Bahrani is the new great American director. He never steps wrong. In *Goodbye Solo* he begins with a situation that might unfold in a dozen different ways and makes of it something original and profound. It is about the desire to help and the desire to not be helped.

In Winston-Salem, North Carolina, a white man around seventy gets into the taxi of an African immigrant. He offers him a deal. For $1,000, paid immediately, he wants to be driven in ten days to the top of a mountain in Blowing Rock National Park, to a place so windy that the snow falls up. He says nothing about a return trip. The driver takes the money but is not happy about this fare. He asks some questions and is told to mind his own business.

Now look at these actors. They aren't playing themselves, but they evoke their characters so fully that they might as well be. Red West plays William, the white man. His face is a map of hard living. He was a Marine and a

boxer. He became a friend of Elvis in high school. He was his bodyguard and driver from 1955—a charter member of the "Memphis Mafia." He split with Elvis after breaking the foot of the cousin who was bringing Elvis drugs and telling him he would work his way up to his face.

Souleymane Sy Savane plays Solo, the taxi driver. He is from the Ivory Coast, although the character is from Senegal. Savane was a flight attendant for Air Afrique. Solo is studying for just such a job. Solo lives in Winston-Salem, is married to a Mexican-American woman, adores the woman's young daughter, and acts as her father. William's face was made to look pissed off. Solo's face was made to smile. We are not speaking of an odd couple here. We're speaking of human nature. You can't learn acting like this.

Bahrani worked with these actors for months. Savane drove a taxi in Winston-Salem. Red West spent a lifetime rehearsing William (although in real life he is said to be kind and friendly). Bahrani and his cinematographer, Michael Simmonds, discussed every shot. Although *Goodbye Solo* is an independent film in its heart and soul, it is a classical film in its style. It is as pure as something by John Ford. Only its final shot might call attention to itself—but actually, we aren't thinking about the shot, we're thinking about what has happened, and why.

Don't get the idea the whole film takes place in the taxi. It takes place in Winston-Salem, a city it wears with familiarity because Bahrani was born and raised there. We feel the rhythms of Solo's life. Of his relationship with his wife, Quiera (Carmen Leyva), and their pride in her daughter, Alex (Diana Franco Galindo). Like many taxi drivers, Solo knows where you can find drugs or a sexual partner. But he isn't a pusher or a pimp; he's a one-man service industry, happy to help.

The film sees cars being repaired in front yards, a few customers at a downtown movie theater on a weekday night, a lonely motel room, a bar. The next few times William calls a cab, he begins to notice the driver is always Solo. What's up with that? With almost relentless good cheer, Solo insinuates himself into William's life—becomes his chauffeur, his protector, his adviser, even for a few nights his roommate and almost his friend. It occurred to me that Red West may have performed similar functions for Elvis, another man pointed to doom.

Neither William nor Solo ever once speaks about their real subject, about what William seems to be about to do. It hangs in the air between them. Alex, the stepdaughter, comes to love old William, who has the feel of a grandfather about him. But no, Alex is not one of those redeeming movie children. She doesn't understand everything and brings in an innocence that Solo and William both respect.

Goodbye Solo is not finally about what William and Solo do. It is about how they change, which is how a great movie lifts itself above plot. These two lives have touched, learned, and deepened. Not often do we really *care* this much about characters. We sense they're not on the automatic pilot of a plot. They're feeling their way in life. This is a great American film.

This is Bahrani's third feature, after *Man Push Cart* (2005) and *Chop Shop* (2007). His films are about outsiders in America: a Pakistani who operates a coffee-and-bagel wagon in Manhattan, Latino kids who scramble for a living in an auto parts bazaar in the shadow of Shea Stadium. Now a Senegalese who wants to help an American whose weathered face belongs in a Western. Bahrani, whose parents immigrated from Iran, felt like an outsider when he was growing up in Winston-Salem: "There were blacks, whites and my brother and me." He loves the city, and you can tell that in this film. He is curious about people, and you can tell that from all his films. He told me he asks the same question of all of his characters: How do you live in this world?

A film like this makes me wonder if we are coming to the end of the facile, snarky indie films. We live in desperate times. We are ready to respond to films that ask that question. How do you live in this world? Bahrani knows all about flashy camera work, tricky shots, visual stunts. He teaches film at Columbia. But like his fellow North Carolinian David Gordon Green, he is drawn to a more level gaze, to a film at the service of its characters and their world. Wherever you live, when this film opens, it will be the best film in town.

The Good Guy ★★★
R, 90 m., 2010

Scott Porter (Tommy), Alexis Bledel (Beth), Bryan Greenberg (Daniel), Anna Chlumsky (Lisa), Aaron Yoo (Steve-O), Andrew McCarthy (Cash), Andrew Stewart-Jones (Shakespeare). Directed by Julio DePietro and produced by DePietro, Rene Bastian, and Linda Moran. Screenplay by DePietro.

The Good Guy creates the interesting notion that Wall Street trading involves a gang of hard-partying goofs who pass their days playing video games with our money. They trade too fast to know much about the stocks they're selling—and besides, they mostly trade funds and may only vaguely know how the portfolios are weighted.

That at least is the impression given by *The Good Guy*, which contains not a moment in which any trader knows much about the fundamentals of a stock, but much about the dance of the numbers on a screen and the mind games he's playing with other traders. At the end of the day, all that matters is the score. Well, I guess that's the way it works.

At Morgan & Morgan, no relation to JPMorgan or Morgan Stanley, we meet a team of traders bossed by the legendary Cash (Andrew McCarthy). His team leader is Tommy (Scott Porter), who's making money hand over fist while leading the pack on sorties into bars that have a high babe count. These guys get drunk and play adolescent games and plow through conquests and keep laughing so it doesn't get quiet. There is charm in being seventeen, and pathos in being twenty-seven and acting as if you're seventeen.

The crew includes Shakespeare (Andrew Stewart-Jones), a black guy with a British accent who may realize, but doesn't care, that any babe impressed by a British accent belongs on Jaywalking. There's Steve-O (Aaron Yoo), master trader. And there's the new guy, Daniel (Bryan Greenberg), who, odd as it may seem, prefers not to horse around but stay home, fix himself some dinner, and read a good novel. You know, maybe by Dickens, whom many people don't know is about as much fun as any novelist who ever lived.

The section's top hotshot bails out to join

another firm, and Cash orders Tommy to fill his chair. On a hunch, Tommy promotes Daniel. Everyone including Daniel is disbelieving. Under the delusion that a star trader must party hard and conquer the dollies, Tommy takes Daniel into the field for training; the Forty-Year-Old Virgin becomes a Twenty-Seven-Year-Old Reader.

During this process Daniel meets Beth (Alexis Bledel), Tommy's girlfriend. Beth isn't precisely Tommy's type; she belongs to a book club. Tommy is like one of those guys who might read if the library weren't always closed. Beth is a serious Green and believes Tommy's line that he is, too, but he has a line for every girl and is a serious liar. Daniel observes this dynamic.

Young men, let your old dad here impart some advice. If a woman has a choice of a man who makes sacks of money on the trading floor and a man who likes to stay home at night reading *Lolita*, and she's more attracted to the reader, choose that woman. She needs to pass one more test: Does she believe (a) *Lolita* is a sex novel, or (b) it's one of the greatest works of modern literature? Find that out on the second date. If she answers (b), there's your girl.

The Good Guy could have been just a dumb comedy, but actually it has a nice feel to it. It looks carefully at a lifestyle many people might thoughtlessly envy. The writer-director, Julio DePietro, is a former trader from Chicago, and he convinces us he knows that world. I hasten to add that I know some traders who are nice guys. I also add that I would trade the same way the guys in the movie do, because their clients care less about how much money they'll retire with than how rich they'll be tomorrow. Investing myself, I've trusted value guys over performance. That and buying Apple, just because I loved Macs, has turned out all right.

Readers may pick up on the clue that the title and some of the story are inspired by Ford Madox Ford's novel *The Good Soldier.* It opens with a famous line that makes it impossible to stop reading: "This is the saddest story I have ever heard." Tommy's story is another one.

I keep drifting off course. Will you like *The Good Guy*? I think you might. It has smart characters and is wise about the ones who try to tame their intelligence by acting out. And Beth and her friends are the women all these guys should be so lucky as to deserve.

Good Hair ★★★

PG-13, 95 m., 2009

A documentary featuring Chris Rock, Maya Angelou, A'Lelia Bundles, Vanessa Bell Calloway, Joe Dudley, Eunice Dudley, Eve, Meagan Good, Vijay Madupali Gupta, Andre Harrell, Ice-T, Nia Long, Paul Mooney, Willie Morrow, Valerie Price, Tracie Thoms, Salli Richardson, Salt-n-Pepa, Al Sharpton, and Raven-Symone. Directed by Jeff Stilson and produced by Stilson, Kevin O'Donnell, and Jenny Hunter. Screenplay by Stilson, Chris Rock, Lance Crouther, and Chuck Sklar.

Good Hair is a documentary about black women and their hair. Chris Rock, the host and narrator, is a likable man, quick, truly curious, with the gift of encouraging people to speak openly about a subject they usually keep private. He conveys a lot of information, but also some unfortunate opinions and misleading facts. That doesn't mean the movie isn't warm, funny, and entertaining.

The film had its start for Rock when his little daughter asked him, "Daddy, how come I don't have good hair?" He wonders how she got that idea. He discovers that some children even younger than her are already having their hair straightened—and that for children that is a bad idea. He talks to a great many black women about their hair, beginning with the matriarch Maya Angelou and including such celebrities as Nia Long, Eve, Tracie Thoms, Salli Richardson, Salt-n-Pepa, and Raven-Symone.

He discovers that for some black women, attaining "good hair" means either straightening or extensions. Straightening involves the application of products containing sodium hydroxide, which a dermatologist and a chemist describe as potentially dangerous to the scalp and even to inhale in quantity (your lungs might get straightened). Leave it on too long, and your scalp or face can be burned—something that has happened to some of the women here.

I imagine a good many black women would tell Chris Rock that having "good hair" simply means having hair that is healthy and strong. For African-American women, that can mean versatile hair that can be worn in a variety of styles: natural, Afros, braids, dreads, African knots, pressed, chemically relaxed, or with extensions. They look great. Often they go back and forth among hairstyles; that is the way of women, unlike us male clods who settle on a hairstyle in grade school and stick with it like Rod Blagojevich.

Extensions involve braiding long hair to rows of existing hair. Think Beyonce. Where does this hair come from? India, mostly, where some women cut off their hair before marriage or for religious purposes, and can sell it for amounts that mean a lot in a poor nation.

What about the hazards of straightening? Rock shows a hair-raising demonstration of an aluminum Coke can literally being eaten up in a bath of sodium hydroxide. It may help to recall that another name for sodium hydroxide is "lye." God forbid a woman should put that on her head! What Rock doesn't mention is that few women do. If he had peeked at Wikipedia, he would have learned: "Because of the high incidence and intensity of chemical burns, chemical relaxer manufacturers have now switched to other alkaline chemicals." Modern relaxers can also burn if left on too long, but they won't eat up your Coke cans.

The popularity of Afros in the 1960s and '70s asserted that natural hair was beautiful just the way it grew (and was styled, cut, and shaped, of course; Angela Davis didn't look that good without effort). Classic Davis-style Afros have grown rare, but another "natural" style, braiding, is seen all the time. Many black men also use braids and dreads as a fashion statement.

The use of the word "natural hair" is, in any event, misleading. Take a stroll down the hair products aisle of a drugstore, or look at the stock price of Supercuts. Few people of any race go without hair grooming. If they did, we would be a nation of Unabombers.

Black hair is a $9 billion industry. Rock plunges in. He visits Dudley Products in Atlanta, a black-owned hair products empire, and is fascinated by the Bronner Bros. International Hair Show, an annual convention in Atlanta. Here a vast convention hall is jammed with the booths of hair-care companies, and there's an annual competition to name the hairdresser of the year. The contest is fascinating, not least because it seems to have little to do with actually taking care of someone's hair. Would you want your hair done by a stylist hanging upside down from a trapeze? Or joining you inside a giant aquarium? Showmanship is everything; one of the four finalists is a young white man who is treasured by his clients.

What Rock does is create a film with much good feeling and instinctive sympathy for our desire to look as good as we can. He asks direct questions, but doesn't cross-examine; he reacts with well-timed one-liners, and he has a hilarious, spontaneous conversation with some black men in a barber shop that gets into areas that are rarely spoken about. The movie has a good feeling to it, but why do I know more about this subject than Chris Rock does? Smile.

The Good Heart ★ ½
R, 98 m., 2010

Brian Cox (Jacques), Paul Dano (Lucas), Isild Le Besco (April). Directed by Dagur Kari and produced by Skuli Fr. Malmquist and Thor Sigurjonsson. Screenplay by Kari.

Every once in a while a movie comes along and you watch it and the credits come up and you sit there feeling a certain sadness. The actors are good ones and they work hard and the look and feel of the film are evocative—but good gravy! Where did that plot come from? The actors cast themselves adrift on the sinking vessel of this story and go down with the ship.

Few people know the name of Horatio Alger anymore. He was long outdated when I heard of him, but in those ancient times people still referred to "a Horatio Alger story." That would be a story sopping wet with cornball sentimentalism, wrapped up in absurd melodrama, and telling some version of the rags-to-riches story. Poor farm boy stops runaway carriage carrying banker's daughter, they fall in love, he inherits bank. I believe Alger used that actual plot.

The Good Heart isn't that obvious, but it's that corny. Poor homeless lad named Lucas (Paul Dano) lives in cardboard shack under the freeway, befriends forlorn kitten. Kitten is found hanged, lad attempts suicide, wakes up in intensive care next to nasty old banker. Sorry! Nasty old tavern owner. This barkeep, named Jacques (Brian Cox), has just had his fifth heart attack and is so foul-tempered even the nurses hate him. Jacques finds out the lad is homeless, brings him home, gives him a garret room above the bar, and tells him he can have the bar after he dies.

In my extensive research into the world of bars, I have observed that they survive by selling drinks at retail. The House of Oysters doesn't follow this time-tested model. Jacques has three business policies he drums into Lucas: (1) No walk-ins from the street. (2) No women allowed—and BTW it's not a gay bar. (3) No being nice to the customers.

Rule No. 1 seems paradoxical. If no walk-in customers are allowed, how does anybody ever get to be a regular? Presumably the regulars have all been there since Jacques got the place from a man who sold oysters. One of the oysters killed someone, the guy sold out, Jacques took over, discontinued food, and inherited the regulars.

They are a group who need fumigating. The bar itself is a skanky dump. Jacques throws customers out regularly, but they come back, maybe because they're barred everywhere else. One day the beautiful April (Isild Le Besco) walks in and orders champagne. She has a sad story. No, she's not a fallen woman with a heart of gold. She's a flight attendant from France, who can't go home again or find a job because, I kid you not, she's afraid to fly.

Lucas and April fall in love, Jacques hates her for violating all the rules, and now I am biting my hand hard enough to make it bleed in order to prevent myself from blurting out more plot details. No, I will not—I must not—tell you what happens at the end of this movie, except to say I was stupefied that anyone in modern times (i.e., since 1910) would have the gall to sell such cornball at retail.

So now my review must end. But wait. I haven't even mentioned the bar's pet goose. This goose is kept in a sturdy cage, but escapes from time to time and must be chased down by Lucas. The ending of *The Good Heart* is supposed to be sad, but for me the saddest thing in this movie is that Lucas didn't chop off the head of that goose when he had the chance. No animals are harmed during the filming of a picture, and look where it gets you.

The Goods: Live Hard, Sell Hard ★★★
R, 90 m., 2009

Jeremy Piven (Don Ready), Ving Rhames (Jibby Newsome), James Brolin (Ben Selleck), David Koechner (Brent Gage), Kathryn Hahn (Babs Merrick), Ed Helms (Paxton Harding), Jordana Spiro (Ivy Selleck), Craig Robinson (DeeJay), Charles Napier (Dick Lewiston), Ken Jeong (Teddy Dang), Rob Riggle (Peter Selleck), Alan Thicke (Stu Harding). Directed by Neal Brennan and produced by Adam McKay, Will Ferrell, Kevin Messick, and Chris Henchy. Screenplay by Andy Stock and Rick Stempson.

The Goods: Live Hard, Sell Hard is a cheerfully, energetically, very vulgar comedy. If you're OK with that, you may be OK with this film, which contains a lot of laughs and has studied political correctness only enough to make a list of groups to offend. It takes place after a failing car dealer calls in a hired gun and his team to move goods off the lot over the Fourth of July.

The hotshot is Don Ready (Jeremy Piven), a hard charger who lives on the road and exists only to close deals. On his team: Babs (Kathryn Hahn), a lustful slut; Jibby (Ving Rhames), a sweet man who has never been in love; and Brent (David Koechner), who does not respond well when the failing auto dealer caresses his thigh.

They walk into a seething hotbed of problems in the small-town dealership of Ben Selleck (James Brolin). Let's see. His son, Peter, is ten years old, but because of a hormonal problem looks thirty. His daughter, Ivy (Jordana Spiro), is engaged to the air-headed son (Ed Helms) of his hated rival (Alan Thicke). His sales team includes Dick Lewiston (Charles Napier), who swears at customers and goes after them with a baseball bat, and Teddy Dang (Ken Jeong), a Korean-American who is assaulted by Dick, who blames him for Pearl Harbor.

Romantic entanglements and personal crises spring up overnight, including Don Ready's conviction that he has met the son he fathered with the third runner-up in the local beauty contest twenty-three years earlier. Babs becomes infatuated by the fully grown, lightly bearded ten-year-old. Jibby experiences love for the first time. Ben pursues the hostile Brent. Flashbacks involve an orgy on an airplane and the tragic death of Don's best friend (an uncredited Will Ferrell).

That's all another way of saying the screenplay moves at a breakneck pace. If a gag doesn't work, another one is on its heels. There are also countless details about auto sales scams, and a definition of the most awesome possible feat of salesmanship, named in honor of Nigeria, which in this film and *District 9* seems to be taking a place as a world leader in con games.

Jeremy Piven might not seem the obvious choice to play the ringleader of this menagerie, but he shows a side of himself I haven't seen before: the pep-talking, superconfident, ultracynical salesman. With no life of his own, as Ivy correctly informs him, he lives only to sell cars. It isn't even the money. It's the imposition of his will on a reluctant customer. His triumph of salesmanship at the end of the film is, at least on its own terms, almost even plausible.

I liked Kathryn Hahn as the potty-mouthed teammate, and Brolin's work as the deeply confused but ever-hopeful car dealer. And it was fun to see Chuck Napier, whose career began as a member of the Russ Meyer stock company, in a mad dog role that gets the film off to a rip-roaring start. He still looks like he could fight a wolf for a T-bone.

Gran Torino ★ ★ ★ ½
R, 116 m., 2008

Clint Eastwood (Walt Kowalski), Bee Vang (Thao Lor), Ahney Her (Sue Lor), Christopher Carley (Father Janovich). Directed by Clint Eastwood and produced by Robert Lorenz and Bill Gerber. Screenplay by Nick Schenk.

I would like to grow up to be like Clint Eastwood. Eastwood the director, Eastwood the actor, Eastwood the invincible, Eastwood the old man. What other figure in the history of the cinema has been an actor for fifty-three years, a director for thirty-seven, won two Oscars for direction, two more for Best Picture, plus the Thalberg Award, and at seventy-eight can direct himself in his own film and look meaner than hell? None, that's how many.

Gran Torino stars Eastwood as an American icon once again—this time as a cantankerous, racist, beer-chugging retired Detroit autoworker who keeps his shotgun ready to lock and load. Dirty Harry on a pension, we're thinking, until we realize that only the autoworker retired; Dirty Harry is still on the job. Eastwood plays the character as a man bursting with energy, most of which he uses to hold himself in. Each word, each scowl, seems to have broken loose from a deep place.

Walt Kowalski calls the Asian family next door "gooks" and "chinks" and so many other names he must have made it a study. How does he think this sounds? When he gets to know Thao, the teenage Hmong who lives next door, he takes him down to his barber for a lesson in how Americans talk. He and the barber call each other a Polack and a Dago and so on, and Thao is supposed to get the spirit. I found this scene far from realistic and wondered what Walt was trying to teach Thao. Then it occurred to me Walt didn't know it wasn't realistic.

Walt is not so much a racist as a security guard, protecting his own security. He sits on his porch defending the theory that your right to walk through this world ends when your toe touches his lawn. Walt's wife has just died (I would have loved to meet *her*), and his sons have learned once again that the old bastard wants them to stay the hell out of his business. In his eyes they're overweight meddlers working at meaningless jobs, and his granddaughter is a self-centered greed machine.

Walt sits on his porch all day long, when he's not doing house repairs or working on his prized 1972 Gran Torino, a car he helped assemble on the Ford assembly line. He sees a lot. He sees a carload of Hmong gangstas trying to enlist the quiet, studious Thao into their thuggery. When they threaten Thao to make him try to steal the Gran Torino, Walt catches him red-handed and would just as soon shoot him as not. When Thao's sister, Sue (Ahney Her, likable and sensible), comes over to apologize for her family and offer Thao's services for odd jobs, Walt accepts only reluctantly. When Sue is threatened by some black bullies, Walt's eyes narrow, and he growls and gets involved because it is his nature.

What with one thing and another, his life becomes strangely linked with these people, although Sue has to explain that the Hmong are mountain people from Vietnam who were U.S. allies and found it advisable to leave their homeland. When she drags him over to join a family gathering, Walt casually calls them all "gooks" and Sue a "dragon lady," they seem like awfully good sports about it, although a lot of them may not speak English. Walt seems unaware that his role is to embrace their common humanity, although he likes it when they stuff him with great-tasting Hmong food and flatter him.

Among actors of Eastwood's generation, James Garner might have been able to play this role, but my guess is, he'd be too nice in it. Eastwood doesn't play nice. Walt makes no apologies for who he is, and that's why, when he begins to decide he likes his neighbors better than his own family, it means something. *Gran Torino* isn't a liberal parable. It's more like out of the frying pan and into the melting pot. Along the way, he fends off the sincere but very young parish priest (a persuasive Christopher Carley), who is only carrying out the deathbed wishes of the late Mrs. Kowalski. Walt is a nominal Catholic. Hardly even nominal.

Gran Torino is about two things, I believe. It's about the belated flowering of a man's better nature. And it's about Americans of different races growing more open to one another in the new century. This doesn't involve some kind of grand transformation. It involves starting to see the gooks next door as people you love. And it helps if you live in the kind of neighborhood where they *are* next door.

If the climax seems too generic and preprogrammed, too much happening fairly quickly, I like that better than if it just dribbled off into sweetness. So would Walt.

The Great Buck Howard ★ ★ ★ ½
PG, 90 m., 2009

John Malkovich (Buck Howard), Colin Hanks (Troy Gable), Emily Blunt (Valerie Brennan), Steve Zahn (Kenny), Griffin Dunne (Jonathan Finerman), Ricky Jay (Gil Bellamy), Tom Hanks (Mr. Gable). Directed by Sean McGinly and produced by Tom Hanks and Gary Goetzman. Screenplay by McGinly.

Is there anyone better than John Malkovich at barely containing his temper? He gravitates toward characters who do not suffer fools lightly, and that would include the Great Buck Howard, who once was Johnny Carson's favorite guest. Buck was dropped from Johnny's guest list and now tours the provinces, taking his magic act from small stages to smaller ones, but he still has his dignity.

"I LOVE this town!" he shouts with outstretched arms in Akron, and Akron still loves him. He is famous for his "signature effect," in which his evening's fee is given to an audience member and he uses his psychic powers to find it. He has never failed, and no one has ever discovered how he does it.

Buck was named "the Great" by Carson and still maintains a facade of greatness, even in front of Troy (Colin Hanks, Tom's son), his newly hired road manager. Malkovich invests him with self-importance and yet slyly suggests it's not all an act; you believe at some level Buck really does love that town, and also when he says, as he always does, "I LOVE you people!"

The story is told from Troy's point of view. His father (Tom Hanks) fervently wants him to enter law school, but he wants to test showbiz, and this is his first contact with any degree of fame. He never penetrates the Great Buck Howard's facade (and neither do we), but he sure does learn a lot about showbiz, some of it intimately from Valerie (Emily Blunt), a new PR person hired for Buck's spectacular new illusion in Cincinnati. Troy learns to carry bags, open doors, deal with local reps, and supply mineral water, not distilled ("I'm not an iron," Buck crisply tells Troy's eventual replacement).

We see Buck as Troy does, as an impenetrable mystery. Buck is far from forgotten (he guests on shows hosted by Regis Philbin and Kelly Ripa, Jon Stewart, and Martha Stewart, all playing themselves). He can still fill a room, even if it's a smaller room. His manager, Gil (Ricky Jay, who always seems to know the inside odds), even gets him a Las Vegas booking.

What happens there, and how it happens, is perceptive about showbiz and even more perceptive about Buck and his "signature effect."

Well, how *does* he find the person in the room holding the money—every time? Rumors are common that he uses a hidden spotter, whispering into a mike hidden in his ear. When Troy tells him this, Buck invites two doctors on stage to peer into his ears, then turns his back to the room and covers his head with a black cloth. Does he still find the money?

If he does, it can't be because of psychic powers, can it? I firmly believe such illusions are never the result of psychic powers, but I am fascinated by them anyway. The wisdom of this film, directed and written by Sean McGinly, is to never say. Troy practically lives with the man and doesn't have a clue. He's asked if Buck is gay, and he replies truthfully, "I don't know. I've never seen him with anybody." Colin Hanks is affecting as a man young enough and naive enough to be fascinated by whatever it is Buck represents. Emily Blunt is sweetly kind to him. No one else could have played Buck better than Malkovich. I LOVE this guy.

I've read one review that complains we never meet the real Buck Howard. Of course we don't. There may *be* no real Buck Howard. But the film is funny and perceptive in the way it shows the humiliations for a man with Buck's tender vanity. The ladies singing on stage. The many who have no idea who he is. Being bumped off the news by Jerry Springer. Being bumped off Jay Leno for Tom Arnold. Distilled water.

Note: McGinly's screenplay is based on his observations as road manager for the Amazing Kreskin, to whom the film is dedicated.

The Greatest ★★
R, 100 m., 2010

Pierce Brosnan (Allen Brewer), Susan Sarandon (Grace Brewer), Carey Mulligan (Rose), Johnny Simmons (Ryan), Aaron Johnson (Bennett), Zoe Kravitz (Ashley), Michael Shannon (Jordan Walker). Directed by Shana Feste and produced by Lynette Howell and Beau St. Clair. Screenplay by Feste.

The Greatest includes a great performance and a very good one at the center of vagueness and confusion. The film's people and situation are perfectly clear, and with this cast might have made a powerful film, but the screenplay contains baffling omissions, needless confusions, and questions we should not be thinking of.

The film opens with two teenagers deeply, joyously in love. It's the kind of love where they've flirted with their eyes and their hearts since they started school, and now, on the last day of their senior year, he finally finds the courage to speak to her, and her face lights up, and this is all they dreamed of, and they make love, and then he's killed when their car is hit by a truck.

Not a spoiler. It's the setup for the whole film. The girl is Rose (Carey Mulligan, the Oscar nominee from *An Education*). The boy is Bennett (Aaron Johnson, on screen briefly but with all the presence necessary to make their love significant). We cut to the funeral, and then to an extraordinary shot of three people in the backseat of a funeral limousine: Bennett's father, Allen (Pierce Brosnan), his mother, Grace (Susan Sarandon), and his kid brother, Ryan (Johnny Simmons).

They do not speak. They do not look at one another. They do not offer comfort. The shot lasts maybe a minute. It establishes that these people are grieving in their own private ways. Bennett was a wonderful boy, known as "the Greatest" since grade school because . . . well, he was. Grace is inconsolable. They all are, but she's the most intense, and Allen tries to hold the family together while Ryan disappears into his room and drugs and who knows.

Three months pass in this way. Rose appears at their door and tells Allen she is pregnant. It was the first time for both Rose and Bennett. She didn't even know you could get pregnant the first time. She moves in with them because—well, I don't know exactly. Apart from one enigmatic phone call late in the film, perhaps involving a mother, she seems to have no one. She attended high school in an affluent neighborhood for three years, she was a gifted pianist, she's in a fatal crash, and now she has no one? No family, no friends, not one single person, and this is never explained?

Maybe she comes from a troubled background? Hard to see. Carey Mulligan plays

Rose as upbeat, cheerful, able to cope. Grace is cold and distant; Sarandon plays her as unforgiving. Rose overhears her saying she wishes it was Rose, and not Bennett, who had been killed. She doesn't give a damn about Bennett's child. She wants her own child back.

Allen tries to be friendly. There are a couple of scenes, indeed, that are oddly handled because there's no question of Allen and Rose growing intimate, but the film's staging allows such a question to occur. Meanwhile, Ryan starts attending a grief support group where the leader does what no support group leader should ever do, and offers a diagnosis and recommendation to members after one comment.

In this group, a young woman named Ashley (Zoe Kravitz) reaches out to Ryan, and he responds and improves emotionally, and they like each other, and a romance seems to be in the works, and then he knocks on her door and her sister (I guess) answers and says something (I'm not sure what) and he runs off, and Ashley runs after him but that's the end of that subplot. What's that about?

And what about the scene where Ryan consumes what may be Ecstasy and then smokes pot. OK . . . and then? Nothing. He gets high and comes down, I guess. Meanwhile, Grace sits at the bedside of Jordan (Michael Shannon), the truck driver who hit her son's car. She knows her son lived for seventeen minutes after the crash and that Jordan spoke to him, and she's obsessed to know what he said. But after the conversation Jordan went into coma. Some months later, we see her at his bedside, hearing the story of the seventeen minutes.

I will omit certain additional details involving Allen and Rose (separately), and I suppose I shouldn't describe the melodrama of the closing scenes, except to say they're an anthology of clichés. And there's a car ride in which way too much communication takes place, at long last, in a much too facile fashion.

So the screenplay is a soap operatic mess, involving distractions, loose ends, and sheer carelessness. Yet Sarandon creates a wrenching performance of a woman torn apart by grief, and Brosnan is convincing as a man holding it together as long as he can. As for Mulligan and Simmons, what can I say? There is nothing they do wrong, but this film written

and directed by Shana Feste leaves both characters deprived of explanation, development, and revelation. And you can't get me to believe that after you have sex one time and get pregnant, and your lover is killed, and you have absolutely *nobody* to turn to except his parents, and his mother hates you, a teenage girl can have this much self-confidence. Even Juno would have disintegrated under the pressure.

Greenberg ★★★ ½
R, 107 m., 2010

Ben Stiller (Roger Greenberg), Greta Gerwig (Florence Marr), Rhys Ifans (Ivan Schrank), Jennifer Jason Leigh (Beth), Brie Larson (Sara), Juno Temple (Muriel), Chris Messina (Phillip Greenberg), Susan Traylor (Carol Greenberg), Mark Duplass (Eric Beller). Directed by Noah Baumbach and produced by Jennifer Jason Leigh and Scott Rudin. Screenplay by Baumbach.

When you're angry with the world and yourself to the same degree, you're running in place. It takes a great deal of energy. It can be exhausting. You lash out at people. You're hard on yourself. It all takes place in your head. After a time people give up on you. They think you don't give a damn and don't care about yourself. If they only knew.

That's Roger Greenberg. I never knew who Ben Stiller was born to play, but now I do. I don't mean he *is* Greenberg, but that he makes him a convincing person and not a caricature. The hero of Noah Baumbach's new film was once, years ago, part of a rock band on the brink of a breakthrough. He walked away from it, stranding his bandmates, and never explained why. He fled Los Angeles and became a carpenter in New York.

He's been struggling. There has been some sort of vague period in an institution. Now he's returned to L.A. to house-sit his brother's big home and look after the dog. He glares out of the windows like old man Fredricksen in *Up*. He can live alone no more successfully than with others. He calls Florence Marr (Greta Gerwig), his brother's family assistant, who knows where everything is and how everything works. And the dog knows her.

Florence is someone we know. A bright, pleasant recent college graduate for whom the job market, as they say, has no use. We see her interacting with the family of Greenberg's brother; she does all the planning for them that she should be doing for herself. In a more conventional movie, Florence would be the love interest, and Greenberg would be fated to marry her. But Florence isn't looking for a man. She just broke up. "I don't want to go from just having sex to sex to sex," she says. "Who's the third 'sex'?" asks Greenberg. "You."

I have a weakness for actresses like Greta Gerwig. She looks reasonable and approachable. Some actresses are all edges and polish. This one, you could look up and see her walking dreamily through a bookstore, possibly with a Penguin Classic already in her hand. Greenberg treats her badly. He has no notion of his effect on people. When they end up having sex, and they do, it's like their right hands don't know what their left hands are doing.

Noah Baumbach made the inspired film *The Squid and the Whale* (2005), about a formidably articulate family torn apart by a divorce. Both parents were at fault to various degrees, and both sons could have done more in their own way to help the situation. Everyone obsessed on their grievances. Greenberg takes this a step further: He obsesses on the grievances against him.

He has a reunion with a former bandmate, Ivan (Rhys Ifans), a calm Brit, troubled by a trial separation, happy enough to see Greenberg and help him if he can. But Ivan is troubled that Greenberg *still* doesn't get it, doesn't understand how he crushed the dreams of his bandmates. Then there's Beth (Jennifer Jason Leigh), whom Greenberg once loved and was loved by. Life has moved on. She has a family. Does he recognize the look a woman gets in her eyes when she's thinking how that just would have never, ever worked out? Does he have enough self-knowledge to see how impossible he is?

The important relationship is the one between Greenberg and Florence. We look upon her and see wholesome health and abundant energy. She's happy when she has a purpose. She wishes she had a direction in life, but can be happy enough in the moment. It's as if when Greenberg moves a little in the direction

of happiness, he gets jealous because that draws attention away from his miserable uniqueness. People driven to be constantly unique can be a real pain in the ass.

This is an intriguing film, shifting directions, considering Greenberg's impossibility in one light and then another. If he's stuck like this at forty, is he stuck for good? What Ben Stiller does with the role is fascinating. We can't stand Greenberg. But we begin to care about him. Without ever overtly evoking sympathy, Stiller inspires identification. You don't have to like the hero of a movie. But you have to understand him—better than he does himself, in some cases.

Green Zone ★★★★
R, 114 m., 2010

Matt Damon (Roy Miller), Jason Isaacs (Briggs), Brendan Gleeson (Martin Brown), Greg Kinnear (Clark Poundstone), Amy Ryan (Lawrie Dayne), Khalid Abdalla (Freddy), Igal Naor (General Al Rawi). Directed by Paul Greengrass and produced by Tim Bevan, Eric Fellner, and Lloyd Levin. Screenplay by Brian Helgeland, inspired by the book *Imperial Life in the Emerald City* by Rajiv Chandrasekaran.

Green Zone looks at an American war in a way almost no Hollywood movie ever has: We're not the heroes, but the dupes. Its message is that Iraq's fabled "weapons of mass destruction" did not exist, and that neocons within the administration fabricated them, lied about them, and were ready to kill to cover up their deception.

Is this true? I'm not here to say. It's certainly one more element in the new narrative that has gradually emerged about Iraq, the dawning realization that we went to war under false premises. It's a thriller that makes no claim to be based on fact, but provides characters and situations that have uncanny real-life parallels. Its director made two of the Bourne films, and imports his approach to Baghdad, starring Matt Damon as an unstoppable action hero.

But this isn't merely a thriller. It has a point to argue: Critical blunders at the outset made a quick and easy victory impossible, and turned Bush's "Mission Accomplished" photo-op into a historic miscalculation. *Green Zone* argues, as many observers have, that the fatal error of the United States was to fire the officers and men of the Iraqi army and leave them at large with their weapons. The army had no great love of Saddam, and might have been a helpful stabilizing force. Instead, it was left unemployed, armed, and alienated.

Damon, playing Chief Warrant Officer Roy Miller, is seen at the outset leading a raid on a suspected storage site for WMDs. Nothing there. Another raid, intended to find weapons of chemical warfare, turns up years-old pigeon droppings. Because some of the raids produce casualties, he begins to question the intelligence reports the raids are based on. He speaks out at a briefing, and rather improbably finds himself face-to-face with a U.S. intelligence agent named Poundstone (Greg Kinnear). He's fed the usual line and told to perform his duty, but is overheard by Brown, a hulking, grizzled CIA man who's an old Middle East hand. Soon he's meeting with Brown to pass on his doubts. *Green Zone* indicates that the CIA, which lacked (as in real life) any evidence to back up the WMD claims, has been cut out of the loop, and that Poundstone is not only the architect of the neocon fictions, but their enforcer; he even has a military group answering directly to him.

Chief Miller also meets a New York newspaperwoman named Lawrie Dayne (Amy Ryan), whose reports about a secret Iraqi informer have given credence to the WMD claims. From her he discovers that General Al Rawi (Igal Naor) of the Iraqi army met with Poundstone in Jordan, but unlike the source Poundstone cited, flatly told him Saddam had no WMDs. So the bad intel was cooked up to justify the war the neocons desired.

Have I made the plot sound complex? Greengrass works with the screenwriter, Brian Helgeland, to tell it with considerable clarity. By limiting the characters and using typecasting, he makes a web of deceit easy to understand. Also a great help to Chief Miller is a local named Freddy (Khalid Abdalla), who risks his life to help him, acts as a translator, and is given the film's key line of dialogue.

The action in *Green Zone* is followed by Greengrass in the queasycam style I've found distracting in the past: lots of quick cuts between handheld shots. It didn't bother me here. That may be because I became so involved in the story. Perhaps also because unlike the Bourne films, this one contains no action sequences that are logically impossible. When we see a car chase that couldn't take place in the real world, we naturally think about the visual effects. When they could take place, and it's a good movie, we're thinking about the story.

Green Zone will no doubt be under fire from those who are still defending the fabricated intelligence we used as an excuse to invade Iraq. Yes, the film is fiction, employs far-fetched coincidences, and improbably places one man at the center of all the action. It is a thriller, not a documentary. It's my belief that the nature of the neocon evildoing has by now become pretty clear. Others will disagree. The bottom line is: This is one hell of a thriller. ☞

The Grocer's Son ★ ★ ★

NO MPAA RATING, 96 m., 2008

Nicolas Cazale (Antoine Sforza), Clotilde Hesme (Claire), Daniel Duval (Monsieur Sforza), Jeanne Goupil (Madame Sforza), Liliane Rovere (Lucienne), Paul Crauchet (Pere Clement), Stephan Guerin-Tillie (Francois Sforza). Directed by Eric Guirado and produced by Milena Poylo and Gilles Sacuto. Screenplay by Guirado and Florence Vignon.

The term "coming of age" always seems to apply to teenagers. But you can come of age in your twenties, thirties, or forties, or maybe never. I define it as beginning to value other people for who they are, rather than what they can do for you.

Antoine (Nicolas Cazale) is thirty-ish, lives in a cluttered room in Paris, and left home ten years ago promising never to return to the village where his parents ran the only grocery store. His father has a heart attack, and that forces him to go to the hospital for a reunion with his brother and mother, whom he has avoided. She comes home to his room to spend the night, and what with one thing and another he reluctantly returns to the village to help her with the business.

That means taking over his father's daily

route with a van packed with groceries, produce, and provisions. He already knows the route—probably learned it going along as a kid. It takes him through the painterly landscape of Provence, stopping at particular homes or crossroads where old people depend on the service. A popular item seems to be tinned peas. Antoine is not the model of friendliness. He curtly advises one old-timer to pay his tab and rejects his father's long-standing arrangement to barter with another for eggs.

Madame Sforza, his mother (Jeanne Goupil), is a sunny woman with a lovely smile and wisely doesn't push him too hard. His brother, Francois (Stephan Guerin-Tillie), visits, and they fight, as usual. And there is another visitor. This is Claire (Clotilde Hesme), who lives across the hall from him in Paris. "And this would be my room?" she asks Madame Sforza. "You're not sleeping with Antoine?" she asks. "We don't sleep together," Claire explains. "That's good," the mother says. "Rare, but good."

It is clear that his mother is curious about the exact relationship between Antoine and Claire, who is taking a correspondence course to be admitted to a Spanish university. The two young people obviously like each other and would be a good match, but Antoine is too self-centered and selfish to open himself to her. Nor is he any good with customers, he is informed by his Paris friend Hassan, who also runs a grocery. Antoine seems to find it difficult to release the words "Thank you."

You can probably guess the trajectory of the story. But it's not really the destination that makes this a charmer; it's the journey there, mostly by grocery van. The side of the truck opens and is propped up to display the goods inside. When the side falls down and flattens old Lucienne (Liliane Rovere), who is none too pleased with Antoine's prices anyway, she walks out to the van at the next visit wearing a bowl on her head.

The film was directed and co-written by Eric Guirado, who reportedly followed and observed country grocers on their routes. He works gently. The summer unfolds slowly. Claire goes back to Paris. The father arrives from Paris. The countryside is calm and seductive. The mother soldiers on, keeping the store open late "to help people." And Antoine comes of age. That's all the film is, apart from having humor, warmth, kindness, insight, and scenery. That's enough.

Grown Ups ★★
PG-13, 102 m., 2010

Adam Sandler (Lenny Feder), Kevin James (Eric Lamonsoff), Chris Rock (Kurt McKenzie), David Spade (Marcus Higgins), Rob Schneider (Rob Hilliard), Maria Bello (Sally Lamonsoff), Salma Hayek (Roxanne Chase-Feder), Maya Rudolph (Deanne McKenzie), Joyce Van Patten (Gloria), Ebony Jo-Ann (Mama Ronzoni), Di Quon (Nanny Rita), Steve Buscemi (Wiley). Directed by Dennis Dugan and produced by Jack Giarraputo and Adam Sandler. Screenplay by Sandler and Fred Wolf.

Grown Ups is a pleasant, genial, good-hearted, sometimes icky comedy that's like spending a weekend with well-meaning people you don't want to see again any time real soon. They're the kind of people where, in the car driving home, you ask, "What was that all about?" Try to imagine the Three Stooges slapping one another's faces with dehydrated reconstituted bananas. No, really.

The pretense for the story: Five kids were on a basketball team in middle school. Their beloved old coach has died. To mourn him they return to the lakeside cabin where they celebrated their victory all those years ago. Wouldn't you know, the five kids on the team they beat are at the same lake for the same weekend.

The five buddies are played by Adam Sandler, Rob Schneider, Kevin James, Chris Rock, and David Spade. Sandler's wife is a famous designer (Salma Hayek). Schneider's much older wife is Joyce Van Patten. Rock's pregnant wife is Maya Rudolph. His Madea-style mother is Ebony Jo-Ann. James's wife is Maria Bello, who is still breast-feeding their four-year-old at every opportunity. Spade is unmarried, which, given the size of the cast, is just as well, since the characters have five children (I think), and there are also roles for Steve Buscemi as a guy who ends up in a body cast, Di Quon as Sandler's Asian nanny, and, of course, Schneider's three daughters from two previous marriages, two of them towering models, the third short and stout. There are so many characters in the movie that some scenes look like everyone lined up for a group shot.

The physical humor is not sophisticated. One character ends up with her face in a cake, and another has his face pushed twice into doggy-doo. The nursing mother squirts milk here and there, and her son is warned that if he doesn't wean himself soon he'll have a "got milk?" mustache with real hair. The gang all goes to a water park. There's a basketball game to settle old scores. And so on.

What's strange is how laid-back it all is. The five old pals at times sound positively like they're idly remembering old times. Lots of stuff seems intended only to be pleasant. When it looks like Sandler and his wife will be given the bedroom with the water mattress, for example, he says, naw, let the kids all share it. Does that sound like the set-up for a joke? There isn't one.

Joyce Van Patten (who is seventy-five) and Rob Schneider (who is forty-six) play a married couple, which generates some laughs, mostly on the nice side, and no vulgarities. See, they really like each other. And during the obligatory scene where every character makes a confession or relates one of life's lessons, she makes a warm and genuine speech that is well delivered, but hardly seems to belong in this movie.

The comedy talent here is seen but not much heard, given the human traffic jam of the cast. Chris Rock and Kevin James are underutilized. Maria Bello is reduced to breast-feeding and milk-pumping scenes. The character of Ebony Jo-Ann, with her farts, bunions, and pratfalls, comes perilously close to an insulting caricature. Maya Rudolph spends much of her time reacting to others and caressing her pregnancy. Adam Sandler plays a good guy who never does much more than be a good guy.

The direction by Dennis Dugan never overcomes the ungainly size of the cast. It's such a challenge to keep all the characters alive that he sometimes does round-robins of reaction shots—a fatal strategy when it comes to timing. Some of the dialogue is broken down into one-shots; some of the characters spend stretches of merely responding. It's all, as I said, pleasant and good-natured, but it feels too much as if all these nice people are trying to keep the conversation going. A comedy it is, but *The Hangover* or *Death at a Funeral* it isn't.

H

Hamlet 2 ★ ★ ★
R, 92 m., 2008

Steve Coogan (Dana Marschz), Joseph Julian Soria (Octavio), Elisabeth Shue (Elisabeth Shue), Skylar Astin (Rand), Phoebe Strole (Epiphany), Marshall Bell (Mr. Rocker), Catherine Keener (Dana's Wife), David Arquette (Gary the Boarder), Amy Poehler (Cricket Feldstein), Shea Pepe (The Critic). Directed by Andrew Fleming and produced by Eric D. Eisner, Leonid Rozhetskin, and Aaron Ryder. Screenplay by Fleming and Pam Brady.

The problem with a sequel to *Hamlet* is that everybody interesting is dead by the end. That doesn't discourage Dana Marschz, a Tucson high school drama teacher, from trying to save the school's theater program with a sequel named *Hamlet 2*. The shop class builds him a time machine, and he brings back the dead characters, plus Jesus, Einstein, and the very much alive Hillary Clinton. Music is by the Tucson Gay Men's Chorus.

Hamlet 2 stars the British comedian Steve Coogan, who with this film and *Tropic Thunder* may develop a fan base in America. He's sort of a gangling, flighty, manic Woody Allen type, but without the awareness of his neurosis. Oh, he knows he has problems. He's a recovering alcoholic, so broke he and his wife have to take in a boarder, and when his drama class is thrown out of the school lunchroom they have to meet in the gym during volleyball practice.

Anyone who has ever been involved in high school theatrical productions will recognize a few elements from *Hamlet 2*, here much exaggerated. There are the teacher's pets who usually play all the leads. The rebellious new student who's sort of an ethnic Brando. The pitiful costumes. The disapproving school board, which wants to discontinue the program. The community uproar over the shocking content (gay men singing "Rock Me, Sexy Jesus"?). The ACLU lawyer, named Cricket (Amy Poehler), who flies to the rescue but seems to have a tendency toward anti-Semitism. And above all the inspired, passionate, more than slightly mad drama teacher.

Mr. Marschz (to pronounce it, you have to sort of buzz at the end) has seen too many movies like *Dead Poets Society* and *Mr. Holland's Opus*, and tries to inspire his students with his bizarre behavior. This takes little effort, especially after he starts wearing caftans to school because his wife (Catherine Keener) thinks he's impotent because jockey shorts cut off his circulation. Principal Rocker (Marshall Bell) is his unremitting enemy, and Octavio (Joseph Julian Soria) is the brilliant but rebellious student (he comes across as street tough but is headed for Brown). Rand (Skylar Astin) and Epiphany (Phoebe Strole) are his special pets, now feeling left out.

And then there is Elisabeth Shue. Yes, the real Elisabeth Shue, Oscar nominee for *Leaving Las Vegas*. When Dana goes to the hospital for treatment of his broken f-you finger, he tells the nurse she looks like his favorite actress, Elisabeth Shue. "That's because I am Elisabeth Shue," she says, explaining that she got tired of all the BS in showbiz and decided to help people by becoming a nurse. She agrees to visit his class. You can imagine the questions she gets.

Chaotic rehearsals and legal maneuvers by Cricket succeed in getting the play staged—not in the school, but in an abandoned railroad shed. Some of the characters may have the same names as characters in *Hamlet*, but that's about as far as the resemblance goes. No danger of plagiarism charges. The Gay Men's Chorus is very good, Dana himself not so good in the role of Jesus, moon-walking on the water.

Much depends on the verdict of my favorite character in the movie, the critic of the high school paper (Shea Pepe), a freshman who is about five feet tall. Having eviscerated Dana's previous production, he helpfully gives him advice (he should stop remaking movies like *Erin Brockovich* and do something original). *Hamlet 2* is original, all right. But will the kid like it?

The movie is an ideal showcase for the talents of Coogan, whom you may remember from *A Cock and Bull Story* (2005), the film about a film of *Tristram Shandy*, where only one person involved in the production had ever read the book. He is a TV legend in the UK, but not so uber-Brit that he doesn't travel well. He seems somewhat at home in Tucson, which, let it be said, has got to be a nicer town than anybody in this movie thinks it is.

Hancock ★ ★ ★
PG-13, 92 m., 2008

Will Smith (John Hancock), Charlize Theron (Mary Embrey), Jason Bateman (Ray Embrey), Eddie Marsan (Red), Jae Head (Aaron Embrey), David Mattey (Man Mountain). Directed by Peter Berg and produced by Akiva Goldsman, Michael Mann, Will Smith, and James Lassiter. Screenplay by Vy Vincent Ngo and Vince Gilligan.

I have been waiting for this for years: a superhero movie where the actions of the superheroes have consequences in the real world. They always leave a wake of crashed cars, bursting fire hydrants, exploding gas stations, and toppling bridges behind them, and never go back to clean up. But John Hancock, the hero of *Hancock*, doesn't get away with anything. One recent heroic stunt ran up a price tag of seven million dollars, he's got hundreds of lawsuits pending, and when he saves a stranded whale by throwing it back into the sea, you can bet he gets billed for the yacht it lands on.

Hancock, the latest star showcase for Will Smith, has him playing a Skid Row drunk with superpowers and a super hangover. He does well, but there are always consequences, like when he saves a man whose car is about to be struck by a train, but causes a train wreck. What he needs is a good PR man. Luckily, the man whose life he saved is exactly that. He's Ray Embrey (Jason Bateman, the adopting father in *Juno*), and Ray has a brainstorm: He'll repay Hancock by giving him a complete image makeover. If this sounds like a slapstick comedy, strangely enough it isn't. The movie has a lot of laughs, but Smith avoids playing Hancock as a goofball and shapes him as serious, thoughtful, and depressed.

Embrey the PR whiz brings Hancock home to dinner to meet his wife, Mary (Charlize Theron), and son, Aaron (Jae Head). The first time she meets him, Mary gives Hancock an odd, penetrating look. Also the second time, and also the third time. OK, OK, already: We get it. One odd, penetrating look after another. They have some kind of a history, but Hancock doesn't know about it, and Mary's not talking.

She has a lot to keep quiet about, although thank goodness she eventually opens up, or the movie wouldn't have a second half. I will not reveal what she says, of course, because her surprise is part of the fun. I am willing to divulge some of the setup, with Ray coaching Hancock to start saying "thank you" and "you did a good job here," and stop flying down out of the sky and crushing $100,000 cars. Ray also gets him a makeover: Gone is the flophouse wardrobe, replaced by a slick gold and leather costume, and Hancock gets a shave, too. Does it himself, with his fingernails.

He appeared some eighty years ago in Miami, as far as he knows. He doesn't know very far. He has no idea where his powers came from, or why he never grows any older. He can fly at supersonic speeds, stop a speeding locomotive, toss cars around, and in general do everything Superman could do, but not cleanly, neatly, or politely. Part of his reform involves turning himself in to the law and serving a prison term, although the chief of police has to summon him from prison to help with a bank hostage crisis. (In prison, there's a guy named Man Mountain who must not read the papers, or he would never, ever try to make Hancock his victim.)

It's not long after the bank hostage business that Mary reveals her secret, Hancock starts asking deep questions about himself, and the movie takes an odd, penetrating turn. This is the part I won't get into, except to say that the origin stories of superheroes consistently underwhelm me, and Hancock's is one of the most arbitrary. Even Mary, who knows all about him, doesn't know all that much, and I have a shiny new dime here for any viewer of the movie who can explain exactly how Hancock came into being.

Not that it matters much anyway. I guess he had to come into being *somehow*, and this movie's explanation is as likely as most, which is to say, completely preposterous. Still, *Hancock* is a lot of fun, if perhaps a little top-heavy with stuff being destroyed. Will Smith makes the character more subtle than he has to be, more filled with self-doubt, more willing to learn. Jason Bateman is persuasive and helpful on the PR front, and it turns out Charlize Theron has a great deal to feel odd and penetrating about.

The Hangover ★ ★ ★ ½
R, 100 m., 2009

Bradley Cooper (Phil), Ed Helms (Stu), Zach Galifianakis (Alan), Heather Graham (Jade), Justin Bartha (Doug), Jeffrey Tambor (Sid). Directed by Todd Phillips and produced by Phillips and Dan Goldberg. Screenplay by Jon Lucas and Scott Moore.

Now this is what I'm talkin' about. *The Hangover* is a funny movie, flat out, all the way through. Its setup is funny. Every situation is funny. Most of the dialogue is funny almost line by line. At some point we actually find ourselves caring a little about what happened to the missing bridegroom—and the fact that we almost care is funny, too.

The movie opens with bad news for a bride on her wedding day. Her fiancé's best buddy is standing in the Mohave Desert with a bloody lip and three other guys, none of whom is her fiancé. They've lost him. He advises her there's no way the wedding is taking place.

We flash back two days to their road trip to Vegas for a bachelor party. Her future husband, Doug (Justin Bartha), will be joined by his two friends, the schoolteacher Phil (Bradley Cooper) and the dentist Stu (Ed Helms). Joining them will be her brother, Alan (Zach Galifianakis), an overweight slob with a Haystacks Calhoun beard and an injunction against coming within two hundred feet of a school building.

The next morning, Doug will be missing. The other three are missing several hours: None of them can remember a thing since they were on the roof of Caesars Palace, drinking shots of Jagermeister. They would desperately like to know: How in the hell do you wake up in a $4,200-a-night suite with a tiger, a chicken, a crying baby, a missing tooth, and a belly button pierced for a diamond dangle? And when you give your parking check to the doorman, why does he bring around a police car? And where is Doug?

Their search provides a structure for the rest of the movie, during a very long day that includes a fact-finding visit to a wedding chapel, a violent encounter with a small but very mean Chinese mobster, a sweet hooker, an interview with an emergency room doctor, and an encounter with Mike Tyson, whose tiger they appear to have stolen, although under the circumstances he is fairly nice about it. There is never an explanation for the chicken.

Despite these events, *The Hangover* isn't simply a laff riot. I won't go so far as to describe it as a character study, but all three men have profound personality problems, and the Vegas trip works on them like applied emergency therapy. The dentist is rigidly ruled by his bitchy girlfriend. The schoolteacher thinks nothing of stealing the money for a class trip. And Alan . . .

Well, Zach Galifianakis's performance is the kind of breakout performance that made John Belushi a star after *Animal House*. He is short, stocky, wants to be liked, has a yearning energy, was born clueless. It is a tribute to Galifianakis's acting that we actually believe he is sincere when he asks the clerk at the check-in counter: "Is this the real Caesar's palace? Does Caesar live here?"

The film is directed by Todd Phillips, whose *Old School* and *Road Trip* had their moments but didn't prepare me for this. The screenplay is by Jon Lucas and Scott Moore, whose *Ghosts of Girlfriends Past* certainly didn't. This movie is *written*, not assembled out of off-the-shelf parts from the Apatow Surplus Store. There is a level of detail and observation in the dialogue that's sort of remarkable: These characters aren't generically funny, but specifically funny. The actors make them halfway convincing.

Phillips has them encountering a mixed bag of weird characters, which is standard, but the characters aren't. Mr. Chow (Ken Jeong), the vertically challenged naked man they find locked in the trunk of the police car, is strong, skilled in martial arts, and really mean about Alan being fat. He finds almost anything a fat man does to be hilarious. When he finds his clothes and his henchmen, he is not to be trifled with. Jade (Heather Graham), a stripper, is forthright: "Well, actually I'm an escort, but stripping is a good way to meet clients." She isn't the good-hearted cliché, but more of a sincere young woman who would like to meet the right guy.

The search for Doug has them piecing together clues from the ER doctor, Mike Tyson's security tapes, and a mattress that is impaled on the uplifted arm of one of the Caesars Palace statues. The plot hurtles through them. If the movie ends somewhat conventionally, well, it almost has to: Narrative housecleaning requires it. It began conventionally, too, with uplifting music and a typeface for the titles that may remind you of *My Best Friend's Wedding*. But it is not to be. Here is a movie that deserves every letter of its R rating. What happens in Vegas stays in Vegas, especially after you throw up.

The Happening ★ ★ ★
R, 91 m., 2008

Mark Wahlberg (Elliot Moore), Zooey Deschanel (Alma Moore), John Leguizamo (Julian), Betty Buckley (Mrs. Jones), Ashlyn Sanchez (Jess), Spencer Breslin (Josh). Directed by M. Night Shyamalan and produced by Shyamalan, Sam Mercer, and Barry Mendel. Screenplay by Shyamalan.

If the bee disappears from the surface of the Earth, man would have no more than four years to live.
—Albert Einstein

An alarming prospect, and all the more so because there has been a recent decline in the honeybee population. Perhaps it is comforting to know that Einstein never said any such thing—less comforting, of course, for the bees. The quotation appears on a blackboard near the beginning of M. Night Shyamalan's *The Happening*, a movie that I found oddly touching. It is no doubt too thoughtful for the summer action season, but I appreciate the quietly realistic way Shyamalan finds to tell a story about the possible death of man.

One day in Central Park people start to lose their trains of thought. They begin walking backward. They start killing themselves. This behavior spreads through Manhattan, and then all of the northeastern states. Construction workers throw themselves from scaffolds.

Policemen shoot themselves. The deaths are blamed on a "terrorist attack," but in fact no one has the slightest clue, and New York City is evacuated.

We meet Elliot Moore (Mark Wahlberg), a Philadelphia high school science teacher; the quote was on his blackboard. We meet his wife, Alma (Zooey Deschanel), his friend Julian (John Leguizamo), and Julian's daughter, Jess (Ashlyn Sanchez). They find themselves fleeing on a train to Harrisburg, Pennsylvania, although people learn from their cell phones that the plague, or whatever it is, may have jumped ahead of them.

Now consider how Shyamalan shows the exodus from Philadelphia. He avoids all the conventional scenes of riots in the train station, people killing one another for seats on the train, etc., and shows the population as quiet and apprehensive. If you don't know what you're fleeing, and it may be waiting for you ahead, how would you behave? Like this, I suspect.

Julian entrusts his daughter with Elliot and Alma, and goes in search of his wife. The train stops permanently at a small town. The three hitch a ride in a stranger's car and later meet others who are fleeing, from what or to what, they do not know. Elliot meets a man who talks about a way plants have of creating hormones to kill their enemies, and he develops a half-baked theory that man may have finally delivered too many insults to the grasses and the shrubs, the flowers and the trees, and their revenge is in the wind.

By now the three are trekking cross-country through Pennsylvania, joined by two young boys, whom they will eventually lose. They walk on, the wind moaning ominously behind them, and come to the isolated country home of Mrs. Jones (Betty Buckley), a very odd old lady. Here they eat and spend the night, and other events take place, and Elliot and Alma find an opportunity to discuss their love and reveal some secrets and speculate about what dread manifestation has overtaken the world.

Too uneventful for you? Not enough action? For me, Shyamalan's approach was more effective than smash-and-grab plot-mongering. His use of the landscape is disturbingly effective. The performances by Wahlberg and Deschanel bring a quiet dignity to their characters. The *strangeness* of starting a day in New York and ending it hiking across a country field is underlined. Most of the other people we meet, not all, are muted and introspective. Had they been half-expecting some such "event" as this, whatever its description?

I know I have. For some time the thought has been gathering at the back of my mind that we are in the final act. We have finally insulted the planet so much that it can no longer sustain us. It is exhausted. It never occurred to me that vegetation might exterminate us. In fact, the form of the planet's revenge remains undefined in my thoughts, although I have read of global deserts and starvation, rising sea levels and the ends of species.

What I admired about *The Happening* is that the pace and substance of its storytelling allowed me to examine such thoughts, and to ask how I might respond to a wake-up call from nature. Shyamalan allows his characters space and time as they look within themselves. Those they meet on the way are such as they might indeed plausibly meet. Even the television and radio news is done correctly, as convenient clichés about terrorism give way to bewilderment and apprehension.

I suspect I'll be in the minority in praising this film. It will be described as empty, uneventful, meandering. But for some it will weave a spell. It is a parable, yes, but it is also simply the story of these people and how their lives and existence have suddenly become problematic. We depend on such a superstructure to maintain us that one or two alterations could leave us stranded and wandering through a field, if we are that lucky.

Happy-Go-Lucky ★ ★ ★ ★
R, 118 m., 2008

Sally Hawkins (Poppy), Eddie Marsan (Scott), Alexis Zegerman (Zoe), Samuel Roukin (Tim). Directed by Mike Leigh and produced by Simon Channing Williams. Screenplay by Leigh.

Mike Leigh's *Happy-Go-Lucky* is the story of a good woman. As simple as that. We first see Poppy pedaling her bike through London and smiling all the time to herself. She stops at a bookshop and tries to cheer up the dour proprietor. No, that isn't right. She doesn't want to change him, just infect him with her irrepressible good nature. She may not even be aware of how she operates. Then her bike is stolen. She takes that right in stride.

Poppy (Sally Hawkins) is one of the most difficult roles any actress could be assigned. She must smile and be peppy and optimistic at (almost) all times, and do it naturally and convincingly, as if the sunshine comes from inside. That's harder than playing Lady Macbeth. Sally Hawkins has been in movies before, including Leigh's *Vera Drake* and Woody Allen's *Cassandra's Dream*, but this is her star-making role. She was named best actress at Berlin 2008. I will deliberately employ a cliché: She is a joy to behold.

At first, that seems to be all there is to it. The movie will be about Poppy and her job as an elementary school teacher, and the lessons she is taking in flamenco dancing, and her flatmate Zoe, and her sister Suzy, and how she starts to feel about Tim, the school counselor who comes to assist her with a troubled little boy. That would almost be enough. But *Happy-Go-Lucky* is about a great deal more and goes very much deeper.

As she works with the little boy, we see that she's not at all superficial but can listen, observe, empathize, and find the right note in response. In another scene, which may not seem to fit but is profoundly effective, she comes across a homeless man in the shadows under a rail line, and talks with him. He's one of those people who chants the same thing, ferociously, over and over. She listens to him, speaks with him, asks if he's hungry. She is not afraid. She's worried about him. I think he's aware of that, and it soothes him. It is possible nobody has spoken to him in days or weeks.

So we get these glimpses into Poppy's deeper regions. Then she decides to take driving lessons and meets Scott, the instructor. He is played brilliantly by Eddie Marsan, an English comedian who as an actor often finds morose, worrywart roles. Consider him as the pessimistic Jewish father in *Sixty Six*. Scott is an angry man. Oddly for a driving instructor, he seems to channel road rage. His system for helping her remember the rearview mirror and the two side mirrors involves naming them after fallen angels. He screams at her. No one could drive with Scott at their side.

Any other person would quit working with Scott after one lesson. Not Poppy. Does she think she can help him? Their relationship descends into an extraordinary scene during which we suddenly see right inside both of them and understand better what Poppy's cheerfulness is all about. We also see Scott's terrifying insecurity and self-loathing; Marsan is spellbinding.

This is Mike Leigh's funniest film since *Life Is Sweet* (1991). Of course, he hasn't ever made a *completely* funny film, and *Happy-Go-Lucky* has scenes that are not funny, not at all. There are always undercurrents and oddness. His films feel as if they're spontaneously unfolding; he has a vision of his characters that is only gradually revealed. He almost always finds remarkable performances, partly because he casts actors, not stars, and partly because he and the actors rehearse for weeks, tilting the dialogue this way and that, contriving back stories, finding out where the characters came from before the movie began, predicting where they will go after it's over.

I had seen Sally Hawkins in movies before. She was the rich girl who went to the private clinic in *Vera Drake*. No role could be more different than Poppy. Leigh, who spent years working for the stage, was able to imagine her as Poppy, a role very few women could play. Maybe Meryl Streep could sustain that level of merriness, but then, what can't she do? And now I must ask, what can't Hawkins do? There are countless ways she might have stepped wrong. But she breezes in on her bicycle and engages our deepest sympathy. Poppy has a gift, as I said, for not running but standing there, reading the situation, understanding other people, and acting helpfully. And by that I do not mean she cheers them up.

Happy Tears ★★★

R, 95 m., 2010

Parker Posey (Jayne), Demi Moore (Laura), Rip Torn (Joe), Ellen Barkin (Shelly), Christian Camargo (Jackson). Directed by Mitchell Lichtenstein and produced by Joyce M. Pierpoline. Screenplay by Lichtenstein.

In *Happy Tears*, two sisters—one poor, one rich, one steady, one obsessed with posses-

sions—deal with their old dad's approach to senility and his girlfriend's approach to his money. This story takes on an eerie resonance with the performance by Rip Torn as the aging father. He was recently in the news for being arrested, at the age of seventy-eight, for breaking into a bank while intoxicated and carrying a firearm.

To be sure, it was late at night, he had apparently forgotten he had the firearm, and after all, the bank looked a lot like a house. Nor is senility his problem. He is now in alcohol rehab, and I wish him good fortune because he is a fine actor. Ann Landers wrote about the danger signals of alcoholism. His arrest in the bank is surely one of them. Still, to stir up such a scandal at seventy-eight is perhaps even a tiny accomplishment, when so many his age are no longer physically able to break into banks.

Even more worthy is Torn's work here as Joe, cantankerous, stubborn as a mule, and oblivious to the fact that his "nurse," Shelly (Ellen Barkin), does not practice medicine but a far older profession. This is evident to his daughter Laura (Demi Moore), who has flown in from San Francisco to decide what should be done with him. Of course he insists he's perfectly fine and will stay right at home, thank you.

As the film opens, Laura is on the phone with her sister, Jayne (Parker Posey), telling her it's her duty to fly east and help with Joe. Jayne is a shopaholic, and we see her buying a pair of boots so expensive that if it were my money I'd just buy a car. Posey is an actress with a nice line in flightiness, and here she blends it interestingly with selfishness and irresponsibility. Soon after her arrival, the need to tidy up after Joe's problems with number two becomes the first of several life lessons she'll learn.

Happy Tears centers on these two women, who have been opposites all their lives and yet like each other, and share a fondness for pot. Jayne can be infuriating, but Laura deals with it. Demi Moore is interesting here. In the role of a dialed-down, capable woman, she suggests dramatic possibilities for future roles. She projects a kind of calm, and it's attractive.

I was also intrigued by Ellen Barkin's work as the "nurse" Shelly, who optimistically believes that by wearing a stethoscope around her neck she can pass herself off. It's abundantly clear to Jayne and Laura that she learned her nursing on TV, but Joe is sold on her and cannot comprehend the possibility that he won't get his way. Instead of keeping Shelly at Level One of character complexity, writer-director Mitchell Lichtenstein wisely makes her a little more than she might seem. Barkin, a force of nature in such films as *Sea of Love*, here wades into a character role with zeal.

We assume the movie will mostly concern what the daughters should do with Joe. These scenarios are common enough, when estranged siblings are brought back together for the one reason it's hard to deny: the shared responsibility of family.

It's as well, too, that Joe is seen as a fairly clear-cut case. You want my opinion? He belongs in a home. In many films considering this question, the parents don't actually *need* such care, but it's such a convenience, you see, for their children. Joe presents not so much a problem for Jayne and Laura as an opportunity. It's time to grow up and be daughters and sisters. They've waited long enough. All of this, I must add, is done with a nice, screwy, sometimes stoned humor.

Harry Brown ★★★
R, 103 m., 2010

Michael Caine (Harry Brown), Emily Mortimer (D. I. Frampton), Charlie Creed-Miles (D. S. Hicock), Ben Drew (Noel Winters), Liam Cunningham (Sid Rourke), Iain Glen (S. I. Andrew Childs), David Bradley (Leonard Attwell), Jack O'Connell (Marky Hathaway). Directed by Daniel Barber and produced by Keith Bell, Matthew Brown, Kris Thykier, and Matthew Vaughn. Screenplay by Gary Young.

Harry Brown is a revenge thriller poised somewhere between *Death Wish* and *Gran Torino*. All three depend on the ability of an older actor to convince us he's still capable of violence, and all three spend a great deal of time alone with their characters, whose faces must reflect their inner feelings. Charles Bronson, Clint Eastwood, Michael Caine. Those are faces sculpted by time.

Caine plays an old man with a dying wife. He lives in a London housing estate used by a drug gang as its own turf. Pedestrians are terrorized and beaten, drugs are openly sold, there are some areas understood as no-go. From his high window, Harry hears a car alarm and looks down to see the car's owner come out and be beaten by thugs. This is the daily reality.

Caine is a subtle actor who builds characters from the inside out. His voice has become so familiar over the years that it's an old friend. In this film he begins as a lonely, sad geezer, and gradually an earlier persona emerges, that of a British marine who served in Northern Ireland. All of that has been put in a box and locked away, he says, and thinks.

There's a pub on the estate, quiet in the daytime, where he and his old friend Leonard (David Bradley) meet for studious games of chess. The thugs have been shoving dog mess through Leonard's mail slot. His life is miserable. He shows Harry a gun. One day when the gang pushes burning newspapers through the slot, he goes to confront them in an underpass they control. Later Frampton, a young police inspector (Emily Mortimer), comes to tell Harry that Leonard has been killed.

The inspector is human, and sympathetic. Harry tells her the police have no control over the area, and she cannot disagree. Her superior officer has his own notions. And then the film takes the turn that we expect, and in the process takes on aspects of a more conventional police procedural.

What Caine is successful at, however, is always remaining in character. Like Eastwood, and unlike Bronson, he is always his age, always in the same capable but aged body. The best scene in the movie involves his visit to the flat of a drug dealer, where Harry plans to buy a gun. There's a semi-comatose girl on the sofa. The situation is fraught. How Harry handles it depends not on strength but on experience and insight. He carefully conceals his cards.

The police investigation is misdirected for political motives. Frampton has an excellent notion of who may be responsible for the killings of neighborhood hoods, but cannot get a hearing. It would not do for a geezer to outdo the police. Vigilante activity is, of course, not the answer to urban crime, but what is? In Chicago, Mayor Richard Daley floods one area with cops, and shootings continue nearby. It's all fueled by drugs and drug money, of course. You know, one of the areas where I think Libertarians may be right is about the legalization of drugs. There would be less of them with no profit motive for their sale. Less money for guns. Fewer innocent bystanders would die. Who knows?

This movie plays better than perhaps it should. Directed as a debut by Daniel Barber, it places story and character above manufactured "thrills," and works better. We are all so desperately weary of CGI that replaces drama. With movies like this, humans creep back into crime films. There is a clear thread connecting this Michael Caine and the Caine of *The Ipcress File*. You may not be able to see it, but it's there.

Harry Potter and the Half-Blood Prince ★★★

PG, 153 m., 2009

Daniel Radcliffe (Harry Potter), Rupert Grint (Ron Weasley), Emma Watson (Hermione Granger), Jim Broadbent (Horace Slughorn), Helena Bonham Carter (Bellatrix Lestrange), Robbie Coltrane (Rubeus Hagrid), Michael Gambon (Albus Dumbledore), Alan Rickman (Severus Snape), Maggie Smith (Minerva McGonagall), Tom Felton (Draco Malfoy), Evanna Lynch (Luna Lovegood), Bonnie Wright (Ginny Weasley). Directed by David Yates and produced by David Heyman and David Barron. Screenplay by Steve Kloves, based on the novel by J. K. Rowling.

The climactic scene in *Harry Potter and the Half-Blood Prince* takes place in one of those underground caverns with a lake and an ominous gondola as the means of transportation, popularized by *The Phantom of the Opera*. At first I thought—no gondola! But then one appeared, dripping and hulking. In another movie I might have grinned, but you know what? By that point, I actually cared.

Yes, this sixth chapter is a darker, more ominous Harry Potter film, with a conclusion that suggests more alarmingly the deep dangers Harry and his friends have gotten themselves into. There was always a disconnect between

Harry's enchanting school days at Hogwarts and the looming threat of Voldemort. Presumably it would take more than skills at Quidditch to defeat the dreaded Dark Lord.

In one of the opening scenes, we find Harry (Daniel Radcliffe) late at night in a café of the London Underground, reading a copy of the *Daily Prophet*, which poses the question: Is Harry Potter the Chosen One? By the film's end, he acknowledges that he has, indeed, been chosen to face down Voldemort (whose name should properly rhyme with the French word for death, *mort*. Also, since their word *vol* can have meanings such as "thief" and "steal," Lord Voldemort is most ominously named).

Harry is distracted from his paper, however, by an instant flirtation with the young waitress, a saucy cutie who informs him, although he asked only with his eyes, that she gets off work at eleven. She indeed waits for him on the platform, but the Chosen One must respond to his higher calling from Dumbledore (Michael Gambon), who either materializes, gets off a train, or has a pied-a-terre right there in the Underground. I for one will be disappointed if that waitress (I think her name is Elarica Gallagher) doesn't turn up again in *Harry Potter and the Deathly Hallows*, whose two parts will conclude the series in 2010 and 2011.

That will be none too soon if Harry doesn't want to steal up on the *Twilight* franchise, since he and his friends, especially poor Ron Weasley, have definitively entered adolescence. Even now he seems to be entertaining thoughts of snoggling with Ron's sister, Ginny (Bonnie Wright). Yes, Harry, so recently a round-eyed little lad, will soon be one of Hogwarts's Old Boys.

Director David Yates suggests the transition in subtle ways, one of them by making Hogwarts itself seem darker, emptier, and more ominous than ever before. Its cheery corridors are now replaced by gloomy Gothic passages, and late in the film an unspeakable fate befalls the beloved dining hall at the hands of Bellatrix Lestrange (Helena Bonham Carter), who seems to function principally as a destructive vixen but no doubt has more ominous goals.

The mission for which Dumbledore summoned Harry at the outset was to visit the London home of Professor Horace Slughorn (Jim Broadbent), who has become reclusive since his

Hogwarts days, but is now urgently needed along with his memories of the young student Tom Riddle, who grew up to become the man whose name should rhyme with Death. Dumbledore hopes they can discover a secret vulnerability of Voldemort's, and that is why they find themselves in the underground cavern. When this possible key is discovered, I promise you I'm not spoiling anything by observing that its basic message is "to be continued."

There are really two story strands here. One involves the close working relationship of Dumbledore and Harry on the trail of Voldemort. The other involves everything else: romance and flirtation, Quiddich, a roll call of familiar characters (Hagrid, Snape, McGonagall, Wormtail, Lupin, Filch, Flitwick, and Malfoy, whose name could be French for "bad faith"). With names like that, how do they get through commencement without snickering?

Some of these characters are reprised just as reminders. The giant Hagrid (Robby Coltrane), for example, turns up primarily to allow us to observe, "Look who's turned up!" Snape, as played by Alan Rickman, is given much more dialogue, primarily I suspect because he invests it with such macabre pauses. Radcliffe's Potter is sturdy and boring, as always; it's not easy being the hero with a supporting cast like this. Michael Gambon steals the show as Dumbledore, who for a man his age certainly has some new tricks, so to speak, up his sleeve.

I admired this Harry Potter. It opens and closes well, and has wondrous art design and cinematography as always, only more so. "I'm just beginning to realize how beautiful this place is," Harry sighs from a high turret. The middle passages spin their wheels somewhat, hurrying about to establish events and places not absolutely essential. But those scenes may be especially valued by devoted students of the Potter saga. They may also be the only ones who fully understand them; ordinary viewers may be excused for feeling baffled some of the time.

The Haunting in Connecticut ★ ★
PG-13, 92 m., 2009

Virginia Madsen (Sara Campbell), Kyle Gallner (Matt Campbell), Martin Donovan (Peter Campbell), Amanda Crew (Wendy), Elias Koteas (Reverend Popescu). Directed by Peter Cornwell and produced by Paul Brooks, Daniel Farrands, Wendy Rhoads, and Andrew Trapani. Screenplay by Adam Simon and Tim Metcalfe.

The Haunting in Connecticut isn't based on just any old true story. No, it's based on *the* true story. That would be the case of the Snedeker family, who in the 1970s moved into a ghost-infested house in Southington, Connecticut, and had no end of distress. We know their story is true because it was vouched for by Ed and Lorraine Warren, the paranormal sleuths, who also backed up Bill Ramsey, a demonic werewolf who bit people, *The Amityville Horror,* and the story of Jack and Janet Smurl, who inspired the movie *The Haunted.*

Even so, I doubt it's "based on." More likely it was "loosely inspired by" a story. At the end of the movie, the Snedeker house is consumed by flames, and yet we're told before the credits that it was restored, rehabbed, and lived in happily ever after. So much for any hopes of a sequel. Of course, *Amityville* inspired a prequel, so I may not be safe. I don't believe a shred of this movie is true. Ray Garton, the author of *In a Dark Place,* a book including the case, observed that the Snedekers couldn't get their stories straight. When he reported this to the investigators, Wikipedia says, he was instructed to "make the story up" and "make it scary."

But what does that matter if all you're looking for is a ghost story? *The Haunting in Connecticut* is a technically proficient horror movie, well acted by good casting choices. We have here no stock characters, but Virginia Madsen and Martin Donovan in a troubled marriage, Kyle Gallner as their dying son, and Elias Koteas as a grim priest. They make the family, now known as the Campbells, about as real as they can be under the circumstances.

The movie has an alarming score and creepy photography, and a house that doesn't look like it has been occupied since the original inhabitants . . . died, let's say. So all the elements are there, and one of my fellow critics said he "screamed like a girl three times," although he is rather known for doing so. There are two scream-able elements: (1) surprises and (2) specters.

The surprises are those moments when a hand, a face, a body, a body part, or (usually) a cat leaps suddenly into the frame, and you jump in your seat and then say, "Aw, it was only a cat." Or a face, a body part, a vampire bat, etc. The specters involve some ghostly apparitions that may or may not be physical. There are so many of them that the movie, set in Connecticut but filmed in Canada, has credits for "ghost coordinators" in both Vancouver and Winnipeg. Having seen Guy Maddin's brilliant *My Winnipeg*, I believe the ghosts coordinate themselves there.

Matt, the Campbells' son, is dying of cancer and must be driven many miles for his radiation treatments. Madsen, playing his mother, makes an "executive decision" to buy a house in the distant town so Matt, with radiation burns and nausea, doesn't have to drive so far. She gets a really good deal. Let me ask you something. If you found a terrific price on a three-story Victorian mansion with sun-porches, lots of bedrooms, original woodwork, and extensive grounds in Connecticut, and it hadn't been lived in since events in the 1920s, how willing would *you* be to laugh off those events?

If the movie has a flaw, and it does, it's too many surprises. Every door, window, bedroom, hallway, staircase, basement area, attic, and crawl space is packed with surprises, so that it is a rare event in the house that takes place normally. The Campbells are constantly being surprised, so often they must be tuckered out at day's end from all of that running, jumping, and standing real still.

But I must not be too harsh, because surprises are what a movie like this trades in. I also thought Elias Koteas did a great job as the priest, who was not a ghostbuster in a Roman collar but a fellow radiation patient who never looked like he was confident good would win out in the end. (It is noteworthy that the Catholic Church does what it can to discourage exorcism, even though it could have done a lot of business in the boom times after *The Exorcist*.)

So. A preposterous story, so many scares they threaten to grow monotonous, good acting and filmmaking credits, and what else? Oh, what's with the ectoplasm? Didn't Houdini unmask that as a fraud? And the Amazing Randi? And what's it doing still being treated as real in *the* true story?

Hellboy II: The Golden Army ★ ★ ★ ½
PG-13, 120 m., 2008

Ron Perlman (Hellboy), Selma Blair (Liz Sherman), Doug Jones (Abe Sapien), Jeffrey Tambor (Tom Manning), Luke Gross (Prince Nuada), John Hurt (Trevor Bruttenholm), Seth McFarlane (Johann Kraus [voice]), Anna Walton (Princess Nuala). Directed by Guillermo del Toro and produced by Lawrence Gordon, Mike Richardson, and Lloyd Levin. Screenplay by del Toro, based on the comic book by Mike Mignola.

Imagine the forges of hell crossed with the extraterrestrial saloon on Tatooine and you have a notion of Guillermo del Toro's *Hellboy II: The Golden Army*. In every way the equal of his original *Hellboy* (2004), although perhaps a little noisier, it's another celebration of his love for bizarre fantasy and diabolical machines. The sequel bypasses the details of Hellboy's origin story but adds a legend read to him as a child by his adoptive father (John Hurt), in which we learn of an ancient warfare between humans and, well, everybody else: trolls, monsters, goblins, the Tooth Fairy, everybody.

There was a truce. The humans got the cities and the trolls got the forests. But humans have cheated on our end of the deal by building parking lots and shopping malls, and now Prince Nuada (Luke Gross) defies his father, the king, and hopes to start the conflict again. This would involve awakening the Golden Army: seventy times seventy slumbering mechanical warriors. Standing against this decision is his twin sister, Princess Nuala (Anna Walton).

And so on. I had best not get bogged down in plot description, except to add that Hellboy (Ron Perlman) and his sidekicks fight for the human side. His comrades include Abe Sapien (Doug Jones), sort of a fish-man, the fire-generating Liz Sherman (Selma Blair), a Teutonic adviser named Johann Kraus (Seth McFarlane), and of course Princess Nuala. Tom Manning (Jeffrey Tambor) from the secret center for extrasensory perception tags along but isn't much help except for adding irrelevancies and flippant asides.

Now that we have most of the characters onstage, let me describe the sights, which are almost all created by CGI of course, but how else? There's a climactic showdown between Hellboy and the prince, with the Golden Army standing dormant in what looks like the engine room of hell. Enormous interlocking gears grind against each other for no apparent purpose, except to chew up Hellboy or anything else that falls into them. Lucky they aren't perfectly calibrated.

There are also titanic battles in the streets of Manhattan, involving gigantic octo-creatures and so on, but you know what? Although they're well done, titanic battles in the streets of Manhattan are becoming commonplace in the movies these days. What was fascinating to me was what the octo-creature transformed itself into, which was unexpected and really lovely. You'll see.

The towering creatures fascinated me less, however, than some smaller ones. For example, swarms of tens of thousands of calcium-eaters, who devour humans both skin and bone and are the source of the Tooth Fairy legend. They pour out of the walls of an auction house and attack the heroes, and in my personal opinion Hellboy is wasting his time trying to shoot them one at a time.

I also admired the creativity that went into the Troll Market (it has a secret entry under the Brooklyn Bridge). Here I think del Toro actually was inspired by the Tatooine saloon in *Star Wars*, and brings together creatures of fantastical shapes and sizes, buying and selling goods of comparable shapes and sizes. It would be worth having the DVD just to study the market a frame at a time, discovering what secrets he may have hidden in there. The movies only rarely give us a genuinely new kind of place to look at; this will become a classic.

There are, come to think of it, other whispers of the *Star Wars* influence in *Hellboy II*. Princess Nuala doesn't have Princess Leia's rope of hair (just ordinary long blond tresses), but she's not a million miles distant from her. And Abe Sapien looks, moves, and sort of sounds so much like C3PO that you'd swear the robot became flesh and developed gills. I also noticed hints of John Williams's *Star Wars* score in the

score by Danny Elfman, especially during the final battle. Not a plundering job, you understand, more of an evocation of mood.

What else? Two love stories, which I'll leave for you to find out about. And the duet performance of a song that is rather unexpected, to say the least. And once again a strong performance by Ron Perlman as Hellboy. Yes, he's CGI for the most part, but his face and voice and movements inhabit the screen figure, and make him one of the great comic heroes. Del Toro, who preceded *Hellboy II* with *Pan's Labyrinth* (2006) and the underrated *Blade II* (2002) is warming up now for *Doctor Strange* and *The Hobbit*. He has an endlessly inventive imagination and understands how legends work, why they entertain us, and that they sometimes stand for something. For love, for example.

Hell Ride ★

R, 83 m., 2008

Larry Bishop (Pistolero), Michael Madsen (The Gent), Eric Balfour (Comanche), Vinnie Jones (Billy Wings), Dennis Hopper (Eddie Zero). Directed by Larry Bishop and produced by Michael Steinberg, Larry Bishop, and Shana Stein. Screenplay by Bishop.

I read an article the other day saying the average age of motorcyclists is going up. Judging by *Hell Ride*, the average age of motorcycle gang members is approaching the Medicare generation, not that many will survive to collect the benefits. Some of the "plot" involves revenge for the torching of the girlfriend of the gang president. That took place in the bicentennial year of 1976, which was, let's see, thirty-two years ago. By the time they kill the guy who did it, he's a geezer with so many chin whiskers they can barely cut his throat.

The movie was written and directed by Larry Bishop, who also stars as Pistolero, president of an outlaw club named the Victors. Bishop starred in a motorcycle movie named *The Savage Seven* in 1968, which was, let's see, forty years ago. He was also in *The Devil's 8, Angels Unchained*, and *Chrome and Hot Leather*. It's a wonder he doesn't have a handicapped placard for his hog.

In between searching for a killer, he leads a gang whose members are sort of hard to tell apart, except for The Gent (Michael Madsen), so called because instead of leathers he wears a ruffled formal shirt under a tux jacket with his gang colors stitched on the back. Why does he do that? The answer to that question would require character development, and none of the cast members develop at all. They spring into being fully created and never change, like Greek gods.

There are cameo roles for two icons of biker movies, Dennis Hopper and David Carradine, who play old-timers—that is, contemporaries of the other gang members. Madsen, at fifty, may be the youngest cast member, and also brings along expertise in doing The Walk. That would be the scene made famous from *Reservoir Dogs* and a zillion other movies where three or four tough guys lope along in unison away from something that is about to blow up and don't flinch when it does.

Wait a minute. Maybe the guy who gets blown up was the killer and not the grizzled old-timer. I dunno. The enemy gang of the Victors are the 666ers, but I couldn't tell them apart except for the close-ups of the colors on their backs, which had the disadvantage of not showing their faces. There is a character named Deuce, but I don't know why. Or maybe he is a gang.

The movie was executive-produced by Quentin Tarantino. Shame on him. He intends it no doubt as another homage to grindhouse pictures, but I've seen a lot of them, and they were nowhere near this bad. *Hell's Angels on Wheels*, for example: pretty good.

All these guys do is shoot one another and roll around in bars with naked girls with silicone breasts—who don't seem to object to the bikers' smelly grime. The girls look about twenty-five, tops, but the only reference to age in the movie is when a biker names his bike after the horse Trigger, and is asked, "How old is Trigger in horse-bike years?" Quick—whose horse was Trigger? Can anyone under twenty-five answer? OK, then: Silver? Champion? Topper?

Henry Poole Is Here ★ ★ ★ ½
PG, 101 m., 2008

Luke Wilson (Henry Poole), Radha Mitchell (Dawn), Adriana Barraza (Esperanza), George Lopez (Father Salazar), Cheryl Hines (Meg), Richard Benjamin (Dr. Fancher), Morgan Lily (Millie), Rachel Seiferth (Patience), Beth Grant (Josie). Directed by Mark Pellington and produced by Tom Rosenberg, Gary Lucchesi, Richard Wright, Gary Gilbert, and Tom Lassally. Screenplay by Albert Torres.

Henry Poole Is Here achieves something that is uncommonly difficult. It is a spiritual movie with the power to emotionally touch believers, agnostics, and atheists—in that descending order, I suspect. It doesn't say that religious beliefs are real. It simply says that belief is real. And it's a warmhearted love story.

It centers on a man named Henry Poole (Luke Wilson), who has only one problem when he moves into a house. He is dying. Then he acquires another problem. His neighbor Esperanza (Adriana Barraza) sees the face of Jesus Christ in a stain on his stucco wall. Henry Poole doesn't see the face, and indeed neither do we most of the time, even if we squint. It's a hit-or-miss sort of thing.

Wilson plays Henry as hostile and depressed. Well, he has much to be depressed about. "We hardly ever see this disease in the States," the doctor tells him. "It steamrolls through your system." Patience (Rachel Seiferth), the nearly blind checkout girl at the supermarket, gives him dietary hints when she notices he buys mostly vodka and frozen pizza. Although her glasses are half an inch thick, she's observant: "Why are you sad and angry all the time?"

Henry starts hearing voices in his backyard. There is a rational reason for this. He is being secretly recorded by Millie (Morgan Lily), the five-year-old who lives next door on the other side from Esperanza. Millie's mother is the lovely Dawn (Radha Mitchell), who apologizes for her daughter, brings cookies, and also notices how sad and angry Henry is. He is especially angry with Esperanza, warning her to stay out of his yard and stop praying to his bad stucco job. But she has seen Jesus and cannot be stopped. She brings in Father Salazar (George Lopez), who explains that the church does not easily declare miracles but keeps an open mind.

There are more details, which I must not reveal, including certain properties of the wall. I will observe that the director, Mark Pellington, uses some of the most subtle special effects you've probably seen for some time to fine-tune the illusion that the face of Christ is really there, or really not there. I will now think of this movie every time I drive through the Fullerton Avenue underpass of the Kennedy Expressway in Chicago, where since April 2005 people have said they can see the Virgin Mary in a wall stain. There are always flowers there.

The thing is, certain miraculous events take place, and the people involved believe it is because they touched Henry's wall. Patience the checkout girl even quotes the formidable intellectual Noam Chomsky, who, she informs Henry, said some things cannot be explained by science. One critic of this film believes it is antiscience and pounds you over the head to believe. Not at all. It is simply that Chomsky is right, as any scientist will tell you. What do I believe? I believe science can eventually explain everything, but only if it gets a whole lot better than it is now and discovers realms we do not even suspect. You could call such a realm God. You could, of course, call it anything you wanted; it wouldn't matter to the realm.

Another critic, or maybe it is the same critic, believes the movie is a Hollywood ploy to reach the Christian market. Not at all. Esperanza sees Jesus because the face of Jesus is ready in her mind, supplied by holy cards and paintings. You might see the face of Uncle Sam. No one knows what Jesus looked like. It is also strange that the Virgin's appearances always mirror her holy card image. People from biblical lands at that time would have been a good deal darker and shorter. The movie gets that right: The image is so low on the wall that Jesus must have stood less than five feet tall.

But I stray, and I do injustice to this film. I fell for it. I believed the feelings between Henry and Dawn. I cared about their tenderness and loneliness. I thought Millie was adorable. I thought Father Salazar had his head on straight. I loved Esperanza's great big heart. And I especially admired the way that Henry stuck to his guns. He doesn't believe there's a face on his stucco, and that's that. And no, he doesn't undergo a deathbed conversion. That's because . . . but find out for yourself.

He's Just Not That Into You ★ ★
PG-13, 129 m., 2009

Ben Affleck (Neil), Jennifer Aniston (Beth), Drew Barrymore (Mary), Jennifer Connelly (Janine), Kevin Connolly (Conor), Bradley Cooper (Ben), Ginnifer Goodwin (Gigi), Scarlett Johansson (Anna), Justin Long (Alex). Directed by Ken Kwapis and produced by Nancy Juvonen. Screenplay by Abby Kohn and Marc Silverstein, based on the book by Greg Behrendt and Liz Tuccillo.

Ever noticed how many self-help books are limited to the insight expressed in their titles? You look at the cover, you know everything inside. The rest is just writing. I asked Amazon to "surprise me" with a page from inside the best-seller He's Just Not That Into You, and it jumped me to page 17, where I read: "My belief is that if you have to be the aggressor, if you have to pursue, if you have to do the asking out, nine times out of 10, he's just not that into you."

I personally would not be interested in a woman who needed to buy a book to find that out. Guys also figure out that when she never returns your calls and is inexplicably always busy, she's just not that into you. What is this, brain surgery? I have tried, but I cannot imagine what was covered in the previous sixteen pages of that book. I am reminded of the book review once written by Ambrose Bierce: "The covers of this book are too far apart."

The movie version of He's Just Not That Into You dramatizes this insight with comic vignettes played by actors who are really too good for this romcom. Jennifer Aniston in particular has a screen presence that makes me wonder why she rarely takes on the kinds of difficult roles her costars Jennifer Connelly, Scarlett Johansson, and Drew Barrymore have played. There are depths there. I know it.

The movie takes place in modern-day Baltimore, where those four, and Ginnifer Goodwin, play women who should ask themselves: Is he really that into me? Aniston, for example, plays Beth, who has been living for years with Neil (Ben Affleck), who is perfect in every respect except that he is disinclined to marry her. "We're happy just the way we are," he argues. The old "if it's not broke, don't fix it" routine.

239

But if a woman knows her loved one won't ever want to marry her, it's her heart that's broke, and there is only one way to fix it. There are even evolutionary theories to explain this.

Gigi (Goodwin), on the other hand, doesn't have a perfect boyfriend, or any at all, and sits by her phone like a penguin waiting for the damn egg to hatch. Why hasn't that dreamy guy who asked for her number called back? Maybe, just maybe, it's because he doesn't want to. I haven't read the book, but I know that much. There was once a girl I didn't call, and she mailed me a book titled *The Dance-Away Lover.* How did I instinctively know the book was about me? Why did I know everything in it without having to read it? Because the book was intended for her, that's why.

Janine (Connelly) is married to Ben (Bradley Cooper), who doesn't share her ideas about home decoration, which are that you always make the more expensive choice. Not a lot of guys are into that. If you get one who is, he may make it a general policy and decide to trade you in for an advanced model. Look for a guy who treats you not as an acquisition but as an angel of mercy, the answer to the prayers of the rat he knows he is.

Mary (Barrymore) is surrounded by great guys, but they're all gay. They're from that subspecies of gay men who learned everything they know about life from Bette Davis. This is true even if they've never seen one of her movies. Then there's Anna (Johansson), who is courted fervently by Conor (Kevin Connolly), who would marry her in a second, except she's "committed" to a married man, who is committed to not marrying her, which is maybe what she likes about him, along with getting the right to constantly be the wronged one in a relationship she, after all, freely walked into.

The problem with most of the movie's women is that they are only interested in (a) the opposite sex, (b) dating, and (c) marriage. Maybe that's because the screenplay only has so much time. But a movie about one insecure woman talking to another can be monotonous, unless you're a masochist looking to share your pain. If you consider a partner who has no more compelling interests than a, b, or c, you're shopping for boredom.

There is one superb monologue in the movie, by Drew Barrymore, who complains that she is driven crazy by the way guys always seem to be communicating in another medium. She calls at home but he doesn't pick up. She calls on his cell, and he e-mails her. She texts him. He Twitters back and leaves coded hints on MySpace. She tries snail mail. He apparently never learned how to open one. She yearns for the days when people had one telephone and one answering machine, and a guy had either definitely called you, or he had not.

This is a very far from perfect movie, and it ends on an unsatisfactory note. Stop reading *now* because I am going to complain that most of the stories have happy endings. Not in the real world, they don't. In the real world, the happy endings come only with a guy who's really into you. I should write a self-help book: *If Some Guy Says He Loves You, Check It Out.*

Holy Rollers ★★
R, 80 m., 2010

Jesse Eisenberg (Sam Gold), Justin Bartha (Yosef), Ari Graynor (Rachel), Danny A. Abeckaser (Jackie), Q-Tip (Ephraim), Mark Ivanir (Mendel Gold), Elizabeth Marvel (Elka Gold). Directed by Kevin Asch and produced by Danny A. Abeckaser, Jen Gatien, Per Melita, and Tory Tunnell. Screenplay by Antonio Macia.

One function of any traditional religious costume is to enforce the wearer's separation from the greater community. Those male Hasidic Jews who choose to dress in black and wear distinctive hats never seem to be anything else than Hasidic Jews. When they dress in the morning, they're making a decision to set themselves apart. This is not required in Jewish law, but is a sign of their devotion.

Apart from the hats, the side curls, and their religious beliefs, Hasidim are, well, a lot like everybody else. Sam Gold (Jesse Eisenberg) is a kid about twenty who is devout, naive, shy around women, loves his mom, respects his dad, and plans to go into the family business. Then his best friend's brother takes advantage of those qualities—and very specifically his dress style—to trick him into being a drug courier.

Holy Rollers is said to be based on a true story, circa 1990, of how Hasidic Jews from Brooklyn Heights were used to smuggle millions of Ecstasy pills from Amsterdam to New York. They weren't stopped by customs because they were so far from the profile of drug runners. In the movie, Sam is frustrated in his plans to build his father's business and accepts $1,000 from the brother to fly to Amsterdam and return with some "medicine."

Come on, you're thinking: How innocent can this kid possibly be? You should see him tongue-tied, sitting at the other end of a sofa from the girl he hopes to marry. Or even in Amsterdam, trying to avoid any body contact with women in a disco. Yes, the first trip he really does think the pills are medicine, and doesn't ask himself how what he's doing could possibly be legal.

He's a sweet kid as played by Eisenberg, who specializes in that line of work. The brother, Yosef (Justin Bartha), is persuasive, smooth, and hard to refuse. In Amsterdam, Sam meets a man named Jackie (Danny A. Abeckaser) and his girlfriend, Rachel (Ari Graynor), and is brought into their world of late-night clubs and loose living. On his second trip, things click into place, and he begins to put his good business sense to work.

It's that click that throws the movie off. Sam is moral and law-abiding, then changes seemingly overnight into a canny player in the drug trade. Before long he's instructing new Hasidim recruits on how to get past customs: "Act normal and look Jewish." It becomes apparent to his father and indeed his community what he's up to, but he's making good money and it seems so easy. For a long time he never even experiences Ecstasy.

The story may sound sensational, and you're possibly picturing traditional crime scenes: shoot-outs, chases, that sort of thing. But *Holy Rollers* is surprisingly matter-of-fact. Nobody gets shot, nobody gets chased, and Sam's anguish is internal.

The film's failure is to get from A to B. We buy both good Sam and bad Sam, but we don't see him making the transition. The film expects us to assume too much. Eisenberg is convincing as an essentially nice person who sounds confident but turns into a kid again when things start going wrong. But Kevin Asch, the director, keeps his distance from too many scenes; there's no particular suspense involved in getting past customs, for example.

The movie relates to its story as Sam relates to women: look, talk, but don't get too close.

Home ★★★ ½
NO MPAA RATING, 98 m., 2010

Isabelle Huppert (Marthe), Olivier Gourmet (Michel), Adelaide Leroux (Judith), Madeleine Budd (Marion), Kacey Mottet Klein (Julien). Directed by Ursula Meier and produced by Denis Delcammpe, Denis Freyd, Thierry Spicher, and Elena Tatti. Screenplay by Meier, Antoine Jaccoud, Raphaelle Valbrune, Gilles Taurand, and Olivier Lorelle.

There are two questions never answered in *Home*. How did this family come to live here? And why does the mother fiercely refuse to leave, even after a four-lane freeway opens in her front yard? Both are more satisfactory remaining as questions. In any event, as the film opens, they live in a comfortable small home in the middle of vast fields and next to the highway, which hasn't been used for ten years. So much is the road their turf that the story begins with them playing a family game of street hockey on its pavement.

Then big trucks arrive to lay down a fresh coating of asphalt, and steel guardrails are installed on each side and down the middle. Workmen wordlessly clear the highway of their hockey sticks, inflatable swimming pool, satellite dish, charcoal grill, and so on. On the radio, they hear breathless coverage of the road's grand opening, and eventually the first car speeds past their house.

The family seems ordinary enough, if not quite conventional. The parents snuggle, the small boy plays, the sister in her early twenties sunbathes and smokes in the front yard, the teenage daughter wears mostly black and sulks. Michel, the father (Olivier Gourmet), goes off to work every morning in the green Volvo station wagon. Marthe, the mother (Isabelle Huppert), does the laundry ("today is whites day"). There's horseplay in the bathtub, which the family seems to share rather freely.

The opening of the highway wasn't a surprise for them. Maybe they got the house cheap because it was coming. The heavy, unceasing traffic is a big problem. The two younger kids always ran across the bare pavement to cut through a field for school. Dad parked on the other side. Now even getting to the house is a problem. Marion, the smart younger sister (Madeleine Budd) is concerned about CO_2 poisoning. Young Julien (Kacey Mottet Klein) can't safely get to his pals. Judith (Adelaide Leroux) continues to sunbathe in the front yard and gives the finger to honking truck drivers.

Something will have to give, and it does, as the movie grows more and more dark. It's the skill of Ursula Meier, the director and cowriter, to bring us to those fraught passages by rational stages. What happens would not make sense in many households, but in this one it represents a certain continuity, and confirms deep currents we sensed almost from the first.

Do you remember Olivier Gourmet from his performance in the Dardenne brothers' movie *The Son* (2003)? Balding, middle-aged, nimble, and quick. Many secrets. Troubled. Isabelle Huppert you know since forever, usually looking fundamentally the same, always assuming a new character from the inside out. Intriguing us. There's thought in that face, but it's inscrutable. They work with the young actors here to face what it means when a home is not a house.

Honeydripper ★ ★ ★ ½
PG-13, 123 m., 2008

Danny Glover (Tyrone Purvis), Lisa Gay Hamilton (Delilah Purvis), Yaya DaCosta (China Doll), Charles S. Dutton (Maceo Green), Gary Clark Jr. (Sonny Blake), Mable John (Bertha Mae Spivey), Vondie Curtis Hall (Slick), Stacy Keach (Sheriff Pugh). Directed by John Sayles and produced by Maggie Renzi. Screenplay by Sayles.

John Sayles's *Honeydripper* is set at the intersection of two movements that would change American life forever: the civil rights movement, and rhythm and blues. They may have more to do with each other than you might think, although that isn't his point. He's more concerned with spinning a ground-level human comedy than searching for pie in the sky. His movie is rich with characters and flowing with music.

The time, around 1950. The place, Harmony, Alabama. The chief location, the Honeydripper Lounge, which serves a good drink but is feeling the competition from a juke joint down the road. The proprietor, Pine Top Purvis (Danny Glover), is desperately in debt. The wife, Delilah (Lisa Gay Hamilton), is causing him some concern: Will she get religion and disapprove of his business? The best friend, Maceo (Charles S. Dutton), is a sounding board for his problems. The nightmare, the local sheriff (Stacy Keach), is a racist, but doesn't go overboard like most. Club characters: blues singer (Mable John) and her man (Vondie Curtis Hall).

Into Harmony one day comes a footloose young man named Sonny, played by Gary Clark Jr., in real life a rising guitar phenom. He drifts into the Honeydripper looking for a job or a meal and carrying something no one has ever seen before: a homemade electric guitar carved out of a solid block of wood. Pine Top has no work for him, and the youth is soon arrested by the sheriff (his crime: existing while unemployed) and put to work picking cotton for a crony.

Meanwhile, in desperation, Pine Top books the great Guitar Sam out of New Orleans and puts up posters all over town. Sure, he can't afford him, but the plan is, Guitar Sam will bring in enough business on one Saturday night to pay his own salary and also the lounge's worst bills. Pine Top finds out what real desperation is when Guitar Sam doesn't arrive on the train. He wonders if the kid with the funny guitar can play a little. After all, no one in Harmony knows what Guitar Sam really looks like.

Now all the pieces are in place for an unwinding of local race issues, personal issues, financial issues, and some very, very good music, poised just at that point when the blues were turning into rhythm and blues, which after all is what rock and roll is only an alias for. Because after all, yes, the kid can play a little. More than a little.

John Sayles has made nineteen films, and none of them is a two-character study. As the writer of his own work, he instinctively embraces the communities in which they take place. He's never met a man who was an island. Everyone connects, and when that includes black and white, rich and poor, young and old, there are lessons to be learned, and his generosity to his characters overflows into affection.

Danny Glover is well cast to stand at the center of this story. A tall, imposing, grave presence as Pine Top, he is not so much a music lover as a survivor. This is his last chance to save the Honeydripper and his means of making a living. And Gary Clark Jr. is the right man to be told: Tonight, you are Guitar Sam. He may be a prodigy, but he is broke, scared, young, and far from home. So this isn't one of those showbiz stories where a talent scout is in the audience, but a story where the audience looks at him with great suspicion until his music makes them smile.

As for the sheriff's role: As I suggested, lots of Alabama sheriffs were more racist than he is, which is not a character recommendation, but means that he isn't evil just to pass the time and would rather avoid trouble than work up a sweat. At that time, in that place, he was about the best you could hope for. Within a few more years, the Bull Connors would be run out of town, one man would have one vote, and the music of the African-American South would rule the world. That all had to start somewhere. It didn't start on Saturday night at the Honeydripper, but it didn't stop there, either.

The Horse Boy ★★★
NO MPAA RATING, 94 m., 2009

Featuring Rupert Isaacson, Kristin Neff, Rowan Isaacson, Simon Baron-Cohen, Temple Grandin, Roy Richard Grinker, Tulga, and Ghoste. A documentary directed by Michel O. Scott.

The Horse Boy tells a remarkable story. A four-year-old Texas boy with autism has angry seizures, isn't potty-trained, is often distant and hostile. His parents fly with him to Mongolia, drive nine hours into the steppes, and then journey by horseback, with the boy sharing their saddles, to a sacred mountain in reindeer country. There he undergoes a miraculous cure at the hands of shamans.

I have many inclinations, but no reason, to doubt this. At the end of the treatment, the shamans tell the parents that on the next day their boy will stop soiling his pants and throwing tantrums. This happens. Today, back home, little Rowan is now six and for the first time plays with friends his own age.

"Is he cured? No," says Rupert Isaacson, his father. "Is he still autistic? Yes." What happened "seems miraculous," but he is skeptical enough to wonder if the trip itself was part of the cure. Rowan has a strong empathy with animals, especially with horses, but also, we see, with goats—who are docile and affectionate with him. Perhaps the enormity of a long horseback journey with his parents in clearly daunting conditions overwhelmed his defenses and calmed him.

There seems no reason to question that he has improved. In the footage taken after the healing, we never see Rowan except when he is happily playing with his new friends or smiling with his parents. Is that the whole story? You decide. To their credit, Isaacson and his wife, Kristin Neff, a University of Texas psychology professor, do not recommend that parents of other autistic children take them to the wilds of Siberia. All they know is what happened to Rowan.

With any documentary, there is another story that goes unreported: the story of the making of the film. *The Horse Boy* didn't make itself. The parents and their son were accompanied to Siberia by the director/cinematographer Michel Orion Scott, apparently a second cameraman, and sound technicians and a support staff. This cost money, up-front on the bottom line. Airfares, food, lodging, not least insurance for everyone and a completion bond for the film itself.

You may know that the book of the experience, *The Horse Boy*, became a best-seller. The trip and the film were financed by a million-dollar advance on the book Isaacson proposed to write about this experience. He's the author of a successful previous book, *The Healing Land: The Bushmen and the Kalahari Desert*, which includes shamans on another continent. He had heard that the shamans of Mongolia, especially one legendary shaman, had unusual powers.

The stakes are high in such a venture. What if the trip turns into a fool's errand? What if Rowan becomes worse, not better? It was obviously crucial that Rowan undergo some kind of dramatic improvement or there would be no film. It's well to keep that in mind.

The whole enterprise seems to be Isaacson's project. He narrates the film. The wife, Kristin, seems fully in accord with him, and they're both courageous, but I would have liked more insights from the side of her that teaches psychology. I imagine many parents of autistic children, while identifying with the strains autism places upon their marriage, would appreciate more information about his exact state at present.

The film includes expert testimony from autism experts, including the famous Temple Grandin, an autistic professor at Colorado State, who has designed most of the environments used to handle cattle in the worldwide meatpacking industry. Her genius was to be able to identify with the point of view of the cattle.

I've met her. A remarkable woman. She talks in the film about autism in general. The newspaperman in me would have asked her: "Do you feel autistics feel a special empathy and calm with animals? Could the horseback journey itself have brought about some of the improvement?"

Hotel for Dogs ★ ★ ½
PG, 100 m., 2009

Emma Roberts (Andi), Jake T. Austin (Bruce), Kyla Pratt (Heather), Lisa Kudrow (Lois), Kevin Dillon (Carl), Don Cheadle (Bernie), Johnny Simmons (Dave), Troy Gentile (Mark). Directed by Thor Freudenthal and produced by Lauren Shuler Donner, Jonathan Gordon, Ewan Leslie, and Jason Clark. Screenplay by Leslie, Jeff Lowell, Bob Schooley, and Mark McCorkle, based on the book by Lois Duncan.

Hotel for Dogs is a sweet, innocent family movie about stray dogs that seem as well-trained as Olympic champions. Friday, the Jack Russell terrier who's the leader of the pack, does more acting than most of the humans and doesn't even get billing. I know, because I searched for one, hoping to mention him by name and call him a good doggie.

What can Friday do? Let himself up and down from a fire escape landing, using a pulley-and-counterweight system. Find his masters anywhere in the city. Steal hot dogs and possibly a whole gyros wheel. Get out of his collar and back in again. Outrace dogs five times his size in a sprint down city streets. And

join dozens of other dogs in mastering these abilities: feeding himself, using a doggie fire hydrant, sitting on a toilet, running on a treadmill, activating a bone-throwing mechanism. I'm only scratching the surface.

Friday belongs to Andi (Emma Roberts) and Bruce (Jake T. Austin), a brother and sister in foster care. He is kept a secret from their foster parents, two obnoxious would-be rock musicians (Lisa Kudrow and Kevin Dillon). The kids saved him from the streets, and he has been their secret pal through three years and five foster homes. One day he leads them into an abandoned downtown hotel occupied by two dogs he makes friends with, and soon the kids find themselves running an unofficial animal shelter.

In this they're assisted by Dave (Johnny Simmons) and Heather (Kyla Pratt), two Nickelodeon-cute employees at a pet shop, which they can apparently abandon on a moment's notice to use the store's van on rescue missions. Since they can't possibly care for all those dogs, little Bruce rigs up Rube Goldberg devices to automate the tasks. There's even an automatic door knocker to send the dogs into frenzies of barking and jumping. Good exercise, although sooner or later these dogs will get wise to it.

Don Cheadle plays the dedicated social worker in charge of the kids, who bails them out when they get in trouble with cops and meany attendants at the animal pound. He even has a big speech on the Dog Hotel steps, during which I did my best not to think of *Hotel Rwanda*. What I thought instead was, Marley could learn a lot from these dogs.

Hot Tub Time Machine ★★★
R, 100 m., 2010

John Cusack (Adam), Rob Corddry (Lou), Craig Robinson (Nick), Clark Duke (Jacob), Crispin Glover (Phil), Lizzy Caplan (April), Chevy Chase (Repairman). Directed by Steve Pink and produced by John Cusack, Grace Loh, Matt Moore, and John Morris. Screenplay by Morris, Josh Heald, and Sean Anders.

Hot Tub Time Machine may sound almost by definition like a bad comedy. I mean, how good can a movie named *Hot Tub Time*

Machine possibly be? Yes? That's not what I thought. I saw the stand-up display in a movie lobby and perked up. With a title like that, the filmmakers aren't lacking in confidence. There was also the item of John Cusack in the lead. As a general rule, he isn't found in bad films.

I wasn't disappointed. This is a step or two below *The Hangover,* but occupying similar turf. It's another guy picture, which is like a buddy picture except usually without cops. The guys bond, they seek to relive their misspent youth, there are women and even wives around but they're strictly in supporting roles.

A forty-something party animal named Lou (Rob Corddry) gets drunk and passes out after he unwisely guns his car engine in time to the music while parked in his garage and listening to Mötley Crüe. This is interpreted as a suicide attempt by his best friends Adam (John Cusack) and Nick (Craig Robinson), and although he tells him they're mistaken, they're not so sure. They're worried about their friend. He's a full-bore, full-time alcoholic without a shred of maturity or caution. What this boy obviously requires is a return to the ski lodge where they all got blasted together in the 1980s. Over Lou's protests, they drag along Jacob (Clark Duke), Adam's nephew. Adam wants to keep him out of trouble (hollow laugh).

Today, this lodge is so shabby it looks not only like a poor excuse for a ski resort but even like a poor excuse for a movie set. That's part of the movie's charm. Did the Marx Brothers ever lavish money on sets? (Well, yes, but never mind.) The check-in routine is from Motel Hell, and the surly one-armed bellboy (Crispin Glover) kicks their luggage around, dumps it on the floor, and sticks out his remaining hand for a tip.

They get the same big room they had before. It's gone downhill. The hot tub seems to harbor growth from the Planet of Mold. But there's a cheerful repairman (Chevy Chase), who plays the role that George Burns used to play when you needed a guy who just looked like he knew the secrets of the universe. Chevy fixes the tub and it starts to bubble with an inner glow, like beer on the simmer. The guys jump in and are magically transported back in

time to their youth in the 1980s. Jacob hadn't been born then, but never mind; it's their present selves who are transported.

This then becomes the premise for a comedy contriving more or less every possible problem and paradox, of which the high point is possibly Nick's boozy phone call to his wife, who at the time is still in grade school. A pretty girl named April (Lizzy Caplan) catches Adam's eye, although strict logic suggests they have little future together. And Corddry essentially steals the movie as Lou.

Remember how Corddry was always so earnest and sincere when assuring Jon Stewart of outrageous facts on *The Daily Show*? He brings the same focus to getting drunk. Comedy is a delicate art, with nothing so important as the performer never seeming to believe anything he does is funny. Corddry here achieves a level of comic confidence that seems almost uncanny; Cusack, as coproducer, and Steve Pink, the director (who wrote Cusack's *High Fidelity* and *Grosse Point Blank*), must have intuited this gift and been willing to give him free rein.

I can't be sure, but I think the density of the f-word reaches the saturation point in *Hot Tub Time Machine.* I may have heard it employed as three different parts of speech in the same sentence. One wonders if American spoken English could survive without it. What did we say in the old days? It must have been a quiet land.

The bottom line is, gross-out guy comedies open twice a month, and many of them are wretched excesses. *Hot Tub Time Machine,* which wants nothing more than to be a screwball farce, succeeds beyond any expectations suggested by the title, and extends John Cusack's remarkable run: Since 1983, in fifty-five films, he's never made a bad one. Well, I never saw *Grandview, USA.* ☞

Hounddog ★ ★
R, 93 m., 2007

Dakota Fanning (Lewellen), Cody Hanford (Buddy), Robin Wright Penn (Stranger Lady), David Morse (Daddy), Piper Laurie (Grammie), Afemo Omilami (Charles), Jill Scott (Big Mama Thornton). Directed by Deborah Kampmeier and produced by Kampmeier, Scott Franklin,

Raye Dowell, Terry Leonard, Roberta Hanley, Jen Gatien, and Lawrence Robins. Screenplay by Kampmeier.

Dakota Fanning takes an impressive step forward in her career, but that's about the only good thing about *Hounddog*. The reigning child star, now fourteen, handles a painful and complex role with such assurance that she reminds me of Jodie Foster in *Taxi Driver*. But her character is surrounded by a swamp of worn-out backwoods Southern clichés that can't be rescued even by the other accomplished actors in the cast.

She plays Lewellen, a barefoot tomboy who lives in a shack with her father (David Morse), a slovenly drunk and self-pitying whiner. Next door is Grammie (Piper Laurie), who keeps house well but is a hard-drinking slattern. Lewellen prowls the woods and frequents the swimming hole with her best friend, Buddy (Cody Hanford), as they trade awkward kisses and examine each other's private parts with great curiosity.

The poverty of her family is indicated by the usual marker: rusting trucks in the lawn. Her father operates a tractor, which during a rainstorm is struck by lightning. This hurls him to the ground and makes him even more dramatically loony. He is seized by anxiety that his daughter will abandon him, and one night he walks into the local tavern seeking her, having failed to notice that he is stark naked. The pool players prod him with their cues. Lewellen stalks in and drags him home.

Somehow amid this chaos the young girl succeeds in being playful and high-spirited, until she is raped by an older teenager. She grows silent and morose, even comatose, and one night is visited by dozens of (imaginary?) snakes, who crawl in through her bedroom window and perform a function, whether demonic or healing, that is understood by her friend and protector Charles (Afemo Omilami), a black man who works in the stables of the local gentry. He brings her back to health and lectures her about making people treat her with respect.

Moving around the edges of the story is a character known in the credits as Stranger Lady (Robin Wright Penn). Her identity and function are left unclear, except for the fact that it will be immediately obvious to any sentient viewer exactly who she is. It has been some time since I quoted from Ebert's Little Movie Glossary, but the Stranger Lady perfectly fits the Law of Economy of Characters, which teaches us that whenever an important star appears in a seemingly unexplained role, that character will represent the solution to a plot question.

Now about *Hounddog*. Lewellen is a passionate fan of Elvis and has some small local fame for her Elvis impersonations. Her life may be transformed when she hears Charles and his friends, including Jill Scott as Big Mama Thornton, performing in the rhythm and blues tradition that inspired Elvis. Lewellen is obsessed with the news that Elvis will be performing in a local concert and is cruelly tricked when she thinks she can get a ticket. One moonlit night, Elvis himself drives past in a pink Cadillac and blows her a kiss. Yes. Elvis would have driven himself to the concert, alone, down back roads, of course.

Hounddog is assembled from the debris of countless worn-out images of the Deep South, and is indeed beautifully photographed. But the writer-director, Deborah Kampmeier, has become inflamed by the imagery and trusts it as the material for a story, which seems grotesque and lurid. David Morse's Daddy, well-played as the character may be, is a particularly dreary presence, pitiful instead of sympathetic. Having seen so many of these fine actors in other roles, my heart goes out for them. Still, the discovery here is the remarkable Dakota Fanning, opening the next stage in her career and doing it bravely, with presence, confidence, and high spirits.

The House of the Devil ★★★
R, 93 m., 2009

Jocelin Donahue (Sam), Greta Gerwig (Megan), Mary Woronov (Mrs. Ulman), Tom Noonan (Mr. Ulman), A. J. Bowen (Victor), Danielle Noe (Mother), Dee Wallace (Landlady). Directed by Ti West and produced by Josh Braun, Larry Fessenden, Roger Kass, and Peter Phok. Screenplay by West.

Has there ever been a movie where a teenage babysitter enjoyed a pleasant evening? And a nondemonic child? Sam gets a break in *The House of the Devil.* She discovers there isn't a baby at all. Only the aged mother of Mr. Ulman, a sinister man played by Tom Noonan, who is my choice to portray The Judge in Cormac McCarthy's *Blood Meridian,* and if you have read that gruesome masterpiece, there is nothing more I need say about Mr. Ulman.

Sam (Jocelin Donahue) is a perky college student saving money for a deposit on her own apartment. She puts up signs around the campus offering her babysitting services, and Mr. Ulman takes one of them. In fact, he takes all of them.

Sam's friend Megan (Greta Gerwig) gives her a lift to the Ulman household, which they find way, way down at the end of a long, long road in the middle of a dark, dark forest. It looks like the House of the Seven Gables with three gables amputated. Mr. Ulman and his wife, Mrs. Ulman (Mary Woronov), greet Sam with hospitality laced with . . . commiseration. The house is furnished in a way to remind you of aged maiden aunts who haven't changed a thing since their parents died.

Mother Ulman is upstairs in her room, Mr. Ulman explains. He only told Sam there was a baby because some babysitters balk at the difficulties of old folks. But not to worry. Mr. Ulman more or less promises she'll be no more problem than Norman Bates's mom. Then the Ulmans depart because they want to observe the full eclipse of the moon and you can't even see the moon so deep in the dark, dark forest, you see.

Left alone on her own (Mother's upstairs in her room and doesn't make a sound), Sam pokes around. It's sort of creepy. Good thing she only snaps on the TV briefly; if *The Addams Family* came on, it might look familiar. And it might come on: This is the mid-1980s, when babysitters had more to fear from their employers than vice versa.

The House of the Devil has been made almost by hand by Ti West, who wrote, directed, and edited. He's an admirer of classic horror films and understands that if there's anything scarier than a haunted house, it's a *possibly* haunted house. The film may provide an introduction for some audience members to the Hitchcockian definition of suspense: It's the anticipation, not the happening, that's the fun.

This is the kind of movie that looks lighted by the full of the moon, which is a good trick during an eclipse. Sam is relieved when Mr. and Mrs. Ulman return, until they don't seem prepared to give her the traditional ride home. She also meets Mother (Danielle Noe), who is considerably more spry than advertised. And there's the family—handyman?—named Victor (A. J. Bowen). And Mother's room turns out to be far, far different than you might expect, and dark, dark.

House of the Sleeping Beauties ★
NO MPAA RATING, 99 m., 2009

Vadim Glowna (Edmond), Angela Winkler (Madame), Maximilian Schell (Kogi), Birol Unel (Mister Gold), Mona Glass (Secretary), Marina Weiss (Maid). Directed by Vadim Glowna and produced by Glowna and Raymond Tarabay. Screenplay by Glowna, based on the novella by Yasunari Kawabata.

House of the Sleeping Beauties has missed its ideal release window by about forty years. It might—*might*—have found an audience in that transitional period between soft- and hard-core, when men would sit through anything to see a breast, but even then, I dunno. It's discouraging to see a movie where the women sleep through everything. They don't even have the courtesy to wake up and claim to have a headache.

I know I am being disrespectful to what is obviously intended to be a morose meditation about youth, age, men, women, children, mothers, hookers, johns, life, death, and the endless possibilities I thought of at sixteen when I heard that song "Behind the Green Door." The movie has been inspired by a 1961 novella by Yasunari Kawabata, who explores the now-obsolete Japanese theory that a woman should be seen but not heard. Even then, they were supposed to wake up sometimes and speak submissively.

The film centers on five scenes in which Edmond, a dying man in his sixties (Vadim Glowna, the director), lies in bed next to sleeping nude women of about twenty, all breathtakingly beautiful, and utters a mournful interior soliloquy about his age, their perfection, his mother, a childhood sexual

247

experience, and his own misery. This is an intensely depressing experience for Edmond and for us, intensified by his robotic smoking habit. Sometimes he shakes a woman or slaps her on her butt, but if anything is going to wake her up, his breath will.

Surrounding these scenes is a plot more intriguing than they deserve, involving Edmond's old friend Kogi (Maximilian Schell), who advised him to visit the brothel in the first place. Kogi is concerned that Edmond is depressed by the death of his wife and young daughter in an auto accident. This happened fifteen years ago. I think the human ability to heal ourselves is such that, after fifteen years, you can expect to be sad and deeply regretful, but if you are still clinically depressed, you need medical attention.

It is also a wonder that this shambling sad sack and secret drinker is still apparently the head of a big corporation and has a full-time driver for his stretch BMW. Here is one tycoon who could definitely not be played by Michael Douglas. We've seen ultrarich Masters of the Universe before, but now we get the first Masturbator of the Universe.

The brothel is a one-bedroom operation supervised by Madame (Angela Winkler), a handsome woman of a certain age, who explains that the women have been "prepared" to sleep the whole night through, and the man is invited to sleep next to them (sleeping pills provided) and feast his eyes, or perhaps caress, but no funny business like sticking his finger in her mouth. Since Madame goes away all night, there's no telling what could happen to these helpless women, of course.

Do you find this premise anything but repugnant? It offends not only civilized members of both sexes, but even dirty old men, dramatizing as it does their dirtiness and oldness. Obvious questions arise, but, no, Madame will not explain why the women sleep so soundly, and the house rules strictly forbid any contact with the women outside the house. How does she find the women? Who are they? Why do they seem to sleep peacefully instead of as if they are drugged? How do they keep their hair and makeup impeccable? Why don't they snore?

Does Edmond get up to nastiness? There is a close-up of his tumescence, which looks younger and healthier than the rest of him, but no explicit sex. It hardly matters; the film is intended as allegory, although I am unsure what the allegory teaches us. Perhaps the message is: "You see what can happen to you if you direct and star yourself in a movie like this."

How to Lose Friends and Alienate People ★ ★ ★ ½

R, 110 m., 2008

Simon Pegg (Sidney Young), Kirsten Dunst (Alison Olsen), Megan Fox (Sophie Maes), Jeff Bridges (Clayton Harding), Gillian Anderson (Eleanor Johnson), Danny Huston (Lawrence Maddox). Directed by Robert B. Weide and produced by Stephen Woolley and Elizabeth Karlsen. Screenplay by Peter Straughan, based on the memoir by Toby Young.

When a film begins with the proud claim that it was "inspired by real events," the word "inspired" usually translates as "heavily rewritten from." I can't remember if *How to Lose Friends and Alienate People* even makes the claim. But it could fairly claim to be "inspired by real events so much more outrageous than anything in this movie that you wouldn't believe it."

I have been a follower of the real Toby Young for years. He is much more preposterous than "Sidney Young," the hero of this film, which is based on Toby's memoir. He first came to fame in the early '90s as coeditor of *Modern Review,* a British magazine devoted to fierce criticism of everything but itself. The magazine ended in tabloid headlines after Young shut it down and traded savage insults with his coeditor, the equally famous Julie Burchill, who had left her husband and announced she was a lesbian. Young went on to fail sensationally as a writer for *Vanity Fair* and as a Hollywood screenwriter. He is currently back in London as drama critic for the *Spectator.* If I were a producer, I would hire security to keep him away from my opening nights or any other nights. However, I gather that, at forty-five, he has settled down a little.

I'm fond of British eccentrics. Consider Young's Wiki entry. He is the son of a baron, could legally call himself "the Honorable," studied at Oxford, Harvard, and Cambridge, went on to become Britain's favorite drunk since Jeffrey Bernard, and was described by *Private Eye* magazine as looking like "a peeled quail's egg dipped in celery salt." He has starred in West End comedies, one based on his book. He is a very funny writer, often providing inspiring material for himself. His father, a sociologist, created the term "meritocracy." The son defined demeritocracy. He's the kind of man you might enjoy having dinner with, but you wouldn't risk staying for dessert.

How to Lose Friends and Alienate People is "based on" his tumultuous employment at *Vanity Fair* magazine, where, yes, he really did send a strip-o-gram to the office on Bring Your Daughter to Work Day ("a regrettable mistake"). He blew through deadlines, vomited on people, wrecked parties, brushed with libel, suggested offensive story ideas, alienated the very celebrities he was paid to celebrate, and pulled off the neat trick of being shunned by most of the publicists in America.

How to Lose Friends and Alienate People is possibly the best movie that could be made about Toby Young that isn't rated NC-17. It stars Simon Pegg, who was born to play Young, just as Peter O'Toole was destined to play Jeffrey Bernard. On Young's first day at work at *Sharp's* magazine, he wears a T-shirt emblazoned: "Young, Dumb & Full of ——." (No dashes in the movie.) His editor, Clayton Harding (Jeff Bridges), hires him after he tries to sneak into a *Sharp's* party carrying a famous pig. I've known editors that tolerant. When a reporter at the *Sun-Times* tried to hurl a chair through the editor's office window, the editor quietly asked him, "Any complaints about the interior decorating, Paul?" Full disclosure: That was the same editor who hired me. The rest of the story: The window was made of unbreakable plastic, and the chair rebounded, striking the reporter.

Back to the movie. Harding puts up with incredible behavior by Young, which can only be explained by drink, drugs, spectacularly bad judgment, lust, rampaging ambition, or a need to be the center of attention, however appalled. There is one woman at the office who can tolerate him. This is Alison Olsen (Kirsten Dunst), who writes the captions on photos (an important job at *Sharp's*). Young is too blinded by a fifteen-minutes-of-fame sex-

pot named Sophie (Megan Fox) to give Alison the time of day. Meanwhile, Alison is being manhandled by another editor, the unsavory and back-stabbing Maddox (Danny Huston, as oily as his old man could be).

What you'd expect from the upward-bound-young-man formula would be a Machiavellian schemer. What you get in *How to Lose Friends* is a flywheel who embarrasses his magazine at every opportunity. Why? He detests the celebrity culture he has been hired to write about and has some half-baked idea that he is attacking it through acts of self-destruction.

In a boring old world, such people are to be prized. I have met only one man I would back to be more outrageous than Toby Young, even though he is handicapped by not using drugs. His name is Jay Robert Nash. Those who know him would agree with me. He once walked into a saloon in a tiny mountain town in Colorado, where cowboys were not only drinking around the fire but had tethered their horses outside, and serenaded them with "Rhinestone Cowboy," and *meant well* by it. I saw this. It should be said that both Nash and Young are good fathers and nice men. I can't speak for Crosby and Stills.

How to Train Your Dragon ★★★
PG, 98 m., 2010

Jay Baruchel (Hiccup), Gerard Butler (Stoick), Craig Ferguson (Gobber), America Ferrara (Astrid), Jonah Hill (Snotlout), Christopher Mintz-Plasse (Fishlegs), Kristen Wiig (Ruffnut), T. J. Miller (Tuffnut). Directed by Chris Sanders and Dean DeBlois and produced by Bonnie Arnold. Screenplay by Sanders and DeBlois, based on the book by Cressida Cowell.

Some movies seem born to inspire video games. All they lack is controllers and a scoring system. *How to Train Your Dragon* plays more like a game born to inspire a movie. It devotes a great deal of time to aerial battles between tamed dragons and evil ones, and not much to character or story development. But it's bright, good-looking, and has high energy. Kids above the easily scared age will probably like the movie the younger they are.

This is another action animation with an

improbable young hero. Remember when the heroes in this genre were teenagers? Now it's usually some kid who is ten at the most, revealing himself as stronger, wiser, and braver than older people, and a quick learner when it comes to discovering or mastering a new form of warfare. We are born knowing how to command dragons and spaceships, and we forget as up we grow.

Our hero is Hiccup Horrendous Haddock III (voice by Jay Baruchel), a young Viking who lives in Berk, a mountainside village surrounded by the crags and aeries of hostile dragons. Hiccup tells us that his village is very old, but all of the houses are new. An alarming omen. Led by his father, Stoick (Gerard Butler), and the dragon master, Gobber (Craig Ferguson), the villagers have been in combat with the dragons since time immemorial. It would seem to be an unequal struggle; the dragons are enormous and breathe fire, and the Vikings, while muscular, have only clubs, swords, and spears. They may, however, be smarter than the dragons, although you wouldn't know that just by listening to them.

Butler seems to be channeling his character from *300*, beefed up by many a hearty Viking feast. He joins Ferguson and others in muscular Scottish accents, since as we all know, that dialect of English was widely used among the Vikings. In appearance, the Vikings seem victims of a testosterone outbreak causing enormous sprouty growths of hair. Even the hair from their nostrils might knit up into a nice little sock. Oh, how I tried not to, but as I watched these brawlers saddled up on great flying lizards, I kept thinking, "*Asterix* meets *Avatar*."

The plot: Little Hiccup is ordered to stay inside during a dragon attack. But the plucky lad seizes a cannon, blasts away at the enemy, and apparently wings one. Venturing into the forest to track his prey, he finds a wounded little dragon about his age, already chained up. He releases it, they bond, and he discovers that dragons can be perfectly nice. With his new friend, Toothless, he returns to the village, and an alliance is formed with good dragons against the bad dragons, who are snarly holdouts and grotesquely ugly.

One evil beast is covered all over with giant warlike knobs, and has six eyes, three on either side, like a classic Buick. In one scene, a Viking hammers on an eyeball with his club. Not very appetizing. The battle ends as all battles must, with the bad guys routed and the youngest hero saving the day. The aerial battle scenes are storyboarded like a World War I dogfight, with swoops, climbs, and narrowly missed collisions with craggy peaks and other dragons. For my taste, these continued way too long, but then I must teach myself that I do not have a six-year-old's taste.

Note: The movie is in both 3-D and 2-D. The 3-D adds nothing but the opportunity to pay more in order to see a distracting and unnecessary additional dimension. Paramount has threatened theaters that if they don't clear screens for Dragon *despite the current glut of 3-D films, the studio won't let them show it in 2-D. This displays real confidence in 3-D.* ☞

The Human Centipede no stars
NO MPAA RATING, 90 m., 2010

Dieter Laser (Dr. Heiter), Ashley C. Williams (Lindsay), Ashlynn Yennie (Jenny), Akihiro Kitamura (Katsuro). Directed by Tom Six and produced by Tom Six and Ilona Six. Screenplay by Tom Six.

It's not death itself that's so bad. It's what you might have to go through to get there. No horror film I've seen inflicts more terrible things on its victims than *The Human Centipede*. You would have to be very brave to choose this ordeal over simply being murdered. Maybe you'd need to also be insane.

I'm about to describe what happens to the film's victims. This will be a spoiler. I don't care, because (1) the details are common knowledge in horror film circles, and (2) if you don't know, you may be grateful to be warned. This is a movie I don't think I should be coy about.

OK. Dr. Heiter is a mad scientist. He was once a respected surgeon, but has now retreated to his luxurious home in the forest, which contains an operating room in the basement. His skin has a sickly pallor, his hair is dyed black, his speech reminds us of a standard Nazi, and he gnashes his teeth. He is filled with hatred and vile perversion.

He drugs his victims and dumps them into

his Mercedes. When they regain consciousness, they find themselves tied to hospital beds. He provides them with a little slide show to brief them on his plans. He will demonstrate his skills as a surgeon by—hey, listen, now you'd really better stop reading. What's coming next isn't so much a review as a public service announcement.

Heiter plans to surgically join his three victims by sewing together their mouths and anuses, all in a row, so the food goes in at the front and comes out at the rear, you see. They will move on their hands and knees like an insect with twelve limbs. You don't want to be part of the human centipede at all, but you most certainly don't want to be in the middle. Why does Dr. Heiter want to commit such an atrocity? He is insane, as I've already explained.

He also wants to do it because he is in a movie by Tom Six, a Dutch director whose previous two films average 4 out of 10 on the IMDb scale, which is a score so low very few directors attain it. Six has now made a film deliberately intended to inspire incredulity, nausea, and hopefully outrage. It's being booked as a midnight movie, and is it ever. Boozy fanboys will treat it like a thrill ride.

And yet within Six there stirs the soul of a dark artist. He treats his material with utter seriousness; there's none of the jokey undertone of a classic Hammer horror film like *Scream and Scream Again* (1970), in which every time the victim awoke, another limb had been amputated. That one starred the all-star trio of Vincent Price, Christopher Lee, and Peter Cushing, and you could see they were having fun. Dieter Laser, who plays Dr. Heiter, takes the role with relentless sincerity. This is his sixty-third acting role, but, poor guy, this is seemingly the one he was born to play.

Tom Six is apparently the director's real name. I learn his favorite actor is Klaus Kinski, he is an AK-47 enthusiast, and wears RAF sunglasses and Panama hats. Not the kind of guy you want to share your seat on a Ferris wheel. He has said, "I get a rash from too much political correctness." I promise you that after this movie his skin was smooth as a Gerber baby's.

I have long attempted to take a generic approach. In other words, is a film true to its genre and does it deliver what its audiences presumably expect? *The Human Centipede* scores high on this scale. It is depraved and disgusting enough to satisfy the most demanding midnight movie fan. And it's not *simply* an exploitation film.

The director makes, for example, an effective use of the antiseptic interior of Heiter's labyrinthine home. Doors and corridors lead nowhere and anywhere. In a scene where the police come calling, he wisely has Heiter almost encourage their suspicions. And there is a scene toward the end, as the human centipede attempts escape, that's so piteous it transcends horror and approaches tragedy.

The members of the centipede are Ashley C. Williams, Ashlynn Yennie, and Akihiro Kitamura. The Japanese actor screams in subtitled Japanese, perhaps because he will broaden the film's appeal among Asian horror fans. In the last half of the film, the two American actresses don't scream at all, if you follow me.

I am required to award stars to movies I review. This time, I refuse to do it. The star rating system is unsuited to this film. Is the movie good? Is it bad? Does it matter? It is what it is, and occupies a world where the stars don't shine.

Humpday ★★★ ½

R, 94 m., 2009

Mark Duplass (Ben), Joshua Leonard (Andrew), Alycia Delmore (Anna). Directed and produced by Lynn Shelton. Screenplay by Shelton.

Humpday, a film by a woman about the limits of male bonding, blows the whistle on buddy movies. After the buddies in those movies finish with pounding each other on the back, giving each other Dutch rubs, and chanting, "I love you, man!"—how far are they prepared to take their love? Just about exactly that far, perhaps, and then they draw the line.

The film is a perceptive comedy about how many men, if not homophobic in theory, shudder in practice about the prospect of getting it on with their own sex. It's also about how close friends in school can drift far apart in a decade. That's what has happened to Ben and Andrew. Ben (Mark Duplass) is a married man, using fertility methods to conceive a child with his wife, Anna. Andrew (Joshua Leonard) is a shaggy college friend, who turns up in the middle of the night after living the life of a free spirit in India, Cambodia, Mexico, and other faraway places.

Anna (Alycia Delmore) has never heard of this old buddy. But she's a good sport and invites him to spend the night. Andrew spends more than the night, and Ben, now a straight arrow, feels a certain wistfulness about the freedom he has lost to marriage. Andrew takes him to a party of swingers no longer in the first bloom of youth, where booze, drugs, and sex toys are thrown into the pot, so to speak.

When they're fairly drunk, the two friends hear about a Seattle event named Humpfest, in which amateurs compete to produce the best short porn film. They decide to enter. They will win, they predict, because they have the most daring idea: They will have sex with each other. Two straight guys doing it for the first time. "That's beyond gay!"

As is sometimes the way with drunken vows, these are taken seriously, and Ben and Andrew set about making plans to make the film in a rented hotel room. Meanwhile, Anna grows increasingly uncomfortable with Andrew's omnipresence and his influence on her reliable husband. Anna, you understand, is in no way a conventional movie spouse, but has been imagined by the writer-director, Lynn Shelton, as an open-minded, sex-loving woman who is nevertheless mature and reasonable and expects from Ben an attentive husband and a dependable father.

Anna is, of course, never to learn the truth about what is described as "Andrew's art project." Andrew, of course, lets it slip. Anna's reaction is more complex than you might imagine, and it's at such a moment you appreciate the woman in the writer-director's chair. Women, I suspect, are more likely than men to view sex from the overall perspective of what we may call their lives. In a country like Saudi Arabia, whose citizens express discomfort about men and women even attending movies together, I have little doubt which gender is more concerned.

Ben and Andrew advance doggedly on a trajectory leading them to their Humpfest entry, and there's a rather remarkable scene in the hotel room that involves great perception of word choices, vocal intonations, and body language (what does it mean as both men clasp pillows to their tummies?). I understand most of the dialogue was improvised after extensive discussion, and it sounds real—uncertain, tentative, even bashful. For starters, who's going to pitch and who's going to catch? Not an easy question to answer.

Humpday is funny, yes, but observant and thought-provoking. Buddy movies like *I Love You, Man,* which I loved, can intrigue us with the possibility of an attraction between two men that could threaten a heterosexual romance. But when all bets are called, most guys just don't want to go there. It could be the end of a beautiful platonic friendship.

We will leave Ben and Andrew in their hotel room and pull back to consider Humpfest itself, which I discover is an actual annual event in Seattle. Unlike the porn films described in this film, its entries must be hump films—in other words, depicting an activity common in dogs and Transformers. In fact, the festival has only one rule: "Penetration equals disqualification."

You can find its Web site, which includes a chart of recommended drinking levels, if you want to enter. In the meantime, here is a Humpfest entry of less than sixty seconds. It contains no nudity and no explicit sex, and of course only one protagonist. Be sure to watch until the end: www.youtube.com/watch?v=nRM89nVHyl4.

Hunger ★ ★ ★ ½
NO MPAA RATING, 92 m., 2009

Michael Fassbender (Bobby Sands), Liam Cunningham (Father Dominic Moran), Stuart Graham (Raymond Lohan), Brian Milligan (Davey Gillen), Liam McMahon (Gerry Campbell). Directed by Steve McQueen and produced by Laura Hastings-Smith and Robin Gutch. Screenplay by McQueen and Enda Walsh.

It was a desperate business, and *Hunger* is a desperate film. It concerns the fierce battle between the Irish Republican Army and the British state, which in 1981 led to a hunger strike in which ten IRA prisoners died. The first of them was Bobby Sands, whose agonizing death is seen with an implacable, level gaze in the closing act of the film.

If you do not hold a position on the Irish Republican cause, you will not find one here. *Hunger* is not about the rights and wrongs of the British in Northern Ireland, but about inhuman prison conditions, the steeled determination of IRA members such as Bobby Sands, and a rock and a hard place. There is hardly a sentence in the film about Irish history or politics, and only two extended dialogue passages: one a long debate between Sands and a priest about the utility or futility of a hunger strike, the other a doctor's detailed description to Sands's parents about the effect of starvation on the human body.

There is not a conventional plot to draw us from beginning to end. Instead, director Steve McQueen, an artist who employs merciless realism, strikes three major chords. The first involves the daily routine of a prison guard (Stuart Graham), who is emotionally wounded by his work. The second involves two other prisoners (Brian Milligan and Liam McMahon), who participate in the IRA prisoners' refusal to wear prison clothes or bathe. The third involves the hunger strike.

This is clear: Neither side will back down. Twice we hear Prime Minister Margaret Thatcher describing the inmates of the Maze prison in Belfast as not political prisoners but criminals. The IRA considers itself political to the core. The ideology involved is not even mentioned in the extraordinary long dialogue scene, mostly in one shot, between Sands and a priest (Liam Cunningham) about whether a hunger strike will have the desired effect. The priest, worldly, a realist, on very civil terms with Sands, never once mentions suicide as a sin; he discusses it entirely in terms of its usefulness.

Sands thinks starvation to death will have an impact. The priest observes that if it does, Sands will by then be dead. His willingness to die reflects the bone-deep beliefs of Irish Republicans; recall the Irish song lyric, "And always remember, the longer we live, the sooner we bloody well die."

Sands's death is shown in a tableau of increasing bleakness. It is agonizing, yet filmed with a curious painterly purity. It is alarming to note how much weight the actor Michael Fassbender lost; he went from 170 to 132 pounds. His dreams or visions or memories toward the end, based on a story he told the priest, would have been more effective if handled much more briefly.

Did the hunger strike succeed? After the remorseless death toll climbed to ten, Thatcher at last relented, tacitly granting the prisoners political recognition, although she refused to say so out loud. She was called the Iron Lady for a reason. Today there is peace in Northern Ireland. The island nation is still divided. Bobby Sands is dead. The priest has his conclusions, the dead man has his, or would if he were alive.

The Hurt Locker ★★★★
R, 127 m., 2009

Jeremy Renner (Staff Sergeant William James), Anthony Mackie (Sergeant J. T. Sanborn), Brian Geraghty (Specialist Owen Eldridge), Ralph Fiennes (Contractor Team Leader), Guy Pearce (Sergeant Matt Thompson), David Morse (Colonel Reed), Evangeline Lilly (Connie James). Directed by Kathryn Bigelow and produced by Bigelow, Nicolas Chartier, and Greg Shapiro. Screenplay by Mark Boal.

A lot of movies begin with poetic quotations, but *The Hurt Locker* opens with a statement presented as fact: "War is a drug." Not for everyone, of course. Most combat troops want to get it over with and go home. But the hero of this film, Staff Sergeant William James, who has a terrifyingly dangerous job, addresses it like a daily pleasure. Under enemy fire in Iraq, he defuses bombs.

He isn't an action hero, he's a specialist, like a surgeon who focuses on one part of the body over and over, day after day, until he could continue if the lights went out. James is a man who understands bombs inside out and has an almost psychic understanding of the minds of the bombers. This is all the more remarkable because in certain scenes it seems fairly certain that the bomb maker is standing in full view—on a balcony or in a window overlooking the street, say, and is as curious about his bomb as James is. Two professionals, working against each other.

253

Staff Sergeant James is played by Jeremy Renner, who immediately goes on the short list for an Oscar nomination. His performance is not built on complex speeches but on a visceral projection of who this man is and what he feels. He is not a hero in a conventional sense. He cares not for medals. He could no doubt recite patriotic reasons for his service, but does that explain why he compulsively, sometimes recklessly, puts himself in harm's way? The man before him in this job got himself killed. James seems even cockier.

The Hurt Locker is a spellbinding war film by Kathryn Bigelow, a master of stories about men and women who choose to be in physical danger. She cares first about the people, then about the danger. She doesn't leave a lot of room for much else. The man who wrote "War is a drug" was Chris Hedges, a war correspondent for the *New York Times*. Mark Boal, who wrote this screenplay, was embedded with a bomb squad in Baghdad. He also wrote the superb movie *In the Valley of Elah* (2007), with Tommy Lee Jones as a professional army man trying to solve the murder of his son who had just returned from Iraq. Also based on fact.

Bigelow and Boal know what they're doing. This movie embeds itself in a man's mind. When it's over, nothing has been said in so many words, but we have a pretty clear idea of why James *needs* to defuse bombs. I'm going to risk putting it this way: (1) bombs need to be defused; (2) nobody does it better than James; (3) he knows exactly how good he is; and (4) when he's at work, an intensity of focus and exhilaration consumes him, and he's in that heedless zone when an artist loses track of self and time.

The most important man in his life is Sergeant J. T. Sanborn (Anthony Mackie), head of the support team that accompanies James. Sanborn and his men provide cover fire, scan rooftops and hiding places that might conceal snipers, and assist James into and out of his heavy protective clothing. Sanborn gives constant audio feedback that James hears inside his helmet. It is Sanborn, who has his eye on everything, who is nominally in charge, and not the tunnel-visioned James.

Sanborn is a skilled, responsible professional. He works by the book. He follows protocol. James drives him nuts. Sometimes James seems to almost deliberately invite trouble, and Sanborn believes that by following the procedure they'll all have a better chance of going home. He isn't a shirker, and he doesn't have weak nerves. He's a realist and thinks James is reckless.

Certainly James behaves recklessly at times, even in his use of protective clothing. He takes risks boldly. But in the actual task of defusing a bomb, he is as careful as if he were operating on his own heart. Bigelow uses no phony suspense-generating mechanisms in this film. No false alarms. No gung-ho. It is about personalities in terrible danger. The suspense is real, and it is earned. Hitchcock said when there's a bomb under a table and it explodes, that's action. When we know the bomb is there, and the people at the table play cards and it doesn't explode, that's suspense.

The Hurt Locker is a great film, an intelligent film, a film shot clearly so that we know exactly who everybody is and where they are and what they're doing and why. The camera work is at the service of the story. Bigelow knows that you can't build suspense with shots lasting one or two seconds. And you can't tell a story that way, either—not one that deals with the mystery of why a man like James seems to depend on risking his life. A leading contender for Academy Awards.

I

I Am Love ★★★★
R, 120 m., 2010

Tilda Swinton (Emma), Flavio Parenti (Edoardo Jr.), Edoardo Gabbriellini (Antonio), Alba Rohrwacher (Elisabetta), Pippo Delbono (Tancredi), Maria Paiato (Ida), Gabriele Ferzetti (Edoardo Recchi Sr.), Marisa Berenson (Allegra). Directed by Luca Guadagnino and produced by Guadagnino, Francesco Melzi d'Eril, Marco Morabito, Tilda Swinton, Alessandro Usai, and Massimiliano Violante. Screenplay by Barbara Alberti, Ivan Cotroneo, Walter Fasano, and Guadagnino.

Did she understand when she married her husband what sort of family she was joining? She knew they were rich Italian aristocrats, operators of textile mills in Milan. But did she understand that as a wife from Russia she would serve and provide and even be loved, but would never truly be a member?

When we see Emma (Tilda Swinton), she is preparing the Recchi house for the birthday party of the patriarch. She seems to relate more as a caterer than as a hostess. At the head of the table is the grand old Edoardo (Gabriele Ferzetti). Among those gathered are his son, Emma's husband, Tancredi (Pippo Delbono). The old man makes an unexpected announcement: He is retiring and putting Tancredi in charge. But not Tancredi alone. His grandson, their son, Edo (Flavio Parenti), will also share the responsibility.

Is Emma filled with joy? Her husband and son will inherit the dynasty? She is so calm and expert, it's hard to say. Tilda Swinton is a daring actress who doesn't project emotions so much as embody them. *I Am Love* provides an ideal role for her, in that her actions speak instead of words. We learn she has her own private space, that after launching a family event she likes to leave it running smoothly and retire to her room upstairs.

The opening act of Luca Guadagnino's film establishes the stature of the Recchi family as surely as the Corleones are established in *The Godfather,* or the Salinas in Visconti's *The Leopard.* It may be impossible to write about this film without evoking *The Leopard,* not simply because they both involve Italian aristocrats, but because they involve matters of succession, and the way that love and lust can breach the walls aristocrats live behind. Guadagnino makes the connection inescapable by naming Tancredi; in *The Leopard,* Alain Delon pays the Salina nephew of that name.

The Recchi family has been living in a particular way for a long time. Cushioned by great wealth, working in an industry associated with style, never challenged, well educated, its hungers cloaked in tradition, it occupies its place of privilege effortlessly. Emma speaks Italian fluently, but with a Russian accent, a reminder that she is not . . . quite one of them.

Few actresses can embody urgent sexual desire so well as Swinton. She is realistic about such feelings. When she learns her daughter, Elisabetta (Alba Rohrwacher), is a lesbian, she reacts not as a mother, possibly with shock, but as a woman, in surprise and curiosity. She has heard of such things. The heart has its reasons.

The feast opening the film was prepared by Antonio (Edoardo Gabbriellini), a friend of her Edo's. She consults with this young chef, and a feeling passes into her. Later, on a visit to her daughter in San Remo, she happens to see Antonio, and with decision follows him through the streets. This is all done without dialogue. The camera is pursuer and pursued. The longer she follows him, the more certain they must meet.

Of course they make love. Actresses are often called upon to enact sex in the movies. Swinton does it differently with each character, understanding that sexuality is as distinctive as speech or taste. Emma is urgent as if a dam has burst, releasing not passion but happiness. Of course this affair threatens her relationship with her husband, her son, and her family. But most long-established families have overcome the inconveniences of adultery. Continuity is more important than commitment. The film now observes the ways, not predictable, in which this new sexual fact affects Emma's role.

All this time, Guadagnino has been paying

due attention to other important members of the family. There is Allegra (Marisa Berenson), gatekeeper of her husband. There is the long-serving housekeeper, Ida (Maria Paiato), who sees and understands everything and in many ways is Emma's refuge in the household. There is the personality of her son, Edo, as yet untouched by the ordeals of business life, more open in his personal feelings. And there is the overarching sense in which the Recchi family embodies a tradition that, like a church, requires devotion if not belief.

I Am Love is an amazing film. It is deep, rich, human. It is not about rich and poor but about old and new. It is about the ancient war between tradition and feeling. For this role Tilda Swinton learned to speak Italian with a Russian accent, as Tilda Swinton would, but her performance is nothing as trivial as a feat of learning. She evokes Emma as a woman who for years has accepted the needs of the Recchis, and discovers in a few days to accept her own needs. She must have been waiting a long time for Antonio, whoever he would be.

Ice Age: Dawn of the Dinosaurs ★★★ ½
PG, 93 m., 2009

With the voices of: Ray Romano (Manny), Queen Latifah (Ellie), John Leguizamo (Sid), Denis Leary (Diego), Simon Pegg (Buck), Seann William Scott (Crash), Josh Peck (Eddie), Bill Hader (Gazelle), Kristen Wiig (Pudgy Beaver Mom), Chris Wedge (Scrat), Karen Disher (Scratte). Directed by Carlos Saldanha and produced by Lori Forte and John C. Donkin. Screenplay by Michael Berg, Peter Ackerman, Mike Reiss, and Yoni Brenner.

Ice Age: Dawn of the Dinosaurs is the best of the three films about our friends in the inter-species herd of plucky prehistoric heroes. And it involves some of the best use of 3-D I've seen in an animated feature. It also introduces a masterstroke that essentially allows the series to take place anywhere: There is this land beneath the surface of the earth, you see . . .

Well, if there can be one land, there can be any number of lands, including not only this one, where dinosaurs still roam, but maybe a portal in time leading to the future, or one in space, leading to another planet. We can maybe expect Manny and Ellie in Vegas, or Scrat on Mars. This particular land looks a great deal like a primeval jungle, if such a wilderness had lava falls as well as waterfalls. As it is subterranean, it has sort of a rock roof, although indirect lighting comes from somewhere and sustains lush vegetation.

All of our friends are back, and some new ones, including a ferocious T-Rex and a sexy rival for Scrat the squirrel, named Scrattè, accent grave over the *e*. As befits this land before time, Scrat and Scrattè are saber-toothed squirrels. No wonder the big teeth died out. They're of more use to a carnivore than a vegetarian. But logic like this is of no use in a movie where Sid the sloth (voice by John Leguizamo) adopts three dinosaur eggs and plans to raise the babies.

That's how they all end up underground in the Hollow Earth, the land Edgar Rice Burroughs name Pellucidar, and I guess with a place like that, you can name it anything you want. The mother dinosaur comes looking for her hatchlings, grabs them and Sid, and disappears under the surface. An all-for-one, one-for-all spirit has grown among our friends, who give chase: Manny and Ellie the woolly mammoths (Ray Romano and Queen Latifah), Diego the saber-toothed tiger (Denis Leary), and the possums Eddie and Crash (Josh Peck and Seann William Scott). They meet Buck the weasel (Simon Pegg), who has an eye patch instead of a peg leg and is obsessed with his quest for a Great White Dinosaur, unfortunately not named Moby Dino.

In the Ice Age films the tiger has learned to coexist with such edible species as sloths and gazelles, but dinosaurs aren't covered by the terms of the truce, and this one is so big it could eat even a woolly mammoth in one chomp. That sets us up for the staple of the series—chase scenes involving dizzying falls, catapults into the sky, close shaves, and possible digestion. This is pure invention, and unlike the monotonous chase sequences in some family animation, *Ice Age: Dawn of the Dinosaurs* is tirelessly inventive visually.

Carlos Saldanha, writer of the 2002 film and codirector of the (disappointing) *Ice Age: The Meltdown* (2006), is the director this time, and many of his sequences are in the spirit of the brilliant Scrat-and-acorn scene that opened the first *Ice Age*. That includes one in which Scrat, Scrattè, and the acorn are trapped inside floating bubbles, which is no big deal to the acorn. Still, this is a talented acorn, which sings a tune from the Gilbert O'Sullivan songbook to express how alone an acorn must sometimes feel. An acorn that smart, you don't want to eat all at once.

I thought the 3-D was done well. I remain unconvinced by the process. You have to fool with the glasses, the brightness is dimmed, and so on. But I was surprised how well *Dawn of the Dinosaurs* implements it. It creates much less of a distracting superfluous dimension, and more skillfully makes the whole image seem to belong together. The movie is also widely being shown in 2-D, and if you want to save a few bucks, that's the way to go.

Note: Here's a nice, bright 2-D scene including the new character Buck: www.apple. com/trailers/fox/iceagedawnofthedinosaurs/ large_clip. html/.

I Hate Valentine's Day ★ ½
PG-13, 90 m., 2009

Nia Vardalos (Genevieve Gernier), John Corbett (Greg Gatlin), Judah Friedlander (Dan O'Finn), Stephen Guarino (Bill), Amir Arison (Bob), Zoe Kazan (Tammy Greenwood), Rachel Dratch (Kathy Jeemy). Directed by Nia Vardalos and produced by William Sherak, Jason Shuman, and Madeleine Sherak. Screenplay by Vardalos, Ben Zook, and Stephen David.

I Hate Valentine's Day is a romantic comedy with one peculiarity: The heroine is stark staring mad. I will tell you how I arrived at this diagnosis. Genevieve has an unbreakable policy regarding men: Five dates, and she's out the door. She even specifies exactly what each of the dates must be like, leading up to number five, during which she doesn't say so, but going all the way is a possibility.

Why does she impose these draconian measures? Because she likes only the falling in love part of an affair and not the inevitable breaking up. She expects a guy to jump through the hoops and then disappear after number five, remaining, of course, a "friend." When a woman says, "We should stay friends," it trans-

lates as, "Take your genitals to a faraway place and limit our contact to sending me flowers on my birthday."

Let's assume conservatively that Genevieve started dating when she was twenty, and that she has met on average three men a year willing to accept her strictures. And that after completing all the requirements, half of them have triumphantly arrived at home plate. Given her age, which a gentlemen does not mention, that works out to thirty-nine sex partners. According to surveys reported by ABC News and the *New York Times,* which I don't necessarily believe, the average American woman has between four and seven sex partners in a lifetime. That means Genevieve is not only an obsessive-compulsive, but a nympho.

Yet she looks so sweet. And knows she does. Yes, this is the second movie in a month, after *My Life in Ruins,* in which Nia Vardalos goes through the entire film smiling brightly and almost continuously. Nobody smiles that much unless they suffer from the rare giocondaphobia, or Constantly Smiling Syndrome, a complaint more often seen among listeners of Bill O'Reilly and field hands in *Gone With the Wind.*

Genevieve is a woman beloved by all who encounter her, when in life I would be terrified of her. She is considered a source of great wisdom about romance, although Dr. Phil might advise protective custody. In *I Hate Valentine's Day,* she runs the cutest little florist's shop in Brooklyn and dispenses invaluable advice to men uncertain about a Valentine's Day gift ("flowers"). She has two gay assistants who think she is about the best thing since Maria Callas. And this cute guy opens a tapas bar next door, named Get on Tapas, ha ha.

The cute guy is played by John Corbett, her costar in *My Big Fat Greek Wedding.* He is way too desirable to have to settle for the five-date rule. The women from *Sex and the City* would be camped out in pup tents on his sidewalk. It should have occurred to someone, maybe Vardalos, the writer and director, that it would have been funnier and way more plausible to make the hero a needy schlub who is lovestruck by her and would agree to waterboarding for even one date. The movie is set up as a valentine to Vardalos. She should try sending herself flowers.

Il Divo ★★★ ½

NO MPAA RATING, 117 m., 2009

Toni Servillo (Giulio Andreotti), Anna Bonaiuto (Livia Andreotti), Giulio Bosetti (Eugenio Scalfari), Flavio Bucci (Franco Evangelisti), Carlo Buccirosso (Paolo Cirino Pomicino), Giorgio Colangeli (Salvo Lima). Directed by Paolo Sorrentino and produced by Nicola Giuliano, Francesca Cima, and Andrea Occhipinti. Screenplay by Sorrentino.

They would seem to be opposites, but on the basis of two recent films, the longtime Italian prime minister Giulio Andreotti and the longtime fashion emperor Valentino were surprisingly similar. Both are seen as intensely private, rarely happy, single-minded in pursuit of their ambitions, cool in their personal relationships, and ruling as if by divine right. A difference is that Valentino was never accused of criminal activities.

Another difference is that they've inspired radically different films. *Valentino: The Last Emperor* is reverential; *Il Divo* is fascinated by what it presents as Andreotti's lifelong career of skullduggery. Still serving the Italian state as a senator for life at the age of ninety, he entered politics in 1946 and was prime minister during most of the years between 1972 and 1992. During much of that time he was widely believed to have associations with the mafia, and *Il Divo* shows him imagining a confession to his wife in which he links himself to 236 deaths. One of those might include the murder of Aldo Moro, his election rival, who was kidnapped by the Red Brigades and killed after fifty-four days when Andreotti shockingly refused to negotiate a ransom.

What you would not guess from this history is that *Il Divo* is a deadpan, horrified comedy. The writer-director Paolo Sorrentino is fascinated by Andreotti's wicked intelligence, his awareness that so many believe the worst of him, his enigmatic mask. He fascinated his contemporaries; Margaret Thatcher once said of him: "He seemed to have a positive aversion to principle, even a conviction that a man of principle was doomed to be a

figure of fun." He said of himself: "Power is a disease one has no desire to be cured of." He knew where all the strings were attached, and once told a pope: "Your Holiness, forgive me, but you don't know the Vatican like I do."

What is astonishing is that a film like this could be made about a man still living. One imagines Andreotti reflecting that it only enhances his larger-than-life image. His Christian Democrats ruled postwar Italy until 1992, by which time the party was in such disrepute that it no longer survives. Yet he prevails. He prevails, and the legend is only enhanced by the great performance here by Toni Servillo, an actor who succeeds in making him hypnotizing by supplying him with an almost cheerful lack of the slightest magnetism. Here was a man who suppressed the usual charm of a politician, perhaps aware he worked better as an enigma. Was he thinking of himself when he famously said, "You sin in thinking bad about people; but often, you guess right"?

The film proceeds like a black comedy version of *The Godfather*, crossed with Oliver Stone's *Nixon*. It assembles a roll call of figures in postwar Italian politics, society, and crime, uses an abundance of names and dates in captions, and makes us despair of keeping track until we realize we're not intended to—the purpose of all these facts is simply to evoke the sheer scope and breadth of Andreotti's machinations. The more we learn, the more fascinated we become, as Servillo portrays him as poker-faced, hunched, impassive, observing all, revealing little, wise, and cynical beyond measure. Imagine Dick Cheney without the jolly charisma.

After I saw *Il Divo*, I suppose I should have felt indignation. I suppose I should also have felt that way after *The Godfather*. But such films present such mesmerizing figures that I simply regard them, astonished. I wonder if just before a snake strikes you, you think, "What an amazing snake!" The Italians, you have to admit, get good value for their money. Who could possibly follow Andreotti as prime minister? Try Silvio Berlusconi.

Note: "Il Divo" was also the nickname of Julius Caesar, a name suggesting "the divine one." Andreotti's other nicknames, per Wikipedia: Beelzebub, the Hunchback, the Sphinx, and the Black Pope.

I Love You, Beth Cooper ★★
PG-13, 102 m., 2009

Hayden Panettiere (Beth Cooper), Paul Rust (Denis Cooverman), Jack Carpenter (Rich Munsch), Lauren London (Cammy Alcott), Lauren Storm (Treece Kilmer). Directed by Chris Columbus and produced by Columbus, Michael Barnathan, and Mark Radcliffe. Screenplay by Larry Doyle, based on his novel.

The writer of *I Love You, Beth Cooper* says the story is based on a dream. I believe him. This is one of the very few movies where I *wanted* the hero to wake up and discover it was only a dream. But it's a dream all the way through—a dream evoking just another teen romcom.

The situation is so universal. The high school nerd harbors a secret crush on the most popular girl in school. He chooses the occasion of his valedictory speech to publicly proclaim this love. We can believe that, all the way up to the valedictory speech. But, yes, this is another movie hailing a hero with the courage to say what he really believes and accept the consequences.

Sometimes, as in a dream, doing that will pay off abundantly by focusing the popular girl's attention on how unique and special you are. Sometimes the popular girl will reveal herself as actually a warm and cuddly human being. Sometimes. More often, the nerd will confirm everyone's belief in his nerdhood, humiliate himself, selfishly derail the whole graduation exercise, and discover that the most popular girl really *is* a bitch. Lots of wonderful girls fall in love with nerds. They may not become the most popular girl in school, but they don't care. That honor carries with it a terrible lifetime price tag.

So what I wish is that *I Love You, Beth Cooper* had awakened from its dream and been a smart high school comedy, even one subscribing to an alternate set of clichés in which the hero discovers he really loves the nerdy girl once she takes off her glasses.

I am also tiring of the way high school movies insist that all nonheroic characters travel in posses of three. All Most Popular Girls arrive flanked by two girlfriends who follow them by half a step. And all macho villains have two underlings who follow their or-ders. In *I Love You, Beth Cooper,* the girlfriends are nice enough, because the heroine is. But the villain, "Muncher" Munsch (Jack Carpenter), is a uniformed ROTC officer who, along with his sidekicks, is a muscular master of the martial arts, a skilled gymnast, and a vicious bully. When he whistles, his minions snap to attention. And they attack with coordination worthy of a dance troupe.

The movie also goes over the top with special effects, where the theory "less is more" must be in an incomprehensible language. I know that fierce struggles over romance can break out in high school, but with these kids, I doubt they would threaten to be lethal. Nor is driving an SUV into a house commonplace. Scene after scene is on autopilot.

I'm thinking of films that remember what it's like to be a teenager with a hopeless love. *Almost Famous, Lucas, Say Anything, The Man in the Moon.* If I were a filmmaker like Chris Columbus, who has directed two of the Harry Potter films, I don't know if I'd bother with this genre unless I felt I could make a film aspiring to that kind of stature.

Of the two costars, what I can say is that I'm looking forward to their next films. Hayden Panettiere (Beth) is professional and lovable and convincingly projects emotions and has a face the screen loves. Paul Rust (Denis the valedictorian) can be very earnest and sincere, and seems to actually take the plot seriously, which is more than I could do. ☞

I Love You, Man ★ ★ ★ ½
R, 104 m., 2009

Paul Rudd (Peter Klaven), Jason Segel (Sydney Fife), Rashida Jones (Zooey), Andy Samberg (Robbie), J. K. Simmons (Oz), Jane Curtin (Joyce), Jon Favreau (Barry), Jaime Pressly (Denise). Directed by John Hamburg and produced by Hamburg and Donald De Line. Screenplay by Hamburg and Larry Levin.

I would like to have a friend like Sydney Fife. I think a lot of guys would. Even though it's funny, charming, and lighthearted, that may be the basic appeal of *I Love You, Man.* Sydney represents the freedoms most men hesitate to give themselves, maybe through fear of ending up alone, arrested, or locked inside behavior that looks fun when you're young but crazy when you're older. The great thing about Sydney is that he lives your fantasies so you don't have to yourself.

Peter needs a Sydney (Jason Segel) in his life. He has been told this by Zooey (Rashida Jones), the girl he plans to marry. She would, however, have preferred a less extreme case than *this* Sydney. Peter (Paul Rudd) is a Realtor who is hopelessly, even touchingly, clueless when it comes to seeming the least bit cool. One of those really nice guys who, when the chips are down, has no idea where to look, what to say, how to move, or how to extricate himself gracefully from an impossible situation. He gets along great with women but has no male best friend, and actually needs to find one to be best man at his wedding.

Because this is a romcom, various obligatory scenes are necessary; Peter goes shopping for a best friend on some man-dates with guys met on the Internet, with predictable results. The movie feels locked into formula until the appearance of Sydney, met while scarfing free food at Peter's open house for the home of Lou Ferrigno. Jason Segel brings sunshine into the movie; we like his character even more quickly than Peter does.

Sydney lives in a little frame cottage a block up the street from the Venice Beach boardwalk. This house was cheap in, oh, say, the Depression. Now it only looks cheap. We never see its interior; Sydney escorts Peter directly to his "man cave," a converted garage in the backyard where he keeps all his toys: drum set, guitars, music system, flat-screen TV, movie posters, lava lamps, weird souvenirs, recliner chairs, wet bar, fridge, wall hangings, even an area dedicated to . . . well, never mind.

Jason Segel plays Sydney as a man thoroughly comfortable within his own skin, an unapologetic hedonist who uses his intelligence as a comic weapon. Essentially, the whole movie is based on the fact that he is able to create an actually plausible, human best friend. Incredibly, this is the first time I'm aware of seeing him in a movie. I apparently saw him in *SLC Punk!* and *Slackers* (zero stars), but never saw his recent *Forgetting Sarah Marshall*. I think he's a natural for Walter Matthau, and both Segel and Rudd would be perfect for a SoCal retread of the classic British one-upmanship comedy *School for Scoundrels.*

Rudd is also very good and very funny, using delicate timing to create a man who is never quite right for the room. Observe his attempts to look loose and casual. He even pulls off sincere scenes with the lovely Rashida Jones, and sincerity, as we know, is the downfall of many a romcom and almost all buddy movies. I believe my Little Movie Glossary even contains an entry about an obligatory moment in all buddy movies in which one of the characters says, you guessed it, "I love you, man."

John Hamburg, who cowrote and directed, populates his film with many other gifted comedy actors, including J. K. Simmons as Peter's father, Jane Curtin as his mother, Andy Samberg as his gay brother, and Jon Favreau and Jaime Pressly as a married couple from hell—their own. Lou Ferrigno finds the right note as the client about to fire his Realtor, who has asked himself the question, "How many people want to buy a mansion in Beverly Hills with a statue of the Incredible Hulk in the garden?"

I Love You, Man is above all just plain funny. It's funny with some dumb physical humor, yes, and some gross-out jokes apparently necessary to all buddy movies, but also funny in observations, dialogue, physical behavior, and Sydney Fife's observations as a people watcher. I heard a lot of *real* laughter from a preview audience, not the perfunctory laughter at manufactured payoffs. You feel good watching the movie. That's what comedies are for, right? Right?

The Imaginarium of Doctor Parnassus ★★★
PG-13, 122 m., 2010

Heath Ledger (Tony), Johnny Depp (Imaginarium Tony 1), Jude Law (Imaginarium Tony 2), Colin Farrell (Imaginarium Tony 3), Christopher Plummer (Dr. Parnassus), Andrew Garfield (Anton), Verne Troyer (Percy), Lily Cole (Valentina), Tom Waits (Mr. Nick). Directed by Terry Gilliam and produced by Amy Gilliam, Terry Gilliam, Samuel Hadida, and William Vince. Screenplay by Terry Gilliam and Charles McKeown.

The traditional motto at Second City is Something Wonderful Right Away, and maybe Terry Gilliam has the words displayed on his mirror when he shaves every morning. He has never faltered. *The Imaginarium of Doctor Parnassus* could be seen as a sideshow version of his own life, with him playing the role of the pitchman who lures you into his fantasies. That they may seem extravagant and overheated, all smoke and mirrors, is, after all, in the nature of a pitchman's fantasies.

The story in Gilliam's fevered new film is all over the map as usual, but this time there's a reason for it. His wild inventions in character, costumes, and CGI effects are accounted for by a plot that requires revolving worlds. Elements of this plot were made necessary by the tragic death of Heath Ledger halfway into the shooting, but the plot itself, I think, was in place from the first.

It involves a bizarre, threadbare traveling show that unfolds out of a rickety old wagon in rundown pockets of London occupied mostly by drunks and grotesques. The show consists of the (very, very) old Dr. Parnassus (Christopher Plummer) perching ominously on a stool while his barker, Anton (Andrew Garfield), his daughter, Valentina (Lily Cole), and his angry dwarf, Percy (Verne Troyer), try to perform for an unruly handful of lager louts.

Percy and Anton save the life of a man hanging from a bridge. Why only they can perform this task is wisely not explained. The man on the rope is Tony (Heath Ledger). I know. He joins the show, is appalled by its archaic form, and suggests updates. The reason it's creaky is that Dr. Parnassus is many centuries old, having made a pact with Satan (Tom Waits, as usual) to live forever on condition that Satan can possess his daughter when she turns sixteen. You have to admit, Dr. Parnassus didn't rush into reproduction. Of course, he wants out of the deal. Satan frequently runs into credit payment risks.

Tony, it develops, can enter/evoke/control/create strange worlds on the other side of a looking glass on the shabby stage. In these worlds anything goes, which is always to Gilliam's liking. CGI allows the director and his designers to run riot, which they do at a gallop, and some wondrous visions materialize.

I believe Ledger was intended to be the guide through all of these. But Gilliam apparently completed filming all the outer-world London scenes, Ledger returned to New York for R&R, and the rest is sad history. Gilliam replaced him by casting Johnny Depp, Jude Law, and Colin Farrell as the Tonys of Imaginariums 1 through 3 and offering no other explanation, as indeed with Imaginariums he isn't required to do. Depp looks the most like Ledger, but it's a melancholy fact that Farrell steals the role.

My problem with Terry Gilliam's pictures is that they lack a discernible story line. I don't require A-B-C, Act 1–2–3, but I do rather appreciate having some notion of a film's own rules. Gilliam indeed practices Something Wonderful Right Away, and you get the notion that if a bright idea pops into his head, he feels free to write it into his screenplay under the Cole Porter Rule (Anything Goes). Knowing my history with Gilliam, whom I always want to like more than I do, I attended the Cannes screening of *Dr. Parnassus* in order to be baffled, which I was, and then the Chicago press screening, where I had an idea what was coming and tried to reopen my mind. Gilliam is, you understand, a nice man, and has never committed the sin of failing to amaze.

Now what I see are a group of experienced actors gamely trying to keep their heads while all about are losing theirs. Can it be easy to play one-third of a guide to one-third of an arbitrary world? You just have to plunge in. Ledger himself, who makes Tony relatively grounded in the "real" world, must have been prepared to do the same, and would have lent the story more continuity. Still, this movie is an Imaginarium indeed. The best approach is to sit there and let it happen to you: See it in the moment and not with long-term memory, which seems to be what Dr. Parnassus does. It keeps his mind off Satan's plans for his daughter.

Imagine That ★ ★ ½
PG, 107 m., 2009

Eddie Murphy (Evan Danielson), Thomas Haden Church (Johnny Whitefeather), Yara Shahidi (Olivia Danielson), Nicole Ari Parker (Trish), Ronny Cox (Tom Stevens), Martin Sheen (Dante D'Enzo), DeRay Davis (John Strother). Directed by Karey Kirkpatrick and produced by Ed Solomon and Lorenzo di Bonaventura. Screenplay by Solomon and Chris Matheson.

Eddie Murphy's new family comedy is a pleasant and unassuming fantasy in which a high-powered investment adviser gets advice from his daughter's imaginary friends. We never see the friends, but we see a great deal of the daughter, and it's a charming performance from newcomer Yara Shahidi.

She plays Olivia, seven years old, who doesn't see nearly enough of her daddy. He is Evan Danielson (Murphy), who is competing for a big promotion at his Denver investment firm. Olivia is being raised by his former wife, Trish (Nicole Ari Parker), who insists it is time for the child to spend some quality time with her father.

Evan is not well equipped to handle this, or much of anything else apart from his job. He can't find babysitters, takes the kid to the office, and to his horror discovers she has drawn with water paints all over his notes and charts for a crucial meeting. It does not go well. He's upstaged by Johnny Whitefeather (Thomas Haden Church), a Native American who evokes the great spirits and Indian legends to convince the clients the force is with him.

In response, Murphy does one of his semi-comic riffs, desperately improvising advice from the stories Olivia told him about her drawings. He returns to his office expecting to be fired but amazingly the advice turns out to be solid gold. But how did he do that? What did Olivia know? She knew what a fairy princess told her, and she can see her imaginary world when she has her precious blue blankie over her head. Evan doesn't know what else to do, so he starts turning to Olivia for more investment tips, and she's right again and again.

The movie is amusing without ever being break-out funny—except for one scene, loudly appreciated by the kiddies in the audience, when he makes pancakes and Olivia insists he eat them covered with gobs of ketchup, mustard, chocolate sauce, and hot sauce. Kids may not get all the verbal jokes, but playing with food, they understand.

Murphy stays interestingly in character, not going over the top. He does his usual rapid-fire dialogue and desperate invention, but

more sanely than usual. The film is really about the father-daughter relationship, and Murphy comes through as sincere, confused, lonely, and with a good heart.

The key to the chemistry between them is Yara Shahidi's work as the daughter. Apparently she really is seven, and her previous experience is limited to three episodes of *In the Motherhood*. She's a natural. I never caught her trying to be "cute." She played every scene straight and with confidence, and she's filled with personality. I've been noticing recently how good the child actors are in movies. Maybe they grow up inputting acting from TV. I wonder why not all young actors can bring this gift with them into adulthood. To paraphrase e.e. cummings: And down they forgot as up they grew.

The third major role, by Thomas Haden Church, is an interesting invention: an Indian con man, trading on his background to score points in the boardroom, steamrollering the clients with his people's lore. This is funny. Is it offensive? Not when we find out more about Johnny Whitefeather.

So all of these elements are present in the film and supply nice moments, but director Karey Kirkpatrick, the writer of animated films such as *Chicken Run* and *Over the Hedge*, never brings them to takeoff velocity. They rest on the screen, pleasant, amusing, but too predictable for grown-ups and not broad enough for children. I couldn't believe *Imagine That* counts on one of the most exhausted clichés in the movies, the parent making a dramatic late entrance to a child's big concert.

Still, think about this: If the investment gurus of Wall Street had turned to their kids for advice, we might not be in such a mess.

IMAX: Hubble 3-D ★★★
G, 45 m., 2010

Leonardo DiCaprio (Narrator). Featuring the astronauts Scott D. Altman, Andrew J. Feustel, Michael T. Good, John M. Grunsfeld, Gregory C. Johnson, Michael J. Massimino, and K. Megan McArthur. Directed, written, and produced by Toni Myers.

When I think of space travel, I get a sort of mental tingle. It intrigues and frightens me. I have nightmares, possibly illustrated by *2001*, in which the astronaut Poole has his tether clipped by HAL 9000 and goes tumbling away into the immensity. Mercifully, his oxygen tube has been cut, so he will quickly be dead. I remember, too, a science fiction story that curdled my blood about an astronaut who is lost in space *with* a full tank of oxygen, and drifts into the void, his vision field filled with the universe.

Then you would know how small you were, how powerless and insignificant. When the end comes, it would be good to be set adrift into space, I think, with time for reflection, or perhaps madness. Fatal, yes, but so much less boring than the ceiling of a hospital room. I have always been intensely interested in thoughts of space.

IMAX: Hubble 3-D offers two categories of images, both awesome. One involves footage filmed on board the space shuttle Atlantis on a mission to repair the Hubble Space Telescope one last time. The other involves a 3-D rendering of some of Hubble's photographs of the cosmos. It's remarkable how casual the astronauts are, joking and performing for the camera. Then we see space walks in which they drift weightless to replace, adjust, and tune up Hubble. There is nothing there but the shuttle, Hubble, Earth, and the abyss. If they lose a tool, it is lost . . . forever, or until it is found millions and millions of years from now in a galaxy far away.

The fact that this footage exists at all is enough to justify it. Someone like me would need to see it. I would be happier if the astronauts had been less confident and casual. I suppose that's the astronaut culture. Could they have acted? Pretended to be tense, scared, deadly serious? They're like the crew on the *Star Trek* command deck, which most of the time might as well be controlling the traffic grid of a subway system.

The important thing to understand about the 3-D photography of stars is that they are too far away to give any true idea of their distance. Almost all of the objects in the universe are very, very far apart. What they did was take Hubble photographs of small and old (therefore young) slices of the sky and use spectrum analysis and a computer to separate the stars according to their distance. Although the nar-

ration by Leonardo DiCaprio doesn't mention this, the third dimension we're regarding is really time, not space. As the viewpoint moves forward toward galaxies, we are hurtling at unimaginable speed toward light that originated longer and longer ago.

Beyond the most distant stars, at the end of our ability to see, there is black nothingness. If you stood there and looked outward, what would you see? A logical question. The answer is: more universe. Not another universe, but this one, because space is curved, you see, and therefore has no edge. This answer satisfies me, although I do not understand it and cannot picture how space can be curved. I understand how a circle has no beginning and no end, and that helps.

So these are thoughts I had while watching *IMAX: Hubble 3-D*. A movie like this can get you thinking.

In Bruges ★ ★ ★ ★
R, 107 m., 2008

Colin Farrell (Ray), Brendan Gleeson (Ken), Ralph Fiennes (Harry), Clemence Poesy (Chloe), Jeremie Renier (Erik), Thekla Reuten (Marie), Jordan Prentice (Jimmy). Directed by Martin McDonagh and produced by Graham Broadbent and Pete Czernin. Screenplay by McDonagh.

You may know that Bruges, Belgium, is pronounced *broozh*, but I didn't, and the heroes of *In Bruges* certainly don't. They're Dublin hit men, sent there by their boss for two weeks after a hit goes very wrong. One is a young hothead who sees no reason to be anywhere but Dublin; the other, older, gentler, more curious, buys a guide book and announces: "Bruges is the best-preserved medieval city in Belgium!"

So it certainly seems. If the movie accomplished nothing else, it inspired in me an urgent desire to visit Bruges. But it accomplished a lot more than that. This film debut by the theater writer and director Martin McDonagh is an endlessly surprising, very dark human comedy, with a plot that cannot be foreseen but only relished. Every once in a while you find a film like this that seems to happen as it goes along, driven by the peculiarities of the characters.

Brendan Gleeson, with that noble shambles of a face and the heft of a boxer gone to seed, has the key role as Ken, one of two killers for hire. His traveling companion and unwilling roommate is Ray (Colin Farrell), who successfully whacked a priest in a Dublin confessional but tragically killed a little boy in the process. Before shooting the priest, he confessed to the sin he was about to commit. After accidentally killing the boy, he reads the notes the lad made for his own confession. You don't know whether to laugh or cry.

Ken and Ray work for Harry, apparently a Dublin crime lord, who for the first two-thirds of the movie we hear only over the phone, until he materializes in Bruges and turns out to be a worried-looking Ralph Fiennes. He had the men hiding out in London, but that wasn't far enough away. Who would look for them in Bruges? Who would even look for Bruges? Killing the priest was business, but "blowing a kid's head off just isn't done."

The movie does an interesting thing with Bruges. It shows us a breathtakingly beautiful city without ever seeming to be a travelogue. It uses the city as a way to develop the characters. When Ken wants to climb an old tower "for the view," Ray argues, "Why do I have to climb up there to see down here? I'm already down here." He is likewise unimpressed by glorious paintings, macabre sculptures, and picturesque canals, but is thrilled as a kid when he comes upon a film being shot.

There he meets two fascinating characters: First he sees the fetching young blonde Chloe (Clemence Poesy, who was Fleur Delacour in *Harry Potter and the Goblet of Fire*). Then he sees Jimmy (Jordan Prentice), a dwarf who figures in a dream sequence. He gets off on a bad footing with both, but eventually they're doing cocaine with a prostitute Jimmy picked up and have become friends, even though Ray keeps calling the dwarf a "midget" and having to be corrected.

Without dreaming of telling you what happens next, I will say it is not only ingenious but almost inevitable the way the screenplay brings all of these destinies together at one place and time. Along the way, there are times of great sadness and poignancy, times of abandon, times of goofiness, and that kind of humor that is *really funny* because it grows

out of character and close observation. Colin Farrell in particular hasn't been this good in a few films, perhaps because this time he's allowed to relax and be Irish. As for Brendan Gleeson, if you remember him in *The General*, you know that nobody can play a more sympathetic bad guy.

Martin McDonagh is greatly respected in Ireland and England for his plays; his first film, a short named *Six Shooter* starring Gleeson, won a 2006 Oscar. In his feature debut, he has made a remarkable first film, as impressive in its own way as *House of Games*, the first film by David Mamet, whom McDonagh is sometimes compared with. Yes, it's a "thriller," but one where the ending seems determined by character and upbringing rather than plot requirements. Two of the final deaths are, in fact, ethical choices. And the irony inspiring the second one has an undeniable logic, showing that even professional murderers have their feelings.

The Incredible Hulk ★ ★ ½
PG-13, 114 m., 2008

Edward Norton (Bruce Banner), Liv Tyler (Betty Ross), Tim Roth (Emil Blonsky), Tim Blake Nelson (Samuel Sterns), Ty Burrell (Dr. Samson), William Hurt (General Ross), Lou Ferrigno (Voice of Hulk). Directed by Louis Leterrier and produced by Avi Arad, Kevin Feige, and Gale Anne Hurd. Screenplay by Zak Penn and Edward Norton, based on the Marvel comic books by Stan Lee and Jack Kirby.

The Incredible Hulk is no doubt an ideal version of the Hulk saga for those who found Ang Lee's *Hulk* (2003) too talky or, dare I say, too thoughtful. But not for me. It sidesteps the intriguing aspects of Hulkdom and spends way too much time in, dare I say, noisy and mindless action sequences. By the time the Incredible Hulk had completed his hulk-on-hulk showdown with the Incredible Blonsky, I had been using my Timex with the illuminated dial way too often.

Consider the dilemma of creating a story about the Hulk, who is one of the lesser creatures in the Marvel Comics stable. You're dealing with two different characters: mild-mannered scientist Dr. Bruce Banner and the rampaging, destructive Hulk, who goes into frenzies of aggression whenever he's annoyed, which is frequently, because the army is usually unloading automatic weapons into him. There is even the interesting question of whether Dr. Banner is really conscious inside the Hulk. In the Ang Lee version, he was, more or less, and confessed to Betty Ross: "When it happens, when it comes over me, when I totally lose control . . . I like it." In this 2008 version by Louis Leterrier, the best Banner can come up with is that being the Hulk is like a hyperthyroid acid trip, and all he can remember are fragments of moments.

It's obvious that the real story is the tragedy that Bruce Banner faces because of the Hulk-inducing substance in his blood. If Banner never turned into the Hulk, nobody would ever make a movie about him. And if the Hulk were never Banner, he would be like Godzilla, who tears things up real good but is otherwise, dare I say, one-dimensional.

The Ang Lee version was rather brilliant in the way it turned the Hulk story into matching sets of parent-child conflicts: Betty Ross (Jennifer Connelly) was appalled by her father the general (Sam Elliott), and Bruce Banner (Eric Bana) suffered at the hands of his father, a scientist who originally created the Hulk genes and passed them along to his child. (Nick Nolte had nice scenes as the elder Dr. Banner.)

In the new version, Betty (Liv Tyler) still has big problems with her father the general (William Hurt); she's appalled by his plans to harness the Hulk formula and create a race of super-soldiers. In both films, Banner (Ed Norton) and Ross are in love but don't act on it because the Hulk business complicates things way too much, although I admit there's a clever moment in *Hulk* 2008 when Bruce interrupts his big chance to make love with Betty because when he gets too excited, he turns into the Hulk, and Betty is a brave girl but not that good of a sport.

Consider for a moment General Ross's idea of turning out Hulk soldiers. They would be a drill sergeant's worst nightmare. When they weren't Hulks, why bother to train them? You'd only be using them in the fullness of their Hulkdom, and *then* how would you train them? Would you just drop thousands of Ed

Nortons into enemy territory and count on them getting so excited by free fall that they became Hulks? (This transformation actually happens to Banner in *Hulk* 2008, by the way.)

So. What's to like in *The Incredible Hulk*? We have a sound performance by Ed Norton as a man who desperately does not want to become the Hulk and goes to Brazil to study under a master of breath control in order to curb his anger. And we have Liv Tyler in full, trembling sympathy mode. Banner's Brazilian sojourn begins with an astonishing shot: From an aerial viewpoint, we fly higher and higher above one of the hill cities of Rio, seeing hundreds, thousands, of tiny houses built on top of one another, all clawing for air. This is the *City of God* neighborhood, and as nearly as I could tell, we were looking at the real thing, not CGI. The director lets the shot run on longer than any reasonable requirement of the plot; my bet is, he was as astonished as I was, and let it run because it was so damned amazing.

The scenes involving Banner in Brazil are well conceived, although when he accidentally contaminates a bottled soft drink with his blood, the movie doesn't really deal with the consequences when the drink is consumed in the United States. The contamination provides General Ross with his clue to Banner's whereabouts, and army troops blast the hell out of the City of God; all through the movie, the general deploys his firepower so recklessly that you wonder if he has a superior, and if he ever has to account for the dozens, hundreds, thousands, who die while his guys are blasting at the Hulk with absolutely no effect.

Enter Emil Blonsky (Tim Roth), a marine General Ross recruits because he's meaner and deadlier than anyone else. Blonsky leads the chase in Rio. Later, Banner's research associate Dr. Samuel Sterns (Tim Blake Nelson) is forced to inject Blonsky with a little Hulkie juice, setting up a titanic rooftop battle in Harlem between Hulk and Blonsky. And this battle, as I have suggested, pounds away relentlessly, taking as its first victim our patience. *Iron Man*, the much better spiritual partner of this film, also ended with a showdown between an original and a copycat, but it involved two opponents who knew who they were and why they were fighting. When you get down to it, as a fictional creature, the

265

Incredible Hulk is as limited as a bad drunk. He may be fun to be around when he's sober, but when he drinks too much, you just feel sorry for the guy.

Indiana Jones and the Kingdom of the Crystal Skull ★ ★ ★ ½
PG-13, 124 m., 2008

Harrison Ford (Indiana Jones), Cate Blanchett (Irina Spalko), Karen Allen (Marion Ravenwood), Ray Winstone (George "Mac" McHale), John Hurt (Professor Oxley), Jim Broadbent (Dean Stanforth), Shia LaBeouf (Mutt Williams). Directed by Steven Spielberg and produced by Frank Marshall. Screenplay by David Koepp.

Indiana Jones and the Kingdom of the Crystal Skull. Say it aloud. The very title causes the pulse to quicken, if you, like me, are a lover of pulp fiction. What I want is goofy action—lots of it. I want man-eating ants, swordfights between two people balanced on the backs of speeding jeeps, subterranean caverns of gold, vicious femme fatales, plunges down three waterfalls in a row, and the explanation for flying saucers. And throw in lots of monkeys.

The Indiana Jones movies were directed by Steven Spielberg and written by George Lucas and a small army of screenwriters, but they exist in a universe of their own. Hell, they created it. All you can do is compare one to the other three. And even then, what will it get you? If you eat four pounds of sausage, how do you choose which pound tasted the best? Well, the first one, of course, and then there's a steady drop-off of interest. That's why no Indy adventure can match *Raiders of the Lost Ark* (1981). But if *Crystal Skull* (or *Temple of Doom* from 1984 or *Last Crusade* from 1989) had come first in the series, who knows how much fresher it might have seemed? True, *Raiders of the Lost Ark* stands alone as an action masterpiece, but after that the series is *compelled* to be, in the words of Indiana himself, "same old same old." Yes, but that's what I *want* it to be.

Crystal Skull even dusts off the Russians, so severely underexploited in recent years, as the bad guys. Up against them, Indiana Jones is once again played by Harrison Ford, who is now sixty-five but looks a lot like he did at fifty-five or forty-six, which is how old he was when he made *Last Crusade.* He has one of those Robert Mitchum faces that don't age; it only frowns more. He and his sidekick, Mac McHale (Ray Winstone), are taken by the cool, contemptuous Soviet uber-villainess Irina Spalko (Cate Blanchett) to a cavernous warehouse to seek out a crate he saw there years ago. The contents of the crate are hyper-magnetic (lord, I love this stuff) and betray themselves when Indy throws a handful of gunpowder into the air.

In ways too labyrinthine to describe, the crate leads Indy, Mac, Irina, and the Russians far up the Amazon. Along the way they've gathered Marion Ravenwood (Karen Allen), Indy's girlfriend from the first film, and a young biker named Mutt Williams (Shia LaBeouf), who is always combing his ducktail haircut. They also acquire Professor Oxley (John Hurt), elderly colleague from the University of Chicago, whose function is to read all the necessary languages, know all the necessary background, and explain everything.

What happens in South America is explained by the need to create (1) sensational chase sequences and (2) awe-inspiring spectacles. We get such sights as two dueling jeep-like vehicles racing down parallel roads. Not many of the audience members will be as logical as I am and wonder who went to the trouble of building *parallel* roads in a rain forest. Most of the major characters eventually find themselves at the wheels of both vehicles; they leap or are thrown from one to another, and the vehicles occasionally leap right over each other. And that Irina, she's something. Her Russian backups are mostly just atmosphere, useful for pointing their rifles at Indy, but she can fight, shoot, fence, drive, leap, and kick, and keep on all night.

All leads to the discovery of a subterranean chamber beneath an ancient pyramid, where they find an ancient city made of gold and containing . . . but wait, I forgot to tell you they found a crystal skull in a crypt. Well, sir, it's one of thirteen crystal skulls, and the other twelve are in that chamber. When the set is complete, amazing events take place. Professor Oxley carries the thirteenth skull for most of the time, and finds it repels man-eating ants. It also represents one-thirteenth of all knowledge about everything, leading Irina to utter the orgasmic words, "I want to *know*!" In appearance, the skull is a cross between the aliens of the special edition of Spielberg's *Close Encounters of the Third Kind* and the hood ornaments of 1950s Pontiacs.

What is the function of the chamber? "It's a portal—to another dimension!" Oxley says. Indy is sensible: "I don't think we wanna go that way." It is astonishing that the protagonists aren't all killed twenty or thirty times, although Irina will become The Woman Who Knew Too Much. At his advanced age, Professor Oxley tirelessly jumps between vehicles, survives fire and flood and falling from great heights, and would win on *American Gladiators*. Relationships between certain other characters are of interest, since (a) the odds against them finding themselves together are astronomical, and (b) the odds against them *not* finding themselves together in this film are incalculable.

Now what else can I tell you, apart from mentioning the blinking red digital countdown, and the moving red line tracing a journey on a map? I can say that if you liked the other Indiana Jones movies, you will like this one, and that if you did not, there is no talking to you. And I can also say that a critic trying to place it in a hierarchy with the others would probably keep a straight face while recommending the second pound of sausage.

The Informant! ★★★★
R, 108 m., 2009

Matt Damon (Mark Whitacre), Scott Bakula (Brian Shepard), Joel McHale (Robert Herndon), Melanie Lynskey (Ginger Whitacre), Patton Oswalt (Ed Herbst), Allan Havey (Dean Paisley), Tom Papa (Mick Andreas). Directed by Steven Soderbergh and produced by Gregory Jacobs, Jennifer Fox, Michael Jaffe, Howard Braunstein, and Kurt Eichenwald. Screenplay by Scott Z. Burns, based on the book by Eichenwald.

Mark Whitacre was the highest-ranking executive in U.S. history to blow the whistle in a case of corporate fraud. He ended up with a prison sentence three times longer than any of the criminal executives he exposed. To be sure, there was the detail of the $9 million he embezzled along the way for his personal use. What we discover toward the end of *The Informant!* may help explain that theft, although he apparently didn't want that used in his defense.

Whitacre, persuasively played by Matt Damon in Steven Soderbergh's new thriller, was a top vice president of Archer Daniels Midland in Decatur, Illinois, one of the fifty largest corporations in America. Sprawling at the edge of the small central Illinois city, it is surrounded by miles of soybean fields, and if you buy Japanese tofu at Whole Foods, it probably passed through ADM on its way to Japan. It's also involved in several other crops, produces sweeteners, sells ethanol.

Whitacre knew that ADM and its competitors were engaged in global price fixing that cost consumers billions. This largesse was passed on invisibly to executives and stockholders, yet created a surprisingly small footprint in central Illinois. Yes, executives lived in very nice houses (Soderbergh shot in Whitacre's mansion in tiny Moweaqua, Illinois), but they were low profile compared to Manhattan high rollers, and ate at the local restaurants just like ordinary folks.

Whitacre is put under pressure to discover the source of contamination, possibly industrial sabotage, in one of ADM's operations. He engages in unofficial conversations with key competitors overseas and thinks he may be onto something. Then FBI agents swoop down as part of an espionage probe. He clears himself, but as the agents (Scott Bakula and Joel McHale) are leaving, he calls after them.

He has something he wants to say. They're blindsided. He tells them ADM has been fixing prices for years, that he has been involved, that he has the details and wants to clear his conscience. His wife, Ginger (Melanie Lynskey), helped him arrive at the decision to do the right thing.

The FBI recruits him as an informant, taps phones, teaches him to wear a wire, and even videotapes price-fixing meetings, building an airtight case. Eventually three officials, including vice chairman Michael Andreas, son of the founder, were found guilty; the company was fined $100 million and paid another $400 million in a class action lawsuit.

If only it were that simple, *The Informant!* might have been a corporate thriller like Michael Mann's *The Insider* (1999), with Russell Crowe as a whistle-blower in the tobacco industry. But during the investigation Mark Whitacre reveals himself as a man of bewildering contradictions. Who would think to attempt an embezzlement and phony check-cashing scheme while literally working under the noses and at the side of FBI accountants? What was the full story of the industrial espionage he halted? Did he really expect that by exposing those above him, it would clear the way for him, one of the key price fixers, to take command of the company?

What did Whitacre think about *anything?* Not even his wife was sure. All is explained, sort of, in *The Informant!* and as Soderbergh lovingly peels away veil after veil of deception, the film develops into an unexpected human comedy. Not that any of the characters are laughing.

The film is fascinating in the way it reveals two levels of events, not always visible to each other or to the audience. A second viewing would be rewarding, knowing what we find out. Matt Damon's performance is deceptively bland. He comes from a world of true-blue downstate people, without affectations, surrounded by some of the richest farmland in the world. Whitacre's determination to wear the wire leads to situations where discovery seems inevitable, but he's seemingly so feckless that suspicion seems misplaced. What he's up to is in some ways so very simple. Even if it has the FBI guys banging their heads against the wall.

Mark Whitacre, PhD, released a little early after FBI agents called him "an American hero," is now an executive in a high-tech start-up in California and is still married to Ginger. Looking back on his adventure, he recently told his hometown paper, the *Decatur Herald and Review*: "It's like I was two people. I assume that's why they chose Matt Damon for the movie because he plays those roles that have such psychological intensity. In the *Bourne* movies, he doesn't even know who he is." ☞

The Informers ★ ★ ½
R, 98 m., 2009

Billy Bob Thornton (William Sloan), Kim Basinger (Laura Sloan), Winona Ryder (Cheryl Moore), Mickey Rourke (Peter), Jon Foster (Graham Sloan), Amber Heard (Christie), Austin Nichols (Martin), Lou Taylor Pucci (Tim Price), Brad Renfro (Jack), Chris Isaak (Les Price), Mel Raido (Bryan Metro), Rhys Ifans (Roger). Directed by Gregor Jordan and produced by Marco Weber. Screenplay by Bret Easton Ellis and Nicholas Jarecki, from the novel by Ellis.

The Informers is about dread, despair, and doom, and its characters are almost all about to be hit with more reasons for dread and despair, and a shared doom. It takes place in the Los Angeles showbiz drug subculture circa 1983, when AIDS didn't have a name and cocaine looked like the answer to something. It demonstrates the eerie ways that music and movies connect people from vastly different lives in a subterranean way where desire is the common currency.

What do they desire? Drugs, sex, power, wealth, and fame or its proximity. These things have made their lives hollow daily punishments, treatable only by oblivion. One character, in a moment of desperate need, says, "All I want is someone to tell me what is good, and someone to tell me what is bad." Hemingway told him, if he had been listening: "What is moral is what you feel good after, and what is immoral is what you feel bad after."

As nearly as I can recall, none of the characters ever feels happy. They're all pitiful, some are evil, the rest are helpless. There may be a few who are bystanders, like the anchorwoman, but even she's guilty of sleeping with a married studio chief primarily because of who he is. Almost everyone in this film is connected by sexual partners, sometimes in ways they never suspect.

The film, based on work by Bret Easton Ellis, takes place in his usual world of hedonistic excess. It tells many interweaving stories and is skillfully cast with actors who embody precisely what their roles call for. What common needs can link characters played by Billy Bob Thornton, Kim Basinger, Mickey Rourke, Winona Ryder, Lou Taylor Pucci, Amber Heard, Chris Isaak, Jon Foster, Brad Renfro, and Rhys Ifans? See paragraph two.

The scenes cycle through parties, famous restaurants, studio offices, TV news sets, Mulholland Drive, beaches, and beds. A lot of beds, often populated by bisexual three-somes. Thornton is the studio head, Basinger is his pill-popping wife, Ryder is the newswoman. Basinger uses a male prostitute who is one of the threesomes. Thornton's children despise him.

There is a wasted rock singer in the film (Mel Raido) who thinks he might once have lived in L.A. He vaguely realizes at times where he is and what he is doing. A father (Isaak) who takes his son to Hawaii, suspects the kid might be gay, approves when he invites a girl to dinner, then tries to pick her up. A wasted night clerk (Brad Renfro) who hopes to be an actor ends up being victimized by his loathsome uncle (Rourke) into possibly (not certainly) committing a monstrous act. A young girl (Heard) who sleeps with anyone, more or less out of indifference.

There is no hope in this world. No frogs falling from the sky. I have met a few people like this and imagine they tend to meet one another. Their humanity has been burnt right out. Bret Easton Ellis is sometimes described as the poet of beautiful blond people whose lives are devoted to making themselves and others miserable. True enough. The most intimate, and startling, scene between Thornton and Basinger involves him requesting something disgusting (not sexual) and her providing it, while they're both preoccupied with whether they can ever live together again, or even want to. The fact that this service she provides takes place without discussion suggests the numbness of their souls.

If *The Informers* doesn't sound to you like a pleasant time at the movies, you are right. To repeat: dread, despair, and doom. It is often, however, repulsively fascinating, and has been directed by Gregor Jordan as a soap opera from hell, with good sets and costumes. If he finds no depths in the characters, well, what depths are there? What you see is what you get. Sometimes less than that. Some viewers of *The Informers* criticize it for lacking a third act, but these lives are all two-act plays.

Note: Brad Renfro, who once played Huck Finn, died of a heroin overdose on January 15, 2008. He was twenty-five. He is actually very good here, in a role he possibly never dreamed of playing.

Inglourious Basterds ★★★★

R, 152 m., 2009

Brad Pitt (Lieutenant Aldo Raine), Christoph Waltz (Colonel Hans Landa), Michael Fassbender (Lieutenant Archie Hicox), Eli Roth (Sergeant Donny Donowitz), Diane Kruger (Bridget von Hammersmark), Daniel Bruhl (Frederick Zoller), Til Schweiger (Sergeant Hugo Stiglitz), Melanie Laurent (Shosanna Dreyfus), B. J. Novak (Private First Class Smithson Utivich), Samm Levine (Private First Class Hirschberg). Directed by Quentin Tarantino and produced by Lawrence Bender. Screenplay by Tarantino.

Quentin Tarantino's *Inglourious Basterds* is a big, bold, audacious war movie that will annoy some, startle others, and demonstrate once again that he's the real thing, a director of quixotic delights. For starters (and at this late stage after the May 2009 premiere at Cannes, I don't believe I'm spoiling anything), he provides World War II with a much-needed alternative ending. For once the bastards get what's coming to them.

From the title, ripped off a 1978 B-movie, to the Western sound of the Ennio Morricone opening music to the key location, a movie theater, the film embeds Tarantino's love of the movies. The deep, rich colors of 35 mm film provide tactile pleasure. A character at the beginning and end, not seen in between, brings the story full circle. The "Basterds" themselves, savage fighters dropped behind Nazi lines, are an unmistakable nod to the Dirty Dozen.

And above all there are three iconic characters, drawn broadly and with love: the Hero, the Nazi, and the Girl. These three, played by Brad Pitt, Christoph Waltz, and Melanie Laurent, are seen with that Tarantino knack of taking a character and making it a Character, definitive, larger than life, approaching satire in its intensity but not—quite—going that far. Let's say they feel bigger than most of the people we meet in movies.

The story begins in Nazi-occupied France, early in the war, when the cruel, droll Nazi Hans Landa (Christoph Waltz) arrives at an isolated dairy farm where he believes the farmer (Denis Menochet) is hiding Jews. He's right, and a young woman named Shosanna (Melanie Laurent) flees into the woods. It is for this scene, and his performance throughout the movie, that Christoph Waltz deserves an Oscar nomination to go with his Best Actor award from Cannes. He creates a character unlike any Nazi—indeed, anyone at all—I've seen in a movie: evil, sardonic, ironic, mannered, absurd.

The Hero is Brad Pitt, as Lieutenant Aldo Raine, leader of the Basterds. Tarantino probably wants us to hear "Aldo Ray," star of countless war films and B pictures. Raine is played by Pitt as a broad caricature of a hard-talking Southern boy who wants each of his men to bring him one hundred Nazi scalps. For years his band improbably survives in France and massacres Nazis, and can turn out in formal evening wear at a moment's notice. Pitt's version of Italian is worthy of a Marx brother.

The Girl is Shosanna, played by Laurent as a curvy siren with red lipstick and, at the end, a slinky red dress. Tarantino photographs her with the absorption of a fetishist, with close-ups of shoes, lips, a facial veil, and details of body and dress. You can't tell me he hasn't seen the work of the Scottish artist Jack Vettriano and his noir paintings of the cigarette-smoking ladies in red. Shosanna calculatingly flirts with Frederick Zoller (Daniel Bruhl), a Nazi war hero and now movie star, who convinces Joseph Goebbels to hold the premiere of his new war film in her theater. This sets up a plot that includes Tarantino breaking several rules in order to provide documentary footage about how flammable nitrate film prints are.

A Tarantino film resists categorization. Inglourious Basterds is no more about war than Pulp Fiction is about—what the hell is it about? Of course nothing in the movie is possible, except that it's so bloody entertaining. His actors don't chew the scenery, but they lick it. He's a master at bringing performances as far as they can go toward iconographic exaggeration.

After I saw Inglourious Basterds at Cannes, although I was writing a daily blog, I resisted giving an immediate opinion about it. I knew Tarantino had made a considerable film, but I wanted it to settle and to see it again. I'm glad I did. Like a lot of real movies, you relish it more the next time. Immediately after Pulp Fiction played at Cannes, QT asked me what I thought. "It's either the best film of the year, or the worst

film," I said. I hardly knew what the hell had happened to me. The answer was: the best film. Tarantino films have a way of growing on you. It's not enough to see them once.   ☞

Inkheart ★ ★
PG, 105 m., 2009

Brendan Fraser (Mo Folchart), Paul Bettany (Dustfinger), Helen Mirren (Elinor Loredan), Jim Broadbent (Fenoglio), Andy Serkis (Capricorn), Eliza Hope Bennett (Meggie), Rafi Gavron (Farid), Sienna Guillory (Resa). Directed by Iain Softley and produced by Softley, Cornelia Funke, and Diana Pokorny. Screenplay by David Lindsay-Abaire, based on the novel by Funke.

I never knew reading was so dangerous. No child seeing Inkheart will ever want to be read to again, especially if that child loves its mother, as so many do. Here is a film about a man named Mo who, when he reads aloud, has the power of liberating fictional characters into the real world. The drawback is that real people are trapped within the same book. Tit for tat. A law of physics must apply.

The film opens with its best scene, for me, anyway: the professional book buyer Mo (Brendan Fraser) and his twelve-year-old daughter, Meggie (Eliza Hope Bennett), poking through an open-air book market. As always I was trying to read the titles on the spines. Not realizing that Inkheart is based on a famous fantasy novel, I had the foolish hope the movie might be about books. No luck. Wait till you hear what it's about.

At the edge of the market is a dark little bookstore presided over by a dark little man. As Mo prowls its aisles, he hears the faint chatter of fictional characters calling to him. (Dictionaries must be almost impossible to shut up.) Sixth sense leads him to discover, on an obscure shelf, the novel Inkheart, in the format of a Penguin mystery from the 1950s. He buys it, slips it into his pocket, and the two of them are followed by a mysterious skulking man.

We discover this is the very book Mo was reading when his wife, Meggie's mother (Sienna Guillory), was sucked into its pages, and that is the true story, Meggie, of how your mom suddenly disappeared when you were little. Yeah, right, Dad. At the same time, various demonic creatures were liberated from the book's pages. They have now set up shop in a mountaintop castle and are conspiring to command Mo's power now that he has discovered their book again. Do they want to return to its pages, or be reunited with old chums in the real world? And how do you get a mortgage to buy a castle when you're a demonic creature and your résumé mentions only fictional adventures in an out-of-print book? The banks must have been lending carelessly there awhile back.

Mo and Meggie take refuge in a cliffside mansion occupied by her great-aunt Elinor (Helen Mirren). Mansion? Looks to me like a dreamy tourist hotel from a Merchant-Ivory production. Elinor is a nasty scold who always wears a turban, the reliable standby of the actress tired of having her hair fussed over every second. I hope good Dame Helen passed this tip along to young Eliza Hope Bennett, who shows every sign of becoming an accomplished actress.

The movie now descends into the realm of your basic good guys vs. wrathful wraiths formula, with pitched battles and skullduggery. The villains are Dustfinger (Paul Bettany) and the ambitious Capricorn (Andy Serkis), and there is always the threat of Mo and Meggie being transmogrified into the pages of the book. There they'd at least have the company of the missing mom and the shabby author Fenoglio (Jim Broadbent), who wrote the novel within *Inkheart*, and apparently was only set free to rise up one level, to the novel containing his novel. Thanks for nothing.

Lots of screams, horrible fates almost happening, close scrapes, cries for help, special effects, monomania, quick thinking, pluck, fear, and scrambling. You know the kinds of stuff. I learn there are two more novels in this series by Cornelia Funke, both of which will remain just as unread by me as the first. It is hard to guess what they will involve, however, because this one closes with a curiously cobbled-together ending that seems to solve everything, possibly as a talisman against a sequel.

In Search of a Midnight Kiss ★ ★ ★ ½
NO MPAA RATING, 100 m., 2008

Scoot McNairy (Wilson), Sara Simmonds (Vivian), Brian Matthew McGuire (Jacob), Katy Luong (Min), Twink Caplan (Wilson's Mom), Nic Harcourt (Radio DJ). Directed by Alex Holdridge and produced by Seth Caplan and Scoot McNairy. Screenplay by Holdridge.

Let's begin with the actors. Sara Simmonds is a pretty girl, and Scoot McNairy is a good-looking guy. But neither one is improbably attractive. In their story, which begins before sunset and ends after sunrise, if you get my drift, they're no Julie Delpy and Ethan Hawke. If they were, they wouldn't be looking for a date on the afternoon of December 31. Simmonds and McNairy look, act, speak, and have thoughts that uncannily resemble life: We believe these could be real people. Yes, Delpy and Hawke are real people, too, but not anyone we'd ever hope to be.

McNairy plays Wilson, who begins New Year's Eve on an unpromising note by masturbating before a Photoshopped computer image of his roommate's girlfriend. He is discovered by the roommate and the girlfriend. Awkward. Min (Katy Luong) claims she's sort of flattered. Jacob (Brian Matthew McGuire) decides Wilson clearly needs a date and suggests a posting on Craigslist. "Misanthrope seeks misanthrope," Wilson bitterly types. He gets a call from Vivian (Simmonds). She is interviewing candidates because she doesn't want to spend the Eve with a loser.

In the sidewalk café where Wilson's audition begins, Vivian comes across as a furiously smoking, aggressive put-down artist. She claims she's seventeen, then accuses Wilson of being a mental statutory rapist, then says she's twenty-seven. Their conversation goes sort of OK after that, and she gives him until 6 p.m. before she calls in another candidate.

At this point we think their date will be very short and blood may be shed. Then begins a long day's journey through the night, choreographed with delicacy, some humor, some pathos by writer-director Alex Holdridge, and photographed in glorious black-and-white by Robert Murphy. Taking the subway, they wander around downtown L.A., including the Sheridan Square area haunted by abandoned and shuttered movie palaces. On the stage of one of them, Vivian, who wants to be an actress, dreams of reopening all the theaters and re-creating a golden age. Wilson, who moved to L.A. three months ago from Texas, had a screenplay, of course, but it was lost when his laptop was stolen.

Black-and-white is the correct medium for this material. Holdridge finds locations that, paradoxically, look just like Los Angeles, but like no part of the city you've ever seen before. A decaying business district is no place to begin a date, but Wilson, who has warmed up, even finds romance in a sign painted on an old building: *Los Angeles Sanitary District—1927.* They talk. I wouldn't call it flirting. Both are painfully earnest. They reveal secrets. You might be able to guess one of them. They talk about her abusive redneck ex-boyfriend, and they go together to steal her possessions out of her ex-apartment. She accuses Wilson of planning to have sex on their first date and asks, "You're carrying a condom, aren't you?" He denies it. She discovers he's carrying five. He can explain it. In a sense, he's carrying them for his roommate.

The night unfolds and the movie never steps wrong. We increasingly admire the quality of the acting: Both actors take their characters through a difficult series of changes, without ever seeming to try or be aware of it. We sense them growing closer. We also sense they were not created for each other. We sense those things because they do, too.

The story is obviously influenced by Richard Linklater's *Before Sunrise* and *Before Sunset.* He is thanked in the end credits. Anne Walker, producer of this film, also produced *Sunrise.* But *In Search of a Midnight Kiss* isn't an homage or a recycling job. It's a film with its own organic existence, its own reason for being. It is ultimately a very true and moving story. I came to care about Wilson and Vivian. I hope they had a happy new year.

The International ★ ★ ★
R, 118 m., 2009

Clive Owen (Louis Salinger), Naomi Watts (Eleanor Whitman), Armin Mueller-Stahl (Wilhelm Wexler), Brian F. O'Byrne (The Consultant). Directed by Tom Tykwer and produced by Charles Roven, Richard Suckle, and Lloyd Phillips. Screenplay by Eric Warren Singer.

Not since the days of silent movies have bankers as a group been cast so ruthlessly as

villains. They used to wear waxed mustaches and throw widows and orphans out into the storm. Now the mustaches are gone. "Banker" has been incorporated into the all-embracing term "Wall Street." The bankers in *The International* broker arms deals, sell missiles under the counter, and assassinate anyone who gets too snoopy. First they throw you out into the storm, then they blow you up.

Whether this is a fair portrait is not the purpose of a movie review to determine. It is accurate of the bankers on view here, and given the face of Armin Mueller-Stahl, once familiar as a good guy, now enjoying a new career as a ruthless villain. His bank, based in Luxembourg, as so many schemes are, has been assassinating Nosy Parkers for getting too close to their operations, which involve investing in African rebels and nuclear weaponry, and arming both sides of the Israeli-Palestinian conflict.

Does it seem to you that a bank with headquarters in Luxembourg is asking for it, just as a nice girl shouldn't rent a room in a whorehouse? In the opening scenes we meet the Interpol agent Louis Salinger (Clive Owen), keeping watch in Berlin as his partner meets with an insider of the bank. The partner is killed by mysterious means, and that, as they say, makes it personal. Salinger is joined by Eleanor Whitman (Naomi Watts), a district attorney from Manhattan, for cloudy law enforcement reasons but excellent dramatic ones: It's great to have a plucky blonde in the plot.

The movie has a scene in it Hitchcock might have envied, a gun battle ranging up and down the ramps of the Guggenheim Museum in New York. Why there? Because the visuals are terrific. After Salinger and Whitman follow their quarry there, how do dozens of the bank's killers turn up? Because they're needed. Why do assassination squads in the movies always dress in matching uniforms? Makes them easier to identify. You don't ask questions like that. You simply enjoy the magnificent absurdity of the scene. (It was filmed, by the way, on an enormous interior set in Germany.)

A lot of the remainder of the movie involves dialogue and plotters skulking around colorful international locales including even Istanbul, that traditional setting for intrigue. I found the unfolding of the plot sort of fascinating. The ads will no doubt play up the shoot-out, but you may be relieved to discover this isn't another hyperkinetic exercise in queasy-cammery. It's more interested in demonstrating that a bank like this transcends national boundaries and corrupts everyone it deals with.

How does it do this? With money. As David Mamet so usefully informs us: "Everybody needs money. That's why they call it money." In the film, everything is secondary to the bank's profits, and an Italian political candidate, not unlike Berlusconi, is shot during a speech. Why the bank, so efficient, isn't better at going after Salinger and Whitman isn't hard to explain: They're needed for the whole movie. The Berlusconi type has a big dialogue scene in which he explains, succinctly and objectively, how banks, armies, and governments interact. Apparently our Wall Street was a babe in the woods, being motivated merely by arrogance, avarice, and ego.

I enjoyed the movie. Clive Owen makes a semi-believable hero, not performing too many feats that are physically unlikely. He's handsome and has the obligatory macho stubble, but he has a quality that makes you worry a little about him. I like heroes who *could* get killed. Naomi Watts wisely plays up her character's legal smarts and plays down the inevitable possibility that the two of them will fall in love.

The director is Tom Tykwer (*Run, Lola, Run*). Here he's concerned not merely with thriller action but with an actual subject: the dangers of a banking system that operates offshore no matter where your shoreline is. We're gradually getting it into our heads that in the long run your nuclear capability may not be as important as your bank balance. Banks are not lending much money these days, but if you want to buy some warheads, they might take a meeting.

The Invention of Lying ★★★ ½
PG-13, 99 m., 2009

Ricky Gervais (Mark Bellison), Jennifer Garner (Anna McDoogles), Jonah Hill (Frank), Louis C.K. (Greg), Jeffrey Tambor (Anthony), Fionnula Flanagan (Martha Bellison), Rob Lowe (Brad Kessler), Tina Fey (Shelley). Directed by Ricky Gervais and Matthew Robinson and produced by Gervais, Dan Lin, Lynda Obst, and Oly Obst. Screenplay by Gervais and Robinson.

In its amiable, quiet PG-13 way, *The Invention of Lying* is a remarkably radical comedy. It opens with a series of funny, relentlessly logical episodes in a world where everyone always tells the truth, and then slips in the implication that religion is possible only in a world that has the ability to lie. Then it wraps all of this into a sweet love story.

Ricky Gervais plays a pudgy everyman named Mark, who's a writer for a company that produces movies of stunning tedium. There's no comedy or drama in its productions because, of course, fiction requires lies. Mark fails to turn the Black Plague into box office and is fired, but not before his secretary (Tina Fey) tells him she has loathed every day she worked for him. Mark takes this agreeably enough; one is not easily insulted when everyone tells the truth all the time.

What would such a world be like? In *The Invention of Lying*, a retirement home is called "A Sad Place Where Homeless Old People Come to Die." Pepsi ads say: "For when they don't have Coke." When Mark goes on a blind date with Anna (Jennifer Garner), she opens the door and starts right off with a hilarious line that Garner reportedly improvised on the spot. Then she says she finds him unattractive, there will never be any possibility of sex, and he is too short and fat to make a good genetic sperm source. At a restaurant, the waiter tells them he hates working there, and that Anna is out of Mark's league. Mark and Anna agree.

You see how it goes. Mark lives in a typical little city with bland people and no anger. Everyone always believes everyone else. I wonder if politics are even possible. We see this isn't an ideal situation. There are no consolations. Nothing eases the way.

Mark is a nice man, in that sneaky-smooth Gervais way, and would like to console his mother (Fionnula Flanagan), who is dying in a Sad Place Where Old People, etc. One day he undergoes an astonishing revelation. He knows his bank balance is $300. The camera zooms into his brain to show mental lightning bolts, and he tells the teller he has $800. She hands him the money and apologizes for the bank's computer.

He can lie! His world lacks even a word for this. Nor does it have the word "truth." Something is either "so," or "not so." With his new power, Mark is able to tell his mother that death doesn't lead to oblivion, but to a wonderful afterlife. Of course she, and everyone else, believes him. The word races around the world, and people beg for more details. Anna tells him how happy he could make everyone.

Then, in one of the funniest satirical scenes I can remember, Mark stands on his front steps and informs the world there is a Man in the Sky, and they will be happy up there with him after death. The world is ecstatic. This Man, Mark explains, is responsible for everything. "Even my cancer?" a woman asks. Yes, that too, but Mark asks his audience not to get bogged down in the details.

What we have here, in microcosm, is the paradox of a benevolent god creating a world of evil. Mark is hard-pressed to explain it, but greater men than he have tried. Think of the power you'd possess if everything you said was believed without question. Mark, under the circumstances, behaves reasonably well.

I saw the movie with a large audience, which laughed a lot and had a good time. I have no idea what they thought of its implications. It isn't strident, ideological, or argumentative; it's simply the story of a guy trying to comfort his mother and perhaps win the woman he loves. Gervais, who codirected and cowrote with Matthew Robinson, walks a delicate tightrope above hazardous chasms.

He's helped greatly in his balancing act by Jennifer Garner's inspired, seemingly effortless, performance as a great beauty who isn't conceited or cruel but simply thinks Mark, with his pug nose, is the wrong genetic match for her children. She plans to marry Brad (Rob Lowe), who is as conventionally handsome (and boring) as Clark Kent. The film has one of those scenes at the altar ("Do you, Brad, agree to stay with Anna as long as you can?") that avoids obvious clichés by involving profound philosophical conclusions.

I saw the trailer for *The Invention of Lying* and expected to dislike it. It's a much better movie than the trailer dares to admit. Today's trailers would make *Sophie's Choice* into a

feel-good story. Watching the movie, I thought—oh, yeah, that's right: It's October. Good movies are allowed again.

Invictus ★★★ ½
PG-13, 134 m., 2009

Morgan Freeman (Nelson Mandela), Matt Damon (Francois Pienaar), Jason Tshabalala (Tony Kgoroge), Louis Minnaar (Springbok Coach), Shakes Myeko (Minister of Sport), Patrick Lyster (Francois's Father), Leleti Khumalo (Mary). Directed by Clint Eastwood and produced by Eastwood, Robert Lorenz, Lori McCreary, and Mace Neufeld. Screenplay by Anthony Peckham, based on the book by John Carlin.

Morgan Freeman has been linked to one biopic of Nelson Mandela or another for at least ten years. Strange that the only one to be made centers on the South African rugby team. The posters for Clint Eastwood's *Invictus* feature Matt Damon in the foreground, with Freeman looming behind him in shadowy nobility. I can imagine marketing meetings during which it was lamented that few Americans care much about Mandela, and Matt Damon appeals to a younger demographic.

Screw 'em, is what I would have contributed. The achievement of Nelson Mandela is one of the few shining moments in recent history. Here is a man who was released after twenty-four years of breaking rocks in prison and sleeping on the floor to assume leadership of the nation that jailed him. His personal forgiveness of white South Africa was the beacon that illuminated that nation's Truth and Reconciliation Commissions, one of the very few examples in history of people who *really* had much to forgive, and forgave it. Let us not forget that both black and white had reasons to grieve, and reasons to forgive, and that in many cases they were facing the actual murderers of their loved ones.

Compared to that, what really does it matter that an underdog Springbok team, all white with one exception, won the World Cup in rugby in the first year of Mandela's rule? I understand that in a nation where all the races are unusually obsessed by sport, the Cup was an electrifying moment when the pariah state stood redeemed before the world—even if soccer is the black man's game there, and rugby is the white's. It was important in the way the Beijing Olympics were important to China.

Clint Eastwood I believe understood all of these things and also sought to make a film he believed he could make, in an area where he felt a visceral connection. Eastwood is too old and too accomplished to have interest in making a film only for money. He would have probably read the screenplays for the previous Mandela projects. They all had one thing in common: They didn't get made. It was universally agreed that Morgan Freeman was the right actor (Mandela and he met and got along famously), but the story, financing, and deal never came together. Eastwood made the film that did get made.

It is a very good film. It has moments evoking great emotion, as when the black and white members of the presidential security detail (hard-line ANC activists and Afrikaner cops) agree with excruciating difficulty to serve together. And when Damon's character Francois Pienaar, as the team captain, is shown the cell where Mandela was held for those long years on Robben Island. Chaz and I were taken to the island early one morning by Ahmed Kathrada, one of Mandela's fellow prisoners, and yes, the movie shows his very cell, with the thin blankets on the floor. You regard that cell and you think, here a great man waited in faith for his rendezvous with history.

The World Cup was a famous victory. The Springboks faced a New Zealand team so dominant it had crushed every opponent—Japan by around ninety points, which in rugby is a *lot*. South Africa won in overtime. About that team name. The South African national teams have been called the Springboks since time immemorial (New Zealand is known as the All Blacks). A springbok is on the tail of every South African Airlines airplane. It's the national logo. Would Mandela change the name to one less associated with the apartheid regime? He would not. Join me in a thought experiment. An African-American is elected mayor of Boston. He is accepted, grudgingly in some circles. How would it go over if he changed the name of the Red Sox?

Freeman does a splendid job of evoking the man Nelson Mandela, who is as much a secular saint as Gandhi. He shows him as genial, confident, calming—over what was clearly a core of tempered steel. The focus is on his early time in office. I believe there may be one scene with a woman representing Winnie Mandela, but the dialogue is vague. Damon is effective at playing the captain Francois, an Afrikaner, child of racist parents, transformed by his contact with "the greatest man I've ever met." Clint Eastwood, a master director, orchestrates all of these notes and has us loving Mandela, proud of Francois, and cheering for the plucky Springboks. A great entertainment. Not, as I said, the Mandela biopic I would have expected. ☞

I.O.U.S.A. ★ ★ ★ ½
PG, 85 m., 2008

Featuring David M. Walker, Robert Bixby, Paul Volker, Ron Paul, Warren Buffett, Paul O'Neill, and others. A documentary directed by Patrick Creadon and produced by Christine O'Malley and Sarah Gibson. Screenplay by Creadon, O'Malley, and Addison Wiggin.

A letter to our grandchildren, Raven, Emil, and Taylor:

I see you growing up into such beautiful people, and I wish all good things to you as you make the leap into adulthood. But I have just seen a film named *I.O.U.S.A.* that snapped into sharp focus why your lives may not be as pleasant as ours have been. Chaz and I had the blessing of growing up in an optimistic, bountiful America. We never fully realized that we were paying for many of our comforts with your money.

Let me explain. There is something called the "national debt." In the movie's interviews with ordinary people, it has a hard time finding anyone who knows exactly what that is. Well, I've never exactly known, either. I thought I knew, but it never came up in conversation, and it became a meaningless abstraction, even though in 2009 the debt will pass nine *trillion* dollars. You might think of those as dollars our nation has spent without having them.

What will this mean to you? It will mean

275

you will live in a country no longer able to pay for many of the services and guarantees we take for granted. In forty years, when you are still less than my age, it looks like the government will be able to pay for only three things: interest on the national debt, *some* Social Security, and *some* Medicare. It will not be able to afford any of the other functions it now performs.

How did we get into this situation? With a federal government that has been throwing bad money after good. Of all the presidents in the last century, the only one who was able to achieve a balanced budget and produce a surplus was Bill Clinton. He did that by bravely raising taxes and cutting spending. Our current president, George W. Bush, is now finishing up eight years of throwing around money like a drunken sailor. His fellow conservatives, like Rush Limbaugh, like to talk about "tax-and-spend Democrats." But they seem to be "don't-tax-and-spend-even-more Republicans."

Not that this film takes sides. It is nonpartisan and includes many Republicans who agree with its argument that the country is headed for disaster within the lifetimes of many now living. It centers on David M. Walker, until recently the U.S. comptroller general, and Robert Bixby, the head of the nonpartisan Concord Coalition, who have been on a national Fiscal Wake-Up tour that will last until the November elections. They are trying to sound the alarm, but they speak to half-empty town halls and captive Rotarians and get pushed off the local news by a story of a man who swallowed a diamond.

I don't really believe this review will inspire enormous numbers of people to go see the film. But if they do, they'll find it accomplishes an amazing thing. It *explains* the national debt, the foreign trade deficit, the decrease in personal savings, how the prime interest rate works, and the weakness of our leaders. No, not only George W. Bush, but politicians of both parties who know if they vote against a tax cut they will be lambasted by their opponents and could lose their jobs. In the film we see President Bush asked about the debt and replying: "Ask the economists. I think I only got a B-minus in economics." Then he gives that little chuckle. "But I got an A-plus in cutting taxes."

Yes, he cut taxes while our spending mushroomed. What we have to do is bite the bullet and pay higher taxes while spending less. The war in Iraq is a much sexier issue. But no matter what happens in Iraq, the real crisis we face is the debt. The movie includes testimony by former Fed chairman Paul Volker, former treasury secretary Paul O'Neill, billionaire Warren Buffett, Congressman Ron Paul, and others on both sides of the fence who all agree: Don't buy what you can't pay for. Any politician who tries to win votes by promising to cut taxes is digging our country's grave.

Here's an interesting statistic. I remember when "Made in China" meant cheap and shabby merchandise. No longer. In the ranking of the trade imbalance among all the world's nations, China is first with the highest surplus, and the United States is last with the largest deficit. The Chinese now hold a huge chunk of our debt. If they ever call in the loan, it would destroy our economy. In the presidential debate earlier in the year, Ron Paul was a lonely voice talking about the debt; the others on both sides paid lip service to the problem and moved on.

So here's the bottom line, kids. The United States is probably going to go broke during your lifetimes. Actually, it's already broke, but getting deeper into debt allows it to keep running on thin air, like the Road Runner. My advice? Start savings accounts. Don't buy what you can't afford. Learn Chinese.

Irene in Time ★ ½
PG-13, 95 m., 2009

Tanna Frederick (Irene Jensen), Andrea Marcovicci (Helen Dean), Victoria Tennant (Eleanor Jensen), Karen Black (Sheila Shiwers), Lanre Idewu (Jacob), Jack Maxwell (Mikey). Directed by Henry Jaglom and produced by Rosemary Marks. Screenplay by Jaglom.

Henry Jaglom's new film, *Irene in Time*, is dedicated to "my daughter." A curious note to end on, since it is about a woman whose personality and selfhood have been destroyed by an absent, unreliable father. So much is she obsessed by this long-gone parent that her life is consumed by talking about her father, relating her childhood memories, hanging around with his old friends, and dating men she hopes will fill the gap in her life.

Irene's dating strategy is so inept and needy, however, it's a wonder one guy lasted for what she says is three months but he precisely times at two and a half months. Another poor guy, an architect, doesn't last though their first dinner together. She asks if he uses a protractor and compass in his drawing, and he says he does. And pencils and erasers? Yes, he says, all the tools. "And what is your favorite tool?" He doesn't have one. "Come on," she says, "close your eyes and concentrate! Name your favorite tool!" By now he's looking desperate, and asks: "What is your problem?"

Her Daddy's Little Girl act isn't helped by the books she studies about how to behave on dates, attract men, and so forth. If any of you, my dear readers, are women studying such books as *The Rules*, I offer this free advice: A wise man will stay far away from a woman playing him like a fish, and only a needy one will respond well if you are coy about returning his calls.

Irene (Tanna Frederick) is such an insecure flywheel that any man (repeat, any man) should know enough to start edging away after two minutes of conversation. A woman's stock of small talk shouldn't center on how magical her father was, especially when she's in her thirties and hasn't seen him since she was young.

Irene in Time follows Jaglom's "women's trilogy" of films about women's issues such as childbearing, weight, and compulsive shopping. I guess it's the women's quartet now. Irene hangs around with a posse of female friends who gossip, offer sometimes heartfelt advice, receive massages, have lunch, and attend parties. They're all apparently independently wealthy, well divorced, or kept women, since work never seems to interrupt their busy schedules. True, Irene has a job of sorts, making a recording with a band, but their woeful material seems well suited for the lounge of a cruise ship.

There's a dramatic revelation in the film, inspired by a trail of clues in the form of messages that Irene's father apparently left behind years ago for her to discover only now. Good thing she finds them. Note to disappearing fathers: If you want to communicate in twenty

years with a daughter, write it down in a letter and leave it with your lawyer.

The revelation does, however, lead to two of the better scenes in the movie, involving older women played by Victoria Tennant and Andrea Marcovicci. Tennant plays her mother, and I must not tell you whom Marcovicci plays.

Jaglom has been producing his own films since 1971 and has made some good ones, notably *Deja Vu* (1997). This is not a good one. It offers certain pleasures, but suffers from an inability to structure events or know when to end a shot. And it has an ending that is simply, perhaps ridiculously, incomprehensible. That's if it means what I think it means, and I fear it does.

Note: Strolling around the Internet, I found a review of Irene *in* Time *by Tommy Garrett of the* Canyon News. *He compares Jaglom with Wilder and Hitchcock, then writes: "In Frederick's case, he has given her a vehicle which has propelled her into a category that no actress in the past 50 years could be placed. Frederick makes the list of very talented women in Hollywood: Garbo, Davis, Crawford and Hepburn."*

(I'm grateful to Tommy Garrett, who has achieved the feat of writing praise so astonishing we at last have someone to compare to the critic who said I Am Legend *was one of the greatest movies ever made.)*

Iron Man ★ ★ ★ ★
PG-13, 126 m., 2008

Robert Downey Jr. (Tony Stark/Iron Man,) Terrence Howard (Colonel Rhodes), Jeff Bridges (Obadiah Stane/Iron Monger), Gwyneth Paltrow (Pepper Potts). Directed by Jon Favreau and produced by Ari Arad. Screenplay by Mark Fegus and Hank Ostby.

When I caught up with *Iron Man*, a broken hip had delayed me and the movie had already been playing for three weeks. What I heard during that time was that a lot of people loved it, that they were surprised to love it so much, and that Robert Downey Jr.'s performance was special. Apart from that, all I knew was that the movie was about a big iron man. I didn't even know that a human occupied it and halfway thought that the Downey character's brain had been transplanted into a robot, or a fate equally weird.

Yes, I knew I was looking at sets and special effects—but I'm referring to the reality of the illusion, if that makes any sense. With many superhero movies, all you get is the surface of the illusion. With *Iron Man,* you get a glimpse into the depths. You get the feeling, for example, of a functioning corporation. Consider the characters of Pepper Potts (Gwyneth Paltrow), Stark's loyal aide, and Obadiah Stane (Jeff Bridges), Stark's business partner. They don't feel drummed up for the occasion. They seem to have worked together for a while.

Much of that feeling is created by the chemistry involving Downey, Paltrow, and Bridges. They have relationships that seem fully formed and resilient enough to last through the whole movie, even if plot mechanics were not about to take them to another level. Between the two men, there are echoes of the relationship between Howard Hughes and Noah Dietrich in Scorsese's *The Aviator* (2004). Obadiah Stane doesn't come onscreen waving flags and winking at the camera to announce he is the villain; he seems adequately explained simply as the voice of reason at Stark's press conference. (Why did "Stark," during that scene, make me think of "raving mad"?) Between Stark and Pepper, there's that classic screen tension between "friends" who know they can potentially become lovers.

Downey's performance is intriguing and unexpected. He doesn't behave like most superheroes: He lacks the psychic weight and gravitas. Tony Stark is created from the persona Downey has fashioned through many movies: irreverent, quirky, self-deprecating, wisecracking. The fact that Downey is allowed to think and talk the way he does while wearing all that hardware represents a bold decision by the director, Jon Favreau. If he hadn't desired that, he probably wouldn't have hired Downey. So comfortable is Downey with Tony Stark's dialogue, so familiar does it sound coming from him, that the screenplay seems almost to have been dictated by Downey's persona.

There are some things that some actors can safely say onscreen, and other things they can't. The Robert Downey Jr. persona would find it difficult to get away with weighty, profound statements (in an "entertainment movie," anyway—a more serious film like *Zodiac* is another matter). Some superheroes speak in a kind of heightened, semiformal prose, as if dictating to *Bartlett's Familiar Quotations.* Not Tony Stark. He could talk that way and be Juno's uncle. *Iron Man* doesn't seem to know how seriously most superhero movies take themselves. If there is wit in the dialogue, the superhero is often supposed to be unaware of it. If there is broad humor, it usually belongs to the villain. What happens in *Iron Man,* however, is that sometimes we wonder how seriously even Stark takes it. He's flippant in the face of disaster, casual on the brink of ruin.

It's prudent, I think, that Favreau positions the rest of the characters in a more serious vein. The supporting cast wisely does not try to one-up him. Gwyneth Paltrow plays Pepper Potts as a woman who is seriously concerned that this goofball will kill himself. Jeff Bridges makes Obadiah Stane one of the great superhero villains by seeming plausibly concerned about the stock price. Terrence Howard, as Colonel Rhodes, is at every moment a conventional straight arrow. What a horror show it would have been if they were all tuned to Tony Stark's sardonic wavelength. We'd be back in the world of *Swingers* (1996), which was written by Favreau.

Another of the film's novelties is that the enemy is not a conspiracy or spy organization. It is instead the reality in our own world today: Armaments are escalating beyond the ability to control them. In most movies in this genre, the goal would be to create bigger and better weapons. How unique that Tony Stark wants to disarm. It makes him a superhero who can think, reason, and draw moral conclusions, instead of one who recites platitudes.

The movie is largely founded on its special effects. When somebody isn't talking, something is banging, clanging, or laying rubber. The armored robotic suits utilized by Tony and Obadiah would upstage lesser actors than Downey and Bridges; it's surprising how much those two giant iron men seem to reflect the personalities of the men inside them. Everything they do is preposterous, of course, but they seem to be doing it, not the suits. Some of their moments have real grandeur—

as when Tony tests his suit to see how high it will fly, and it finally falls back toward Earth in a sequence that reminded me of a similar challenge in *The Right Stuff.*

The art direction is inspired by the original Marvel artists. The movie doesn't reproduce the drawings of Jack Kirby and others, but it reproduces their feeling, a vision of out-scaled enormity, seamless sleekness, secret laboratories made not of nuts and bolts but of . . . vistas. A lot of big budget f/x epics seem to abandon their stories with half an hour to go and just throw effects at the audience. This one has a plot so ingenious it continues to function no matter how loud the impacts, how enormous the explosions. It's an inspiration to provide Tony with that heart-saving device; he's vulnerable not simply because Obadiah might destroy him, but because he might simply run out of juice.

That leaves us, however, with a fundamental question at the bottom of the story: Why must the ultimate weapon be humanoid in appearance? Why must it have two arms and two legs, and why does it matter if its face is scowling? In the real-world competitions between fighting machines, all the elements of design are based entirely on questions of how well they allow the machines to attack, defend, recover, stay upright, and overturn their enemies. It is irrelevant whether they have conventional eyes, or whether those eyes narrow. Nor does it matter whether they have noses, because their oxygen supply is obviously not obtained by breathing. The solution to such dilemmas is that the armored suits look the way they do for entirely cinematic reasons. The bad iron man should look like a mean machine. The good iron man should utilize the racing colors of Tony Stark's favorite sports cars. It wouldn't be nearly as much fun to see a fight scene between two refrigerators crossed with the leftovers from a boiler room.

At the end of the day it's Robert Downey Jr. who powers the liftoff separating this from most other superhero movies. You hire an actor for his strengths, and Downey would not be strong as a one-dimensional mightyman. He is strong because he is smart, quick, and funny, and because we sense his public persona masks deep private wounds. By building on that, Favreau found his movie, and it's a good one.

Iron Man 2 ★★★
PG-13, 124 m., 2010

Robert Downey Jr. (Tony Stark), Gwyneth Paltrow (Pepper Potts), Don Cheadle (Lieutenant Colonel "Rhodey" Rhodes), Scarlett Johansson (Natasha Romanoff), Sam Rockwell (Justin Hammer), Mickey Rourke (Ivan Vanko), Samuel L. Jackson (Nick Fury), Clark Gregg (Paul Coulson), Garry Shandling (Senator Stern). Directed by Jon Favreau and produced by Kevin Feige. Screenplay by Justin Theroux, based on the Marvel comic by Stan Lee, Don Heck, Larry Lieber, and Jack Kirby.

Iron Man 2 is a polished, high-octane sequel, not as good as the original but building once again on a quirky performance by Robert Downey Jr. The superhero genre doesn't necessarily require good acting, but when it's there (as in *Iron Man* and *The Dark Knight*), that takes it up a level. Downey here gives us a Tony Stark who is cockier and more egotistical than ever. Or, and here's the key, he seems to be.

All heroes have a fatal flaw. That's one of the rules of the road in fiction. Tony Stark's flaw is that he is dying. The megalomaniac act comes naturally, but now it's useful as a cover-up. His chest-mounted battery pack, or life source, or whatever it is, is running low and poisoning his blood. It works by using the rarest element in the periodic table, and to renew it would require discovering or inventing a new element. Not easy.

So Tony stands aside at big events and uses a little blood monitor—helpfully named the "Stark Blood Monitor," in case anybody sees it—that tells him his blood toxicity is relentlessly climbing toward death. This is his private fear, not even shared with the loyal Pepper Potts (Gwyneth Paltrow), who is running his company.

Stark is sponsoring a Stark Expo at the site of the New York World's Fair, and he flies in for an appearance in the Iron Man suit and promises world peace. The arena is thronged with adoring fans. Imagine Steve Jobs announcing iPad 3. But trouble is brewing. His archrival Justin Hammer (Sam Rockwell) plans an army of rival iron suits. A congressional committee headed by the fatuous Senator Stern (Garry Shandling) wants Stark to make Iron Man the exclusive property of the Defense Department. And in Russia, the bitter Ivan Vanko (Mickey Rourke) believes Stark's father stole the Iron Man secrets from his own father.

Hammer hires Vanko to design a better suit than Stark's, the two suit designs go to war, we get half an hour of sensational special effects, and Bob's your uncle. But you also have a niece, a sexy martial arts expert played by Scarlett Johansson, who may be more than she seems. The character was named Black Widow in the comic books, never a good sign. Fighting at Stark's side is his comrade Lieutenant Colonel "Rhodey" Rhodes (Don Cheadle); while rocketing through a blizzard of enemy missiles, the two find time to talk. How slow must a missile be moving if your buddy has time to warn you to dodge it?

The best CGI sequence in the movie comes at midpoint, when Tony Stark decides to drive his own car in the Monaco Grand Prix, and Ivan Vanko stands fearlessly in the middle of the race, dressed like a kinky gladiator and wielding electric whips that can slice a car in two. He nearly destroys Stark, which is so exciting that we forget to wonder how he knew that Tony was driving his own car. It's after this race that Hammer signs him up.

Mickey Rourke gives us all the Ivan Vanko we could possibly wish for, unless he had a third arm to provide space for more tattoos. His performance features flashing his gold teeth in mirthless laughter, and lots of growling. Sam Rockwell gives a wry comic performance as Hammer, a querulous whiner who seems in over his head in the super weapons business.

You want a sequel, you got a sequel. *Iron Man 2*, directed like the first one by Jon Favreau, gets the job done. Since both movies have essentially the same story arc, there aren't a lot of surprises, however, which started me to wondering how the guys survive inside those suits. Sure, the suits are armored, but their bodies aren't. How many dizzying falls and brutal blows and sneaky explosions can you survive without breaking every bone in your body? Just askin'. At the end of a long day, those suits should be filled with bloody pulp.

Is Anybody There? ★ ★ ½
PG-13, 92 m., 2009

Michael Caine (Clarence), Bill Milner (Edward), Anne-Marie Duff (Mum), David Morrissey (Dad), Elizabeth Spriggs (Prudence), Leslie Phillips (Reg), Ralph Raich (Clive), Rosemary Harris (Elsie). Directed by John Crowley and produced by David Heyman, Marc Turtletaub, and Peter Saraf. Screenplay by Peter Harness.

Sir Michael Caine makes acting look as natural as running water. I have never sensed an ounce of egotism in his makeup. The videos he made to teach film acting are plain-spoken and practical. Of course, you need inspiration and talent. But what can he tell you about that? He tells you that you have to look out of the same eye all during a close-up. Or if you don't, that's what they mean by shifty-eyed.

Look at him here in *Is Anybody There?* Caine is seventy-six years old, but this is the first movie where he looks it. He doesn't give a damn. He's supposed to be old. That's why he has checked himself, reluctantly, into an old folks' home. It's called Lark Hall; it's close to the sea and inhabited by dotty seniors who have little to entertain them apart from territorial battles and simmering resentments.

He plays a retired magician named the Amazing Clarence, who drives up in a van painted like an ice cream wagon and almost runs down Edward (Bill Milner), who is about ten and whose parents run the operation. Edward likes living in Lark Hall because he's fascinated by ghosts, and he reasons that a home for the aged would be a good place to find some. He sneaks his tape recorder under the bed of a dying patient, hoping to capture some spirit manifestations.

The Amazing Clarence is spiteful, hostile, and unfriendly. Edward doesn't much notice. He's a force of nature and bowls over Clarence with his curiosity. The old magician is persuaded to put on a magic show for the other retirees; he pretends great reluctance, but I doubt it because if you're still tooling around the countryside in a van and doing one-night stands at seventy-six, it may be because you like to.

The rest of *Is Anybody There?* doesn't measure up to the Amazing Clarence and his young acolyte. Lark Hall seems less like a retirement home than a failed pilot for a sitcom, with old folks who behave in relentlessly obvious comic shtick. It reminded me nostalgically of *Mrs. Palfrey at the Claremont* (2005), with Joan Plowright and Anna Massey among the inhabitants of an establishment where the evening meals were an exercise in thrilling nonverbal communication. The folks in Lark Hall should spend more time eyeing one another and less time acting out.

I can't really recommend the film, unless you admire Caine as much as I do, which is certainly possible. Let's say I somehow found myself retired, and I was informed that the movie was shallow, clunky, and sitcomish, but that Michael Caine played an old magician named the Amazing Clarence in it. I would take the remnants of my latest Social Security check and hobble down to the theater, because my sixth sense would tell me Caine would be worth the price of admission. I would, however, demand a full refund if the Amazing Clarence didn't attempt at least one magic trick that went spectacularly wrong. Reader, the theater would be able to keep my money.

I Served the King of England ★ ★ ★
R, 118 m., 2008

Ivan Barnev (Young Jan Dite), Oldrich Kaiser (Old Jan Dite), Julia Jentsch (Liza), Martin Huba (Skrivanek), Marian Labuda (Walden), Milan Lasica (Professor), Josef Abrham (Hotelier Brandejs). Directed by Jiri Menzel and produced by Petr Dvorak, Helena Uldrichova, Dusan Kukal, Vit Komrzy, and Luba Feglova. Screenplay by Menzel, based on the novel by Bohumil Hrabal.

I first got to know the Czech director Jiri Menzel through his whimsical 1966 Oscar winner, *Closely Watched Trains.* Looking up my old review, I found a sentence that could also apply to his latest film: "If you're charged up emotionally, you'd better lie down for an hour or two before going to see it. It requires an audience at peace with itself."

Don't assume, however, that Menzel's *I Served the King of England* is a snoozer; for that matter, don't assume it has anything to do with the king of England. It's a film filled with wicked satire and sex both joyful and pitiful. But Menzel doesn't pound home his points. He skips gracefully through them, like his hero. He takes the velvet glove approach.

Here is a film with a hatred of Nazis and a crafty condemnation of communist bureaucracy and cronyism. It seems to be a comic tale of the long and somewhat uneventful life of Jan Dite, who worked as a waiter, bought a hotel with stolen postage stamps, and was jailed because he wasn't quick enough to figure out what the communists, when they came to power, really wanted from him. Even that story has a happy ending: He was sentenced to fifteen years, but because of an "amnesty," was released after only fourteen years and eleven months.

Menzel loves that kind of deadpan detail. In *Closely Watched Trains*, the hero's grandfather was crushed while trying to hypnotize the German army. *I Served the King of England* is a life story told by the old and gray Jan Dite (Oldrich Kaiser) about the adventures of the young and clueless Jan Dite (Ivan Barnev). The youth was easily impressed by uniforms, pomp, theatrical displays of grandness, hotel dining rooms jammed with chandeliers, mirrors, candles, curtains, finery. It all came together for him when he was hired as a waiter in Prague's grandest hotel.

Parts of his life story are told in the style of a silent film because Menzel, like all good directors, does not depend entirely on what the characters say. *I Served the King of England* could probably be enjoyed about as much without the English subtitles—although you'd want to keep the playful piano score, of course. The characters are like those in a Buster Keaton comedy: immediately evident, looking just as they should, absorbed by themselves, sometimes doing things simply to amuse themselves, exhibiting grace.

Jan Dite is in awe of the majestic headwaiter, who floats among the tables like a dancer in *Swan Lake,* all the while balancing a heavy tray stacked with meals. Jan treats him like a god. Where did the man learn such grandeur? He served the king of England. One day the man is tripped, drops a tray, and goes on a rampage. The other waiters agree: It was the only decent thing for him to do. Jan ascends to headwaiter, and "ascend" may be the correct word, since he is a very small man.

Menzel apparently sees the pecking order in the dining room as mirroring the Nazi Party's. Jan soon wants more than to serve; he wants to own and accumulate. He marries a fiercely Aryan woman who enlists in the German army, leaving him a box of rare stamps she has looted from the homes of Jews. He happily uses them to buy the hotel. Do we see a pattern here? Didn't the communists appropriate the Jewish wealth, factories, businesses, and art that were stolen by the Nazis?

There is a sequence where the hotel is used by the Nazis as a luxurious resort for a pool full of bodacious Aryan beauties whose duty is to become impregnated by soldiers on leave. How this works out I will leave for you to discover. You see the velvet glove slipping. A metaphor for the Jan Dite character runs through the film after he discovers to his amusement that anyone, even a millionaire, will stoop to pick up loose change from the sidewalk. Dite is a shallow man in a society that becomes a very deep hole.

We will not soon see a comedy like this made in America. Even if it were entirely translated into American characters and terms, audiences would wonder what it was about. We have lost the delight in the irony that Mark Twain and H. L. Mencken practiced. The movie must come to us bearing the answers to its questions. When I say "we," of course, I do not include anyone who has read this far. We would not ask: A Czech comedy? Sly? No appearance by the king of England? An iron fist inside the glove?

Many more things happen here than I have described, including Jan Dite's own sex life and the erotic image beloved by his wife. But enough, although I should add that the name Dite means "child."

It's Complicated ★★ ½

R, 120 m., 2009

Meryl Streep (Jane), Steve Martin (Adam), Alec Baldwin (Jake), John Krasinski (Harley), Lake Bell (Agness), Mary Kay Place (Joanne), Rita Wilson (Trisha). Directed by Nancy Meyers and produced by Meyers and Scott Rudin. Screenplay by Meyers.

It's Complicated is perfectly plausible if you are only willing to believe that Meryl Streep sells a whole lot of muffins. She plays a bakery and restaurant owner who lives in a sprawling hacienda on a bluff overlooking the Pacific in Santa Barbara, set on grounds approached by a sweeping circular drive. I've been to Oprah's place, which is only a little nicer. Life is sweet, although she hires an architect to give her a new kitchen. Her current one tragically has only two ovens.

Give the sainted Meryl a lot of credit. Living alone, she occupies this space as if it makes perfect sense for her. There's an actress for you. Her children love her, her son-in-law adores her, and life would be perfect if it weren't that her husband, Jake (Alec Baldwin), left her ten years ago. You'd think she'd be able to get over the loss of Baldwin in ten years. A lot of women have.

Jake married the much younger Agness (Lake Bell), another of those people who mess with the spelling of their names to make it hard on everybody. Agness (rhymes with "ssss") has a perfect body but a petulant expression, and for the life of us we can't figure out why Jake left the merry Meryl for her. Neither can he. Running into his first wife at their son's graduation, he's moved by memories of their past. At the bar of her hotel, she unwisely orders a Tanqueray martini, dry, with a lemon twist, just before Jake walks in. That's like disarming before the battle.

They experience something between love and tantric rapture. She's not merely more exciting than he remembered, she's the next generation of Viagra. Alec Baldwin, it must be said, was born to play a man blissful in bed, and few other actors could so perfectly deliver his line, "Home, sweet home." Miss Streep, in one of her rare (and nonexplicit, of course) sex scenes, inspires as so often our belief that she's good at everything she does. Maybe she does bake great muffins.

Adam (Steve Martin), her architect, is meanwhile forging ahead with plans for the new addition on a house already spacious enough to accommodate a youth hostel. He visits a lot, and it is clear he's smitten. But he's recovering from a painful breakup and fearful of starting something new. Jane finds herself in the position of starting to like this architect while at the same time carrying on an affair with a married man, her ex-husband. She keeps this a personal secret, confiding only in her best girlfriends, which is accurate enough about the way women keep secrets.

It's Complicated was written and directed by Nancy Meyers, who after *Something's Gotta Give* (2003), *What Women Want* (2000), and *The Holiday* (2006), has established a cottage industry in movies about romantically inclined middle-aged people. Pairing Diane Keaton and Jack Nicholson, Mel Gibson and Helen Hunt, and now Streep, Baldwin, and Martin, she favors tush-baring scenes from her stars, although it's a sign of the times that Baldwin finds himself hooked up with Martin via iChat, with the camera and screen-sharing options unfortunately enabled.

There's funny stuff here. We like everybody. We enjoy the way Harley the future son-in-law (John Krasinski) finds himself in possession of much more information than he desires. At the same time, we're aware that the scene of a character sneaking up to peek through a window, losing his footing, and crashing to the ground was not fresh when it was used so well in *The Lady Eve* (1941). And while it can be funny when a respectable lady gets stoned on pot, it's difficult for even Streep to make it funny for ten minutes.

It's Complicated is a rearrangement of the goods in Nancy Meyers's bakery, and some of them belong on the day-old shelf. Oh, how I hate food analogies in reviews. In a season of blessings, there are several better choices than this one. Truth in criticism: I must report that I expect *It's Complicated* will be terrifically popular with its target demographic, which includes gal pals taking a movie break after returning Christmas presents. Not everybody is in a mood for *Avatar*.

I've Loved You So Long ★ ★ ★ ½
PG-13, 117 m., 2008

Kristin Scott Thomas (Juliette), Elsa Zylberstein (Lea), Serge Hazanavicius (Luc), Laurent Grevill (Michel), Frederic Pierrot (Faure), Lise Segur (P'tit Lys), Jean-Claude Arnaud (Papy Paul). Directed by Philippe Claudel and produced by Sylvestre Guarino. Screenplay by Claudel.

I've Loved You So Long begins with a situation similar to *Rachel Getting Married*. One sister is released from an institution for a homecoming with another sister who is not overjoyed to see her. Both of the sisters are believed responsible for a tragic death some years in the past. There are subtle questions about whether either one can be "trusted," even now. But the two films are otherwise completely different, and if you've seen one, you haven't seen the other.

Rachel is as American as apple pie. *I've Loved You So Long* is as French as *tarte de pomme*. Hackneyed expressions, but there you are. One of the most French elements in *Loved You* is Juliette, played by Kristin Scott Thomas. Yes, from *The English Patient*. One of those actors who can move effortlessly between English and French, like Jacqueline Bisset or, with a charming accent, Jeanne Moreau, who had a British mother.

French seems to agree with Scott Thomas. In her English-language roles, she sometimes seems a little cool, ever so slightly aloof. In French, she warms, is more free with emotions, more easily reaches joy and sorrow. Watch her here falling in love with the two adopted Vietnamese daughters of her sister, Lea (Elsa Zylberstein). It's a love that seems spontaneous and not faked.

She also comes home to her sister's husband, Luc (Serge Hazanavicius), and his father, Papy Paul (Jean-Claude Arnaud). Luc doesn't welcome her with open arms. He's nervous about her being with the children. Papy Paul has lost the power to speak and spends all of his time reading books. In an American movie, this trait might make his character eccentric, a practitioner of dark arts, or unnecessary. *Zut!* In France, he just likes to read.

The film explores the past at arm's length; everyone is afraid to discuss it except indirectly. No one dares ask her straight-out questions. Families are like that. There's an elephant in a lot of living rooms. At a dinner party that begins on a cheerful but somewhat uneasy note, one of the guests takes almost sadistic pleasure in asking Juliette questions it is clear she will not answer. This is social sadism in the guise of innocent curiosity.

One of the few in Juliette's corner is her probation officer (Frederic Pierrot), who understands, as the others do not, what Juliette has gone through and what fifteen years in prison really do to the human spirit. She has to learn to be released, to be free, to live her life without the unconscious air of someone afraid of being locked up again. Some people appear to be friends but only want to help her up to a point, for example, at her first job after prison.

Everything centers on Juliette. Her transgression was more unforgivable than what Rachel's sister did. Her feelings run even deeper. She has been away for longer and finds it more difficult to gather up the threads of life. This is one of Kristin Scott Thomas's most inspired performances. Maybe she could have been up for Academy consideration. Pity she speaks French.

J

JCVD ★ ★ ½
R, 92 m., 2008

Jean-Claude Van Damme (JCVD), Herve Sogne (Lieutenant Smith), Francois Damiens (Bruges), Norbert Rutili (Perthier), Olivier Bisback (Doctor), Karim Belkhadra (Vigile). Directed by Mabrouk El Mechri and produced by Sidonie Dumas. Screenplay by Frederic Benudis, El Mechri, and Christophe Turpin.

I remember the global high point of Jean-Claude Van Damme's career. That would have been at the 1992 Cannes Film Festival, when he and his *Universal Soldier* costar Dolph Lundgren got into a shoving match on the grand staircase leading up to the festival's Auditorium Lumiere. The festival's entrances are documented by every TV network in Europe and by a melee of paparazzi. Think how humiliating it was for their scuffle to be so widely seen. Doing research on the Web, I went to Lundgren's own site, only to find myself quoted: "Some said it was a publicity stunt. I say if you can do one thing and do it well, stick to it."

It says something peculiar about the nature of celebrity that on your own Web site you are still quoting a snarky remark about your sixteen-year-old publicity stunt. But wait. There may be hope. Here's a press release from early 2008: Lundgren insists he can "overcome scheduling difficulties" and reunite with Van Damme. "You know, I was thinking today, it would be great to make a movie with the '80s action Rat Pack—Jean Claude and a few others."

I'm trying to think of a few others. I remember it more as the Rat Whack. But that's just me. If my theme today is the fleeting passage of time, so is Van Damme's. The new film from the Muscles from Brussels is the surprisingly transgressive *JCVD*, which trashes his career, his personal life, his martial arts skills, his financial stability, and his image. He plays himself, trapped in a misunderstood hostage crisis, during which we get such a merciless dissection of his mystique that it will be hard to believe him as a Universal Soldier ever again. On the other hand, it will be easier to like him. This movie almost endearingly savages him.

Van Damme obviously was a good sport to make this movie, which is like every self-parodying Bruce Willis cameo rolled into one. The movie opens with a virtuoso single take in which Van Damme fights, chops, shoots, and kick-boxes his way down an endless street while dozens of stunt men topple from high places, cars explode, and at some point it becomes very funny. The CGI is so evident and the fights so choreographed that it confirms something I've long believed: The most difficult thing an action star does during a battle scene is to hit his marks.

Cut to Los Angeles, where the Muscles loses a child custody battle. His ex-wife wins after his wee daughter tells the judge she gets teased by the kids at school after one of her daddy's movies plays on TV. In the real America, it would be incredibly cool to have JCVD as your dad. In Los Angeles, meanies from third grade would be gossiping that your dad had the wrong agent. "Tell him to sign with Morris," that Britneyette who thinks she's so cute would taunt.

Back home in Brussels after years abroad, JCVD has his card rejected at an ATM and goes into a bank to get some money. Alas, he walks in on a stickup, and the fanboys at the video store across the street call the cops and report he's the one committing the crime. Soon the police have the area surrounded, while behind the barricades a (smallish) crowd of his fans chants its support. It's like *Dog Day Afternoon* with hamsters.

The suspense in the hostage crisis is pretty much a dud, and the standoff ends as it must, but it's funny when JCVD's old parents tearfully implore him to release his prisoners and express concern about the turn his career has taken. Van Damme says worse things about himself than critics would dream of saying, and the effect is shockingly truthful. I sorta enjoyed myself. I could have done without the scene where he floats in anguished reverie, making Hamlet sound like an extrovert.

And that's that, except on Wikipedia I discovered that JCVD is "known throughout the French-speaking world" for his "picturesque aphorisms." Man, oh, man, they're picturesque, all right. I'm going to tack on a bunch and let the editors decide how many they have room for.

"You don't need a flash to photograph a rabbit that already has red eyes."

"If you work with a jackhammer during an earthquake, stop, otherwise you are working for nothing."

"If you phone a psychic and she doesn't answer the phone before it rings, hang up."

"My wife is not my best sexual partner, but she's good with the housework."

"Obviously I've taken drugs."

"When I walk across my living room from my chimney to my window, it takes me ten seconds, but for a bird it takes one second, and for oxygen zero seconds!"

"I am fascinated by air. If you remove the air from the sky, all the birds would fall to the ground. And all the planes, too."

"Air is beautiful, yet you cannot see it. It's soft, yet you cannot touch it. Air is a little like my brain."

Jellyfish ★ ★ ★

NO MPAA RATING, 78 m., 2008

Sarah Adler (Batya), Nikol Leidman (Little Girl), Gera Sandler (Michael), Noa Knoller (Keren), Ma-nenita De Latorre (Joy), Zharira Charifai (Malka). Directed by Etgar Keret and Shira Geffen and produced by Amir Harel, Ayelet Kait, Yael Fogiel, and Laetitia Gonzalez. Screenplay by Geffen.

Jellyfish tells the stories of three young women whose lives, for a change, do not interlock so much as coexist. It never quite explains why these three were chosen and not three others. I found that refreshing because with some films based on entwined lives, you spend more time untangling the plot than caring about it.

In *Jellyfish,* one character is a waitress for a wedding catering firm, another is a new bride, and the third is a home care worker for elderly women. To be sure, there is a mystical vision (or memory) at the end of the film, but I'm not sure I understand the logic behind it, and I don't think I require one. It inexplicably spans a generation but works just as it is.

The film is set in Tel Aviv, but it's not an "Israeli film." That's where it was made, but it's not about anything particularly Israeli. It could take place in countless cities, and it's not "about" anything at all, in the way of a message, a theme, or a revelation. What it offers is a portrait of some time in these lives, created with attentive performances and an intriguing way of allowing them to emerge a little at a time.

The film also gives us sharply defined supporting characters. The most enigmatic, sufficient to be the center of a movie of her own, is an angelic little girl who wanders up to Batya (Sarah Adler) at the beach. She has an inner tube around her middle, which she refuses to be parted from. There are no parents in sight. Batya takes the girl to the police, who aren't much interested. They advise her to care for her over the weekend, while they wait to see if a missing-persons report comes in.

That seems a strange police decision (are there no social agencies in Israel?), but it allows a scene where Batya takes the child to her catering job, and the little girl gets her fired, and in the process she meets a woman who is a freelance wedding photographer, and so on. The photographer is fired, too, and the women end up smoking on a loading dock, discussing turns of fate. Batya has problems, and water is one of their common themes: (a) the little girl seemingly emerged from the sea, and (b) the leak in her apartment ceiling has covered the floor with about four inches of water. A tenuous link, but there you have it.

Another lead character is Keren (Noa Knoller), who breaks her ankle in a particularly ignominious way at her own wedding: She's locked into a toilet cubicle and tries to climb over the door. She and her husband have to cancel their plans for a cruise, end up in a hotel room they hate, and what's worse, the elevator goes out, and at one point it seems that her husband might have bodily carried her up twelve flights of stairs. Maybe only six. Try that sometime. The husband meets a mysterious woman from the top-floor suite, and they spend way too much time together because they're both smokers. The woman says she is a writer, but there's more to it than that.

The most realistic, down-to-earth woman in the film is Joy (Ma-nenita De Latorre), from the Philippines, who works as a minder. Her latest client, dumped on her by the woman's actress daughter, is a short-tempered case study who shouts at her to speak Hebrew or German. The girl does speak English, which is enough in many situations around the world, is learning Hebrew as fast as she can, isn't being paid much, and has a good heart. She convinces the old woman to see her daughter as Ophelia in a decidedly peculiar *Hamlet* (it seems to be written not in iambic pentameter, but in chanted repetition).

These stories have as their justification the fact that they are intrinsically interesting. I think that's enough. *Jellyfish* won the Camera d'Or at Cannes 2007 for best first feature. Given all the temptations that lure gifted first-time filmmakers with three stories to tell, each story with its own story within it, I think director Etgar Keret and his codirector and writer, Shira Geffen, are commendable, since they bring it in at seventy-eight minutes. You can easily see how it could have overstayed its welcome, especially if it ever got around to explaining that little girl, and if she's who she seems to be in the dream or vision or hallucination or whatever. Rather than an explanation in a case like that, I prefer the vision to appear, make its impact, and leave unexplained.

Jennifer's Body ★★★

R, 102 m., 2009

Megan Fox (Jennifer Check), Amanda Seyfried (Needy Lesnicky), Johnny Simmons (Chip Dove), Adam Brody (Nikolai Wolf), J. K. Simmons (Mr. Wroblewski), Amy Sedaris (Toni Lesnicky), Chris Pratt (Officer Duda), Juno Ruddell (Officer Warzak), Kyle Gallner (Colin Gray). Directed by Karyn Kusama and produced by Daniel Dubiecki, Mason Novick, and Jason Reitman. Screenplay by Diablo Cody.

Just what we were waiting for, *Twilight* for boys, with Megan Fox in the Robert Pattinson role, except that I recall Pattinson was shirtless. Diablo Cody's next screenplay after *Juno* is a 180-degree reversal, with the heroine now transformed into a fiend who eats the flesh of teenage boys. Can you imagine Juno's poor boyfriend, Michael Cera, with steak sauce?

The film opens on a deceptively light note in high school, introducing Jennifer Check (Fox) and Needy Lesnicky (Amanda Seyfried) as lifelong best friends. Jennifer is the hottest and most popular babe in school, and Needy is—well, needy. Surely that's her nickname. What parents would name a child Needy?

Jennifer is your classic teen queen who rules the school. Boys lust after her, she's the head cheerleader, and maybe it does her ego good to have needy Needy trailing along. But then she's transformed into, not a vampire exactly, although she does go after throats with bared teeth. She's some kind of demon or monster, sort of undefined, whose mission in life becomes attacking teenage boys.

Her image gives her a valuable weapon in satiating her unwholesome appetites. Timid lads who would never dream of dating Jennifer now find her unexpectedly friendly, even seductive. One kid even gets invited to her home. This turns out to be a creepy empty house. Why do characters always enter creepy empty houses and feel their way in the dark, when they should stand outside on the sidewalk and whistle?

Jennifer gets away with murder because, well, who would expect the sexy and popular cheerleader to be a secret drinker of blood and quite possibly a devourer of flesh? Only Needy suspects the horrifying reality, and finally it is she who stands between Jennifer and more victims, including a nice kid like Chip Dove (Johnny Simmons), who you know is a nice kid because his name, after all, is Chip Dove, and what kind of name is that for a villain?

It's easy to go on like this, but I'd be missing something. There is within Diablo Cody the soul of an artist, and her screenplay brings to this material a certain edge, a kind of gleeful relish that's uncompromising. This isn't your assembly line teen horror thriller. The portraits of Jennifer and Needy are a little too knowing, the dialogue is a little too off-center, the developments are a little too quirky. After you've seen enough teen thrillers, you begin to appreciate these distinctions. Let's put it this way: I'd rather see *Jennifer's Body* again than *Twilight*.

Megan Fox is an interesting case. We think of her as a star, but this is actually her first leading role. She didn't get named number 18 on *Maxim*'s Hot 100 list of 2007 for acting.

(The top post went to Lindsay Lohan. How quickly times change.) She is also famous for her many tattoos, but in researching that aspect of her image I made an encouraging discovery. Anyone can have a tattoo of a butterfly. Been there, done that. But Megan Fox has a tattoo that quotes *King Lear*: "We will laugh at gilded butterflies." How cool is that? Plus, so far, there are no tiresome rumors about booze and drugs.

Fox did her career a lot of good with the two *Transformer* movies, but this is her first chance to really perform, and you know what? She comes through. She has your obligatory projectile vomiting scene and somehow survives it, she plays the role straight, and she looks great in a blood-drenched dress with her hair all straggly. Amanda Seyfried makes a plucky heroine.

The film is directed by Karyn Kusama, who in the splendid *Girlfight* (2000) introduced Michelle Rodriguez. She handles this material efficiently and with a certain relish. It's not art, it's not *Juno*, it's not *Girlfight* for that matter, but as a movie about a flesh-eating cheerleader, it's better than it has to be.

Jerichow ★ ★ ★
NO MPAA RATING, 91 m., 2009

Benno Furmann (Thomas), Nina Hoss (Laura), Hilmi Sozer (Ali), Andre M. Hennicke (Leon), Claudia Geisler (Administrator), Marie Gruber (Cashier), Knut Berger (Policeman). Directed by Christian Petzold and produced by Florian Koerner von Gustorf and Michael Weber. Screenplay by Petzold.

In a district where unemployment and poverty are common, it may not seem like wealth to own a snack shop. But if you own a string of them, you've got it made. Ali owns a string. He also owns a beautiful blond wife, whom he acquired by paying off her debts, just like he got the snack shops and a shiny new Mercedes.

Yet Ali is not a happy man. Born in Turkey but raised in East Germany, he moans, "I am in a country where nobody wants me, with a wife I bought." He needs a friend. Also a driver, after he loses his license for drunk driving. He hires Thomas, who has troubles of his own: He has been dishonorably discharged

from the German forces in Afghanistan, his wife has just died, his savings have been stolen in a settlement of a gambling debt, he was knocked out in the process, and he is homeless and broke. Sure, he'd like to be Ali's driver.

This is the setup for Christian Petzold's *Jerichow*, named for the East German locale. Petzold may ring a bell for you from last year's weirdly intriguing thriller *Yella*, about a woman on the lam from an abusive husband and hoping to embezzle a fortune in her new job. Yella was played by Nina Hoss, who plays Ali's wife, Laura, here. She would be sexy if she didn't have that quality of edgy desperation. Ali (Hilmi Sozer), who looks a little like a Turkish Bob Hoskins, is a very untrusting man, convinced he is being cheated for an excellent reason: He is.

Thomas (Benno Furmann), who shows in one scene he is very confident with brutal hand-to-hand fighting, is the kind of man Ali is looking for—a collector, enforcer, spy, and dependent on Ali. He is also taller than Ali, younger, and better-looking, which doesn't escape Laura's attention. We can see trouble coming.

Ali likes to flash his money and hint at big plans, but he leads a narrow life. He and Laura live at the end of a forest road, next to the warehouse where they load a van with milk, soda, chips, and candy for daily deliveries. He is half-crazy with paranoia, sneaking around corners to catch his shop managers stealing. He also fears catching Laura and Thomas together, and when he makes a business trip to Turkey, is he almost setting them up?

It may not be that simple. Nothing in this movie may be that simple. Petzold doesn't make level-one thrillers, and his characters may be smarter than us or dumber. It's never just about the plot, anyway. It has to do with random accidents, dangerous coincidences, miscalculations, simple mistakes. And the motives are never simple.

It's easy to compare *Jerichow* with the films of *The Postman Always Rings Twice*, with the grimy gas station owner, the sexy wife, and the rugged drifter, but people have a way of not behaving according to their superficial qualities. And there may be something going on here about the complexities of being a stranger in a very strange land.

Joan Rivers: A Piece of Work ★★★ ½
R, 84 m., 2010

Featuring Joan Rivers. A documentary directed by Ricki Stern and Annie Sundberg and produced by Seth Keal and Sundberg.

No one is ever too old. You may have that idea about Joan Rivers, who is seventy-five in this film and never tires of reminding us of that fact. Is that too old? It's older than she would prefer, but what are you gonna do? She remains one of the funniest, dirtiest, most daring and transgressive of stand-up comics, and she hasn't missed a beat.

Joan Rivers: A Piece of Work covers the events in about a year of her life. If the filmmakers didn't have total access, I don't want to see what they missed. In one stretch in this film she closes a show in Toronto, flies overnight to Palm Springs, does a gig, flies overnight to Minneapolis and performs another one. Try that sometime.

She has the energy, stamina, and aggression that a great stand-up needs. She assaults the audience. She pounds laughter out of us. If you've seen her only on television, you have no idea. I saw her in Vegas, and she had people weeping with laughter. I saw her at a memorial service in Toronto for a friend of hers, and she brought down the house. Was that wrong at a memorial service? Brian Linehan, her friend, wouldn't have expected anything less, and she knew it. If you need devout solemnity, Joan Rivers is not your girl.

The way she is funny is, she tells the truth according to herself. She hates some people. She has political opinions. Her observations are so merciless and her timing so precise that even if you like that person, you laugh. She is a sadist of comedy, unafraid to be cruel—even too cruel. She doesn't know fear. She seems to be curious about how far she can go and still get a laugh. That must feel dangerous on a stage with a live audience. Maybe she feeds on that danger.

This documentary began filming before she had her latest fifteen minutes of fame on Donald Trump's *Celebrity Apprentice*. God help Rod Blagojevich if he'd been on the show that season. Rivers has had hours of those fifteen minutes of fame. Her life is like a comeback tour. She is frank about her setbacks. She was

Johnny Carson's resident cohost (and gave young Siskel & Ebert their first spot on *The Tonight Show*). She left Carson to begin her own nightly show on Fox. Carson never spoke to her again. NBC banned her from all of its shows until two years ago. The Fox show eventually failed, and it was discovered that her husband, Edgar, the show's manager, had been stealing from her. He killed himself. She never forgave him—for the suicide, not the other stuff.

She was down. She was up. Her daughter, Melissa, says, "Her career was like me having a sister." I wonder if Melissa appears with her on red carpet shows because it's a chance for some quiet time with Mom. She hardly mentions the red carpets for which she is now widely known. For her, it all comes down to this week: Does she have bookings? She looks at blank pages in her engagement calendar and says they're so white she needs sunglasses to read them.

What makes Joannie run? They say if a shark stops swimming, it dies. She's not a shark. She's a woman who for various reasons depends on making audiences laugh. They walk in knowing all of her problems, knowing her age, eagle-eyed for the plastic surgery, ready to complain, and she *forces* them to laugh because she's so damned funny. I admire that. Bernard Shaw called it the Life Force. We see her in the film's first shot, without makeup. A minute later, *Joan Rivers* is before us. Her life is a performance of herself.

Yes, she's had plastic surgery. Well, why not? I think it's wrong for most people. But show business is cruel and eats its old, and you do what you have to do. She talks about it. She talks about everything. A portrait emerges of a bright little girl who walked onto a stage and never wanted to get off. If she can't have a network show, she'll work a dinner club.

There's that need in a lot of comics. Once in the Merchandise Mart, I was riding down in an elevator with Henny Youngman. The doors opened at the private club on the second floor, and there was a big placard there pointing to the room for a wedding. Henny didn't miss a beat. He walked off, asked to be introduced to the father of the bride, and told him, "My name is Henny Youngman. I'll do ten minutes for two hundred dollars."

289

I think *Joan Rivers: A Piece of Work* is fascinating and has a lot of laughs in it. It's more than that. It's the portrait of a woman who will not accept defeat, who will not slow down, who must prove herself over and again. A brave and stubborn woman, smart as a whip, superbly skilled. You want to see what it looks like to rage, rage against the dying of the light? Joan Rivers will not go gentle into that good night.

Jonah Hex ★★
PG-13, 80 m., 2010

Josh Brolin (Jonah Hex), John Malkovich (Quentin Turnbull), Megan Fox (Lilah), Michael Fassbender (Burke), Will Arnett (Lieutenant Grass), Michael Shannon (Doc Cross Williams). Directed by Jimmy Hayward and produced by Akiva Goldsman and Andrew Lazar. Screenplay by Mark Neveldine and Brian Taylor, based on the DC Comics characters by John Albano and Tony Dezuniga.

Jonah Hex is a Western set around the town of Stunk Crick, although that doesn't entirely explain why the climactic scene involves an attack on the U.S. Capitol building in Washington. Using my powers of logic, I deduce that the characters traveled there from Stunk Crick. The movie is not precise in its geography. Most of the location filming was in Louisiana, which is not named, perhaps because that might make it hard to explain its vast deserts and dusty frontier town.

The thriller involves a man named Jonah Hex (Josh Brolin), who is bent on vengeance. During the Civil War, the evil Quentin Turnbull (John Malkovich) strapped him to a cross and made him watch as a house containing his family was set afire. Then Turnbull branded Jonah's face with a hot iron, causing difficulties with leaks when he tries to throw back a shot of whiskey. You can see why Jonah would want his revenge. To be sure, Turnbull mutters something about Jonah having previously murdered HIS family, meaning he isn't entirely without motive.

Stunk Crick is your standard frontier town with a wide Main Street, a saloon, and a room over the saloon occupied by Lilah, a sexy hooker. The presence of Lilah in the film is easily explained: She is played by Megan Fox. If you want a woman in an old western town, there are only three occupations open to her, hooking, schoolmarming, and anyone called Ma.

Lilah and Jonah are in love, for reasons unexplained. It certainly isn't because of the quality of their conversation. The only hooker in a Western I've ever believed in was in *Lonesome Dove*, but I've seen *Lonesome Dove*, and *Jonah Hex* is no *Lonesome Dove*.

It's based on some DC Comics characters, which may explain the way the plot jumps around. We hear a lot about graphic novels, but this is more of a graphic anthology of strange occult ideas. Consider, for example, that Jonah was once so close to death that he wandered around on the Other Side and made valuable contacts there. He can even talk to the dead, and one corpse revives long enough to tell him precisely where Quentin Turnbull can be found.

In what is possibly a confused stab at allegory, Jonah finds himself trying to prevent Turnbull from blowing up the Capitol building with a terrorist super weapon. In scenes set in the Oval Office, the U.S. president is concerned about this threat by Turnbull, who is an embittered Confederate general, and decides that the wanted outlaw Hex is the only man who can prevent the plot from being carried out.

A climactic battle scene takes place in the Potomac River between two ironclad ships. In U.S. history, you will recall, there was such a battle between the USS *Monitor* and the Confederate ship *Virginia*. One of these ships looks like the *Monitor*, but I'm unclear. Anyway, Turnbull is onboard, directing the Weapon, which is a big cannon. He's previously tested it by blowing up a Western town. Now he trains it on the Capitol, depicted in special effects that suggest the Capitol and the Washington Monument were the only two structures in Washington at that time, at least for purposes of being fired on.

After Hex saves the day, he's invited into the Oval Office, thanked, and then presented with a big badge. What is this badge? The president tells Hex: "America needs a sheriff." This provided the audience with a big laugh, which sounded like it might have been bottled up for a while.

The Joneses ★★
R, 96 m., 2010

Demi Moore (Kate Jones), David Duchovny (Steve Jones), Amber Heard (Jennifer Jones), Ben Hollingsworth (Mick Jones), Gary Cole (Larry), Glenne Headly (Summer), Lauren Hutton (KC). Directed by Derrick Borte and produced by Borte, Doug Mankoff, Andrew Spaulding, and Kristi Zea. Screenplay by Borte.

Everyone wants to keep up with the Joneses. They're good-looking, friendly, popular, affluent, and they always seem ahead of the curve when it comes to what they drive, wear, play, and consume. They never boast. They never have to. People just plain want to be just like them. And you had better stop reading now, because it's impossible to say more without out a spoiler.

OK, for those still in the room, I wonder how many will really be surprised by the big plot "reveal." From the first moments of dialogue, there seems to be something off about the Joneses. Nothing is made explicit for a time, but they don't seem to relate to one another as family members. There's something they understand and we don't.

The fact is, they aren't a family; they're a marketing unit. Marketing people talk about "early adopters": People who influence a peer group by being the first to know about, use, wear, or attend something. At a conference I attended in Boulder, Colorado, total strangers followed Andy Ihnatko and his iPad around like a man with a T-bone at a dog pound. The Joneses are professional early adopters, paid to impersonate a family unit and consume the sponsor's products.

Among other advantages to this story idea, it makes product placement necessary, not merely venal. If you don't leave this movie more aware of the new Audi models, you slept through it. The Joneses never make a point of anything. It's just that Steve Jones (David Duchovny) makes great shots with his new golf clubs. Kate Jones (Demi Moore) entertains so brilliantly. Their teenagers, Jennifer (Amber Heard) and Mick (Ben Hollingsworth), wear such cool stuff. If the Joneses don't have a dog, maybe that's because there's not enough money in dog retailing.

It would seem to be a comfortable existence, consuming the best products ahead of the market and never having to pay for them. It's not that easy. It means denying your own impulses to be honest and confiding. Suppressing your own tastes. Not feeling genuine. Ask yourself who in your crowd insisted you had to see *How to Train Your Dragon* in 3-D, when you wanted to see it in 2-D, and what you *really* wanted to see was *My Son, My Son, What Have Ye Done*. That person is a Jones.

You, on the other hand, are a Larry or Summer (Gary Cole and Glenne Headly), the next-door neighbors who are always playing catch-up. You have ceded control of your taste to someone you admire for superficial reasons. This is a doomed enterprise, for you will never, ever catch up, and by definition you can never take the lead because the Joneses define the race.

The Joneses not surprisingly finds troubling flaws in the lives of this professional family. Try as they will to be disciplined and on message, they have emotions of their own. Some of them involve sex. Others involve a feeling of inner worthlessness. The strongest is Kate, played by the great-looking Demi Moore as a capable team leader aiming for a promotion. Steve is a former golf pro, so no stranger to the challenge of playing a role model, but his decency runs deeper than Kate's.

As for the kids, Jennifer and Mick, well, even their names are popular; Jennifer is the sixty-seventh most popular name in the nation and Michael is the third. But they're teenagers, and you know how that goes. So many raging hormones, either to follow or suppress. That Jennifer and Mick are so attractive, and so . . . advanced . . . for their age complicates their inner lives. At that age, you haven't been completely tamed by the corporate mind-set.

The Joneses was directed and cowritten by Derrick Borte, an advertising man, and contains a good deal of dark cynicism. It also hopes to entertain, and those two goals don't fit together easily. Either this is a tragic family or a satirical one, and the film seems uncertain which way to jump. In a perfect film, the noose of their inauthentic lives would draw more tightly, more swiftly, around the Joneses, and the movie might be angrier.

Still, Demi Moore is good as a corporate team player with no conscience (she could have played the George Clooney role in *Up in the Air*), and the others adequately act around the problems of the screenplay. It's just that somehow this movie should acknowledge how very close to life it is, and how in our society you don't have to pay the Joneses. They learn their roles from television and work for free.

Journey to the Center of the Earth ★ ★
PG, 92 m., 2008

Brendan Fraser (Trevor Anderson), Josh Hutcherson (Sean), Anita Briem (Hannah). Directed by Eric Brevig and produced by Charlotte Huggins, Beau Flynn, and Cary Granat. Screenplay by Michael Weiss, Jennifer Flackett, and Mark Levin, inspired by the novel by Jules Verne.

There is a part of me that will always have affection for a movie like *Journey to the Center of the Earth*. It is a small part and steadily shrinking, but once I put on the 3-D glasses and settled into my seat, it started perking up. This is a fairly bad movie, and yet at the same time maybe about as good as it could be. There may not be an eight-year-old alive who would not love it. If I had seen it when I was eight, I would have remembered it with deep affection for all these years, until I saw it again and realized how little I really knew at that age.

You are already familiar with the premise, that there is another land inside of our globe. You are familiar because the Jules Verne novel has inspired more than a dozen movies and countless TV productions, including a series, and has been ripped off by such as Edgar Rice Burroughs, who called it Pellucidar and imagined that the earth was hollow and there was another world on the inside surface. (You didn't ask, but yes, I own a copy of *Tarzan at the Earth's Core* with the original dust jacket.)

In this version, Brendan Fraser stars as a geologist named Trevor, who defends the memory of his late brother, Max, who believed the center of the earth could be reached through "volcanic tubes." Max disappeared on a mysterious expedition, which, if it involved vol-

canic tubes, should have been no surprise to him. Now Trevor has been asked to spend some time with his nephew, Max's son, who is named Sean (Josh Hutcherson). What with one thing and another, wouldn't you know they find themselves in Iceland, and peering down a volcanic tube. They are joined in this enterprise by Hannah (Anita Briem), whom they find living in Max's former research headquarters near the volcano he was investigating.

Now begins a series of adventures, in which the operative principle is: No matter how frequently or how far they fall, they will land without injury. They fall very frequently and very far. The first drop lands them at the bottom of a deep cave, from which they cannot possibly climb, but they remain remarkably optimistic: "There must be a way out of here!" Sure enough, they find an abandoned mine shaft and climb aboard three cars of its miniature railway for a scene that will make you swear the filmmakers must have seen *Indiana Jones and the Temple of Doom*. Just like in that movie, they hurtle down the tracks at breakneck speeds; they're in three cars, on three more or less parallel tracks, leading you to wonder why three parallel tracks were constructed at great expense and bother, but just when such questions are forming, they have to (1) leap a chasm, (2) jump from one car to another, and (3) crash. It's a funny thing about that little railway: After all these years, it still has lamps hanging over the rails, and the electricity is still on.

The problem of lighting an unlit world is solved in the next cave they enter, which is inhabited by cute little birds that glow in the dark. One of them makes friends with Sean and leads them on to the big attraction—a world bounded by a great interior sea. This world must be a terrible place to inhabit; it has man-eating and man-strangling plants, its waters harbor giant-fanged fish and fearsome sea snakes that eat them, and on the farther shore is a Tyrannosaurus rex.

So do the characters despair? Would you despair if you were trapped miles below the surface in a cave and being chased by its hungry inhabitants? Of course not. There isn't a moment in the movie when anyone seems frightened, not even during a fall straight down for thousands of feet, during which they link hands like skydivers and carry on a conversation. Trevor gets the ball rolling: "We're still falling!"

I mentioned 3-D glasses earlier in the review. Yes, the movie is available in 3-D in "selected theaters." Select those theaters to avoid. With a few exceptions (such as the authentic IMAX process), 3-D remains underwhelming to me—a distraction, a disappointment, and more often than not offering a dingy picture. I guess setting your story inside the earth is one way to explain why it always seems to need more lighting.

The movie is being shown in 2-D in a majority of theaters, and that's how I wish I had seen it. Since there's that part of me with a certain weakness for movies like this, it's possible I would have liked it more. It would have looked brighter and clearer, and the photography wouldn't have been cluttered up with all the leaping and gnashing of teeth. Then I could have appreciated the work of the plucky actors, who do a lot of things right in this movie, of which the most heroic is keeping a straight face.

The Joy of Singing ★★★
NO MPAA RATING, 96 m., 2010

Marina Fois (Muriel), Lorant Deutsch (Philippe), Jeanne Balibar (Constance), Julien Baumgartner (Julien), Nathalie Richard (Noemie), Caroline Ducey (Anna), Guillaume Quatravaux (Joseph), Evelyne Kirschenbaum (Eve). Directed by Ilan Duran Cohen and produced by Anne-Cecile Berthomeau and Edouard Mauriat. Screenplay by Cohen and Philippe Lasry.

Don't get the wrong idea. *The Joy of Singing* could also be titled *The Joy of Singing Rather Than Being Murdered*. One of the meetings of Madame Eve's voice class begins with her tearful announcement that two of the group have been found dead. Her students eye one another uneasily. Who will be killed next? We wonder, too.

This is the goofiest thrill-sex-music-spy movie in many a moon, with a surprising amount of nudity and an even more surprising amount of singing, ranging from opera to "Amazing Grace" to "I'll Stand by You." Its MacGuffin is a missing USB memory stick containing unspecified uranium secrets.

I fully believe no one in the movie has any idea what these secrets could consist of, where they came from, and how they went missing, but never mind. The information belonged to the late husband of Constance (Jeanne Balibar), a student in the class. Therefore, French undercover agents *and* terrorists *and* possible Israeli and Russian agents enroll in the class to keep an eye on her. I'm trying to remember if anyone in the class has enrolled to improve their voice.

This is all done with a straight face. The students with their nefarious secrets all have to sing. Some aren't half bad. A couple are damn fine. Maybe there's something about singing in a small group of fellow spies that elevates the libido. Soon many, if not all, of these people (except for Madame Eve) are screwing like rabbits. Even the young hustler Julien (Julien Baumgartner), who doesn't give freebies for ethical reasons, is astonished to find himself growing tender about Noemie (Nathalie Richard). If there's one thing fatal to spying, it's sincerity.

At a different velocity this could be a screwball comedy, especially with those big apartments where people are always coming into and going out of rooms, but then it would be less fun. Death and sex are sort of serious, you see, and these people don't treat them lightly. They also have underlying concerns about growing old and never having children. The French agents, Muriel (Marina Fois) and Philippe (Lorant Deutsch), have a problem: She wants him to sleep with her, and he wants to be respected for more than his body. If Inspector Clouseau wandered in, he'd be out of his league and soon out of his pants.

I'll award a shiny new dime to anyone who watches the film once and can tell me who is doing what and to whom and for what reason. It just doesn't matter. We get the basic idea, and realize we know more about what's happening than anyone on the screen. I doubt if anyone in the movie, in the audience, or among the filmmakers can offer a plausible explanation for why all these people have to attend music class, especially considering its fatality rate.

Julia ★★★★
R, 140 m., 2009

Tilda Swinton (Julia), Saul Rubinek (Mitch), Kate del Castillo (Elena), Aidan Gould (Tom), Jude Ciccolella (Nick), Bruno Bichir (Diego), Horacio Garcia Rojas (Santos), Gaston Peterson (Miguel). Directed by Erick Zonca and produced by Francois Marquis and Bertrand Faivre. Screenplay by Zonca and Aude Py.

Tilda Swinton is fearless. She'll take on any role without her ego, paycheck, vanity, or career path playing a part. All that matters, apparently, is whether the movie interests her, and whether she thinks she can do something interesting with the role. She almost always can. She hasn't often been more fascinating than in *Julia*, a nerve-wracking thriller with a twisty plot and startling realism.

We have not seen this Tilda before—but then, we haven't seen most of the Tildas before. This one is an alcoholic slut who lacks what we are pleased to call normal feminine emotions. She's just been fired from another job. Her pattern is to get sloppy drunk every night and drag a strange man to bed. She needs money. Her neighbor Elena (Kate del Castillo) comes to her with an offer. Elena's young son is now living with his millionaire grandfather, who won't allow her to see him. She needs somebody to help her kidnap the child.

This is the beginning of Julia's nightmare journey through a thorn thicket of people you do not want to meet. If there's one thing consistent about her behavior, it's how she lies to all of them. This is not one of those tough heroines you sort of like. You don't like her. She makes not the slightest effort to be liked. She doesn't give a damn. She cuts back on the drinking, however, perhaps because she is constantly fleeing—both away from and toward.

You have to give a lot of credit to Erick Zonca, the fifty-two-year-old French director who cowrote the film with Aude Py. He makes it move relentlessly. He skillfully buries it in seedy American and Mexican locations that never, ever, feel like sets. He uses a child actor and uses him well. He makes no attempt to sentimentalize the kid, who is spoiled and

hostile. He puts Tilda Swinton at the center of this, and she plays Julia as a tough broad who is in way over her head, and desperately invents stories to mislead those who want the money involved—which starts out at $50,000 before she cheats her way up to $2 million.

The plot of *Julia*, its twists and turns and surprises and rotten luck, is, shall we say, not very plausible. I believed it. That's because everything that happens seems inevitable, not contrived—the inescapable outcome of what has gone before, growing out of the greed and evil of the characters, which Julia, who is herself greedy and evil, is blindsided by. I could summarize the plot for you in one sentence, but I don't think I will, and when you see the film you will understand why.

Do we hate this woman Julia? When you see how she treats the boy Tom (Aidan Gould), we want to, except that she's all that stands between Tom and much worse things, including death. No matter what her motive for keeping him alive, there comes a moment when she shields him with her body from a man with a gun, and an utterly amoral woman would have made a deal.

Oh, she offers lots of deals. She's not to be trusted. There are times here when only her quick powers of invention keep her and the boy alive, and Swinton does a magnificent job with a tough acting challenge: letting us see how desperate she is without another character being able to tell. This movie lives on the edge all the way through, right up until an astonishing final scene on the median strip of a superhighway. What she does then shows that she's a better woman than she was when she started out, but you can't call it a false happy ending because it's more wrung-out than happy, and after all, what choice did she have?

This movie should have a big ad campaign and be making a lot of noise, stirring up word of mouth. It's being treated as an art film. It's good enough to be an art film, but don't let anyone pigeonhole it for you. It's one doozy of a great thriller. And the acting here is as good as it gets—not just from Swinton but from Saul Rubinek as her one remaining friend, and by Bruno Bichir as Diego, whom she meets in Tijuana. You want to be careful who you meet in Tijuana. Swinton here is amazing. She goes for broke and wins big time.

Julie and Julia ★★ ½

PG-13, 123 m., 2009

Meryl Streep (Julia Child), Amy Adams (Julie Powell), Stanley Tucci (Paul Child), Chris Messina (Eric Powell), Linda Emond (Simone Beck), Mary Lynn Rajskub (Sarah), Jane Lynch (Dorothy McWilliams), Frances Sternhagen (Irma Rombauer). Directed by Nora Ephron and produced by Ephron, Laurence Mark, Amy Robinson, and Eric Steel. Screenplay by Ephron, based on books by Julie Powell and Julia Child.

Did you ever want to take a three-day bus trip sitting next to Julia Child? Just asking. In thirty-minute programs on TV, she was priceless. But to live with her, I suspect, must have taken the patience of a saint. Her husband, Paul, in *Julie and Julia* is portrayed as a saint, so that explains her marriage.

Now about Julie Powell. That's the woman who wrote a blog documenting her vow to cook all the way through Child's *Mastering the Art of French Cooking,* 524 recipes in 365 days. She is also married to a patient man, although he retains enough self-respect to walk out for a few days halfway through her project. Together, they make just about enough money to live above a pizza parlor in Queens. How do they pay for all those groceries?

The performances go a long way toward selling the characters. Meryl Streep creates an uncanny version of Julia Child, of course with a spot-on accent. She seems to have grown several inches to play the great six-foot-two-inch chef. Stanley Tucci, playing her diplomat husband, stands five foot eight in real life. The movie somewhat diminishes this difference, but at no point, however, does he seem capable of denying anything to his beloved goddess.

Amy Adams could make anyone lovable, but with Julie Powell it's sometimes a stretch. Julie is so single-minded about her obsession that it comes to dominate her married life. Having cooked a few of Julia's recipes myself, I doubt there are many you can start on after getting home, some nights, as late as eight or nine. The dinner bell seems to have rung at the Powell household after midnight, although the wait was mellowed by a remarkable number of martinis.

The film, written and directed by Nora Ephron, cuts back and forth between the two women, showing how their dedication to cuisine shaped their lives and marriages. A fair number of no doubt delicious recipes are prepared and served, but there is never a moment our mouths water as they did over the Japanese noodle soup in *Tampopo.*

Nor are the leads seen as great eaters. They put a forkful in their mouth, close their eyes, and say "Mmmm," and that's about it. If Paul likes a dish, it is because it gives him the opportunity to tell Julia what a genius she is. Poor Eric simply gobbles everything like pizza after a softball game; having to wait so late for his meals perhaps gives him anxiety.

Julia Child was a rarity, an American woman studying haute cuisine at a French school for professional chefs, and was obviously a gifted student and a natural chef, even if she was driven to cooking because of her impatience with bridge. Ephron chooses to show her education in scenes so broad we could be watching *I Love Lucy.* If you came home and found your wife savagely dicing so many onions she had a pyramid two feet high, would you wonder about her?

As for Julie Powell, her project is undertaken to boost her self-esteem; she's a telephone call taker in a cubicle, dealing with insurance questions involving 9/11, although "really" she's a novelist. Someone once said, "What you do all day instead of your real job *is* your real job."

This movie is not lacking in entertainment value, especially from the Streep performance. But if the men had been portrayed as more high-spirited, it might have taken on intriguing dimensions. Both husbands are, frankly, a little boring: They've been assigned their supporting roles in their marriages and are reluctant to question the single-mindedness of their wives.

All the same, credit is due. Julia Child really did write a cookbook that changed American culinary history. And Julie Powell really did cook her way through 524 recipes in 365 days. I am currently writing a cookbook titled *The Pot and How to Use It,* about how you can cook almost anything in a rice cooker. Take my word for it, it's not going to take anyone a year to cook their way through this one. ☞

Just Another Love Story ★ ★ ★ ½
NO MPAA RATING, 104 m., 2009

Anders W. Berthelsen (Jonas), Rebecka Hemse (Julia), Nikolaj Lie Kaas (Sebastian), Charlotte Fich (Mette), Dejan Cukic (Frank), Karsten Jansfort (Poul), Flemming Enevold (Overlaege Dichmann), Bent Mejding (Hr. Castlund). Directed by Ole Bornedal and produced by Michael Obel. Screenplay by Bornedal.

Apart from a little nudity, *Just Another Love Story* could have been inspired, almost shot by shot, from a 1940s film noir from RKO, when it would have started with Robert Mitchum dying on the sidewalk in the rain. This is a vigorous thriller from Denmark that tells the classic noir story of a flawed cop trapped between a good wife and a bad woman. The twist is, the woman doesn't know she's been bad, since she has amnesia. It gets better.

Jonas is a Copenhagen homicide scene photographer, happily married, two kids. One day his car stalls, another car slams into him, runs head-on into a third car, and flips into the ditch. The other driver, Julia, is critically injured. He visits her in the hospital and is greeted with joy by her family, who assumes he must be the Sebastian she told them about, the new fiancé she met in Vietnam. He had to return on a later flight.

At this point, if Jonas (Anders W. Berthelsen) had seen any noirs at all, he would say: "I don't know who Sebastian is, but my name is Jonas." He pauses for a fatal instant and is swept into another life. Because Julia (Rebecka Hemse) doesn't remember much and can't see well, she has no choice but to agree with her family that this is Sebastian. Her father gives him a blank check, her family embraces him, and Jonas topples into a double life.

Oh, but it's more than that. Most noirs are. One thing about them is that they're rigidly moralistic. If you cheat on your wife, you're going to pay for it. This is true even if your wife knows nothing about it, the other woman can scarcely be blamed, and you start out only trying to accommodate an accident victim and her worried family.

Ole Bornedal, the film's writer and director, works at a considerably quicker pace than traditional noirs and ingeniously introduces

ironies and complications I will not even hint at. The closing scenes of the plot spring one surprise after another. They seem laid on thick, but we have to admit, given all that leads up to them, they make sense.

Just Another Love Story works in nice little touches. I liked Jonas's partner in photographing crime scenes, who deals with the violence and gore by laughing about it. There's a scene where a horrifying situation is described, and the guy shakes, he's chuckling so hard. Why is this shown? Well, if you photograph murder scenes, you deal with it the best you can. The whole movie flavors its plot with quirky observations and asides.

It's interesting that two of the best thrillers of the last several months, *Tell No One* and *Just Another Love Story*, have come from Europe. Both movies gain because they star actors unfamiliar to us. They gain because there's room in them for close observation of the characters. They gain most of all because they don't slow down the plot for unnecessary special effects scenes—fights, chases, things like that. Unless such scenes are necessary or very well-done, essentially they just put the plot on hold while the filmmakers flex their muscles. Here the plotting has all the muscle that's required.

Just Wright ★★★
PG, 99 m., 2010

Queen Latifah (Leslie Wright), Common (Scott McKnight), Paula Patton (Morgan Alexander), James Pickens Jr. (Lloyd Wright), Phylicia Rashad (Ella McKnight), Pam Grier (Janice Wright). Directed by Sanaa Hamri and produced by Debra Martin Chase, Shakim Compere, and Queen Latifah. Screenplay by Michael Elliot.

One reason people like Queen Latifah is that she likes herself. In most of her roles, she radiates cheer. She can play grim, as in *Bringing Out the Dead*, but she has a natural sunniness that makes me, at least, feel good. And she is a real woman, not a skinny woman with too many sharp angles. Jennifer Aniston, who looks perfectly great, makes me worry about her mental health when she publicizes her new baby food diet.

Latifah has never been fat. She has always been plus size. There is a difference. She is healthy, fit, carries herself with confidence, and looks terrific in *Just Wright* in the kind of clothing a physical therapist might feel comfortable wearing. If you're dragging around feeling low about yourself, you want to know her secret.

This is not a discussion of the Queen's body, however; it's about the whole gestalt. One of the reasons she's the star of *Just Wright* is that few people, and certainly no one in this film, can hold the screen against her. In common with many other stars, when she's in a shot, it's about her.

Sure, we go along with the fiction that Scott (Common), the handsome pro basketball player in the movie, is going to marry Morgan (Paula Patton), Queen Latifah's BFF. Sure, we think Patton looks terrific and is a beauty. But, come on. Once Scott injures his knee and hires Miss Wright (Latifah) as his live-in physical therapist, we know he's going to fall in love with her. It's so much easier to fall in love with someone who is necessary to you than someone you are necessary to.

The plot involves Leslie Wright and Morgan as obsessed fans of the New Jersey Nets— Leslie because she loves basketball, and Morgan because she wants to be a player's wife. After Leslie has a Meet Cute with the handsome Nets star Scott McKnight at a gas station, she gets invited to his birthday party, and, of course, takes Morgan along. Scott zooms in on Morgan. Leslie, as loyal best friend, is accustomed to this.

After Scott gets a knee injury and Leslie becomes his special duty therapist, the trick is to not rush in the direction the movie is obviously moving. Director Sanaa Hamri accomplishes this. She and writer Michael Elliot add enough detail and actual dialogue (you know, people talking about things in more than one syllable) that we enjoy the growing-closer process. Paula Patton's Morgan is a self-centered egotist and no good at caregiving, but hey, that's built into the role.

Sanaa Hamri is herself an actor-director, with an interesting background; she directed two of Prince's TV specials and the very good *Something New* (2006), starring Sanaa Lathan (no relation). That was another film about a woman and man gradually discovering they're in love, which is always more fun than the first-sight deal. Here Common isn't called upon to do much heavy lifting in the acting department, but he plays well with Queen Latifah. Sure, the movie is a formula. A formula that works reminds us of why it became a formula.

K

The Karate Kid ★★★ ½
PG, 131 m., 2010

Jaden Smith (Dre Parker), Jackie Chan (Mr. Han), Taraji P. Henson (Sherry Parker), Han Wenwen (Mei Ying), Wang Zhenwei (Cheng), Rongguang Yu (Master Li). Directed by Harald Zwart and produced by James Lassiter, Jada Pinkett Smith, Will Smith, Ken Stovitz, and Jerry Weintraub. Screenplay by Christopher Murphey.

If you've seen *The Karate Kid* (1984), the memories will come back during this 2010 remake of the original. That's a compliment. The original story was durable enough to inspire three sequels, and now we have an entertaining version filmed mostly on location in China, with fifty-six-year-old Jackie Chan in the role of Mr. Miyagi.

The original film was one of its year's best movies. The new one lacks the perfect freshness of that one; there aren't many surprises as it follows the 1984 almost point by point. But here is a lovely and well-made film that stands well on its own feet. The Chinese locations add visual interest, there are scenes of splendor in mountains and on the Great Wall, and the characters are once again engaging.

The original film's greatest asset was the Oscar-nominated performance by Pat Morita as Mr. Miyagi. Jackie Chan is so famous that it can come as no surprise here when Mr. Han, a reclusive janitor, reveals a hidden talent for the martial arts. But Chan has never been a strutting, macho fighter onscreen; his charm comes from a self-kidding quality. Here he does a good job of cooling down his usual cheerfulness and keeping his cards hidden.

In the role of his young pupil, Jaden Smith, son of Will and Jada Pinkett Smith, has a natural screen presence that glows. Dre Parker is calmer than the skitterish kid played by Ralph Macchio, but so much smaller than his opponents that we can well believe his fear of a bully at school. And when that happens, we can forget obsessing about the 1984 film and enjoy this one. That was then; this is now.

The story once again involves a kid being packed up by his divorced mom and forced to leave his hometown and friends and move far away—from Detroit to Beijing, this time. He hates it. Then a cute young violinist named Mei Ying (Han Wenwen) smiles at him, and life looks more promising—if it weren't for the school bully, Cheng (Wang Zhenwei). This creature is so hateful and sadistic it's hard to explain, until we meet his brutal kung fu coach, Master Li (Rongguang Yu). The monstrous Li teaches a new form of child abuse: kids beating up on each other.

The story proceeds, as it must, with Dre slowly softening the heart of Mr. Han, who saves him from a beating by Cheng and agrees to teach him the secrets of kung fu. Training goes well, and Dre and Mei Ying make a pact to attend each other's big days: his kung fu tournament, her recital. There's the usual nonsense about her parents disapproving of him. Gee, why in the world would the parents of a world-class classical musician disapprove of a kung fu student from Detroit who doesn't speak Chinese?

Luckily for Dre and the movie, everyone in China who needs to speak English can do so, even the little monster Cheng. Many Americans not only have small interest in learning another language, they have small interest in reading subtitles of their own. We believe, as Mark Twain put it in *The Innocents Abroad*, that any foreigner can speak English if only it is spoken slowly enough and loudly enough.

It goes without saying that the whole film leads up to a climactic kung fu tournament, and that Dre is pitted against Cheng for the championship. The lineage of the film is distinguished; the '84 version was directed by John Avildsen, director of *Rocky*. This film's climax is unusually well handled; the tension is constructed in a careful way, the characters are developed, and use of a scoreboard makes it seem orderly, not rushed. It's one of the better Obligatory Fight climaxes I've seen.

The director, Harald Zwart, has not been one of my favorites; he made last year's *Pink Panther 2*. But here, with a robust script by Christopher Murphey and cinematography by Roger Pratt (who filmed two Harry Potters), he makes a handsome, absorbing movie. It runs a little long, but during the championship, that's the last thing you're thinking of.

Katyn ★★★ ½

NO MPAA RATING, 121 m., 2009

Maja Ostaszewska (Anna), Artur Zmijewski (Andrzej), Andrzej Chyra (Jerzy), Jan Englert (General), Danuta Stenka (General's Wife), Magdalena Cielecka (Agnieszka), Agnieszka Glinska (Irena). Directed by Andrzej Wajda and produced by Michal Kwiecinski. Screenplay by Wajda, Wladyslaw Pasikowski, and Przemyslaw Nowakowski.

In 1940, some fifteen thousand officers of the Polish army were rounded up, transported in sealed buses to a forest named Katyn, shot in the back of the head by the Russian KGB, and buried in mass graves. That is the simple truth. When the nation was occupied by both the Nazis and Soviets, their deaths were masked in silence. Then the Nazis dug up the graves and blamed the deaths on the Soviets. After the defeat of Hitler and the Soviet occupation of Poland, history was rewritten and the official version blamed the massacre on the Nazis.

One of the officers murdered that day was Jakub Wajda, whose son Andrzej would become a leading Polish film director and one of the chroniclers of the Solidarity movement. Now eighty-two, Andrzej has evoked what happened that day and how it infected Polish society for fifty years. Reflect that everyone in Poland knew the truth of the massacre, but to lie about it became an official requirement under the Soviet-controlled regime. Thus, in some cases, to gain immunity or advancement in postwar Poland required parents and children, brothers and sisters of the dead to remain silent about their fates.

This poor bruised nation, trapped by time and geography between the two dark evils of twentieth-century Europe, has prevailed, and its survival is embodied in the career of Wajda, who in key films starting in the 1950s found a way to say what he needed even with Communist national film censorship. His early films *Kanal* (1957), about the Warsaw Uprising, and *Ashes and Diamonds* (1958), about the Polish Resistance during the war, involved Poland's two oppressors.

A single image at the beginning of *Katyn* expresses the nation's dilemma. A bridge is crowded by fleeing civilians—from both ends. Some flee advancing Nazis. Some flee advancing Russians. As the two armies, in concert under the Hitler-Stalin pact, acted together, such situations took place. The refugees are not tattered stragglers, but ordinary civilians, torn so quickly from domestic security that they carry suitcases, although they could have little idea of the journey ahead for them.

Wajda tells his story through a few characters. We meet Anna (Maja Ostaszewska), traveling in search of her husband, Andrzej (Artur Zmijewski), a Polish officer. They are clearly intended as Wajda's parents; movingly, he has named his father after himself. His father, like many of the Polish officer corps, was not a professional military man, but a reservist, called up from the professional, scientific, educational classes. The 1940 massacre would exterminate many of a generation's best and brightest.

Lives hang by a thread. Anna succeeds in finding her husband at a deployment camp and begs him to escape with her. He feels his place is with his fellow officers. Neither of them suspect he will be executed. Wajda broadens his canvas to include others, including Andrzej's own father; his mother, like his wife, waits for word. We meet two other women: the wife of an executed general, who refuses to toe the Soviet line, and the sister of a dead officer, who commissions a plaque in his memory. Her crime is to add the date of the Katyn massacre, since the Soviets played with time to make it correspond to a later period when the Nazis were enemies, not friends.

The actresses playing these roles are all well-known in Poland, where I assume they are easy to distinguish. To an outsider like myself, they tended to resemble one another, and I was able to follow them by story and plot more easily than facially. This is not really a problem because all are facets of the same experience.

Anna remains the central figure, refusing to accept that her husband is dead until she finally receives the truth from an eyewitness to his remains. So did many loved ones cling to hope, as the POW/MIA relatives do in this country. The dead had no peace. They were dug up by the Nazis to expose Soviet crimes,

299

then dug up again, and metaphorically dug up in revisionist history.

The film ends with a scene of relentless horror, showing the assembly line of execution. Men are taken from the sealed buses one by one, their names checked off a list, then quickly walked to their place of death and killed with a bullet to the back of the skull. Their bodies fall or are heaved into mass graves in orderly progress, falling side by side and buried by bulldozer. Now Wajda has brought some small measure of rest to their names, to Poland, and to history.

Note: Katyn was one of 2008's Oscar nominees for best foreign language film.

Kick-Ass ★

R, 117 m., 2010

Aaron Johnson (Dave/Kick-Ass), Christopher Mintz-Plasse (Chris/Red Mist), Mark Strong (Frank D'Amico), Chloe Grace Moretz (Mindy/Hit Girl), Nicolas Cage (Damon/Big Daddy). Directed by Matthew Vaughn and produced by Vaughn, Adam Bohling, Tarquin Pack, Brad Pitt, David Reid, and Kris Thykier. Screenplay by Vaughn and Jane Goldman, based on the comic book by Mark Millar and John S. Romita Jr.

Shall I have feelings, or should I pretend to be cool? Will I seem hopelessly square if I find *Kick-Ass* morally reprehensible, and will I appear to have missed the point? Let's say you're a big fan of the original comic book, and you think the movie does it justice. You know what? You inhabit a world I am so very not interested in. A motion picture camera makes a record of whatever is placed in front of it, and in this case it shows deadly carnage dished out by an eleven-year-old girl, after which an adult man brutally hammers her to within an inch of her life. Blood everywhere. Now tell me all about the context.

The movie's premise is that ordinary people, including a high school kid, the eleven-year-old, and her father, try to become superheroes in order to punish evil men. The flaw in this premise is that the little girl *does* become a superhero. In one scene, she faces a hallway jammed with heavily armed gangsters and shoots, stabs, and kicks them all to death,

while flying through the air with such power it's enough to make Jackie Chan take out an AARP membership.

This isn't comic violence. These men, and many others in the film, are really stone-cold dead. And the eleven-year-old apparently experiences no emotions about this. Many children that age would be, I dunno, *affected* somehow, don't you think, after killing eight or twelve men who were trying to kill them?

I know, I know. This is a satire. But a satire of what? The movie's rated R, which means in this case that it's doubly attractive to anyone under seventeen. I'm not too worried about sixteen-year-olds here. I'm thinking of six-year-olds. There are characters here with walls covered in carefully mounted firearms, ranging from handguns through automatic weapons to bazookas. At the end, when the villain deliciously anticipates blowing a bullet hole in the child's head, he is prevented only because her friend, in the nick of time, shoots him with a bazooka shell at ten-foot range and blows him through a skyscraper window and across several city blocks of sky in a projectile of blood, flame, and smoke. As I often read on the Internet: Hahahahaha.

The little girl is named Mindy (Chloe Grace Moretz). She adopts the persona of Hit Girl. She has been trained by her father, Big Daddy (Nicolas Cage), to join him in the battle against a crime boss (Mark Strong). Her training includes being shot at point-blank range while wearing a bulletproof vest. She also masters the martial arts—more, I would say, than any other movie martial artist of any age I can recall. And she's gifted with deadly knife-throwing skill; a foot-long knife was presented to her by her dad as, I guess, a graduation present.

Big Daddy and Mindy never have a chat about, you know, stuff like how when you kill people they are really dead. This movie regards human beings like video game targets. Kill one, and you score. They're dead, you win. When kids in the age range of this movie's home video audience are shooting each other every day in America, that kind of stops being funny.

Hit Girl teams up with Kick-Ass (Aaron Johnson), the narrator of the film, a lackluster high school kid who lives vicariously through comic books. For reasons tedious to explain, he orders a masked costume by mail order and sets about trying to behave as a superhero, which doesn't work out well. He lacks the training of a Big Daddy. But as he and Hit Girl find themselves fighting side by side, he turns into a quick learner. Also, you don't need to be great at hand-to-hand combat if you can just shoot people dead.

The early scenes give promise of an entirely different comedy. Aaron Johnson has a certain anti-charm, his problems in high school are engaging, and so on. A little later, I reflected that possibly only Nic Cage could seem to shoot a small girl point-blank and make it, well, funny. Say what you will about her character, but Chloe Grace Moretz has presence and appeal. Then the movie moved into dark, dark territory, and I grew sad.

The Killer Inside Me ★★ ½
R, 109 m., 2010

Casey Affleck (Lou Ford), Kate Hudson (Amy Stanton), Jessica Alba (Joyce Lakeland), Ned Beatty (Chester Conway), Elias Koteas (Joe Rothman), Tom Bower (Sheriff Bob Maples), Simon Baker (Howard Hendricks), Bill Pullman (Billy Boy Walker). Directed by Michael Winterbottom and produced by Andrew Eaton, Chris Hanley, and Bradford L. Schlei. Screenplay by John Curran, based on the novel by Jim Thompson.

What we desire is not a happy ending, so much as closure. That often means simply that a film knows what it thinks about itself. *The Killer Inside Me* is expert filmmaking based on a frightening performance, but it presents us with a character who remains a vast, empty, lonely, cold space. The film finds resolution there somewhere, perhaps, but not on a frequency I can receive.

Michael Winterbottom's film is inspired by a 1952 pulp novel by Jim Thompson, perhaps the bleakest and most unrelenting of American crime novelists. The book is considered by some his finest work; other Thompson novels were filmed as *The Grifters, The Getaway, After Dark, My Sweet,* and *Coup de Torchon.* Stephen King wrote: "Big Jim didn't know the meaning of the word stop. There are three

brave *lets* inherent in the forgoing: He let himself see everything, he let himself write it down, then he let himself publish it."

What Thompson saw in his character Lou Ford (Casey Affleck) was a mild-spoken, intellectual psychopath with no understanding of good and evil. He murders people he loves, *while* loving them, and has no idea why. The story's insights into this seem limited to the title. There is a killer inside him. The killer is not him. He doesn't understand that killer. He has no control over him and no doubt sincerely regrets the killer's crimes.

The story is set in West Texas in the early 1950s. Lou Ford, narrating his own story, is a deputy sheriff in a small town. He still lives in the home where he was raised. In the evenings he plays classical piano, reads books from his father's library, plays opera recordings. His voice, high-pitched but rough, bespeaks innocence. He has a girlfriend named Amy (Kate Hudson). He has the respect and affection of his alcoholic boss, Sheriff Bob Maples (Tom Bower). He is unfailingly calm and pleasant.

One day Maples gives him a job: Drive a few miles outside town and have a word with a prostitute, Joyce (Jessica Alba). A powerful local developer, Chester Conway (Ned Beatty), is concerned about her influence on his son, Elmer (Jay R. Ferguson). Ford pays the visit, has some words, and soon the two of them are urgently having rough sex. Why? Because this is the pulp universe, where a woman may be a prostitute with other men but she finds *you* irresistible. Female psychology is not the strong point with many pulp writers. Psychology in general is sketchy, based on simplified and half-understood Freudian notions. With Lou Ford, for example, we're given fragmented glimpses of childhood sexual abuse. Not the sort of abuse we've seen before: His mother liked Lou to slap her.

Indeed, Lou seems to attract women who like to be beaten. One apparently even likes to be nearly killed. The film attempts to account for this no more than it explains Lou's own nature. The best explanation probably is: When you buy a cheap paperback with a lurid cover, these are the sorts of events that will be described inside. In prose, the focus is through the point of view. In the film, we see the violence happening, and the first time it comes as a gut punch because we're not remotely expecting it.

Not from Lou Ford, anyway. Casey Affleck, an effective actor, is so convincing with his innocent, almost sweet facade that the movie sets us up to expect he'll be solving a crime, not causing one. He maintains that facade in the face of the most compelling challenges, not only from his own violence, but from two people with excellent reasons to suspect him: a labor leader (Elias Koteas) and the county attorney (Simon Baker). When Lou actually confesses to a kid who admires him (Liam Aiken), even what happens then doesn't faze him.

There is a point beyond which his implacability brings diminishing returns. While I admire Affleck's performance, I believe Winterbottom and his writer, John Curran, may have miscalculated. The reader of a pulp crime thriller might be satisfied simply with the prurient descriptions, and certainly this film visualizes those and has as its victims Jessica Alba and Kate Hudson, who embody paperback covers, but the dominant presence in the film is Lou Ford, and there just doesn't seem to be anybody at home.

Kit Kittredge: An American Girl ★ ★ ★ ½

G, 100 m., 2008

Abigail Breslin (Kit), Julia Ormond (Mrs. Kittredge), Chris O'Donnell (Mr. Kittredge), Max Thieriot (Will), Zach Mills (Stirling Howard), Joan Cusack (Miss Bond), Stanley Tucci (Jefferson J. Berk), Willow Smith (Countee), Madison Davenport (Ruthie Smithens), Jane Krakowski (Miss Dooley), Glenne Headley (Mrs. Howard), Wallace Shawn (Mr. Gibson). Directed by Patricia Rozema and produced by Elaine Goldsmith-Thomas, Lisa Gillan, Ellen L. Brothers, and Julie Goldstein. Screenplay by Ann Peacock, based on the stories by Valerie Tripp.

Considering that it is inspired by one of the dolls in the American Girl product line, *Kit Kittredge: An American Girl* is some kind of a miracle: an actually good movie. I expected so much less. I was waiting for some kind of banal product placement, I suppose, and here is a movie that is just about perfect for its tar-

get audience and more than that. It has a great look, engaging performances, real substance, and even a few whispers of political ideas, all surrounding the freshness and charm of Abigail Breslin, who was eleven when it was filmed.

The movie is set in Cincinnati at the dawn of the Great Depression; perfectly timed, it would appear, as we head into another one. Kit pounds furiously on the typewriter in her tree house, determined to become a girl reporter, while a big story is happening right downstairs in her family house: Its mortgage is about to be foreclosed. Her dad (Chris O'Donnell) has lost his car dealership and gone to Chicago seeking work, her mom (Julia Ormond) is taking in boarders, and there's local hysteria about muggings and robberies allegedly committed by hoboes.

Kit meets a couple of hoboes. Will (Max Thieriot) is about her age, and his sidekick Countee (Willow Smith) is a little younger. They live in the hobo camp down by the river, along with as nice a group of hoboes as you'd ever want to meet, and Kit tries selling their story and photos to the editor of the local paper (snarling Wallace Shawn). No luck. But other adventures ensue: She adopts a dog, her mom acquires chickens, Kit sells the eggs, and the new boarders are a colorfully assorted lot. And she sees such unthinkable sights as neighbors' furniture being moved to the sidewalk by deputies. Will that happen at her address?

The boarders include a magician (Stanley Tucci), a nurse (Jane Krakowski), the erratic driver (Joan Cusack) of a mobile library truck, and assorted others, eventually including even a monkey. Kit's mom hides her treasures in a lock box, but it is stolen, and unmistakable clues point to the hoboes. A footprint found under a window, for example, has a star imprint that exactly matches the boots found in Will's tent, and the sheriff names him the prime suspect. But hold on! Kit and her best friends, Stirling and Ruthie (Zach Mills and Madison Davenport), develop another theory, which would clear Will and implicate someone (dramatically lowered voice) a lot closer to home.

All of this (the missing loot, Kit's ambitions, Important Clues) is, of course, the very lifeblood of the Nancy Drew and Hardy Boys books, and *Kit Kittredge* not only understands that genre but breathes life into it. This movie, intelligently and sincerely directed by Patricia Rozema (*Mansfield Park*) does not condescend. It does not cheapen or go for easy laughs. It is as serious about Kit as she is about herself and doesn't treat her like some (indignant exclamation) dumb girl.

If you have or know or can borrow a girl (or a boy) who collects the American Girl dolls, grab onto that child as your excuse to see this movie. You may enjoy it as much as the kids do—maybe more, with its period costumes, settings, and music. The kids may be astonished that banks actually foreclosed on people's homes in the old days (hollow laugh). And there may be a message lurking somewhere in the movie's tolerance of hoboes. The American Girl dolls have already inspired TV movies about Molly, Felicity, and Samantha. What's for sure is that if *Kit Kittredge* sets the tone for more upcoming American Girl movies, we can anticipate some wonderful family films.

Knight and Day ★★★
PG-13, 109 m., 2010

Tom Cruise (Roy Miller), Cameron Diaz (June Havens), Peter Sarsgaard (Fitzgerald), Viola Davis (Director George), Jordi Molla (Antonio), Paul Dano (Simon Feck), Maggie Grace (April Havens), Marc Blucas (Rodney), Celia Weston (Molly). Directed by James Mangold and produced by Todd Garner, Cathy Konrad, Steve Pink, and Joe Roth. Screenplay by Patrick O'Neill.

Knight and Day aspires to the light charm of a romantic action comedy like *Charade* or *Romancing the Stone*, but would come closer if it dialed down the relentless action. The romance part goes without saying after a Meet Cute contrived in an airport, and the comedy seems to generate naturally between Tom Cruise and Cameron Diaz. But why do so many summer movies find it obligatory to inflict us with CGI overkill? I'd sorta rather see Diaz and Cruise in action scenes on a human scale, rather than have it rubbed in that for long stretches they're essentially replaced by animation.

Have summer audiences been so hammered down by special effects that they require noise and fragmented visuals to hold their interest? Is it still possible to delight in a story unfolding with charm and wit? How many machine guns do you need in a romantic comedy? If you have charismatic stars like Cruise and Diaz and an A-list director, do you have to hedge your bet?

The movie is entertaining but could have been better. The director is James Mangold, whose previous two films were *Walk the Line* and *3:10 to Yuma*. I have a hunch there was an early draft of Patrick O'Neill's screenplay that was more in the Cary Grant romcom tradition, and then somebody decided the effects had to be jacked up. From the ads, you could get the notion this was a Michael Bay film.

The wonder is that Cruise and Diaz are effective enough in their roles that they're not overwhelmed by all the commotion surrounding them. They make the movie work because they cheerfully project that they know it's utter nonsense and pitch in to enjoy the fun. I've been reading that movie stars can no longer "sell" a blockbuster movie. Audiences buy the concept, brand name, packaging, whatever. If that's true, which I doubt, it would mean a victory of technology over humans. If it comes true, it will be because movies have lost interest in creating and shaping characters we care about—because they're using actors as insert shots in special effects.

The plot makes splendid use of a MacGuffin, the device that explains everything by explaining nothing. Roy Miller, the Cruise character, has something and there are bad guys who want it. I could tell you what it is, but what difference does it make? That's the whole point of a MacGuffin. Anyway, Roy *happens* to run into June Havens, the Diaz character, at an airport, for reasons you will discover. That's the manipulated Meet Cute. Now this next part you will want to follow closely.

They both end up on the same airplane, which has no other passengers except some men scattered here and there. She goes to the rest room. He kills all the men and both pilots, and sits the dead passengers upright, *Weekend at Bernie's* style. She comes out of the rest room, not having heard the gunshots. He

303

crash-lands the plane in a field, and urges her to follow him in escaping FBI agents who are after them.

But . . . but . . . was there no other way for the bad guys to get the MacGuffin than by taking over a scheduled flight? Maybe, I dunno, snatch him on the ground? How did the FBI know the plane would crash—and where? Also, if you track who has possession of the MacGuffin during various times at the airport, you'll go crazy. Mind you, I'm not complaining. The movie knows this sequence is monumentally silly, and so do Cruise and Diaz, and Cruise keeps up a reassuring line of patter all during it, even while trying to crash-land safely.

That stuff is entertaining. There's also a running joke about how much ground they cover in an international chase. The movie was shot on location in Massachusetts, Spain (where they are chased by bulls), California, Jamaica, Austria, and Kankakee, Illinois, which has an excellent Steak 'n Shake out on I-57. Whether the actors were actually there on all those locations is a good question. Maybe only the green screen stuff was shot on location.

Such matters are irrelevant in a movie that makes not the slightest pretense of realism. Cruise and Diaz are fully scripted throughout with nonstop bantering and one-liners. They never seriously discuss their situation. They spend half the movie in dire danger. Thousands of bullets miss them. By motorcycle, car, train, airplane, and parachute, they survive anything.

That girl June, she's a trouper. She follows Roy everywhere and believes everything he says. But . . . but . . . why does she need to come along? Roy has the MacGuffin. She was a witness, you say? To what? I'll tell you why she has to be along. It's because this is a romantic action comedy starring Tom Cruise and Cameron Diaz, that's why.

So all of that I accept and even applaud, and I observe that Diaz has one of the most winning grins in the movies. Basically, what I wanted was more of it. Some of that Cary Grant dialogue. More flirtation. More of a feeling the characters, not the production, were the foreground. More of the stars. Because movie stars really do make a difference. I insist on it.

Knowing ★ ★ ★ ★
PG-13, 122 m., 2009

Nicolas Cage (John Koestler), Rose Byrne (Diana Wayland), Chandler Canterbury (Caleb Koestler), Lara Robinson (Lucinda Embry/Abby Wayland), Ben Mendelsohn (Phil Beckman). Directed by Alex Proyas and produced by Proyas, Todd Black, Jason Blumenthal, and Steve Tisch. Screenplay by Proyas, Ryne Pearson, Juliet Snowden, and Stiles White.

Knowing is among the best science fiction films I've seen—frightening, suspenseful, intelligent, and, when it needs to be, rather awesome. In its very different way, it is comparable to the great *Dark City*, by the same director, Alex Proyas. That film was about the hidden nature of the world men think they inhabit, and so is this one.

The plot involves the most fundamental of all philosophical debates: Is the universe deterministic or random? Is everything in some way preordained, or does it happen by chance? If that question sounds too abstract, wait until you see this picture, which poses it in stark terms: What if we could know in advance when the earth will end?

Nicolas Cage, in another wound-up, edgy performance, plays Koestler, a professor of astrophysics at MIT. He votes for deterministic; as he tells his class, he believes "shit happens." His wife has died, and he's raising his young son, Caleb (Chandler Canterbury). A time capsule is opened at Caleb's grade school, containing the drawings of students in 1959 predicting the sights of 2009. But the sheet Caleb gets isn't a drawing; it's covered with rows of numbers. In a prologue, we've seen the girl with haunted eyes, Lucinda (Lara Robinson), who so intensely pressed the numbers into the paper.

What do these numbers mean? You already know from the TV ads, but I don't believe I should tell you. I'll write another article that will contain spoilers. Let me say that Koestler discovers almost by accident a pattern in the numbers, and they shake his scientific mind to its core. His obsession is scoffed at by his MIT colleague, a cosmologist named Beckman (Ben Mendelsohn), who warns Koestler against the heresy of numerology—the finding of imaginary patterns in numbers. Beckman's passionate arguments in the film, which are not technical yet are scientifically sound, raise the stakes. This is not a movie about psychic mumble-jumble; Koestler is a hard-headed scientist, too, or always thought he was, until that page of numbers came into his hands.

By "scientifically sound," I don't mean anyone at MIT is going to find the plot other than preposterous. So it is—but not while the movie is playing. It works as science fiction, which often changes one coordinate in an otherwise logical world just to see what might happen. For Koestler, it leads to a rejection of what he has always believed, to his serious consideration of the paranormal, and to his discovery of Diana (Rose Byrne), the daughter of little Lucinda who wrote down the numbers, and Abby, the granddaughter (Lara Robinson again).

He believes the two children are somehow instrumental in the developing scenario, and he bonds with Diana to protect them from evil Strangers in the woods—who are mostly kept far enough away in long shots to prevent them from seeming more Strange than they must. The logic of the story leads us to expect something really spectacular at the end, and I was not disappointed visually, although I have logical questions that are sort of beside the point.

With expert and confident storytelling, Proyas strings together events that keep tension at a high pitch all through the film. Even a few quiet, human moments have something coiling beneath. Pluck this movie, and it vibrates. Even something we've seen countless times, like a car pursuit, works here because of the meaning of the pursuit and the high stakes.

There are sensational special effects in the film, which again I won't describe. You'll know the ones I mean. The film is beautifully photographed by Simon Duggan, the Marco Beltrami score hammers or elevates when it needs to, and Richard Learoyd's editing is knife-edged; when he needs to hurtle us through sequences, he does it with an insistence that doesn't feel rushed.

You may have guessed from the TV ads that something very bad is unfolding for the earth, and you may ask, not unreasonably, how these two nice parents and their lovable kids can possibly have any effect on it. Ah, but that would be in a random universe, and *Knowing* argues that the universe is deterministic. Or . . . *does* it? Your papers will be due before class on Monday.

Kung Fu Panda ★ ★ ★
PG, 91 m., 2008

With the voices of: Jack Black (Po), Dustin Hoffman (Master Shifu), Angelina Jolie (Tigress), Ian McShane (Tai Lung), Jackie Chan (Monkey), Seth Rogen (Mantis), Lucy Liu (Viper), David Cross (Crane), Randall Duk Kim (Oogway), James Hong (Mr. Ping), Michael Clarke Duncan (Commander Vachir), Dan Fogler (Zeng). Directed by John Stevenson and Mark Osborne and produced by Melissa Cobb. Written by Jonathan Aibel and Glenn Berger.

Kung Fu Panda is a story that almost tells itself in its title. It is so hard to imagine a big, fuzzy panda performing martial arts encounters that you intuit (and you will be right) that the panda stars in an against-all-odds formula, which dooms him to succeed. For the panda's target audience, children and younger teens, that will be just fine, and the film presents his adventures in wonderfully drawn Cinemascope animation. It was also shown in some IMAX venues.

The film stars a panda named Po (voice by Jack Black), who is so fat he can barely get out of bed. He works for his father, Mr. Ping (James Hong), in a noodle shop, which features Ping's legendary Secret Ingredient. How Ping, apparently a stork or other billed member of the avian family, fathered a panda is a mystery, not least to Po, but then the movie is filled with a wide variety of creatures who don't much seem to notice their differences.

They live in the beautiful Valley of Peace with an ancient temple towering overhead, up zillions of steps, which the pudgy Po can barely climb. But climb them he does, dragging a noodle wagon, because all the people of the valley have gathered up there to witness the choosing of the Dragon Warrior who will engage the dreaded Tai Lung (Ian McShane) in kung fu combat. Five contenders have been selected, the "Furious Five": Monkey (Jackie Chan), Tigress

(Angelina Jolie), Mantis (Seth Rogen), Viper (Lucy Liu), and Crane (David Cross).

Tigress looks like she might be able to do some serious damage, but the others are less than impressive. Mantis in particular seems to weigh about an ounce, tops. All five have been trained (for nearly forever, I gather) by the wise Shifu, who with Dustin Hoffman's voice is one of the more dimensional characters in a story that doesn't give the others a lot of depth. Anyway, it's up to the temple master, Oogway (Randall Duk Kim), an ancient turtle, to make the final selection, and he chooses—yes, he chooses the hapless and pudgy Po.

The story then becomes essentially a series of action sequences, somewhat undermined by the fact that the combatants seem unable to be hurt, even if they fall from dizzying heights and crack stones open with their heads. There's an extended combat with Tai Lung on a disintegrating suspension bridge (haven't we seen that before?), hand-to-hand-to-tail combat with Po and Tai Lung, and, upstaging everything, an energetic competition over a single dumpling.

Kung Fu Panda is not one of the great recent animated films. The story is way too predictable and, truth to tell, Po himself didn't overwhelm me with his charisma. But it's elegantly drawn, the action sequences are packed with energy, and it's short enough that older viewers will be forgiving. For the kids, of course, all this stuff is much of a muchness, and here they go again.

L

La France ★ ★ ½
NO MPAA RATING, 102 m., 2008

Sylvie Testud (Camille), Pascal Greggory
(Lieutenant), Guillaume Verdier (Cadet),
Francois Negret (Jacques), Laurent Talon
(Antoine), Pierre Leon (Alfred). Directed
by Serge Bozon and produced by Philippe
Martin and David Thion. Screenplay by
Axelle Ropert.

Here is one of the strangest and most original
war movies I've seen. Whether it is successful
is a good question. *La France* centers on the
story of Camille (Sylvie Testud), wife of a
French soldier during World War I. She lives
within a long walk of the Western Front, and
after receiving an alarming letter from him,
she boldly sets out to find him.

To do this, she cuts her hair and disguises
herself as a boy. She encounters a group of
about a dozen soldiers, who accept her as
male, which is one of the first hints that the
film will not be rigidly realistic. The men are
led by a friendly lieutenant (Pascal Greggory).
Their uniforms are ragged. After wounding
Camille in the hand when they mistake her for
an enemy, they find her a cast-off uniform
with the smell of death about it. They explain
they were separated from their main unit and
are looking for it.

They engage in a long trek through forest
and field. Sometimes distant guns are heard,
but there are no signs of war except for a
trench they walk down later in the film. The
scenery is suspiciously pastoral, sylvan, and
deserted for being so close to a war. At a time
when, needless to say, we are not expecting it,
the soldiers produce musical instruments
and burst into song. Yes. Guitars, a banjo, an
accordion, a clarinet, a violin, what may be a
dulcimer. When marching, they show no
sign of carrying these instruments, which
mysteriously appear all four times they need
to sing. At one point, they sing their way past
a sentry.

Does Camille look like a teenage boy? Not
to me. Testud has an angular face that is at
least not soft and rounded, and she has
pluck, as when she climbs a watchtower and

kills a threatening lookout. But she looks like
a girl. That the soldiers do not recognize this
is consistent with their inability to fear that
enemy troops might hear their songs. They
are walking not through a war, but through a
fantasy.

This is an intriguing idea, consistent with
the moment when Camille's missing husband
appears out of the woods and walks straight
toward her. The film has had little action, except for a scene involving a farmer and his son
who give them food and refuge. Refuge? Yes,
these soldiers are deserters, looking for Belgium. Along the way they conduct deep, sad
conversations about a soldier's life and tell a
parable about a comrade named Pierre; they
even read poetry. This must be the song and
story squad.

I had a problem with the film's visual strategy. At least half of the scenes take place at
night. No, not "day for night," but pitch-black
night, where the soldiers appear and disappear from view. I learn from IMDb.com that
the director, Serge Bozon, and his cinematographer (his sister Celine) employed a special
film stock to get what they consider the
"aquarium feeling" of the night scenes. Rather
than seeing faces swimming out of the murk,
I would rather have had a fair chance of seeing
more of the characters.

Not that they are deeply developed. In
keeping, I guess, with the decision to make
a fantasy, they are all as consistent as the
figures in a myth. They don't change. I can
imagine deep, personal interaction, suspicion, revelation in the story of a disguised
woman among men, but all of these characters seem swept along by the same narrative
tide.

Yes, the music is intriguing and odd. The
songs are more modern than the period, and
have a certain bluegrass feel. There is no joy
in their singing, but that is the point: These
are sad, exhausted men. There is a point
being made about war, in a very unexpected
way. *La France* won the coveted Prix Jean
Vigo as the best feature of 2007. It is inventive and unconventional, to be sure, and I
credit Bozon for his daring, but personally
I was not convinced.

Lakeview Terrace ★ ★ ★ ★
PG-13, 110 m., 2008

Samuel L. Jackson (Abel Turner), Patrick Wilson (Chris Mattson), Kerry Washington (Lisa Mattson), Jay Hernandez (Javier Villareal). Directed by Neil LaBute and produced by James Lassiter and Will Smith. Screenplay by David Loughery and Howard Korder.

Neil LaBute's *Lakeview Terrace* is a film about a black cop who makes life hell for an interracial couple that moves in next door. It will inspire strong reactions among its viewers, including outrage. It is intended to. LaBute often creates painful situations that challenge a character's sense of decency. This time he does it within the structure of a thriller, but the questions are there all the same.

For example, the neighbor, Abel Turner, is a bitter racist. He has his reasons, but don't we all. It is one mark of a sociopath to try to cure his wounds by harming others. The decent person does not visit his obsessions and prejudices upon his neighbor but is enjoined to love him as he does himself. Since Turner (Samuel L. Jackson) may hate himself, of course that is a problem.

But take a step back. What if all the races were switched? If the neighbor were white, the husband next door black, his wife white? Same script. It would be the story of a sociopathic white racist. It might be interesting, but it would have trouble getting made. The casting of Jackson as the neighbor creates a presumption of innocence that some will hold onto longer than the story justifies. Don't think for a moment that LaBute doesn't know audience members will be thinking about that switch of identities. He wants us to. All of his films feature nasty people who challenge nasty thoughts or fears within ourselves. Is this movie racist for making the villain black, or would it be equally racist by making the villain white? Well? What's your answer?

Jackson, a Los Angeles police veteran, lives on Lakeview Terrace, a crescent of comfortable suburbia in the hills of the city. The lots are pie-shaped, so the houses are placed close together, but the lots open out into big back yards. Into the house next door, newcomers

arrive: Chris Mattson (Patrick Wilson) and his wife, Lisa (Kerry Washington). They seem fairly recently married, happy. Turner starts slow, dropping some subtly hostile remarks, and then escalates his war on this couple. I will not describe his words and actions, except to say he pushes buttons that make the Mattsons first outraged, then fearful, then angry—at him and each other.

Take another step back. Mattson's father-in-law, a successful attorney, is cool and civil toward his daughter's white husband. Mattson's own parents, his wife observes, "are always making a point of telling me how much they love me." Why make that a special point? Because they do or because they don't? What do you think? Lisa's father asks Chris point-blank: "Are you planning to have children with my daughter?" Is he eager to become a grandfather? Doesn't sound like it.

Well, are they having kids? Lisa wants to get pregnant right now. Chris says, "We have an agreement to wait a while." Why wait a while? Because that makes sense while they're getting their feet on the ground? Or because he's ambivalent about his wife? You decide. Even if waiting does "make sense," are his feelings worthy of their marriage? Even while making a superb thriller, LaBute makes the film more than that. It deals with one of his themes, the difficult transition from prolonged adolescence to manhood, a journey Chris takes in the film. It is not easy. Many of the steps are contrary to his nature.

LaBute ingeniously poses moral choices in all of his films. In his first great picture, *In the Company of Men,* about a cruel office worker who plays a trick on a deaf woman, does the villain gain more pleasure by hurting her or forcing his passive male coworker to act against his own better nature? Both? Why does the coworker go along? Timidity? Buried aggression? Homoerotic feelings for his buddy? See?

On top of all these questions, LaBute constructs a tightly wound story that also involves crude male bonding at an LAPD bachelor party, sexual humiliation, attempted rape (not by Chris or Turner), a cat-and-mouse game with cell phones, and a violent conclusion during which we must decide if Chris is right about Turner, or wrong, or just discovering how to push *his* buttons. I'm surprised by the PG-13 rating.

It's a challenging journey LaBute takes us on. Some will find it exciting. Some will find it an opportunity for an examination of conscience. Some will leave feeling vaguely uneasy. Some won't like it and will be absolutely sure why they don't, but their reasons will not agree. Some will hate elements that others can't even see. Some will only see a thriller. I find movies like this alive and provoking, and I'm exhilarated to have my thinking challenged at every step of the way.

The effect is only intensified by the performances, especially by Jackson, who for such a nice man can certainly play vicious. Kerry Washington's character, in my mind, takes the moral high ground, although it's a little muddy. Her beauty and vulnerability are called for. Patrick Wilson plays a well-meaning man who is challenged to his core and never thought that would happen. I think I know who is good and bad or strong and weak in this film. But here's the brilliance of it: I don't know if they do.

Note: Lake View Terrace is the name of the street where Rodney King was arrested and beaten. This film mentions King and uses the street name, but not the location.

Land of the Lost ★ ★ ★
PG-13, 93 m., 2009

Will Ferrell (Dr. Rick Marshall), Danny McBride (Will Stanton), Anna Friel (Holly Cantrell), Jorma Taccone (Chaka). Directed by Brad Silberling and produced by Jimmy Miller and Sid and Marty Krofft. Screenplay by Chris Henchy and Dennis McNicholas.

Land of the Lost is a seriously deranged movie. That's not to say it's bad, although some of its early critics consider it a hanging offense ("a pot of ersatz dinosaur piss"—Peter Keough, *Boston Phoenix*). Marshall Fine even apologizes for prematurely predicting that *Night at the Museum: Battle of the Smithsonian* would be "the most witless, humor-challenged movie of the summer." The release inspires fervent hatred, which with the right kind of movie can be a good thing. Amid widespread disdain, I raise my voice in a bleat of lonely, if moderate, admiration.

The film involves a gloriously preposterous premise, set in a series of cheerfully fake landscapes that change at the whim of the art director. How else to explain a primeval swamp within walking distance of a limitless desert? Or to explain a motel sign from another dimension that appears there, with all of the motel missing but plenty of water still in the pool? And dinosaurs walking the earth at the same time as early man, just like in *Alley Oop* and *The Flintstones?*

Will Ferrell plays Dr. Rick Marshall, a scientist who assures Matt Lauer of the *Today* show that he has discovered a way to solve the energy crisis by importing fossil fuels from a parallel dimension. Lauer informs him that respectable scientists think he's mad. Like who? "Stephen Hawking," Lauer says. Dr. Rick goes nuclear: "You promised you wouldn't mention that!"

Marshall has, in fact, invented a machine that will transport him to one of those other worlds, and he is encouraged to try it by the only scientist in the world who agrees with him, Holly Cantrell (Anna Friel), who was thrown out of Cambridge for saying so. For reasons far too complicated to enumerate, they are joined in their journey by a fireworks salesman and part-time guide to a mysterious cave named Will (Danny McBride). Their cave tour strangely includes a river that seems to originate in thin air and flow into an artificial mountain before sucking them into a vortex and depositing them in . . . the Land of the Lost.

There they become friends with Chaka (Jorma Taccone), who belongs to a tribe of Missing Links and offers convincing evidence that in his land the straightening of teeth had not been developed. Luckily, Holly speaks his language. Yes, speaks his language, indicating that the movie will do anything to get to the next scene.

There are many jokes about dinosaur manure, dinosaur urine, dinosaur intelligence, dinosaur babies, and dinosaurs' hurt feelings. Also blood-sucking insects, carnivorous trees, and the sound track from *A Chorus Line*. The use of the songs is utterly wacky, of course, which is why I liked it.

The movie is inspired by the 1974 TV series and has the same producers, Sid and Marty

Krofft. The two will never be confused, but they share one thing in common: deliriously fake locations, props, and special effects. The dinosaurs are so obviously not really there in shots where they menace humans that you could almost say their shots are *about* how they're not really there. Confronted with such effects, the actors make not the slightest effort to appear terrified, amazed, or sometimes even mildly concerned. Some might consider that a weakness. I suspect it is more of a deliberate choice, and I say I enjoyed it.

I guess you have to be in the mood for a goofball picture like this. I guess I was. Marshall Fine says it's worse than *Night at the Museum*, but I've seen *Night at the Museum*, and Marshall, this is no *Night at the Museum*.

Last Chance Harvey ★ ★ ★

PG-13, 92 m., 2009

Dustin Hoffman (Harvey Shine), Emma Thompson (Kate Walker), Eileen Atkins (Maggie), Liane Balaban (Susan), James Brolin (Brian), Kathy Baker (Jean). Directed by Joel Hopkins and produced by Tim Perell and Nicola Usborne. Screenplay by Hopkins.

Last Chance Harvey is a tremendously appealing love story surrounded by a movie not worthy of it. For Dustin Hoffman, after years of character roles (however good) and dubbing the voices of animated animals, it provides a rare chance to play an ordinary guy. For Emma Thompson, there is an opportunity to use her gifts for tact and insecurity. For both, their roles project warmth and need.

When the film gets out of their way and leaves them alone to relate with each other, it's sort of magical. Then the lumber of the plot apparatus is trundled on, and we wish it were a piece for two players. One subplot, scored with funny-bumpy-scary music, is entirely unnecessary. And even with the two stars on screen, there is too much reliance on that ancient standby, the Semi-Obligatory Lyrical Interlude.

But what's good is very good. Hoffman plays Harvey, a failed jazz pianist who has found success writing jingles for TV ads. Thompson plays Kate, an airport interviewer for a British agency. Hoffman flies to London to attend his daughter's wedding, and in the space of twenty-four hours he learns that he has been fired and that his daughter would prefer her stepfather gave her away. At the same time, Thompson is ignored on a blind date and has to deal with a mother who fears her new neighbor is a vivisectionist.

They met briefly when Harvey was rude to her at the airport. The next day, when both are deep in misery, they find themselves the only two people in a pub. Harvey recognizes her, apologizes, and out of desperation tries to start a conversation. She resists. But notice the tentative dialogue that slowly allows them to start talking easily. It's not forced. It depends on his charm and her kindness.

Pitch perfect. But then the dialogue fades down and the camera pulls back and shows them talking and smiling freely, and the music gets happier, and there is a montage showing them walking about London with lots and lots of scenery in the frame. The movie indulges the Semi-OLI more than once; it uses the device as shorthand for scenes that should be fully transcribed. In *Before Sunrise* and *Before Sunset*, Richard Linklater sent Ethan Hawke and Julie Delpy talking all through a night in Vienna and all through a day in Paris, and never let them stop, and kept his camera close. Why didn't Joel Hopkins, the writer-director of *Last Chance Harvey*, try the same? He had the right actors.

He gets one thing right. They stay outdoors. Going to his hotel or her flat would set the stage for body language neither one is ready for. They avoid the issue by walking around London, although unfortunately Hopkins sends them mostly up and down the Victoria Embankment and the South Bank, so he can hold the Thames vista in the background. We get more montages of them walking and talking, as substitutes for listening to a conversation we've become invested in.

One subplot works well. After she starts him talking about why his relationship with his daughter failed, she tells him he *must* attend her wedding reception. He says she must go with him. He will buy her a dress. There is a gratuitous and offensive montage of her trying on dresses, including one frilly gown that looks perfect for a fancy dress ball in *Gone with the Wind.* Not only is this montage an exhausted cliché, they're in a hurry, remember? But when they get to the reception, Harvey is touching in a carefully worded speech.

The subplot that doesn't work involves Kate's mother (Eileen Atkins). She peers through the curtains at the suspicious neighbor, thinks she sees him carrying a body to the woodshed, and speed-dials her daughter every five minutes. Every time we cut to her, we get that peppy suspense music, as the movie confuses itself with light comedy.

Last Chance Harvey has everything it needs and won't stop there. It needs the nerve to push all the way. It is a pleasure to look upon the faces of Hoffman and Thompson, so pleasant, so real. Their dialogue together finds the right notes for crossing an emotional minefield. They never descend into tear-jerking or cuteness. They are all grown up and don't trust love nearly as much as straight talk. Hopkins deserves credit for creating these characters. Then he should have stood back and let them keep right on talking. Their pillow talk would have been spellbinding.

The Last House on the Left ★ ★ ½
R, 100 m., 2009

Tony Goldwyn (John Collingwood), Monica Potter (Emma Collingwood), Sara Paxton (Mari Collingwood), Garret Dillahunt (Krug), Spencer Treat Clark (Justin), Riki Lindhome (Sadie), Aaron Paul (Francis), Martha MacIsaac (Paige). Directed by Dennis Iliadis and produced by Wes Craven, Sean Cunningham, and Marianne Maddalena. Screenplay by Adam Alleca and Carl Ellsworth, based on the 1972 film by Craven.

I have seen four films inspired by the same thirteenth-century folk ballad: Ingmar Bergman's *The Virgin Spring* (1960), Wes Craven's *The Last House on the Left* (1972), David DeFalco's *Chaos* (2005), and now Dennis Iliadis's remake of the 1972 film, also titled *The Last House on the Left*.

What I know for sure is that the Bergman film is the best. Beyond that, it is a confusion of contradictions. I gave the 1972 film 3½ stars, describing it as "a tough, bitter little sleeper of a movie that's about four times as good as you'd expect." I gave the 2005 film zero stars, describing it as "ugly, nihilistic, and cruel—a film I regret having seen." What do I think about the latest story about a girl who goes walking in the woods, is raped and in some versions is killed, and whose attackers then seek shelter in the house of her parents, who realize who they are and take revenge?

Would I still admire 1972 today? Can I praise 2009 after savaging 2005? Isn't it all more or less the same material? Not quite. In the Bergman film, the father asks God's forgiveness for taking vengeance and says: "I promise You, God, here on the dead body of my only child, I promise you that, to cleanse my sins, here I shall build a church. On this spot. Of mortar and stone . . . and with these, my hands."

And such a church was built in the 1300s, and still stands at Karna in Sweden. No churches will be built because of the other films, no parents will ask forgiveness, and few members of the audience will think they should. These are in the horror genre, which once tried to scare the audience but now invites the audience to share the fear and pain of the characters. It is the one genre that can lead the box office without name stars, perhaps because its fans know that big stars very rarely appear in one (I'm not thinking of films where story is first but those in which graphic violence is first).

Horror films have connoisseurs, who are alert to gradations in violence. The well-informed critic "Fright" at the Web site Horror Movie a Day writes: "In the original, EVERYTHING was just so depraved, the rape barely stuck out as anything worse than the other things they endured. Not the case here, and so while some may cry foul that the movie is too toned down, I think it's a good decision." Not many unseasoned audience members will find the 2009 rape scene "toned down," and indeed I found it painful to watch. In the 2005 film, it was so reprehensibly and lingeringly sadistic I found it unforgivable. So now my job as a film critic involves grading rape scenes.

I don't think I can. I wrote that original *Last House* review thirty-seven years ago. I am not the same person. I am uninterested in being "consistent." I approach the new film as simply a filmgoer. I must say it is very well made.

The rape scene appalled me. Other scenes, while violent, fell within the range of contemporary horror films, which strive to invent new ways to kill people so the horror fans in the audience will get a laugh.

This film, for example, which as I write has inspired only one review (by "Fright"), has generated a spirited online discussion about whether you can kill someone by sticking their head in a microwave. Many argue that a microwave won't operate with the door open. Others cite an early scene establishing that the microwave is "broken." The question of whether one *should* microwave a man's head never arises.

Let's set that aside and look at the performances. They're surprisingly good, and I especially admired the work of Monica Potter and Tony Goldwyn as the parents of one of two girls who go walking in the woods. It is no longer only the father who takes revenge; both parents work together, improvising, playing a deadly chess game in their own home, which they know better than the villains. We are only human, we identify with the parents, we fear for them, and we applaud their ingenuity.

There is also sound work by Krug (Garret Dillahunt), the convincingly evil leader of a pack of degenerates. He isn't just acting scary. He creates a character. And Sara Paxton, who has been acting since eight and was twenty when the movie was made, shows, as so many sexy young blondes do, that they are better than the bubblehead roles they are mostly given.

It is also true that director Dennis Iliadis and his cinematographer, Sharone Meir, do a smooth job of handling space and time to create suspense. The film is an effective representative of its genre, and horror fans will like it, I think, but who knows? I'm giving it a 2½ on the silly star rating system and throwing up my hands.

The Last Mistress ★ ★ ★ ½

NO MPAA RATING, 114 m., 2008

Asia Argento (Vellini), Fu'ad Ait Aattou (Ryno de Marigny), Roxane Mesquida (Hermangarde), Claude Sarraute (Marquise de Flers), Yolande Moreau (Comtesse d'Artelles), Michael Lonsdale (Vicomte de Prony). Directed by Catherine Breillat and produced by Jean-Francois Lepetit. Screenplay by Breillat, based on the novel by Jules Barbey d'Aurevilly.

In *The Last Mistress*, a passionate and explicit film about sexual obsession, everything pauses for a scene depicting a wedding. It is 1835, in a church in Paris. Vows are exchanged between Ryno de Marigny, a notorious young libertine, and the high-born Hermangarde, whose wealth will be a great comfort to the penniless Ryno. The film opens with two gossipy old friends wondering why the Marquise de Flers would sacrifice her beloved granddaughter to this rake.

I wondered why time was devoted to the ceremony, in a film where Hermangarde speaks scarcely one hundred words and the great passion is between Ryno and his mistress of ten years, the disreputable Vellini. Then I realized it was an excuse to work in the Biblical readings ("requested by the bride and groom"—surely a modern touch?). The Gospel contains God's strictures about man and wife, divorce and adultery, letting no man put asunder, etc. The epistle is Paul to the Corinthians, venting his admonishments to women, who must always take second place, cover their heads in the sight of the Lord, obey their masters, and so on.

These readings enter the film precisely to be contradicted by Vellini (Asia Argento) in every atom of her being. Born out of wedlock to an Italian princess and a Spanish matador, she is technically wed to an English aristocrat but in fact is the most impetuous courtesan in Paris. When she overhears young Ryno (Fu'ad Ait Aattou) describe her as a "mutt," she permits herself the smallest smile before taking another lick of her ice cream (shaped like what we now call a torpedo).

Their relationship begins with her hatred, or what she convinces Ryno is her hatred; it inspires his uncontrollable desire and leads to a duel with her husband during which Ryno is nearly killed with a bullet near his heart. As he lingers near death, so inflamed is Vellini that she bursts into his bedchamber and licks the blood from his wound. The doctor growls about "infection," but never mind: She has been inspired by his sacrifice. Any man who would suffer that much for her love would surely suffer more.

The Last Mistress is the latest film from the French director Catherine Breillat, famous for the explicit eroticism of such films as *Fat Girl* and *Romance*. Here she makes an elegant period piece, with all the costumes, carriages, servants, chateaus, and mannered behavior we would expect, and then explodes its decorum with a fiery performance by Argento. Does she love her young prize, with his lips full as a woman's? Does he love her, with her two front teeth tilted inward like a vampire's? Love has nothing to do with it. They are in the grip of erotomania.

That in itself could be fairly routine, if it were not for the way Breillat frames her story. Understand that Ryno sincerely loves Hermangarde (Roxane Mesquida). Two days before the marriage, he says his formal farewell to Vellini, which is followed by helpless sex. Later the same night, he pays a courtesy call on the old Marquise de Flers (Claude Sarraute), who arranged the marriage and considers it her "masterpiece," so sure is she about Ryno.

Alas, she has been informed of his affair with Vellini and now asks for a confession. This he supplies in tender and earnest terms. Then she asks for details. These he supplies in lurid flashbacks. The marquise prides herself on being a liberated woman of the previous century. "Damn this herb tea!" she says. "A little port will warm us up." Soon she is stretched out full length in her chair, her feet propped on a divan, drinking in the details of his story.

It is Claude Sarraute's performance that I loved most of all in the film. I can easily imagine spending the night in the salon of this old lady and telling her everything she wants to hear. Her face is so intelligent, her manner so direct that my only fear would be to disappoint her. Astonished, I discover from *Variety* that Sarraute is a "distinguished journalist and commentator who last dabbled in acting more than fifty years ago." She gives dimension and meaning to Ryno's long story of powerless surrender.

Argento's performance is also remarkable. Dressed to flaunt her immorality (in one costume, she is the devil), she puffs on cigars, draws blood, follows the newlyweds to their remote coastal hideaway. Ryno hates himself for being unable to resist her. In one shot, Breillat fills the screen with naked flesh and two items of jewelry: his wedding ring and Vellini's bracelet in the shape of a serpent.

One of the old gossips is played by the immortal Michael Lonsdale, who predicted that Ryno would never be able to stay away from Vellini and takes some satisfaction in being proven right, but not as much as he takes in a properly roasted chicken. Of all the vices, he observes, gluttony lasts the longest and never disappoints. As for debauchery, poor Ryno is desperately overserved, and it is hard for us, even as he surrenders to devouring need, not to feel sorry for him.

The Last Song ★★ ½
PG, 107 m., 2010

Miley Cyrus (Ronnie Miller), Greg Kinnear (Steve Miller), Liam Hemsworth (Will Blakelee), Bobby Coleman (Jonah Miller), Kelly Preston (Kim Miller). Directed by Julie Anne Robinson and produced by Jennifer Gibgot and Adam Shankman. Screenplay by Nicholas Sparks and Jeff Van Wie, based on a novel by Sparks.

Now that Miley Cyrus is seventeen, it's about time she played a sixteen-year-old. That she does fetchingly in *The Last Song*, and wins the heart of a beach volleyball champion a foot taller than she is. Well, actually 12.5 inches. She also learns to love her dad, played by Greg Kinnear, whose aura suggests a man easier to love than, say, Steve Buscemi. She does this on an idyllic island paradise offshore from Savannah, Georgia, where her dad is a classical composer whose pastime is restoring stained glass windows.

I was trying to remember the last time I felt the way about a girl that Miley Cyrus's fans feel about her. That would have been in 1959, when I saw Hayley Mills in *Tiger Bay*. Oh, she was something. A brave tomboy. She was twelve, but I could wait. It's a bit much to ask for the same innocence from Miley, who has already had her first world tour, but the fact is, she does a good job of making her character, Ronnie, engaging and lovable. That's despite her early Alienated Teen scenes. You know it's an Alienated Teen when it's a lovely day on an island paradise, but she has her hands pulled up inside the sleeves of her sweater and huddles against the chill of the cold, cruel world.

I like Miley Cyrus. I like her in spite of the fact that she's been packaged within an inch of her life. I look forward to the day when she squirms loose from her handlers and records an album of classic songs, performed with the same sincerity as her godmother, Dolly Parton. I think it'll be a long, long time until she plays a movie character like the freestanding, engaging heroines of Ashley Judd, but I can wait.

The Last Song is about how Ronnie (Miley) and her little brother, Jonah (Bobby Coleman), are taken by their mother (Kelly Preston) to spend the summer with their dad, Steve (Kinnear). She blames her dad for the divorce, is sullen and withdrawn. Ten minutes after she hits the beach (dressed in Gothic black), her milk shake is spilled by a flying volleyball player named Will (Liam Hemsworth). Talk about your Meet Cutes. Gradually she overcomes her hostility to men and realizes Will is a nice and honorable kid, even though he lives in a vast Southern mansion with insufferable rich parents.

Ronnie and Will make an attractive couple, possibly because Miley is standing on a box below camera range. I suspect Hemsworth may have been cast for his appeal to fangirls, rather like Robert Pattinson in *Twilight*. He's a little too tall, blond, blue-eyed, and hunky to be super plausible. He can definitely become a star, but it may be in the Peter O'Toole tradition; I can more easily imagine him in a remake of *Lawrence of Arabia* than as a settled spouse in a domestic drama.

Miley Cyrus, on the other hand, is attractive in the way of a girl you might actually meet. Her acting is unaffected, she can play serious, and she works easily with a pro like Kinnear, whose light comedy skills are considerable and undervalued. She even seems sincere in the face of a plot so blatantly contrived it seems like an after-school special. Would you believe that she and Will bond over sea turtle eggs?

Yes, she scares off a raccoon trying to raid a nest of eggs buried in the sand and mounts an all-night vigil over them. Then she calls the aquarium, and who do you think is the hand-some volunteer who responds to the call? Standing watch together the second night, Ronnie and Will start talking, and it's only a matter of time until they regard together the itty bitty turtles hurrying toward the sea.

The other big crisis of her summer is that she's a trained classical pianist, but has just turned down a scholarship to Juilliard because her dad, you see, is such a snake. In a world containing divorce, what's the use of Mozart? The film's title relates to this situation, I believe, in some obscure way. Miley does, however, sing in the movie. She's mad at her dad, but not her fans.

The Last Song is based on the novel by Nicholas Sparks, who also wrote the screenplay. Sparks recently went on record as saying he is a greater novelist than Cormac McCarthy. This is true in the same sense that I am a better novelist than William Shakespeare. Sparks also said his novels are like Greek tragedies. This may actually be true. I can't check it out because, tragically, no really bad Greek tragedies have survived. His story here amounts to soft porn for teenage girls, which the acting and the abilities of director Julie Anne Robinson have promoted over its pay scale.

The movie is intended, of course, for Miley Cyrus admirers, and truth compels me to report that on that basis alone, it would get four stars. But we cannot all be Miley Cyrus fans, and these days you rarely hear Hayley Mills mentioned. Yet I award the film two and a half stars.

To be sure, I resent the sacrilege Nicholas Sparks commits by even mentioning himself in the same sentence as Cormac McCarthy. I would not even allow him to say, "Hello, bookstore? This is Nicholas Sparks. Could you send over the new Cormac McCarthy novel?" He should show respect by ordering anonymously. But it seems unfair to penalize Miley Cyrus fans, Miley, and the next Peter O'Toole for the transgressions of a lesser artist.

The Last Station ★★★
R, 110 m., 2010

Helen Mirren (Sofya), Christopher Plummer (Tolstoy), Paul Giamatti (Chertkov), Anne Marie Duff (Sasha), Kerry Condon (Masha), James

McAvoy (Valentin). Directed by Michael Hoffman and produced by Bonnie Arnold, Chris Curling, and Jens Meurer. Screenplay by Hoffman, based on the novel by Jay Parini.

Watching *The Last Station*, I was reminded of the publisher Bennett Cerf's story about how he went to Europe to secure the rights to James Joyce's *Ulysses*.

"Nora, you have a brilliant husband," he told Joyce's wife.

"You don't have to live with the bloody fool."

If Joyce was a drunk and a roisterer, how different was the Russian novelist Leo Tolstoy, who was a vegetarian and pacifist, and recommended (although did not practice) celibacy? *The Last Station* focuses also on *his* wife, Sofya, who after bearing his thirteen children thought him a late arrival to celibacy and accused him of confusing himself with Christ. Yet it's because of the writing of Joyce and Tolstoy that we know about their wives at all. Well, the same is true of George Eliot's husband.

The Last Station focuses on the last year of Count Tolstoy (Christopher Plummer), a full-bearded Shakespearian figure presiding over a household of intrigues. The chief schemer is Chertkov (Paul Giamatti), his intense follower, who idealistically believes Tolstoy should leave his literary fortune to the Russian people. It's just the sort of idea that Tolstoy might seize upon in his utopian zeal. Sofya (Helen Mirren), on behalf of herself and her children, is livid.

Chertkov, who as the quasi-leader of Tolstoy's quasi-cult, hires a young man named Valentin (James McAvoy) to become the count's private secretary. In this capacity, he is to act as a double agent, observing moments between Leo and Sofya when Chertkov would not be welcome.

It may be hard for us to understand how seriously Tolstoy was taken at the time. To call him comparable in stature to Gandhi would not be an exaggeration, and indeed, Gandhi adopted many of his ideas. Tolstoy in his eighty-second year remained active and robust, but everyone knew his end might be approaching, and the Russian equivalent of paparazzi and gossips lurked in the neighborhood. Imagine Perez Hilton staking out J. D. Salinger.

Tolstoy was thought a great man and still is, but in a way his greatness distracts from how good he was as a writer. When I was young the expression "reading *War and Peace*" was used as a synonym for idly wasting an immense chunk of time. Foolishly believing this, I read Dostoyevsky and Chekhov but not Tolstoy, and it was only when I came late to *Anna Karenina* that I realized he wrote page-turners. In *Time* magazine's compilation of 125 lists of the ten greatest novels of all time, *War and Peace* and *Anna Karenina* placed first and third. (You didn't ask, but *Madame Bovary* was second, *Lolita* fourth, and *Huckleberry Finn* fifth.)

The Last Station has the look of a Merchant-Ivory film, with the pastoral setting, the dashing costumery, the roomy old country house, the meals taken on lawns. But did Merchant and Ivory ever deal with such a demonstrative family? If the British are known for suppressing their emotions, the Russians seem to bellow their whims. If a British woman in Merchant-Ivory land desires sex, she bestows a significant glance in the candlelight. Sofya clucks like a chicken to arouse old Leo's rooster.

The dramatic movement in the film takes place mostly within Valentin (James McAvoy), who joins the household already an acolyte of Tolstoy. Young and handsome, he says he is celibate. Sofya has him pegged as gay, but Masha (Kerry Condon), a nubile Tolstoyian, pegs him otherwise. Valentin also takes note that Tolstoy, like many charismatic leaders, exempts himself from his own teachings. The thirteen children provide a hint, and his private secretary cannot have avoided observing that although the count and countess fight over his will, a truce is observed at bedtime, and the enemies meet between the lines.

As the formidable patriarch, Christopher Plummer avoids any temptation (if he felt one) to play Tolstoy as a Great Man. He does what is more amusing; he plays him as a Man Who Knows He Is Considered Great. Helen Mirren plays a wife who knows his flaws, but has loved him since the day they met. To be fair, no man who wrote that fiction could be other than wise and warm about human nature.

Some women are simply sexy forever. Helen Mirren is a woman like that. She's sixty-four. As she enters her seventies, we'll begin to develop a fondness for sexy septuagenarians.

Mirren and Plummer make Leo and Sofya Tolstoy more vital than you might expect in a historical picture. Giamatti has a specialty in seeming to be up to something, and McAvoy and Condon take on a glow from feeling noble while sinning. In real life, I learn, Tolstoy provided Sofya with more unpleasant sunset years, but could we stand to see Helen Mirren treated like that?

Late Bloomer ★ ★ ★ ½
NO MPAA RATING, 83 m., 2008

Masakiyo Sumida (Sumida), Mari Torii (Nobuko), Naozo Horita (Take), Ariko Arita (Oba-chan), Sumiko Shirai (Aya). Directed by Go Shibata and produced by Toshiki Shima. Screenplay by Shibata.

I see so many references to Go Shibata's *Late Bloomer* as a thriller or horror film. That may be true, but it's beside the point. Here is a film about the despair and rage building up within a man whose body has betrayed him. It fearlessly regards the dark side of severe disability, and would be offensive if we didn't know it represents only this single character, who is going mad.

Sumida (Masakiyo Sumida) is dealing with what seems to be muscular dystrophy. He is aided by a care giver, has some sort of job at a disability center, speaks with a computerized voice, gets drunk regularly, and has a scrawny beard, tangled hair, and thick, permanently smudged eyeglasses. He uses an electric wheelchair. His pastimes are drinking, watching pornography, and going to underground rock concerts with his friend Take (Naozo Horita). On the whole, people seem happy to spend time with him, and he takes many meals with Take, who is a counselor.

In the ways that he can be, Sumida is a party animal. I remember a guy in his twenties who hung out at O'Rourke's in the 1970s. I think he had MS. He'd be warmly greeted when he came in. He liked to booze, too, but he was still walking and knew he had his limit. He threw a party once. You should have seen his pad. Psy-

chedelic posters, glo-lights, sound system cranked up high, a water bed, an open bar, pot. He braced his jaw as he spoke, but it wasn't hard to understand him. He was friendly with the girls. Once when we were wondering if he was getting any, a couple of girls who were regulars traded private little smiles.

The thing to realize when you see a person like that is: There's somebody at home! He doesn't automatically have a mental disability. It's OK to go ahead and say what's on your mind. You don't have to end every sentence with "Right?" and "OK?" and "You know what I mean?" so that he has to nod and nod and nod. It's easy to imagine how a man like Sumida, who might be a barfly even if he were unimpaired, could develop a lot of pent-up frustration.

A young woman named Nobuko (Mari Torii) volunteers to serve as his companion. Part of a school project. She's sweet and friendly, but not gifted with the unique abilities of a true care giver. She brightens his day. Then he begins to suspect she is seeing Take. Sumida tells a bedridden friend in a similar condition that he is in love. The friend warns him: Nothing good will come of that for you. Spare yourself.

And now *Late Bloomer* begins its journey into the pain and anger of Sumida's mind. What happens, you will discover. This is not a movie about the essential humanity of a good-hearted disabled person. Someone with MD can be as dangerous as someone without. There's somebody at home, all right, and he's hurting.

You have to meet the film's visual style halfway. It's shot in contrasty black and white, slo-mo, fast-mo, sometimes jagged cutting, sometimes an erratic handheld camera that suggests the jerky way Sumida must view the world. You watch for a while, and the movie is tough going. Then it takes hold, and you begin identifying with Sumida. He is a bad, bad man. You can sort of understand that.

Law-Abiding Citizen ★★★
R, 122 m., 2009

Jamie Rice (Nick Rice), Gerard Butler (Clyde Shelton), Colm Meaney (Detective Dunnigan), Bruce McGill (Jonas Cantrell), Leslie Bibb (Sarah Lowell), Michael Irby (Detective Garza),

Gregory Itzin (Warden Iger), Regina Hall (Kelly Rice), Emerald-Angel Young (Denise Rice), Christian Stolte (Darby), Annie Corley (Judge Laura Burch), Viola Davis (Mayor). Directed by F. Gary Gray and produced Gerard Butler, Lucas Foster, Mark Gill, Robert Katz, Alan Siegel, and Kurt Wimmer. Screenplay by Wimmer.

Law-Abiding Citizen is a taut thriller about a serial killer in reverse: He's already in prison when he commits all but one of his many murders, and in solitary for most of that time. So the story is a locked-room mystery: How does he set up such elaborate kills? Does he have an accomplice outside the walls, or what?

Jamie Foxx stars as Nick, the Philadelphia district attorney, and Gerard Butler is Clyde, the ingenious killer. He begins the film as a loving husband and father, but then his wife and daughter are savagely murdered. Nick arranges a plea bargain: One of the guilty men will be executed, and the other, in return for his testimony, will get a murder conviction but not death.

Clyde can't believe this. He saw his family murdered. Both men are guilty. On this everyone agrees. Why is one allowed to live? Because, Nick explains, the case isn't airtight without the testimony, and if they lose, both men walk free. That's not good enough for Clyde, who has ten years to plot, plan, and simmer in his hatred.

That's the prologue. I won't go into detail about what happens next, except to observe that Clyde's first killing involves his penetration of the death row execution chamber itself—and that's before he's in prison. Is this guy Houdini, or does he have supernatural powers?

As his methods are uncovered, it's clear he's a nonmagical human being, but a clever one with remarkable resources. So remarkable, in fact, that they fly in the face of common sense. Movie super villains have a way of correctly predicting what everyone will do and making their plans on that basis. The explanation of Clyde's methods is preposterous, but it comes late enough that F. Gary Gray, the director, is first able to generate considerable suspense and a sense of dread.

Foxx and Butler make a well-matched pair in their grim determination. Colm Meaney is underused as Foxx's partner; we suspect he may be the accomplice, given the Law of Economy of Characters, but perhaps he has a different role to play. Leslie Bibb works well as Foxx's partner, Regina Hall as his wife, Annie Corley as the judge who experiences some surprises in her courtroom, and the powerful Viola Davis as the city mayor.

Law-Abiding Citizen is one of those movies you like more at the time than in retrospect. I mean, *come on*, you're thinking. Still, there's something to be said for a movie you like well enough at the time.

Leap Year ★★★
PG, 97 m., 2010

Amy Adams (Anna), Matthew Goode (Declan), Adam Scott (Jeremy), John Lithgow (Jack). Directed by Anand Tucker and produced by Gary Barber, Chris Bender, Roger Birnbaum, and Jake Weiner. Screenplay by Deborah Kaplan and Harry Elfont.

Amy Adams and Matthew Goode have the charm necessary to float a romantic comedy like *Leap Year*, and this is a story that needs their buoyancy. A sort of conspiracy forms between the audience and the screen: We know what has to happen, and the movie knows what has to happen, and the point is to keep us amused. *Leap Year* did better than that: It made me care. It did that by not being too obvious about what it was obviously trying to do.

Let's start off on the same page. A sweet but over-organized young woman named Anna (Amy Adams) has been dating a high-powered heart surgeon named Jeremy (Adam Scott) for four years. He's pleasant, attentive, presentable, and shares her goal of buying a condo in the best building in Boston. He does nothing, absolutely nothing wrong. For veteran filmgoers, he has one fatal flaw: He has a healthy head of hair, and every strand is perfectly in place. No modern movie hero can have his hair combed.

When, oh when, will Jeremy ask Anna to marry him? After dashing her hopes once again, he hurries off to Dublin for a cardiologists' convention because as we all know it's a professional necessity for cardiologists to meet in faraway places. Anna is told that in Ireland on Leap Day, every four years, a woman can ask a man to marry her. Anna double-checks on the Web, somehow not discovering that this is believed nearly everywhere, and if a man in Denmark turned her down, he would have to buy her a pair of gloves.

Anna flies off to Ireland. The flight lasts only long enough for her to survive severe turbulence. The plane is diverted to Cardiff. Is there *anyone* in the theater surprised that she didn't arrive in Dublin on schedule? Despite canceled ferry boats, she makes her way to Ireland by hiring a tugboat. The skipper says they can't land at Cork but must head for Dingle. Dingle in Ireland is more or less as far as you can get from Wales (or Dublin), but never mind.

We know what's coming. Anna must meet her costar, Declan, played by Matthew Goode as the owner of the local pub. I suspect business has fallen off there ever since Robert Mitchum left after filming *Ryan's Daughter* in 1969. Anna is now wet and tired, but still plucky. In the pub, she asks Declan how she can get to Dublin. Turns out Declan is not only the publican but the taxi driver and runs the local hotel. They get a good smile out of this, but wouldn't you be asking yourself why neither one mentions "Local Hero"?

OK, enough fooling with the plot. Let's agree it stays firmly on course, and that Anna and Declan argue all the way to Dublin through adventures that, by law, must include getting all muddy and being forced to share a bedroom together. Therefore, the success of the film depends on the acting and direction.

Amy Adams and Matthew Goode sell it with great negative chemistry and appeal. Adams has an ability to make things seem fresh and new; everything seems to be happening to her for the first time, and she has a particularly innocent sincerity that's convincing. (Who was it that said if you can fake sincerity, you can fake anything?) Goode is wisely not made too handsome. Oh, you could shoot him as handsome; he's good-looking, let's face it. But the director, Anand Tucker, shoots him as annoyed, rude, and scruffy. Hair not too well combed.

Then take another look at Jeremy (Adam

Scott). I'm not going to say he's too handsome. All I have to say is that in a silent movie he could simply walk on the screen and you'd know he's not going to get the girl. The movie carefully avoids making him a heavy. It's rather clever: He smoothly does more or less exactly what she's trained him to do, and what he doesn't understand is that she no longer believes in that version of him.

Bottom line: This is a full-bore, PG-rated, sweet romantic comedy. It sticks to the track, makes all the scheduled stops, and bears us triumphantly to the station. And it is populated by colorful characters, but then, when was the last time you saw a boring Irishman in a movie?

Le Doulos ★ ★ ★ ½
NO MPAA RATING, 108 m., 1962 (rereleased 2008)

Jean-Paul Belmondo (Silien), Serge Reggiani (Maurice), Jean Dessailly (Inspector Clain), Fabienne Dali (Fabienne), Michel Piccoli (Nuttheccio), Monique Hennessy (Therese). Directed by Jean-Pierre Melville and produced by Georges de Beauregard and Carlo Ponti. Screenplay by Melville, based on the novel by Pierre Lesou.

Near the end of *Le Doulos*, Jean-Paul Belmondo reinterprets everything that has gone before, his words illustrated by flashbacks to the film we have seen. That is essentially a wink by the writer-director, Jean-Pierre Melville, suggesting that he was misleading us all along. This goes with his territory: "I take care never to be realistic," he said in a 1963 interview. Does it matter that what we're seeing is not necessarily what we're getting? Not at all. The movie is entirely about how it looks and feels.

I am an admirer of Melville; his *Bob le Flambeur* and *Le Samourai* are in my Great Movies collection. He helped introduce film noir to the New Wave generation and was such a lover of all things American that he renamed himself after Herman Melville. His heroes tend to drive Detroit cars that look huge on the streets of Paris; when one character in this film parks three spaces down from the car of another, how can he *not* notice the twenty-footer and be tipped off the other guy is already there? Melville was also a fetishist of American men's clothing styles, he said, and you will scarcely see a beret in his films. Indeed, *le doulos,* which means "the finger man" in Parisian criminal slang, is the name for the small-brimmed fedora that most of the men wear.

The film is made of elements Melville said he came to love in the black-and-white American crime movies of the 1930s: shadows, night, trench coats, guns, tough guys, cigarettes, slinky dames, cocktail bars, crooked cops, betrayal, loot, and a plot shutting out the world and confining the characters within their own lives and space. It looks gorgeous in the newly restored 35 mm print by Rialto Pictures, which will no doubt issue it as a DVD.

The film opens with a newly released prisoner (Serge Reggiani) calling on a man who set up a diamond heist for him. He later has good reason to believe the Belmondo character fingered him, in a plot that leads through nightclubs, whisky bars (no wine for Melville), dark underpasses, and deserted suburban wastelands. There are three lovely lady friends, including Therese (Monique Hennessy), who is attached to Nuttheccio (Michel Piccoli), a shady nightclub owner. Belmondo ties her up and gags her, which is perhaps what she deserves, depending on what we choose to believe. (The movie drew some criticism for its treatment of women, leading Melville to defend himself: He did not mistreat the women; his characters did.)

To see both Belmondo and Piccoli in 1962 is to be reminded how early they embodied their distinctive screen presences: Piccoli, the balding, saturnine slickster with the five o'clock shadow, and Belmondo, the oily outlaw punk. One trick that Melville plays is to dress them, and others, in essentially identical trench coats and hats, and then shoot them in shadows or from behind, so that we are misled for a while about who we're watching. This, coupled with a habit that some of them have of straightening their hats before a mirror, perhaps suggests they are interchangeable, playing different games by the same rules. See, too, how meticulously Alain Delon treats his hat in *Le Samourai,* about a hit man who lives with a code as rigid as a samurai's. The Belmondo character here has a code, too, but he

keeps it so concealed it doesn't do him much good.

The plot is, as I've suggested, baffling. I'll give a shiny new dime to anyone who understands Belmondo's illustrated lecture at the end. It is designed to explain that he is *not* the finger man everyone (and the film until then) thinks he is—but can he be believed? It really matters not, as we enjoy plunging into an underworld of deadly confusion.

Letters to Juliet ★★★
PG, 101 m., 2010

Amanda Seyfried (Sophie), Vanessa Redgrave (Claire), Christopher Egan (Charlie), Gael Garcia Bernal (Victor), Franco Nero (Lorenzo Bartolini). Directed by Gary Winick and produced by Ellen Barkin, Mark Canton, Eric Feig, Caroline Kaplan, and Patrick Wachsberger. Screenplay by Jose Rivera and Tim Sullivan.

I know *Letters to Juliet* is soppy melodrama, and I don't mind in the least. I know the ending is preordained from the setup. I know the characters are broad and comforting stereotypes. In this case, I simply don't care. Sometimes we have personal reasons for responding to a film.

Letters to Juliet is about Sophie (Amanda Seyfried), an American girl who visits Verona with the man she's engaged to marry (Gael Garcia Bernal). He's always leaving her behind to investigate wine and truffles for his New York restaurant. She visits the house allegedly inhabited by Shakespeare's Juliet. Below the balcony there, lovelorn women for years have posted "letters to Juliet" asking for advice.

Sophie finds a letter fifty years old, written by a young British girl about a Tuscan boy she met, fell in love with, and allowed to fall out of her life. Sophie writes to the girl, the letter amazingly finds its way, and soon Claire (Vanessa Redgrave) and her grandson, Charlie (Christopher Egan), arrive in Verona. So now, if we're experienced moviegoers, we know what must happen by the end of the story.

All of this is wrapped up in unimaginably beautiful shots of the Italian countryside, the warmth of the friendship between Sophie and Claire, and visits to many men named Lorenzo Bartolini, which was the name of the boy Claire loved so long ago. A hard-hearted realist would suggest that Sophie help Claire check out the possible Lorenzo Bartolinis on the phone, but no. *Letters to Juliet* requires the three of them to visit the candidates in person, leading to a series of false leads and at last, of course, to the real Lorenzo Bartolini (Franco Nero).

As it happens, this story stirred romantic memories in my own life. Once in a small hill town outside Rome, under a full moon, I stood before the balcony being used by Franco Zeffirelli for his great film *Romeo and Juliet* (1968), and heard Nino Rota hum his theme music to Zeffirelli. Some years later, I stood beneath Juliet's balcony in Verona itself with a woman dear to my heart, and saw the notes pinned to the wall.

And the very first movie set I ever visited, before I was yet a movie critic, was *Camelot* (1967). On that set I met and interviewed Vanessa Redgrave, who was not yet thirty, and Franco Nero, who was twenty-six. They played Guenevere and Lancelot. They fell in love on the set and had a child. They took separate paths for years, but on New Year's Eve 2006, they married. Even earlier, Franco walked Vanessa's daughter Natasha Richardson down the aisle when she married Liam Neeson.

So you see, when Vanessa marries Franco forty years after falling in love with him, and they are playing characters who meet after fifty years, and this all has to do with Juliet's balcony—reader, what am I to do? I am helpless before such forces.

Vanessa Redgrave recently lost her sister, Lynn. I met Lynn once in London. I went to her house for tea. This was not long after the success of *Georgy Girl*. My interview has been lost in the past, but I remember the feeling of the day, Lynn sitting cross-legged on the carpet beside her coffee table, smoking and jolly, a famous actress friendly to an unknown kid her own age.

I have strayed far from the film. But I've told you what you need to know about it. I also want to observe that our response to every film depends on the person we bring to it. Pauline Kael said she went to a movie, and the movie happened, and she wrote about what changed within her after she saw it. This

is quite valid. Sometimes, however, we go to a movie, and our lives have happened, and we write about what hasn't changed.

Let the Right One In ★ ★ ★ ½
R, 114 m., 2008

Kare Hedebrant (Oskar), Lina Leandersson (Eli), Per Ragnar (Hakan), Henrik Dahl (Erik), Karin Bergquist (Yvonne), Peter Carlberg (Lacke). Directed by Tomas Alfredson and produced by John Nordling and Carl Molinder. Screenplay by John Ajvide Lindqvist, based on his novel.

I look at young people who affect the Goth look. I assume they want to keep a distance and make a statement. The leather can be taken off, the tattoos not so easily. It is relatively painless to pierce many body areas, not all. But what would it feel like to be pierced by a vampire's fangs? That would be more than a look, wouldn't it? And you wouldn't want to advertise yourself as a vampire.

Let the Right One In is a "vampire movie," but not even remotely what we mean by that term. It is deadly grim. It takes vampires as seriously as the versions of *Nosferatu* by F. W. Murnau and Werner Herzog do, and that is very seriously indeed. It is also a painful portrayal of an urgent relationship between two twelve-year-olds on the brink of adolescence. It is not intended for twelve-year-olds.

It opens with the reflection of Oskar (Kare Hedebrant) looking soberly out a window. He may remind you of the boy in Bergman's *The Silence*, looking out of the train window. They will both have much to be sober about. There will be many reflections in the film, not all from mirrors, but this is not one of those vampire stories that drags out the crosses and the garlic.

Oskar is lonely. His parents have separated, neither one wants him, he is alone a lot. He hangs around outside in the snowy Swedish night. One night he meets a kid named Eli (Lina Leandersson), who is about his age. Eli is lonely too, and they become friends. Oskar is at that age when he accepts astonishing facts calmly because life has given up trying to surprise him. Eli walks through the snow without shoes. Eli has a faint scent almost of a corpse. "Are you a vampire?" Oskar asks Eli. Yes. Oh.

They decide to have a sleepover in his bed. Sex is not yet constantly on Oskar's mind, but he asks, "Will you be my girlfriend?" She touches him lightly. "Oskar, I'm not a girl." Oh.

Oskar is cruelly bullied at school by a sadistic boy who travels with a posse of two smaller thugs and almost drowns him in a swimming pool. At a time like this it is useful to have a vampire as your best pal. A girl vampire or a boy vampire, it doesn't really matter.

I have not even started to describe this film, directed by Tomas Alfredson and written by John Ajvide Lindqvist, based on his novel. I will not go into the relationship Eli has with an unsavory middle-aged man named Hakan (Per Ragnar). Maybe he is her familiar, maybe he just likes blood. Nor will I talk about the iron rod and the knife, or Oskar's horrible parents. I've already made it sound grim enough, and the fact is, there are some funny moments. Vampire-funny, you know. "Are you really my age?" Oskar asks Eli. "Yes. But I've been this age for a very long time."

Remove the vampire elements, and this is the story of two lonely and desperate kids capable of performing dark deeds without apparent emotion. Kids washed up on the shores of despair. The young actors are powerful in draining roles. We care for them more than they care for themselves. Alfredson's palette is so drained of warm colors that even fresh blood is black. We learn that a vampire must be invited into a room before it can enter. Now the title makes sense.

Note: Jeremy Knox of Film Threat likes the film as much as I do, but comes from a different place. He writes: "I'd even go so far as to say this would make a great date film. Women will melt watching this. Not only that, but it'd also make a fine film to show to the ten- to sixteen-year-old crowd. Little kids, especially girls, will love this. Yeah, there's some blood and one really quick shot of nudity, but just because they're young doesn't mean they're stupid. Kids will totally get this."

They'll get it, all right. In the neck.

Lights in the Dusk ★ ★ ★ ½
NO MPAA RATING, 78 m., 2008

Janne Hyytiainen (Koistinen), Maria Jarvenhelmi (Mirja), Ilkka Koivula (Lindholm).

Directed and produced by Aki Kaurismaki. Screenplay by Kaurismaki.

More and more I am learning to love the films of Aki Kaurismaki, that Finnish master of the stories of sad and lonely losers. Like very few directors (such as Tati, Fassbinder, Keaton, Fellini), he has created a world all his own, and you can recognize it from almost every shot. His characters are dour, speak little, expect the worst, smoke too much, are ill-treated by life, are passive in the face of tragedy. Yes, and they are funny.

It is a deadpan humor. Kaurismaki never signals us to laugh, and at festivals there is rarely a roar of laughter, more often the exhalation people make when they are subduing a roar of laughter. His characters are lovable, but nobody seems to know that. *Lights in the Dusk* is the third film in his "loser trilogy," preceded by *Drifting Clouds*, the story of an unemployed couple hopelessly in debt, and *The Man Without a Past*, the story of a homeless man who has no idea who he is. How can I convince you these stories are deeply amusing? I can't. Take my word for it.

In *Lights in the Dusk*, everybody on the screen smokes more than ever, perhaps because it is the highlight of their day. We meet Koistinen (Janne Hyytiainen), a night watchman who says "I have no friends" because it is true: He has no friends. Well, there is the woman who runs the late-night hot dog stand. She is nice to him, but he is cold to her.

Koistinen is shunned at work by his fellow security guards. After three years, the manager cannot remember his name. People stare at him in restaurants. One night he is approached at his solitary table in a cafe by an attractive blonde who asks, "Is this seat taken?" He asks her why she sat there when the café is empty. "Because you looked like you needed company."

They date, if that is the word. They sit rigidly through a movie, almost silently through a dinner, and he stands in the corner at a disco. He invites her to dinner in his basement flat, which has large pipes running through it. He offers her a fresh bagel: "The roast is in the oven." She says, "Koistinen, I have to make a trip. My mother is ill." He asks,

"When?" She says, "Right now," and stands up and leaves.

He protests to three bruisers that their dog has been tied outside a bar for days, without water. They take him offscreen and he returns beaten. Most of Kaurismaki's beatings are offscreen, mercifully. There is a plot behind all of his misfortune, which leads to jail time and then a cot in a homeless shelter. He disastrously tries to take action against those who have used him. The hot-dog girl seeks him out. The dog finds a new owner. There is a happy ending, lasting about thirty seconds.

It isn't what happens, it's how it happens. You'll have a hard time finding Kaurismaki in a theater in most cities (and states), but he's waiting for you on DVD. Put a Kaurismaki in your Netflix queue. Most any film will do. You will start watching it and feel strangely disoriented because none of the usual audience cues are supplied. You're on your own. You will watch it engrossed and fascinated right up until the very end, which will not feel much like an ending. You will for some reason feel curious to see another Kaurismaki film. If by any chance you dislike the film and turn it off, let it wait a day, and start it again. You were wrong.

The Limits of Control ★ ½
R, 116 m., 2009

Isaach De Bankole (Lone Man), Alex Descas (Creole), Jean-Francois Stevenin (French), Luis Tosar (Violin), Paz de la Huerta (Nude), Tilda Swinton (Blonde), Youki Kudoh (Molecules), John Hurt (Guitar), Gael Garcia Bernal (Mexican), Hiam Abbass (Driver), Bill Murray (American). Directed by Jim Jarmusch and produced by Stacey Smith and Gretchen McGowan. Screenplay by Jarmusch.

I am the man in *The Limits of Control.* I cannot tell you my name because the screenplay has not given me one. There's only room for so many details in 116 minutes. Call me The Man With No Name. I wander through Spain saying as little as possible, as Clint Eastwood did in films I enjoyed as a boy. Now I am a man, handsome, exotic, cool, impenetrable, hip, mysterious, quiet, coiled, enigmatic, passive, stoic, and hungry.

On my journey, I enter cafés and always specify the same order: "Two espressos, in two separate cups." In each café, I am met by a contact. I exchange matchboxes. The one I hand over is filled with diamonds. The one I am given contains a note on a small piece of paper, which I eat. I meet strange people. I do not know them. They know me. I am the one with two espressos in two separate cups. One is a beautiful young woman, always nude, whom I would like to get to know better, but not in this movie.

The writer and director of the film is Jim Jarmusch. I've seen several of his movies and even appeared in a couple. This one takes the cake. He is making some kind of a point. I think the point is that if you strip a story down to its bare essentials, you will have very little left. I wonder how he pitched this idea to his investors.

As an actor, my name is Isaach De Bankole. I have the opportunity to appear in scenes with actors who are known for the chances they take. Sometimes an actor like that will prove nothing except that he is loyal to his friends or a good sport. Bill Murray is appearing so frequently in such films I think it is time for him to star in a smutty action comedy. The other good sports include Tilda Swinton, Gael Garcia Bernal, John Hurt, and Paz de la Huerta, who is nude all the time. That's a good sport and a half.

My acting assignment was not so hard. I costarred with Mathieu Amalric in *The Diving Bell and the Butterfly.* He played a man whose movement was restricted to one eye. Now there was a tough assignment. I acted in Lars von Trier's *Manderlay,* where the locations were suggested by chalk lines on the floor of a sound stage. Not as much fun as Spanish cafés. I starred in the Quebec film *How to Make Love to a Negro Without Getting Tired,* and I played the Negro, but I was the one who got tired.

So I'm not complaining. We actors enjoyed Spain. Often we would gather for a dinner of paella and sangria. One night Bill Murray quoted Gene Siskel: "I ask myself if I would enjoy myself more watching a documentary of the same actors having dinner." We all sat and thought about that, as the night breeze blew warm through the town and a faraway mandolin told its tale.

We were pretty sure it would be a good-looking movie. Jarmusch was working with the cameraman Christopher Doyle, and they spent a lot of time discussing their palette, figuring their exposure, and framing their compositions. That reminded me of a silent film named *Man with a Movie Camera,* which some people think is the best film ever made. It shows a man with a movie camera, photographing things. Was Jarmusch remaking it without the man and the camera?

Little Ashes ★ ★ ★
R, 112 m., 2009

Javier Beltran (Federico García Lorca), Robert Pattinson (Salvador Dalí), Matthew McNulty (Luis Buñuel), Marina Gatell (Magdalena), Arly Jover (Gala). Directed by Paul Morrison and produced by Carlo Dusi, Jonny Persey, and Jaume Vilalta. Screenplay by Philippa Goslett.

It was a ripe time to live at the Students' Residence in Madrid and study at the School of Fine Arts. When he arrived from Catalonia in 1922, Salvador Dalí met the future poet Federico García Lorca and future filmmaker Luis Buñuel. Dalí was a case study, dressed as a British dandy of the previous century with a feminine appearance. No doubt he was a gifted painter. He was to become a rather loathsome man.

Little Ashes focuses on an unconsummated romantic attraction between Dalí (Robert Pattinson) and García Lorca (Javier Beltran), who in the flower of youthful idealism and with the awakening of the flesh began to confuse sexuality with artistry. Not much is really known about their romance, such as it was, but in the conservative Catholic nation of the time and given Dalí's extreme terror of syphilis, it seems to have been passionate but platonic.

It found release in their roles in the developing Surrealist movement, in which church, state, ideology, landowners, parents, authorities, and laws were all mocked by deliberately outlandish behavior. In 1929, Dalí wrote and Buñuel directed probably the most famous of all Surrealist works, the film *Un Chien Andalou* (*The Andalusian Dog*), with its notorious images of a cloud slicing through the moon and a knife slicing through a woman's eyeball. In a time before computer imagery, it was a real eyeball (belonging to a pig, not a woman, but small comfort to the pig).

By 1936, García Lorca was dead, murdered by Spanish fascists. The story is told in the film *The Disappearance of García Lorca* (1997). Buñuel fled Spain to Mexico, then later returned as one of the world's greatest filmmakers. Dalí betrayed his early talent, embraced fascism, Nazism, and communism, returned repentant to the Church, and become an odious caricature of an artist, obsessed by cash. "Each morning when I awake," he said, "I experience again a supreme pleasure—that of being Salvador Dalí." Yes, but for a time he was a superb painter.

Little Ashes is a film that shows these personalities being formed. Because most audiences may not know much about Dalí, García Lorca, and Buñuel, it depends for its box-office appeal on the starring role of Robert Pattinson, the twenty-three-year-old British star of *Twilight.* He is the heartthrob of the teenage vampire fans of *Twilight* but here shows an admirable willingness to take on a challenging role in direct contrast to the famous Edward Cullen. Is it too much to hope that *Twilight* fans will be drawn to the work of García Lorca and Buñuel? They'd be on the fast track to cultural literacy.

Biopics about the youth of famous men are often overshadowed by their fame to come. *The Motorcycle Diaries,* for example, depended for much of its appeal on our knowledge that its young doctor hero would someday become Che Guevara. *Little Ashes* is interested in the young men for themselves.

It shows unformed young men starting from similar places but taking different roads because of their characters. García Lorca, who is honest with himself about his love for another man, finds real love eventually with a woman, his classmate Magdalena (Marina Gatell). Dalí, who presents almost as a transvestite, denies all feelings, and like many puritans ends as a voluptuary. Buñuel, the most gifted of all, ends as all good film directors do, consumed by his work. I am fond of his practical approach to matters. Warned that angry mobs might storm the screen at the Paris premiere of *Un Chien Andalou,* he filled his pockets with stones to throw at them.

The film is absorbing but not compelling. Most of its action is inward. The more we know about the three men the better. Although the eyeball-slicing is shown in the film, many audiences may have no idea what it is doing there. Perhaps Dalí's gradual slinking away from his ideals, his early embrace of celebrity, and his preference for self-publicity over actual achievement makes better sense when we begin with his shyness and naivete; is he indeed entirely aware that his hair and dress are those of a girl, or has he been coddled in this way by a strict, protective mother who is hostile to male sexuality?

Whatever the case, two things stand out: He has the courage to present himself in quasi-drag, and the other students at the Residence, inspired by the fever in the air, accept him as "making a statement" he might not have been fully aware of.

I have long believed that one minute of wondering if you are about to be kissed is more erotic than an hour of kissing. Although a few gay sites complain *Little Ashes* doesn't deliver the goods, I find it far more intriguing to find how repressed sexuality expresses itself, because the bolder sort comes out in the usual ways and reduces mystery to bodily fluids. Orgasms are at their best when still making big promises, don't you find?

Lola Montes ★ ★ ★ ½
NO MPAA RATING, 110 m., 1955 (rereleased 2008)

Martine Carol (Lola Montes), Peter Ustinov (Ringmaster), Anton Walbrook (King Ludwig I), Henri Guisol (Maurice), Lise Delamare (Mrs. Craigie), Paulette Dubost (Josephine), Oskar Werner (Student). Directed by Max Ophuls and produced by Albert Caraco. Screenplay by Ophuls.

One of the signs of a great director is his ability to sustain a consistent personal tone throughout a film. The work of certain directors can be recognized almost at once; a few hundred feet of Godard or Fellini are sufficient. Max Ophuls was such a director, and his *Lola Montes* has as much unity of tone as any film I can remember.

It is all of a piece from beginning to end: the mood, the music, the remarkably fluid camera movement, the sets, the costumes. It is a director's film. The actors are in Ophuls's complete control, an additional element in his examination of the romantic myth.

His story involves the infamous Lola Montes, "The Most Scandalous Woman in the World," the mistress of Franz Liszt and King Ludwig of Bavaria, of students and artists, of soldiers and ringmasters. We find her in a New Orleans circus, the star attraction in a review of her sensational career. Peter Ustinov, the ringmaster, narrates her past as Lola revolves on a platform. Later the customers will have their chance to spend a dollar and kiss her hand.

The device of the circus is as successful as it is daring. Using it to supply his narrative thread, Ophuls slides through a series of flashbacks with as much ease and psychological completeness as Welles exhibited in *Citizen Kane*. The structure of the film is terribly artificial—flashbacks suspended from a fantasy circus—and the style itself is a highly mannered romanticism. But it works; Ophuls understands and justifies his method.

He is not so successful, unfortunately, with the performance of the late Martine Carol in the title role. Famous in the 1950s as a sort of prototype Bardot, Miss Carol was a third-rate actress, and she comes across as wooden, shallow, not even very attractive.

Ophuls apparently needed Miss Carol's box-office name to help justify his $1.5 million budget (this was the most expensive French film to date when it was completed in 1955). He tries to make an advantage of her weakness by directing her almost as a doll; her function is to watch impassively while her lovers save her scenes. The best performance in the film is by Anton Walbrook as the deaf, touching old king. Peter Ustinov is typically excellent. Oskar Werner, as a young student, is not much better than ever.

Lola Montes was a commercial flop when Ophuls released it in 1955, shortened against his will. He died two years later, still engaged in a battle with the film's producers. An even more savagely butchered version was in circulation for a few years. Through the efforts of the *Village Voice*'s Andrew Sarris and other lovers of the film, a somewhat restored version was shown at the first New York Film Festival in 1963 and in an improved version in 1968. In reviews at the time, Sarris called it "the greatest film of all time."

Now, thanks to the discovery of additional footage and new digital technology, the film has finally been restored to Ophuls's original version, which was thought lost after the cuts in the 1950s. It showed for the third time at the 2008 New York Film Festival in October. It is now complete and looks better than at any time in its viewing history. In fact, it is breathtaking, an extravaganza of bright circus colors and Ophuls's fluid camera in wide-screen Cinemascope.

The Longshots ★ ★ ★
PG, 94 m., 2008

Ice Cube (Curtis Plummer), Keke Palmer (Jasmine Plummer), Tasha Smith (Claire), Jill Marie Jones (Ronnie), Dash Mihok (Cyrus), Miles Chandler (Damon), Matt Craven (Coach Fisher). Directed by Fred Durst and produced by Ice Cube, Matt Alvarez, and Nick Santora. Screenplay by Santora and Doug Atchison.

If I've seen one movie about a team of underdogs from a small town, I've seen a dozen. But I hadn't seen *The Longshots* before. It's based on the true story of eleven-year-old Jasmine Plummer, from the Chicago suburb of Harvey, who in 2003 became the first female to play quarterback in the Pop Warner football tournament.

Her story is remarkable, especially if you factor in her national wrestling title and her grades as an honor student. But the film is remarkable in other ways. It includes some of the expected elements of any film from this genre, but without the usual Hollywood supercharging. It's not all pumped up with flash and phoniness. Its stars play their characters with a quiet conviction, warm and touching. Its heroine is not the usual young girl who is required to be smarter and talk faster and correct adults in their faulty thinking. She has humility, shyness, and a certain sadness.

And that is all the more impressive because Jasmine is played by Keke Palmer, who seems absolutely convincing in the role. Yet consider that this is the same actress (thirteen when the movie was shot) who played Queen Latifah's

niece in *Barbershop 2*, held her own in an exchange with Cedric the Entertainer in that film, has starred in Medea projects by Tyler Perry, and was the youngest actress ever nominated for best actress by the Screen Actors Guild.

That means this is real acting. Her Jasmine has *not* always wanted to play boys' football. In fact, she doesn't want to. But she has a good eye and a strong throwing arm, and is pushed into it by her Uncle Curtis (Ice Cube), who was a star years ago on the same team. Curtis has been unemployed since the town's factory closed, has no aim in life, loves his niece, and acts like a father to her because her own dad abandoned the family. He teaches her all he knows about quarterbacking, and more or less forces the coach (Matt Craven) to put her in a game. She's small but smart and quick, and soon her story is picked up by the press, and she quarterbacks the team into Pop Warner history.

Some facts have been changed. Harvey becomes Minton, Illinois, a small town with a sizable African-American population. Since the factory closed, Main Street has a lot of empty storefronts and there's not much civic spirit. But the team revives hope and pride. And Ice Cube and Keke Palmer create a believable uncle-niece relationship that is right down to the ground in honesty and sincerity.

It's also nice that the team accepts her pretty quickly. They like her, she plays well, and that's that. No practical jokes or hazing, although some of the other girls in school are jealous and snippy. Some of the best things about this film are what it doesn't do. The director, Fred Durst (lead singer for Limp Bizkit), and his writers, Nick Santora and Doug Atchison, are actually interested in these human beings, not in all the semi-obligatory clichés.

No team bully. No seemingly tragic injuries. Not many fans in the stands, although more trickle in when the team starts to win. There's a little romance between Curtis and a schoolteacher (Jill Marie Jones), but it's mostly low-key conversation. Jasmine's mother (Tasha Smith) runs the town diner and is not in personal crisis. The movie even lacks that old groaner, the scene where the kid spots a parent in the crowd and is suddenly inspired. And the ending will surprise you by being true to life.

The movie, in short, is absolutely sure what it wants to be, right down to the worn-out grass on the football field, so realistically photographed by Conrad W. Hall. Even the signs Jasmine's fans hold up look homemade, when a lot of teen sports movies seem to have employed sign painters. And Jasmine dresses exactly like an ordinary girl her age and doesn't seem to be auditioning for a role as an American Girl doll. The more the movie builds, the more it grows on you. And would you believe this? Keke Palmer was also born in Harvey.

Looking for Eric ★★
NO MPAA RATING, 116 m., 2010

Steve Evets (Eric Bishop), Eric Cantona (Himself), Stephanie Bishop (Lily), Gerard Kearns (Ryan), John Henshaw (Meatballs), Lucy-Jo Hudson (Sam), Stefan Gumbs (Jess). Directed by Ken Loach and produced by Rebecca O'Brien. Screenplay by Paul Laverty.

Looking for Eric is the last film I would have expected from Ken Loach, the great British director of films about working-class lives. His strength is social realism and a critique of the limited options within a class system. He works close to the earth and to his characters.

Here now is a most unexpected comedy, appealing to world soccer fans and based on a common enough daydream: A man's sports hero appears in his life and carries on friendly conversations with him. I call it a fantasy, but Loach approaches it as if it were quite real. He uses Eric Cantona, a famed star of Manchester United, and places him right there in the room with Eric Bishop (Steve Evets), a Manchester postal worker badly in need of encouragement.

The outlines of Eric's life are grim. The film begins after he survives a car crash and involves his two worthless grown sons, Ryan and Jess, and his lingering feelings for his estranged wife, Lily (Stephanie Bishop), who has refused to speak to him in seven years.

Into this sad man's life steps Cantona, a superstar in all the soccer-playing world, who becomes his confidant and confessor. Cantona, it must be said, is quite successful in his role: warm, persuasive, a source of common sense. He diagnoses Eric's problem: He should get back together with Lily. This is also the plan of Sam (Lucy-Jo Hudson), Eric and Lily's grown daughter.

This counsel provides a reason for flashbacks showing Eric and Lily's romance in earlier years, very touching, causing us to hope they'll fall in love all over again. But, excuse me, why does this require brokering by an imaginary sports star? Cantona himself produced the film and may have been involved in the financing, which could explain how it came to be made. What I can't explain is why Loach chose to make it. Maybe after so many great films he simply wanted to relax with a genre comedy. It has charm and Loach's fine eye and an expected generic payoff. But it doesn't make any sense.

I had another problem I'm almost ashamed to admit. Loach has always made it a point to use actors employing working-class accents, reflecting the fact that accent is a class marker. I've usually been able to understand the characters in his movies; it's the music as much as the words to begin with, and then I start to hear the words. This time his star, Steve Evets, uses a Manchester accent so thick many of the English themselves might not be able to understand it. Ironically Eric Cantona, who is French, is easier to understand.

Looking for Eric is inexplicable. It has elements of a Loach social drama, which might have been better used as the entire story. Cantona is nice enough, but so what? If there seem to be any comic possibilities in the story, Loach doesn't find them. If your world doesn't revolve around Eric Cantona, he'll come over as just a nice enough guy, no big deal. And can the great Ken Loach actually have fallen prey to the Obligatory Action in the Third Act virus?

Lorna's Silence ★★★ ½
R, 105 m., 2009

Arta Dobroshi (Lorna), Jeremie Renier (Claudy), Fabrizio Rongione (Fabio), Alban Ukaj (Sokol), Morgan Marinne (Spirou). Directed by Jean-Pierre Dardenne and Luc Dardenne, and produced by Jean-Pierre Dardenne, Luc

Dardenne, and Denis Freyd. Screenplay by Jean-Pierre Dardenne and Luc Dardenne.

The Dardenne brothers focus intently on individuals in their films, which are among the best in recent years. In such films as *Rosetta* (1999), *Le Fils* (*The Son,* 2002), and *L'Enfant* (*The Child,* 2005), their cameras scarcely allow the protagonists to escape the frame. *Lorna's Silence* begins that way but allows shots in which Lorna is not even present. A plot begins to unfold that she isn't aware of.

Lorna (Arta Dobroshi) is a young woman of about thirty from Albania, now living in Belgium. She is a beneficiary and exploiter of the marriage-for-sale racket. A pathetic drug addict named Claudy has married her for money, a vermin named Fabio has arranged this marriage, Fabio plans to arrange Claudy's death, a Russian will pay Lorna to marry him so he can obtain a passport, and then, Lorna believes, she will be free to marry her lover, Sokol. They even know the little storefront where they talk of opening a café.

It is all so shabby and sad. And dominating the early scenes is the character of Claudy (Jeremie Renier), who wants to quit heroin cold turkey and is a wretched, needy, trembling creature. Renier's performance is the best thing in the movie, although all the actors, cast partly for their faces, are part of creating this desperate world.

Lorna treats Claudy coldly. He telephones her incessantly. He is afraid to be left alone. Eventually his pathos wears her down; she's not an evil woman, just an opportunist. She wonders if it might not be possible for her to divorce Claudy, rather than clear the stage with an overdose—Fabio's plan.

The gift of Jean-Pierre and Luc Dardenne is to show their characters as trapped in personal human situations; they're not creatures of a plot. Fabio (Fabrizio Rongione), for example, isn't a "villain"; he is simply a man, brutal and heartless by nature and driven entirely by money. He has a callow flunky named Spirou (Morgan Marinne), who is as servile as a cur. Both Rongione and Marinne have the hard faces of bullies; you would feel wary of them on sight.

That's not to say they're that way in person. They may be jolly good chaps for all I know.

Here they are reptilian. That's partly because the Dardennes shoot them mostly in profile; a full face seems open to us, but a side shot from an oblique angle can seem sinister. If everyone has a "good side," the Dardennes must figure out which it is, in order to avoid it.

All centers on Lorna. She is a pleasant-enough young woman, crisp, direct. I've seen photos of Arta Dobroshi with a warm smile. In *Lorna's Silence,* she plays a woman who is deprived of her bodily integrity even more than a prostitute might be; she hasn't been bought and sold because of sex, but simply because of her gender. Claudy married her for money, the Russian doesn't care if he sleeps with her, and Sokol is a snaky man who is out of the country most of the time. His qualities exist mostly in her mind.

The Dardennes do something I haven't seen them do before. There is a considerable time lapse in the story, while basic changes take place with the characters. Lorna's nature shifts. I'm not saying this is bad, but it releases the tension they generate when they stay close in time and space. Still, what power is here. What affecting acting by Dobroshi, Renier (who in *L'Enfant* played the father who sold and desperately tried to rebuy his child), and Marinne (who was the apprentice with the dark past in *The Son*). In the cold, harsh world of the Dardennes, they feel sympathy but can grant little mercy.

The Losers ★★★ ½
PG-13, 98 m., 2010

Zoe Saldana (Aisha), Jeffrey Dean Morgan (Clay), Chris Evans (Jensen), Idris Elba (Roque), Columbus Short (Pooch), Oscar Jaenada (Cougar), Jason Patric (Max). Directed by Sylvain White and produced by Kerry Foster, Akiva Goldsman, and Joel Silver. Screenplay by Peter Berg and James Vanderbilt.

The Losers is a classical action movie based on a comic strip. It does just enough nodding toward the graphics of drawn superheroes, and then gets that out of the way and settles down into a clean, efficient, and entertaining thriller. It's a reminder of how exhausting this kind of material can be when it's brought to a manic level by overwrought directors. It looks, feels, and plays like a real movie. There is another reason to be grateful: It's not in 3-D. You have to treasure movies like this before they're entirely eaten away by the marketing gimmicks.

Story, straightforward, no gargoyles. Five tough guys on a mission against a drug lord in Bolivia. They abort the mission when they see a bus full of little kids arrive at the target. No luck. A voice named "Max" orders a plane to carry out a bombing run. The tough guys break in and rescue the kids just in time. A helicopter is sent for them. No room on the copter except for the kids. The copter is shot down, the kids die.

"That was supposed to be us," they say, regarding the smoldering wreckage. Close-up of flames still licking at a toy bear that was established earlier as belonging to a cute kid. Note: Whenever a kid gets on a copter in an action film and is told to take good care of his bear, the kid and the bear will go down in flames.

The tough guys rip off their dog tags and throw them on the flames. Now they're The Losers, dedicated to bringing the mysterious Max to justice. Who is he? They guess maybe CIA–Special Forces–Black Ops . . . nobody knows. Meanwhile, they're officially dead and stranded in Bolivia with no passports and no money.

Think I'm giving away too much? That's only the pre-title sequence. Then we meet them one by one: Clay (Jeffrey Dean Morgan), Jensen (Chris Evans), Roque (Idris Elba), Pooch (Columbus Short), and Cougar (Oscar Jaenada). Each has a specialty: command, ordnance, rockets, sniper, etc. They're rugged, macho, wisecracking. Clay is the highest-ranking officer, but he keeps saying, "We're not in the military now." Later, of course, he pulls rank.

Then we meet Aisha (Zoe Saldana). Saldana is a seriously beautiful woman. You didn't notice that so much in *Avatar*. She poses as a bar girl to seduce her way into Clay's room, and then they have a deadly fight, destroy the room, and burn down the hotel, and after that they're friends on the same side and Clay is convincing the others to trust her. I didn't quite follow this every step of the way.

Aisha knows who Max really is, where he is, and how to get him. And she has the resources to get The Losers into the United States, arm them, rent them helicopters, and so on. They want to avenge those kids. Can Aisha be trusted? It's not always clear. Nor is it clear at first exactly what Max is up to, although here's a first: He demonstrates the first green weapon of mass destruction. It totally destroys a target, yet adds no pollution to the atmosphere. How's that for progress? How he plans to use the weapon and what his super-secret computer files are for provide the movie's MacGuffin.

Max is played by Jason Patric, who can make a very snaky snark. The director, Sylvain White, contrives a nice little scene on the beach where Max's curvaceous servant shades him with an umbrella. The wind blows the umbrella aside for a second, and the shot becomes a perfect steal of that butler on the beach in the Jack Vettriano painting that became the largest-selling poster in British history. Then Max shoots her. That's not in the Vettriano.

The Losers knows what it's doing and how to do it. Sylvain White doesn't have a lot of credits, but he knows how to direct and not trip over his own feet. The movie gets the job done, and the actors show a lot of confidence in occupying that tricky middle ground between controlled satire and comic overkill. It's fun.

I noted that Zoe Saldana is beautiful. I noted something else. In keeping with the current popularity of cafe au lait complexions, the movie uses lighting and filters to bathe the romantic scenes in a kind of golden glow, so that Saldana and Morgan come out looking about the same. We're no longer making people of color look whiter in the movies; we're tinting people of whiteness. Time marches on.

The Loss of a Teardrop Diamond ★★★
PG-13, 102 m., 2010

Bryce Dallas Howard (Fisher Willow), Chris Evans (Jimmy Dobyne), Ellen Burstyn (Miss Addie), Mamie Gummer (Julie), Ann-Margret (Aunt Cornelia), Will Patton (Old Man Dobyne), Jessica Collins (Vinnie). Directed by Jodie Markell and produced by Brad Michael Gilbert. Screenplay by Tennessee Williams.

Soft summer nights, the moon low above the river, "Alice Blue Gown" drifting on the breeze, a rich Southern girl who tasted freedom in Paris and now pretends to desire Memphis society, a poor but honest boy, bitchy debutantes in pastel gowns, wary old ladies in wide-brimmed hats, an opium addict in agony, a good but drunken father, and down by the levee the ghosts of sharecroppers drowned by a rich man's dynamite.

The voice of Tennessee Williams calls to us across the twenty-six years since his death. It is not strong and fierce, but it is his. *The Loss of a Teardrop Diamond* is an original screenplay he wrote in the 1950s, never produced, long forgotten. It has been filmed in a respectful manner that feels like a touring production of an only moderately successful Broadway play. Understand that, accept it, and the film has its rewards and one performance of great passion.

That would be by Ellen Burstyn, Miss Addie, who plays it all in bed in her sickroom in a Tennessee country mansion with a debutante party going on downstairs. She has snared Fisher Willow (Bryce Dallas Howard) away from the party and ordered her to lock the doors. Addie lived for many years in Hong Kong, consoled by opium for her lost dreams. She remembers Fisher from a brief visit home. The girl struck her as hard and brave. Now she asks her to do something for her. Give her the pills that will allow her to die.

Fisher is very agitated, a word Tennessee might have liked. She has hired Jimmy Dobyne (Chris Evans), the good-looking poor boy whose alcoholic father manages her father's commissary, to be her escort to the party. She even measured him for his evening wear. Jimmy's grandfather was governor, but the family has fallen back to its knees. Addie senses all has not gone well on their date, discovers Jimmy didn't want to kiss Fisher when she parked on the riverbank, advises her to escape and go back to Europe.

These are all Williams tropes. The paralyzing stupidity of genteel society. The lure of Europe and the "arts," and escape itself. The drink, the drugs, the decay. The not-as-young woman hiring a gentleman caller and hoping for the kindness of strangers. Bryce Dallas Howard is affecting as Fisher, but not electri-

fying because the material doesn't have it in it. Chris Evans, as Jimmy, is reserved to the point of oddness: a straight arrow without the arrowhead. He may think he's channeling Paul Newman, but he evokes instead the new male lead on a soap opera.

There are extended scenes involving the party downstairs, everyone perfectly dressed. No one talks unless they have dialogue provided. They stand around murmuring like extras. Remember the party scene in Visconti's *The Leopard*, all told in one shot, establishing characters and relationships? This party is as lifeless as the "pageant" staged earlier in a garden by drilled girls for bored old ladies.

And yet I relax and take it for what it is. I feel Tennessee's yearnings. I saw something of his life indirectly, at a remove. His brother Dakin lived in Chicago and was a frequent player on the newspaper drinking circuit; he announced his candidacy for governor at a press conference at Riccardo's. He wore a white pinstripe suit and a Panama hat. He had a platform, but the only plank you ever heard about was that he was the brother of Tennessee—and of Rose, you remember, the sister. He was a friendly man, courteous, sharing I suspect the joke of his several runs for office. He was the comedy, Rose was the tragedy, and Tennessee was the recording angel.

You will want to see this film if Tennessee means anything to you. Does he, to most people, anymore? And do Albee and Miller? A nonmusical play can hardly open on Broadway these days, and the twentieth century's playwriting history flourishes elsewhere in places like Chicago. But this *is* a Tennessee Williams screenplay. And in it one of the great Williams women, Miss Addie, and one of the great Williams actresses, Ellen Burstyn. That ought to mean something. Well, shouldn't it?

The Love Guru ★
PG-13, 87 m., 2008

Mike Myers (Guru Pitka), Jessica Alba (Jane Bullard), Justin Timberlake (Jacques Grande), Romany Malco (Darren Roanoke), Meagan Good (Prudence), Omid Djalili (Guru Satchabigknoba), Ben Kingsley (Guru Tugginmypuddha), Verne Troyer (Cherkov). Directed by Marco Schnabel and produced by

Michael De Luca and Mike Myers. Screenplay by Myers and Graham Gordy.

What is it with Mike Myers and penis jokes? Having created a classic funny scene with his not-quite-visible penis sketch in the first Austin Powers movie, he now assembles, in *The Love Guru*, as many more penis jokes as he can think of, none of them funny except for one based on an off-screen *thump*. He supplements this subject with countless other awful moments involving defecation and the deafening passing of gas. Oh, and elephant sex.

The plot involves an American child who is raised in an Indian ashram (never mind why) and becomes the childhood friend of Deepak Chopra. Both come to America, where Chopra becomes a celebrity, but Guru Pitka (Myers) seems doomed to anonymity. That's until Jane Bullard (Jessica Alba), owner of the Toronto Maple Leafs, hires him to reconcile her star player, Darren Roanoke (Romany Malco), with his estranged wife, Prudence (Meagan Good). Just at the time of the Stanley Cup play-offs, Prudence has left her husband for the arms and other attributes of star Los Angeles player Jacques "Le Coq" Grande (Justin Timberlake), said to have the largest whatjamacallit in existence.

And what *don't* they call it in *The Love Guru*? The movie not only violates the Law of Funny Names (usually not funny), but rips it from the Little Movie Glossary and tramples it into the ice. Yes, many scenes are filmed at the Stanley Cup finals, where we see much of the Maple Leafs' dwarf coach (Verne Troyer), also the butt of size jokes (you will remember him as Mini-Me in the Powers films). There is also a running gag involving the play-by-play commentators and occasional flashbacks to the guru's childhood in India, where he studied under Guru Tugginmypuddha (Ben Kingsley). One of the guru's martial arts involves fencing with urine-soaked mops. Uh-huh.

Myers, a Canadian, incorporates some Canadian in-jokes; the team owner's name, Bullard, evokes the Ballard family of Maple Leaf fame. At the center of all of this is Guru Pitka, desperately trying to get himself on *Oprah* and finding acronyms in some of the most unlikely words. He has a strange manner of delivering punch lines directly into the camera and then laughing at them—usually, I must report, alone.

Myers is a nice man and has made some funny movies, but this film could have been written on toilet walls by callow adolescents. Every reference to a human sex organ or process of defecation is not automatically funny simply because it is naughty, but Myers seems to labor under that delusion. He acts as if he's getting away with something, but in fact all he's getting away with is selling tickets to a dreary experience. There's a moment of invention near the beginning of the film (his flying cushion has a back-up beeper), and then it's all into the Dumpster. Even his fellow actors seem to realize no one is laughing. That's impossible because they can't hear the audience, but it looks uncannily like they can, and do.

The Lovely Bones ★ ½
PG-13, 136 m., 2010

Mark Wahlberg (Jack Salmon), Rachel Weisz (Abigail Salmon), Susan Sarandon (Grandma Lynn), Stanley Tucci (George Harvey), Michael Imperioli (Len Fenerman), Saoirse Ronan (Susie Salmon), Rose McIver (Lindsey Salmon). Directed by Peter Jackson and produced by Jackson, Carolynne Cunningham, and Fran Walsh. Screenplay by Jackson, Walsh, and Philippa Boyens, based on the novel by Alice Sebold.

The Lovely Bones is a deplorable film with this message: If you're a fourteen-year-old girl who has been brutally raped and murdered by a serial killer, you have a lot to look forward to. You can get together in heaven with the other teenage victims of the same killer and gaze down in benevolence upon your family members as they mourn you and realize what a wonderful person you were. Sure, you miss your friends, but your fellow fatalities come dancing to greet you in a meadow of wildflowers, and how cool is that?

The makers of this film seem to have given slight thought to the psychology of teenage girls, less to the possibility that there is no heaven, and none at all to the likelihood that if there is one, it will not resemble a happy gathering of new Facebook friends. In its version of the events, the serial killer can almost be seen as a hero for liberating these girls from the tiresome ordeal of growing up and dispatching them directly to the Elysian Fields. The film's primary effect was to make me squirmy.

It's based on the best-seller by Alice Sebold that everybody seemed to be reading a couple of years ago. I hope it's not faithful to the book; if it is, millions of Americans are scary. The murder of a young person is a tragedy, the murderer is a monster, and making the victim a sweet, poetic narrator is creepy. This movie sells the philosophy that even evil things are God's will and their victims are happier now. Isn't it nice to think so. I think it's best if they don't happen at all. But if they do, why pretend they don't hurt? Those girls are dead.

I'm assured, however, that Sebold's novel is well-written and sensitive. I presume the director, Peter Jackson, has distorted elements to fit his own "vision," which involves nearly as many special effects in some sequences as his *Lord of the Rings* trilogy. A more useful way to deal with this material would be with observant, subtle performances in a thoughtful screenplay. It's not a feel-good story. Perhaps Jackson's team made the mistake of fearing the novel was too dark. But its millions of readers must know it's not like this. The target audience may be doom-besotted teenage girls—the *Twilight* crowd.

The owner of the lovely bones is named Susie Salmon (Saoirse Ronan, a very good young actress, who cannot be faulted here). The heaven Susie occupies looks a little like a Flower Power world in the kind of fantasy that, murdered in 1973, she might have imagined. Seems to me that heaven, by definition outside time and space, would have neither colors nor a lack of colors—would be a state with no sensations. Nor would there be thinking there, let alone narration. In an eternity spent in the presence of infinite goodness, you don't go around thinking, "Man! Is this great!" You simply *are*. I have a lot of theologians on my side here.

But no. From her movie-set Valhalla, Susie gazes down as her mother (Rachel Weisz) grieves and her father (Mark Wahlberg) tries to solve the case himself. There's not much of a case to solve; we know who the killer is al-

most from the get-go, and, under the Law of Economy of Characters, that's who he has to be because (a) he's played by an otherwise unnecessary movie star, and (b) there's no one else in the movie he *could* be.

Here's something bittersweet. Weisz and Wahlberg are effective as the parents. Because the pyrotechnics are mostly upstairs with the special effects, all they need to be are convincing parents who have lost their daughter. This they do with touching subtlety. We also meet one of Susie's grandmothers (Susan Sarandon), an unwise drinker who comes on to provide hard-boiled comic relief, in the Shakespearean tradition that every tragedy needs its clown. Well, she's good, too. This whole film is Jackson's fault.

It doesn't fail simply because I suspect its message. It fails on its own terms. It isn't emotionally convincing that this girl, having had these experiences and destined apparently to be fourteen forever (although cleaned up and with a new wardrobe), would produce this heavenly creature. What's left for us to pity? We should all end up like her, and the sooner the better; preferably not after being raped and murdered. ☞

The Lucky Ones ★ ★ ★
R, 113 m., 2008

Tim Robbins (Fred Cheaver), Rachel McAdams (Colee Dunn), Michael Pena (T.K. Poole). Directed by Neil Burger and produced by Burger, Brian Koppelman, David Levien, and Rick Schwartz. Screenplay by Burger and Dirk Wittenborn.

Three soldiers, home on a month's leave from Iraq, find themselves on an odyssey from New York to Las Vegas in *The Lucky Ones*. That's the setup. The journey involves your standard rest stops: friendly diners, dubious mechanics, fervent church people, roadside hookers, redneck saloons, lonely motels, tornadoes, casinos, those sorts of things. This formula is fraught with pitfalls, but the characters and the actors redeem it with a surprising emotional impact.

Tim Robbins plays the father figure, a fiftysomething career army sergeant who received a back injury and is returning home to

St. Louis. After a blackout shuts down JFK, he rents a car and ends up taking the others on board. Rachel McAdams plays Private Colee Dunn, who has a leg injury and is heading for Vegas to return a guitar belonging to her boyfriend, who was killed in the war. Michael Pena plays Sergeant T.K. Poole, injured by shrapnel in the groin, who wants to go to Vegas to find hookers who can reawaken his equipment before he meets his stateside girlfriend.

Don't laugh when I say this: These three resemble in broad outline the three returning servicemen in the classic *The Best Years of Our Lives* (1946). That film had an alcoholic older man returning to a loyal wife, one younger man returning to a sluttish wife, and another afraid to marry his girlfriend because he had lost his hands. Change one man to a woman, shuffle a little, and you see what I mean.

That doesn't mean the film is an "homage"; director and cowriter Neil Burger told me he hasn't seen the 1946 film. It means the underlying structure and character group is somewhat archetypal. What distinguished *Best Years* was its gravitas. What made *The Lucky Ones* so gratifying to me was anything but gravitas; these three characters are simply likable, warm, sincere, and often funny. The performances are so good they carry the film right along.

Consider the events during the road trip. They are far from original. Many road movies are *about* what happens on the road. In *The Lucky Ones*, the events are somewhat inconsequential backdrops to the three-way relationship and the sympathy we feel for the characters. Yes, there are some considerable payoffs at the end, although not exactly unforeseen. There are also some plot contrivances at the end that seem hauled in. I noted this but didn't much mind.

Rachel McAdams (*The Notebook, Mean Girls*) comes into her own here. Previously she has been seen mostly as a hot chick (the title of her worst film) or an idealized sweetheart. Here she is feisty, vulnerable, plucky, warm, and funny. This is her coming-of-age as an actress. She provides yet another lesson that you can't judge acting ability until you see an actor given a chance to really stretch. Watch the poignancy of the scene when she meets her boyfriend's family.

Michael Pena plays a type I recognize: young, earnest, prudent, brimming with unsolicited advice. The opposite of stereotypes. T.K. needs to grow up some more, of course. He is so obsessed with his groin injury because without sex, he says, he and his girlfriend have nothing in common. This is an upbeat film, which explains, I suppose, why the shrapnel after-effects could be cured not by a doctor but by a hooker. If he and his girl have only sex in common, maybe she could have done the healing freelance. Along the way, Pena's T.K. provides a nudging counterpoint.

Tim Robbins's army lifer is, above all, a decent man and honest enough to reveal how he received his back injury in less-than-heroic circumstances. We sense he's been shepherding younger soldiers for most of his career, and now, during his leave, he's doing it again. He is not stupid, but he isn't the brightest bulb in the chandelier. He has a plan to finance his son's college tuition by winning in Vegas. This shows a touching but unwise fatherly love. Because we know how smart and quick Robbins is, it's uncanny how convincing he is as a steady and dependable calming hand.

Movies about the war in Iraq have not been popular—not even such a good one as *In the Valley of Elah*, with its Tommy Lee Jones performance. But as I wrote after seeing *The Lucky Ones* at Toronto, it is *not* an Iraq war movie. These three characters could be returning home from anywhere, for countless reasons. That might be a weakness in a film that wanted to make a statement about Iraq, but these three good and brave soldiers see the war in personal, not ideological, terms and the film clearly focuses on their personalities more than their experiences. There were some reviews from Toronto that seemed to focus on its departure from some theoretical, serious war film. I believe audiences will be moved by the characters. I was.

Lymelife ★ ★ ★ ½
R, 95 m., 2009

Alec Baldwin (Mickey Bartlett), Kieran Culkin (Jimmy Bartlett), Rory Culkin (Scott Bartlett), Jill Hennessy (Brenda Bartlett), Timothy Hutton

(Charlie Bragg), Cynthia Nixon (Melissa Bragg), Emma Roberts (Adrianna Bragg). Directed by Derick Martini and produced by Steven Martini, Barbara DeFina, Jon Cornick, Alec Baldwin, Michele Tayler, and Angela Somerville. Screenplay by Derick Martini and Steven Martini.

Lymelife sometimes cuts to the tiny buildings and inhabitants of a model suburb, the kind you might find on display in a Realtor's office. Just as frequent are its shots of actual homes in a Long Island suburb, of the sort occupied by the Bartlett and Bragg families. The film is about the distance between the ideal and the real.

Unhappy suburban families are more familiar in the movies than real ones—perhaps because, as Tolstoy believed, all happy families are the same. The sickness of these two families emanates from the parents. Two are committing adultery with each other. A third has Lyme disease and regards life with fatigue and depression.

The movie isn't about Lyme disease, but it serves as a theme: "Isn't it amazing that your whole life can be changed by a bug the size of a pimple on your ass?" A tick has destroyed the spirit of Charlie Bragg (Timothy Hutton) and left his sluttish wife, Melissa (Cynthia Nixon), open to the predations of her business partner, Mickey Bartlett (Alec Baldwin). Mickey's wife, Brenda Bartlett (Jill Hennessy), knows what's going on but tries to stand above it.

Their children are directly affected, and much of the film is seen through the eyes of two kids around fifteen, Scott Bartlett (Rory Culkin) and Adrianna Bragg (Emma Roberts). In a film of good actors, these are two finely realized performances. Scott has an inarticulate crush on Adrianna and is wounded when he sees her with an older, more studly boy. Adrianna likes him—they've been lifelong friends—but likes to date "more mature" men, which at that age may mean seventeen. Both of them know what Mickey and Melissa are doing. Adrianna is cynical; he's betrayed.

But those are only the outlines of a tender, sometimes painful, sometimes blackly comic story. The film's characters are not types but

particular people, and if the adults protect themselves in one way or another, the children are wide open. That includes Scott's older brother, Jimmy (Kieran Culkin), who is getting out while he can and has enlisted in the service. (The film has misplaced the Falkland Islands conflict in the 1970s, but how many even remember it? Nor was it a U.S. war.)

Rory Culkin's performance is the mainspring. Apart from the misfortune that they all look angelic, the Culkin family is rich in gifted actors. Here Rory plays a sexually inexperienced, bullied, sensitive kid, wounded by the loud arguments of his parents. His mother, played by Hennessy, is a strong, good woman, keeping a brave face for her kids, loathing her husband. He lives through his work (a new suburban home development), buys a new home for them without even mentioning it to her, and has sex with Melissa because she is there.

Now look at the Timothy Hutton character, the sick one. Exhausted, emasculated, hopeless, he stares at a blank television screen, watches unseen as his wife and Mickey have sex in the basement, develops a strange obsession with a deer he often sees in a forest near his house. Such a low-energy character might seem to offer little for an actor to "do," but Hutton brings the film a level of defeat and despair that shadows everything. They could all end up like him; Brenda wraps Scott's neck, wrists, and ankles with duct tape and searches his hair for ticks.

The film is by Derick Martini, written with his brother Steven. I met them at Toronto 1999, with their screenplay for the quirky indie *Goat on Fire and Smiling Fish*. This is their first feature—showing confidence enough, despite a heavyweight cast, to build carefully to their unexpectedly appropriate conclusion. Martini is especially good with Alec Baldwin, an actor whose power is used here to create an intense mano a mano with Jimmy. He and Hennessy are lacerating together in a scene of mutual hate.

A buried subject is parenting. There are two good parents here. Brenda has a warm scene with Scott the morning after his confirmation (and, she doesn't know, his first sexual experience); Adrianna, the young girl, who knows more about life than Scott, sees him with sympathy, and handles him with almost maternal care. Emma Roberts's performance is far deeper than the sexpot we first seem to see.

Lymelife doesn't have the sheer power of *The Ice Storm*, but it's not just another recycling of suburban angst. By allowing their characters complexity, the Martinis spill open those tiny model homes as thoroughly as a dropped Monopoly game.

M

Madagascar: Escape 2 Africa ★ ★ ★
PG, 88 m., 2008

With the voices of: Ben Stiller (Alex), Chris Rock (Marty), David Schwimmer (Melman), Jada Pinkett Smith (Gloria), Sacha Baron Cohen (King Julien), Cedric the Entertainer (Maurice), Andy Richter (Mort), Bernie Mac (Zuba), Alec Baldwin (Makunga), Sherri Shepherd (Alex's Mom), will.i.am (Moto Moto). Directed by Eric Darnell and Tom McGrath and produced by Mireille Soria and Mark Swift. Screenplay by Darnell, McGrath, and Etan Cohen.

These poor animals. First, they're hauled away from the comforts of the Central Park Zoo to be stranded on Madagascar. Then they find a crashed Cargo Cult airplane from WWII, tape the plane together, and try to fly it back home. Why would they rather be in New York? Can't get a cab in Madagascar? They all belong to separate species, but they're comfortable with diversity. These guys would have turned themselves in to Noah.

It doesn't look like that plane is gonna make it. That doesn't mean across the Atlantic from Africa. It means across Africa to the Atlantic. Do they (or their audience) realize Madagascar is *east* of Africa, in the Indian Ocean? How I know, I had a friend from Madagascar once. Beat me at chess.

Some people are probably wondering about the title *Madagascar: Escape 2 Africa,* because they think the animals escaped 2 Africa in the first place. Now shouldn't they be escaping 4rom Africa? So they take off, and (spoiler?) crash in Africa. Now they are faced with exactly the same dilemma as in the first film: Can wild animals survive in the wild?

They do a pretty funny job, which is the point. This is a brighter, more engaging film than the original *Madagascar.* I'll bet Dreamworks cofounder Jeffrey Katzenberg was hands-on. When he was at Disney, he made friends with a lion during the filming of *The Lion King.* He even appeared with it on a leash at the junket. He looked more relaxed than the members of the press. Usually at a junket, they're the ones who do the eating.

All of the original voice talents are back, doing their original characters. What an all-star cast: Ben Stiller, Chris Rock, David Schwimmer, Jada Pinkett Smith, Sacha Baron Cohen, Cedric the Entertainer, Andy Richter, Bernie Mac, Alec Baldwin, and will.i.am, who has one of those names like his mother was frightened during pregnancy by a typographer.

The look of *Madagascar: Escape 2 Africa* is open and sunlit. Better the wild savannah than the dense jungle. The action is thrilling (sacrifices to a volcano, a struggle for water), and there is a touching romance between Gloria the hippo and Melman the giraffe. I want to think Melman is not named after Larry (Bud) Melman, but I don't have the strength of character. Anyway, the prospect of a giraffe making love to a hippo is enough to set me writing limericks. Can it be done? I think it might be safer than a hippo making love to a giraffe.

So OK, kids, if you liked the first one, this is better. Your parents may like it, too, although they may have to dash out for just a second to see *Soul Men.*

Mad Money ★ ½
PG-13, 104 m., 2008

Diane Keaton (Bridget Cardigan), Queen Latifah (Nina Brewster), Katie Holmes (Jackie Truman), Ted Danson (Don Cardigan), Adam Rothenberg (Bob Truman). Directed by Callie Khouri and produced by James Acheson, Jay Cohen, and Frank DeMartini. Screenplay by Glenn Gers and John Mister.

There is something called "found poetry." The term refers to anything that was not written as poetry but reads as if it was. I would like to suggest a new category: found reviews. These are not really reviews but serve the same function. I found one just now, and after a struggle with myself, I have decided to share it with you. It is about *Mad Money,* a movie in which Diane Keaton, Queen Latifah, and Katie Holmes are lowly workers who team up to rob a Federal Reserve Bank.

I was noodling around Rotten Tomatoes, trying to determine who played the bank's security chief, and noticed the movie had not yet been reviewed by anybody. Hold on! In the "Forum" section for this movie, "islandhome" wrote at 7:58 a.m. January 8: "review of this movie . . . tonight i'll post." At 11:19 a.m. January 10, "islandhome" was finally back with the promised review. It is written without capital letters, flush-left like a poem, and I quote it spelling and all:

hello sorry i slept when i got back
well it was kinda fun
it could never happen in the way it was
    portraid
but what ever its a movie
for the girls most will like it
and the men will not mind it much
i thought it was going to be kinda like
    how tobeat the high cost of living
kinda the same them but not as much fun
ill give it a 4 Out of 10

I read this twice, three times. I had been testing out various first sentences for my own review, but somehow the purity and directness of islandhome's review undercut me. It is so final. "for the girls most will like it / and the men will not mind it much." How can you improve on that? It's worthy of Charles Bukowski.

Anyway, here's how I was going to start out: *Mad Money* is astonishingly casual for a movie about three service workers who steal millions from a Federal Reserve Bank. There is little suspense, no true danger, their plan is simple, the complications are few, and they don't get excited much beyond some high-fives and hugs and giggles. If there was ever a movie where Diane Keaton would be justified in bringing back "la-di-da," this is that movie.

Keaton costars with Queen Latifah and Katie Holmes. She's set up as a rich wife whose husband (Ted Danson) gets downsized. They owe a mountain of debt, their house is being repossessed, and she thinks she might as well (gulp) get a job. The best she can do is emptying the garbage at the Federal Reserve.

That's when she spots a loophole in the bank's famous security system. She figures out a way to steal used bills on the way to the shredder and smuggle them out of the building stuffed into her bra and panties, and those of her partners in crime, Katie and the Queen. This system works. And the beauty is, the money isn't missed because it has supposedly

already been destroyed. All they're doing is spending it one more time on its way to the shredder. A victimless crime, unless it brings down the economy, of course.

I would have gone on to observe that the movie makes it all look so easy and painless that it's a good thing it opens with a flash-forward showing them in a panic mode, so we know that sooner or later something exciting will happen. In the meantime, we get more scenes starring Ted Danson, with a hairstyle that makes him look alarmingly like a cross between David Cronenberg and Frankenstein's monster. And there's of course a chief of security who is constantly being outwitted. And so on.

Mad Money is actually a remake of a 2001 TV movie, I discovered on IMDb. Britain's Granada made it about a team of cleaners who pull the same scam on the Bank of England. Two character first names are the same (Bridget and Jackie), but the last name of the Keaton and Danson characters is changed from Watmore to Cardigan. Go figure. Or don't. The bottom line is, some girls will like it, the men not so much, and I give it 1½ stars out of 4.

Malls R Us ★★★
NO MPAA RATING, 78 m., 2009

A documentary directed by Helene Klodawsky and produced by Ina Fichman and Luc Martin-Gousset. Screenplay by Klodawsky.

Is a shopping mall a sacred place? Not a question often asked. A provocative new documentary named *Malls R Us* seriously argues that malls serve similar functions today that cathedrals, temples, parliaments, arenas, and town squares did in earlier times. Then it slowly works its way around to the possibility that they may be a plague upon the earth.

One thing is clear. From its uncertain beginnings in the 1950s, led by a developer named Victor Gruen, the mall concept has expanded relentlessly until it is essentially the template for a city-state such as Dubai, in the United Arab Emirates. They've become so omnipresent, we learn, that in all of North America there remains only a single location suitable for a new megamall—outside Montreal. In China and Japan they're reshaping cities and traditional ways of life, and in India they've inspired class conflicts and street protests in Delhi. You can buy Nikes, Sony TVs, and Louis Vuitton luggage in pretty much all of them, and dine at McDonald's.

I'm conflicted. I like malls. My favorite is the Ala Moana in Honolulu. I never buy much of anything. I like to sit in the enormous food court and feel the hum of the city. On the other hand, I love meandering through the busy local streets of London, Paris, or Toronto, where one little shop after another is lined up, often with a real live owner on the premises.

Ray Bradbury shares my conflict, I learn in *Malls R Us*. The great science fiction writer is interviewed in the film. He likes the futuristic vision of the new supermalls, and at the same time yearns for a simpler time when he was growing up in Waukegan and folks walked downtown to do their shopping and see a movie.

Helene Klodawsky, the director, is also of two minds. She's traveled the globe to assemble footage of malls so spectacular that we in North America have little idea of their scope. In Osaka, Delhi, Warsaw, they sprawl across city blocks and devour traditional neighborhoods. They center on fountains, spires, waterfalls, roller coasters, nature preserves.

Rubin Stahl, who is developing the Montreal project, is like a kid delighting in his gargantuan existing projects, like the Scottsdale Galleria, where he take us on a tour of its nature diorama, including a real (i.e., stuffed) polar bear. He says his Montreal project will be the world's first environmentally friendly mall, complete with fully stocked trout streams; he hopes Al Gore will visit to open it.

Thinking even bigger than Stahl is Eric Kuhne, an American architect who finds malls an outlet for his fantasies. He's building a million-square-foot project in Dubai. At a brainstorming session, we see him seeking inspiration in the Tower of Babel and an artichoke.

If Minneapolis and St. Paul have the Mall of America, Dubai is proposing itself as the Mall of the World. Jets fly in from everywhere loaded with affluent consumers, who wander through an air-conditioned desert oasis with wall-to-wall luxury brands. Thousands of workers are imported from Third World countries to build these fantasies. Their average wage: forty-five cents an hour.

It's that income disparity that concerns Klodawsky. She considers India as a case study of a land where malls may not be a perfect fit. She interviews Vikram Soni, an environmentalist who walks us through the Delhi Ridge Wilderness Preserve, a watershed that renews itself annually and provides drinking water better than in bottles. Now it is being destroyed for a mall. There don't seem to be permits, but Indian bureaucracy is notoriously unreliable, and the developers are bulldozing anyway.

Anyone who has been to India pictures the endless streets of small shops piled upon shops, each one with an owner and a family to support. Seeking to modernize, or something, Delhi has condemned tens of thousands of these little stores and torn them down. Klodawsky has footage of an event not much covered in the news: Thousand of Indians blocked the city streets for days in protest. In a land where 50 percent lack reliable drinking water, most will never be able to afford to enter a mall.

There seems to be a life cycle for malls. Most run down after about thirty years. There's even a Web site, deadmalls.com, devoted to the thousands that have closed. What happens to them? Apparently they just sit there empty. This used to be the most wonderful fountain, says a nostalgic visitor to one of them.

Mamma Mia! ★ ★
PG-13, 98 m., 2008

Meryl Streep (Donna), Pierce Brosnan (Sam), Colin Firth (Harry), Stellan Skarsgård (Bill), Julie Walters (Rosie), Dominic Cooper (Sky), Amanda Seyfried (Sophie), Christine Baranski (Tanya). Directed by Phyllida Lloyd and produced by Judy Craymer and Gary Goetzman. Screenplay by Catherine Johnson, based on the stage musical.

I saw the stage version of *Mamma Mia!* in London, where for all I know it is now entering the second century of its run, and I was underwhelmed. The film version has the advantage of possessing Meryl Streep, Pierce Brosnan, Amanda Seyfried, Colin Firth, and Julie Walters—but they are assets stretched fairly thin. And there are the wall-to-wall songs by ABBA, if you like that sort of thing. I don't, not much, with a few exceptions.

But here's the fact of the matter. This movie wasn't made for me. It was made for the people who will love it, of which there may be a multitude. The stage musical has sold thirty million tickets, and I feel like the grouch at the party. So let me make that clear and proceed with my minority opinion.

The action is set on a Greek isle, where the characters are made to slide down rooftops, dangle from ladders, enter and exit by trapdoors, and frolic among the colorful local folk. The choreography at times resembles calisthenics, particularly in a scene where the young male population, all wearing scuba flippers, dance on the pier to "Dancing Queen" (one of the ABBA songs I do like).

It would be charity to call the plot contrived. Meryl Streep plays Donna, who runs a tourist villa on the island, where she has raised her daughter, Sophie (Seyfried), to the age of twenty. Sophie, engaged to Sky (Dominic Cooper), has never known who her father is. But now she's found an old diary and invited the three possible candidates to her forthcoming wedding. She'll know the right one at first sight, she's convinced. They are Sam (Pierce Brosnan), Bill (Stellan Skarsgard), and Harry (Colin Firth), and if you know the first thing about camera angles, shot choice, and screen time, you will quickly be able to pick out the likely candidate—if not for sperm source, then for the one most likely to succeed in one way or another.

Meryl Streep's character of course knows nothing of her daughter's invitations, but even so, it must be said she takes a long time to figure out why these particular men were invited. Wouldn't it be, like, obvious? She has earnest conversations with all three, two of whom seem to have been one-night stands; for them to drop everything and fly to Greece for her after twenty years speaks highly of her charms.

The plot is a clothesline on which to hang the songs; the movie doesn't much sparkle when nobody is singing or dancing, but that's rarely. The stars all seem to be singing their own songs, aided by an off-screen chorus of, oh, several dozen, plus full orchestration. Meryl Streep might seem to be an unlikely choice to play Donna, but you know what? She can play anybody. And she can survive even the singing of a song like "Money, Money, Money." She has such a merry smile, and seems to be actually having a good time.

Her two best friends have flown in for the occasion: Tanya (Christine Baranski, an often-married plastic surgery subject) and Rosie (Julie Walters, plainer and pluckier). With three hunks their age like Brosnan, Firth, and Skarsgard on hand, do they divvy up? Not exactly. But a lot of big romantic decisions do take place in just a few days.

The island is beautiful. Moviegoers will no doubt be booking vacations there. The energy is unflagging. The local color feels a little overlooked in the background; nobody seems to speak much Greek. And then there are the songs. You know them. You may feel you know them too well. Or maybe you can never get enough of them. Streep's sunshine carries a lot of charm, although I will never be able to understand her final decision in the movie—not coming from such a sensible woman. Never mind. Love has its way.

Mammoth ★★★
NO MPAA RATING, 125 m., 2009

Gael Garcia Bernal (Leo), Michelle Williams (Ellen), Marife Necesito (Gloria), Run Srinikornchot (Cookie), Sophie Nyweide (Jackie). Directed by Lukas Moodysson and produced by Lars Jonsson. Screenplay by Moodysson.

Our health care rests to a sizable degree upon the shoulders of Filipino doctors, nurses, patient care specialists, and caregivers. There is a reason for this. Medical schools in the Philippines produce many graduates whose eyes are set on such jobs in North America, where there is a perennial shortage. During my adventures since 2006, I've been helped by a great many Filipinos, who were without exception cheerful, hardworking, and skilled—not least when on three occasions they were racing me to emergency surgery in the middle of the night.

One of the central stories in *Mammoth* involves a Filipino nanny who cares for rich children in Manhattan while her own children at home live in relative poverty and tell her on the phone how much they miss her. The film is intended to make us feel guilty that such people care for us and not for their own. I don't buy that. At least in the case of the Filipinos I've known, they worked hard to win jobs over here, are sending much of their income back home, are saving to bring over their kids, and are urging them to get an education to help them find jobs when they get here. It certainly helps that English is one of the national languages.

In a world of massive inequality, they're at least taking those direct measures available to them to improve their family situations. Only superficial thinking about global reality would lead a Swedish-born director such as Lukas Moodysson to offer the sentimental simplifications in *Mammoth,* which cuts back and forth between a lucky American kid at the planetarium and her nanny's children telling her they love her in a phone call. This is hard, but it's harder to be unable to feed your children or offer them a future.

These matters don't make this a bad movie. It's very well-acted and is about a good deal more than the nanny. As the parents, Leo and Ellen, it stars Gael Garcia Bernal and Michelle Williams (in her first lead since *Wendy and Lucy*). The two other leads are Gloria (Marife Necesito), as the nanny, and Cookie (Run Srinikornchot), as a bar girl Leo meets while on a business trip to Thailand.

Understand Leo isn't looking for trouble. He's a happily married video game author, very rich, in Bangkok to sign off on details of a major deal. But his business partner handles the negotiations, he's bored and lonely, he jets off to a coastal resort for a break, and he meets Cookie—who is very nice. No, really. In Thailand some parents know their children are working in the sex industry and happily accept the money. That's sad, but it's the way things are.

Nor does Leo mistreat or exploit Cookie (an adult), other than accepting her basic situation. Suppose he doesn't do business with her. Will she then leave prostitution? She may well be better off with a nice guy like him than

the next sex tourist who wanders into the bar. Money has a way of dictating our decisions. If Leo weren't rich, for example, maybe he'd be back home where he's needed.

His wife, Ellen, is a surgeon specializing in pediatrics, which brings her into touch with a young patient who—but you can guess how this world simply isn't fair. There are so many reasons to be outraged and depressed in this film, indeed, that it all but distracts from the real and immediate qualities of the four fine actors.

Lukas Moodysson, working for the first time in English, has made some good films, including *Together* (2000), *Lilja 4-Ever* (2002), and *Show Me Love* (1998), which used a little English in its Swedish title (cough). What he finds from Michelle Williams here is interesting. *Wendy and Lucy* was so effective at establishing her as a helpless innocent that it's sort of a shock to see her here as a cool and competent ER surgeon. It shows her range at a time when many actresses are cast over and over in the same role. *Mammoth* is a perfectly decent film. Too bad it isn't a little more thoughtful. It's easy to regret misfortune, if all you do is regret it.

Note: What does the title mean? If refers to the movie's $3,000 fountain pen made from ivory from a frozen mammoth. Not coincidentally, it's also the word for "mother" in Tagalog, a national language of the Philippines.

Management ★ ★ ★
R, 93 m., 2009

Steve Zahn (Mike), Jennifer Aniston (Sue), Woody Harrelson (Jango), Fred Ward (Jerry), Margi Martindale (Trish). Directed by Stephen Belber and produced by Marty Bowen, Wyck Godfrey, and Sidney Kimmel. Screenplay by Belber.

Sometimes casting has everything to do with a movie. In the usual course of events, a high-powered company sales executive wouldn't have much to do with Mike, the hapless loser who works and lives at the Arizona motel where she plans to spend one night. But cast Steve Zahn as the loser and it becomes thinkable.

The sales rep is Sue, played by Jennifer Aniston, who is upward-bound, successful, sharply dressed, and reduced to spending her evenings in remote motels, playing games on her laptop. Sue is every woman Mike has ever wanted but has never had, which is easy because he wants all women and has never had any. He's a nice guy, often stoned, under the thumbs of his parents, who own the motel, and looks at her with the love-struck eyes of a wet puppy.

Why and how they end up in the laundry room doing the rumpy-pumpy on a dryer is something *Management* takes for granted. Sometimes, apparently, high-powered Manhattan career women swoon in the presence of a guy who looks like he should be pumping their gas. His courtship technique is cute: He checks her in, carries her bags, brings her flowers, knocks again with the "customary" house bottle of champagne, uncorks it, gets two plastic-wrapped glasses from the bathroom, and struggles to say several coherent words in a row.

We can more or less predict where all of this will lead. Mike is obviously the fish out of water, so he must travel to New York to dramatize his unsuitability. Then Sue must travel to Washington, where she sees Jango (Woody Harrelson), a former punk rocker who has become a yogurt millionaire (for Harrelson, this is typecasting). Then Mike must follow her there.

He's not a stalker, you understand. He only wants to lick her hand, curl up at her feet, and be thrown a Milk Bone when he's been a good boy. It is Aniston's task to make us believe Sue might be won over by this, and because she succeeds, the movie works as a sweet romcom with some fairly big laughs.

What's nice is to see Zahn playing a guy who's not the dimmest bulb in the chandelier. For some reason he's often typecast as a stoner dimwit, maybe because he was so good at playing such roles early in his career. Here he's smart enough, just extremely socially challenged. Watch Aniston play off him with her pert intelligence; she could demolish him but is touched by his lack of defenses.

Fred Ward has a good role here as Mike's father, a perfectionist stuck with a slacker as an heir. Eventually he, too, is touched. That only leaves one question, which first-time writer-director Stephen Belber wisely doesn't mine for a subplot: Why did Sue's office travel manager book her into this motel?

Man on Wire ★ ★ ★ ★
PG-13, 94 m., 2008

Featuring Philippe Petit, Paul McGill, Annie Allix, Ardis Campbell, Jean-Louis Blondeau, David Demato, Jean-Francois Heckel, Aaron Haskell, and David Frank. A documentary directed by James Marsh and produced by Simon Chinn.

I am afraid of heights. Now you know. That is one reason I was helplessly engrossed in *Man on Wire,* the story of how Philippe Petit crossed *eight times* on a tightwire between the two towers of the World Trade Center on August 7, 1974. Another reason is that the documentary, a hybrid of actual and restaged footage, is constructed like a first-rate thriller.

Early in the film, we see what we think is sadly familiar footage: construction workers and huge trucks and cranes at work in the footprint of one of the WTC towers. At first I thought this was a film of the cleanup after 9/11. As the scene develops, I realized I was watching an early stage in the construction of the towers. The film shows the towers growing, huge steel beams being lifted, the puzzle being put together. As it happens, 9/11 is not even mentioned in the film, which is the right decision, I think. *Man on Wire* is about the vanquishing of the towers by bravery and joy, not by terrorism.

We meet Philippe Petit, a French wire walker, magician, unicyclist, and street performer, who tells us he was sitting in a dentist's office when he saw a drawing of the proposed towers and knew he was destined to conquer them. He drew a pencil line between them. His wire. The film will follow his campaign, as he enlists an unlikely cadre of helpers, draws inspiration from his girlfriend, Annie, and becomes obsessed with those two magnets acting on his personality.

Man on Wire, directed by James Marsh (*Wisconsin Death Trip*), has access to all of Petit's film, video, and photographs of the assault on the towers. But there is more than that. Ingeniously using actors and restaging events, Marsh fleshes out the story with scenes that could never have been filmed, such as the episode when Petit and a partner crouched motionless under tarps on a beam near the top floor as a security guard nosed around. He has gathered a motley crew, including a pot-addled musician and an executive who actually works in an office in one tower. He trains these amateurs on how to rig a high wire. Properly, he hopes.

This new footage is integrated seamlessly into the old; I gave up trying to decide which was which by the look of the picture, although a few sequences (shadows climbing a staircase) are obviously CGI. Marsh is dealing with an event that is almost thirty-five years old, and when he shows the same people at two stages of their lives, I assume either the younger or the older one is the actor, but I couldn't always be sure which. Philippe Petit is himself, both now and then, speaking fluent English, excited, passionate, voluble.

Even as a child he liked to climb things. No telling why. He taught himself to walk on a wire, practiced endlessly, dreamed of conquering the clouds. He rehearsed on wire strung up in country fields. His first great feat was to walk on a wire between the two bell towers of Notre Dame. Then he walked between the towers of the Sydney Harbour Bridge in Australia. As the World Trade Center was growing, so were his ambitions.

He never just *walked* on a wire. He lay down, knelt, juggled, ran. Every wire presented its own problems, and in rehearsing for the WTC, he built a wire the same distance in France. To simulate the winds, the movements of the buildings and the torsion of the wire, he had friends jiggle his wire, trying to toss him off. His balance was flawless. He explains how a wire can move: up and down, sideways, laterally, and it can also sometimes twist.

The installation of a wire between the two towers was as complicated as a bank heist. He and his friends scouted the terrain, obtained false ID cards, talked their way into a freight elevator reaching to the top—above the level of the finished floors. Incredibly, they had to haul nearly a ton of equipment up there. You may have heard how they got the wire across and how they guy-wired it, but if you don't know, I won't tell you.

They did it, anyway. Their plan worked. And on the morning of that August 7, Petit took the first crucial step that shifted his weight from the building to the wire, and stood above a drop of 1,350 feet. Many people know he crossed successfully. I had no idea he went back and forth eight times, the police waiting on both sides. His friends shed tears as they remember it happening. It was dangerous, foolhardy, glorious. His assistants feared they could be arrested for trespassing, manslaughter, or assisting a suicide. Philippe Petit was arrested and found guilty. The charge: disturbing the peace.

The Marc Pease Experience ★
PG-13, 84 m., 2009

Ben Stiller (Jon Gribble), Jason Schwartzman (Marc Pease), Anna Kendrick (Meg Brickman), Jay Paulson (Gerry), Zachary Booth (Craig), Ebon Moss-Bachrach (Gavin), Gabrielle Dennis (Tracey). Directed by Todd Louiso and produced by Michael London, Bruna Papandrea, and David Rubin. Screenplay by Louiso and Jacob Koskoff.

The Marc Pease Experience is a cheerless and almost sullen experience. Not even its staging of a high school production of *The Wiz* can pep it up. It's badly written and inertly directed, with actors who don't have a clue about what drives their characters. This is one of those rare films that contains no chemistry at all. None. The actors scarcely seem to be in the same scenes together.

For that matter, I can't think of many titles that are worse. "Marc Pease" is a name that looks like a typo, and Marc has no "experience" other than allegedly existing during the events of this film. Oh, at the end he becomes more philosophical and human, but that's just the screenplay jerking his chain. There is no sense that a human is involved.

The movie involves two unpleasant men. There is a young woman who is intended as pleasant but lacks all dimension on the screen, so she is simply filling a blank space labeled "pleasant character." Both unpleasant men are attracted to this young woman, but there is not a single scene between her and either of them that has the slightest joy, playfulness, affection, credibility, or humanity. All three are like bad witnesses who have been coached.

Eight years ago, when he was in high school, Marc Pease (Jason Schwartzman) panicked on stage while playing the Tin Man, and ran off stage and out of the school screaming. His drama coach, who has the Dickensian name of Mr. Gribble (Ben Stiller), has never forgiven him. Both have designs on Meg Brickman (Anna Kendrick), who is a little young for Marc and inappropriately young for Mr. Gribble. She has a nice singing voice and is coached by Gribble, the letch.

Marc Pease, now a limo driver, lives with the dream that his eight-member a cappella singing group, now reduced to four members, will cut a demo tape and become famous. He believes Mr. Gribble will produce this demo. He sells his condo to finance the recording session. The people who made this movie presumably know someone in the recording business, who could have advised them that even in this housing market, you don't have to sell a condo to pay for a demo. Don't you kind of guess every member of the audience can figure that out?

This year Mr. Gribble is producing *The Wiz* again. Same costumes, etc. There is a crisis on opening night, involving behavior bordering on lunacy by Marc Pease and on the malevolent by Mr. Gribble. Nevertheless, Marc Pease saves the production, in a way I will not spoil for you in case someone kidnaps you, takes you to a theater, straps you to a seat, props your eyes open with toothpicks, and forces you to watch this film.

I learn that Ben Stiller had another job coming up and shot all of his scenes in two weeks. Perhaps he suspected this film was not his shot at an Academy nomination. Stiller, Schwartzman, and Anna Kendrick will all work again. My advice: as soon as possible.

Marley and Me ★ ★ ★
PG, 120 m., 2008

Owen Wilson (John Grogan), Jennifer Aniston (Jenny Grogan), Eric Dane (Sebastian Tunney), Alan Arkin (Arnie Klein), Kathleen Turner (Ms. Kornblut). Directed by David Frankel and produced by Gil Netter and Karen Rosenfelt. Screenplay by Scott Frank and Don Roos, based on the book by John Grogan.

The second greatest headline in the history of the *Onion* is "Millions of Pet Owners Demand to Know: 'Who's a Good Boy?'"

This line is not frequently used in the Grogan household. There is a reason for that. Marley is not a good boy. I'd love to have a dog around the house, but not Marley. We have, you know, stuff we like. Books, dishes, tables, chairs, rugs, curtains. You know how it is. Marley considers such objects to be food, playthings, or enemies.

There was a real Marley. He belonged to John and Jennifer Grogan and was the subject of a 2005 best-seller that has been adapted into this film. I hope the book earned enough to pay for Marley's overhead. Marley has the behavior pattern of a manic wrecking crew and the appetite of a science fiction monster, but you gotta love him. At least, the Grogans gotta love him. They may be as crazy as their dog. Here is a useful lesson. When you go to the pet lady and she shows you a group of Labrador puppies and one is cheaper than all the others, this is not the time to go bargain hunting.

Marley and Me is a cheerful family movie about a young couple starting out in life with a new house, new jobs, a new dog, and then three children, whom the dog doesn't eat or it wouldn't be rated PG. Owen Wilson and Jennifer Aniston play the Grogans as brave and resourceful. Every couple has to survive ups and downs in their marriage, but Louis XVI and Marie Antoinette might be alive today if they'd adopted Marley, he had eaten the crown jewels, and they'd fled the palace and abdicated.

You would think the dog would supply the playful, upbeat elements in this movie. Not exactly. Marley supplies the Sturm und Drang, 24-7. It is Grogan's professional life that supplies the fantasy. He gets a job as a cub reporter on a newspaper and is soon *ordered* by his editor (Alan Arkin) to become a columnist. "Nothing doing!" he says. He'd rather cover school board meetings and sewer inspectors. Arkin counters: "I'll double your salary!"

In today's newspaper world, this plays like escapist porn. Grogan would be ordered to carry a route on his way to work and Arkin would be replaced by Uncle Scrooge. But Grogan makes the canny decision to write a column about the dog, and it is a great success. Soon the column and the dog are beloved.

Marley becomes as useful to Grogan as Slats Grobnik was to Mike Royko: always good for a column on a slow day. Come to think of it, Marley has all the earmarks of having been trained by Slats, starting out as a puppy by eating bar stools and spittoons.

This may be the first family film I've seen that will frighten more adults than children. The Marley kids, Conor, Patrick, and Colleen, all love Marley. Their parents are appalled. At one point, Jenny actually despairs and tells John that either the dog goes or she does. No, actually, she doesn't force him to choose. She's outta there. But she relents and returns to the doggie from hell. The thing about Marley, see, is that he has an uncanny way of knowing exactly when to pause in eating the garbage and gaze soulfully upon his masters with unconditional love.

When Marley is not on the screen, Wilson and Aniston demonstrate why they are gifted comic actors. They have a relationship that's not too sitcomish, not too sentimental, mostly smart and realistic. That's because she plays a newspaper reporter, too. Marley would have been a welcome break after a day in the riotous city rooms of the good old days. In today's city rooms, reporters hide in their cubicles praying to escape extermination. I say lock Scrooge in a cage and throw in Marley.

Marmaduke ★★
PG, 87 m., 2010

Lee Pace (Phil Winslow), Judy Greer (Debbie Winslow), William H. Macy (Don Twombly). With the voices of: Owen Wilson (Marmaduke), Emma Stone (Mazie), George Lopez (Carlos), Christopher Mintz-Plasse (Giuseppe), Steve Coogan (Raisin), Stacy Ferguson (Jezebel), Kiefer Sutherland (Bosco). Directed by Tom Dey and produced by Dey and John Davis. Screenplay by Tim Rasmussen and Vince di Meglio, based on the comic strip by Brad Anderson and Phil Leeming.

Dogs cannot talk. This we know. Dogs can talk in the movies. This we also know. But when we see them lip-synching with their dialogue, it's just plain grotesque. The best approach is the one used by *Garfield* in which we saw the cat and heard Bill Murray, but there was no nonsense about Garfield's mouth moving.

The moment I saw Marmaduke's big drooling lips moving, I knew I was in trouble. There is nothing discreet about a Great Dane with a lot on his mind, especially when he's the narrator of the film and never shuts up. And when his master, Phil, moves the Winslow family from Kansas to Orange County and he joins the crowd at the dog park of a vegetarian pet food company, well, what can I say about a movie that has more speaking parts for dogs (and a cat) than for humans?

This is a congenial PG-rated animal comedy. If you like the comic strip, now in its fifty-sixth year, maybe you'll like it, maybe not. Marmaduke's personality isn't nearly as engaging as Garfield's. Then again, if personality is what you're in the market for, maybe you shouldn't be considering a lip-synched talking-animal comedy in the first place.

The plot. In California, Marmaduke likes his new backyard, but gets in hot water with his family for a dumb reason and runs away. Mazie, the collie he's been romancing at the park, goes searching for him, and it rains, and Marmaduke gets lost, and his family piles in the station wagon and searches, and—long story made short—they all end up where a burst sewer has caused a big sink hole (although not as big as the one in Guatemala). Mazie falls in, Marmaduke leaps in after her, they're swept into a sewer, they come out in an aqueduct, Phil Winslow (Lee Pace) leaps in, and so on and so forth.

Great Danes can be your best friends, but they are not gifted comedians. Mazie is typecast as a sexy collie; just once couldn't a pug play the female lead, in a little nontraditional casting? And speaking of that, what's with William H. Macy as the owner of the pet food company? If you admire Macy as I do, you can imagine dozens of ways he could be funny as a pet food tycoon. The movie sidesteps all of them and has him play the role right down the middle as a businessman. Then why hire Macy in the first place?

And then . . . but enough. Why am I writing, and why are you reading, a review of a talking-animal movie? Little kids may like it. It's not offensive. I don't find Marmaduke particularly photogenic, but that's just me. Great Danes look like they have extra elbows. The movie gets two stars. It could have done a little better if Marmaduke had kept his mouth shut.

Married Life ★ ★ ★
PG -13, 90 m., 2008

Pierce Brosnan (Richard Langley), Chris Cooper (Harry Allen), Patricia Clarkson (Pat Allen), Rachel McAdams (Kay Nesbitt). Directed by Ira Sachs and produced by Steve Golin, Sachs, Sidney Kimmel, and Jawal Nga. Screenplay by Sachs and Oren Moverman, based on the novel *Five Roundabouts to Heaven* by John Bingham.

Remember the time businessmen were expected to drink martinis at lunch, and the time they were expected not to? Ira Sachs's *Married Life* begins with Harry taking Richard into his confidence at a martinis-and-cigarettes lunch that confirms the movie is set in 1949. Harry (Chris Cooper) is a buttoned-down, closed-in respectable type. Richard (Pierce Brosnan) is more easygoing. You can tell by the way they smoke. Harry is painfully earnest as he tells his friend that he plans to leave his wife for a much younger woman. The younger woman truly and deeply loves him. All his wife wants is sex.

Why does Harry share this information? I think he wants understanding and forgiveness from a man he respects. He has arranged for the young woman to join them at lunch. Here she comes now. She is Kay (Rachel McAdams). She has the bottle-blond hair and the bright red lipstick, the Monroe look. But don't get the wrong idea. She's a sweet kid, and she really does love Harry. The movie has a voice-over narration by Richard, but we don't need it to tell from the look in his eyes that Richard desires Kay, and that from the moment he sees her he wants to take her away from the dutiful Harry.

How dutiful is Harry? So devoted to his wife that he can't stand the thought of telling her he wants a divorce. He decides to take pity on her, spare her that pain, and murder her instead. Sort of a mercy killing. He's serious about this. He knows how devoted his wife is to him and how this news would shatter her, and he doubts she could stand it.

This story, which crosses film noir with the look and feel of a Douglas Sirk film, balances between its crime element and its social commentary: Everything Harry does is within the terms of a circa-1950 middle-class suburban marriage, with what we have been taught are all of its horrors. Marriage is always bad in these dark movies. I personally think it was better than in 1950s comedies, but then that's just me. We have the same problems, but we smoke less and use more jargon. And no generation thinks its fashions look funny, although Gene Siskel used to amuse himself by watching people walking down the street and thinking to himself, "When they left home this morning, they thought they looked good in that."

But enough. What about Harry's wife? She is Pat, played by Patricia Clarkson, who is so expert at portraying paragons of patient domestic virtue: so trusting, oblivious, or preoccupied that she never thinks to question Harry's absences when he's seeing Kay. Richard observes all of this in a low-key, factual way; it's as if he's telling us the story over martinis. He even addresses us directly at times.

Will Harry really try to kill his wife? Many men have killed their wives for less, shall we call them, considerate motives. Sachs and his cowriter, Oren Moverman, have based their screenplay on the pulp novel *Five Roundabouts to Heaven* by John Bingham, who, I learn from the critic Keith Uhlich, was a British intelligence agent and the original for John Le Carre's character George Smiley. Smiley, however, would be the Richard character here, not the Harry. The story has been ported from the land of roundabouts to the land of four-way stops, all except for Richard, who is British and urbane, which with Harry possibly passes for trustworthy.

Pierce Brosnan is becoming a whole new actor in my eyes, after this film, *The Matador, Evelyn,* and *The Tailor of Panama.* It's the kiss of death to play James Bond, but at least it gives you a chance to reinvent yourself. Chris Cooper reinvents himself in every film; can this be the same actor from *Adaptation?* Here he seems so respectable. Rachel McAdams does a nice job of always seeming honest and sincere, even when she makes U-turns, but Patricia Clarkson, as always, has a few surprises behind that face that can be so bland, or scornful, or in between. Still housewives run deep.

There is so much passion in this story that it's a wonder how damped down it is. Nobody shouts. And we discover that Harry is not the only person in the story who can surprise us. The lesson, I think, is that the French have the right idea, and adultery is no reason to destroy a perfectly functioning marriage. But is the movie about marriage, or sex, or murder, or the murder plot, or what? I'm not sure. It deals all those cards, and fate shuffles them. You may not like it if you insist on counting the deck after the game and coming up with fifty-two. But if you get fifty-one and are amused by how the missing card was made to vanish, this may be a movie to your liking.

Me and Orson Welles ★★★★
PG-13, 109 m., 2009

Zac Efron (Richard Samuels), Claire Danes (Sonja Jones), Christian McKay (Orson Welles), Zoe Kazan (Gretta Adler), James Tupper (Joseph Cotton), Leo Bill (Norman Lloyd), Eddie Marsan (John Houseman), Ben Chaplin (George Coulouris), Al Weaver (Sam Leve), Kelly Reilly (Muriel Brassler). Directed by Richard Linklater and produced by Ann Carli, Linklater, and Marc Samuelson. Screenplay by Holly Gent Palmo and Vince Palmo, based on the novel by Robert Kaplow.

Remember that Orson Welles himself didn't always look like Orson Welles. He was a master of makeup and disguise, and even when appearing in the first person liked to use a little putty to build up a nose he considered a tad too snubbed. The impersonation of Welles by Christian McKay in *Me and Orson Welles* is the centerpiece of the film, and from it all else flows. We can almost accept that this is the Great Man.

Twenty-four years after his death at seventy, Welles is more than ever a Great Man. There is something about his manner, his voice, and the way he carries himself that evokes greatness, even if it is only his own conviction of it. He is widely thought of as having made one masterpiece, *Citizen Kane,* and several other considerable films, but flaming out into false starts, uncompleted projects, and failed promise. Yet today even such a film as *The Magnificent Ambersons,* with its ending destroyed by the studio, often makes lists of the greatest of all time.

Oh, he had an ego. He once came to appear at Chicago's Auditorium Theater. A historic snowstorm shut down the city, but he was able to get to the theater from his nearby hotel. At curtain time he stepped before the handful of people who had been able to attend. "Good evening," he said. "I am Orson Welles—director, producer, actor, impresario, writer, artist, magician, star of stage, screen, and radio, and a pretty fair singer. Why are there so many of me, and so few of you?"

Richard Linklater's new film is one of the best movies about the theater I've ever seen, and one of the few to relish the resentment so many of Welles's collaborators felt for the Great Man. He was such a multitasker that while staging his famous Mercury Theater productions on Broadway he also starred in several radio programs, carried on an active social life, and sometimes napped by commuting between jobs in a hired ambulance. Much of the day for a Welles cast member was occupied in simply waiting for him to turn up at the theater.

Most viewers of this film will not necessarily know a lot about Welles's biography. There's no need to. Everything is here in context. The film involves the Mercury's first production, a *Julius Caesar* set in Mussolini's Italy. It sees this enterprise through the eyes of Richard Samuels (Zac Efron), a young actor who is hired as a mascot by Welles and somehow rises to a speaking role. He is starstruck and yet self-possessed, and emboldened by a sudden romance that overtakes him with a Mercury cohort, Sonja Jones (Claire Danes).

The film is steeped in theater lore. The impossible hours, the rehearsals, the gossip, the intrigue, the hazards of stage trapdoors, the quirks of personalities, the egos, the imbalance of a star surrounded entirely by supporting actors—supporting on stage, and in life.

Many of the familiar originals are represented here, not least Joseph Cotten (James Tupper), who costarred with Welles in *Citizen Kane* and *The Third Man.* Here is John Houseman (Eddie Marsan, not bulky enough but evocative), who was Welles's long-suffering producer. And the actor George Coulouris (Ben Chaplin), who played Mr. Thatcher in

345

Kane. All at the beginning, all in embryo, all promised by Welles that they would make history. They believed him, and they did.

McKay summons above all the unflappable self-confidence of Welles, a con man in addition to his many other gifts, who was later able to talk actors into appearing in films that were shot over a period of years, as funds became available from his jobs in other films, on TV, on the stage, and in countless commercials ("We will sell no wine before its time."). Self-confidence is something you can't act; you have to possess it, and McKay, in his first leading role, has that in abundance.

He also suggests the charisma that swept people up. People were able to feel it even in his absence; I recall having lunch several times at the original Ma Maison in Beverly Hills, where no matter whom I was interviewing (once it was Michael Caine), the conversation invariably came around to a mysterious shadowy figure dining in the shade—Welles, who ate lunch there every single day.

Efron and Danes make an attractive couple, both young and bold, unswayed by Welles's greatness but knowingly allowing themselves to be used by it. Linklater's feel for on stage and backstage is tangible, and so is his identification with Welles. He was thirty when he made his first film, Welles of course twenty-five, both swept along by unflappable fortitude. *Me and Orson Welles* is not only entertaining but an invaluable companion to the life and career of the Great Man.

Medicine for Melancholy ★ ★ ★ ½
NO MPAA RATING, 88 m., 2009

Wyatt Cenac (Micah), Tracey Heggins (Joanne). Directed by Barry Jenkins and produced by Justin Barber. Screenplay by Jenkins.

Medicine for Melancholy is nothing more or less than the story of a man and a woman spending twenty-four hours together. It has no other agenda, which is part of its charm. Haven't we all spent some interesting time together with a stranger, talking a little about our lives, sharing a certain communion, with no certainty that we will ever see them again?

Micah and Joanne are African-Americans in their late twenties who wake up next to each other in a bed in an expensive home on San Francisco's Nob Hill. They are hung over. They don't know each other's names. She wants to go home and forget. He persuades her to have breakfast. In a perhaps symbolic walk across a hill into a less posh neighborhood, he tries to cheer her up. It becomes clear that in a city with a 7 percent black population, he sees her as intriguing: a single, hip black woman in what he describes as the "indie world."

They talk. They take a taxi to her neighborhood—not to her door. She leaves her wallet in the cab. He discovers she is Joanne, not "Angela." He tracks her down on his bike. He kids her. They bike to an art gallery. Then they go through a couple of museums. They're getting to like each other.

Micah is interested in stereotypes. He observes that two black people spending Sunday at art museums does not fit the stereotype. Whose? His, I think. She asks what race has to do with it. He says his identity, in the eyes of the world, is as a black man. "That's what people see." Who would speculate he supplies and maintains upscale private aquariums? And Joanne? Her expensive condo in the Marina belongs to her lover, a white man now in London on business. He is an art curator, although Micah observes there is not a single artwork in the condo.

"Does it matter that he's white?" she asks. "Yes and no," Micah says. A good answer. The day does not continue their discussion of interracial dating. It becomes more of a test-drive of a possible life together. Neither seriously expects to lead such a life, but it's intriguing to play. At one point they go to Whole Foods. When a newly met couple go grocery shopping together, they're playing house.

Micah is concerned with demographics and residential patterns. He passionately loves San Francisco and has seen gentrification push out the populations and neighborhoods that gave it flavor. All men need a lecture topic when trying to impress a woman, and this is his. At one point the film drops in on a completely unrelated discussion group about housing policy; it's the sort of detour you might find in *Waking Life.*

The actors are effortlessly engaging. Tracey Heggins plays skittish at first, then warmer and playful. Is she having a better time than she usually has with her white lover? Yes. Well, maybe yes and no. She doesn't talk enough about him for us to be sure. Wyatt Cenac plays a smart charmer; the urban facts he cites are a reminder of his comedy alter ego, the "Senior Black Correspondent" on Jon Stewart's *The Daily Show.*

Medicine for Melancholy is a first, but very assured, feature by Barry Jenkins, who has the confidence to know the precise note he wants to strike. This isn't a statement film or a bold experiment in style; it's more like a *New Yorker* story that leaves you thinking, yes, I see how they feel. The film is beautifully photographed by James Laxton; much of the color is drained, making it almost black and white. The critic Karina Longworth writes: "I guessed that the entirety of the film had been desaturated 93 percent to match the racial breakdown, but in a recent interview, Jenkins said the level of desaturation actually fluctuates." The visual effect is right; McLuhan would call this a cool film.

The Men Who Stare at Goats ★★★ ½
R, 93 m., 2009

George Clooney (Lyn Cassady), Jeff Bridges (Bill Django), Ewan McGregor (Bob Wilton), Kevin Spacey (Larry Hooper), Stephen Lang (General Hopgood), Nick Offerman (Scotty Mercer), Tim Griffin (Tim Kootz). Directed by Grant Heslov and produced by Heslov, George Clooney, and Paul Lister. Screenplay by Peter Straughan, based on the book by Jon Ronson.

Bear with me here. Imagine *Ghostbusters* is based on a true story. Imagine the Big Lebowski as a real-life U.S. Army general. All factual, right? That's what *The Men Who Stare at Goats* sort of wants us to believe. I think I sort of do—to a small degree, sort of. "More of this is truer than you would believe," the movie says in an opening title. I'm waiting for the review of this one in *Skeptic* magazine.

We begin with a newspaperman named Wilton (Ewan McGregor) from Ann Arbor. That's a poignant note because Ann Arbor recently lost its daily newspaper. He interviews a goof who tells him he was a member of the New Earth Army, a supersecret army team of paranormals who were being trained as stealth weapons. In theory, they could spy at a distance, kill by the power of their sight alone, and penetrate enemy lines in spirit, not in body.

Wilton hungers to hunt where the headlines are. In 2002 he flies to Kuwait, hoping to cross into the war zone. He runs into a legendary guy he heard about from the crackpot back home. This is Lyn Cassady (George Clooney), said to be the best of the New Earth trainees. Wilton pumps him and learns of an acidhead Vietnam veteran named Bill Django (Jeff Bridges), who sold the army the notion of fighting men who could transcend physical limitations. We see Django in flashbacks; Bridges essentially plays him *as* the Big Lebowski. Members of the Church of Lebowskism will be able to enjoy this film as apocrypha.

The movie flashes between the recent Middle East and events twenty years earlier, when Cassady trained under Django to become, he explains, a Jedi Warrior. Clooney doesn't overplay and is persuasive, playing Cassady as a sensible, sane man who has seen the impossible and has no choice but to believe it. He shows Wilton videos of a goat and a hamster killed by brain power. In theory, mind power can even allow men to run through walls—if, of course, they believe they can.

The two of them unwisely journey into wartime Iraq, where they run into hostility. Cassady attempts to deal with it using paranormal techniques. He explains his theory of Jedi Warriordom to Wilton, who has apparently never seen *Stars Wars* episodes I, II, and III. Little joke. Their troubles are intercut with scenes of Cassady's early training, which included such self-persuasion exercises as fire walking. *I think* it is impossible that a flywheel like Bill Django could survive in the army, but then again, he has top-security clearance in a crucial secret program, so maybe he gets a pass. It may be that psychotropic drugs are justified as a pathway to higher powers. Whatever.

Kevin Spacey, who has been absorbed recently in London theatrical adventures, comes back in a good role as Hooper, who hates everything that Cassady stands for, whatever that is. All of the actors play without winks and spins, unless you consider Lebowskism

347

itself a wink and spin. And then we're faced with the fact that the movie is based on the 2004 book by Jon Ronson, a writer for the *Guardian*, who wrote it humorously but (he said) truthfully about an army experiment. It was this real program, he says, that inspired playing the *Barney the Dinosaur* theme as a torture technique.

It actually doesn't matter if the book is truthful. It doesn't claim the paranormal powers are real. Ronson simply says some officials thought they might be—and that if they were, we had to get there first. The movie is funny either way.

But figure this out. The book inspired a BBC-TV series that interviewed the real retired general Albert Stubblebine III, who explains on camera exactly how men could walk through walls.   ☞

The Merry Gentleman ★ ★ ★ ½
R, 99 m., 2009

Michael Keaton (Frank Logan), Kelly Macdonald (Kate Frazier), Tom Bastounes (Dave Murcheson), Bobby Cannavale (Michael), Darlene Hunt (Diane), Guy Van Swearingen (Billy Goldman), William Dick (Mr. Weiss). Directed by Michael Keaton and produced by Ron Lazzeretti, Steven A. Jones, and Tom Bastounes. Screenplay by Lazzeretti.

Good actors sometimes despair of finding worthy opportunities. They cheerlessly attend a premiere of their new film and think, "I could direct better than this dingbat." Sometimes they're right. I give you Michael Keaton, whose *Merry Gentleman* is original, absorbing, and curiously moving in ways that are far from expected. Michael Keaton once starred in *Jack Frost* as a boy's father imprisoned in a snowman. Think about that.

Keaton is one of the most intelligent men I have met in the acting profession, where you don't have much success these days if you're dumb. His mind is alive and present in many of his characters, and sometimes you get the impression the character is thinking, "I could say a lot more if the screenplay allowed me." What is uncanny about *The Merry Gentleman* is the way he implies that his character sometimes wishes he had said less.

Keaton plays Frank Logan, a Chicago hit man who is efficient and deadly, but suicidal. But no, this isn't a crime movie. Nothing as easy as that. It's a character study as Georges Simenon might have written, and Logan isn't the most important character. That is Kate Frazier, an abused wife newly employed in an office. A crime movie requires a skillful actress, but *The Merry Gentleman* requires a gifted one, and Keaton as director correctly places his focus on Kelly Macdonald, who played Josh Brolin's small-town wife in *No Country for Old Men*. Keaton wisely allows her to use a mid-Atlantic version of her Scots accent, because why not? She gets another aspect to her character for free.

These two first encounter each other through what is technically a Meet Cute, but they don't collide while entering a revolving door. Logan has just used a sniper scope to murder a man in an office window across the street. The job performed, he stands on the ledge of a rooftop and prepares to jump off. Kate, emerging from the street door of the building, looks up, sees him, and screams. He is startled and falls back onto the roof. He knows she has seen him. Now they will have to meet.

Is the movie about his intention to kill her before she can identify him? It's legitimate for us to think so. Although Logan goes through the motions of preparing for that, there is the possibility that he might have murdered for the last time. Yet how can we know? Kate reports the incident to the police, who file a routine report. Then the dead man is found, and a policeman named Murcheson (Tom Bastounes) realizes she must have seen the killer.

Murcheson, a recovering alcoholic, is immediately attracted to her. He invites her for "a coffee or something." Recovering from marriage, she is not eager to make a new friend. Murcheson, who is not a bad person, persists. Logan must realize the woman who saw him is dating the policeman on the case. There are other elements in play, but discover for yourself.

What is so good about the movie is the way Kate relates to these two men, who both hunger for care and sympathy. The screenplay is by Ron Lazzeretti, who writes dialogue of a very high order: subtle, cautious, aware. We understand this will not be a movie about a triangle and will not hurry to a neat conclusion. It will be about a worthwhile woman trying to relate to two difficult puppies left on her doorstep.

The Merry Gentleman isn't jolly. There are undercurrents of sadness and dread. Both men are frightened of their flaws. What will happen may be unforeseeable. Watch Keaton. His is a complex performance, evoking a damaged man who has, somewhere inside, ordinary emotions. As a director, he is attentive to the inner feelings of all three main characters, and it is there that a lot of the film really resides.

Of Lazzeretti I know little, except that he directed a feature in 1999 named *The Opera Lover,* and it also starred Tom Bastounes, an intriguing actor. I believe they met through Second City. Lazzeretti set out to write a film about humans, not genre stereotypes, and I suspect that's what attracted Keaton. The hit man–possible victim situation provides a reason for this unsocial man to need to meet her and adds potential suspense, but I was pleased the movie ended in the way it did.

The Messenger ★★★ ½
R, 112 m., 2009

Ben Foster (Will Montgomery), Woody Harrelson (Tony Stone), Samantha Morton (Olivia Pitterson), Jena Malone (Kelly), Steve Buscemi (Dale Martin). Directed by Oren Moverman and produced by Benjamin Goldhirsh, Mark Gordon, Lawrence Inglee, and Zach Miller. Screenplay by Oren Moverman and Alessandro Camon.

Maybe the only way to do it is by the book. You walk up to the house of a total stranger, ring the bell, and inform them their child has been killed in combat. When they open the door and see two uniformed men, they already know the news. Some collapse. Some won't let you finish before they beat their fist on your chest, crying for you to shut up, Goddamn it, that can't be true. Some seem to fall into a form of denial, polite, inviting you in as if this is a social situation. Some tell you it's a mistake. It isn't a mistake.

The Messenger is an empathetic drama about two men who have that job. One is Captain Tony Stone (Woody Harrelson), an old hand at breaking the news. The other is Staff Sergeant Will Montgomery (Ben Foster), who was wounded in combat in Iraq and is serving out the last three months of his tour. Stone, who has never experienced combat, is the more soldierly. Montgomery, in his first days on the job, has a tendency to care about the people—mostly parents—he's informing.

That's a very bad idea, Stone tells him. It is always necessary to go by the book. Don't have physical contact with anyone, let alone hug them. Better for you, better for them. These are their lives. They need the news, not a new best friend. Stone is another of Woody Harrelson's penetrating performances. His hair shaved almost as short as a kid in boot camp, his eyes behind dark glasses, his manner the stubborn fragility of the newly recovering alcoholic, he doesn't care that much about Montgomery, either. This may not be the first soldier he's had to break in on this hard assignment.

Ben Foster has usually played tough guys (*Alpha Dog, 3:10 to Yuma,* the Alaskan vampire thriller *30 Days of Night*). It is a wonderment to me how some actors seem defined by their credits and reinvent themselves in the right role. Here in countless subtle ways he suggests a human being with ordinary feelings who has been through painful experiences and is outwardly calm but not anywhere near healed.

Both of them are time bombs. How close is Stone to taking another drink? Will posttraumatic stress disorder bring down Montgomery? They drive in their rental car through the ordinary streets of America, so recently left by those they bring news of. Stone takes the lead. He sticks to the script. "The Secretary of Defense deeply regrets informing you that your [son, daughter], [military rank], [name], has been killed while on duty."

Everyone takes it differently, and the film develops the two characters as they meet survivors, notably Samantha Morton as a new widow, and Steve Buscemi as an angry father. Following the army way, they would never see these people again. It doesn't work out that way. Montgomery encounters Olivia (Morton) again. He sensed she was hurting.

A tender, frightened romance slowly begins to grow between them, in a series of scenes that are not simply about two people but about these two, and all that we know about them and continue to learn. They meet the angry father again, and Buscemi, as he sometimes does, plays an almost impossible scene in a way we didn't anticipate and cannot improve.

The Messenger is the first film directed by Oren Moverman, a combat veteran in the Israeli army, whose earlier screenplays included the Bob Dylan biopic *I'm Not There* (2007) and the extraordinary *Jesus' Son* (1999). This is a writer's picture, no less than a visceral experience that approaches its subject as tactfully as the messengers do. No fancy camerawork. It happens; we absorb it.

An important element is Kelly (Jena Malone), the girl Montgomery left behind when he shipped out to Iraq. She hasn't remained committed. She isn't heartless; that's her trouble. Her heart found other occupations. Malone treads a careful, not unkind, path with him. Her absence has created a vacuum; he may be too willing for Olivia to fill it.

The Messenger knows that even if it tells a tear-jerking story, it doesn't have to be a tear-jerker. In fact, when a sad story tries too hard, it can be fatal. You have to be the one coming to your own realization about the sadness. Moverman and his screenwriter, Alessandro Camon, born in Italy, have made a very particularly American story, alert to nuances of speech and behavior. All particular stories are universal, inviting us to look in instead of pandering to us. This one looks at the faces of war. Only a few, but they represent so many.

Micmacs ★★ ½
R, 104 m., 2010

Dany Boon (Bazil), Andre Dussollier (De Fenouillet), Omar Sy (Remington), Dominique Pinon (Buster), Julie Ferrier (Elastic Girl), Nicolas Marie (Francois Marconi), Marie-Julie Baup (Calculator), Michel Cremades (Tiny Pete), Yolande Moreau (Mama Chow), Jean-Pierre Marielle (Slammer). Directed by Jean-Pierre Jeunet and produced by Jeunet, Frederic Brillion, and Giles Legrand. Screenplay by Jeunet and Guillaume Laurant.

Here's a movie with visual invention and imagination up the wazoo. *Micmacs* is a whimsical fantasy about how a weapons manufacturer is set upon by a man with a bullet in his head and a motley crew of weirdos who live in a cave inside a junkyard. It may be a little too much for one meal.

I say this with reluctance, because this kind of visual energy is rarely found in the movies. I should be grateful for the change after several recent films in which the camera freezes in its tracks and stares stupefied at the action. I suppose I am. But the invention upstages the story without seeming necessary to it.

The director is Jean-Pierre Jeunet. Recall his magical *Amelie* (2001) and *A Very Long Engagement* (2004) and you'll understand its fancies. Recall his *The City of Lost Children* (1995) and you'll understand its problems. In an age when special effects can show us almost anything, there can come a tipping point when a movie is essentially only showing off. I'm not flatly against that, but in general I like to delude myself that the story is in the foreground. It's a judgment call. You may enjoy *Micmacs* more than I did.

The story is about a sad-sack clerk in a video store, named Bazil (Dany Boon). His father was killed with a land mine. As a child, opening a box of his father's effects, he finds the trademark of the manufacturer. He grows up into a feckless young man who passes his time in the video store by reciting the dialogue of movies in synch. One day, after a series of, shall we say, improbable events, he's shot in the middle of the forehead. The bullet lodges. The doc flips a coin and decides to leave it in, even though he could die at any moment.

Naturally, he's replaced at work. He's taken under the wing of a band of scavengers who live in a sort of Aladdin's Cave inside a mound of junk. This may sound sordid, but it's not. Imagine steampunk heaven. These people have the resources of a troupe of itinerant troubadours. They could start their own circus.

There's the contortionist named Elastic Girl (Julie Ferrier). The Guinness book–obsessed type named Buster (Dominique Pinon). A master thief named Slammer (Jean-Pierre Marielle), perhaps because of where he's spent a lot of time. A woman Calculator (Marie-Julie Baup), whose mind does mathematical wonders. A sage from the Congo (Omar Sy), who speaks Fortune Cookie. And Mama Chow

(Yolande Moreau), who feeds and mothers them. Oh, and a human cannonball.

These oddballs enlist in Bazil's cause so quickly he hardly realizes he has a cause, and conspire with him to destroy the enterprises of the munitions experts. They zero in on the chief malefactor, Nicolas Thibault de Fenouillet (Andre Dussollier), and conspire against him with schemes so improbably labyrinthine that Rube Goldberg would have advised them to dial down.

The production values of the film are splendid. Jeunet's camera is so liberated that *Micmacs* might as well be animated. But there's a lack of urgency. The characters seem defined by the requirements of the plot. Dany Boon, in the lead, seems to be mostly along for the ride. The villain de Fenouillet is the most compelling character, particularly because of his fondness for collecting spare parts from the cadavers of evil men.

I look at a film like this and must respect it for its ingenuity and love of detail. Then I remember *Amelie* and its heroine played by Audrey Tautou, and I understand what's wrong: There's nobody in the story who much makes us care.

Milk ★ ★ ★ ★
R, 127 m., 2008

Sean Penn (Harvey Milk), Emile Hirsch (Cleve Jones), Josh Brolin (Dan White), James Franco (Scott Smith), Diego Luna (Jack Lira), Alison Pill (Anne Kronenberg), Lucas Grabeel (Danny Nicoletta). Directed by Gus Van Sant and produced by Dan Jinks and Bruce Cohen. Screenplay by Dustin Lance Black.

Sean Penn amazes me. Not long before seeing *Milk*, I viewed his work in *Dead Man Walking* again. Few characters could be more different, few characters could seem more real. He creates a character with infinite attention to detail and from the heart out. Here he creates a character who may seem like an odd bird to mainstream America and makes him completely identifiable. Other than the occasional employment of Harvey Milk's genitals, what makes him different? Some people may argue there is a gay soul, but I believe we all share the same souls.

Harvey Milk became in 1977 the first openly gay man elected to public office in America. Yes, but I have become so weary of the phrase "openly gay." I am openly heterosexual, but this is the first time I have ever said so. Why can't we all be what we prefer? Why can't gays simply be gays and "unopenly gays" be whatever they want to seem? In 1977, it was not so. Milk made a powerful appeal to closeted gays to come out to their families, friends, and coworkers, so the straight world might stop demonizing an abstract idea. But so powerful was the movement he helped inspire that I believe his appeal has now pretty much been heeded, save in certain backward regions of the land that a wise gay or lesbian should soon deprive of their blessings.

Gus Van Sant's film begins with Harvey Milk at forty-eight, reflecting into his tape recorder about a personal journey that began at forty. At that watershed age he grew unsatisfied with his life and decided he wanted to really *do* something. A researcher at Bache & Co. and a Goldwater Republican, Milk became involved with a hippie theater company in Greenwich Village and began to edge the closet door ajar and wave out tentatively. He was in love with Scott Smith (James Franco), they moved to San Francisco, they opened a camera shop in the shadow of the Castro theater, and saw that even America's largest and most vocal gay community was being systematically persecuted by homophobic police.

Milk didn't enter politics as much as he was pushed in by the evidence of his own eyes. He ran for the Board of Supervisors three times before being elected in 1977. He campaigned for a gay rights ordinance. He organized. He acquired a personal bullhorn and stood on a box labeled "SOAP." He forged an alliance including liberals, unions, longshoremen, teachers, Latinos, blacks, and others with common cause. He developed a flair for publicity. He became a fiery orator. Already known as the Mayor of Castro Street, he won public office. It was a bully pulpit from which to challenge rabble-rousers like the gay-hating Anita Bryant.

Milk, from an original screenplay by Dustin Lance Black, tells the story of its hero's rise from disaffected middle-aged hippie to national symbol. Interlaced are his romantic adventures. He remained friendly with Scott

Smith after they drifted apart because of his immersion in politics. He had a weakness for befriending wet puppies: at first, Cleve Jones (Emile Hirsch), who became another community organizer. Then Jack Lira (Diego Luna), a Mexican-American who became neurotically jealous of Milk's political life. The prudent thing would have been to cut ties with Lira, but Milk was almost compulsively supportive.

His most fateful relationship was with Dan White, a seemingly straight member of the Board of Supervisors, a Catholic who said homosexuality was a sin and campaigned with his wife, kids, and the American flag. An awkward alliance formed between Milk and White, who was probably gay and used their areas of political agreement as a beard. "I think he's one of us," Milk confided. The only gay supervisor, Milk was also the only supervisor invited to the baptism of White's new baby. White was an alcoholic, all but revealed his sexuality to Milk during a drunken tirade, became unbalanced, resigned his position, wasn't allowed back on the board by Mayor George Moscone, and on November 27, 1978, walked into city hall and assassinated Milk and Moscone.

Milk tells Harvey Milk's story as one of a transformed life, a victory for individual freedom over state persecution, and a political and social cause. There is a remarkable shot near the end, showing a candlelight march reaching as far as the eyes can see. This is actual footage. It is emotionally devastating. And it comes as the result of one man's decisions in life.

Sean Penn never tries to show Harvey Milk as a hero and never needs to. He shows him as an ordinary man: kind, funny, flawed, shrewd, idealistic, yearning for a better world. He shows what such an ordinary man can achieve. Milk was the right person in the right place at the right time, and he rose to the occasion. So was Rosa Parks. Sometimes, at a precise moment in history, all it takes is for one person to stand up. Or sit down.

Millions (A Lottery Story) ★ ★ ★ ½

NO MPAA RATING, 101 m., 2008

Featuring Phylis Breth, Barb and Dwain Nelson, Donna Lange, Curtis Sharp, Susan and Donny Breth, and Lou Eisenberg. A documentary directed by Paul La Blanc and produced by La Blanc and Jordon Katon.

Millions (A Lottery Story) is not so much about six lottery winners as about six people whom I watched with growing fascination and affection. What did I expect when the movie began? Former millionaires now on Skid Row, I suppose, contrasted with misers counting their compound interest and intercut with bizarre misadventures. What I found were people who, if I may say so, are utterly unfazed by their sudden wealth, and who have developed strategies for coping not with wealth or poverty, but with life. They all seem happy, and it has nothing to do with the lottery.

The movie follows four kitchen workers from a Minnesota high school and two New Yorkers who were once famous because they were the first to win $5 million at the dawn of the lottery and became the stars of television ads. The Minnesotans, sixteen altogether, split up $95,450,000 on a shared Powerball ticket, which works out to $5,965,625 apiece, a figure none of them ever once mentions.

They're from Holdingford, Minnesota, a town that Garrison Keillor himself once called "the Lake Wobegonest town in Minnesota." The town is so typical of his monologues that not only are the high schoolers' grades above average, but the interstate highway makes a four-mile detour just to avoid it. Of the four women we meet, all come from large families (I'm talking like eleven or sixteen kids), all worked hard on family dairy farms, many still keep dairy cattle as a second job, and none of them quit their jobs in the high school kitchen.

Phylis Breth is most eloquent about staying on the job. "These are my best friends, and I love my work." She is a dishwasher, and uses a little laugh to end many sentences. "I've got bad knees, I've had four surgeries, and this job keeps you going. On days when they serve mashed potatoes or cheese, it gets pretty hectic." Like some of the others, she bought a new house, not a mansion, just comfy, and she finally has what she long dreamed of, a refrigerator with an ice-cube maker. She still hits all the garage sales, pouncing on a two-dollar ice cream scoop.

Of the New Yorkers, who won in the early

1970s, Lou Eisenberg lives in retirement in West Palm Beach, in a very basic condo. All of his winnings are gone, and he gets by on Social Security and a small pension. But he has a girlfriend, knows people everywhere he goes, bets at the dog track daily. He spent every lottery check almost as it came in. Why didn't he invest for the future? "I never thought I would live to be seventy-six."

The other, Curtis Sharp, has also run through his winnings. Some of them went to invest in a company claiming to make an electric automobile that could run forever without ever being recharged. At one point the company was valued at "billions," he assures us, before the government came in and charged the organizer with selling fraudulent stock. Curtis still believes the guy was on the level: "Someday that investment is going to pay off." Having been a "drinker and fornicator," he moved to Nashville to buy a beer joint. Then he saw the light, found Jesus, and is a preacher.

The two of them became famous for their New York Lotto commercials. "A Jew and a black man," Lou says. "A good fit." Curtis was known for his bowler hats and collected one hundred. Before winning, Lou had owned a beauty shop, but something came over him one day, he developed panic attacks, and found he could not speak or look people in the eye. He got a job at $240 a week, screwing in lightbulbs. The Lotto saved him: "It was like a shot in the arm." It sure was. We see clips of him gabbing away on TV with Johnny Carson, Regis Philbin, Ted Koppel, Sammy Davis Jr.

There are times in this documentary that I was reminded of work by Errol Morris. The director, Paul La Blanc, has the same ear for the American vernacular and the same eye for obsessions. Take Phylis Breth, for example. Many women clean house for days before letting a camera crew into their homes, but let's say her housekeeping is not Wobegonian. But then we meet her daughter, Susan, the opposite. As she provides a tour of her orderly pantry shelves, ticking off "1994 pickles . . . last year's tomato juice," she proudly shows us that most of her preserves are in jars that originally held the retail version of the same substances. Her homemade salsa is in a salsa jar, for example, with the original label still on.

If there is one thing the Holdingford ladies are sure of, it's that their winnings will send their children through college. Apart from that, they carry on as before. Susan's husband, Donny, is known as the "wood man," because if you have a fallen tree, he comes around and cuts it into firewood. With pride he shows a shed jammed with logs. They heat their home all winter with wood, in a climate that goes to thirty below. "I've burned wood all my life, and I will keep on burning wood as long as the good Lord lets me," he says.

Getting to know these people, I realized I knew others exactly like them. The women could come from my downstate Illinois family. Giving me a recipe once, my Aunt Mary said, "One tater for everybody, one for the pot, and one for fear of company." For fear. Perfect. I wrote it down as part of the recipe.

Miracle at St. Anna ★ ★ ★
R, 160 m., 2008

Derek Luke (Aubrey Stamps), Michael Ealy (Bishop Cummings), Laz Alonso (Hector Negron), Omar Benson Miller (Sam Train), Matteo Sciabordi (Angelo), John Leguizamo (Enrico), Joseph Gordon-Levitt (Tim Boyle), Valentina Cervi (Renata), Pierfrancesco Favino (Peppi Grotta). Directed by Spike Lee and produced by Roberto Cicutto and Luigi Musini. Screenplay by James McBride, based on his novel.

Spike Lee's *Miracle at St. Anna* contains scenes of brilliance, interrupted by scenes that meander. There is too much: too many characters, too many subplots. But there is so much here that is powerful that it should be seen no matter its imperfections. There are scenes that could have been lost to more decisive editing, but I found after a few days that my mind did the editing for me, and I was left with lasting impressions.

The story involves four African-American soldiers behind enemy lines in Italy in World War II. It's a story that needed telling. It begins with an old black man looking at an old John Wayne movie on TV and murmuring, "We fought that war, too." The next day he goes to work at the post office and does something that startles us. The movie will eventually

353

explain who he is and why he did it. But in a way, we don't need that opening scene, and we especially don't need the closing scene, not the way it plays, when a man walks slowly toward a seated man on a beach. The problem is, the wrong man is doing the walking.

You may disagree. There is one "extraneous" scene that is absolutely essential. While in the Deep South for basic training, the four soldiers are refused service in a local restaurant, while four German POWs relax comfortably in a booth. Such treatment was not uncommon. Why should blacks risk their lives for whites who hate them? The characters argue about this during the movie, after boneheaded decisions and racist insults from a white officer. One has the answer: He's doing it for his country, for his children and grandchildren, and because of his faith in the future. The others are doing it more because of loyalty to their comrades in arms, which is what all wars finally come down to during battle.

Miracle at St. Anna has one of the best battle scenes I can remember, on a par with *Saving Private Ryan* but more tightly focused on a specific situation rather than encompassing a huge panorama. The four soldiers find themselves standing in a river, with a Nazi loudspeaker blasting the sultry voice of "Axis Sally," who promises them sexy women and racial equality in Germany. Their white superior officer orders artillery strikes on their position because he can't believe any blacks could possibly have advanced so far. Then the Nazis open fire. The visceral impact of the episode is astonishing.

The four who survive find themselves in a small hill village. They are Stamps (Derek Luke), cool and collected; Cummings (Michael Ealy), a skirt chaser; Negron (Laz Alonso), a Puerto Rican; and Train (Omar Benson Miller), a towering man with the gentle simplicity of a child. Train has picked up the head of a statue from Florence and carries it with him because he believes that it makes him invulnerable.

Among the Italians they meet are three important ones: Angelo (Matteo Sciabordi), a young boy whom Train saves from death; Renata (Valentina Cervi), a daring and attractive village woman; and Peppi (Pierfrancesco Favino), known as the Great Butterfly, who is

a leader of the region's anti-Nazi partisans. All the characters and all the villagers are involved in another battle scene fought in the steep pathways and steps of the village. Both firefights are choreographed with immediate visceral effect.

The story of the bond between Train and the boy Angelo seems like material for a different movie. Yes, it involved me, but it seemed to exist on the plane of parable, not realism. It involved a shift of the emotions away from the surrounding action. The acting is superb. Omar Benson Miller (not actually as tall as the movie makes him seem) feels responsible for the boy because he saved his life, and the two form a bond across the language barrier. Matteo Sciabordi, in his first performance, is a natural the camera loves. I can imagine an entire feature based on these two, but I am not sure this story, seen this way, could have taken place in the reality of this film.

Another scene I doubted was an extended one involving a dance in the local church, music playing loudly, GIs standing illuminated in an open doorway, just as if they weren't behind enemy lines and the hills weren't possibly crawling with Nazis. The romantic developments during that scene would have seemed more at home in a musical.

In a sense, the scenes I complain about are evidence of Lee's stature as an artist. In a time of studios and many filmmakers who play it safe and right down the middle, Spike Lee has a vision and sticks to it. The scenes I object to are not evidence of any special perception I have. They're the kind of scenes many studio chiefs from the dawn of film might have singled out in the interest of making the film shorter and faster. But they're important to Lee, who must have defended them. And it's important to me that he did. When you see one of his films, you're seeing one of *his* films. And *Miracle at St. Anna* contains richness, anger, history, sentiment, fantasy, reality, violence, and life. Maybe too much. Better than too little.

Mister Lonely ★ ★

NO MPAA RATING, 112 m., 2008

Diego Luna (Michael Jackson), Samantha Morton (Marilyn Monroe), Denis Lavant

(Charlie Chaplin), Anita Pallenberg (The Queen), James Fox (The Pope), Esme Creed-Miles (Shirley Temple), Richard Strange (Abraham Lincoln), Werner Herzog (Father Umbrillo). Directed by Harmony Korine and produced by Nadja Romain. Screenplay by Harmony Korine and Avi Korine.

I wish there were a way to write a positive two-star review. Harmony Korine's *Mister Lonely* is an odd, desperate film, lost in its own audacity, and yet there are passages of surreal beauty and preposterous invention that I have to admire. The film doesn't work, and indeed seems to have no clear idea of what its job is, and yet (sigh) there is the temptation to forgive its trespasses simply because it is utterly, if pointlessly, original.

All of the characters except for a priest played by Werner Herzog and some nuns live as celebrity impersonators. We can accept this from the Michael Jackson clone (Diego Luna), and we can even understand why when, in Paris, he meets a Marilyn Monroe impersonator (Samantha Morton), they would want to have a drink together in a sidewalk café. It's when she takes him home with her that the puzzlements begin.

She lives in a house with the pretensions of a castle in the Highlands of Scotland. It is inhabited by an extended family of celebrity impersonators, and they portray, to get this part out of the way, Charlie Chaplin (Denis Lavant), the Pope (James Fox), the Queen (Anita Pallenberg), Shirley Temple (Esme Creed-Miles), Abraham Lincoln (Richard Strange), Buckwheat, Sammy Davis Jr., and, of course, the Three Stooges. Now consider. How much of a market is there in the remote Highlands for one, let alone a houseful, of celebrity impersonators? How many pounds and pence can the inhabitants of the small nearby village be expected to toss into their hats? How would it feel to walk down the high street and be greeted by such a receiving line? What are the living expenses?

But such are logical questions, and you can check credibility at the door. This family is not only extended but dysfunctional, starting with Marilyn and Charlie, who are a couple, although she says she thinks of Hitler when she looks at him, and he leaves her out

in the sun to burn. Lincoln is foul-mouthed and critical of everyone, Buckwheat thinks of himself as foster parent of a chicken, and the Pope proposes a toast: They should all get drunk in honor of the deaths of their sheep.

Perhaps that's how they support themselves: raising sheep. However, there seem scarcely two dozen sheep, which have to be destroyed after an outbreak of one of those diseases sheep are always being destroyed for. They're shotgunned by the Three Stooges. Or maybe there are chickens around somewhere that we don't see. The chickens would probably be in the movie in homage to Werner Herzog, who famously hates chickens.

Now you are remembering that I mentioned Herzog and some nuns. No, they do not live on the estate. They apparently live in South America, where they drop sacks of rice on hungry villages from an altitude of about two thousand feet. Rinse well. When one of the nuns survives a fall from their airplane, she calls on all of the nuns to jump, to prove their faith in God. I would not dream of telling you if they do.

Herzog feels a bond with Korine, who was still a teenager when he wrote the screenplay for Larry Clark's great *Kids* (1995). Korine is visionary and surrealistic enough to generate admiration from Herzog, who also starred in his *Julien Donkey-Boy* (he plays a schizophrenic's father, who listens to bluegrass while wearing a gas mask). In addition to the chickens, *Mister Lonely* has another homage to Herzog, a shot of an airplane taking off, which you would have to be very, very familiar with the director's work to footnote.

Various melodramatic scenarios burrow to the surface. Marilyn is fraught with everything a girl can be fraught with. Lincoln has anger-management problems. The Pope insists he is not dead. Everyone works on the construction of a theater, in which they will present their show, expecting to—what? Stand in a spotlight and do tiny bits evoking their celebrities? Then fulsome music swells, and the underlying tragedy of human existence is evoked, and the movie is more fascinating than it has any right to be, especially considering how fascinating it is that it was made at all.

Mongol ★ ★ ★ ½
R, 126 m., 2008

Tadanobu Asano (Temudgin), Honglei Sun (Jamukha), Khulan Chuluun (Borte), Odnyam Odsuren (Young Temudgin), Amarbold Tuvshinbayar (Young Jamukha), Bayartsetseg Erdenabat (Young Borte), Amadu Mamadakov (Targutai). Directed by Sergei Bodrov and produced by Sergey Selyanov. Screenplay by Arif Aliyev and Bodrov.

Mongols need laws. I will make them obey— even if I have to kill half of them.
—Genghis Khan

Sergei Bodrov's *Mongol* is a ferocious film, blood-soaked, pausing occasionally for passionate romance and more frequently for torture. As a visual spectacle, it is all but overwhelming, putting to shame some of the recent historical epics from Hollywood. If it has a flaw, and it does, it is expressed succinctly by the wife of its hero: "All Mongols do is kill and steal."

She must have seen the movie. That's about all they do in *Mongol.* They do not sing, dance, chant, hold summit meetings, have courts, hunt, or (with one exception) even cook or eat. They have no culture except for a series of sayings: "A Mongol does, or does not . . ." a long list of things, although many a Mongol seems never to have been issued the list, and does (or does not) do them anyway. As a result, the film consists of one bloody scene of carnage after another, illustrated by hordes of warriors eviscerating one another while bright patches of blood burst upon the screen.

At the center of the killing is invariably the khan, or leader, named Temudgin (Tadanobu Asano), who is not yet Genghis Kahn, but be patient: This film is the first of a trilogy.

The film opens with Temudgin (Odnyam Odsuren) at the age of nine, taken by his father to choose a bride from the Merkit clan. This will settle an old score. But along the way they happen upon a smaller clan, and there Temudgin first sets eyes on ten-year-old Borte (Bayartsetseg Erdenabat), who informs him he should choose her as his bride. He agrees, and thus is forged a partnership that will save his life more than once.

Years pass, the two are married, and Borte (played as an adult by Khulan Chuluun) makes a perfect bride but one hard to keep possession of. She is kidnapped by another clan, bears the first of two children claimed by Temudgin despite reasons to doubt, and follows her man into a series of battles that stain the soil of Mongolia with gallons of blood.

It happens that I have seen another movie about Mongols that suggests they do more than steal and kill. This is the famous nine-hour, three-part documentary *Taiga* (1995) by Ulrike Ottinger, who lived with today's yurt dwellers, witnessed one of their trance-evoking religious ceremonies, observed their customs and traditions, and learned in great detail how they procure and prepare food. There is also a wrestling match that is a good deal more cheerful than the contests in *Mongol.* But you do not have the time for a nine-hour documentary on this subject, I suppose, nor does *Mongol.* The nuances of an ancient and ingeniously developed culture are passed over, and it cannot be denied that *Mongol* is relentlessly entertaining as an action picture.

It left me, however, with some questions. Many involve the survival of the young Temudgin. Having inherited all his father's enemies, he is captured more than once, and we actually see him being fed so he can grow tall enough to kill ("Mongols do not kill children"). His neck and hands are imprisoned in a heavy wooden yoke, and when he escapes, he has the energy to run for miles across the steppe. On another occasion, he falls through the ice of a lake, and the movie simply ignores the question of how he is saved, unless it is by Tengri, God of the Blue Sky. Yes, I think it was Tengri, who also appears as a wolf and saves him more than once. If you want to be Genghis Khan, it helps to have a god in your corner.

Finally Temudgin is imprisoned in a cell surrounded by a moat populated by savage dogs. No such arrangement can hold him, of course, and he leads his clan into yet another series of battles, as gradually it occurs to him that this is no way to live, and the Mongols need to be united under a strong leader who will enforce less anarchistic battle practices. It's at about that point the movie ends, and we reflect that Temudgin has to survive two more such films to become Genghis Khan. And we think our election campaigns run on too long.

Monsters vs. Aliens ★ ★ ½
PG, 96 m., 2009

With the voices of: Reese Witherspoon (Susan/Ginormica), Seth Rogen (B.O.B.), Hugh Laurie (Dr. Cockroach, PhD), Will Arnett (The Missing Link), Kiefer Sutherland (Gen. W.R. Monger), Rainn Wilson (Gallaxhar), Stephen Colbert (President Hathaway), Paul Rudd (Derek Dietl). Directed by Rob Letterman and Conrad Vernon and produced by Lisa Stewart. Screenplay by Letterman, Maya Forbes, Wallace Wolodarsky, Jonathan Aibel, and Glenn Berger.

Monsters vs. Aliens is possibly the most commercial title of the year. How can you resist such a premise, especially if it's in 3-D animation? Very readily, in my case. I will say this first and get it out of the way: 3-D is a distraction and an annoyance. Younger moviegoers may think they like it because they've been told to, and picture quality is usually far from their minds. But for anyone who would just like to be left alone to SEE the darned thing, like me, it's a constant nudge in the ribs saying, *Never mind the story. Just see how neat I look.*

The film was made in Tru3D, the Dream-Works process that has been hailed by honcho Jeffrey Katzenberg as the future of the cinema. It is better than most of the 3-D I've seen (it doesn't approach the work on *The Polar Express* and *Beowulf*). But if this is the future of movies for grown-ups and not just the kiddies, saints preserve us. Billions of people for a century have happily watched 2-D and imagined 3-D. Think of the desert in *Lawrence of Arabia*. The schools of fish in *Finding Nemo*. The great hall in *Citizen Kane*.

Now, that flawless screen surface is threatened with a gimmick, which, let's face it, is intended primarily to raise ticket prices and make piracy more difficult. If its only purpose was artistic, do you think Hollywood would spend a dime on it? The superb MaxiVision process is available for $15,000 a screen, and the Hollywood establishment can't even be bothered to look at it. Why invest in the technology of the future when they can plunder the past?

Speaking of the past, *Monsters vs. Aliens* retreads some of the monsters that starred in actual 1950s B-movies: a blob, the fifty-foot woman, and no end of aliens with towering foreheads on their dome-shaped heads. Whether the average kid will get all of the connections is beside the point; if kids could accept Pokemon and the Teenage Mutant Ninja Turtles, these monsters are going to seem like masterpieces of manic personality.

The plot: On her wedding day, sweet Susan (Reese Witherspoon) is mutated by a meteorite; just as she walks down the aisle, she grows to (I learn) just an inch short of fifty feet, maybe because Disney wanted to respect the copyright. Her husband (Paul Rudd) was no match for her anyway, and now he really has small-man complex. After she wreaks havoc with every step, the military names her Ginormica, no doubt sidestepping *Amazonia* so as not to offend the lesbian lobby. She's snatched by the feds and deposited in a secret government prison holding other monsters, who have been languishing since the 1950s. They're old enough that, if they escape, they could terrorize the subway on a senior pass.

Earth is invaded by a robot that has one big eyeball in the middle of its head, like a giant Leggs pantyhose container bred with an iSight camera. Gen. W.R. Monger (Kiefer Sutherland) and the president (Stephen Colbert) are helpless to deal with this threat, and in desperation release the monsters to save the earth. Springing, leaping, skittering, or oozing into battle we have Ginormica at the head of an army including B.O.B., Insectosaurus, Dr. Cockroach, and The Missing Link.

With the exception of Susan, who is perky, these creatures have no personalities in the sense of the distinctive characters in Dream-Works' *Shrek* movies. Basically they express basic intentions, fears, and desires in terms of their physical characteristics. There is a lot of banging, clanging, toppling, colliding, and crumbling in the movie, especially when San Francisco is attacked by Gallaxhar, a squid that is the master of the robot. Conventional evolutionary guidelines are lost in the confusion.

I didn't find the movie rich with humor, unless frenetic action is funny. Maybe kids have learned to think so. Too bad for them. Think of the depth of *Pinocchio*. Kids in those

357

days were treated with respect for their intelligence. *Monsters vs. Aliens* is also lacking in wit. What is wit? Well, for example, the spirit in which I am writing this review. The dictionary defines it as *analogies between dissimilar things, expressed in quick, sharp, spontaneous observations.* A weak point with the monsters, and way outside Gallaxhar's range.

I suppose kids will like this movie, especially those below the age of reason. Their parents may not be as amused, and if they have several children, may ask themselves how much it was worth for the kids to wear the glasses. Is there a child who would see this movie in 2-D (which has brighter colors than 3-D) and complain?

Moon ★ ★ ★ ½

R, 97 m., 2009

Sam Rockwell (Sam Bell), Kevin Spacey (Gerty), Dominique McElligott (Tess Bell). Directed by Duncan Jones and produced by Stuart Fenegan and Trudie Styler. Screenplay by Nathan Parker.

Is *Moon* evoking *2001*, or does its mining outpost on the far side of the moon simply happen to date back to the *2001* era (which was, of course, more than eight years ago)? I lean toward the second theory. After the mission carrying Dave Bowman disappeared beyond Jupiter, mankind decided to focus on the moon, where we were already, you will recall, conducting operations. The interior design of the new moon station was influenced by the *2001* ship, and the station itself was supervised by Gerty, sort of a scaled-down HAL 9000 that scoots around.

At some point in the future (we can't nail down the story's time frame), this station on the far side is manned by a single crew member, Sam Bell (Sam Rockwell). He's working out the final days of a three-year contract and is close to cracking from loneliness. Talking to loved ones via video link doesn't satisfy. The station is largely automated; it processes lunar rock to extract helium-3, used to provide Earth with pollution-free power from nuclear fusion. My guess is, the station is on the far side because you don't want to go gazing at the Man in the Moon some night and see a big zit on his nose.

The station is large and well-appointed, and has entertainment resources and adequate supplies. Sam communicates frequently with the home office . . . and so does Gerty. Sam doesn't do any actual mining, but his human hands and brain are needed for repairs, maintenance, and inspection. One day he's outside checking up on something, and his lunar rover smashes up. He's injured and awakens in the station's medical facility. And that, I think, is all I need to say. A spoiler warning would mean secrets are revealed—and you'd look, wouldn't you, no matter what you say.

I want to take a step back and discuss some underlying matters in the film. In an age when our space and distance boundaries are being pushed way beyond the human comfort zone, how do we deal with the challenges of space in real time? In lower gravity, how do our bodies deal with loss of bone and muscle mass? How do our minds deal with long periods of isolation?

The *2001* vessel dealt with the physical challenges with its centrifuge. Dave and Frank had each other—and HAL. Sam is all on his own, except for Gerty, whose voice by Kevin Spacey suggests he was programmed by the same voice synthesizers used for HAL. Gerty seems harmless and friendly, but you never know with these digital devils. All Sam knows is that he's past his shelf date and ready to be recycled back to Earth.

Space is a cold and lonely place, pitiless and indifferent, as Bruce Dern's character grimly realized in Douglas Trumbull's classic *Silent Running*. At least he had the consolation that he was living with Earth's last vegetation. Sam has no consolations at all. It even appears that a new guy may have entered the orbits of his wife and daughter. What kind of a man would volunteer for this duty? What kind of a corporation would ask him to? We, and he, find out.

Moon is a superior example of that threatened genre, hard science fiction, which is often about the interface between humans and alien intelligence of one kind or other, including digital. John W. Campbell Jr., the godfather of this genre, would have approved. The movie is really all about ideas. It only seems to be about emotions. How real are our emotions, anyway? How real are we? Someday I will die. This laptop I'm using is patient and can wait.

Note: The capable director, Duncan Jones, was born Duncan Zowie Heywood Jones. Easy to understand if you know his father is David Bowie, rhymes with Zoe, not Howie. Jones a successful UK commercial director; this is his debut feature. ☞

Moscow, Belgium ★ ★ ★
NO MPAA RATING, 106 m., 2009

Barbara Sarafian (Matty), Jurgen Delnaet (Johnny), Johan Heldenbergh (Werner), Anemone Valcke (Vera), Sofia Ferri (Fien), Julian Borsani (Peter). Directed by Christophe van Rompaey and produced by Jean-Claude van Rijckeghem. Screenplay by van Rijckeghem and Pat van Beirs.

She backs up her car. His big truck runs into it. She should have looked first. A truck that size shouldn't have been in a parking lot. They get out and start screaming insults at each other. This is in a Flemish-speaking city in Belgium. We quickly learn that the f-word sounds exactly the same in English and Flemish.

Now here is the intriguing element. They are both livid with anger. Their insults escalate from their driving abilities to their genders. Women are bloodsuckers. Men are—never mind what men are. At some point, very subtle and hard to define, their insults turn into play. No, they don't start grinning. They still both seem angry. But they grow verbally inventive, and we sense, and they sense, a shift in the weather. It ends with him asking her out for coffee.

The buried emotions in this scene play out all through *Moscow, Belgium*, an uncommon comedy that is fairly serious most of the time. She is Matty (Barbara Sarafian), forty-one years old. He is Johnny (Jurgen Delnaet), in his late twenties. Matty's husband has walked out on her and her three kids. Johnny's girlfriend left him for some rich dude. Johnny has fallen helplessly in love with her, possibly because he has met his match in insults, possibly because a woman who can think that fast on her feet can—never mind what she can do.

Their working-class neighborhood of Ghent is named Moucou, with high rises,

heavy traffic, rough bars. Johnny lives here in the sleeping compartment of his truck cab. He is friendly, has eyes that smile, hair she would probably love to take a brush to. Her hair is a slightly tidier mess. She has no desire to meet a man, especially one so much younger. Her husband, Werner (Johan Heldenbergh), an art teacher, left her for a little tart who was one of his students. One cradle robber is enough for her family.

Now about her kids. They are individuals intent on their own lives and indifferent to the fact that they are in a movie. Here's what I mean by that. Ever notice how in a lot of movies the family members are playing Family Members? The kids are arrayed around the dinner table smoothly fitting in their dialogue. Matty's kids are Vera, about seventeen, who regards her mother with weary insight; a younger daughter, Fien, who is going through a stage of reading everyone's Tarot cards and relating to you as if you're the Hanging Man or The Fool; and a still younger son, Peter, who is obsessed by airplanes. Johnny comes for dinner, but they're indifferent to him or, in Vera's case, tactfully withdrawn.

Werner turns up when he hears about his wife's young boyfriend, and they all share a family meal that I suspect owes something to Mike Leigh's family occasions of awkward, weird embarrassment. Matty has to choose: the faithless husband who is a handsome jerk, or the love-struck truck driver with a disturbing past and good reasons to never, ever drink again. The audience would advise her against both.

Underneath everything rolls the rhythm of Matty's real life. Men can come and go, but someone needs to put food on the table, do the shopping, be a parent. Matty has a job in the post office, where half the customers seem to know her. This is not the greatest job, but it's what she has. She understands Johnny's pride in his truck. It is all he has, but it is *his*. He can come and go with the freedom of a ranch hand. Werner, on the other hand, sometimes seems like one of the kids. Well, both men do. By the virtue of their continuity through family crises, women maintain a home, which serves as a powerful attraction.

The performances make these characters work. Barbara Sarafian, first seen in a long shot as she looks painfully hostile and withdrawn, is weather-beaten but attractive. Johnny must be the despair of his mother: an unkempt charmer who looks like trouble. Werner is a creep. The only grown-up in the movie is Vera. She puts her mother to an unexpected test, and Matty, after a double take, shows she has instinctive love for her daughter.

I will not be revealing a thing if I say we're not too sure Matty has made the right choice at the end. That's because neither choice would be the right choice. But notice how deeply the director, Christophe van Rompaey, has drawn us into these lives, how much we finally care, and with what sympathy all the actors enter into the enterprise.

The Most Dangerous Man in America ★★★
NO MPAA RATING, 94 m., 2010

Featuring Daniel Ellsberg (Narrator), Patricia Ellsberg, Anthony Russo, Howard Zinn, Janaki Natajaran, Randy Koehler, Tom Oliphant, Egil Krogh, Max Frankel, John Dean, Leonard Weinglass, Hendrick Smith, and Mike Gravel. A documentary directed and produced by Judith Ehrlich and Rick Goldsmith. Screenplay by Goldsmith, Ehrlich, Lawrence Lerew, and Michael Chandler, partly based on Daniel Ellsberg's *Secrets: A Memoir of Vietnam and the Pentagon Papers.*

I thought I was pretty much familiar with the story about how the Pentagon Papers were leaked to the press in 1971. I knew that Daniel Ellsberg, a high-level analyst at the Pentagon and the Rand Corporation, had Xeroxed the Pentagon's secret history of the war in Vietnam and leaked it to the press, notably the *New York Times*. I recalled his arrest and trial. Ironically, his case was dismissed because White House plumbers broke into his psychiatrist's office and Nixon offered to make Ellsberg's judge head of the FBI. Said Judge William Matthew Byrne Jr.: "The bizarre events have incurably infected the prosecution of this case."

I knew all that. What I never realized was what a high-ranking employee Ellsberg really was, and how secret the Pentagon Papers really were. Locked in safes, their existence was a

secret even from President Lyndon B. Johnson, who, it was believed, would have been infuriated by such a history. Ellsberg didn't merely leak the papers; he played a key role in contributing to them.

His first day on the job, cables came in from the celebrated Gulf of Tonkin incident, used by LBJ to justify escalating the war in Vietnam. Later the same day, cables from the commodore in command over the "attacked" ships said there was a "problem" with the reports—which turned out to be false. Johnson didn't want to hear it. He was ready to escalate the war, and he escalated.

His was the latest in a series of presidential decisions beginning with Truman, and continuing through Kennedy, Johnson, and Nixon, who financed France in its Indochinese war, propped up corrupt regimes in South Vietnam, prevented free elections, and eventually wreaked destruction in an unwinnable war.

Ellsberg, a marine company commander in the 1950s, wanted firsthand information. He went to Vietnam personally, shouldered a weapon, and led a patrol. What he learned convinced him that a false portrait of U.S. success was being painted. On a flight back to Washington with Robert McNamara, the defense secretary agreed the war could not be won, and we see the two men leaving the aircraft together before McNamara lied to the press that America was winning it. Later McNamara resigned, for reasons he didn't make clear at the time, nor even later in his confessional Errol Morris documentary, *The Fog of War*.

Ellsberg, in short, could not be dismissed as merely a sneak and a snitch, but a man who had direct knowledge of how the American public had been misled. He saw himself not as a peacenik war protester, but as a government servant exercising a higher moral duty. The documentary *The Most Dangerous Man in America*, by Judith Ehrlich and Rick Goldsmith, traces his doubts about authority back to a childhood tragedy and forward to the influence of young men who went to prison for their convictions.

It is a skillful, well-made film, although, since Ellsberg is the narrator, it doesn't probe him very deeply. We see his version of himself.

A great deal of relevant footage has been assembled, and is intercut with stage re-creations, animations, and the White House tapes of Richard Nixon, who fully advocated the nuclear bombing of Hanoi. Kissinger was apparently a voice of restraint. If you can think of another war justified by fabricated evidence, and another cabinet secretary who resigned without being very clear about his reasons, you're free to, but the film draws no parallels.

Mother ★★★ ½
R, 128 m., 2010

Kim Hye-ja (Mother), Won Bin (Do-joon), Jin Goo (Jin-tae). Directed by Bong Joon-ho and produced by Choi Jae-won, Park Tae-joon, and Seo Woo-sik. Screenplay by Park Eun-gyo and Bong Joon-ho.

The strange, fascinating film *Mother* begins with what seems like a straightforward premise. A young man of marginal intelligence is accused of murder. A clue with his name on it and eyewitness testimony tie him to the crime. His mother, a dynamo, plunges into action to prove her son innocent. So there we have it, right? He's either guilty or not, and his mom will get to the bottom of things. Or not.

Is it that I've seen so many movies? Is that why I grow impatient with formulas, and am grateful for films that upset my expectations? If you faithfully remade *Mother* for a mass American audience (let's say with Helen Mirren and Ed Norton), mainstream moviegoers would likely be furious because: (a) "You can't do that!" and (b) "Uh, what is it that you did, exactly?"

This is a new South Korean film by Bong Joon-ho, his first after *The Host* (2006). That was a popular thriller about a giant squid created by toxic waste who dragged away a victim. Her family members learn she's still alive, but can't get the authorities to listen. Once again, in *Mother*, blood ties go up against the state.

The mother of the title, played by a respected South Korean actress named Kim Hye-ja, is a force of nature. In a village, she runs a little shop selling herbs, roots, and spices. Her sideline is prescribing herbal cures. Her son, Do-joon (Won Bin), in his late twenties, lives at home and they sleep in the same bed. He's a few slices short of a pie. Early in the film, he's saved from death in traffic when his mother races to the rescue.

Do-joon has a best friend named Jin-tae (Jin Goo). Jin-tae can easily manipulate him, persuade him to his will. Do-joon's mental fogginess may be his most attractive quality. In the town, a shocking murder takes place. A young girl's body is left where all can see. A golf ball with Do-joon's name on it is found near the death site.

Did he do it? We can't be sure. Did Jin-tae do it and plant the evidence? Or persuade Do-joon to do it when he was drunk? Again, we can't be sure. Under the Law of Economy of Characters, Jin-tae must have been involved because there are no other eligible characters. You can't simply produce a killer out of your hat. Of course, Do-joon could be guilty and Jin-tae had no involvement. Or, at least technically, the mother could have done it.

Mother (she's given no other name) marches tirelessly around the village, doing her own detective work. She questions people, badgers them, harasses the police, comforts her son, hires a worthless lawyer. We learn everything she learns. It seems she's getting nowhere. And it's at this point that the movie might become upsetting for a mass audience, because *Mother* creates not new suspects from off the map, but new levels in the previously established story.

The film is labyrinthine and deceptive, and not in a way we anticipate. It becomes a pleasure for the mind. Long after a conventional thriller would have its destination in plain sight, *Mother* is still penetrating our assumptions. So much depends on Kim Hye-ja's performance as a remorseless parent defending her fledgling. Likely she has spent years helping her clueless son escape one dilemma after another, and now she rises to the great occasion of her life. Her struggle is made more difficult because the police found it child's play to extract a confession from him.

Mother, and South Korean films in general, provide a case study of the situation of alternative films in this country. Many Americans have never seen a South Korean film and never will. I once spoke to a class for would-be foreign correspondents at the University of Illinois, and only two of them had ever seen a subtitled film from anywhere.

A film like *Mother*, and the recent *Chaser*, are adult films, not in the sense that they contain x-rated material, but in the sense that they appeal to intelligent grown-ups. A bright ten-year-old can understand most of today's Hollywood films. Disney recently announced it will make only 3-D "event" movies, comic hero stories, and extensions of franchises like *Pirates of the Caribbean*. It has essentially abandoned movies about plausible human beings. It isn't a luxury to see indie and alternative films. It's a necessity.

Mother will have you discussing the plot, not entirely to your satisfaction. I would argue: The stories in movies are complete fictions and can be resolved in any way the director chooses. If he actually cheats or lies, we have a case against him. If not, no matter what strange conclusions he arrives at, we can be grateful that we remained involved and even fascinated. Why do we buy a ticket? To confirm that a movie ends just the way we expect it to?

Mother and Child ★★★ ½
R, 126 m., 2010

Naomi Watts (Elizabeth), Annette Bening (Karen), Kerry Washington (Lucy), Jimmy Smits (Paco), Samuel L. Jackson (Paul), S. Epatha Merkerson (Ada), Cherry Jones (Sister Joanne), Elpidia Carrillo (Sofia), Shareeka Epps (Ray). Directed by Rodrigo Garcia and produced by Lisa Maria Falcone and Julie Lynn. Screenplay by Garcia.

Three mothers in need of a child. Three children, one not yet born. Three lives that are obscurely linked. Rodrigo Garcia has made his career of films sympathetic to the feelings of women, and *Mother and Child* is so emotionally affecting because it is concerned only with their feelings. The story lines coil and eventually join, but that's just a narrative device. If these characters had no connection, their lives would be equally evocative.

The film is founded on three performances by Annette Bening, Kerry Washington, and Naomi Watts. All have rarely been better. Bening plays Karen, a caregiver at work, where she's a physical therapist, and at home, where she cares for her mother (Eileen Ryan). There will be no one to care for her: When she was fourteen, she gave up a child for adoption, and now she yearns to have that child back. This is not a film about the wisdom of adoption, however, but about Karen's desire for her child.

Kerry Washington plays Lucy, happily married, childless, trying to adopt a child. She finds one she loves, but the baby's birth mother, Ray (Shareeka Epps), is a piece of work. She considers it a seller's market, and is fiercely determined that her unborn baby will find a good home with worthy parents. She's more exacting than an adoption agency. Epps is very good, very focused here.

Naomi Watts plays Elizabeth, a lawyer who is focused not so much on her career but on her power, and how her sexuality can be a part of that. She goes to work for a Los Angeles law firm and makes it her business to have an affair with one of the partners (Samuel L. Jackson). She calls the shots, perhaps because she never knew her own parents, and fears a feeling of abandonment.

A quiet, nurturing person at the intersection of these lives is Sister Joanne (Cherry Jones), a nun at a church adoption bureau. She is childless, of course, but content; she accepts her state as part of her service to God, and is devoted to her clients. The nun is one of several important supporting characters who give *Mother and Child* richness. There is a large cast here, but the actors are gifted and well cast, down to the smaller roles, and each one is important to the development of the story—not just added for diversion or variety.

These include Sofia (Elpidia Carrillo), Karen's maid, who has a daughter who sometimes comes to work with her and embodies some of Karen's regrets. Paul, the Samuel Jackson character, has daughters of his own, as does Paco (Jimmy Smits), Karen's friend at work. They have what she doesn't. Lucy's mother (S. Epatha Merkerson) is a nurturing example of motherhood; not so her mother-in-law, who is cruel about the absence of a grandchild.

Garcia, whose credits include *Things You Can Tell Just by Looking at Her* (2000) and

Nine Lives (2005), has created an interwoven plot here, not just for the purpose of being clever. Each facet revolves to illuminate the others. The characters reflect aspects of the central dilemma of mothers without children. It doesn't argue that all mothers require children, and indeed the nun may be the happiest woman here. It simply argues that these mothers believe that they do.

Of all the performances, Samuel L. Jackson's is the most surprising. It sometimes appears that the busy Jackson will take almost any role to stay working (remember *Black Snake Moan*?). This film provides a reminder of his subtlety. He is a powerful, successful man, relatively helpless with a demanding and sexually skilled woman. They like the sex, there is no love, she doesn't want to be involved in his personal life, and there is something there that disturbs him.

Bening, Watts, and Washington create three distinct beings with three distinct lives. They don't all "share the same problem," but they believe they share the same solution. Garcia embeds their needs in the details of their lives, so we don't emerge with ideas about them, but feelings.

Motherhood ★★
PG-13, 89 m., 2009

Uma Thurman (Eliza), Anthony Edwards (Avery), Minnie Driver (Sheila), Daisy Tahan (Clara), David and Matthew Schallipp (Lucas). Directed by Katherine Dieckmann and produced by Rachel Cohen, Jana Edelbaum, Pamela Koffler, Christine Vachon, and John Wells. Screenplay by Dieckmann.

Motherhood is about a conventional family living a conventional life in a conventional way. This life isn't perfect, but whose life is? The father is absent-minded but means well, the kids are normal, the mother is trying to juggle parental duties and her plans for a career. This could be countless families. Why do we require a movie about this particular one?

The film stars Uma Thurman, doing her best with a role that may offer her less than any other in her career, even though she's constantly on-screen. She's Eliza, who takes her laptop along to the playground to work on her blog, which is just a blog. She's not cooking her way through Julia Child or anything. Her husband is played by Anthony Edwards. I didn't remember the character's name after seeing the movie, so I checked with IMDb and he doesn't seem to have one. That tells you something.

The kids are six-year-old Clara (Daisy Tahan) and two-year-old Lucas (twins David and Matthew Schallipp). The tooth-challenged Daisy is pitch-perfect at that demanding age when kids become fixated on their convictions. Watching the movie, it occurred to me that child actors are invariably terrific. Maybe we are all born as great actors, but after a certain age most of us morph into bad ones.

Some effort is made to introduce interest to the cast. Minnie Driver plays a best friend who has an unsatisfactory personal life; the two women go to a sale of women's clothing during which they have tugs-of-war with other women who want the same frocks. Did I mention the movie takes place in Manhattan? That would also explain the crotchety neighbor (Alice Drummond), who is annoyed that a movie crew is using their street as a location. It would also explain Jodie Foster's cameo as a mom being followed by paparazzi. Don't you sort of imagine that if you lived in Greenwich Village you would sometimes have a Jodie Foster sighting?

The movie suggests two directions that might fruitfully have been employed by Katherine Dieckmann, the writer and director. One is in the person of an East Indian delivery man (Arjun Gupta) who begins an intriguing conversation with Eliza. Indian-Americans are appearing in movies much more frequently—for one reason, I suspect, because we like their accents. (An Indian friend told me, "We have been speaking English longer than you have.") Could this meeting have been developed into a subplot?

The other direction might have been fundamental. Instead of jumping through hoops to make Eliza somehow seem unique, special, and besieged by her (utterly commonplace) problems, how about making her desperate with boredom and the desire to break out into the extraordinary? Maybe her blog dives off the high board and she becomes a media creature? I dunno.

The movie is billed as a comedy, but at no point will you require oxygen. There are some smiles and chuckles and a couple of actual laughs, but the overall effect is underwhelming. Meh.

Moving Midway ★ ★ ★
NO MPAA RATING, 98 m., 2008

Featuring Charlie Hinton Silver, Robert Hinton, Elizabeth "Sis" Cheshire, Al Hinton, Abraham Lincoln Hinton. A documentary directed by Godfrey Cheshire and produced by Cheshire, Jay Spain, and Vincent Farrell. Screenplay by Cheshire.

SPOILER WARNING: *Moving Midway* tells three stories, each one worthy of a film of its own. (1) It records the journey home to North Carolina of the film critic Godfrey Cheshire and his discovery of his family's secret history. (2) It documents the ordeal of moving a 160-year-old Southern plantation house to a new location miles away, not by road but overland. (3) It demolishes the myth of the Southern plantation.

Movie critics are always asked if they've ever wanted to make a movie of their own. A handful, like Peter Bogdanovich and Rod Lurie, have had success with features. Others, like Todd McCarthy, have made good documentaries. Godfrey Cheshire's first film follows the first rule of both kinds of films: Start with a strong story that you feel a personal connection with. His story grows stronger, and the connections deeper.

Like many critics (the Alabama-born Jonathan Rosenbaum comes to mind), Cheshire was a small-town boy who moved to the big city. First it was Raleigh, and now New York. In North Carolina, his youth revolved around Midway Plantation, outside of Raleigh, the family seat since 1848. In 2006 the ravages of progress overran Midway. It was boxed in by two expressways. Best Buy was across the street. Target and Home Depot were moving in. Godfrey's brother Charlie hired experts to jack up the house, put it on wheels, and move it to sixty or seventy acres deep into the country.

Godfrey went south to film this undertaking. It stirred family memories and stories about the ghosts many people thought they had seen in Midway. Then he heard from an NYU professor of African-American studies named Robert Hinton, who said he was related to the family; Hinton is the ancestral name. Robert was an African-American. Godfrey invited him to come to North Carolina, visit the house, and watch the move.

Hinton had written about a much-publicized North Carolina family reunion that reunited the black and white members of the same plantation family. Now he received an e-mail from a Brooklyn teacher named Al Hinton, who said his ninety-six-year-old grandfather, Abraham Lincoln Hinton, had some memories to share.

Abraham, visited by Godfrey and Robert, his mind clear as a bell, recalled his father, born in 1848, taking him past a big white two-story house and saying it was his birthplace. That was Midway. Oral tradition in the African-American branch of the family recorded that they were descended from a Hinton patriarch and a cook who was a black slave. There seems no doubt, both in genealogy and physical evidence: Every Hinton, white and black, has the same distinctive nose, which can clearly be seen in the portrait of their common ancestor.

Godfrey made these discoveries while filming, and Robert became coproducer. He considers the myth of the idyllic plantation as formed in works like *Birth of a Nation* and *Gone with the Wind,* and demolished by *Roots.* Robert Hinton, whose slave ancestors constructed Midway and picked cotton there, is a succinct and sometimes droll observer. He surprises Godfrey by telling him he considers Midway part of his own heritage, and again when he says it doesn't bother him at all that the original land will be buried beneath a parking lot. Robert on Civil War reenactments: "I'm comfortable with the idea that they keep refighting it, as long as they keep losing it."

Invited by Al and Abraham to a Hinton family reunion, Godfrey finds he has more than one hundred African-American cousins, all of whom know exactly who they are descended from. "It is becoming clearer," he says, "that the South is a mixed-race society." Robert reveals to him: "I found after I came north that I was more comfortable with Southern whites than with young blacks up here." When Cheshire's lively mother, Sis, and the stately Abraham meet, they are instantly at ease, even kidding with each other. Not that Sis doesn't believe the slaves, by and large, were taken good care of.

This is a deceptive film. It starts in one direction and discovers a better one. Cheshire is a dry, almost dispassionate narrator, and that is good; preaching about his discoveries would sound wrong. Robert Hinton, whose feelings run deep, brings the story into focus: "I always wanted to meet a white Hinton. I was hoping I would hate him. The problem is, I like you, so I can't lay a lot of stuff on you." He is philosophical, but not resigned. There is a difference.

Meanwhile, at the new Shoppes of the Midway Plantation mall, there is a restaurant named Mingo's. That was the name of Midway's first slave. The local mayor, bursting with civic pride about the new development, explains how we have all moved on and outgrown the troubles of the past. The mayor is black. We are now in the twenty-first century.

The Mummy: Tomb of the Dragon Emperor ★ ★ ★
PG-13, 112 m., 2008

Brendan Fraser (Rick O'Connell), Jet Li (Emperor Han), Maria Bello (Evelyn O'Connell), Michelle Yeoh (Zi Juan), Luke Ford (Alex O'Connell), John Hannah (Jonathan Carnahan), Isabella Leong (Lin), Anthony Wong Chau-Sang (General Yang), Russell Wong (Ming Guo), Liam Cunningham (Mad Dog Maguire). Directed by Rob Cohen and produced by Sean Daniel, Bob Ducsay, James Jacks, and Stephen Sommers. Screenplay by Alfred Gough and Miles Millar.

Moviegoers who knowingly buy a ticket for *The Mummy: Tomb of the Dragon Emperor* are going to get exactly what they expect: There is a mummy, a tomb, a dragon, and an emperor. And the movie about them is all that it could be. If you think *The Mummy: Tomb of the Dragon Emperor* sounds like a waste of time, don't waste yours.

I, as it happens, have time to waste, and cannot do better than to quote from my review of *The Mummy* (1999): "There is hardly a thing I can say in its favor, except that I was cheered by nearly every minute of it. I cannot

argue for the script, the direction, the acting, or even the mummy, but I can say that I was not bored and sometimes I was unreasonably pleased. There is a little immaturity stuck away in the crannies of even the most judicious of us, and we should treasure it."

I was not, however, pleased by *The Mummy Returns* (2001), although it inspired one of my funnier reviews. But *The Mummy: Tomb of the Dragon Emperor* is the best in the series and, from the looks of it, the most expensive. And once again it presents the spectacle of undead warriors who are awakened from the slumber of ages only to be defeated in battle—this time, by the skeletons of the slaves buried beneath the Great Wall after constructing it (which is a neat trick).

Rick O'Connell (Brendan Fraser) and his wife, Evelyn (Mario Bello), are back, having come out of retirement to race to the aid of their now-adult son Alex (Luke Ford), who has inadvertently awakened the mummy of the Dragon Emperor (Jet Li). In a prologue, we learn he was cursed by the sorceress Zi Juan (Michelle Yeoh), who incurred his wrath by spurning his love, and later, we learn, bearing the daughter of General Ming (Russell Wong). Both daughter and mother are immortal. So is the emperor, although it is a mixed blessing when you are immortal but mummified inside a thick cocoon of terracotta. Where's the benefit?

Now the emperor has awakened, and he unleashes his army of ten thousand slumbering warriors to feed his ambition to conquer the world, which is going to take more than ten thousand spear carriers, but he's operating on B.C. time. To counter him, the sleeping slave-skeletons are awakened by the sorceress and are sort of funny: One misplaces his head and screws it back on. The battle between these two sides is won by the side with the fewest missing heads.

Before that climactic event, however, Rick, Evelyn, Alex, and Evelyn's supercilious brother Jonathan (John Hannah) penetrate the underground city of the mummy, survive a perilous series of booby traps, and in several other ways remind us of Indiana Jones, the obvious inspiration for this series, which has little—no, nothing—to do with Boris Karloff's *The Mummy* (1932). They even make it into the Himalayas, and . . . could that be the lost city of Shangri-La?

The emperor is a shape-shifter, able to turn himself into a three-headed fire-breathing dragon, which coils, twists, turns, and somehow avoids scorching itself. He speaks in a low bass rumble, just like Imhotep, the mummy in the two earlier pictures, whose name continues to remind me of an Egyptian house of pancakes. But moving the action from Egypt to China allows a whole new set of images to be brought into play, and the movie ends by winking at us that the next stop will be Peru.

Now why did I like this movie? It was just plain dumb fun is why. It is absurd and preposterous, and proud of it. The heroes maintain their ability to think of banal clichés even in the most strenuous situations. Brendan Fraser continues to play Rick as if he is taking a ride at Universal Studios, but Maria Bello has real pluck as she uses a handgun against the hordes of terra-cotta warriors. The sacrifice of the sorceress in relinquishing not only her own immortality but that of her daughter permits love to bloom, although would you really want a bride who was four thousand years old, even if she was going to die?

Munyurangabo ★★★★

NO MPAA RATING, 97 m., 2009

Jeff Rutagengwa (Munyurangabo), Eric Ndorunkundiye (Sangwa), Jean Marie Nkurikiyinka (Papa Sangwa), Narcicia Nyirabucyeye (Mama Sangwa), Jean Pierre Harerimana Mulomda (Gwiza), Edouard B. Uwayo (Poet), Etienne Rugazora (Ngabo's Father). Directed and produced by Lee Isaac Chung. Screenplay by Chung and Samuel Gray Anderson.

Perhaps the best way to approach a subject of bewildering complexity is with simplicity. *Munyurangabo* considers the genocide in Rwanda entirely through the lives of two boys who are ten or eleven years old. They are not symbols. They are simply boys, who have been surviving on their own in a big city but are not toughened and essentially good. That's all.

Its story involves one of those miracles that can illuminate the cinema. It was directed by Lee Isaac Chung, thirty, a first-generation Korean-American who grew up on a small farm in rural Arkansas. It was shot on location in Rwanda in two weeks. It involved only local actors. It is the first film in the Kinyarwanda language (with few, excellent, and easy-to-see subtitles). It is in every frame a beautiful and powerful film—a masterpiece.

An opening shot shows Sangwa and Munyurangabo, called Ngabo, as friends embarking on a cross-country journey. They trek through a pastoral landscape, stricken by drought. There are no dangers along the way. They have been in Kigali, the capital city. They will stop at Sangwa's family farm. He hasn't seen his mother for three years. All seems well, although weighing in our mind is the machete Ngabo carries in his knapsack. Sangwa's mother is joyful to see him, his father reserved and stern: What kind of a boy runs away from home for three years? Why did he not stay to help his family raise his younger siblings? What kind of a thing is that? Who is this boy he is traveling with?

The answers to those questions come in the unfolding of the story, an experience you should have without viewing the trailer, which provides an item of information you don't require. I will discuss instead the rural society Sangwa (Eric Ndorunkundiye) rejoins, and the city boy, Ngabo (Jeff Rutagengwa), sees for the first time. These people are poor. They catch water in plastic jugs from a trickle on the hillside. They till the soil by hand. They live in a house made from mud bricks. But this is not the wretched poverty you imagine. These people possess dignity and have a life they accept on its own terms, which is all they have known. Children run and laugh. Everything is done in its own time.

Sangwa's mother (Narcicia Nyirabucyeye) cherishes her boy and finds food for him when there is none. His father (Jean Marie Vianney Nkurikiyinka) is stern and not quick to forgive, but speaks to his son in reasoned words that obviously sink in. He knows what life is likely to bring Sangwa.

Chung, who cowrote with Samuel Gray Anderson as well as directing, is a born filmmaker. You see that in his eye, his cinematography, and his editing. He avoids pointless reaction shots and obvious payoffs; his strategy is to view a scene, give it weight, and let it stand. Everything is perfectly clear, but nothing is hammered home. We get the point. He knows we do.

The timing and precision of the way Chung explains the boys' journey, and the way he spaces out the information, is so much more effective than crude narrative storytelling. Since all is known between the boys, they never have to tell each other anything simply so we can listen. All dialogue is to the moment, and therefore we understand everything. The playing out of Ngabo's big decision is handled with a perfect sense of the time he takes to arrive at it, and the way it was prepared for and comes about.

There is an extraordinary passage outside a little roadside restaurant. When Ngabo approaches, an older boy is sitting outside in the shade. He sees the machete in the knapsack. He takes a swig from his beer and observes that tomorrow is National Independence Day. He has been asked to recite a poem he wrote. "Would you like to hear me say it?"

He doesn't wait for a reply. He begins with confidence and pride. It is all there, the whole canvas, Rwanda, its past, its future. The poet is played by Edouard B. Uwayo, and this is his own poem. Chung's decision to use it as he does is the right one, and the young poet's face evokes depths of wisdom.

Munyurangabo played in the Un Certain Regard section of Cannes 2007, where *Variety*'s Robert Koehler called it "flat-out, the discovery of this year's batch." It won the Grand Jury Prize at the AFI film festival. The Tomatometer stands at 100. If it seems like I'm trying to convince you on this film, I am. It is rolling out across the country in those few theaters where a film like this is welcomed. You can find it on DVD, and it went to Film Movement subscribers, who receive and can keep a film a month. They certainly got their money's worth.

Must Read After My Death ★ ★ ★

NO MPAA RATING, 76 m., 2009

A documentary directed, produced, and written by Morgan Dews.

Here is a cry from the grave. A woman who died some eight years ago at the age of eighty-nine left behind about fifty hours of audiotapes, two hundred home movies, and three hundred pages of documents, a record that all ended, thirty years before that, on the death of her husband. The cache was labeled, in bold marker on a manila envelope, *Must Read After My Death*. What an anguished story it tells, of a marriage from hell.

The woman was named Allis. Her grandson, Morgan Dews, has created this film from her archives and understandably represses her family name. She met her husband Charley when they were both married to others. What she wanted was a nice little house with a white picket fence, where she would bear his children, whether or not they were married, because she knew they would have beautiful children together. They were married, and until death did not part.

It was an "open marriage." Charley was away much of the year on business, often to Australia. They decided to exchange Dictaphone recordings, and later tape recordings, and Allis saved hours of taped telephone messages. Charley is forthright about his adventures with "interesting women" he has met in Australia, "good dancers" and obviously good at more than that, "but the international operators listen in." Allis tells only of one weekend affair. She says she thinks she "helped" the man rebuild his self-confidence.

Charley is such a perfect bastard. His dry voice objectively slices through everything. He speaks of love and travel arrangements in the same tone. When he's home, there is always fighting. Always. Not about sex; he sees the real problems in their marriage as housekeeping and finances. Allis says she was meant to be a good mother but was never a housekeeper. She speaks four languages, went to college, was married first to a European, did some kind of unspecified singing. We hear not a word about Charley's first marriage.

Charley and Allis have three sons and a daughter. Charley is relentless with them about their "chores." He's an alcoholic, and it seems to make him a perfectionist. He's tall, balding, handsome in that Harry Smith way. Allis is small, tidy, worried. There are tapes of screaming rages involving Charley and his sons; their daughter, Morgan's mother, not much heard, leaves home at sixteen, following the advice in Philip Larkin's famous poem

367

about destructive families, "This Be the Verse": "Get out as early as you can."

The first line of that poem certainly describes the marriage of Charley and Allis. All four children are angry, miserable, neurotic in various ways. The family falls into the clutches of a psychiatrist named Lenn, who wrongly sends one son to a mental institution, diagnoses Charley as "the worst inferiority complex I've ever seen," and strews misery and anguish as freely as his advice. What we learn of the children later in life is that three of them, anyway, grew up into apparently happy married adults with children.

It was the family itself that was toxic. They needed to get out. Charley is hated by the children, and Allis thinks of herself as not meant for such a life. She and Charley never have a real talk about "open marriage," but it certainly suits good-time Charley, a man without a single moment of introspection in this film.

Home movies and now the ubiquitous videotape mean that everyday lives are now recorded with a detail not dreamed of earlier. We will never hear all of Allis's recordings and see all her images, but this distillation by Morgan Dews might have been what she had in mind when she stored away those records of pain. They act as her justification of her life, her explanation of the misery of her children. I watched this film horrified and fascinated. There is such raw pain here. Allis might have read or seen *Revolutionary Road* and by comparison envied that marriage.

There are things you will see here that will lead you to some conclusions. I will leave you to them. All I can say is that I believe the daughter's guess at the end is correct. We learn that after Charley died, Allis moved to her own small cottage in Vermont and "continued her volunteer work." She lived another thirty years. She never mentioned Charley again.

My Life in Ruins ★ ½

PG-13, 95 m., 2009

Nia Vardalos (Georgia), Richard Dreyfuss (Irv), Alexis Georgoulis (Poupi), Rachel Dratch (Kim), Maria Adanez (Lena), Maria Botto (Lala), Harland Williams (Big Al), Alistair McGowan (Nico). Directed by Donald Petrie and produced

by Michelle Chydzik Sowa and Nathalie Marciano. Screenplay by Mike Reiss.

Nia Vardalos plays most of *My Life in Ruins* with a fixed toothpaste smile, which is no wonder because her acting in the film feels uncomfortably close to her posing for a portrait. Rarely has a film centered on a character so superficial and unconvincing, played with such unrelenting sameness. I didn't hate it so much as feel sorry for it.

Vardalos plays Georgia, an American tour guide in Athens, in rivalry with Nico (Alistair McGowan), who always gets assigned the new bus with the well-behaved Canadians, while our girl gets the beater containing a group of walking human clichés who were old when *If It's Tuesday, This Must Be Belgium* was new. You got your loud Yankees, your boozy Aussies, your prowling Spanish divorcees, your ancient Brits, and, of course, your obligatory Jewish widower who is laughing on the outside and mourning on the inside.

These characters are teeth-gratingly broad and obvious, apart from Richard Dreyfuss, who brings life, maybe too much life, to Irv, who tells bad jokes even though he is old enough to have learned funnier ones. To him, I recommend the delightful Web site www.oldjewstellingjokes.com, where every single old Jew is funnier than he is. Irv, of course, eventually reveals a sentimental side and does something else that is required in the Screenplay Recycling Handbook. (Interested in reading it? Send in five dollars. I won't mail it to you, but thanks for the money. Rim shot, please.)

The central question posed by *My Life in Ruins* is, what happened to the Nia Vardalos who wrote and starred in *My Big Fat Greek Wedding*? She was lovable, earthy, sassy, plumper, more of a mess, and the movie grossed more than $300 million. Here she's thinner, blonder, better dressed, looks younger, and knows it. She's like the winner of a beauty makeover at a Hollywood studio. She has that "Don't touch my makeup!" look. And if anyone in Hollywood has whiter, straighter, more gleaming teeth, we'll never know it, because like most people they'll usually keep their lips closed.

To speculate on people's motives is risky

and can be unfair. Let me gently suggest that when Nia Vardalos made *My Big Fat Greek Wedding* she was an unlikely, saucy movie star who didn't take herself seriously. She was also an incomparably better screenwriter than Mike Reiss, the autopilot sitcom veteran who cobbled together this lousy script.

Now she is rich, famous, and perhaps taking herself seriously after being worked over for one too many magazine covers. She has also made the mistake of allowing herself to be found in one of those situations that only happen in trashy romance novels. The driver of her bus is a surly Greek named Poupi (Alexis Georgoulis), who has a beard that looks inspired by the Smith Brothers. After he shaves it off, he emerges as an improbably handsome, long-locked Adonis of the sort that customarily only dates older women if he has reason to think they are rich. This romance is embarrassing.

There is, in short, nothing I liked about *My Life in Ruins*, except some of the ruins. The tourists are even allowed to consult the Oracle at Delphi. That scene reminded me of when Chaz and I visited an ancient temple at Ise in Japan. Outside the gates, monks sat on platforms inscribing scrolls. "You may ask anything you want," our guide told us. "Will there be peace in our time?" asked Chaz. The monk gave a look at our guide. Our guide said, "Ah . . . I think maybe better question be more like, 'How many monks live in temple?'"

Note: "Poupi" is pronounced "poopy." That would never get past the editor of a romance novel.

My Name Is Bruce ★ ★
R, 86 m., 2008

Bruce Campbell (Bruce Campbell), James J. Peck (Guan-Di), Taylor Sharpe (Jeff), Ted Raimi (Mills Toddner), Grace Thorsen (Kelly). Directed by Bruce Campbell and produced by Campbell and Mike Richardson. Screenplay by Mark Verheiden.

Many's the actor who has brooded in his trailer and pondered: "Maybe I could direct better than this idiot." With Bruce Campbell that is often true, with the exceptions of such directors as Sam Raimi, with whom he has worked eleven times, and the Coen brothers (four). You know you're in trouble when your top-user-rated title at IMDb is a video game, although the gameboys are such generous raters they place the game *Evil Dead: Regeneration* right above the film *Fargo*.

In that Coen brothers' film, Campbell played an uncredited soap opera actor on a TV set in the background, but that was as a favor, because he and the Coens have long been friends. They met him on *Crimewave* (1985), their first writing credit, which was directed by, no surprise, Sam Raimi. Campbell has appeared in horror and exploitation movies without number, has always provided what the role requires, has inspired fondness in the genre's fans, and has been in some movies where I've been the lonely voice protesting they are good, such as *Congo* (1995), which featured a martini-sipping gorilla, volcanoes, earthquakes, and the always economical scene in which an actor looks over his shoulder, sees something, screams, and the screen turns black.

Also please consult my review of *Bubba Ho-Tep* (2002). In that film, which is set in recent times, Elvis and JFK did not die but are roommates in an East Texas nursing home. Campbell plays Elvis. Ossie Davis plays JFK. "But you're black," Elvis observes. JFK nods: "After Lyndon Johnson faked my assassination, they dyed me."

You see that Bruce Campbell often returns value for money. And in that spirit, I welcome his first work as a director since *The Man with the Screaming Brain* (2005). He plays himself in a lampoon of his career, his movies, his genres, and everything else he stands for. Maybe it's only "one-note insider navel-gazing," writes one of its critics, but if the navel has been there, done that, and had unspeakable horrors wreaked onto it, the navel has paid its dues.

The plot involves a movie star helping to save Gold Lick, Oregon, from an ancient Chinese god named Guan-Di, played by James J. Peck, although that could be anybody inside the suit. I know Dave Prowse, who wore the Darth Vader suit, and a lot of good that did him. Guan-Di, the god of war, for reasons best known unto himself, inhabits a falling-apart shanty-board crypt in the decrepit local cemetery that looks like the set for a grade-school production of a haunted graveyard movie. His eyes are flaming coals. Hard to see the evolutionary advantage there.

Campbell depicts himself as a drunken slob behind on his alimony, a vain, egotistical monster, a phony, a poseur, and a man in flight from his most recent movie, *Cave Alien 2*. This movie would make the perfect lower half of a Bruce Campbell double feature. If you don't already know who Bruce Campbell is, it will set you searching for other Bruce Campbell films on the theory that they can't all be like this. Start with *Evil Dead II*, is my advice. Not to forget *Bubba Ho-Tep*. In fact, start with them before *My Name Is Bruce*, which is low midrange in the Master's ouvre.

My One and Only ★★★ ½

PG-13, 107 m., 2009

Renee Zellweger (Ann Devereaux), Logan Lerman (George Devereaux), Kevin Bacon (Dan Devereaux), Eric McCormack (Charlie), Chris Noth (Dr. Harlan Williams), Mark Rendall (Robbie), Nick Stahl (Bud), Steven Weber (Wallace McAllister), David Koechner (Bill Massey), Robin Weigert (Hope). Directed by Richard Loncraine and produced by Aaron Ryder and Norton Herrick. Screenplay by Charlie Peters.

I have no idea how closely *My One and Only* follows the facts of George Hamilton's teenage years, but it tells a story that goes a good way toward explaining his years of celebrity and his lifelong attachment to his mother. It's also an appealing comedy, a road movie set in the 1950s and starring Renee Zellweger as his mom, the irrepressible Ann Devereaux.

She's a blond Southern belle, married to Dan, a bandleader (Kevin Bacon) who loves her, after his fashion, but is a compulsive womanizer. Finding him in bed with one woman too many, Ann leaves him, taking her two sons: George (Logan Lerman) and Robbie (Mark Rendall), half brothers from her two marriages. In a sky-blue Cadillac convertible, they set off on an odyssey to find Ann a new husband. That's the only way she can imagine to support them.

Ann is fortyish, comely, attractive to men, but no longer this year's model. Their journeys take them to a series of her old beaus, in Boston, Pittsburgh, and St. Louis, and these hunting expeditions are seen through George's dubious eyes. One is an ex-military sadist, one a playboy, all not suitable candidates. She tries actually working, but being a waitress is beyond her, and then she apparently strikes pay dirt with a proposal from a man whose family owns a big house-paint business.

The paint tycoon is entertaining. As played by the invaluable David Koechner, he sits beside George on a pier and confides that Ann has asked him to have a man-to-man talk with him about women. He explains to the boy that women have a problem with body temperature. They're always too warm or too cool. On a date, always bring along a sweater you can lend them. End of advice. I can't say why, but I suspect George Hamilton really was told this at one time or another in his youth.

Hamilton is the film's executive producer, and although the screenplay is by Charlie Peters, Hamilton must have had substantial input at the story level. His mother was really named Ann. His father was really a bandleader. He had a brother something like the one here. He did get into movies somewhat improbably. The one detail in the film I doubt is that he ever said, "There's too much sun here in L.A. It's not depressing enough."

This is essentially Renee Zellweger's picture, and she glows in it. We've seen the type before, but she's able, beneath Ann's pluck, to suggest her sadness and the love she had for her boys. Yes, she was a lousy mother, as George assures her, but she had a good heart and was determined to provide for them. It struck some as notable that Hamilton remained so close to his mother, even living with her, but this film is a worthy memory, including both her ditzyness and her bravery.

The director, Richard Loncraine, achieves a seemingly effortless early-1950s look, down to the details of Ann's wardrobe and hair, which today look more like costuming than fashion: No matter what she goes through and how much she endures, she's always well turned out. The relationship between her two sons is a little enigmatic, considering Robbie is presented as gay. They never refer to that, except very discreetly. Maybe it was like that in the 1950s.

Basing psychological speculation on a biopic is notoriously risky. All I can say is that after seeing *My One and Only*, Hamilton's persona somehow clicked into place for me. He had the example of a woman who was concerned with making a good impression. I met him only once, in 1971 when he had starred in *Evel Knievel*, and I still recall how nice he seemed.

My Sister's Keeper ★ ★ ★ ½
PG-13, 108 m., 2009

Cameron Diaz (Sara Fitzgerald), Abigail Breslin (Anna Fitzgerald), Alec Baldwin (Campbell Alexander), Jason Patric (Brian Fitzgerald), Sofia Vassilieva (Kate Fitzgerald), Joan Cusack (Judge De Salvo), Heather Wahlquist (Aunt Kelly), Thomas Dekker (Taylor Ambrose), Evan Ellingson (Jesse Fitzgerald), David Thornton (Dr. Chance). Directed by Nick Cassavetes and produced by Mark Johnson, Chuck Pacheco, and Scott L. Goldman. Screenplay by Cassavetes and Jeremy Leven, based on the novel by Jodi Picoult.

My Sister's Keeper is an immediate audience grabber, as we learn that an eleven-year-old girl was genetically designed as a source of spare parts for her dying sixteen-year-old sister. Yes, it's possible: In vitro fertilization ensured a perfect match. And no, this isn't science fiction like Kazuo Ishiguro's novel *Never Let Me Go*, with its cloned human replacements. It's just a little girl subjected to major procedures almost from birth to help her sister live.

So far they have succeeded, and Kate (Sofia Vassilieva) is alive long after her predicted death at five. Her sister, Anna (Abigail Breslin), has donated blood, bone marrow, and stem cells, and now is being told she must donate one of her kidneys. She's had it. It dismays her to know she was conceived as an organ bank, and she wants her chance at a normal life without round trips to the operating room. She may be young but she's bright and determined, and she decides to file a lawsuit against her parents for "medical emancipation."

Hers would be a model family if not for her sister's death sentence. Her mom, Sara (Cameron Diaz), is a successful Los Angeles lawyer. Her dad, Brian (Jason Patric), is a fire chief. Her older brother, Jesse (Evan Ellingson),

is a good student but feels ignored. Anna and Kate love each other dearly. But always there is Sara's relentless drive to keep her daughter alive. Like some successful attorneys, she also wants to win every case in her private life.

Anna goes to an attorney who boasts a 90 percent success rate in his TV ads. This is the polished Campbell Alexander (Alec Baldwin), who drives a Bentley convertible and is known for bringing his dog into courtrooms. Anna offers her savings of seven hundred dollars. This is far under his fee, but he listens and accepts the case.

Although *My Sister's Keeper*, based on the best-seller by Jodi Picoult, is an effective tear-jerker, if you think about it, it's something else. The movie never says so, but it's a practical parable about the debate between pro-choice and pro-life. If you're pro-life, you would require Anna to donate her kidney, although there is a chance she could die and her sister doesn't have a good prognosis. If you're pro-choice, you would support Anna's lawsuit.

The mother is appalled by the lawsuit. Keeping her daughter alive has been a triumph for her all of these years. The father is shocked, too, but calmer and more objective. He can see Anna's point. She has her own life to live, and her own love to demand. The performances don't go over the top, although they can see it from where they're standing. Cameron Diaz has the greatest challenge because her determination is so fierce, but she makes her love evident—more for Kate, it must be said, than for Anna and Jesse. Jason Patric, too, rarely gets sympathetic roles, and he embodies thoughtfulness and tenderness. The young actors never step wrong.

Nicely nuanced, too, is Alec Baldwin as the hotshot attorney. He doesn't have a posh office, and his photo is plastered on billboards, but he's not a fly-by-night, and he has a heart. He also has a sense of humor; in several supporting roles recently, he has stepped in with lines enriched by unexpected flashes of wit. Also navigating around clichés here is Joan Cusack as the judge. She takes that impossible case and convinces us she handles it about as well as possible. The enigma is the underdeveloped brother, Jesse, who runs away for three days.

We're never told what that was all about; in the film, it serves merely to distract us when

Taylor (Thomas Dekker), Kate's fellow cancer patient, seems to disappear. The hospital romance between Taylor and Kate is one of the best elements of the movie, tender, tactful, and very touching.

The screenplay by Jeremy Leven and Nick Cassavetes (who directed) is admirable in trusting us to figure things out. Because it's obvious in one beautiful scene that Kate is wearing a wig, they didn't ask, "Will the audience understand that?" and add a jarring line. Routine courtroom theatrics are avoided. We learn of the verdict in the best way. We can see the wheels turning, but they turn well. ☞

My Son, My Son, What Have Ye Done ★★★
NO MPAA RATING, 87 m., 2010

Willem Dafoe (Detective Hank Havenhurst), Michael Shannon (Brad McCullum), Chloe Sevigny (Ingrid), Michael Pena (Detective Vargas), Udo Kier (Lee Meyers), Brad Dourif (Uncle Ted), Grace Zabriskie (Mrs. McCullum), Irma P. Hall (Mrs. Roberts), Loretta Devine (Miss Roberts), Verne Troyer (Midget). Directed by Werner Herzog and produced by Eric Bassett. Screenplay by Herzog and Herbert Golder.

Werner Herzog's *My Son, My Son, What Have Ye Done* is a splendid example of a movie not on autopilot. I bore my readers by complaining about how bored I am by formula movies that recycle the same moronic elements. Now here is a film where Udo Kier has his eyeglasses snatched from his pocket by an ostrich, sees them yanked from the ostrich's throat by a farmhand, gets them back all covered with ostrich mucus, and tells the ostrich, "Don't you do that again!"

Meanwhile, there is talk about how the racist ostrich farmer once raised a chicken as big as, I think, forty ordinary birds. What did he do with it? "Ate it. Sooner pluck one than forty." Knowing as I do that Herzog hates chickens with a passion beyond all reason, I flashed back to an earlier scene in which the film's protagonist talks with his scrawny pet flamingoes. Is a theme emerging here? And the flamingo who regards the camera with a dubious look: Is it inspired by the staring iguana in Herzog's *Bad Lieutenant*?

For me it hardly matters if a Herzog film provides conventional movie pleasures. Many of them do. *Bad Lieutenant*, for example. *My Son, My Son, What Have Ye Done*, on the other hand, confounds all convention and denies the usual expected pleasures, providing instead the delight of watching Herzog feed the police hostage formula into the Mixmaster of his imagination. It's as if he began with the outline of a stunningly routine police procedural and said to hell with it, I'm going to hang my whimsy on this clothesline.

He casts Willem Dafoe as his hero, a homicide detective named Hank Havenhurst. Dafoe is known for his willingness to embrace projects by directors who work on the edge. He is an excellent actor, and splendid here at creating a cop who conducts his job with tunnel vision and few expected human emotions. It is difficult to conceive of a police officer showing a more measured response to a madman ostrich farmer.

His case involves a man named Brad McCullum, played by Michael Shannon as a man with an alarming stare beneath a lowering brow. He kills his mother with a wicked antique sword as she sits having coffee with two neighbors. He likes to repeat "razzle dazzle," which reminded me of "helter skelter," and yes, the movie is "inspired by a true story." His mother (Grace Zabriskie) is a woman who is so nice she could, possibly, inspire murder, especially in a son who has undergone life-altering experiences in the Peruvian rain forest, as this one has—and why, you ask? For the excellent reason, I suspect, that Herzog could with great difficulty revisit the Urubamba River in Peru, where he shot much of *Aguirre, the Wrath of God* (1972) and part of *Fitzcarraldo* (1982). Perhaps whenever he encounters an actor with alarming eyes, like Klaus Kinski or Shannon, he thinks, "I will put him to the test of the Urubamba River!"

Detective Havenhurst takes over a command center in front of the house where Brad is said to be holding two hostages (never seen), and interviews Brad's fiancée, Ingrid (Chloe Sevigny), and a theater director, Lee Meyers (Udo Kier). Both tell him stories that inspire flashbacks. Indeed, most of the film involves flashbacks leading up to the moment when Brad slashed his mother. Ingrid is played by

Sevigny as a dim, sweet young woman lacking all insight and instinct for self-protection, and Meyers is played by Kier as a man who is incredibly patient with Brad during rehearsals for the Greek tragedy *Elektra*. That's the one where the son slays his mother.

The memories of Lee Meyers inspire the field trip to the ostrich farm run by Uncle Ted (Brad Dourif). If you've been keeping track, the film's cast includes almost *only* cult actors often involved with cult directors: Dafoe, Shannon, Sevigny, Kier, Dourif, Zabriskie, and I haven't even mentioned Oscar nominee Irma P. Hall and Verne Troyer. Havenhurst's partner is played by Michael Pena, who is not a cult actor but plays one in this movie. Little jest. For that matter, the film's producer is David Lynch, one of the few producers who might think it made perfect sense that a cop drama set in San Diego would require location filming on the Urubamba River.

There is a scene in this movie that involves men who appear to be yurt dwellers from Mongolia, one with spectacular eyebrow hairs. I confess I may have had a momentary attention lapse, but I can't remember what they had to do with the plot. Still, I'll not soon forget those eyebrows, which is more than I can say for most scenes at the 60 percent mark in most cop movies. I am also grateful for two very long shots, one involving Grace Zabriskie and the other Verne Troyer, in which they look at the camera for thirty or forty seconds while flanked with Shannon and another one of the actors. These look like freeze frames, but you can see the actors moving just a little. What do these shots represent? Why, the director's impatience with convention, that's what.

Herzog is endlessly fascinating and always surprising. I have now performed an excellent job of describing the movie. Can you sense why I enjoyed it? If you don't like it, you won't be able to claim I misled you. I rode on an ostrich once. Halfway between Oudtshoorn and the Cango Caves, it was.

The Mysteries of Pittsburgh ★ ★
R, 95 m., 2009

Jon Foster (Art Bechstein), Peter Sarsgaard (Cleveland), Sienna Miller (Jane), Nick Nolte (Joe Bechstein), Mena Suvari (Phlox). Directed by Rawson Marshall Thurber and produced by Michael London and Jason Ajax Mercer. Screenplay by Thurber, based on the novel by Michael Chabon.

After that summer, nothing would ever be the same again. Where have we seen that movie before? Most recently in *Adventureland*, another movie set in 1980s Pittsburgh. If you think about it, after every summer nothing will ever be the same again. But *The Mysteries of Pittsburgh* has an unusually busy summer, in which a hero who is a blank slate gets scrawled all over with experiences.

The movie is all the more artificial because it has been made with great, almost painful, earnestness. It takes a plot that would have been at home in a 1930s Warner Bros. social melodrama, adds sexuality and a little nudity, and Bob's your uncle. It's based on a 1988 novel by Michael Chabon, still much read and valued, but to call it "inspired by" would be a stretcher. Hardly a thing happens that doesn't seem laid on to hurry along the hero's coming of age.

That hero is Art (Jon Foster), whose voiceover narration does not shy away from the obvious. He is the son of Joe Bechstein (Nick Nolte), a mobster of such stature that he has his own FBI shadows. Joe would like Art to follow him into the family business, but Art wants nothing to do with it. He'll become a broker, which in the 1980s was an honest trade. For the summer he takes a job at a vast surplus bookstore, where the minimum wage allows him to lose himself.

Life comes racing after him. Phlox (Mena Suvari), the store manager, pages him on the intercom for sex on demand in the stock room. At a party, he meets the winsome blonde Jane (Sienna Miller), whose boyfriend, Cleveland (Peter Sarsgaard), is both friendly and disturbing. These two mess with his mind: Jane although she doesn't mean to, Cleveland because he is a sadistic emotional manipulator. The first little "joke" Cleveland plays on Art should have sent Art running as far from Cleveland as he could get. But Art is pathologically passive; the summer happens to him, but he can't be said to happen to it.

Complications from countless other movies. The fraught relationship with his father. Phlox's possessiveness. Jane's ambivalence.

Cleveland's odd promotion of an emotional, if not at first sexual, ménage à trois. Then a crime-driven climax that arrives out of thin air and involves a very small world indeed. Finally a bittersweet closing narration that seems to tie up loose ends but really answers nothing about Art except whether he still lives in Pittsburgh.

Complicating this are some well-developed performances for such an underdeveloped screenplay. Peter Sarsgaard is intriguing as the seductive, profoundly screwy Cleveland. Mena Suvari is pitch-perfect in a finally thankless role. Nick Nolte, in expensive suits, hair slicked back, takes no nonsense as the hard mob boss. Sienna Miller is sweet but is never allowed to make clear why she is attracted to either man. Jon Foster, as the feckless protagonist, is the latest in a long line of manipulated male ingénues going back beyond Benjamin in *The Graduate*. This is a guy who hardly deserves the attention of the other characters in the story, with his closed-in, inarticulate, low self-esteem.

At the end, Art is supposed to have learned lessons in life from his "last summer before life begins." The melancholy likelihood is, however, that he learned nothing except the punch line to the old joke, "Don't do that no more." At summer's end he seems poised to graduate directly into the Lonely Crowd. There is an old word: nebbish. It is still a good word.

My Winnipeg ★ ★ ★
NO MPAA RATING, 80 m., 2008

Darcy Fehr (Guy Maddin), Ann Savage (Mother), Amy Stewart (Janet Maddin), Louis Negin (Mayor Cornish), Brendan Cade (Cameron Maddin), Wesley Cade (Ross Maddin), Fred Dunsmore (Himself). Directed by Guy Maddin and produced by Jody Shapiro and Phyllis Laing. Screenplay by Maddin.

If you love movies in the very sinews of your imagination, you should experience the work of Guy Maddin. If you have never heard of him, I am not surprised. Now you have. A new Maddin movie doesn't play in every multiplex or city or state. If you hear of one opening, seize the day. Or search where obscure films can be found. You will be plunged into the mind of a man who thinks in the images of old silent films, disreputable documentaries, movies that never were, from eras beyond comprehension. His imagination frees the lurid possibilities of the banal. He rewrites history; when that fails, he creates it.

First, a paragraph of dry fact. Maddin makes films that use the dated editing devices of old movies: Iris shots, breathless titles, shock cutting, staged poses, melodramatic acting, recycled footage, camera angles not merely dramatic but startling. He uses these devices to tell stories that begin with the improbable and march boldly into the inconceivable. My paragraph is ending now, and you have seen how difficult it is to describe his work. I will end with two more statements: (1) Shot for shot, Maddin can be as surprising and delightful as any filmmaker has ever been, and (2) he is an acquired taste, but please, sir, may I have some more?

Consider his film *My Winnipeg*. The city fathers commissioned it as a documentary, to be made by "the mad poet of Manitoba," as a Canadian magazine termed him. Maddin has never left his hometown, although, judging by this film, it has left him. It has abandoned its retail landmarks, its sports traditions, and even the daily local soap opera, *Ledge Man*, which ran for fifty years and starred Maddin's mother. As every episode opened, a man was found standing on a ledge and threatening to jump, and Maddin's mother talked him out of it.

Is that true? It's as true as anything else in the film. My friend Tony Scott of the *New York Times* thought he should check out some of the facts in *My Winnipeg* but decided not to. Why should he doubt the film? I certainly believe that after a stable fire at the racetrack, terrified horses stampeded into a freezing river and were frozen into place—their heads rising from the ice for the rest of the winter, for skaters to picnic on. I believe there are two taxi companies, one serving streets, and the other back lanes shown on no map. I believe Guy Maddin himself was born in the Winnipeg Arena during a game, nursed in the women's dressing room, and brought back a few days later for his first hockey match.

I also believe this because it is shown in the film: After Manitoba joined the hated (American-controlled) National Hockey League, the arena was enlarged to hold larger crowds.

When the tragic decision was made to destroy the beloved arena by demolition, only the new parts collapsed, leaving the bones of the old arena still standing. "Demolition is one of our few growth industries," he says, acting as his own narrator.

Maddin was raised in this city, which he says has "ten times the sleepwalking rate" of any other. His childhood occurred in a house built as three white squares, one for his mother's beauty parlor, one for his aunt's family, one for his own. The scents of the parlor drifted up into his bedroom, and "every word of conversation swirled up out of that gynocracy." He attended a convent school named the Academy of the Super Vixens, ruled by "ever-opiating nuns."

Many of these facts are glimpsed through the windows of a train that seems headed out of town but never gets there. The narration is hallucinatory: "Old dreamy addresses, ad-dresses, addresses, dreamy river forks. We see maps of the rivers fading into the fork of a woman's loin and back again." We are told that shadow-rivers flow beneath the visible ones. That the local madams were highly respected and streets were named after them and their brothels. That white-bearded Mayor Cornish (Louis Negin) personally judged the city's annual Golden Boy pageant, measuring biceps and thighs before scandal forced him out: too many Golden Boys on the city payroll!

I try to evoke, but I have failed! Failed! Disaster! I have tried to evoke the opiations of Guy Maddin, only to discover that the mother in the film is played by Ann Savage, star of *Detour*. Yes! A film in the Great Movies Collection of my Web site! Detour! Rocky road ahead! Savage! Maddin's father lies in state under a rug in the living room! Dead—not forgotten. Savage stepping around him! Watch your step. Savage! See this film!

N

New in Town ★ ★
PG, 96 m., 2009

Renee Zellweger (Lucy Hill), Harry Connick Jr. (Ted Mitchell), J. K. Simmons (Stu Kopenhafer), Siobhan Fallon Hogan (Blanche Gunderson), Frances Conroy (Trudy Van Uuden). Directed by Jonas Elmer and produced by Paul Brooks, Darryl Taja, Tracey Edmonds, and Peter Safran. Screenplay by Kenneth Rance and C. Jay Cox.

We open on a gathering of the Scrappers Club, four women around a kitchen table pasting things into scrapbooks. The moment we hear one of them talking, we're not too surprised to find her name is Blanche Gunderson. Her sister Marge, the trooper, must have been the ambitious one. Not that Blanche isn't, just that she's relentlessly nice.

So are most of the folks in the small town of New Ulm, Minnesota, which is so cold in the winter that scrapping warms you up. Old Ulm (I know you were wondering) is the town on the Danube where Einstein was born. To this frigid outpost flies Lucy Hill, a high-powered exec from Miami, whose mission is to downsize the local food products plant more or less out of existence.

Lucy is the cute-as-a-button Renee Zellweger, so we know she's only kidding when she pretends to be a heartless rhymes-with-witch who hammers around on her stiletto heels and won't smile. That doesn't scare Blanche (Siobhan Fallon Hogan), Lucy's assistant, who invites her home for dinner ("We're only havin' meat loaf"). So uncannily does her accent resemble Marge in *Fargo* that I was trying to remember where I had heard it recently, doncha know?

The extra man at Blanche's table turns out to be Ted Mitchell (Harry Connick Jr.), the widowed dad of a thirteen-year-old girl, whom Blanche obviously thinks would be a great match for Lucy. That Ted, the union guy at the plant Lucy plans to downsize, is perhaps not a perfect match never even occurs to Blanche, who like all Minnesotans and most Dakotans, is just plain nice. I mean that. I've been to Fargo. You should go sometime.

Ted doesn't seem nice at first, but then, jeez, he's originally from out of town, y'know. Ted and Lucy get in such a fight at the table that they both stalk out, which means they miss out on Blanche's famous tapioca pudding. Glossary Rule: Whenever a recipe is much discussed in the first act, it will be tasted in the third.

So firmly do we believe Lucy is visiting relatives of the *Fargo* cast that it's a surprise to learn *New in Town* was actually filmed in Winnipeg, which here looks nothing like the glittering metropolis in Guy Maddin's masterpiece. New Ulm consists of some houses, a VFW hall with a Friday fish fry, the food plant, and not a whole lot else except snow. But the people are friendly, hardworking, and proud of their plant, and soon Lucy softens, begins to like them, and reveals she was Renee Zellweger all along.

Because this is a romcom with no ambition in the direction of originality, Lucy is single, and Ted is the only eligible unmarried man in the cast, so do the math. The only remaining question is whether Lucy can save the plant, if you consider that much of a question. Am I giving too much away? This is the kind of movie that gives itself away. I've used that line before.

The real question is, do you like this sort of romcom? It's a fair example of its type, not good, but competent. The plant workers seem to function like the chorus in an opera, shutting down the line for Lucy's arias from a catwalk and moving as a unit with foreman Stu Kopenhafer (J. K. Simmons) always in the front. Simmons has grown a bushy beard and is wearing a fat suit (I hope), so you may not recognize him as Juno's dad. Let the bushy beard be a lesson: A bushy beard is the enemy of an actor's face unless he is playing Santa or attacking with a chainsaw.

The only question remaining after *New in Town* is, how come there's never a movie where a small-town girl leaves the snarly, greedy, job-ladder-climbing people behind and moves to the big city, where she is embraced by friendly folks, fed meat loaf and tapioca, and fixed up with Harry Connick Jr.?

The New Year Parade ★★★

NO MPAA RATING, 87 m., 2009

Greg Lyons (Jack), Jennifer Welsh (Kat), Andrew Conway (Mike McMonogul), MaryAnn McDonald (Mike's Wife), Tobias Segal (Curtis), Irene Longshore (Jack's Girlfriend), Paul Blackway (Kat's B.F.), and the South Philadelphia String Band. Directed by Tom Quinn and produced by Quinn and Steve Beal. Screenplay by Quinn.

I'm pretty much paraded out. The high point for me was the Fourth of July twenty-five years ago in Three Oaks, Michigan, where Shriners performed an intricate choreography while riding their power mowers. But I now believe the Philadelphia Mummers Parade must be worth attending every year. The marchers aren't hauling ads for Pepsi or anchoring giant inflated Ronald McDonald balloons. They march because of fierce generational pride.

This I learn from Tom Quinn's movie *The New Year Parade*, an appealing indie feature that weaves together the traditions of the parade and an Irish-American family. If that sounds contrived, it's not; the two flow together in a convincing way. The film, which won top prizes at Slamdance 2009 and (understandably) Philadelphia, introduces us to the McMonogul family, who have been part of the South Philadelphia String Band for three generations.

Mike (Andrew Conway), the father, is captain of the band. He discovers his wife (MaryAnn McDonald) has cheated on him and moves out in a rage. There are subtle hints that she may have had her reasons. Their children, Jack (Greg Lyons), in his early twenties, and Kat (Jennifer Welsh), about sixteen, are devastated—Kat especially, but she decides to stay with her mom. Jack accuses Mike of choosing to destroy the family instead of forgiving his mom, and he contemplates the unspeakable: leaving the band and enlisting with its traditional arch-competitors.

Quinn photographed his film over four years, and yet as his own editor has mastered what must have been hours of material into a story so convincingly embedded in the band and parade that it would have been impossi-

ble to create just for a film. His characters all seem to be much of that world; whether his actors are, I can't say. But we see them rehearsing, marching, hanging out, *caring* about the band. For Jack to join the opposition is the most hurtful thing he could do to his father.

On top of that is the enormity of the parade itself. I vaguely imagined it as a bunch of people dressed up funny and playing "Yankee Doodle." The costumes and props cannot even be described. The year's work and no doubt the money involved is almost unimaginable. Yet Quinn does not make the plot rest on that weary old device of who wins the big parade/game/match/bout/election. This is not about winning but about striving.

The New Year Parade is a tad frayed around the edges, no doubt because of the scope of the reality presented. But the story holds strong, the indie approach is more moving than a polished production plugging in big stars, and this is the sort of film a civic resource such as Facets exists to show.

New York, I Love You ★★★

R, 104 m., 2009

With Hayden Christensen, Andy Garcia, Rachel Bilson, Natalie Portman, Irrfan Khan, Orlando Bloom, Christina Ricci, Maggie Q, Ethan Hawke, Chris Cooper, Robin Wright Penn, Anton Yelchin, James Caan, Olivia Thirlby, Blake Lively, Drea de Matteo, Bradley Cooper, Julie Christie, John Hurt, Shia LaBeouf, Taylor Geare, Carlos Acosta, Jacinda Barrett, Ugur Yucel, Shu Qi, Burt Young, Eli Wallach, and Cloris Leachman. Directed by Jiang Wen, Mira Nair, Shunji Iwai, Yvan Attal, Brett Ratner, Allen Hughes, Shekhar Kapur, Natalie Portman, Fatih Akin, Joshua Marston, and Randy Balsmeyer, and produced by Emmanuel Benbihy and Marina Grasic.

The rules: No more than two days' shooting time. One week of editing. An eight-minute time limit. Ten directors, and one more to consider the ten short films and create transitions. *New York, I Love You* is the second installment in an ambitious project that began with *Paris, Je T'aime* (2006), an anthology with thirteen directors. Rio is said to be next.

Inevitably, the film is a jumble sale, but you

can make some nice discoveries. It's not one of those films where all the separate characters come together at the end in a miraculous co-incidence, although a few people do turn up, still as themselves, in one another's segments.

I suspect the title isn't intended as a simple declaration, but should be pronounced in a wondering tone, with a wry shake of the head, as in, "Oh, you kid." The film assembles a collection of colorful characters, who find that eight minutes is quite enough to make an impression, as so many New Yorkers would agree.

The very first segment, directed by Jiang Wen and starring Hayden Christensen, Andy Garcia, and Rachel Bilson, begins the film with a deft touch worthy of O. Henry, the master of New York short stories. Bilson and Christiansen meet in a bar, where he finds a cell phone she left behind. He opens a seductive conversation, interrupted by Garcia as her boyfriend, who immediately reads the other guy. The two of them elevate their confrontation to a level of sly expertise, in a way that is rather remarkable.

Another O. Henry twist is in Yvan Attal's segment starring Maggie Q and Ethan Hawke, as two people who meet outside a club. He is determined to seduce her, and launches an impressive improvisation involving his sexual skills and uses. This spiel could work one of two ways: as a serious come-on, or as a display of sheer wit. It fails at both, for reasons he entirely failed to suspect—although it must be admitted he does get her phone number.

In these days after my fractured hip, Joshua Marston's segment starring Eli Wallach and Cloris Leachman struck a chord. They've been married since forever, and now they're taking a walk at Coney Island. "Pick up your feet!" she tells him. "I *am* picking them up!" he says. "You're shuffling!" We intuit this conversation has been going on a very long time. My wife and I exchanged a little smile. Do you have any idea how hard it is to pick up your feet after you've broken your hip? It's not as if shufflers are merely lazy. And it's not as if this is the first time they've been lectured to pick up their feet.

Not all of the stories end in a surprise ending, thank goodness. Some are small slices of life. Mira Nair's segment stars Natalie Portman as a Hassidic woman in dealings with an Indian diamond merchant (Irrfan Khan). She's about to be married and confides that on that day she'll cut off all of her hair. Such a practice is not unknown in India, but the merchant now is simply a man admiring beautiful hair. And she . . . how does she feel?

Look at the cast and credits to form an idea of the directors and actors at work here. By its nature, *New York, I Love You* can't add up. It remains the sum of its parts. If one isn't working for you, wait a few minutes, here comes another one. New Yorkers, I love you.

Next Day Air ★ ★ ★
R, 90 m., 2009

Donald Faison (Leo), Mike Epps (Brody), Wood Harris (Guch), Omari Hardwick (Shavoo), Darius McCrary (Buddy), Yasmin Deliz (Chita), Mos Def (Eric), Emilio Rivera (Bodega), Cisco Reyes (Jesus), Debbie Allen (Ms. Jackson). Directed by Benny Boom and produced by Scott Aronson and Inny Clemons. Screenplay by Blair Cobbs.

Next Day Air is a bloody screwball comedy, a film of high spirits. It tells a complicated story with acute timing and clarity, and it gives us drug-dealing lowlifes who are almost poetic in their clockwork dialogue. By that I mean they not only use the words, they know the music.

Donald Faison stars in a cast of equals, as a pothead delivery man for the Next Day Air firm, who hurls around packages marked "Fragile!" as if he has never seen that word. Drifting in a cloud of weed, he delivers a package to the wrong apartment. Because it contains ten bricks of cocaine, this is a mistake, although perhaps not as fundamental as shipping it from L.A. to Philadelphia in the first place. FedEx and UPS have never lost anything of mine, but then, I've never shipped ten bricks of cocaine, which are likely to attract more attention than a signed copy of *Roger Ebert's Movie Yearbook 2009*.

The drugs are intended for a Latino couple (Cisco Reyes and Yasmin Deliz) and shipped by a cigar-smoking drug lord (Emilio Rivera) who is very annoyed when they are lost. He comes with his sidemen to pound some questions into Faison, who finally leads them to the apartment, where they find a gang of lousy bank robbers (Mike Epps, Wood

Harris, Omari Hardwick) who got the shipment, and three men who plan to buy the drugs from them.

This puts, I dunno, nine or ten heavily armed men in a room of limited size. One reason the cops don't respond to the eventual gunfire is that the room simply couldn't hold them. Since a shotgun and an automatic rifle are included with their handguns and one of those gourmet carving knife sets, I'm not sure why the MPAA's R rating mentions "some violence." In the MPAA's coded terminology, the word "some" means "violence, but nothing to get too worked up about." I guess that's fair; there are none of those 3-D X-ray shots showing a bullet inching its way in slow motion through human organ meats.

A plot this complex, with so many characters to keep alive, could easily go astray. Indeed, I could make no sense of this week's *Perfect Sleep* despite a fulsome narration. But the director, Benny Boom, a music video director, knows what he's doing and skillfully intercuts the story strands. The first-time screenplay by Blair Cobbs has a lot of dire dialogue, very sunny, and presents the world's most inept bank robbers along with its most inept delivery man and most imprudent drug lord.

Nice surprise: Debbie Allen plays the manager of the delivery company, and gets a big laugh; no, not just because the audience sees she's Debbie Allen.

Nick and Norah's Infinite Playlist ★ ★
PG-13, 90 m., 2008

Michael Cera (Nick), Kat Dennings (Norah), Aaron Yoo (Thom), Rafi Gavron (Dev), Ari Graynor (Caroline), Alexis Dziena (Tris), Jonathan Wright (Lethario), Zachary Booth (Gary), Jay Baruchel (Tal). Directed by Peter Sollett and produced by Kerry Kohansky, Andrew Miano, Chris Weitz, and Paul Weitz. Screenplay by Lorene Scafaria, based on the novel by Rachel Cohn and David Levithan.

There is one merciful element to *Nick and Norah's Infinite Playlist*. The playlist is not infinite. The movie trudges around the Lower East Side of Manhattan in pursuit of a group of seventeen-somethings who are desperately seeking a mysterious band named Where's Fluffy.

Clues are posted on the walls of toilet stalls, which are an unreliable source of information.

Nick and Norah have no relationship to the hero and heroine of *The Thin Man*, which I urgently advise you to watch instead of this film. That movie stars William Powell as a man who steadily drinks martinis and is never more than half-percolated. This one has a best friend character named Caroline (Ari Graynor) who drinks, I forget, I think it was banana daiquiris, and gets so drunk she ends up near Times Square in a toilet in the bus terminal, where she is fishing, not for Where's Fluffy clues, but for her gum, which fell into the toilet while she was vomiting. Didn't Ann Landers warn that this was one of the danger signals of alcoholism?

Nick and Norah are played by Michael Cera, best remembered as Juno's boyfriend, and Kat Dennings, best known for *The 40-Year-Old Virgin*, where she played anything but. They work well together, are appealing, and desperately require material as good as those films. Here they're not stupid; it's just that they're made to act stupidly. There's not much to recommend an all-night search through the dives of Manhattan for a lost friend who makes Britney Spears seem like a stay-at-home.

The two meet at a club, when Norah needs Nick to pose as her boyfriend to make her ex-boyfriend jealous. He is named Tal (Jay Baruchel). My first Chicago girlfriend was named Tal, which is Hebrew for "the morning dew." I don't think he knows that. So then, let's see, the plot requires an ex-girlfriend for Nick. This is Tris (Alexis Dziena), a blond vixen of the type that in most teeny movies is infinitely unattainable for nice kids like Nick.

Give Nick credit, he knows all about playlists. Tris has broken up with him as the movie opens, and he cuts many custom CDs for her in an attempt to win her back. These fall into the hands of Norah, who adores them, and What a Coincidence that Tris's ex is the very same guy she picked to play her pretend boyfriend. Ohmigosh. How Norah never previously saw Tris and Nick together is a good question since every character in this movie has built-in GPS equipment that allows them to stumble across any other character whenever the plot requires it.

I was relieved to observe that Nick doesn't drink as he pilots his battered Yugo around Manhattan. Ever notice how Yugos look like stretch Gremlins? People spot its bright yellow paint job and hail him, thinking it's a cab. This is impossible, since he doesn't have an illuminated sign for an Atlantic City casino on his roof.

Nick & Norah's Infinite Playlist lacks some of the idiocy of your average teenage romcom. But it doesn't bring much to the party. It sort of ambles along, with two nice people at the center of a human scavenger hunt. It's not much of a film, but it sort of gets you halfway there, like a Yugo.

Nick Nolte: No Exit ★★
NO MPAA RATING, 74 m., 2010

Featuring Nick Nolte, Jacqueline Bisset, Rosanna Arquette, Barbara Hershey, Ben Stiller, Paul Mazursky, Alan Rudolph, Powers Boothe, James Gammon, F. X. Feeney, Mike Medavoy. A documentary directed and produced by Thomas Thurman.

Nick Nolte is an interesting actor. Perhaps too interesting to appear in an independent documentary about himself. Perhaps too interesting to be interviewed by someone else. In *Nick Nolte: No Exit*, he interviews himself. The way he does this does what it can to assist a fairly pointless documentary.

Seated behind a silver laptop, well-groomed and wearing a big white Stetson, Nolte asks questions. Seated behind a black desktop computer and looking disheveled and squinty-eyed (well, all right, hung over), Nolte replies to them. It would be going too far to say he "answers" them.

Here is a fine actor who has made many very good films. On the wall behind him is the poster for Paul Schrader's *Affliction* (1997), the one he and James Coburn both won Oscar nominations for (Coburn won). His credits include *Hotel Rwanda*, *The Thin Red Line*, *Who'll Stop the Rain*, *North Dallas Forty*, *Lorenzo's Oil*, *Q&A*, and many others.

He mentions several of these films, and others, but doesn't really discuss them. He's proud of them, and of his work, as he should be. He admires Marlon Brando, who encour-

aged him. He has nothing to say about his private life. He mentions "the most famous celebrity mug shot," which he posed for after a DUI arrest in 2006, but doesn't go into details.

Nolte is intercut with sound bites about him by Nick Nolte, Jacqueline Bisset, Rosanna Arquette, Barbara Hershey, Ben Stiller, Paul Mazursky, Alan Rudolph, Powers Boothe, James Gammon, F. X. Feeney, Mike Medavoy. He's worked with them all, but doesn't go into detail. Most of them he doesn't mention.

Yet despite everything, the film has a certain fascination because Nolte is such a charismatic enigma. I've interviewed him several times, including at Telluride, which he attended in a bathrobe, and at Cannes, where we did a Q&A that was light on the A's. I enjoyed his company. Can't say that he confided many secrets.

Night at the Museum: Battle of the Smithsonian ★ ½
PG, 105 m., 2009

Ben Stiller (Larry Daley), Amy Adams (Amelia Earhart), Owen Wilson (Jedediah Smith), Hank Azaria (Kahmunrah/The Thinker), Christopher Guest (Ivan the Terrible), Alain Chabat (Napoleon Bonaparte), Ricky Gervais (Dr. McPhee), Steve Coogan (Octavius), Bill Hader (General Custer), Robin Williams (Teddy Roosevelt). Directed by Shawn Levy and produced by Levy, Chris Columbus, and Michael Barnathan. Screenplay by Robert Ben Garant and Thomas Lennon.

Don't trust me on this movie. It rubbed me the wrong way. I can understand, as an abstract concept, why some people would find it entertaining. It sure sounds intriguing: *Night at the Museum: Battle of the Smithsonian*. If that sounds like fun to you, don't listen to sourpuss here.

Oh, did I dislike this film. It made me squirmy. Its premise is lame, its plot relentlessly predictable, its characters with personalities that would distinguish picture books, its cost incalculable (well, $150 million). Watching historical figures enact the clichés identified with the most simplistic versions of their images, I found myself yet once again echoing the frequent cry of Gene Siskel: Why not just give us a documentary of the same actors having lunch?

One actor surpasses the material. That would be Amy Adams, as Amelia Earhart, because she makes Amelia sweet and lovable, although from what I gather, in real life that was not necessarily the case. I found myself looking forward to the upcoming biopic about Earhart with Hilary Swank. Over the closing credits, Bonnie Koloc could sing Red River Dave McEnery's "Amelia Earhart's Last Flight":

> Just a ship out on the ocean, a speck
>   against the sky,
> Amelia Earhart flying that sad day;
> With her partner, Captain Noonan, on
>   the second of July
> Her plane fell in the ocean far away.

(Chorus)

> There's a beautiful, beautiful field
> Far away in a land that is fair,
> Happy landings to you, Amelia Earhart,
> Farewell, first lady of the air.

Sigh. Sort of floats you away, doesn't it? But then I crash-landed in the movie, where Amelia Earhart has to become the sidekick of Larry Daley (Ben Stiller), who has faked his résumé to get hired as a security guard and rescue his buddies from *Night at the Museum* (2006).

What has happened, see, is that the Museum of Natural History is remodeling. They're replacing their beloved old exhibits, like Teddy Roosevelt mounted on his horse, with ghastly new interactive media experiences. His friends are doomed to go into storage at the National Archives, part of the Smithsonian Institution. We see something of its sterile corridors stretching off into infinity; it looks just a little larger than Jorge Luis Borges's Library of Babel, and you remember how big *that* was.

However, Larry is able to manage one last night of freedom for them before the crates are filled with plastic popcorn. This is thanks to, I dunno, some kind of magic tablet of the villainous Pharaoh Kahmunrah (Hank Azaria). Among the resurrected are Teddy Roosevelt (Robin Williams), General Custer (Bill Hader), Ivan the Terrible (Christopher Guest), Octavius (Steve Coogan), and Albert Einstein (Eugene Levy). Also, the stuffed monkey from our first manned (or monkeyed)

satellite, on a flight where the mission controller is played, of course, by Clint Howard, who has played mission controllers in something like half a dozen movies, maybe a dozen. When he gets a job, he already knows all of the lines. I could give you the exact number of the mission controllers he has played, but looking up Clint Howard's IMDb credits for a review of *Night at the Museum: Battle of the Smithsonian* seems like dissipation.

What is the motivation for the characters? Obviously, the video game they will inspire. Wilbur Wright is here with the first airplane, and Amelia pilots the plane she went down in on that sad second of July. Rodin's Thinker (Hank Azaria) is somewhat distracted, his chin leaning on his hand, no doubt pondering such questions as: "Hey, aren't I supposed to be in the Musee Rodin in Paris?"

The reanimated figures are on three scales. Some are life-size. Some are larger-than-life-size, like the statue in the Lincoln Memorial on the National Mall. Some are the size of tiny action figures, and they're creepy, always crawling around and about to get stepped on. Nobody asks Abe Lincoln any interesting stuff like, "Hey, you were there—what did Dick Nixon really say to the hippies during his midnight visit to your memorial?"

I don't mind a good dumb action movie. I was the one who liked *The Mummy: Tomb of the Dragon Emperor*. But *Night at the Museum: Battle of the Smithsonian* is such a product. Like ectoplasm from a medium, it is the visible extrusion of a marketing campaign.

A Nightmare on Elm Street ★
R, 95 m., 2010

Jackie Earle Haley (Freddy Krueger), Kyle Gallner (Quentin Smith), Rooney Mara (Nancy Holbrook), Katie Cassidy (Kris Fowles), Thomas Dekker (Jesse Braun), Kellan Lutz (Dean Russell). Directed by Samuel Bayer and produced by Michael Bay, Andrew Form, and Bradley Fuller. Screenplay by Wesley Strick and Eric Heisserer.

Forget about the plot, the actors, and the director. What you require to make a new *Nightmare on Elm Street* are these three off-the-shelf sound effects:

1. A sudden, loud clanging noise mixed with a musical chord.
2. Snicker-snack sounds, which Freddy Krueger's steel finger claws make every time they are seen.
3. A voice deepener, to drop Freddy's speaking voice to an ominous level.

On top of that, you need your sudden cuts, your lighting from below, your thump-thump-thumps, and, of course, a dog that barks at something unseen in the night, so that your teenage heroine can go out onto the lawn in bare feet and flimsy PJs and call, "Rufus! Rufus! Here, boy!" You know in your bones that Rufus is now checking into Doggie Heaven.

Oh, and actors. Lots of Dead Teenagers, seen in the last moments of their lives, when they enjoy a farewell Moment of Deceptive Safety just before there's a sudden, loud clanging noise and the snicker-snack claws disembowel them and Freddy rumbles, "You have nothing to worry about. This won't hurt one . . . little . . . bit."

The 2010 edition of *A Nightmare on Elm Street* is number 8½ in the series. I arrive at that number not out of a desperate desire to be seeing the Fellini film instead, but because *Freddy vs. Jason* (2003) should in all fairness count for half a film on this list, and half a film on the *Friday the 13th* list.

It is sad to think of all those Dead Teenagers. They were played by ambitious, talented young actors, some of them now in their forties, who survived grueling auditions for the honor of being slashed by Freddy. Some of them are now successful: Johnny Depp, for example. Robert Englund became famous playing Freddy, but where can that lead when you're always wearing a mask of makeup? Now Jackie Earle Haley plays the role. For what purpose? He might as well play Santa Claus.

It was twenty-six long years ago when Freddy first began to haunt the nightmares of the children of Elm Street in Springwood, Ohio. At least 137 victims have been claimed by Freddy in the years since then, but the shady little street is still lined with handsome homes and hasn't been leveled, covered with ashes and sprinkled with holy water. The franchise was founded by Wes Craven, the Ray

Kroc of horror, who made the excellent *Wes Craven's New Nightmare* (1994), about Freddy haunting the dreams of the *makers* of the *Nightmare* movies.

Freddy is not a good argument for a supernatural existence. He can live inside wallpaper, appear anywhere, and has no need of physical existence except, arguably, when he inflicts actual physical damage. Yet he's such a bore, always growling away with his deep-voiced *hahahahaha*. If a man leads an interesting life he ought to be able to make good conversation, is what I say.

I stared at *A Nightmare on Elm Street* with weary resignation. The movie consists of a series of teenagers who are introduced, haunted by nightmares, and then slashed to death by Freddy. So what? Are we supposed to be scared? Is the sudden clanging chord supposed to evoke a fearful Pavlovian response? For Rufus, maybe, but not for me. Here, boy.

Nights in Rodanthe ★ ½

PG-13, 97 m., 2008

Richard Gere (Dr. Paul Flanner), Diane Lane (Adrienne Willis), Scott Glenn (Robert Torrelson), Christopher Meloni (Jack Willis), Viola Davis (Jean). Directed by George C. Wolfe and produced by Denise Di Novi. Screenplay by Ann Peacock and John Romano, based on the novel by Nicholas Sparks.

Nights in Rodanthe is what *Variety* likes to call a "weeper." The term is not often intended as praise. The movie attempts to jerk tears with one clunky device after another, in a plot that is a perfect storm of cliché and contrivance. In fact, it even contains a storm—an imperfect one.

The movie stars Richard Gere and Diane Lane, back again, together again, after *Unfaithful* (2002). I have no complaints about their work here. Admiration, rather, as they stay afloat in spite of the film's plot, location, voice-overs, and not-very-special effects. They are true movie stars and have a certain immunity against infection by dreck.

He plays Paul, a surgeon. She plays Adrienne, a mother of two, separated from her snaky husband. To help out a friend, she is taking care of a rustic inn on an island of the

Outer Banks of North Carolina. He is the only weekend guest. He has booked it to "be by myself," he says, and also "to find someone to talk to." To summarize: These two beautiful, unhappy people are alone in a romantic beachfront inn. If the inn is really where it seems to be, on the edge of the water in a vast stretch of deserted, high-priced beach frontage, then it is not CGI and will soon be listed as *This Week* magazine's "steal of the week."

A hurricane is approaching. Hurricane warnings are issued just hours before it arrives. A grizzled old-timer at the local grocery wisely says it's gonna be real big. Adrienne stocks up on white bread. Having spent days watching CNN as little whirling twos and threes inched across the Gulf Coast, I would say this warning was belated. Paul doesn't evacuate because of some dialogue he is made to say. Adrienne doesn't because she promised her friend to look after the inn. They put up some shutters and have a jolly game of indoor basketball while tossing spoiled canned goods into a garbage can. "Ratatouille! Spam! Lard!"

The hurricane strikes. If it has a name, they don't know it. It blows off some shutters and cuts off the power. Do they face "certain death"? They cling to each other while sitting on the floor next to a bed. Then they cling to each other after getting into the bed. Have you ever made love during a hurricane that is shaking the house? I haven't. How did it go for you?

The hurricane bangs the shutters like *The Amityville Horror*. It must have no eye, so the wind only blows once. In the morning after the storm, the sun is shining and the inn is still standing. Remarkable, really, considering the photos from Galveston. It is a three- or four-story clapboard building, taller than it is wide, standing on stilts at the veritable water's edge. We see damage: a skateboard and a bike blown up. Some trees blown over. Just the most wonderful gnarly old piece of driftwood.

Reader, they fall in love. They deal with the real reason Paul came to Rodanthe, which I will say nothing about, except that it involves a grieving man who is well-played by Scott Glenn. Paul and Adrienne have found true love for the first time in their lives. Paul has an estranged son who has opened a clinic on a mountainside in Ecuador. He must go there.

They exchange letters. The mountainside has no telephones but excellent mail service. The letters serve the function of the notebook in the (much better) adaptation of Sparks's *Notebook*. These letters are read aloud in voice-overs that would not distinguish a soap opera. Does Paul find his son? Does Adrienne reunite with her snaky husband? Does her troubled and hostile teenage daughter turn into a honey bun from one scene to the next? Does the movie depend upon a deus ex machina to propel itself toward the lachrymose conclusion? Yes, no, yes, and yes.

9 ★★★

PG-13, 79 m., 2009

With the voices of: Elijah Wood (No. 9), Jennifer Connelly (No. 7), Christopher Plummer (No. 1), Crispin Glover (No. 6), Martin Landau (No. 2), Fred Tatasciore (No. 8), John C. Reilly (No. 5). Directed by Shane Acker and produced by Tim Burton, Timur Bekmambetov, and Dana Ginsburg. Screenplay by Pamela Pettler and Jim Lemley.

The first images are spellbinding. In close-up, thick fingers make the final stitches in a roughly humanoid little rag doll, and binocular eyes are added. This creature comes to life, walks on tottering legs, and ventures fearfully into the devastation of a bombed-out cityscape.

This visionary world was first created as a short subject by Shane Acker, a student at UCLA, and was nominated for a 2006 Oscar. At the time I found it "an atmosphere of creeping, crashing, menace . . . elaborated as a game of hide-and-seek, beautifully animated and intriguingly unwholesome." So it is still, as the first figure, named 9, meets his similar predecessors, No. 1 through No. 8, and they find themselves in battle against a Transformer-like red-eyed monster called the Beast.

One might question the purpose of devising a life-form in a world otherwise without life, only to provide it with an enemy that wishes only to destroy it. The purpose, alas, is to create a pretext for a series of action scenes, an apocalyptic battle that is visually more interesting than, but as relentless as, similar all-action-all-the-time movies. This is a disappointment. Remembering the promise of his original short, I looked forward to what Acker would do at feature length, especially with a producer like Tim Burton to watch his back.

The characters look similar but are easy enough to tell apart, not least because they have their numbers stitched on their backs. They also have different visual characteristics and are voiced by distinctive actors, including Christopher Plummer as their fearful leader, No. 1, and Jennifer Connelly as the token female, No. 7. The usefulness of gender in a species without genitalia is not discussed, not even wistfully.

Nine is the youngest, probably the smartest, and certainly the most daring, leading the others, against No. 1's wishes, to poke around the ruins. These look left over from a city from the past, not the future, and a 1940ish newsreel reports on a devastating global war triggered by a Hitleresque dictator. Was the Beast left behind to wipe out any survivors and assure final victory even in the absence of victors?

Such questions, I submit, are intriguing. But the dialogue is mostly simplified Action Speak, with barked warnings and instructions and strategy debates of the most rudimentary kind. Since this movie is clearly targeted not at kiddies but at teens and up, is it now Hollywood theory that eloquence and intelligence are no longer useful in action dialogue?

One of the benefits of the pre-CGI era was that although action scenes might be manifestly artificial, they had to be composed of details that were visually intelligible. Modern CGI artists, intoxicated by their godlike command of imagery, get carried away and add confusing complexity. If I were pressed to provide the cops with a detailed description of the Beast, the best I could do would be: "You'll know it when you see it. Also, it has a big glowing red eye."

Contrast that to the enormous construction in Miyazaki's *Howl's Moving Castle*. It is awesomely complex, but I have a large print of one of Miyazaki's still drawings from the film, and you can clearly see that it's all *there*.

9 is nevertheless worth seeing. It might have been an opportunity for the sort of challenging speculation that sci-fi is best at, however, and the best reason to see it is simply because of the creativity of its visuals. They're entrancing.

Nine ★★
PG-13, 112 m., 2009

Daniel Day-Lewis (Guido Contini), Marion Cotillard (Luisa), Penelope Cruz (Carla), Judi Dench (Lilli), Stacy Ferguson (Saraghina), Kate Hudson (Stephanie), Nicole Kidman (Claudia), Sophia Loren (Mamma). Directed by Rob Marshall and produced by Marshall, John DeLuca, Marc Platt, and Harvey Weinstein. Screenplay by Michael Tolkin and Anthony Minghella, based on the book for the musical *Nine* by Arthur Kopit.

My problem may be that I know Fellini's *8½* too well. Your problem may be that you don't know it well enough. Both of us may be asking, who exactly was *Nine* made for? This is a big-scale version of the 1982 Broadway production, which won the Tony for best musical. It's likely that most who saw it had either seen the Fellini or made that their business.

I didn't see the musical, but I'm sure it greatly benefited from being live and right there on stage, where the energy in the performance compensated for its lack of a single great song. All the songs sound exactly like standard boilerplate Broadway show tunes, except for composer Maury Yeston's "Finale," which evokes the original Nino Rota sound track for Fellini, which is the problem.

Fellini's great films are essentially musicals. Like most Italian directors of his generation, he didn't record live dialogue and sound. He depended on dubbing. On a set, he usually had an orchestra playing and asked his actors to move, not in time with the music, but "in sympathy." Everyone in a Fellini film evokes an inner body rhythm. Then there's Rota's music itself, my favorite sound tracks. I could watch a Fellini film on the radio.

The story, recycled by Rob Marshall for *Nine*, involves aspects of Fellini's own life: his vagueness about screenplays and deadlines, his indifference to budgets, his womanizing, the guilt about sex instilled by his Catholic upbringing, his guilt about cheating on his wife and about bankrupting his producers. It was said that *8½* wasn't so much a confessional as an acting-out of the very problems he was having while making the film, including how to use a gigantic outdoor set he constructed for no clear purpose.

It's a great film, some say his best. *Nine* the musical "adapts" it, true enough, but doesn't feel it. Consider Fellini's most famous scene. The many women in the life of the hero, Guido (played by Marcello Mastroianni), assemble in a fantasy harem and greet him: the Swedish air stewardess, his wife, his mistress, his mother, Saraghina the local whore of his childhood, and above all his muse (Claudia Cardinale), a reassuringly perfect woman, encouraging, never critical. In the harem they caress him, bathe him, soothe him—and then reveal complaints and criticisms, so that he has to take up a whip and threaten them like a lion tamer.

In *Nine* this scene is, of course, reprised, but with an unclear focus. It's less like a vengeful dream, more like a reunion. There's no urgency, no passion, most of all no guilt. In fact, the subtext of Catholic guilt, which is central to Fellini, is only hinted at in *Nine*. But then *Nine* pays homage to a Broadway musical, and not Fellini at all.

In this connection, consider the odd casting of Daniel Day-Lewis in the Fellini/Mastroianni role, played on stage by Raul Julia. Of course he isn't Marcello; who could be? But he also isn't romantic, musical, comic, baffled, exasperated—and not (even though he apprenticed under a Florentine shoemaker) in the slightest degree Italian. What current movie star could play the role? I think Javier Bardem could. Gael Garcia Bernal? Maybe Alec Baldwin? You need a man who is handsome and never seems to have given it a thought. I'm crazy? Then you tell me.

Nine is just plain adrift in its own lack of necessity. It is filled wall-to-wall with stars (Marion Cotillard as the wife figure, Penelope Cruz as the mistress, Judi Dench as the worrying assistant, Nicole Kidman as the muse, the sublime Sophia Loren as the mother). But that's what they are, stars, because the movie doesn't make them characters. My closing advice is very sincere: In the life of anyone who loves movies, there must be time to see 8½. You can watch it instantly right now on Netflix or Amazon. What are you waiting for?

Nobel Son ★ ★ ★
R, 110 m., 2008

Alan Rickman (Eli Michaelson), Bryan Greenberg (Barkley Michaelson), Shawn Hatosy (Thaddeus James), Mary Steenburgen (Sarah Michaelson), Eliza Dushku (City Hall), Bill Pullman (Max Mariner), Danny DeVito (George Gastner). Directed by Randall Miller and produced by Miller and Jody Savin. Screenplay by Savin and Miller.

When Alan Rickman portrays an egomaniacal, self-preening, heartless SOB, he seems to have found himself an autobiographical role. Since Rickman the human being (yes, there is such a thing) is kind, genial, and well-loved, he is in fact acting in *Nobel Son,* but who else could seem so utterly at home as a supercilious, snide, hurtful snake? I'm thinking maybe Richard E. Grant. The late Terry-Thomas, certainly. There isn't a long list.

Rickman plays a brilliant chemist named Eli Michaelson, the kind of man who, when he wins the Nobel Prize, those who know him best exclaim, "$#!t!" His wife loves her work as a forensic pathologist, perhaps because when she is disassembling the victim of a run-in with an auto crusher, she can imagine it is her husband. Eli belittles his son in all things. He considers his colleagues inferiors at best, insectoid at worst.

In *Nobel Son,* just when Eli is preparing to fly to Sweden and favor the crown with his presence, his son, Barkley (Bryan Greenberg), is kidnapped. The ransom: his $2 million prize money. I am reminded of the day I called my mother to tell her I had won the Pulitzer, and she said, "Oh, honey, does it pay anything?" She meant well. She just didn't see how I could make a living just . . . going to the movies, you know. Eli's inclination is to tell the kidnappers: "You keep my son, and I'll keep my money." Then a severed thumb arrives in the mail. Never a harbinger of good.

Nobel Son is a mercilessly convoluted version of a Twister, that genre in which the plot whacks us as if it's taking batting practice. I will not hint at anything that happens. I will simply observe that it's all entertaining. The plot by itself could have become tiresome; no audience enjoys spending all evening walking into stone walls. But the acting is another matter.

Rickman supplies the crown jewel in the cast, but Mary Steenburgen is no less amusing as his wife, Sarah. A woman can be married to a man like Eli only by being a masochist, insane, or in possession of a highly developed sense of sardonic irony. She doesn't talk like Alice Kramden on *The Honeymooners*, but you know what I mean. And Steenburgen's appearance is a pleasant surprise. She's so often cast as comic goofballs that it's good to be reminded that in a normal style and sensible clothes, she's a beauty and a charmer. This movie makes up for *Four Christmases*.

Shawn Hatosy plays the kidnapper, who gets up to more than we expect and less than he understands. Danny DeVito is a "recovering obsessive-compulsive" gardener, which is just as well because imagine how often you'd want to wash your hands in *that* line of work. Bill Pullman is a cop who thinks the whole setup stinks, and he's only sniffing at one corner of it.

These characters are, in order, Eli, Sarah, Barkley, Thaddeus, Max, and Gastner. All names right at home in a novel by Dickens. But then there's the brilliant writer played by Eliza Dushku, whom Barkley meets at a poetry reading. Her name is City Hall. Marry her, and every time you make a call from a bar it will sound important.

I have studiously avoided plot description because everything I said would be a lie or misleading. Assume these actors have not chosen this screenplay as a waste of their time. That would be *Four Christmases*. The plot is ingenious, the schemes are diabolical, and it is not every day that a character needs to inform us, "It is more cruel to eat the living than the dead," although now that I think about it, I agree. If you cannot follow every loop and coil of the plot, relax: Neither can the plot. At the end, by my calculations, the leftovers include one dead body and a hand without its thumb.

North Face ★★★

NO MPAA RATING, 126 m., 2010

Benno Fuermann (Toni Kurz), Johanna Wokalek (Luise Fellner), Florian Lukas (Andi Hinterstoisser), Simon Schwarz (Willy Angerer), Georg Friedrich (Edi Rainer), Ulrich Tukur (Henry Arau). Directed by Philipp Stoelzl and produced by Benjamin Herrmann, Gerd Huber, Danny Krausz, Rudolf Santschi, Boris Schonfelder, Kurt Stocker, and Isabelle Welter. Screenplay by Stoelzl, Christoph Silber, Rupert Henning, and Johannes Naber.

The movies have long been convinced that any story can be improved by adding a romance. Not true. Any story can be improved by leaving out as much as you reasonably can. Consider *North Face*, the bone-chilling, superbly mounted record of an assault on the north face of the Eiger, which is known by the grim understatement as "the last remaining problem in the Alps."

Mountain climbing terrifies me because it has such a ruthless digital simplicity. It is either zero or one: (1) You are holding on. (Zero) You are falling. Time's arrow flies in one direction. Once you aren't holding on, there is nothing you can do. No skill, no courage, no training, nor any rope or piton.

These fears explain why in its scenes on the Eiger itself *North Face* starts strongly and ends as unbearably riveting. They also explain why it was a strategic error to believe this story needed romantic and political subplots. You know something has gone wrong when a story about mountain climbers gives the sorta girlfriend of one of them second billing.

North Face is based on the true story of a May 1936 attempt on the Eiger by four climbers—two Germans and two Austrians who meet on the mountain in the movie but began together in real life. All four are experienced and confident. One is not very wise. Using the long-tested rope-and-piton method, they hope to reach the top after spending only one night in sleeping bags secured to the mountain. They have little petrol burners to heat tea or broth. They are very fit.

One of the Germans has doubts about making an attempt on a peak that has never been scaled and that froze two Germans to death the year before. The Eiger is known for its weather shifts and avalanches of snow and rocks. Meanwhile in Berlin, the Nazi editor (Ulrich Tukur) of a daily newspaper wants to produce German heroes for Hitler in the run-up to the Olympics. The two Germans, Toni Kurz and Andi Hinterstoisser (Benno Fuermann and Florian Lukas), both in the army, are such lackluster Nazis that they're assigned to cleaning latrines.

The editor's secretary, Luise Fellner (Johanna Wokalek), was sweet on Toni when they were young; Toni and Andi took her climbing with them. When her editor discovers she knows them, he orders her to go to the Eiger and convince them it's their patriotic duty to climb. Toni is convinced more by Luise than by Hitler. Setting off from the base, they eye two Austrians, Willy Angerer (Simon Schwarz) and Edi Rainer (Georg Friedrich). Higher up, their climbs will intersect.

The director, Philipp Stoelzl, is uncanny in his ability to convince us these four are actually climbing a mountain. Because the four actors could hardly be climbing themselves, he must use doubles for some shots. That is easier because of sunglasses, hoods, and blowing snow. Some of the shots must have been made on sets. None of that matters. I was on the side of that mountain all the way.

If the film had stayed there, it might have been devastatingly good. It's powerful enough as it is. But consider the 2004 film *Touching the Void*, about a climber who broke his leg, driving a bone through a knee socket, and later fell into an ice crevice, and agonizingly, unbelievably, made his way alone back down the mountain. That semi-documentary by Kevin Macdonald showed only the two climbers. That was more than enough.

In *North Face*, Stoelzl cuts to the luxury hotel at the base and even back to Berlin. There's a lot about the editor's ego and his desire to please Hitler. And much about Luise's fears for her friends and her determination to bring help to them after they disappear from view before the second night. We learn that railway tunnels through the mountain have occasional openings to the surface to admit air, and that the climbers might be approached by that means. Sounds reasonable, although some of her later decisions are dubious.

I believe audiences will enjoy this film. I did. But there's too much baggage along for the ride. It involves not only Luise but also the Nazis. A love story is not needed here, particularly when the reputed lovers got along perfectly well apart for ten years. And as for the

Nazis, must every German film set in the '30s involve Nazism? Do you climb a mountain for Hitler and think about him all the way up? Not these climbers. They don't give a damn about Hitler.

Note: Speaking of mountains and special effects, when Clint Eastwood made The Eiger Sanction, *he personally performed in a scene showing him dangling at the end of a rope three thousand feet in the air. A telephoto lens zoomed in on him from a distance to prove it was really him. He told me he attended a sneak preview in disguise and overheard: "It really looked like it was Clint up there. I wonder how they did that."*

Nothing but the Truth ★ ★ ★ ½
R, 106 m., 2009

Kate Beckinsale (Rachel Armstrong), Vera Farmiga (Erica Van Doren), Matt Dillon (Patton Dubois), Angela Bassett (Bonnie Benjamin), Alan Alda (Albert Burnside), David Schwimmer (Ray Armstrong), Floyd Abrams (Judge Hall). Directed by Rod Lurie and produced by Lurie, Bob Lari, and Marc Frydman. Screenplay by Lurie.

Alan Alda has a scene in *Nothing but the Truth* where he reads a dissenting Supreme Court opinion defending the right of journalists to protect confidential sources. I assumed the speech was genuine and was surprised to learn that the case inspiring the film was not heard by the Supreme Court. In fact the speech was written by Rod Lurie, the writer and director of the film, who would make an excellent Supreme if writing opinions were the only requirement. It was so soundly grounded in American idealism that I felt a patriotic stirring.

The film is obviously inspired by the case of Judith Miller, a *New York Times* reporter who served eighty-five days in prison for refusing to name her source in the Valerie Plame affair. That was the case in which Vice President Cheney's top aide blew the cover of a CIA agent in order to discredit the agent's husband, who investigated reports that Niger sold uranium to Saddam Hussein. He found no such evidence. The uranium story was part of the web of Bush-Cheney lies about WMDs that were used to justify the Iraq war.

The case is complicated, but if you know the general outlines, you can easily interpret Lurie's fictional story as a direct parallel to Miller/Valerie Plame/Joseph Wilson, though the names and specific details have been changed. In real life, Miller's reporting, accuracy, and objectivity were sharply questioned, and Lurie wisely sidesteps history to focus on the underlying question: Which is more important, the principle of confidentiality or national security? Trying to deal with the real Miller story would have trapped the film in a quicksand of complications.

I'm sure some readers are asking, why don't I just review the movie? Why drag in politics? If you are such a person, do not see *Nothing but the Truth*. It will make you angry or uneasy, one or the other. That Bush lied to lead us into Iraq is a generally accepted fact, and the movie regards a few of the consequences.

Lurie, however, has more on his mind than a political parable. The movie is above all a drama about the people involved, and his actors are effective at playing personalities, not symbols. Kate Beckinsale is Rachel Armstrong, the reporter for the *Capital Sun-Times*. Vera Farmiga is Erica Van Doren, the outed spy. Matt Dillon plays prosecutor Patton Dubois, obviously intended as U.S. prosecutor Patrick Fitzgerald, now so involved in the case of our fascinating former Illinois governor. Alda is the high-priced Washington lawyer hired by the newspaper to defend Rachel. Angela Bassett is the newspaper's editor, under pressure to tart up coverage, trying to stand firm. And this is interesting: There is a wonderful performance by Floyd Abrams as the federal judge; in real life, he was Miller's attorney.

Armstrong and Van Doren are suburban Washington soccer moms whose children attend the same school. They know each other by sight. In possession of the leak, the reporter asks the agent point-blank if it is true, and the agent replies in terms Justice Scalia does not believe decent people use in public. It is a fierce scene.

Dubois, the prosecutor, calls Armstrong as a witness in his investigation of the leak, and she refuses to name her source. That begins her harrowing ordeal in jail, where eventually she has been behind bars longer than any sister prisoner. She will not tell, even though this decision estranges her husband (David Schwimmer), alienates her young son, and paints her as a heartless mother who places job above family.

How she is treated seems to go beyond reasonable punishment. Dillon, as Dubois, is positioned as the villain, but objectively he is only doing his job, and Dillon says he played the role as if he were the film's good guy. Alda comes on strong as a man not above boasting of his expensive Zegna suit, but grows so involved that he goes pro bono. The dire costs to both women are at the heart of things.

Lurie, who is a powerful screenwriter, is freed by fiction to do two very interesting things. (1) He presents the issues involved with great clarity. (2) He shows that a reporter's reasons for concealing a source may be more compelling than we guess. What is deeply satisfying about *Nothing but the Truth* is that the conclusion, which will come as a surprise to almost all viewers, is not a cheat, is plausible, and explains some unresolved testimony.

Nothing but the Truth is a finely crafted film of people and ideas, of the sort more common before the movie mainstream became a sausage factory. It respects the intelligence of the audience, it contains real drama, it earns its suspense, and it has a point to make. In the ordinary course of events, it would have had a high-profile release and plausibly won nominations. But the economic downturn struck down its distributor, the film missed its release window, and its life must be on DVD. It is far above the "straight-to-DVD" category, and I hope filmgoers discover that.

Notorious ★ ★ ★ ½
R, 122 m., 2009

Jamal "Gravy" Woolard (Notorious B.I.G.), Angela Bassett (Voletta Wallace), Derek Luke (Sean Combs), Anthony Mackie (Tupac Shakur), Antonique Smith (Faith Evans), Naturi Naughton (Lil' Kim). Directed by George Tillman Jr. and produced by Voletta Wallace, Wayne Barrow, Mark Pitts, Robert Teitel, and Trish Hofmann. Screenplay by Reggie Rock Bythewood and Cheo Hodari Coker.

He was known as Notorious B.I.G., a man-mountain of rap, but behind the image was

Christopher Wallace, an overgrown kid who was trying to grow up and do the right thing. The image we know about. The film *Notorious* is more interested in the kid. He was born in Brooklyn, loved his mother—a teacher who was studying for a master's degree—got into street-corner drug dealing because he liked the money, performed rap on the street, and at twenty was signed by record producer Sean "Puffy" Combs. Four years later, he was dead.

Documentaries about B.I.G. have focused on the final years of his life. *Notorious* tells us of a bright kid who was abandoned by his father, raised by a mother from Jamaica who laid down the rules, and told the kids on the playground he would be famous someday. "You too fat, too black, and too ugly," a girl tells him. He just looks at her. He is sweet-tempered, even after being seduced into the street-corner crack business, but he sounds tough in his rap songs—he is tough, introspective, autobiographical, and a gifted writer.

His demo tape is heard by Sean Combs (Derek Luke), who is seen in the film as a good influence, in part perhaps because he's the executive producer. Combs draws a line between the street as a market and a place where he wants his artists to be seen. B.I.G. leaves the drug business and almost overnight becomes a huge star, an East Coast rapper to match the West Coast artists such as Tupac Shakur.

Tupac was shot dead not long before B.I.G. was murdered, and the word was they died because of a feud between the East and West Coast dynasties and onetime friends B.I.G. and Tupac (Anthony Mackie). Another version, in Nick Broomfield's 2002 documentary *Biggie and Tupac,* is that both shootings were ordered by rap tycoon Suge Knight and carried out by off-duty LAPD officers in his hire. Broomfield produces an eyewitness and a bag man who says on camera that he delivered the money. The film, perhaps wisely, sidesteps this possibility.

Notorious is a good film in many ways, but its best achievement is the casting of Jamal Woolard, a rapper named Gravy, in the title role. He looks uncannily like the original, and Antonique Smith is a ringer for B.I.G.'s wife,

Faith Evans. Woolard already knew how to perform but took voice lessons for six months at Juilliard to master B.I.G.'s sound. He performs a lot of music in the film, all of it plot-driven, sure to become a best-selling sound track. As an actor, he conveys the singer's complex personality: a mother's boy, a womanizer, an artist who accepts career guidance from his managers, a sentimentalist, an ominous presence.

The real B.I.G. may have had a harder side, but we don't see it here. Instead, director George Tillman Jr. and his writers, Reggie Rock Bythewood and Cheo Hodari Coker, craft an understated message picture in which B.I.G. eventually decides to accept responsibility for the children he has fathered, and as his mother, Voletta (Angela Bassett), urges him to do, become a man. Shortly before his death, he announces a new direction for his music.

Bassett doesn't play Voletta as a conventional grasping mamma. She believes in tough love and throws her son out of their apartment after she finds cocaine under the bed. Few actors are better at fierce resolve than Bassett, and she provides a baseline for her son's fall and eventual rise. The real Voletta is in the Broomfield documentary, where in 2002 she looks like . . . an older Angela Bassett.

George Tillman and his producing partner, Robert Teitel, are Chicagoans who have, together and separately, been involved in some of the best recent films about African-American and minority characters: *Nothing Like the Holidays, Soul Food, Men of Honor,* both *Barbershop* pictures, *Beauty Shop.* None of these films is sanctimonious, none preaches, but in an unobtrusive way they harbor positive convictions. In *Notorious,* they show how talent can lift a kid up off the street corner but can't protect him in a culture of violence. The whole gangsta rap posture was dangerous, as B.I.G. and Tupac proved.

Note: Tupac: Resurrection, *an extraordinary 2002 documentary, uses hours of autobiographical tapes left behind by Shakur to allow him to narrate his own life story. He also proved his acting ability in* Gridlock'd, *Vondie Curtis-Hall's 1997 film where he costarred with Tim Roth.*

O

October Country ★★★
NO MPAA RATING, 80 m., 2010

Featuring members of the Mosher family. A documentary directed by Michael Palmieri and Donal Mosher and produced by Palmieri. Screenplay by Palmieri and Mosher.

"We wouldn't know normal if it fell on us," Donald Mosher says. He sits and smokes on the front porch of one of two adjacent houses that are home to four generations of his family. The Moshers are a sad and dysfunctional family, which they are curiously willing to explain, as if they've spent years rehearsing their mistakes. "Bad taste in men runs in the family," observes Desiree, Donald's eleven-year-old granddaughter.

The Moshers live in the beautiful Mohawk Valley in upstate New York. "Here is where we were born, and here, I guess, is where we'll die," says Dottie Mosher, the matriarch. She and Donald are the enduring centers of a family of a daughter, Donna, who has a history of abusive men; a granddaughter, Daneal, who seems to be following the same pattern; her sister, Desiree, who explains, "I'm a lot smarter than the rest of them"; and Daneal's daughter, Ruby. There is also Don's sister, Denise, who dresses in a black cape, haunts cemeteries to videotape ghosts, and is a Wiccan.

None of the husbands are seen in the film. The only male apart from Donald is Chris, a foster child he and Dottie took in. He's been in jail, explains in one scene how he likes Walmart because it's "easy to steal from," warns the Moshers he'll be trouble for them, and proves it by stealing two computers. Dottie wipes aside a tear as Chris goes back behind bars.

What happened to this family? One of the two codirectors is Donal Mosher, another son, who is never mentioned in the film. His photographs of his family inspired the film, made with his partner, Michael Palmieri, a director of TV commercials. The film is often lovely to regard, and sees the Moshers surrounded by the beauty of the seasons between one Halloween and the next.

The legacy of sadness started when Donald went to serve in Vietnam. Dottie remembers him as a cheerful, upbeat kid when he went away. Something happened there to change him forever. He never talks about it—or about much of anything else. He watches old war movies on TV, makes doll house furniture in his attic workshop, and watches with dour passivity as the generations go awry.

He worked at first in the Remington Arms Factory, the chief employer in the valley, but found his job so boring "an ape could do it." He observes, "Remington executives get an eight-hundred-thousand-dollar Christmas bonus, and the workers get a damn belt buckle after thirty years." He quit, went to work as a police officer, and on his first day on the job covered a suicide that left brains all over a garage wall.

Donna and Daneal seem to move through a cloud of gloom. They know all about abusive men, but seem to feel that is their fate. The spark of hope is Desiree—"Desi"—who is spirited and sarcastic, and seems to have gotten the family's entire allotment of senses of humor. Even at her age, she sees the problems and refuses to enlist in them. I hope her school can set her on a good path in life; she seems ready for one.

One understands how Donal Mosher could obtain access to these moments of stark honesty and bleak truth. One wonders what the family thought of the film when they saw it. This is the face of dysfunction. Apparently alcohol and drugs are not involved, except perhaps with some of the missing men. The drug here is despair. They seem to treat it with cigarettes.

Note: The photographs that inspired the film are here: http://donalmosher.com/.

Of Time and the City ★ ★ ★ ½
NO MPAA RATING, 77 m., 2009

A documentary directed by Terence Davies and produced by Solon Papadopoulos and Roy Boutler. Screenplay by Davies.

The streets of our cities are haunted by the ghosts of those who were young here long ago.

In memory we recall our own past happiness and pain. Terence Davies, whose subject has often been his own life, now turns to his city, Liverpool, and regrets not so much the joys of his youth as those he did not have. Central to these are the sexual experiences forbidden by the Catholic Church to which he was most devoted.

Liverpool was once a shipbuilding capital of the world, later a city broken by unemployment and crime, and now a recovering city named the European Capital of Culture in 2008. For many people, Liverpool's cultural contribution begins and ends with the Beatles, and Davies does little to update that view except to focus on its postwar architecture, which is grotesque, and its modern architecture, much improved, but still lacking the grandeur of the city's Victorian glory.

The way Davies and his cinematographer, Tim Pollard, regard heritage buildings and churches, their domes and turrets worthy of an empire, suggests that he, like me, prefers buildings that express a human fantasy and not an abstract idea. What is it that makes the Hancock magnificent and Trump Tower appalling? Not just the Trump's bright, shiny tin appearance, the busy proportions of its facade, or its see-through parking levels, but a lack of modesty and confidence. It insists too much. On the other hand, there is nothing modest about the grandiloquent civic structures of Liverpool, but their ornate cheekiness is sort of touching. They had no idea they were monuments to the end of an era.

In this city Davies was born into modest circumstances, was shaped and defined by the Church, was tortured by his forbidden homosexual feelings, and gradually grew to reject the Church and the British monarchy. He remembers a boy who put a hand on his shoulder "and I didn't want him to take it away." In his parish, Church of the Sacred Heart, "I prayed until my knees bled," but release never came.

These memories are mixed with those of the city, suggested with remarkable archival footage collated from a century: crowds in the streets and at the beach, factories, shipyards, faces, movie theaters, snatches of song, long-gone voices, an evocation of a city tuned in to the BBC for the Grand National, a long-gone horse and rider falling at the first hurdle, the wastelands surrounding new public housing, children and dogs at play, and, yes, the Beatles.

The sound track includes classical music and pop tunes, and the deep, rich voice of Davies, sometimes quoting poems that match the images. The film invites a reverie. It inspired thoughts of the transience of life. It reminded me sharply of Guy Maddin's *My Winnipeg* (2008), which combined old footage and new footage that looked even older into the portrait of a city that existed only in his imagination. I imagine the city fathers in both places were astonished by what their sons had wrought, although in Winnipeg they would have found a great deal more to amuse them.

O'Horten ★ ★ ★ ½
PG-13, 89 m., 2009

Baard Owe (Odd Horten), Espen Skjonberg (Trygve Sissener), Githa Norby (Mrs. Thogersen), Bjorn Floberg (Flo), Kai Remlov (Steiner Sissener), Henny Moan (Svea). Directed, written, and produced by Bent Hamer.

The thing about a deadpan comedy is it has to think. It must involve us in the lives of its characters so we can understand why they are funny while at the same time so distant. *O'Horten*, a bittersweet whimsy by the Norwegian director Bent Hamer, finds that effortless. It is about a retiring railroad engineer named Odd Horten. *Odd* is a common enough first name in Norway, but reflect that English is widely used in Scandinavia.

O'Horten is a quiet, reflective man, a pipe smoker who lives alone but is not lonely and sets his life by the railroad timetable. He is baffled by retirement. He's not sure when he should be anywhere. After the retirement party thrown by his fellow engineers, who sing him a "choo-choo-choo woo-woo-woo" song, he is uncertain. An evening begins on an inauspicious note when he is unable to get into a colleague's apartment, climbs a scaffolding in freezing weather, lets himself into someone else's window, and finds himself in conversation with a small boy.

O'Horten has his consolations. One is Mrs. Thogersen (Githa Norby), a sweet, silvery-haired widow who lives at the end of the Oslo–Bergen run. He is accustomed to overnighting in her arms. "So . . . this is the end?" she asks on his last run. Apparently so. It doesn't occur to him that they could rendezvous without him driving a train there.

Left to his own devices, O'Horten allows himself to be drawn into uncertain circumstances. There is the case of Trygve Sissener (Espen Skjonberg), a curious old man who informs O'Horten, "Ever since I was young, I have been able to see with my eyes closed." To prove it, he takes O'Horten on a drive through Oslo with a black hood pulled over his head. You would think this would be terrifying for an engineer who once hit a moose on the tracks, but no. He puffs his pipe, interested.

His Oslo resembles the macabre Stockholm of the director Roy Andersson, whose *Songs from the Second Floor* we showed at Ebertfest a few years ago. Inexplicable events seem to be a matter of course. Why, for example, would well-dressed businessmen slide on their fannies down an icy incline? O'Horten is probably wondering the same thing but doesn't inquire.

Odd is played by Baard Owe, a trim, fit man with a neat mustache, who may cause you to think a little of James Stewart, Jacques Tati, or Jean Rochefort. He has some regrets. He was never an Olympic ski jumper like his mother. Too afraid. He never really developed any hobbies. He has few friends. He was on the rails too much. He prides himself in perfection on the job but has no need for perfection in his life. At least a pipe smoker can always count on his pipe.

Old Dogs ★
PG, 88 m., 2009

John Travolta (Charlie), Robin Williams (Dan), Seth Green (Craig), Kelly Preston (Vicki), Matt Dillon (Barry), Rita Wilson (Jenna), Lori Loughlin (Amanda), Ella Bleu Travolta (Emily), Conner Rayburn (Zach), Bernie Mac (Jimmy Lunchbox). Directed by Walt Becker and produced by Peter Abrams, Robert L. Levy, and Andrew Panay. Screenplay by David Diamond and Davis Weissman.

Old Dogs is stupefyingly dimwitted. What were John Travolta and Robin Williams *think-*

ing of? Apparently, their agents weren't perceptive enough to smell the screenplay in its advanced state of decomposition, but wasn't there a loyal young intern in the office to catch them at the elevator and whisper, "You've paid too many dues to get involved with such crap at this stage in your careers"?

Williams and Travolta play business partners trying to float a big deal with Japan. Meanwhile, they're saddled with baby-sitting six-year-old twins. Be sure your seat belt is visible on the outside of your blanket; you will be awakened for breakfast when this flight is about to land.

The film makes a big business meeting with Japanese investors a study in laugh-avoidance. The Japanese line up on one side of a table in a Las Vegas Japanese restaurant, and Travolta, Williams, their partner Seth Green, and a translator are on the other. Travolta tries to warm them up with the funny story of how Williams just got divorced twice in the last twenty-four hours. The Japanese sit stony-faced. So do we. Then Travolta gets to his big finish, and the Japanese break into helpless laughter. My theory: Since almost all Japanese businessmen in Vegas speak English, they've been playing a practical joke.

This film seems to have lingered in post-production while editors struggled desperately to inject laugh cues. It obviously knows no one will find it funny without being ordered to. How else to explain reaction shots of a dog responding to laugh lines? Or the painfully obvious use of music as glaring as a yellow highlighter to point out comedy? Example: Rita Wilson gets her hand slammed by a car trunk, and the sound track breaks into "Big Girls Don't Cry."

Another clue is when characters break into bad sitcom dialogue. After the Old Dogs end up at camp with their young charges, a muscular counselor (Matt Dillon) asks them, "You girls ready to play a little Ultimate Frisbee?" Williams: "I think so, Mr. Testosterone."

Another clue: "Funny moments" repeated in case we missed them. Example: Robin Williams test-drives a buckled-on, back-mounted device that allows him to fly. It loses power and he drops into a pond. Wow, that was funny! Wait! Here it is again! Same drop, new angle! Twice as funny! Oh, no! A third drop! Ohmigod! Wait—wait—a *fourth* time? Usher, quick! Bring me oxygen!

Seth Green is not a tall man. But hell, he's only three inches shorter than Robin Williams. In this movie, you'd think he was Danny De-Vito. He ends up wrapped in the arms of a go-rilla. Never mind why. Doesn't matter. First Law of Movie Gorillas: Guy in a gorilla suit is never funny, unless the joke is on him.

To save himself from the enormous beast, Green sings a soothing lullaby. The gorilla dozes off peacefully. Hey, that's good! That's very good! Green gently tries to extricate him-self from the gorilla's embrace. Nothing doing! Green desperately starts crooning again. Just think. If the gorilla wakes up, Green will be crushed to death! Man, oh, man!

The release of *Old Dogs* was delayed from April until now because of the death of an-other of its costars, Bernie Mac. I can think of another way they might have respected his memory. ☞

Orphan ★★★ ½
R, 123 m., 2009

Vera Farmiga (Kate Coleman), Peter Sarsgaard (John Coleman), Isabelle Fuhrman (Esther), CCH Pounder (Sister Abigail), Jimmy Bennett (Daniel Coleman), Aryana Engineer (Max Coleman). Directed by Jaume Collet-Serra and produced by Joel Silver, Susan Downey, Jennifer Davisson Killoran, and Leonardo Di Caprio. Screenplay by David Johnson.

After seeing *Orphan*, I now realize that the Omen was a model child. The Demon Seed was a bumper crop. Rosemary would have been happy to have this baby. Here is a shame-lessly effective horror film based on the most diabolical of movie malefactors, a child.

Pity. Esther is such a bright child. So well-behaved. Her paintings are so masterful. She sits down at the piano and rips off a little Tchaikovsky. So why does her adoptive mother have such a fearful attitude toward her? Could it be because Kate, the mom, got drunk and almost let her son Daniel drown? Had Max, a darling daughter, but then mis-carried a third child? Is an alcoholic trying to stay sober? Just doesn't like the little orphan girl's looks?

There is something eerie about her. Some-thing too wise, too knowing, too penetrating. And why won't she remove those ribbons she always wears? And why does she dress like Lit-tle Bo Peep to go to school? Daniel is cool to-ward her. Max is too young to be sure. Only John, the father, is convinced she's a bright kid and blameless in a series of unfortunate events.

Vera Farmiga is at the film's core as Kate, a onetime Yale music professor who feels she is unfairly targeted by her therapist, her hus-band, and eventually the authorities. Peter Sarsgaard plays John, the kind of understand-ing husband who doesn't understand a damned thing except that he is understand-ing. And Esther, the orphan, is played by Is-abelle Fuhrman, who is not going to be convincing playing a nice child for a long, long time.

The movie hinges on a classic thriller de-vice: the heroine who knows the truth and in-sists on it even though everyone is convinced she's mad and wants to ship her off to rehab or even a mental institution. It's frustrating to know you're right when no one can see the truth you find so obvious.

Things happen around Esther. A child falls from a playground slide. A car rolls down a hill. A nun comes into harm's way. She spreads disinformation. She's secretive. And some-times she's so perfect you want to wring her neck. When it turns out the orphanage has faulty info on her Russian origins, Kate starts sniffing around in what her husband dis-misses as paranoia.

Orphan begins like your usual thriller, with Scare Alerts and False Alarms. You know, like a nice, peaceful shot until suddenly the sound blares and something rushes past the camera and—hey, it's only kids. We even get the old standby when Kate is looking in the medicine cabinet and closes it and—ohmigod!—there's another face in the mirror! But hey, it's only her smiling husband.

Sarsgaard is well cast in the role. He looks normal, sounds pleasant, and yet can suggest something a little twitchy. Not that he's evil. Simply that he really should trust his wife more. Really.

How the movie handles the other children, Daniel and Max, would probably have offended Gene Siskel, who had a thing about movies exploiting children in danger. This one sure does. What with the tree house and the pond and the runaway SUV, it's amazing these kids are still able to function.

The climax of the film is rather startling, combining the logic of the situation with audacity in exploiting its terror. Yet you have to hand it to *Orphan*. You want a good horror film about a child from hell, you got one. Do not, under any circumstances, take children to see this. Take my word on this.

OSS 117: Cairo, Nest of Spies ★ ★ ★
NO MPAA RATING, 99 m., 2008

Jean Dujardin (Hubert Bonisseur de la Bath), Berenice Bejo (Larmina El Akmar Betouche), Aure Atika (Princess Al Tarouk), Philippe Lefebvre (Jack Jefferson), Constantin Alexandrov (Setine). Directed by Michel Hazanavicius and produced by Eric Altmayer and Nicolas Altmayer. Screenplay by Jean-Francois Halim, based on the novels by Jean Bruce.

Well, to begin with, *OSS 117: Cairo, Nest of Spies* is a terrific title. Better than the film, but there you are. Watching it, I began to shape a review about how its hero, French agent 117, was influenced by James Bond out of Inspector Clouseau and Austin Powers (try not to picture that). But then I discovered from *Variety* that the character Agent 117 actually appeared in a novel in 1949; its author, Jean Bruce, wrote no less than 265 novels about him, qualifying for second place, I guess, behind Georges Simenon's Inspector Maigret. And the agent appeared in seven earlier movies.

The books and movies, I gather (not having read or seen any of them), were more or less straightforward action, so although Ian Fleming may have created 007 with a debt to 117, what he brought new to the table was the idea of comedy. And if the Bond movies are themselves quasi-serious on some level, Mike Myers went completely over the top with Austin Powers, inspiring the makers of this new film to try to make *him* seem laid-back. Their agent is now the subject of a parody so far over the top that, well, it's not every day

you see two spies fighting by throwing dead chickens at each other.

The movie stars Jean Dujardin as Agent 117 (real name: Hubert Bonisseur de la Bath), whom in 1955 is sent by the French secret service to Egypt to deflect the impending Suez crisis, bring peace among the Americans, Russians, and Egyptians, and settle the problems of the Arab world. No problem-o. Jean Dujardin, who looks more than a little like the young Sean Connery, is in a Bondian film that begins with an extreme action sequence, has titles based on the view through a roving gun sight, and cuts directly to Rome and 117 in a tuxedo, making out with a beauty garbed in satin, who tries to stab him in the back.

The movie travels familiar ground, with a nod as well to *Top Secret, Airplane!* and that whole genre. Even compared to them, it pushes things just a little—not too far, but toward the loony. For example, Agent 117's cover role in Cairo is as the owner of a wholesale chicken business. When he discovers that the chickens cluck and the roosters crow when the lights are on, but not when they're off, he has no end of fun playing with the light switch. This is a guy who's short some bulbs.

How stupid is he? Leaving Rome for Cairo, he meets his local contact, a lithesome beauty named Larmina El Akmar Betouche (Berenice Bejo) and on the trip from the airport complains about how much dust there is in the desert. Shown the Suez Canal, he congratulates the Egyptians for having the foresight to dig it four thousand years ago. He assures her that Arabic is a ridiculous language, and she is dreaming if she thinks millions of people speak it. And his sleep is interrupted one morning by a call to prayer from a muezzin in the tower of a nearby mosque. "Shut the **** up!" he bellows out the window, and then climbs the tower and silences the troublemaker.

The movie relishes its 1955 look, not just in the costumes and locations, but in such details as special effects and fight scenes. Remember hand-to-hand combat pre–Bruce Lee? No end of tables and chairs get trashed, while the distinctly Bondian musical score pounds away relentlessly. One nice 1950s touch: "Cigarette?" he's asked. "I'm trying to start," he replies.

For a parody, the movie is surprisingly competent in some of the action scenes, when the dim-witted hero turns out to have lightning improvisational skills. And there is an escape scene that develops in unforeseen ways. Dujardin is somehow able to play his clueless hero as a few degrees above the doofus level, mixing in a little suave seductiveness and then effortlessly drifting into charmingly crafted comments that are bold insults, if only he understood that.

My only problem is, there's a little too much of 117. Only ninety-nine minutes long, it nevertheless seems to go on more than necessary. There is a limit to how long such a manic pitch can be maintained. It's the kind of film that might seem funnier if you kept running across twenty minutes of it on cable. Yet I suppose that is not a fatal fault, and I have developed the same kind of affection for 117 that I have for Austin Powers. Who else would tell that lithesome beauty, "You're not a Lebanese reporter posted to Rome! You're actually the niece of Egypt's King Farouk!" It was the "Egypt's King Farouk" part that got me. Like she didn't know who he was. And like he didn't know Farouk had been deposed by Nasser. Well, that I can believe.

OSS 117: Lost in Rio ★★★
NO MPAA RATING, 101 m., 2010

Jean Dujardin (Hubert Bonisseur de la Bath), Louise Monot (Delores), Alex Lutz (Heinrich), Rudiger Vogler (Von Zimmel), Reem Kherici (Carlotta), Ken Samuels (Trumendous). Directed by Michel Hazanavicius and produced by Eric Altmeyer and Nicholas Altmeyer. Screenplay by Michel Hazanavicius and Jean-Francois Halin, inspired by the OSS 117 novels by Jean Bruce.

Hubert Bonisseur de la Bath, French Agent OSS 117, looks like a parody of James Bond, British Agent 007, but it may be the other way around. Pretty much unknown over here, he first appeared in print in 1949. I haven't read a single OSS 117 novel (there are more than 250!), but it appears Ian Fleming may have found some inspiration from Jean Bruce, the creator of 117.

The OSS man first appeared in a film in 1957, and was once played by John Gavin, of all people. The character was revived in OSS 117: Cairo, Nest of Spies (2006), but while the orig- inal stories were played straight, Cairo and now OSS 117: Lost in Rio are parodies—of the James Bond movies, appropriately enough.

The star is Jean Dujardin, who in some shots looks something like Sean Connery, and who has the same gift of understatement and drollery. He's also surrounded by babes, in particular a sexy Mossad agent named Delores Koulechov (Louise Monot). The movie is set in the early 1960s, and 117 is sent to Brazil to retrieve a secret list of French collaborators with the Nazis. This leads to an action climax atop the right arm of the immense statue of Christ that towers above Rio de Janeiro. Hitchcock set Notorious in Rio, but didn't quite have the nerve to use that location.

Imagine that the film looks exactly like a slightly faded thriller from 1967. The makers have gone to a great deal of trouble to get not only the costumes, the sets, the props, and the cars right, but even the film stock; some audience members may wonder if they wandered into a revival house. The stunts are as stagy as 007, the villains as absurd, and 117 as unflappable.

One thing that will strike North American audiences as odd is that 117 is cheerfully racist. Working with an Israeli agent gives him plenty of opportunities to voice his anti- Semitism, which is not intended to hurt, but grows directly out of his ignorance. I think (or hope) the filmmakers are making a commentary on the everyday anti-Semitism of the De- Gaulle era.

But 117 is an equal-opportunity offender and makes unbelievably gross statements to women. He somehow gets away with it because Dujardin is a polite charmer with an eager smile and a quick laugh, and you see he doesn't mean to offend; he's only trying to make conversation. That he is clueless is the joke.

There's too much of that for my taste, but the movie depends mostly on wild exaggerations of 007, and here it does something right: It shows stunts and special effects that look like they might have been staged in 1967. The movie almost goes out of its way to reveal it's using rear projection on a studio set. The music is appropriate, too: that kind of cheesy pop that has a good time no matter what's happening on the screen. The sound track reminded me of nothing so much as a forced laugh.

I sort of liked the 2006 film, and I sort of like this one, too. I may like it a little more because Dujardin grows on you. The film opens with him singing "Everybody Loves Somebody" in a voice that sounds so much like Dean Martin that maybe it is. But the way he smiles and moves . . . well, surely you've heard of the Trololo Man?

If you haven't, Google him.

Our Family Wedding ★★
PG-13, 101 m., 2010

Forest Whitaker (Brad Boyd), America Ferrera (Lucia Ramirez), Carlos Mencia (Miguel Ramirez), Regina King (Angela), Lance Gross (Marcus Boyd), Diana Maria Riva (Sonia Ramirez). Directed by Rick Famuyiwa and produced by Edward Saxon and Steven J. Wolfe. Screenplay by Famuyiwa, Wayne Conley, and Malcolm Spellman.

Our Family Wedding is a perfectly good idea for a comedy: A wedding between a Mexican-American woman and an African-American man leads to culture clash. The film, unfortunately, deals with the situation at the level of a middling sitcom. You almost miss the laugh track. Difficult problems are sidestepped, arguments are overacted, and there are three food fights involving wedding cakes. Well, two, actually, and the destruction of a third cake.

At the center of the wedding are Lucia Ramirez (America Ferrera), who was a law student at Columbia, and Marcus Boyd (Lance Gross), a Columbia med school graduate. The young couple plan to move to Laos, where he will work with Doctors Without Borders. They've been living together in New York, but keeping it a secret from her parents because her mom, Sonia (Diana Maria Riva), expects her to remain a virgin before marriage, and her father, Miguel (Carlos Mencia), would be crushed if he learned she had dropped out of law school. In a plot twist of startling originality, she is not pregnant.

A slimmed-down Forest Whitaker plays Marcus's father, Brad, a popular Los Angeles all-night DJ. He's doing all right and inhabits a huge house in the hills with a pool, stairs leading to a terrace, and a lawn big enough to hold a wedding party. Plus his ride is a Jaguar. Not bad for an all-night DJ.

Miguel is also well off, with the daughter at Columbia, the big luxurious house, and the passion for restoring classic cars. He owns a towing service, which is how he and Brad have a Meet Cute: All his drivers call in sick. Miguel fills in, and he and Brad meet when he tows the Jag.

The dads meet again at dinner when their children pop the big news and are immediately screaming insults and shaking each other by the throat. This scene, like all the stagy arguments between the fathers, is completely unconvincing. Their fights are drummed up for the purposes of the screenplay, and the actors hardly seem to believe them. Their families flutter their hands and beg them to calm down. Their running feud feels phony to begin with, and painfully forced by the end.

All of the family difficulties seem trumped up. Although Lucia is terrified that her mother will discover she had sex before marriage, that revelation, when it comes, is almost a throwaway. Marcus is embarrassed that his dad dates much younger women, but when he turns up at the family dinner with a girl who was Lucia's softball teammate, there's barely a mild stir. Lucia's grandmother faints when she sees Lucia's fiancé is a black man, but when she comes to, this is forgotten. (Didn't anyone tell her?) Oh, and speaking of softball, the game played between the two family teams is so badly staged, I wasn't sure which side many of the players were on, nor who won the game.

The bright spots are America Ferrera, the kind of cuddly beauty who plunges right in and kisses a guy without worrying about her makeup, and Lance Gross as the guy, who has a thankless task as the Perfect Fiancé but doesn't overplay it. Regina King steals many scenes as Brad's longtime lawyer and secret admirer; her character is smart, focused, and sympathetic, and King's costumes showcase those Michelle Obama arms.

Our Family Wedding is a pleasant but inconsequential comedy, clunky, awkward for the actors, and contrived from beginning to end. Compare it with *Nothing Like the Holidays* (2008) to see how well a movie can handle similar material.

Outlander ★ ★
R, 115 m., 2009

Jim Caviezel (Kainan), Sophia Myles (Freya), Jack Huston (Wulfric), Ron Perlman (Gunnar), John Hurt (Rothgar). Directed by Howard McCain and produced by Chris Roberts. Screenplay by McCain and Dirk Blackman.

I am tempted to describe the plot of Outlander as preposterous, but a movie about an alien spaceship crashing into a Viking fjord during the Iron Age is likely to be preposterous. Two alien life forms survive the crash: Kainan and a monster known as "the Moorwen." Kainan, played by Jim Caviezel, looks exactly like a human being. The Moorwen looks like a giant, speedy, armored hippo-beetle with a toothy front end designed in the same forges of hell that produced the alien in Alien.

Kainan was returning from the Moorwen's home planet, which his race had terraformed, not quite wiping out all the Moorwens. The creatures counterattacked, wiping out most of Kainan's fellow settlers; what he doesn't realize is that one Moorwen was onboard ship when he blasted off. Kainan uses a handy device to pump the local Earth language (Viking, spoken in English) into his mind through his eyeball and soon encounters the nearest Viking village.

Having seen more than a few movies, we intuit that this village will contain a venerable king (Rothgar, played by John Hurt), his bodacious daughter (Freya, played by Sophia Myles), a jealous young warrior (Wulfric, played by Jack Huston), and a menacing dissident (Gunnar, played by Ron Perlman). There are also numerous villagers who stand around in the background looking intensely interested.

The village is suspicious of this strange "outlander." Then Vikings start to disappear in the forest, and Kainan realizes he has brought along a passenger. After he saves Rothgar from the Moorwen, he wins royal favor and organizes the village in a plan to lure the beast into a deep pit with stakes at the bottom and burn it alive.

I began my study of science fiction at the age of nine, with Tom Corbett, Space Cadet. I grew to love the authors who incorporated as much science as possible: Clarke, Asimov,

Heinlein. They would have had questions about Kainan. For example, is he as human as he appears? It seems unlikely from a Darwinian point of view that two human species should evolve independently and contemporaneously on separate worlds. Even more so that they would share common sexual feelings and be able to mate, although that is precisely what Kainan and Freya propose.

But yes, their love flowers, against a backdrop of Arthurian romance. The Moorwen is the dragon, of course. And much depends on a sword mighty enough to pierce its armor. To forge this Excalibur, Kainan dives into the fjord and retrieves scrap steel from the wreckage of his ship, thus bringing the Iron Age to a quick close—in this village, anyway. The climax involves the usual violent and incoherent special effects scenes, after which Rothgar gives Kainan the hand of his daughter, and Kainan and Freya presumably retire to discover if separate evolutionary paths have outfitted them with compatible fixtures.

Outlander is interesting as a collision of genres: The monster movie meets the Viking saga. You have to give it credit for carrying that premise to its ultimate (if not logical) conclusion. It occurs to me, however, that the Moorwen had legitimate reason to be grieved. First Kainan's race appropriated the Moorwen planet for its own purposes, then it massacred the Moorwens, now it was picking off a survivor. Do you think genocide or colonialism are concepts to be found in Outlander? Not a chance. That's because Kainan is so human, and the Moorwens are, well, just not our sort.

Over Her Dead Body ★ ★
PG-13, 95 m., 2008

Eva Longoria Parker (Kate), Paul Rudd (Henry), Lake Bell (Ashley), Lindsay Sloane (Chloe), Stephen Root (Sculptor), Jason Biggs (Dan), William Morgan Sheppard (Father Marks). Directed by Jeff Lowell and produced by Paul Brooks, Scott Niemeyer, Peter Safran, and Norm Waitt. Screenplay by Lowell.

Why is nobody utterly in awe of ghosts in Over Her Dead Body and so many other ghostcoms? Here is a supernatural manifestation from another realm, and everybody treats it as a plot device. The movie even drags in a Catholic priest, who seems bewilderingly ignorant of his church's beliefs about ghosts (they don't exist) and treats the situation as an opportunity for counseling.

The setup: It's the wedding day of Henry and Kate (Paul Rudd and Eva Longoria). She's a Type A perfectionist who races manically around the reception venue, straightening place settings, adjusting decorations, and flying into a rage at the ice sculptor (Stephen Root) who has delivered an ice angel—without wings! She orders him to take it back and bring her one with wings, which, as everybody knows, all angels possess. He argues reasonably that you can't just stick wings on an ice sculpture. In a tragic accident involving the sculpture, Kate is killed.

Flash forward a decent amount of time and Henry, still in mourning, is informed by his sister, Chloe (Lindsay Sloane), that it's time for his life to begin again. He should start dating. He won't hear of it. He's still in love with Kate. She persuades him to visit Ashley (Lake Bell), a psychic she knows. He does so. Is she a real psychic? Sometimes. She begins to get vibes. So does he. Neither one needs to be psychic to realize they are falling in love with each other.

I guess it's all right for psychics (as opposed to psychiatrists) to date their clients, but Ashley seeks advice. She gets it from Dan (Jason Biggs), her partner in a catering business. Also from Father Marks (William Morgan Sheppard), who also doesn't know that his church doesn't believe in psychics. (Was he ordained by mail order? The Church teaches that consulting a psychic is a sin, although it doesn't totally rule out info from the other side, suggesting it could be disinformation from Satan.) Anyway, meanwhile . . . eek! The ghost of Kate appears, none too pleased that an-

other woman has designs on her man. She intends to sabotage their romance.

What happens then? Kate looks completely real, although she has no material presence and can walk through walls, etc. I always wonder why walls are meaningless to such beings, but they never fall through floors. Do elevators go up without them? Never mind. The plot plays out as you would expect it to, as the amazing presence of a ghost is effortlessly absorbed into the formula plot. If it were me and a ghost, I'd put my personal agenda on hold and ask all sorts of questions about the afterlife. Wouldn't you?

Heaven, in this movie, is represented in the standard way: Everything is blindingly white, and everyone is garbed in white, even an angel (Kali Rocha) who has, by the way, no wings. Well, of course it doesn't. Being a pure spirit, it has no need to fly. Kate switches back to a conventional wardrobe for her sojourns here below. How would I depict heaven? As a featureless void with speaking voices. I haven't decided about subtitles.

Even in a movie with a ghost, the hardest thing to believe is a revelation that Dan makes to Ashley. They have worked together five years, and yet she is astonished. I will leave the revelation for you to discover, only adding that I believe it would be impossible for Dan to work five years in the catering industry without his secret being obvious to everyone.

Consider for a moment how this movie might play if it took itself seriously. Would it be better than as a comedy? I suspect so. Does the premise "her ghost turns up and fights the new romance" make you chuckle? Me neither. It's the kind of angle that could seem funny only at a pitch meeting. Not only have we been there, done that, we didn't want to go there, do that in the first place.

P

Paper Heart ★★★
PG, 88 m., 2009

Charlyne Yi (Herself), Michael Cera (Himself), Jake Johnson (Nicholas Jasenovec). Directed by Nicholas Jasenovec and produced by Sandra Murillo and Elise Salomon. Screenplay by Jasenovec and Charlyne Yi.

To describe Charlyne Yi as a whimsical comedian doesn't quite capture the full flavor. She may be the first female in the history of MySpace to claim she is ten years older than she really is. She appears naive, clueless, a little simple, but she's playing us. She embodies that persona in *Paper Heart,* a quasi-documentary about love that is sweet, true, and perhaps a little deceptive.

Yi is a performance artist who makes standup comedy only one facet of her act. She's short, cute, likes sweat clothes, wears hornrim glasses, isn't assertive, is a poster child for the melting pot: Filipino, Spanish, Korean, Irish, German, French, and Native American. She always seems to be trying to figure things out. *Paper Heart* is about how she has never been able to figure out love.

The movie takes the form of a documentary about her partnership with director Nicholas Jasenovec to travel America seeking insights into romance from all sorts of possible authorities, all of them obviously real, many of them touching, and one of them an inspired choice. That would be the Elvis impersonator who runs a Las Vegas wedding chapel. These people share their own stories, drawn out by Yi's disarming persona.

But wait. Although Nicholas Jasenovec appears in the film, that's not the real Nicholas Jasenovec. It's an actor, Jake Johnson, who is taller and darker and in my opinion more handsome than the real Jasenovec. Photographs reveal the real Jasenovec is shorter, cute, likes sweat clothes, wears horn-rim glasses. Then you have his good friend, the actor Michael Cera (*Juno*'s boyfriend), who looks much more like Jasenovec than Johnson. When Yi goes to a party with Jasenovec, she meets Cera and it's love at first sight.

We see them meeting, and it feels absolutely real: You wonder which of these two diffident and soft-spoken people summoned the energy to speak first. But wait. In real life, before shooting on this film began, Charlyne Yi and Michael Cera were *already* girlfriend and boyfriend, and were celebrated by such gossip sites as Gawker as "America's Twee-hearts." Therefore, their courtship in the film is scripted, although it feels uncannily real, perhaps because Cera and Yi have such enveloping personas that little they do is acting.

These matters give *Paper Heart* an intriguing quality on top of its intrinsic appeal. And the onscreen presence of "Nick," as the director, is uncannily well acted by Johnson, who embodies a hungry young L.A. filmmaker who thinks all human considerations are secondary to his film. There are moments when he insists on violating the privacy of Charlyne and Michael with his camera, and these scenes are so well-acted and handled that, in retrospect, you realize this is a very well-made film indeed. There's more than meets the eye.

But wait! In real life, the heartless Cera has just dumped Yi! Right in the middle of their national publicity tour for this film! Can this possibly be true, or is it a publicity stunt? Surely he would have been decent enough to keep it private for a couple more weeks? No? Or is it possible that Cera and Yi, like many seemingly passive people, are, in fact, passive-aggressive, and have anger seething just beneath the surface?

Don't ask me. But if the heartbreak is true, I have advice for Charlyne Yi about how to cheer herself up wonderfully: Just go to your MySpace page and take off ten years.

Paranormal Activity ★★★ ½
R, 96 m., 2009

Katie Featherston (Katie), Micah Sloat (Micah), Michael Bayouth (The Psychic). Directed by Oren Peli and produced by Peli and Jason Blum. Screenplay by Peli.

Paranormal Activity is an ingenious little horror film, so well made it's truly scary, that arrives claiming it's the real thing. Without any form of conventional opening or closing credits, it begins by thanking "the families of Micah Sloat and Katie Featherston" and closes with one of those "current whereabouts unknown" title cards and a screen of copyright notices. This was apparently a film made without a director, a writer, a producer, grips, makeup, sound, catering, or a honey wagon.

All of the footage is presented as if it had been discovered after the fact. The story device is that Micah shot it himself. There isn't a single shot that violates that presumption, although a few seem technically impossible without other hands on the camera. Those are hard to notice.

Katie is a graduate student of English. Micah is a day trader. They've been together three years and have now moved into a house in San Diego that doesn't seem much lived in. It's well enough furnished, but everything looks new and there's no clutter. Micah greets Katie out front one day by filming her on his new video camera, which she observes looks bigger than his other one.

They've been bothered by indications of some sort of paranormal activity in an upstairs bedroom. Micah's bright idea is to film in the house, leaving the camera running as a silent sentinel while they sleep. Like any man with a new toy, he becomes obsessed with this notion—the whole point, for him, isn't Katie's fear but his film. After one big scare, she asks him incredulously, "Did you actually go back to pick up your camera?"

One benefit of the story device is that for long periods of time the camera is ostensibly left on with no one running it. It's on a tripod at the end of their bed while they sleep, and we see events while their eyes are closed. Some of these events are very minor, and I won't describe any of them. The fact that they happen *at all* is the whole point. That they seem to happen by themselves, witnessed by a static camera, makes them eerie, especially since there are some shots that seem impossible without special effects, and there's no visible evidence of f/x, looking as closely as we can.

He is frequently off camera. She is on cam for almost every shot, and of Katie Featherston's performance it's enough to say it is flawless for the purposes of this film. We're not talking Meryl Streep here; we're talking about a young woman who looks and talks absolutely like she might be an ordinary college student who has just moved in with her boyfriend. There's not a second of "acting."

Micah behaves, shall I say, just like a man. You know, the kind who will never stop and ask directions. Katie has been bothered by some sort of paranormal presence since she was a child, and now she's seriously disturbed, and Micah's response isn't sympathy but a determination to get it all down on film.

They do call in a "psychic expert" (Michael Bayouth), but he's no help. He specializes in ghosts, he explains, and he knows by walking in the door that what's haunting them isn't a ghost but some sort of demonic presence. He recommends a demonologist, but alas this man is "away for a few days." That's the plot's most unrealistic detail. Having spent some time in my credulous days hanging about the Bodhi Tree bookstore in L.A., I would suggest that California is a state with more practicing demonologists than published poets.

I learn from IMDb that *Paranormal Activity* does indeed have a writer-director, Oren Peli, and other technical credits. But like *The Blair Witch Project*, with which it's routinely compared, it goes to great lengths to seem like a film found after the event. It works. It illustrates one of my favorite points, that silence and waiting can be more entertaining than frantic fast-cutting and berserk f/x. For extended periods here, nothing at all is happening, and believe me, you won't be bored. ☞

Paris ★★★ ½
R, 128 m., 2009

Juliette Binoche (Elise), Romain Duris (Pierre), Fabrice Luchini (Roland), Albert Dupontel (Jean), Francois Cluzet (Philippe), Karin Viard (Shop Owner), Julie Ferrier (Caroline), Melanie Laurent (Laetitia), Zinedine Soualem (Mourad). Directed by Cedric Klapisch and produced by Bruno Levy. Screenplay by Klapisch.

At the end of *Paris*, a character whose future is uncertain rides in a taxi through the city and glimpses some of the film's other characters going about their lives. He doesn't know them, but we do, and seeing them so briefly is enough to make the film's point: We are here, we strive, we love, we laugh, we fail, we are sad, sometimes we look at the world and smile for no particular reason.

Here is a film about a group of Parisians. It opens with a sweeping shot of Paris from atop the Eiffel Tower. The characters don't have interlocking lives; it's not that kind of film. They have parallel lives. The purpose of Cedric Klapisch, the writer-director, is to make a symphonic tribute to the city he loves, and each character is a movement.

That said, every character has life and depth. It's unusual for an episodic film to involve us so well in individual lives; as the narrative circles through their stories, we're genuinely curious about what will happen next.

The central character is Pierre (Romain Duris), who is a dancer in his thirties told that he has little time left. Only a heart transplant can save him. His sister Elise (Juliette Binoche) brings her two daughters and comes to live with him, and they try to cheer each other. He spends much time standing on his balcony, observing life in the street. She's rebounding from a bad marriage and considers herself finished with men.

We also meet a famous Parisian historian named Roland (Fabrice Luchini), whose lectures are so literate and certain he seems to be reading from a TelePrompTer scrolling in his mind. He is very alone. Well into his fifties, he becomes obsessed with a pretty student and anonymously sends her florid romantic compliments by text. Then he lurks nearby to watch her reading them. Creepy. Meanwhile, he's starring in a TV documentary series about the city.

His younger brother is Philippe, played by Francois Cluzet, the Dustin Hoffmanish star of *Tell No One* (2006). Philippe is an architect, a father-in-waiting, an encourager who senses Roland's discontent. Elise finds herself attracted to Jean (Albert Dupontel), a vendor in one of the many Paris street-food markets. Jean is divorced from Caroline (Julie Ferrier), but they're still friendly. Still, they don't seem to have a future.

There are several smaller characters, including a bakery owner (Karin Viard) who has outspoken prejudices about people from any part of France that is not Paris, and yet is open-minded enough to praise a young employee from North Africa who is a reliable worker. I've met French people like that: not racist, but tactlessly opinionated—or particular, as they might prefer.

All of these stories are told against the backdrop of Paris, a city Klapisch loves with a passion. He hasn't made a travelogue with beauty shots, however, but set his story in very specific places: streets, a university, cafés, restaurants, dawn at the vast Rungis, the wholesale food market that replaced Les Halles. There is even a scene set in the catacombs, the bones and skulls of Parisians past neatly stacked behind the professor.

The characters have love, fear it, or seek it. Only one has a desperate problem. None is quite satisfied. They have a daily reprieve from illness or death but never think in those terms—except for Pierre, who is forced to. They go to work, home again, to their spouses or lovers or empty flats. They move easily through the city, and we are reminded that in Paris, traditionally a city of tiny apartments, the cafés serve as living rooms. You're not buying a coffee, you're renting a table, and it's yours for as long as you sit there.

I love Paris in the same way Klapisch does, for the concentration and intensity of its daily life and street theater. A modern place like downtown Houston seems to me an unlovely prospect, all concrete, no shadows. Why do modern corporations envision their headquarters as freestanding tombstones instead of friendly neighbors?

Viewing the film's city, I was reminded of another film, *When the Cat's Away* (1996). That was the one about the young woman who leaves town and entrusts her cat with a neighboring cat lady. When she returns, this old lady is heartbroken: The cat has run away. The entire neighborhood gets caught up in the search, including a simple-minded fellow who helpfully risks his life on rooftops, usually in search of the wrong cat. I looked up the film, and discovered it was by Cedric Klapisch. There you go.

Paris 36 ★ ★ ½
PG-13, 120 m., 2009

Gerard Jugnot (Pigoil), Clovis Cornillac (Milou), Kad Merad (Jacky), Nora Arnezeder (Douce),

Pierre Richard (Monsieur TSF), Bernard-Pierre Donnadieu (Galapiat), Maxence Perrin (Jojo), Elisabeth Vitali (Viviane). Directed by Christophe Barratier and produced by Nicolas Mauvernay and Jacques Perrin. Screenplay by Barratier.

Sometimes you get the feeling that if a movie had been made years ago, it would now be considered a classic. *Paris 36* is like that—an old-fashioned story set around a music hall. Cutting-edge, it's not. But if taken in the right spirit, enjoyable.

In the 1930s, in no particular neighborhood in Paris, an ancient music hall named the Chansonia wheezes along with performers who are past their sell-by dates. It's a time of social upheaval in France; the Popular Front, a left-wing coalition, has taken power, and the rise of Hitler is stirring up French right-wingers. The Chansonia's cast and crew are solidly socialist.

For Pigoil (Gerard Jugnot), the left-wing stage manager, things are going badly. The Chansonia's fascist landlord has padlocked the doors for rent in arrears, Pigoil and his friends are all out of work, his wife has left him, and a silence has fallen upon the neighborhood. The burden, he feels, rests on his shoulders. Jacky (Kad Merad), a man who wears a sandwich board for the theater but believes he can do impressions, becomes a supporter. Also Milou (Clovis Cornillac), a young radical, who helps him to reopen the doors again. But it is not enough to have the doors open; customers must use them.

The day is saved by the miraculous appearance of Douce (Nora Arnezeder), a chantoozie who is not only said to be a future star, but actually has the charisma to prove it. She's an overnight success, the show comes together, but the day is only apparently saved. The situation is fraught with complications. There is the problem of Pigoil's gifted young son Jojo (Maxence Perrin), an accordionist now in the custody of his faithless mother, and the schemes of the fascist landlord Galapiat (Bernard-Pierre Donnadieu).

Paris 36 takes place in a neighborhood known locally simply as the Faubourg (the street). Remarkably, I learn, this entire neighborhood—streets, facades, cafés—was built as a set outside Prague. It's one of those movie neighborhoods not crowded with extras. Like the street in Spike Lee's *Do the Right Thing*, it's a place where everyone knows one another; the street's a stage, and the neighbors are players on it. And they all know about Monsieur TSF (Pierre Richard), nicknamed after a French broadcasting station. He never leaves his room, but the jazz on his radio keeps everyone humming.

It is inevitable that the movie ends with a smashing song-and-dance number starring Douce and, of course, young Jojo. It's one of those numbers where the size of the cast (even including Pigoil) seems improbable. Not to mention the sound of the orchestra. The theater is too small to possibly support such a production, but never mind: Hey, gang, let's rent the old Chansonia and put on a show!

The movie otherwise lacks a certain energy, advances somewhat creakily through its plot, and contains mostly obligatory surprises. Still, it's pleasant and amusing. If I had seen it before I was born, I would have loved it.

Passing Strange ★★★★
NO MPAA RATING, 135 m., 2009

De'Adre Aziza (Edwina/Marianna/Sudabey), Daniel Breaker (The Youth), Eisa Davis (Mother), Colman Domingo (Mr. Franklin/Joop/Mr. Venus), Chad Goodridge (Reverend Jones/Terry/Christophe/Hugo), Rebecca Naomi Jones (Sherry/Renata/Desi), Stew (Narrator). Directed by Spike Lee and produced by Elizabeth Ireland McCann. Screenplay by Stew, based on his stage play.

Passing Strange is one of the best musicals I've seen. It tells the story of a young black man from Los Angeles, rebelling against a loving, churchgoing family and breaking out on his own in the late 1960s to follow the call of art, or "art," to Amsterdam and Berlin. Starting with a garage band, he moves through psychedelic, punk, and rock stages in a journey toward the meaning of life. But can that meaning be found in art? His life builds toward that question.

The movie is moving and exciting not only because of the book, music, and performances, but because of its intelligence, passion, and heart. A Tony Award winner from the Public Theater and on Broadway, it has been filmed by Spike Lee, whose work is the very model of how to record a live performance.

This is the semi-autobiographical story of the rock musician Stew, who wrote the book and lyrics and is onstage throughout as the Narrator. He is surrounded by a gifted, high-energy cast, in a production that certainly works as a musical but also, particularly, as a drama. Often the story of a musical will be only a clothesline to hang the songs from. This story has depth and weight.

The hero is a young man known only as The Youth (Daniel Breaker), who when we meet him is being sent by his loving mother (Eisa Davis) to try out for a church choir. He joins after a comely choir member catches his eye, but church doesn't turn out as his mother intended, after he samples pot for the first time under the tutelage of the pastor's son (Colman Domingo). The son, who calls himself a coward under his father's thumb, instills in The Youth a vision of Europe and its freedoms, art films and cafés, a refuge for such black American exiles as James Baldwin.

Once in Amsterdam, embraced (sometimes literally) by a more color-blind society, The Youth finds not only personal freedom but a new understanding of his own roots. The scenes in Holland and Germany are rich with satire of the times, as the hash bars of Amsterdam are replaced by the radicalism of Berlin. The Dutch and Germans are played with droll accents by the cast members De'Adre Aziza, Rebecca Naomi Jones, Chad Goodridge, and Domingo, who, with a few costume details and attitude changes, effortlessly evoke three characters apiece.

Stew's lyrics, sometimes funny, sometimes edgy, come with a twist. Having warmed the fleshpots of Amsterdam, The Youth encounters a new kind of sex in Berlin. "Celibacy," he is informed by a female German erotic entrepreneur, "is the only sane response to a world gone wild. My porno films feature fully clothed men making business deals."

The hero feels he has embarked on a new kind of life in the Old World, and when entreated by his mother to come home for Christmas, he hems and haws and says that "maybe after" his next show he can "start thinking about" visiting home. Her song advises him "don't forget your own people." And indeed, he poses as culturally much "blacker" in Europe than he really is, because it works for him. It's as foretold by the preacher's son: "We're blacks passing as blacks."

This progress from youthful rebellion to eventual disillusionment and a search for deeper meaning is one that Stew himself possibly made. Today a forty-eight-year-old guitarist, studiously nonhip, he transforms himself with his guitar into the whole catalog of musical poses but emerges as a man who has learned something. Toward the end he makes this devastating observation: "Some of us spend our entire adult lives acting on the decisions of a teenager."

Spike Lee attended the opening night of *Passing Strange* at the Public, determined to film it, and shot at several performances at the Belasco Theater on Broadway, including closing night. With great skill and craft, he allows the material to speak for itself. He uses several cameras for many simultaneous angles, and with his editor, Barry Alexander Brown, seamlessly composes close-ups and longer shots to convey both character emotion and the exuberance of the choreography.

I can't single out a performance. This is a superb ensemble, conveying that joy actors feel when they know they're good in good material. This is not a traditional feature, but it's one of Spike Lee's best films.

Paul Blart: Mall Cop ★ ★ ★
PG, 87 m., 2009

Kevin James (Paul Blart), Jayma Mays (Amy), Keir O'Donnell (Veck Sims), Bobby Cannavale (Commander Kent), Stephen Rannazzisi (Stuart), Shirley Knight (Mom Blart), Raini Rodriguez (Maya Blart). Directed by Steve Carr and produced by Adam Sandler, Jack Giarraputo, Barry Bernardi, Todd Garner, and Kevin James. Screenplay by James and Nick Bakay.

Paul Blart: Mall Cop is a slapstick comedy with a hero who is a nice guy. I thought that wasn't allowed anymore. He's a single dad, raising his daughter with the help of his mom; he takes his job seriously; he may be chubby but he's brave and optimistic. And he's in a PG-rated film with no nudity except for a bra strap, and no jokes at all about bodily functions.

What's even more amazing, the movie isn't "wholesome" as a code word for "boring." It's as slam-bang preposterous as any R-rated comedy you can name. It's just that Paul Blart and the film's other characters don't feel the need to use the f-word as the building block of every sentence. They rely on the rest of the English language, which proves adequate.

Kevin James stars as Officer Blart, who looks like the result of an experiment combining the genomes of Jackie Gleason and Nathan Lane. He dreams of making it into the state police, and indeed is in great physical shape but tends to collapse because of hypoglycemia. He carries around little sugar packets the way some people pack nitro for angina. He's a veteran security officer at a giant mall in West Orange, New Jersey, which he patrols aboard a Segway, a vehicle he has so mastered that he can even go in reverse without looking.

It is Black Friday, the day after Thanksgiving, busiest shopping day of the year. He turns up pitifully hung over. Paul doesn't drink, but the night before, assaulted by hot sauce during a nacho-eating contest, he chugged a pitcher he mistakenly thought contained virgin margaritas. His behavior alienated a pretty mall salesclerk named Amy (Jayma Mays), and his heart has been broken, far from the first time.

The mall is seized by a tightly organized crew of thieves, and customers are ordered outside, but Blart was playing free video games and didn't notice. Now he's locked inside, the only person who might be able to save Amy, his daughter, Maya (Raini Rodriguez), and their fellow prisoners. Yes, it's a hostage situation, with the mall already surrounded by cops and a SWAT team. The plan of the thieves is sensationally stupid, guaranteed to call attention to their scheme, easy to thwart, and possibly inspired by watching *Dog Day Afternoon* while drunk.

Everything is a sitcom until Officer Blart goes into action in an astonishingly inventive cat-and-mouse chase past myriad product placements, all of which find uses. The movie even discovers a new angle on the old hiding-in-the-ventilation-shaft routine.

Paul Blart emerges as a hero and something

else: Kevin James illustrates how lighting and camera angles can affect our perception of an actor. In the early scenes, he's a fat schlub, but after he goes into action, the camera lowers subtly, the lighting changes, and suddenly he's a good-looking action hero, ready for business. He demonstrates what fat men have secretly believed for a long time. Should Daniel Craig someday retire, I am supporting Kevin James for the next James Bond.

Percy Jackson and the Olympians: The Lightning Thief ★★★
PG, 119 m., 2010

Logan Lerman (Percy), Alexandra Daddario (Annabeth), Brandon T. Jackson (Grover), Uma Thurman (Medusa), Sean Bean (Zeus), Pierce Brosnan (Chiron), Steve Coogan (Hades), Catherine Keener (Sally Jackson), Joe Pantoliano (Gabe Ugliano), Melina Kanakaredes (Athena), Rosario Dawson (Persephone), Kevin McKidd (Poseidon). Directed by Chris Columbus and produced by Michael Barnathan, Thomas M. Hammel, Guy Oseary, Mark Radcliffe, and Karen Rosenfelt. Screenplay by Craig Titley, based on the novel by Rick Riordan.

Every movie involving superheroes requires an origin story, and *Percy Jackson and the Olympians: The Lightning Thief* has a doozy. The Greek gods on Mount Olympus sometimes descend to Earth to have children, you see, and these half-god, half-humans are demigods. They live among us. One is Percy Jackson (Logan Lerman), who is the teenage son of Poseidon and Sally Jackson (Catherine Keener). He doesn't know this. I wonder if his mom noticed. Kind of a letdown to discover Greek gods are runaway dads.

Percy finds he can think best when underwater for ten minutes at a time. Poseidon was the god of the sea, you will recall. His best buddy is Grover (Brandon T. Jackson), who is revealed as a sort of assistant-demigod assigned to watch over him. His teacher is Mr. Brunner (Pierce Brosnan), who is actually Chiron, a centaur. Give Brosnan a lot credit for wearing the back half of a horse as if he'd been doing it for years.

The movie, based on a novel by Rick Riordan, has fun working out modern parallels for Greek mythology. Percy, for example, thinks he is dyslexic, but it's only that his eyes instinctively turn English into Greek letters. No help in class. After learning of his real identity, he goes off to Chiron's demigod training camp with Grover, and he becomes friends with Annabeth (Alexandra Daddario), a demigoddess if ever I've seen one.

The plot heats up. Zeus (Sean Bean) and Poseidon (Kevin McKidd) meet atop the Empire State Building to discuss Zeus's missing lightning bolt, which he believes Poseidon's son Percy has stolen. (The story requires a certain suspension of disbelief.) Why, when, or how he allegedly might have done so begins as a mystery to Percy, but eventually the situation leads to slam-bam special effects sequences, as the gods and demigods do battle.

Undoubtedly the biggest attraction among the gods is Medusa, and Uma Thurman demonstrates she can wear a snake-filled head as gracefully as Pierce Brosnan can trot around with a horse's netherlands. There is also the advent of Steve Coogan as Hades. Yes, Steve Coogan. Hades, you recall, is the brother of Zeus and Poseidon.

Or maybe you don't recall. It's one of my weaknesses that I was never able to work up much of an interest in the Greek gods, who made for discouraging fiction because they were entirely defined by their attributes. They had no personalities to speak of, but simply went about doing what they did. You can understand why Zeus is so upset about losing his lightning bolt. That's what he does, is hurl that lightning bolt. What is Zeus without his bolt?

Director Chris Columbus has fun with this goofy premise, but as always I am distracted by the practical aspects of the story. Does it bother the Greek gods that no one any longer knows or cares that they rule the world? What are the genetic implications of human-god interbreeding? And, forgive me, I'll have to double back to Sally Jackson, Percy's mother. How did she meet Poseidon? At the beach, I suppose. Did he reveal his true identity? If a guy picks you up at the beach and says he's Poseidon, do you say, fine, let's not date, let's just mate? And then when the bastard dumps you and disappears leaving you pregnant, what way is that for a god to behave?

My remaining question involves the title. Call me foolish, but I don't consider *Percy Jackson and the Olympians: The Lightning Thief* an ideal title. The movie's original title was *Percy Jackson and the Lightning Thief,* which at least has the advantage of sounding less like a singing group.

Note: This is the first film I recall with end credits including the names of the actors who played Parthenon Janitors. I know, it's the Parthenon in Nashville, but even so.

The Perfect Game ★★★

PG, 118 m., 2010

Clifton Collins Jr. (Cesar Faz), Cheech Marin (Padre Estaban), Jake T. Austin (Angel Macias), Ryan Ochoa (Norberto), Emilie de Ravin (Frankie), Moises Arias (Mario), Patricia Manterola (Maria), Louis Gossett Jr. (Cool Papa Bell), Bruce McGill (Tanner). Directed by William Dear and produced by Daniel de Liege, Michael O. Gallant, Mark W. Koch, David Salzberg, Christian Tureaud, and W. William Winokur. Screenplay by Winokur.

Once upon a very long time, a film "based on a true story" was both true and almost too good to be a story. Perhaps anticipating any suspicion, William Dear intercuts newsreel footage from 1957 with *The Perfect Game,* frequently piping into the past for black-and-white and then segueing into the color of the present day. These players really lived, and this game was really played.

The film begins in Monterrey, Mexico, seen here as an impoverished town with many baseball fans, who follow the Brooklyn Dodgers on the radio with nearly religious intensity. We meet young Angel Macias (Jake T. Austin), who aims at a bucket fastened to a wall as a strike zone and dreams of greatness on the mound. His father is not so enthusiastic.

The setup is traditional. The town's boys have time on their hands and need an activity to keep them out of mischief. Enter wise, gentle Padre Estaban (Cheech Marin), who thinks a baseball team might help. Newly returned to town is Cesar Faz (Clifton Collins Jr.), who was a prospect for the St. Louis Cardinals but was devalued and shunted aside, possibly because he was Mexican. Unable to take more of the racism of management, he returned home and is recruited by Padre Estaban, not without difficulty, to coach the kids' team.

Because the film is titled *The Perfect Game,* you expect one to be pitched. You do not expect it to be pitched in Monterrey. You sort of know how these underdog sports movies turn out. Doesn't matter. *The Perfect Game* so expertly uses the charisma and personalities of the actors, especially the young ones, that it's thrilling anyway.

The scenes at the Little League World Series in Williamsport, Pennsylvania, make the contrast seem so dramatic between the teams in the final game—the Mexicans seemingly a foot shorter on average than their American counterparts. William Dear cannot, by the very nature of his story, avoid certain clichés, but the way he orchestrates the big game is sure and confident, and there's that life we often feel at the end of an underdog story.

In the years since, the Little League World Series has become blown out of proportion, verging on the exploitation of the players. They're trained within an inch of their lives, placed under enormous pressure, and subjected to punishing media scrutiny. It's not a game anymore. In 1957, these kids were *playing.* And it was a perfect game.

A Perfect Getaway ★★★

R, 97 m., 2009

Steve Zahn (Cliff), Timothy Olyphant (Nick), Milla Jovovich (Cydney), Kiele Sanchez (Gina), Marley Shelton (Cleo), Chris Hemsworth (Kale). Directed by David Twohy and produced by Robbie Brenner, Mark Canton, Ryan Kavanaugh, and Tucker Tooley. Screenplay by Twohy.

Man, am I glad I knew nothing about *A Perfect Getaway* going in. There are two things Hollywood can't resist in making a trailer: showing the best jokes in a comedy, and revealing the secrets of thrillers. Oops, did I say "thriller"? If you see ads on TV, I suppose you already knew that, but I didn't, and on the basis of the opening minutes, I thought this was a comedy. Honest.

So here was a thriller that worked for me. I didn't see revelations approaching because I didn't expect any. At one point in the film, I wondered about something, and then thought, "Nahhh, couldn't be." Could be.

The movie is about two couples and a suspicious third couple. The two main couples are Cliff and Cydney, honeymooners in Hawaii, and Nick and Gina, hikers. They meet on a difficult wilderness trail on the beautiful island of Kauai. The trail is spotted with signs warning of narrow paths, steep drops, sudden rains, and falling rocks. I love warnings about falling rocks. How do you avoid them? The Hawaii Park Service is famous for its helpful signs. My favorite is "Caution: Lava flow."

Cliff and Cydney (Steve Zahn and Milla Jovovich) are burdened with half the contents of an outdoor store for their couple of days of camping. Nick and Gina (Timothy Olyphant and Kiele Sanchez) travel lighter; indeed, the first time we see Nick he's carrying only a canteen, although later he produces a tent and a hunting bow. The third couple (Marley Shelton and Chris Hemsworth) are hitchhikers; she's friendly, he sends out bad vibes to both of the other men.

News comes of the brutal murder of a honeymooning couple in Honolulu. But Kauai should be safe, right? Maybe not. It's a rule of a thriller that if you warn the audience about a brutal killing, the killer(s) must turn up. This would be true if hikers in Iceland learned of a brutal killing in Hawaii. You don't bring the gun onstage unless it fires.

The director, David Twohy, allows creepiness to steal into the film slowly, but soon the jungle shadows seem filled with menace. Also, there is a narrow path with a steep drop, although Nick helps the newlyweds to negotiate it. Nick is a former Special Ops man, first into Iraq; Gina helpfully mentions he's "impossible to kill." Soon his macho posture begins to eat away at the less capable Cliff. They all travel together, which may or may not be a good idea, although—are they being followed? Whether they are or not I will leave you to decide. I will also leave the obligatory murderer(s) unrevealed. Let me just mention that Cliff says he's a screenwriter, and Nick finds out the screenplay is being rewritten and busts his chops about that, and then Nick mentions "red snappers" and Cliff says the correct term is "red herrings," and let us say that although the dinner menu includes mountain goat and macaroni and cheese, there is no fish course.

I enjoyed the acting. Steve Zahn is at last being liberated from the doofus characters he specialized in and allowed into the I.Q. mainstream. Milla Jovovich sure does a mighty fine rural Georgia accent for a girl from Ukraine. Timothy Olyphant is convincing as a man who is impossible to kill, and Kiele Sanchez as a woman who likes that aspect of his character.

The plot will require some discussion after the film is over. Is it misleading? Yes. Does it cheat? I think not. It only seems to cheat. That's part of the effect. All's fair in love and war, and the plots of thrillers.

The Perfect Sleep ★ ½
R, 105 m., 2009

Anton Pardoe (Narrator), Roselyn Sanchez (Porphyria), Patrick Bauchau (Nikolai), Peter J. Lucas (Ivan), Tony Amendola (Dr. Sebastian), Sam Thakur (The Rajah). Directed by Jeremy Alter and produced by Alter, Keith Kjarval, and Anton Pardoe. Screenplay by Pardoe.

The Perfect Sleep puts me in mind of a flywheel spinning in the void. It is all burnished brass and shining steel, perfectly balanced as it hums in its orbit; yet because it occupies a void, it satisfies only itself and touches nothing else. Here is a movie that goes about its business without regard for an audience.

Oh, it is well-crafted, I grant you that. The cinematography contains fine compositions, looking down steeply on angled shadows and seeking down lost corridors. It has interiors that look like nineteenth-century landmarks of architecture just after the movers left with the furniture. It has grim men, a seductive woman, guns, knives, garrotes, scalpels, needles, cudgels, feet, fists, and baseball bats. It even has Patrick Bauchau, with the most insinuating voice since Orson Welles. But what in God's name is it about?

The Perfect Sleep does not lack explanation; in fact, the unnamed hero (Anton Pardoe) provides a narration that goes on and on and on, perhaps because the screenplay is by Anton Pardoe. He has returned to an unnamed city after ten years of fleeing men who would kill him, one who may be his father, a woman named Porphyria (Roselyn Sanchez), whom he loves and who has always loved him, a child he raised or fathered—or is an orphan, I'm unclear—an ambitious crime boss named The Rajah, a sinister physician named Dr. Sebastian (Tony Amendola), empty streets, wicked staircases, not many cars, and lots of streetlights.

It's all here. And after telling you so much about what's in it, wouldn't you think I could tell you the plot? I know the Narrator is back, he wants revenge, people want revenge on him, everybody is getting killed, and he personally is beaten, stabbed, kicked, thrown down stairs, skewered, hammered with karate, strangled, whipped, and shot point-blank in the head, and, what a guy, he just keeps on narrating, narrating, and narrating.

There are many unique ways of delivering mayhem in the film, some of them described in clinical detail by Dr. Sebastian while he is administering them. "Jugular . . . carotid? Carotid . . . jugular?" he debates with himself, his scalpel poised. At another point, he walks cheerfully up to two guys and stabs them in a lung apiece. Then he explains to them that they each have a collapsed lung. Dreadfully painful but not fatal.

He suggests it would be appalling for one to have two collapsed lungs. And he delivers this speech: "Our very biological structure promises us that, if it be now, 'tis not to come; if it be not to come, it will be now; if it be not now, yet it will come: Good sirs, the readiness is all." If this sounds like part of a famous speech, you are correct. I fancy the two collapsed lung guys are trying to remember where they heard it when he stabs them in the remaining two lungs. Now I know a lot about collapsed lungs, but I'm not entirely sure who Dr. Sebastian is.

Maybe it doesn't matter. Maybe if it did, the plot would give us a place to dig in our claws and hold on. The movie seems more interested in behavior. Many scenes take place in vast empty spaces like abandoned rehearsal halls or hotel function rooms. Major characters are discovered along an office corridor behind glass doors with their names stenciled on (more fun than captions). There are shadows on top of shadows. It's the film noir universe, all right. What does the title refer to? Perhaps to what you will enjoy during the film.

Persepolis ★ ★ ★ ★
PG-13, 95 m., 2008

Chiara Mastroianni (Marjane), Catherine Deneuve (Tadji [Mother]), Danielle Darrieux (Grandmother), Simon Abkarian (Ebi [Father]), Francois Jerosme (Uncle Anouche), Gabrielle Lopes (Young Marjane). Directed by Marjane Satrapi and Vincent Paronnaud and produced by Marc-Antoine Robert and Xavier Rigault. Screenplay by Satrapi and Paronnaud, based on Satrapi's graphic novels.

I attended the Teheran film festival in 1972 and was invited to the home of my guide and translator to meet her parents and family. Over tea and elegant pastries, they explained proudly that Iran was a "modern" country, that they were devout Muslims but did not embrace the extremes of other Islamic nations, that their nation represented a new way. Whenever I read another story about the clerical rule that now grips Iran, I think of those people and millions of other Iranians like them, who do not agree with the rigid restrictions they live under—particularly the women. Iranians are no more monolithic than we are, a truth not grasped by our own zealous leader. Remember, on 9/11 there was a huge candlelight vigil in Teheran, in sympathy with us.

That was the Iran that Marjane Satrapi was born into in 1969, and it was the Iran that ended in the late 1970s with the fall and exile of the shah. Yes, his rule was dictatorial; yes, his secret police were everywhere and his opponents subjected to torture. But that was the norm in the Middle East and in an arc stretching up to the Soviet Union. At least most Iranians were left more or less free to lead the lives they chose. Ironically, many of them believed the fall of the shah would bring more, not less, democracy.

Satrapi remembers the first nine or ten years of her life as a wonderful time. Surrounded by a loving, independently minded family, living in a comfortable time, she resembled teenagers everywhere in her love for

pop music, her interest in fashion, her Nikes. Then it all changed. She and her mother and her feisty grandmother had to shroud their faces from the view of men. Makeup and other forms of western decadence were forbidden. At her age she didn't drink or smoke, but God save any woman who did.

Satrapi, now living in Paris, told her life story in two graphic novels, which became best-sellers and have now been made into this wondrous animated film. The animation is mostly in black and white, with infinite shades of gray and a few guest appearances, here and there, by colors. The style is deliberately two-dimensional, avoiding the illusion of depth in current animation. This approach may sound spartan, but it is surprisingly involving, wrapping us in this autobiography that distills an epoch into a young woman's life. Not surprisingly, the books have been embraced by smart teenage girls all over the world, who find much they identify with. Adolescence is fueled by universal desires and emotions, having little to do with government decrees.

Marjane, voiced as a child by Gabrielle Lopes and as a teenager and adult by Chiara Mastroianni, is a sprightly kid, encouraged in her rambunctiousness by her parents (voiced by Catherine Deneuve and Simon Abkarian), and applauded by her outspoken grandmother (Danielle Darrieux). She dotes on the stories of her spellbinding Uncle Anouche (Francois Jerosme), who has been in prison and sometimes in hiding but gives her a vision of the greater world.

In her teens, with the Ayatollah Khomeini under full steam, Iran turns into a hostile place for the spirits of those such as Marjane. The society she thought she lived in has disappeared, and with it much of her freedom as a woman to define herself outside of marriage and the fearful restrictions of men. Sometimes she fast-talks herself out of tight corners, as when she is almost arrested for wearing makeup, but it is clear to her parents that Marjane will eventually attract trouble. They send her to live with friends in Vienna.

Austria provides her with a radically different society, but one she eventually finds impossible to live in. She was raised with values that do not fit with the casual sex and drug use she finds among her contemporaries there, and after going a little wild with rock and roll and acting out, she doesn't like herself, is homesick, and returns to Iran. But it is even more inhospitable than she remembers. She is homesick for a nation that no longer exists.

In real life, Marjane Satrapi eventually found a congenial home in France. I imagine Paris offered no less decadence than Vienna, but her experiences had made her into a woman more sure of herself and her values, and she grows into—well, the author of books and this film, which dramatize so meaningfully what her life has been like. For she is no heroine, no flag-waving idealist, no rebel, not always wise, sometimes reckless, but with strong family standards.

It might seem that her story is too large for one ninety-eight-minute film, but *Persepolis* tells it carefully, lovingly, and with great style. It is infinitely more interesting than the witless coming-of-age western girls we meet in animated films; in spirit, in gumption, in heart, Marjane resembles someone like the heroine in *Juno*—not that she is pregnant at sixteen, of course. While so many films about coming of age involve manufactured dilemmas, here is one about a woman who indeed does come of age, and magnificently.

Note: Persepolis shared the jury prize at Cannes 2007 and has been selected by France as its official Oscar entry in the foreign-language category, a rare honor for any animated film.

Pineapple Express ★ ★ ★ ½
R, 111 m., 2008

Seth Rogen (Dale Denton), James Franco (Saul Silver), Danny McBride (Red), Gary Cole (Ted Jones), Rosie Perez (Carol), Amber Heard (Angie Anderson), Bill Hader (Private Miller), James Remar (General Bratt). Directed by David Gordon Green and produced by Judd Apatow and Shauna Robertson. Screenplay by Seth Rogen and Evan Goldberg.

David Gordon Green, that poet of the cinema, is the last person you'd expect to find directing a Judd Apatow male-buddy comedy about two potheads who start a drug war. But he does such a good job there's a danger he'll become in demand by mainstream Hollywood and tempted away from the greatness he showed in *George Washington* and *Undertow*. (I can imagine his agent hiding this review from him.)

Pineapple Express has all the elements you'd expect from the genre: male bonding, immature sexual desires, verbal scatology, formidable drug abuse, fight scenes, gunfire, explosions. Yawn? Not this time. It's a quality movie even if the material is unworthy of the treatment. As a result, yes, it's a druggie comedy that made me laugh.

The heroes are a process server named Dale (Seth Rogen) and his drug dealer, Saul (James Franco). Both are stoned in every single scene. Dale has a romance going with Angie (Amber Heard), who I hope is of legal age, although physical sex isn't necessarily involved. I think Dale is still at the age of emotional development where going all the way means asking a girl to go steady. Saul is even more pathetic, hiding in his apartment filled with electronic gizmos and merchandise.

Dale drops in on Saul one day to buy some weed, and Saul gives him a sample of a new product just imported by his connection. This is Pineapple Express, a blend of marijuana so sublime, he says, that even smoking it is a crime "like killing a unicorn." Dale gets high on the aroma alone. Floating away from Saul's after a hallucinatory conversation, he goes to serve a summons on Ted Jones (Gary Cole), the very man Saul gets his pot from.

Parked in front of the house for one last toke, Dale is horrified to see a squad car parked behind him and throws away the joint. Then he has a front-row seat to witness, through a huge glass wall, a man being shot dead by Ted and a female cop (Rosie Perez). He speeds away, leaving Ted to find the joint, sample it, identify it, and know that the murder witness bought it from Saul. The buddies know Ted will make this connection and begin a desperate flight from Ted's incompetent hit men. This leads them into a funny stumble through a forest preserve, the loss of their car, and Dale's attempt to plausibly sit through dinner with Angie's parents (Ed Begley Jr. and Nora Dunn) while stoned, bleeding, torn, disheveled, and in need of being hosed down.

The critic James Berardinelli observes: "A lot of buddy films aren't fundamentally that different from romantic comedies. The relationships are often developed in the same fashion, only with male bonding replacing sexual chemistry." Does that make Dale and Saul gay, even if they're not aware of it? I think that describes the buddies in a lot of buddy movies produced by Judd Apatow, including the recent *Step Brothers*. Especially in the obligatory happy ending, there's a whole lot of hugging and chanting of "I love you, man!"

A third major character enters the scene when Dale and Saul visit Saul's buddy, Red (Danny McBride), who has already betrayed them to the hit men. All of this leads, don't ask how, to a full-scale war between Ted's men and a rival drug empire, "the Asians," who attack conveniently dressed in matching black uniforms, which makes them easy targets under the sunlamps of Ted's indoor pot farm. Many, many people die horribly, none more thoroughly than poor Rosie Perez.

Two teams have met to make this picture: the Apatow production line, and Green and his cameraman, Tim Orr, soundman Chris Gebert, actor Danny McBride, and others he met at the North Carolina School of the Arts. As always, even in their zero-budget first effort, they use widescreen compositions with graceful visual instincts, although you may be excused for not noticing them, considering what happens. The movie has the usual chase, this time between two squad cars, but to my amazement I found it exciting and very funny, especially the business about Saul's leg.

Pineapple Express is the answer to the question, "What would happen if a movie like this was made by a great director?" This question descends directly from those old rumors that Stanley Kubrick was going to make a porn film. Give it a moment's thought. And I suspect Green of foiling Apatow's vow to include at least one penis in every one of his comedies. This time, it's not a penis but a finger, and a good thing, too.

Note: Despite a "warning," the movie is enthusiastically pro-pot.

The Pink Panther 2 ★ ★
PG, 92 m., 2009

Steve Martin (Jacques Clouseau), Jean Reno (Ponton), Emily Mortimer (Nicole), Andy Garcia (Vincenzo), Alfred Molina (Pepperidge), Yuki Matsuzaki (Kenji), Aishwarya Rai Bachchan (Sonia), John Cleese (Dreyfus), Lily Tomlin (Mrs. Berenger). Directed by Harald Zwart and produced by Robert Simonds. Screenplay by Scott Neustadter, Michael H. Weber, and Steve Martin.

I was smiling all the way through the opening credits of *The Pink Panther 2*. They made me miss the golden age of credits, when you actually found out who the actors were going to be and maybe saw a little cartoon in the bargain: this time, one about the misadventures of the Pink Panther, of course. And then the names in the cast!

Imagine these appearing one after another: Steve Martin, Jean Reno, Emily Mortimer, Andy Garcia, Alfred Molina, Aishwarya Rai Bachchan, John Cleese, Lily Tomlin, Jeremy Irons, Johnny Hallyday . . . wait a minute! Aishwarya Rai Bachchan! That's the Indian actress Aishwarya Rai! The most beautiful woman in the world!

As the movie began, my smile faded. The actors are let down by the screenplay and direction, which don't really pop the supporting characters out into strong comic focus. Maybe the cast is simply too star-studded? There's sometimes the feeling they're being cycled onscreen by twos and threes, just to keep them alive.

Then there's the albatross of the Blake Edwards and Peter Sellers films. Edwards was a truly inspired director of comedies (*The Party, SOB, Victor/Victoria*). Peter Sellers was a genius who somehow made Inspector Clouseau seem as if he really were helplessly incapable of functioning in the real world, and somehow incapable of knowing that. Steve Martin is a genius, too, but not at being Inspector Clouseau. It seems more like an exercise.

The plot: "The Tornado" has stolen the Magna Carta, the Japanese emperor's sword, and the Shroud of Turin. Next may be the Pink Panther, the pink diamond that is, for some reason, the symbol of France's greatness and not merely an example of carbon under great pressure. Clouseau is chosen, despite the apoplectic agitation of Chief Inspector Dreyfus (John Cleese), to join an international police Dream Team to thwart the possible deed.

Also onstage is Clouseau's assistant, Nicole (Emily Mortimer), a fragrant rose; she and Jacques are so in love with each other they cannot even bring themselves to admit it. The Italian team member, Vincenzo (Andy Garcia), family name Doncorleone, moves in on Nicole and tells Clouseau that Sonia (Aishwarya Rai) likes him. That creates a romcom situation that's sort of muted because of Jacques and Nicole's shyness, and because the film seems reluctant to foreground Sonia very much. Aishwarya Rai is breathtaking in Bollywood films, where they devote a great deal of expertise to admiring beauty, but here she's underutilized and too much in the background.

Molina plays Pepperidge, a Sherlockian type who claims to be a great deducer of clues. Clouseau takes one look at him and they start a deducing showdown, sort of funny. Reno is Ponton, Clouseau's associate inspector, whose considerable presence never really pays off. Yuki Matsuzaki, as the Japanese cop Kenji, seems to be projecting ideas about the character that were edited out or never written in. Tomlin is the departmental expert on P.C. behavior, whom Clouseau argues with ("But . . . blondes *are* dumb!").

Opportunities to better develop all of these characters are lost, and we're left with the sight and stunt gags, which are central to the Panther movies, of course, but feel recycled: This time, little kids are the kung fu experts, for example, instead of Cato.

Too many of the stunt gags are performed without payoffs; Buster Keaton, the master, always gave you reaction shots. When Clouseau is mistaken for the pope, for example, and seems to fall from his balcony to his death, why isn't there a crowd to contemplate the fallen Frenchman with his black moustache, maybe lurching to his feet, blessing them, and intoning *dov'e la toilette*? Or after Clouseau sets the restaurant on fire, why not make him struggle to get back inside, telling the firemen he insists on paying his check?

The first two Panther movies, *The Pink Panther* (1963) and *A Shot in the Dark* (1964), were a serendipitous coming together of Edwards and Sellers. Truth to tell, none of their others were as inspired. The moment had passed. And it still hasn't come back round again. Zut!

Pirate Radio ★★★
R, 116 m., 2009

Philip Seymour Hoffman (The Count), Bill Nighy (Quentin), Rhys Ifans (Gavin), Tom Sturridge (Carl), Kenneth Branagh (Dormandy), Emma Thompson (Charlotte). Directed by Richard Curtis and produced by Curtis, Hilary Bevan Jones, Tim Bevan, and Eric Fellner. Screenplay by Curtis.

Before we get to the movie, let's assume you're near a computer that has iTunes. Go to "radio," look under "alternative rock," and go down to Radio Caroline. I'll tell you why in a moment. Don't turn it up so loud that it drowns out my review.

Incredible but true: From the birth of rock 'n' roll, through the rise of the Beatles and the Stones, all the way until the late 1960s, the BBC used to broadcast only about thirty minutes per day of pop music. "Thought for the Day" did almost as well. The old maids on the BBC board of governors thought it was, in the words of a Conservative minister depicted in this movie, "immoral."

Boredom abhors a vacuum. From pirate radio stations anchored offshore, a steady stream of rock was broadcast from powerful transmitters to the British mainland, where at a given moment, more than half of the radios may have been tuned in. The most famous of these pirates was Radio Caroline. Yes, the very station we're listening to right now. Webcasting is sort of piratical, no? (Right now on Radio Caroline: Bob Dylan's "Just Like a Woman.")

Caroline is the inspiration for Radio Rock, the floating transmitter in *Pirate Radio*. Richard Curtis, who wrote and directed the film, was ten years old in Radio Caroline's heyday, but he must know people who worked on board because the film has a real feel for the shipboard combination of excitement and desperation. Think about it. You're at the cutting edge of a cultural revolution, but you're anchored outside the U.K. territorial waters. It's the Swinging '60s, but the only woman on board is a lesbian. Nobody is swinging, anyway. (Now playing: The Who, "Won't Get Fooled Again.")

The shipboard culture involves a mixed bag

of oddballs and egomaniacs who hold sway over millions of listeners and then go back to their grotty cabins and smoke weed. Well, it's not a crime outside territorial waters. Life really only happens for them when they're on the air. The best known of them is The Count (Philip Seymour Hoffman), an American who has a focus on his work that can only be described as reverential. The ranks of his rivals are peopled by a menagerie of British character actors, led by the Steve Buscemis of England, Bill Nighy and Rhys Ifans. Hold on, Ifans is Welsh. ("I Want You All to Myself," Joan Armatrading.)

Shifts on Rock Radio are long: More than a month, I think, and I get the impression some DJs never went ashore. Everybody is stir-crazy. Nobody is a happy camper. ("Free Bird," Lynyrd Skynyrd.)

Aboard this ship of fools arrives one day a young man named Carl (Tom Sturridge), who is the godson of the station's aloof and preoccupied manager, Quentin (Nighy). What's Carl doing aboard here? He's on summer holiday and is rather uncertain in the midst of this hotbed. It's possible he may find the solution to a personal question on board. ("Complicated," Avril Lavigne.)

Richard Curtis is good at handling large casts, establishing all the characters, and keeping them alive. His credits include *Love Actually* and the scripts for *Four Weddings and a Funeral, Notting Hill,* and *Bridget Jones's Diary.* Here the plot doesn't require a reason for the characters to keep running into one another; there's nowhere they can hide. No coincidences means more development. And the wall-to-wall '60s rock keeps things bright.

Meanwhile, back in Parliament, a tight-arsed Sir Alistair Dormandy (Kenneth Branagh) denounces pirate radio as "a sewer of dirty commercialism and no morals." As the threat of a shutdown looms, the prospect grows dire, and we begin to realize that among these pirates, as among the original ones, the shipboard community holds their identity and validates their stubborn dreams.

The government vows to sink the pirates and finally forces through the required legislation. This is highly unpopular. Just imagine an American administration turning off your rock and forcing you to listen only to NPR.

Wow, I'm sorry I wrote that. There are probably fringers who think Obama is plotting to do just that.

No Beatles. No, I don't mean Obama would outlaw the Beatles. I mean I noticed Radio Caroline didn't play their records.   ☞

Planet 51 ★★ ½
PG, 91 m., 2009

With the voices of: Dwayne Johnson (Captain Chuck Baker), Justin Long (Lem), Jessica Biel (Neera), Gary Oldman (General Grawl), Seann William Scott (Skiff), John Cleese (Professor Kipple), Freddie Benedict (Eckle), Alan Marriott (Glar). Directed by Jorge Blanco and codirected by Javier Abad and Marcos Martinez; produced by Guy Collins and Ignacio Pérez Dolset. Screenplay by Joe Stillman.

The 1950s Hollywood tradition was that an alien spaceship landed on Earth and was surrounded fearfully by military troops. *Planet 51* is true to the tradition, but this time the ship comes from Earth, and it lands on a planet inhabited by little green men. It's still the 1950s, however.

Yes, on *Planet 51* they speak English, "Lollipop" is on the jukebox, and they speed around in little cars that look like a cross between '50s gas guzzlers and those bubble-domed cars of the future. Planet 51, in fact, is a lot like the black-and-white parts of *Pleasantville.* Everybody is sweet and friendly, except for militaristic warmongers like General Grawl (Gary Oldman), and it's hard to figure out who he's afraid of because as far as we can tell, this is a civilization without any enemies.

Although not bowling me over, this is a jolly and good-looking animated feature in glorious 2-D. It doesn't make the slightest effort to explain why an English-speaking clone of the world of *American Graffiti* could exist elsewhere in the universe. How could it? Besides, under the emerging theory of the multiverse, I think (but am not sure) such a thing is entirely possible. Somewhere. As long as it's consistent with the laws of physics. I am not sure how they explain that the rain is made of rocks. You'd think the rocks would eventually bury everything. Maybe they melt?

Not that science on Planet 51 has reached

the level of explaining such things. Its hero, Lem (Justin Long), has just won a job as a lecturer at the astronomical observatory, where he explains the universe is "hundreds of miles wide." He is gently filled in by Chuck Baker (Dwayne Johnson), an American astronaut who lands on the planet. At first he and Lem are frightened of each other, but after they bond and Chuck discovers he can breathe Planet 51's atmosphere, he settles down to the puzzle of using his lander to return to its orbiter. He has arrived with Rover, possibly intended to stay and look around, who is a cross between a Mars lander, WALL-E, and a friendly dog, and he loves to scamper around and collect rocks, as all good Rovers do.

Apparently there is no way a family animated cartoon can avoid ending in action scenes, and General Grawl leads his troops against the menacing Chuck. At least the battle is slapstick and not very violent. And all ends happily. Oops, was that a spoiler?

The movie was written by Joe Stillman, who wrote *Shrek*. It was beautifully animated in Spain and uses the voice talents of Jessica Biel, Seann William Scott, and John Cleese. It's perfectly pleasant as kiddie entertainment, although wall-to-wall with pop references to the American 1950s. I believe there may be millions of kiddies who, hard as this is to conceive, have never heard of Elvis. As that decade recedes in our rearview mirror, it more and more seems to signify something big and enduring. What, I am not sure.

Play the Game ★★
PG-13, 105 m., 2009

Andy Griffith (Grandpa Joe), Paul Campbell (Dave), Liz Sheridan (Edna Gordon), Doris Roberts (Rose Sherman), Marla Sokoloff (Julie), Clint Howard (Dick), Rance Howard (Mervin), Geoffrey Owens (Rob), Juliette Jeffers (Carrie). Directed, written, and produced by Marc Fienberg.

The Andy Griffith Show meets *Seinfeld* in the sack, in *Play the Game*, which shows Andy is not too old to star in a sex comedy. I guess. Griffith plays Grandpa Joe, who lost his beloved wife two years ago. Now his grandson Dave (Paul Campbell) thinks it's time for him to start dating again. After all, he isn't getting any younger.

Grandpa Joe is pretty much on standby in his retirement home. He'd like to get cozy with Rose (Doris Roberts). But he's unprepared for the wiles of Edna (Liz Sheridan, who played Seinfeld's mom). She supplies Joe with Viagra, and he more or less seduces her on autopilot.

Dave considers himself a babe magnet. He's a genius at fast-talking himself into relationships that, alas, have a way of ending once he's run through his prepared material. He's also a whiz at selling cars, but at least when he makes a sale the victim drives it off the lot.

The screenplay, written by first-time director Marc Fienberg, fervently stays true to an ancient sitcom tradition. We somehow suspect Grandpa Joe will end up with the adorable Rose, and whaddaya know, Dave finds genuine love with Rose's granddaughter, Julie (Marla Sokoloff).

And that's about it, except for a close-up of Andy Griffith that I could easily have lived without. I've admired Griffith ever since *No Time for Sergeants*, but the one thing I must admit I've never wanted to do was regard his face while he's enjoying oral sex from Seinfeld's mom. I have a good friend whose own dad discovered Viagra in a retirement home and would call his son almost daily to recount his latest adventures. He called once when I was in the room with my friend, who urgently told him, "Dad, I've told you, I don't want to know!" I told him the old one about the old lady who runs naked into the TV room of her retirement village shouting, "Super sex! Super sex!" One of the guys perks up and says, "I'll have the soup, please."

Please Give ★★★ ½
R, 91 m., 2010

Catherine Keener (Kate), Amanda Peet (Mary), Oliver Platt (Alex), Rebecca Hall (Rebecca), Ann Morgan Guilbert (Andra), Sarah Steele (Abby). Directed by Nicole Holofcener and produced by Anthony Bregman. Screenplay by Holofcener.

There is an evil-tempered old woman in *Please Give* whose greatest accomplishment is having survived into her nineties without being pushed down a steep flight of stairs. She finds fault with everyone and everything, is ungrateful, is a whiner, and brings nothing to the party. How do people like this live with themselves?

Her next-door neighbors are waiting for her to die so that her apartment will become available and they can break down some walls. This is in New York, the city that drains a cruel price per square foot of living space from its inhabitants. I know New Yorkers happy to find an apartment that for a somewhat poor Chicagoan would be the bedroom. It is one of the pleasures of Nicole Holofcener's new film that everyone, including the old lady, knows this.

The couple next door are Kate and Alex (Catherine Keener and Oliver Platt). They run an antique-furniture store specializing in furniture from the 1950s—you know, the kind your family accumulated at great expense, which sat there in the house looking superior. They often obtain their stock from grandchildren who consider a 1952 coffee table to be the graceless blotch it surely is, but which metrosexuals consider an ironic statement on how cool they are.

The old lady, Andra, is played by Ann Morgan Guilbert with exact cunning: She makes Andra expert at seeming unaware of her monstrous selfishness. Andra is looked after by two granddaughters, Mary (Amanda Peet) and Rebecca (Rebecca Hall). Rebecca is constant and kind, Mary is a distracted heavy drinker, both are attractive, and they live together in one of those roommate arrangements that can be explained only by madness or the cost of apartments.

Kate is another of those Catherine Keener characters you feel like you've known somewhere before. She and her husband have a nice life as a couple who seem to be winning their own version of *Antiques Roadshow*. They have a daughter, Abby (Sarah Steele), who is pudgy, has skin problems, and is a little antisocial right now but is smart, has good timing, and will eventually get life sorted out. Abby is incredulous at the way her mom is a pushover for street beggars, as if she's making some kind of amends. Kate can hardly enjoy a meal without taking a doggie bag to a homeless man. She's an innocent; she's shocked to find that another dealer bought a table from her and marked it up in his own store.

Kate and Alex are reasonably happy. They run errands for old Andra to calm their consciences, and decide to have a dinner party for the old lady and her granddaughters. This scene shows Holofcener demonstrating that recognizable life is almost always more engrossing than fantasy; it's an exercise in social embarrassment, one of those Bunuelian scenes in which people unexpectedly tell the truth and say what should not be said.

Nicole Holofcener, who made the great *Lovely and Amazing*, pays close attention to women. She doesn't define them by their relationships with men. In a Holofcener movie, women actually have their *own* reasons for doing things—and these are even allowed to be bad reasons, and funny ones. The movie is about imperfect characters in a difficult world, who mostly do the best they can under the circumstances, but not always. Do you realize what a revolutionary approach that is for a movie these days?

Police, Adjective ★★★
NO MPAA RATING, 115 m., 2009

Dragos Bucur (Cristi), Vlad Ivanov (Anghelache), Irina Saulescu (Anca), Ion Stoica (Nelu), Marian Ghenea (Prosecutor). Directed, written, and produced by Corneliu Porumboiu.

Police, Adjective is a peculiar title for a film. The posters at Cannes 2009 read "*Politist, adjectiv.*" With a period and a gun on top of a dictionary. A critic from Romania, sitting next to us before the screening, explained that the purity of the language is enforced as fervently in Romania as in France, and "police," of course, is properly a noun.

And there you have the movie. Its hero is a young cop assigned to nab drug users, and its surprisingly effective key scene involves an argument with his captain over the dictionary definitions of the words "conscience" and "justice." This may not sound exciting, but it was welcome after legions of cop movies in which such arguments are orchestrated with the f-word (good luck finding that in the dictionary).

The cop's name is Cristi (Dragos Bucur), and he's been assigned to follow a sixteen-year-old schoolboy suspected of smoking pot. The kid does smoke pot. He often smokes it with a pal and a girlfriend. Does he "supply" it? If he has it and offers a toke to them, I suppose the definition of that would be supplying.

The cop is recently married, and he and his wife spent their honeymoon in Prague. He doesn't want to follow this kid. If he arrests him, the kid gets locked up for eight to sixteen years. "That would ruin his life," he tells the captain. "Did you force him to smoke pot?" No, the cop says, but in Prague it's smoked openly on the streets and the cops look the other way.

The captain patiently explains that in Romania smoking pot is against the law, and the duty of the police is to enforce the law. "I don't want to arrest him," Cristi says. "It's against my conscience." Then the dictionary comes out. My dictionary, which I believe the captain was also using, although in Romanian, has only one definition: *conscience. noun. An inner feeling or voice viewed as acting as a guide to the rightness or wrongness of one's behavior.*

You know the rest. It isn't a policeman's job to act on his inner voices and feelings. It's his job to enforce the law.

This movie I suspect comes with a lot of baggage. Romania under the Ceausescu regime (1965–89) started out promisingly but grew into a repressive police state under which perhaps two million people were killed. Ceausescu's police were often only enforcing the law. Romania has a population of twenty-one million, but it's in the nature of things that many people knew the cops, who were sometimes arresting them or their neighbors. What choice did a cop have?

I speculate that Corneliu Porumboiu, born 1975, who wrote and directed the film, grew up in a nation shadowed by those memories, and that his film to some degree is about that time. It is also a low-key, observant record of a universal dilemma among people in authority: How do you do your duty when your inner voice tells you it's wrong?

The visual style, foregrounding drab areas of a small industrial city, is flat and realistic. We never really meet the young suspect. Cristi doesn't confide in his wife. His office mate knows what he feels but stays out of it. Only the captain and a prosecutor will discuss it with him. Both are more than willing. Both are of an age when they would have started their careers under Ceausescu. They depend on the strict definition of the law because they can use that as a refuge from their inner voices. Cristi understands this, and that's why the debate over the dictionary is so intense. They aren't talking about definitions. They're talking about the past, present, and future of their nation.

Note: The film won both the Un Certain Regard jury prize and the Critics' Prize at Cannes 2009.

Ponyo ★★★★
G, 101 m., 2009

With the voices of: Noah Cyrus (Ponyo), Frankie Jonas (Sosuke), Matt Damon (Koichi), Cate Blanchett (Gran Mamare), Tina Fey (Lisa), Kurt Knutsson (Newscaster), Cloris Leachman (Yoshie), Liam Neeson (Fujimoto), Jennessa Rose (Kumiko), Lily Tomlin (Toki), Betty White (Noriko). Directed by Hayao Miyazaki and produced by Steve Alpert, Kathleen Kennedy, and Frank Marshall. Screenplay by Miyazaki.

There is a word to describe *Ponyo*, and that word is "magical." This poetic, visually breathtaking work by the greatest of all animators has such deep charm that adults and children will both be touched. It's wonderful and never even seems to try: It unfolds fantastically.

The G-rated feature tells a story both simple and profound. Sosuke, a five-year-old who lives in a house on a seaside cliff, finds a goldfish trapped in a jar on the beach. This is Ponyo. Freeing her, he is rewarded by a lick on a finger that heals a cut. And by tasting human blood, we learn, Ponyo gains the ability to transform between fish and human.

This begins a friendship. Sosuke (voice by the Jonas brother Frankie) protects Ponyo (Noah Cyrus, Miley's kid sister) in a pail until arms and legs pop spontaneously from her body and she becomes a little girl who speaks his language. He takes her to school and to the nursing home next door where his father works, and all is wonderful until we discover that by crossing the divide between land and sea, Ponyo has triggered ecological changes that unleash a dangerous tsunami that floods Sosuke's village right up to the doorstep of his house.

This begins an exciting escape in a toy boat that Ponyo magically enlarges, and a dream-like journey among flooded treetops in search of Sosuke's mother. From the surface they can see giant prehistoric fish, awakened by the great wave, that cruise the highways his mother once drove.

This cannot help but sound like standard animated fare. But I have failed to evoke the wonder of Hayao Miyazaki's artistry. This sixty-eight-year-old Japanese master continues to create animation *drawn by hand*, just as *Snow White* and *Pinocchio* were. There is a fluid, organic quality to his work that exposes the facile efficiency of CGI. And, my God!— his imagination!

The film opens with a spellbinding, wordless sequence beneath the sea, showing floating jellyfish and scampering bottom-dwellers. The pastels of this scene make *Ponyo* one of the very rare movies where I want to sit in the front row, to drown in it. This is more than "artistry." It is art.

And consider Miyazaki's imagination as he creates a human protector of this seascape, Fujimoto (Liam Neeson). He is the father of Ponyo and her countless baby sisters (the biology involved is wisely not explained). And although he seems sinister at first, his desire to keep Ponyo in the sea is eventually explained because of his concern for the balance of Earth's nature.

Already it is threatened by the debris of human civilization; we see a bottom-scooping ship dredge up tons of waste. Sosuke's happy life on the cliff top and the peace of his friends at the old folks' home are belied by the pollution so near at hand. Of course, it is up to Ponyo and Sosuke to set things back in balance.

Miyazaki is the Japanese creator of *My Neighbor Totoro, Spirited Away, Howl's Moving Castle,* and many other beloved films. Already I have heard from a few people who don't want to see it "because it's Japanese." This is solid gold ignorance. "Is it only dubbed?" I was asked. You dummy! *All* animated films are dubbed! Little Nemo can't really speak! Miyazaki is known as the god of American animators, and Disney has supplied *Ponyo* with an A-list cast of vocal talents, including also Cate Blanchette, Matt Damon, and Tina Fey. The English-language version has been adapted by John Lasseter (*Toy Story, Up*) and, believe me, he did it for love, not money. There are so few movies that can delight both a small child and the adult in the next seat. Here is one of them.

Post Grad ★★★
PG-13, 89 m., 2009

Alexis Bledel (Ryden Malby), Zach Gilford (Adam Davies), Rodrigo Santoro (David Santiago), Jane Lynch (Carmella Malby), Fred Armisen (Pitchman), Bobby Coleman (Hunter Malby), Michael Keaton (Walter Malby), Carol Burnett (Grandma Maureen). Directed by Vicky Jenson and produced by Jeffrey Clifford, Joe Medjuck, and Ivan Reitman. Screenplay by Kelly Fremon.

The Malbys are just plain nice. That's the only word for them. They're a goofy, strange California suburban family who love one another and share the same sunny sense of humor and nothing terrible ever happens to them and it's all for one and one for all.

Post Grad, the story of how Ryden Malby graduates from college and tries to enter the job market, shows them coping with hard times with good cheer. It's a screwball comedy. It's also, I have to say, a feel-good movie that made me smile a lot. The Malbys are just so darned lovable.

Take Ryden. She's played by Alexis Bledel, who is beautiful in a blue-eyed, open-faced kind of way, and awfully hopeful she'll get a job in publishing because she likes to read more than anything. Dad is Walter (Michael Keaton), the district manager for a luggage retailer, who isn't worried that things will work out fine for her, and even offers her a job helping him sell mail-order belt buckles that he doesn't know are stolen goods.

Ryden's mom, Carmella (Jane Lynch), is sort of the sane center of gravity. Her grandma (Carol Burnett) is a hip baby boomer who gives her frank sex advice. Her much younger little brother, Hunter (Bobby Coleman), is a cuddly goof. Her best friend,

Adam (Zach Gilford), is admiring and loyal, and accepts that she's not in love with him. Even David (Rodrigo Santoro), Adam's sexy older Brazilian rival from across the street, is not a letch and doesn't take advantage of her.

To these good people happen unfortunate things. A job is lost. A cat is mashed. Coffins are damaged. Dad is arrested. The brakes fail on Hunter's car in the soap box derby, and it runs into the lake. But the mashed cat is successfully buried, not without a struggle, which brings to mind the observation of a pet grave digger in *Gates of Heaven*: "Make it too small, and you can't get 'em in there."

There's no doubt Alexis Bledel is the star of this show, an adorable young woman. You may recall her from the *Sisterhood of the Traveling Pants* movies or *Bride & Prejudice*. Hard to believe she was in *Sin City*. Keaton and Lynch somehow seem like the logical parents for this phenomenon of niceness.

Apart from a few words and attitudes, this movie, directed by Vicky Jenson and written by Kelly Fremon, could be a throwback to more innocent times. It contains no drugs, no angst, no bitterness, no generation gap, no big family problems, and it doesn't even seem to know how blessed it is. Sometimes you get out of a movie and feel like you've just worked a desperate overnight shift on homicide. You get out of this movie and you have a good feeling.

Oh, it's not a great movie. It won't alter the course of cinema. It won't make any best ten lists. If you're cynical or jaded, it might not get past you. But here is the first movie in a long time that had me actually admitting I wouldn't mind seeing a sequel.

Precious: Based on the Novel *Push* by Sapphire ★★★★
R, 109 m., 2009

Gabourey "Gabby" Sidibe (Precious), Mo'Nique (Mary), Paula Patton (Ms. Rain), Mariah Carey (Ms. Weiss), Lenny Kravitz (Nurse John), Sherri Shepherd (Cornrows). Directed by Lee Daniels and produced by Daniels and Sarah Siegel-Magness. Screenplay by Geoffrey Fletcher, based on the novel *Push* by Sapphire.

Precious has shut down. She avoids looking at people, she hardly ever speaks, she's nearly illiterate. Inside her lives a great hurt, and also her child, conceived in a rape. She is fat. Her clothes are too tight on her. School is an ordeal of mocking cruelty. Home is worse. Her mother, defeated by life, takes it out on her daughter. After Precious is raped by her father, her mother is angry not at the man, but at the child for "stealing" him.

There's one element in the film that redeems this landscape of despair. That element is hope. Not the hope of Precious, but that of two women who want better for her. It's not that Precious "shows promise." I think it's that these women, having in their jobs seen a great deal, can hardly imagine a girl more obviously in pain.

That is the starting point for *Precious*, a great American film that somehow finds an authentic way to move from these beginnings to an inspiring ending. Gabourey "Gabby" Sidibe, a young actress in her debut performance as Precious, says: "I know this girl. I know her in my family, I know her in my friends, I've seen her, I've lived beside this girl." We may have seen her, too, if we looked. People often don't really look. They see, evaluate, dismiss.

Sidibe is heartbreaking as Precious, that poor girl. Three other actresses perform so powerfully in the film that Academy voters will be hard-pressed to choose among them. Audiences may be hard-pressed to recognize them. Mo'Nique plays Mary, Precious's chain-smoking couch potato of a mother, treating her daughter like a domestic servant and turning a blind eye on years of abuse. Paula Patton is Ms. Rain, Precious's teacher, who is able to see through the girl's sullen withdrawal and her vulgarities and wonder what pain it may be masking. Mariah Carey is Ms. Weiss, a social worker.

This casting looks almost cynical on paper, as if reflecting old Hollywood days when stars were slipped into "character roles" with a wink. But Lee Daniels, the director, didn't cast them for their names and actually doesn't use any of their star qualities. He requires them to act. Somehow he was able to see beneath the surface and trust they had within the emotional resources to play these women, and he was right. Daniels began his career by producing *Monster's Ball*, in which Halle Berry shed

417

her glamour and found such depths that she won an Oscar. Daniels must have an instinct for performances waiting to flower.

Carey and Patton are equal with Sidibe in screen impact; the film holds the girl in the center of their attempt to save her future. Why would a teacher and a social worker go to such lengths to intervene? They must see tragic victims of abuse every day. Mary, the mother, is perhaps not a bad woman but simply one defeated by the forces she now employs against her daughter. Mo'Nique is frighteningly convincing.

The film is a tribute to Sidibe's ability to engage our empathy. Her work is still another demonstration of the mystery of some actors, who evoke feelings in ways beyond words and techniques. She so completely creates the Precious character that you rather wonder if she's very much like her. You meet Sidibe, who is engaging, outgoing, and ten years older, and you're almost startled. She's not at all like Precious, but in her first performance she not only understands this character but knows how to make her attract the sympathy of her teacher, the social worker—and ourselves. I don't know how she does it, but there you are.

Pride and Glory ★ ★
R, 125 m., 2008

Edward Norton (Ray Tierney), Colin Farrell (Jimmy Egan), Jon Voight (Francis Tierney Sr.), Noah Emmerich (Francis Tierney Jr.), Jennifer Ehle (Abby Tierney). Directed and produced by Gavin O'Connor. Screenplay by O'Connor and Joe Carnahan.

Pride and Glory is the kind of film where you feel like you know the words and ought to be singing along. It follows the well-worn pathways of countless police dramas before it. We find a drug deal gone bad, corruption on the force, brother against brother, alcoholic dad who is both their father and their superior officer, family friend as a traitor, plus one dying wife and another one who is fed up. There's a stroke of originality: A baby seems about to be branded by a hot steam iron.

If you set this in New York, provide all the characters with strong ethnic identities, film

under glowering skies, add a lot of dead bodies right at the start, and have characters shout at one another, all you'd have to do is change the names and hire different actors, and you could do this all again and again.

The setup: Four cops are killed in a drug bust gone wrong. They are under the command of Francis Tierney Jr. (Noah Emmerich). The moment you bring a Junior onstage, the formula requires a Senior, in this case played by Jon Voight as a high-maintenance boozer. Senior confronts his other son, Ray Tierney (Edward Norton), who has fled the streets for a low-risk assignment after Something Very Bad happened a few years ago, and persuades him to rejoin the tough guys: After all, he has to help out Junior.

Also involved is the Tierney brother-in-law, Jimmy Egan (Colin Farrell). Oh, and Junior's wife, Abby (Jennifer Ehle), is dying of cancer and has lost her hair to chemo. And Ray's wife, Tasha (Carmen Ejogo), has split with him and, in the tradition of all cop wives, accuses him of neglecting his family and, on Christmas, receiving a visit from a guy who would be the first one you would pick out of a lineup, whether or not you recognized him, because he looks like he has just done Something Very Bad.

The plot involves how and why the four cops were killed. This may not come as a shock to veteran filmgoers: There is a culture of corruption in the department, and one character is guilty, one is innocent, and one is conflicted in his loyalties. Once we know this, we know there will be a series of angry and desperate confrontations among the three, interlaced with violent face-downs with criminals, cops being slammed up against walls in the basement of headquarters, and Senior drinking even more because he is horribly confused about whether he values truth above family loyalty, and either one above loyalty to the department. Jon Voight is a fine actor, but putting him in a role like this is like hanging him out to dry.

My friend McHugh used to be fond of suddenly announcing, "Clear the bar! I want to drink by myself!" Such a moment supplies the sensationally bad ending to *Pride and Glory*, when one brother enters the bar where the other brother is drinking, flashes his badge, and tells everyone to scram. Why? So he and his brother can settle everything with a brutal fistfight. As we know, under the Macho Code, this means that after two people who love each other end up beaten and bloody, they will somehow arrive at a catharsis. How that solves this tangled web of loyalty, deceit, and corruption, I can't be exactly sure.

Prince of Persia: The Sands of Time ★★
PG-13, 116 m., 2010

Jake Gyllenhaal (Dastan), Gemma Arterton (Tamina), Ben Kingsley (Nizam), Alfred Molina (Sheikh Amar), Steve Toussaint (Seso), Toby Kebbell (Garsiv), Richard Coyle (Tus), Ronald Pickup (King Sharaman). Directed by Mike Newell and produced by Jerry Bruckheimer. Screenplay by Boaz Yakin, Doug Miro, and Carlo Bernard, based on the video game by Jordan Mechner.

Prince of Persia: The Sands of Time is a children's story beefed up to appeal to young teens. It's based on a video game, but don't make me play it, let me guess: The push-button magic dagger is used in the game to let you rewind and try something again, right? Since anything in the story (any death, for example) can be reversed, the stakes are several degrees below urgent. And there's a romance in which the boy and girl spend endless moments about to kiss for every nanosecond they actually do. If I were the Prince of Persia, I'd push the button, go back in time, and plant a wet one on Tamina's luscious lips.

The movie is set in ancient Persia, which is now named Iran. This is a land with truly astonishing landscapes: deserts, canyons, craggy monument valleys, and a mountain range that resembles the Himalayas. Fair enough, since Persia reaches "from the steppes of China to the shores of the Mediterranean," but even more impressive since it's all within a day's journey of the capital city.

That city, whose name escapes me, is ruled by the noble King Sharaman (Ronald Pickup). One day in the marketplace he sees a brave young urchin defend a boy being beaten and escape pursuit by running across rooftops. This is Dastan, who will grow up to be played by Jake Gyllenhaal. He's an orphan; his birth

parents are two movies, the Douglas Fairbanks (1924) and Michael Powell (1940) versions of *The Thief of Bagdad*.

Dastan is adopted by the king and raised with two brothers, Garsiv (Toby Kebbell) and Tus (Richard Coyle). The names of the movie's characters seem to have been created by a random-word generator. The king has a brother named Nizam (Ben Kingsley), first seen in a sinister close-up that could be subtitled, "I will turn out to be the villain." He has a Vandyke beard and eyes that glower smolderingly.

Dastan is good at running on rooftops. He can also leap from back to back in a herd of horses, jump across mighty distances, climb like a monkey, and spin like a top. This is all achieved with special effects, ramped up just fast enough to make them totally unbelievable. Fairbanks has a 1924 scene where he hops from one giant pot to another. He did it in real time, with little trampolines hidden in the pots, and six pots in that movie are worth the whole kitchen in this one.

Anyway, the evil Nizam insists that the Persian army invade the peaceful city of Alamut. This is a beautiful city surrounding a towering castle. King Sharaman has ordered the city not be sacked, but nooo. Nizam has secret information that Alamut is manufacturing weapons of mass destruction for Persia's enemies. Poor Dick Cheney. He can't even go to a Disney swashbuckler without running into finger wagging.

Anyway, Dastan climbs the city walls, pours flaming oil on its guards, etc., and then encounters the beautiful Princess Tamina (Gemma Arterton). She possesses the Dagger of Time, which is an honest-to-God WMD, since if it's switched on too long, all the sands of time will run out, and it's back to the Big Bang.

The plot involves portentous dialogue ("The only way to stop this Armageddon is for us to take the Dagger to the Secret Guardian Temple"), which separates tiresome CGI sequences in which clashing warriors do battle in shots so brief we can see people getting whacked, but have no conception of actual physical space. Of course, this must all lead to Tamina and Dastan fleeing from the evil Nizam, who has framed the lad for regicide.

Their flight brings them under the sway of

419

the film's obligatory Comic Supporting Character, Sheikh Amar (Alfred Molina), a con man who runs rigged ostrich races, and those who have tried to fix an ostrich race will know that the bloody ostriches are impossible to reason with. My interest perked up with the prospect that Dastan and Tamina might try to flee by ostrich-back, but no luck. Imagine the scene! Gemma in foreground, Jake right behind her, compressed by telephoto, jerking up and down at terrific speed while sand dunes whiz past on the green screen in the background.

The irritating thing about special effects is that *anything* can happen, and often you can't tell what the hell it is. Dastan, for example, seems to fall into a vast sinkhole as the sand is sucked from beneath him at dizzying speed. Exactly how he is saved of this predicament isn't exactly clear.

Other key events are obscure. It looked to me as if Garsiv was killed on two occasions, yet is around for the end of the movie, and I don't think the Dagger of Time was involved in either of them. The workings of the Dagger are in any event somewhat murky; when you push the button in its base, it makes you light up like Sylvester the Puddy Cat sticking a paw in an electric socket, and everyone fast-reverses into their starting positions. How do people in movies always know how to do this stuff without practice?

The two leads are not inspired. Jake Gyllenhaal could make the cover of a muscle mag, but he plays Dastan as if harboring Spider-Man's doubts and insecurities. I recall Gemma Arterton as resembling a gorgeous still photo in a cosmetics ad. If the two actors had found more energy and wit in their roles (if they'd ramped up to the Alfred Molina level, say), that would have been welcome. Oh, almost forgot: Molina's ostrich racer is outraged at government taxes. If big government can't leave a man alone to race his ostriches, they're all Alamutist sympathizers.

The Princess and the Frog ★★★
G, 95 m., 2009

With the voices of: Anika Noni Rose (Tiana), Bruno Campos (Prince Naveen), Keith David (Dr. Facilier), Michael-Leon Wooley (Louis), Jennifer Cody (Charlotte), Jim Cummings (Ray), Peter Bartlett (Lawrence), Jenifer Lewis (Mama Odie), Oprah Winfrey (Eudora, Tiana's Mother), Terrence Howard (James, Tiana's Father), John Goodman ("Big Daddy" La Bouff). Directed by John Musker and Ron Clements and produced by Peter Del Vecho. Screenplay by Musker, Clements, and Rob Edwards.

The opening scenes of Disney's *Princess and the Frog* are like a cool shower after a long and sweaty day. This is what classic animation was like! No 3-D! No glasses! No extra ticket charge! No frantic frenzies of meaningless action! And . . . good gravy! A story! Characters! A plot! It's set in a particular time and place! And it uses (calm me down here) lovingly hand-drawn animation that proceeds at a human pace, instead of racing with odd smoothness. I'm just gonna stand here and let it pour over me.

The movie, which is sweet and entertaining, doesn't quite live up to those opening scenes. But it's a demonstration that the Walt Disney Studios still shelters animators who know *how* to make a movie like that, in an age when too many animated films are like fast food after memories of Mom's pot roast. My guess is that afterward the poor kids won't feel quite so battered by input overload. It dances on the screen and doesn't come into the audience and shake you to make you like it.

The story is set mostly in an African-American community in New Orleans, America's most piquant city, before and after World War I. We meet a young girl named Tiana, who is cherished by her mother Eudora (voice by Oprah Winfrey) and father James (Terrence Howard). Her mom is a seamstress, her dad a hardworking restaurant owner who stirs up a mighty gumbo. He goes off to the army and . . . doesn't return. For Tiana as an adult (Anika Noni Rose), life is a struggle, but she holds fast to her dream of opening a restaurant and serving up her dad's gumbo (with just a soupçon more red sauce).

This is all shown in flowing, atmospheric animation and acted with fetching voices, but the songs by Randy Newman are—I dunno, do you think he's getting sort of Randy Newmaned out? And the absence of a couple of terrific musical numbers is noticeable, I think, although younger viewers will probably be drawn into the story.

SPOILER WARNING: You've heard it before. A princess kisses a frog, and it turns into her handsome Prince Charming. But what if instead she turns into a frog? That's what happens. So now Tiana and the visiting Prince Naveen of Malvonia (Bruno Campos) are both amphibians, although they retain, of course, all of their moral principles and do not perform that act of which frogs are more fond than anything apart from croaking and eating flies.

They're captives of a spell cast by the evil voodoo villain Dr. Facilier (Keith David). But life in the swamp is enlivened by two friends, Louis (Michael-Leon Wooley), an alligator who plays jazz saxophone, and Ray (Jim Cummings), a firefly who fills the Jiminy Cricket slot. They seek the occult Mama Odie (Jenifer Lewis), who may have the power to offset Facilier, and whether Tiana and Prince Naveen are restored and settle down to happy lives of slurping gumbo, I will leave for you to discover.

It is notable that this is Disney's first animated feature since *Song of the South* (1946) to feature African-American characters, and if the studio really never is going to release that film on DVD, which seems more innocent by the day, perhaps they could have lifted "Zip-a-Dee-Do-Dah" from it and plugged it in here. Although the principal characters are all black (other than the rich man Big Daddy and the prince, who is of undetermined race), race is not an issue here because Disney adroitly sidesteps all the realities of being a poor girl in New Orleans in the early 1920s. And just as well, I suppose.

The Princess and the Frog inspires memories of Disney's Golden Age that it doesn't quite live up to, as I've said, but it's spritely and high-spirited and will allow kids to enjoy it without visually assaulting them.

Princess Kaiulani ★★ ½
PG, 97 m., 2010

Q'orianka Kilcher (Princess Ka'iulani), Barry Pepper (Thurston), Will Patton (Sanford Dole), Shaun Evans (Clive Davies), Jimmy Yuill (Archie), Julian Glover (Theo Davies). Directed by Marc Forby and produced by Forby, Lauri Apelian, Ricardo S. Galindez, Nigel Thomas, and Roy Tijoe. Screenplay by Forby.

In the late nineteenth century, American corporations backed by U.S. Marines overthrew the legitimate monarchy of Hawaii. One of the conspirators was Sanford B. Dole, of pineapple fame.

Princess Ka'iulani, niece of King David Kalakaua, was in England at the time, getting a thorough Victorian education. After Kalakaua's death, Queen Lydia Lili'uokalani became his successor to the throne and resisted the outsiders. Then Ka'iulani returned and took up the doomed struggle.

Princess Ka'iulani (Q'orianka Kilcher) is much remembered in Hawaii, much forgotten on the mainland, and the subject of this interesting but creaky biopic. She was the child of a Hawaiian mother who died when she was young, and a Scottish father, Archibald Cleghorn (Jimmy Yuill). It was he who feared his young daughter's life was in danger from the Americans, and returned her to Britain and to the household of his friend Theo Davies (Julian Glover). In the United Kingdom she attended a rigorous boarding school, where there was some rudeness but the children of foreign royalty were not unknown. And she fell in love with Davies's son, Clive (Shaun Evans).

News of the uprising was withheld from her, but when she learned, she blamed the Davies family for concealing telegrams, hurried home, and moved into the Iolani Palace. (The film opens with her throwing a switch to illuminate the place and bring electricity to Honolulu; it had electric lighting before the White House.)

The real Iolani Palace, usually closed to the public but handsomely maintained, was made available to the filmmakers, and is one of a wealth of Hawaiian locations that make the film effortlessly authentic. Indeed, in production values the film is flawless. But it plays too sedately, moves too slowly, and contemplates the occupation of a sovereign kingdom with a curious impassivity.

The presence of Q'orianka Kilcher in the lead is a suggestion of what might have been. You may recall her as the tall, grave fourteen-year-old playing the somewhat similar historical figure Pocahontas in Terrence Malick's *The New World* (2005). In both films a native princess sees her nation conquered by Europeans and is removed to England, educated, and falls in love with a Brit. The difference is that Malick finds mystery, poetry, and beauty in his film, and *Princess Kaiulani* plays more like a history lesson.

When the film was premiered at the 2009 Hawaiian Film Festival, there was much complaint about its original title, *The Barbarian Princess.* For so she was called, just as Pocahontas was sometimes described as a savage. She seems to have been a woman of uncommon intelligence and strength of will, and so loyal to her land that in the film she breaks off with Clive Davies and chooses Hawaii over love.

Princess Kaiulani shows the European business community conspiring against King David's efforts to secure Hawaiians' title to their own land, and indeed the rights were stripped away and the Doles and other old white families converted much of Hawaii into their own private plantation. The film's treatment of these results seems somewhat muted; more drama would have been welcome.

Q'orianka Kilcher seems an intriguing Ka'iulani, as she was a Pocahontas. Of Peruvian and German descent, she was raised in Hawaii, was a hula dancer by five and a student of classical voice at the University of Hawaii by six. Unlike a standard young starlet, she evokes great depth and sympathy in her role, and seems to have created Ka'iulani from the inside out. That she has admired the character since childhood is a help. It's a shame more help didn't come from greater passion in the filmmaking.

The Promotion ★ ★
R, 85 m., 2008

Seann William Scott (Doug), John C. Reilly (Richard), Jenna Fischer (Jen), Lili Taylor (Laurie), Fred Armisen (Scott), Gil Bellows (Board Exec), Bobby Cannavale (Dr. Timm), Rick Gonzalez (Ernesto). Directed by Steve Conrad and produced by Steven A. Jones and Jessika Borsiczky Goyer. Screenplay by Conrad.

The Promotion is a human comedy about two supermarket employees who are always ill at

ease. It's their state of being. I felt a little ill at ease watching it because I was never quite sure whether I was supposed to be laughing at them or feeling sorry for them. It's one of those off-balance movies that seems to be searching for the right tone.

The setting: a Chicago supermarket. The central characters: Doug (Seann William Scott), thirty-three, a loyal employee, and Richard (John C. Reilly), mid-thirties, a Canadian who has immigrated to America with his Scottish wife, Laurie (Lili Taylor), and their daughter. Doug is recently married to Jen (Jenna Fischer). When their supermarket chain decides to open a new store, the two men are in line for a promotion to store manager.

They both desperately desire and need this job. Doug has convinced his wife he's a "shoo-in," and they invest all of their savings in a nonrefundable deposit on a house. Richard is a recovering alcoholic and drug addict, now in AA, trying to prove he is a trustworthy husband and father. The two men fight for the job not in a slapstick way but in an understated, underhanded way that Doug feels bad about, Richard not so much. ("We're all just out here to get some food," Richard philosophizes. "Sometimes we bump into each other.")

The movie is unusually quiet and introspective for a comedy. Doug provides a narration, and Richard gets one of his own in the form of a self-help tape he obsessively listens to. Doug decides Richard is a "nice guy" and observes, "all Canadians are nice." That's before Richard fakes an injury to lodge a dreaded "in-store complaint" that could cost Doug his job.

Richard himself is on a self-destruct mission. Consider an episode when Doug hits a young black man who has thrown a bottle of Yoo-Hoo at him in the parking lot. Doug apologizes to a "community forum," backed up by a panel including Richard and the store's board of directors. He says something about a "few bad apples." Apology accepted. Afterward, however, when they're all standing around relieved, Richard tells one of the community leaders, "You are not a black apple to me." Explaining this digs him in deeper, until he's reduced to speechlessness. He has a gift for saying the wrong things at the wrong times.

Richard actually is nice at times, however. As a member of a motorcycle gang, he once watched his fellow members roar through a toll gate without paying, and then sheepishly told the collector, "I'll pay for them all." Doug empathizes with Richard, even to the point of defending him to the board, but he feels rotten inside: Having lied to his wife that he has the job, he finds a present of long-sleeve shirts they can't afford. He's afraid he's stuck in the ranks of the short-sleeve guys.

I was interested in the fates of these two men, but mildly. I was expected to laugh, but I only smiled. Some of the race-based situations made me feel uncomfortable. All of the characters, especially the straight-arrow chairman of the board (Gil Bellows), needed to be pushed further into the realms of comedy. More could have been done with the store's other employees. At the end of *The Promotion*, I wondered what the atmosphere was like on the set every day. How does it feel to make a movie where the characters don't seem sure who they are?

A Prophet ★★★★

R, 154 m., 2010

Tahar Rahim (Malik el Djebena), Niels Arestrup (Cesar Luciani), Adel Bencherif (Ryad), Reda Kateb (Jordi le Gitan), Hichem Yacoubi (Reyeb), Jean-Philippe Ricci (Vettorri). Directed by Jacques Audiard and produced by Lauranne Bourrachot, Martine Cassinelli, and Marco Cherqui. Screenplay by Audiard and Thomas Bidegain.

There is a murder at the center of Jacques Audiard's *A Prophet* that is unlike most murders I've seen in films. It's clumsy, messy, and brutal, and leaves the killer shaking. Whether he shakes with grief, relief, or anger we cannot say. That's the key to this film. We look, we see, but we cannot say. It often must be that way when we witness violence. Those capable of murdering live in another country.

The movie follows the life of Malik, a young Frenchman of Arab descent, who enters prison as a naive outsider and is shaped into an evil adult criminal. He wasn't born evil; he was born a shy, passive loser. Prison made him all that he can be. He seems an unlikely protagonist for a prison movie. Played by Tahar Rahim, he's skinny, insecure, trying to raise a mustache. He's behind bars for unclear reasons; he says he's innocent, although it doesn't matter. Prison efficiently strips him of privacy and self-respect and serves him over to the Corsican gang that controls everything behind bars through violence and bribes.

This gang is run by Cesar Luciani (Niels Arestrup), a man who has the presence of Don Corleone but colder eyes. He walks everywhere followed by bodyguards. His spies see all that happens. He gives an order, and it is followed out. He makes it his business to intimidate the new man, who is useful because he provides entrée into the wing housing the Arabic prisoners.

There is a prisoner there (Hichem Yacoubi) whom Cesar wants killed. This man must not live to testify. Malik is instructed by Cesar's lieutenant how to conceal a razor blade in his mouth and slit the man's throat. It is very simple. If Malik doesn't do this, he will die. When Malik seeks help from the warden, he quickly sees that Cesar is right: Kill or die.

Well, it's an unforgiving Darwinian choice. Malik has never killed. He makes a botch of it. There is a horrible struggle. Everything is covered in blood. Malik escapes only because Cesar has had the wing cleared out. It is a baptism. Now that he has killed, he is not a "man," but he is a survivor who will do what is necessary.

In the years to come, Malik undergoes a transformation. He's a quick learner. Outside society never got a chance to fashion him. Now he learns how to observe, how to measure motives, how to devise strategy, how to rise. He also learns to read, although that's more important for his self-confidence than for anything he learns. It's not as if he becomes Jean Genet. He is an outsider to the Corsicans, a "dirty Arab," but there is no purpose in resenting that. He keeps his own counsel.

Eventually he becomes Cesar's most trusted confidant, perhaps because he is Arab, cannot band with the other Arabs, and has no other place to turn. Prisoners sometimes are given a few days' leave. He performs a task for Cesar on the outside, and it also allows him to better position himself. *A Prophet* becomes a young man's bleak, remorseless coming-of-age story.

The best performance in the film is by Niels Arestrup, as Cesar Luciani. You may remember

423

Aerstrup from Audiard's *The Beat That My Heart Skipped* (2005), where he played a seedy but confident father who psychically overshadows his son. That one was very loosely inspired by James Toback's *Fingers,* with Harvey Keitel as the vulnerable son of a gangster.

Aerstrup sees but does not want to be perceived. He keeps his own deep counsel. He rules by passive aggression. He has held absolute power over life and death for so long that he acts as if it's innate. Most of his big moments involve silent reaction shots: decisions and realizations.

The newcomer Tahar Rahim is an enigma. What is he thinking? I believe that's the quality Jacques Audiard wants. He's a newly poured man, and when the mold sets, it happens inside. He learns from Cesar to reveal nothing. Many movies and actors are too ready to inform us what everyone is thinking, and why. It's more absorbing for us to read significance from mystery. An actor who reveals nothing, like Alain Delon in Melville's *Le Samourai,* is fascinating.

But what does go on inside Malik? That's the frightening part. We can only judge by what he does. Now he is prepared to kill. If we must be killed, don't we all rather hope it will be by someone for whom the act has meaning? For whom our life has importance? Malik was such a man once, but that ended in the bloody mess of the prison cell. Now prison has prepared him to return to the streets.

Note: A Prophet *swept all major categories in this year's Cesar Awards, the "French Oscars." It won the Grand Jury Prize at Cannes 2009.*

The Proposal ★ ★ ★

PG-13, 107 m., 2009

Sandra Bullock (Margaret Tate), Ryan Reynolds (Andrew Paxton), Mary Steenburgen (Grace Paxton), Craig T. Nelson (Joe Paxton), Betty White (Grandma Annie), Denis O'Hare (Mr. Gilbertson), Malin Akerman (Gertrude), Oscar Nunez (Ramone). Directed by Anne Fletcher and produced by David Hoberman and Todd Lieberman. Screenplay by Pete Chiarelli.

The Proposal is a movie about a couple who start out hating each other and end up liking each other. It's a funny thing about that. I started out hating the movie and ended up liking it.

It opens on a rather cheerless note, as the portrait of Margaret (Sandra Bullock), a tyrannical book editor, and Andrew (Ryan Reynolds), her long-suffering assistant. Known on office instant messages as The Witch, she terrorizes underlings, fires the man who wants her job, and orders Andrew to marry her.

How that happens is, she's a Canadian in danger of being deported, she imperiously ignored the law, and now she figures if she gets married she'll get her green card. They blackmail each other in their prenuptial hostage negotiations and fly off to Sitka, Alaska, to meet his folks. Sitka turns out to be a charming waterfront town, filled with chic little shops like the Fudgery, no fast-food stores or franchise chains, and a waterfront that looks less like a working fishing harbor than a tourist resort. Perhaps that's because the movie was filmed not in Alaska, but in Massachusetts and Rhode Island. Alaska might have been too real for this fantasy.

So I was sitting there cringing, knowing with uncanny certainty where the story was going. No movie begins with scenes of a man and a woman who are utterly incompatible unless it ends with them in love, unless perhaps it might be one about Hitler and Eleanor Roosevelt. They will fly to Alaska, she will be charmed by his family, she will be moved by the community spirit, she will love the landscape after the skyscraper towers of Manhattan, and they will have misadventures, probably involving unintended nudity and someone falling off a boat. So it is written.

But slowly, reluctantly, disbelievingly, they will start to warm up to each other. And it was about at that point when reluctantly, disbelievingly, I began to warm up to them. Bullock is a likable actress in the right roles, which she has been avoiding frequently since *Speed 2: Cruise Control* (1997), which I liked more than she did. She is likable here because she doesn't overdo it and is convincing when she confesses that she has warmed to his family's embrace—and who would not, since Andrew's mother is the merry Mary Steenburgen and his grandmother is the unsinkable Betty White. His father, Craig T. Nelson, is not quite so embraceable, but only because he is protective.

The key scene involves Steenburgen and White fitting Granny Annie's wedding dress for Bullock, and the presentation of a family heirloom. I don't care how much of a witch a woman is, when she sees herself in the mirror wearing her grandmother-in-law's gown, she's going to cave in. For that matter, Bullock was never that convincing as the office witch; she couldn't have touched Meryl Streep's work in *The Devil Wears Prada*.

The Proposal is much enhanced by all of the supporting performances. Betty White, at eighty-seven, makes her character eighty-nine and performs a Native American sunrise ceremony beside a campfire in the forest, which is not easy, especially in the Alaskan summer when the sun hardly sets. And look for a character named Ramone (Oscar Nunez), who will remind you of an element in *Local Hero*.

The Proposal recycles a plot that was already old when Tracy and Hepburn were trying it out. You see it coming from a great distance away. As it draws closer, you don't duck out of the way because it is so cheerfully done you don't mind being hit by it.

The Providence Effect ★★★
PG, 92 m., 2009

With Paul Adams III, Jeanette DiBella, John W. Fountain. A documentary produced and directed by Rollin Binzer.

One of the great success stories in American education is Providence St. Mel Catholic High School, at 119 S. Central Park on Chicago's West Side. This is a far from advantaged area where gangs and drugs are realities, and yet the school reports that for twenty-nine straight years, it has placed 100 percent of its graduates in colleges. Of course, this figure benefits from the school's policy of expelling troublemakers, but it also reflects its commitment to providing deserving students with a quality education.

The Providence Effect, a new documentary, charts the school's growth from a time when an existing Catholic high school was scheduled for closure by the Archdiocese of Chicago. A remarkable educator named Paul J. Adams III began at the school as a counselor, was named principal, and raised funds to keep the school open as a private academy dedicated to college prep. It boasts that in the most recent seven years, half its students have gone to first-tier, even Big Ten and Ivy League, schools.

About five years ago, Providence St. Mel opened Providence Englewood Charter School, starting at kindergarten to begin on students at the dawn of their school days. The results are impressive. They draw from the same neighborhood pool. Their test scores are above the state average.

A documentary about this achievement is certainly appropriate. The new film *The Providence Effect* is impressive, although not quite the film it could have been. It asks few hard questions. It's concerned primarily with charting the school's achievements through a series of testimonials from current and former teachers, community leaders, and national figures (Ronald Reagan visited the school twice). These witnesses are impressive, but the film's lack of traditional documentary footage leads to a certain beneficent monotony. The doc observes but doesn't probe.

How do the students survive the toxic neighborhood in their personal lives? What is the process by which a misbehaving or counterproductive child can be expelled? What is the selection process? How are non-Catholic students regarded? How do teacher salaries rank? Do gangs take a negative interest in the school or its children?

The film's powerful message is that inner-city black and Hispanic children are fully capable of competing with anyone on an intellectual level. But potential and practice are two different things. What kinds of homes do the students come from? Presumably their parents are highly motivated on their behalf and maintain family discipline. Can the process of becoming a Providence St. Mel success story be said to begin at birth?

What prevents the public school system from producing results such as these? The film suggests that public schools spend too many resources on administration and bureaucracy, and not enough on education itself. Also, of course, they have to take all applicants—those suited for school and those already temperamentally not suited. Guns and drugs are a problem. Self-image and school spirit are also.

425

If there's one thing we learn for sure about Prov-St. Mel's in this film, it's that the students and teachers are united in a fierce belief in the school.

Public Enemies ★ ★ ★ ½
R, 140 m., 2009

Johnny Depp (John Dillinger), Christian Bale (Melvin Purvis), Marion Cotillard (Billie Frechette), Billy Crudup (J. Edgar Hoover), Stephen Dorff (Homer Van Meter), Stephen Lang (Charles Winstead), Branka Katic (Anna Sage). Directed by Michael Mann and produced by Mann and Kevin Misher. Screenplay by Mann, Ronan Bennett, and Ann Biderman, based on the book *Public Enemies: America's Greatest Crime Wave and the Birth of the FBI, 1933–34* by Bryan Burrough.

"I rob banks," John Dillinger would sometimes say by way of introduction. It was the simple truth. That was what he did. For the thirteen months between the day he escaped from prison and the night he lay dying in an alley, he robbed banks. It was his lifetime. Michael Mann's *Public Enemies* accepts that stark fact and refuses any temptation to soften it. Dillinger was not a nice man.

Here is a film that shrugs off the way we depend on myth to sentimentalize our outlaws. There is no interest here about John Dillinger's childhood, his psychology, his sexuality, his famous charm, his Robin Hood legend. He liked sex, but not as much as robbing banks. "He robbed the bankers but let the customers keep their own money." But whose money was in the banks? He kids around with reporters and lawmen, but that was business. He doesn't kid around with the members of his gang. He might have made a very good military leader.

Johnny Depp and Michael Mann show us that we didn't know all about Dillinger. We only thought we did. Here is an efficient, disciplined, bold, violent man, driven by compulsions the film wisely declines to explain. His gang members loved the money they were making. Dillinger loved planning the next job. He had no exit strategy or retirement plans.

Dillinger saw a woman he liked, Billie Frechette, played by Marion Cotillard, and courted her, after his fashion. That is, he took her out at night and bought her a fur coat, as he had seen done in the movies; he had no real adult experience before prison. They had sex, but the movie is not much interested. It is all about his vow to show up for her, to protect her. Against what? Against the danger of being his girl. He allows himself a tiny smile when he gives her the coat, and it is the only vulnerability he shows in the movie.

This is a very disciplined film. You might not think it was possible to make a film about the most famous outlaw of the 1930s without clichés and "star chemistry" and a film-class screenplay structure, but Mann does it. He is particular about the way he presents Dillinger and Billie. He sees him and her. Not them. They are never a couple. They are their needs. She needs to be protected because she is so vulnerable. He needs someone to protect in order to affirm his invincibility.

Dillinger hates the system, by which he means prisons, which hold people, banks, which hold money, and cops, who stand in his way. He probably hates the government, too, but he doesn't think that big. It is him against them, and the bastards will not, *cannot*, win. There's an extraordinary sequence, apparently based on fact, where Dillinger walks into the "Dillinger Bureau" of the Chicago Police Department and strolls around. Invincible. This is not ego. It is a spell he casts on himself.

The movie is well researched, based on the book by Bryan Burrough. It even bothers to try to discover Dillinger's speaking style. Depp looks a lot like him. Mann shot on location in the Crown Point jail, scene of the famous jailbreak with the fake gun. He shot in the Little Bohemia Lodge in the same room Dillinger used, and Depp is costumed in clothes to match those the bank robber left behind. Mann redressed Lincoln Avenue on either side of the Biograph Theater and laid streetcar tracks; I live a few blocks away and walked over to marvel at the detail. I saw more than you will; unlike some directors, he doesn't indulge in beauty shots to show off the art direction. It's just there.

This Johnny Depp performance is something else. For once, an actor playing a gangster does not seem to base his performance on movies he has seen. He starts cold. He plays Dillinger as a fact. My friend Jay Robert Nash says 1930s gangsters copied their styles from the way Hollywood depicted them; screenwriters like Ben Hecht taught them how they spoke. Dillinger was a big movie fan; on the last night of his life, he went to see Clark Gable playing a man a lot like him, but he didn't learn much. No wisecracks, no lingo. Just military precision and an edge of steel.

Christian Bale plays Melvin Purvis in a similar key. He lives to fight criminals. He is a cold realist. He admires his boss, J. Edgar Hoover, but Hoover is a romantic, dreaming of an FBI of clean-cut young accountants in suits and ties who would be a credit to their mothers. After the catastrophe at Little Bohemia (the FBI let Dillinger escape but killed three civilians), Purvis said to hell with it and made J. Edgar import some lawmen from Arizona who had actually been in gunfights.

Mann is fearless with his research. If I mention the Lady in Red, Anna Sage (Branka Katic), who betrayed Dillinger outside the Biograph when the movie was over, how do you picture her? I do, too. We are wrong. In real life she was wearing a white blouse and an orange skirt, and she does in the movie. John Ford once said, "When the legend becomes fact, print the legend." This may be a case where he was right. Mann might have been wise to decide against the orange and white and just break down and give Anna Sage a red dress.

This is a very good film, with Depp and Bale performances of brutal clarity. I'm trying to understand why it is not quite a great film. I think it may be because it deprives me of some stubborn need for closure. His name was John Dillinger, and he robbed banks. But there had to be more to it than that, right? No, apparently not. ☞

The Punisher: War Zone ★ ★
R, 101 m., 2008

Ray Stevenson (Frank Castle), Dominic West (Billy Russo/Jigsaw), Julie Benz (Angela Donatelli), Doug Hutchison (Loony Bin Jim), Colin Salmon (Paul Budiansky), Wayne Knight (Microchip), Dash Mihok (Martin Soap), Stephanie Janusauskas (Grace). Directed by Lexi Alexander and produced by Gale Ann Hurd. Screenplay by Nick Santora, Art Marcum, and Matt Holloway, based on the Marvel comic books.

You used to be able to depend on a bad film being poorly made. No longer. *The Punisher: War Zone* is one of the best-made bad movies I've seen. It looks great, it hurtles through its paces, and it is well-acted. The sound track is like elevator music if the elevator were in a death plunge. The special effects are state of the art. Its only flaw is that it's disgusting.

There's a big audience for disgusting, and I confidently predict the movie will "win the weekend," if not very many hearts and minds. Here you will see a man's kidney ripped out and eaten, a chair leg pushed through a head via the eyeball, a roomful of men wiped out by the Punisher revolving upside-down from the chandelier and firing machine guns with both hands, a widow and her wee girl threatened with mayhem, heads sliced off, victims impaled and skewered, and the villain thrown into a machine that crushes glass bottles in much the same way concrete is mixed.

The glass-crushing machine caught my eye. Billy (Dominic West) is socked into it by the Punisher (Ray Stevenson) and revolves up to his neck in cutting edges while screaming many, many four-letter words, which, under the circumstances, are appropriate.

What confused me is that nearby in the same factory there is a conveyor belt carrying large lumps of hamburger or something. I expected Billy to emerge as ground round, but then I thought, how much ground glass can you really add to ground round? It's not often that you see meat processing and bottle crushing done in adjacent operations in the same factory. I was looking for the saltwater taffy mixer.

Billy survives his ordeal and announces to his henchmen, "From now on, my name is Jigsaw." This is after he has had operations, apparently lasting only minutes by the movie's time line, to stitch up his face with twine. He now looks like the exhibit in the entrance lobby of the Texas Chainsaw Museum, and one eye looks painfully introspective.

The movie is not heavy on plot. By my Timex Indiglo, there was no meaningful exposition at all during the first fifteen minutes, just men getting slaughtered. Then things slow down enough to reveal that the Punisher, aka Frank Castle, who avenged the murder of his family in an earlier film, has now killed a

427

good guy who was father to little Grace (Stephanie Janusauskas) and husband to Angela (Julie Benz), who will Never Be Able to Forgive Him for What He's Done, nor should she, but she will.

The city, Montreal playing New York, has a small population, consisting only of good guys and bad guys and not much of anybody else. I'd get out, too. It's the kind of violence the president should fly over in Air Force One and regard sadly through the window. It goes without saying that the bad guys are unable to shoot the Punisher with their machine guns. That's consistent with the epidemic of malfunctioning machine guns in all recent super-violent films. Yet the Punisher kills a couple dozen hoodlums with his machine guns, while spinning upside-down under that chandelier.

Now pause to think with me. Everyone around the table is heavily armed. More armed men bust in through the door. The revolving Punisher is suspended in the center of the room. Because of the logic of the laws of physical motion, most of the time he is shooting away from any individual bad guy. How can they possibly miss hitting him? It's so hard these days, getting good help.

The Punisher: War Zone is the third in a series of Punisher movies. It follows *The Punisher* (1989), starring Dolph Lundgren, and *The Punisher* (2004), starring Thomas Jane and John Travolta. Since the second film has the same title as the first, it's hard to tell them apart, but why would you want to? My fellow critic Bill Stamets, settling down for the screening, shared with me that he watched the 2004 movie for his homework. I did my algebra.

Push ★ ½
PG-13, 111 m., 2009

Chris Evans (Nick Gant), Dakota Fanning (Cassie Holmes), Camilla Belle (Kira Hudson), Cliff Curtis (Hook Waters), Djimon Hounsou (Henry Carver). Directed by Paul McGuigan and produced by Bruce Davey, William Vince, and Glenn Williamson. Screenplay by David Bourla.

Push has vibrant cinematography and decent acting, but I'm blasted if I know what it's about. Oh, I understand how the characters are paranormals, and how they're living in a present that was changed in the past, among enemies who are trying to change the future. I know they can read minds and use telekinesis to move things. I know they're a later generation of a Nazi experiment gone wrong, and the U.S. Army wants them for super-soldiers.

But that's all simply the usual horsefeathers to set up the situation. What are they *doing*? The answer to that involves a MacGuffin that would have Hitchcock harrumphing and telling Alma, "Oh, dear, they really have allowed themselves to get carried away." The MacGuffin is a briefcase. Yes, like in *Pulp Fiction*, but this time we know what's in it. It's a drug or serum that (is the only thing that?) kills paranormals. And the Division desperately wants it.

I'm not sure if the Division is part of the army or against it. I know that the telekinetic Nick (Chris Evans) is hiding from it in Hong Kong, and that the Pusher Cassie (Dakota Fanning) finds him there and brings along the briefcase (I think), and that she's followed there by most of the other characters, including Kira (Camilla Belle) and the Division agent Henry (Djimon Hounsou), who is another Pusher. Pushing involves not drugs but Pushing into other people's minds.

Kira is said to be the only paranormal who ever survived the deadly serum. But why did they want her dead? And who are they? And why is it so urgent to find the briefcase, which contains a syringe filled with the serum? This is an especially perplexing question for me because when the syringe was being filled to kill Kira, it looked to me like the label on the bottle of medicine clearly said "B-12," an excellent curative for anemia, which none of the characters has a problem with.

Apart from the MacGuffin, the movie is wall to wall with the Talking Killer Syndrome. Never have more people pointed more guns at more heads and said more words without anyone getting shot. Even if they are telekinetic and can point the guns without holding them.

All of these people, and others, speak very earnestly about Pushing, and they plot to outwit and outthink enemy Pushers, and clearly they are in a lot deeper than the audience is ever likely to get. It's like you're listening to shop talk in a shop that doesn't make anything you've ever seen.

Dakota Fanning's Cassie claims at one point that she's "older than twelve," but I dunno. Her mother would probably not have allowed her to fly off to Hong Kong alone, wearing a miniskirt and with purple streaks in her hair, but her mother has been killed, which is part of her problem. She does get a little drunk, which provides the movie's only laugh. Dakota's real mother probably told her, "Dakota, honey, why don't you take the role and get to see Hong Kong?" If that's what happened, she has the best reason of anybody for being in this movie.

Putty Hill ★★★★
NO MPAA RATING, 85 m., 2010

Sky Ferreira (Jenny), Zoe Vance (Cory's older sister), James Siebor Jr. (Cory's brother), Dustin Ray (Cory's best friend), Cody Ray (Dustin's brother), Charles Sauers (Tattooist), Cathy Evans (Cory's mom), India Streeter (Cory's girlfriend). Directed by Matthew Porterfield and produced by Eric Bannat, Steve Holmgren, Joyce Kim, and Jordan Mintzer. Screenplay by Mintzer and Porterfield.

In a way rarely seen, *Putty Hill* says all that can be said about a few days in the lives of its characters without seeming to say very much at all. It looks closely, burrows deep, considers the way in which lives have become pointless and death therefore less meaningful. It uses fairly radical filmmaking techniques to penetrate this truth and employs them so casually that they seem quite natural.

Matthew Porterfield's film, which takes place in a poor, wooded suburb of Baltimore, involves the death by overdose of a young man named Cory. We never meet him, although we see his portrait at a memorial service. The portrait tells us nothing: He projects no personality for the camera. His family and friends gather for his funeral, and we meet them in unstructured moments that tell us much about them but little about Cory.

The sad truth is, nobody knew Cory that well. There seems to have been little fierce love for him, even from his girlfriend (whose identity I only learned from the Web site), because little is made of her in the film as she sits quietly at a memorial gathering, impassive.

Everyone knows he died from an overdose of heroin; no one is much surprised. One conversation is philosophical about how he "wasn't able to handle it."

Sometimes Porterfield's camera steps aside with some of the characters, and an off-screen voice (his?) is heard interviewing them. How old are you? Do you have brothers and sisters? Have you come back for the funeral? Have you attended many funerals? This voice seems to come from outside; it doesn't necessarily know who these characters are. The illusion is that the film is an ongoing narrative, and the interviewer is asking characters questions in order to clarify it for himself. Oddly, this seems perfectly natural.

So do all the actors. None of them, I learn, are professionals. Only the lead, Sky Ferreira, as Cory's sister Jenny, has any performing experience; she's a C&W singer. Few experienced actors could be this convincing, sound this authentic, seem to be there in the moment and not in any way acting. The dialogue isn't "written"; everything feels spontaneous, and it *just sounds right*, if you know what I mean.

Cory lived in a mostly lower-class white neighborhood, although at his memorial service there are a fair number of blacks, including his unidentified girlfriend, a woman possibly her mother, and others. His mourners mostly seem people without resources. The only occupation we see on screen is held by a tattoo artist, who learned his trade while in prison for second-degree murder after revenging the rape of his wife ("and you can fill in the rest").

The film opens with contemplative shots inside a barren apartment we later learn was Cory's. It returns there at the end, as two of the mourners break in, sit in the dark and smoke, and are surprised he could live like that. Where is all his stuff? Probably sold to buy drugs, we suppose. Only a miserable life could have been lived in these rooms.

Casually, we meet Jenny as she arrives back in town. She hasn't seen Cory much in recent years. Doesn't miss home: "God, no." We follow four girlfriends as they hang out in an aboveground pool, go walking in a woods, meet two cops with rifles, watch TV, smoke, are bored. Later they go to a swimming hole but don't seem to have as much fun as they should. Notice the body language as a boy and girl lie on a rock, hands idly entwined; why do we feel eroticism is behind them and has been played out?

The most extraordinary scene is the memorial service. Everyone sits crowded together passing around pitchers of beer. A professional karaoke emcee has been employed along with his equipment. Family members sing standard songs—in Cory's memory, I guess. Some of the mourners say a few awkward words about the deceased. The karaoke man asks, "Does anyone else want to say something at this time?" His words "at this time," reflecting a dutiful solemnity, attempt to lend a sense of ceremony. Tributes are inarticulate and trail off into uncompleted thoughts.

No one seems to know exactly where Cory was or what he was doing. He made little impression. No one has learned anything from his death other than, perhaps, that it was to be expected. None of these people seem to have hopes and plans. A grandmother in "sheltered living" won't attend the funeral because "I simply can't take it. I want to remember things as they were."

Porterfield takes no cheap shots. He respects these people, their lives, their unspoken hopelessness. He doesn't go for dire colorful dialogue. He has no social commentary. *Putty Hill* makes no statement. It looks. It looks with as much perception and sympathy as it is possible for a film to look. It is surprisingly effective. I know what the budget was, but the figure is irrelevant. He had all the money he needed to make this film, his cinematography by Jeremy Saulnier always simply and evocatively visualizes; there is not one wrong shot. He has internalized his characters, knows them, understands them, shows them in just such a way that we can, too. If there had been a real Cory, this would be his memorial. Watching *Putty Hill*, we don't have to be told there are real Corys.

Q

Quantum of Solace ★ ★
PG-13, 105 m., 2008

Daniel Craig (James Bond), Olga Kurylenko (Camille), Mathieu Amalric (Dominic Greene), Judi Dench (M), Jeffrey Wright (Felix Leiter), Gemma Arterton (Agent Fields). Directed by Marc Forster and produced by Michael G. Wilson and Barbara Broccoli. Screenplay by Paul Haggis, Neal Purvis, and Robert Wade.

OK, I'll say it. Never again. Don't ever let this happen again to James Bond. *Quantum of Solace* is his twenty-second film, and he will survive it, but for the twenty-third it is necessary to go back to the drawing board and redesign from the ground up. Please understand: James Bond is not an action hero! He is too good for that. He is an attitude. Violence for him is an annoyance. He exists for the foreplay and the cigarette. He rarely encounters a truly evil villain. More often a comic opera buffoon with hired goons in matching jumpsuits.

Quantum of Solace has the worst title in the series save for *Never Say Never Again,* words that could have been used by Kent after King Lear utters the saddest line in all of Shakespeare: "Never! Never! Never! Never! Never!" The movie opens with Bond involved in a reckless car chase on the tollway that leads through mountain tunnels from Nice through Monte Carlo and down to Portofino in Italy, where Edward Lear lies at rest with his cat, Old Foss. I have driven that way many a time. It is a breathtaking drive.

You won't find that out here. The chase, with Bond under constant machine-gun fire, is so quickly cut and so obviously composed of incomprehensible CGI that we're essentially looking at bright colors bouncing off one another, intercut with Bond at the wheel and POV shots of approaching monster trucks. Let's all think together. When has an action hero ever, even once, been killed by machine-gun fire, no matter how many hundreds of rounds? The hit men should simply reject them and say, "No can do, Boss. They never work in this kind of movie."

The chase has no connection to the rest of the plot, which is routine for Bond, but it's about the movie's last bow to tradition. In *Quantum of Solace* he will share no cozy quality time with the Bond girl (Olga Kurylenko). We fondly remember the immortal names of Pussy Galore, Xenia Onatopp, and Plenty O'Toole, who I have always suspected was a drag queen. In this film, who do we get? Are you ready for this? Camille. That's it. Camille. Not even Camille Squeal. Or Cammy Miami. Or Miss O'Toole's friend, Cam Shaft.

Daniel Craig remains a splendid Bond, one of the best. He is handsome, agile, muscular, dangerous. Everything but talkative. I didn't count, but I think M (Judi Dench) has more dialogue than 007. Bond doesn't look like the urge to peel Camille has even entered his mind.

He blows up a hotel in the middle of a vast, barren, endless Bolivian desert. It's a luxury hotel, with angular W Hotel–style minimalist room furniture you might cut your legs on and a bartender who will stir or shake you any drink, but James has become a regular bloke who orders lager. Who are the clients at this highest of high-end hotels? Lawrence of Arabia, obviously, and millionaires who hate green growing things. Conveniently, when the hotel blows up, the filmmakers don't have to contend with adjacent buildings, traffic, pedestrians, skylines, or anything else. Talk about your blue screen. Nothing better than the azure desert sky.

Why is he in Bolivia? In pursuit of a global villain, whose name is not Goldfinger, Scaramanga, Drax, or Le Chiffre, but . . . Dominic Greene (Mathieu Amalric). What is Dominic's demented scheme to control the globe? As a start, the fiend desires to corner the water supply of . . . Bolivia. Ohooo! Nooo! This twisted design, revealed to Bond after at least an hour of death-defying action, reminds me of the famous laboratory mouse who was introduced into a labyrinth. After fighting his way for days through baffling corridors and down dead ends, finally, *finally,* parched and starving, the little creature crawled at last to the training button and hurled his tiny body against it. And what rolled down the chute as his reward? A licorice gum ball.

Dominic Greene lacks a headquarters on

the moon or on the floor of the sea. He operates out of an ordinary shipping warehouse with loading docks. His evil transport is provided by forklifts and pickup trucks. Bond doesn't have to creep out to the ledge of an underground volcano to spy on him. He just walks up to the chain-link fence and peers through. Greene could get useful security tips from Wal-Mart.

There is no Q in *Quantum of Solace,* except in the title. No Miss Moneypenny at all. M now has a male secretary. That Judi Dench, what a fox. Bond doesn't even size him up. He learned his lesson with Plenty. This Bond, he doesn't bring much to the party. Daniel Craig can play suave, and he can be funny, and Brits are born doing double entendre. Craig is a fine actor. Here they lock him down. I repeat: James Bond is not an action hero! Leave the action to your Jason Bournes. This is a swampy old world. The deeper we sink in, the more we need James Bond to stand above it.

R

Race to Witch Mountain ★ ★ ½
PG, 98 m., 2009

Dwayne Johnson (Jack Bruno), AnnaSophia Robb (Sara), Alexander Ludwig (Seth), Carla Gugino (Dr. Alex Friedman), Ciaran Hinds (Henry Burke), Garry Marshall (Dr. Donald Harlan), Tom Everett Scott (Matheson). Directed by Andy Fickman and produced by Andrew Gunn. Screenplay by Matt Lopez and Mark Bomback.

Before the sneak preview of *Race to Witch Mountain,* they had a little quiz show and gave away T-shirts. One question: "Who plays Jack Bruno?" Half the audience roared, "The Rock!" Not one lonely vote for Dwayne Johnson. The other famous movie "Rock" was born Roy Harold Scherer Jr. It's a name that stays in the mind.

I think Dwayne Johnson has a likable screen presence and is a good choice for an innocuous family entertainment like this, and also he once sent me some Hawaiian Macadamia Nut Brickle. I would have mailed it back because film critics are not supposed to accept gifts from movie stars, but I accidentally ate it first. What Johnson does here is provide a credible tough-guy action hero in a nonthreatening mode. He rules over chases, fights, explosions, and an Ooze Monster, yet never seems nasty, so the kids can feel safe around him.

Young audiences will like the kids in the movie, played by AnnaSophia Robb and Alexander Ludwig. And in using kids as the costars, the movie has its cake and eats it too, because Sara and Seth may look like they're fifteen or sixteen, but actually, you see, they're aliens whose flying saucer crash-landed and is being held at a secret government UFO facility inside Witch Mountain—so secret, the mountain is not shown on Google Maps. I suspected right away it was a mountain made for this movie because it is shaped like a sawed-off version of the mashed potato sculpture that Richard Dreyfuss kept sculpting in *Close Encounters of the Third Kind*—the one that resembled, you remember, the outcrop where the flying saucer landed.

Anyway, Dwayne Johnson plays a former driver for a Las Vegas mob boss who goes straight after he gets out of prison and starts driving a taxi. In his backseat one day, Sara and Seth materialize, explain they are aliens, and ask him to drive them to a remote desert location. They talk like an artificial intelligence program that got a D in English, although later they gradually start to sound more like Disney teenagers. They're later joined by Dr. Alex Friedman (Carla Gugino), an expert who was in Vegas lecturing to fanboys and girls at a combination UFO convention and costume party.

On their tail is a pursuit team of federal agents led by a hardnose named Burke (Ciaran Hinds). Burke moves in a caravan of three black SUVs with tinted glass, although when necessary he can materialize dozens of heavily armed SWAT team members. The chase leads deep into Witch Mountain, although not before the kids enter a buried chamber beneath a miner's shack and there obtain some kind of extraterrestrial cell phone extracted by Seth after plunging his arm up to the elbow into a pulsating mass of gelatinous goo.

Further details I will leave for your discovery. Since Seth and Sara only appropriated the bodies of human teenagers, I was left with a couple of questions. (1) Did they displace real teenagers, or only clone themselves? (2) They're cute, but what do they actually look like as aliens? Not quivering gobs of mucilaginous viscidity, I trust.

Rachel Getting Married ★ ★ ★ ★
R, 111 m., 2008

Anne Hathaway (Kym), Rosemarie DeWitt (Rachel), Bill Irwin (Paul), Tunde Adebimpe (Sidney), Mather Zickel (Kieran), Anna Deavere Smith (Carol), Anisa George (Emma), Debra Winger (Abby). Directed by Jonathan Demme and produced by Demme, Neda Armian, and Marc Platt. Screenplay by Jenny Lumet.

The rules say that critics don't discuss movies after screenings. After I saw Jonathan Demme's *Rachel Getting Married* for the second time, however, a friend asked: "Wouldn't you love to attend a wedding like that?" In a way, I felt I had. Yes, I began to feel absorbed in the experience. A few movies can do that, can slip you out of your mind and into theirs.

Rachel (Rosemarie DeWitt) does indeed get married. There is an engrossing plot involving her sister, Kym (Anne Hathaway). But I believe the film's deep subject is the wedding itself: how it unfolds, who attends, the nature of the ceremony, and what it has to observe about how the concept of "family" embraces others, and how our multicultural society is growing comfortable with itself.

The story centers on Kym (Hathaway), a recovering drug addict, who after being in and out of rehab for ten years is now several months into a treatment that seems to be working. She's given a day pass to attend her sister's wedding. Her family lives in a big old country house in Connecticut, filled with memories, family, future in-laws, and the friends of bride and groom. Sidney (Tunde Adebimpe), Rachel's intended, is a classical musician, and all kinds of music fills a film that has no formal score. The wedding party is what we call "diverse." I'm not going to identify characters by race because such a census would offend the whole spirit of the film. These characters love one another, and that's it.

Notice the visual strategy of Demme and his cinematographer, Declan Quinn. Some shots are dealt with in a traditional way (establishing, close-ups, etc). More shots plunge right into the middle of the characters; some may be hand-held, or maybe not, but for me they reproduced an experience we've all had. That's when we wander through a party looking first here and then there, noticing who is where and why, connecting threads, savoring. Sometimes we walk outside and look through doorways and windows. This visual approach is how they populate the film with a large number of characters, establish them, familiarize us, and don't pause for redundant identifications. We don't meet everyone at a wedding, but we observe everyone.

Consider in this context the former and present wives of the father, Paul (Bill Irwin). His first wife, Abby (Debra Winger), is the mother of Kym, Rachel, and a younger brother who drowned. She is of intense importance to Kym. Their private conversation

is filmed in a traditional, powerful way, underlining dialogue and emotion. Then consider Paul's second wife, Carol (Anna Deavere Smith). She has limited dialogue and no big dramatic scenes. But without being obvious about it, Demme and Quinn make her very present. As we wander through the house and sit through the rehearsal dinner, the wedding, and the party, we are always aware of her.

This is exactly right and observant of the way a loved and comfortable "second wife" functions at an event where the bride's parents have higher billing. She knows everyone, watches everything, is pleased or concerned, stands quietly behind her husband, loves his daughters, smoothes the waves. To give her a foreground role would have been a mistake. But you will not forget her.

One of the reasons Smith works so well, as an unobtrusive soothing element, is typecasting. She *looks* like she would be the kind of person she plays. Whether she really is or not, I wouldn't know. But that's not the point of typecasting. Why have I given so much attention to a relatively minor character? Because she represents the film's approach to all the characters. When Robert Altman is thanked in the end credits, I imagine it is not only because he was Demme's friend, but because his instinct for ensemble stories was an example. Demme owes much to his editor, Tim Squyres, who also edited Altman's *Gosford Park,* another film that kept track of everyone at a big house party. That might have been the very reason he was hired.

Demme's achievement is shared with the original screenplay by Sidney Lumet's daughter, Jenny Lumet. This is her first writing credit, but the story might have felt like second nature to her. She is descended from artists; her grandparents on her mother's side were the singer Lena Horne and the jazz legend Louis Jordan Jones; her grandparents on her father's side were Baruch and Eugenia Lumet, an actress and an actor-director. Her father is the director Sidney Lumet, and her mother the writer Gail Lumet Buckley. The apple did not fall far from those trees. I don't have to be told that her life has included countless gatherings of the nature of Rachel's wedding. And although I do not know Sidney Lumet well, I know enough to say he is kind and warm; I suspect he was an inspiration for the character Paul, who can hear Carol even when she isn't talking.

Jenny Lumet has a sister, the sound editor Amy Lumet. That's interesting. Is the film autobiographical? I have no way of knowing. Demme demonstrates something he shares with Altman: He likes to be surrounded by his own extended family. The gray-bearded man who performs the ceremony is his cousin, Reverend Robert Castle, subject of Demme's doc *Cousin Bobby* (1992). His daughter Josephine is in the film. And so on. Apart from the story, which is interesting enough, *Rachel Getting Married* is like theme music for an evolving new age.

Radical Disciple:
The Story of Father Pfleger ★★★
NO MPAA RATING, 58 m., 2009

Featuring Father Michael Pfleger, Carol Marin, Reverend Jeremiah Wright, and Tom Roeser. A documentary directed by Bob Hercules and produced by Hercules and Terrie Pickerill.

The most significant image of Fr. Michael Pfleger may be an old snapshot taken in the basement of his childhood home. It shows him in front of an altar made of orange crates and a white sheet, with candles and a Bible on it. My mother used to implore me to pray for a vocation to the priesthood. With little Mike Pfleger, there was never any doubt.

Michael Pfleger is well known in Chicago and elsewhere as an outspoken liberal and civil rights advocate. The Roman Catholic hierarchy doesn't concern itself with his politics but in the very public way he weaves them into his priesthood. He advocates politics in his sermons, shares his pulpit with others, leads demonstrations, speaks out. He invited the controversial Reverend Jeremiah Wright to speak from his altar before a reading by the poet Maya Angelou. At the height of the controversy in autumn 2008, he preached from Wright's altar.

Politics are not to be discussed from the pulpit. Nobody but a Catholic priest is to give a sermon. There is another problem. In the archdiocese of Chicago, a priest is assigned to a parish for six years, renewable once. Pfleger has been the pastor at St. Sabina's Church on Chicago's South Side since 1981. When he went there he was the youngest Catholic pastor in Chicago. Now he has been there longer than any other priest has served in one parish in America. That has made a series of cardinals increasingly unhappy. Now sixty, Pfleger seems to consider St. Sabina's a lifetime pastorate, and his congregation agrees. He walks a tightrope. "Somebody is in my church every Sunday waiting to trip me," he says in this doc.

Pfleger feels a deep affinity with his parishioners. When he first came to the parish, the church was desolate, run-down, sparsely attended, scheduled for closure. Soon it was packed for services. He led campaigns to restore the church. He rebuilt St. Michael's Academy, opened an employment resource center and social services center, and built residences for senior citizens.

The elder housing is on land once occupied by bars, porno stores, and hookers. Pfleger led campaigns against such stores, singling out merchants who sold alcohol or tobacco to minors, leading campaigns against billboards targeting teenagers, selling malt liquor and cigarettes. He was behind twenty Chicago billboards advising "Stop Listening to Trash," and attacking several rappers for their songs, often violent, that were disrespectful to women. He and the Reverend Jesse Jackson led demonstrations against gun shop owners selling to inner-city youths.

I have attended Mass at St. Sabina's three or four times. The South Side congregation is predominantly African-American, with a good sprinkling of other races. Father Pfleger is a gifted, impassioned orator. A black parishioner in this documentary says when she started going to the church she sat in the back and couldn't see him. By his voice, she thought he sounded black.

Pfleger was an outspoken supporter of Barack Obama. It's not that he told his congregation it would be a sin to vote against him, it's more that he considered it unthinkable. The archdiocese fears his sermons will threaten its tax-exempt status. He has been reprimanded more than once by the current Francis Cardinal George, who would dearly love to reassign him and once put him on leave for two weeks to "meditate and reconsider."

435

"He keeps a distance" from the official church, says *Sun-Times* columnist Carol Marin in the doc. She covered Pfleger for years as a TV reporter. He also doesn't bond readily with other priests. His focus is on his pastorate, not the church structure. However, Pleger's theology remains orthodox. He is arguably the most loved white man in the Chicago African-American community. Among mainstream Catholics, not so much. "He is a follower of Marx," says Tom Roeser, head of the Catholic Citizens of Illinois.

This documentary by Bob Hercules assembles archival and new footage and interviews into a comprehensive portrait. If you've heard of Father Pfleger and want to know more, here is the place. What seems to be lacking is a fuller examination of the church's differences with its priest. Archdiocesan spokesmen are judicial. Roeser seems more concerned with his politics than his theology. The most helpful view comes from Marin, who has covered him for thirty years, approves of him, but questions some of his choices and strategies.

One thing seems certain. More than most priests, he has brought material change to the community and transformed his parish. Some of his most passionate actions can be seen as practicing the teachings of Jesus quite literally.

The Rape of Europa ★ ★ ★
NO MPAA RATING, 117 m., 2008

Joan Allen (Narrator). A documentary written, produced, and directed by Richard Berge, Nicole Newnham, and Bonni Cohen, based on the book by Lynn H. Nicholas.

We know the Nazis looted art from the nations they overran. Maybe we've seen *The Train* (1964) and know how one shipment was thwarted. But how many important paintings, sculptures, and other artworks would you say the Nazis made off with? Hundreds? Thousands?

The Rape of Europa, a startling documentary, puts the number rather higher: *one-fifth* of all the known significant works of art in Europe—millions. Incredibly, Hitler maintained shopping lists of art for every country he invaded and dispatched troops to secure (i.e., plunder) the works and ship them back to Germany. He had plans to build a monumental art museum in Linz, his Austrian birthplace, and was working on models of the structure even during his final days in the Berlin bunker. His right-hand man Goering was no less keen as a collector.

That Hitler was mad is well known. That he was mad about art, not so well. He was, in his youth, an ambitious painter and applied to an art school in Vienna but was rejected. The general outline of his early art career, somewhat fictionalized, can be seen in *Max*, a little-noticed 2002 film starring Noah Taylor as Hitler and John Cusack as a one-armed Jewish art dealer in Munich who befriends Hitler, his liquor deliveryman.

Hitler's art was not good (we see some landscape watercolors), and his taste in art was terrible. He had a weakness for heroic Nordic supermen and women in a style of uber-kitsch, and he believed modern art was Jewish and decadent. In addition to the artworks he looted, he ordered the destruction of countless others; not all of those Nazi bonfires consumed only books.

This absorbing documentary begins with one painting, Gustav Klimt's *Gold Portrait of Adele Bloch-Bauer,* which, like countless other paintings, was stolen from Jews, disappeared, and then mysteriously reappeared in galleries and museums in Europe and America with shadowy provenance. Maria Altmann, the niece of the man who commissioned the painting, waged a long legal battle to have possession returned to her and won; when the painting was later sold at auction, its price of $135 million set a record.

But until recently, many possessors of stolen artworks have chosen to ignore claims by their original owners, and only now is an international tracing operation under way. It is believed that countless priceless works languish in the shadows of private homes, discreetly kept out of sight. Work is only beginning on a central clearinghouse of information.

Many other works of sculpture and architecture were destroyed by the bombing raids of both sides, although an occasional exception was made; the city of Venice, for example was spared by American bombers. Much praise is given to the Monument Men, American art experts enlisted into the Army and deployed under the orders of Eisenhower to identify and protect the surviving heritage of liberated nations. In stark contrast, American bombs destroyed museums in Baghdad and throughout Iraq, and others were looted; no effort was made by our commanders to preserve the treasures.

The Reader ★ ★ ★ ½
R, 123 m., 2008

Kate Winslet (Hanna Schmitz), Ralph Fiennes (Michael Berg), David Kross (Young Michael Berg), Lena Olin (Rose Mather/Ilana Mather), Bruno Ganz (Professor Rohl). Directed by Stephen Daldry and produced by Anthony Minghella, Sydney Pollack, Donna Gigliotti, and Redmond Morris. Screenplay by David Hare, based on the novel by Bernhard Schlink.

The crucial decision in *The Reader* is made by a twenty-four-year-old youth, who has information that might help a woman about to be sentenced to life in prison but withholds it. He is ashamed to reveal his affair with this woman. By making this decision, he shifts the film's focus from the subject of German guilt about the Holocaust and turns it on the human race in general. The film intends his decision as the key to its meaning, but most viewers may conclude that *The Reader* is only about the crimes of the Nazis and the response to them by postwar German generations.

The film centers on a sexual relationship between Hanna (Kate Winslet), a woman in her midthirties, and Michael (David Kross), a boy of fifteen. That such things are wrong is beside the point; they happen, and the story is about how it connected with her earlier life and his later one. It is powerfully, if sometimes confusingly, told in a flashback framework, and powerfully acted by Winslet and Kross, with Ralph Fiennes coldly enigmatic.

The story begins with the cold, withdrawn Michael in middle age (Fiennes) and moves back to the late 1950s and a day when young Michael is found sick and feverish in the street and taken back to Hanna's apartment to be cared for. This day, and all their days together, will be obsessed with sex. Hanna makes little pretense of genuinely loving Michael, whom she calls "kid," and although Michael has a helpless crush on Hanna, it should not be confused with love. He is swept away by the discovery of his own sexuality. What does she get from their affair? Sex, certainly, but it seems more important that he read aloud to her: "Reading first. Sex afterwards." The director, Stephen Daldry, portrays them with a great deal of nudity and sensuality, which is correct, because for those hours, in that place, they are about nothing else.

One day Hanna disappears. Michael finds her apartment deserted, with no hint or warning. His unformed ego is unprepared for this blow. Eight years later, as a law student, he enters a courtroom and discovers Hanna in a group of Nazi prison guards being tried for murder. Something during this trial suddenly makes another of her secrets clear to him and might help explain why she became a prison guard. His discovery does not excuse her unforgivable guilt. Still, it might affect her sentencing. Michael remains silent.

The adult Michael has sentenced himself to a lonely, isolated existence. We see him after a night with a woman, treating her with remote politeness. He has never recovered from the wound he received from Hanna, nor from the one he inflicted on himself eight years after. She hurt him; he hurt her. She was isolated and secretive after the war; he became so after the trial. The enormity of her sin far outweighs his, but they are both guilty of allowing harm because they reject the choice to do good.

At the end of the film, Michael encounters a Jewish woman in New York (Lena Olin), who eviscerates him with her moral outrage. She should. But she thinks he seeks understanding for Hanna. Not so. He cannot forgive Hanna's crimes. He seeks understanding for himself, although perhaps he doesn't realize that. In the courtroom he withheld moral witness and remained silent, as she did, as most Germans did. And as many of us have done or might be capable of doing.

There are enormous pressures in all human societies to go along. Many figures involved in the Wall Street meltdown have used the excuse, "I was only doing my job. I didn't know what was going on." President Bush led us into war on mistaken premises and now says he was betrayed by faulty intelligence.

U.S. military personnel became torturers because they were ordered to. Detroit says it was only giving us the cars we wanted. The Soviet Union functioned for years because people went along. China still is.

Many of the critics of *The Reader* seem to believe it is all about Hanna's shameful secret. No, not her past as a Nazi guard. The earlier secret she essentially became a guard to conceal. Others think the movie is an excuse for soft-core porn disguised as a sermon. Still others say it asks us to pity Hanna. Some complain we don't need yet another "Holocaust movie." None of them think the movie may have anything to say about them. I believe the movie may be demonstrating a fact of human nature: Most people, most of the time, all over the world, choose to go along. We vote with the tribe.

What would we have done during the rise of Hitler? If we had been Jews, we would have fled or been killed. But if we were one of the rest of the Germans? Can we guess, on the basis of how most white Americans, north and south, knew about racial discrimination but didn't go out on a limb to oppose it? Philip Roth's great novel *The Plot Against America* imagines a Nazi takeover here. It is painfully thought-provoking and probably not unfair. *The Reader* suggests that many people are like Michael and Hanna and possess secrets that we would do shameful things to conceal.

Recount ★ ★ ★
NO MPAA RATING, 115 m., 2008

Kevin Spacey (Ron Klain), John Hurt (Warren Christopher), Laura Dern (Katherine Harris), Tom Wilkinson (James Baker), Denis Leary (Michael Whouley), Ed Begley Jr. (David Boies), Bob Balaban (Ben Ginsburg). Directed by Jay Roach and produced by Kevin Spacey. Screenplay by Danny Strong.

Katherine Harris was a piece of work. The Florida secretary of state during the 2000 elections is not intended as the leading role in *Recount,* an HBO docudrama about that lamentable fiasco, but every time Laura Dern appears on the screen, she owns it. Watch her stride into a room of powerful men, pick up a little paper packet of sugar for her coffee, and shake it with great sweeping arm gestures as if she were a demonstrator in an educational film.

As much as anyone, Harris was responsible for George W. Bush being declared the winner of the state, and thus of the presidency. In a bewildering thicket of controversy about chads, hanging chads, dimpled chads, military ballots, voting machines, and nearsighted elderly voters, it was her apparent oblivion that prevented a meaningful recount from ever taking place. Don't talk to me about the Florida Supreme Court, the U.S. Supreme Court, or even the hero of the film, a Democratic Party strategist named Ron Klain (Kevin Spacey). They had a great influence on events, but it was Katherine Harris who created a shortage of time that ultimately had a greater effect than anything else.

And this is the fascinating part, the part that Laura Dern exploits until her performance becomes mesmerizing: Harris did it *without seeming to know what she was doing.* Although she was the head of Bush's Florida campaign, she bats her eyes in innocence while announcing a "firewall" isolating her office from anyone, Democrat or Republican, lest they affect her worship of the power of law. After that announcement, it is the merest detail that the film portrays two GOP strategists moving into her office and giving her suggestions. They include her when talking about what "we" have to do.

But even in the privacy of her office, she never quite seems to know what they are doing or why. She signals that her mind is operating in more elevated, more long-range dimensions. She sees it all as an adventure starring herself, and sometimes seems to be thanking her classmates for electing her homecoming queen. "Ten years ago," she tells her minders in a wondering voice, "I was teaching the chicken dance to seniors, and now I've been thrust into a political tempest of historical dimensions."

She sure has. *Recount,* an efficient and relentless enactment of the strategists on both sides of the Florida controversy, shows an accident that was waiting to happen. So confusing was the state's "butterfly ballot" (how such terms resound in memory) that large numbers of senior citizens from liberal districts apparently cast mistaken votes for

Pat Buchanan, a right-wing independent. Buchanan himself went on CNN to doubt that his support was quite that strong in Palm Beach County. If their chads alone had been correctly punched, Al Gore might have been elected president. But a chad is a chad. And the film follows all the jaw-dropping developments that kept us so enthralled during that confusing season.

The point of view is largely Klain's, played as a weary and dogged idealist by Spacey. As the film opens and it looks like Gore will win the election, he turns down a job offer from Gore because he thinks he deserves better. Yet soon he is the engine behind the Democrats' legal challenges, persisting even more than Gore himself probably would have. "You know what's funny about all this?" he asks his teammate Michael Whouley (Denis Leary). "I'm not even sure I *like* Al Gore." Klain's GOP opponent is James Baker (Tom Wilkinson), written and played as a man who does what any reasonable politician would have done under the circumstances. Often enough these ultimate insiders seem to get most of their information from CNN; aides frequently run in and tell them to watch the TV, as when both supreme courts drop their bombshells.

You might assume the movie is pro-Gore and anti-Bush, but you would not be quite right. Dave Grusin's almost eerie score evokes a journey into uncharted territories and haunted lands, but that's as close as it comes to making a statement (other than the incredulity voiced by the losers). The Democratic Party figures portrayed in the film have been the loudest in protest, especially Warren Christopher (John Hurt), who was the first head of the Gore team, and is portrayed as a wimp ready to cave in to the GOP. Whether the film is fair to him, I cannot say.

Recount portrays a lot of Democrats as being in favor of an "orderly transition of power" at whatever cost, and a lot of Republicans as being in favor of winning, in an orderly transition or any other kind. At least, as an exhausted Warren Christopher says when all is over and his man has lost: "The system worked. There were no tanks in the streets." Of course, at that time he would not have been thinking of the streets of Baghdad.

Redbelt ★ ★ ★
R, 98 m., 2008

Chiwetel Ejiofor (Mike Terry), Alice Braga (Sondra Terry), Emily Mortimer (Laura Black), Tim Allen (Chet Frank), Joe Mantegna (Jerry Weiss), Rodrigo Santoro (Bruno Silva), Max Martini (Joe Collins), Ricky Jay (Marty Brown). Directed by David Mamet and produced by Chrisann Verges. Screenplay by Mamet.

David Mamet's *Redbelt* assembles all the elements for a great Mamet film, but they're still spread out on the shop floor. It never really pulls itself together into the convincing, focused drama it promises, yet it kept me involved right up until the final scenes, which piled on developments almost recklessly. So gifted is Mamet as a writer and director that he can fascinate us even when he's pulling rabbits out of an empty hat.

The movie takes place in that pungent Mamet world of seamy streets on the wrong side of town, and is peopled by rogues and con men, trick artists and thieves, those who believe and those who prey on them. The cast is assembled from his stock company of actors whose very presence helps embody the atmosphere of a Mamet story, and who are almost always not what they seem, and then not even what they seem after that. He is fascinated by the deceptions of one confidence game assembled inside another.

At the center of a story, in a performance evoking intense idealism, is Mike Terry (Chiwetel Ejiofor), a martial arts instructor who runs a storefront studio on a barren city street. His is not one of those glass and steel fitness emporiums, but a throwback to an earlier time; the sign on his window promises jujitsu, and he apparently studied this art from those little pamphlets with crude illustrations that used to be advertised in the back pages of comic books. I studied booklets like this as a boy; apparently one embodies the philosophy of The Professor, a Brazilian martial arts master who is like a god to Mike.

Mike has few customers, is kept afloat by the small garment business of his wife, Sondra (Alice Braga), and is seen instructing a Los Angeles cop named Joe Collins (Max Martini). When you seem to be your studio's only instructor, the impression is fly-by-night, but there's a purist quality to Mike's dedication that has Joe completely convinced, and they both seriously believe in the "honor" of the academy.

Now commences a series of events it would be useless to describe, and which are eventually almost impossible to understand, involving a troubled lawyer (Emily Mortimer), a movie star (Tim Allen), the star's shifty manager (Joe Mantegna), and the world of a pay-TV fight promoter (Ricky Jay). All of these characters seem like marked-down versions of the stereotypes they're based on, and the pay-for-view operation feels more like local access cable than a big-bucks franchise.

In a bewildering series of deceptions, these people entrap the idealistic Mike into debt, betrayal, grief, guilt, and cynical disappointments, all leading up to a big televised fight sequence at the end that makes no attempt to be plausible and is interesting (if you are a student of such things) for its visual fakery. We've seen a lot of crowd scenes in which camera angles attempt to create the illusion of thousands of people who aren't really there, but *Redbelt* seems to be offering a crowd of hundreds (or dozens) who aren't really there. At a key point, in a wildly impossible development, the action shifts out of the ring, and the lights and cameras are focused on a man-to-man showdown in a gangway. The conclusion plays like a low-rent parody of a Rocky victory. The last shot left me underwhelmed.

So now you're wondering why you might want to see this movie at all. It might be because of the sheer art and craft of Mamet himself. For his dialogue, terse and enigmatic, as if in a secret code. For his series of "reveals" in which nothing is as it seems. For his lost world of fly-by-night operators. For his actors like Ricky Jay, who would be familiar with the term "suede shoe artist." For his bit parts for unexplained magicians. Especially for a sequence when Mike Terry, as baffled as we are, essentially asks for someone to explain the plot to him.

If you savor that sort of stuff, and I do, you may like *Redbelt* on its own dubious but seductive terms. It seems about to become one kind of movie, a conventional combination of con games and action, and then shadow-

boxes its way into a different kind of fight, which is about values, not strength. It's this kind of film: Some of the characters at the end, hauled in to provide a moral payoff, seem to have been airlifted from Brazil—which, in fact, they were.

Red Riding Trilogy ★★★★
NO MPAA RATING, 302 m., 2010

Andrew Garfield (Eddie Dunford), Paddy Considine (Peter Hunter), Mark Addy (John Piggott), David Morrissey (Maurice Jobson), Warren Clarke (Bill Molloy), Sean Bean (John Dawson), Peter Mullan (Martin Laws), Robert Sheehan (BJ), Rebecca Hall (Paula Garland), Sean Harris (Bob Craven). Directed by Julian Jarrold (*1974*), James Marsh (*1980*), and Anand Tucker (*1983*) and produced by Wendy Brazington, Andrew Eaton, and Anita Overland. Screenplay by Tony Grisoni, based on the novels by David Peace.

Red Riding Trilogy is an immersive experience like *Best of Youth, Brideshead Revisited,* or *Nicholas Nickleby.* Over the course of 302 minutes, we sink into a virtual world: the corrupt police and establishment figures of West Yorkshire in England, at the time of the real-life Yorkshire Ripper. Peter Sutcliffe, the Ripper, was convicted of killing thirteen women, and may have killed more. The fictional Ripper here enjoys the same inexplicable immunity to police investigation.

This is the sort of undertaking the UK's Channel 4 excels at and is approached in the United States only by ambitious cable TV series. The experience could give you the impression that the three parts were filmed at separate times. The visual style proceeds from 16 mm to 35 mm to high-def video, different actors play some of the characters at different times, and there are three directors, each with a distinctive style. But that was all part of the Channel 4 plan, and the completed trilogy aired in March 2009.

There's a large cast of characters involved in a complex series of events. Few viewers could be blamed for failing a test on what happens and who (in addition to the Ripper) is guilty. Strict continuity is sidestepped to such a degree that some characters do not quite seem to remain dead. This is a way to reflect the shifting nature of reality in which there are many concealed motives and the police version of events is fabricated entirely for their own convenience.

The police have their reasons, chillingly dramatized in a scene where conspirators drink a toast to "the North!" Yorkshire is in northern England, traditionally hostile to the South (London), but what does that have to do with a license for corruption? The toast is an example of the human willingness to excuse behavior by evoking meaningless abstractions (The South! The Young! Party Time! Der Fuhrer!). Where they are is irrelevant to what they do.

They are in a society that seems, to our North American eyes, clearly distinct from other parts of Britain. In some segments, the Yorkshire accents are so pronounced that Channel 4 wisely adds subtitles. We are inhabiting a subculture. In the early scenes, our attention is focused on an investigative reporter, new in town, Eddie Dunford (Andrew Garfield), who looks deeper into the murders, but is unlucky enough to get personally involved with a woman linked to a separate series of crimes. Their intimate scenes together are the closest the trilogy will come to human kindness.

Dunford is an unalloyed hero. Much of the rest of the story involves conspirators who plot among and against themselves. Any sense of objective morality is lacking. We get the sense that no one rises high in the police without knowing the rules and playing by them. They arrange for their own immunity.

There is a public outcry as the Ripper continues to kill and evade capture. It was the same in real life. Scotland Yard was brought in, represented indirectly here by a veteran cop named Peter Hunter (Paddy Considine). He makes little progress, in large part because the officers he's working with have guilt to conceal and much to cover up.

Without revealing anything crucial, the reality is that the Ripper murders are invisibly connected to a police cover-up of a deadly real estate conspiracy, and if you pull a string from the Ripper, the whole ball of yarn of the larger conspiracy may unravel. A central figure becomes a vile chief of police, played by David Morrissey, who is so alarming that one searches the Web to discover he looks a nice

enough man in real life. The casting here and throughout is essential to the trilogy's effect.

All this time a mentally challenged suspect has been held as the alleged Ripper. He has even confessed, which after police interrogation in Yorkshire, is a foregone conclusion. His guilt is convincingly challenged, which leads to a reopening of the case, as well it might, because the murders didn't stop with his imprisonment.

One wants to believe no police department in North America has ever been as corrupt as this one from Yorkshire. That may not be true, but the chances of a television trilogy about it are slim. *Red Riding Trilogy* hammers at the dark souls of its villains until they crack open, and it is a fascinating sight. We're in so deep by the final third that there can hardly be a character whose hidden evil comes as a surprise: Can innocence exist in this environment?

The directors, who worked on their segments more or less simultaneously, have impressive credits that do not, however, suggest the different feels they bring to their segments. *Red Riding 1974* is by Julian Jarrold, whose *Brideshead Revisited, Becoming Jane,* and *Kinky Boots* are all some distance from the immediacy of his 16 mm. *Red Riding 1980* is by James Marsh, whose documentaries *Man on Wire* and *Wisconsin Death Trip* don't suggest the 35 mm feature feel of his segment. And *Red Riding 1983*'s Anand Tucker (*Shopgirl, Hilary and Jackie*) is a specialist in clearly delineated ambiguity, at odds with the moral anarchy of his segment. I gather they were not hired to reproduce their strengths, but to find the right approach for this material.

I have given only the sketchiest of plot outlines here. The trilogy isn't so much about what happens objectively (which can sometimes be hard to determine), but about the world in which it takes place, a miasma of greed and evil. I have no idea whether the real Yorkshire police were led by monsters such as these. Someone must have thought so. Channel 4 aired these segments as they stand.

Religulous ★ ★ ★ ½
R, 101 m., 2008

Featuring Bill Maher. A documentary directed by Larry Charles and produced by Jonah Smith,

Palmer West, and Bill Maher. Screenplay
by Maher.

I'm going to try to review Bill Maher's *Religulous* without getting into religion. Is that OK with everybody? Good. I don't want to fan the flames of a holy war.

The movie is about organized religions: Judaism, Christianity, Islam, Mormonism, TV evangelism, and even Scientology, with detours into pagan cults and ancient Egypt. Bill Maher, host, writer, and debater, believes they are all crazy. He fears they could lead us prayerfully into mutual nuclear doom. He doesn't get to Hinduism or Buddhism, but he probably doesn't approve of them either.

This review is going to depend on one of my own deeply held beliefs: It's not what the movie is about; it's how it's about it. This movie is about Bill Maher's opinion of religion. He's very smart, quick, and funny, and I found the movie entertaining, although sometimes he's a little mean to his targets. He visits holy places in Italy, Israel, Great Britain, Florida, Missouri, and Utah, and talks with adherents of the religions he finds there, and others.

Or maybe "talks with" is not quite the right phrase. It's more that he lines them up and shoots them down. He interrupts, talks over, slaps on subtitles, edits in movie and TV clips, and doesn't play fair. Reader, I took a guilty pleasure in his misbehavior. The people he interviews are astonishingly forbearing, even most of the truckers in a chapel at a truck stop. I expected somebody to take a swing at him, but nobody did, although one trucker walked out on him. Elsewhere in the film, Maher walks out on a rabbi who approvingly attended a Holocaust denial conference in Iran.

Maher had a Jewish mother and a Catholic father, and was raised as a Catholic until he was thirteen, when his father stopped attending services. He speaks with his elderly mother, who tells him: "I don't know why he did that. We never discussed it." He asks her what the family believed, before and after that event. "I don't know what we believed," she says. No, she's not confused. She just doesn't know.

Most everybody else in the film knows what they believe. If they don't, Maher does. He impersonates a Scientologist at London's Speakers' Corner in Hyde Park and says Scientology teaches that there was a race of thetans several trillion years old (older than the universe, which is only 13.73 billion years) and that we are born with thetans inside us, which can be detected by an E-Meter, on sale at your local Scientology center, and driven out by "auditing," which takes a long time and unfortunately costs money.

Many of Maher's confrontations involve logical questions about holy books. For example, did Jonah really live for three days in the belly of a large fish? There are people who believe it. Is the end of days at hand? A U.S. senator says he thinks so. Will the Rapture occur in our lifetimes? Widespread agreement. Mormons believe Missouri will be the paradise ("Branson, I hope," says Maher). There are even some people who believe Alaska has been chosen as a refuge for the saved after Armageddon. In Kentucky, Maher visits the Creation Museum, which features a diorama of human children playing at the feet of dinosaurs.

His two most delightful guests, oddly enough, are priests stationed in the Vatican. Between them, they cheerfully dismiss wide swathes of what are widely thought to be Catholic teachings, including the existence of hell. One of these priests almost dissolves in laughter as he mentions various beliefs that I, as a child, solemnly absorbed in Catholic schools. The other observes that when Italians were polled to discover who was the first person they would pray to in a crisis, Jesus placed sixth.

Maher meets two representations of Jesus. One is an actor at the Holy Land Experience theme park in Orlando. He stars in a reenactment of the Passion, complete with crown of thorns, wounds, a crucifix, and Roman soldiers with whips. I suppose I understand why Florida tourists would take snapshots of this ordeal, but when Jesus stumbles, falls, and is whipped by soldiers, I was a little puzzled why they applauded.

The other Jesus, Jose Luis de Jesus Miranda, believes he actually is the Second Coming—that is, Jesus made flesh in our time. He explains how the bloodline traveled from the Holy Land through Spain to Puerto Rico. He has one hundred thousand followers.

Why have I focused on the Christians? Maher also has interesting debates with Muslims about whether the Quran calls for the death of infidels. And he interviews an Israeli manufacturer who invents devices to sidestep the bans on Sabbath activity. Since the laws prohibit you from operating machines, for example, they've invented a "negative telephone." Here's how it works: All the numbers on the touch-pad are constantly engaged. All you do is insert little sticks into holes beside the numbers you *don't* want to work.

I have done my job and described the movie. I report faithfully that I laughed frequently. You may very well hate it, but at least you've been informed. Perhaps you could enjoy the material about other religions and tune out when yours is being discussed. That's only human nature.

Remember Me ★★★

PG-13, 113 m., 2010

Robert Pattinson (Tyler Hawkins), Emilie de Ravin (Ally Craig), Chris Cooper (Sergeant Neil Craig), Pierce Brosnan (Charles Hawkins), Lena Olin (Diane Hirsch), Tate Ellington (Aidan Hall), Ruby Jerins (Caroline Hawkins). Directed by Allen Coulter and produced by Trevor Engelson and Nick Osborne. Screenplay by Will Fetters.

Remember Me tells a sweet enough love story, and tries to invest it with profound meaning by linking it to a coincidence. It doesn't work that way. People meet, maybe they fall in love, maybe they don't, maybe they're happy, maybe they're sad. That's life. If a refrigerator falls out of a window and squishes one of them, that's life, too, but it's not a story many people want to see. We stand there looking at the blood seeping out from under the Kelvinator and ask with Peggy Lee, "Is that all there is?"

You can't exactly say the movie cheats. It brings the refrigerator onscreen in the first scene. It ties the action to a key date in Kelvinator history, one everybody knows even if that's all they know about refrigerators. But, come on. This isn't the plot for a love story; it's the plot for a Greek tragedy. It may be true, as *King Lear* tells us, that "As flies to wanton boys are we to th' gods." But we don't want to think of ourselves as flies, or see fly love stories. Bring on the eagles.

The fact is, *Remember Me* is a well-made movie. I cared about the characters. I felt for them. Liberate them from the plot's destiny, which is an anvil around their necks, and you might have something.

The film opens on a New York subway platform. A young girl witnesses the senseless murder of her mother. We meet her again as a young woman. She is Ally Craig (Emilie de Ravin, from *Lost*), the daughter of a police sergeant (Chris Cooper). She's in college. Having lost his wife, he is intensely protective of her.

We meet a feckless young man named Tyler Hawkins (Robert Pattinson). He slouches about trying to look like a dissipated Robert Pattinson. Drinks too much, smokes too much, has the official four-day stubble on his face, hair carefully messed up, bad attitude. He lives in a pigpen of an apartment with a roommate named Aidan (Tate Ellington), who might have been played by Oscar Levant back in the days when roommates were obnoxious, OK, but bearable.

Tyler gets drunk one night, is thrown out of a club, gets in a fight, the cops are called, and when it's almost all over, he shoves one of the cops—Sergeant Craig, of course. Young drunks: It is *extremely unwise* to shove the cop who is about to let you off with a warning. Tyler is thrown in the slammer. Not long after in school, the snaky Aidan tells Tyler that their pretty classmate Ally is the daughter of that very cop. He dares Tyler to ask her out and then dump her in revenge.

Aidan is a jerk, but logically Tyler is too, because this is morally reprehensible. However, to the surprise of no one in the audience, Tyler falls for Ally and neglects to break up with her. Their courtship is a sensitive, well-acted progression through stages of mutual trust and Tyler's gradual rediscovery of his own real feelings.

There's an intriguing subplot. Tyler's parents are divorced. His father is the immensely wealthy Charles Hawkins (Pierce Brosnan), whose office looks larger than small airplane terminals. His mother, Diane (Lena Olin), has remarried. Tyler's beloved kid sister, Caroline (Ruby Jerins), lives with her. Only with Caroline can Tyler relax and drop the sullen facade, showing warmth and love. Until he meets Ally—and then there are two safe harbors, and his rebirth begins.

Pierce Brosnan plays a key role in the process.

He has only a few significant scenes in the movie, but plays them so well that he convincingly takes a three-step character development and makes it into an emotional evolution. Meanwhile, Ally and Tyler encounter fierce opposition to their relationship from her dad, who can't be blamed because as a cop he saw Tyler at his drunken worst.

These people and their situation grow more involving as the movie moves along. Then there's a perfect storm of coincidences to supply the closing scenes. That's what I object to.

If we invest in a film's characters, what happens to them should be intrinsically important to us. We don't require emotional reinforcement to be brought in from outside. The movie tries to borrow profound meaning, but succeeds only in upstaging itself so overwhelmingly that its characters become irrelevant. I'm guessing the message is: Parents, when you have a rebel child who hates you, someday you will learn what a good person that child really was. It's the dream of every tormented adolescent. Many of them become parents themselves and get their turn at being resented. Such is life.

Repo Men ★★

R, 111 m., 2010

Jude Law (Remy), Forest Whitaker (Jake), Liev Schreiber (Frank), Alice Braga (Beth), Carice van Houten (Carol). Directed by Miguel Sapochnik and produced by Mary Parent and Scott Stuber. Screenplay by Eric Garcia and Garrett Lerner, based on Garcia's novel *The Repossession Mambo*.

Repo Men makes sci-fi's strongest possible case for universal health care. In a world of the near future, where they still drive current cars, a giant corporation named the Union will provide you with a human heart, kidney, liver, or other organ. Let's say a pancreas costs you, oh, $312,000. No, it's not covered by insurance, but the sales guy says, "You owe it to yourself and your family." For a guy in need of a pancreas, this is an eloquent argument. Interest rates are around 19 percent.

Now let's say you can't make the payments. If you fall behind more than three months, they send around a repo man who shoots you with a stun gun, slices open your body, reaches in, and repossesses the organ. To be sure, he puts on latex gloves first. I don't believe the gun kills you, but after they leave you on the floor with an organ missing, your prognosis is poor.

Let's say you were conscious during such a procedure. Would it hurt? You bet it would. At one point in the film, our heroes Remy and Beth (Jude Law and Alice Braga) decide the only way to outwit the company's computer is to repossess themselves. He has a donor heart, and as for Beth, her heart is her own, but it is surrounded by guest organs. They don't actually carve themselves open and *remove* the organs. No, that would be fatal. But they have to reach inside each other with a bar-code scanner and scan them in. As Remy carves into his chest with a big old knife, you oughta see the way his fist clenches and he grits his teeth. He's thinking, I wish I had the public option.

I don't know if the makers of this film intended it as a comedy. A preview audience regarded it with polite silence, and left the theater in an orderly fashion. There are chases and shootouts, of course, and a standard overwrought thriller sound track, with the percussion guy hammering on cymbals and a big bass drum. Even then, you wonder.

Remy and Beth find themselves locked in a corridor with a dozen guys from the evil corporation who are well-armed. They dodge the bullets and wham some guys with karate, and then Remy pauses, strips off his shirt, reveals his bare (pre-repo) chest, and is wearing kinky leather pants with buckles. From scabbards in the back, he withdraws two long knives that help explain why he wasn't seated earlier in the scene. He slices some other guys. Then he shouts "Hacksaw!" to Beth and she slides it to him on the floor, and he whirls around and *decapitates* three guys, it looked like, although it happened real fast.

What are people supposed to think? Is this an action scene, or satire? Does it make any difference? I dunno. I know the actors play everything with deep, earnest seriousness. The head of the Union corporation is Frank (Liev Schreiber), who demands complete dedication from his repo men and is humorously not humorous. Maybe he's not the head of the whole Union, but only their immediate boss. The

Union's headquarters building is maybe one hundred stories high, and Remy stumbles into a room with guys in white suits working at tables that stretch farther than a football field. There are enough props in this movie to clean out the organ department at Moo & Oink's. When I say they're up to their elbows in blood, I mean it. This work takes its toll. Remy's friend at work is a repo man named Jake, played by Forest Whitaker. Like most Forest Whitaker characters and Whitaker himself, he is a warm, nice man. I noticed for the second time in a week (after *Our Family Wedding*) that Whitaker has lost a lot of weight and looks great. I hope the extra pounds weren't repo'ed.

Reprise ★ ★

R, 105 m., 2008

Espen Klouman Hoiner (Erik), Anders Danielsen Lie (Phillip), Viktoria Winge (Kari), Odd Magnus Williamson (Morten), Pal Stokka (Geir), Christian Rubeck (Lars). Directed by Joachim Trier and produced by Karin Julsrud. Screenplay by Eskil Vogt and Trier.

If there was ever a movie that seems written and directed by its characters, that movie is Joachim Trier's *Reprise*. Here is an ambitious and romantic portrait of two young would-be writers that seems made by ambitious and romantic would-be filmmakers. In the movie, the young heroes idolize Norway's greatest living writer, who tells one of them his novel is good and shows promise, except for the ending, where he shouldn't have been so poetic. The movie itself is good and shows promise, except for the ending, when Trier shouldn't have been so poetic. Not only does *Reprise* generate itself, it contains its own review.

The twenty-three-year-old heroes are Erik and Phillip. They seem to be awfully nice boys who have some growing-up to do. It opens with the two of them simultaneously dropping the manuscripts of their first novels into a post box. Then an anonymous narrator takes over and describes some possible futures of the characters and their novels. We will be hearing a lot from that narrator, and he, along with Erik and Phillip and Phillip's girlfriend, Kari, remind us inescapably of Francois Truffaut's *Jules and Jim*.

The movie is set in Oslo, with a visit to Paris. I have been to Oslo, and it's nowhere near the gray arrangement of apartment blocks and perfunctory landscaping that we see in the movie. (Nor is it Paris.) I have met Norwegians, who are nowhere near the bland, narcissistic Erik and Phillip. The big problem with the movie is our difficulty in working up much real interest in the characters. They're not compelling. Even when Phillip becomes so obsessed with Kari that he has to be accommodated in a mental institution, and even after (back on the streets) he takes her to Paris on the exact anniversary of their first trip there, it's impossible to see him as passionate. His emotions never seem to be at full volume.

The high point, passion-wise, comes during their Paris trip. His mother has confiscated his photos of Kari, fearing they will trigger a relapse. So in Paris he poses her to take them again, Kari even helpfully hitching up her skirt to more closely match the original. They visit the same café (I think). Then they check into the same hotel and make love in (one assumes) much the same way.

The movie finds it necessary to do something I'm growing weary of: It depicts their love-making at greater length than depth. They're seen in profile, in dim lighting, with a sound track that reminded me of the Hondells ("First gear—it's all right. Second gear—hold on tight").

After their breathing reaches overdrive, they disengage and she soon enough says, "You don't still love me." That word *love* is such a troublemaker. For characters like those in the movie, it represents an attainment like feeling patriotic or missing your dog. It's a state not consuming, not transcendent, but obligatory.

I also wearied of Phillip's countdowns. At a party, he bets himself Kari will turn and look at him at "zero" when he counts down from "ten." He tempts fate on his bicycle, in traffic, by closing his eyes while counting down. It's the kind of numerology that was charming in *Me and You and Everyone We Know*, when the heroine imagines that the sidewalk stretching ahead of her represents the life span of herself and the guy she likes, and they're halfway to the corner. It was fanciful and fetching in that film, but disposable in this one—indeed, bordering on

445

idiotic, because Phillip isn't that kind of person. For him the counting down not only seems to represent (a) something meaningful, but also (b) age-appropriate. If I were Kari, I'd jump ship at "seven," and actually she does tell Phillip, "I can't take it any more." Bonus points for taking it as long as she does.

Erik has a girlfriend, too, the seldom-seen (by his friends) Lillian, whom he pulls apart from because he fears she might not fit in with his friends, who therefore seldom see her. The characters meet in cafés, restaurants, one another's apartments, lakesides, and punk concerts. They take music very seriously, or say they do, but with fans like these, punk audiences would applaud politely.

Then there is the matter of their novels and the title of one of them, *Prosopopeia*. Well, Norway's greatest living writer thinks it's a good title, just as the book is a "good" book. You get the impression that, at his age, "great" would trigger a seizure. I never got any clear idea of what the novels were about, not even during a torturous television chat show that later triggers the greatest living writer's observation that TV is not the ideal medium for discussing literature. The cinema is an ideal medium for considering characters like those in *Reprise*, but you'd have to see *Jules and Jim* to find out why.

Revanche ★★★ ½

NO MPAA RATING, 121 m., 2009

Johannes Krisch (Alex), Irina Potapenko (Tamara), Ursula Strauss (Susanne), Hannes Thanheiser (Grandfather), Andreas Lust (Robert), Hanno Poschl (Konecny). Directed by Gotz Spielmann and produced by Mathias Forberg, Heinz Stussak, and Sandra Bohle. Screenplay by Spielmann.

Revanche involves a rare coming together of a male's criminal nature and a female's deep needs, entwined with a first-rate thriller. It is also perceptive in observing characters, including a proud old man. Rare is the thriller that is more about the reasons of people instead of the needs of the plot.

Alex and Tamara are a sad couple. In a trashy Vienna brothel, she is a prostitute from Ukraine; he is an ex-con who works as a bouncer for the reprehensible pimp Konecny. They are having a secret affair. Neither has the nerve to cross the pimp, the ruler of their world. Konecny has his eye on Tamara, and at one point visits her for sexual purposes while Alex hides humiliatingly under her bed.

Both Alex (Johannes Krisch) and Tamara (Irina Potapenko) are pitiful. They steal moments of love in their grubby rooms, and Alex plots a bank robbery. He brings her along in the getaway car. It will be easy, he says. Nobody will get hurt. Look—his gun isn't even loaded. But it does go wrong, and a cop turns up just as they're driving away.

Alex takes refuge at the only place he can think of, his grandfather's humble farm. And it is here that the story transcends crooks and hookers and bank jobs and becomes so surprisingly human. The catalyst I think is the character of the grandfather, played by Hannes Thanheiser.

He's a proud old man, living alone, mourning his wife, feeding his friends the cows, resisting well-meaning attempts to move him into a "home." When he dies, he wants to be carried out of his farmhouse. He has seen little of his grandson. Alex goes to work, chopping a mountain of firewood for the winter. They eat simple meals of sausage, cheese, and bread. I liked the old man and wanted to give him some mustard.

Susanne (Ursula Strauss), a neighbor's wife, visits him with offers of help. He appreciates her friendliness but not her help. Alex is distant and unfriendly. She takes good notice of him, and out of the blue asks him to visit her that night, when her husband is away. He does. No formalities. They have sex on her kitchen table.

Of course she is the wife of the cop who happened upon the bank robbery, but none of them can know this. We do. We also know that the cop cannot give her a child, and she wants to become pregnant. In this limited world, the old man's son is the only eligible father; she loves the old man and sees the son working hard for him.

The suspense at first involves whether the cop will happen upon them having sex. Then *Revanche* begins to involve a great deal more. It's here that the film's power resides. It seamlessly brings together the possibility of violence, of Alex's exposure, of threats to her marriage, of harm to the old man's well-being, in a way that doesn't seem to manipulate these things for advantage. Instead, it simply tells a good story, very well. Susanne becomes the protagonist. She is taking dangerous risks. All three of the men are unhappy and touchy. In a way, she represents their only hope.

As I watched the film I became grateful that I didn't know the actors. American films often involve actors well known to me, which is fine—but also sometimes stars are chosen primarily because they're "bankable." Few bankable stars could work in this material. The Austrian actors look normal. Unglamorous. Plausible. Ursula Strauss, as Susanne, looks sweet and pleasant but is careworn and not a great beauty. Johannes Krisch, as Alex, looks like a loser marginalized by crime and prison. As the prostitute, Irina Potapenko retails what beauty she has in a buyer's market.

All of these actors create characters who are above all people, not performances. That's why the film is peculiarly effective; it's about their lives, not their dilemmas. And the bedrock is old Hannes Thanheiser, born 1925, as a strong, stubborn, weathered old man who doesn't live through his grandson, his neighbors, or anyone else, but on his own terms, in daily mourning of the wife who shared his long life. That harm or loss could come to him would be a great misfortune.

How often, after seeing a thriller, do you continue to think about the lives of its characters? If you open up most of them, it's like looking inside a wristwatch. Opening this one is like heart surgery.

Note: Revanche was a 2008 Oscar nominee for Best Foreign Language Film.

Revolutionary Road ★ ★ ★ ★

R, 119 m., 2009

Leonardo DiCaprio (Frank Wheeler), Kate Winslet (April Wheeler), Kathy Bates (Helen Givings), Michael Shannon (John Givings), Kathryn Hahn (Milly Campbell), David Harbour (Shep Campbell), Zoe Kazan (Maureen Grube), Dylan Baker (Jack Ordway), Jay O. Sanders (Bart Pollock), Richard Easton (Howard Givings). Directed by Sam Mendes and produced by John N. Hart, Scott Rudin, and Bobby Cohen. Screenplay by Justin Haythe, based on the novel by Richard Yates.

Life is what happens to you while you're busy making other plans.

—John Lennon

Revolutionary Road shows the American Dream awakened by a nightmare. It takes place in the 1950s, the decade not only of Elvis but of *The Man in the Gray Flannel Suit*. It shows a young couple who meet at a party, get married, and create a suburban life with a nice house, a manicured lawn, "modern" furniture, two kids, a job in the city for him, housework for her, and martinis, cigarettes, boredom, and desperation for both of them.

The Wheelers, Frank and April, are blinded by love into believing life together will allow them to fulfill their fantasies. Their problem is, they have no fantasies. Instead, they have yearnings—a hunger for something *more* than a weary slog into middle age. Billy Wilder made a movie in 1955 called *The Seven Year Itch* about a restlessness that comes into some marriages when the partners realize the honeymoon is over and they're married for good and there's an empty space at the center.

Frank (Leonardo DiCaprio) and April (Kate Winslet) can't see inviting futures for themselves. Frank joins the morning march of men in suits and hats out of Grand Central and into jobs where they are "executives" doing meaningless work—in Frank's case, he's "in office machines." He might as well be one. April suggests he just quit so they can move to Paris; she can support them as a translator at the American Embassy, and he can figure out what he really wants to do. Translating will not support their Connecticut lifestyle, but Paris! What about their children? Their children are like a car you never think about when you're not driving somewhere.

Frank agrees, and they think they're poised to take flight, when suddenly he's offered a promotion and a raise. He has no choice, right? He'll be just as miserable, but better paid. In today's hard times, that sounds necessary, but maybe all times are hard when you hate your life. Frank and April have ferocious fights about his decision, and we realize that

447

April was largely motivated by her own needs. Better to support the neutered Frank in Paris with a job at the embassy, where she might meet someone more interesting than their carbon-copy neighbors and the "real estate lady," Helen Givings (Kathy Bates).

Helen makes a tentative request. Can she and her husband bring their son John (Michael Shannon) over for a meal? He's in a mental institution, and perhaps some time with a nice normal couple like the Wheelers would be good for him. John comes for dinner, and we discover his real handicap is telling the truth. With cruel words and merciless observations, he chops through their facade and mocks their delusions. It is a wrecking job.

Remember, this is the 1950s. A little after the time of this movie, *Life* magazine would run its famous story about the beatniks, "The Only Rebellion Around." There was a photo of a beatnik and his chick sitting on the floor and listening to an LP record of modern jazz that was cool and hip, and I felt my own yearnings. I remember on the way back from Steak 'n Shake one night, my dad drove slow past the Turk's Head coffeehouse on campus. "That's where the beatniks stand on tables and recite their poetry," he told my mom, and she said, "My, my," and I wanted to get out of that car and put on a black turtleneck and walk in there and stay.

The character John is not insane, just a beatnik a little ahead of schedule. He's an early assault wave from the 1960s, which would sweep over suburbia and create a generation its parents did not comprehend. What he does for the Wheelers is strip away their denials and see them clearly. Do you know these John Prine lyrics?

> *Blow up your TV, throw away your paper,*
> *Go to the country, build you a home.*
> *Plant a little garden, eat a lot of peaches,*
> *Try an' find Jesus on your own.*

Frank and April are played by DiCaprio and Winslet as the sad ending to the romance in *Titanic,* and all other romances that are founded on nothing more than . . . romance. They are so good, they stop being actors and become the people I grew up around. Don't think they smoke too much in this movie. In the 1950s everybody smoked everywhere all the time. Life was a disease, and smoking held it temporarily in remission. And drinking? Every ad executive in the neighborhood would head for the Wrigley Bar at lunchtime to prove the maxim: One martini is just right, two are too many, three are not enough.

The direction is by Sam Mendes, who dissected suburban desperation in *American Beauty,* a film that after this one seems merciful. The screenplay by Justin Haythe is drawn from the famous 1961 novel by Richard Yates, who has been called the voice of the postwar Age of Anxiety. This film is so good it is devastating. A lot of people believe their parents didn't understand them. What if they didn't understand themselves?

Ricky ★★

NO MPAA RATING, 89 m., 2010

Alexandra Lamy (Katie), Sergi Lopez (Paco), Melusine Mayance (Lisa), Arthur Peyret (Ricky), Andre Wilms (Doctor), Jean-Claude Bolle-Reddat (Journalist). Directed by Francois Ozon and produced by Chris Bolzli, Claudie Ossard, and Vieri Razzini. Screenplay by Ozon, based on the short story "Moth" by Rose Tremain.

Parables are stories about other people that help us live our own lives. The problem with *Ricky* is that the lesson of the parable is far from clear, and nobody is likely to encounter this situation in their own life. That would be pretty much impossible. The story begins in gritty realism, ends in pure fantasy, and leaves out most of the alphabet as it makes its way from A to Z.

The story begins with Katie (Alexandra Lamy), a morose French factory worker who has been abandoned, she thinks, by the man she lives with. It's hard to pay the rent. We flash back to the beginning, see her living with her peppy seven-year-old daughter, Lisa (Melusine Mayance), and working in a French chemical factory. There she meets a Spanish worker named Paco (Sergi Lopez). He's warm and attracted, they smile, they live together and have a baby.

These events take place in a series of time jumps that are momentarily jolting, but easy enough to follow. Not so easy is what happens to their son, Ricky (Arthur Peyret), as he grows up. In appearance he seems at first like an outtake from *Babies,* but then when Paco cares for him at home alone, Katie discovers bruises on his shoulders. Paco is enraged to be accused of child beating and stalks out, explaining Katie's opening scene.

These scenes are absorbingly created and well acted, and we settle in for a French slice of life. I can hardly deal with any more of the film without revealing details. Here goes, after a spoiler warning.

Those aren't bruises, they're the beginning of wings. Yes. Little wings, which at first look so much like poultry parts that Katie tape-measures a turkey wing at the supermarket, just to get an idea. One night, in slow-mo, the wings begin to sprout tiny feathers, which in close-up look like one of those life forms you don't want to make friends with. Soon the little lad has flapped his way to the top of an armoire.

No, he isn't an angel. Maybe more likely the result of his parents working at the chemical factory, although the movie doesn't make that a point. It doesn't much make anything a point. Katie and Lisa are about as amazed as if the child had a lot of hair on its head. You'd think babies with wings were born every day. Later, after Paco rejoins the family, baby Ricky gets a little injury, and the family doctor seems, to me, insufficiently amazed. Surely this is an OMG case?

Because the film is directed by the esteemed Francois Ozun (*Swimming Pool, Under the Sand, See the Sea*), I waited to see where it would take me. At the end, I wasn't sure. The ending has the form of a statement, but not the content of one. Its last half seems to be building to a life lesson, and perhaps the lesson is: "Parents! If you have a baby with wings, don't be this calm about it!"

I couldn't help myself. All during the film I was distracted by questions of aeronautics. In early scenes, those wings are way too small to allow a healthy baby to fly. Even later, the ratio of wingspan to baby weight seems way off. A scene where Ricky breaks free and flies around a supermarket seems designed for comedy, but doesn't play that way. And what kind of a cockamamie idea is it to hold a press conference and let Ricky fly with only Katie holding a string around its ankle? This is worse than the hot air balloon kid, if there had been one.

The film is bewildering. I don't know what its terms are, and it doesn't match any of mine. I found myself regarding it more and more as an inexplicable curiosity. It's so curiously flat in tone that when a baby grows wings and flies (think about that!), people in the film and in the audience seem to watch with no more than mild interest. *Ricky* makes a good case for lurid melodrama.

The Road ★★★ ½
R, 119 m., 2009

Viggo Mortensen (The Man), Kodi Smit-McPhee (The Boy), Charlize Theron (The Woman), Robert Duvall (Old Man), Guy Pearce (The Veteran), Michael K. Williams (The Thief), Garret Dillahunt (Gang Member), Molly Parker (Motherly Woman). Directed by John Hillcoat and produced by Paula Mae Schwartz and Steve Schwartz. Screenplay by Joe Penhall, based on the novel by Cormac McCarthy.

The Road evokes the images and the characters of Cormac McCarthy's novel but lacks the same core of emotional feeling. I am not sure this is any fault of the filmmakers. The novel itself would not be successful if it were limited to its characters and images. Its effect comes above all through McCarthy's prose. It is the same with all of McCarthy's work but especially this one, because his dialogue is so restrained, less baroque than usual.

The story is straightforward enough: America has been devastated. Habitations have been destroyed or abandoned, vegetation is dying, crops have failed, the infrastructure of civilization has disappeared. It has happened in such recent memory that even The Boy, so young, was born into a healthy world. No reason is given for this destruction, perhaps because no reason would be adequate. McCarthy evokes the general apprehension of post-9/11. The Boy and The Man make their way toward the sea, perhaps for no better reason than that the sea has always been the direction of hope in this country.

The surviving population has been reduced to savage survivalists, making slaves of the weaker, possibly using them as food. We've always done that, employing beef cattle, for example, to do the grazing on acres of pasture so we can consume the concentrated calories of their labor. In a land where food is scarce, wanderers seek out canned goods and fear their own bodies perform this work for the cannibals.

Although we read of those who stockpile guns and ammunition for an apocalypse, weapons stores on the Road have grown low. The Man has a gun with two remaining bullets. He is a wary traveler, suspecting everyone he sees. He and The Boy have a few possessions in a grocery cart. He encourages his son to keep walking but holds out little hope for the end of their journey.

I am not sure the characters could be played better, or differently. Viggo Mortensen plays The Man as dogged and stubborn, determined to protect his boy. Kodi Smit-McPhee is convincing as a child stunned by destruction, depending on his father in a world where it must be clear to him that any man can die in an instant. The movie resists any tendency toward making the child cute or the two of them heartwarming.

Flashback scenes star Charlize Theron as the wife and mother of the two in earlier, sunnier days. They show the marriage as failing, and these memories haunt The Man. I'm not sure what relevance this subplot has to the film as a whole; a marriage happy or sad—isn't it much the same in this new world? It has a lot of relevance to The Man and The Boy. In times of utter devastation, memories are all we have to cling to.

The external events of the novel have been boldly solved, and this is an awesome production. But McCarthy's prose has the uncanny ability to convey more than dialogue and incident. It's as dense as poetry. It is more spare in *The Road* than in a more ornate work like *Suttree*; in *The Road* it is evocative in the way Samuel Beckett is. If it were not, *The Road* might be just another film of sci-fi apocalypse. It's all too easy to imagine how this material could be vulgarized into the 2007 version of *I Am Legend*.

How could the director and writer, John Hillcoat and Joe Penhall, have summoned the strength of McCarthy's writing? Could they have used more stylized visuals instead of relentless realism? A grainy black-and-white look to suggest severely limited resources?

I have no idea. Perhaps McCarthy, like Faulkner, is all but unfilmable. The one great film of his work is the Coens' *No Country for Old Men*, but it began with an extraordinary character and surrounded him with others. *The Road* is not fertile soil but provides a world with the life draining from it.

McCarthy's greatest novels are *Suttree* and *Blood Meridian*. The second, set in the Old West, is about a fearsome, bald, skeletal man named Judge Holden, who is implacable in his desire to inflict suffering and death. It is being prepared by Todd Field (*In the Bedroom*). The Judge has not been cast; I see him as Tom Noonan—tall, grave, soft-spoken, almost sympathizing with you about your fate. Certainly not as a major star. As for a film based on *Suttree*, the director of *The Road*, John Hillcoat, made a film in 2005 named *The Proposition*, and I wrote in my review:

"Have you read *Blood Meridian*, the novel by Cormac McCarthy? This movie comes close to realizing the vision of that dread and despairing story. The critic Harold Bloom believes no other living American novelist has written a book as strong and compares it with Faulkner and Melville, but confesses his first two attempts to read it failed, 'because I flinched from the overwhelming carnage.'

"That book features a character known as the Judge, a tall, bald, remorseless bounty hunter who essentially wants to kill anyone he can, until he dies. His dialogue is peculiar, the speech of an educated man. *The Proposition* has such a character in an outlaw named Arthur Burns, who is much given to poetic quotations. He is played by Danny Huston in a performance of remarkable focus and savagery."

Perhaps it is significant that Hillcoat's next film would be based on *The Road*. Something in McCarthy's work draws him to it, and you must be a brave director to let that happen. Writing this, I realize few of the audience members can be expected to have read *The Road*, even though it was a selection of Oprah's Book Club. Fewer still will have read his other work. I've been saying for years that a film critic must review the film before him, and not how *faithful* the film is to the book—as if we're married to the book and screen adaptation is adultery. I realize my own fault is in being so very familiar with Cormac McCarthy. That may affect my ability to view the film afresh. When I know a novel is being filmed, I make it a point to not read the book. Yet I am grateful for having read McCarthy's.

Robin Hood ★★

PG-13, 131 m., 2010

Russell Crowe (Robin Longstride), Cate Blanchett (Marion Loxley), Mark Strong (Godfrey), William Hurt (William Marshal), Mark Addy (Friar Tuck), Oscar Isaac (Prince John), Danny Huston (Richard the Lionheart), Eileen Atkins (Eleanor of Aquitaine), Kevin Durand (Little John), Scott Grimes (Will Scarlet), Alan Doyle (Allan A'Dayle), Max von Sydow (Sir Walter Loxley). Directed by Ridley Scott and produced by Scott, Russell Crowe, and Brian Grazer. Screenplay by Brian Helgeland.

Little by little, title by title, innocence and joy is being drained out of the movies. What do you think of when you hear the name of Robin Hood? I think of Errol Flynn, Sean Connery, and the Walt Disney character. I see Robin lurking in Sherwood Forest, in love with Maid Marian (Olivia de Havilland or Audrey Hepburn), and roistering with Friar Tuck and the Merry Men. I see a dashing swashbuckler.

That Robin Hood is nowhere to be found in Ridley Scott's new *Robin Hood,* starring Russell Crowe as a warrior just back from fighting in the Third Crusade. Now Richard is dead, and Robin is essentially an unemployed mercenary. This story is a prequel. It takes place entirely *before* Robin got to be a folk hero. The idea of taking from the rich and giving to the poor was still in storyboard form. Grieving Richard the Lionheart and now faced with the tyrant King John, he leads an uprising.

This war broadens until, in the words of the movie's synopsis, "it will forever alter the balance of world power." That's not all: "Robin will become an eternal symbol of freedom for his people." Not bad for a man who, by general agreement, did not exist. Although various obscure bandits and ne'er-do-wells inspired ancient ballads about such a figure, our image of him is largely a fiction from the nineteenth century.

But so what? In for a penny, in for a pound. After the death of Richard, Robin Hood raises, arms, and fields an army to repel a French army as it lands on an English beach in wooden craft that look uncannily like World War II troop carriers at Normandy. His men, wielding broadswords, backed by archers, protected from enemy arrows by their shields, engage the enemy in a last act devoted almost entirely to nonstop CGI and stunt carnage in which a welter of warriors clashes in confused alarms and excursions, and Russell Crowe frequently appears in the foreground to whack somebody.

Subsequently, apparently, Robin pensioned his militia and retired to Sherwood Forest to play tag with Friar Tuck. That's my best guess; at the end the film informs us, "and so the legend begins," leaving us with the impression we walked in early.

Ah, you say, but what of Maid Marian? In this telling, Marion (Cate Blanchett) is not a maid but a widow, and not a merry one. At one point she threatens to unman Robin with her dagger, which is unlike the Maid Marians I've known and loved. Blanchett plays the role with great class and breeding, which is all wrong, I think. She's the kind of woman who would always be asking Robin, "Why do you let that smelly so-called friar hang around you like a fanboy?"

If you listen closely to the commercials, you may hear of a royal edict being issued against "Robin of the Hood." A hood, in medieval English, was, of course, a wood, or forest—a point that may be lost on many of the commercial's viewers.

Robin Hood is a high-tech and well-made violent action picture using the name of Robin Hood for no better reason than that it's an established brand not protected by copyright. I cannot discover any sincere interest on the part of Scott, Crowe, or the writer Brian Helgeland in any previous version of Robin Hood. Their Robin is another weary retread of the muscular macho slaughterers who with interchangeable names stand at the center of one overwrought bloodbath after another.

Have we grown weary of the delightful aspects of the Robin Hood legend? Is witty dialogue no longer permitted? Are Robin and Marion no longer allowed to engage in a spirited flirtation? Must their relationship seem like high-level sexual negotiations? How many people need to be covered in boiling oil for Robin Hood's story to be told these days? How many parents will be misled by the PG-13 rating? Must children go directly from animated dragons to skewering and decapitation, with no interval of cheerful storytelling?

The photography is, however, remarkable, and Crowe and the others are filled with fierce energy. Ridley Scott is a fine director for work like this, although in another world Hollywood would let him make smarter films. God, he must be tired of enormous battle scenes.

Note: The film was the opening night attraction at the 2010 Cannes Film Festival. There must be a reason for that. ☞

RocknRolla ★ ★ ★

R, 117 m., 2009

Gerard Butler (One Two), Tom Wilkinson (Lenny Cole), Thandie Newton (Stella), Mark Strong (Archy), Idris Elba (Mumbles), Tom Hardy (Handsome Bob), Toby Kebbell (Johnny), Jeremy Piven (Roman), Ludacris (Mickey). Directed by Guy Ritchie and produced by Ritchie, Joel Silver, Susan Downey, and Steve Clark-Hall. Screenplay by Ritchie.

I'm looking at *RocknRolla* and I'm thinking, why make a movie about stealing a parcel of London real estate, when you could make a movie about stealing a trillion bucks of real estate? British gangsters may dress better than Wall Street overlords and be more colorful, but they just don't think big. After watching Richard S. Fuld, CEO of Lehman Brothers, squirm before the House Oversight and Government Reform Committee (HOG-REFORM) as he explained why he deserved $350 million for guiding his company into bankruptcy, I found it refreshing to watch hoodlums squirm because they might get *personally* kneecapped without even so much as a golden hang-glider.

Guy Ritchie's new movie is about some very hard cases from the London and Russian underworlds who are all trying to cheat one another, and about an accountant whom the term "femme fatale" has been hanging around waiting to describe. It's one of those rare circular con jobs where you can more or less figure out what's going on, and you can more or less understand why nobody else

does, although at various times they all think they do, and at other times you're wrong. While they engage in these miscalculations, they act terrifically dangerous to one another—so smoothly you'd swear they were in the second year of a repertory tour.

You know who Tom Wilkinson is. You may not recognize him here, for reasons I won't describe because then you would. He's funny and terrifically dangerous as Lenny Cole, a gangster with the memory of a tax collector. He owns or has leveraged great swathes of London, including one swath urgently required by a Russian gangster named Uri Obamavich (Karel Roden), who comes to Cole. Now follow this attentively. One Two (Gerard Butler), Handsome Bob (Tom Hardy), and Mumbles (Idris Elba), whose parents may have been Dick Tracy fans, borrow $7 million from Cole to buy some land. Cole secretly owns the land and won't sell it to them, and arranges to steal the money back and demands to be paid. So he has the money and still has his land. Ken Lay would be proud.

But that's the simple part. Now Uri pays Cole $7 million to put the fix in on his own swath deal through Cole's tame London councilman, offering Cole his "good luck painting" as security. The femme fatale (Thandie Newton), Uri's accountant, sees a way to sidetrack the money herself. She hires One Two and Mumbles to steal Cole's $7 million, which she doesn't know was briefly their $7 million, from which they can pay $2 million to Cole and he won't kill them, but they lose the money and Cole doesn't have the $7 million to pay Uri, and meanwhile the invaluable "good luck painting" has been stolen, so at this point I'm not sure who has the money, maybe the femme fatale, but Cole needs it to give Uri, and Uri desperately needs it for harrowing reasons of his own, and the councilman needs it to save his career. Uri may not give a damn about his priceless painting, but Cole doesn't know that and sends Archy (Mark Strong) and Mickey (Ludacris) to find out who stole the painting, and—ohmigod!—it's in the hands of Cole's own stepson, the druggie rocknrolla Johnny Quid (Toby Kebbell), and Cole discovers that if there's anyone harder to deal with than a Russian mafioso, it's a druggie rocknrolla stepson.

Now don't go medieval on me because I gave away the whole plot, because (1) that's only the first time around the block, (2) right now you can't remember what I said, and (3) I may have gotten large parts of it wrong, although my fingers were bleeding from scribbling notes. The bottom line is, all these people chase the same money around with the success of doggie tail-biting, and it's a lot of fun, and it's not often in these con films that *everybody* is conning *everybody*, and they're all scared to death, and nobody knows which cup the pea is under.

RocknRolla (which is how they say *rock and roller* in the East End) isn't as jammed with visual pyrotechnics as Ritchie's *Lock, Stock and Two Smoking Barrels* (1998), but that's OK, because with anything more happening the movie could induce motion sickness. It never slows down enough to be really good and never speeds up enough to be the Bourne Mortgage Crisis, but there's one thing for sure: British actors love playing gangsters as much as American actors love playing cowboys, and it's always nice to see people having fun.

Role Models ★ ★ ★
R, 99 m., 2008

Seann William Scott (Wheeler), Paul Rudd (Danny), Christopher Mintz-Plasse (Augie), Jane Lynch (Sweeny), Bobb'e J. Thompson (Ronnie), Elizabeth Banks (Beth). Directed by David Wain and produced by Mary Parent, Scott Stuber, and Luke Greenfield. Screenplay by Wain, Paul Rudd, Ken Marino, and Timothy Dowling.

Role Models is the kind of movie you don't see every day, a comedy that is funny. The kind of comedy where funny people say funny things in funny situations, not the kind of comedy that whacks you with manic shocks to force an audible Pavlovian response.

Now that we've cleared the room by using "Pavlovian," let's enjoy *Role Models*. This is a fish-out-of-water plot with no water. The characters are all flopping around in places they don't want to be. Paul Rudd and Seann William Scott play Danny and Wheeler, teammates who drive a Minotaur-mobile super truck from school to school, touting a Jolt-like drink as the high-octane energy boost that will get you high without a jail sen-

tence: "Just say no to drugs, and 'YES!' to Minotaur!"

They get in trouble and are assigned to community service. Sweeny (Jane Lynch), the woman in charge of the program, could have been your usual Nurse Ratched type, but instead she's a brilliant comic invention, a former big-time cokehead from the Village with tattoos on her arm. I don't know why, but I have always found it pleasing to hear a pretty middle-aged woman saying, "You can't bullshit a bullshitter."

Danny and Wheeler are assigned to be mentors in a Big Brother kind of program for young troublemakers. Here the film is inventive. The heroes are assigned a potty-mouth and a nerd, but not like any you've seen before. Danny gets Augie (Christopher Mintz-Plasse), whose life is entirely absorbed in a medieval fantasy game where bizarrely costumed "armies" do battle in parks with fake swords. There are mostly younger teenagers and lonely men with mountain-man beards. Sort of a combination of Dungeons and Dragons and pederasty. Wheeler draws Ronnie (Bobb'e J. Thompson), a sassy rebel who looks about ten and hasn't had his growth yet. Not only does Ronnie know all the bad words, he can deliver them with the loud confidence of Chris Rock at full speed. Bobb'e J. Thompson will have his own show on Comedy Central before he's twenty-five.

So these two terrific young actors go through all the steps of a formula plot, but a formula plot works if you're laughing at the plot and not noticing the formula. There are nicely drawn supporting characters, including the pompous King Argotron (Ken Jeong). He rules this universe, and its members take him very, very seriously, even going so far as to fork-feed him and wipe his chin with a napkin at a pancake house.

Then there is Beth (Elizabeth Banks, Miri to Zack), Danny's girlfriend, who breaks up with him after he insults an Italian coffeehouse waitress. He shouts at her for calling a taller coffee a *vingt*. That's not Italian! (It's French, but she may have been saying *venti*.) Twenty ounces, you see. Anyway, Beth is sick of his anger and his dark moods. Augie helps to bring them back together after he accidentally gazes upon her "boobies." He is ecstatic. Earlier, he and Danny had started to bond for the first time when Danny told him: "Remember, for every man in the world, there are two boobies, more or less." A troubled young man needs all the encouragement he can get.

What's interesting about the fantasy medieval warfare is that the players take it with deadly seriousness. This is not a game. It is the game of their very lives. When they are tagged by a sword, they are dead, and what is unbearable is that they are still alive to know they are dead and listen to their enemies' scorn. The punishment is they can't play anymore. Oh, this is heavy stuff. Remember that story a few years ago about some college students who were playing a fantasy game in the tunnels and sewers beneath a campus, and a few of them got lost or killed, I forget which?

Everything is satisfactorily resolved in the end, as the formula requires. But since their problems were a little deeper than usual in this genre, our pleasure is increased a little. Not to the point where we're cheering, you understand. But to the point where we're thinking, hey, I sort of liked that.

I was mentioning little Ronnie's attitude. I like this exchange:

Ronnie: Suck it, *Reindeer Games!*
Danny: I'm not Ben Affleck.
Ronnie: You white, then you Ben Affleck.

The Romance of Astrea and Celadon ★ ★ ½
NO MPAA RATING, 109 m., 2009

Andy Gillet (Celadon), Stephanie Crayencour (Astrea), Cecile Cassel (Leonide), Veronique Reymond (Galathee), Rosette (Sylvie), Rodolphe Pauly (Hylas), Jocelyn Quivrin (Lycidas). Directed by Eric Rohmer and produced by Philippe Liegeois and Jean-Michel Rey. Screenplay by Rohmer, based on the novel by Honore d'Urfe.

The French New Wave began circa 1958 and influenced in one way or another most of the good movies made ever since. Some of its pioneers (Melville, Truffaut, Malle) are dead, but the others (Godard, Chabrol, Rivette, Resnais, Varda) are still active in their late seventies and up, and Eric Rohmer, at eighty-eight, has only just announced that *The Romance of Astrea and Celadon* may be his last film.

It doesn't look like a typical Rohmer. He

frequently gives us contemporary characters, besotted not so much by love as by talking about it, finding themselves involved in ethical and plot puzzles, at the end of which he likes to quote a proverb or moral. His films are quietly passionate and lightly mannered.

But then, so is *Astrea and Celadon,* even if it's set in fifth-century Gaul and involves shepherds, shepherdesses, druids, and nymphs. The story was told in a novel by Honore d'Urfe, marquis of Valromey and count of Chateauneuf, who published it in volumes between 1607 and 1627—running, I learn, some five thousand pages. The film version must therefore be considerably abridged at 109 minutes, although it leaves you wondering if the novel ran on like this forever.

The movie does rather run on, although it is charming and sweet, and perhaps too languid. It is about two lovers obsessed with love's codes of honor. That is, curiously, the same subject as Rivette's 2007 film *The Duchess of Langeais,* made when he was seventy-nine. The characters seem perversely more dedicated to debating the fine points than getting down to it. Rivette has them talking to one another; Rohmer has them fretting while separated.

The story is told in pastoral woodlands and pastures and along a river's banks. We meet the handsome Celadon (Andy Gillet) and the beautiful Astrea (Stephanie Crayencour), shepherds and in love, not long before a tragic misperception breaks Astrea's heart, and Celadon hurls himself into the river in remorse. Believed by Astrea to be dead, he is fished out by the statuesque nymph Galathee (Veronique Reymond) and her handmaidens and kept all but captive in her castle. He pines, sworn never to be seen by Astrea's eyes again, while the two lovers debate the loopholes in romantic love with their friends. They also debate such matters as whether the Trinity corresponds to the Roman gods and sing, quote poetry, and mostly seem to ignore sheep.

A druid priest convinces Celadon to disguise himself as a girl and infiltrate Astrea's inner circle, creating much suspense, mostly on my part, as I kept expecting Astrea to exclaim, "Celadon, do you actually think you can fool anyone with that disguise?" But they play by the rules, and then things pick up nicely when they break them.

This would not be the Rohmer film you would want to start with. I've seen most of his films, and my first was *My Night at Maud's* (1969), about a long conversation about everything but love—which is to say, about love. Rohmer, I think, delights in these dialogue passages as allowing him to see his characters more carefully than in your usual formula, where courtships seem to be conducted via hormonal aromas. Sometimes his approach is sexier. The knee in *Claire's Knee* (1970) fascinated me more than entire bodies in countless films. Why Rohmer decided to end with this film I cannot say. Perhaps after forty-five years of features, he had heard it all.

Roman de Gare ★ ★ ½
R, 103 m., 2008

Dominique Pinon (Pierre Laclos/Louis), Fanny Ardant (Judith Ralitzer), Audrey Dana (Huguette), Cyrille Eldin (Paul). Directed, written, and produced by Claude Lelouch.

Roman de Gare is French for what we call an "airport novel," but it's virtually the opposite. In a good airport novel, the plot plows you through safety-belt demonstrations, five-dollar "snacks," and lists of connecting flights. In *Roman de Gare*, the plot has a way of braking to a halt and forcing us to question everything that has gone before. What can we believe, and when can we believe it? Directed by Claude Lelouch, that inexhaustible middlebrow whose *A Man and a Woman* (1966) monopolized art house screens for months and months, it's so clever that finally that's all it is: clever.

It begins with a flash-forward to the end (or, as it turns out, not quite the end), featuring a famous novelist being questioned by the cops for murder. This is Judith Ralitzer, played by the elegant Fanny Ardant, Francois Truffaut's widow. She's idolized by the next character we meet, Huguette (Audrey Dana). We join her and her boyfriend, Paul (Cyrille Eldin), in a car on an expressway at 3 a.m. They're having a fight that seems to be about her smoking but is actually about their entire relationship, which ends when Paul abandons her at a highway café, taking with him her purse, money, keys, everything. What a lousy trick.

Watching this happen is a man (Dominique Pinon) drinking coffee in the café. He offers her a ride and keeps sipping his coffee until she agrees. The movie hints this is actually Jacques Maury, a pedophile who has escaped from prison. Nicknamed "The Magician," he performs magic tricks to entrance his victims. On the other hand, he may be Judith Ralitzer's ghost writer, as he claims. And what about a worried wife we meet talking to a cop? She thinks her husband, a schoolteacher, has abandoned her. Lelouch constructs a story in which this same man could be one, but not, *I think*, all of the above.

Dominique Pinon is a fascinating actor to watch. With a stepped-on face, a scrawny beard, and a low-key, insinuating manner, he is not blessed by the gods, but he seems able to fascinate women. As he and Huguette drive through the night, he drops the bombshell that he's the ghost writer of her favorite novelist. Then he says things that may synch with news reports of the Magician. All the time, he chews gum in lots of fast little chomps. I was going to say he looks like he's chewing his cud, but he's not like a cow; he's like an insect.

At this point, the movie had me rather fascinated. Turns out Huguette and Paul were driving to the country so she could introduce her parents to Paul for the first time. "Would you do me a huge favor?" she asks her new friend. She wants him to impersonate her fiancé. This leads us into a sly domestic comedy, when Huguette's mother wonders who this little man really is, and Huguette's daughter (who lives on the farm) takes him trout fishing; they're gone for hours, while Huguette reflects she knows nothing about the man except that he said he was a ghost writer and then he said he wasn't. And now the *real* Paul turns up at the farmhouse.

It's here that the movie goes wrong, starting with Huguette's method of facing this situation. Then we learn more about the novelist, her ghost writer, the wife with the missing husband, the cop she's talking to, one of his relatives, and magic tricks. I've invested countless words denouncing plots as retreads! Standard! Obligatory! Here's a plot that double-crosses itself at every opportunity. I should be delighted with it, especially since it visits two of my favorite places, Cannes and

Beaune, home of a medieval hospital that made a deep impression on me. Lined up along the walls of an enormous arching room, the patients are bedded in alcoves with a clear view of the altar where Mass is celebrated; the Beaune cure is prayer.

Offshore from Cannes in her luxurious yacht, Judith floats with whomever the hell Dominique Pinon is playing now. He has unexpected plans for her next novel, leading to the question that generates the flash-forward at the beginning. The closing scenes of the movie are dominated by Fanny Ardant, who has the kind of sculptured beauty Truffaut must have recognized when he desired to make her his wife and his star.

When a movie like *Roman de Gare* works, it's ingenious, deceptive, and slippery. When it doesn't, it's just jerking our chains. I think I understand the alternative realities of the plot, and I concede the loose ends are tied up, sort of, but I didn't care. One of the characters played by Pinon would have been enough for this movie. I would have been interested in the escaped pedophile or the ghost writer. But not in both of them interchangeably, and that pesky missing husband. Come on, I'm thinking, give us a place to stand. Do we care about Huguette because her favorite novelist is a fraud, or because her daughter may be sleeping with the fishes?

Roman Polanski:
Wanted and Desired ★ ★ ★ ½
NO MPAA RATING, 100 m., 2008

A documentary directed by Marina Zenovich and produced by Jeffrey Levy-Hinte and Lila Yacoub. Screenplay by Zenovich, Joe Bini, and P. G. Morgan.

The tragic story of Roman Polanski, his life, his suffering, and his crimes, has been told and retold until it assumes the status of legend. After the loss of his parents in the Holocaust, after raising himself on the streets of Nazi-controlled Poland, after moving to America to acclaim as the director of *Chinatown,* after the murder by the Manson Family of his wife and unborn child . . . what then?

He was arrested and tried for unlawful sexual intercourse with a thirteen-year-old girl, the least of several charges including supplying her with drink and drugs. Then he fled the country to avoid a prison sentence and still remains in European exile for that reason. That is what everybody remembers, and it is all here in Marina Zenovich's surprising documentary, *Roman Polanski: Wanted and Desired.*

But there is so much more, and the story she builds, brick by brick with eyewitness testimony, is about crimes against the justice system carried out by the judge in Polanski's case, Laurence J. Rittenband. So corrupt was this man that the documentary finds agreement among the three people (aside from Polanski) most interested in the outcome: the defense attorney, Douglas Dalton; the assistant district attorney who prosecuted the case, Roger Gunson; and Samantha Gailey Geimer, who was the child involved.

Their testimony nails Rittenband as a shameless publicity seeker who was more concerned with his own image than arriving at justice. Who broke his word to attorneys on both sides. Who staged a fake courtroom session in which Gunson and Geimer were to go through the motions of making their arguments before the judge read an opinion he had already prepared. Who tried to stage such a "sham" (Gunson's term) a second time. Who juggled possible sentences in discussions with outsiders, once calling a Santa Monica reporter, David L. Jonta, into his chambers to ask him, "What the hell should I do with Polanski?" Who discussed the case with the guy at the next urinal at his country club. Who held a press conference while the case was still alive. Who was removed from the case on a motion by *both* prosecution and defense.

The most significant fact of the film is that the prosecutor Gunson, a straitlaced Mormon, agrees with the defender Dalton that justice was not served. Both break their silences for this film after many years, Gunson saying, "I'm not surprised that he left the country under those circumstances." Samantha Geimer, whose family asked at the time that Polanski not be prosecuted or jailed, came public in 1997 to forgive him, and now says she feels Rittenband was running the case for his own aggrandizement, "orchestrating some little show that I didn't want to be in."

And in 2003, I learn from the *New York Times,* she published a statement concluding: "Who wouldn't think about running when facing a fifty-year sentence from a judge who was clearly more interested in his own reputation than a fair judgment or even the well-being of the victim?"

It is her own well-being that leaves her bitter about the judge and the press, when as a child she became the center of an international media circus. Finally, she says, "I just stayed in my room." Now an intelligent and well-spoken adult, she represents herself with quiet dignity.

Polanski's ordeal with the press began after the 1969 Manson murders. Before the case was linked to Manson, Polanski was widely reported to be a Satanic drug addict who probably orchestrated the killings himself. That was a crushing irony for a man who had suffered so much as a child and had now lost so much as an adult.

Yes, what he did with the thirteen-year-old girl was very wrong. That there were mitigating circumstances should not concern us. He confessed his guilt in a plea bargain arranged by the judge and both attorneys. He turned up at Chino State Prison to serve a ninety-day "evaluation" sentence. When Chino agreed with the parole board and two court-appointed psychiatrists (one is in the film) that he should be given parole, Rittenband decided to ignore those opinions because he was getting a bad image, he complained in chambers, while trying to orchestrate the second of his sham sessions (Dalton calls them "like a mock trial").

Zenovich uses file footage of Polanski at the time, TV news bites, newspaper clippings, even scenes from Polanski's films (*Rosemary's Baby* made such an impact that some thought it was made under Satanic inspiration). There are no current interviews with Polanski - himself—just older TV interviews. But she has achieved extraordinary access to the other still-living players in the case, and they all seem to be in agreement: Polanski is correct in saying the judge played with him as a cat might play with a mouse. The corruption in Rittenband's courtroom was worthy of *Chinatown.*

Note: On July 15, 2008, Polanski and Dalton asked the L.A. district attorney's office to review his case based on new evidence disclosed in the film, including alleged improper communication between a member of the prosecutor's office (not Gunson) and Rittenband.

Rudo y Cursi ★ ★ ★
R, 103 m., 2009

Gael Garcia Bernal (Tato), Diego Luna (Beto), Guillermo Francella (Batuta), Dolores Heredia (Elvira), Adriana Paz (Tona), Jessica Mas (Maya). Directed by Carlos Cuaron and produced by Alfonso Cuaron, Alejandro Gonzalez Inarritu, Guillermo del Toro, and Frida Torresblanco. Screenplay by Carlos Cuaron.

I am gradually discovering that soccer is superior to American football: quicker, more athletic, depending on improvisation more than planning. In South and Central America, where American baseball has been embraced, soccer is a way of life. A movie like *Rudo y Cursi* helps explain why: One day, peons on a banana plantation; the next day, playing for big bucks in Mexico City. Just bring your shorts, your shoes, your shirt, and your ability. No shoulder pads.

The movie is a rags-to-beeyaches comedy about two half brothers from a poor rural background who are spotted one day by a talent scout. Why was he even watching their small-town game on a vacant lot? He was stranded there, along with his disabled red sports convertible and his trophy squeeze, by a slow-moving auto shop. He sees them playing and offers them an audition, which hinges ironically on the ancient confusion between audience right and stage right.

This is not a deep movie, but it's a broad one. It reunites three talents who had an enormous hit with *Y Tu Mama Tambien* in 2001: the actors Gael Garcia Bernal and Diego Luna, and Carlos Cuaron, who wrote that film and writes and directs this one. Instead of trying to top themselves with life and poignancy, they wisely do something for fun.

Tato (Bernal) plays the accordion and dreams of a future as a musical star, although nothing about his singing and playing suggests much of a future. Beto (Luna) has a wife and kids and has recently been promoted to foreman of a banana-picking crew. He dreams of being a pro goalie in much the same way we all dream of being Susan Boyle, although without her talent.

Batuta (Guillermo Francella), the talent scout, is a smooth-talking slickster who considers himself a historian and philosopher of soccer. He is the film's narrator and shares the surprising news that soccer was invented by ancient Aztecs while kicking around the severed heads of their enemies. So much for the belief that it originated in China in about 200 B.C. I'm not surprised. To hear them tell it, everything originated in China in about 200 B.C.

The boys travel eagerly to Mexico City, leaving behind Beto's family, their mother, and their mother's assorted worthless husbands. They pick up nicknames. Tato is "Cursi," meaning cornball. Beto is "Rudo," meaning rough-edged. They're dazzled by the bright lights, the big city, and, in Rudo's case, the joys of high-stakes poker. Tato realizes his fantasy of meeting a sexy spokesmodel he's worshipped on TV and tapes his first music video, which, on the basis of its outcome, seems likely to be the last.

Curiously, and wisely, there's not a lot of soccer action in the movie, although it goes without saying there's a Big Match. This isn't a sports movie but a human comedy, and it depends on the effortless chemistry between Luna and Bernal, who evoke, like real brothers, the ability to love and hate each other and push all the right buttons. We are happy for their sudden good fortune, but somehow doubtful it will amount to much; they want success, but not enough to commit their entire lives to the quest.

The movie is the first from the newly formed Cha Cha Cha Productions, a collaboration of the top Mexican directors Alejandro Gonzalez Inarritu (*Amores Perros*), Guillermo del Toro (*Pan's Labyrinth*), and Alfonso Cuaron (brother of Carlos and director of *Y Tu Mama Tambien*). It comes at the end of an exciting decade for the Mexican cinema, which because of its high quality and the growing indie, foreign, and Spanish-speaking markets in the United States, is finding significant success. *Rudo y Cursi* is the sort of high-level buddy movie every national cinema needs for export—along with its masterpieces, to be sure.

Rumba ★★ ½
NO MPAA RATING, 77 m., 2009

Dominique Abel (Dom), Fiona Gordon (Fiona). Directed by Dominique Abel, Fiona Gordon, and Bruno Romy, and produced by Abel, Gordon, Charles Gillibert, Marin Karmitz, and Nathanael Karmitz. Screenplay by Abel, Gordon, and Romy.

Rumba is a peculiar deadpan comedy from Belgium, sort of sweet, sort of macabre, about a couple who are out of step with life but not with each other. It's not terrifically funny, but then how could it be? The influence of Jacques Tati abides in the material, without his sunniness.

Dom and Fiona (Dominique Abel and Fiona Gordon) are schoolteachers and competitive rumba dancers, and dangerously out to lunch. Arriving at the dance contest, they realize they've forgotten their costumes, race home to get them, and drive back at top speed while changing their clothes, Dom at one point upside down in the driver's seat while Fiona tugs at his socks. It's one time you're relieved to be able to see it's back projection.

Their luck worsens. Just for starters, they're in a car crash on their way home and Dom loses his memory and Fiona her leg. This doesn't much depress them; they're loving and ebullient and have each other. But then one catastrophe after another besets them, only one of which I will reveal. Abel and Gordon, I learn, have long worked together in cabaret, tilting toward physical comedy. They're essentially silent comedians with no need of a movie with a sound track, and *Rumba* has a bare minimum of dialogue.

They're skilled. A scene when Dom tries to rescue Fiona after a mishap with a trash fire reminded me of that Buster Keaton bit where he tries to help the drunken woman into her bed.

The movie is pleasing and amusing. I think it's intended to be funnier, but it's too laid back to achieve takeoff. Yes, laid back, even after they burn the house down. Those damned wooden legs. Nothing but fire hazards.

The Runaways ★★★
R, 100 m., 2010

Kristen Stewart (Joan Jett), Dakota Fanning (Cherie Currie), Michael Shannon (Kim Fowley),

Stella Maeve (Sandy West), Scout Taylor-Compton (Lita Ford), Alia Shawkat (Robin), Riley Keough (Marie Currie). Directed by Floria Sigismondi and produced by Art Linson, John Linson, and William Pohlad. Screenplay by Sigismondi, based on the book *Neon Angel: The Cherie Currie Story* by Cherie Currie.

An all-girl rock band is named and trained by a rock manager of dubious sexuality, goes on the road, hits the charts, has a lesbian member and another who becomes a sex symbol but crashes from drugs. This is the plot of a 1970 film named *Beyond the Valley of the Dolls*, which inadvertently anticipated the saga of the Runaways five years later. Life follows art.

The Runaways tells the story of a hard-rock girl band that was created more or less out of thin air by a manager named Kim Fowley. His luck is that he started more or less accidentally with performers who were actually talented. Guitarists Joan Jett and Lita Ford are popular to this day, long after the expiration of their sell-by dates as jailbait. The lead singer, Cherie Currie, costarred in the very good *Foxes* (1980) with Jodie Foster, had drug problems, rehabbed, and "today is a chainsaw artist living in the San Fernando Valley." The ideal art form for any retired hard rocker.

The movie centers on the characters of Jett (Kristen Stewart), Currie (Dakota Fanning), and the manager Fowley (Michael Shannon). Jett was the original driving force, a Bowie fan who dreamed of forming her own band. Fowley, known in the music clubs of Sunset Strip as a manager on the prowl for young, cheap talent, told her to give it a shot, and paired her with Currie, whose essential quality is apparently that she was fifteen. That fit Fowley's concept of a jailbait band who would appeal because they seemed so young and so tough. He rehearses them in a derelict trailer in the Valley, writing their early hit "Cherry Bomb" on the spot.

Shannon is an actor of uncanny power. Nominated for a role as an odd dinner guest in *Revolutionary Road* (2008), he was searing as he turned paranoid in William Friedkin's *Bug* (2006). Here he's an evil Svengali, who teaches rock 'n' roll as an assault on the audience; the girls must batter their fans into submission or admit they're losers. He's like a Marine drill sergeant: "Give me the girl. I'll give you back the man." He converts Cherie, who begins by singing passively, into a snarling tigress.

The performance abilities of the Runaways won respect. The rest was promotion and publicity. The film covers the process with visuals over a great deal of music, which helps cover an underwritten script and many questions about the characters. We learn next to nothing about anyone's home life except for Currie, who is provided with a runaway mother (Tatum O'Neal), a loyal but resentful sister (Riley Keough), and a dying alcoholic father. Although this man's health is important in the plot, I don't recall us ever seeing him standing up or getting a clear look at his face.

So this isn't an in-depth biopic, even though it's based on Currie's 1989 autobiography. It's more of a quick overview of the creation, rise, and fall of the Runaways, with slim character development, no extended dialogue scenes, and a whole lot of rock 'n' roll. Its interest comes from Shannon's fierce and sadistic training scenes as Kim Fowley, and from the intrinsic qualities of the performances by Stewart and Fanning, who bring more to their characters than the screenplay provides.

Another new movie this week, *The Girl with the Dragon Tattoo* from Sweden, has a role for a young, hostile computer hacker. Stewart has been mentioned for the inevitable Hollywood remake. Reviewing that movie, I doubted she could handle such a tough-as-nails character. Having seen her as Joan Jett, I think she possibly could.

Note: Many years ago, while I was standing at a luggage carousel at Heathrow Airport, I was approached by a friendly young woman. I'm Joan Jett, she told me. I liked Beyond the Valley of the Dolls.

Just sayin'.

S

Saint John of Las Vegas ★★
R, 85 m., 2010

Steve Buscemi (John Alighieri), Romany Malco (Virgil), Sarah Silverman (Jill), Peter Dinklage (Mr. Townsend), Emmanuelle Chriqui (Tasty D Lite), Tim Blake Nelson (Ned). Directed by Hue Rhodes and produced by Mark Burton, Lawrence Mattis, Kelly McCormick, and Matt Wall. Screenplay by Rhodes, based on the story by Dante Alighieri.

If you were to view the trailer of *Saint John of Las Vegas*, it would probably look like a good time. It seems to have so much great stuff. Promise me a movie with Steve Buscemi, Sarah Silverman, Peter Dinklage, and Tim Blake Nelson, and I'm there. But this movie is all elbows. Nothing fits. It doesn't add up. It has some terrific free-standing scenes, but they need more to lean on.

Consider the burning man. This is a sideshow performer who wears a suit designed to burst into flames. Unfortunately, the suit has malfunctioned and he can't take it off until the fuel is exhausted. He waits it out on a folding chair behind the carnival midway, consumed in flames every thirty seconds. That's funny, especially when he's dying for a cigarette. But . . . what? He exists only to be existing.

Well, not quite. The flaming also seems to fit into the movie's overall symbolism. The screenplay, we learn, was written by the director Hue Rhodes, based on the story by Dante Alighieri. That name may not ring a bell with a lot of moviegoers and had better not be a question on the Tea Baggers' literacy test. We all recall that Dante's *Inferno* told the story of a journey into hell, with the poet Virgil as the tour guide.

In the movie, Steve Buscemi plays John Alighieri, an insurance claims adjuster who is assigned a partner named Virgil (Romany Malco) and sets off on a journey through the desert to Las Vegas (hell).

Let's have some fun. Dante's First Circle of Hell was Limbo. In the movie, that would be the main office of the insurance company. People in Limbo have trouble controlling their weaknesses. John's weakness is compulsive gambling. Second Circle is Lust. He lusts for Jill (Silverman), a chirpy coworker who labors in the next cubicle. Later, in a lap-dance bar, he undergoes but resists temptation from a stripper (Emmanuelle Chriqui), who sprained her neck in a car crash but tries to give him a lap dance from her wheelchair. It's her crash the insurance company doesn't want to pay the claim on.

Third Circle, Gluttony. In this circle are rain and hail, which the two drive through. Fourth Circle, Avarice. John dreams of winning the lottery and spends every dollar on scratch cards. Virgil also has greed, revealed later. Fifth Circle, Anger. They argue with a cop and arrive at a senseless flaming gateway in the desert, guarded by Tim Blake Nelson and other naked men with guns. Sixth Circle, Heresy. Virgil seems not to take the insurance company seriously.

Seventh Circle, Violence. In a used car lot, they are led into a trap and John, knocked senseless, barely escapes with his life. The lot is guarded by a savage dog, no doubt based on Cerberus, the watchdog of Hell. Eighth Circle, Fraud. John discovers the nature of a scheme to defraud the insurance company. Ninth and last Circle, Treason against God—or, in this case, Mr. Townsend (Dinklage), who is their boss at the insurance company.

If you recall Dante very well, or jot some reminders on your palm with a ballpoint, you can possibly follow the movie in this way. But if like most people your command of the *Inferno* is shaky, the film may seem disjointed and pointless. There is also this inescapable storytelling dilemma: Once you arrive in the Ninth Circle of Hell, what do you do for an encore?

The acting is first-rate. Buscemi is an apologetic loser who fled Vegas after losing his net worth, and now unwisely returns. Malco's Virgil, now that we think of it, is a guide who seems to have been this way before. Silverman's Jill is part temptress, part saint. It must have taken all of Rhodes's willpower to avoid naming her character "Beatrice," although of course Beatrice was Dante's guide into heaven. That would be the sequel.

And who is Saint John of Las Vegas? That would be John the Baptist or "John of the desert," divine messenger, not to be confused with the brother of Jesus. Why is he "of Las Vegas"? I think the answer must relate to John's gambling history. When Anna Dudak, my landlady on Burling Street, would take a trip to Las Vegas, her husband, Paul, would tell me she had gone to Lost Wages.

Sangre de Mi Sangre ★ ★ ★
NO MPAA RATING, 100 m., 2008

Jorge Adrian Espindola (Pedro), Armando Hernandez (Juan), Jesus Ochoa (Diego), Paola Mendoza (Magda), Eugenio Derbez (Anibal), Israel Hernandez (Ricardo), Leonardo Anzure (Simon). Directed by Christopher Zalla and produced by Benjamin Odell and Per Melita. Screenplay by Zalla.

Sangre de Mi Sangre, the grand jury prize winner at Sundance 2007, gives us wonderful actors struggling in a tangled web of writing. The film is built around two relationships, both touching, both emotionally true. But time after time, we're brought up short by absolute impossibilities and gaping improbabilities in the story. To give one example: A newly arrived Mexican immigrant struggles to find his father in New York City. All he has is the seventeen-year-old information that the man works in (or perhaps owns) a French restaurant. Working his way through the yellow pages listings of French restaurants, he successfully finds his father. Uh-huh.

Let's back up to earlier screenplay questions. We meet the hero, Pedro, as he escapes from Mexico by quickly scaling a fence along the U.S. border. Is it that easy to cross? Never mind; waiting on the other side (not miles away, or hidden) is a truck waiting to take immigrants to New York. Wouldn't U.S. customs patrols notice it, in full view in an urban area? Pedro is hustled inside, the doors are slammed, and the truck begins a 2,500-mile journey that can apparently be survived on half a taco and a small bottle of water. More surprising still is that no effort is made to charge Pedro for the trip. He rides free.

Pedro (Jorge Adrian Espindola) is young, earnest, trusting. On the journey he makes a friend of Juan (Armando Hernandez), and tells him his story: He hopes to find his father in New York and carries a letter to the old man from his mother. When Pedro wakes up at the end of the trip, Juan has already disappeared with the letter.

Juan is enterprising and decides to pose as Pedro; maybe it's true, as Pedro's mother claimed, that the father owned the restaurant where he earned money, which he sent home for several years. But why a French restaurant? Using the address on the envelope, Juan easily finds the shabby apartment of old Diego (Jesus Ochoa), who has never seen him and has no desire to acquire a son. But Juan is ingratiating and tells a convincing story; after all, he has read the letter and Diego refuses to.

Meanwhile, the *real* Pedro wanders the streets, remembering only his father's street address (still accurate after seventeen years). He enlists Magda, a hard-worn Mexican girl who does drugs, makes a living by her wits and her body, and wants nothing to do with Pedro. They nevertheless become confederates, picking up fifty dollars here or there by performing sex for men who want to watch.

At this point you're rolling your eyes and wondering how the grand jury at Sundance, or any jury, could have awarded such a story its prize. But you would have missed what makes the film special: the relationships. Juan does such a good job of playing Pedro that he convinces Diego he really is his son. And the real Pedro gets a quick series of lessons in surviving the mean streets and comes to care about (not for) Magda.

The truest of these relationships, paradoxically, is the false one. Jesus Ochoa, a much-honored Mexican actor, creates a heart-breaking performance as Diego, the "old man," as Juan always calls him. He was once in love in Mexico, left, sent money home, returned, and then (after apparently fathering the real Pedro) returned to New York seventeen years ago. Maybe he told his wife he owned a restaurant, or maybe she lied about that to her son. No matter. He is a dishwasher and vegetable slicer, who earns extra money by sewing artificial roses. He has money stashed away. He is big, burly, very lonely. He comes to care for this "son." And despite Juan's deception, Juan comes to care for him—almost, you could say, as a father.

Magda is a tougher case. She does not bestow her affection lightly, nor is the real Pedro attracted to prostitution as a way for them to earn money. But Zalla, the director, does a perceptive, concise job of showing us how Magda lives on the streets and nearly dies. Magda and Pedro are together as a matter of mutual survival.

Pedro, Juan, and Diego have paths that must eventually cross, we think. See for yourself if they do. And try not to ask why the police, planning to break down a door by surprise, would announce their approach with five minutes of sirens. The story's conclusion is rushed and arbitrary, but so perhaps it has to be. *Sangre de Mi Sangre* (*Blood of My Blood*) is a film that stumbles through a maddening screenplay but nevertheless generates true emotional energy.

Savage Grace ★ ★ ½

NO MPAA RATING, 97 m., 2008

Julianne Moore (Barbara Daly), Stephen Dillane (Brooks Baekeland), Eddie Redmayne (Tony Baekeland), Elena Anaya (Blanca), Unax Ugalde (Jake), Hugh Dancy (Sam Green). Directed by Tom Kalin and produced by Iker Monfort, Katie Roumel, Pamela Koffler, and Christine Vachon. Screenplay by Howard Rodman, based on the book by Natalie Robins and Steven M. L. Aronson.

When a movie's story ends and words appear on the screen telling us what happened then, they are sometimes inspirational, sometimes triumphant, sometimes sad. But I don't think I've ever seen an outcome more pathetic than the one described at the end of *Savage Grace*. They describe the ultimate destiny of Tony Baekeland, whose misfortune it was to be the heir of a great fortune. His fate is all the more appalling because it hardly seems inevitable. He is a very disturbed young man, as who might not be after the life he led? But life took him to tragic extremes.

The movie tells the true story of the marriage of Barbara Daly (Julianne Moore) and Brooks Baekeland (Stephen Dillane), who glittered erratically in the social circles of the

1940s through the 1960s. Brooks's grandfather invented Bakelite, used in everything, we learn, from cooking utensils to nuclear bombs. By the third generation the fortune has produced Brooks, a vapid clotheshorse who nevertheless perhaps deserves better than a wife who is all pose and attitude, all brittle facade, deeply rotten inside. Their son, Tony (Eddie Redmayne), who narrates much of the story, is raised as her coddled darling but feels little real love from either parent and grows into a narcissistic, hedonistic, inverted basket case.

Oh, but they all look so elegant! They know how to dress and how to behave (and misbehave) in the high society watering holes of New York (1950s), Paris (1960s), Majorca and London (into the 1970s). They are known everywhere, loved nowhere, except for a few hangers-on like Sam (Hugh Dancy), a gay "walker" who accompanies Barbara after Brooks has left.

It's not simply that Brooks has left. He left with Blanca (Elena Anaya), the Spanish beauty Tony brought home from the beach one day, only to watch his father seduce her from right under his nose. Tony is of indeterminate sexuality from the beginning and now tilts over into homosexuality, with such friends as Jake (Unax Ugalde), a pot-smoking beach creature. Sam, an art dealer, is also in the mix, and indeed mother, son, and walker all end up in bed together.

The tone of the film is set by Julianne Moore, in what I suppose must be described as a fine performance, although she has little enough to work with. Barbara was so shallow. She was all clothes and hair and endless cigarettes, and conversation that was never really adequate for the level she was aiming for. She also had a nasty habit of saying rude things to break up social events, and you can hardly blame Brooks for leaving—although he, too, was so lacking in ordinary human qualities.

Decadence, of course, is the word to describe this world, but nothing really prepares us for its final descent. I will not describe what happens at the end, except to say nothing has really prepared us for it. It's hard to take. Very hard. And then those stark white letters on the black background.

This is the first film in fifteen years by Tom Kalin, who made *Swoon* in 1992. That was about another famous scandal, the murder of Bobby Franks by Richard Loeb and Nathan Leopold Jr. Both films are about protagonists without ordinary moral values; they find the unacceptable to be thinkable, even a pleasure. Or a compulsion.

But what we miss in the film is insight into Barbara and Brooks and Tony. In his letters and diaries, Tony makes a great effort toward understanding his life but doesn't come up with much. Living these lives, for these people, must have been sad and tedious, and so, inevitably, is their story and, it must be said, the film about it.

A Secret ★ ★ ★

NO MPAA RATING, 105 m., 2008

Cecile de France (Tania), Patrick Bruel (Maxime), Ludivine Sagnier (Hannah), Julie Depardieu (Louise), Mathieu Amalric (Francois), Nathalie Boutefeu (Esther), Yves Jacques (George), Valentin Vigourt (Francois [age seven]), Quentin Dubuis (Francois [age fourteen]). Directed by Claude Miller and produced by Yves Marmion. Screenplay by Miller and Natalie Carter, based on the novel by Philippe Grimbert.

Let's set aside for the moment the idea that the characters in A Secret are Jewish. If you were Catholic, Protestant, Muslim, Hindu, Buddhist, atheist, whatever, and the country had been occupied by ruthless forces determined to track you down and exterminate you, what would you do? How would you protect your family?

Would you put a sign on the door saying, "Please exterminate us first to demonstrate our moral courage and bring shame down upon you?" Or would you attempt to conceal your identity, change your name, obtain forged papers, move to a safe haven? It wouldn't take me long to puzzle that one out.

But what if something went horribly wrong with your plans? What if you survived but others died? Would you feel guilt? How would you deal with that? Would you blame yourself if there was nothing you could have done? What would you keep secret? What if a whole generation shared your feelings and fears?

In France during the Nazi occupation, hun-

dreds of thousands of Jews were deported and killed. Some of the French were collaborators and prospered. Some of the French were in the Resistance and risked their lives as anti-Nazi terrorists. Most of the French kept their heads low and their opinions to themselves. Jews were included in all three categories. See Truffaut's 1980 film of the wartime theater in Paris, *The Last Metro*. After the war, astonishing numbers of French claimed to have been in the Resistance all along.

Claude Miller's *A Secret* is inspired by a French best-seller by Philippe Grimbert, who has the same family name as the family in his novel. More precisely, they share the family name Grinberg. As it became clear the Nazis would occupy vast areas of France, including Paris and Lyon, they changed it. After the war, they preserved their secret from those who had not known them before. During the war we sympathize with their decision. But by maintaining it, what torments did they feel?

This film is about the torments and how they were visited on later generations. It centers on the story of a teenager who is a disappointment to his parents because he has no skill at athletics. This is crushing to young Francois (Quentin Dubuis) and continues to haunt the adult Francois (Mathieu Amalric, star of *The Diving Bell and the Butterfly*). When he was fourteen, a family friend who lived across the courtyard (Julie Depardieu) told him some things he seemed to be the last to know.

This is a sad and lonely boy. He feels inadequate and unloved by his parents (Cecile de France and Patrick Bruel). In his fantasies, they were an ideal couple, hopelessly in love. In his solitude as a child (Valentin Vigourt), unable to join in the play of others, he imagines a brother who is taller, athletic, charming, and loved. His invisible companion is with him everywhere, even at the dinner table. His father is furious about the shadow brother.

Miller, a gifted veteran French director (*Class Trip, The Accompanist, The Little Thief*) and a French Jew born in 1942, seems to feel a special urgency in this material, as does Grimbert, the author of the book. They are telling a story less uncommon in France than it might seem. The film, they say, "is based on real people." People we care for, worry about, sympathize with, and pity. Who can cast the first stone?

The Secret in Their Eyes ★★★★
R, 129 m., 2010

Ricardo Darin (Benjamin Esposito), Soledad Villamil (Irene Menendez Hastings), Guillermo Francella (Pablo Sandoval), Pablo Rago (Ricardo Morales), Javier Godino (Isidoro Gomez). Directed by Juan Jose Campanella and produced by Campanella, Mariela Besuievski, and Carolina Urbieta. Screenplay by Campanella, based on the novel by Eduardo Sacheri.

The Secret in Their Eyes opens with the meeting, after many years, of Benjamin (Ricardo Darin) and Irene (Soledad Villamil). She is a judge. He is a retired criminal investigator. They are just a little too happy to see each other. Twenty-five years ago, when she was assistant to a judge and he was an investigator under her, they were involved in a brutal case of rape and murder. Benjamin visited the crime scene, and the corpse of the dead woman spoke eloquently of the brutality of the crime. Two workmen were arrested and convicted. Benjamin was never convinced of their guilt. Now he tells Irene that on his own time he wants to write about the case.

This commences an absorbing back-and-forth journey through time, between Buenos Aires in 1974 and 2000, which reopens both the crime and the unacknowledged feeling that has remained all these years between Irene and Benjamin. That's where their personal appeal comes into play. The actress Soledad Villamil is, forgive me, my idea of a Woman. Grown-up, tallish, healthy, brunette, sane, and perhaps she was cast for her eyes because the film contains a lot of close-ups and they're required to conceal secrets. Think of Anne Archer. Playing Irene at ages twenty-five years apart, she is never too young or too old, but standing right there.

Ricardo Darin makes her a worthy partner as Benjamin. His rank was too low, his pay too small, her presence too assured for him to trust the signals he must have known she was sending. He's one of those men on whom a beard seems inevitable. There is a sadness about him. He has never stopped thinking about the murder case, and we understand— although the movie is indirect about this— that the investigation was mishandled at the time because of Argentina's diseased right-wing politics.

Without being too obvious about it, the film reassembles the strands of two stories, the murder case and the unfinished emotions between Benjamin and Irene. It is filled with vivid characters. Sandoval (Guillermo Francella) is Benjamin's alcoholic assistant in the investigation, one of those drunks who may be incompetent but is not useless. He and Benjamin, and all the legal side, engage in the droll formality of addressing one another by fanciful titles. Morales (Pablo Rago) is the husband of the dead woman, still obsessed with her death. Gomez (Javier Godino) has always been Benjamin's real suspect, and there is a scene involving him in a soccer stadium that I have no idea how it could have been filmed, special effects or no.

Juan Jose Campanella is the writer-director, and here is a man who creates a complete, engrossing, lovingly crafted film. He is filled with his stories. *The Secret in Their Eyes* is a rebuke to formula screenplays. We grow to know the characters, and the story pays due respect to their complexities and needs. There is always the sense that they exist in the *now*, and not at some point along a predetermined continuum. Sometimes I watch a film unspool like a tape measure, and I can sense how far we are from the end. Sometimes my imagination is led to live right along with it.

The Secret in Their Eyes surprised many by winning the 2010 Academy Award for best foreign-language film. Michael Haneke's *The White Ribbon,* another considerable film, was thought to be the front-runner. The Academy did a good thing when it reformed the foreign language voting, requiring all voters to see all five finalists. In 2009, with the Japanese winner *Departures,* and again in 2010, the voters had an advantage over the rest of us. Who is to say whether they were right? They voted as they felt, and in today's unhappy distribution scene, the Oscar means your chances of seeing this film are much increased. You won't regret it. This is a real movie, the kind they literally don't make very much anymore.

The Secret Life of Bees ★ ★ ★ ½
PG-13, 110 m., 2008

Queen Latifah (August Boatwright), Dakota Fanning (Lily Owens), Jennifer Hudson (Rosaleen Daise), Alicia Keys (June Boatwright), Sophie Okonedo (May Boatwright), Nate Parker (Neil), Tristan Wilds (Zach Taylor), Hilarie Burton (Deborah Owens), Paul Bettany (T. Ray Owens). Directed by Gina Prince-Bythewood and produced by James Lassiter, Ewan Leslie, Joe Pichirallo, Lauren Shuler Donner, and Will Smith. Screenplay by Prince-Bythewood, based on the novel by Sue Monk Kidd.

As a realistic portrayal of life in rural South Carolina in 1964, *The Secret Life of Bees* is dreaming. As a parable of hope and love, it is enchanting. Should it have been painful or a parable? Parable, I think, so it will please those who loved the novel by Sue Monk Kidd.

One critic has described it as sappy, syrupy, sentimental, and sermonizing, and those are only the S's. The same review admitted it is also "wholesome and heartwarming," although you will never see "wholesome" used in a movie ad.

I go with heartwarming. There is such a thing as feeling superior to your emotions, but I trust mine. If I sense the beginnings of a teardrop in my eye during a movie, that is evidence more tangible than all the mighty weight of Film Theory. "The immediate experience," one of the wisest of critics called it. That's what you have to acknowledge. I watched the movie, abandoned history and plausibility, and just plain fell for it. If it had been a bad movie, it would have been ripe for vivisection. But it is not a bad movie.

Above all, it contains characters I care for, played by actors I admire. If a script doesn't get in the way, a movie like that just about has to work. Queen Latifah, who combines conviction, humor, and a certain majesty, plays August Boatwright, a woman about as plausible as a fairy godmother and so what. She lives outside town in a house painted the color of the Easter Bunny and gathers honey for a living. Famous honey, from happy bees. Living with her are her two sisters: June (Alicia Keys), a classical cellist and civil rights activist, and May (Sophie Okonedo), whom you don't want to startle with anything sad.

In a shack many miles away, fourteen-year-old Lily Owens (Dakota Fanning) lives with her cruel father (Paul Bettany). Her best friend and defender, the black housekeeper Rosaleen (Jennifer Hudson), endures the wrath of the father because she will not abandon Lily. One day Rosaleen is so bold as to attempt to register to vote and is beaten by racists in the nearby town. This results, of course, in her arrest. Lily helps her escape the town, and they set off on a journey to the town of Tiburon, which Lily knows about because of something she found in her late mother's possessions: the label for a honey jar.

As Lily helps Rosaleen flee from virtual slavery, it's impossible not to think about Huck and Jim, unless Political Correctness has prevented you from reading that greatest of all novels about black and white in America. From what little we see of the folks in Tiburon, they're as nice as the folks in Lily's hometown were mean.

They land on August's doorstep. She takes them in, over resistance from the militant June. And there the proper story begins, involving discoveries about the past, problems in the present, and hopes for the future. These are well-handled melodramatic events that would not benefit from being revealed here.

Dakota Fanning comes of age in this film and in the somewhat similar but less successful *Hounddog*. She's not a kid anymore. She has always been a good actress, and she is only growing deeper and better. I expect her to make the transition from child to woman with the same composure and wisdom that Jodie Foster demonstrated. Here she plays a plucky, forthright, and sometimes sad and needy young teen with the breadth this role requires and a depth that transforms it.

Then observe Sophie Okonedo, the London-born, Cambridge-educated actress who has no trouble at all playing a simple-minded, deeply disturbed country girl. The English have little trouble with Southern accents. Michael Caine explained it to me once. Has to do with Appalachia being settled by working-class Brits. Her May is the heart of the film, because her heart is so open. She has some delicate emotional transitions to traverse here and convinces us of them. Remember her in *Hotel Rwanda*?

The Alicia Keys character, June, is really too complex for a supporting role. In the workings of the story, she functions as an eye opener for Rosaleen, who has never guessed black women could be so gifted and outspoken. The three sisters live in an idyllic household that must have taken a powerful lot of honey sales, even then, to maintain. That isn't an issue. We believe it, because Queen Latifah as August beams watchfully on all before her, and nobody can beam like Latifah. If ever there was a woman born to be christened Queen, she's the one.

I have great affection for this film because it honors a novel that many people loved for good reasons. It isn't superior, nor does it dumb it down. It sees what is good and honors it. The South was most likely not like this in 1964. That was the year the Voting Rights Act and Civil Rights Act were passed. The Boatwright farm, as I said, is really a dream. But in those hard days, people needed dreams.

The Secret of Kells ★★★
NO MPAA RATING, 75 m., 2010

With the voices of: Evan McGuire (Brendan), Christen Mooney (Aisling), Mick Lally (Brother Aidan), and Brendan Gleeson (Abbot Cellach). Directed by Tomm Moore, codirected by Nora Twomey, and produced by Moore, Didier Brunner, Viviane Vanfleteren, and Paul Young. Screenplay by Fabrice Ziolkowski.

When I went to Ireland to visit the set of *Ryan's Daughter*, the studio sent a car to ferry me and my cohort McHugh to the Dingle Peninsula. As we drove along we crossed an old bridge and the driver said, "Leprechauns made their home under this bridge." We stopped for petrol, and I quietly said to McHugh, "He doesn't know you're Irish and is giving us the tourist treatment." "Ebert," said McHugh, "he means it."

Did he mean it? Did McHugh believe that he meant it? With the Irish, the answer is yes and no. McHugh and his brothers told me how as lads they picked up change by discovering the Irish surnames of Yankee tourists and offering to show them where their ancestors lived. They always led them to the same shop in a little cottage, where the owner gave

them a "consideration" for any purchases made.

What does this possibly have to do with *The Secret of Kells*, the new film that was one of this year's Oscar nominees for best animation? Quite a bit, I think. Here is a film about a young and very brave medieval monk named Brendan, a sacred book, a storied monastery, a fairy girl, and an alarming creature, a forest containing little nuts that make brilliant green inks. The fairy girl is quite real, as Brendan can see for himself. If there are any leprechauns, she no doubt knows them. If there are not, how does she know for sure?

The Irish are a verbal people, preserving legends in story and song, and although few Chicagoans may know there's a First Folio of Shakespeare in the Newberry Library, few Dubliners do NOT know that the Book of Kells reposes in Trinity College. I viewed it once. It is a painstakingly illuminated medieval manuscript preserving the four Gospels, and every page is a work of art. Many monks created it over many years.

Perhaps little Brendan was one of them. Perhaps some of that brilliant emerald green was his, extracted from nuts he gathered in the forest. Brendan (voice by Evan McGuire), the youngest and pluckiest monk in the walled monastery, befriends old Brother Aidan (Mick Lally), a traveler who has arrived bearing the precious book. Some pages remain to be created, and Aidan says Brendan must help. He can start by disobeying the Abbot (Brendan Gleeson), venturing outside the walls, and gathering the nuts.

This and his further adventures are related in Tomm Moore's film, which is a little like an illuminated manuscript itself. Just as every margin of the Book of Kells is crowded with minute and glorious decorations, so is every shot of the film filled with patterns and borders, arches and frames, doodads and scrimshaw images. The colors are bold and bright, the drawings are simplified and 2-D. That reflects the creation of the original book in the centuries before the discovery of perspective in the Renaissance.

Like the people in Nina Paley's *Sita Sings the Blues*, these move mostly back and forth within the same plane, which is only correct since perspective hasn't yet created spatial dimension. But there's no feeling of limitation. Indeed, in a season where animated images hurl themselves from the screen with alarming recklessness, I was grateful that these were content merely to be admired.

The movie has a wide appeal, with a gap in the middle. I think it will appeal to children young enough to be untutored in boredom, and to anyone old enough to be drawn in, or to appreciate the artistry. For those in between, the *Transformers*-damaged generation, it will seem to be composed in a quaint, unknown language.

The Secret of the Grain ★ ★ ★ ½
NO MPAA RATING, 151 m., 2009

Habib Boufares (Slimane Beiji), Hafsia Herzi (Rym), Faridah Benkhetache (Karima), Abdelhamid Aktouche (Hamid), Bouraouia Marzouk (Souad), Hatika Karaoui (Latifa), Alice Houri (Julia). Directed by Abdellatif Kechiche and produced by Claude Berri. Screenplay by Kechiche.

A nineteen-year-old actress named Hafsia Herzi steps into the cinema in this film. I have a feeling it will be, like the first film of Isabelle Huppert, not simply a debut, but an announcement: "Here I am, and I am the real thing." She is the energy at the heart of a life-filled portrait of a big family of second-generation immigrants in a shabby French port city, a family that nourishes love, jealousy, discouragement, ambition, and a whole lot of dining and talking.

The Secret of the Grain is the wrong title for this movie. In France, where it was honored for best film, director, screenplay, and most promising actress, the title translates as "Fish Couscous." In England, it opened as *Couscous*. The only secret involving the grain is why it's so late being served. What were you expecting, Napoleon's toenails?

The wave of immigrants from former French colonies such as Tunisia, Morocco, and Algeria began in the late 1950s and continues, but most of the early arrivals are now grandparents, their offspring speaking only a few words of Arabic. We land in the middle of such a family, its patriarch the grave, taciturn Slimane Beiji (Habib Boufares). He's in the process of losing his job at a shipyard and negotiating uneasily between his first wife, Souad (Bouraouia Marzouk), and his lover, Latifa (Hatika Karaoui), who owns a little hotel. He has two sons, one always in lust, but saves his deepest affection for Latifa's daughter, Rym (Hafsia Herzi). We have to gather these facts from the others, because Slimane doesn't confide.

The Tunisian-born writer-director, Abdellatif Kechiche, isn't interested in a formal story, although he does provide a cliff-hanging third act. He wants us to see these people live. Early in the film, he has a dinner table scene of such virtuosity that we feel we know everyone, even those we haven't seen before. This scene only incidentally sets up plot points; its purpose is to show strong opinions, deep feelings, humor, and a sincere interest in the food. The cook is the first wife, renowned for her couscous; she always sends a plate home to Slimane, who lives in a little room in Latifa's hotel. She also, as a ritual, gives a plate from every meal to the nearest homeless man she can find.

Still waters run deep. Slimane reveals plans to use his severance pay to open a restaurant aboard a rusty ship in the harbor, serving Souad's couscous. His strongest supporter is Rym, and as she talks with Slimane and a group of old musicians who live at the hotel, and to her mother, she reveals herself as an instinctive actress who tells each what they need to hear. She never gets angry, never pushes too hard, and doesn't insist, but it's almost impossible to keep her from having her way.

The film arrives at a big free dinner thrown by Slimane for the town big shots, in hopes of getting planning permission for the restaurant. Here we see race and class discrimination in France; the big shots are happy to wine and dine for free, but in their minds immigrants are not . . . quite . . . French. The younger generation all seem quintessentially French to us, but what do we know?

There are two amazing dialogue scenes in the movie. One involves Rym pleading with her mother to attend Slimane's opening night, despite the couscous being prepared by the other woman. The other involves Alice Houri as Julie, who is married to Slimane's womanizing son and explains with astonishing passion why he is a liar, a worthless scumbag, and a failure as husband and father.

This verbal assault comes to poor Slimane as the latest in a series of disasters, including the delivery of the dinner. Help comes, not from an unexpected source, but certainly in an unexpected way. We leave the movie as we entered, in the middle of things. *The Secret of the Grain* never slows, always engages, may continue too long, but ends too soon. It is made of life itself. Hafsia Herzi has four more films in the can and two in production. Remember her name.

The Secrets ★ ★ ★ ½
NO MPAA RATING, 127 m., 2009

Fanny Ardant (Anouk), Ania Bukstein (Naomi), Michal Shtamler (Michelle), Adir Miller (Yanki), Guri Alfi (Michael). Directed by Avi Nesher and produced by Nesher and David Silber. Screenplay by Nesher and Hadar Galron.

Naomi is a great disappointment to her father. She is his student, the most learned, the most devout student of the respected old rabbi. But she hasn't learned the most important lesson: how to be a submissive woman, to submit herself to the will of her father and her future husband. Even worse, she wickedly thinks she could someday be a rabbi herself.

There are hints in *The Secrets* that she knows well how her father's beliefs worked in the life of her mother: "Often when I came into this kitchen, I found her weeping." Naomi submits to her father the rabbi but not to her father the man. The rabbi has decided that his student Michael will marry Naomi. Naomi has no feeling for this man: She knows more than he does, but he treats her as a silly girl and piously asserts his narrow view of a woman's role.

Naomi buys time. After the death of her mother, she postpones the wedding and convinces her father to let her spend some time in a seminary in a secluded town in Israel. Here she will come into her own as a natural spiritual leader, as a woman, and as someone who discovers the difference between convenient and romantic love.

Avi Nesher's *The Secrets*, a deeply involving melodrama, has all the devices to draw us into this story. In some ways it is a traditional narrative. But it is more. It is gently and powerfully acted. And it is thoughtful about its characters, so that even though they follow a somewhat predictable arc, they contain surprises for us. They keep thinking for themselves.

Naomi (Ania Bukstein) seems at first a subdued, intellectual young woman, who believes explicitly in her father's orthodoxy. But as she sees how it worked in her mother's life and is working in hers, she experiences the basic feminist insight: Why a man but not a woman? It fascinates me that in some religions, men subscribe so eagerly to a dogma that oppresses women, and some women agree with it. Naomi does not agree.

At the seminary, one of her roommates doesn't even think of agreeing. This is Michelle (Michal Shtamler), from Paris, with a chip on her shoulder. The two find themselves assigned to make daily meal deliveries to Anouk (Fanny Ardant), a very ill French woman, just released from prison and living in the town. Michelle discovers on the Internet that Anouk's sentence was for murder. The details of the crime are left murky, but the woman desperately wants to be cleansed and appeals to Naomi and Michelle to help her.

Their help for Anouk is the crux of the film. Even though she is not Jewish, Anouk seeks Jewish healing, and Naomi essentially acts as a rabbi in trying to help her. These scenes are the most moving in the film, involving a secret visit to an ancient cleansing pool, which, of course, is off-limits to women.

Through this process Naomi and Michelle grow close romantically, tension grows between Naomi and the loathsome Michael, Naomi's father reacts with towering rage, and the movie becomes an argument against some elements of his style of Judaism. It will help clarify for some viewers that Judaism incorporates beliefs that are not all in agreement.

The Secrets is, first of all, continuously absorbing, which most good films must be. The performances by the three leading actresses are compelling, although Ardant is required to sustain the note of fatal illness perhaps too long. There's a subplot involving a klezmer clarinetist that's delightful. And one about the older woman in charge of the seminary that evokes an earlier generation's beliefs about the limitations of women.

So *The Secrets* plays as a melodrama and much more: a film about religious and sexual intolerance, about reconciling opposed beliefs, about matching the fervor of feminism against religious patriarchy, and even in some ways a social comedy. It contains an object lesson for the whole genre involving romance and the battle of the generations: Such films can actually be serious about something.

The September Issue ★★★
PG-13, 89 m., 2009

With Anna Wintour, Thakoon Panichgul, Andre Leon Talley, Grace Coddington, Mario Testino, Patrick Demarchelier, Oscar de la Renta, Stefano Pilati, Vera Wang, Jean Paul Gaultier. A documentary directed by R. J. Cutler and produced by Eliza Hindmarch and Sadia Shepard.

The magazine rack at 7-Eleven doesn't have many real magazines. No *Economist, Vanity Fair, Discover,* or the *New Yorker.* It's mostly pseudo-magazines, about celebrities, diets, video games, and crossword puzzles. Except for one: *Vogue.* The other day I bought the September 2009 issue, which ran to a little under six hundred pages. That may sound like a lot to you, but actually it's a marker of hard times for the economy.

The September Issue is a documentary about the magazine's September 2007 issue, which set a record at well over eight hundred pages. *Vogue* is ruled by the famous Anna Wintour, who is said to be the single most important person in the world of fashion. When she says yes, it happens. When she says no, it doesn't. She says no frequently. She rarely deigns to explain why, but it would appear that most people believe she is right. She is *always* right about her own opinion, and in fashion, hers is the opinion that matters most.

The documentarian R. J. Cutler followed Wintour for months during the preparation for September 2007, which was expected to set a record. There cannot have been a page in it she wasn't involved with. This seems to be a woman who is concerned with one thing above all: the implementation of her opinion.

She is not the monster depicted by Meryl Streep in *The Devil Wears Prada* (2006), but then how could she be? I expect that one to have a sequel titled *Return of the Bitch.*

Perhaps it was *The Devil Wears Prada,* based on a novel by one of her former assistants, that motivated Wintour to authorize this documentary. She doesn't otherwise seem like the kind of woman who craves attention, since after all she is the focus of the eyes of everyone who matters to her. She doesn't throw handbags at her assistants here, as Streep does in the 2006 movie, but then, she knows too much about cameras to make that mistake.

What comes across is that she is, after all, a very good editor. Like Hugh Hefner, William Shawn, Harold Hayes, or Graydon Carter, she knows exactly what she wants, and her readers agree with her. When she cringes at the sight of a dress, we're inclined to cringe along with her. The question arises: What possible meaning is there in haute couture for the vast majority of humans who have ever lived? None, of course. And few of these costumes must actually ever be worn, and then often for photo opportunities like Cannes or the Oscars or charity balls in Palm Beach. A woman cannot live in them. She can only wear them.

Yet there is a very great deal of money involved, because these inconceivably expensive dresses serve as the show cars of designers whose ideas are then taken down-market at great speed by multinational corporations, as was shown happening to Valentino in the 2009 documentary about him. Today Paris, tomorrow Bloomingdale's.

Wintour rules *Vogue* with a regal confidence. No one dares to disagree with her, except for a Julia Childian former British model named Grace Coddington, who has been on the staff as long as Wintour and is as earthy as Wintour is aloof. The two women have a grudging respect for each other, perhaps because each realizes they need someone to push back. Coddington's gift is conceiving many of *Vogue*'s wildly fantastical photo spreads. Wintour's gift is knowing how to moderate her enthusiasm.

We meet other members of her staff, including the court jester, Andre Leon Talley, the editor at large, who specializes in spotting young talent. He's very funny, but I didn't see Wintour smiling at him or very much at anyone else. I think she'd look pretty when she did. Old photographs show she has worn the same hairstyle since time immemorial, perhaps because to change it would be a fatal admission that she cares what people think. In public she always wears the same dark glasses, which provide maximum concealment; "armor," she calls it.

Although we see her taste constantly at work, the only definite things we learn about it are that she approves of fur and disapproves of black. She shows great affection in a scene with her bright daughter, Kathryn. Otherwise, like the Sphinx, she regards.

Seraphine ★ ★ ★
NO MPAA RATING, 126 m., 2009

Yolande Moreau (Seraphine), Ulrich Tukur (Wilhelm Uhde), Anne Bennent (Anne Marie), Genevieve Mnich (Madame Duphot), Nico Rogner (Helmut), Adelaide Leroux (Minouche), Serge Lariviere (Duval), Francoise Lebrun (Mere Superieure). Directed by Martin Provost and produced by Milena Poylo and Gilles Sacuto. Screenplay by Provost and Marc Abdelnour.

You might not look twice at her. Seraphine is a bulky, work-worn housecleaner who gets down on her knees in a roomy print dress and fiercely scrubs the floor. She slips away from work to steal turpentine from the church votive candles, blood from the butcher, and clay from the fields, and these she combines with other elements to mix the paints she uses at night, covering panels with fruits and flowers that seem to look at us in alarm.

Seraphine de Senlis, who died in a French mental institution in 1942, today has her paintings in many museums. She did not paint for money or fame, although she grew heady when they began to come. She painted because she was instructed to by her guardian angel. Sometimes while painting she would loudly sing in praise of the Holy Virgin. In this miraculous film we learn nothing of her low birth or early life; we see only her daily toil and nightly ecstasy.

Seraphine arrives from France as the year's most honored film, winner of seven Cesars from the French Academy, including best film and best actress. The actress is Yolande Moreau, who combines, as some people do, a plain face with moments of beauty. Notice her fleeting little smile of complicity as she steals fuel from candles before the Virgin. Moreau plays Seraphine as a straight-ahead charger, a little stooped, marching always with energy, plunging into work, not saying much, shy, but very much who she is. Her physical bearing tells us what we need to know about her mental state.

Her life is changed forever when Wilhelm Uhde (Ulrich Tukur) comes as a boarder to the home she works in; it offers a pastoral setting near Chantilly, and she observes that Uhde needs relief from stress. He's a famous German art critic and a Paris gallery owner, already well-known as an early champion of Picasso and Braque; he discovered Rousseau. He glimpses one of Seraphine's little paintings of apples, asks to see more, is convinced she is a primitive genius. (In the film, we appear to see her actual paintings.)

She observes everything, worries about Uhde, sees he is sad, offers him some of her homemade "power wine," tells him that when she is sad, she walks in the forest and touches the trees. We even see her climbing one, in her late fifties, for the view.

She lives in bitter poverty, hounded by her landlady, doing laundry for a few francs, doling out her coins at the local store to buy canvas and the paints she cannot mix herself. Uhde admires her work, which she cannot believe, gives her some money, makes her some promises, and then disappears: As a German, he flees France at the outset of World War I. Ten years after the war, he and his sister return to Senlis. He assumes Seraphine is dead. At a town hall exhibition by local artists, he sees a work that is unmistakably hers, but larger and more finished. He is overwhelmed, as many others would be.

Seraphine is not a rags-to-riches story. The director, Martin Provost, who wrote it with Marc Abdelnour, focuses intently on Seraphine's delusions, on the manic state that overtakes her at the prospect of fame and fortune, about how she hides far inside so that Uhde cannot reach her. I've seen many films hoping to understand the nature of great artists; one that comes close is *Vincent*, by Paul Cox. This is another. It "explains" nothing but feels everything. It reminded me of two other films: Bresson's *Mouchette*, about a poor girl victimized by a village, and Karen Gehre's *Begging Naked*, shown at Ebertfest this year, about a woman whose art is prized even as she lives in Central Park.

People like these are not entirely to be pitied. Their art is a refuge. All artists fall into a reverie state while working. Some experience a joy that obliterates their circumstances. The problem is that when they're not creating, they have to go right on living.

Serbis ★ ★ ½
R, 91 m., 2009

Gina Pareno (Nanay Flor), Jaclyn Jose (Nayda), Julio Diaz (Lando), Coco Martin (Alan), Kristofer King (Ronald), Dan Alvaro (Jerome), Mercedes Cabral (Merly), Roxanne Jordan (Jewel). Directed by Brillante Mendoza and produced by Ferdinand Lapuz. Screenplay by Armando Lao.

Although *Serbis* spends a great deal of time following its characters through the corridors and up and down the stairs of a shabby Filipino porno movie theater, we never get a clear idea of the interior layout. And the auditorium looks rather small considering the hulking exterior of the Family Theater. But maybe that's the idea, because the film is a labyrinth of lost and wandering lives.

An extended family runs this failing old theater, lives in it, too, and is even raising a cute little son. The movies on the screen are hetero, but nobody is watching. The dark seats and the bright corridors and staircases are home to gay hustlers and their clientele, everybody knows it, nobody cares, many of them seem to be waiting around for something to relieve their boredom. There is some gratitude when a goat gets loose inside the theater. How it climbed so high without being seen on the stairs is a good question; maybe it's a mountain goat.

Up and down the staff and customers go, like ants in a hill. We get to know the members of the Pineda family of Angeles City pretty well, especially Nayda (Jaclyn Jose), the

daughter, whose son is the little boy, and whose mother, Nanay Flor (Gina Pareno), is due in court for her husband's divorce hearing. A strong matriarch, she fiercely wants to be rid of the man. And there is another worry: Merly (Mercedes Cabral), girlfriend of the cousin/projectionist Alan (Coco Martin), has announced she is pregnant, so there will be the expense of a wedding no one wants.

In a film so immersed in sex, there is little actual sex. *Serbis* (the word means "service") is about a closed world in which sex is a commodity and it's a buyer's market. Sexual encounters are hurried, hidden, and never lingered on by the camera of director Brillante Mendoza, who is more absorbed by faces, routine, work, and the passage of time. The body part that receives the most attention is the projectionist's butt, where there is a painful boil. His self-treatment for this affliction reportedly drew groans at the Cannes 2008 press screening, but it seems a quick and relatively painless solution, and I will file it away.

The film opens with a curious scene: Nayda bathes, dresses herself, and applies lipstick in front of a mirror, while telling her reflection, "I love you." Later there is a scene of her mother applying lipstick in preparation for her court appearance. Given the seedy surroundings, there is something touching about these two women preparing their faces to bravely face the world.

This is not a film most people will enjoy. Its qualities are apparent only if one appreciates cinematic style for itself. I enjoyed it because I got into Mendoza's visual use of the corridors and staircases and their life rhythms. Most people will find that annoying. Anyone hoping to see sex will be badly disappointed. Let's put it this way: If you see only one art film this month, this shouldn't be the one. If you see one every week, you might admire it.

A Serious Man ★★★★
R, 104 m., 2009

Michael Stuhlbarg (Larry Gopnik), Richard Kind (Uncle Arthur), Fred Melamed (Sy Ableman), Sari Lennick (Judith Gopnik), Adam Arkin (Divorce Lawyer), Amy Landecker (Mrs. Samsky), Alan Mandell (Rabbi Marshak), David Kang (Clive Park), Fyvush Finkel (Dybbuk),

Allen Lewis Rickman (Shtetl Husband), Yelena Shmulenson (Shtetl Wife). Directed, written, and produced by Joel and Ethan Coen.

We learn from the Book of Job: *Man that is born of a woman is of few days, and full of trouble.* Such a man is Larry Gopnik. He lectures on physics in front of a blackboard filled with bewildering equations that are mathematical proofs approaching certainty, and in his own life, what can he be sure of? Nothing, that's what.

His wife is leaving him for his best friend. His son is listening to rock 'n' roll in Hebrew school. His daughter is stealing money for a nose job. His brother-in-law is sleeping on the sofa and lurking in unsavory bars. His gun-nut neighbor frightens him. A student tries to bribe him and blackmail him at the same time. The tenure committee is getting unsigned libelous letters about him. The wife of his other neighbor is sex crazy. God forbid this man should see a doctor.

"This is the kind of picture you get to make after you've won an Oscar," writes Todd McCarthy in *Variety.* I cannot improve on that. After the seriously great *No Country for Old Men,* the Coen brothers have made the not greatly serious *A Serious Man,* which bears every mark of a labor of love.

It is set in what I assume to be a Minneapolis suburb of their childhood, a prairie populated by split-level homes with big garages but not enough trees around them. In this world, Larry Gopnik (Michael Stuhlbarg) earnestly desires to be taken as a serious man and do the right thing, but does God take him seriously? "I read the book of Job last night," Virginia Woolf said. "I don't think God comes out well in it." Someone up there doesn't like Larry Gopnik.

Beginning with a darkly comic prologue in Yiddish, *A Serious Man* inhabits a Jewish community where the rational (physics) is rendered irrelevant by the mystical (fate). Gopnik can fill all the blackboards he wants and it won't do him any good. Maybe because an ancestor invited a dybbuk to cross his threshold, Larry is cursed. A dybbuk is the wandering soul of a dead person. You don't want to make the mistake of inviting one into your home. You don't have to be Jewish to figure that out.

Much of the success of *A Serious Man* comes from the way Michael Stuhlbarg plays the role. He doesn't play Gopnik as a sad sack or a loser, a whiner or a depressive, but as a hopeful man who can't believe what's happening to him. What else can go wrong? Where can he find happiness? Whom can he please? In the sex department, why are even his wet dreams, starring his brazen neighbor (Amy Landecker), frightening? Why does Sy Ableman (Fred Melamed), his so-called best friend who is taking away his wife, speak to him in terms of such sadness, sympathy, and understanding? Does Fred know Larry is doomed?

Why do his children dismiss him? Why is his no-account brother-in-law (Richard Kind) such a shiftless leech? Why can no rabbi provide him with encouragement or useful advice? Why would a student (David Kang) clearly fail an exam, leave bribe money on his desk, and then act to destroy him?

Why, why, why? I'm sure you've heard the old joke where Job asks the Lord why everything in his life is going wrong. Remember what the Lord replies? If you don't remember the joke, ask anyone. I can't prove it, but I'm absolutely certain more than half of everyone on Earth has heard some version of that joke.

Have I mentioned *A Serious Man* is so rich and funny? This isn't a laugh-laugh movie, but a wince-wince movie. Those can be funny, too. The Coens have found mostly unfamiliar actors, or those like Stuhlbarg, Kind, and Melamed you've seen before, but you're not quite sure where. I imagine (but do not know) that Joel and Ethan have been kicking this story around for years, passing time by reminding each other of possible characters, seeing an actor and observing, "There's our Mrs. Samsky." Their actors weren't cast; they were preordained.

In some ways my favorite is Melamed as Sy Ableman. It's not a big role, but he's so good he establishes a full presence in his first scene, when he's only a voice on the telephone. This is the traitor who has stolen away Gopnik's wife, and he believes it will be good if they have a long, helpful talk. Ableman is not only the grief, but the grief counselor. Such chutzpah, you have to admire.

Amy Landecker, too, is perfect as Mrs. Samsky. She makes the character sexy in a strictly logical sense, but any prudent man would know on first sight to stay clear. Judith Gopnik, as Larry's wife, is able to suggest in only a few scenes that she's leaving him not for passion or out of anger, but because she senses his ship going down and Sy Ableman is a lifeboat.

There is a story told in *A Serious Man* that may seem out of place. I believe it acts as a parable reflecting the film, Gopnik's life, and indeed the Book of Job. It's the one about the Jewish dentist who discovers the words "Help me" naturally occurring in Hebrew on the back of a gentile's lower front teeth. Remember that many parables contain their message in their last lines.

Seven Pounds ★ ★ ★
PG-13, 100 m., 2008

Will Smith (Ben Thomas), Rosario Dawson (Emily Posa), Woody Harrelson (Ezra Turner), Michael Ealy (Ben's Brother), Barry Pepper (Dan). Directed by Gabriele Muccino and produced by Todd Black, James Lassiter, Jason Blumenthal, Steve Tisch, and Will Smith. Screenplay by Grant Nieporte.

I am fascinated by films that observe a character who is behaving precisely, with no apparent motivation. A good actor brings such a role into focus, as Will Smith does in the enigmatically titled *Seven Pounds*. Who is he, what does he want, why is he behaving so oddly for an IRS agent? And why won't he kiss Rosario Dawson when they both so obviously want that to happen?

As Ben Thomas, the man from the IRS, he can get in anywhere and ask any question. But surely the IRS doesn't require him to punch a nursing home supervisor for not allowing an old lady her bath? And why, after he intuits he is speaking to a blind man on the phone, is he so needlessly cruel to him? And why then does he follow the same man (Woody Harrelson) into a restaurant and engage him in conversation?

And why does he check into a fleabag hotel? Doesn't the IRS pay him a salary? And what favor does his lifelong friend Dan (Barry Pepper) owe him? And why is he looking for people who need their own favors? And so on. For much of the first hour of *Seven Pounds*, Ben Thomas acts according to a plan that seems perfectly clear, but

only to himself. The reason it goes unexplained is that he has no need to explain it to himself and no way to explain it to anyone else.

I am reminded of a film you should see someday, Melville's *Le Samourai*, about a man who lies on a bed in a dark hotel room and smokes, and gets up, and pays meticulous attention to his appearance, and goes out into the night, and we have no idea who this man is. I find this more interesting than a movie about a man whose nature and objectives are made clear in the first five minutes in a plot that simply points him straight ahead.

Will Smith displays a rather impressive range of emotional speeds here. He can be a tough, merciless IRS man. He can bend the rules on some cases. He can have a candlelight dinner with a beautiful woman named Emily Posa (Dawson) and go home afterward. She can sense his deep sadness. He is angry with people sometimes, but he seems angriest of all at himself. It's quite a performance. And Dawson makes Emily not simply a woman confused, maybe offended, by his behavior, but a woman of instinctive empathy who does an emotional dance with him, following his lead when he needs to be treated like an IRS agent, or like a perfect gentleman, or like a man who needs understanding even if she doesn't know what she's supposed to understand.

I haven't even hinted about the hidden motives in this film. Miraculously, for once even the trailers don't give anything away. I'll tell you one thing: I may have made Ben sound like an angel, but he is very much flesh and blood, and none of his actions are supernatural. He has his reasons.

The director is Gabriele Muccino, who also directed Smith in *The Pursuit of Happyness*. He is effective at timing the film's revelations so that they don't come suddenly like a U-turn; they're revealed at the last necessary points in the story. Some people will find it emotionally manipulative. Some people like to be emotionally manipulated. I do, when it's done well.

17 Again ★ ★ ★
PG-13, 98 m., 2009

Zac Efron (Mike O'Donnell), Matthew Perry (Adult Mike), Leslie Mann (Scarlet), Thomas

Lennon (Ned Gold), Michelle Trachtenberg (Maggie), Sterling Knight (Alex), Melora Hardin (Jane Masterson). Directed by Burr Steers and produced by Adam Shankman and Jennifer Gibgot. Screenplay by Jason Filardi.

Mike O'Donnell's wife wants a divorce, his kids are remote, he didn't get the job promotion he expected, and everything else in his life has gone wrong since that magic year when he was seventeen, a basketball star, in love, and looked like Zac Efron instead of Matthew Perry. He's obviously a case for treatment by a Body Swap Movie.

Revisiting the trophy case at his old high school, Mike encounters a janitor who, from the way he smiles at the camera, knows things beyond this mortal coil. If only Mike could go back to seventeen and not make all the same mistakes. In *17 Again*, he can. He falls into a Twilight Zone vortex and emerges as Zac Efron. They say be careful what you wish for, because you might get it. Mike should have been more specific. Instead of wishing to be seventeen again, he should have wished to go back twenty years in time.

Yes, he becomes himself trapped inside his own seventeen-year-old body. Same wife, same kids, same problems. As Old Mike was getting divorced, he'd moved in with his best friend, Ned (Thomas Lennon), and now he throws himself on Ned's mercy: Will Ned pose as his father, so Young Mike can be his son and help out his kids by enrolling in the same high school again? Ned, who is a software millionaire and middle-aged fanboy, agrees, especially after he falls helplessly in love with the high school principal, Jane (Melora Hardin).

Young Mike becomes the new best friend of his insecure son, Alex (Sterling Knight). Then he meets Alex's mom, Scarlet (Leslie Mann), who, of course, before the vortex was his wife, and before that his high school bride (Allison Miller). She thinks it's strange that he looks *exactly* like the boy she married at seventeen. He explains he is the son of an uncle, who I guess would have to be Old Mike's brother, so it's curious Old Scarlet never met him, but if she doesn't ask that, why should I?

In high school, Young Mike again becomes a basketball star, befriends Alex, and attempts to defend his Gothish daughter, Maggie (Michelle Trachtenberg), against the predations of her jerk boyfriend, who as a hot-rodding jock traveling with a posse is, of course, the *last* guy in school who would date, or be dated by, a moody girl who wears black.

I've seen Body Swaps before (Tom Hanks in *Big*). The first act of this movie seemed all retread. Then it started to dig in. There are twin romances; as Shakespeare demonstrated, one must be serious and the other farcical. Young Mike is still seriously in love with his wife, Old Scarlet, and she is powerfully attracted to this boy who's a double for her first love. She thinks that's wrong. He knows it isn't, but how can he explain?

Meanwhile, best buddy Ned courts Principal Masterson, who for the first time in his life has Taught Him What Love Means. Before her, ecstasy was owning Darth Vader's costume. I will not describe what happens the first time they go out to dinner, except to say that it's comic genius, perfectly played by Melora Hardin and Thomas Lennon.

I attended a screening held by a radio station, which attracted mainly teenage girls who left their boyfriends behind. When Zac Efron took off his T-shirt, the four in front of me squealed as if there were buzzers in their seats. Now that he's a little older, Efron has a Tom Cruiseish charm and a lot of confidence. Why Matthew Perry was cast as his adult self is hard to figure; does your head change its shape in twenty years?

17 Again is a pleasant, harmless PG-13 entertainment, with a plot a little more surprising and acting a little better than I expected. Mike is dispatched into that vortex by the bearded old janitor with a delighted smile. The janitor (Brian Doyle Murray) is quite a convenience, supplying vortexes when needed. If his smile reminds you of anyone, he's played by Bill Murray's brother.

Sex and the City ★ ★
R, 145 m., 2008

Sarah Jessica Parker (Carrie Bradshaw), Kim Cattrall (Samantha Jones), Kristin Davis

(Charlotte York), Cynthia Nixon (Miranda Hobbes), Chris Noth (Mr. Big), Jennifer Hudson (Louise), Candice Bergen (Enid Frick), David Eigenberg (Steve Brady), Evan Handler (Harry Goldenblatt), Jason Lewis (Smith Jerrod). Directed by Michael Patrick King and produced by King, Sarah Jessica Parker, John Melfi, and Darren Star. Screenplay by King, based on the novel by Candace Bushnell and the TV series.

I am not the person to review this movie. Perhaps you will enjoy a review from someone who disqualifies himself at the outset, doesn't much like most of the characters, and is bored by their bubble-brained conversations. Here is a 145-minute movie containing one (1) line of truly witty dialogue: "Her forties is the greatest age at which a bride can be photographed without the unintended Diane Arbus subtext."

That line might not reverberate with audience members who don't know who Diane Arbus was. But what about me, who doesn't reverberate with the names on designer labels? There's a montage of wedding dresses by world-famous designers. I was lucky I knew who Vivienne Westwood was, and that's because she used to be the girlfriend of the Sex Pistols' manager.

The movie continues the stories of the four heroines of the popular HBO series, which would occasionally cause me to pause in my channel surfing. They are older but no wiser, and all facing some kind of a romantic crossroads. New Line has begged critics not to reveal plot secrets, which is all right with me, because I would rather have fun with plot details. I guess I can safely say: Carrie (Sarah Jessica Parker) is in the tenth year of her relationship with Mr. Big (Chris Noth) when they sort of decide to buy a penthouse they name "Heaven on Fifth Avenue." Publicist Samantha (Kim Cattrall) has moved to Los Angeles, where her client Smith (Jason Lewis) has become a daytime TV star. Charlotte (Kristin Davis) and her husband, Harry (Evan Handler), have adopted a Chinese daughter. And Miranda (Cynthia Nixon) is in a crisis with her husband, Steve (David Eigenberg).

What with one thing and another, dramatic developments cause the four women to join

each other at a luxurious Mexican resort, where two scenes take place that left me polishing my pencils to write this review. The girls go sunbathing in crotch-hugging swimsuits, and Miranda is ridiculed for the luxuriant growth of her pubic hair. How luxuriant? One of her pals describes it as *the National Forest*, and there's a shot of the offending proliferation that popped the Smith Brothers right into my head.

A little later, Charlotte develops a tragic case of *turista* and has a noisy accident right there in her pants. This is a key moment, because Carrie has been so depressed she has wondered if she will ever laugh again. Her friends say that will happen when something really, really funny happens. When Charlotte overflows, Carrie and the others burst into helpless laughter. Something really, really funny has finally happened! How about you? Would you think that was really, really funny?

Sex and the City was famous for its frankness, and we expect similar frankness in the movie. We get it, but each *frank* moment comes wrapped in its own package and seems to stand alone from the story. That includes (1) a side shot of a penis, (2) sex in positions other than the missionary, and (3) Samantha's dog, which is a compulsive masturbator. I would be reminded of the immortal canine punch line ("because he can"), but Samantha's dog is a female. "She's been fixed," says the pet lady, "but she hasn't lost the urge." Samantha can identify with that. The dog gets friendly with every pillow, stuffed animal, ottoman, and towel, and here's the funny thing, she ravishes them male-doggy-style. I went to AskJeeves.com and typed in "How do female dogs masturbate?" and did not get a satisfactory answer, although it would seem to be: "Just like all dogs do, but not how male dogs also do."

On to Mr. Big, the wealthy tycoon and victim of two unhappy marriages, who has been blissfully living in sin with Carrie for ten years. I will supply no progress report on their bliss. But what about Mr. Big himself? As played by Chris Noth, he's so unreal he verges on the surreal. He's handsome in the Rock Hudson and Victor Mature tradition, and has a low, preternaturally calm voice that delivers stock reassurances and banal clichés right on time. He's so . . . passive. He stands there (or lies there) as if consciously posing as The Ideal Lover. But he's . . . kinda slow. Square. Colorless. Notice how, when an old friend shouts rude things about him at an important dinner, he hardly seems to hear them, or to know he's having dinner.

The warmest and most human character in the movie is Louise (Jennifer Hudson), who is still in her twenties and hasn't learned to be a jaded consumerist caricature. She still believes in True Love, is hired as Carrie's assistant, and pays her own salary on the first day by telling her about a Netflix of designer labels (I guess after you wear the shoes, you send them back). Louise is warm and vulnerable and womanly, which does not describe any of the others.

All of this goes on for nearly two and a half hours, through New Year's Eve, Valentine's Day, and other bonding holidays. The movie needs a Thanksgiving bailout opportunity. But this is probably the exact *Sex and the City* film that fans of the TV series are lusting for. I know some nurses who are going to smuggle flasks of cosmopolitans into the theater on opening night and have a Gal Party. "Do you think that's a good idea?" one of them asked me. "Two flasks," I said.

Sex and the City 2 ★
R, 146 m., 2010

Sarah Jessica Parker (Carrie Bradshaw), Kim Cattrall (Samantha Jones), Kristin Davis (Charlotte York), Cynthia Nixon (Miranda Hobbes), Chris Noth (Mr. Big), John Corbett (Aidan Shaw), David Eigenberg (Steve Brady), Evan Handler (Harry Goldenblatt), Jason Lewis (Smith Jerrod), Willie Garson (Stanford Blatch), Mario Cantone (Anthony Marantino). Directed by Michael Patrick King and produced by King, John P. Melfi, Sarah Jessica Parker, and Darren Star. Screenplay by Patrick King.

Some of these people make my skin crawl. The characters of *Sex and the City 2* are flyweight bubbleheads living in a world that rarely requires three sentences in a row. Their defining quality is consuming things. They gobble food, fashion, houses, husbands, children, vitamins, and freebies. They must plan their wardrobes on the phone, so often do

they appear in different basic colors, like the plugs of a Playskool workbench.

As we return to the trivialities of their lives for a sequel, marriage is the issue. The institution is affirmed in an opening sequence at a gay wedding in Connecticut that looks like a Fred Astaire production number gone horribly over-budget. There's a sixteen-man chorus in white formal wear, a pond with swans, and Liza Minnelli to perform the ceremony. Her religious or legal qualifications are unexplained; perhaps she is present merely as the patron saint of gay men. After the ceremony, she changes to a Vegas lounge outfit and is joined by two look-alike backups for a song-and-dance routine possibly frowned upon in some denominations.

Then it's back to the humdrum married life of our gal Carrie Bradshaw (Sarah Jessica Parker) and the loathsome Mr. Big (Chris Noth). Carrie, honey, how can you endure life with this purring, narcissistic, soft-velvet idiot? He speaks loudly enough to be heard mostly by himself, his most appreciative audience. And he never wants to leave the house at night, preferring to watch classic black-and-white movies on TV. This leads to a marital crisis. Carrie thinks they should talk more. But sweetheart, Mr. Big has nothing to say. At least he's provided you with a Manhattan apartment that looks like an *Architectural Digest* wet dream.

Brief updates. Miranda Hobbes (Cynthia Nixon) is a high-powered lawyer who is dissed by her male chauvinist pig boss. Samantha Jones (Kim Cattrall) is still a sexaholic. Charlotte York (Kristin Davis) has the two little girls she thought she wanted, but now discovers that they actually expect to be raised. Mothers, if you are reading this, run this through your head. One little girl dips her hands in strawberry topping and plants two big handprints on your butt. You are on the cell to a girlfriend. How do you report this? You moan and wail out: "My vintage Valentino!" Any mother who wears her vintage Valentino while making muffin topping with her kids should be hauled up before the Department of Children and Family Services.

All of this is pretty thin gruel. The movie shows enterprise and flies the entire cast away to the emirate of Abu Dhabi, where the girls are given a $22,000-a-night suite and matching Maybachs and butlers, courtesy of a sheikh who wants to have a meeting with Samantha and talk about publicity for his hotel.

This sequence is an exercise in obscenely conspicuous consumption, which the girls perform in so many different outfits they must have been followed to the Middle East by a luggage plane. I don't know a whole lot about fashion, but I know something about taste, and these women spend much of the movie dressed in tacky, vulgar clothing. Carrie and Samantha also display the maximum possible boobage, oblivious to Arab ideas about women's modesty. There's more cleavage in this film than at a pro wrestling wedding.

And crotches, have we got crotches for you. Big close-ups of the girls themselves and some of the bulgers they meet. And they meet some. They meet the Australian World Cup team, for example, which seems to have left its cups at home. And then there's the intriguing stranger Samantha meets at the hotel, whose zipper-straining arousal provokes the fury of an offended Arab guest and his wife. This prodigy's name is Rikard Spirt. Think about it.

Samantha is arrested for kissing on the beach, and there's an uncomfortable scene in which the girls are menaced by outraged men in a public market, where all they've done is dress in a way more appropriate for a sales reception at Victoria's Secret. They're rescued by Arab women so well-covered only their eyes are visible, and in private these women reveal that underneath the burka they're wearing Dior gowns and so forth. Must get hot.

I wondered briefly whether Abu Dhabi had underwritten all this product placement, but I learn that *SATC2* was filmed in Morocco, which must be Morocco's little joke. That nation supplies magnificent desert scenes, achieved with CGI, I assume, during which two of the girls fall off a camel. I haven't seen such hilarity since *Abbott and Costello in the Foreign Legion*.

The movie's visual style is arthritic. Director Michael Patrick King covers the sitcom by dutifully cutting back and forth to whoever is speaking. A sample of Carrie's realistic dialogue in a marital argument: "You knew when I married you I was more Coco Chanel than coq au vin." Carrie also narrates the film, providing useful guidelines for those challenged by its intricacies. Sample: "Later that day, Big and I arrived home."

Truth in reviewing: I am obliged to report that this film will no doubt be deliriously enjoyed by its fans, for the reasons described above. Male couch potatoes dragged to the film against their will may find some consolation. Reader, I must confess that while attending the sneak preview with its overwhelmingly female audience, I was gob-smacked by the delightful cleavage on display. Do women wear their lowest-cut frocks for one another?

Note: From my understanding of the guidelines of the MPAA Classification and Rating Administration, Samantha and Mr. Spirt have one scene that far, far surpasses the traditional MPAA limits for pumping and thrusting. ☞

Sex Drive ★ ★

R, 101 m., 2008

Josh Zuckerman (Ian), Clark Duke (Lance), James Marsden (Rex), Amanda Crew (Felicia), Alice Greczyn (Mary), Seth Green (Ezekiel). Directed by Sean Anders and produced by Bob Levy, Leslie Morgenstein, and John Morris. Screenplay by Anders and Morris.

Sex Drive is an exercise in versatile vulgarity. The actors seem to be performing a public reading of the film's mastery of the subject. Not only are all the usual human reproductive and excretory functions evoked, but new (and I think probably impossible) ones are included. This movie doesn't contain "offensive language." The offensive language contains the movie.

Was I offended? I'm way over that. I was startled. The MPAA ratings board must have been scribbling furiously in the dark, to come up with: "Rated R, for strong crude and sexual content, nudity, language, some drug and alcohol use, all involving teens." What did they forget? Violence. Nothing much blows up real good, and there is a lack of vivisection and disembowelment.

The plot involves Ian (Josh Zuckerman), who is that tragic creature, a virgin eighteen-year-old boy, deeply fascinated by an online girlfriend who calls herself Ms. Tasty (Katrina Bowden). This suggests several topics: (1) Since when is an eighteen-year-old's virginal status *automatically* assumed to be tragic? Never mind. Forget about it. I was going to dig up some statistics proving many eighteen-year-olds are virgins, but when I Googled the topic, the top hits involved eighteen-year-olds complaining about it. (2) Most of the people you meet in chat rooms are much older than they claim, of a different gender, a cop, or your so-called buddy who is goofing on you, ha ha. (3) Every female named Ms. Tasty is either a hooker or take your choice from (2).

Ian has a best buddy suitably named Lance (Clark Duke), who is pudgy, has zits, and only has to smile at a girl to have her offer herself. This is not unrealistic. The unrealistic part is that Ian himself is not pudgy and does not have zits. The two friends live in Wisconsin, and Ms. Tasty, who lives in Tennessee, wants Ian to drive down for guaranteed sex. Personal to Ian: When having sex with anyone named Ms. Tasty, in addition to a nice block of smoked cheddar, take along protection. Ian is in love with a hometown girl named Felicia (Amanda Crew), who is in love with Lance, as all females are. She comes along for the ride, essentially because she is needed to allow the in-car triangle to function.

Ian steals his brother's most prized possession, a perfectly restored 1969 GTO, to impress Ms. Tasty. Ian, Ian, Ian! Anyone calling herself Ms. Tasty who promises you sex doesn't *have* to be impressed. As they motor south, they pass through Amish country. Luckily it's the day of the annual Amish sex orgy, and Ian meets sexy Mary (Alice Greczyn), who falls in love with him, flashes her boobs, etc. The director, Sean Anders, should be ashamed of himself. Lucky the Amish don't go to movies, or he'd be facing a big lawsuit. Better be nice to the Amish. In a year we'll be trading gold bars for their food, ha ha.

What happens in Tennessee, stays in Tennessee. The movie has some laughs, to be sure, even a few big ones, but is so raunchy and driven by its formula that you want to cringe. Let's see. What else . . . Oh, I just noticed the pun in the title, ha ha.

Shall We Kiss? ★ ★ ½
NO MPAA RATING, 102 m., 2009

Virginie Ledoyen (Judith), Emmanuel Mouret (Nicolas), Julie Gayet (Emilie), Michael Cohen (Gabriel), Frederique Bel (Caline), Stefano Accorsi (Claudio), Melanie Maudran (Penelope), Marie Madinier (Eglantine). Directed by Emmanuel Mouret and produced by Frederic Niedermayer. Screenplay by Mouret.

The characters in *Shall We Kiss?* are attractive, wear impeccable clothes, and move easily through minimalist rooms, hotel lobbies, social gatherings, restaurants, and their lives. The sound track is by Schubert and Tchaikovsky. There are discreet paintings on the walls and drawings of composers. They are French, articulate, composed, and dumber than a box of rocks.

That is the only way I can account for their behavior, and since their behavior is the subject of the film, that must be counted as a flaw. They approach the subjects of sex and romance with a naivete so staggering it must be an embarrassment in the greater world. Inside their hermetically sealed complacency, I suppose it's a little exciting.

Gabriel and Emilie are strangers when they have a chance encounter in Nantes. Their eyes meet, there is a connection, they have dinner, and when Gabriel moves as if to kiss Emilie she seems willing, but then pulls back. She is afraid to kiss. Why? She will tell him a story.

Flashbacks to the story involve most of the film, with occasional returns to Emilie (Julie Gayet) relating it to Gabriel (Michael Cohen) in her hotel room. It is about her friends Judith (Virginie Ledoyen) and Nicolas (Emmanuel Mouret, the film's director). They have been best friends since childhood. Judith is happily married. Nicolas has just broken up with a lover of some duration. He is unhappy because he believes he is incapable of fully entering into physical love.

Judith suggests . . . a prostitute? Nicolas tried that. She was perfectly nice but wouldn't kiss him, and without kissing, his engine refused to turn over. What to do? He appeals to Judith. As a dear friend, his very dearest, would she consider . . . you know . . . to . . . She does. They proceed with the shy hesitation of a first game of spin-the-bottle. May I feel? asks he. May I touch here? And here? Shall we undress? I am on record as calling for more foreplay in the movies, but this isn't foreplay; it's the whole spring training season. And the problem is, they both enjoy it. That won't do. The answer is to do it again right away, roughly, on the floor, to break the spell. They enjoy that even more.

Now *Shall We Kiss?* enters into a complex plot involving deception, role-playing, her husband, his new girlfriend, and a twist I won't even hint at. All performed without the slightest concession to actual human nature as many of we humans understand it. In its long, exploratory conversations, the movie plays very much like a film by Eric Rohmer, who, having now allegedly retired at eighty-eight, has left the field free. But Rohmer used artifice to find truth, and Mouret uses it to find artifice.

You say, but perhaps the French—they are like that? And I reply, nooo, I don't think so. What do I really know about French attitudes toward such matters? Very little, although I once knew a French girl who talked no end about romance. We weren't even in spring training. We seemed to be in the Little League. If actual sex had ever entered the picture, I am convinced she would have regarded it as more than a theoretical exercise in platonic friendship.

Is *Shall We Kiss?* without merit? Not entirely. It has a grace, a languid charm, a pictorial elegance. The plot, when it winds up and unwinds, is ingenious. But are we expected in any sense to find these people realistic? What do we learn from them? All I learned was that that will never work. I already knew that.

Sherlock Holmes ★★★
PG-13, 128 m., 2009

Robert Downey, Jr. (Sherlock Holmes), Jude Law (Dr. John Watson), Rachel McAdams (Irene Adler), Mark Strong (Lord Blackwood), Eddie Marsan (Inspector Lestrade), Kelly Reilly (Mary Morstan). Directed by Guy Ritchie and produced by Susan Downey, Dan Lin, Joel Silver, and Lionel Wigram. Screenplay by Michael Robert Johnson, Anthony Peckham, and Simon Kinberg, based on the stories by Sir Arthur Conan Doyle.

The less I thought about Sherlock Holmes, the more I liked *Sherlock Holmes*. Yet another classic hero has been fed into the f/x mill, emerging as a modern superman. Guy Ritchie's film is filled with sensational sights, over-the-top characters, and a desperate struggle atop Tower Bridge, which is still under construction. It's likely to be enjoyed by today's action fans. But block bookings are not likely from the Baker Street Irregulars.

One of the comforts of the Arthur Conan Doyle stories is their almost staid adherence to form. Villains and cases come and go up the staircase at 221B Baker Street, but within that refuge life stays the same: Holmes all-knowing and calm, Watson fretful and frightened, clues orderly, victims distraught, never a problem not seemingly insoluble. Outside is the fabled Edwardian London, a city we all know in our imaginations. I think I became an Anglophile on those winter nights when I sat curled up in my dad's big chair, a single lamp creating shadows in the corners of the room, reading the Modern Library edition of the stories while in the basement I heard the comforting sounds of my parents doing the laundry.

Every Holmes story is different and each one is the same, just as every day has its own saint but the Mass is eternal. *Sherlock Holmes* enacts the strange new rites of hyperkinetic action and impossible CGI, and Holmes and Watson do their best to upgrade themselves. Holmes tosses aside the deerstalker hat and meerschaum calabash, and Watson has decided once and for all to abandon the intimacy of 221B for the hazards of married life. Both of them now seem more than a little gay; it's no longer a case of, "Oh, the British all talk like that." Jude Law even seemed it be wearing lipstick when he promoted the movie on Letterman.

Well, Holmes, like Hamlet, has survived countless interpretations. The character has been played by Basil Rathbone, Jeremy Brett, Frank Langella, Peter Cushing, John Barrymore, James D'Arcy, Michael Caine, John Cleese, Peter Cook, Rupert Everett, William Gillette, Stewart Granger, Charlton Heston, Anthony Higgins, Raymond Massey, Roger Moore, John Neville, Leonard Nimoy, Christopher Plummer, Jonathan Pryce, Nicol Williamson . . . and now Robert Downey Jr., who is not the least of these.

Downey's Holmes is at once more dissolute and more fit than previous incarnations.

Holmes's canonical devotion to the opium pipe is here augmented by other drugs and a great deal of booze. Yet Holmes has the body of a lithe athlete, the skills of a gymnast, and the pugilism of a world champion. He and Watson (who is, you recall, only a doctor, although one with clients who must be puzzled about his office hours) spring readily into action like Batman and Robin.

In a really very good opening sequence, the two burst in upon the fiendish Satanist Lord Blackwood (Mark Strong) in the act of committing a dastardly act. Blackwood is sent to the gallows and sealed in his tomb, only to reappear (to Holmes's undeniable satisfaction) seemingly still alive. This sets off a series of action set pieces in the streets of London, which have never seemed more looming, dark, and ominous; I had the impression Jack the Ripper had just darted out of view.

After the initial apprehension of Blackwood, Holmes retreats to his digs. In Conan Doyle, this is often explained as "a period of study" and implied opium reveries. In Ritchie's version, he trashes his rooms like a drunken undergraduate; they lack only empty pizza boxes. This will not do. My Sherlock is above all fastidious. But never mind. Blackwood's resurrection gives him a new reason for living.

There is also interest from two women: Irene Adler (Rachel McAdams), of course, said to be the only woman to ever touch Holmes's heart, and Mary Morstan (Kelly Reilly), Watson's intended, who may be in for more than she knows. The advent of Mary on the scene sends Holmes into fits of petulance; how dare the doctor prefer a woman to his own fascinating company? Watson has always maintained quarters elsewhere, but in this film the cozy confines of 221B make his other rooms seem more than ever like a beard.

The Conan Doyle stories are still read and probably always will be. Most readers get to at least a few. But among moviegoers on Christmas night (traditionally one of the busiest movie nights of the year), probably not so many. They will be unaware that this *Sherlock Holmes* is cheerfully revisionist. They will be entertained, and so was I. The great detective, who has survived so much, can certainly shrug off a few special effects.   ☞

She's Out of My League ★★★
R, 106 m., 2010

Jay Baruchel (Kirk), Alice Eve (Molly), T. J. Miller (Stainer), Mike Vogel (Jack), Nate Torrence (Devon), Krysten Ritter (Patty), Geoff Stults (Cam), Lindsay Sloane (Marnie). Directed by Jim Field Smith and produced by Eric Gold, David B. Householter, and Jimmy Miller. Screenplay by Sean Anders and John Morris.

Molly is a perfect ten. Kirk is a five. This scoring is provided by his best friends, who sadly inform him, "You can't jump more than two." Because of reasoning like that, Aristotle Onassis remains a hero to fours and fives everywhere. *She's Out of My League,* which is sortofa good comedy, tells the story of a five who meets a ten who believes there is a ten inside of him fighting to get out.

Kirk (Jay Baruchel) works as a TSA security screener at the Pittsburgh airport. He's competent enough, but the behavior of his colleagues should all by itself raise the national security level to red. Apparently unsupervised, they brighten up their jobs by trying to pick up every cute girl who comes through security. This is made more possible because there never seem to be five hundred impatient passengers waiting in line.

Baruchel looks as if he could indeed be a five, but he has that essential quality of turning into a ten with his attitude alone. Here he will find what I have long observed, that everyone is beautiful when they're looking at you with love in their eyes. Kirk has recently become the victim of the sort of perfect storm that strikes the heroes of movies like this. His girlfriend, Marnie (Lindsay Sloane), has broken up with him. But having lacked a warm family relationship, she latched onto Kirk's family, and now hangs out at his house with her new boyfriend, whom Kirk's parents approve of. Think about that.

Molly is also fresh from romantic disaster. When she loses her iPhone and Kirk finds it and returns it, she asks him out to dinner. He's stunned because, yes, she's out of his league. But it turns out Molly is ready to play in a different league, one where being a ten on the outside is less important than being a ten on the inside. Kirk's innate decency melts her heart.

Jay Baruchel has that quality of seeming like someone we might actually have known outside of a movie. He plays Kirk as apologetic, easily embarrassed, with low self-esteem—plain and simple, a nice guy. Alice Eve, who is despite all evidence British, is pretty, yes, but not actually quite a ten. A 9.5, easy. Isn't that scoring system loathsome? Her best friend, Patty (Krysten Ritter), thinks Kirk is beneath her, possibly because Patty likes to bask in the reflected glow of Molly's tenhood. Kirk's own three best buddies include two party animals and one nice pudgy guy, whose combined wisdom on women is a perfect two.

There are some funny set pieces here, one involving guys rummaging through each other's netherlands, one involving a family trip to Branson, Missouri, in matching sweatshirts. Do you ever get the feeling you're the last American alive who hasn't been to Branson? That *Titanic* attraction sounds great to me. Anyway, much depends on whether Kirk will actually make this journey.

The movie is not a comedy classic. But in a genre where so many movies struggle to lift themselves from zero to one, it's about, oh, a 6.5.

Shine a Light ★ ★ ★ ★
PG-13, 122 m., 2008

Featuring Mick Jagger, Keith Richards, Ron Wood, Charlie Watts, Buddy Guy, Christina Aguilera, Jack White, and Bill Clinton. A documentary directed by Martin Scorsese and produced by Steve Bing, Michael Cohl, Zane Weiner, and Victoria Pearman.

Martin Scorsese's *Shine a Light* may be the most intimate documentary ever made about a live rock 'n' roll concert. Certainly it has the best coverage of the performances onstage. Working with cinematographer Robert Richardson, Scorsese deployed a team of nine other cinematographers, all of them Oscar winners or nominees, to essentially blanket a live September 2006 Rolling Stones concert at the smallish Beacon Theater in New York. The result is startling immediacy, a merging of image and music, edited in step with the performance.

In the brief black-and-white footage opening the film, we see Scorsese drawing up shot charts to diagram the order of the songs, the order of the solos, and who would be where on the stage. This was the same breakdown approach he used with his documentary *The Last Waltz* (1978), which he hoped would enable him to call his shots through the earpieces of the cameramen, as directors of live TV did in the early days. The challenge this time was that Mick Jagger toyed with the song list in endless indecision; we look over his shoulder at titles scratched out and penciled back in, and hear him mention casually that of course the whole set might be changed on the spot. Apparently after playing together for forty-five years, the Stones communicate their running order telepathically.

This movie is where Scorsese came in. I remember visiting him in the postproduction loft for *Woodstock* in 1970, where he was part of a team led by Thelma Schoonmaker that was combining footage from multiple cameras into a split-screen approach that could show as many as three or four images at once. But the footage they had to work with was captured on the run, while *The Last Waltz* had a shot map and outline, at least in Scorsese's mind. *Shine a Light* combines his foreknowledge with the versatility of great cinematographers so that it essentially seems to have a camera in the right place at the right time for every element of the performance.

It helped, too, that the Stones' songs had been absorbed by Scorsese into his very being. "Let me put it this way," he said in a revealing August 2007 interview with Craig McLean of the *London Observer*. "Between '63 and '70, those seven years, the music that they made I found myself gravitating to. I would listen to it a great deal. And ultimately, that fueled movies like *Mean Streets* and later pictures of mine, *Raging Bull* to a certain extent, and certainly *GoodFellas* and *Casino* and other pictures over the years."

Mentioning that he had not seen the Stones in concert until late 1969, he said the music itself was ingrained: "The actual visualization of sequences and scenes in *Mean Streets* comes from a lot of their music, of living with their music and listening to it. Not just the songs I use in the film. No, it's about the tone and the mood of their music, their attitude. . . . I just kept listening to it. Then I kept imagining scenes in movies. And interpreting. It's not just imagining a scene of a tracking shot around a person's face or a car scene. It really was [taking] events and incidents in my own life that I was trying to interpret into filmmaking, to a story, a narrative. And it seemed that those songs inspired me to do that. To find a way to put those stories on film. So the debt is incalculable. I don't know what to say. In my mind, I did this film forty years ago. It just happened to get around to being filmed right now."

The result is one of the most engaged documentaries you could imagine. The cameras do not simply regard the performances; in a sense, the cameras are performers, too, in the way shots are cut together by Scorsese and his editor, David Tedeschi. Even in their sixties, the Stones are the most physical and exuberant of bands. Compared to them, watching the movements of many new young bands on Leno, Letterman, and *SNL* is like watching jerky marionettes. Jagger has never used the mechanical moves employed by many lead singers; he is a dancer and an acrobat and a conductor, too, who uses his body to conduct the audience. In counterpoint, Keith Richards and Ron Wood are loose-limbed and angular, like way-cool backup dancers. Richards in particular seems to defy gravity as he leans so far over; there's a moment in rehearsal when he tells Scorsese he wants to show him something, and leans down to show that you can see the mallet of Charlie Watts's bass drum, visible as it hits the front drumhead. "I can see that because I'm down there," he explains.

The unmistakable fact is that the Stones love performing. Watch Ron lean an arm on Keith's shoulder during one shared riff. Watch the droll hints of irony, pleasure, and quizzical reaction shots, which so subtly move across their seemingly passive faces. Notice that Keith smokes onstage not simply to be smoking, but to use the smoke cloud, brilliant in the spotlights, as a performance element. He knows what he's doing. And then see it all brought together and tied tight in the remarkably acrobatic choreography of Jagger's performance. I've seen the Stones in Chicago in venues as large as the United Center and as small as the Double Door, but I've never experienced them this way, because the cameras are as privileged as the performers onstage.

And the music? What do I have to say about the music? What is there *left* to say about the music? In that interview, Scorsese said, "'Sympathy for the Devil' became this score for our lives. It was everywhere at that time; it was being played on the radio. When 'Satisfaction' starts, the authority of the guitar riff that begins it is something that became anthemic." I think there is nothing useful for me to say about the music except that if you have been interested enough to read this far, you already know all about it, and all I can usefully describe is the experience of seeing it in this film.

A Shine of Rainbows ★★ ½
PG, 101 m., 2010

Connie Nielsen (Maire O'Donnell), Aidan Quinn (Alec O'Donnell), John Bell (Tomas), Jack Gleason (Seamus), Niamh Shaw (Katie), Tara Alice Scully (Nancy). Directed by Vic Sarin and produced by James Flynn, Tina Pehme, and Chris Rudolph. Screenplay by Sarin, Catherine Spear, and Dennis Foon, from the novel by Lillian Beckwith.

As you can possibly guess from the title, *A Shine of Rainbows* is a feel-good movie. Hey, what's not to like about cute orphans, baby seals, sweet moms, and gruff dads with hearts of gold? And rainbows? If your heart is going thumpety-thump at such a prospect, here is the movie for you.

No, I'm serious. And kids may really love it. It's too much of an emotional heart tugger for me, but then I prefer my orphans by Dickens, where the little rascals pick pockets for a living. I'll admit one thing: I wish there were still an Ireland (or anywhere else) where a couple looking like Connie Nielsen and Aidan Quinn could live in an isolated and charming home on a high meadow overlooking the sea, operate a small family farm, and make a living.

The film is set on Corrie Island, off the western coast of Ireland, and I'll grant you one thing: You can find dozens of photos of it at http://j.mp/cnQWBU, and it looks just about the way it does in the film. It is a wonderful place for small Tomas (John Bell), who has become a punching bag for bullies at the orphanage, but is swept up by the heaven-sent Maire O'Donnell (Connie Nielsen), popped aboard a ferry, and carried across to this idyllic setting.

All is fine, except . . . why does his new dad, Alec (Aidan Quinn), glower at him so darkly? Alec confides to his wife that the boy doesn't look sturdy enough. Why didn't she pick a brawnier model? Alec is possibly in the Dickens tradition of a cruel stepfather who demands only a brisk twenty-hour day of hard labor in return for the lad's bowl of gruel. Good thing Tomas is Irish. If he'd been Russian, there'd be no telling.

Maire unfortunately contracts Ali MacGraw's Disease, defined in an ancient edition of the Glossary as that disease of young women whose only symptom is that after they take to a hospital bed they grow more and more beautiful. That leaves Tomas with Alec. Oh, but Tomas finds a new friend, a baby seal stranded down on the beach. He knows another orphan when he sees one.

As Tomas and Alec slowly bond over the seal, Alec's heart melts, as it must. It's the seal I'm worried about. Tomas brings him fish to wolf down, but I dunno . . . how long can a young seal lie helpless on a beach in full sun and remain happy? Couldn't he, like, you know, sort of crawl into the sea? Isn't that kind of programmed into seals? The movie offers some reason for his immobility, which didn't lock into my memory bank. Essentially he stays there day after day because the plot requires him.

I know, I know. I'm being unsentimental. I should make this clear: *A Shine of Rainbows* is a sweet, good-looking film about nice people in a beautiful place, and young John Bell is an appealing performer in the tradition of the Culkins. Quinn and Nielsen are pros who take their roles seriously, and Vic Sarin's direction gets the job done. If I were six . . . but then I'm not, am I?

Shotgun Stories ★ ★ ★ ★
PG-13, 92 m., 2008

Michael Shannon (Son Hayes), Douglas Ligon (Boy Hayes), Barlow Jacobs (Kid Hayes), Michael Abbott Jr. (Cleaman Hayes), Travis Smith (Mark Hayes), Lynnsee Provence (Stephen Hayes), David Rhodes (John Hayes), Natalie Canerday (Nicole Hayes), Glenda Pannell (Annie Hayes). Directed by Jeff Nichols and produced by David Gordon Green, Lisa Muskat, and Nichols. Screenplay by Nichols.

Jeff Nichols's *Shotgun Stories* is shaped and told like a revenge tragedy, but it offers an unexpected choice: The hero of the film does not believe the future is doomed by the past. If it were, most of the key characters would be dead by the end, an outcome that seems almost inevitable. Here is a tense and sorrowful film where common sense struggles with blood lust.

The movie takes place in a "dead-ass town" where three brothers exist. "Hang out" is the only term for what they do. They were named Son, Kid, and Boy by an alcoholic father and, in Son's words, "a hateful woman." Son (Michael Shannon) sprinkles the feed at a local fish farm and loses all his money trying to perfect a "system" he thinks can beat the local casino. His wife has just walked out, taking their son. His brother Kid (Barlow Jacobs) would like to get married, but "I worry about taking care of her. I mean, I don't have a truck. I don't have a house. I sleep in a damn tent." The youngest, Boy (Douglas Ligon), lives in his van and is struggling to beat the heat by persuading a home air conditioner to run off his cigarette lighter.

If this sounds like the setup for a redneck joke, it isn't. The brothers are quiet, lonely, still suffering from abusive childhoods. And consider the remarkable scene where their mother knocks on the door to tell them their father, now married to another woman and with four more sons, has died.

"When's the funeral?" Son asks.

"You can find out in the newspaper."

"You going?"

"No."

Son, Kid, and Boy attend. Since abandoning them, their father had sobered up in rehab, found Jesus, and started a prosperous middle-class family. Now Son chooses to say a few words over the coffin before spitting on it, and a fight breaks out. This fight will escalate into a blood feud in which lives are lost and blood is shed, and yet the enemies are so unprepared that after one buys a shotgun in a pawn shop, he has to be shown how to assemble and load it.

The film is by no means entirely grim and implacable. There are moments of quiet humor, as when Boy finally figures out a way to run the air conditioner off his car battery, and rigs it to blow at him on a river bank and to run a blender for his margaritas. Annie (Glenda Pannell) is fed up with Son's gambling habit but is a gentle woman who loves him. Son himself has hopes for his own son and wants to break the cycle of violence. So does the oldest son of the other family, although the dead father seems to have done a better job of raising those boys than the first three.

Jeff Nichols, the writer and director, is working in the same world where David Gordon Green sets his films; indeed, Green is a coproducer of this film, which uses his cinematographer, Adam Stone. The photography, of course, is wide-screen; these people live surrounded by distant horizons, the vista broken only by the occasional tree or broken-down tractor. Like Green, Nichols uses sleight of hand to sneak in plot details; Shotgun Stories uses the most subtle dialogue I can imagine to reveal, by implication, that Boy has, or had, an African-American wife, or girlfriend.

This film has literally been saved by the festival circuit. After being rejected by major distributors, it found a home in smaller festivals, where word of mouth propelled it into its current wider release. It has qualities that may not come out in a trailer or in an ad, but that sink in when you have the experience of seeing it. Few films are so observant about how we relate with one another. Few as sympathetic.

The film is as spare as the landscape. Classical drama comes condensed to a harshness: "You raised us to hate those boys, and we do. And now it's come to this." In a movie where so much violence obviously takes place, we actually see very little of it. Nichols sidesteps the problem of the intrinsic interest of violence by looking away from it and focusing on its effect. We don't get to know the second family very well, but Son, Kid, and Boy are closed up within their melancholy. Although some orange flowers and gentle music try to do their work at the end, we can only hope Son finds the life he desires for his own son.

Shrink ★★ ½

R, 110 m., 2009

Kevin Spacey (Henry Carter), Saffron Burrows (Kate Amberson), Jack Huston (Shamus), Keke Palmer (Jemma), Dallas Roberts (Patrick), Robin Williams (Jack), Pell James (Daisy), Mark Webber (Jeremy), Robert Loggia (Robert Carter), Laura Ramsey (Keira). Directed by Jonas Pate and produced by Michael Burns, Braxton Pope, and Dana Brunetti. Screenplay by Thomas Moffett.

Shrink gives us a high-profile Los Angeles psychiatrist whose life has been reduced to smoking as much pot as he possibly can. If the movie contains a surprise, it's that he doesn't find his way to cocaine. Kevin Spacey brings another of his cynical, bitter characters to life—very smart and fresh out of hope—but the movie doesn't give him much of anywhere to take it.

The idea of rich, famous, drug-addled Hollywood flotsam is not precisely original, and this sort of story has rarely been more strongly told than in Hurlyburly (1998), with Sean Penn as a cokehead and Spacey himself as a bemused, supercilious witness to the wreckage. As for the behind-the-scenes Hollywood stuff, you can't much improve on Altman's The Player.

What director Jonas Pate and his writer, Thomas Moffett, do is sidestep deep characterization and bring in a rather conventional assortment of clients for Spacey's shrink, named Henry Carter. We meet a movie star past his sell-by date (Robin Williams, unbilled), who thinks his problem is sex addiction, although Henry assures him it is alcoholism (the sex addict's running mate). Dallas Roberts plays Patrick, an agent driven by hyperactive compulsions; Patrick's assistant Daisy (Pell James) is preggers; Shamus (Jack Huston) is an Irish actor who is an alcoholic just for starters; and the actress Kate (Saffron Burrows) is a trophy wife who finds her husband's trophy shelf is not yet complete.

These characters are intriguing in their own ways, especially when we sense Williams restraining himself from bolting headlong into his descriptions of sexual improbabilities, but each one is essentially a walk-on act, and even when their lifelines cross it seems an event in the screenplay, not their lives.

One actress who does create a free-standing character is Keke Palmer (Jemma), mourning her mother, finding refuge in the movie revivals she attends as a form of escape. Palmer was the young star of *Akeelah and the Bee* (2006), and is still only sixteen; remember her name.

Directing emotional traffic amid these problems, the Spacey character is coming to pieces. His wife has recently committed suicide, he can barely focus on his clients, and although he's excellent at spotting addiction in others, he rationalizes his own. It takes his father (Robert Loggia) to talk straight to him, and he is stunned to find himself the recipient of an intervention.

Working within the range we frequently find him, Kevin Spacey is a master. Yes, there is a pattern to many of his roles, but there are characters he is suited to and others that would be improbable. Many critics find fault with him for not repeating *American Beauty* in every film, or maybe even for making it in the first place. I sense an acute intelligence at work. When he found few interesting Hollywood projects, he went to the London stage, took over management of the Old Vic, and reinvented himself. Why are some critics snarky toward such an actor? Is it the price they pay for trying?

That said, *Shrink* contains ideas for a film, but no emotional center. A group of troubled characters is assembled and allowed to act out, not to much purpose. Jemma, the young girl, is the most authentic, and Henry relates to her most movingly. Two actors have found something to dig into.

Shutter Island ★★★ ½

R, 138 m., 2010

Leonardo DiCaprio (Teddy Daniels), Mark Ruffalo (Chuck Aule), Ben Kingsley (Dr. Cawley), Michelle Williams (Dolores), Emily Mortimer (Rachel 1), Patricia Clarkson (Rachel 2), Max von Sydow (Dr. Naehring). Directed by Martin Scorsese and produced by Scorsese, Brad Fischer, Mike Medavoy, and Arnold Messer. Screenplay by Laeta Kalogridis, based on the novel by Dennis Lehane.

Shutter Island starts working on us with the first musical notes under the Paramount mountain, even before the film starts. They're ominous and doomy. So is the film. This is Martin Scorsese's evocation of the delicious shuddering fear we feel when horror movies are *about* something and don't release all the tension with action scenes.

In its own way it's a haunted house movie, or make that a haunted castle or fortress. Shutter Island, we're told, is a remote and craggy island in Boston bay, where a Civil War fort has been adapted as a prison for the criminally insane. We approach it by boat through lowering skies, and the feeling is something like the approach to King Kong's island: Looming in gloom from the sea, it fills the visitor with dread.

To this island in rainy weather in 1954 travel U.S. Marshal Teddy Daniels (Leonardo DiCaprio) and his partner, Chuck Aule (Mark Ruffalo). They're assigned to investigate the disappearance of a child murderer (Emily Mortimer). There seems to be no way to leave the island alive. The disappearance of one prisoner might not require the presence of two marshals unfamiliar with the situation, but we never ask that question. Not after the ominous walls of the prison arise. Not after the visitors are shown into the office of the prison director, Dr. Cawley, played by Ben Kingsley with that forbidding charm he has mastered.

It's clear that Teddy has no idea what he's getting himself into. Teddy—such an innocuous name in such a Gothic setting. Scorsese, working from a novel by Dennis Lehane, seems to be telling a simple enough story here; the woman is missing, and Teddy and Chuck will look for her. But the cold gray walls clamp in on them, and the offices of Cawley and his colleagues, furnished for the Civil War commanding officers, seem borrowed from a tale by Edgar Allan Poe.

Scorsese the craftsman chips away at reality piece by piece. Flashbacks suggest Teddy's traumas in the decade since World War II. That war, its prologue and aftermath, supplied the dark undercurrent of classic film noir. The term "post-traumatic stress disorder" was not then in use, but its symptoms could be seen in men attempting to look confident in their facades of unstyled suits, subdued ties, heavy smoking, and fedoras pulled low against the rain. DiCaprio and Ruffalo both effect this look, but DiCaprio makes it seem more like a hopeful disguise.

The film's primary effect is on the senses. Everything is brought together into a disturbing foreshadow of dreadful secrets. How did this woman escape from a locked cell in a locked ward in the old Civil War fort, its walls thick enough to withstand cannon fire? Why do Cawley and his sinister colleague Dr. Naehring (Max von Sydow, ready to play chess with Death) seem to be concealing something? Why is even such a pleasant person as the deputy warden not quite convincingly friendly? Why do the methods in the prison trigger flashbacks to Teddy's memories of helping to liberate a Nazi death camp?

These kinds of questions are at the heart of film noir. The hero is always flawed. Scorsese showed his actors the great 1947 noir *Out of the Past*, whose very title is a noir theme: Characters never arrive at a story without baggage. They have unsettled issues, buried traumas. So, yes, perhaps Teddy isn't simply a clean-cut G-man. But why are the others so strange? Kingsley in particular exudes menace every time he smiles.

There are thrilling visuals in *Shutter Island*. Another film Scorsese showed his cast was Hitchcock's *Vertigo*, and we sense echoes of its hero's fear of heights. There's the possibility that the escaped woman might be lurking in a cave on a cliff or hiding in a lighthouse. Both involve hazardous terrain to negotiate, above vertiginous falls to waves pounding on the rocks below. A possible hurricane is approaching. Light leaks out of the sky. The wind sounds mournful. It is, as they say, a dark and stormy night. And that's what the movie is about: atmosphere, ominous portents, the erosion of Teddy's confidence and even his identity. It's all done with flawless directorial command. Scorsese has fear to evoke, and he does it with many notes.

You may read reviews of *Shutter Island* complaining that the ending blindsides you. The uncertainty it causes prevents the film from feeling perfect on first viewing. I have a feeling it might improve on second. Some may believe it doesn't make sense. Or that, if it does, then the movie leading up to it doesn't. I asked myself: OK, then, how *should* it end? What would be more satisfactory? Why can't I be one of those critics who informs the director what he should have done instead?

Oh, I've had moments like that. Every moviegoer does. But not with *Shutter Island*.

This movie is all of a piece, even the parts that don't appear to fit. There is a human tendency to note carefully what goes before and draw logical conclusions. But—what if you can't nail down exactly what went before? What if there were things about Cawley and his peculiar staff that were hidden? What if the movie lacks a reliable narrator? What if its point of view isn't omniscient but fragmented? Where can it all lead? What does it mean? We ask, and Teddy asks, too. ☞

Shuttle ★

R, 107 m., 2009

Peyton List (Mel), Cameron Goodman (Jules), Tony Curran (Driver), Cullen Douglas (Andy), Dave Power (Matt), James Snyder (Seth). Directed by Edward Anderson and produced by Mark Williams, Todd Lemley, Allan Jones, Michael Pierce, and Mark Donadio. Screenplay by Anderson.

Why do I have to watch this movie? Why does anyone? What was the impulse behind this sad, cruel story? Is there, as they say, "an audience for it"? I guess so. The critic *Tex Massacre* at bloodydisgusting.com rates it four skulls out of five and says, "While gorehounds might not be doing back flips over the blood loss, they should appreciate that director Edward Anderson makes the kills relatively painful and wholly grounded in reality."

I'm not sure if the gorehounds will think there is too much blood loss or too little. Never mind. At least the killings are relatively painful. There's that to be said for it. But I think it's a cop-out to review this movie only as an entry in the horror/slasher genre and not pull back for a larger context. Do images have no qualities other than their technical competence?

Shuttle opens with two young women arriving at an almost empty airport at 2 a.m. It's raining. They can't get a cab. A guy in a van says he'll take them downtown for fifteen dollars. He already has one passenger. Now two young guys also want a ride. Guy says, nothing doing. One girl says, they're with us. Two guys get on board.

Under the driver's window is painted, "No more than three stops." That's strange. Looks like there's room for sixteen, twenty people in the van. The driver takes them on a strange route into no-man's land, pulls a gun, takes all five passengers hostage. OK, so far we're in standard horror territory.

It's what comes next that grows disturbing. The women, played by Peyton List and Cameron Goodman, are resourceful and try to fight back. The young guys help but are neutralized. The other passenger is a crybaby. The film seems set up to empower women. I won't say more about the plot except to say that it leads to utter hopelessness and evil.

That things happen as they do in *Shuttle* I suppose is true, however rarely. But a film can have an opinion about them. This one simply serves them up in hard, merciless detail. There is no release for the audience, no "entertainment," not even much action excitement. Just a remorseless march into the dark.

There is good work here. Peyton List, now twenty-two, working on TV since 2000, is effective as Mel, the more resourceful of the girls. She has a Neve Campbell quality. Tony Curran, as the driver, isn't your usual menacing monster but has more of a workaday attitude inflicting suffering. And the writer-director, Edward Anderson, is reasonably skilled at filmmaking, although it becomes a major distraction when he has the van drive through miles of empty streets when, as the plot reveals, there is little reason.

Last week I reviewed the latest version of *The Last House on the Left*. It had qualities, too, including more developed characters and more ingenious action sequences. But *Shuttle* is uninterested in visual style; it wants to appear nuts-and-bolts, unsentimental, pushing our faces in it. I know the horror genre is a traditional port of entry for first-time directors on low budgets, and I suppose that is Anderson's purpose. All right, he has proven himself. Now let him be less passionately infatuated with despair.

Note: The R rating proves once again that it is impossible for a film to be rated NC-17 on violence alone.

Silent Light ★ ★ ★ ★

NO MPAA RATING, 136 m., 2009

Cornelio Wall Fehr (Johan), Miriam Toews (Esther), Maria Pankratz (Marianne), Peter Wall (Padre), Elisabeth Fehr (Madre), Jacobo Klassen (Zacarias). Directed by Carlos Reygadas and produced by Reygadas and Jaime Romandia. Screenplay by Reygadas.

Sometimes we are helpless in the face of love, and it becomes a torment. It is a cruel master. We must act on it or suffer, and sometimes because we act, others suffer. *Silent Light* is a solemn and profound film about a man transfixed by love, which causes him to betray his good and faithful wife.

How he fell into this love, we do not know. Certainly Johan isn't the kind of man to go straying. Nor is Marianne, the woman he loves, a husband stealer. That they are both good to the core is the source of their pain. Yes, Johan and Marianne have sex, but it is the strength of the film that not for a second do we believe they are motivated by sex—only by love.

Esther, Johan's wife and the mother of their six children, knows Marianne and knows about the affair. Johan has told her. He is a religious man and has also confessed to his father and his best friend. There is the sense that he will never leave Esther and never stop loving Marianne. He and Esther say they love each other, and they mean it. You see how love brings its punishment.

The director Carlos Reygadas sets this story among the one hundred thousand or so Mennonites living in Mexico. He does not choose such a sect casually. His story involves people who deeply hold their values and try to act upon them and yet who do not seem to be zealots. (It says much about the Mennonites that their clergy are unpaid.) In fact, the film never mentions the word "Mennonite," there are no church services, and all the characters act from their hearts and not simply their teachings.

Reygadas cast the film entirely from the actual Mennonite community, which I believe will feel he played fair with them. If you didn't know these were untrained actors, you would assume they had years of experience. There is not a false instance in the film, and the performances assume an almost holy reality. Cornelio Wall Fehr as Johan, Miriam Toews as his wife, and Maria Pankratz as Marianne are so focused they gather interior power. They take a story of extreme emotions and make it believable. The father (Wall's real father), the friend, all of the actors, are unshakable.

Silent Light has a beauty based on nature and the rhythms of the land. It opens with a sunrise and closes with a sunset, both in long-held shots, and we see corn being gathered by a harvester, wheat being stacked, long dusty roads between soy fields. The cinematographer, Alexis Zabe, evokes some of the unadorned beauty of a film by Bresson or Bergman, and of the Dreyer film this one in some ways resembles, *Ordet*. He keeps a distance that sometimes suggests awe. When Marianne comes to Johan at a critical time near the end, the camera sees them as distant figures across a field. It is not a time for close-ups.

And look at a scene where Marianne tenderly kisses Esther. First we see them from the side, Marianne bending over. Then from directly overhead. When Marianne stands, the camera remains fixed on Esther's face, and we, but only after a time, see that there is a tear on her cheek. Marianne's. What actually happens next is open to discussion. I was reminded of a similar puzzle in Bergman's *Cries and Whispers*.

This film is not short, and it is not fast. There is no score, location sounds seem hard-edged, and when a hymn is sung, it is not a tune but a dirge. The film's rhythm imposes itself. Curious, how a slow and deep film can absorb, and a fast and shallow one can tire us.

"The world is too much with us," Wordsworth says. "Late and soon, getting and spending, we lay waste our powers: little we see in nature that is ours." It is Reygadas's inspiration to set this film among a people whose ways are old and deeply felt, and to cast it with actors who believe in those ways. To set it in "modern times," most places in today's world, would make it seem artificial and false. What the film is really about is people who see themselves and their values as an organic whole. There are no pious displays here. No sanctimony, no preaching. Never even the word "religion." Just Johan, Esther, and Marianne, all doing their best.

A Single Man ★★★
R, 101 m., 2009

Colin Firth (George Falconer), Julianne Moore (Charley), Matthew Goode (Jim), Nicholas

Hoult (Kenny). Directed by Tom Ford and produced by Ford, Andrew Miano, Robert Salerno, and Chris Weitz. Screenplay by Ford, based on the novel by Christopher Isherwood.

Hemingway wrote something years ago that returns to my memory from time to time: "Isn't it pretty to think so." Never mind what he was referring to. The words apply for me to those situations where we imagine the reality to be quite different than it really is. Perhaps our imagination is a protective strategy.

A Single Man is told from the point of view of its hero, George (Colin Firth), the single man. He is single because unmarried and single because homosexual; the phrase was used at one time with a lifted eyebrow. It has been eight months since his lover died, and he still grieves. He is empty. His only friendship is with Charley (Julianne Moore), a sad alcoholic of a certain age with whom he once, briefly, had a try at a heated affair. She gives him gin and sympathy, but it's more ritual than comfort. She tries to kiss him, says maybe "we could still make a go of it," but that's a lie neither one believes.

A Single Man begins on what may be the last day of George's life, in 1962. The sight of a revolver waiting in a drawer makes this unmistakable. He performs his morning toilet of grooming and dressing in impeccable taste, and turns out to the world as the very model of flawless perfection. He teaches a college class on Aldous Huxley (is he still taught?). He works in a subtext about those who do not conform. No student is interested except Kenny (Nicholas Hoult), who may be less interested in the lecture than the lecturer.

Firth plays George superbly, as a man who prepares a face to meet the faces that he meets. He betrays very little emotion, and certainly his thoughts cannot be read in his eyes. He's so good at this it must have been rehearsed since youth. No one will ever see anything in George to complain about. Growing up in Britain as he did in the 1920s and 1930s he must have found few people with whom he could share his true nature. Now, in California, he had only his lover, and his lover is dead. Life is stale and profitless.

His evening is spent with Charley, who is always a little drunk or a little drunker. She has prepared for their date. Her hair is piled up and cemented in place, her makeup perfect, their dinner elegant. They talk in a code long-practiced. She offers sympathy she barely means and he barely feels. It is horrible that this may be the most meaningful relationship right now in either of these lives.

More happens later in the evening, but you will see for yourself. I want to return to those six words. I assume the film faithfully reflects George's idea of who he is, how he behaves, and what it means. The first-time director Tom Ford, the famous fashion designer, has been faulted for over-designing the film, but perhaps that misses the point. Perhaps George has over-designed his inner vision.

He sees himself as impeccable, reserved, ironic, resigned, detached. He projects a cool, impenetrable facade. Charley is seen in his way, which may not be hers. When events take place to interrupt his routine, he tries to maintain his demeanor unchanged. His game plan is apparently to complete this day in an orderly way, and then shoot himself, still above reproach.

Isn't it pretty to think so. It may work for George, but it didn't work for me. I sensed there were shrieks of terror and anger inside, bottled up for years. The last eight months must have been hell. Firth wisely doesn't try to signal this because any attempt to do so would break the facade and reduce his rather awesome performance to acting-out. I think it was Ford's responsibility to suggest it, perhaps through violations of the facade: a stain left overlooked on a tie, a careless remark, a car badly parked. A disintegration.

As Ford's first film, this story, based on a novel by Christopher Isherwood, must have had special meaning. He has another life and wasn't driven to the rigors of filmmaking. Many designers are known for their own faultless appearances. If Ford doesn't scream inside, and I have no reason to believe he does, perhaps the film faithfully reflects his idea of himself and George. Such a man will never kill himself.

Sin Nombre ★ ★ ★ ★
R, 96 m., 2009

Paulina Gaitan (Sayra), Edgar Flores (Willy/Casper), Kristyan Ferrer (Smiley), Tenoch Huerta Mejia (Lil' Mago), Diana Garcia (Martha Marlene), Luis Fernando Pena (Sol), Hector Jimenez (Leche/Wounded Man). Directed by Cary Fukunaga and produced by Amy Kaufman. Screenplay by Fukunaga.

El Norte. The North. It is a lodestar for some of those south of our border, who risk their lives to come here. *Sin Nombre,* which means "without name," is a devastating film about some of those who try the journey. It contains risk, violence, a little romance, even fleeting moments of humor, but most of all it sees what danger and heartbreak are involved. It is riveting from start to finish.

The film weaves two stories. One involves Sayra (Paulina Gaitan), a young woman from Honduras who joins her father and uncle in an odyssey through Guatemala and Mexico intended to take them to relatives in New Jersey. The other involves Casper (Edgar Flores), a young gang member from southern Mexico who joins with his leader and a twelve-year-old gang recruit to rob those riding north on the tops of freight cars. Their paths cross.

This is an extraordinary debut film by Cary Fukunaga, only thirty-one, who shows a mastery of image and story. He knows the material. He apparently spent time riding on the tops of northward trains; hundreds of hopeful emigrants materialize at a siding and scramble onboard, and the railroad apparently makes little attempt to stop them. He is also convincing about the inner workings of the terrifying real-life gang named Mara Salvatrucha.

Before turning to the story, I want to say something about the look and feel of the film. It was photographed by Adriano Goldman, who used not hi-def video as you might suspect, but 35 mm film, which has a special richness. Fukunaga's direction expresses a desire that seems to be growing in many young directors to return to classical compositions and editing. Those norms establish a strong foundation for storytelling; no queasy-cam for Fukunaga. Bahrani is another member of the same generation whose shots call attention to their subject, not themselves.

The story of Sayra, her father, and her uncle is straightforward: They are driven to improve their lives, think they have a safe haven in New

Jersey, and want to go there. Some elements of their journey reminded me of Gregory Nava's great indie epic *El Norte* (1983). The journey in that film was brutal; in this one, it is forged in hell.

That hell is introduced by Fukunaga in the club rooms of the gang, whose members are fiercely tattooed, none more than Lil' Mago (Tenoch Huerta Mejia), the leader, whose face is covered like a war mask. Casper is a member of the gang, more or less by force; he brings twelve-year-old Smiley (Kristyan Ferrer) to a meeting, and the kid is entranced by the macho BS. The three board one of the northbound trains to rob the riders, and that's when Casper meets Sayra and their fates are sealed.

Smiley, so young, with a winning smile, is perhaps the most frightening character because he demonstrates how powerful an effect, even hypnotic, gang culture can have on unshielded kids. In his eyes Lil' Mago looms as a god, the gang provides peer status, and any values Smiley might have had evaporate. The initiation process includes being savagely beaten and kicked by gang members, and then proving himself by killing someone. Smiley is ready and willing.

There are shots here of great beauty. As the countryside rolls past and the riders sit in the sun and protect their small supplies of food and water, there is sometimes the rhythm of weary camaraderie. I was reminded of Hal Ashby's *Bound for Glory*. Kids along the tracks are happy to see the riders getting away with something, and at one place throw them oranges. At stations, the riders jump off and detour around the guards to board the train again as it leaves town.

Sin Nombre is a remarkable film, showing the incredible hardships people will endure in order to reach El Norte. Yes, the issue of illegal immigration is a difficult one. When we encounter an undocumented alien, we should not be too quick with our easy assumptions. That person may have put his life on the line for weeks or months to come here, searching for what we so easily describe as the American Dream. What inspired Fukunaga, an American, to make this film, I learn, was a 2003 story about eighty illegals found locked in a truck and abandoned in Texas. Nineteen died.

The Sisterhood of the Traveling Pants 2 ★ ★ ★
PG-13, 117 m., 2008

America Ferrera (Carmen), Alexis Bledel (Lena), Blake Lively (Bridget), Amber Tamblyn (Tibby), Rachel Nichols (Julia), Tom Wisdom (Ian), Leonardo Nam (Brian), Michael Rady (Kostas), Blythe Danner (Greta), Jesse Williams (Leo). Directed by Sanaa Hamri and produced by Debra Martin Chase, Kira Davis, Denise Di Novi, Broderick Johnson, and Andrew A. Kosove. Screenplay by Elizabeth Chandler, based on the novels by Ann Brashares.

The Sisterhood of the Traveling Pants 2, which you will agree has one of the more ungainly titles of recent years, is everything that *Sex and the City* wanted to be. It follows the lives of four women, their career adventures, their romantic disasters and triumphs, their joys and sadness. These women are all in their early twenties, which means they are learning life's lessons; *SATC* is about forgetting them.

The traveling pants, you will recall, are a pair of jeans that the four best friends tried on in a clothing store in the 2005 movie. Magically, they were a perfect fit for all four. So they agree that each one can wear the jeans for a week of the coming summer and then FedEx them to the next name in rotation. Following the jeans, in both movies, we follow key moments in the girls' lives.

Carmen is my favorite. Played by the glowing America Ferrera (*Real Women Have Curves*), she has followed her tall blond friend Julia (Rachel Nichols) to Vermont, where Julia will spend the summer at the Village Playhouse. Carmen sees herself as a stagehand but is dragged into an audition by a talented British actor named Ian (Tom Wisdom) and amazingly gets the female lead in *A Winter's Tale*. Not so amazingly, she falls in love with Ian, and the jealous Julia tries to sabotage her happiness. Meanwhile, her remarried mother produces a baby brother for her.

Alexis Bledel plays Lena, spending the summer at the Rhode Island School of Design and still in love with the Greek guy she met in the previous picture. Amber Tamblyn is Tibby, possibly the most contentious video store clerk in history. She's going through a shaky period in her romance with Brian (Leonardo Nam). Blake Lively is Bridget, who goes on an archaeological dig in Turkey, adopts the supervising professor (Shohreh Aghdashloo) as a mother-figure, then flies home to seek out her grandmother (Blythe Danner) and learn for the first time the details of her own mother's death. It's worth noticing that all four heroines are involved in relationships that are cross-cultural and/or interracial.

The movie intercuts quickly but not confusingly from one story to another, is dripping with seductive locations, is not shy about romantic clichés, and has a lot of heart. These women are all sincere, intelligent, vulnerable, sweet, warm. That's in contrast to *SATC* with its narcissistic and shallow heroines. The *SATC* ladies should fill their flasks with Cosmopolitans, go to see *The Sisterhood of the Traveling Pants 2*, and cry their hearts out with futile regret for their misspent lives.

Because the four leads spend the summer in different places, the movie has an excuse to drop in interesting supporting characters. Blythe Danner is splendid as the Alabama grandmother who knows the whole story of Bridget's mom. Leonardo Nam is a kind and perceptive boyfriend for Lena, Shohreh Aghdashloo (*The House of Sand and Fog*) is a role model for Bridget, Kyle MacLachlan has fun as the wine-sipping director of the summer playhouse, Tom Wisdom does a lot with the small role of the playhouse star. And Rachel Nichols as Julia proves a principle that should be in the Little Movie Glossary: If a short, curvy, sun-kissed heroine has a tall, thin blonde as a roommate, that blonde is destined to be a bitch. No way around it.

As for the pants themselves, they've gathered a lot of patches and embroideries over the three years since the last installment, and they still fit. But not so much is made about them in this film, and by the end they've disappeared, sparing us *The Sisterhood of the Traveling Pants 3* and *The Sisterhood of the Traveling Pants 4*. The movies are inspired by the novels of Ann Brashares, but this one, I learn, combines plot details from novels 2, 3, and 4, and so the sisters can go their separate ways, no doubt keeping in touch by e-mail and congratulating themselves on being infinitely better than the Ya-Ya Sisterhood.

Sita Sings the Blues ★ ★ ★ ★
NO MPAA RATING, 82 m., 2009

Directed, written, and produced by Nina Paley.

I got a DVD in the mail, an animated film titled *Sita Sings the Blues*. It was a version of the epic Indian tale of Ramayana set to the 1920s jazz vocals of Annette Hanshaw. Uh, huh. I carefully filed it with other movies I will watch when they introduce the eight-day week. Then I was told I *must* see it.

I began. I was enchanted. I was swept away. I was smiling from one end of the film to the other. It is astonishingly original. It brings together four entirely separate elements and combines them into a great whimsical chord. How did Paley's mind work?

She begins with the story of Ramayana, which is known to every schoolchild in India but not to me. It tells of a brave, noble woman who was made to suffer because of the foibles of an impetuous husband and his mother. Paley depicts this story with exuberant drawings in bright colors. It is about a prince named Rama who treated Sita unfairly, although she loved him and was faithful to him. There is more to it than that, involving a monkey army, a lustful king who occasionally grows ten heads, synchronized birds, a chorus line of gurus, and a tap-dancing moon.

It coils around and around, as Indian epic tales are known to do. Even the Indians can't always figure them out. In addition to her characters talking, Paley adds a hilarious level of narration: Three voice-over modern Indians, Desis, ad-libbing as they try to get the story straight. Was Sita wearing jewelry or not? How long was she a prisoner in exile? How did the rescue monkey come into the picture? These voices are as funny as an *SNL* skit, and the Indian accent gives them charm: "What a challenge, these stories!"

Sita, the heroine, reminds me a little of the immortal Betty Boop, but her singing voice is sexier. Paley synchs her life story and singing and dancing with recordings of the American jazz singer Annette Hanshaw (1901–1985), a big star in the 1920s and 1930s who was known as "the Personality Girl." Sita lived around 1000 BCE, a date that inspires lively debate

491

among the three Indians discussing her. When her husband outrageously accuses her of adultery and kicks her on top of a flaming pyre, we know exactly how she feels when Annette Hanshaw sings her big hit, "Mean to Me."

There is a parallel story. In San Francisco, we meet an American couple, young and in love, named Dave and Nina, and their cat, named Lexi. Oh, they are in love. But Dave flies off to take a "temporary" job in India, Nina pines for him, she flies to join him in India, but he is cold to her, and when she returns home she receives a cruel message: "Don't come back. Love, Dave." Nina despairs. Lexi despairs. Cockroaches fill her apartment but she hardly notices. One day in her deepest gloom she picks up the book *Ramayana* and starts to read. Inspiration begins to warm the cold embers of her heart.

There are uncanny parallels between her life and Sita's. Both were betrayed by the men they loved. Both were separated by long journeys. Both died (Sita really, Nina symbolically) and were reborn—Sita in the form of a lotus flower, Nina in the form of an outraged woman who moves to Brooklyn, sits down at her home computer for five years, and creates this film. Yes, she reveals in her bio that her then-husband "terminated" their marriage while he was in India. No ex-husband has inspired a greater cultural contribution since Michael Huffington.

One remarkable thing about *Sita Sings the Blues* is how versatile the animation is. Consider Sita's curvaceous southern hemisphere. When she sings an upbeat or sexy song, it rotates like a seductive pendulum. Look at those synchronized birds overhead. When they return they have a surprise, and they get a surprise. Regard the marching graybeards. Watch Hanuman's dragging tail set a palace on fire.

The animation style of the scenes set in San Francisco and Brooklyn is completely different, essentially simple line drawings alive with personality. See how Paley needs only a few lines to create a convincing cat. Paley works entirely in 2-D with strict rules, so that characters remain within their own plane, which overlaps with others. This sounds like a limitation. Actually, it becomes

the source of much amusement. Comedy often depends on the device of establishing unbreakable rules and then finding ways to break them. The laughs Paley gets here with 2-D would be the envy of an animator in 3-D. She discovers dimensions where none exist. This is one of the year's best films.

Sixty Six ★ ★ ★
PG-13, 94 m., 2008

Helena Bonham Carter (Esther Rubens), Eddie Marsan (Manny Rubens), Gregg Sulkin (Bernie Rubens), Peter Serafinowicz (Uncle Jimmy), Catherine Tate (Aunt Lila), Ben Newton (Alvie Rubens), Richard Katz (Rabbi Linov), Stephen Rea (Dr. Barrie). Directed by Paul Weiland and produced by Tim Bevan, Eric Fellner, and Elizabeth Karlsen. Screenplay by Peter Straughan and Bridget O'Connor.

The year 1966, as few Americans can be expected to know, is the year England won the World Cup. It is also the year that twelve-year-old Bernie Rubens is going to be celebrating his bar mitzvah in London. This will be an event lasting two days, his blind rabbi tells him. He will become a man, catch the eye of God, be showered with presents, and climax when he is the center of the universe at his own party. In what the director, Paul Weiland, calls "a tru-ish story" based on his own life, Bernie has the rotten luck to select for his party July 30, 1966, the day England won the World Cup.

Of course, England has no chance to get into the finals, right? They're like the Cubs. But in 1966, against all odds, England somehow did win the final game, and as for the Cubs, who knows? Bernie is placed in the peculiar position of being the only person in the nation who hopes England loses. Devout Jew that he is, he sneaks in a book of heathen chants and spells and evokes demon spirits against the national team.

Sixty Six is a warmhearted story about a boy coming of age in a particularly tragic way: Who in the world would rather come to his party than watch the final match on the telly? Bernie is crushed. He has always been the underdog, the last to be picked, the one with glasses, the butt of jokes by his brother Alvie.

Before he discovers the fateful date coincidence, he maps out his party: a formal dinner for 350, a full orchestra. He even invites Frankie Vaughan to sing (for free, I think), and writes to the famous criminals the Kray brothers for their assistance. Then bad luck steps in. His father, Manny (Eddie Marsan), and Uncle Jimmy (Peter Serafinowicz) are forced to sell their grocery store when a supermarket opens next door. A fireworks rocket set off after an England victory starts a fire in the Rubenses' attic and burns up his dad's life savings. The party has to be scaled way back, held at home, and catered by his aunt, who makes a canapé they cannot identify as potato, chicken, or fish.

Yes, the movie is predictable. England will play in the final game, and the party will be far from Bernie's dreams. But Weiland somehow extracts the real meaning of a bar mitzvah from the wreckage. Central to the whole story is the love of Bernie's mother, Esther (Helena Bonham Carter, surprising us by seeming born to the role). She encourages her hangdog husband during a series of setbacks. She puts a good face on things. And she unveils an astonishing vocabulary as one family friend after another telephones with a bogus excuse for not being able to attend.

The story line sounds plain and simple, but the movie is enlightened by Bernie's impassioned narration and by a gallery of small comic details. While Manny is a morose loser, for example, his brother Jimmy is a popular back-slapper and specialist in Jewish humor. Example: "Ask me how I am." "How are you?" "Don't ask!" The blind rabbi (Richard Katz) excels at answering Bernie's questions about God's position on the World Cup ("I don't think it's covered in the Old Testament"). And Stephen Rea, as Bernie's asthma doctor, has a nice scene where he and Bernie puff through straws at a tabletop soccer ball, and their game is intercut with a real one.

Sixty Six isn't a great movie, but it's confident of its material and lucky in its casting. Eddie Marsan, for example, has more ways of looking discontented than most repertory companies. One question: Bernie is a bright kid. Why doesn't he shift the date of his party?

Skin ★★★★
PG -13, 107 m., 2009

Sophie Okonedo (Sandra Laing), Sam Neill (Abraham Laing), Alice Krige (Sannie Laing), Tony Kgoroge (Petrus Zwane), Ella Ramangwane (Young Sandra), Faniswa Yisa (Nora Molefe), Hannes Brummer (Leon Laing). Directed by Anthony Fabian and produced by Fabian, Genevieve Hofmeyr, and Margaret Matheson. Screenplay by Helen Crawley, Jessie Keyt, and Helena Kriel.

I remember the story of Sandra Laing. I lived in Cape Town in 1965, the year this film begins, and it was all over the South African newspapers. Sandra (Ella Ramangwane as a child) was the daughter of white Afrikaners, the descendants of the original Dutch settlers. There was no question they were her parents. She didn't look white. They cherished her and were proud of her. She was bright as a button. They enrolled her in school, and there was trouble. The white parents didn't want their children going to school with a black girl.

Given the insanity of the apartheid system, it was unthinkable that white parents could have a black child. Her parents reassure her: Of course she's white. They run a little shop with a black clientele, but that doesn't make them liberal. When Sannie Laing (Alice Krige) gets too friendly with the customers, her husband, Abraham (Sam Neill), tells her, "Be friendly with them, but don't adopt them!"

He's outraged by any suggestion of African blood in his family. Sandra looks "coloured" to the people white and black who see her, but not to her parents. He fights all the way to the Supreme Court to have Sandra officially classified as white. Among his witnesses is a geneticist from Witwatersrand University in Johannesburg who testifies, "many and perhaps most Afrikaners have some non-white blood."

This was a *very* touchy subject in South Africa. I was aware of an Afrikaner student who hit another student when he was offered a pencil. That was an unmistakable reference to the infamous "pencil test": Stick a pencil through your hair and shake your head. The pencil will usually fall out of white hair, but not from black.

From being a cheerful child, Sandra grows

into a troubled adolescent (Sophie Okonedo) who tries to bleach her skin. Her parents set up two disastrous dates with white boys. She falls in love with Petrus (Tony Kgoroge), a young black gardener, and her father chases him away with a rifle. Pregnant, she runs away from home, but now it is a crime for her to live with a black man.

The story of Sandra Laing (her real name) played out into the 1970s and fascinated South Africa like no other. It cut directly into the official fiction that the races were separate and would never meet. She was proof they'd been meeting a lot in the four hundred years since the Dutch landed at Cape Town.

Sophie Okonedo you may remember from *Hotel Rwanda* in 2004, which won her an Oscar nomination. Born in London of a white mother and African father (which is very relevant here), she was in *Dirty Pretty Things* (2002) and *The Secret Life of Bees* (2008)—remember the childlike May Boatwright?—and has completed playing the title role in *Mrs. Mandela*. Here she's magnificent, convincingly spanning Sandra's ages from sixteen into adulthood, and her buffeting by a society where race dictated who you could love, where you could live, how you could work, whether you could study, and who society thought you were. Consider how she handles a scene where she applies to the same clerk who issued her a "white card" and now demands a "black card." Her very existence reveals her society is based on no more than a piece of paper.

This great film by Anthony Fabian tells this story through the eyes of a happy girl who grows into an outsider. This isn't one of those potted stories of uplift and doesn't end quite the way we expect, although we do get to see the real Sandra Laing right at the end. It's not giving away anything to say the film's first scene takes place on the day South Africa elected Nelson Mandela as its first African president. Sandra is cornered by a TV crew that asks for her reaction. She says, "It comes too late for me."

Slumdog Millionaire ★ ★ ★ ★
R, 116 m., 2008

Dev Patel (Jamal Malik), Freida Pinto (Latika), Madhur Mittal (Salim Malik), Anil Kapoor (Prem), Irrfan Khan (Inspector). Directed by Danny Boyle and produced by Christian Colson. Screenplay by Simon Beaufoy, based on the novel *Q&A* by Vikas Swarup.

Danny Boyle's *Slumdog Millionaire* hits the ground running. This is a breathless, exciting story, somehow heartbreaking and exhilarating at the same time, about a Mumbai orphan who rises from literal rags to literal riches, all on the strength of his lively intelligence. So universal is the film's appeal that it will present a portrait of the real India to millions of moviegoers for the first time.

The real India, supercharged with a plot as reliable and eternal as the hills. The film's surface is so dazzling that you hardly realize how traditional it is underneath. But it's the buried structure that pulls us through the story like a big engine on a short train.

By the real India, I don't mean an unblinking documentary like Louis Malle's *Calcutta* or the recent documentary *Born Into Brothels*. I mean the real India of social levels that seem to be separated by centuries. What do many people think of when they think of India? On the one hand, Mother Teresa, *Salaam Bombay!* and the wretched of the earth. On the other, the Masterpiece Theater–style images of *A Passage to India*, *Gandhi*, and *The Jewel in the Crown*.

The India of Mother Teresa still very much exists. Because it is side by side with the new India, it is easily seen. People living in the streets. A woman crawling from a cardboard box and adjusting her sari. Men bathing themselves at a fire hydrant. Men relieving themselves at the roadside (you never see women doing that—where do they go?). You stand on one side of the Hooghly River, a branch of the Ganges that runs through Kolkata, and your friend tells you, "On the other bank millions of people live without a single sewer line."

On the other hand, the world's largest middle class, mostly lower-middle, but all the more admirable. The India of *Monsoon Wedding*. Millionaires. Mercedes Benzes and Audis. Traffic like Demo Derby. Luxurious condos. Comfortable suburbs. Exploding education. A computer segment that supplies the world with programming, researchers, and educators. A fountain of medical professionals. So much of the most exciting modern English literature. A Bollywood to rival Hollywood.

Slumdog Millionaire bridges these two Indias by cutting between a world of poverty and the Indian version of *Who Wants to Be a Millionaire*. It tells the story of an orphan from the slums of Mumbai who is born into a brutal early existence. A petty thief, impostor, and survivor, mired in the most dire poverty, he improvises his way up through the world and remembers everything he has learned.

His name is Jamal (played as a teenager by Dev Patel). He is Oliver Twist. High-spirited and defiant in the worst of times, he survives. For example, he scrapes out a living at the Taj Mahal, which he did not know about but discovers by being thrown off a train. How? He pretends to be a guide, invents *facts* out of thin air, advises tourists to remove their shoes, and then steals them. He eventually finds a bit part in the Mumbai underworld and even falls in idealized romantic love, that most elusive of conditions for a slumdog.

His life until about the age of twenty is told in flashbacks intercut with his appearance as a contestant on the quiz show. Pitched as a slumdog, he supplies the correct answers to question after question and becomes a national hero as the suspense builds. The flashbacks show why he knows the answers. He doesn't volunteer this information. It is beaten out of him by the show's security staff as he stands poised on the eve of winning the top prize. They are sure he must be cheating.

The film uses dazzling cinematography, breathless editing, driving music, and headlong momentum to explode with narrative force, somehow stirring in a romance at the same time. For Danny Boyle, it is a personal triumph. If you have seen some of his earlier films (*Shallow Grave, Trainspotting, 28 Days Later,* the lovable *Millions*), you know he's a natural. Here he combines the suspense of a game show with the vision and raw energy of *City of God* and never stops sprinting.

When I saw *Slumdog Millionaire* at Toronto, I was witnessing a phenomenon: dramatic proof that a movie is about how it tells itself. I walked out of the theater on the second day of the festival and flatly predicted it would win the Audience Award. Seven days later, it did.

And that it was a definite possibility for an Oscar best picture nomination. We will see. It is one of those miraculous entertainments that achieves its immediate goals and keeps climbing toward a higher summit.

Solitary Man ★★★ ½
R, 90 m., 2010

Michael Douglas (Ben Kalmen), Mary-Louise Parker (Jordan Karsch), Jenna Fischer (Susan Porter), Jesse Eisenberg (Cheston), Imogen Poots (Allyson Karsch), Susan Sarandon (Nancy Kalmen), Danny DeVito (Jimmy Merino). Directed by Brian Koppelman and David Levien and produced by Heidi Jo Markel, Paul Schiff, and Steven Soderbergh. Screenplay by Koppelman.

For an actor with so many films, Michael Douglas hasn't played many conventional heroes. Yes, he did those *Romancing the Stone* roles, and he's been more memorable as a villain (*Wall Street*), but his strongest roles are as sinners: not big or bad enough to be villains, more ordinary men, smart, glib, conniving, trying to get by on short dues. Here is where he best uses his considerable screen presence. And he gets better at it as he grows older because his characters keep on sinning when they just don't have the stamina for it anymore.

In *Solitary Man,* he plays Ben Kalmen, once a regional celebrity as "New York's Honest Car Dealer." Ben is good-looking, still has that great head of hair, and is as persuasive as—well, as a good car dealer. In business he can sense what car to put you in. In sex he can sense what mood to put you in. He closes a lot of deals.

He isn't solitary by choice but by default. He cheated on his good wife, Nancy (Susan Sarandon). He disappointed their daughter, Susan (Jenna Fischer), one time too many. He cheats on his current companion, Jordan (Mary-Louise Parker), in a particularly unforgivable way. He uses the offer of his experience in life to charm Cheston (Jesse Eisenberg), a college student, and then betrays him. He has lied to his customers so often that, as everyone knows, "Honest Ben Kalmen" spent time behind bars.

495

Yet he's charming and persuasive. He looks like a winner until you look too close. *Solitary Man* follows him for several days after he agrees to accompany Jordan's daughter, Allyson (Imogen Poots), as she goes to Boston to settle in for her freshman year at college. This is the same school he attended. He knows the dean, which may be a help.

You want to like Ben. He works on encouraging that. When he was younger and less of a sinner, he must have been good to know, and there's an effective character in *Solitary Man* who suggests that. This is his old school-years buddy (Danny DeVito) who still runs a greasy spoon diner. On campus, Ben befriends the sophomore Cheston with man-of-the-world advice about sex, success, and how to sell yourself. With women, his approach is solicitous: Do some men misunderstand you? Are your qualities recognized? What are you getting out of the transaction?

The film is all about Ben Kalmen, but one of the strengths of Michael Douglas's performance is that he isn't playing a character. He's playing a character who is playing a character. Ben's life has become performance art. You get the feeling he never goes offstage. He sees few women he doesn't try seducing. As a car dealer, he was also in the seduction trade. His business was selling himself. At a dealership, it's hard to move a lemon. What about in life when you need a recall?

What happens with Ben and the people in his life, especially the women, I should not hint at here. The movie depends on our fascination as we see what lengths this man will go to. Reading in the gossip sheets that Douglas in years past was led astray by lust, we suspect that some of his performance is based on experience. Why is a man a serial seducer? To prove to himself that he can, which to a woman is not a compelling reason to be seduced.

This is a smart, effective film, a comedy in many ways even though it's bookended with reasons for Ben to see it as a potential tragedy. It's a serious comedy, perceptive, nuanced, with every supporting performance well calibrated to demonstrate to Ben that he can run but he can no longer hide. One of the best is by DeVito, who has been standing behind his counter for years and is perfectly content. He doesn't have that hunger that gnaws at Ben.

Imogen Poots is good, too, as the girl going away to school. She could sell Honest Ben the Brooklyn Bridge, and he would think he was talking her into it. As the trip upstate begins to fall apart, so does Ben's shaky financial future, and he has a meeting with a banker (Richard Schiff) that plays out with relentless logic.

Here is one of Michael Douglas's finest performances. Because the other characters, no matter what they think, never truly engage Ben Kalmen, he's on that stage by himself. Everyone else is in the audience. Douglas plays Ben as charismatic, he plays him as shameless, he plays him as brave, and very gradually, he learns to play him as himself. That's the only role left.

The Soloist ★ ★ ½
PG-13, 117 m., 2009

Jamie Foxx (Nathaniel Ayers), Robert Downey Jr. (Steve Lopez), Catherine Keener (Mary Weston), Tom Hollander (Graham Claydon), Lisa Gay Hamilton (Jennifer Ayers-Moore). Directed by Joe Wright and produced by Gary Foster and Russ Krasnoff. Screenplay by Susannah Grant, based on the book by Steve Lopez.

The Soloist has all the elements of an uplifting drama, except for the uplift. The story is compelling, the actors are in place, but I was never sure what the filmmakers wanted me to feel about it. Based on a true story, it stars Jamie Foxx as Nathaniel Ayers, a homeless man who was once a musical prodigy, and Robert Downey Jr. as Steve Lopez, the *Los Angeles Times* columnist who writes about him, bonds with him, makes him famous, becomes discouraged by the man's mental illness, and—what? Hears him play great music?

"Explaining madness is the most limiting and generally least convincing thing a movie can do," Pauline Kael once wrote. *The Soloist* doesn't even seem sure how to depict it. Unlike Russell Crowe's mathematician in *A Beautiful Mind,* whose madness was understood through his own eyes, the musician here seems more of a loose cannon, unpredictable in random ways. Yes, mental illness can be like that, but can successful drama? There comes a point when Lopez has had enough, and so, in sympathy, have we.

That is no fault of Jamie Foxx's performance creating a man who is tense, fearful, paranoid, and probably schizophrenic. We can almost smell his terror, through the carnival clown clothing and hats he hides behind. When Foxx learned of this role, he might reasonably have sensed another Academy Award. Unfortunately, the screenwriter and director don't set up a structure for Oscar-style elevation, nor do they really want to make a serious and doleful film about mental illness. But those are the two apparent possibilities here, and *The Soloist* seems lost between them.

As the film opens, Lopez is troubled. His marriage has problems, he feels burned out at work, he's had a bike accident. He encounters Ayers almost outside the *Times* building, attracted by the beautiful sounds he's producing on a violin with only two strings. The man can play. Lopez tries to get to know him, writes a first column about him, learns he once studied cello at Juilliard. A reader sends Lopez a cello for him (this actually happened), and the columnist becomes his brother's keeper.

This is a thankless and possibly futile task. *The Soloist* does a very effective job of showing us a rehab center on Skid Row, and the reason so many homeless avoid such shelters. It's not what happens inside, but the gauntlet of street people necessary to run just to get to its doors. Indifference about adequate care for our homeless population was one of the priorities of the Selfish Generation.

As a mentally ill man, Ayers is unpredictable and explosive, yes, but almost as if responding to the arc of the screenplay. Characters have arcs in most movies, but the trick is to convince us we're watching them really behave. Here Foxx is let down, and the disappointment is greater because of the track records of director Joe Wright (*Atonement*) and writer Susannah Grant (*Erin Brockovich*). We see a connection between the two men, but not communication.

As a newspaper columnist, Downey is plausible as his overworked, disillusioned character, finding redemption through a story. And Catherine Keener, like Helen Mirren in *State of Play,* convinces me she might really be an editor. Both actresses bring a welcome change of pace from the standard Lou Grant type. Talk about disillusionment; the old-timers can't be-

lieve their eyes these days. The *Los Angeles Times* of this movie is at least still prospering.

As for the music, Beethoven of course is always uplifting, but the movie doesn't employ him as an emotional show-stopper, as Debussy's "Clair de Lune" is used in *Tokyo Sonata.* There's no clear idea of what it would mean should Ayers triumph in a public debut; would it be a life-changing moment or only an anomaly on his tragic road through life? Can he be salvaged? Does he want to be? Or will he always be a soloist, playing to his demons in the darkness under a bridge?

Son of Rambow ★ ★ ★
PG-13, 96 m., 2008

Bill Milner (Will Proudfoot), Will Poulter (Lee Carter), Jessica Stevenson (Mary), Neil Dudgeon (Brother Joshua), Jules Sitruk (Didier Revol), Ed Westwick (Laurence Carter), Anna Wing (Grandmother). Directed by Garth Jennings and produced by Nick Goldsmith. Screenplay by Jennings.

The two friends in *Son of Rambow* hang out in a backyard shack that rewards close study. It's made of rough lumber, hammered together into not quite parallel lines; it's out of plumb. It could be drawn, but not easily built. Since the eleven-year-old hero, Will Proudfoot (Bill Milner) is himself a cartoonist and sketch artist, his inventions seem to be seeping into his life. He leads an existence that's strictly limited by his family's religious sect, making him a vacuum for fantasy and escapism, and when his friend Lee Carter (Will Poulter) shows him a pirated copy of *First Blood,* the adventures of Rambo ignite him like fireworks whose time have come.

Set in an English village in the early 1980s, *Son of Rambow* is a gentle story that involves a great deal of violence, but mostly the violence is muted and dreamy, like a confrontation with a fearsome scarecrow that looks horrifying but is obviously not real—or real enough, but not alive. The two boys meet one day in the corridor outside their grade school classroom. Will has been sent there because his religion forbids him to watch TV, even educational videos (it also forbids music, dancing, and so on). Lee has been booted out of his classroom, spots

Will, and immediately beans him with a hard-thrown tennis ball. This is the beginning of a strange but lasting friendship.

Lee takes Will into his garage, which looks like a toolkit for inventive kids. A rowboat hangs suspended from the ceiling, and there's equipment for pumping out videotape copies of the movies that Lee pirates at the local cinema, while puffing somewhat uncertainly on a filter-tip (yes, you could smoke in the movies in England in those days).

Electrified by his introduction to Rambo, Will joins Lee in making their own home video remake of the film. This involves Will enacting literally death-defying stunts: He's catapulted high into the air, for example, and swings on a rope to drop into a lake, neglecting to tell Lee he can't swim. The special effects are cobbled together from household items, purloined booty, and Will's sketches and flip-book animation.

All is not well at home, where Will lives with his mom (Jessica Stevenson), a sister, and his drooling grandma (Anna Wing). There's an unwelcome visitor in the house most of the time, Brother Joshua (the perfectly named Neil Dudgeon), who covets the role of Will's absent father and enjoys being stern and forbidding to the lad. The intimacy of his relationship with the mother seems limited mostly to significant nods when he says goodbye at the end of the evening.

Will and Lee find their world unsettled when a busload of French exchange students descends on their school, and Didier (Jules Sitruk) captures their admiration. Taller and older, he takes charge of their indie production and their lives. Meanwhile, their stunt work escalates: They steal a life-sized dog from the Guide Dogs for the Blind people, hook it to a parasail, and inadvertently set off fire alarms at their school. And a runaway Jeep causes a load of scrap metal to fall on Will and Lee, with surprisingly limited results.

All of this takes place in a pastoral countryside and a benign city, where the boys move more or less invisibly. They're not simply growing up, but expanding: their horizons, their imaginations, their genius for troublemaking. Since it is made clear at the start that little fatal or tragic is likely to happen, the movie becomes like a fable—maybe too fabulous for its own

good. The plot unspools with nothing really urgent at stake, the boys live in innocence and invulnerability, and the settings and action have a way of softening the characters.

I liked *Son of Rambow* in a benign sort of way, but I was left wanting something more. Drama, maybe? No, that would simply be manufactured. Comedy? It is technically a comedy, although the limited laughs are incredulous. Fantasy? That it is, in a bittersweet way. After the movie, I imagined its writer-director, Garth Jennings (*The Hitchhiker's Guide to the Galaxy*), being more than a little like Will, and the movie uncannily similar to one of Will's comic epics.

Soul Men ★ ★ ★
R, 103 m., 2008

Samuel L. Jackson (Louis Hinds), Bernie Mac (Floyd Henderson), Sharon Leal (Cleo Whitfield), Adam Herschman (Phillip Newman), Sean Hayes (Danny Epstein), Affion Crocket (Lester), Jennifer Coolidge (Rosalee), Isaac Hayes (Himself), John Legend (Marcus Hooks). Directed by Malcolm D. Lee and produced by Charles Castaldi, David T. Friendly, and Steve Greener. Screenplay by Robert Ramsey and Matthew Stone.

Soul Men is the one that's really going to make you miss Bernie Mac. He's so filled with life and energy here that it's hard to believe . . . well, anyway. It will make you miss him. He found his comfort zone in mainstream comedies, of which I have liked nine of twelve. When an edgy director like Terry Zwigoff came into the picture with *Bad Santa* (2003), he allowed Bernie Mac a little more depth.

In *Soul Men*, there are scenes that hint at what he might have done in a dramatic role. It's a formula comedy, but there are real feelings here that we suspect would exist in this troubled struggle between musicians who haven't played together in twenty years. In the end credits, there are generous tributes to Bernie Mac and Isaac Hayes, also in the film, both gone from us within two days last August. Bernie gets the last, touching word. And you know, even if I mentioned a possible heavy dramatic role, I never felt he was a comedian with a sad man inside. In the credit cookies, he talks about his good luck while thanking a theater audience (of extras) for his career, and we believe him. He seems like a comedian with a happy man inside.

Anyway, years ago Louis (Samuel L. Jackson), Floyd (Bernie Mac), and Marcus (John Legend) were a trio of big-time musicians. But Marcus split for superstardom, and the other two took separate paths to relative anonymity. Now Marcus has died, and Floyd and Louis are desperately needed to appear in a memorial concert at the Apollo in Harlem. They're not even speaking to each other. Fight over a woman.

For the money, Louis agrees to join Floyd in a cross-country road trip to New York. That's the formula: two incompatible guys, long trip, one car. *Planes, Trains and Automobiles*, etc. It's Floyd's car. An El Dorado convertible. But of course it is. Ever notice how often cross-country road trips in the movies involve classic convertibles? Two reasons: The rag top makes it easier for the camera to see them, and recent cars don't look like cars.

In the 1950s, kids used to stand on the corner and spot cars approaching from one or two blocks away. First kid to ID one scored a point. Chevy. Dodge. Chrysler Imperial. Studebaker. Ford. That far away and they could even ID the model: Rocket 88. Fairlane. Golden Hawk. To kids today from a block away, unless it's a Hummer, all cars look the same. Camry. Camry. Camry. Fifty years from now, movie characters will be crossing the country in one-hundred-year-old cars.

Floyd and Louis rehash all their old differences and encounter some remarkably friendly women (including Jennifer Coolidge, Stifler's mom). They have adventures. The beloved Caddy, with absolute inevitability, is damaged. Their spirits lift, and they do one of their old routines. The trio is re-formed by adding a young singer, Cleo (Sharon Leal), who may have more to do with the trio's history than anybody realizes. At the Apollo, the reunion with Marcus and their big stage entrance are interestingly linked.

This movie has a lot of good music in it, some on the sound track, some on the screen. Jackson and Bernie Mac have enormous fun doing intricate dance moves together. Isaac Hayes has a farewell role worthy of our memories. Of the actors, only John Legend is a lit-

tle stiff, although he goes through a timeline of costumes and hairstyles in the flashbacks. You want a good time? *Soul Men* will provide it. You want to say good-bye to Bernie Mac? He wants to say good-bye to you.

Space Chimps ★ ★ ★
G, 80 m., 2008

With the voices of: Andy Samberg (Ham III), Cheryl Hines (Luna), Omid Abtahi (Titan Jagu), Jeff Daniels (Zartog), Kristin Chenoweth (Kilowatt), Stanley Tucci (Senator). Directed by Kirk De Micco and produced by Barry Sonnenfeld and John H. Williams. Screenplay by De Micco and Robert Moreland.

Space Chimps is delightful from beginning to end: a goofy space opera that sends three U.S. chimptronauts rocketing to a galaxy, as they say, far, far away. Although it's aimed at a younger market and isn't in the same science fiction league as *WALL-E*, it's successful at what it wants to do: take us to an alien planet and present us with a large assortment of bugeyed monsters, not to mention a little charmer nicknamed Kilowatt who lights up when she gets excited, or afraid, or just about anything else.

The story starts with the circus career of the chimp Ham III (voice by Andy Samberg), the grandson of the first chimp launched by NASA into space (and, yes, that first chimp really was named Ham). Ham III works at being shot out of a cannon and never quite landing where he should. Once, when he goes really high, he considers the beauty of the moon and outer space, and has a *Right Stuff* moment, of which there are several. He feels keenly that he hasn't lived up to the family tradition.

Meanwhile, the U.S. space program faces a crisis. One of its deep space probes has disappeared into a wormhole. It is perhaps a measure of the sophistication of younger audiences that no attempt is made to explain what a wormhole is. Perhaps that's because wormholes are only conjecture anyway, and if you can't say there is one, how can you say what it is?

What with one thing and another, Ham III finds himself enlisted in the crew of a space flight to follow the probe into the wormhole and see what happened to it. Joining the mission is a big chimp named Titan (Patrick Warburton) and the cute (in chimp terms) Luna (Cheryl Hines). Hurtling through what looks like a dime-store version of the sound-and-light fantasy in *2001*, they land on a planet where the local creatures are ruled by a big, ugly tyrant named Zartog (Jeff Daniels).

He has commandeered the original NASA probe and uses its extendable arms to punish his enemies by dipping them into a supercold bath so they freeze in an instant. This is a cruel fate, especially since the eyeballs of his victims continue to roll, which means they must be alive inside their frozen shells, which implies peculiarities about their metabolism.

The chimps, of course, have lots of adventures, including being chased through a cave by a monster of many teeth and being rescued by the plucky Kilowatt, who eventually sees more of the monster than she really desires. Then there's a showdown with Zartog, some business about the planet's three suns (night lasts only five minutes), and a most ingenious way to blast off again.

On Earth, there's an unnecessary subplot about an evil senator (Stanley Tucci) who wants to disband the space program and replace it with something you really have to hear to believe. On second thought, maybe the subplot is necessary, just so we get to hear his idea.

I ponder strange things during movies like this. For example, there seem to be only five forms of life on the planet. Zartog is one, his obedient subjects are another, some flying creatures are a third, the toothy monster is the fourth, and Kilowatt is the fifth. I suppose a planet where evolution has produced only five species is possible. But what do they eat? The planet looks like Monument Valley, is covered with sand, and has no flora or fauna. Could they all be silicon-based? And since Zartog, the tooth monster, and Kilowatt each seem to be one of a kind, who do they mate with? Or do silicon beings need to mate? And have they invented the hourglass?

The Spiderwick Chronicles ★ ★ ★ ½
PG, 96 m., 2008

Freddie Highmore (Jared/Simon Grace), Mary-Louise Parker (Helen Grace), Nick Nolte

(Mulgarath), Joan Plowright (Aunt Lucinda), David Strathairn (Arthur Spiderwick), Seth Rogen (Hogsqueal), Martin Short (Thimbletack/Boggart), Sarah Bolger (Mallory Grace). Directed by Mark Waters and produced by Karey Kirkpatrick, Mark Canton, Larry Franco, and Ellen Goldsmith-Vein. Screenplay by Kirkpatrick, David Berenbaum, and John Sayles, based on the books by Tony DiTerlizzi and Holly Black.

The Spiderwick Chronicles is a terrific entertainment for the whole family, except those below a certain age, who are likely to be scared out of their wits. What is that age? I dunno; they're your kids. But I do know the PG classification is insane, especially considering what happens right after a father says he loves his son. This is a PG-13 movie for sure. But what will cause nightmares for younger kids will delight older ones, since here is a well-crafted family thriller that is truly scary and doesn't wimp out.

Based on a well-known series of five books, the movie involves a soon-to-be divorced mom and her three children who come to live in a creepy old mansion. This is Spiderwick, named after her great-uncle, Arthur Spiderwick, who disappeared under mysterious circumstances. The house itself is one of the stars of the movie, looking Victorian Gothic with countless nooks and crannies and shadows and scary sounds. Is it haunted? Nothing that comforting. It's . . . inhabited.

The mother is Helen Grace (Mary-Louise Parker), who is battling with the rebellious Jared (Freddie Highmore), one of her twin sons. He doesn't like being away from his dad, is homesick, doesn't want anything to do with this dusty and spiderwebby old ruin that was left to his mom by her aunt. Jared's brainy twin, Simon, looks remarkably identical, no doubt because he is also played by Freddie Highmore, born 1992, a gifted young actor best known for *Finding Neverland, August Rush*, and *The Golden Compass*. The twins' sister is the plucky Mallory (Sarah Bolger), a fencer who seldom goes anywhere without her sword, which is just as well in this movie. You may remember how good she was in *In America* (2002).

Jared is the kind of kid who is always getting blamed for everything. When stuff starts disappearing, for example, he gets the rap. When he hears noises in the wall and punches holes in it, he's being destructive. But he's brave, and when he finds a hidden dumbwaiter, he hauls himself up to a hidden room—his grandfather's study, left undisturbed after all these years. This room fairly reeks of forbidden secrets.

Don't read further unless you already know, as the Web site makes abundantly clear, that he finds a "field guide" to the unseen world left by his great-great-uncle (David Strathairn), and that with its help and a Seeing Stone, Jared can see goblins, sprits, hobgoblins, ogres, trolls, and griffins, which themselves can take many shapes. Some of them are amusing, like Thimbletack (voice by Martin Short), some alarming, like Boggart (Short again), some helpful but undependable, like Hogsqueal (voice by Seth Rogen). And some of the newly visible creatures are truly alarming, like Mulgarath. The credits say his voice is by Nick Nolte, but I gotta say that all of Mulgarath looks a lot like the real Nick Nolte to me.

Anyway, Jared finally convinces his brother, and then his sister and mother, that what he reports is real, and then, after pages from the field guide get into Mulgarath's hands, the Circle of Protection around the house is threatened, and the Graces are faced with dire threats. This is all done with a free mixture of lighthearted action, heavy action, and some dramatic scenes that, as I said, are pretty heavy going for younger imaginations. The movie is distinguished by its acting, not least by the great Joan Plowright as old Aunt Lucinda. Strathairn is completely credible as a spirit-world investigator, although exactly where the sparkling points of light take him, and what he does there, is a little murky.

They say be careful what you ask for because you might get it. I've often hailed back to the really creepy moments in Disney classics, like what happens to Dumbo and Bambi and the witch in *Snow White,* and I've complained that recent family movies are too sanitized. This one, directed by Mark Waters (*The House of Yes, Freaky Friday*), doesn't skip a beat before its truly horrific moments, so if you're under eight or nine years old, don't say you weren't warned.

The Spirit ★
PG-13, 102 m., 2008

Gabriel Macht (The Spirit), Samuel L. Jackson (The Octopus), Eva Mendes (Sand Saref), Scarlett Johansson (Silken Floss), Jaime King (Lorelei), Sarah Paulson (Ellen), Dan Lauria (Commissioner Dolan), Paz Vega (Plaster of Paris). Directed by Frank Miller and produced by Deborah Del Prete, Gigi Pritzker, and Michael E. Uslan. Screenplay by Miller, based on the comic book series by Will Eisner.

The Spirit is mannered to the point of madness. There is not a trace of human emotion in it. To call the characters cardboard is to insult a useful packing material. The movie is all style—style without substance, style whirling in a senseless void. The film's hero is an ex-cop reincarnated as an immortal enforcer; for all the personality he exhibits, we would welcome Elmer Fudd.

The movie was written, directed, and fabricated largely on computers by Frank Miller, whose *300* and *Sin City* showed a similar elevation of the graphic novel into fantastical style shows. But they had characters, stories, a sense of fun. *The Spirit* is all setups and posing, muscles and cleavage, hats and ruby lips, nasty wounds and snarly dialogue, and males and females who relate to one another like participants in a blood oath.

The Spirit (Gabriel Macht) narrates his own story with all the introspection of a pro wrestler describing his packaging. The Octopus (Samuel L. Jackson) heroically overacts, devouring the scenery as if following instructions from Gladstone, the British prime minister who attributed his success to chewing each bite thirty-two times. The Spirit encounters a childhood girlfriend, Sand Saref (Eva Mendes), pronounced like the typographical attribute, who made good on her vow of blowing off Central City and making diamonds her best friend. The Octopus has an enigmatic collaborator named Silken Floss (Scarlett Johansson), pronounced like your dentist.

These people come and go in a dank, desolate city, where always it's winter and no one's in love and their duty is to engage in impossible combat with no outcome, because The

Octopus and The Spirit apparently cannot slay each other, for reasons we know (in a certainty approaching dread) will be explained with melodramatic, insane flashback. In one battle in a muddy pond, they pound each other with porcelain commodes and rusty anchors, and The Spirit hits The Octopus in the face as hard as he can twenty-one times. Then they get on with the movie.

The Octopus later finds it necessary to bind The Spirit to a chair so that his body can be sliced into butcher's cuts and mailed to far-off zip codes. To supervise this task, he stands in front of a swastika attired in full Nazi fetish-wear, whether because he is a Nazi or just likes to dress up, I am not sure. A monocle appears in his eye. Since he doesn't wear it in any other scene, I assume it is homage to Erich von Stroheim, who wasn't a Nazi but played one in the movies.

The objective of Sand Saref is to obtain a precious vial containing the blood of Heracles or Hercules; she alternates freely between the Greek and Roman names. This blood will confer immortality. Fat lot of good it did for Heracles or Hercules. Still, maybe there's something to it. At one point, The Spirit takes three bullets in the forehead, leans forward, and shakes them out. At another, he is skewered by a broadsword. "Why, oh why, do I never die?" he asks himself. And we ask it of him.

I know I will be pilloried if I dare end this review without mentioning the name of the artist who created the original comic books. I would hate for that to happen. Will Eisner.

Splice ★★★

R, 107 m., 2010

Adrien Brody (Clive Nicoli), Sarah Polley (Elsa Kast), Delphine Chaneac (Dren), Brandon McGibbon (Gavin Nicoli), Simona Maicanescu (Joan Chorot), David Hewlett (William Barlow), Abigail Chu (Child Dren). Directed by Vincenzo Natali and produced by Steven Hoban. Screenplay by Natali, Antoinette Terry Bryant, and Douglas Taylor.

Well-timed to open soon after Craig Venter's announcement of a self-replicating cell, here's a halfway serious science fiction movie about two researchers who slip some human DNA into a cloning experiment and end up with an unexpected outcome, or a child, or a monster, take your pick. The screenplay blends human psychology with scientific speculation and has genuine interest until it goes on autopilot with one of the chase scenes Hollywood now permits few pictures to end without.

In the laboratory of a genetic science corporation, we meet Clive and Elsa (Adrien Brody and Sarah Polley), partners at work and in romance, who are trying to create a hybrid animal gene that would, I dunno, maybe provide protein while sidestepping the nuisance of having it be an animal first. Against all odds, their experiment works. They want to push ahead, but the corporation has funded quite enough research for the time being, and can't wait to bring the "product" to market.

Elsa rebels and slips some human DNA into their lab work. What results is a new form of life, part animal, part human, looking at first like a rounded SpongeBob and then later like a cute kid on Pandora, but shorter and not blue. This creature grows at an astonishing rate, gets smart in a hurry, and is soon spelling out words on a Scrabble board without apparently having paused at the intermediate steps of learning to read and write. Clive thinks they should terminate it. Elsa says no. As the blob grows more humanoid, they become its default parents, and she names it Dren, which is nerd spelled backward, so don't name your kid that.

Dren has a tail and wings of unspecific animal origin, and hands with three fingers, suggesting a few sloth genes, although Dren is hyperactive. She has the ability common to small monkeys and CGI effects of being able to leap at dizzying speeds around a room. She's sweet when she gets a dolly to play with, but don't get her frustrated.

The researchers keep Dren a secret, both because they ignored orders by creating her, and because, although Elsa wanted no children, they begin to feel like her parents. This feeling doesn't extend so far as to allow her to live with them in the house. They lock her into the barn, which seems harsh treatment for the most important achievement of modern biological science.

Dren is all special effects in early scenes,

and then quickly grows into a form played by Abigail Chu when small and Delphine Chaneac when larger. She also evolves more attractive features, based on the Spielberg discovery in *E.T.* that wide-set eyes are attractive. She doesn't look quite human, but as she grows to teenage size, she could possibly be the offspring of Jake and Neytiri, although not blue.

Brody and Polley are smart actors, and the director, Vincenzo Natali, is smart, too; do you remember his *Cube* (1997), with subjects trapped in a nightmarish experimental maze? This film, written by Natali with Antoinette Terry Bryant and Douglas Taylor, has the beginnings of a lot of ideas, including the love that observably exists between humans and some animals. It questions what "human" means, and suggests it's defined more by mind than body. It opens the controversy over the claims of some corporations to patent the genes of life. It deals with the divide between hard science and marketable science.

I wish Dren had been more fully developed. What does she think? What does she feel? There has never been another life form like her. The movie stays resolutely outside, viewing her as a distant creature. Her "parents" relate mostly to her mimetic behavior. Does it reflect her true nature? How does she feel about being locked in the barn? Does she "misbehave" or is that her nature?

The film, alas, stays resolutely with human problems. The relationship. The corporation. The preordained climax. Another recent film, *Ricky,* was about the French parents of a child who could fly. It also provided few insights into the child, but then Ricky was mentally as young as his age, and the ending was gratifyingly ambiguous. Not so with Dren. Disappointing, then, that the movie introduces such an extraordinary living being and focuses mostly on those around her. All the same, it's well done and intriguing.

The Spy Next Door ★ ½
PG, 92 m., 2010

Jackie Chan (Bob Ho), Amber Valletta (Gillian), Madeline Carroll (Farren), Will Shadley (Ian), Alina Foley (Nora), Magnus Scheving (Poldark), Katherine Boecher (Creel), Lucas Till (Larry), Billy Ray Cyrus (Colton James), George Lopez (Glaze). Directed by Brian Levant and produced by Robert Simonds. Screenplay by Jonathan Bernstein, James Greer, and Gregory Poirier.

Let's see. Jackie Chan is a spy working for China and the CIA, who falls in love with a widow with three kids. He retires to be with them, but his job follows him home. Mom goes to be with her sick dad. Evil Russians have a plot to control the world's oil supply, and this requires them to chase Jackie and the kids through shopping malls, large empty factories, and so on. Jackie's character is named Bob Ho, which reminds me of someone.

Truth in reviewing requires me to report that *The Spy Next Door* is precisely what you would expect from a PG-rated Jackie Chan comedy with that plot. If that's what you're looking for, you won't be disappointed. It's not what I was looking for.

There are things you learn from movies like this. (1) All kids know how to use weapons better than Russian mobsters. (2) A villainess in a spy movie always dresses like a dominatrix. (3) Hummers are no help. (4) Kids always hate the guy their mom is dating until they survive in battle with him, and then they love him. (5) Whenever an adult turns away, a small child will instantly disappear. The smaller the child, the more agile. (6) Even in New Mexico, Russian gangsters wear heavy long black leather coats, which they just bought in customs at Heathrow. These, added to their six-foot-five-inch heights and goatees, help them blend in. (7) The mole in the CIA is always the white boss, never the Latino.

What else? Oh, (8) if you put a cell phone under a rock with iron in it, it cannot be traced. Only such a rock miles into the desert will work. No good putting it in the stove. (9) Little girls would rather dress in a pink princess outfit than wear a Hulk mask. (10) Spies always have fiery kitchen disasters the first time they cook for kids, and the second time produce perfect French toast with powdered sugar on it. Oh, and (11) no spy has the slightest idea of a reasonable ratio of oatmeal to water.

Such sights made a young Saturday morning audience happy. Nothing to a kid is quite as funny as a food fight. A cat trapped on a roof is a suspense builder. They don't like the guy dating their mom until they save him with their well-timed action moves. And all young audiences find it perfectly reasonable that when a kid runs away from a residential neighborhood on a bike, that kid will, of course, pedal into the large empty factory where Jackie Chan is facing the Russian mob giants.

Jackie Chan is fifty-five. Just sayin'. He no longer runs up walls by using the leverage of a perpendicular surface. Back in the days before CGI, he used to really do that. OK, maybe some wires were involved, but you try running up a two-story wall with wires. I wouldn't even want to be winched up.

Chan was famous for doing his own stunts. He had so many accidents it's a wonder he can walk. Everybody knew to wait for the outtakes during the closing credits because you'd see him miss a fire escape or land wrong in the truck going under the bridge. Now the outtakes involve his use of the English language. What's that? Your name *isn't* Bob Hope?

The Square ★★★ ½
R, 116 m., 2010

David Roberts (Ray), Claire van der Boom (Carla), Joel Edgerton (Billy), Anthony Hayes (Smithy), Peter Phelps (Jake), Bill Hunter (Gil Hubbard). Directed by Nash Edgerton and produced by Louise Smith. Screenplay by Joel Edgerton and Matthew Dabner.

The Square moves with implacable logic toward catastrophe, as its desperate heroes try to squirm out of a tightening noose. Step by step, mistake by mistake, their delusion is trampled on by reality. More horrible things happen in this film than are probable in any scenario short of a large anvil falling from the sky and flattening the town, but it remains mostly plausible from scene to scene.

Crime doesn't pay. This we all know. Adultery has a way of making itself known. Adulterers who hope to steal cash and live happily ever after are really asking for trouble. Note to adulterers with such a plan: Never try to carry it out until you first join your partner in sin on a seventy-two-hour bus ride.

In a small Australian town, Ray (David Roberts) works as the harried supervisor of a housing development. Carla (Claire van der Boom) is married to Smithy (Anthony Hayes), a lowlife. Ray and Carla, both unhappily married, have been having an affair for quite some time. In each other's arms they console themselves with the dream that someday they will run away from their lives and live happily ever after—in hiding, I guess.

Carla dreams that this will happen. Ray plays along with it. Note to other women, if younger and without resources: A gray-haired married man with a good job is lying when he says he'll surrender everything for you. Lying. But Carla calls his bluff. She discovers that Smithy has a lot of cash hidden in the house. Enough to finance their flight. It's undoubtedly illegal cash. If they steal it, how can the theft be reported?

Well, sure, yeah, great, Ray says, possibly hoping for something to come up. You know, like maybe Smithy will move the money. Nothing comes up, and Ray finds himself involved in a plan that goes wrong and wronger and wrongest.

The delight of this film, directed by Nash Edgerton and written with his brother Joel Edgerton and Matthew Dabner, is that it never pushes too hard or moves too fast. It lovingly, almost sadistically, lays out the situation and deliberately demonstrates all the things that can go wrong. And I mean *all* the things.

At the center of these things is a very large hole filled with concrete, the "square" of the title. Note to people with dead bodies on their hands: If you cover a corpse with several feet of concrete, it is difficult to dig it up discreetly. It is also hard to keep all of your stories straight, to control what people may notice, to deal with the moment when the cash is found missing, and to say thanks but no thanks when the police try to be helpful.

One of the best elements of *The Square* is how well it establishes the rhythms and layout of its small town, which is in New South Wales, cane toad country. I was waiting for a cane toad to figure in the plot, but Edgerton is admirably disciplined. That's why the movie is so effective. The acting is convincing, the characters are realistic, nobody is looking for trouble, fate plays a role, and we clearly understand who everybody is. There is a shot from a high bluff down to a house on fire, and we already know whose that house is.

The Square has been compared to *Blood Simple* and *A Simple Plan*. High praise, but not undeserved. It's so good to find filmmakers with quiet, firm confidence in story and character. An unseemly number of people die here, but never in "thrilling" scenes, which are so rarely even interesting. They die because, despite their best efforts, something happens to them. Note to thieves and adulterers: Live so as to prevent things from happening to you.

Standard Operating Procedure ★ ★ ★ ½
R, 121 m., 2008

A documentary written and directed by Errol Morris and produced by Morris and Julie Bilson Ahlberg.

Errol Morris's *Standard Operating Procedure,* based on the infamous prison torture photographs from Abu Ghraib, is completely unlike anything I was expecting from such a film—more disturbing, analytical, and morose. This is not a political film or yet another screed about the Bush administration or the war in Iraq. It is driven simply, powerfully, by the desire to understand those photographs.

There are thousands of them, mostly taken not from the point of view of photojournalism, but in the spirit of home snapshots. They show young Americans, notably Lynndie England, posing with prisoners of war who are handcuffed in grotesque positions, usually naked, heads often covered with their underpants, sometimes in sexual positions. Miss England, who was about twenty at the time and weighed scarcely one hundred pounds, often has a cigarette hanging from her mouth in a show of tough-guy bravado. But the effect is not to draw attention to her as the person who ordered these tableaux, but as a part of them. Some other force, not seen, is sensed as shaping them.

This invisible presence, we discover, is named Charles Graner, a staff sergeant Lynndie was in love with, who is more than fifteen years her senior. She does what he suggests.

She doesn't question. But then, few questions are asked by most of the Americans in the photographs, who are not so much performing the acts as being photographed performing them.

"Pictures only show you a fraction of a second," says a Marine named Javal Davis, who was a prison guard but is not seen in any of them. "You don't see forward, and you don't see backward. You don't see outside the frame." He is expressing the central questions of the film: Why do these photos exist, why were they taken, and what reality do they reflect? What do we think about these people?

Those are the questions at the heart of many of Morris's films, all the way back to his first, *Gates of Heaven* (1978), in which to this day I am unable to say what he feels about his subjects or what they think of themselves. The answers would be less interesting anyway than the eternally enigmatic questions. Morris's favorite point of view is the stare. He chooses his subjects, regards them almost impassively, and allows their usually strange stories to tell themselves.

There is not a voice raised in *S.O.P.* The tone is set by a sad, elegiac, sometimes relentless score by Danny Elfman. The subject, in addition to the photographs, is Morris's interview subjects, seen in a mosaic of close-ups as they speak about what it was like to be at Abu Ghraib. Most of them speak either in sorrow or resentment, muted, incredulous. How had they found themselves in that situation?

Yes, unspeakable acts of cruelty were committed in the prison. But not personally, if we can believe them, by the interviewees. The torturers seem to have been military intelligence specialists in interrogation. They, too, are following orders and choose to disregard the theory that the information is useless since if you torture a man enough he will tell you anything.

I cannot imagine what it would be like to be suspended by having my hands shackled behind my back so tightly I might lose them. Or feeling I am being drowned. And so on—this need not be a litany of horrors.

More to the point of this film is that the prison wardens received their prisoners after the tortures were mostly committed, and then posed with them in ghastly "human pyramids," in "dog piles," or in scenes with sexual innuendo. Again, why? "For the picture." The taking of the photos seems to have been the motivation for the instants they reveal. And, as a speaker observes in the film, if there had been no photos, the moments they depict would not have existed, and the scandal of Abu Ghraib would not have taken place.

Yes, some of those we see in *Standard Operating Procedure* were paid for their testimony. Morris acknowledges that. He did not tell them what to say. I personally believed what they were telling me. What it came down to was, they found themselves under orders that they did not understand, involved in situations to provide a lifetime of nightmares.

They were following orders, yes. But whose? Any orders to torture would have had to come from those with a rank of staff sergeant or above. But all of those who were tried, found guilty, and convicted after Abu Ghraib were below that rank. At the highest level, results were demanded—find information on the whereabouts of Saddam Hussein (whose eventual capture did not result from any information pried loose by torture). At lower levels, the orders were translated into using torture. But there was a deliberate cutoff between the high level demanding the results and the intermediate level authorizing the violation of U.S. and international law by the use of torture.

At the opening of the film, Defense Secretary Donald Rumsfeld is seen, his blue blazer hooked over one shoulder, his white dress shirt immaculate, "touring" Abu Ghraib. He is shown one cell, then cancels his tour. He doesn't want to see any more.

And so little Lynndie England is left with her fellow soldiers as the face of the scandal. And behind the photos of her and others lurks the enigmatic figure of Sergeant Charles Graner, who was not allowed by the military to be interviewed for this film. I imagine him as the kind of guy we all knew in high school, snickering in the corner, sharing thoughts we did not want to know with friends we did not want to make. If he posed many of the photos (and gave away countless copies of them), was it because he enjoyed being at one remove from their subjects? The captors were seen dominating their captives, and he was in the role, with his camera, of dominating both.

Remember the photo of Lynndie posing with the prisoner on a leash? His name, we learn, was Gus. Lynndie says she wasn't dragging him: "You can see the leash was slack." She adds: "He would never have had me standing next to Gus if the camera wasn't there."

Star Trek ★ ★ ½
PG-13, 126 m., 2009

Chris Pine (James Tiberius Kirk), Zachary Quinto (Spock), Leonard Nimoy (Spock Prime), Eric Bana (Captain Nero), Bruce Greenwood (Captain Christopher Pike), Karl Urban (Leonard "Bones" McCoy), Zoe Saldana (Uhura), Simon Pegg (Montgomery "Scotty" Scott), John Cho (Sulu), Anton Yelchin (Chekov), Ben Cross (Sarek), Winona Ryder (Amanda Grayson). Directed by J. J. Abrams and produced by Abrams and Damon Lindelof. Screenplay by Roberto Orci and Alex Kurtzman.

Star Trek as a concept has voyaged far beyond science fiction and into the safe waters of space opera, but that doesn't amaze me. The Gene Roddenberry years, when stories might play with questions of science, ideals, or philosophy, have been replaced by stories reduced to loud and colorful action. Like so many franchises, it's more concerned with repeating a successful formula than going boldly where no *Star Trek* has gone before.

The 2009 *Star Trek* film goes back eagerly to where *Star Trek* began, using time travel to explain a cast of mostly the same characters, only at a younger point in their lives, sailing the starship *Enterprise*. As a story idea, this is sort of brilliant, and saves on invention because young Kirk, Spock, McCoy, Uhuru, Scotty, and the rest channel their later selves. The child is father to the man, or the Vulcan, and all that.

Don't get me wrong. This is fun. And when Leonard Nimoy himself returns as the aged Spock, encountering another Spock (Zachary Quinto) as a young man, I was kind of delighted, although as customary in many sci-fi films, nobody is as astonished as they should be. "Holy moley! Time travel exists, and this may be me!" It's more like a little ambiguous dialogue is exchanged and they're off to battle the evil Romulan captain Nero (Eric Bana).

Time travel, as we all know, is impossible in

the sense it happens here, but many things are possible in this film. Anyone with the slightest notion of what a black hole is, or how it behaves, will find the black holes in *Star Trek* hilarious. The logic is also a little puzzling when they can beam people into another ship in outer space, but they have to physically parachute to land on a midair platform from which the Romulans are drilling a hole to Vulcan's core. And after they land there, they fight with two Romulan guards using fists and swords? The platform is suspended from Arthur C. Clarke's "space elevator," but instead of fullerenes, the cable is made of metallic chunks the size of refrigerators.

But stop me before I get started. I mention these details only to demonstrate that the movie raises its yo-yo finger to the science, while embracing the fiction. Apart from details from the youths of the characters and the Spock reunion, it consists mostly of encounters between the *Enterprise* and the incomparably larger and much better armed Romulan spaceship from the future. It's encouraging to learn that not even explosions and fires can quickly damage a starship. Also that lifeboats can save the crew, despite the vast distance from home base.

That would be because of warp speed, which for present purposes consists of looking through an unnecessary window at bright lights zapping past. This method of transportation prevents any sense of wonder at the immensity of outer space and is a convenience not only for the starship but also for the screenwriters, who can push a button and zap to the next scene. The concept of using warp speed to escape the clutches of a black hole seems like a recycling of the ancient dilemma of the rock and the hard place.

There are affecting character moments. Young Spock is deliberately taunted in hopes he will, as a Vulcan, betray emotion. Because Zachary Quinto plays him as a bit of a self-righteous prig, it's satisfying to see him lose it. Does poor young Spock realize he faces a lifetime of people trying to get a rise out of him? Nimoy, as the elderly Spock, must have benefited because he is the most human character in the film.

Chris Pine, as James Tiberius Kirk, appears first as a hot-rodding rebel who has found a Corvette in the twenty-third century and drives it into a pit resembling the Grand Canyon. A few years later, he's put in suspension by the academy and smuggled on board the *Enterprise* by "Bones" McCoy (Karl Urban) before he becomes the ship's captain. There are times when the command deck looks like Bring Your Child to School Day, with the kid sitting in Daddy's chair.

Uhura (Zoe Saldana) seems to have traveled through time to the prefeminist 1960s, where she found her miniskirt and go-go boots. She seems wise and gentle and unsuited to her costume. Scotty (Simon Pegg) seems to have begun life as a character in a Scots sitcom. Eric Bana's Nero destroys whole planets on the basis of faulty intelligence, but the character is played straight and is effective.

The special effects are slam-bam. Spatial relationships between spaceships are unclear because the Romulan ship and the *Enterprise* have such widely unmatched scales. Battles consist primarily of jumpsuited crew members running down corridors in advance of smoke, sparks, and flames. Lots of verbal commands seem implausibly slow. Consider, at light-warp speeds, how imprecise it would be to say, "At my command . . . three . . . two . . . one."

I understand that *Star Trek* science has never been intended as plausible. I understand that this is not science fiction but an ark movie using a starship. I understand that character types are as familiar as your favorite slippers. But the franchise has become much of a muchness. The new movie essentially intends to reboot the franchise with younger characters and carry on as before. The movie deals with narrative housekeeping. Perhaps the next one will engage these characters in a more challenging and devious story, one more about testing their personalities than reestablishing them. In the meantime, you want space opera, you got it.

Star Wars: The Clone Wars ★ ½
PG, 98 m., 2008

With the voices of: Matt Lanter (Anakin Skywalker), James Arnold Taylor (Obi-Wan Kenobi), Ashley Eckstein (Ahsoka Tano), Catherine Taber (Padme Amidala), Anthony

Daniels (C-3PO), Christopher Lee (Count Dooku), Nika Futterman (Asajj Ventress), Tom Kane (Yoda), Ian Abercrombie (Palpatine), Samuel L. Jackson (Mace Windu). Directed by Dave Filoni and produced by Catherine Winder. Screenplay by Henry Gilroy, Steve Melching, and Scott Murphy.

Has it come to this? Has the magical impact of George Lucas's original vision of *Star Wars* been reduced to the level of Saturday morning animation? *Star Wars: The Clone Wars,* which is a continuation of an earlier animated TV series, is basically just a ninety-eight-minute trailer for the autumn launch of a new series on the Cartoon Network.

The familiar *Star Wars* logo and the pulse-pounding John Williams score now lift the curtain on a deadening film that cuts corners on its animation and slumbers through a plot that (a) makes us feel like we've seen it all before, and (b) makes us wish we hadn't. The action takes place between the events in the "real" movies *Episode II: Attack of the Clones* and *Episode III: Revenge of the Sith.* The Republic is still at war with the Separatists, its access to the Galactic Rim is threatened, and much depends on pleasing the odious Jabba the Hutt, whose child has been kidnapped—by the Jedi, he is told.

It's up to Anakin Skywalker and his new Padawan pupil, Ahsoka Tano, to find the infant, as meanwhile Obi-Wan Kenobi and Yoda lead the resistance to a Separatist onslaught. And if all of this means little to you, you might as well stop reading now. It won't get any better.

This is the first feature-length animated *Star Wars* movie, but instead of pushing the state of the art, it's retro. You'd think the great animated films of recent years had never been made. The characters have hair that looks molded from Play-Doh, bodies that seem arthritic, and moving lips on half-frozen faces—all signs that shortcuts were taken in the animation work.

The dialogue in the original *Star Wars* movies had a certain grace, but here the characters speak to each other in simplistic declamation, and Yoda gets particularly tiresome with his once-charming speech pattern. To quote a famous line by Wolcott Gibbs, *Backward ran sentences until reeled the mind.*

The battle scenes are interminable, especially once we realize that although the air is filled with bullets, shells, and explosive rockets, no one we like is going to be killed. The two armies attack each other, for some reason, only on a wide street in a towering city. First one army advances, then the other. Why not a more fluid battle plan? To save money on backgrounds, I assume. The trick that Anakin and his Padawan learner use to get behind the enemy force field (essentially, they hide under a box) wouldn't even have fooled anybody in a Hopalong Cassidy movie—especially when they stand up and run with their legs visible but can't see where they're going.

Ahsoka Tano, by the way, is annoying. She bats her grapefruit-sized eyes at Anakin and offers suggestions that invariably prove her right and her teacher wrong. At least when we first met Yoda, he was offering useful advice. Which reminds me, I'm probably wrong, but I don't think anyone in this movie ever refers to the Force.

You know you're in trouble when the most interesting new character is Jabba the Hutt's uncle. The big revelation is that Jabba has an infant to be kidnapped. The big discovery is that Hutts look like that when born, only smaller. The question is, who is Jabba's wife? The puzzle is, how do Hutts copulate? Like snails, I speculate. If you don't know how snails do it, let's not even go there. The last thing this movie needs is a Jabba the Hutt sex scene.

State of Play ★ ★ ★
PG-13, 127 m., 2009

Russell Crowe (Cal McAffrey), Ben Affleck (Stephen Collins), Rachel McAdams (Della Frye), Helen Mirren (Cameron Lynne), Robin Wright Penn (Anne Collins), Jason Bateman (Dominic Foy), Jeff Daniels (George Fergus). Directed by Kevin Macdonald and produced by Tim Bevan, Eric Fellner, and Andrew Hauptman. Screenplay by Matthew Michael Carnahan, Tony Gilroy, and Billy Ray, based on the BBC series created by Paul Abbott.

State of Play is a smart, ingenious thriller set in the halls of Congress and the city room of a newspaper not unlike the *Washington Post.* It's also a political movie, its villain a shadowy corporation that contracts with the government for security duties and mercenaries in Iraq. The name is PointCorp. Think Blackwater. If an outfit like that would kill for hire, the plot wonders, would it also kill to protect its profits?

Here is Russell Crowe playing an ace investigative reporter for the *Washington Globe*. All the cops and most of the people on Capitol Hill seem to know him; he's one of those instinctive newsmen who connect the dots so quickly that a 127-minute movie can be extracted from a six-hour BBC miniseries. This keeps him so occupied that he has little time for grooming, and doesn't seem to ever wash his hair.

Crowe stepped into the role after Brad Pitt dropped out. Pitt, I suspect, would have looked more clean-cut, but might not have been as interesting as Crowe in this role, as Cal McAffrey, a scruffy hero in a newspaper movie that is acutely aware of the crisis affecting newspapers. He becomes part of a team that involves not two experienced reporters, as in *All the President's Men*, but Della (Rachel McAdams), one of the paper's plucky bloggers. He tries to teach her some ancient newspaper wisdom, such as: If you seem to be on the edge of uncovering an enormous political scandal, don't blow your cover by hurrying online with some two-bit gossip.

In a short span of time, a man is shot dead in an alley, a passing bicyclist, also a witness, is killed, and a woman is shoved or jumps under a subway train. Cal, of course, covers all of these deaths in person. The dead woman was a researcher for Representative Stephen Collins (Ben Affleck), who breaks into tears during a congressional hearing into Point-Corp and confesses to conducting an affair with her. His wife, Anne (Robin Wright Penn), plays the brave politician's wife and says their family will stay together. Anne and Cal were lovers in college. The dead man turns out to be carrying a briefcase stolen from PointCorp. Now we connect the dots.

There are many other surprises in the film, which genuinely fooled me a couple of times and maintains a certain degree of credibility for a thriller. The implication is that Point-Corp and the administration are locked in an unholy alliance to channel millions of taxpayer dollars into unsavory hands. That this can all be untangled by one reporter who looks like a bum and another who looks like Rachel McAdams (which is no bad thing) goes with the territory.

An important role in their investigation is played by the *Globe*'s editor, Cameron Lynne (Helen Mirren). The paper's new corporate owners are on her neck to cut costs, redesign the venerable front page, get more scoops, and go for the gossip today instead of waiting for the Pulitzer tomorrow. There is, in fact, an eerie valedictory feeling to the film; mother of God, can this be the last newspaper movie? (The answer is no, because no matter what happens to newspapers, the newspaper movie is a durable genre. Shouting, "Stop the presses!" is ever so much more exciting than shouting, "Stop the upload!")

It is a reliable truth that you should never ask an expert how a movie deals with his field of knowledge. Archaeologists, for example, have raised questions about *The Mummy: Tomb of the Dragon Emperor*. When Cal races out of the office at deadline and shouts over his shoulder, "Tell Cameron to kill the story," it is just possible that she would tear up the front page, if the story was so important the paper could not risk being wrong. But when Cal and his sidekick the perky blogger solve the mystery and are back in the office and it is noted, "Cameron has been holding the presses four hours!"—I think her new corporate bosses will want to have a long, sad talk with her, after which she will discover if the company still offers severance packages.

State of Play, directed by Kevin Macdonald (*The Last King of Scotland*), is well-assembled and has some good performances. Crowe pulls off the Joaquin Phoenix look-alike; McAdams doesn't overplay her blogger's newbieness; Helen Mirren convinced me she could be a newspaper editor. Robin Wright Penn always finds the correct shadings. If Ben Affleck, as he plays this role, were to have his face carved into Mount Rushmore, people would ask which was the original.

The thing is, though, that the movie never quite attains altitude. It has a great takeoff, levels nicely, and then seems to land on autopilot. Maybe it's the problem of resolving so much plot in a finite length of time, but it seems a little too facile toward the end. Questions are answered, relationships revealed, and mysteries solved too smoothly. If a corporation like PointCorp could have its skullduggery exposed that easily, it wouldn't still be in business.

Step Brothers ★ ½
R, 95 m., 2008

Will Ferrell (Brennan Huff), John C. Reilly (Dale Doback), Mary Steenburgen (Nancy Huff), Richard Jenkins (Robert Doback), Adam Scott (Derek Huff), Kathryn Hahn (Alice Huff). Directed by Adam McKay and produced by Jimmy Miller and Judd Apatow. Screenplay by McKay and Will Ferrell.

When did comedies get so mean? *Step Brothers* has a premise that might have produced a good time at the movies, but when I left I felt a little unclean. The plot: Will Ferrell and John C. Reilly play Brennan and Dale, two never-employed fortyish sons who still live at home, eating melted cheese nachos and watching TV. When their parents (Mary Steenburgen and Richard Jenkins) get married, they become stepbrothers and have to share the same room. This causes them to inflict agonizing pain upon each other and use language that would seem excessive in the men's room of a truck stop.

Is this funny? Anything can be funny. Let me provide an example. I am thinking of a particular anatomical act. It is described in explicit detail in two 2008 movies, *Step Brothers* and *Tropic Thunder*. In *Step Brothers* it sounds dirty and disgusting. In *Tropic Thunder*, described by Jack Black while he is tied to a tree and undergoing heroin withdrawal, it's funny.

Same act, similar descriptions. What's the difference? It involves the mechanism of comedy, I think. The Jack Black character is desperately motivated. He will offer to do *any-thing* to be released. In *Step Brothers*, the language is simply showing off by talking dirty. It serves no comic function and just sort of sits there in the air, making me cringe.

I know, I know, four-letter language is the currency of a movie like this and many of the other films Judd Apatow produces. I would be lying if I said I was shocked. I would also be lying if I said I had no taste or judgment of comic strategy. I'm sure I've seen movies with more extreme language than *Step Brothers*, but here it seems to serve no purpose other than simply to exist. In its own tiny way, it lowers the civility of our civilization.

Now what about the violence? These two adult children do horrible things to each other. The movie must be particularly proud of one scene because they show part of it in the trailer. Dale thinks he has killed Brennan by slamming him with the cymbal of his drum set. He rolls him in a rug and prepares to bury him in the lawn. Brennan comes to, bangs Dale with the shovel, and starts to bury him alive.

I dunno. Maybe it sounds funny when you read it. Coming at the end of a series of similar cruelties, it was one living burial too many. There is also an attempted drowning. And never mind.

Mary Steenburgen and Richard Jenkins, two gifted actors, do what they can. They despair of their grown-up, unemployed brats. They lay down the law. They realize their sons are destroying their marriage. But they exist in another dimension than Brennan and Dale—almost in another movie. Their reaction shots are almost always curious because the only sane reaction would be sheer horror, followed by calls to the men with the butterfly nets.

Sometimes I think I am living in a nightmare. All about me, standards are collapsing, manners are evaporating, people show no respect for themselves. I am not a moralistic nut. I'm proud of the x-rated movie I wrote. I like vulgarity if it's funny or serves a purpose. But what is going on here?

Back to the movie. I suppose it will be a success. Will Ferrell and John C. Reilly have proven how talented they are in far better movies. If it makes millions, will they want to wade into this genre again? I hope not. Ferrell actually cowrote the movie with Adam McKay, the director. Maybe he will. But why not a comedy with more invention, with more motivation than hate at first sight? There is one genuinely funny moment in the movie: The blind man who lives next door has a guide dog that misbehaves, snarls, and bites people. Bad taste, yes. But . . . I'm desperate here.

Do you see why the dog doing it is funny, but Will Ferrell doing it to John C. Reilly is not funny?

Still Walking ★★★★
NO MPAA RATING, 114 m., 2009

Hiroshi Abe (Ryota), Yui Natsukawa (Yukari), You (Chinami), Kazuya Takahashi (Nobuo), Shohei Tanaka (Atsushi), Kirin Kiki (Toshiko), Yoshio Harada (Kyohei). Directed by Hirokazu Kore-eda and produced by Yoshihiro Kato and Hijiri Taguchi. Screenplay by Kore-eda.

Most family dramas contain too much drama. In most families, the past and present don't meet and find resolution during a twenty-four-hour period, no matter how many American films you've seen about Thanksgiving. Painful family issues are more likely to stay beneath the surface, known to everyone but not spoken of. *Still Walking*, a magnificent new film from Japan, is very wise about that, and very true.

A dozen years ago, the prized possession of this family was Junpei, the eldest son, doted on by his parents and admired by his younger brother and sister. But Junpei drowned while saving a life, and every year the family gathers, as many Japanese families do, to visit his grave and memory.

These occasions are hated by Ryota (Hiroshi Abe), the second son. His father (Yoshio Harada) almost blames him for not being the one who died. On the drive to his hometown at the seaside, Ryota tells his new wife, Yukari (Yui Natsukawa), they must not even stay the night. This will be her first meeting with the parents; she is a widow with a young son.

The father is a retired physician, slowed with age, still marching joylessly on his daily walk. He stays mostly closed off in his office and greets his son brusquely. The mother has her doubts about this marriage; it is better to marry a divorced woman than a widow because at least the divorcee *chose* to leave her husband.

Also together for this day are Ryota's sister, Chinami, and her husband. It is only slowly that we pick up the suppressed currents of feeling in the family; on the surface, the mother stays cheerful, although the old doc-

tor's bitterness is obvious: The wrong son drowned.

The day arrives at some sort of centerpiece when they welcome a luncheon guest, who is never named. This is the man Junpei died while saving. He is homely, fat, ill at ease, squirmy, apologetic, bursting from his white dress shirt. The doctor clearly doesn't regard him as having been worth saving. Ryota has spent a lifetime feeling shunned by his father and considered inferior to his brother. He has been wounded time and again, and so he is alert to the discomfort of the saved man. Why do they even invite him? He's obviously suffering during these annual visits. They invite him, he learns offhandedly, *because* he suffers.

If anyone can be considered an heir of the great Yasujiro Ozu, it might be Hirokazu Kore-eda, the writer and director of *Still Walking*. In *Maborosi* (1995), *After Life* (1998), and *Nobody Knows* (2004), his first three features released in North America, and now in this film, he has produced profoundly empathetic films about human feelings. He sees intensely and tenderly into his characters. Like Ozu, he pays meticulous attention to composition and camera placement. Acting as his own editor, he doesn't cut for immediate effect but for the subtle gathering of power. His actors look as if they could be such people as they portray.

He feels a strong connection with spouses separated by death or circumstances, and the children who are involved. *Maborosi* involves a widow with a young son, who goes to a new seaside town to marry a virtual stranger. *After Life*, a serious fantasy, is about newly dead people who spend a week in a heavenly waiting room to prepare a film of the one memory they want to carry through eternity. *Nobody Knows* is about the children of a quasi-prostitute who leaves them to fend for themselves in a city apartment.

None of these films elevates the temperature with melodrama. They draw us inward with concern. Kore-eda is a tender humanist, and that fits well with his elegant visual style. In *Still Walking*, he shares something valuable with Ozu: what I call Ozu's "pillow shots," named after the "pillow words" in Japanese poetry, which separate passages with just a word or two, seemingly unconnected, for a pause in the rhythm. These shots may show passing trains (a favorite of both directors) or a detail of architecture or landscape. It isn't their subject that matters; it's their composure.

The Stoning of Soraya M. ★ ★ ★
R, 114 m., 2009

Shohreh Aghdashloo (Zahra), Mozhan Marno (Soraya), Jim Caviezel (Sahebjam), Navid Negahban (Ali), Parviz Sayyad (Hashem), Ali Pourtash (Mullah), David Diaan (Ebrahim). Directed by Cyrus Nowrasteh and produced by Stephen McEveety and John Shepherd. Screenplay by Cyrus Nowrasteh and Betsy Griffen Nowrasteh, based on the book by Freidoune Sahebjam.

The Islamic practice of stoning women and the Christian practice of burning them as witches are both born not from religious reasons but of a male desire to subjugate women and define them in terms of sexuality. Is this in dispute? Are there any theologians who support such actions? Of all the most severe punishments of both religions, this is the one most skewed against women, and the one most convenient for men.

To be sure, no witches have been burned at the stake in many long years, and few ever were. But women are still stoned to death in some Islamic countries, including Iran, where this film is set. The practice survives in backward rural areas, and the law turns a blind eye. It is rare, and Iran denies it, but French journalist Freidoune Sahebjam's best-selling The Stoning of Soraya M. (1994) appears to be quite authentic. A woman really was stoned to death on trumped-up adultery charges, brought for the convenience of her husband, who desired to marry a young girl.

Cyrus Nowrasteh's The Stoning of Soraya M. does not dramatize this story in a subtle way. You might argue that the stoning of a woman to death is not a subtle subject. But it would be helpful to have it told in a way that shows how almost the entire population of a village allows it to happen, even though most of them know of the woman's innocence and her husband's vile motives. How does a lynch mob form? Instead, we're given a village pop-

ulated primarily by overacted villains and moral cowards.

Against them is one strong voice: the widow Zahra, Soraya's aunt. She's played by Shohreh Aghdashloo, the Oscar nominee from House of Sand and Fog (2004). She knows all the players and all the motives and publicly calls them on it, to no avail. She's a "crazy woman," says the husband, Ali (Navid Negahban). The phrase "crazy woman" can fall easily from the tongue, and it's worth remembering that in Victorian England a wife could be locked in an asylum for life on only her husband's signature (see the great novel The Quincunx).

Ali the husband is an immoral monster. His intended child bride has not been asked if she wants to marry him; the marriage has been arranged. The village mullah goes along because Ali threatens to blackmail him about an old prison sentence. The mayor knows it is wrong and doubts Allah desires it, but lacks the courage to do much more than mutter.

The stoning sequence itself is one of the most unbearable experiences I have had at the movies. I learn it lasts nearly twenty minutes. Soraya is buried in a hole up to the waist. Village boys collect stones of a good throwing weight in a wheelbarrow. We see blow after blow, as blood pours from her face and body. She accepts this as her fate, as indeed it is. She did nothing that was not innocent and kind.

The stoning took place in 1986, after the Islamic Revolution. Fundamentalists were in power and enforced their strictures; the measures they introduced are being challenged today in the streets of Iran, and similar extremism is the practice in our dear friend Saudi Arabia. Those with objections fear crushing reprisal. The enforcers have power, position, and wealth to gain, and dare their enemies to go against what they say is God's will.

The message is that if a religion requires practices that seem evil to its members, they should resign from that religion. If it condones a death penalty that is visited unequally on members of a specific gender, race, or class, it is immoral. There cannot be a reward for following it blindly because only a thoughtful choice has meaning. At heaven's gate you cannot say, "I always followed the herd."

The Stoning of Soraya M. has such a powerful stoning sequence that I recommend it if only for its brutal ideological message. That the pitiful death of Soraya is followed by a false Hollywood upbeat ending involving tape recordings and silliness about a car that won't start is simply shameful. Nowrasteh, born in Colorado, attended the USC Film School. Is that what they teach there? When you are telling the story of a woman being stoned to death, you may not be able to use everything you learned in class.

The Strangers ★ ½
R, 90 m., 2008

Liv Tyler (Kristen McKay), Scott Speedman (James Hoyt), Gemma Ward (Dollface), Kip Weeks (Man in the Mask), Laura Margolis (Pin-Up Girl), Glenn Howerton (Mike). Directed by Bryan Bertino and produced by Doug Davison, Roy Lee, and Nathan Kahane. Screenplay by Bertino.

My mistake was to read the interview with the director. At the beginning of my review of *The Strangers,* I typed my star rating instinctively: "One star." I was outraged. I wrote: "What a waste of a perfectly good first act! And what a maddening, nihilistic, infuriating ending!" I was just getting warmed up.

And then, I dunno, I looked up the movie on IMDb, and there was a link to an interview with Bryan Bertino, the writer and director, and I went there, read it, and looked at his photo. He looked to be in his twenties. This was his first film. Bertino had been working as a grip on a peanuts-budget movie when he pitched this screenplay to Rogue Pictures and was asked to direct it. He gave a friend his grip tools and thought: "Cool, I'm never going to need this anymore! I'm never using a hammer again." Then he tells the interviewer: "I still had to buy books on how to direct."

So I thought, Bryan Bertino is a kid, this is his first movie, and as much as I hate it, it's a competent movie that shows he has the chops to be a director. So I gave it 1½ stars instead of one. Still harsh, yes. I think a lot of audience members will walk out really angry at the ending, although it has a certain truthfulness and doesn't cheat on the situation that has been building up. The movie deserves more stars

for its bottom-line craft, but all the craft in the world can't redeem its story.

Yes, Bertino can direct. He opens on a dark night in a neighborhood of deserted summer homes with two people in a car. These are Kristen (Liv Tyler) and James (Scott Speedman). They are coming from a wedding reception. They go inside James's summer home. We learn that he proposed to her, but she "isn't ready." The camera focuses on a 33 rpm turntable that, along with their Volvo, are the easiest two props I can imagine to create a 1970s period look.

I am intrigued by these people. Will they talk all night? Will they do things they'll regret forever? Will they . . . *there is a knock on the door!* Not the sound of a human hand hitting wood. The sound of something hard hitting wood. It is very loud, and it echoes. To evoke an infinitely superior film, it creates the same sense of alarm and danger as the planks do, banging against each other in *Le Fils* (*The Son*), by the Dardenne brothers.

They open the door and find a young girl. They tell her she has the wrong house. She goes and stands in the yard. And then, all night long, their sense of security is undercut by more knocks, breaking glass, scraping, smashing. The sound track is the third protagonist. After a time, Bertino creates an empty space in one of his compositions, and it attracts a . . . figure . . . that casually fills it, wearing a mournful, shroudlike mask. We will see the mask again. Also two figures wearing little-doll masks that are not sweet, but ominous. We recall the opening credits telling us, "This film is inspired by true events." Never a good sign.

Is *The Strangers* inspired by other movies? Asked by Moviesonline.ca if he was influenced "by the film" (never named), Bertino answers, as only someone young and innocent could answer: "I don't *necessarily* think that I looked at it, you know." The *necessarily* is a masterstroke. He adds: "I'm definitely influenced by, like, '70s genre stuff in general, structure wise. . . . I read *Helter Skelter* when I was, like, eleven. That was where I first started getting interested in the idea of people just walking into a house that you didn't know. I lived in a house in the middle of nowhere in Texas on this road where you could call out in the middle of the night and nobody would hear you."

There have been great movies about home invasion, like *In Cold Blood*, that made more of it than gruesome events. *The Strangers* is a well-shot film (the cinematographer is the veteran Peter Sova). It does what it sets out to do. I'm not sure that it earns the right to do it. I will say that Bertino shows the instincts and choices of a good director; I hope he gets his hands on worthier material. It's a melancholy fact that he probably couldn't have found financing if his first act had lived up to its promise. There's a market for the kind of movie that inspires the kinds of commercials and trailers that *The Strangers* inspires, ending with a chilling dialogue exchange:

"Why are you doing this to us?"

"Because you were home."

Sugar ★ ★ ★ ½

R, 118 m., 2009

Algenis Perez Soto (Miguel Santos), Rayniel Rufino (Jorge Ramirez), Andre Holland (Brad Johnson), Michael Gaston (Stu Sutton), Jaime Tirelli (Osvaldo), Jose Rijo (Alvarez), Ellary Porterfield (Anne Higgins), Ann Whitney (Helen Higgins), Richard Bull (Earl Higgins). Directed by Anna Boden and Ryan Fleck and produced by Paul Mezey, Jamie Patricof, and Jeremy Kipp Walker. Screenplay by Boden and Fleck.

Sugar approaches with tender care the story of a kid from the Dominican Republic who has a strong pitching arm and a good heart. Miguel Santos, known as "Sugar" because of his sweet personality, is recruited from the fields of dreams in his homeland by Major League Baseball and assigned to an Iowa farm club that is very, very far from home.

I thought I could guess the story. But I couldn't. There isn't a single scene in this film where it really matters which side wins a game, and it doesn't end with a no-hitter. It looks with care at Sugar, and there are a thousand Sugars for every Sammy Sosa. Probably more. Baseball players have become an important export for the Dominican Republic, and poor families like Miguel's dream of the day when sons will be sending home paychecks. A minor league salary represents wealth.

The film is knowledgeable about how the system works. American teams maintain elaborate training facilities in the D.R., send talent scouts to local leagues, and keep recruits under close watch: Room and board is provided, there are security guards to enforce discipline, the kids get a few days off once in a while. This is heaven for them. For years their dreams have been filled with visions of big-time baseball.

Sugar isn't filled with melodramatic developments and a hard landing on American soil. Baseball seems, in fact, a friendly if realistic destination, an income where there was none before. If very few players ever make it into a major league starting lineup, well, they know that going in. What's special about the film—and this is a very special film—is how closely it observes the emotional uncertainties of a stranger in a strange land, not speaking the language, not knowing the customs, beset with homesickness and the dread of disappointing his family.

Algenis Perez Soto, a young baseball player in his acting debut, embodies Sugar with a natural sincerity. The movie regards him with sympathy. Sugar isn't "torn with conflict," as movie ads like to say, but weighed with worry. He finds himself boarding in the friendly Iowa farm home of Helen and Earl Higgins (Ann Whitney and Richard Bull), who have taken in a generation of new players for the local farm club. They know their baseball ("You've been dropping your arm," Helen tells him, and Sugar doesn't disagree).

There is also the presence of their granddaughter Anne (Ellary Porterfield), who sends out mixed messages; she's obviously attracted to him and invites him to meet her friends, evangelicals who would like to get him on board. On the team, he bonds with Jorge (Rayniel Rufino), a more seasoned player from the Republic, and Brad Johnson (Andre Holland), who is the same color but from a different world; if baseball doesn't pan out, he'll go back for an advanced degree from Stanford.

For Sugar, who mumbles he's had "a little" high school, everything depends on baseball panning out. On their regular phone calls, his mother fears she can sense something troubling in his voice. He finds the farm system is supportive, and he gets help from coaches who care, but there is always another player waiting behind him in line.

Anna Boden and Ryan Fleck, who wrote and directed *Sugar*, are serious filmmakers who have no desire to make a "sports movie." They've obviously done their research on the major league farm system and the men who pass through it; at some level, this entire tryout process is for the benefit of a fan in the grandstands with a wise-ass opinion about the "new kid." Remembering a day when Sammy Sosa was booed at Wrigley Field, I see it now in a wholly new light.

The true subject of *Sugar* is the immigrant experience in America. Boden and Fleck are interested in newcomers to this country, doing what they can to make a living and succeed. Whether this happens for Sugar, or how it might happen, you will see for yourself. The filmmakers are too observant to settle for a quick, conventional payoff. For them this film is a chapter in the more interesting story of the lifetime Sugar has ahead of him. Algenis Perez Soto plays the character so openly, so naturally, that an interesting thing happens: Baseball is only the backdrop, not the subject. This is a wonderful film.

Note: The R *rating is for relatively inconsequential reasons.*

Summer Hours ★ ★ ★

NO MPAA RATING, 103 m., 2009

Juliette Binoche (Adrienne), Charles Berling (Frederic), Jeremie Renier (Jeremie), Edith Scob (Helene), Dominique Reymond (Lisa), Isabelle Sadoyan (Eloise), Kyle Eastwood (James). Directed by Olivier Assayas and produced by Marin Karmitz, Nathanael Karmitz, and Charles Gillibert. Screenplay by Assayas.

Sometimes what holds a family together is custom and guilt. *Summer Hours* begins on the seventy-fifth birthday of Helene, a woman who is joined in the French countryside by her three children and their families. Much of the talk is about how far two of the children had to travel—one from New York, the other from China—and there's the sense they're eager to be going home. Sure, they love their mother. They really do. But you know how it is. They visit less because they should visit more.

Helene understands this. She understands a great deal. She pulls aside Frederic (Charles Berling), her only child still living in France, to talk about the handling of her estate. This makes him unhappy, but she produces an inventory of the sort women often keep, of her valued possessions. Tea sets, vases, paintings.

The house belonged to her uncle, a fairly well-known painter. She has kept it unchanged since his death, as almost a shrine. She has little of his work, but many of his valuable pieces, including a desk. In less than a year, she's dead, and the children gather again. She predicted to Frederic that the house would have to be sold—indeed, she knew them all well enough to foresee everything—but he assumes his sister, Adrienne (Juliette Binoche), and brother, Jeremie (Jeremie Renier), will want to keep it in the family.

He is wrong. Adrienne is getting married to her New York boyfriend (Kyle Eastwood). Jeremie has been offered a promotion in Hong Kong. The film, which has no false sentimentality, is matter-of-fact about how the valuable works are disposed of. They're all sorry they couldn't keep and maintain the house, but, well . . .

There are two long-standing facts of the family that are discussed, really, for the first time. What exactly was the nature of the long relationship between Helene and her uncle? And how is Eloise to be treated—Eloise, the family's cook and housekeeper since time immemorial? Olivier Assayas, the writer-director, doesn't treat these subjects as melodrama but as the sorts of things adult children naturally discuss. They're much more effective that way.

What happens is that the film builds its emotional power by stealth, indirectly, refusing to be a tear-jerker, always realistic, and yet observing how very sad it is to see a large part of your life disappear. A parent, for example. In Errol Morris's *Gates of Heaven*, these perfect words are spoken: "Death is for the living, and not for the dead so much."

The actors all find the correct notes. It is a French film, and so they are allowed to be adult and intelligent. They are not the creatures of a screenplay that hurries them along. The film is not about what will happen. It is about them. The recent American film that most resembles this one is Jonathan Demme's

515

Rachel Getting Married. Some audience members didn't know what to think of it because it didn't tell them. Sometimes you just have to figure out what you think for yourself. *Summer Hours* ends on the perfect note, the more you think about it.

Sunshine Cleaning ★ ★

R, 102 m., 2009

Amy Adams (Rose Lorkowski), Emily Blunt (Norah Lorkowski), Alan Arkin (Joe Lorkowski), Jason Spevack (Oscar Lorkowski), Steve Zahn (Mac), Mary Lynn Rajskub (Lynn), Clifton Collins Jr. (Winston). Directed by Christine Jeffs and produced by Glenn Williamson, Jeb Brody, Marc Turtletaub, and Peter Saraf. Screenplay by Megan Holley.

Sunshine Cleaning is a little too sunny for its material. Its heroine, Rose, is a single mom in desperate need of income, trapped in a one-way affair with her high school boyfriend, who fathered her son but married someone else. Her son is always in trouble at school. Her sister, Norah, is a hard-living goofball. Rose starts a new business cleaning up messy crime scenes.

Does this sound sunny to you? The material might have promise as a black comedy, but its attempt to put on a smiling face is unconvincing. That despite the work by Amy Adams as Rose and Emily Blunt as Norah, two effortless charmers who would be terrific playing these characters in a different movie. And Alan Arkin is back, and engaging, in what is coming dangerously close to "the Alan Arkin role." He's their father, Joe, forever hatching new get-poor-quick schemes.

Rose is a good mom. She understands her seven-year-old son, Oscar (Jason Spevack), who is not really troubled but simply high-spirited. I wonder how many little boys are accused of misbehaving simply because they are boys. Why does she still sleep with Mac, the faithless high school quarterback (Steve Zahn) who seduced and abandoned her? She asks herself the same question.

It's Mac, at least, who tips her off on a possible business. He's a cop and notices that people get paid well for mopping up after gruesome murders. So is born Rose and Norah's

Sunshine Cleaning, which will clean up the rugs and scrape the brains off the wall, etc. This job by its nature allows them to witness the aftermath of lives unexpectedly interrupted; an ID in a dead woman's purse leads them to make an awkward new acquaintance.

This is promising material. Gene Siskel loved movies about what people actually do all day long. There is even a documentary subject here. But not this film that compromises on everything it implies, because it wants to be cheerful about people who don't have much to be cheerful about. How can you make a feel-good movie about murder-scene cleanups? "Life's a messy business," the poster says. Yes, and death is messier.

There are times when the movie works, but those are the times it (and even we) forget what it's really about. If you could plot it on a curve, it might look like a cross-section of a roller-coaster. The poster also evokes *Little Miss Sunshine*, by the same producers, also with Alan Arkin, and the presence of Amy Adams evokes the sublime *Junebug*. Those were both movies with more consistent tones and, although based on contrivance, felt more natural.

There's one element in the film that does work, and it's sort of off to the side, apart from the rest of the plot. It involves Winston (Clifton Collins Jr.), a one-armed hardware store owner, who babysits Oscar in an emergency and provides an oasis of warmth and common sense. You may remember him as Perry, one of the killers Truman wrote the book about in *Capote* (2005). An actor like this works a lot but doesn't always get ideal roles. Now he's beginning to emerge, with seven more films in postproduction.

You won't have a bad time seeing *Sunshine Cleaning*. You may get a little frustrated waiting for it to take off. It keeps heading down different runways. There's a movie here somewhere. Not this one.

Surfwise ★ ★ ★

R, 93 m., 2008

A documentary directed and narrated by Doug Pray and produced by Graydon Carter, Tommy Means, Matthew Weaver, and Jonathan Paskowitz.

Surfwise sounds, of course, like a surfing documentary. It contains surfers and surfing all right, but in fact it's about the strange and problematical Paskowitz family, "the first family of surfing." We meet Dorian "Doc" Paskowitz at eighty-five years old, doing exercises in the nude and then providing a full body inventory: arthritis, muscular degeneration, but nothing that keeps him from surfing. "And I don't take a single pill!" he boasts. This from a 1940s graduate of the Stanford Medical School.

Young Dr. Paskowitz was on a standard post-college career track, I guess, through two failed marriages. Then he sold everything, went on a quest for meaning, found that he loved surfing more than anything else, introduced the sport to Israel, and took to himself a wife named Juliette, with whom he had eight sons and a daughter. These eleven people lived a nomadic life together in a twenty-four-foot camper during the years when the kids were growing up.

We see the campers—there were three, all purchased used, all the same size. A little crowded for two people. Not for the Paskowitz family. As Doc drove from one surfing mecca to another, they crowded in the back, slept together "like puppies," had to listen to their parents make loud, energetic love every single night, ate a lot of gruel and organic soups, and had just about enough clothing to muster eight clothed children, but not always nine. There was nothing at all like formal education.

What are we to make of this existence? Doc sees himself as a messiah of surfing, clean living, and healthy exercise. We might be more inclined to see him as a narcissistic monster, ruling his big family with an iron fist. Sounds like fun, driving from one beach to another, unless you're crowded in the back of the camper with eight other kids and not much of a view. One son recalls the day he discovered other people had eggs for breakfast.

Doc finally found a more stable way to support his family by starting a surfing camp near San Diego. Graydon Carter, editor of *Vanity Fair* and one of the producers of this film, was an early camper. The Paskowitz Surfing Camp inspired devotion, although one of Doc's children after another drifted away from the camper "home." Doc saw each bail-out as treachery.

Remarkably, the film's director, Doug Pray, has been able to track down each and every Paskowitz child, and he weaves their memories together with old home movies, still photos, and news clippings to create an evocative portrait of their lives. The kids are no more screwed up than any other nine kids—maybe less so. They have survived the absence of formal education. One says, "I love my father, but I don't understand him." And at the end they all bury their differences and gather for a family reunion in Hawaii (staged at least in part for the camera, one suspects). In the center of everything, there's Doc, his weather-beaten skin now a deep bronze, and his wife, Juliette, kissing and hugging and looking completely serene about the lives they built for themselves and their children.

Surrogates ★★ ½
PG-13, 88 m., 2009

Bruce Willis (Thomas Greer), Radha Mitchell (Jennifer Peters), Rosamund Pike (Maggie Greer), Boris Kodjoe (Andrew Stone), James Francis Ginty (Young Canter), James Cromwell (Dr. Lionel Canter), Ving Rhames (The Prophet), Jack Noseworthy (Strickland), Devin Ratray (Bobby), Michael Cudlit (Colonel Brendon). Directed by Jonathan Mostow and produced by Max Handelman, David Hoberman, and Todd Lieberman. Screenplay by John Brancato and Michael Ferris, based on the graphic novel by Robert Venditti and Brett Weldele.

In the future world of *Surrogates,* most of the human population reclines at home without moving, while living vicariously through robot avatars controlled by their minds. They present themselves to the world as younger and more attractive than they really are—and more fit, I assume, since the avatars work out at gyms instead of their owners. No one you meet is really there.

Bruce Willis, looking about thirty-eight and with a healthy mop of hair, stars as Greer, an FBI agent. He and his partner, Jennifer Peters (Radha Mitchell), are assigned to investigate a messy murder late one night outside a club, and are astonished to find that the victim is the son of Dr. Lionel Canter (James Cromwell), the inventor of surrogate technology. But wait a minute, you're thinking. Who dies if only your surrogate is killed? The unsettling answer is that the murder device works by frying the brain of its controller. I hate it when that happens.

Dr. Canter, no longer associated with the corporation that makes surrogates, has indeed grown disillusioned with his invention. As Agent Greer's investigation continues, it leads him into the world of the Dreads—actual human beings who reject surrogates and live on "reservations" with other flesh-and-blood people. The Dread leader is The Prophet (Ving Rhames of the eerie presence), who preaches against avatars as an abomination.

As indeed they are. It's a relief when something goes wrong with Greer's avatar and he must venture onto the streets as himself: middle-aged, bald, and looking, I must say, considerably more attractive than his creepy surrogate.

Unfortunately, *Surrogates*, while more ambitious than it has to be, descends into action scenes too quickly. Why must so many screenplays reduce their ideas to chases and shoot-outs? The concept here, based on a graphic novel by Robert Venditti and Brett Weldele, would lead naturally to intriguing considerations.

Consider plastic surgery. To what extent is Joan Rivers a seventy-six-year-old woman inhabiting a fifty-six-year-old avatar? Consider the problem of sex. After two attractive people meet, flirt, and desire to have sex, there are two possibilities: (1) their avatars have some sort of mechanical encounter while their owners, at home, masturbate; or (2) two real people, God forbid, have to discover how the other really looks. Since evolution suggests that we evaluate potential mates for their reproductive potential, this could lead to setbacks in the process of natural selection.

In this future world, we learn, surrogates mean that crime and racism have been all but eliminated. If anybody can be of any race, that takes care of racism, all right. But crime? How do those humans who are poor and unemployed *pay* for their surrogates? What if you decide you want to trade up to a better model? Sure, your surrogate may have a job, but why would salaries be any better? Especially since robots make poor consumers. What process

actually takes place when they have a meal together in a restaurant? Can they eat or drink?

Avatars first came into general consciousness by way of computer games and chat boards. It's well known that people you meet online may not be who they pretend to be. Surrogates sound like an ideal solution for transsexuals. Don't go through the surgery, just switch your avatar's gender. But would that satisfy your hormonal feelings? There are real bodies involved here, and that gets into another issue: If you spend your life reclining, your muscles will atrophy surprisingly quickly, and it will become physically impossible for you to get out of bed and walk, let alone go into action like Bruce Willis does here.

These are areas *Surrogates*, perhaps wisely, doesn't explore. Such a film might have required a Spike Jonze or Guy Maddin. *Surrogates* is entertaining and ingenious, but it settles too soon for formula. One other thing: It ends with the wrong shot. The correct shot would have been the overhead exterior of the street, about four shots earlier. You'll know the one I mean. 🖙

Survival of the Dead ★★
R, 90 m., 2010

Alan Van Sprang (Sarge Crocket), Kenneth Welsh (Patrick O'Flynn), Kathleen Munroe (Jane O'Flynn), Richard Fitzpatrick (Seamus Muldoon), Devon Bostick (Boy). Directed by George A. Romero and produced by Paula Devonshire. Screenplay by Romero.

For the purposes of watching *Survival of the Dead*, I'm perfectly willing to believe in zombies. It's a stretch, however, to believe in an island off the coast of Delaware where life looks like outtakes from *Ryan's Daughter*, everyone speaks with an Irish accent, and there's a bitter feud between those who believe in capital punishment for zombies, and those who call for their rehabilitation and cure.

How can you kill *or* rehabilitate a zombie, since by definition it is dead? Here's my reasoning: If it can attack you and dine on your throbbing flesh, it isn't dead enough. George A. Romero is our leading researcher in this area, having reinvented zombies for modern times with *Night of the Living Dead* (1968), and returned to them from time to time, most successfully in the excellent *Dawn of the Dead* (1978).

Zombies, as I have noted before (and before, and before), make excellent movie creatures because they are smart enough to be dangerous, slow enough to kill, and dead enough we need not feel grief. Romero has not even begun to run out of ways to kill them. My favorite shot in this film shows a zombie having its head blown apart, with the skullcap bouncing into the air and falling down to fit neatly over the neck. If that doesn't appeal to you, nothing will.

I've seen a whole lot of zombies killed. I've been cordial over the years with Romero, who in addition to reinventing zombies demonstrated how horror movies were a low-cost point of entry for independent filmmakers. To him we possibly owe such directors as David Cronenberg and John Carpenter. *Dawn of the Dead* was a biting indictment of the culture of the shopping mall, with most of its action in a landscape of modern retailing and merchandising. It was also funny.

All true. But after you've seen, oh, I dunno, twenty or thirty zombie movies, you sort of stop caring very much, unless something new is going on, as in *Zombieland*. At this point, I find myself watching primarily to spot and appreciate entertaining new ways to slaughter zombies. That's why the skullcap moment appealed to me. It was new.

Not much else is new in *Survival of the Dead*. After a vaguely explained plague of zombies has broken out, America has descended into post-apocalyptic warfare. The zombie disease is spreading. If one bites you, you become a zombie. That ability to infect others was once the special gift of vampires, and I suspect it has now been bestowed on zombies by gene-splicing at the genetic level. All zombies share one characteristic: They take a lickin' and keep on tickin'.

On the island off Delaware, we meet the O'Flynns and Muldoons, who are in the dependable tradition of the Hatfields and McCoys. The O'Flynns believe zombies exist to be destroyed. The Muldoons, more humane, want to chain them up and keep them around until a cure is discovered. How do you vote? How would you feel if the Muldoon scheme

worked, and you were a cured zombie? Would your flesh still look a little decomposed? Would you mention it in your entry on Match.com?

The leader of the O'Flynns is exiled to the mainland via rowboat, and in Philadelphia we encounter paramilitaries who are fighting off zombies and considering going to . . . the island off the Delaware coast. I was unable to stir up the slightest interest in the O'Flynns and Muldoons, the military types reminded me of the better *28 Days Later*, and finally, all that kept my attention were the ingenious ways Romero killed the zombies. The man is a fount of imagination. Scarcely a zombie dies in a boring way. So there's that.

Swing Vote ★ ★ ★
PG-13, 119 m., 2008

Kevin Costner (Bud Johnson), Madeline Carroll (Molly Johnson), Paula Patton (Kate Madison), Kelsey Grammer (Andrew Boone), Dennis Hopper (Donald Greenleaf), Nathan Lane (Art Crumb), Stanley Tucci (Martin Fox). Directed by Joshua Michael Stern and produced by Jim Wilson and Kevin Costner. Screenplay by Stern and Jason Richman.

Kevin Costner's new movie is about a presidential election that literally comes down to one man, one vote. The vote belongs to Bud Johnson, an alcoholic egg inspector from New Mexico, who finds himself the focus of the eyes of the world. Costner plays him as a hungover loser who cares about only one pair of eyes, those of his twelve-year-old daughter, Molly. When he realizes he has become an embarrassment to her, he begins to change.

The idea of an entire election coming down to one man's vote is admittedly just a tad difficult to accept. But the movie makes a plucky stab at explaining how it comes to happen—and it almost sounds plausible. Everything depends on Molly. From the opening scene (Bud too hungover to get Molly to school) we see she's trying her best to be loyal to him, although he's a daily problem. This day, as it turns out, is Election Day, and she is determined at all costs that her dad will turn up at the polling place and vote.

It doesn't turn out that way. Bud gets laid

off at the egg works, gets drunk, passes out. Molly waits impatiently at the polling place, where he promised to turn up on time. He doesn't, but an ingenious plot strategy makes it appear that he did, and that his vote was not counted, and when the whole election comes down to that one vote in New Mexico, which is tied, well, then you've got your movie.

The media descend on the town like a locust swarm. TV cameras and reporters are camped permanently outside the Johnson house trailer. Molly, who knows what really happened, keeps it to herself. And we meet people like Kate Madison (Paula Patton), the ace TV reporter who makes friends with Molly, and Sweeney (George Lopez), who will do anything for a scoop.

We also meet the two presidential candidates. Yes, they both fly to New Mexico to court Bud Johnson's decisive vote, and promise him the sun, the moon, and the stars. Kelsey Grammer is the Republican incumbent, President Andrew Boone. Dennis Hopper plays the Democratic challenger, Donald Greenleaf. Each has a campaign manager: Nathan Lane for the Democrat, and Stanley Tucci for the Republican. Oddly enough, there are times when the managers seem to have more ethics than the candidates.

The movie is a genial comedy, but it has significant undertones. Like some of Frank Capra's pictures (*Mr. Smith Goes to Washington* comes to mind), it shows a little guy up against the establishment—except this time it's a little girl, encouraging her dad to do the right thing. This works, because if there's one thing Bud Johnson doesn't want to do, it's embarrass Molly.

It all comes down to a crucial speech before his deciding vote. It's a Capraesque speech, incorporating big ideas into everyday language, and Costner delivers it with dignity, avoiding various pitfalls easily imagined. The speech doesn't make anyone very happy, but that's the idea. Kevin Costner makes a convincing everyman, even handling the transition from drunk to diplomat in one week flat. The turning point comes when he and the president relax in lawn chairs, contemplating Air Force One, and Bud pours out a margarita instead of drinking it. Sober, he turns out to be a pretty smart guy.

Molly always knew that. Young Madeline Carroll is splendid in the role, which during some stretches of the film is really the lead. She's clear-eyed and outspoken, has faith in her dad, and despite his drinking loves living with him. Once we get a glimpse of her mom (Mare Winningham), we understand why. The whole film is strongly cast, and I especially liked Stanley Tucci as a campaign manager who has steered one campaign after another into defeat.

The movie is determined to be bipartisan. It doesn't take sides. Both candidates would sell their mothers to win the election. That's the message, really: Our political system doesn't encourage politicians to tell the truth, but to say what they think voters want to hear. And the press assists them in that process. The movie is actually surprisingly realistic in portraying reporters on the campaign trail. They're a bunch of jackals, with the exception of sweet Kate Madison, who sacrifices the scoop of a lifetime because she has a good heart. That's one detail I really couldn't believe.

Synecdoche, New York ★ ★ ★ ★
R, 124 m., 2008

Philip Seymour Hoffman (Caden Cotard), Samantha Morton (Hazel), Michelle Williams (Claire Keen), Catherine Keener (Adele Lack), Emily Watson (Tammy), Dianne Wiest (Ellen/Millicent), Jennifer Jason Leigh (Maria), Hope Davis (Madeleine Gravis), Tom Noonan (Sammy Barnathan). Directed by Charlie Kaufman and produced by Sidney Kimmel, Anthony Bregman, Ray Angelic, and Spike Jonze. Screenplay by Kaufman.

I think you have to see Charlie Kaufman's *Synecdoche, New York*, twice. I watched it the first time and knew it was a great film and that I had not mastered it. The second time because I needed to. The third time because I will want to. It will open to confused audiences and live indefinitely. A lot of people these days don't even go to a movie once. There are alternatives. It doesn't have to be the movies, but we must somehow dream. If we don't "go to the movies" in any form, our minds wither and sicken.

This is a film with the richness of great fiction. Like *Suttree*, the Cormac McCarthy novel I'm always mentioning, it's not that you have to return to understand it. It's that you have to return to realize how fine it really is. The surface may daunt you. The depths enfold you. The whole reveals itself, and then you may return to it like a talisman.

Wow, is that ever not a "money review." Why will people hurry along to what they expect to be trash, when they're afraid of a film they think may be good? The subject of *Synecdoche, New York*, is nothing less than human life and how it works. Using a neurotic theater director from upstate New York, it encompasses every life and how it copes and fails. Think about it a little and, my god, it's about you. *Whoever* you are.

Here is how life is supposed to work. We come out of ourselves and unfold into the world. We try to realize our desires. We fold back into ourselves, and then we die. *Synecdoche, New York*, follows a life that ages from about forty to eighty on that scale. Caden Cotard (Philip Seymour Hoffman) is a theater director, with all of the hang-ups and self-pity, all the grandiosity and sniffles, all the arrogance and fear typical of his job. In other words, he could be me. He could be you. He could be Joe the Plumber. The job, the name, the race, the gender, the environment all change. The human remains pretty much the same.

Here is how it happens. We find something we want to do, if we are lucky, or something we need to do, if we are like most people. We use it as a way to obtain food, shelter, clothing, mates, comfort, a First Folio of Shakespeare, model airplanes, American Girl dolls, a handful of rice, sex, solitude, a trip to Venice, Nikes, drinking water, plastic surgery, child care, dogs, medicine, education, cars, spiritual solace, whatever we think we need. To do this, we enact the role we call *me*, trying to brand ourselves as a person who can and should obtain these things.

In the process, we place the people in our lives into compartments and define how they should behave to our advantage. Because we cannot *force* them to follow our desires, we deal with projections of them created in our minds. But they *will* be contrary and have

wills of their own. Eventually new projections of us are dealing with new projections of them. Sometimes versions of ourselves disagree. We succumb to temptation—but, oh, father, what else was I gonna do? I feel like hell. I repent. I'll do it again.

Hold that trajectory in mind and let it interact with age, discouragement, greater wisdom, and more uncertainty. You will understand what *Synecdoche, New York*, is trying to say about the life of Caden Cotard and the lives in his life. Charlie Kaufman is one of the few truly important writers to make screenplays his medium. David Mamet is another. That is not the same as a great writer (Faulkner, Pinter, Cocteau) who writes screenplays. Kaufman is writing in the upper reaches with Bergman. Now for the first time he directs.

It is obvious that he has only one subject, the mind, and only one plot, how the mind negotiates with reality, fantasy, hallucination, desire, and dreams. *Being John Malkovich*. *Eternal Sunshine of the Spotless Mind*. *Adaptation*. *Human Nature*. *Confessions of a Dangerous Mind*. What else are they about? He is working in plain view. In one film, people go inside the head of John Malkovich. In another, a writer has a twin who does what he cannot do. In another, a game show host is, or thinks he is, an international spy. In *Human Nature*, a man whose childhood was shaped by domineering parents trains white mice to sit down at a tiny table and always employ the right silverware. Is behavior learned or enforced?

Synecdoche, New York, is not a film about the theater, although it looks like one. A theater director is an ideal character for representing the role Kaufman thinks we all play. The magnificent sets, which stack independent rooms on top of one another, are the compartments we assign to our life's enterprises. The actors are the people in roles we cast from our point of view. Some of them play doubles assigned to do what there's not world enough and time for. They have a way of acting independently, in violation of instructions. They try to control their own projections. Meanwhile, the source of all this activity grows older and tired, sick and despairing. Is this real or a dream? The world is but a stage, and we are mere actors upon it. It's all a play. The play is real.

This has not been a conventional review. There is no need to name the characters, name the actors, assign adjectives to their acting. Look at who is in this cast. You know what I think of them. This film must not have seemed strange to them. It's what they do all day, especially waiting around for the director to make up his mind.

What does the title mean? It means it's the title. Get over it.

T

Take ★ ★
R, 99 m., 2008

Minnie Driver (Ana), Jeremy Renner (Saul), Bobby Coleman (Jesse), Adam Rodriguez (Steven), David Denman (Marty Nicols). Directed by Charles Oliver and produced by Chet Thomas. Screenplay by Oliver.

Well, you can't fault the actors. That must mean it's the fault of the writer and director. *Take* is a monotonous slog through dirge land, telling a story that seems strung out beyond all reason, with flashbacks upon flashbacks delaying interminably the underwhelming climax.

Minnie Driver and Jeremy Renner star, and both of their performances would distinguish a better screenplay. She is Ana, a house cleaner, the wife of an elementary school-teacher, the mother of a hyperactive little boy named Jesse (Bobby Coleman). Renner plays Saul, a loser at a very low level, who owes two thousand dollars to a lowlife and works for a storage company. He gets fired by stealing possessions from one locker and planting them in a locker where the contents will be auctioned. He pockets the extra cash. Neat, right? I don't know how the boss finds out about it. Just Saul's rotten luck.

It's one of those days for him. After getting fired, he splits his knuckles while breaking the window of his car, which won't start. Then he begs a pal for the two thousand dollars, and is lent a car and assigned to steal a Range Rover. Then the owner of the Range Rover beats him to a pulp. He finds a gun in the loaner car, slips it in his pocket, and goes to a drugstore to get his ailing dad's prescription filled. Seeing the cashier's window, he decides on the spot to rob the store, and in the process shoots the cashier and takes little Jesse as hostage. If only he hadn't been fired, a lot of people would have been saved a lot of trouble.

These events are doled out parsimoniously by Charles Oliver, who wrote and directed, intercutting with Ana driving her own broken-down car and towing a trailer. She is driving to the prison where Saul is scheduled to be executed, and wants to talk to him before he dies.

Although there is an enigmatic phone call over the opening credits that may explain this, I am not at all sure how by this point she seems to have misplaced her husband.

Meanwhile (the whole movie takes place meanwhile), we see Saul sitting chained to a chair, being walked down corridors, being prepared for death, and then having a long theological chat with the prison chaplain. The chaplain is certainly a good sport, trying to convince the murderer that everything is part of God's plan. Saul is not too bright, but he cannot quite see how what he has done and what is being done to him represent good planning.

Ana and Saul do indeed meet and talk, but if you're hoping for a conversation along the lines of *Dead Man Walking*, you'll be disappointed. I spent more time wondering how long it takes to try to execute a prisoner in whatever state this is, since Saul still has a not-quite healed scar from the Range Rover beating, and a Band-Aid from the window smashing.

One critic of the movie accuses it of having a sneaky ending that suggests it might all have been a dream. I guess that would explain the emphasis placed on close-ups showing Ana and Saul staring at each other's ID patches on their uniforms. Maybe they imagined each other's lives? But then why would they meet? The backseat shot that may have misled the critic is obviously only in Ana's imagination. Little Jesse can't really be there. After all that's happened, do you think she would walk off and leave her son unattended in a prison parking lot?

Taken ★ ★ ½
PG-13, 91 m., 2009

Liam Neeson (Bryan Mills), Famke Janssen (Lenore), Maggie Grace (Kim). Directed by Pierre Morel and produced by Luc Besson. Screenplay by Besson and Robert Mark Kamen.

If CIA agents in general were as skilled as Bryan Mills in particular, bin Laden would have been an American prisoner since late September 2001. *Taken* shows him as a one-man rescue squad, a master of every skill, a laser-eyed, sharpshooting, pursuit-driving, pocket-picking, impersonating, knife-fighting, torturing, karate-fighting killing machine who can cleverly turn over a petrol tank with one pass in his car and strategically ignite it with another.

We meet Mills (Liam Neeson) in "sort of retirement" in Los Angeles, grilling steaks with old CIA buddies and yearning to spend more time with his seventeen-year-old daughter, Kim (Maggie Grace). Kim now lives with her mom, Mills's ex-wife (Famke Janssen), and her effortlessly mega-rich husband (Xander Berkeley), whose idea of a birthday present is giving Kim, not a pony, but what looks like a thoroughbred.

Mills has seen action in Afghanistan and apparently everywhere else and knows it's a dangerous world for a naive teenage girl. He is against Kim spending the summer in Paris with her girlfriend, even though "cousins" will apparently chaperone. He's right. Kim and her pal succeed in getting themselves kidnapped the afternoon of the same day they get off the plane, although Kim has time for one terrified phone call to Dad before she's taken.

Now listen to this. Using CIA contacts at Langley, Mills is able to use his garbled tape of their conversation to determine the name of his girl's kidnapper (Marko), that he is Albanian, that his ring kidnaps young tourists, drugs them, and runs them as prostitutes; the virgins are auctioned off to Arab sheiks and so on. Headquarters also tells Mills he has ninety-six hours to rescue his daughter before she meets a fate worse than death, followed by death.

With this kind of intelligence, the CIA could be using bin Laden's Visa card in every ATM in Virginia. It's the setup for a completely unbelievable action picture where Mills is given the opportunity to use one element of CIA spy craft after another, read his enemies' minds, eavesdrop on their telephones, spy on their meetings, and, when necessary, defeat roomfuls of them in armed combat. At one point a former colleague in the Paris police says he has left seven bodies behind. Mills is just getting warmed up. How this man and his daughter could hope to leave France on a commercial flight doesn't speak highly of the French police—and the new

Pink Panther doesn't open for a week. Oh, why does he have only ninety-six hours? To provide the movie with a handy deadline, that's why.

It's always a puzzle to review a movie like this. On the one hand, it's preposterous. But who expects a Bourne-type city-wrecking operative to be plausible? On the other hand, it's very well made. Liam Neeson brings the character a hard-edged, mercilessly focused anger, and director Pierre Morel hurtles through action sequences at a breathless velocity. If Kim is an empty-headed twit, well, she's offscreen most of the time, and the villains are walking showcases for testosterone gone bad. The only tiny glitch is that if one chase scene doesn't use the same ramp down to a construction site that the opening of *Quantum of Solace* did, it sure looks like it does.

The film reopens a question I've had. A lot of movies involve secret clubs or covens of rich white men who meet for the purposes of despoiling innocent women in despicable perversity. The men are usually dressed in elegant formal wear, smoke cigars, and have champagne poured for them by discreet servants. Do such clubs actually exist? Since every member would be blackmailable, how can they survive? If you lost everything in a Ponzi scheme, would you betray your lodge members? Just wondering.

The movie proves two things: (1) Liam Neeson can bring undeserved credibility to most roles just by playing them, and (2) Luc Besson, the cowriter, whose action assembly line produced this film, turns out high-quality trash, and sometimes much better (*The Fifth Element, Taxi, The Transporter, La Femme Nikita*, even *The Three Burials of Melquiades Estrada*). The bottom line is, if you can't wait for the next Bourne thriller, well, you don't have to. I can easily wait, but Truth in Reviewing compels me to confess that if the movie I was describing in the first paragraph sounded as if you'd like this, you probably will.

The Taking of Pelham 1 2 3 ★ ★ ½
R, 106 m., 2009

Denzel Washington (Walter Garber), John Travolta (Ryder), John Turturro (Camonetti), Luis Guzman (Phil Ramos), Michael Rispoli

(John Johnson), James Gandolfini (Mayor). Directed by Tony Scott and produced by Scott, Todd Black, Jason Blumenthal, and Steve Tisch. Screenplay by Brian Helgeland, based on the novel by John Godey.

There's not much wrong with Tony Scott's *The Taking of Pelham 1 2 3* except that there's not much really right about it. Nobody gets terrifically worked up except the special effects people. Oh, John Travolta is angry and Denzel Washington is determined, but you don't sense passion in the performances. They're about behaving, not evoking.

The story, you already know from cable re-runs. There are a few changes: The boss hijacker is now an ex-con instead of a former mercenary. The negotiator is now a transit executive, not a cop. The ransom has gone up from $1 million to $10 million. The special effects are much more hyperkinetic and absurd than before, which is not an improvement. When a police car has a high-speed collision, the result is usually consistent with the laws of gravity and physics. It does not take flight and spin head over heels in the air.

The Washington and Travolta roles were played the first time around by Walter Matthau and Robert Shaw. They fit into them naturally. Matthau in particular had a shaggy charm I am nostalgic for. Shaw brought cold steel to the film. Denzel is . . . nice. Sincere. Wants to clear his name. Travolta is so ruthless it comes across as more peremptory than evil.

Since time immemorial, Vehicular Disaster Epics have depended on colorful and easily remembered secondary passengers: nuns with guitars, middle-aged women with swimming medals, a pregnant woman about to go into labor, etc. This time the passengers on the Pelham line disappoint. There's a nice woman who's worried about her child, and an ex–Army Ranger who comes to her aid. That's about it. Few of the juicy ethnic stereotypes of the original.

In fact, the whole film is less juicy. The 1974 version took place in a realistic, well-worn New York City. This version occupies a denatured action movie landscape, with no time for local color and a transit system control room that humbles Mission Control. That may also explain its lack of time to establish the supporting characters, even Travolta's partners. These sleek modern actioners don't give the audience credit for much patience and curiosity. One star or the other has to be on the screen in almost every scene. The relentless pace can't be slowed for much dialogue, especially for supporting characters. It all has to be mindless, implausible action.

Say what you will about the special effects of the 1970s, at least I was convinced I was looking at a *real train*. Think this through with me: Once you buy in to the fact that the train is *there*, the train becomes a given. You're thinking, ohmigod, what's going to happen to the train? With modern CGI, there are scenes where a real train is obviously not on the screen, at least not in real time and space, and you're thinking, ohmigod, real trains can't go that fast. And when cars crash, cars should crash. They shouldn't behave like pinballs.

Note: Here's an interesting thing. Looking up my 1974 review, I found that four of the characters were named Blue, Green, Grey, and Brown. Could it be that when Quentin Tarantino was writing about Mr. White, Mr. Orange, Mr. Blonde, and Mr. Pink in Reservoir Dogs, *he was . . . naw, it's gotta be just a coincidence.*

Taking Woodstock ★★★
R, 120 m., 2009

Demetri Martin (Elliot Teichberg), Dan Fogler (Devon), Henry Goodman (Jake Teichberg), Jonathan Groff (Michael Lang), Eugene Levy (Max Yasgur), Jeffrey Dean Morgan (Dan), Imelda Staunton (Sonia Teichberg), Paul Dano (VW Guy), Kelli Garner (VW Girl), Mamie Gummer (Tisha), Emile Hirsch (Billy), Liev Schreiber (Vilma). Directed by Ang Lee and produced by Lee, James Schamus, and Celia Costas. Screenplay by Schamus, based on the book *Taking Woodstock: A True Story of a Riot, a Concert, and a Life* by Elliot Tiber with Tom Monte.

Luckily I saw *Woodstock* again in April, so it was fresh in my mind while watching *Taking Woodstock*, Ang Lee's entertaining new film about the kid who made it all possible—in Woodstock, anyway. This was Elliot Teichberg, a young interior designer who leaves a New York City career to return home to upstate New York and help his parents bail out their failing and shabby motel.

He's already held outdoor "music festivals" at the motel, which have involved people sitting on the grass and listening to him play records. Now he learns a nearby town has refused a permit to the organizers of a proposed August 1969 rock concert. As the head of the tiny Bethel Chamber of Commerce, near Woodstock, he calls the organizers and offers a permit. And history is made. What if Woodstock had been named after the town that turned it down, Wallkill?

Lee's movie is so deliberately backstage that we never see any of the performances, although we hear them sometimes in the background. All is seen through the eyes of Elliot, who ignores local fears of a hippie riot and persuades local dairy farmer Max Yasgur (Eugene Levy) to make his acres available as the venue. Max and other people in the film, such as the Port-O-San man and a local couple with one son at Woodstock and another in Vietnam, are familiar from the Woodstock film.

But Lee and his writer, James Schamus, aren't making a historical pastiche. This is a comedy with some sweet interludes and others that are cheerfully over the top, such as a nude theatrical troupe living in Elliot's barn, and Vilma, his volunteer head of motel security, a transvestite ex-Marine played by Liev Schreiber. How does Schreiber, looking just as he usually does except for a blond wig and a dress, play a transvestite? Completely straight. It works.

The backstage cast of characters includes concert organizer Michael Lang (Jonathan Groff) and Elliot's buddy Billy (Emile Hirsch), a returned and strung-out Vietnam veteran. Also loud and omnipresent are Elliot's mother, Sonia (Imelda Staunton), and her long-suffering husband, Jake (Henry Goodman). Sonia, a Russian immigrant paralyzed by fears of poverty, has run the motel into the ground with lack of maintenance and such policies as charging a dollar for a towel. Descended upon by a busload of organizers, she converts rooms into "triples" by hanging sheets from the ceiling. Her shrill greed cuts through all the peace and love until, finally, even she warms up.

Instead of showing much more than glimpses and edges of the concert, Lee shows the local impact as "Woodstock Nation" swamps little Bethel. He also shows the good will of most of the locals and police, who join in the spirit. There's a remarkable shot, which must have been hard to stage, of Elliot getting a ride on a police motorcycle past a backup of hundreds of cars, vans, and pedestrians; this reminded me of the famous traffic jam in Godard's *Weekend*.

I was reminded, too, of another film, Phil Kaufman's *The Unbearable Lightness of Being*. That film made remarkable use of pre-CGI special effects to seamlessly insert its characters into actual footage of the Prague demonstrations against the Russian occupation.

What Lee does, apparently, is use footage from Michael Wadleigh's *Woodstock* (1970) and insert Elliot and others into it. I say "apparently," because the end titles don't mention the Warner Bros. picture. Who knows? It looks remarkably convincing. Perhaps they found some of the miles of additional footage shot by Wadleigh and his big crew. The poignancy of Wadleigh's closing shots of the cleanup effort are mirrored here as Elliot joins in.

Not many events of forty years ago would inspire a feature comedy. Seeing the 1970 film on a big screen in 70 mm in April at Ebertfest, with an audience including many who had never seen it before, was an affirmation of how timeless those "three days of peace and music" have become. *Taking Woodstock* has the freshness of something being created, not remembered. I saw a photo the other day of the young couple shown on the original album jacket. Still married, still with their arms around each other.

The Tale of Despereaux ★ ★ ★
G, 93 m., 2008

Matthew Broderick (Despereaux), Dustin Hoffman (Roscuro), Emma Watson (Princess Pea), Tracey Ullman (Miggery Sow), Kevin Kline (Andre), William H. Macy (Lester), Stanley Tucci (Boldo), Ciaran Hinds (Botticelli), Robbie Coltrane (Gregory). Directed by Sam Fell and Rob Stevenhagen and produced by Gary Ross and Allison Thomas. Screenplay by Ross, based on the book by Kate DiCamillo.

The Tale of Despereaux is one of the most beautifully drawn animated films I've seen, rendered in enchanting detail and painterly colors by an art department headed by Olivier Adam. A story centering around a big-eared little mouse named Despereaux, a sniffy rat named Roscuro, and various other members of the animal and vegetable kingdoms, it is a joy to look at frame by frame, and it would be worth getting the Blu-ray to do that.

I am not quite so thrilled by the story, which at times threatens to make *Gormenghast* seem straightforward. There are three societies with interconnections (mouse, rat, and human), plus a man made of vegetables who possibly runs his social life out of the produce market, and maybe dates dates. Very old joke:

"You got dates?"

"I got no dates, mister."

"Then you got nuts?"

"Hey, mister! If I had nuts, I'd have dates!"

Roscuro (with a Ratso voice by Dustin Hoffman) is first on the scene, racing from a ship in port to sniff at the kingdom's annual spring festival, celebrated by the royal chef Andre (Kevin Kline) by creating a new soup to be shared by every citizen. Alas, Roscuro falls in the soup of the queen, who then falls in the soup herself and puts the king in mourning. He then banishes soup and rats from his realm, which is little matter to the rats, who have a highly evolved civilization somewhere below stairs.

The movie then intercuts between the plights of Princess Pea (Emma Watson) and the wretched scullery maid Miggery Sow (Tracey Ullman) upstairs; the big-eared Despereaux and his parents and teacher midstairs; and a rivalry between Roscuro and the scheming Botticelli (Ciaran Hinds) in the cellars.

Their antagonism leads to a gladiatorial combat, suggesting that the rats have a history as rich as the humans, and also that by this point some kids are going to want the nice mouse back again. The movie is based on a Newbery Award–winning novel by Kate DiCamillo, unread by me, but somehow puts me in mind of another wonderful mouse story, *Ben and Me,* by the great Robert Lawson.

I suppose the plot will be easier for DiCamillo's readers to untangle, and that those too young or too old to have read it will nevertheless appreciate the look of the film.

What I'd like to see is this same team take on a better-organized screenplay. Has anyone read the *Gormenghast* trilogy? There's a classic that would seem just about right with this look.

Taxi to the Dark Side ★ ★ ★ ★
R, 106 m., 2008

Featuring Alex Gibney (Narrator), Moazzam Begg, William Brand, Jack Cloonan, Damien Corsetti, Ken Davis, Carlotta Gall, Tim Golden, Scott Horton, Tony Lagouranis, Carl Levin, Alfred McCoy, Alberto Mora, Anthony Morden, Glendale Walls, Lawrence Wilkerson, Tim Wilner, John Yoo. A documentary written and directed by Alex Gibney and produced by Gibney, Eva Orner, and Susannah Shipman.

"We have to work the dark side."

So said Dick Cheney a few days after 9/11, discussing the war on terror. Is this what he meant? In December 2002, an Afghan named Dilawar had scraped together enough money to buy a taxi. He was fingered by a paid informant as a terrorist connected with a rocket attack. Taken to the American prison at Bagram, he was tortured so violently that he died after five days. An autopsy showed that his legs were so badly mauled they would have had to be amputated, had he lived. Later, the informant who collected U.S. money for fingering him was proven to be the terrorist actually responsible for the crime the innocent Dilawar was charged with.

An official report said Dilawar died of "natural causes." The *New York Times* found an autopsy report describing the death as a homicide. After a belated investigation, a few U.S. soldiers were accused of the murder. No officers were involved. Dilawar was the first casualty after we started to work the dark side. In all the torture scandals since, few officers have ever been charged. If all of these crimes took place without their knowledge, they would appear to be guilty of dereliction of duty, if nothing else.

Alex Gibney's horrifying documentary *Taxi to the Dark Side* uses the death of Dilawar as an entry point into a remorseless indictment of the Bush administration's unofficially condoned policy of the torture of suspects, which is forbidden by American constitutional and

527

military law and international agreements, but justified under the "necessity" of working the dark side. Gibney interviews U.S. soldiers who participated in such torture sessions (under orders, they thought, although their superiors claimed innocence, all the way up to Bush, who claimed ignorance of torture even after he had seen official Pentagon and intelligence reports). They seem sorry, sobered, and confused.

The film, one of this year's Oscar nominees for best documentary, has TV footage of administration officials demonstrably lying about what they knew and when they knew it. And it leads to Gibney's conversation with his own father, who was an interrogator of prisoners in World War II, and says not only was such behavior forbidden, but it wouldn't have worked anyway. If you torture a man long enough, he will tell you anything to make you stop. If you act on that "information," you are likely on a fool's errand.

Gibney is the same filmmaker who made the merciless *Enron: The Smartest Guys in the Room* (2005), a documentary where he produced actual tape recordings of Enron operatives *creating* the California "power shortage" by ordering power plants shut down and joking that a few grandmothers might have to die without air conditioning in order for Enron to make more millions. By the same logic, lives may have to be lost to torture to produce intelligence, although there is precious little evidence that the strategy has worked. And besides, is that what we do, as Americans? Are those our values? Then what do we stand for?

Gibney widens the net to include the illegal detainees at Guantanamo, most of whom have never been charged with any crime. He talks with former administration officials and spokesmen who didn't like what they were seeing and resigned. His conversations with the American torturers themselves are the most heartbreaking; young kids for the most part, they thought they were doing their duty. And he includes never-before-seen photos and images of torture at work. One tactic: Prisoners have their hands tied above their heads and are made to balance on boxes in pools of electrified water. Would they really be electrocuted if they fell off? Would you like to try? John McCain, who endured unimagin-

able torture, is among the most outspoken critics of this strategy.

There are those, their numbers shrinking every day, who would agree we have to "work the dark side." Growing numbers of us are yearning for the light. This movie does not describe the America I learned about in civics class or think of when I pledge allegiance to the flag. Yet I know I will get the usual e-mails accusing me of partisanship, bias, only telling one side, etc. What is the other side? See this movie and you tell me.

Tell No One ★ ★ ★ ½
NO MPAA RATING, 125 m., 2008

Francois Cluzet (Alexandre Beck), Andre Dussollier (Jacques Laurentin), Marie-Josee Croze (Margot Beck), Kristin Scott Thomas (Helene Perkins), Nathalie Baye (Elysabeth Feldman), Francois Berleand (Eric Levkowitch), Jean Rochefort (Gilbert Neuville), Guillaume Canet (Philippe Neuville), Gilles Lellouche (Bruno), Marina Hands (Anne Beck). Directed by Guillaume Canet and produced by Alain Attal. Screenplay by Canet and Philippe Lefebvre, based on a novel by Harlan Coben.

Tell No One will play as a terrific thriller for you if you meet it halfway. You have to be willing to believe. There will be times you think it's too perplexing, when you're sure you're witnessing loose ends. It has been devised that way, and the director knows what he's doing. Even when it's baffling, it's never boring. I've heard of airtight plots. This one is not merely airtight, but hermetically sealed.

The setup is the simple part. We meet a married couple, sweethearts since childhood: Alex (Francois Cluzet) and Margot (Marie-Josee Croze). They go skinny-dipping in a secluded pond and doze off on a raft. They have a little quarrel, and Margot swims ashore. Alex hears a scream. He swims to the dock, climbs the ladder, and is knocked unconscious.

Flash forward eight years. Alex is a pediatrician in a Paris hospital. He has never remarried and still longs for Margot. Two bodies are found buried in the forest where it is believed she was murdered, and the investigation is reopened. Although Margot's case was believed solved, suspicion of Alex has never entirely died out. He was hit so hard before falling back into the water that he was in a coma for three days. How did he get back on the dock?

Now the stage is set for a dilemma that resembles in some ways *The Fugitive*. Evidence is found that incriminates Alex: a murder weapon, for example, in his apartment. There is the lockbox that contains suspicious photographs and a shotgun tied to another murder. Alex is tipped off by his attorney (Nathalie Baye) and flees out the window of his office at the hospital just before the cops arrive. "You realize he just signed his own confession?" a cop says to the lawyer.

Alex is in very good shape. He runs and runs, pursued by the police. It is a wonderfully photographed chase, including a dance across both lanes of an expressway. His path takes him through Clignancourt, the labyrinthine antiques market, and into the mean streets on the other side. He shares a Dumpster with a rat. He is helped by a crook he once did a favor for; the crook has friends who seem to be omnipresent.

Ah, but already I've left out a multitude of developments. Alex has been electrified by cryptic e-mail messages that could only come from Margot. Is she still alive? He needs to elude the cops long enough to make a rendezvous in a park. And *still* I've left out so much—but I wouldn't want to reveal a single detail that would spoil the mystery.

Tell No One was directed and coscripted by Guillaume Canet, working from a novel by American author Harlan Coben. It contains a rich population of characters but has been so carefully cast that we're never confused. There are Alex's sister (Marina Hands), her lesbian lover (Kristin Scott Thomas), the rich senator whose obsession is racehorses (Jean Rochefort), Margot's father (Andre Dussollier), the police captain who alone believes Alex is innocent (Francois Berleand), the helpful crook (Gilles Lellouche), and the senator's son (Guillaume Canet himself). Also a soft-porn fashion photographer, a band of vicious assassins, street thugs, and on and on. And the movie gives full weight to these characters; they are necessary and handled with care.

If you give enough thought to the film, you'll begin to realize that many of the key roles are twinned, high and low. There are two cops closely on either side of retirement age. Two attractive brunettes. A cop and a crook who have similar personal styles. Two blondes who are angular professional women. Two lawyers. One of the assassins looks a little like Alex but has a beard. Such thoughts would never occur during the film, which is too enthralling. But it shows what love and care went into the construction of the puzzle.

One of the film's pleasures is its unexpected details. The big dog Alex hauls around. The Christian Louboutin red-soled shoes that are worn on two most unlikely occasions. The steeplechase right in the middle of everything. The way flashbacks are manipulated in their framing so that the first one shows less than when it is reprised. The way solutions are dangled before us and then jerked away. The computer technique. The tortuous path taken by some morgue photos. The seedy lawyer, so broke his name is scrawled in cardboard taped to the door. Alex patiently tutoring a young child. That the film clocks at only a whisper above two hours is a miracle.

And then look at the acting. Francois Cluzet is ideal as the hero: compact, handsome in a fortyish Dustin Hoffman sort of way, believable at all times (but then, we know his story is true). Marie-Josee Croze, with enough psychic weight she's present even when absent. Kristin Scott Thomas, not the outsider she might seem. Legendary Jean Rochefort, in a role legendary John Huston would have envied. Legendary Francois Berleand as a senior cop who will make you think of Inspector Maigret. And legendary Andre Dussollier sitting on the bench until the movie needs the bases cleared. Here is how a thriller should be made.

Terminator: Salvation ★ ★
PG-13, 115 m., 2009

Christian Bale (John Connor), Sam Worthington (Marcus Wright), Anton Yelchin (Kyle Reese), Bryce Dallas Howard (Kate Connor), Moon Bloodgood (Blair Williams), Common (Barnes), Jadagrace Berry (Star), Helena Bonham Carter (Dr. Serena Kogan), Jane Alexander (Virginia). Directed by McG and produced by Moritz Borman, Jeffrey Silver, Victor Kubicek, and

Derek Anderson. Screenplay by John Brancato and Michael Ferris.

One of Hollywood's oldest axioms teaches us: The story comes first. Watching *Terminator Salvation*, it occurred to me that in the new Hollywood, the story board comes first. After scrutinizing the film, I offer you my summary of the story: Guy dies, finds himself resurrected, meets others, fights. That lasts for almost two hours.

The action scenes, which is to say, 90 percent of the movie, involve Armageddon between men and machines ten years in the future. The most cheerful element of the film is that they've perfected Artificial Intelligence so quickly. Yes, Skynet is self-aware and determines to wipe out humankind for reasons it doesn't explain. A last-ditch resistance is being led by John Connor, or "J.C." for you Faulkner fans.

Christian Bale plays the role of Connor, in a movie that raises many questions about the lines between man and machine. Raises them and leaves them levitating. However, it has many fights between a humanoid cyborg and robotic Skynet men made of steel. How do these antagonists fight? Why, with their fists, of course, which remains a wonderfully cinematic device. They also shoot at each other, to little effect. In fact, one metal man is covered in molten ore and then flash-frozen, and keeps on tickin'. And listen, Skynet buddies, what Bale thought about that cameraman is only the tip of the iceberg compared to what he thinks about you.

There is nothing visible in this world but a barren wasteland. No towns, no houses, no food, no farms, no nothing. Maybe they live on Spam. The Resistance is run from a submarine commanded by General Ashdown (Michael Ironside), who wants to destroy Skynet and all of its human POWs. Connor, who is not even human, vows to save them. Wait. That's Marcus Wright (Sam Worthington), the guy from the past, who looks so much like Connor that maybe he only thinks he's Wright. Marcus is a convicted murderer from the past, awakened from cryogenic sleep.

I know with a certainty approaching dread that all of my questions will be explained to me in long, detailed messages from *Terminator* experts. They will also charge me with not seeing the movie before I reviewed it. Believe me, I would have enjoyed traveling forward through time for two hours, starting just before I saw the movie. But in regard to the answers to my questions: You know what? I *don't care.*

I regret (I suppose) that I did not see the first *Terminator* movie. *Terminator 2: Judgment Day* (1991) was a fairly terrific movie, set in the (then) future, to prevent the nuclear holocaust of 1997. You remember that. It was *about something.* In it, Edward Furlong was infinitely more human as John Connor than Christian Bale is in this film. Think about that.

Schwarzenegger, indeed, reappears in this fourth film, thanks to a body double and a special effects face, which makes him, I think, a cyborg of a cyborg. His famous line "I'll be back" is uttered by one John Connor or another, and I hope it draws more chuckles than it did at the screening I attended. Why, those immortal words are chiseled into granite, or at least into the lobby floor at the AMC River East theaters.

If there is one wholly sympathetic character in this film, that would be Blair Williams, played by the fragrant Moon Bloodgood. She murmurs some tender words at the forty-fiveminute mark, representing the most complex dialogue up to that point. Dr. Serena Kogan (Helena Bonham Carter) has a longer speech, but you can't be sure it's really her, and she may have been lying.

Anyway, most of the running time is occupied by action sequences, chase sequences, motorcycle sequences, plow truck sequences, helicopter sequences, fighter plane sequences, towering android sequences, and fistfights. It gives you all the pleasure of a video game without the bother of having to play it.

Terribly Happy ★★★
NO MPAA RATING, 100 m., 2010

Jakob Cedergren (Robert), Lene Maria Christensen (Ingelise Buhl), Kim Bodnia (Jorgen Buhl), Lars Brygmann (Dr. Zerlang), Anders Hove (Kobmand Moos), Mathilde Maack (Dorthe). Directed by Henrik Ruben Genz and produced by Tina Dalhoff and Thomas Gammeltoft. Screenplay by Genz and Gry Dunja Jensen, based on a novel by Erling Jepsen.

The cow gave birth to a calf with two heads, and they weren't just any two heads. Into the bog it went. All sorts of village problems sink in the bog. No telling what's rotting down there. This beginning may make *Terribly Happy* sound like a modern-day *Motel Hell*, where Farmer Vincent buried people to their necks and fattened them like geese. But no, this is a dour and deadpan film noir from Denmark, and a good one.

Robert (Jakob Cedergren), a young policeman from Copenhagen, has been exiled as punishment to a dismal village in South Jutland. He's about thirty, single, and made a "terrible mistake" he doesn't talk about. The town doesn't look like some cheery Danish hamlet, but more like a rundown grain elevator town in the Old West. When he steps into the bar, he's made to feel not only unwelcome, but in some subtle way threatened. The drinkers regard him with a level, cold gaze. They laugh at him behind his back. When he goes to get a bicycle repaired, he finds the repairman missing. He's told it's not uncommon for folks to go missing.

He asks a young woman for directions. This is Ingelise (Lene Maria Christensen). She has that Shirley MacLaine gamine look. She's not a raving beauty but has undeniable sex appeal. Robert senses it—he feels an attraction—but no, that would be wrong. But what happens when wrong starts to look right?

Something very wrong is happening in this town. The guys in the bar were unfriendly because they have every reason to believe Robert is kidding himself if he thinks he can get anything accomplished as the new town marshal. It gradually develops that Jorgen (Kim Bodnia), the husband of Ingelise, is feared by everyone, not least Ingelise, whom he beats. The film's most eerie detail involves their little daughter. When she parades alone down the abandoned main street with her baby buggy and its squeaky wheels, everyone knows domestic violence is taking place at Jorgen's house.

Bodnia, who plays Jorgen, is alarming in appearance and manner. He isn't one of those jumped-up ex-bouncers who stands six foot six and has big arms and a shaved head. He's alarming not for how he looks but for what he signals he's capable of. If Robert was a bad cop before, he's in way over his head now.

But there's another level. The townspeople seem to have little reason to fear if they'll just go along. They keep their heads low and their thoughts to themselves. Is this intended by the director, Henrik Ruben Genz, as some sort of a parable? I have no idea. It works well enough just at creating an intimidating atmosphere for Robert, who is disoriented when people don't just naturally accept him as, you know, the law.

Genz creates a distinctive look and feel in the film. The town is drab, the people wrung out, and the moments of passion are smoothed back down into the tired routine. You could almost get to feel comfortable in a town like this. Play ball and you won't be disturbed. Jakob Cedergren plays the marshal as a man born to be ordered around. He could only be a policeman in a town where people take cops seriously. Whatever happened to him in Copenhagen has him still in shock, and it's almost like he feels he deserves the way the town treats him. Even in his romantic transgression he seems to be going with the flow.

Terribly Happy at heart plays like a classic Western: the frontier town, the local bad man, the new marshal, the townspeople, cute and vulnerable Ingelise. I've only been to Denmark twice and have no idea if this is even remotely a Danish situation, but it could fit right fine in the Old West.

Tetro ★ ★ ★

NO MPAA RATING, 127 m., 2009

Vincent Gallo (Tetro), Alden Ehrenreich (Bennie), Maribel Verdu (Miranda), Klaus Maria Brandauer (Carlo/Alfie), Carmen Maura (Alone). Directed, written, and produced by Francis Ford Coppola.

Tetro may be the most autobiographical film Francis Ford Coppola has made. He said at Cannes, "Nothing in it happened, but it's all true." I guess I know what that means. He could be describing any "autobiographical" film or novel. The pitfall is in trying to find parallels: Coppola had a father who was a famous conductor, he has a brother he has sometimes argued with, his sister Talia Shire somewhat resembles the heroine of this film, his nephew Nicolas Cage somewhat resembles the character Tetro, and on and on. All meaningless.

Better to begin with a more promising starting point: The film is boldly operatic, involving family drama, secrets, generations at war, melodrama, romance, and violence. I'm only guessing, but Coppola, considering his father and his Italian-American heritage, may be as opera-besotted as any living American director, including Scorsese. His great epic *Apocalypse Now* is fundamentally, gloriously operatic. The oedipal issues in the *Godfather* trilogy are echoed again in *Tetro*. The emotions are theatrical, not realistic.

For that, he has the right actor, Vincent Gallo, who devotes himself to the title role with heedless abandon. There is nothing subtle about his performance, and nothing should be. He is the son of a famous conductor, he lives in exile in Buenos Aires, he has a wife who loyally endures his impossibilities. There are events in his past that damaged him, and he is unhappy that his younger brother, Bennie (Alden Ehrenreich), knocks unexpectedly at the door. He never wanted to see him again.

Tetro's wife, Miranda (Maribel Verdu), welcomes the young man, who works as a waiter on a cruise ship now in port for repairs. She wishes she knew more about Tetro's family and the reasons for his unhappiness. Tetro is uniformly hostile to almost everyone except Miranda, perhaps because he needs at least one person to speak with. Bennie bunks down in their apartment, is kept at arm's length from Tetro, is left alone in the flat, finds an unfinished play by Tetro, finishes it, and submits it to a festival run by the nation's most powerful critic, Alone (Carmen Maura). Argentina here is a nation that still has a powerful critic.

All hell breaks loose with Tetro, inspiring a series of flashbacks involving his father, Carlo (Klaus Maria Brandauer), a conductor who carries himself as a grand man. There are, of course, terrible secrets in the family past, known to Tetro but not to Bennie, and they are revealed in a final act worthy of Verdi.

Coppola and his cinematographer, Mihai Malaimare Jr., have photographed the central story in black and white, which made me hopelessly desire that more features could be made in this beautiful format. People who dislike b&w movies are, in their sad way, colorblind. The flashbacks are in color, presided over by Brandauer, as a sleek and contended

reptile. In a way, this is what his amoral character in *Mephisto* could have turned out like. Without straining or being given a lot of evil dialogue, he communicates egomania and selfishness.

Bennie has always idealized his older brother, picturing him as a brilliant writer in a faraway land, and is shaken to find the reality; Tetro's first entrance, on crutches, flailing at the furniture, is not promising. Gallo is not naturally given to playing ingratiating characters. He brings an uneasy edge to his work, and it's valuable here in evoking the deep wounds of his youth. Alden Ehrenreich, the newcomer playing Bennie, in his first major role, is confident and charismatic, and inspires such descriptions as "the new Leonardo DiCaprio," which remind me of the old showbiz joke.

Perhaps it was because of the b&w photography, but while watching the film I was reminded for the first time in years of Sidney Lumet's *A View from the Bridge* (1962) and Raf Vallone. It has the same feel of too much emotion trapped in a room, and Gallo channels Vallone's savage drive. It was a good memory. Here is a film that, for all of its plot, depends on characters in service of their emotional turmoil. It feels good to see Coppola back in form.

That Evening Sun ★★★ ½
PG-13, 110 m., 2010

Hal Holbrook (Abner Meecham), Ray McKinnon (Lonzo Choat), Walton Goggins (Paul Meecham), Mia Wasikowska (Pamela Choat), Carrie Preston (Ludie Choat), Barry Corbin (Thurl Chesser), Dixie Carter (Ellen Meecham). Directed by Scott Teems and produced by Terence Berry, Walton Goggins, Ray McHinnon, and Laura D. Smith. Screenplay by Teems, based on the story "I Hate to See That Evening Sun Go Down" by William Gay.

One of the reasons *That Evening Sun* works so well is that the good character isn't all good and the bad character isn't all bad, although they both come close. That leads to a drama set on a Tennessee farm that begins by looking like your standard old-codger story and turns out, as Clint Eastwood's *Gran Torino* did, to be a lot more.

Hal Holbrook, that rock-steady actor with a face off Mount Rushmore, stars as Abner Meecham, an eighty-something who up and walks out of a retirement home one day and takes a taxi to his farm outside of town. It is his farm as far as he's concerned, anyway, although his lawyer son has power of attorney and has rented it to the Choat family. This family is well-known to Abner, who dislikes them. He and his neighbor Thurl (Barry Corbin) agree that Lonzo Choat (Ray McKinnon) doesn't amount to much.

While his son, Paul (Walton Goggins), busy with a court case, issues ineffectual commands into his cell phone, Abner sets up an outpost in the bare-boards sharecropper cabin and keeps a hostile eye on the house. Lonzo's sixteen-year-old daughter, Pamela (Mia Wasikowska), comes to visit, is instinctively nice, and sort of disregards Abner's hostility. When she confides that her father hates barking dogs, Abner adopts one of Thurl's barkingest dogs and moves him into the cabin.

Choat has been living on disability, can't make payments on the house, is in no shape to work the farm, and usually has a beer in his hand. If the inside of the farmhouse looks warm and inviting, that's because of two women: Choat's long-suffering wife, Ludie (Carrie Preston), and Abner's own dead wife, Ellen (Dixie Carter). There is poignancy in that role now that Carter, Holbrook's wife, has herself died.

Ellen fixed up the house, Ludie keeps it up, and the two men snarl at each other in the yard. Abner cheerfully calls Choat a white trash redneck, which seems true as we see him drunkenly whipping his wife and daughter with a garden hose. Abner brings this to a stop with a couple of pistol shots. But this situation isn't as simple as who has the gun.

We begin to sense that Choat acts mean but is scared and uncertain inside. By flashbacks and other means, we learn that Abner hasn't always been a sterling husband and father himself. Because both men are flawed, the story takes on an interest and complexity that the setup doesn't hint.

It's a story confined by time and space, adapted by the director, Scott Teems, from the story "I Hate to See That Evening Sun Go Down" by William Gay. Although the setting is a gentle Tennessee landscape and the houses look like illustrations for a calendar of farm life, the situation owes more to Eugene O'Neill or Tennessee Williams. The actors are more than successful at creating deeply plausible characters. There may have been temptations to go broad, but they're all subtle, even McKinnon, in a role that could have gone over the top.

Watching Hal Holbrook, I was reminded again of how steady and valuable this man has been throughout his career. I saw his famous *Mark Twain Tonight* three times in the 1960s, I remember him and Dixie one night at the Royal Court Theater in London where a lamp came crashing to the stage and they handled it with perfect grace and humor, and I remember him most recently as the old man who cares and worries about the doom-seeking hero of *Into the Wild*. Here he incorporates everything he knows about getting to the age of eighty (he's actually eighty-five) and conveys it without the slightest sign of effort. This isn't a performance; it's an embodiment. You know, I think he's about old enough to play Mark Twain.

Note: That Evening Sun *won the Audience Award and a jury prize for ensemble acting at the 2010 SXSW film festival.*

Theater of War ★ ★ ½

NO MPAA RATING, 96 m., 2009

Featuring Meryl Streep, Tony Kushner, George C. Wolfe, Kevin Kline, Jay Cantor, Austin Pendleton, Barbara Brecht-Schall, Oskar Eustis, Jeanine Tesori, Carl Weber. A documentary directed by John Walter and produced by Nina Santisi.

Meryl Streep strikes me as one of the nicest people you'd ever want to meet. Also one of the great actresses, but her down-to-earth quality is what struck me in *Theater of War*, a documentary about the Public Theater's 2006 production of Bertolt Brecht's *Mother Courage and Her Children* in Central Park. She rehearses, she works with the composer, she never raises her voice, she endures full-dress rehearsals during a heat wave. The only complaint she has is that it's not a good idea for audiences to see a performance in "process" because the work looks like "bad acting."

Theater of War, directed by John Walter, does have access to all the rehearsals and intercuts them with documentary material about Brecht, his theatrical career, his life in exile, and his adventures with the House Un-American Activities Committee. There are also interviews with Streep, translator Tony Kushner, Brecht's daughter Barbara Brecht-Schall, and the director George C. Wolfe, a friend of Brecht's, who witnessed the historic 1949 production in East Berlin.

All of this makes an interesting, if not gripping, film about the play, the playwright, and the lead-up work to a stage production. It also leaves me wanting a great deal more. Perhaps in an attempt to emulate Brecht's antiwar theme, Walter devotes too much screen time to footage of antiwar protests during Vietnam, the Israeli invasion of Lebanon, and the war in Iraq. TV news footage means little and still less when it is sometimes seen integrated into graphics representing 1950s all-American families. Nor do we need to see again that familiar footage of U.S. schoolchildren practicing "duck and cover" in case of a nuclear attack.

Walter is trying to make an antiwar doc on top of his primary subject. Not needed, not effective. There could be more of Streep actually changing a stage moment in rehearsal. More from her costar Kevin Kline. Another costar, Austin Pendleton, appears in many shots but is not even mentioned—and he, I believe, would have talked more openly about "process."

The film recounts Brecht's development as a Marxist playwright who deliberately avoided engaging the audience on an emotional level or encouraging it to identify with his characters. He wanted them to rise above the immediate experience to the level of thought and ideology. We are to realize: "War is bad and everyone loses!" At this he is so successful that I suspect the play is impossible to make truly involving. It is sort of a passion play of the left, a work that inspires more piety than enthusiasm.

One peculiar element involves college lectures on Marxism by the novelist Jay Cantor (*The Death of Che Guevara*). If it is explained why he was necessary in the film, I missed it. His comments are generalized and not perti-

nent. But, oddly, his students are always seen with black bars over their eyes, like patrons being arrested in a brothel. Brecht was famous for distancing strategies that prevented audiences from getting so swept up in his stories that they didn't focus on their messages. Perhaps these distracting and seemingly unnecessary black bars are, dare I say, a Brechtian device?

The doc lacks the usual scene of the company gathered to read their reviews; just as well, because the production was not well received. Oskar Eustis, artistic director of the Public Theater, has said *Mother Courage and Her Children* is the greatest play of the twentieth century. My money's on *Waiting for Godot.*

There Will Be Blood ★ ★ ★ ½
R, 158 m., 2008

Daniel Day-Lewis (Daniel Plainview), Paul Dano (Paul/Eli Sunday), Kevin J. O'Connor (Henry), Ciaran Hinds (Fletcher), Dillon Freasier (H. W. Plainview). Directed by Paul Thomas Anderson and produced by Anderson, JoAnne Sellar, and Daniel Lupi. Screenplay by Anderson, based on the novel *Oil!* by Upton Sinclair.

The voice of the oil man sounds made of oil, gristle, and syrup. It is deep and reassuring, absolutely sure of itself and curiously fraudulent. No man who sounds this forthright can be other than a liar. His name is Daniel Plainview, and he must have given the name to himself as a private joke, for little that he does is as it seems. In Paul Thomas Anderson's brutal, driving epic *There Will Be Blood,* Plainview begins by trying to wrest silver from the earth with a pick and shovel, and ends by extracting countless barrels of oil whose wealth he keeps all for himself. Daniel Day-Lewis makes him a great, oversize monster who hates all men, including, therefore, himself.

Watching the movie is like viewing a natural disaster that you cannot turn away from. By that I do not mean that the movie is bad, any more than it is good. It is a force beyond categories. It has scenes of terror and poignancy, scenes of ruthless chicanery, scenes awesome for their scope, moments echoing with whispers, and an ending that in some peculiar way this material demands because it could not conclude on an appropriate note—there has been nothing appropriate about it. Those who hate the ending, and there may be many, might be asked to dictate a different one. Something bittersweet, perhaps? Grandly tragic? Only madness can supply a termination for this story.

The movie is very loosely based on *Oil!*, Upton Sinclair's 1927 novel about a corrupt oil family—based so loosely you can see the film, read the book, and experience two different stories. Anderson's character is a man who has no friends, no lovers, no real partners, and an adopted son he exploits mostly as a prop. Plainview comes from nowhere, stays in contact with no one, and when a man appears claiming to be his half brother, it is not surprising that they have never met before. Plainview's only goal in life is to become enormously wealthy, and he does so, reminding me of *Citizen Kane* and Mr. Bernstein's observation, "It's easy to make a lot of money, if that's all you want to do, is make a lot of money."

There Will Be Blood is no *Kane*, however. Plainview lacks a "Rosebud." He regrets nothing, misses nothing, pities nothing, and when he falls down a mine shaft and cruelly breaks his leg, he hauls himself back up to the top and starts again. He gets his break in life when a pudding-faced young man named Paul Sunday (Paul Dano) visits him and says he knows where oil is to be found and will share this information for a price. The oil is to be found on the Sunday family ranch, where Standard Oil has already been sniffing around, and Plainview obtains the drilling rights cheaply from old man Sunday. There is another son, named Eli, who is also played by Paul Dano, and either Eli and Paul are identical twins or the story is up to something shifty, since we never see them both at once.

Eli is an evangelical preacher whose only goal is to extract money from Plainview to build his church, the Church of the Third Revelation. Plainview goes along with him until the time comes to dedicate his first well. He has promised to allow Eli to bless it, but when the moment comes, he pointedly ignores the youth, and a lifelong hatred is founded. In images starkly and magnificently created by cinematographer Robert Elswit and set designer Jack Fisk, we see the first shaky wells replaced by vast fields, all overseen by Plainview from the porch of a rude shack where he sips whiskey more or less ceaselessly. There are accidents. Men are killed. His son is deafened when a well blows violently, and Plainview grows cold toward the boy; he needs him as a prop, but not as a magnet for sympathy.

The movie settles down, if that is the word, into a portrait of the two personalities, Plainview's and Eli Sunday's, striving for domination over their realms. The addition of Plainview's alleged half brother (Kevin J. O'Connor) into this equation gives Plainview, at last, someone to confide in, although he confides mostly his universal hatred. That Plainview, by now a famous multimillionaire, would so quickly take this stranger at his word is incredible; certainly we do not. But by now Plainview is drifting from obsession through possession into madness, and at the end, like Kane, he drifts through a vast mansion like a ghost.

The performance by Day-Lewis may well win an Oscar nomination, and if he wins, he should do the right thing in his acceptance speech and thank the late John Huston. His voice in the role seems like a frank imitation of Huston, right down to the cadences, the pauses, the seeming to confide. I interviewed Huston three times, and each time he spoke with elaborate courtesy, agreeing with everything, drawing out his sentences, and each time I could not rid myself of the conviction that his manner was masking impatience; it was his way of suffering a fool, which is to say, an interviewer. I have heard Peter O'Toole's famous imitation of Huston, but channeled through O'Toole he sounds heartier and friendlier and, usually, drunk. I imagine you had to know Huston pretty well before he let down his conversational guard.

There Will Be Blood is the kind of film that is easily called great. I am not sure of its greatness. It was filmed in the same area of Texas used by *No Country for Old Men*, and that is a great film, and a perfect one. But *There Will Be Blood* is not perfect, and in its imperfections (its unbending characters, its lack of women or any reflection of ordinary society, its ending, its relentlessness) we may see its reach exceeding its grasp. Which is not a dishonorable thing.

Thirst ★★★
R, 133 m., 2009

Song Kang-ho (Sang-hyun), Kim Ok-vin (Tae-ju), Kim Hae-sook (Madame Ra), Shin Ha-kyun (Kang-woo), Park In-hwan (Priest Noh), Oh Dal-soo (Young-du), Song Young-chang (Seung-dae). Directed by Park Chan-wook and produced by Park and Chung Seo-kyung. Screenplay by Park and Jeong Seo-gyeong, inspired by Emile Zola's novel *Therese Raquin*.

Park Chan-wook of South Korea is today's most successful director of horror films, perhaps because there's always more than horror to them. He seems to be probing alarming depths of human nature. Maybe that's why he can simultaneously be celebrated on fanboy horror sites and win the Jury Prize at this year's Cannes Film Festival.

His best-known film is the masterful *Old Boy*, about a man who is taken captive and locked up for years for no reason he can guess and none he is supplied with. Now comes *Thirst*, a blood-drenched vampire film about, unexpectedly, a Roman Catholic priest. The priest is a deeply good man, which is crucial to the story: He dies in the first place because he volunteered as a subject for a deadly medical experiment.

That he is resurrected as a vampire after receiving a transfusion of tainted blood is certainly not his fault. Nor does he set about sinking his fangs into the necks of innocent victims. Given his access to a hospital, he can slurp much of the blood he needs from IV drips leading into unconscious patients, who will hardly complain about a missing pint or two. His slurping, by the way, is very audible; Park has the knack of making the activities of his characters tangible.

This priest, played by the South Korean star Song Kang-ho, is youthful and, despite his vow of chastity, awakened to an urgent carnality by the interloper vampire blood. Perhaps vampires fascinate us because they act not out of a desire to do evil—but by a need. The priest is powerfully attracted to the young

wife of a childhood friend of his. We've already seen how willing he is to help the unfortunate, and now his mercy is inspired by this poor girl, who is mistreated by her sick husband and his shrewish mother.

She loves him, too, and is so grateful to him she forgives anything, even the detail of his vampirism. The priest fights against his new undead nature and tries to cause little harm. The girl has no hesitation: in for a dime, in for a dollar. Soon they're so blood-soaked that the film tilts into comedy of a gruesome flavor.

The eventual effect is not as great as it could have been. To begin with a responsible priest is to promise, in some way, to grapple with the philosophical dilemma of vampirism—as *Let the Right One In*, the best modern vampire movie, did. Park descends too enthusiastically into sensation and carnal excess, and it's a disappointment, although it's interesting to see what a quick and willing convert the young wife becomes.

There have long been vampire movies, and Murnau's masterpiece *Nosferatu* (1922) set a high standard for the genre right at the start. What's so attractive about vampires? Perhaps it helps that they tend to be regal in their detachment, familiar with the way of the night, and usually so well-dressed. An unflinchingly realistic vampire would be as unattractive as a late-stage addict. There's nothing terrific about living forever if you must do it with the blood of innocents.

No matter. Movies exist to cloak our desires in disguises we can accept, and there is an undeniable appeal to *Thirst*. Park Chan-wook deserves points for mentioning the source of his story, which is *Therese Raquin*, an 1867 French novel by Emile Zola, filmed in 1953 by Marcel Carne and starring Simone Signoret and Raf Vallone. I'll bet if Park hadn't mentioned the Zola novel, no one would have guessed, particularly since it contains no priests and no vampires.

35 Shots of Rum ★★★★
NO MPAA RATING, 99 m., 2010

Alex Descas (Lionel), Mati Diop (Josephine), Gregoire Colin (Noe), Nicole Dogue (Gabrielle), Julieth Mars Toussaint (Rene), Ingrid Caven (Jo's Aunt). Directed by Claire Denis and produced by Karl Baurmgartner and Bruno Pesery. Screenplay by Denis and Jean-Pol Fargeau.

Here is a movie about four people who have known each other for a long time, and how their relationships shift in a way that was slow in the preparation. The film makes us care for them, and so our attention is held. I've seen films where superheroes shift alliances, and I only yawned. It's not the scope of a story; it's the depth.

Part of the pleasure in Claire Denis's *35 Shots of Rum* is working out how these people are involved with each other. Two couples live across a hallway from each other in the same Paris apartment building. Neither couple is "together." Gabrielle and Noe have the vibes of roommates, but the way Lionel and Josephine obviously love each other, it's a small shock when she calls him "papa."

Lionel (Alex Descas) is a French train engineer. Jo (Mati Diop) works in a music store. Gabrielle (Nicole Dogue) drives her own taxi. Noe (Gregoire Colin) is of uncertain plans. He claims only his much-loved cat is preventing him from moving to Brazil. The four people are in and out of both apartments, and we sense they're a virtual family. Small events take place. A guy flirts with Jo at her store. Gabrielle deals with a talkative customer. Lionel and Jo both bring home rice cookers, so Jo puts hers aside so as not to hurt his feelings.

At work, Lionel attends a retirement party for a longtime engineer, Rene. His fellow workers love him, but Rene is miserable. He has no desire to retire. Afterward on a bus, he confesses to Lionel he has no idea how he got into his life to begin with. He has no desire to be an engineer. Spending his life on trains and buses is no way to live.

Lionel seems content. All four of the neighbors seem content, yes, but not completed. One night they head out together in Gabrielle's taxi to attend a concert. The taxi breaks down, they get out of the rain in a Jamaican café, there's good music on the jukebox, they dance with one another, the woman who owns the café, and others.

And in that long scene with its familiar music, Clare Denis achieves the shift. She does it not with dialogue, not with plot points, but with the eyes. This is what movies are for.

They begin happy enough, but . . . incomplete. During the dancing and kidding around, it becomes clear to them, and to us, what must happen for the parts to fall into place.

Denis has long been interested in the former French colonies of West Africa, and in those who came from there to France. Lionel did, and married a German woman; she has died, but they go to visit her sister, Jo's aunt (Ingrid Caven). It is part of Lionel taking care to raise his daughter well and launch her into life. Lionel is handsome, Jo is beautiful, neither one cares.

Nicole Dogue glows in a quiet way as Gabrielle, in her forties, once no doubt stunning, now beautiful in a comfortable way. It's clear she has long been in love with Lionel. No pressure. It's clear Lionel has put that side of his life on hold to be a good father. What does he think about his job? It is a job; he's good at it. The tragedy of the retired Rene will not be his.

You can live in a movie like this. It doesn't lecture you. These people are getting on with their lives, and Denis observes them with tact. She's not intruding; she's discovering. We sense there's not a conventional plot, and that frees us from our interior moviegoing clock. We flow with them. Two are blessed; two are problematic. Will all four be blessed at the end? This is a wise movie and knows that remains to be seen.

This Is It ★★★★
PG, 112 m., 2009

A documentary directed by Kenny Ortega and produced by Ortega, Paul Gongaware, and Randy Phillips.

"This is it," Michael Jackson told his fans in London, announcing his forthcoming concert tour. "This is the final curtain call." The curtain fell sooner than expected. What is left is this extraordinary documentary, nothing at all like what I was expecting to see. Here is not a sick and drugged man forcing himself through grueling rehearsals, but a spirit embodied by music. Michael Jackson was something else.

The film has been assembled from rehearsals from April through June 2009 for a concert tour scheduled for last summer. The footage was "captured by a few cameras," an opening screen tells us, but they were professional high-def cameras and the sound track is full-range stereo. The result is one of the most revealing music documentaries I've seen.

And it's more than that. It's a portrait of Michael Jackson that belies all the rumors that he would have been too weak to tour. That shows not the slightest trace of a spoiled prima donna. That benefits from the limited number of cameras by allowing us to experience his work in something closer to realistic time, instead of fracturing it into quick cuts. That provides both a good idea of what the final concert would have looked like, and a portrait of the artist at work.

Never raising his voice, never showing anger, always soft-spoken and courteous to his cast and crew, Michael, with his director, Kenny Ortega, micromanages the production. He corrects timing, refines cues, talks about details of music and dance. Seeing him always from a distance, I thought of him as the instrument of his producing operation. Here we see that he was the auteur of his shows.

We know now that Michael was subjected to a cocktail of drugs in the time leading up to his fatal overdose, including the last straw, a drug so dangerous it should only be administered by an anesthesiologist in an operating room. That knowledge makes it hard to understand how he appears to be in superb physical condition. His choreography, built from such precise, abrupt, and perfectly timed movements, is exhausting, but he never shows a sign of tiring. His movements are so well synchronized with the other dancers on stage, who are much younger and highly trained, that he seems one with them. This is a man in such command of his physical instrument that he makes spinning in place seem as natural as blinking his eye.

He has always been a dancer first, and then a singer. He doesn't specialize in solos. With the exception of a sweet love ballad, his songs all incorporate four backup singers and probably supplementary tracks prerecorded by himself. It is the whole effect he has in mind.

It might have been a hell of a show. Ortega and special effects wizards coordinate prefilmed sequences with the stage work. There's a horror-movie sequence with ghouls rising from a cemetery (and ghosts that were planned to fly above the audience). Michael is inserted into scenes from Rita Hayworth and Humphrey Bogart movies, and through clever f/x even has a machine-gun battle with Bogie. His environmental pitch is backed by rain forest footage. He rides a cherry-picker high above the audience.

His audience in this case consists entirely of stagehands, gaffers, technicians, and so on. These are working people who have seen it all. They love him. They're not pretending. They love him for his music and perhaps even more for his attitude. Big stars in rehearsal are not infrequently pains in the ass. Michael plunges in with the spirit of a coworker, prepared to do the job and go the distance.

How was that possible? Even if he had the body for it, which he obviously did, how did he muster the mental strength? When you have a doctor on duty around the clock to administer the prescription medications you desire, when your idea of a good sleep is reportedly to be unconscious for twenty-four hours, how do you wake up into such a state of keen alertness? Uppers? I don't think it quite works that way. I was watching like a hawk for any hint of the effects of drug abuse, but couldn't see any. Perhaps it's significant that of all the people in the rehearsal space, he is the only one whose arms are covered at all times by long sleeves.

Well, we don't know how he did it. *This Is It* is proof that he did do it. He didn't let down his investors and colleagues. He was fully prepared for his opening night. He and Kenny Ortega, who also directed this film, were at the top of their game. There's a moving scene on the last day of rehearsal when Jackson and Ortega join hands in a circle with all the others and thank them. But the concert they worked so hard on was never to be.

This is it.

A Thousand Years of Good Prayers ★ ★ ★ ½
NO MPAA RATING, 83 m., 2008

Henry O (Mr. Shi), Faye Yu (Yilan), Vida Ghahremani (Madame), Pasha Lychnikoff (Boris). Directed by Wayne Wang and produced by Wang, Yukie Kito, and Rich

Cowan. Screenplay by Yiyun Li, based on her short story.

I suppose you could say that Wayne Wang is our leading Chinese-American filmmaker, but I despise categories like that. He's a fine filmmaker, no labels needed. I bring it up only because his new film, *A Thousand Years of Good Prayers*, is the first Wang movie since 1997 to deal with Chinese themes. His previous feature, *Last Holiday* (2006), was the lovable comedy starring Queen Latifah at a posh Czech spa.

When I asked Wang about this hiatus in subject matter, he said: "I'm sorry that over the last ten years, the kinds of films that the audience likes to watch have changed, but I will continue to make these films about Chinese-Americans, and in my own way." And that is what he has done in *A Thousand Years of Good Prayers*.

The critic Todd McCarthy is correct in calling the film Ozu-like. It is an intensely observed, small-scale family drama, involving disagreement between generations. A father from China arrives in America for his first visit in years with his daughter. Their values have grown apart, their lifestyles are opposite, they suppress what they're feeling. This in microcosm is Ozu's *Tokyo Story*, the only film I ever showed my film class that made some of them cry.

Mr. Shi (Henry O) gets off his flight in San Francisco and looks around for a daughter who should be waiting for him. Yilan (Faye Yu) is a little tardy. She has not seen her father in years, yet does not kiss him. She takes him home to her antiseptic condo. As they have dinner, silences threaten to overwhelm them. He is reluctant to pry too much. She is guarded.

As the film develops, he will pry more, and she will reveal some long-hidden feelings. He will begin to shop for food and cook meals, as an attempt to turn her apartment into a place that feels more like home. She will find excuses to be absent more and more. He will wander around and try to have conversations in his imperfect English.

We see this corner of America through his eyes. He speaks to people he finds around the condo pool and is surprised they don't have to go to work. They are courteous to him, but uninterested. They have never met a "real" Chinese person in their lives, and so what? One day on a park bench he strikes up a conversation with Madame (Vida Ghahremani). She is about his age, is from Iran, which she thinks of as Persia, and is living with her Iranian-American daughter.

Her English is a little better than Mr. Shi's. But they speak the same language, of people who grew up in cultures that value, even venerate, the older generation. Families stayed together across the years. Parents lived at home until they died. Their children did not have "sex lives" until they were in an approved marriage. It was like this here in North America until two or three generations ago. It would have been unthinkable for my Grandmother Anna to live in a nursing home. She lived with a son and a daughter, and her other children visited regularly, my mother every day.

The legendary professor Howard Higman of Boulder once described to me the difference between American and European society: We are horizontal; they are vertical. An American spreads widely into his own generation and times. A European is more conscious of his place on the family tree. Of course, consumerism and television and a laundry list of other factors are making the developing world more horizontal every day.

A Thousand Years of Good Prayers has moments of truth that should have taken place years earlier. They solve almost nothing. How could they? Mr. Shi is genuinely worried about his daughter's happiness. She grows defensive, even angry, when he gives voice to his concerns. So do we all. Quit prying into my life. You don't understand. This is my life, and it's none of your business. "But I'm only trying to help." I don't need any help. I know what I'm doing. Leave me alone.

In observing the reality of this relationship, Wang contemplates the "generation gap" in modern societies all over the world. His film quietly, carefully, movingly observes how these two people of the same blood will never be able to understand each other, and the younger one won't even care to. The term "generation gap" was not used until the 1960s. It hasn't been very helpful. As Wordsworth wrote:

*The world is too much with us; late
  and soon,
Getting and spending, we lay waste our
  powers;*

Little we see in Nature that is ours;
We have given our hearts away, a sordid
  boon!

Three Monkeys ★★★
NO MPAA RATING, 109 m., 2009

Yavuz Bingol (Eyup), Hatice Aslan (Hacer), Ahmet Rifat Sungar (Ismail), Ercan Kesal (Servet). Directed by Nuri Bilge Ceylan and produced by Zeynep Ozbatur. Screenplay by Ebru Ceylan, Ercan Kesal, and Nuri Bilge Ceylan.

Nuri Bilge Ceylan's *Three Monkeys* begins on a lonely country road at night in the rain. A middle-aged driver grows sleepy at the wheel. His eyelids droop lower, and then suddenly there is a body in the road behind him, and he is awake now and weeping with fear. That's more action than took place in the whole of *Distant* (2002), Ceylan's oddly seductive film about a cousin who moves in and won't leave. This film is as steamy as the other was dry, an elegant exercise in four characters trapped by class, guilt, and greed.

There is about enough plot here to furnish a thirty-minute TV crime show, if they still made them anymore. What makes the film fascinating is its four central characters. Each one is locked within, hidden from the others, driven by private needs that all come together after the death in the forest. Ceylan films them in painterly widescreen compositions that impose a spectacular landscape, one of lowering clouds, indifferent skies, and lonely vistas. In this world, their best companions are their desires.

The sleepy man at the wheel is a politician named Servet (Ercan Kesal). He's in the middle of an election campaign. In a panic, he wakes his driver, Eyup (Yavuz Bingol), in the middle of the night and asks him to take the rap. If Eyup says he was at the wheel, Servet promises he'll get a short prison sentence, his salary will continue, and there will be cash waiting for him on his release. He agrees.

We meet Eyup's wife, Hacer (Hatice Aslan), and son, Ismail (Ahmet Rifat Sungar). They live in a spartan flat on a top floor of a strikingly narrow building with such a great view they can hardly be bothered to look indoors.

She's an attractive woman of not quite a certain age, stuck for life on hold. He is a good-looking kid at an age when poor young men often find there is money to be made from crime. He comes home one night bloodied and beaten, and she decides she needs more money to help him on a career path.

Eyup is opposed to any idea of asking the politician for an advance. His reluctance is that of an employee reluctant to offend a rich and powerful man—even if he holds Servet's reputation in his hands. His wife is not swayed by such class insecurity, approaches Servet, and soon, to their mutual surprise, is having an affair with him. Sounds like the plot of a 1930s pulp crime story, especially when her son finds out.

But Ceylan is intrigued by more than just the spinning out of the story. There is something more going on. His characters are crowded for room. There's no place to escape to in their lives. They're always running up against one another's motives, needs, problems. And when Eyup gets out of prison, everything grows that much more complicated, especially as we learn more about the shaky foundations of the politician's career. Nor must we assume that his affair with the other man's wife happened only because of cash. He and his stature offer her a way out of her dead end.

These themes are always there under the surface, possibly not perceived by his characters. They come into play when the plot takes an ironic direction that places Eyup and his son in a position similar to the one the politician placed them in. That's the kind of moral scorekeeping that film noir specializes in.

The film has extraordinary beauty. Indeed, the visuals by cinematographer Gokhan Tiryaki are so awesome that the characters almost seem belittled, which may be Ceylan's purpose. They scramble about looking for ways out that life has closed to them, while the overarching sky remains indifferent. Words cannot do justice, but there are still photos at http://outnow.ch/Movies/2008/UecMaymun/Bilder/ that will blow your socks off. Click on "Ansehen" to enlarge.

The title? About the monkeys who could see no evil, hear no evil, and speak no evil, of course. Look how far that got them. The film won the Best Director Award at Cannes 2008.

Timecrimes ★ ★ ★
R, 88 m., 2009

Karra Elejalde (Hector), Candela Fernandez (Clara), Barbara Goenaga (Girl), Nacho Vigalondo (Scientist). Directed by Nacho Vigalondo and produced by Esteban Ibarretxe, Eduardo Carneros, and Javier Ibarretxe. Screenplay by Vigalondo.

Time travel in the movies is always about paradox. And it always drives me nuts. Sometimes I enjoy that, in the same way I enjoy chess—and that's a compliment. My mind gets seduced in chess by trains of thought that are hypnotic to me but, if they could be transcribed, would be unutterably boring to anyone else, since you always think of a chess piece in terms of its function, not its name: If this goes here and he moves there and I take that and he takes me back, and I reveal the check and he . . . And if you're a grand master, I don't imagine you think in many words at all. It's more like, "Hmmmm . . . aha!"

Timecrimes is like a temporal chess game with nudity, voyeurism, and violence, which makes it more boring than most chess games, but less boring than a lot of movies. It begins by introducing us to an ordinary sort of Spanish guy named Hector (Karra Elejalde), who is sitting on the lawn of his country place using his binoculars and sees a babe stripping in the woods. Now this is important. What he is witnessing is the outset of an event he has already participated in because of time travel. And when he goes to investigate, he runs the risk of running into himself, which, for paradoxical reasons, he already knows. Not this "he." The other "he."

I guess you can make up the rules of time travel as you go along, but whatever they are, they have to be inexorable, and there have to be dire consequences when a mere mortal rips the fabric of the space-time continuum. The reason we don't get more warnings of this danger, you understand, is that travelers into the past tend to do things that inalterably change the future, so that their present no longer exists for them to return to. I love this stuff.

Hector has a main squeeze named Clara (Candela Fernandez), but leaves her to go into the woods and find the Girl (Barbara Goenaga), who has been assaulted by a certain someone—don't get ahead of me here—and then a little later he meets the Scientist (Nacho Vigalondo, the movie's director), who puts him into what turns out to be a time travel machine, which had earlier or maybe later—now you're getting behind me—done something to lead Hector to sit on the lawn, or maybe see himself sitting on the lawn, or maybe—but now I'm ahead *and* behind—and now (earlier or later?) Hector wraps his bloody head (which I have explained in a review I still haven't written) so he will not be recognized by two of the three Hectors, although I am not sure whether this is Hector One, Two, or Three.

I apologize for the 147-word sentence. In time travel, bad things can happen if you stop for very long. One of the crucial requirements is apparently not to meet yourself coming or going, although if you are physically present twice at the same time, what difference does it make if you see yourself, unless it drives you mad? If I were to see myself walk into this room right now, I would simply nod to myself and ask, "Have you finished writing that review yet?" If I replied no, then I would say, "Well, I have, so why don't we eliminate the middle man and you kill yourself?"

That's not too harsh, because I would only be dying in the past of the unfinished review, see, and be here with my work all done. But then again, in that case, how could I have written it before walking into the room in the first place? I couldn't have, that's how, so that means I couldn't walk into the room, and I would continue writing the review just as I am now, which means the paradox would be solved because nothing happened, which, as nearly as I can tell, would be positive proof that time travel exists.

These problems are dealt with in *Timecrimes* in a thrilling scenario involving possible death by falling off of a roof after getting up there in an unorthodox way, and trying to save the life of a woman one of them loves, maybe two, maybe all three. This is all done in an ingenious and entertaining way. As you might imagine, *Timecrimes* is not a character study. Hector doesn't have the time for that, ha ha. In a time travel saga, by the way, it is considered bad form to wonder what makes somebody tick.

(If, after watching *Timecrimes,* you have the strangest feeling that you have seen some of these problems explored before, you are (a) merely experiencing déjà vu, which is the low-cost and safe alternative to time travel, or (b) remembering Shane Carruth's splendid *Primer* (2004), which, if it didn't drive you nuts, this one will, or has, or vice versa.)

The Time Traveler's Wife ★★ ½
PG-13, 107 m., 2009

Rachel McAdams (Clare), Eric Bana (Henry), Arliss Howard (Richard DeTamble), Ron Livingston (Gomez), Stephen Tobolowsky (Dr. Kendrick), Jane McLean (Charise), Brooklynn Proulx (Clare as a Child). Directed by Robert Schwentke and produced by Nick Wechsler and Dede Gardner. Screenplay by Bruce Joel Rubin, based on the novel by Audrey Niffenegger.

Clare is in love with a man who frequently disappears into thin air, leaving behind his clothing in a pile on the floor. "It can be a problem," she observes. Henry is a time traveler, and his trips are out of his control. Another problem is that whenever he arrives at another time, or even returns to the present (whenever that may be for him), he is naked. Well, that makes sense. You wouldn't expect his clothes to travel.

The dilemma of Henry (Eric Bana) and Clare (Rachel McAdams) becomes, in *The Time Traveler's Wife,* a bittersweet love story. The warmth of the actors makes it surprisingly tender, considering the premise that is blatantly absurd. If you allow yourself to think for one moment of the paradoxes, contradictions, and logical difficulties involved, you will be lost. The movie supports no objective thought.

So, OK. It's preposterous. Lots of movies are. What we're given is a lifelong love story that begins when a little girl (Brooklynn Proulx) gives her blanket to a naked man who has appeared in the shrubbery of her family's idyllic meadow. He tells her his name, that he's her friend, and that they'll see each other again. And so they do. When she's grown, she encounters him in a library and introduces

herself because at this point in his life he doesn't know who she is. I know what you're asking yourself. Don't even go there.

They fall in love. They get married. Their wedding ceremony is threatened with disaster when he evaporates with minutes to go, but Henry is a stand-up guy and materializes from the future just in the nick of time to stand in for himself. His disappearances strike instantly, for example while he's carrying the dishes to their dinner table. Clare finds herself cleaning up a lot of spills. Although she gets pregnant, if he ever disappears during sex, we don't see it. From a strictly logical point of view, that would be the opposite of *ejaculatio praecox.*

Henry consults Dr. Kendrick (Stephen Tobolowsky), a genetics expert, who finds he has a genetic condition named chrono-impairment. Apparently since this trait is in all of his genes, they travel in time simultaneously, which is just as well, lest he be scattered hither and yon. One thing's for sure. It's hard to explain how a gene for time travel could develop in the Darwinian model, since it's hard to see how an organism could ever find out that was an advantage.

You have to hand it to director Robert Schwentke and screenwriter Bruce Joel Rubin (*Ghost*). They deal with these difficulties by not dealing with them at all. McAdams and Bana play their roles straight and seriously, have a pleasant chemistry, and sort of involved me in spite if myself. They're just so . . . nice. She does get around to asking a logical question: Why did he appear in the first place to that little girl in the meadow and set all of this in motion? Well, maybe he did for the simple reason that he already had, if you see what I mean.

What's remarkable is how upbeat and romantic he's able to remain, considering the difficulties of always rematerializing naked. You'd think he'd be worn down and demoralized. I guess he has some control over where that happens, as in the meadow. But in a crucial opening scene with himself as a child, how does he find two blankets by the side of a road?

He turns up regularly in Chicago—on bridges, on elevated platforms, in alleys—and always breaks and enters to grab clothes, or steals wallets (if a naked man asks you for your wallet, what do you do?). He keeps getting arrested and disappearing from the backs of police cars. The cops should put out a bulletin with an artist's rendition of his face: "If you catch this guy, don't arrest him. It's a waste of time." ☞

Tokyo! ★ ★ ½
NO MPAA RATING, 112 m., 2009

A film in three segments: *Interior Design,* with Ayako Fujitani, Ryo Kase, and Ayumi Ito. Directed by Michel Gondry. Screenplay by Gondry and Gabrielle Bell. *Merde,* with Denis Lavant. Directed by Leos Carax. Screenplay by Carax. *Shaking Tokyo,* with Teruyuki Kagawa, Yu Aoi, and Naoto Takenaka. Directed by Bong Joon-ho. Screenplay by Bong.

Three directors, three films, three reasons to rethink moving to Tokyo: You can't find a place to live, there are earthquakes, and a weird goblin may leap from a sewer and grab your sandwich. *Tokyo!* assigns the French filmmakers Michel Gondry and Leos Carax and the Korean Bong Joon-ho to create their own visions of the megalopolis, which would seem to spawn oddly adapted inhabitants.

The best of the three is *Merde,* the centerpiece by Carax, a director whose films are willfully, sometimes successfully, odd. He stars Denis Lavant as a haywire subterranean denizen who pops off a sewer lid, scrambles to the sidewalk, lurches down the street, and rudely assaults pedestrians. He grabs cigarettes, sandwiches, and arms, alarms a baby, terrorizes the populace, and disappears into another manhole.

He is captured and hauled into court, where a translator is found who allegedly speaks his unknown language. Here he wickedly reviles Japan, its citizens, and specifically its women. It remains unclear why he has chosen to live in sewers. This segment is, oddly enough, similar to some Japanese reality shows, such as *The Screamer,* where a man with an ear-piercing scream is photographed by hidden cameras while he sneaks up behind people and lets loose. What a scream.

Shaking Tokyo, directed by Bong Joon-ho,

stars Teruyuki Kagawa as a *hikikomori,* a type so familiar the Japanese have a name for it. A hikikomori, usually male, decides to stay inside one day and essentially never leaves. Some have been reported as hermits for up to ten years, living mostly on pizza deliveries. In America we call these people "software engineers." One day the hero is jarred loose from his isolation by a pretty pizza delivery girl, not to mention an earthquake, which sends others into the unpopulated and barren streets for the first time in months.

Michel Gondry's *Interior Design,* an only slightly more conventional tale, stars Ayako Fujitani and Ryo Kase as young lovers new in Tokyo, who undergo personal and physical changes during the ordeal of apartment hunting. Much more I should not say.

Do these films reflect actual aspects of modern Tokyo? The hikikomori epidemic is apparently real enough, but the other two segments seem more deliberately fantastical. The entertainment value? Medium to high (*Merde*). Tokyo? Still standing.

Tokyo Sonata ★ ★ ★ ½
PG-13, 119 m., 2009

Teruyuki Kagawa (Ryuhei Sasaki), Kyoko Koizumi (Megumi Sasaki), Yu Koyanagi (Takashi Sasaki), Kai Inowaki (Kenji Sasaki), Haruka Igawa (Kaneko), Kanji Tsuda (Kurosu), Koji Yakusho (Thief). Directed by Kiyoshi Kurosawa and produced by Yukie Kito and Wouter Barendrecht. Screenplay by Kurosawa, Max Mannix, and Sachiko Tanaka.

Just as the economic crisis has jolted everyday life, so it shakes up *Tokyo Sonata,* which begins as a well-behaved story and takes detours into the comic, the macabre, and the sublime. All you know about three-act structure is going to be useless in watching this film, even though, like many sonatas, it has three movements.

It opens on a note of routine, of a family so locked into their lives that they scarcely know one another. Ryuhei is a salaryman in a management job. His wife, Megumi, is a source of predictable domesticity, centering on cleaning, sewing, and the preparation of meals. His older son, Takashi, and younger son, Kenji, are filled with unhappiness but seemingly well-disciplined, although Kenji gets in trouble at school: The teacher unfairly blames him for passing along a manga, or graphic novel, and Kenji defiantly says he saw the teacher reading a porno manga on the train. Many men in Japan do the same, no big deal, but hypocrisy is the point.

In the opening scene, Ryuhei (Teruyuki Kagawa) is fired. He comes home, hands over his week's wages, says nothing. He is an autocratic father, filled with anger. The older son, Takashi (Yu Koyanagi), announces he has enlisted for the U.S. Army as a way to gain citizenship, as he sees no future for himself in Japan. His father forbids him.

Unable to lose face by admitting his job loss, Ryuhei leaves "for the office" every day and lingers in a cheerless concrete oasis with other jobless men. There is a soup kitchen. His wife sees him there, knows everything, stays quiet. Young Kenji (Kai Inowaki), no longer attending school, spends his money on piano lessons with the beautiful Kaneko (Haruka Igawa). His father, breaking with the Japanese tradition of encouraging children to study, has already forbidden piano lessons. Why? Perhaps he feels so inadequate he's threatened by any success involving his family.

What we seem to have are the outlines of a traditional family drama, in which tensions are bottled up, revelations will occur, and a crisis will result in either tragedy or resolution. But that's not what we're given by director Kiyoshi Kurosawa, best known for upscale horror films. He almost misleads us in the early scenes, by framing the family dinners in sedate and orderly compositions. We believe we know where *Tokyo Sonata* is going. We are wrong.

No, it doesn't turn into another horror film, or a murder-suicide. It simply shows how lives torn apart by financial emergencies can be revealed as being damaged all along. Unemployment is the catalyst—an unspoken reality that makes everyone in the family angrier than they already are. All of the performances have perfect pitch; the young son engages us in the same way as the hero of Truffaut's *The 400 Blows*.

The directions the film takes I should not reveal. But notice how Kurosawa (no relation) allows his train to leave the tracks. Dramatic events occur that demonstrate how a routine, once broken, cannot easily be repaired. The entrance of a completely unexpected character results in an instinctive acceptance of the new situation, providing a sad payoff to what at first seems merely arbitrary.

At the same time, Kurosawa observes the agony of unemployment in Japan, which, like the United States, has been beset by outsourcing to cheaper labor pools. (The day when China and India begin outsourcing will be a historic turning point.) Ryuhei joins hopeless queues at an employment office. He finds work cleaning toilets in a shopping mall. His humiliation is underlined when all maintenance workers must change into one-piece coveralls at lockers in full view of passing customers. He has an encounter at work that is bizarre.

And then the film finds a form of release in another unexpected scene. Watch it play out. We are blindsided by its beauty. An extended passage is held in a medium-long shot in which nobody moves, and the effect is uncanny. Is there a happy ending? Nothing as simple as that. Simply a new beginning. Debris has been cleared. Old tapes have been destroyed. Freedom has been asserted. Nothing is for sure.

A sonata is a classical form in which two musical ideas are intercut. In the beginning, they are introduced. In the following sections, they are developed in passages revealing the secrets or potentials of both. The conclusion does not resolve them; instead, we return to look at them, knowing what we know now. The "themes" in this movie are the father and his family. At the end they feel the same tensions as at the beginning, but the facade has been destroyed, and they will have to proceed unprotected.

Tooth Fairy ★★
PG, 101 m., 2010

Dwayne Johnson (Derek Thompson), Ashley Judd (Carly), Stephen Merchant (Tracy), Julie Andrews (Lily), Billy Crystal (Jerry), Destiny Whitlock (Tess), Chase Ellison (Randy). Directed by Michael Lembeck and produced by Jason Blum, Mark Ciardi, and Gordon Gray. Screenplay by Lowell Ganz, Babaloo Mandel,

Joshua Sternin, Jeffrey Ventimilia, and Randi Mayem Singer.

In the pantheon of such legends as Santa Claus and the Bogeyman, the Tooth Fairy ranks down in the minor leagues, I'd say, with Jack Frost and the Easter Bunny. There is a scene in *Tooth Fairy* when the hero is screamed at by his girlfriend for even *beginning* to suggest to her six-year-old that there isn't a Tooth Fairy, but surely this is a trauma a child can survive. Don't kids simply humor their parents to get the dollar?

The film reveals that there's not one Tooth Fairy anyway, but a whole workforce, tightly scheduled and supervised by the strict head fairy (Julie Andrews). This comes as rather an astonishment to a rugged hockey player named Derek, played by Dwayne (The Rock) Johnson, who is sentenced to a term in Fairy Land for almost spoiling the young girl's faith. It happens so abruptly that he finds himself wearing a pink tutu. Oddly, a still photo of this sight is not included in the movie's press materials.

Derek's nickname in pro hockey is "The Tooth Fairy" because he is a specialist in body-slamming opponents so hard that you can fill in the rest. He hasn't scored a goal in ages. The coach puts him in just so he can take someone out. He spends so much time in the penalty box he has his own recliner installed.

The Rock plays this role straight, which is basically the way he plays every role. He's a pleasant, relaxed screen presence, but a Method Actor he's not. His idea of a tone for the Tooth Fairy is sincerity.

The movie's best scenes involve Fairy Land, where a brisk but very tall fairy social worker named Tracy (Stephen Merchant) adds some quirkiness. Merchant is a six-foot-seven British comedian, inheritor of the possibly genetic trait that populated Monty Python. His great regret in life is that he was never issued wings. Also in Fairy Land is Jerry (Billy Crystal), in charge of magic weapons, who issues Derek visibility sprays and suchlike.

Look, I hate to say this, but Billy Crystal has put on a few pounds. I say it not as a criticism but as an observation. Good for him. He seems more avuncular now, more confiding. Maybe he could start looking for dramatic roles as your favorite wise-guy uncle. Anyway, I've noticed in a lot of movies lately that the stars I've grown old with have, good lord, also grown old with me. There's a kind of fascination in how film so accurately records the passage of time. Julie Andrews, by still looking like Julie Andrews, seems to be swimming upstream.

Derek's girlfriend, mentioned above, is played by the divine Ashley Judd, thanklessly. I guess as an actor you know that in a movie named *Tooth Fairy* you're going to have a lot of scenes where you're tucking someone in. Fair enough, but where can you go with them dramatically?

The film is rated PG. I wondered why it didn't make Derek a husband instead of a boyfriend, but parents can relax: He seems to sleep on the couch. Uh, huh. The chemistry between the two suggests that they're together primarily because they work so well together at tucking time.

There's no way I can recommend this movie to anyone much beyond the Tooth Fairy Believement Age, but I must testify it's pleasant and inoffensive, although the violence in the hockey games seems out of place. It must be said in closing that given his nickname and reputation, it's a miracle the Tooth Fairy has been allowed to survive with such a dazzling row of pearlies.

Toots ★ ★ ★
NO MPAA RATING, 84 m., 2008

A documentary directed by Kristi Jacobson and produced by Jacobson, Whitney Dow, and Alicia Sams.

Toots Shor. For twenty years, the most famous saloonkeeper in the world. A huge, towering man with a sloppy grin, a bear hug, a big laugh, a big gut, and a lot of friends. His restaurant at 51 West 51 in Manhattan was where you had to be for the action. The regulars included Jackie Gleason, Sinatra, Mickey Mantle, DiMaggio and Monroe, Babe Ruth. Mobsters like Frank Costello. Boxers like Rocky Graziano and Tony Zale. Walter Cronkite, Mike Wallace, Bogart and Bacall, Hemingway, Yogi Berra, and John Wayne. He wasn't a regular, but Richard Nixon came when he was in town.

A critic trying to explain Astaire and Rogers once said, "He gives her class. She gives him *sex*." That's how the saloon worked. There was no VIP area. Everybody stood at a big circular bar or was clearly visible in booths. Sinatra was maybe a little pleased to nod to Costello, who ran the mob in Manhattan. Costello was maybe pleased to nod back. They were big guys, but they were maybe impressed. It made Costello classier to hang out with Sinatra. It made Sinatra sexier to be the drinking buddy of a godfather. Toots Shor provided a stage for the road company of Damon Runyon's imagination.

New York had eleven newspapers in those days, and all the columnists made a nightly stop. Ed Sullivan, Earl Wilson, Walter Winchell. The best movie ever made about a newspaper columnist, *The Sweet Smell of Success*, was shot on location at Toots Shor. Sportswriters were the newspaper superstars. They sat down with Yogi, Mickey, DiMaggio, Whitey Ford, Frank Gifford. Sportswriters in those days, we learn, were paid as much as the players and could meet them on equal terms. "One of today's baseball stars," Gifford muses in the movie, "makes as much in two weeks as Mickey Mantle made in his entire career."

Toots evokes the era with seductive charm; it's a fascinating memory of a time past, directed by Kristi Jacobson, Toots's granddaughter. She has access to all the archives—an eighteen-hour tape of Shor's memories, video of him on *This Is Your Life* and *What's My Line* and being interviewed by Edward R. Murrow and Mike Wallace, newsreels, photos, newspaper clippings. She draws heavily on eyewitness accounts by Ford, Gifford, Cronkite, Gay Talese, and many others. Her doc plays like a film noir version of *Entertainment Tonight*.

One thing I noticed is that all of the regulars seem to have witnessed famous moments or think they did. They were all there when Toots challenged Gleason to a race around the block, one going one way, one going the other. Gleason lost and paid Toots one thousand dollars. Then he said, "Wait a minute! We never passed each other going around! You stayed right here!" Good story, but then someone says, "Toots took a cab." Unlikely, when he *could* have stayed right

there. And very unlikely that these two men, three hundred pounds or up, would have agreed to race around the block, and that all those famous people just happened to be there that afternoon.

But there were lots of famous people and lots of afternoons. Toots drank with them and then with the evening crowd. His loyal bookkeeper complains that in an evening Toots would pick up thousands of dollars of tabs. A veteran waiter remembers that many of the freebie big shots wouldn't even leave a one-dollar tip. Big shots love to be validated by their friendly saloonkeeper, especially if they're both drunks and he calls you "crumb-bum." He even talked to the mob that way.

It came to an end. In 1970, Toots sold his lease for $1.5 million, and a year later opened a new, larger Toots Shor with a loan from the Teamsters. The old mob had lost power with the rise of independent drug dealers. The new gangsters were not by Damon Runyon, but by Martin Scorsese. People no longer drank all night. They went to discos or the Village. Celebrities no longer liked to be on display. Gone were the days when DiMaggio and Monroe left the restaurant and DiMaggio drove them home *himself*. Toots went broke, the money disappeared, he lived another fifteen years, and he was a ghost of the past. The drinking caught up with him, as it had to. Nobody can really hold his liquor; some just do a better job of standing up and going through their acts.

You see *Toots* and you wish you had been there. The Pump Room was something like that in Chicago, or the old Fritzel's and Riccardo's, with Kup the occupant of Booth No. 1. The columnists from the *Trib*, *Daily News*, and *American*—let 'em sit in the back. For many of us in the 1970s, O'Rourke's on North Avenue was the place where you didn't want to miss anything. Toots would have never understood O'Rourke's. But the night Charlton Heston autographed Michaela Touhy's bra, that he would have understood.

Towelhead ★ ★
R, 128 m., 2008

Aaron Eckhart (Travis Vuoso), Toni Collette (Melina Hines), Maria Bello (Gail Monahan),

Peter Macdissi (Rifat Maroun), Summer Bishil (Jasira Maroun), Chris Messina (Barry). Directed by Alan Ball and produced by Ball and Ted Hope. Screenplay by Ball, based on the novel by Alicia Erian.

Towelhead presents material that cries out to be handled with quiet empathy, and hammers us with it. I understand what the film is trying to do, but not why it does it with such crude melodrama. The tone is all wrong for a story of child sexuality and had me cringing in my seat. It either has to be a tragedy or some kind of dark comedy like Kubrick's brilliant *Lolita*, but here it is simply awkward, embarrassing, and painful.

It tells the story of Jasira, a thirteen-year-old Lebanese-American girl with an obsession about her emerging sexuality. Well, all thirteen-year-olds feel such things. That's why so many of them stop talking to us. They don't know how to feel about themselves. Jasira thinks she does. She's turned on by taxi ads for showgirls, by sexy photos, by her own body. She discovers masturbating more or less by accident, likes it, precociously discusses orgasms.

Her American mother (Maria Bello) lives in Syracuse. Her Lebanese father (Peter Macdissi, of *Six Feet Under*) works for NASA in Houston. Neither is the parent of the year in any conceivable year. Her mother discovers her own boyfriend carefully shaving Jasira's pubic hair and is angry with the girl, not the boyfriend. She ships Jasira off to her father in Houston. He can seem cheerful and ingratiating, but slaps her for wearing a T-shirt to the table, forbids her to wear tampons ("only whores and married ladies wear them"), and is boiling with rage—partly because some of his neighbors think he is an Arab, and he is a Lebanese Christian who hates Saddam even more than they do.

Jasira starts babysitting the younger kid next door, who turns her on to his dad's porno magazines. His dad, known only as Mr. Vuoso, is played by Aaron Eckhart, who was brave enough to take on this slimy role. He actually begins with a variation on the ancient theme "come sit over here on the bed next to me," and escalates to rape. That Jasira is fascinated and to some degree encourages him is mean-ingless; she knows little about what she is encouraging, and apparently thinks of having sex with an adult as merely the sort of thing her reactionary dad would slap her for.

The progress of her journey involves bloody tampons and other details that could be relevant if handled with more sensitivity. She has sex with an African-American fellow student, who seems polite and nice but is experienced enough to know he is doing wrong. Her dad forbids her to see him because he is black. Meanwhile, Mr. Vuoso's son calls her a towelhead, a camel jockey, and worse. Racism is everywhere here.

The movie was written and directed by Alan Ball, who also wrote *American Beauty*. Two movies, two suburban men obsessed with underage beauties. Is there a pattern here? Ball also created and has directed *Six Feet Under*, which specializes in acute embarrassment and spectacular misbehavior. So does the director Todd Solondz, whose *Welcome to the Dollhouse* (1995) also dealt with a troubled adolescent girl. But Solondz knew how to do it, what his intentions were, how to challenge us and yet involve our sympathy. Ball seems to be merely thrashing about in a plot too transgressive for his skills.

The actors were courageous. Another key role is played by Toni Collette, as a pregnant neighbor who suspects what's going on and tries to help Jasira and offer her refuge from both her father and Mr. Vuoso. Trouble is, Jasira thinks she doesn't want to be rescued and has come to love orgasms, as is not uncommon. She's played by an appealing young actress named Summer Bishil, who certainly looks as if she were thirteen, but was eighteen when the film was made. Without showing nudity, Ball plays tricks with lighting and camera angles that sometimes regard her like a cheesecake model. I didn't enjoy that feeling. When Billy Wilder's lighting gives Marilyn Monroe a teasingly low neckline in *Some Like It Hot*, that's one thing. When Ball's framing provides one for a child, that's another.

Yes, the sexual abuse of children is a tragedy. Yes, there are adults who need to be educated, enlightened, warned, or thrashed and locked up. This is not the film to assist that process. The actors labor to be true to their characters and sincere in their work, and they succeed. The movie lets them down. It is more clueless than its heroine.

A Town Called Panic ★★★ ½
NO MPAA RATING, 75 m., 2010

With the voices of: Stephane Aubier (Cowboy), Bruce Ellison (Indian), Vincent Patar (Horse), Jeanne Balibar (Madame Longray), Frederic Jannin (Policeman), Benoit Poelvoorde (Farmer). Directed by Stephane Aubier and Vincent Patar and produced by Philippe Kauffmann and Vincent Tavier. Screenplay by Aubier and Patar.

You know how kids play with little plastic action figures that balance their feet on their own little platforms? And how they're not on the same scale? And how kids move them around while doing their voices and making up adventures for them? And how literally anything is likely to happen in those adventures? Then you have a notion of the goofy charm generated by this new animated comedy from Belgium.

A Town Called Panic is well-named because it takes place in a town where panic is a daily emotion. Here, in a house on a hill much larger inside than out, live the friendly roommates Cowboy, Indian, and Horse. Their neighbor is Farmer. Law is enforced by Policeman.

It is Horse's birthday, and Cowboy and Indian decide his gift must be a brick barbecue. They go online to order fifty bricks, but order fifty million through a computer error, which causes no end of problems, especially when Cowboy and Indian stack them on top of the house, hoping to conceal their foolishness from Horse. I should explain that Horse seems to be the responsible adult.

Everybody talks like little kids. Indian and Horse are on the same scale, about twice as tall as Cowboy, although nobody notices this. They get around fine on their little platforms, even climbing stairs. Horse, who has four legs and can balance without a platform, takes Farmer's kids to Madame Longray's music lessons and falls in love with Madame, who is also a horse and plays the piano with her hooves, pretty well.

The most frequent line of dialogue in this enchanting world is *Oh, no!* One strange thing

happens after another. You wouldn't believe me if I told you how Horse, Indian, and Cowboy all end up perched precariously on a rock slab above a volcano at the center of the earth, or how they get from there to the middle of an ocean and the North Pole, or how they happen upon a mad scientist and his robot, named Penguin, or the excuses Horse uses on his cell phone to explain to Madame Longray why he hasn't turned up for his piano lessons. Or why it rains cows.

A Town Called Panic is the work of Stephane Aubier and Vincent Patar, a Belgian team who first created this world in a group of short films that became enormously popular in 2003 on European television. I've never seen anything like this style. It's stop action, but *really* stop action, you understand, because that's the nature of plastic action figures. Cowboy and Indian can move their arms when they need to, but their platforms keep them upright.

I enjoyed this film so much I'm sorry to report it was finally too much of a muchness. You can only eat so much cake. But I don't think that's a problem. Like all animated family films, this one will find a long life and its greatest popularity on video. And because the plot is just one doggone thing after another without the slightest logic, there's no need to watch it all the way through at one sitting. If you watch it a chapter or two at a time, it should hold up nicely.

Now don't get me wrong. I'm glad I saw it on the big screen. It has an innocent, hallucinatory charm. The friendship of the three pals is sweet. I liked Horse's bashfulness when he's smitten with Madame Longray. And his patience with Indian and Cowboy, who get them into one fine fix after another.

Toy Story 3 ★★★
G, 102 m., 2010

With the voices of: Tom Hanks (Woody), Tim Allen (Buzz Lightyear), Joan Cusack (Jessie), Ned Beatty (Lotso), Don Rickles (Mr. Potato Head), Michael Keaton (Ken), Wallace Shawn (Rex), John Ratzenberger (Hamm), Estelle Harris (Mrs. Potato Head), John Morris (Andy), Jodi Benson (Barbie), Blake Clark (Slinky Dog). Directed by Lee Unkrich and produced by Darla

K. Anderson. Screenplay by Unkrich, Michael Arndt, John Lasseter, and Andrew Stanton.

The first two *Toy Story* movies centered on the relationship between a boy and his toys. In Pixar's *Toy Story 3*, young Andy has grown to college age and the story leaves the toys pretty much on their own. In a third act where they find themselves fighting for life on a conveyor belt to a garbage incinerator, we fear it could be renamed *Toy Story Triage*.

The problems all begin with that most dreaded of commands, "Clean out your room!" No mother in history understands that a boy's room has all of his stuff *exactly where he needs it*, even if he dumped it there ten years earlier. Andy's mom gives him three choices: (1) attic; (2) donation to a day care center; (3) trash. Examining his old toys, his gaze lingers fondly on Woody (voice by Tom Hanks), and he decides to take him along to college.

What with one thing and another the other toys find themselves at the day care center, which they think they'll like because there will be plenty of kids to play with them all day long. There seems to be relatively little grieving about the loss of Andy's affections; he did, after all, sentence them to a toy box for years, and toys by nature are self-centered and want to be played with.

Day care seems like a happy choice, until a dark underside of its toy society emerges in the person of an ominously hug-prone bear (Ned Beatty). They pick up, however, some additions to their little band, including Barbie and Ken dolls with extensive wardrobes. If you ask me, Barbie (Jodi Benson) is anorexic, and Ken (Michael Keaton) is gay, but nobody in the movie knows this, so I'm just sayin'.

Buzz Lightyear (Tim Allen) is back, still in hapless hero mode, but after a reboot he starts speaking Spanish and that leads to some funny stuff. I also enjoyed the dilemma of Mrs. Potato Head (Estelle Harris), whose missing eye continues to see independently of her head. This raises intriguing physiological questions, such as, if Mr. Potato Head lost an ear, would it continue to hear, or if he lost a mouth, would it continue to eat without a body? These are not academic questions; at one point, Mister becomes an uncooked taco

shell. Mr. and Mrs. Potato Head must be old hands at such dilemmas, since children spend most of their time attaching their body parts in the wrong way, like malpracticing little Dr. Frankensteins.

Man, the toys have a dangerous time of it after they eventually find themselves at a garbage collection center. You have no idea what garbage has to go through before becoming landfill, and even an Indiana Jones toy would have trouble surviving the rotating blades. There is a happy ending, of course, but I suspect these toys may be traumatized for eternity.

This is a jolly, slapstick comedy, lacking the almost eerie humanity that infused the earlier *Toy Story* sagas, and happier with action and jokes than with characters and emotions. But hey, what can you expect from a movie named *Toy Story 3*, especially with the humans mostly offstage? I expect its target audience will love it, and at the box office it may take right up where *How to Train Your Dragon* left off. Just don't get me started about the 3-D. ☞

Traitor ★ ★ ★
PG-13, 113 m., 2008

Don Cheadle (Samir Horn), Guy Pearce (Roy Clayton), Neal McDonough (Max Archer), Said Taghmaoui (Omar), Mozhan Marno (Leyla), Jeff Daniels (Carter), Archie Panjabi (Chandra), Aly Khan (Fareed). Directed by Jeffrey Nachmanoff and produced by Don Cheadle, David Hoberman, Jeffrey Silver, and Todd Lieberman. Screenplay by Nachmanoff.

Traitor weaves a tangled web of conspiracy and intrigue, crosses politics with thriller elements, and never quite answers its central question: In the war between good and evil, how many good people is it justifiable for the good guys to kill? Maybe that question has no answer. It is probably not "none."

The film stars Don Cheadle, an actor who excels at inner conflict, as Samir, born in Sudan, later an undercover special op for the United States. As a youth, he witnessed his father killed by a car bomb. For me, at least, it was not immediately clear who was responsible for the bomb, although his father was a committed Muslim. Was he killed by Muslim haters or by Muslims who opposed his politics? That ambiguity works in the film's favor. As Samir enlists on the American side and then is seen as a remarkably effective agent for terrorist jihadists, we are kept wondering where his true loyalties lie.

The film makes it a point that Samir is devout in the practice of his religion. He often quotes the Quran, is observant, seems to have true spirituality in his soul. He is not pretending. Of course, the great majority of Muslims are against terrorism and any form of murder. Others, as we have seen, are not. In paying attention to this division, *Traitor* establishes the mystery of which side Samir is a traitor to. Is he a double agent for the United States or a triple agent?

The film, written and directed by Jeffrey Nachmanoff, uses locations in Africa, the Middle East, Europe, and America, and provides an inside view of both the jihadists and a special FBI counterterrorism unit. Guy Pearce and Neal McDonough play FBI agents who disagree about the handling of the case; Jeff Daniels is a CIA agent who approaches the plot obliquely. Said Taghmaoui is very effective as Omar, leader of a terrorist group that has grave suspicions about Samir, until Samir is able to disprove them by being jailed, escaping with Omar, providing bomb-building expertise, and creating a chilling scenario for a terrorist attack in the United States.

The movie proceeds quickly, seems to know its subject matter, is fascinating in its portrait of the inner politics and structure of the terrorist group, and comes uncomfortably close to reality. But what holds it together is the Cheadle character, whose true motives remain opaque to the terrorists, the Americans, and the audience.

As we have learned from the spies of Graham Greene and John LeCarre, and from countless police movies, to be effective, an undercover agent must to a considerable degree cooperate with those he is targeting. Sometimes transference takes place. He begins to think like his enemies, to sympathize with them. Since working convincingly for either side requires a capacity for the fanatical, agents can grow confused about where their loyalties lie. It is this confusion that makes *Traitor* effective, except for those who like their moral choices laid out in black and white.

That's what makes the film's pure thriller elements work so well. Even in violent action scenes, the participants are forced to make instant decisions, or discoveries, about loyalties. We know from other movies how the violence will unfold, but neither we nor the combatants are sure which side everybody is on. That is true even of the urbane Omar, who is definitely a jihadist, but whose motives and their effect are paradoxical.

Don Cheadle is such a good actor. If he were more of a showboat, he would be a bigger star. But he remains the go-to man for a film like this. Except in his work like the *Ocean's* pictures or his heroic work in *Hotel Rwanda*, we cannot often be certain what we are to think of his characters. He effortlessly seems too intelligent, too complex, to be easily categorized. Perhaps my doubt about the motives of Samir's father's killers was due only to confusion on my part. Even so, who would witness the death of his father by a bomb and then be driven to become a builder of bombs? And why? It is an uncertainty potent enough to drive the entire movie.

Transformers: Revenge of the Fallen ★
PG-13, 149 m., 2009

Shia LaBeouf (Sam Witwicky), Megan Fox (Mikaela Banes), Josh Duhamel (Captain Lennox), Tyrese Gibson (USAF Tech Sergeant Epps), John Turturro (Gent Simmons/Jetfire), Ramon Rodriguez (Leo), Kevin Dunn (Ron Witwicky), Rainn Wilson (Professor Colan), Julie White (Judy Witwicky), Hugo Weaving (Megatron). Directed by Michael Bay and produced by Ian Bryce, Tom DeSanto, Lorenzo di Bonaventura, and Don Murphy. Screenplay by Ehren Kruger, Roberto Orci, and Alex Kurtzman.

Transformers: Revenge of the Fallen is a horrible experience of unbearable length, briefly punctuated by three or four amusing moments. One of these involves a doglike robot humping the leg of the heroine. Such are the meager joys. If you want to save yourself the ticket price, go into the kitchen, cue up a male choir singing the music of hell, and get a kid to start banging pots and pans together. Then close your eyes and use your imagination.

The plot is incomprehensible. The dialogue of the Autobots, Deceptibots, and Otherbots is meaningless word flap. Their accents are Brooklynese, British, and hip-hop, as befits a race from the distant stars. Their appearance looks like junkyard throw-up. They are dumb as rocks. They share the film with human characters who are much more interesting, and that is very faint praise indeed.

The movie has been signed by Michael Bay. This is the same man who directed *The Rock* in 1996. Now he has made *Transformers: Revenge of the Fallen*. Faust made a better deal. This isn't a film so much as a toy tie-in. Children holding a Transformer toy in their hand can invest it with wonder and magic, imagining it doing brave deeds and remaining always their friend. I knew a little boy once who lost his blue toy truck at the movies and cried as if his heart would break. Such a child might regard *Transformers: Revenge of the Fallen* with fear and dismay.

The human actors are in a witless sitcom part of the time, and a lot of the rest of their time is spent running in slo-mo away from explosions, although—hello!—you can't outrun an explosion. They also make speeches like this one by John Turturro: "Oh, no! The machine is buried in the pyramid! If they turn it on, it will destroy the sun!" "Not on my watch!" The humans, including lots of U.S. troops, shoot at the Transformers a lot, although never in the history of science fiction has an alien been harmed by gunfire.

There are many great-looking babes in the film, who are made up to a flawless perfection and look just like real women, if you are a junior fanboy whose experience of the gender is limited to lad magazines. The two most inexplicable characters are Ron and Judy Witwicky (Kevin Dunn and Julie White), who are the parents of Shia LaBeouf, whom Mephistopheles threw in to sweeten the deal. They take their son away to Princeton, apparently a party school, where Judy eats some pot and goes berserk. Later they swoop down out of the sky on Egypt, for reasons the movie doesn't make crystal clear, so they also can run in slo-mo from explosions.

The battle scenes are bewildering. A Bot makes no visual sense anyway, but two or three tangled up together create an incomprehensible confusion. I find it amusing that creatures that can unfold out of a Camaro and stand four stories high do most of their fighting with fists. Like I said, dumber than a box of staples. They have tiny little heads, except for Starscream, who is so ancient he has an aluminum beard.

Aware that this movie opened in England seven hours before Chicago time, and the morning papers would be on the streets, after writing the above I looked up the first reviews as a reality check. I was reassured: "Like watching paint dry while getting hit over the head with a frying pan!" (Bradshaw, *Guardian*); "Sums up everything that is most tedious, crass and despicable about modern Hollywood!" (Tookey, *Daily Mail*); "A giant, lumbering idiot of a movie!" (Edwards, *Daily Mirror*). The first American review, however, reported that it feels "destined to be the biggest movie of all time" (Todd Gilchrist, Cinematical). It's certainly the biggest something of all time.   ☞

Transporter 3 ★ ★ ½
PG-13, 105 m., 2008

Jason Statham (Frank Martin), Natalya Rudakova (Valentina), Francois Berleand (Tarconi), Robert Knepper (Johnson), Jeroen Krabbe (Vasilev). Directed by Olivier Megaton and produced by Luc Besson and Steve Chasman. Screenplay by Besson and Robert Mark Kamen.

Transporter 3 is a perfectly acceptable brainless action thriller, inspiring us to give a lot of thought to complex sequences we would have been better off sucking on as eye candy. Consider this ingenious dilemma faced by the Transporter. He cannot remove a bracelet that is linked to a mighty bomb in his Audi A8. If he goes more than seventy-five feet from the car, the explosion kills him. He and the car and the girl are trapped on a bridge by men with machine guns. He releases the girl. The men are shooting at him. How can he escape?

Remember, this is the Transporter. He completes 100 percent of his deliveries. If he told you his FedEx tracking number, he would have to kill you. Because we know it's impossible to kill an action hero with machine gun fire, no matter how many rounds, he is in no real danger. But as men advance on him from both ends of the bridge, he has to do *something* to keep up appearances. He can't just sit there and wait for them to fire on him point-blank.

For that matter, the bad guys *know* their machine guns are impotent because they have both ends of the bridge blocked and haven't been hit by one another's bullets. But what does the Transporter do? Steers hard to the left, drives through the bridge rail, and plunges into the lake. Now we're talking real trouble. If he swims for the shore, the bomb will kill him. The only answer is to take the car to the shore with him, while holding his breath.

He improvises a way to get air underwater. It's clever but, thinking it over, I wouldn't advise you to try it while underwater. Anyway, the plot involves bad guys who want to bring eight container ships of toxic poisons into a Ukrainian harbor. Odessa has a beautiful harbor, with some nice steps leading down to the water. But the Ukrainian minister (Jeroen Krabbe) doesn't want to give his permission. Meanwhile, the bad guys kidnap the girl (Natalya Rudakova), and the Transporter's job is to transport her for the bad guys, although he violates his policy and begins to care for her.

Rudakova is no Bonnie Hunt when it comes to personality. She skulks, pouts, clams up, looks out the window, and yet falls in love with the Transporter and is able to ask him, "Kiss me—one last time!" Not the words you want to hear when you release her and people start shooting at you. Some perfectionists will no doubt criticize her acting. I say the hell with her acting. Look at those freckles. I can never get enough of freckles. In the movies, they're usually limited to a sprinkling on either side of a moppet nose. When you see beautiful freckles, as for example with the adorable actress Julianne Nicholson, you rejoice.

The director of *Transporter 3*, Olivier Megaton, is named after the bomb at Hiroshima, which was dropped on his birthday. Named not by his parents (the Fontanas) but by himself. French. (The Transporter's real name is the anticlimactic Frank Martin.) Anyway, although Megaton's CGI fight scenes are every bit as chopped up and incomprehensible as the current norm, he mostly avoids the queasy-cam and uses a stable camera while only the *action* moves. How about that.

He also succeeds in clearing every highway in every chase scene so the road is held only by the chasers and the chasees. Except, of course, when two monster trucks are required to speed this way, in which case, although there has been no traffic since the border, they are required to pass each other, and of course loudly toot their Klaxons—ooo-gaah! ooo-gaah!—as if you don't see them.

This movie is not boring. Jason Statham is a splendid action hero, steely eyed, muscular, taciturn, a close-lipped know-it-all with the official three-day stubble. He could do the snowmobile race with two broken arms. The bad guys are suitably reprehensible, the photography is expert, and when you see the Transporter thinking his way out of that problem on the bottom of the lake, you're amazed that later he restarts the engine and uses it to drive onto the top of a speeding train, and then ingeniously calculates a way to use the train's speed to save . . . but see for yourself. That A8, what a car. Solar panels to run the heat and A/C.

Transsiberian ★ ★ ★ ½
R, 111 m., 2008

Woody Harrelson (Roy), Emily Mortimer (Jessie), Kate Mara (Abby), Eduardo Noriega (Carlos), Thomas Kretschmann (Myassa), Ben Kingsley (Grinko). Directed by Brad Anderson and produced by Julio Fernandez. Screenplay by Anderson and Will Conroy.

Transsiberian is—how shall I put this?—one hell of a thriller. It's not often that I feel true suspense and dread building within me, but they were building during long stretches of this expertly constructed film. It takes place mostly on board the Transsiberian Express from Beijing to Moscow, at eight days the longest train journey in the world. And it uses the train as an asset: The characters all have to be on here somewhere, don't they?

The movie stars Emily Mortimer as Jessie and Woody Harrelson as her husband, Roy.

They've just finished working with poor kids in China on behalf of their church group. Roy is a train buff. I've known a couple and they're exactly like this: thinking nothing of going out in the minus twenty-three-degree cold of Siberia to check out an old steam engine. Jessie, we learn, was a wild child when younger but is now clean and sober. Roy is a straight arrow. They love each other.

On board the train they meet another couple. Abby (Kate Mara) is a confused twenty-year-old runaway from Seattle. Carlos (Eduardo Noriega), ten or fifteen years older, is a charming Spanish traveler who knows a lot about customs and passports.

From the moment Carlos sees her, he has his eyes on Jessie. She knows this. When they all get off the train, Roy and Carlos go to look at the steam engine, and Carlos fingers a long iron rod. Back on the train again, Jessie is startled to find her husband not on board. In a panic, she gets off at the next stop to wait for him, hoping he only missed the train. Carlos and Abby get off to be with her.

Already I'm feeling the fears of a stranger in a strange land. Tourists in Russia are welcomed where tourists go, but the Russians they meet in this movie are poor, bitter, and hostile, starting with the venomous woman who is the "hostess" on their railcar. While they're all waiting together at the next town, Carlos persuades Jessie to take a bus ride with him. Then they trek through a deserted, snowy landscape to see an abandoned but indeed pretty Orthodox church. What happens there you will not learn from me, nor will I say much about later events.

Turns out Roy did merely miss the train. While laid over, he made friends with the Russian narcotics detective Grinko (Ben Kingsley, expanding his repertoire of ethnic characters). Grinko is friendly and confiding. But then certain questions arise, and Jessie is shaky at answering them.

The movie, cowritten and directed by Brad Anderson (*The Machinist, Next Stop Wonderland*), is constructed with many of the devices and much of the skill of a Hitchcock. There is an interesting twist on Hitch's *The Lady Vanishes*. Instead of one or more passengers disappearing, most of the train disappears. Jessie gets up, heads for the rear of the train

and almost falls out the back door to her death. From overhead shots we know the train is very long. What happened to all the other cars?

This is one of those trips after which you post dire warnings on the Net and file lawsuits—if you survive. The movie's secrets are manipulated into a clockwork mechanism that grinds to crush Jessie and Roy, and Jessie keeps right on saying the wrong things. She is warned by Grinko: "In Russia, we say that with lies you may go forward in the world, but you may never go back." Eventually, lies are no longer even the point.

Her performance is yet another surprise from Emily Mortimer, that English rose who here comes across as an American survivor of a long, strange trip. She hangs onto her sobriety like a life raft, but she still has a reckless streak. Harrelson, an actor of so many notes, is here earnest and sincere, and too trusting. Kingsley bites like a knife. Noriega persuasively plays Carlos with all of his secrets, and Mara is a wounded runaway who Jessie believes is a "good person."

Although the movie has several action sequences, not one is put in for effect. They all grow from the plot and drive it—even, I would argue, the concluding train sequence, which is certainly improbable but makes a certain sense. Like all the best suspense movies, *Transsiberian* starts in neutral, taking the time to introduce its characters, and then goes from second into high like greased lightning. I was a little surprised to notice how thoroughly it wound me up. This is a good one.

Tropic Thunder ★ ★ ★ ½
R, 106 m., 2008

Ben Stiller (Tugg Speedman), Jack Black (Jeff Portnoy), Robert Downey Jr. (Kirk Lazarus), Nick Nolte (Four Leaf Tayback), Steve Coogan (Damien Cockburn), Danny McBride (Cody), Brandon T. Jackson (Alpa Chino). Directed by Ben Stiller and produced by Stuart Cornfeld, Eric McLeod, and Stiller. Screenplay by Stiller, Etan Cohen, and Justin Theroux.

The documentary *Hearts of Darkness* is about the struggles of filming the great Vietnam War movie *Apocalypse Now*. Ben Stiller's *Tropic*

Thunder plays like the doc's nightmare. A troupe of actors, under the impression they're making a Vietnam War movie, wanders dangerously in the jungle and is captured by a gang of drug lords who think the actors are narcs.

The movie is a send-up of Hollywood, actors, acting, agents, directors, writers, rappers, trailers, and egos, much enhanced by several cameo roles, the best of which I will not even mention. You'll know the one, although you may have to wait for the credits to figure it out.

All but stealing the show, Robert Downey Jr. is not merely funny but also very good and sometimes even subtle as Kirk Lazarus, an Australian actor who has won five Oscars and has now "surgically dyed" his skin to transform himself into a black man. So committed is he to this role that he remains in character at all times, seemingly convinced that he is actually black. This exasperates his fellow actor Alpa Chino (Brandon T. Jackson), a rapper who was born black and blasts Lazarus for his delusions. Alpa Chino (say it out loud) is like many rappers and promotes his own merchandise, notably Booty Sweat, an energy drink that keeps him going in the jungle.

If Chino doesn't buy the Lazarus performance, Lazarus is critical of Tugg Speedman (Stiller), who stars in *Simple Jack,* a movie about a mentally challenged farmer who thinks animals can understand him. Ironically, it is this role that saves their lives when they're taken prisoner. The bored drug lords have only one video, an old *Simple Jack* tape, and think Speedman is Jack himself. In a brilliant comic riff by Downey, Lazarus critiques Speedman's work as over the top: The really big stars, he observes, "never go full retard" when playing such roles.

The movie opens with trailers establishing three of the characters—not only Lazarus and Speedman, but Jeff Portnoy (Jack Black), whose specialty is fart humor. Portnoy is a heroin addict who is in withdrawal for much of the trek through the jungle, and has a funny scene after he begs to be tied to a tree and then begs to be set loose.

The setup involves the actors, director Damien Cockburn (Steve Coogan), and burned-out screenwriter Four Leaf Tayback (Nick Nolte) in the jungle with a huge crew

and explosives expert Cody (Danny McBride). When one of the explosions goes off prematurely (think the opening of *The Party*), Speedman, acting as producer, fires the crew and announces he will direct the movie himself. He explains that hidden cameras have been placed in the jungle and will record everything that happens. Uh, is that possible, especially when they get lost? These actors, even the five-time Oscar winner, almost seem to believe so, a tribute to their self-centered indifference to technical details.

Intercut with the jungle scenes are Hollywood scenes featuring an agent and a studio executive. The movie, written by Justin Theroux, Stiller, and Etan Cohen, is familiar with the ordeals of filmmaking and location work, and distills it into wildly exaggerated scenes that have a whiff of accuracy. Especially interesting is the way the director, Damien Cockburn, leaves the picture, which perhaps reflects the way some actors feel about some directors.

The movie is, may I say, considerably better than Stiller's previous film *Zoolander.* It's the kind of summer comedy that rolls in, makes a lot of people laugh, and rolls onto video. It's been a good summer for that; look at *Pineapple Express.* When it's all over, you'll probably have the fondest memories of Robert Downey Jr.'s work. It's been a good year for him, this one coming after *Iron Man.* He's back, big time.

Trouble the Water ★ ★ ★ ★
NO MPAA RATING, 93 m., 2008

A documentary featuring Scott Roberts and Kimberly Rivers Roberts. Directed and produced by Carl Deal and Tia Lessin.

Do you know what it means? To miss New Orleans?
—lyrics by Louis Armstrong

As I write, the hell storm Ike is battering Texas. I hear of evacuation buses, National Guard troops, emergency supplies, contraflow, Red Cross volunteers, helicopter rescues. It is a different world from the world after Katrina hit New Orleans. Yes, there were noble rescue efforts, but too little and too late, and without enough urgency on the part of the federal ("You're doin' a great job, Brownie!") government.

If you could have witnessed Katrina at ground zero, your blood would have boiled at the treatment of U.S. citizens. The extraordinary documentary *Trouble the Water* had an eyewitness in the city's Ninth Ward, *during* the storm. Her name was Kimberly Roberts. She was twenty-four. A week earlier, she had purchased a video camera from a street hustler for twenty dollars a week. She used it to film the experiences of her family before, during, and after the storm.

Her footage is surrounded by professionally filmed material that deepens and explains what happened. But the eyewitness footage has a desperate urgency that surpasses any other news and doc footage I have seen. Using lessons learned from TV news, she interviews her family, friends, and neighbors, does voice-overs while making shots, even signs off with her stage name as a rapper: "This is Black Kold Madina from the Ninth Ward."

We see the prologue to the storm. Residents have been urged to evacuate, but many do not have the means or the ways to get to evacuation centers, buses, or trains. If they have cars, they don't have gas money. They hunker down and hope to live through it. Kimberly warns a homeless man: "You better take care of yoself or the storm gonna WHUP yo ass!"

Drops of rain start to fall. They watch the TV news. Katrina worsens. Power goes out. The levee near their house is breached. Waters rise. They take refuge in their attic, in pitch darkness. We hear their call to 911. They have women and children up there, even a baby. They're trapped. They're told no rescue teams are working "at this time"—or not for days, in their neighborhood. They escape, helped by a muscular Good Samaritan who found a boat drifting past. Eventually they retreat to shelter in Alexandria, Louisiana, where the makers of this film, Carl Deal and Tia Lessin, found them and her footage. Her film changed all their plans for their film.

The documentary shows outrageous behavior, none more so than when they and many others are directed to a nearby navy base for refuge. The base is being closed. It has an empty housing unit in plain view with hundreds of beds. The gates are locked. They are turned away at gunpoint by sailors with M-16s (who were commended for their "bravery" in guarding the base).

Roberts needs more practice at holding the camera steady and framing shots. It doesn't matter. We feel her footage at the base of our spines. Sometimes she says nothing, just points the camera, and the images speak for themselves. Carl Deal and Tia Lessin, who have worked with Michael Moore, augment her eyewitness account with footage from TV news showing New Orleans mayor Ray Nagin, Louisiana governor Kathleen Babineaux Blanco, and shots of the breached levees and the panorama of destruction.

The film is about Katrina, and even more about the human spirit. Kimberly and her husband, Scott, are the life force personified: smart, funny, undefeated, indignant, determined. Kimberly sings three songs on the sound track. We see her performing one of them. That scene reportedly won a standing ovation at Sundance 2008, where the film won the Grand Jury Prize as best documentary.

Charges were made after Katrina that the federal response was lacking because so many of the victims were poor and black. "We feel like we're not U.S. citizens," Kimberly says at one point. At another, she rails against George Bush in language I will spare you. One of the most affecting scenes is when Kimberly, Scott, and their dog wander down the streets of their neighborhood, remembering: "There was an old lady living in that house. Always on her porch, saying hello to everybody." Her good cheer disappears when she learns that the man she warned was killed. The storm whupped his ass. That was his own fault. What happened to the residents of the Ninth Ward was not their fault.

Roberts was pregnant when she and Scott went to the Sundance premiere. On Monday, January 21, 2008, at the Park City hospital, she gave birth. It was Martin Luther King Jr. Day.

Trucker ★★★★
R, 90 m., 2009

Michelle Monaghan (Diane Ford), Jimmy Bennett (Peter), Nathan Fillion (Runner), Benjamin Bratt (Len), Joey Lauren Adams

(Jenny). Directed by James Mottern and produced by Scott Hanson, Galt Niederhoffer, Celine Rattray, and Daniela Taplin Lundberg. Screenplay by Mottern.

There's one of those perfect moments in *Trucker* when I'm thinking, "This is the moment to end! Now! Fade to black!" And the movie ends. It is the last of many absolutely right decisions by the first-time writer-director James Mottern, who began by casting two actors who bring his story to strong emotional life. Both of them show they're gifted and intelligent artists who only needed, as so many do in these discouraging times, a chance to reveal their deep talents.

Michelle Monaghan was on the brink of inhabiting forever the thankless role of the good-looking, plucky female in action movies about men (*Mission: Impossible III*). She was excellent in *Gone Baby Gone,* and here she confirms her talent. Jimmy Bennett, who was eleven or twelve at the time of shooting, has been good in heavy-duty projects before (*Orphan*) and played the young Captain Kirk in *Star Trek* (2009), but here shows a subtlety and command of tone that is remarkable. (It's time for him to start billing himself as "James." He'll be relieved when he's twenty.) Together these actors create an abrasive relationship that sidesteps all sentimentality, in a film that correctly ends when a lesser film would have added half an hour of schmaltz.

Monaghan is Diane Ford, a trucker who just paid off her own rig. She's thirtyish, cold, hard-drinking, promiscuous, a loner. Bennett plays her son, Peter. She left him with his father, Len (Benjamin Bratt), soon after his birth, has stayed away, doesn't like kids—or men, either, although she uses them. One man (Nathan Fillion) has been her best friend for four years, but that involves getting drunk together and never having sex.

Len gets sick. Colon cancer. He's been living for years with Jenny (Joey Lauren Adams), who now needs time to care for him. It's up to Diane to look after the kid. She doesn't want anything to do with him. "Just for a few weeks," Jenny pleads. Just until Len gets better. Sure.

You are anticipating, as I did, that *Trucker* would turn into one of those predictable

movies where the mother and son grow to love each other. It doesn't end with mutual hate and abandonment, but it damn near does. The kid is as tough as his mom. "Answer me!" she says. "I don't talk to bitches!" he says. Len and Jenny seem nice enough. Where did he learn to talk like that? Little pitchers have big ears.

I concede the story arc is fairly predictable, assuming neither one murders the other. But Mottern and his actors take no hostages. Diane is hard and tough, and stays that way. Her son is angry and bitter, and stays that way. Do they need to love and be loved? Sure. We know that, but they don't. By the end of the film, she hasn't called him "Peter" and he hasn't called her "Mom." He's "kid" or "dude," and she's "you." They have to be together whether they like it or not, and they know it.

That said, Monaghan makes Diane more sad than off-putting. She isn't a caricature. She works hard, values her independence, is making payments on her small suburban home on an unpaved street, is living up to her bargain with herself. The movie spares us any scenes where she's "one of the guys." It opens after a one-night stand with a guy who tries to be nice, but she doesn't need a nice guy in her life. Nor does she need to be nice with Peter, but one thing she does do: She's always honest with him and speaks with him directly, and I think he knows that. Her performance clearly deserves an Academy nomination.

Peter is loved by his father and Jenny. He hasn't been mistreated. He probably senses how sick his dad really is and knows he wasn't parked with Diane because anyone wanted him there. He's been told things about his mother that are, strictly speaking, true. She did leave him and Len soon after his birth. She does want to avoid seeing him. He says something that reveals he knows of her promiscuity, although he may not quite understand it.

What Mottern does is lock these two characters in a story and see what happens. Something will have to give. The supporting performances by Nathan Fillion, Benjamin Bratt, and Joey Lauren Adams are precisely what is needed: direct, open, no "acting," good tone control. They are good people, but very real people, with no illusions about life.

I value films that closely regard specific

lives. I know they usually must have happy endings. Not always. Haven't we all learned to expect certain things in a story about a mother and a son? Aren't those things, in fact, generally true to human nature? I hope to feel elevation at the end. But a film should earn it, not simply evoke it. *Trucker* sets out on a difficult and tricky path, and doesn't put a foot wrong.

Tru Loved ★
R, 104 m., 2008

Najarra Townsend (Tru), Jake Abel (Trevor), Matthew Thompson (Lodell), Tye Olson (Walter), Bruce Vilanch (Daniel/Minister), Alexandra Paul (Leslie), Cynda Williams (Lisa), Nichelle Nichols (Grandmother). Directed by Stewart Wade and produced by Wade, Antonio Brown, and David Avallone. Screenplay by Wade.

Tru Loved as a movie is on about the same level as a not especially good high school play. Student directors could learn from it. I'm sure its heart is in the right place, but it fails at fundamentals we take for granted when we go to the movies. By lacking them, it illustrates what the minimum requirements are for a competent film. Yes, you can clearly see and hear them, especially when they're missing.

1. Line readings. That's what they sound like, readings. Classroom readings. The actors lack the knack of making their dialogue sound spontaneous and realistic. They sound like bright English students who have memorized their lines but find themselves onstage without having had much experience or training.

2. Body language. One of the first things an actor learns is not to gesture to emphasize lines unless the lines really call for it. Insecure actors often seem to punch up dialogue physically as a sort of insurance policy.

3. Framing. When you have five characters at a picnic table, you don't (necessarily) want to block those on the other side with the bodies of those on this side. There are ways to do that or fudge it. Or forget it. But don't have those on side A separated so we can see those on side B centered between persons 1 and 2, and 2 and 3, and then in the reverse shot separate those on side B so we can see those on side A.

4. Don't let the dialogue scream, "I paid at-tention in Gay Lit class!" When a kid comes home from Walt Whitman High School, don't make a point of establishing a lesbian connection to a name.

> Grandmother: *Tru? What kind of a name is that?*
> Lodell: *Short for Gertrude. As in Stein. She's a writer.*
> Grandma: *I know who Gertrude Stein was. "A rose is a rose is a rose."*
> Lodell: *Yeah. Whatever.*

After bringing up the sainted Gertrude, why does Lodell immediately reject her? "Whatever," when used by a teenager to an adult, is a way of dismissing what has been said. Lodell is a bright kid. Since he has *just now come* from a class studying *Romeo and Juliet, maybe* he might have replied, "And by any other name it smells as sweet as sweet as sweet." Grandma seems as if she'd like that.

5. Daydreams. Can be annoying, especially when absurdly stagy. Even more especially when the daydreams are in soft focus and then we cut frequently to the heroine in sharp focus, looking at scenes in her own daydreams and nodding and smiling.

6. Speech patterns. It's my impression most gay men do not "sound like gay men." But we all know exactly what I mean by sounding like gay men. The other side of the rule is, many men who sound gay are gay, and in many cases intend to sound gay. Don't get all homophilic on me. You know I'm right.

7. Cameo appearances. Their use must be carefully controlled to avoid breaking a film's mood with the "Hey! There's Donald Trump!" Syndrome. That is doubly true when the cameo star is famous and appears in a double role, as does Bruce Vilanch, from *Hollywood Squares*. Here he plays "Daniel" and "the Minister." Senator, I know Bruce Vilanch, and he's no Minister.

8. Music. Not necessary to blast in with literal and urgent punch lines and transitions.

The movie is about how Tru moves from idyllic San Francisco to conservative suburbia with her lesbian mothers. This just in: Except for some jocks and those who doth protest too much, today's suburban teens are mostly cool with people who are gay, except in the Palin Belt.

Full disclosure: I lifted the words "San Francisco to conservative suburbia with her lesbian mothers" straight from the plot summary on IMDb.com, because I stopped watching the movie at the 00.08.05 point. IMDb is also where I found out about Bruce Vilanch's dual role. I never did see the lesbian mothers or my friend Bruce. For *Tru Loved*, the handwriting was on the wall. The returns were in. The case was closed. You know I'm right. Or tell me I'm wrong.

Q: How can you give a one-star rating to a movie you didn't sit through?

A: The rating only applies to the first eight minutes. After that you're on your own.

Tulpan ★ ★ ★ ★

NO MPAA RATING, 100 m., 2009

Askhat Kuchinchirekov (Asa), Samal Yeslyamova (Samal), Ondasyn Besikbasov (Ondas), Tulepbergen Baisakalov (Boni), Bereke Turganbayev (Beke), Mahabbat Turganbayeva (Maha). Directed by Sergey Dvortsevoy and produced by Karl Baumgartner and Thanassis Karathanos. Screenplay by Dvortsevoy and Gennady Ostrovskiy.

Tulpan is an amazing film. It shows such an unfamiliar world it might as well be Mars. This is a world where the horizon is a straight line against the sky in every direction. There are no landmarks, no signs, no roads. No vegetation grows much more than a foot or two high. It is dry, dusty, cold, and windy, and nothing seems to be green. This is the world *Tulpan* takes place in, and I can think of only one other story that would feel at home there: *Waiting for Godot.*

Yet the people love it. They are yurt dwellers in Kazakhstan, the largest landlocked nation on Earth. They live on what is named in the credits as the Hungersteppe and raise sheep. We meet a young sailor named Asa, discharged from the Russian navy, who has come here to live with his sister Samal, her husband, Ondas, and their children. As the story opens, Asa, Ondas, and his buddy Boni are negotiating with a poker-faced man and his hostile wife for the hand of their daughter, Tulpan ("Tulip").

Asa enthralls them with tales of the seahorse and octopus. They offer ten sheep and a chandelier. It is to no avail; Tulpan, peeking through the doorway curtains, thinks his ears are too big. There is not one single other potential bride in the district, and how is a man to live here without a wife?

These people are quite familiar with what we call civilization. Their children have been deserting to the cities for years. They do not have electricity, and water must be trucked in. I assume they eat a lot of mutton, and there is a man with an ungainly jeeplike vehicle who comes around selling cucumbers and, I hope, other vegetables. They have a battery-powered radio, which one of the sons listens to eagerly, racing into the yard to announce: "Breaking news! Earthquake in Japan! Seven on the Richter scale!"

They are alarmed that many baby lambs are stillborn. They call out the vet, whose teeth do a thing with his cigarette it is difficult to describe. He travels with a sick baby camel in his motorcycle sidecar. His diagnosis is simple and almost obvious. Asa eventually argues with his taskmaster brother-in-law and walks away from the farm. This consists of disappearing into the void; how do people avoid getting lost here? When Ondas scans the horizon with his binoculars, everything looks the same.

There is humor in the film, some of it involving the cucumber salesman, and tenderness, as when Samal sings a bedtime lullaby to her tired husband and their children. Stark reality, in the difficult birth of a lamb that lives. A shot, long held, of Samal's face, which tells us everything we can ever hope to know about her situation. The film's closing shot is epic in its meaning and astonishing in its difficulty.

This is the first feature by Sergey Dvortsevoy, forty-five, born in Kazakhstan, whose documentaries have been about people in the old Russian republics living between tradition and the future. What does it sound like to you? Ethnographic boredom? I swear to you that if you live in a place where this film is playing, it is the best film in town. You'll enjoy it, not soon forget it, and you'll tell your friends about it and try to convince them to go, but you'll have about as much luck with them as I'm probably having with you. Still, there has to come a time in everyone's life when they see a deadpan comedy about the yurt dwellers of Kazakhstan.

Note: This was the winner of the Un Certain Regard prize at Cannes 2008.

12 ★ ★ ★ ½
PG-13, 153 m., 2009

Sergey Makovetsky (Engineer), Nikita Mikhalkov (Foreman), Sergey Garmash (Cabbie), Valentin Gaft (Elderly Jewish Man), Alexey Petrenko (Transit Worker), Yuri Stoyanov (TV Producer), Sergey Gazarov (Surgeon), Mikhail Efremov (Traveling Actor), Alexander Adabashian (Bailiff), Apti Magamaev (Chechen Accused Man). Directed by Nikita Mikhalkov and produced by Mikhalkov and Leonid Vereschagin. Screenplay by Mikhalkov, Vladimir Moiseenko, and Alexander Novototsky-Vlasov, based on the screenplay by Reginald Rose.

Twelve Angry Men remains a monument of American filmmaking, and more than fifty years after it was made its story is still powerful enough to inspire this Russian version—not a remake, but a new demonstration of a jury verdict arrived at only because one of the men was not angry so much as worried. *12* by Nikita Mikhalkov is a powerful new film inspired by a powerful older one.

You know the story. A jury is sequestered. The men are hot and tired, and impatient to go home. It is assumed that the defendant, a young man accused of murder, is guilty. A quick vote is called for. The balloting shows eleven for convicting, one against. This generates a long and dogged debate in which the very principles of justice itself are called into play.

Perhaps Russia got this film when it needed it. Reginald Rose's original screenplay was written for the CBS drama showcase *Studio One* in 1954 and presented live. Franklin Schaffner (*Patton*) was the director. The telecast took place during the declining days of the hearings held by Senator Joseph McCarthy. CBS also broadcast the army-McCarthy hearings and Edward R. Murrow's historic takedown of the alcoholic witch-hunter. The great film by Sidney Lumet, made in 1957, currently stands at number nine on

IMDb's poll of the greatest films, ahead of *The Empire Strikes Back* and *Casablanca.*

If the original story argued for the right to a fair trial in the time of McCarthy's character assassinations, the Russian version comes at a time when that nation is using the jury system after a legacy of Stalinist purges and Communist Party show trials. It also dramatizes anti-Semitism and hatred for Chechens; the youth on trial is newly arrived in Moscow. The issue of overnight Russian millionaires in a land of much poverty is also on many of the jurors' minds.

None of the jurors is given a name, although director Mikhalkov gives himself the role of the jury foreman. One by one, every member of the jury tells a story or reveals a secret. Their set pieces do the job of swaying fellow jurors to reconsider their votes but are effective on their own as essentially a series of one-man shows. There is not a weak member in the cast, and it's a tribute to the power of the actors that the 2½-hour running time doesn't seem labored. The jury is sequestered in the gymnasium of a school next to the courtroom, and they never leave it, but their stories are performed so skillfully that in our minds we envision many settings; they're like radio plays.

Lumet famously began his film with the camera above eye level and subtly lowered it until the end, when the characters loomed above the camera. Mikhalkov, with a large open space to work in, uses camera placement and movement instead, circling the makeshift jury table and following jurors as they wander the room. A sparrow flies in through a window, and its fluttering and chirping is a reminder that the jurors, too, feel imprisoned.

Going in I knew what the story was about, how it would progress, and how it would end. Mikhalkov keeps all of that (writer Rose shares a screen credit), but he has made a new film with its own original characters and stories, and after all, it's not how the film ends, but how it gets there.

21 and a Wakeup ★ ½
R, 123 m., 2009

Amy Acker (Caitlin Murphy), Faye Dunaway (Major Rose Thorn), Danica McKellar (Jenny

Valentine), Todd Cahoon (Chris Cameron), Ed Begley Jr. (Colonel Ritchie), Ben Vereen (General John Jay Garner), Wes Studi (Doctor). Directed, written, and produced by Chris McIntyre.

I learn that Chris McIntyre served in Vietnam and that *21 and a Wakeup*, set in an army hospital in the waning days of the war, is based on events he experienced and heard about. I'm sure his motivations were heartfelt, but his film is awkward and disjointed, and outstays its welcome.

It stars Amy Acker as a dedicated young army nurse named Caitlin Murphy, assigned to an army combat field hospital. She considers her profession a vocation, as indeed it is. Vocations and an army career don't always go hand in hand, and bureaucracy often wins out. Enforcing the Army Way is the uptight and unfortunately named Major Rose Thorn (Faye Dunaway), who seems opposed to innovation, improvisation, inspiration, and any other inclinations Caitlin might have in mind.

Her character is emblematic of the film's problems. I suspect McIntyre was so happy to enlist a star like Dunaway that it never occurred to him she's inappropriate for the role. God help me if I mention the age of an actress, but let me observe that Dunaway is about my age, and I consider myself beyond the age for optimum combat service.

Even more unfortunately, McIntyre hasn't written a believable character. I doubt Major Thorn as a nurse and as an officer. Her primary function seems to be materializing in a self-contained shot while issuing stiff formal announcements somewhat in the tone of a judge at a debutante charity function. She's stiffly poised in many shots; we can almost hear, "Ready for your close-up, Miss Dunaway."

But let's stop right there. Faye Dunaway is a fine actress and has been miscast in a badly written role. Amy Acker and other leading characters have been well cast in equally badly written roles. In contrast to the energy and life Robert Altman brought to his combat hospital in *M*A*S*H*, this film plays like a series of fond anecdotes trundled onstage without much relationship to one another.

Some of them strain credulity. McIntyre may indeed know about a nurse who went AWOL with a civilian war correspondent (Todd Cahoon) on an unauthorized visit to Cambodia. Such a trip may even have happened. But I didn't believe it.

I also didn't believe the punctuality with which critically wounded soldiers were rushed onscreen at crucial moments in the action in order to punctuate dialogue. These emergencies are tended to by medical personnel who seem like nothing so much as actors impersonating characters they've seen on TV.

McIntyre has enlisted an experienced cast, including Ed Begley Jr., Wes Studi, and Ben Vereen, and while Vereen creates a convincing human, none of them create convincing characters. How can they? They're pawns on a storyboard. The film lacks a sense of time and place. I discover on IMDb that it was actually filmed on location in Vietnam, but its Southeast Asia looks nowhere near as convincing as the locations of Coppola's *Apocalypse Now* and Stone's *Platoon* (shot in the Philippines) or Herzog's *Rescue Dawn* (Thailand).

Maybe I'm being too cynical. Perhaps I'll hear from nurses who served in Vietnam and inform me it was just like this. Even if it was, it plays like an assortment of stories that someone might tell you, "You ought to make a movie about that someday."

2012 ★★★ ½
PG-13, 158 m., 2009

John Cusack (Jackson Curtis), Amanda Peet (Kate Curtis), Chiwetel Ejiofor (Adrian Helmsley), Thandie Newton (Laura Wilson), Oliver Platt (Carl Anheuser), Tom McCarthy (Gordon Silberman), Woody Harrelson (Charlie Frost), Danny Glover (President Wilson), Liam James (Noah Curtis). Directed by Roland Emmerich and produced by Emmerich, Larry J. Franco, and Harald Kloser. Screenplay by Emmerich and Kloser.

It's not so much that the earth is destroyed but that it's done so thoroughly. *2012*, the mother of all disaster movies (and the father and the extended family), spends half an hour on ominous setup scenes (scientists warn, strange events occur, prophets rant, and, of course, a family is introduced) and then unleashes two hours of cataclysmic special events hammering the earth relentlessly.

This is fun. *2012* delivers what it promises, and since no sentient being will buy a ticket expecting anything else, it will be, for its audiences, one of the most satisfactory films of the year. It even has real actors in it. Like all the best disaster movies, it's funniest at its most hysterical. You think you've seen end-of-the-world movies? This one ends the world, stomps on it, grinds it up, and spits it out.

It also continues a recent trend toward the wholesale destruction of famous monuments. Roland Emmerich, the director and cowriter, has been vandalizing monuments for years, as in *Independence Day, The Day After Tomorrow,* and *Godzilla.* I still hold a grudge against him for that one because he provided New York with a Mayor Ebert and didn't have Godzilla step on me and squish me.

In all disaster movies, landmarks fall like dominoes. The Empire State Building is made of rubber. The Golden Gate Bridge collapses like clockwork. Big Ben ticks his last. The Eiffel Tower? *Quel dommage!* Memo to anyone on the National Mall: When the earth's crust is shifting, don't stand within range of the Washington Monument. Chicago is often spared; we aren't as iconic as Manhattan. There's little in Los Angeles distinctive enough to be destroyed, but it all goes anyway.

Emmerich thinks on a big scale. Yes, he destroys regular stuff. It will come as little surprise (because the trailer on YouTube alone has 7,591,413 views) that the aircraft carrier *John F. Kennedy* rides a tsunami onto the White House. When St. Peter's Basilica is destroyed, Leonardo's God and Adam are split apart just where their fingers touch (the ceiling of the Sistine Chapel having been moved into St. Peter's for the occasion). Then when Emmerich gets warmed up, the globe's tectonic plates shift thousands of miles, water covers the planet, and a giraffe walks on board an ark.

Also on board are the humans chosen to survive, including all the characters who have not already been crushed, drowned, or fallen into great crevices opening up in the earth. These include the heroic Jackson Curtis (John Cusack) and his estranged wife, Kate (Amanda Peet); the president (Danny Glover),

his chief science adviser, Adrian Helmsley (Chiwetel Ejiofor); and his chief of staff, Carl Anheuser (Oliver Platt).

Many gigantic arks have been secretly constructed inside the Himalayas by the Chinese, funded by a global consortium, and they're the only chance of the human race surviving. There are also animals on board, and maybe well-named Noah (Liam James). In theory, ark ticket holders represent a cross-section of the globe, chosen democratically. In practice, Carl Anheuser pulls strings to benefit the rich and connected and wants to strand desperate poor people on the dock. I'm thinking, Emmerich often has a twist when he names villains, like Mayor Ebert from *Godzilla.* So how did this villain get his name? What does "Anheuser" make you think of?

Such questions pale by comparison with more alarming events. The tectonic plates shift so violently scientists can almost see it on Google Earth. This havoc requires stupendous special effects. Emmerich's budget was $250 million. It may contain more f/x in total running time than any other film. They're impressive. Not always convincing, because how can the flooding of the Himalayas be made convincing but impressive? And Emmerich gives us time to regard the effects and appreciate them, even savor them, unlike the ADD generation and its quick-cutting "Bay cams."

Emmerich also constructs dramatic real-scale illusions, as when an earthquake fissure splits a grocery store in half. Cusack is the hero in an elaborate sequence involving his desperate attempts to unblock a jammed hydraulic lift that threatens to sink the ark. He does a lot of heroic stuff in this film, especially for a novelist, like leaping a van over a yawning chasm and flying a small plane through roiling clouds of earthquake dust.

The bottom line is: The movie gives you your money's worth. Is it a masterpiece? No. Is it one of the year's best? No. Does Emmerich hammer it together with his elbows from parts obtained from the Used Disaster Movie Store? Yes. But is it about as good as a movie in this genre can be? Yes. No doubt it will inflame fears about our demise on December 21, 2012. I'm worried, too. I expect that to be even worse than Y2K. ☞

Twilight ★ ★ ½
PG-13, 122 m., 2008

Kristen Stewart (Bella Swan), Robert Pattinson (Edward Cullen), Billy Burke (Charlie Swan), Peter Facinelli (Dr. Carlisle Cullen), Elizabeth Reaser (Esme Cullen), Nikki Reed (Rosalie Hale), Ashley Greene (Alice Cullen), Jackson Rathbone (Jasper Hale), Kellan Lutz (Emmett Cullen). Directed by Catherine Hardwicke and produced by Mark Morgan, Greg Mooradian, and Wyck Godfrey. Screenplay by Melissa Rosenberg, based on the novel by Stephenie Meyer.

If you're a vampire, it's all about you. Why is Edward Cullen obsessed to the point of erotomania by Bella Swan? Because she smells so yummy, but he doesn't want to kill her. Here's what he tells her: He must not be around her. He might sink his fangs in just a little and not be able to stop. She finds this overwhelmingly attractive. She tells him he is the most beautiful thing she has ever seen. I don't remember Edward ever saying that to her. Maybe once. He keeps on saying they should stay far, far apart because he craves her so much.

Should a woman fall in love with a man because he desires her so much? Men seem to think so. It's not about the woman; it's about the man's desire. We all know there is no such thing as a vampire. Come on now, what is *Twilight* really about? It's about a teenage boy trying to practice abstinence, and how, in the heat of the moment, it's really, really hard. And about a girl who wants to go all the way with him and doesn't care what might happen. He's so beautiful she would do anything for him. She is the embodiment of the sentiment "I'd die for you." She is, like many adolescents, a thanatophile.

If there were no vampires in *Twilight*, it would be a thin-blooded teenage romance, about two good-looking kids who want each other so much because they want each other so much. Sometimes that's all it's about, isn't it? They're in love with *being* in love. In *Twilight*, however, they have a seductive disagreement about whether he should kill her. She's like, I don't especially want to die, but if that's what it takes, count me in. She is touched by his devotion. Think what a sacrifice he is making on her behalf. On prom night, on the stage of the not especially private gazebo in the public gardens, he teeters right on the brink of a fang job, and then brings all of her trembling to a dead standstill.

The movie is lush and beautiful, and the actors are well-chosen. You may recall Robert Pattinson (Edward) as Cedric Diggory, who on Voldemort's orders was murdered in a graveyard in *Harry Potter and the Goblet of Fire*. Maybe he was already a vampire. Pattinson is not unaware of how handsome he is. When Bella and Edward, still strangers, exchange stern and burning looks in the school cafeteria, he transfixes her with a dark and glowering—nay, penetrating—stare. I checked Pattinson out on Google Images and found he almost always glowers at the camera 'neath shadowed brow. Kristen Stewart's Bella, on the other hand, is a fresh-faced innocent who is totally undefended against his voltage.

Bella has left her mom and stepdad in hot Arizona, clutching a potted cactus, to come live in the clammy, rainy Pacific Northwest, home of Seasonal Affective Disorder. Her dad (Billy Burke) is the chief of police of the very small town of Forks, Washington (population 3,120). His greatest asset: "He doesn't hover." At high school, she quickly notices the preternaturally pale Cullen clan, who in some shots seem to be wearing as much Max Factor Pancake White as Harry Langdon. Edward is 114 years old. He must be really tired of taking biology class. Darwin came in during his watch and proved vampires can't exist.

There are other strange youths around, including American Indians who appear not too distantly descended from their tribe's ancestors, wolves. Great tension between the wolves and vampires. Also some rival vampires around. How small is this town? The Forks high school is so big, it must serve a consolidated district serving the whole table setting. The main local Normal Kid is a nice, sandy-haired boy who asks Bella to the prom. He's out of his depth here, unless he can transmogrify into a grizzly. Also there are four gray-bearded coots at the next table in the local diner, who eavesdrop and exchange significant glances and get big, significant close-ups, but are still just sitting significantly nodding, for all I know.

Edward has the ability to move as swiftly as Superman. Like him he can stop a runaway pickup with one arm. He rescues Bella twice that I remember, maybe because he truly loves her, maybe because he's saving her for later. She has questions. "How did you appear out of nowhere and stop that truck?" Well might she ask. When he finally explains that he is a vampire, he goes up from eight to ten on her Erotometer. Why do girls always prefer the distant, aloof, handsome, dangerous dudes instead of cheerful chaps like me?

Twilight will mesmerize its target audience, sixteen-year-old girls and their grandmothers. Their mothers know all too much about boys like this. I saw it at a sneak preview. Last time I saw a movie in that same theater, the audience welcomed it as an opportunity to catch up on gossip, texting, and laughing at private jokes. This time the audience was rapt with attention. Sometimes a soft chuckle, as when the principal Indian boy has well-developed incisors. Sometimes a soft sigh. Afterward, I eavesdropped on some conversations. A few were saying, "He's so hot!" More floated in a sweet dreaminess. Edward seemed to stir their surrender instincts.

The movie, based on the Stephenie Meyer novel, was directed by Catherine Hardwicke. She uses her great discovery, Nikki Reed, in the role of the beautiful Rosalie Hale. Reed wrote Hardwicke's *Thirteen* (2003) when she was only fourteen. That was a movie that knew a lot more about teenage girls. The girl played by Reed in that movie would make mincemeat of Edward. But I understand who *Twilight* appeals to, and it sure will.

Note: Now playing around the country is the much better and more realistic teenage vampire movie Let the Right One In, *a Swedish import scheduled to be Twilighted by Hollywood. In this one, the vampire girl protects the boy and would never dream of killing him. That's your difference right there between girls and boys. Warning: This is very R-rated.*

The Twilight Saga: Eclipse ★★
PG-13, 124 m., 2010

Kristen Stewart (Bella Swan), Robert Pattinson (Edward Cullen), Taylor Lautner (Jacob Black), Bryce Dallas Howard (Victoria), Billy Burke (Charlie Swan), Dakota Fanning (Jane), Peter Facinelli (Dr. Carlisle Cullen), Elizabeth Reaser (Esme Cullen), Jackson Rathbone (Jasper Hale), Kellan Lutz (Emmett Cullen), Ashley Greene (Alice Cullen), Nikki Reed (Rosalie Hale). Directed by David Slade and produced by Wyck Godfrey, Greg Mooradian, and Karen Rosefelt. Screenplay by Melissa Rosenberg, based on the novel *Eclipse* by Stephenie Meyer.

The price for surrendering your virginity is so high in *The Twilight Saga: Eclipse* that even Edward Cullen, the proposed tool of surrender, balks at it. Like him, you would become one of the undead. This is a price that Bella Swan, the virtuous heroine, must be willing to pay. Apparently when you marry a vampire, even such a well-behaved one as Edward, he's required to bite you.

This romantic dilemma is developed in *Eclipse*, the third installment in this inexhaustible series, by adding a complication that has been building ever since the first. Jacob Black, the shape-shifting werewolf, is also in love with Bella (Kristin Stewart), and she perhaps with him. Jacob (Taylor Lautner) and his tribe are hot-blooded and never wear shirts, inspiring little coos and ripples of delight in the audience. Here is a fantasy to out-steam any romance novel: A sweet young girl is forced to choose between two improbably tall, dark, and handsome men who brood and smolder and yearn for her.

Nothing is perfect. There is a problem. The flame-tressed vampire Victoria (Bryce Dallas Howard) has been active in Seattle initiating new vampires, or Newbies, who in their youth are ravenous for blood and would have superhuman strength, if they were human. Victoria wants to destroy Bella in revenge for the murder of her boyfriend, James. Edward and Jacob both vow to protect the girl they love, and their fellow vampires and werewolves of course are prepared to fight to the death in this cause. This is true buddy love.

The movie contains violence and death, but not really very much. For most of its languorous running time, it listens to conversations between Bella and Edward, Bella and Jacob, Edward and Jacob, and Edward and Bella and Jacob. This would play better if any of them were clever conversationalists, but their ideas are limited to simplistic renderings of their desires. To be sure, there is a valedictory address, reminding us that these kids have skipped school for three movies now. And Edward has a noble speech when he tells Bella he doesn't want to have sex with her until after they're married. This is self-denial indeed for a 109-year-old vampire, who adds a piquant flavor to the category "confirmed bachelor."

Of Taylor Lautner's musculature, and particularly his abs, much has been written. Yes, he has a great build, but I remind you that an abdominal six-pack must be five seconds' work for a shape-shifter. More impressive is the ability of both Edward and Jacob to regard Bella with penetrating gazes from 'neath really heavy eyebrows. When my eyebrows get like Edward's, the barber trims them and never even asks me first.

There is a problem with the special effects. Many of the mountain ranges, which disappear into the far distance as increasingly pale peaks, look suspiciously like landscapes painted by that guy on TV who shows you how to paint stuff like that. The mountain forests and lakes are so pristine we should see Lewis and Clark just arriving. And the werewolves are inexplicable. They look snarly enough, have vicious fangs, and are larger than healthy ponies, but when they fall upon Newbies, they never quite seem to get the job done. One werewolf is nearly squeezed to death, and another, whose identity I will conceal, hears "he has broken bones on one whole side." Luckily, repairing the damage is only a night's work for Dr. Carlisle Cullen (Peter Facinelli). The problem with the effects is that the wolves don't seem to have physical weight and presence.

Much leads up to a scene in a tent on a mountaintop in the midst of a howling blizzard, when Bella's teeth start chattering. Obviously a job for the hot-blooded Jacob and not the cold-blooded Edward, and as Jacob embraces and warms her, he and Edward have a cloying cringe fest in which Edward admits that if Jacob were not a werewolf, he would probably like him, and then Jacob admits that if Edward were not a vampire—well, no, no, he couldn't. Come on, big guy. The two of you are making eye contact. Edward's been a confirmed bachelor for 109 years. Get in the brokeback spirit.

The audience watched this film with rapt attention. They obviously had a deep understanding of the story, which is just as well, because anyone not intimately familiar with the earlier installments could not make heads or tails of the opening scenes. The *Twilight* movies are chaste eroticism to fuel adolescent dreams, and are really about Bella being attracted and titillated and aroused and tempted up to the . . . very . . . BRINK! . . . of surrender, and then, well, no, no, she shouldn't.

The Twilight Saga: New Moon ★
PG-13, 130 m., 2009

Kristen Stewart (Bella Swan), Robert Pattinson (Edward Cullen), Taylor Lautner (Jacob Black), Dakota Fanning (Jane), Ashley Greene (Alice Cullen), Nikki Reed (Rosalie Hale), Jackson Rathbone (Jasper Hale), Kellan Lutz (Emmett Cullen), Peter Facinelli (Dr. Carlisle Cullen), Billy Burke (Charlie Swan). Directed by Chris Weitz and produced by Wyck Godfrey. Screenplay by Melissa Rosenberg, based on the novel by Stephenie Meyer.

The characters in this movie should be arrested for loitering with intent to moan. Never have teenagers been in greater need of a jump-start. Granted, some of them are more than one hundred years old, but still: Their charisma is by Madame Tussaud.

The Twilight Saga: New Moon takes the tepid achievement of *Twilight* (2008), guts it, and leaves it for undead. You know you're in trouble with a sequel when the word of mouth advises you to see the first movie twice instead. Obviously the characters all have. Long opening stretches of this film make utterly no sense unless you walk in knowing the first film, and hopefully both Stephenie Meyer novels, by heart. Edward and Bella spend murky moments glowering at each other and thinking, "So, here we are again."

Bella (Kristen Stewart) is still living at home with her divorced dad (Billy Burke), a cop whose disciplinary policy involves declaring her grounded for the rest of her life and then disappearing so she can jump from cliffs, haunt menacing forests, and fly to Italy so the movie can evoke the sad final death scene from—why, hold on, it's *Romeo and Juliet!* The very play Edward was reciting narcissistically and contemptuously in an opening scene.

Yes, Edward (Robert Pattinson) is back in school, repeating the twelfth grade for the eighty-fourth time. Bella sees him in the school parking lot, walking toward her in slow-motion, wearing one of those Edwardian Beatles jackets with a velvet collar, pregnant with his beauty. How white his skin, how red his lips. The decay of middle age may transform him into the Joker.

Edward and the other members of the Cullen vampire clan stand around a lot with glowering skulks. Long pauses interrupt longer ones. Listen up, lads! You may be immortal, but we've got a train to catch.

Edward leaves because Bella was not meant to be with him. Although he's a vegetarian vampire, when she gets a paper cut at her birthday party, one of his pals leaps on her like a shark on a tuna fish.

In his absence she's befriended by Jake (Taylor Lautner), that nice American Indian boy. "You've gotten all buff!" she tells him. Yeah, real buff, and soon he's never wearing a shirt and standing outside in the winter rain as if he were—why, nothing more than a wild animal. They don't need coats like ours, remember, because God gave them theirs.

SPOILER WARNING: Those not among that 5 percent of the movie's target audience that doesn't already know this will be surprised that Jake is a werewolf.

> *Bella:* "So . . . you're a werewolf?"
> *Jake:* "Last time I checked."
> *Bella:* "Can't you find a way to . . . just stop?"
> *Jake (patiently):* "It's not a lifestyle choice, Bella."

Jake is influenced, or controlled, or something, by Sam, another member of the tribe. He's like the alpha wolf. Sam and his three friends are mostly seen in long shot, shirtless in the rain, hanging around the edges of the clearing as if hoping to dash in and pick off some fresh meat.

Bella writes long letters to her absent vampire friend Alice (Ashley Greene), in which she does nothing to explain why she is helplessly attracted to these sinister, humorless, and vain men. It can't be the sex. As I've already explained in my review of the first film, *The Twilight Saga* is an extended metaphor for teen chastity, in which the punishment for being deflowered I will leave to your imagination.

The movie includes beauteous fields filled with potted flowers obviously buried hours before by the grounds crew, and nobody not clued in on the plot. Since they know it all and we know it all, sitting through this experience is like driving a pickup in low gear through a sullen sea of Brylcreem. ☞

Two Lovers ★ ★ ★ ½
R, 110 m., 2009

Joaquin Phoenix (Leonard Kraditor), Gwyneth Paltrow (Michelle Rausch), Vinessa Shaw (Sandra Cohen), Moni Monoshov (Reuben Kraditor), Isabella Rossellini (Ruth Kraditor), John Ortiz (Jose Cordero), Bob Ari (Michael Cohen), Julie Budd (Carol Cohen), Elias Koteas (Ronald Blatt). Directed by James Gray and produced by Gray, Donna Gigliotti, and Anthony Katagas. Screenplay by Gray and Richard Menello.

I believe Sandra senses something is damaged about Leonard. *Two Lovers* never puts a word to it, although we know he's had treatment and is on medication. It's not a big, showy mental problem; lots of people go through life like this, and people simply say, "Well, you know Leonard." But Sandra does know him, and that's why she tells him she not only loves him but wants to help him.

Leonard (Joaquin Phoenix) is focused on his inner demons. His fiancée left him—dumped him—and he has moved back to his childhood room, still with the *2001* poster on the wall. He makes customer deliveries for his dad's dry cleaning business. Sandra (Vinessa Shaw) is the daughter of another dry cleaner in the same Brighton Beach neighborhood of Brooklyn. Her father plans to buy his father's business, and both families think it would be ideal if Sandra and Leonard married.

But Leonard meets Michelle (Gwyneth Paltrow) and is struck by the lightning bolt.

She's blond, exciting, and in his eyes sophisticated and glamorous. She seems to like him, too. So a triangle exists that might seem to be the makings of a traditional romcom from years ago.

James Gray's *Two Lovers* is anything but traditional, romantic, or a comedy. It is a film of unusual perception, played at perfect pitch by Phoenix, Shaw, Paltrow, and the other actors. It is calm and mature. It understands these characters. It doesn't juggle them for melodrama, but looks inside.

Michelle is the kind of person many of us become fascinated with at some unwise point in our lives. She has enormous charm, a winning smile, natural style. But she is haunted. Leonard is blindsided to discover she has a married lover and that she uses drugs. He is able, like so many men, to overlook these flaws, to misunderstand neediness for affection, to delude himself that she shares his feelings. Sandra, on the other hand, is pretty and nice, but their families have known each other for years, and Michelle seems to offer an entry into a new world across the bridge in Manhattan.

The particular thing about *Two Lovers,* written by Gray and Richard Menello, is that it utterly ignores all the usual clichés about parents in general and Jewish mothers in particular. Both Leonard and Sandra come from loving families, and both of them love their parents. Although Leonard sometimes seems to contain muted, conflicting elements of Travis Bickle and Rupert Pupkin, he tries to get along with people, to be polite, to be sensitive. That he is the victim of his own obsessions is bad luck. It's painful watching him try to lead a secret life with Michelle outside his home, especially when her emergency demands come at the worst possible times.

Leonard's parents are Ruth and Reuben Kraditor (Isabella Rossellini and Moni Monoshov), long-married, staunchly bourgeois, reasonable. Ruth, of course, wants Leonard to find stability in marriage with a nice Jewish girl like Sandra, but her love for him outweighs her demands on him—rare in the movies. Reuben is more narrow in his imagination for his son but not a caricature. And Sandra's father (Bob Ari) wants to buy the Kraditor business and likes the idea of a marriage but would never think of his daughter as part of a business deal. Everyone in the film wants the best for their children.

So the drama, and it becomes intense, involves whether Leonard's demons will allow him to be happy. Michelle represents so many problems she should almost dress by wrapping herself in the yellow tape from crime scene investigations. She has a gift for attracting enablers. We meet her married lover (Elias Koteas), who turns out not to be an old letch, even if he is an adulterer. He's essentially another victim, and a short, tense scene he has with Leonard provides private insights.

Here is a movie involving the kinds of people we know or perhaps have been. It's the third film in which James Gray has directed Joaquin Phoenix (after *The Yards* and *We Own the Night*) and shows them working together to create a character whose manner is troubled but can be identified with. The whole movie is so well-cast and -performed that we watch it unfolding without any particular awareness of "acting." Even the ending, which might seem obligatory in a lesser film, is earned and deserved in this one.

Tyson ★ ★ ★ ★
R, 90 m., 2009

Featuring Mike Tyson. A documentary directed by James Toback.

Some kids beat him up once, and he couldn't stop them. Another kid killed one of his homing pigeons, and he fell upon him with fury. And that is the backstory of Mike Tyson, a boxer known as the Baddest Man on the Planet. When he went into the ring, he was proving he would never be humiliated again and getting revenge for a pigeon he loved. I believe it really is that simple. There is no rage like that of a child, hurt unjustly, the victim of a bully.

James Toback's *Tyson* is a documentary with no pretense of objectivity. Here is Mike Tyson's story in his own words, and it is surprisingly persuasive. He speaks openly and with apparent honesty about a lifetime during which, he believes, he was often misunderstood. From a broken family, he was in trouble at a tender age and always felt vulnerable; his childhood self is still echoed in his lisp, as high-pitched as a child's. It's as if the victim of big kids is still speaking to us from within the intimidating form of perhaps the most punishing heavyweight champion of them all.

Mike Tyson comes across here as reflective, contrite, more sinned against than sinning. He can be charming. He can be funny. You can see why Toback, himself a man of extremes, has been a friend for twenty years. The film contains a great deal of fight footage, of Tyson hammering one opponent after another. We also see a TV interview, infamous at the time, of his ex-wife, Robin Givens, describing him as abusive and manic-depressive. Even then I wanted to ask her, "And who did you think you were marrying?"

Tyson freely admits he has mistreated women and says he regrets it. But he denies the rape charge brought against him by Desiree Washington, which led to his conviction and three years in jail. "She was a swine," he says. He also has no use for boxing promoter Don King, "a slimy reptilian (bleeper)." His shining hero is his legendary trainer Cus D'Amato, the man who polished the diamond in the rough from his early teens and died just before the first heavyweight crown.

"Before the fight even starts, I've won," Tyson says. From Cus he learned never to take his eyes from his opponent's face from the moment he entered the ring. So formidable was his appearance and so intimidating his record that it once seemed he would have to retire before anyone else won the title. But he lost to Buster Douglas in Japan in 1990—the result, he says, of not following Cus's advice to stay away from women before a fight. He went into the ring with a case of gonorrhea. Later losses he attributes to a lack of physical training at a time when he signed up for fights simply for the payday. And there was drug abuse, from which he is now recovering.

This is only Toback's second doc, in a career of directing many fine films (*When Will I Be Loved, Harvard Man, Fingers*). In 1990, he was sitting next to a businessman on a flight and convinced him to finance *The Big Bang,* in which he would ask people about the meaning of life, the possibility of an afterlife, and what they believe in. "Tell me again why I'm financing this cockamamie thing," the man asks him. Toback says, simply, that the film will be remembered long after both he and the man are gone.

Toback is remarkably persuasive. He was offering immortality. It is a tempting offer. In ancient Egypt, an architect named Toback must have convinced a pharaoh to erect the first pyramid. What he offered Tyson was the opportunity to vindicate himself. There is no effort to show "both sides," but, in fact, the case against Tyson is already well-known, and what is unexpected about Tyson is that afterward we feel sympathy for the man, and more for the child inside.

U

The Ugly Truth ★★
R, 95 m., 2009

Katherine Heigl (Abby Richter), Gerard Butler (Mike Chadway), Eric Winter (Colin), John Michael Higgins (Larry), Nick Searcy (Stuart), Kevin Connolly (Jim), Cheryl Hines (Georgia). Directed by Robert Luketic and produced by Tom Rosenberg, Gary Lucchesi, Steven Reuther, Kimberly di Bonaventura, and Deboray Jelin Newmyer. Screenplay by Nicole Eastman, Karen McCullah Lutz, and Kirsten Smith.

Katherine Heigl and Gerard Butler are so pleasant in *The Ugly Truth* that it's a shame to spoil their party. But toil and try as they do, the comedy bogs down in relentless predictability and the puzzling overuse of naughty words. Once, the movies were forbidden to drop the f-word at all, but in this one, it's only an opening salvo in a potty-mouth bombing run.

Heigl plays Abby, producer of the Sacramento early morning news on a station that is operated like no other station in the history of television. Anchored by a bickering married couple, the broadcast is tanking in the ratings, and so she's forced to bring in Mike Chadway (Gerard Butler), a macho local cable personality whose ideas about the battle of the sexes date back to about *Alley Oop*.

On his first appearance, he departs from his script, diagnoses the anchor as the victim of his control-freak wife, and suggests they've probably stopped sleeping together. "This is great!" the station manager enthuses, despite that the segment runs so long it steps on the first five minutes of the network morning slot.

Abby is a raving beauty who, of course, can't find a man, maybe because her standards are so perfectionist. A handsome young orthopedic surgeon (Eric Winter) comes within her sights, after she twists an ankle falling from a tree outside his bedroom window watching him dry off after a shower while she was trying to rescue her cat. That's the sort of thing, wouldn't you agree, that happens all too rarely in life? Mike, the rugged sex-talk guru, tells her she's making all the wrong moves if she ever wants to catch this guy, and starts coaching her.

So which guy does she end up with? Guess. The movie leaves not a stone unturned, including the semi-obligatory Beauty Makeover Montage, during which Mike advises her on the requirements of a push-up bra and tells her to acquire longer hair. Uh, huh. And when the doc takes her to a ball game, Mike broadcasts instructions to her earphone, just as a producer might speak in an anchor's ear.

There's one scene with real comic possibilities, but it doesn't pay off. Mike gives her a pair of remote-controlled battery-powered vibrating panties. (Yes, they actually manufacture such items. Isn't the Web a useful resource?) Abby, the silly girl, foolishly decides to wear these to a business dinner, and takes along the remote controller for reasons it is hard to explain. A kid at a nearby table grabs the vibrator. We all know what's coming, and Heigl makes a real effort, but I'm afraid Meg Ryan's restaurant orgasm in *When Harry Met Sally* remains the gold standard in this rare but never boring genre.

The TV news as portrayed in the film makes *Anchorman: The Legend of Ron Burgundy* look like a documentary. Every segment can run as long as necessary. Macho Mike ad libs everything. Yes, he's good for ratings, but if after a few days he's really pulling in a twelve in the 5 a.m. hour, in prime time he would outscore the Oscars. And TV cameras do not usually follow newsmen out of the studio and into the street and watch whatever they do then—although if it were funnier, we might not mind.

Katherine Heigl and Gerard Butler are awfully nice here. The movie does them in. Amazing that this raunchy screenplay was written by three women. At its conclusion, I am forced to report, it provides abundant evidence of my belief that a good movie has rarely featured a hot-air balloon. ☞

The Uninvited ★ ★ ★
PG-13, 87 m., 2009

Emily Browning (Anna), Elizabeth Banks (Rachel), David Strathairn (Steven), Arielle Kebbel (Alex), Maya Massar (Mom), Kevin McNulty (Sheriff), Jesse Moss (Matt), Dean Paul

Gibson (Dr. Silberling). Directed by Charles Guard and Thomas Guard and produced by Walter F. Parkes, Laurie MacDonald, and Roy Lee. Screenplay by Craig Rosenberg, Doug Miro, and Carlo Bernard.

Emily Browning's face helps *The Uninvited* work so well. She's a twenty-year-old actress from Australia and has a lot of experience, but looks about fourteen. She makes an ideal heroine for a horror movie: innocent, troubled, haunted by nightmares, persecuted by a wicked stepmother, convinced her real mother was deliberately burned to death. She makes you fear for her, and that's half the battle. Yet she's so fresh she's ready for a Jane Austen role.

I recoiled twice in the opening minutes of *The Uninvited,* and that's a good sign. This is a well-crafted first feature by the Guard brothers (Charles and Thomas) from Britain that weaves a story not as predictable as it might seem. Browning plays Anna, who when we meet her is finishing a stay at a psychiatric clinic under the care of chubby, paternal Dr. Silberling (Dean Paul Gibson). Her dad (David Strathairn), darkly ambiguous, drives her home to be welcomed by his girlfriend, Rachel (Elizabeth Banks), who is all sunshine and false friendliness.

But Anna yearns only to see her older sister, Alex (Arielle Kebbel). They dive off from their boathouse, make sister-talk on the raft, and then Alex swims away as young Matt (Jesse Moss) arrives on his grocery delivery boat. Matt, the boy who was getting too insistent with Anna when they were making out at the beach campfire. And that was the night her sick mother died, burned up in the boathouse, which had been converted into a sick room, and now, as Anna has just seen, been rebuilt.

What really happened that night? How did Rachel start as her mother's nurse and become Anna's new stepmom? Don't Rachel and her dad know how it disturbs the girls to see them smooching? And who is Rachel, really? Is that her real name? Google can be an insidious resource.

And more about the story I really cannot say. *The Uninvited* gets under your skin. The cinematography has that classy-horror-movie look, the overhead shots of a lonely car driving through ominous trees, the interiors sometimes shadowed, sometimes uncannily sunny, and the—presences—as Emily Dickinson would punctuate, that are half-seen in a half-sleep.

David Strathairn is well-cast. Nobody can seem more open and affable, and suggest such hooded menace. Who else is so good at telling his daughter there's nothing to worry about, and making us worry? Elizabeth Banks, as Rachel, is almost convincing when she tells Anna she hopes they can be friends. Almost. Hard to imagine that Banks played Laura Bush *and* Miri of Zack and Miri, but that's acting for you. Here she has moments balanced on a knife edge between being cheerful and being a little too quick to start issuing mom-type orders, like telling Matt not to come to the house anymore.

The Uninvited begins with a classically Freudian situation, moves directly into dream analysis, has blood coming from keyholes and corpses speaking from the grave, and is all set, of course, in a huge, rambling New England shore house with gables, attics, long corridors, and places where anyone, or anything, could be hiding. When a movie like this is done well, it's uncommon. *The Uninvited* is done well.

Note: I'm a little surprised by the PG-13, *more evidence the MPAA awards the rating for what a movie doesn't have (nudity, language, sex) than what it does have, images that could be very troubling for some younger viewers.*

The Unknown Woman ★ ★ ★
NO MPAA RATING, 118 m., 2008

Xenia Rappoport (Irena), Michele Placido (Mold), Claudia Gerini (Valeria Adacher), Pierfrancesco Favino (Donato Adacher), Margherita Buy (Irena's Lawyer), Alessandro Haber (Doorman), Piera Degli Esposti (Gina), Clara Dossena (Thea Adacher), Angela Molina (Lucrezia). Directed by Giuseppe Tornatore and produced by Laura Fattori. Screenplay by Tornatore.

The Unknown Woman contains so many secrets that without revealing a few I cannot write a review. Yes, the blond prostitute in the flashbacks is the dark-haired housemaid in the present. Yes, she has a passionate reason for wanting to go to work for the Adacher family. Yes, there is something deeply strange about her behavior toward their little girl, Thea.

The movie was written and directed by Giuseppe Tornatore, still best known for *Cinema Paradiso* (1990). *The Unknown Woman* (*La Sconosciuta*) is being hailed as his best since then and swept Italy's Donatello Awards for best film, actress, director, cinematographer, music, you name it. It's a spellbinder with a lot of Hitchcock touches and an Ennio Morricone score to match. But does it play fair with us?

I have given the plot a lot of thought. I think I know how and why Irena (Xenia Rappoport) arrives in a northern Italian city with a big roll of cash in her pocket, her bankroll already in place before she begins her mysterious surveillance of an apartment across the road from hers. No, it's not a chronological impossibility, given all we later discover. I even think I know what crime (there is a choice) she goes to prison for.

I do not know who rigged the brakes on Mrs. Adacher's car, but I doubt it was Irena because the evidence looks planted. I don't know why Irena was having Gina, the former maid, sign those papers. I don't know how much Gina understood of what Irena was telling her. I believe that DNA testing could resolve a crucial identity in the movie, but if it has, what are we to make of a long, significant glance Irena exchanges with a man late in the film? I don't know if the man is who she thinks he is. I also don't know how anyone could survive those stabbings with the biggest pair of scissors I have ever seen.

These may be questions you share with me, or you may be sure of your answers. I suppose the smiles in the last shot convey nothing but simple human joy and answer nothing. Maybe it doesn't matter, since the film's construction is skillfully devised to prolong suspense as long as possible—maybe too long. It has to sidestep so many questions that it's as much an exercise in footwork as storytelling. But it uses the devices of melodrama to haul us helplessly along, and has a fascinating gallery of characters, beginning with Irena.

She is from the Ukraine. Her twenties were

lost in sexual slavery. It is no accident she gets the job with the Adachers, though an accident leads to it. I believe, because I must, that the bald sadist Mold (Michele Placido) had a way to track her and get her cell number. I suspect, but do not know, that he was one of the two Santas who beat and kicked her on Christmas Eve. Doesn't Mold know if he scares her away, he'll never get what he wants? Does Mold know if what she believes about the Adacher family is true?

These questions build as she steals the Adachers' house keys and security beeper, and goes through every space in the house, even the hidden safe (which has combination numbers big enough to be seen through a keyhole). There are a lot of questions during the disturbing and brutal way she "teaches" little Thea to deal with her rare disease (so rare I have never encountered it, even in fiction, where it is mighty handy). Anyway, all the questions are answered (seemingly, anyway) by the end.

There are a lot of things I can say about *The Unknown Woman*, but I cannot say I was bored or ever let off the hook. Stephen Holden in the *New York Times* questions its integrity. I don't think it has a shred of integrity. Few films of this nature can afford to. It works. Is that enough for you? For me, in a movie like this, it is.

Unmistaken Child ★★ ½
NO MPAA RATING, 102 m., 2009

Featuring Tenzin Zopa. A documentary directed by Nati Baratz and produced by Baratz, Ilil Alexander, and Arik Bernstein. Screenplay by Baratz.

To the mind of a Western rationalist, *Unmistaken Child* raises questions so fundamental that they interfere with the film's purpose. Here is a documentary about a very young child who is believed to be the reincarnation of a Buddhist lama, and is taken from his parents to be raised in a monastery. I know this is a practice of traditional forms of Buddhism, but still: Should it go this smoothly? Should the parents be so agreeable? The child so acquiescent? The monks so certain?

There is a tendency for Westerners to accept

beliefs such as reincarnation more easily than they might accept some of the fundamentalist beliefs of their own Judeo-Christian tradition. This may be a form of exoticism, the willingness to ascribe to the Mysterious East possibilities we would be dubious about in our own culture.

The documentary, made by Nati Baratz, an Israeli who calls himself an "informal Buddhist," accepts everything in the account at face value. It began, he says, during his visit to a monastery, when he met Tenzin Zopa, a thirtyish Nepalese monk who had recently lost his master of twenty-one years. This man, Geshe Lama Konchog, who had lived a life of solitary meditation in a cave for more than two decades, was respected and beloved, and the Dalai Lama placed Tenzin in charge of the search for his reincarnation.

This search involves observations of the direction of the smoke from Geshe Lama's funeral pyre and the reading of his ashes (a footprint pointing east is discerned, although not by me). An astrologer in Taiwan is consulted and advises that there is a 95 percent chance the reincarnated boy's father will have a name beginning with "A," and that he will be found in a place beginning with "TS."

Thus the search focused on the Tsum Valley of Nepal. Tenzin seeks a child of the proper age, believes he has found the right one, and points to his long ears resembling those of Geshe Lama. The parents, a pleasant and loving couple, are surprisingly willing to part with their child for years. The child is tested to see how he responds to possessions of Geshe Lama and if he seems familiar with his cave, and then transported by SUV to Tenzin's monastery, where he is made much of by throngs of the devout.

This is a ritual that has repeated itself over the centuries. Martin Scorsese's *Kundun* (1997) told the story of the discovery and development of the present Dalai Lama. I know I am expected to believe the tenets of a religion on the basis of faith, not common sense, but during this film I found that very difficult. How reliable are wind directions, the interpretation of ashes, and astrological readings? Would you give over your son on such a basis? Would you trust such a chosen one as your spiritual leader?

These matters aside, *Unmistaken Child* has undeniable interest. It is filmed as events occur, in the actual locations, showing a world of great contrasts between an ancient way of life and a society that uses automobiles and helicopters. Baratz doesn't ask any of the obvious questions, preferring to observe uncritically, and if you can do the same, you may find it worth seeing. I could not, and grew restless.

(Untitled) ★★★ ½
R, 96 m., 2009

Adam Goldberg (Adrian Jacobs), Marley Shelton (Madeleine Gray), Eion Bailey (Josh Jacobs), Vinnie Jones (Ray Barko), Ptolemy Slocum (Monroe), Zak Orth (Porter Canby). Directed by Jonathan Parker and produced by Catherine DiNapoli and Matt Luber. Screenplay by Parker and DiNapoli.

(Untitled) picks a fight with its very title, which summarizes the f— you attitude of its hero, a composer of music that sounds like something you'd hear going on in the alley late at night. One of his compositions consists of a chain dropped into a can, loudly ripping paper, a bucket being kicked, the screams of a vocalist, and squawks on a clarinet. He plays the piano with his elbows. Under the circumstances, it seems ungracious for him to complain about an audience member's cell phone.

This musician is named Adrian Jacobs (Adam Goldberg), a bearded thirty-something who seems to have chugged a pint of bile. A good audience for him might consist of two dozen people; some walk out and the rest stare incredulously at the stage. One day, his brother, Josh (Eion Bailey), brings a date to his concert. This is Madeleine Gray (Marley Shelton), who runs a very, very avant-garde art gallery in Soho. Adrian asks if he can borrow her dress. It's made of shiny black plastic, it squeaks when she walks, and he thinks he can use the sound in his music.

(Untitled) is a comedy worthy of the best Woody Allen, and Adrian is not unlike Woody's persona: a sincere, intense, insecure nebbish, hopeless with women, aiming for greatness. He plays classical piano brilliantly and with

contempt. If his "serious" work appeals to very few people, that's too many for him. Josh, on the other hand, is raking in the dough with his canvases, which are snatched up in volume for the lobbies of hotels.

The movie plunges fearlessly but not brainlessly into the world of art so cutting-edge it has run out of edges. Remember Damien Hirst, the British artist who inspired a firestorm when he won the Turner Prize for such works as half a shark preserved in formaldehyde? One of Madeleine's clients is Ray Barko (Vinnie Jones), whose art consists of a dead cat splayed on a wall, a goose apparently buried in a wall up to its wings, and a montage for monkey and vacuum cleaner. A rich client (Zak Orth) eats up this stuff. Lots of people do. I don't know if they enjoy it as much as I love my Edward Lear watercolors. Maybe they love it more.

Madeleine hires Adrian and his musicians to perform at her gallery as "conceptual art." Well, I once attended a poetry reading featuring a revolving fan. Madeleine goes nuts for Adrian, and he finds her hard to resist because everything she wears makes noise. She seems to conceal a sound effects artist in her knickers. Adrian tunes in; the sound track subtly enhances what he hears.

They grow chummy. He attends Madeleine's opening for an artist named Monroe, played by an actor named Ptolemy Slocum, whose own name is a work of art. Meanwhile, Josh's insipid work (pastels of vague shapes adorned by small circles) supports the gallery, but Madeleine keeps them in the back room. He "doesn't need" a gallery opening, she explains. She hates them, is what it is.

It's easy to take cheap shots at conceptual art. *(Untitled)* doesn't do that. It takes expensive shots. Adrian's music has been created for the film by the respected composer David Lang, and Ray Barko's grotesque animals were created by Los Angeles artist Kyle Ng. The thing is, their deliberately (I think) absurd work resembles the real thing, when lesser movies would just ask the art department to drum up something. Barko's "work," given the right setting, would sell. That gives the film plausibility.

Jonathan Parker, who directed and cowrote with Catherine DiNapoli (they collaborated

on *Bartleby*), also respects these artists—in a sense. Adrian can manifestly play the piano in a traditional way, so his music is a choice, not a necessity. Ray Barko has so many problems that his art may be a valid expression of his misery. Doubt remains about Monroe (played by Ptolemy Slocum, you will recall), whose pieces include a label reading *Untitled White Wall*, which is displayed on a white wall. Not any old white wall, you understand. It has to be the *right* white wall. I wonder if he'd need to tear up part of your house for its proper installation.

This is a good film, a smart film. It knows a lot about art and wears its knowledge lightly, dealing with its subject in a way even a student at the Art Institute might not find condescending. As so often, casting decisions help enormously in its success. Marley Shelton's gallery owner is like a lot of bright, formidable young women, ambitious, idealistic, bored by most of the men she meets. Vinnie Jones plays Barko as a reunion of pugnacious British eccentrics. Do not overlook the fetching Lucy Punch, as a member of Adrian's band known only as "The Clarinet." Shelton has the confidence and presence of a born comedienne, and as for Adam Goldberg, he plays the role without a shred of humor, which is exactly right. I have put out a Google alert to see if New York gossips identify the original(s) for the rich collector.

Note: Aspects of the film reminded me of Yasmina Reza's Tony Award–winning play Art— *http://en.wikipedia.org/wiki/%27Art%27_(play).*

Untraceable ★ ★ ★
R, 100 m., 2008

Diane Lane (Jennifer Marsh), Billy Burke (Detective Eric Box), Colin Hanks (Griffin Dowd), Joseph Cross (Owen Reilly), Mary Beth Hurt (Stella Marsh). Directed by Gregory Hoblit and produced by Tom Rosenberg, Gary Lucchesi, Howard Koch Jr., Steven Pearl, and Andy Cohen. Screenplay by Robert Fyvolent, Mark R. Brinker, and Allison Burnett.

Untraceable is a horrifying thriller, smart and tightly told, and merciless. It begins with this premise: A psychopath devises ways to slowly kill people online, in live streaming video. The more hits he gets, the further the process continues, until finally his captive is dead. "You're setting a new record!" he tells one agonized victim, as we see the total growing on a hit counter. Trying to find and stop him are the Cyber Crimes Division of the FBI and the Portland police.

His means of torture and death are sadistic nightmares. Why are so many of us fascinated by horrors in the movies (because, without question, we are)? Maybe it's for the same reason we slow down when we drive past a traffic accident. Maybe because someone else's tragedy is, at least, not ours. It may be hardwired in human nature. I don't have the slightest doubt that if a person were being killed on the Internet, it would draw millions of hits. An FBI spokesman holds a press conference to solemnly warn people that if they log on, they're accessories to murder. Of course that only promotes the site and increases visits.

Diane Lane plays Agent Jennifer Marsh, head of the FBI Portland Cyber Crimes unit. Her partner is Griffin Dowd (Colin Hanks, Tom's son), and her liaison with the Portland police is Detective Eric Box (Billy Burke). They're up against a hacker who uses captive computers of people all over the Net to forward his output and conceal his origins. When you give it a moment's thought, it's sort of a coincidence he's right there in Portland. Maybe that's plot-functional because he can become a threat to Marsh, her daughter, Annie (Perla Haney-Jardine), and her mother (Mary Beth Hurt).

The computer tech jargon in the movie sounds convincing. Whether it's accurate, I have no way of knowing—but that's beside the point, of course. What's ironic is that the key to cracking the case turns out to depend on perhaps our earliest and most basic form of digital communication between remote locations. Diane Lane can play smart, and she does, convincing us she knows her job, while at the same time being a convincing widow, mother, and daughter. The movie is lean and well-acted.

Certain logical questions arise. The killer's ingenuity and unlimited resources are dubious, especially considering what a short turn-around he has between crimes. He has the usual movie villain's ability to know more than he should, move more invisibly than he could, anticipate more than is possible. I think that goes with the territory. Lane's FBI superior is the usual obtuse publicity seeker, making wrong calls. But the through-line of the plot holds firm.

Of course the question occurs: Will the movie inspire copycats? I'm agnostic on this issue. I think a subset of hackers has already demonstrated how ingenious they are at thinking up evil all by themselves, and I doubt a cyber criminal could conceal himself online this successfully: Witness the routine busts of child porn rings.

One detail the movie gets just right. As the current victim dies and the hit-count climbs, we see a scrolling chat room onscreen. The comments are cretinous, stupid, ugly, divorced from all civilized standards. How people with the mentality of the authors of such messages are intelligent enough to get online in the first place is a puzzle. But they do. All you have to do is visit the wrong chat room or bulletin board and see them at their dirty work.

Is there a reason to see this movie? Was there a reason to see *Saw,* or *Se7en*? The purpose and function of the violent movie thriller remains a subject of debate. Yes, I watched fascinated. No, it wasn't art. Its message is visceral. Some people will think: "This is wrong." Others will think: "This is cool." It is the same in countless areas of society.

The movie is made with intelligence and skill. It is a dramatization of the sorts of things that the anonymity of the Internet makes possible, or even encourages. I know that if I learned of a Web site like this one, I, for one, would certainly not log on to it. On the other hand, what did I just do? Type in www.killwithme.com. I found what I expected. But why did I need to find that out? Now what will you do?

Up ★ ★ ★ ★
PG, 96 m., 2009

Edward Asner (Carl Fredricksen), Christopher Plummer (Charles Muntz), Jordan Nagai (Russell), John Ratzenberger (Tom), Bob

Peterson (Dug). Directed by Pete Docter and produced by Jonas Rivera. Screenplay by Docter and Bob Peterson.

Up is a wonderful film, with characters who are as believable as any characters can be who spend much of their time floating above the rain forests of Venezuela. They have tempers, problems, and obsessions. They are cute and goofy, but they aren't cute in the treacly way of little cartoon animals. They're cute in the human way of the animation master Hayao Miyazaki. Two of the three central characters are cranky old men, which is a wonder in this youth-obsessed era. *Up* doesn't think all heroes must be young or sweet, although the third important character is a nervy kid.

This is another masterwork from Pixar, which is leading the charge in modern animation. The movie was directed by Pete Docter, who also directed *Monsters, Inc.*, wrote *Toy Story*, and was the cowriter and first director on *WALL-E* before leaving to devote himself full time to this project. So he's one of the leading artists of this renaissance of animation.

The movie is in 3-D in some theaters, about which I will say nothing except to advise you to save the extra money and see it in 2-D. One of the film's qualities that is likely to be diminished by 3-D is its subtle and beautiful color palette. *Up*, like *Finding Nemo, Toy Story, Shrek,* and *The Lion King,* uses colors in a way particularly suited to its content.

Up tells a story as tickling to the imagination as the magical animated films of my childhood, when I naively thought that because their colors were brighter, their character outlines more defined, and their plots simpler, they were actually more realistic than regular films. It begins with a romance as sweet and lovely as any I can recall in feature animation.

Two children named Carl and Ellie meet and discover they share the same dream of someday being daring explorers. In newsreels, they see the exploits of a daring adventurer named Charles Muntz (Christopher Plummer), who uses his gigantic airship to explore a lost world on a plateau in Venezuela and bring back the bones of fantastic creatures previously unknown to man. When his dis-coveries are accused of being faked, he flies off enraged to South America again, vowing to bring back living creatures to prove his claims.

Nothing is heard from him for years. Ellie and Carl (Edward Asner) grow up, have a courtship, marry, buy a ramshackle house and turn it into their dream home, are happy together, and grow old. This process is silent except for music (Ellie doesn't even have a voice credit). It's shown by Docter in a lovely sequence, without dialogue, that deals with the life experience in a way that is almost never found in family animation. The lovebirds save their loose change in a gallon jug intended to finance their trip to the legendary Paradise Falls, but real life gets in the way: flat tires, home repairs, medical bills. Then they make a heartbreaking discovery. This interlude is poetic and touching.

The focus of the film is on Carl's life after Ellie. He becomes a recluse, holds out against the world, keeps his home as a memorial, talks to the absent Ellie. One day he decides to pack up and fly away—literally. Having worked all his life as a balloon man, he has the equipment on hand to suspend the house from countless helium-filled balloons and fulfill his dream of seeking Paradise Falls. What he wasn't counting on was an inadvertent stowaway—Russell (Jordan Nagai), a dutiful Wilderness Explorer Scout, who looks Asian-American to me.

What they find at Paradise Falls and what happens there I will not say. But I will describe Charles Muntz's gigantic airship that is hovering there. It's a triumph of design and perhaps owes its inspiration, though not its appearance, to Miyazaki's *Castle in the Sky.* The exterior is nothing special: a really big zeppelin. But the interior, now, is one of those movie spaces you have the feeling you'll remember.

With vast inside spaces, the airship is outfitted like a great ocean liner from the golden age, with a stately dining room, long corridors, a display space rivaling the Natural History Museum, and attics spacious enough to harbor fighter planes. Muntz, who must be a centenarian by now, is hale, hearty, and mean, his solitary life shared only by dogs.

The adventures on the jungle plateau are satisfying in a *Mummy/Tomb Raider/*Indiana Jones sort of way. But they aren't the whole point of the film. This isn't a movie like *Mon-*

sters vs. Aliens that's mostly just frenetic action. There are stakes here, and personalities involved, and two old men battling for meaning in their lives. And a kid who, for once, isn't smarter than all the adults. And a loyal dog. And an animal sidekick. And always that house and those balloons.

Up in the Air ★★★★
R, 109 m., 2009

George Clooney (Ryan Bingham), Vera Farmiga (Alex Goran), Anna Kendrick (Natalie Keener), Jason Bateman (Craig Gregory), Danny McBride (Jim Miller), Melanie Lynskey (Julie Bingham). Directed by Jason Reitman and produced by Jeffrey Clifford, Daniel Dubiecki, Ivan Reitman, and Jason Reitman. Screenplay by Jason Reitman and Sheldon Turner, based on a novel by Walter Kirn.

Ryan Bingham is the Organization Man for the 2000s. He never comes to the office. Technically, he doesn't have an office; he has an address where his employer has an office. His life is devoted to visiting other people's offices and firing them. *Up in the Air* takes the trust people once had in their jobs and pulls out the rug. It is a film for this time.

Bingham describes himself as a "termination facilitator." He fires people for a living. When corporations need to downsize quickly but hate the mess, he flies in and breaks the news to the new former employees. In hard times, his business is great.

This isn't a comedy. If it were, it would be hard to laugh in these last days of 2009. Nor is it a tragedy. It's an observant look at how a man does a job. Too many movie characters have jobs involving ruling people, killing them, or going to high school. Bingham loves his work. He doesn't want a home. He doesn't want a family. He gives self-help lectures on how and why to unpack the backpack of your life.

George Clooney plays Bingham as one of those people you meet but never get to know. They go through all the forms, and know all the right moves and you're "friends," but—who's in there? Sitting in a first-class seat one day, asked where he lives, Bingham says, "Here."

He likes his job because he feels he performs a service. Nobody likes to fire someone. Someone has to. He has protocols. In a curious way, he's like the two army men in *The Messenger,* who notify the next of kin after a soldier is killed. Jason Reitman, the director, auditioned real people who had recently been fired to play some of the fired employees (others are played by actors). He asked them to improvise their words on learning the news. Would you want the job of listening to their pain?

There are two women in Bingham's life. Alex Goran (Vera Farmiga) is also a road warrior, and for some time they've been meeting in dreary "suite" hotels in East Moses, Nowhere—having meals, making love, playacting at being the happy couple neither one will commit to. Natalie Keener (Anna Kendrick) is a bright, ambitious new graduate who has taken a job with Bingham's company because it's near her boyfriend. Bingham takes her on the road to teach her the ropes. Alex is him now; Natalie is him then.

Farmiga is one of the warmest and most attractive women in the movies, or at least she plays one. You may not guess all she's thinking. Kendrick's Natalie is so brim-full of joy at the dawn of her career that it shines even on ending those of others. Nothing better than making your boss happy.

The isolation of the road life is threatened by the introduction of firing by Web chat. This is in-sourcing, if you will. It may not be warmer than firing someone in person, but it saves a lot of money on airfare. Notice how Reitman likes to start with the way corporations justify immoral behavior and then apply their rationalizations with perfect logic. That method was at the core of his brilliant debut, *Thank You for Smoking* (2005).

Reitman also made the great *Juno.* Still only thirty-two, the son of the Canadian producer-director Ivan Reitman (*Ghostbusters*), he grew up behind the counter of the family store, so to speak. With these three films at the dawn of *his* career, we can only imagine what comes next. He makes smart, edgy, mainstream films. That's harder than making smart, edgy indies. In a pie chart he compiled of questions he's asked time and again during interviews, "How does your father feel about your success?" ranks high. Bursting with pride is my guess.

V

Valentine's Day ★★
PG-13, 124 m., 2010

Jessica Alba (Morley Clarkson), Kathy Bates (Susan), Jessica Biel (Kara Monahan), Bradley Cooper (Holden), Eric Dane (Sean Jackson), Patrick Dempsey (Dr. Harrison Copeland), Hector Elizondo (Edgar), Jamie Foxx (Kelvin Moore), Jennifer Garner (Julia Fitzpatrick), Topher Grace (Jason), Anne Hathaway (Liz), Carter Jenkins (Alex), Ashton Kutcher (Reed Bennett), Queen Latifah (Paula Thomas), Taylor Lautner (Willy), George Lopez (Alphonso), Shirley MacLaine (Estelle), Emma Roberts (Grace), Julia Roberts (Captain Kate Hazeltine), Bryce Robinson (Edison), Taylor Swift (Felicia). Directed by Garry Marshall and produced by Mike Karz, Wayne Allan Rice, and Josie Rosen. Screenplay by Katherine Fugate.

I've heard of all-star casts, but *Valentine's Day* has a *complete* star cast. What did other movies do for talent when this one was filming? It has twenty-one actors who can be considered stars, and some are very big stars indeed. It's like the famous poster for *It's a Mad Mad Mad Mad World*, with a traffic jam of famous faces.

That's the movie's problem. Gridlock. It needs somebody like that tough traffic warden who stands under the L at Wabash and Randolph and fiercely wags her finger at drivers who don't shape up. The actors in this movie could populate six romantic comedies with reasonable plots, and a couple of sitcoms. Of course you'd need scripts. *Valentine's Day* is so desperate to keep all the characters alive, it's like those Russian jugglers who run around trying to keep all their plates spinning on poles.

I won't even attempt to describe the plot. Nor will I tell you who the characters are and who plays them. Just the names would come to sixty-three words, and if I described each character in twenty words, I'd run out of space way before I got to Captain Kate Hazeltine (Julia Roberts). I will mention it was nice to see Shirley MacLaine and Hector Elizondo as an old married couple, and of interest that two Taylors (Swift and Lautner) had scenes together.

For the rest, words fail me. The structure of the film involves a large number of couples and additional characters who are not in couples. We wake up with them on the morning of February 14, and all of their stories are completed by midnight, and as Ricky told Lucy, there's a lot of 'splainin to do. Several ancient formulas are employed. (1) Best friends who don't realize they're really in love. (2) Guy who thinks she loves him but she doesn't. (3) Girl who thinks he loves her but he's married. (4) People sitting next to each other on an airplane strike up a conversation. (5) Guy misunderstands phone call, draws wrong conclusion. (6) Fifth-grader's first crush.

The most important characters are a florist named Reed (Ashton Kutcher) and his best friend, Julia (Jennifer Garner). They don't have enough screen time to create three-dimensional characters, but at least they get up to two, leaving everyone else stuck at one or below. They're both attractive, but then all twenty-one stars are attractive, especially if, like me, you think George Lopez is handsome, especially when he smiles.

There's one peculiarity. Usually in formula pictures with this huge a cast, maybe one couple will be African-American, one Latino, and one Asian. No such luck. There are no Asians at all. The black characters include a goofy TV sports reporter (Jamie Foxx) and a wise agent (Queen Latifah). Lopez, a Mexican-American, is relegated to the role of Kutcher's sidekick (i.e., the Tonto role). There are a lot of Indians in the movie, at the next table in an Indian restaurant, revealing that when Indians are out to dinner, they act just like Indians in a movie comedy.

The form of the movie may remind you wistfully of a much better one, *Love, Actually,* which created characters we cared a great deal about. None of the characters here ever get beyond the Look—There's (Name of Star) Threshold. You know, when your mind says, Look—There's Patrick Dempsey! Look—There's Anne Hathaway! Look—There's Topher Grace! Wow—That's Jessica Biel!

Valentine's Day is being marketed as a Date Movie. I think it's more of a First Date Movie. If your date likes it, do not date that person again. If you like it, there may not be a second date.

Valentino: The Last Emperor ★ ★ ★

NO MPAA RATING, 96 m., 2009

Featuring Valentino Garavani, Giancarlo Giammetti, and Matteo Marzotto. A documentary directed by Matt Tyrnauer and produced by Tyrnauer and Matt Kapp.

To be sure, we see Valentino only at times of great stress, while he is designing a new collection, presenting it in Paris, and preparing for a monumental Roman celebration of his career. But as seen in this film, he seems to suffer from anhedonia, the inability to feel pleasure. He is a multimillionaire, has ruled his profession for forty-five years, has a personal and business partner who has been with him all that time, has every whim attended to. But he seems gnawed by dissatisfaction.

Valentino: The Last Emperor is a documentary with privileged access to the legendary designer in his studio, workshop, backstage, his homes, even aboard his yacht and private jet (which he shares with his matched pugs). It is clear that he does not enjoy being filmed and regrets ever having agreed to it. That gives the film an innate fascination. I know next to nothing about haute couture, but I became involved in the buried drama: Valentino, at seventy-seven, with his world of elegant dresses being destroyed by the branded marketing of—belt buckles! purses! sunglasses!—is clearly at the end of his career.

Nobody will ask him about anything else. Whenever he appears in public, he is surrounded by reporters chanting, "When will you retire?" What are the odds Valentino will announce his retirement right there on the sidewalk to a baying pack of vultures?

But Valentino is coming to the end, all the same. His company has been purchased by an Italian millionaire named Matteo Marzotto, and a multinational is currently buying up its stock. I once bought a pair of sweat pants at Marshall Field's with a Pierre Cardin label. Crummy pants. The only labels I trust are Brooks Brothers and L.L. Bean. But sunglasses with a sequined "V" on them are so close Valentino can smell them. He wants out first.

He works very hard. His head seamstress drives a team of skilled dressmakers. No sewing machines for Valentino. Every stitch by hand. Always at his side is Giancarlo Giammetti, his business partner and onetime lover, who guesses they haven't been apart two months in forty-five years. Valentino was hopeless at business; Giammetti was not. Right at the start Valentino dressed Jackie Kennedy, and his name was made. "I know what women want," he says. "They want to be beautiful." There is a forty-fifth anniversary exhibit of his iconic dresses. To my eye, they look timeless and lovely.

But I am looking at Valentino. He carries himself like an emperor. He walks and stands as if always on stage. He speaks and everyone listens. In photos, he poses as if above the rabble. He is surrounded by much taller women, and treats them as if they are invisible. He relates to his models as if they were mannequins; there is no interaction, nothing personal. Even Giancarlo receives only an official hug, an occasional very quiet "Thank you."

I have the impression Giancarlo is the only one licensed to tell Valentino the truth. "How did I do?" he asks in the backseat of their limousine.

"Great."

"Tell me the truth."

"A little too tan," Giancarlo says. This to a man who looks deep orange. How can he design such dresses and not see himself in the mirror? Surely there is a browner spray-on?

Valentino as a boy idolized the goddesses of the silver screen. All he ever wanted to do was dress them, and that is all he has ever done. The sets and spectacles for his forty-fifth anniversary celebration in Rome resemble, he complains, Cirque du Soleil. They do. The models fly high above the crowd. Everyone is there. The film is crowded with stars, and they're all in the background: Sophia, Gwyneth, Mick, Elton, Princess This, Countess That.

But when he appears at the end of a show, watch him walk out only halfway and give his cursory little wave. No big smile. No blowing kisses. No hands up in triumph. Why isn't he happier? Is he driven by a work ethic that gives him no mercy? Is he . . . shy?

577

Valkyrie ★ ★ ★
PG-13, 120 m., 2008

Tom Cruise (Colonel Claus von Stauffenberg), Kenneth Branagh (Major General Henning von Tresckow), Bill Nighy (General Friedrich Olbricht), Tom Wilkinson (General Friedrich Fromm), Carice van Houten (Nina von Stauffenberg), Thomas Kretschmann (Major Otto Ernst Remer), Terence Stamp (Ludwig Beck), Eddie Izzard (General Erich Fellgiebel), Jamie Parker (Lieutenant Werner von Haeften), Christian Berkel (Colonel Mertz von Quirnheim). Directed by Bryan Singer and produced by Singer, Christopher McQuarrie, and Gilbert Adler. Screenplay by McQuarrie and Nathan Alexander.

Valkyrie is a meticulous thriller based on a large-scale conspiracy within the German army to assassinate Hitler, leading to a failed bombing attempt on July 20, 1944. At the center of the plot was Colonel Claus von Stauffenberg, played here by Tom Cruise as the moving force behind the attempted coup, which led to seven hundred arrests and two hundred executions, including von Stauffenberg's. Because we know Hitler survived, the suspense is centered in the minds of the participants, who call up the reserve army and actually arrest SS officials before discovering that their bomb did not kill its target.

Considering they were planning high treason with the risk of certain death, the conspirators seem remarkably willing to speak almost openly of their contempt for Hitler. That may be because they were mostly career officers in the army's traditional hierarchy and hated Hitler as much for what he was doing to the army as for what he was doing to the country. Realizing after the invasion of Normandy that the war was certainly lost, they hoped to spare hundreds of thousands of military and civilian lives. Von Stauffenberg was known to be "offended" by the Nazi treatment of Jews in the 1930s, and considered the *Kristallnacht* a disgrace to Germany, which possibly disturbed him as much as the fate of its victims. In any event, little is said among the conspirators about the genocide then under way—although, being alienated from the SS, perhaps they didn't know what was happening. Perhaps.

They repeatedly tell one another that even should they fail, at least the world would know that not all Germans supported Hitler. And so it does. And whatever their deepest motives, they gave their lives in trying to kill the monster. The film, directed by Bryan Singer (*The Usual Suspects*), works heroically to introduce us to the major figures in the plot, to tell them apart, to explain their roles, and to suggest their differences. The two best supporting performances are by Kenneth Branagh, as a general who smuggles a bomb into Hitler's inner circle and then must smuggle it out again, and Tom Wilkinson, as a general who artfully plays both sides of the fence, treating the plot with benign neutrality while covering himself should it fail.

Tom Cruise is perfectly satisfactory, if not electrifying, in the leading role. I'm at a loss to explain the blizzard of negative advance buzz fired at him for the effrontery of playing a half-blind, one-armed Nazi hero. Two factors may be to blame: (a) Cruise has attracted so much publicity by some of his own behavior (Oprah's couch as a trampoline) that anything he does sincerely seems fair game for mockery, and (b) movie publicity is now driven by gossip, scandal, and the eagerness of fanboys and -girls to attract attention by posing as critics of movies they've almost certainly not seen. Now that the movie is here, the buzz is irrelevant but may do residual damage.

If I say that Cruise is not electrifying, I must add that with this character, in this story, he cannot and should not be. This is a film about veterans of officer rank, with all the reserve and probity that officers gather on the way up. They do not scream or hurry and do not care to be seen that way. They have learned not to panic under fire, and they have never been more under fire than now.

A key element of their plot is to use Hitler's Valkyrie plan against him. The reserves were held back to defend Berlin and Hitler in case of an Allied assault, so von Stauffenberg conceived the strategy of killing Hitler, ordering up the reserves to ensure stability, and making the first order of business the immobilization of the SS. We see that the plan might well have worked. Indeed, it did—until the news arrived that Hitler was alive. So much did the führer command the fanatical loyalty of troops and civilians with an almost mystical grip, that merely his voice on the radio could defeat the plot, even with Germany clearly facing ruin.

The July 20 plot is an intriguing footnote to history, one of those "what if" scenarios. If it had succeeded, one of the hopes of the conspirators was said to be an alliance with the Allies against Russia. Given the political realities of the time, when Russia was seen as our ally, that would have been insane, but it shows the plotters continuing to dream of a reborn professional German army with roles for them. The question of the liberation of the death camps is a good one. Even the Allies did not bomb the rail lines leading to them. There were so very, very many people who did not know.

Vicky Cristina Barcelona ★ ★ ★
NO MPAA RATING, 96 m., 2008

Javier Bardem (Juan Antonio), Rebecca Hall (Vicky), Scarlett Johansson (Cristina), Penelope Cruz (Maria Elena), Patricia Clarkson (Judy Nash), Kevin Dunn (Mark Nash), Chris Messina (Doug). Directed by Woody Allen and produced by Letty Aronson. Screenplay by Allen.

The thing about a Woody Allen film is, whatever else happens, the characters are intriguing to listen to. They tend to be smart, witty, not above epigrams. A few days before seeing *Vicky Cristina Barcelona*, I viewed his *Hannah and Her Sisters* again. More than twenty years apart, both with dialogue at perfect pitch. Allen has directed more than forty movies in about as many years and written all of them himself. Why isn't he more honored? Do we take him for granted?

Vicky Cristina Barcelona is typical of a lot of his midrange work. It involves affluent characters at various levels of sophistication, involved in the arts and the intrigues of love. They're conflicted about right and wrong. They're undoubtedly low-level neurotics. In addition, they are attractive, amusing, and living lives we might envy—in this case, during a summer vacation in Barcelona.

Allen's discovery of Europe (of London, Paris, Venice, Barcelona) has provided new opportunities for the poet of Manhattan (and *Manhattan*). In this film we meet two best friends, Vicky (Rebecca Hall) and Cristina (Scarlett Johansson), who decide to spend July and August in the Barcelona home of Vicky's relatives Judy and Mark (Patricia Clarkson and Kevin Dunn). We're briefed by a narrator that Vicky values stable relationships and is engaged to marry Doug (Chris Messina) when she returns. Cristina is more impulsive, more adventurous, not afraid to risk a little turmoil.

Vicky, we learn, is majoring in "Catalan studies," which makes the capital of Catalonia a perfect destination for her. "What will you . . . do with that?" Mark asks over lunch. "Oh," says Vicky, who clearly has no answer. "Maybe teach, or . . . work for a museum?" Her Spanish, it can be observed, could use some work.

They all go to an art gallery show, and Cristina wonders who the man in the red shirt is. Judy explains that he is Juan Antonio (Javier Bardem), an abstract artist, and there was a scandal over his divorce when he tried to kill his wife or she tried to kill him . . . the details are muddled. At midnight in a restaurant (a conventional dinner hour in Barcelona) the two girls see him across the room. "He keeps looking at us!" Cristina says. "That's because you can't take your eyes off of him," says Vicky. He approaches their table, and in quiet, measured tones, offers to fly them in his plane to an interesting city, see the sights, and sleep with him. Both of them.

Vicky is astonished and offended. Cristina accepts, of course, "with no guarantees." Juan Antonio has, in his own words, made a polite, frank, and straightforward offer. And then the film lingers in the complications of the relationships between these three people before introducing a fourth element: the former wife Maria Elena (Penelope Cruz). The tragedy is, she and Juan Antonio are still deeply in love with each other—but they can't live together without violence flaring up. A *ménage à quatre* takes shape—shaky, but fascinating.

Allen is amusing when he applies strict logic to the situation. If everybody knows and accepts what everybody is doing, where's the harm? Cristina is predisposed to such excitement, and Vicky's love for the stable, responsible, absent Doug begins to pale in comparison with this bohemian existence. Judy, the relative, discovers Vicky's secret and

579

urges her to go with her heart, not her prudence. Vicky and Cristina have conversations in which they show they are open-minded, but perhaps not very prudent. There are unexpected arrivals and developments.

And by now we're engrossed in this comedy, which is really a fantasy—beginning with Juan Antonio, who is too cool and good to be true. All the time, Allen gives us a tour of the glories of Barcelona, the city of Gaudi and Miro, the excuse being that Juan Antonio is showing the girls the sights. As Hollywood learned long ago, there's nothing like a seductive location to lend interest to whatever is happening in the foreground.

More surprises than this I must not describe. It is all fairly harmless, although fraught with dire possibilities. Allen has set out to amuse and divert us and discover secrets of human nature, but not tragically deep ones. He is a little like Eric Rohmer here. The actors are attractive, the city is magnificent, the love scenes don't get all sweaty, and everybody finishes the summer a little wiser and with a lifetime of memories. What more could you ask?

Vincent: A Life in Color ★★★ ½
NO MPAA RATING, 96 m., 2010

Featuring Vincent P. Falk. A documentary directed and produced by Jennifer Burns.

You have never heard of Vincent P. Falk, but if you've been near Chicago's Marina City you may have seen him. He's the smiling middle-aged man with a limitless variety of spectacular suits. He stands on the Michigan or Wabash avenue bridges, showing off his latest stupefying suit. He flashes the flamboyant lining, takes the coat off, spins it in great circles above his head, and then does his "spin move," pivoting first left, then right, while whirling the coat in the air. Then he puts it on again and waves to the tourists on the boat, by now passing under the bridge.

You might be forgiven for suspecting that Vincent is a few doughnuts short of a dozen. I know I did. Then I saw the remarkable documentary Vincent: A Life in Color, which unfolds into the mystery of a human personality. Would it surprise you to learn Vincent is a col-

lege graduate? A Cook County computer programmer? A former deejay in gay North Side discos? Paying his own rent in Marina City? Buying his own suits? Legally blind?

All of these things are true. I can believe he buys his own suits. What I can hardly believe is that they are sold. We accompany him on a visit to his customary clothing store, which perhaps caters otherwise to members of the world's second oldest profession.

Jennifer Burns, the producer and director of the film, says that like most Chicagoans, she'd seen Vincent and his colorful suits around for years. How could she not? Then one day she was looking out her office window, watching him performing for a tour boat, "and I was struck by the look of sheer joy I saw on his face. I thought to myself, whatever else you have to say about this guy, he has figured out what makes him happy and he does it, regardless of what anyone else thinks." She approached him, and he agreed to be the subject of a film—not surprising, since his pastime is drawing attention to himself. The subtext of the film is how differently life could have turned out for Vincent.

Vincent, whose surname comes from the last of his foster families, was an orphan abandoned by his mother and raised at St. Joseph's Home for the Friendless. There the nuns discovered that Vincent's problem wasn't intellectual but visual and taught him to read, along with the rest of the class, making sure he was always pushed up against the blackboard so he could see. In high school he was picked on relentlessly, and learned to respond with humor. He was a member of the National Honor Society, the chess club, the debate team, and the diving team, luckily never diving into a pool without water. We meet his diving coach, who was as surprised as we are.

Vincent reads with his good eye held less than an inch from a book or computer screen. Sometimes he uses a magnifying glass. He used a cane in high school, then threw it away and walks freely everywhere in Chicago. It is terrifying to think of him crossing a street.

Vincent, a bright student, was accepted at the University of Illinois, where he studied computer science. He eventually wound up at the Illinois Institute of Technology, studying aeronautical engineering. Yes. He became a popular deejay, first for the go-go boys at Stage 618, and then at the gay disco Cheeks. He didn't exactly fit the image, his old boss recalls, and he held the albums an inch from his face, but he was a great spinner. It was during this time he concluded he was gay. For the past twenty years, he's been a computer programmer for Cook County, helping to track billions of dollars in tax revenue. "He's one of the most brilliant programmers I've ever met," his current boss says.

All of which is admirable, but how does it explain the suits? He started wearing the suits in the 1990s, and says he gave his first bridge show in 2000, adding the "spin move" about a year later. He knows the times when every tour boat passes his bridges, and the guides know his name and point him out somewhere between the Wrigley Building and Marina City. To the guides on the Mercury boats, he is "Riverace" (rhymes with "Liberace"). The captain of one of the Wendella boats says you can set your watch by him. Both of his bridges and both of the TV studios are within a short walk of his home.

There is a great deal of discussion in the documentary about Vincent's motivation. It solves nothing. Vincent himself will say only that he likes to entertain people, to cheer them up a little. One expert in the doc speculates that Vincent has spent a lot of his life being stigmatized and isolated, and the suits are a way of breaking down barriers. I confess that the first time I saw him, I saw a man with unfocused squinting eyes and a weird suit, and leaped to conclusions. Having seen this film, I applaud Vincent. Here is a man who likes to buy Technicolor suits and wave them at tour boats. So why not? What are the people on the boats so busy doing that they don't have time for that?

Note: This review is based on my earlier blog entry.

Vincere ★★★ ½
NO MPAA RATING, 128 m., 2010

Giovanna Mezzogiorno (Ida Dalser), Filippo Timi (Benito Mussolini), Fausto Russo Alesi (Riccardo Paicher), Michela Cescon (Rachele Mussolini), Pier Giorgio Bellocchio (Pietro Fedele), Fabrizio Costella (Young Benito).

Directed by Marco Bellocchio and produced by Mario Gianani. Screenplay by Bellocchio and Daniela Ceselli.

The image of Benito Mussolini has been shifted over the years toward one of a plump buffoon, the inept second fiddle to Hitler. We've seen the famous photo of his ignominious end, his body strung upside down. We may remember his enormous scowling visage trundled out on display in a scene from Fellini's *Amarcord*. What we don't envision is Mussolini as a fiery young man, able to inflame Italians with his charismatic leadership.

That's the man who fascinates Marco Bellocchio, and his *Vincere* explains how such a man could seize a young woman with uncontrollable erotomania that would destroy her life. She was Ida Dalser (Giovanna Mezzogiorno), at first his lover, later his worst nightmare. When she first saw him before World War I, he was a firebrand, dark and handsome, and she was thunderstruck. For Ida, there was one man, and that was Benito (Filippo Timi), and it would always be so.

Her feelings had little to do with his politics. *Vincere* might have been much the same film if Mussolini had been a Christian Democrat. Her feelings spring from a fierce love, which at first is mutual. That he is filled with ideas and ambition makes him all the more attractive, but does she even care what those ideas are? She supports them as a matter of course, selling all she has to support his party newspaper.

They have a son. He leaves to serve in the Italian army in the war. He is possibly lost in combat. She doesn't hear from him. It is an old story. When he reappears after the war, it is impossible for him to lie low; he is Mussolini, in his own mind the chosen one. They are reunited briefly, and the old passion is there. Then she discovers he has a wife. A mistress and a child are decidedly . . . inconvenient for him.

It is revealing how inconvenient Mussolini considers them, and how his values were shaped by bourgeois Catholicism despite his politics. As he makes a strategic alliance with the Vatican, he cannot imagine, and he doesn't believe the public can accept, a leader with a mistress. His wife, Rachele (Michela Cescon), certainly cannot. We might assume Ida could be hidden away or even kept in plain sight, like his friend Hitler's Eva Braun. But no.

If Ida had been capable of staying out of sight and staying quiet, some accommodation can be imagined. A discreet government pension. A home in a city distant from Rome. That is not to be. She considers Mussolini a demigod, and with all the passion of a woman defending her child, she wants her son—hers!—to be acknowledged before all the world as the great man's offspring and heir.

Bellocchio, once himself a fiery young artist (*Fists in the Pocket*), now a legend of the generation of Bertolucci, is concerned with Mussolini's fascism primarily as backdrop. His film is focused on Ida. The last time she sees him in the flesh is the last time we do. Thereafter he's seen only in newsreels—a convenient way for Bellocchio to age and fatten him.

We see Ida's marginal, scorned existence. We see her enacting life scenes that could be staged in opera: She bursts upon Mussolini during public appearances, dragging along the hapless boy as evidence of Benito's heartlessness. The boy himself is bewildered, less concerned with his purported father than with his daily existence with a mother consumed by her obsession.

Was she mad? The term is "erotomania," defined by the conviction that someone is in love with you. It can be a complete delusion, as in the case of celebrity stalkers. But it is not delusional if that person *was* in love with you, held you in his arms night after night, and gave you a son. The fascists instinctively protect Mussolini. When Ida appears in public places, she is surrounded and taken away without Benito even needing to request it. Finally, shamefully, she is consigned to an insane asylum and the boy locked up in an orphanage. She becomes a familiar type: the poor madwoman who is convinced the great man loves her and fathered her child. She writes letters to the press and the pope; such letters are received every day.

Bellocchio bases his film on the performance of Giovanna Mezzogiorno. She is one of those actresses, like Sophia Loren, who can combine passion with dignity. As Mussolini, Filippo Timi avoids any temptation to play

with the benefit of hindsight. He is ambitious, hopeful, sometimes unwise of success. The film's title, which translates as "victory," reflects for much of the film a hope, not a certainty.

The film is beautifully well-mounted. The locations, the sets, the costumes, everything conspire to re-create the Rome of the time. It provides a counterpoint to the usual caricature of Mussolini. They say that behind every great man there stands a great woman. In Mussolini's case, his treatment of her was a rehearsal for how he would treat Italy.

The Visitor ★ ★ ★ ½
PG-13, 103 m., 2008

Richard Jenkins (Walter Vale), Haaz Sleiman (Tarek), Danai Gurira (Zainab), Hiam Abbass (Mouna). Directed by Tom McCarthy and produced by Mary Jane Skalski and Michael London. Screenplay by McCarthy.

Richard Jenkins is an actor who can move his head half an inch and provide the turning point of a film. That happens in *The Visitor*, where he plays a man around sixty who has essentially shut down all of his emotions. A professor, Walter has been teaching the same class for years and cares nothing about it. He coldly rejects a student's late paper without even inquiring about the "personal problems" that made it late. He makes an elderly piano teacher figure out for herself why she will not be needed again. His lips form a straight line that neither smiles nor frowns.

He is forced to travel from his Connecticut campus to New York, to present an academic paper he coauthored. At least he is honest. Protesting the assignment, he tells a colleague he agreed to put his name on the paper as a favor, has not read it, is not competent to present it. He has to go anyway.

He keeps an apartment in Manhattan. Lets himself in. The naked African girl in his bathtub screams. Her boyfriend appears from somewhere. The interlopers are ready to call the police when he explains it is *his* apartment. They'd been renting it from a crafty opportunist. These "roomers" are Tarek (Haaz Sleiman), from Syria, and his girlfriend, Zainab (Danai Gurira), from

Senegal. They immediately pack to leave. He sees them out, then appears at the top of the stairs to tell them they can stay the night. During the film, he will change his mind and appear at the stair-top three times, each time crucial.

Tarek is a virtuoso on an African drum. Walter's late wife was a famous pianist. He loves music but has failed at learning the piano. One day Walter is walking through Washington Square Park and hears two young black boys drumming on the bottoms of plastic buckets. He stops to listen. After a while his head begins to move side to side, half an inch at a time, in response to the rhythm. There you are.

Of course the film, written and directed by Tom McCarthy, is about a great deal more—about illegal U.S. residents and stupid bureaucrats and drums and love and loss. A fourth major character appears, Mouna (Hiam Abbass), who is Tarek's mother and lives in Michigan. She hopes to help her son after he is arrested in an innocent subway incident and threatened with deportation. Walter has already hired a lawyer. He's no bleeding heart, makes no speeches, barely displays emotion, but now for the first time since his wife died, he is feeling things deeply.

This is a wonderful film, sad, angry, and without a comforting little happy ending. But I must not describe what happens because the whole point of serious fiction is to show people changing, and how they change in *The Visitor* is the film's beauty. So much goes unsaid and unseen. Events in Walter's professorial job happen offscreen. We are left to listen to the silences and observe the spaces.

All four actors are charismatic, in quite different ways. Hiam Abbass is one of those actresses who respects small gestures; she knows that when a good cook is using an unfamiliar salt shaker, she shakes the salt first into her hand, and *then* throws it into the pot. And she has other small gestures here that are much more fraught with meaning. Haaz Sleiman and Danai Gurira, as a musician and a jewelry-maker, are young, in love, and simply nice people. The less complicated they are, the better the characters work. And as Walter, Jenkins creates a surprisingly touching, very quiet character study. Not all actors have to call out to us. The better ones make us call out to them.

W

W. ★ ★ ★ ★
PG-13, 131 m., 2008

Josh Brolin (George W. Bush), Elizabeth Banks (Laura Bush), Ellen Burstyn (Barbara Bush), James Cromwell (George H. W. Bush), Richard Dreyfuss (Dick Cheney), Scott Glenn (Donald Rumsfeld), Toby Jones (Karl Rove), Stacy Keach (Reverend Earle Hudd), Bruce McGill (George Tenet), Thandie Newton (Condi Rice), Jeffrey Wright (Colin Powell), Ioan Gruffudd (Tony Blair). Directed by Oliver Stone and produced by Bill Block, Moritz Borman, Paul Hanson, and Eric Kopeloff. Screenplay by Stanley Weiser.

Oliver Stone's *W.*, a biography of President Bush, is fascinating. No other word for it. I became absorbed in its story of a poor little rich kid's alcoholic youth and torturous adulthood. This is the tragedy of a victim of the Peter Principle. Wounded by his father's disapproval and preference for his brother Jeb, the movie argues, George W. Bush rose and rose until he was finally powerful enough to stain his family's legacy.

Unlike Stone's *JFK* and *Nixon,* this film contains no revisionist history. Everything in it, including the scenes behind closed doors, is now pretty much familiar from tell-all books by former Bush aides and reporting by journalists such as Bob Woodward. Although Stone and his writer, Stanley Weiser, could obviously not know exactly who said what and when, there's not a line of dialogue that sounds like malicious fiction. It's all pretty much as published accounts have prepared us for.

The focus is always on Bush (Josh Brolin): his personality, his addiction, his insecurities, his unwavering faith in a mission from God, his yearning to prove himself, his inability to deal with those who advised him. Not surprisingly, in this film, most of the crucial decisions of his presidency were shaped and placed in his hands by the Machiavellian strategist Dick Cheney (Richard Dreyfuss) and the master politician Karl Rove (Toby Jones). Donald Rumsfeld (Scott Glenn) runs an exasperated third.

But what made *them* tick? And what about Colin Powell (Jeffrey Wright) and Condoleezza Rice (Thandie Newton)? You won't find out here. The film sees Bush's insiders from the outside. In his presence, they tend to defer, to use tact as a shield from his ego and defensiveness. But Cheney's soft-spoken, absolutely confident opinions are generally taken as truth. And Bush accepts Rove as the man to teach him what to say and how to say it. He needs them and doesn't cross them.

In the world according to *W.*, Bush always fell short in the eyes of his patrician father (James Cromwell) and outspoken mother (Ellen Burstyn). He resented his parents' greater admiration for his younger brother Jeb. The film lacks scenes showing W. as a child, however—probably wisely. It opens at a drunken fraternity initiation, and "Junior" is pretty much drunk until he finds Jesus at the age of forty. He runs through women, jobs, and cars at an alarming speed and receives one angry lecture after another from his dad.

While running for Congress for the first time, he meets pretty Laura (Elizabeth Banks) at a party, and love blossoms. She was a Gene McCarthy volunteer. Did she turn conservative? I imagine so, but the movie doesn't show them discussing politics. She is patient, steadfast, loving, supportive, and a prime candidate for Al-Anon, the twelve-step program for friends and family of alcoholics. After Bush quits cold turkey, the movie shows him nevertheless often with a beer in his hand, unaware of the jocular AA curse for someone you hate: "One little drink won't kill you." (In an interview, Oliver Stone told me that Bush was not drinking real beer in the later scenes, but the non-alcoholic O'Doul's.)

Dried out, Bush is finally able to hold down jobs. The movie is far from a chronological record, organizing episodes to observe the development of his personality, not his career. Even several spellbinding scenes about the run-up to the Iraq war are not so much critical of his decisions as about how cluelessly, and yet with such vehemence, he stuck with them through thick and thin. At a top-level meeting where he is finally informed that there are no WMDs in Iraq and apparently never were, he is furious for not being informed of this earlier. Several people in the room tried to inform him but were silenced. Colin Powell spends a lot of time softly urging caution and holding his tongue. There is no indication that he will eventually resign.

The movie's Bush is exasperating to work with. At his Texas ranch, he takes the inner circle on a march through the blazing sun, misses a turn, and assures them it's only a half-mile back. Cheney, after three heart attacks, and Rice, wearing inappropriate shoes, straggle along unhappily. His parents are apparently even more disturbed by his decision to run for governor of Texas than by his drinking. Cheney is lectured at a private lunch to remember who is president. He quietly forgets.

Many of the actors somewhat resemble the people they play. The best is Dreyfuss as Cheney, who is not so much a double as an embodiment. The film's portrait of George Senior is sympathetic; it shows him giving Junior the cufflinks that were "the only real thing" his own father, Senator Prescott Bush, ever gave him. The name and the Oedipal Complex were passed down the family tree.

One might feel sorry for George W. at the end of this film, were it not for his legacy of a fraudulent war and a collapsed economy. The film portrays him as incompetent to be president and shaped by the puppet-masters Cheney and Rove to their own ends. If there is a saving grace, it may be that Bush will never fully realize how badly he did. How can he blame himself? He was only following God's will.

The Wackness ★ ★ ★
R, 95 m., 2008

Josh Peck (Luke Shapiro), Ben Kingsley (Dr. Squires), Olivia Thirlby (Stephanie), Method Man (Percy), Mary-Kate Olsen (Union), Famke Janssen (Kristin), Talia Balsam (Mrs. Shapiro), David Wohl (Mr. Shapiro). Directed by Jonathan Levine and produced by Keith Calder, Felipe Marino, and Joe Neurauter. Screenplay by Levine.

The Wackness, which is set in 1994, contains so many drugs it could have been made in the 1970s, along with *Panic in Needle Park* and other landmarks of the psychotropic genera-

tion. The big difference is that drugs have progressed in the years between from cutting-edge material to background music. Both its hero, who has just graduated from high school, and his shrink, forty years his senior, are so constantly stoned that pot and pills are daily, even hourly, fuel.

What saves this from being boring are performances by two actors who see a chance to go over the top and aren't worried about the fall on the other side. Luke Shapiro (Josh Peck) is a college-bound student who deals bushels of marijuana from a battered ice cream pushcart from which no one even attempts to purchase ice cream. Dr. Squires (Ben Kingsley), his psychiatrist, accepts payment in grams and enthusiastically counsels Luke that he needs to get laid. Only when Luke tries to fill the prescription with the doc's stepdaughter Stephanie (Olivia Thirlby, Juno's friend) do ethics come into question.

Peck's performance, for that matter, could have been inspired by Ellen Page's work in *Juno,* assuming he saw the film once and wasn't paying attention. He is cool beyond cool, except when his heart is broken, which happens after he makes the mistake of telling Stephanie he loves her. This is, like, *so* not cool. Meanwhile, Squires's own marriage with Kristin (Famke Janssen) is on the rocks, although both are so spaced out that they don't much care. That leaves space in the story for one meaningful relationship, which is between Luke and Squires.

The Luke character we've seen before, usually not played this well. The psychiatrist is more original. Kingsley, at first unrecognizable with lanky locks and an outdated goatee, is a seriously addicted man, which he must know better than anybody. There's no evidence he has any clients other than Luke, and much of the time he's asking Luke for help. His belief system seems founded on the Beat Generation, and he's acting out his own desires through the younger man. He wants—a laundry list. He wants to be younger, more potent, happily married. He wants to score with hippie chicks (one is played in the movie by Mary-Kate Olsen, who is a superb example of what he has in mind as a hippie chick). He wants to be loved. He wants to love. Everything going wrong in Luke's life right now has been going wrong in the doctor's life for forty years.

It's impossible to not pity this man and carry a reluctant affection for him. He's so screwed up. As a smart, addicted, self-analyzing, secular Jewish intellectual, he could be born of Philip Roth's nightmares. Luke, on the other hand, appears to be a drug-abusing slacker but is, in fact, an *ambitious* drug-abusing slacker, who thinks he might study psychiatry in college. He's in inner turmoil because of problems at home, where the best-laid plans of his father (David Wohl) have run ashore, and the family is being evicted. One motive for Luke's drug-selling spree toward the end of the summer is to bail out his dad, although it appears he would have to turn over the national product of Colombia to succeed.

There's an undeniable pleasure in wallowing in other people's seamy, if entertaining, problems. Even Dr. Squires's descent into despair is accompanied by one-liners and a great sound track (Luke, so retro he's still into cassettes, is always trading custom tracks with both the doctor and his daughter). Toward the end, when Luke summons up the nerve to confess what he truly believes, he has a kind of triumph, heavily laden though it is with qualifiers and apologies. It takes a certain heroism to admit to high feelings and noble instincts of the heart. Drugs are supposed to make that unnecessary, so Luke, I guess, scores more than he realizes. As for the doctor, he achieves all of the benefits of committing suicide, yet suffers none of the drawbacks.

Note: The Wackness *won the audience award at Sundance 2008.*

Waiting for Dublin ★ ★

NO MPAA RATING, 83 m., 2009

Andrew Keegan (Mike), Jade Yourell (Maggie), Hugh O'Conor (Twickers), Guido De Craene (Kluge), Britta Smith (Mrs. Kelleher), Des Braiden (Father Quinlan), Karl Sheils (Vito). Directed by Roger Tucker and produced by Paul Breuls. Screenplay by Chuck Conaway.

As nearly as I can tell, *Waiting for Dublin* is having its world premiere on March 13 in (can you guess?) Chicago, Boston, and New York. The timing could not be better. The St. Patrick's Day parades will be over in time for an afternoon matinee. And if you are the kind of person who marches in or attends the parade, you may enjoy this film. Other kinds of people, not so much.

Waiting for Dublin is like a time capsule, a film that, in every detail, could have been made in the 1940s and starred Bing Crosby, Pat O'Brien, Maureen O'Hara, and Edmund Gwenn as dear old Father Quinlan, who has the narcolepsy something fierce. It takes place in an Irish hamlet that has one telephone, in the post office that is also the pub. A horse and cart is the favored mode of transport, especially because there is no petrol in wartime.

The time is 1945. The hero is Mike (Andrew Keegan), an American pilot. He and his copilot, Twickers (Hugh O'Conor), run out of fuel and make an emergency landing in Ireland, where they are taken in, given lodging, and welcomed at the pub. The village has another guest, the German pilot Kluge (Guido De Craene). Ireland is officially neutral, and so such visitors are welcome, so long as they are not English, of course.

The town is inhabited, as the old movie rules required, by only colorful eccentrics, who spend all of their time in the pub waiting to be entertained by strangers. They move as a unit, decide as a unit, observe as a unit, and go to Sunday Mass as a unit to see whether Father Quinlan can get as far as *"Introibo ad altare Dei"* before falling asleep.

They quickly grow sympathetic to Mike's plight. Back home in Chicago, he made a $10,000 bet that he would shoot down at least five German fighter planes in the war. He needs one more, the war is about to end, and there is another problem: He made the bet with Al Capone's nephew, who in the movie is named Vito but in real life was named Ralph (Risky) Capone Jr. The movie was wise to change his name; in Chicago, you probably wouldn't make a bet you couldn't cover with a man named Risky Capone.

Mike is desperate—to make a fifth kill and to have sex with the lovely local lass Maggie (Jade Yourell), who says nothing doing unless he proposes marriage and means it. He comes up with a plan to get his fifth kill, and how he does that and with which weapons, I will leave for you to discover, pausing only to wonder how petrol was obtained. His solution and how it plays out is of course utterly preposterous, beginning from the moment Twickers begs off because he has a "cold."

Look, this is a perfectly sweet and harmless film, and if it were in black and white on TCM on St. Paddy's Day, you might watch it. It's so old-fashioned it's almost charming. It is constructed entirely with clichés and stereotypes, right down to the brotherhood of pilots, which was not original when Jean Renoir used it in *The Grand Illusion* (1937). The actors are pleasant, the locations (County Galway) are beautiful, but the movie is a wheeze.

Waking Sleeping Beauty ★★★ ½
PG, 86 m., 2010

Featuring Ron Clements, Roy Disney, Jeffrey Katzenberg, Peter Schneider, Rob Minkoff, Michael D. Eisner, Lisa Keene, George Scribner, Gary Trousdale. A documentary directed by Don Hahn and produced by Hahn and Peter Schneider. Screenplay by Patrick Pacheco.

In 1985, when Disney released *The Black Cauldron* to box office disappointment, the animation tradition at the studio was on life support. The studio that began a revolution with *Snow White and the Seven Dwarfs* seemingly no longer knew how to make an animated feature. Roy Disney, Walt's nephew and the largest single stockholder, masterminded an executive shakeup that brought in three men from Paramount: Michael Eisner, Frank Wells, and Jeffrey Katzenberg. That began a second golden age at Disney.

It is enough to name the animated films they made: *Who Framed Roger Rabbit, The Little Mermaid, Beauty and the Beast, Aladdin,* and *The Lion King.* These films proved beyond question that animation was a genre with great international appeal for moviegoers of all ages. Coupled with the home video revolution, they were responsible for literally billions pouring into the studio. Eisner, Katzenberg, and Roy Disney, however, had personal tensions (Michael and Roy thought Jeffrey was getting too much attention as the studio's boy wonder), and after the peacemaker Frank Wells died in a helicopter crash in 1994, the magical period ended.

Waking Sleeping Beauty, made by the studio after all but Disney had left (he died in 2009), is an extraordinary inside look at those ten years. It uses footage and taps into insights, memories, and home movies that only insiders would have access to. Its director and narrator is Don Hahn, who produced *Beauty and the Beast, The Lion King,* and *The Hunchback of Notre Dame,* among others. Another featured narrator is Peter Schneider, who became president of feature animation in 1985, head of Walt Disney Studios in 1999, and left in 2001.

Siskel and Ebert was produced by Disney during all of those years, and I had some contact with these men, and with Rich Frank, studio head before Schneider. Rich would amuse audiences by showing a reel of Siskel and me trashing some of his productions. Michael and Jeffrey insisted that everyone call them—and everyone else at the studio—by their first names. Peter Schneider came on board with a lower profile. One year at Rancho la Puerta, Chaz and I shared a dinner table with a smart, likable young couple from L.A. After a few days, *Siskel and Ebert* came up. "You know I work at Disney," the man said. Really? What do you do? "I'm the president."

It was like that then. I don't know what it's like now. There were rumors that Eisner and Katzenberg didn't get along, and countless articles analyzing why Jeffrey left and/or was pushed after Wells's death. A scene in this film goes a long way to explain the tension. When Jeffrey was in charge of all animation, Eisner announced at a studio meeting that a major new animation building would be constructed. It came as news to Katzenberg.

The most fascinating scenes in *Waking Sleeping Beauty* involve the infamous Disney work ethic. Friends of mine at the studio said the unofficial motto was, "If you didn't come in on Saturday, don't even bother to come in on Sunday." Animators worked so hard they developed anxiety, migraines, carpal tunnel syndrome. The "family studio" required such long hours that some marriages failed. When Katzenberg held a no-holds-barred meeting with the animators, he actually teared up at their stories and relented. But he always came in on Sundays.

The film gives good screen time to the artists who created the films with their own minds and hands and worked in collaboration. There's even a glimpse of young Tim Burton, chained to a drafting board. A tension-breaking Mexican party in the animation department is recalled with the nostalgia of combat veterans given a week of R&R. Whatever happened, happened. The fact remains that those years were revolutionary, and if not for them, it's a good question whether Pixar, DreamWorks, and the other animation production sources—and Disney Animation itself—would still exist. Credit is due.

WALL-E ★ ★ ★ ½
G, 98 m., 2008

With the voices of: Ben Burtt (WALL-E), Elissa Knight (Eve), Jeff Garlin (Captain), Fred Willard (Shelby Forthright), John Ratzenberger (John), Kathy Najimy (Mary), Kim Kopf (Hoverchair Mother), Garrett Palmer (Hoverchair Son), Sigourney Weaver (Ship's Computer). Directed by Andrew Stanton and produced by Jim Morris. Screenplay by Stanton and Jim Reardon.

Pixar's *WALL-E* succeeds at being three things at once: an enthralling animated film, a visual wonderment, and a decent science-fiction story. After *Kung Fu Panda*, I thought I had just about exhausted my emergency supply of childlike credulity, but here is a film, like *Finding Nemo*, that you can enjoy even if you've grown up. That it works largely without spoken dialogue is all the more astonishing; it can easily cross language barriers, which is all the better, considering that it tells a planetary story.

It is the relatively near future. A city of skyscrapers rises up from the land. A closer view reveals that the skyscrapers are all constructed out of garbage, neatly compacted into squares or bales and piled on top of one another. In all the land, only one creature stirs. This is WALL-E, the last of the functioning solar-powered robots. He (the story leaves no doubt about gender) scoops up trash, shovels it into his belly, compresses it into a square, and climbs on his tractor treads up a winding road to the top of his latest skyscraper, to place it neatly on the pile.

It is lonely being WALL-E. But does WALL-E even know that? He comes home at night to a big storage area, where he has gathered a few treasures from his scavengings of the garbage and festooned them with Christmas lights. He wheels into his rest position, takes off his treads from his tired wheels, and goes into sleep mode. Tomorrow is another day. One of thousands since the last humans left Earth and settled into orbit aboard gigantic spaceships that resemble spas for the fat and lazy.

One day WALL-E's age-old routine is shattered. Something new appears in his world, which otherwise has consisted only of old things left behind. This is, to our eye, a sleek spaceship. To WALL-E's eyes, who knows? What with one thing and another, WALL-E is scooped up by the ship and returned to the orbiting spaceship Axiom, along with his most recent precious discovery: a tiny, perfect green plant, which he found growing in the rubble and transplanted to an old shoe.

Have you heard enough to be intrigued, or do you want more? Speaking voices are now heard for the first time in the movie, although all on his own WALL-E has a vocabulary (or repertory?) of squeaks, rattles, and electronic purrs, and a couple of pivoting eyes that make him look downright anthropomorphic. We meet a Hoverchair family, so known because aboard ship they get around in comfy chairs that hover over surfaces and whisk them about effortlessly. They're all as fat as Susie's aunt. This is not entirely their fault, since generations in the low-gravity world aboard the Axiom have evolved humanity into a race whose members generally resemble those folks you see whizzing around Wal-Mart in their electric shopping carts.

There is now a plot involving WALL-E, the ship's captain, several Hoverpeople, and the fate of the green living thing. And in a development that would have made Sir Arthur Clarke's heart beat with joy, humanity returns home once again—or is that a spoiler?

The movie has a wonderful visual look. Like so many of the Pixar animated features, it finds a color palette that's bright and cheerful, but not too pushy and a tiny bit realistic at the same time. The drawing style is comic-book cool, as perfected in the funny comics more than the superhero books: Everything has a stylistic twist to give it flair. And a lot of thought must have gone into the design of WALL-E, for whom I felt a curious affection. Consider this hunk of tin beside the Kung Fu Panda. The panda was all but special-ordered to be lovable, but on reflection I think he was so fat, it wasn't funny anymore. WALL-E, on the other hand, looks rusty and hardworking and plucky, and expresses his personality with body language and (mostly) with the binocular video cameras that serve as his eyes. The movie draws on a tradition going back to the earliest days of Walt Disney, who reduced human expressions to their broadest components and found ways to translate them to animals, birds, bees, flowers, trains, and everything else.

What's more, I don't think I've quite captured the enchanting storytelling of the film. Directed by Andrew Stanton, who wrote and directed *Finding Nemo*, it involves ideas, not simply mindless scenarios involving characters karate-kicking each other into high-angle shots. It involves a little work on the part of the audience and a little thought, and might be especially stimulating to younger viewers. This story told in a different style and with a realistic look could have been a great science-fiction film. For that matter, maybe it is.

Note: The movie is preceded by Presto Chango, *a new Pixar animated short about a disagreement over a carrot between a magician and his rabbit.*

Walt and El Grupo ★★★

PG, 106 m., 2009

Featuring Walt and Lillian Disney and sixteen of Disney's employees in 1941. A documentary directed by Theodore Thomas and produced by Kuniko Okubo. Screenplay by Thomas.

Looking back, Walt Disney felt that 1941 was the worst year of his life. He felt betrayed when his animators went on strike and forced him to shut down the new studio he'd just built with the profits from *Snow White and the Seven Dwarfs, Pinocchio,* and *Fantasia*. As labor negotiations dragged on, Disney did what no other Hollywood studio chief would have done. He packed his wife and sixteen important employees on an airplane and embarked on a goodwill tour of South America.

In large part because of Mickey Mouse, Disney had become the world's most beloved Hollywood moviemaker since Chaplin. He'd been asked to make the tour by President Roosevelt, who on the brink of war was alarmed by Nazi inroads on the continent. Walt took the trip partly for patriotic reasons, and partly, I suspect, to get out of Dodge. The employees he took along weren't mostly executives but creative talent; he hoped they'd get ideas for new films in South America. Included was Frank Thomas, one of the "Nine Old Men" credited with the brilliance of Disney's early animated features. Now, sixty-eight years later, Frank's son Theodore has written and directed this labor of love.

No other Hollywood studio has maintained the same corporate continuity since the day it was founded, and Disney is unparalleled in its archives. Long before film preservation became fashionable, Walt enssured that the studio's work was guarded like the family jewels, and no other studio could produce historical treasure like this from its vaults.

To begin with, there is the footage shot on the trip: black-and-white documentary records of "El Grupo" undertaking what was then not a commonplace journey (they left Miami by Pan American seaplane). The continent is all new to them. The costumes, the music, the folklore, the cities, the fabulous night club shows of Buenos Aires. In 1941, the globe was still immense, and electronic media hadn't started to shrink it.

Thomas shows Disney and his group trying to dance the samba, and Walt looking awkward dressed as a gaucho. It intercuts bright, color footage of the films inspired by the trip, including *Saludos Amigos* and *The Three Caballeros*. Thomas retraced the journey for this film; there's a striking dissolve from the view from a balcony to the drawing it inspired seven decades ago. This trip was one of the inspirations for the U.S. explosion of interest in South American costumes and music, and perhaps the many musicals like *Flying Down to Rio*. Disney even brought back composers to work at his studio.

The subtext of the film is: Walt was young once. He was the Spielberg of his time, the boy genius, a mogul not yet forty, already with the familiar mustache but with a thick head of

589

luxuriant black hair. He's affable, diplomatic, always with a cigarette (which earns the PG rating these days—ohmigod, Walt smoked!). Another message is that animated films, then as now, were far more than "cartoons" and often required more art and music design than conventional features. Always you see members of El Grupo taking photos and making sketches.

At a time when Hollywood doesn't remember last year, is obsessed with the bottom line, and is run by men who often have no sense of history, *Walt and El Grupo* evokes a better time. The great Russian filmmaker Eisenstein, on seeing *Snow White*, called it the greatest film ever made. Walt Disney didn't simply invent Mickey Mouse. He created a new genre of films like nothing anybody had seen before.

Waltz with Bashir ★ ★ ★ ½
R, 87 m., 2009

With the voices of: Ari Folman, Ori Sivan, Ronny Dayag, Shmuel Frenkel, Zahava Solomon, Ron Ben-Yishai, Dror Harazi, Boaz Rein-Buskila, Carmi Cna'an. Directed by Ari Folman and produced by Folman, Yael Nahlieli, Bridgit Folman, Serge Lalou, Gerhard Meixner, and Roman Paul. Screenplay by Folman.

Waltz with Bashir is a devastating animated film that tries to reconstruct how and why thousands of innocent civilians were massacred because those with the power to stop them took no action. Why they did not act is hard to say. Did they not see? Not realize? Not draw fateful conclusions? In any event, at the film's end, the animation gives way to newsreel footage of the dead, whose death is inescapable.

The massacre, well documented, took place during Israel's 1982 invasion of Lebanon. The victims were in Palestinian refugee camps. They were killed by a Christian militia. Israelis were in nominal control of the militia but did not stop the massacre. Blame has never been clearly assigned. Certainly the Christians pulling the triggers were guilty. Were the Israelis enablers?

In war, they say, no one sees the big picture, the men at the top least of all. *Waltz with Bashir* opens with a recurring nightmare had by a friend of Ari Folman, who wrote and directed the film. It is described to Folman in the course of his attempt to reconstruct what actually happened during days when he was present; he has the confused impression that the truth of those days was just outside his grasp. He sets out to interview Israeli army friends who were also there, and his film resembles *Rashomon* in the way truth depends not on facts but on who witnessed them and why.

Folman is an Israeli documentarian who has not worked in animation. Now he uses it as the best way to reconstruct memories, fantasies, hallucinations, possibilities, past and present. This film would be nearly impossible to make any other way. Animation will always be identified, no doubt, with funny animals, but is winning respect as a medium for serious subjects. Consider the great success of *WALL-E*, which was greatly entertaining, yet a radical critique of the consumer society.

The film is structured like a conventional documentary, with Folman visiting old army friends and piecing together what they saw and remember. The freedom of animation allows him to visualize what they tell him—even their nightmares. The title refers to an Israeli soldier losing it and firing all around himself on a street papered with posters of the just-assassinated Lebanese president-elect Bashir Gemayel—thus, waltzing with Bashir.

Folman gradually fits together a puzzle with the massacre at the center and his witnesses in concentric rings at various distances. Who knew what was happening? Which Israeli commanders were in a position to stop it? After it was over, it became simply a thing that had happened, seemingly without decision or choice. Had anyone in fact ordered the Christian militia to shoot or had they spontaneously agreed to kill?

It is impossible to pin down the answers. My impression is that some knew, some could have stopped it, but the connections between the two are uncertain. That is almost always the case with genocide. At this moment, for example, the world fully knows that ethnic slaughter is taking place in the Congo. The world stands aside. Eventually we will regret not having acted, as we regret Rwanda, Bosnia, Somalia, and indeed the Holocaust.

Those pulling the triggers are the immediate murderers. Those in charge of them are morally guilty. Those who could stop them, even more so. That means us.

The debate still continues about the inaction of the Allies in not bombing the rail lines leading to the death camps, although there were bombs to spare for bombing German civilians. Now *Waltz with Bashir* argues that Israel itself is not guiltless in acts of passive genocide, an argument underlined by the disproportionate Israeli response to the provocations of Hamas. We may be confronted here with a fundamental flaw in human nature. When he said, "The buck stops here," Harry Truman was dreaming. The buck never stops.

Wanted ★ ★ ★
R, 110 m., 2008

James McAvoy (Wesley Gibson), Morgan Freeman (Sloan), Terence Stamp (Pekwarsky), Thomas Kretschmann (Cross), Common (The Gunsmith), Angelina Jolie (Fox). Directed by Timur Bekmambetov and produced by Marc Platt, Jim Lemley, Jason Netter, and Iain Smith. Screenplay by Michael Brandt, Derek Haas, and Chris Morgan.

Wanted slams the pedal to the metal and never slows down. Here's an action picture that's exhausting in its relentless violence and its ingenuity in inventing new ways to attack, defend, ambush, and annihilate. Expanding on a technique I first saw in David O. Russell's *Three Kings,* it follows individual bullets (as well as flying warriors) through implausible trajectories to pound down the kills.

The movie is based on comic books by Mark Millar and J. G. Jones. Their origin story involves an anxiety-ridden, henpecked, frustrated office worker named Wesley (James McAvoy), whom you might have glimpsed in a bogus YouTube video trashing his office. In the movie he gets the opportunity to trash a lot more than that. In a plot development that might have been inspired by James Thurber's *The Secret Life of Walter Mitty* (but probably wasn't, because who reads that great man anymore?), Wesley gets the opportunity to find revenge on his tormentors and enter a fantasy world where he can realize his hidden powers as a skilled assassin.

This happens after he is picked up in a bar by Fox (Angelina Jolie), who confides that he is now a member of The Fraternity, a thousand-year-old secret society of assassins who kill bad people. I suppose a lot of people, if they were picked up in a bar by Angelina Jolie, would go along with that story. Although The Fraternity's accuracy rate can be faulted (it missed on Hitler and Stalin, for example), its selection methods must be Really Deep, since orders are transmitted through The Loom of Fate. As demonstrated in the film, if you look at a cloth really, really, *really* closely, you can see that every once in a while a thread is out of line. These threads represent a binary code that is way deeper than my old Lone Ranger Decoder Ring. They also raise questions about the origin, method, and reading of themselves, which are way, way too complicated to be discussed here, assuming they could be answered, which I confidently believe would not be the case.

Never mind. Wesley leaves his office life for a hidden alternative existence in which he masters skills of fighting (by hurtling hundreds of feet) and shooting (around corners, for example). And he is introduced to Sloan (Morgan Freeman), who, the moment I mentioned Morgan Freeman, you immediately knew was deep and wise and in charge of things. He lives in a book-lined library (but Wesley, to my intense regret, never asks him, "Have you really read all these books? Anything by Thurber?"). Sloane explains that Wesley's father was a member of The Fraternity, killed years ago by the man Wesley is now destined to kill. This is Cross (Thomas Kretschmann), who lurks in Europe, where Wesley also meets Pekwarsky (Terence Stamp), another fraternity brother. (Do you suppose The Fraternity's secret handshake is fatal? If brothers give it to each other, do they both die?)

I'd guess there are, oh, ten or fifteen shots in this entire movie without special effects. The rest of the time, we're watching motion-capture animation, CGI, stuff done in the lab. A few of the stunts look like they could not have been faked, but who knows? What do you think your chances are when you run on top of a speeding train? For that matter, if you were assigned to kill someone in Chicago, could you figure out a better way to do it than by standing on top of an El train while it raced past your target's office window? And how did The Fraternity know he would be visible through that window? And how . . . oh, never mind.

Wanted, directed by a hot Russian action-meister named Timur Bekmambetov, is a film entirely lacking in two organs I always appreciate in a movie: a heart and a mind. It is mindless, heartless, preposterous. By the end of the film we can't even believe the values the plot seems to believe, since the plot is deceived right along with us. The way to enjoy this film is to put your logic on hold, along with any higher sensitivities that might be vulnerable, and immerse yourself as if in a video game. That *Wanted* will someday be a video game, I have not the slightest doubt. It may already *be* a video game, but I'm damned if I'll look it up and find out. Objectively, I award it all honors for technical excellence. Subjectively, I'd rather be watching Danny Kaye in the film version of *The Secret Life of Walter Mitty*.

Note: I learn that The Secret Life of Walter Mitty *will be remade next year and will star Mike Myers. Having seen Myers's* The Love Guru, *I think I can predict one of Walter's big secrets.*

War, Inc. ★ ★
R, 106 m., 2008

John Cusack (Brand Hauser), Hilary Duff (Yonica Babyyeah), Marisa Tomei (Natalie Hegalhuzen), Joan Cusack (Marsha Dillon), Dan Aykroyd (Ex–Vice President), Ben Kingsley (Walken/Viceroy), Lubomir Neikov (Omar Sharif). Directed by Joshua Seftel and produced by Les Weldon, Danny Lerner, John Cusack, and Grace Loh. Screenplay by Cusack, Mark Leyner, and Jeremy Pikser.

War, Inc. is a brave and ambitious but chaotic attempt at political satire. The targets: the war in Iraq and the shadowy role of Vice President Cheney's onetime corporate home Halliburton in the waging of the war. Dan Aykroyd plays an "ex–vice president," unmis-

takably Cheney, issuing orders to CIA hit man Brand Hauser (John Cusack) to assassinate a Middle Eastern oil minister (named Omar Sharif, not much of a joke) whose plans to build a pipeline in his own country run counter to the schemes of the supercorporation Tamerlane.

Hauser is an intriguing character, seen chugging shot glasses of hot sauce for reasons that are no doubt as significant as they are obscure. "I feel like a refugee from the island of Dr. Moreau," he confides at one point to the onboard computer on his private plane, a sort of sympathetic HAL 9000. Arriving in the country of Turaqistan, he finds warfare raging everywhere except within a protected area known as the Emerald City, for which of course we are to read Baghdad's Green Zone. Here American corporations are so entrenched that Hauser reaches the secret bunker of the Viceroy (a Tamerland puppet) through a Popeye's Fried Chicken store.

That sort of satire runs through the movie, which is neither quite serious nor quite funny, but very busy with trying to be one or the other. Lots of other brand names (in addition to *brand* Hauser) appear in connection with an expo being staged by public relations whiz Marsha Dillon (Joan Cusack), who becomes Hauser's cynical adviser. Among her plans for the expo: the televised wedding of Middle Eastern pop superstar Yonica Babyyeah (Hilary Duff, but you won't recognize her).

Arriving in Turaqistan at about the same time as Hauser is Natalie Hegalhuzen (Marisa Tomei), a reporter for liberal magazines, whose character and others in the film illustrate my First Law of Funny Names, which teaches us that they are rarely funny. She is a warm, pretty woman who quickly appeals to Hauser, already having second thoughts about his hit-man role. She's smart, too, with an occasional tendency to talk like she's writing (she describes Yonica as "a sad little girl who's been pimped out into a pathetic monstrosity of Western sexuality").

All of the story strands come together into a bewildering series of solutions and conclusions, in which the fictional heritage of the name "Emerald City" plays a prominent role. But the intended satire isn't as focused or merciless as it could be and tries too hard to keep too many balls in the air. The movie's time period is hard to nail down; the opening titles refer to the "21st century," but of course that's the present, and current names are referred to (McLaughlin, Anderson Cooper, Cheney, Katie Couric, 50 Cent, etc). One particularly brilliant invention is Combat-O-Rama, which is a version of a Disney World virtual reality thrill ride allowing journalists to experience battle through what I guess you'd call "virtual embedding."

John Cusack is the power behind the film, as star, top-billed writer, and one of the producers. He deserves credit for trying to make something topical, controversial, and uncompromised. The elements are all here. But the parts never come together. Cusack has made fifty-six films and is only forty-two years old, and his quality control is uncanny. He shies away from unworthy projects and is always available to take a chance. A project like *War, Inc.* must not have been easy to finance, shows a determination to make a movie that makes a statement, and is honorable. Sometimes the best intentions don't pay off. I wanted to like it more than I could.

Watchmen ★ ★ ★ ★
R, 163 m., 2009

Malin Akerman (Laurie Jupiter/Silk Spectre II), Billy Crudup (Jon Osterman/Dr. Manhattan), Matthew Goode (Adrian Veidt/Ozymandias), Carla Gugino (Sally Jupiter/Silk Spectre), Jackie Earle Haley (Walter Kovacs/Rorschach), Stephen McHattie (Hollis Mason/Nite Owl), Jeffrey Dean Morgan (Edward Blake/The Comedian), Patrick Wilson (Dan Dreiberg/Nite Owl II). Directed by Zack Snyder and produced by Lawrence Gordon, Lloyd Levin, and Deborah Snyder. Screenplay by David Hayter and Alex Tse, based on the graphic novel by Alan Moore and Dave Gibbons.

After the revelation of *The Dark Knight,* here is *Watchmen,* another bold exercise in the liberation of the superhero movie. It's a compelling visceral film—sound, images, and characters combined into a decidedly odd visual experience that evokes the feel of a graphic novel. It seems charged from within by its power as a fable; we sense it's not interested in a plot so much as with the dilemma of functioning in a world losing hope.

That world is America in 1985, with Richard Nixon in the White House and many other strange details; this America occupies a parallel universe in which superheroes and masked warriors operate. The film confronts a paradox that was always there in comic books: The heroes are only human. They can only be in one place at a time (with a possible exception to be noted later). Although a superhero is able to handle one dangerous situation, the world has countless dangerous situations, and the super resources are stretched too thin. Faced with law enforcement anarchy, Nixon has outlawed superhero activity, quite possibly a reasonable action. Now the murder of the enigmatic vigilante the Comedian (Jeffrey Dean Morgan) has brought the Watchmen together again. Who might be the next to die?

Dr. Manhattan (Billy Crudup), the only one with superpowers in the literal sense, lives outside ordinary time and space, the forces of the universe seeming to coil beneath his skin. Ozymandias (Matthew Goode) is the world's smartest man. The Nite Owl (Patrick Wilson) is a man isolated from life by his mastery of technology. Rorschach (Jackie Earl Haley) is a man who finds meaning in patterns that may exist only in his mind. And Silk Spectre II (Malin Akerman) lives with one of the most familiar human challenges, living up to her parents, in this case the original Silk Spectre (Carla Gugino). Dr. Manhattan is both her lover and a distant father figure living in a world of his own.

These characters are garbed in traditional comic book wardrobes—capes, boots, gloves, belts, masks, props, anything to make them one of a kind. Rorschach's cloth mask, with its endlessly shifting ink blots, is one of the most intriguing superhero masks ever, always in constant motion, like a mood ring of the id. Dr. Manhattan is contained in a towering, muscular, naked blue body; he was affected by one of those obligatory secret experiments gone wild. Never mind the details; what matters is that he possibly exists at a quantum level, at which particles seem exempt from the usual limitations of space and time. If it seems unlikely that quantum materials could assemble into a tangible physical body, not to worry.

Everything is made of quantum particles, after all. There's a lot we don't know about them, including how they constitute Dr. Manhattan, so the movie is vague about his precise reality. I was going to say Silk Spectre II has no complaints, but actually she does.

The mystery of the Comedian's death seems associated with a plot to destroy the world. The first step in the plot may be to annihilate the Watchmen, who are All That Stand Between, etc. It is hard to see how anyone would benefit from the utter destruction of the planet, but in the movie's world there is a nuclear standoff between the United States and the Soviet Union that threatens exactly that. During the Cuban missile crisis, remember "Better Dead Than Red"? There were indeed cold warriors who preferred to be dead rather than red, reminding me of David Merrick's statement: "It's not enough for me to win. My enemies must lose."

In a cosmic sense it doesn't really matter who pushed the Comedian through the window. In a cosmic sense, nothing really matters, but best not meditate on that too much. The Watchmen and their special gifts are all the better able to see how powerless they really are, and although all but Dr. Manhattan are human and back the home team, their powers are not limitless. Dr. Manhattan, existing outside time and space, is understandably remote from the fate of our tiny planet, although perhaps he still harbors some old emotions.

Those kinds of quandaries engage all the Watchmen and are presented in a film experience of often fearsome beauty. It might seem improbable to take seriously a naked blue man, complete with discreet genitalia, but Billy Crudup brings a solemn detachment to Dr. Manhattan that is curiously affecting. Does he remember how it felt to be human? No, but hum a few bars. . . . Crudup does the voice and the body language, which is transformed by software into a figure of considerable presence.

Watchmen focuses on the contradiction shared by most superheroes: They cannot live ordinary lives but are fated to help mankind. That they do this with trademarked names and appliances goes back to their origins in Greece, where Zeus had his thunderbolts, Hades his three-headed dog, and Hermes his winged feet. Could Zeus run fast? Did Hermes have a dog? No.

That level of symbolism is coiling away beneath all superheroes. What appeals with Batman is his humanity; despite his skills, he is not supernormal. *Watchmen* brings surprising conviction to these characters as flawed and minor gods, with Dr. Manhattan possessing access to godhead on a plane that detaches him from our daily concerns—indeed, from days themselves. In the film's most spectacular scene, he is exiled to Mars and in utter isolation reimagines himself as a human and conjures (or discovers? I'm not sure) an incredible city seemingly made of crystal and mathematical concepts. This is his equivalent to forty days in the desert, and he returns as a savior.

The film is rich enough to be seen more than once. I plan to see it again, this time on IMAX, and will have more to say about it. I'm not sure I understood all the nuances and implications, but I am sure I had a powerful experience. It's not as entertaining as *The Dark Knight*, but like the *Matrix* films, *LOTR*, and *The Dark Knight*, it's going to inspire fevered analysis. I don't want to see it twice for that reason, however, but mostly just to have the experience again.

We Live in Public ★★★★
NO MPAA RATING, 91 m., 2009

With Josh Harris, Jason Calacanis, Missy Galore, Anthony Haden-Guest, Douglas Rushkoff. A documentary directed by Ondi Timoner and produced by Timoner and Keirda Bahruth. Screenplay by Timoner.

I'd never heard of Josh Harris, who is billed in this film as "the greatest Internet pioneer you've never heard of." I can be excused for thinking Josh Harris was the fictional hero of a pseudo-documentary, until the film quickly and obviously became authentic. It's not often you see a doc that's been filmed over a period of fifteen years.

Harris was involved in the early days of Prodigy, back in the Compuserve era, and in 1993 founded Pseudo.com, which forecast audio and video webcasting, YouTube, Hulu, and countless other streamers. He was, to put it kindly, ahead of his time. In 1993, 300-baud modems were commonplace, and 1,200 was fast.

Harris was a myopic visionary, a man who saw the future more vividly than his own life. He was a prototype nerd, a lonely kid who raised himself while planted in front of an old black-and-white TV set, using *Gilligan's Island* as a virtual family to supplement his own remote mother. In the 1990s he became one of the early dot-com millionaires, a celebrity in New York, where he threw lavish parties intended not so much for the famous as to attract brilliant and artistic kids to work for him. Pseudo.com is remembered from that time as Nerd Heaven, offering well-paid positions, loaded with perks, equipped with free creature comforts, demanding only your body and soul.

He sold Pseudo for something like $80 million, and that was the end of his good timing. The filmmaker, Ondi Timoner, had already started to document his life and was on the scene when he began a notorious project named Quiet. Try to imagine this: About one hundred of the best and brightest he could find agreed to live twenty-four hours a day in a cavernous space below street level. They would be under video surveillance every moment. Their lives would be streamed on the Web. They shared dining and recreational facilities and even a shooting range. They were given state-of-the-art computers. They lived in cubicles with the square footage of perhaps six coffins. These were stacked atop one another like sleeping cubicles in a Japanese airport.

Yes. And this was to be the future, in which we will all live virtually on the Internet. The film *Surrogates* perhaps owes something to Harris. Remarkably, no murders claimed any of Quiet's eager volunteers; whether any births resulted is not reported. The fire department closed him down in the first days of 2000, but Harris, not missing a beat, moved with his girlfriend into an apartment where every single room was webcast twenty-four hours a day—every meal, every bowel movement, every sexual event, everything, including their (inevitable) ugly breakup. "She was only a pseudo girlfriend," he explained later. I don't knew if she knew that.

By then Harris had spent most of his $80 million and become disillusioned with living in public. He bought an upstate New York apple farm, and Timoner followed him there to find him in work clothes, having returned to the earth. His friends lost touch. He became forgotten as quickly as he became famous. I wonder, and the film doesn't tell us, what he thinks of YouTube. At the end of the film he's living in Africa.

He did, however, fly to Sundance 2009, where the film won the Grand Jury Prize for best documentary. Sundance has recently become a place where the visitors can barely tear their eyes from texting, surfing, e-mailing, or tweeting in order to look at a movie. What did he make of this? Harris saw it coming in the days when a Tandy 100 transmitted text much more slowly than I could read.

This is a remarkable film about a strange and prophetic man. What does it tell us? Did living a virtual life destroy him? When he had a nervous breakdown after the *We Live in Public* Web experiment collapsed, was it responsible?

Remember Jenny Ringley? She was the pioneer of webcams. From April 1996 until 2003, she lived her life online, getting, it was said, tens of millions of hits a week. She never discussed why she shut down Jennycam. Today she says she doesn't even have a MySpace page. And Josh Harris says Sidamo, Ethiopia, is the best place on Earth to live: "People know each other here."

Wendy and Lucy ★ ★ ★ ½
R, 80 m., 2009

Michelle Williams (Wendy), Will Patton (Mechanic), John Robinson (Andy), Larry Fessenden (Man in Park), Will Oldham (Icky), Walter Dalton (Security Guard). Directed by Kelly Reichardt and produced by Neil Kopp, Anish Savjani, and Larry Fessenden. Screenplay by Reichardt and Jon Raymond, based on the story "Train Choir" by Raymond.

I know so much about Wendy although this movie tells me so little. I know almost nothing about where she came from, what her life was like, how realistic she is about the world, where her ambition lies. But I know, or feel, everything about Wendy at this moment:

stranded in an Oregon town, broke, her dog lost, her car a write-off, hungry, friendless, quiet, filled with desperate resolve.

Kelly Reichardt's *Wendy and Lucy* is another illustration of how absorbing a film can be when the plot doesn't stand between us and a character. There is no timetable here. Nowhere Wendy came from, nowhere she's going to, no plan except to get her car fixed and feed her dog. Played by Michelle Williams, she has a gaze focused inward on her determination. We pick up a few scraps: Her sister in Indiana is wary of her, and she thinks she might be able to find a job in a fish cannery in Ketchikan, Alaska.

But Alaska seems a long way to drive from Indiana just to get a job in a cannery, and this movie isn't about the unemployment rate. Alaska perhaps appeals to Wendy because it is as far away she can drive where they still speak English. She parks on side streets and sleeps in her car, she has very limited cash, her golden retriever, Lucy, is her loving companion. She wakes up one morning somewhere in Oregon, her car won't start, and she's out of dog food, and that begins a chain of events that leads to wandering around a place she doesn't know looking for her only friend in the world.

When I say I know all about Wendy, that's a tribute to Michelle Williams's acting, Kelly Reichardt's direction, and the cinematography of Sam Levy. They use Williams's expressive face, often forlorn, always hopeful, to show someone who embarked on an unplanned journey, has gone too far to turn back, and right now doesn't care about anything but getting her friend back. Her world is seen as the flat, everyday world of shopping malls and storefronts, rail tracks, and not much traffic, skies that the weatherman calls "overcast." You know those days when you walk around and the weather makes you feel in your stomach that something is not right? Cinematography can make you feel like that.

She walks. She walks all the way to the dog pound and back. All the way to an auto shop and back. And back to what? She sleeps in a park. The movie isn't about people molesting her, although she has one unpleasant encounter. Most people are nice, like a mechanic (Will Patton), and especially a security guard of retirement age (Walter Dalton), whose job

is to stand and look at a mostly empty parking lot for twelve hours, to guard against a nonexistent threat to its empty spaces.

Early in the film, the teenage supermarket employee (John Robinson) who busts Wendy for shoplifting won't give her a break. He's a little suck-up who possibly wants to impress his boss with an unbending adherence to "store policy." Store policy also probably denies him health benefits and overtime, and if he takes a good look at Wendy, he may be seeing himself, minus the uniform with the logo and the name tag on it.

The people in the film haven't dropped out of life; they've been dropped by life. It has no real use for them and not much interest. They're on hold. At least searching for your lost dog is a consuming passion; it gives Wendy a purpose and the hope of joy at the end. That's what this movie has to observe, and it's more than enough.

Whatever Works ★ ★ ★
PG-13, 92 m., 2009

Larry David (Boris Yellnikoff), Evan Rachel Wood (Melody), Patricia Clarkson (Marietta), Ed Begley Jr. (John), Conleth Hill (Leo Brockman), Michael McKean (Joe). Directed by Woody Allen and produced by Letty Aronson and Stephen Tenenbaum. Screenplay by Allen.

Woody Allen said in *Manhattan* that Groucho Marx was first on his list of reasons to keep on living. His new film, *Whatever Works*, opens with Groucho singing "Hello, I Must Be Going" from *Animal Crackers*. It serves as the movie's theme song, summarizing in five words the worldview of his hero, Boris Yellnikoff.

Yellnikoff, played with perfect pitch by Larry David, is a nuclear physicist who was once almost nominated for a Nobel Prize, a statement so many of us could make. His field was quantum mechanics, where string theory can be described in the same five words. He's retired now, divorced from a rich wife who was so perfect for him he couldn't stand it. He lives in a walk-up in Chinatown and works part time as a chess instructor to little "inch worms," whom he hits over their heads with the board.

Mostly what he does is hang out at a table in a coffee shop and kvetch with old pals.

These scenes seemed perfectly familiar to me because of my long honorary membership in a group centering on Dusty Cohl at the Coffee Mill in Toronto. Boris doesn't talk with his friends; he lectures them. His speeches spring from the Jewish love of paradox; essentially, life is so fascinating he can't take it any longer.

Midway in his remarkable opening monologue, David starts speaking directly to the camera. His friends think he's crazy. He asks them if they can't see the people out there—us. Allen developed as a standup comic, and the idea of an actual audience often hovers in his work, most literally in *The Purple Rose of Cairo*, where a character climbs down from the screen and joins it.

Boris gets up from the table and walks down the sidewalk, continuing to hector the camera about his own brilliance and the general stupidity that confronts him. It is too great a burden for him to exist in a world of such morons and cretins. He hates everyone and everything—in a theoretical way, as befits a physicist. Later that night he is implored by a homeless waif to give her something to eat, tells her to be about her business, and then relents and invites her in.

This is Melody St. Ann Celestine (Evan Rachel Wood), a fresh-faced innocent from a small town down south, who still believes in the world she conquered in beauty pageants. I've seen Wood in a lot of performances, but nothing to prepare me for this one. She's naivete on wheels, cheerful, optimistic, trusting, infectious. Reader, she wins the old man's heart—and wants it! She proposes marriage, and not for cynical or needy reasons. She believes everything he says, and is perhaps the first person he has ever met who subscribes fully to the theory of his greatness.

This sets in rotation a wheel of characters who all discover for themselves that in life we must accept whatever works to make us happy. Boris and Melody accept each other. Then her parents separately find their way to New York in search of her, and they accept what they discover. They are Marietta (Patricia Clarkson), who is Melody made middle-aged and churchgoing, and John (Ed Begley Jr.), to whom the National Rifle Association ranks just a smidgin higher than the Supreme Court. They are ap-

palled at this human wreckage their daughter has taken to her side.

But whatever works. Both Marietta and John are transformed by the free spirits of New York, as so many have been, although not, it must be noted, Boris Yellnikoff. The New Yorker and the southerners have never met anyone remotely like one another, but the southerners are open to new experiences. More than that I cannot explain.

It might be complained that everything works out for everyone a little too neatly. So it does, because this is not a realistic story but a Moral Tale, like one of Eric Rohmer's. Allen seeks not psychological insight but the demonstration of how lives can be redeemed. To do this he uses Clarkson's innate exuberance and Begley's congenital probity to get them to where they're going. Once they are free to do so, Marietta indulges her feelings, and John reasons it out.

Larry David is the mind of the enterprise, and Evan Rachel Wood is the heart. David is a verbal virtuoso, playing the "Woody Allen role" but with his personal shtick. He'd be lonely if he couldn't confide in his invisible listeners. His opening monologue would be remarkable from any actor, let alone one without training or stage experience. Wood prevents the plot from descending into logic and reason with her character's blind faith that everything is for the better. *Whatever Works* charts a journey for Allen, one from the words of Groucho to the wisdom of Pascal, who informs us, as Allen once reminded us, that the heart has its reasons.

What Just Happened? ★ ★
R, 107 m., 2008

Robert De Niro (Ben), Catherine Keener (Lou Tarnow), Sean Penn (Sean Penn), John Turturro (Dick Bell), Robin Wright Penn (Kelly), Stanley Tucci (Scott Solomon), Kristen Stewart (Zoe), Michael Wincott (Jeremy Brunell), Bruce Willis (Actor). Directed by Barry Levinson and produced by Mark Cuban, Robert De Niro, Art Linson, and Jane Rosenthal. Screenplay by Linson, based on his book *What Just Happened: Bitter Hollywood Tales from the Front Line*.

Julia Phillips's famous autobiography was titled *You'll Never Eat Lunch in This Town Again*. Barry Levinson and Art Linson will. At this point, if you're going to make a film about Hollywood greed, hypocrisy, and lust, you have to be willing to burn your bridges. There's not a whole lot in *What Just Happened?* that would be out of place in a good *SNL* skit.

Linson is an A-list producer (*Fight Club, Into the Wild*) who wrote this screenplay based on his memoir, subtitled *Bitter Hollywood Tales from the Front Line*. He knows where the bodies are buried and who buried them, but he doesn't dig anybody up or turn anybody in. If you want to see a movie that Rips the Lid Off Tinseltown, just go ahead and watch Robert Altman's *The Player* (1992). Altman took no hostages. He didn't give a damn. And the book and screenplay he started with were by Michael Tolkin, who was closer to the front line and a lot more bitter. He didn't give a damn, either.

What Just Happened? stars Robert De Niro as a powerful Hollywood producer who has two troubled projects on his hands and a messy private life. De Niro warmed up for this film in *The Last Tycoon* (1976), in a role inspired by Irving Thalberg. That screenplay was by Harold Pinter, based on the novel by F. Scott Fitzgerald. Levinson himself directed the brilliant *Wag the Dog* (1998), where De Niro played a political spin doctor assigned to fabricate reasons for a war.

Mamet wrote that screenplay, which was astonishingly prescient. The movie, which premiered on December 17, 1997, gave us a U.S. president accused of luring a "Firefly Girl" into an room near the Oval Office and presenting her with unique opportunities to salute her commander in chief. The first hints of the Monica Lewinsky scandal became public in January 1998. For the White House methods used to invent reasons for a phony war, Mamet was six years ahead of Iraq.

So what am I saying? Should Mamet have written *What Just Happened?* Why not? For Mamet's *Heist*, produced by Linson, he gave Danny DeVito one of the funniest lines ever written: "Everybody loves money! That's why they call it money!" For that matter, *Variety*'s Todd McCarthy thinks some of the characters in this film are inspired by the making of Linson's *The Edge*, also written by Mamet. A pattern emerges. But everything I think of is luring me farther away from *What Just Happened?*

Anyway, Ben, the De Niro character, has just had a disastrous preview of his new Sean Penn picture, *Fiercely*. The audience recoils at the end, when a dog is shot. The problem with the footage of *Fiercely* we see is that it doesn't remotely look like a real movie. Meantime, Ben is trying to get his next project off the ground. It will star Bruce Willis as an action hero, but inconveniently Willis has put on a lot of weight and grown a beard worthy of the Smith Brothers.

Ben is still in love with Kelly, his ex-wife number two (Robin Wright Penn), but they just haven't been able to make it work and are now immersed in something I think is called Break-Up Therapy. And their daughter Zoe (Kristen Stewart) is having anguish of her own, which goes with the territory for a rich kid from a shattered home in 90210. And Lou Tarnow (Catherine Keener), Ben's studio chief, is scared to death that *Fiercely* will tank. And the film's mad-dog British director (Michael Wincott) defends the dog's death as artistically indispensable. And the writer of the Bruce Willis thriller (Stanley Tucci) is having an affair with Ben's ex-wife number two.

This isn't a Hollywood satire—it's a sitcom. The flywheels of the plot machine keep it churning around, but it chugs off onto the back lot and doesn't hit anybody in management. Only Penn and Willis are really funny, poking fun not at themselves but at stars they no doubt hate to work with. Wincott is great as the Brit director who wants to end with the dead dog; one wonders if Linson was inspired by Lee Tamahori, the fiery New Zealand director of *The Edge*, who stepped on the astonishing implications of Mamet's brilliant last scene by fading to black and immediately popping up a big credit for Bart the Bear.

What's the Matter with Kansas? ★★★ ½

NO MPAA RATING, 90 m., 2009

With Angel Dillard, Rob Dillard, Pastor Terry Fox, Donn Teske, Brittany Barden, Dawn

Barden, and others. A documentary directed by Joe Winston and produced by Winston and Laura Cohen. Inspired by the book by Thomas Frank.

As a liberal, I agree with about a third of the people in *What's the Matter with Kansas?* A conservative would probably agree with the others. What's interesting is that every single person in this film is seen as themselves, is allowed to speak, and seems to have a good heart. I've rarely seen a documentary quite like it. It has a point to make, but no ax to grind.

This is its point: Conservatives in the heartland have persuaded themselves to vote against their own economic and social well-being because they consider hot-button issues more important than their incomes, economic chances, educations, and the welfare of society at large. Their positions dovetail seamlessly with evangelical Christianity, and they accept hardship as the will of God when it seems more clearly to be the working of a top-loaded economy.

No one in the film says that. The film has no narration at all. It is a fascinating series of portraits of Kansans, all of them good people, shown without judgment. In a subtle way, the accumulation of these portraits adds up to this conclusion: They're doing themselves no favors by voting against their own interests and might hold onto their values while still voting more selectively.

The two most likable people in the film are a Christian mother and farmer named Angel Dillard, and a self-proclaimed populist farmer named Donn Teske, both struggling to keep their family farms afloat after two drought years.

Dillard has a story to win our sympathy. After a bad marriage in Los Angeles, she moved back home to Kansas and bought a small homestead. This she planned to farm by herself and probably never remarry ("I must have had one hundred first dates, but when the guys saw this place . . ."). But she did find the right man and has two pretty daughters, one named Reagan.

We see her manning a right-to-life booth at the state fair. She is a loyal follower of Pastor Terry Fox's six-thousand-member Immanuel Baptist Church in Wichita. When Fox is asked by the church deacons to resign because they were uncomfortable with his political sermons about abortion and homosexuality, his followers follow him to exiled services held in a theater at Wild West World, a new theme park.

Along with Fox and other church members, they ask God for guidance and invest their savings in the park. It goes bankrupt without ever thriving, and there are hints that it may have been a Ponzi scheme. But they accept their loss as God's will. At the end of the film, Angel is selling her CD of Christian music at a local event.

She never has the slightest doubt that God wants her to vote conservative. Although she is a fervent pro-lifer, she tells of a disastrous early pregnancy: After her prolonged labor, a doctor braces his foot and pulls out her son with forceps, crushing his skull; although the boy lives until twelve, he never sees, hears, speaks, or eats, and wears diapers.

It took a long time for the doctors to get a heartbeat, she says calmly. "They should have allowed him to die, but they were afraid of a lawsuit." Has it occurred to her to question the difference between allowing a brain-dead child to die and terminating a pregnancy in a similar case?

Donn Teske, head of the Kansas Farmers' Union, is a Wilford Brimley type, plainspoken, "a redneck," and says he was a Republican committeeman but resigned and now considers himself a populist independent. He is eloquent in testifying before Congress, and in Washington goes to visit the modest Franklin Roosevelt Memorial. It was Roosevelt's New Deal, he says, that created the first, and still the best, farm bill.

Another likable figure in the film is Brittany Barden, a bright teenage campaign worker for GOP candidates. Apparently home-schooled, she goes off to college at Patrick Henry University, a conservative Christian school in Virginia. Her mother explains, "Secular schools teach things like evolution." Brittany explains that our nation is Christian, the founding fathers were all Christian, and Christianity is established in the Declaration of Independence and the Constitution. Perhaps at Patrick Henry she will learn that all three of these beliefs are simply untrue.

Kansas at the start of the twentieth century was a staunchly left-wing state. The town of Girard was the home of the socialist *Appeal to Reason*, then the newspaper with the largest circulation in America. Teske goes to visit the Populist Cemetery and speaks of the state's populist roots.

What's the Matter with Kansas? doesn't connect the dots, nor does it need to. It takes no cheap shots. It is all there to see. These good people are voting against themselves. The current hysteria about health care reform is another example. Meanwhile, we see a state that is draining population, with empty sidewalks and vacant parking spaces, boarded storefronts and foreclosures, and a certainty that all is God's will. A billboard outside one town simply says: "Pray for the Election."

When Did You Last See Your Father? ★ ★ ★
PG-13, 92 m., 2008

Colin Firth (Blake Morrison), Jim Broadbent (Arthur Morrison), Juliet Stevenson (Kim Morrison), Gina McKee (Kathy Morrison), Elaine Cassidy (Sandra), Claire Skinner (Gillian), Matthew Beard (Blake, Teenager), Sarah Lancashire (Auntie Beaty). Directed by Anand Tucker and produced by Elizabeth Karlsen and Stephen Woolley. Screenplay by David Nicholls, based on the memoir by Blake Morrison.

"It's stupid, really," Blake Morrison tells his wife. "You spend a lifetime trying to avoid talking to someone, and then all of a sudden it's too late." He has returned to the Yorkshire town where he was born, and where his father is dying. Surely, his wife says, this is the right time? "He's too doped up."

When Did You Last See Your Father? is based on a 1990s best-seller by Morrison, who redefines the question as, "When did you last *really* see him?" He arrives at an answer for himself, but we're left realizing that he never did really see his father. He was too blinded by anger, and it is only after his death that he forgives him and sees him as a *father*, and not as the focus of resentment.

His father is Arthur (Jim Broadbent), who shares a practice with his wife, Kim (Juliet Stevenson), also a doctor. The son is played by Colin Firth, and it is startling in some scenes how much the two men resemble each other. In an opening where Arthur talks their way into reserved seats at a speedway, Blake tells us his father was a charmer who could talk his way into or out of anything.

The old man does it by bluster, expansive cheerfulness, and bluff. There's a lot of ground to cover. Blake correctly suspects that Arthur is having an affair with his Auntie Beaty (Sarah Lancashire), and even in later years Arthur is able to out-charm his son in the pursuit of a woman they both covet. Blake hated his father for treating his mother so badly, although there are few scenes showing son and mother as particularly close. The person he does confide in is his first love, the family's maid, Sandra (Elaine Cassidy).

The film moves from the 1950s, when Blake is played by Bradley Johnson, to the 1960s, when he's played as a teenager by Matthew Beard. It's episodic, remembering a time when father and son went camping and found that a stream had overflowed into their tent, and a time when Arthur taught Blake how to drive. They make big circles on a deserted beach in the family's elegant Alvis convertible, and the scene ends with smiles on both men's faces.

We see lots of pairs of faces, but they're rarely smiling. The director, Anand Tucker (*Hilary and Jackie*), uses mirrors repeatedly throughout the movie, perhaps as a way of suggesting there's more than one way to see something or someone. The Arthur we see at least has more vitality than his son and wife, who grow increasingly glum. Poor Blake has his own libidinous feelings constantly interrupted by his father, whom he refers to as the "sex police." Why should his dad get away with everything and he with nothing?

It's a sad movie, with a mournful score, romantic landscape photography, and heartbreaking deathbed scenes (his mother weeps while changing the sheets). But it's not very satisfying. Blake and Arthur never really did talk man-to-man, and Arthur had a strange way of showing affection to "Fathead," as in a scene where he embarrasses his son by switching his drink at a party. "April Fool's!" he chortles, and his laugh grows so harsh it seems to be echoing in memory.

The real Blake Morrison was the literary

editor of the *Observer*. Among his resentments were that his father did not respect the literary life and considered it a waste of time and money to study literature at university. His father "never read a single book all the way through," he says. He's been reading *Death on the Nile* for the last forty-two years. That has the sound of an epitaph long rehearsed.

If there is a genre for this sort of film, surely it demands a reconciliation, a moment of truth-telling, an expression of long-delayed love. Although Blake is told by Auntie Beaty that his father worshipped his family, Arthur never says it, and Blake never asks. He has questions still unvoiced near the end of the film, and the way they are finally answered for him is, in a way, perfectly appropriate.

The film did not provide me with fulfillment or a catharsis. Apparently the memoir wouldn't have, either. That's fair enough. How many unanswered questions are we all left with? I have some. This is a film of regret, and judging by what we see of the characters, it deserves to be.

Where the Wild Things Are ★★★
PG, 110 m., 2009

Max Records (Max), Pepita Emmerichs (Claire), Catherine Keener (Mom), Steve Mouzakis (Teacher), Mark Ruffalo (Boyfriend). And the voices of James Gandolfini (Carol), Paul Dano (Alexander), Catherine O'Hara (Judith), Forest Whitaker (Ira), Michael Berry Jr. (The Bull), Chris Cooper (Douglas), Lauren Ambrose (KW). Directed by Spike Jonze and produced by John B. Carls, Gary Goetzman, Tom Hanks, Vincent Landay, and Maurice Sendak. Screenplay by Jonze and Dave Eggers, inspired by the book and illustrations by Sendak.

Where the Wild Things Are reflects so much of a plucky little kid: the flaring up of anger at a parent, the defiant escape into fantasy, the tough talk in a tight situation, the exuberance, and then the fundamental need to return home and be loved and reassured. All of these stages are explored in Maurice Sendak's famous 1963 children's book, which contains only nine sentences. Ah, but what sentences they are when given resonance by his drawings.

Spike Jonze and Dave Eggers have met the challenge of this little masterpiece head-on, by including both a real little boy and the imaginary Wild Things in the same film. It would simply not have done to alter or shrink the monstrous Things, and with an $80 million budget, Jonze has been able to make a movie where any reader of the book should be able to recognize all of the Things in sight.

The creatures in the film are voiced by actors, and given a *great* deal more to say, of course, than in the book. The Things are a considerable technical achievement, combining as they do muppetry and CGI. I don't find them particularly lovely, nor should I; they're not fuzzy toys, but characters in a dream that slides in and out of nightmares.

Max Records, of *The Brothers Bloom*, plays the difficult role of Max, the boy who gets into a stubborn argument with his mom (Catherine Keener) and flees to his room and then to his imagination. In the book, his room transforms itself into a jungle, but the film has him sailing a stormy sea in a little boat that looks like a bathtub toy. It arrives at an island that the Wild Things inhabit in grouchy discontent, and Max finds himself moved to bring the discord under control. Why these creatures, who tower over him, should even consider accepting his leadership is a no-brainer: This is Max's dream.

The plot is simple stuff, spread fairly thin in terms of events but portentous in terms of meaning. It comes down to a question that children often seek answers to: What is right? One of the film's strengths is the way it doesn't soft-pedal sticky situations. For example, Max's mom has a boyfriend (Mark Ruffalo), who isn't painted as an interloper, and affection between the two of them is calmly regarded by Max (whether deeper issues involving his disappeared father are involved in his anger is a good question).

The voice actors and the f/x artists give their fantastical characters personality. When I mention special effects, I don't want to give the impression that the Wild Things are all smoke and mirrors. In close-up they seem tangibly there, and at times I believe human actors are inside costumes. I used to be able to spot this stuff, but f/x have gotten so good that sometimes you just don't know.

601

The voices belong to Catherine O'Hara as the know-it-all Judith, James Gandolfini as the authoritative boss Thing, Lauren Ambrose as KW, Chris Cooper as Douglas, Forest Whitaker as the pleasant and meek Ira, and Paul Dano as Alexander, who is only a few feet taller than Max. Each of these creatures is one of a kind, leaving open the question of how, and with whom, they reproduce their species.

The movie felt long to me, and there were some stretches during which I was less than riveted. Is it possible there wasn't enough Sendak story to justify a feature-length film? In a way I suppose the book tells a feature-length story just in Sendak's drawings, and Jonze and Eggers have taken those for their inspiration. All the same, I suspect the film will play better for older audiences remembering a much-loved book from childhood, and not as well with kids who have been trained on slam-bam action animation.

Whip It ★★★ ½
PG-13, 111 m., 2009

Ellen Page (Bliss Cavendar), Marcia Gay Harden (Brooke Cavendar), Kristen Wiig (Maggie Mayhem), Drew Barrymore (Smashley Simpson), Juliette Lewis (Iron Maven), Jimmy Fallon (Johnny), Daniel Stern (Earl Cavendar), Alia Shawkat (Pash), Landon Pigg (Oliver), Andrew Wilson (Coach Razor), Zoe Bell (Bloody Holly), Eve (Rosa Sparks), Ari Graynor (Eva Destruction). Directed by Drew Barrymore and produced by Barry Mendel. Screenplay by Shauna Cross, based on her novel *Derby Girl*.

Whip It is an unreasonably entertaining movie, causing you perhaps to revise your notions about women's roller derby, assuming you have any. The movie is a coming-together of two free spirits, Drew Barrymore and Ellen Page, and while it may not reflect the kind of female empowerment Gloria Steinem had in mind, it has guts, charm, and a black-and-blue sweetness. Yes, it faithfully follows the age-old structure of the sports movie, but what a sport, and how much the derby girls love it.

Page plays Bliss Cavendar, a small-town Texas girl who shares the rebelliousness of Juno but not the stream-of-consciousness verbal pyrotechnics. She's being coached by

her smothering mother (Marcia Gay Harden) to compete in a Miss Bluebonnet beauty pageant that squeezes Texas girls into a ghastly caricature of Southern womanhood. Bliss despises it. One day she sees an ad for roller derby in Austin, the nearest town of consequence, and with a friend sneaks off to see a game. She is electrified. She was born to be a derby girl.

She begins a series of secret bus trips to Austin that last for an entire season—much too long for her parents not to notice, but never mind. She auditions in her pink Barbie clamp-ons for the Hurl Scouts team. Lying about her age, against all odds she's allowed by the coach, known as Razor (Andrew Wilson), to give it a try. The team veterans are dubious, but she has pluck and speed and doesn't mind getting knocked around. It's worth noting that Page and the other actresses, some of them real derby stars, do almost all their own skating.

She takes the name Babe Ruthless. Other competitors are known as Maggie Mayhem (Kristen Wiig), Smashley Simpson (Barrymore herself), Bloody Holly (Zoe Bell), Rosa Sparks (Eve), and Eva Destruction (Ari Graynor). Juliette Lewis is fiercely competitive as the leader of another team, Iron Maven. Such stage names, or track names, are common in roller derby, and one real-life derby girl is known as Sandra Day O'Clobber.

The screenplay is by a Los Angeles Derby Dolls star named Shauna Cross, the original Maggie Mayhem, based on her novel *Derby Girl*. It neatly balances Bliss's derby career and her situation at home, where her dad (Daniel Stern) turns to pro sports on TV to escape his insufferable wife. Well, OK, she's not insufferable, simply an extreme type of stage mother whose values, as her daughter informs her, are based on a 1950s idea of womanhood. Probably her poor mom was dominated by her own overbearing mother.

Bliss is at a hormonal age when she really likes cute boys and is drawn to a young rock band member named Oliver (Landon Pigg). She experiences this relationship in admirable PG-13 terms, and during her season with the Hurl Scouts learns much about her physical and personality strengths. Odd as it may seem, her roller derby experience is a coming-of-age process.

Ellen Page, still only twenty-two, is the real thing. To see her in this, *Juno,* and *Hard Candy* (2005) is to realize she's fearless, completely in command of her gifts, and will be around for a long time. To learn that she will play the lead in a BBC Films production of *Jane Eyre,* being produced by Alison Owen (*Elizabeth*) seems only natural.

Yes, the movie has clichés. Yes, it all leads up to a big game. Yes, there is a character's validating appearance near the end. Yes, and so what? The movie is miles more intelligent than most of the cream of wheat marketed to teenage girls. Funnier, more exciting, even liberating. Barrymore, in her debut as a director, shows she must have been paying attention ever since Spielberg cast her when she was five. She and her team do an especially effective job in staging the derby showdowns.

There *are* rules to roller derby, but the movie doesn't linger over the details. Basically, you go around as fast as you can, try to stay on your feet, protect your teammates, and clobber your opponents. In the last decade, the optional form of the sport has morphed into a sort of gothic-punk-warrior woman hybrid, with much invention going into the outrageous costumes. Which doesn't mean you don't get hurt when you're slammed.

Note: See my review of Unholy Rollers *(1973) and the great documentary* Derby *(1972) at www.rogerebert.com.*

The White Ribbon ★★★★
R, 145 m., 2010

Ulrich Tukur (Baron), Susanne Lothar (Midwife), Christian Friedel (Schoolteacher), Burghart Klaussner (Pastor), Leonie Benesch (Eva), Josef Bierbichler (Steward), Rainer Bock (Doctor), Ernst Jacobi (Narrator). Directed by Michael Haneke and produced by Stefan Arndt, Veit Heiduschka, Michael Katz, Margaret Menegoz, and Andrea Occhipinti. Screenplay by Haneke.

Something is wrong in the village. Some malevolent force, some rot in the foundation. This wrongness is first sensed in a series of incidental "accidents." Then the murder of a child takes place. This forces the villagers, who all know one another, to look around more carefully. Is one of them guilty? How can that be? One person couldn't be responsible for all of these disturbing events. Have many been seized in an evil contagion?

After the first screening of Michael Haneke's *The White Ribbon* at Cannes, everybody had theories about who "did it." Well, we're trained to see such stories as whodunits. Haneke is never that simple. It all may have been "done," but what if there seems to be no doer? What if bad things happen to good people who are not as good as they think they are? In Haneke's *Caché* (2005), who shot the alarming videos spying on the family? Are you sure? Haneke's feeling is that we can never be sure.

This great film is set in rural Germany in the years before World War I. All has been stable in this village for generations. The baron owns the land. The farmer, the pastor, the doctor, the schoolteacher, the servants, even the children, play their assigned roles. It is a patriarchal, authoritarian society—in other words, the sort of society that seemed ordinary at that time throughout the world.

We are told the story many years after it took place by the schoolteacher (Ernst Jacobi). In the film, we see him young (Christian Friedel). The old man intends to narrate with objectivity and precision. He'll draw no conclusions. He doesn't have the answers. He'll stick to the facts. The first fact is this: While out riding one morning, the doctor was injured when his horse stumbled because of a trip wire. Someone put the wire there. Could they have even known the doctor (Rainer Bock) would be their victim?

Other incidents occur. A barn is burned. A child is found murdered. Someone did each of these things. The same person could not easily have done all of them. There is information about where various people were at various times. It's like an invitation to play Sherlock Holmes and deduce the criminal. But in *The White Ribbon* there are no barking hounds. The clues don't match. Who is to even say something is a clue? It may simply be a fact seen in the light of suspicion.

Life continues in an orderly fashion, as if a gyroscope tilts and then rights itself. The baron steadies his people. The doctor resumes his practice, but is unaccountably cruel toward his mistress. The teacher teaches and the students study, and they sing in the choir. Church services are attended. The white ribbon is worn by children who have been bad but will now try to be good. The crops are harvested. The teacher courts the comely village girl Eva (Leonie Benesch). And suspicion spreads.

I wonder if it's mostly a Western feeling that misfortune is intolerable and, to every degree possible, death must be prevented. I don't hear of such feelings from Asia or Africa. There is more resignation when terrible things happen. Yes, a man must not harm another. He should be punished. But after he causes harm, they don't think it possible to prevent any other man from ever doing the same thing.

In this German town there is a need to solve the puzzle. Random wicked acts create disorder and erode the people's faith that life makes sense. The suspicion that the known facts cannot be made to add up is as disturbing as if the earth gave way beneath our feet.

Haneke has a way of making the puzzle more interesting than its solution. If you saw *Caché*, you'll remember how, after a certain point, a simple shot by an unmoving camera became disturbing even when nothing happened. It wasn't about what we were seeing. It was about the fact that someone was looking, and we didn't know why.

It's too simple to say the film is about the origin of Nazism. If that were so, we would all be Nazis. It is possible to say that when the prevention of evil becomes more important than the preservation of freedom, authoritarianism grows. If we are to prevent evil, someone must be in charge. The job naturally goes to those concerned with enforcing order. Therefore, all disorder is evil and must be prevented, and that's how the interests of the state become more important than the interests of the people.

I wonder if Haneke's point is that we grow so disturbed by danger that we will surrender freedom—even demand to. Do we feel more secure in an orderly state? Many do. Then a tipping point arrives, and the Berlin Wall falls, or we see the Green Revolution in Iran. The problem, as philosophers have noted, is that revolutionaries grow obsessed with enforcing their revolution, and the whole process begins over.

Haneke's genius is to embed these possibilities in films rooted in the daily lives of ordinary people. He denies us the simple solutions of most films, in which everything is settled by the violent victory of our side. His films are like parables, teaching that bad things sometimes happen simply because . . . they happen. The universe laughs at man's laws and does what it will.

The film is visually masterful. It's in black and white, of course. Color would be fatal to its power. Perhaps because b&w film is hard to find, Haneke filmed in color and drained it away. If a color version is ever released, you'll see why it's wrong. Just as it is, *The White Ribbon* tells a simple story in a small village about little people and suggests that we must find a balance between fear and security.

Who Do You Love? ★★ ½
NO MPAA RATING, 90 m., 2010

Alessandro Nivola (Leonard Chess), Jon Abrahams (Phil Chess), David Oyelowo (Muddy Waters), Chi McBride (Willie Dixon), Megalyn Echikunwoke (Ivy Mills), Marika Dominczyk (Revetta Chess), Keb' Mo (Jimmy Rogers), Robert Randolph (Bo Diddley). Directed by Jerry Zaks and produced by Les Alexander, Andrea Baynes, and Jonathan Mitchell. Screenplay by Peter Wortmann and Bob Conte.

The original studios of Chess Records on South Michigan in Chicago are as important to the development of rock 'n' roll as the Sun Records studios in Memphis. You could make a good case, in fact, that without Chess there might have been no Sun, and without Muddy Waters, Willie Dixon, Bo Diddley, and Chuck Berry, there might have been no Elvis Presley, Jerry Lee Lewis, or Carl Perkins. Rock 'n' roll flowed directly, sometimes almost note by note, from rhythm and blues.

Who Do You Love? is the second, and lesser, recent film about the brothers Chess, Leonard and Phil, and the label they founded. It tells the same improbable story of how two Jewish immigrant kids from Poland sold the family junkyard to start a music club on the black South Side, and helped launch the musical styles that have influenced everything since.

Both films are, of course, filled with music.

The Chess catalog must have collected some nice royalties. The basic outlines of the films are roughly the same, although *Cadillac Records* (2008) didn't include Phil, the younger and quieter brother. Leonard (Alessandro Nivola) is hopelessly infatuated with black music, Phil (Jon Abrahams) more interested in the business.

It remains a little unclear exactly what Leonard feels about black people. Yes, he supports their rights. But he underpays them. He was fond of Etta James, called Ivy Mills here and played by Megalyn Echikunwoke. Her drug addiction is greatly fictionalized (she is still very much alive, for one thing) and her great hit "At Last" is shifted in time; the equivalent character in *Cadillac Records* is more moving. Leonard historically decided to back her with violins and a full orchestra.

In this movie's telling, Willie Dixon (Chi McBride, very good) was Leonard's scout in finding the best of a new generation of R&B artists. It's Dixon who introduces Chess to Muddy Waters (David Oyelowo) and lends him a guitar for his audition. But Leonard had a good ear and proved it with the stable he built.

He loved the music. In a no doubt exaggerated scene, his family is all packed up in the car and ready to leave on vacation when he explains he has to go on tour with Muddy instead. His wife, Revetta (Marika Dominczyk), is part long-suffering, part perhaps not fully aware from their suburban home of what's going on in the city.

The Chess Records story is part of modern folklore, and both films treat it too much that way: as a well-rehearsed saga. I think more edge is needed, more reality about the racial situation at the time, more insight into how and why R&B and R&R actually did forever transform societies in America and the world. Who had more to do with bringing down the Berlin Wall? Ronald Reagan or Muddy Waters?

Winter's Bone ★★★★

R, 99 m., 2010

Jennifer Lawrence (Ree Dolly), John Hawkes (Teardrop), Kevin Breznahan (Little Arthur), Dale Dickey (Merab), Lauren Sweetser (Gail), Tate Taylor (Mike Satterfield), Garret Dillahunt (Sheriff Baskin), Sheryl Lee (April), Shelley Waggener (Sonya). Directed by Debra Granik and produced by Alix Madigan and Anne Rosellini. Screenplay by Granik and Rosellini, based on the novel by Daniel Woodrell.

The movie heroes who affect me most are not extroverted. They don't strut, speechify, and lead armies. They have no superpowers. They are ordinary people who are faced with a need and rise to the occasion. Ree Dolly is such a hero.

She is a girl of seventeen who acts as the homemaker for her younger brother and sister. This is in the backlands of the Ozarks. Her mother sits useless all day, mentally absent. Her father, who was jailed for cooking meth, is missing. She tries to raise the kids and feed them, scraping along on welfare and the kindness of neighbors. The children, like all children who are not beaten, are cheerful and energetic and love to play. They have not learned they are disadvantaged.

This world is established with bleak economy in the opening scenes of Debra Granik's *Winter's Bone*, which was a double prize winner at Sundance 2010. Unmistakably filmed on location, this is a society that has been left behind. It looks like Walker Evans's photographs of the rural Depression, brought forward to today. The unanswered question is how Ree Dolly grew up in this world and became strong, self-reliant, and proud. She didn't learn it from her parents.

The sheriff comes to call. Her father, Jessup, has skipped bail. To meet his bond, he put up the house—perhaps the only asset he had. If he doesn't turn himself in within a week, the family will be thrown out. Just like that. "I'll find him," Ree says quietly and firmly. And that's what she sets out to do.

Ree is played by Jennifer Lawrence, a nineteen-year-old newcomer who has already made Jodie Foster's new film. She embodies a fierce, still center that is the source of her heroism. She makes no boasts, issues no threats, depends on a dogged faith that people will do the right thing—even when no one we meet seems to deserve that faith. "Don't ask for what's not offered," she tells her little brother, although the lives of her parents seem to be an exercise in asking and not offering. Did she raise herself?

Everyone in the district knew that Jessup cooked methamphetamine. He is a modern moonshiner. What is obvious is that meth doesn't seem to have made him much money. Perhaps its illegality is its appeal, and its market is among people he feels comfortable with. Ree's travels in search of her father lead her to his brother, Teardrop (John Hawkes), whose existence inflicts a wound on the gift of being alive.

The screenplay, by Granik and Anne Rosellini, based on the novel by Daniel Woodrell, uses the ancient form of an odyssey. At its end will be Ree's father, dead or alive. Most likely dead, she begins to conclude, but unless there is a body her family will be homeless and torn apart. She treks through a landscape scarcely less ruined than the one in Cormac McCarthy's *The Road*. This land seems post-catastrophe. Although it has cars and electricity, running shoes and kitchens, cigarettes and televisions, these seem like relics of an earlier, prosperous time. If thrown-away possessions pile up around the houses of people, it is because they've reached the end of the line. There is no next stop.

There is a hazard of caricature here. Granik avoids it. Her film doesn't live above these people but among them. Ree herself has lived as one of them and doesn't see them as inferior, only ungiving and disappointing. In her father's world everyone is a criminal, depends on a criminal, or sells to criminals. That they are illegal makes them vulnerable to informers and plea-bargainers, so they are understandably suspicious. The cliché would be that they suspect outsiders. These characters suspect insiders, even family members.

As Ree's journey takes her to one character after another, Granik is able to focus on each one's humanity, usually damaged. They aren't attractions in a sideshow but survivors in a shared reality. Do they look at Ree and see a girl in need and a family threatened with eviction? I think they see the danger of their own need and eviction; it's safer to keep quiet and close off.

So the film rests on Ree, counterbalanced by Teardrop, who is aggressive with his hatefulness instead of passive in amorality. A story like this could become mired in despair, but Ree's hope and courage lock us in. How did she get to be the way she is? We are born optimistic, although life can be a great discouragement. In every bad situation, there are usually a few good people. ☞

The Witnesses ★ ★ ★
NO MPAA RATING, 112 m., 2008

Johan Libereau (Manu), Michel Blanc (Adrien), Emmanuelle Beart (Sarah), Sami Bouajila (Mehdi), Julie Depardieu (Julie). Directed by André Téchiné and produced by Said Ben Said. Screenplay by Techine, Laurent Guyot, and Viviane Zingg.

Michel Blanc is that middle-aged French actor with the round bald head and (often enough) round eyeglasses who has played dozens of engaging roles, most notably in Patrice Leconte's masterpiece *Monsieur Hire*. In Andre Techine's *The Witnesses*, he plays Adrien, a doctor, one of an ensemble of five major characters. They are more or less balanced in importance and screen time, but somehow he draws our attention to himself. He doesn't "steal" scenes; what he does simply seems more urgent, more passionate, more driven.

Early in the film, we see him cruising a Paris late-night rendezvous for gays, picking up a young guy and then stalking away from him in anger when he's asked how old he is. The younger man goes into the shrubbery in search of another partner, but first asks Adrien to hold his coat because he's afraid of it being stolen. "I might steal it myself," Adrien says. "I'd be very surprised," says Manu (Johan Libereau). His instinctive trust generates a connection between the two men, but it doesn't blossom into a sexual coupling. It becomes a friendship that will be greatly tested by the end of the story.

The movie begins in 1984 and has sections set in the following year. This is the time that AIDS begins to be recognized in France, and having sex with strangers in the park will soon lack the illusion of safety. Manu is not sexually interested in Adrien anyway, although Adrien is desperately in love with him. Yet Blanc never turns Adrien's love into something needy and pathetic; he shows Manu around Paris, he confides in him, he glows in his company, they grow close as friends.

Manu lives with his sister, Julie (Julie Depardieu), an aspiring opera singer who has no interest in much of anything beyond her work. We also meet Adrien's friend Sarah (Emmanuelle Beart), a wealthy author of children's books, and her husband, Mehdi (Sami Bouajila), who is a policeman and head of a vice squad that targets prostitution. They've just had a baby; Sarah learns through the experience that, despite her books, she does not like children. Her husband despairs when she neglects the child, does what he can to fill in, and sometimes parks the child with his parents.

Now all the pieces are in place for a momentous weekend when Sarah and Mehdi invite Adrien and Manu to her mother's house at the seaside. The two younger men go swimming in the sea, Manu finds himself in trouble, and he nearly drowns. The policeman saves his life, and in pulling him to shore finds to his surprise that he has an erection. The two men, one of whom has never thought of himself as gay, plunge into a physical relationship that becomes all-consuming.

That Mehdi is being unfaithful to Sarah (whether with a man or a woman) is of little concern to her; they have an "open" marriage, which in her case seems to translate into not caring what anyone else does as long as they leave her alone to write her books. One day Adrien sees telltale lesions on Manu's chest and diagnoses him as a victim of the mysterious new disease he has started to see in his practice. Now consider the ramifications of this infection for all five characters, and you have the driving structure of the story.

I will not reveal details. I would rather focus on the Michel Blanc performance. His Adrien is not a perfect man or a noble doctor, but he is a good man who has the courage to do good, although difficult, things. He has been deeply wounded by Manu's "abandoning" him for Mehdi, and is outraged that Mehdi cheated on his wife with, of all people, the man Mehdi knows the doctor loves. Adrien is even the godfather of the child. This outrage leads to a scuffle that is brief, confusing, violent, and without a "winner," revealing how hurt Adrien really is, and how near his emotional wounds are to the surface of his bland exterior.

Adrien becomes a leader in a gay doctors' crusade against AIDS, meanwhile privately taking on Manu's treatment. Mehdi also doesn't shun his friend when he hears the news, although he is terrified that he has AIDS and cannot bring himself to tell his wife. All of this captures the dread and paranoia of the early AIDS years; none of the characters has the benefit of foresight, and even a kiss or a drink from the same water bottle appears as a possible danger.

Techine tells the story with comic intensity for the first hour, and then aching drama. The possibility of having a disease of this sort, especially when you are married, allegedly straight, and even an anti-gay enforcer for the cops, creates secrecy and shame, and can lead to much worse than simply facing the truth. And it is that pain of the double life that concerns Techine in his later scenes.

Johan Libereau, as Manu, does a completely convincing transformation from an effortless young charmer to a dying man; he wasn't meant to die young like this, he despairingly tells Adrien; in fights at school, he didn't even bruise. Beart is mysterious as a remote, cold woman who likes physical sex but not much else apart from her writing. The cop is deeper and more sensitive than the situation might suggest; when he does the laundry for Manu, it is uncommonly touching, especially when the film notices how staring at an automatic washer can become a form of meditation.

But it is, again, Blanc who fascinates. His face, so often used for comedy or parody, here reflects intelligence, concern, and quiet sadness. His love is real enough, but to no purpose. His attempts to replace Manu are depressing even to himself. *The Witnesses* doesn't pay off with a great, operatic pinnacle, but it's better that way. Better to show people we care about facing facts they care desperately about, without the consolation of plot mechanics.

The Wolfman ★★ ½
R, 102 m., 2010

Benicio Del Toro (Lawrence Talbot), Emily Blunt (Gwen Conliffe), Anthony Hopkins (Sir John Talbot), Geraldine Chaplin (Maleva), Hugo Weaving (Inspector Aberline), Antony Sher (Dr. Hoenneger), Gemma Whelan (Gwen's Maid), David Schofield (Constable Nye), Roger Frost

(Reverend Fisk), Clive Russell (MacQueen), Art Malik (Singh). Directed by Joe Johnston and produced by Sean Daniel, Benicio Del Toro, Scott Stuber, and Rick Yorn. Screenplay by Andrew Kevin Walker and David Self.

The Wolfman avoids what must have been the temptation to update its famous story. It plants itself securely in period, with a great-looking production set in 1891. Gothic horror stories seem more digestible when set in once-great British country houses and peopled with gloomy inverts, especially when the countryside involves foggy moorlands and a craggy waterfall. This is, after all, a story set before the advent of modern psychology, back when a man's fate could be sealed by ancestral depravity.

The film's opening and closing shots are of the full moon, which is correct. An early exterior shows Chatsworth in Derbyshire, perhaps the grandest of all English country houses, as a Gothic shriek. Inside it is derelict and unkempt, inhabited by the sinister old Sir John Talbot (Anthony Hopkins) and his faithful manservant Singh (Art Malik). Gas was well-known as a means of illumination in 1891, and indeed electric lights were not uncommon, but Sir John makes do with flickering candles carried from room to room, the better to cast wicked shadows.

Sir John's son Ben and his fiancée, Gwen (Emily Blunt), were living there until recently, when Ben was savagely killed. Gwen writes to his brother Lawrence (Benicio Del Toro), an actor who is appearing in London in *Hamlet* and indeed is holding poor Yorick's skull when we first see him. Lawrence arrives in a foggy, chilly dusk, of course, and his voice echoes in the vast lonely mansion before his father emerges from the shadows.

I love stuff like this. The gloomier and more ominous the better. There is a silent classic named *The Fall of the House of Usher* that actually has dead leaves scuttling across a mansion's floor. Lawrence views his brother's body, which seems to have made a good meal, and then it's off to the obligatory local pub, where the conversations of the locals center on a strange beast marauding in the district. In the nineteenth century, a pub was the evening news.

More plot you do not require. What you might like to know is that *The Wolfman* has been made with care by Joe Johnston, and is well-photographed by Shelly Johnson and designed by Rick Heinrichs. The music by Danny Elfman creeps around the edges. Del Toro makes Lawrence sad, worried, fearful, doomy. It's not just the loss of his brother. It's the earlier loss of his beloved mother. The family manse is haunted by his memories. His father Sir John, however, is played by the bearded Anthony Hopkins as a man holding up perhaps better than you might expect. And he's well turned-out, for a man who lives almost in the dark.

The film has one flaw, and faithful readers will not be surprised to find it involves the special effects by CGI. No doubt there are whole scenes done so well in CGI I didn't even spot them; but when the wolf-creature bounds through the forest, he does so with too much speed. He'd be more convincing if he moved like a creature of considerable weight. In the first Spider-Man movie, you recall, Spidey swung around almost weightlessly. Adding weight and slowing him in the second film was one of the things that made it great. The wolfman moves so lightly here he almost cries out: Look! I'm animated!

I am not sure of the natural history of wolfmen. Is the condition passed through the blood? Apparently. How exactly does one morph from a man into a wolf? By special effects, obviously. The wolfman has much less pseudo-scientific documentation than the vampire. I understand why he sheds his clothes when he expands into a muscular predator. What I don't understand is how he always succeeds in redressing himself in the same clothes. Does he retrace his path back through the dark woods by moonlight, picking up after himself?

In any event, *The Wolfman* makes a satisfactory date movie for Valentine's Day, which is more than can be said for *Valentine's Day*. Truer love hath no woman, than the woman who loves a wolfman. And vice versa, ideally.

A Woman in Berlin ★★★
NO MPAA RATING, 131 m., 2009

Nina Hoss (Anonyma), Yevgeni Sidikhin (Andrei), Roman Gribkov (Lieutenant), Irm Hermann (Widow), Rudiger Vogler (Eckhart),

Ulrike Krumbiegel (Ilse). Directed by Max Faerberboeck, and produced by Gunter Rohrbach. Screenplay by Faeberboeck, based on the diary *Anonyma: A Woman in Berlin.*

In the final weeks of World War II, the conquering Russian army occupied a Berlin in ruins and did what occupying armies often do, raped and pillaged. There was nothing to stop them—least of all their officers, who knew that after years of relentless battle it was useless to try to enforce discipline, even had they wanted to.

A Woman in Berlin is a diary written at that time and published some fifteen years later. Its author, who identifies herself as a journalist, was anonymous. The book's publication in 1959 inspired outrage in Germany, where the idea of German women cooperating somewhat with the Russians was unthinkable, and in Russia, where it soiled the honor of the Red Army.

In that time, in that place, women were raped. "How many times?" asks one of another, and they both know the subject of the question. The diary and film are about how the author attempted to control the terms of her defilement by deliberately seeking out a high-ranking Russian who would act as her protector. Who is to say this was wrong of her?

The woman, Anonyma, is played by Nina Hoss, who in two other films released here in the past year, *Yella* and *Jerichow,* has emerged as a strong, confident new actress with innate star quality. She is seen here in an early shot at a party, elegantly dressed, ruling the room, a proud Nazi, proposing a toast to the brave boys at the front. At the time it appeared Germany would conquer Europe.

By the end of the war, her husband has disappeared in battle and she is camped out with other women in the remnants of a bombed-out building. They are exhausted, dirty, hungry, frightened. They were all raised in the comfortable middle class, and now find themselves scrabbling like animals for food and shelter. The obvious sources of food, and drink, are the Russians. Most of them are crude, even bestial, but then the women cannot be choosers.

Anonyma has luck seducing a lieutenant and then sets her sights on a major, Andrei (Yevgeni Sidikhin), who is the top-ranking officer in sight. He's also by far the most complex. He resists her come-on at first, perhaps because he's fastidious, more likely because he simply doesn't see himself as that kind of man. Something unspoken passes between them. They grow closer. Yes, she profits from their liaison, and yes, he eventually takes up her offer. But for each there is the illusion that this is something they choose to do.

What little I know about war suggests that sometimes it comes down to a choice between two dismaying courses of action. Some people would rather die than lose their honor. Most people would rather not die, particularly if their deaths would change nothing. Anonyma and Andrei are people with similar sensibilities, similar feelings, now divested of the illusions they presumably brought with them into the war.

That is the movie's insight, and the book's, too, I assume. This isn't a love story in any palpable sense. It is a story about how things were. *A Woman in Berlin* finds no particular point in the story, and no one is heroic in any sense. The woman and man make the best accommodation they can with the reality that confronts them. There are several subplots involving other women and other soldiers, and one involves a woman who is subtly pleased by the power her body gives her. Well, she's not the first such woman, or man.

The film is well acted, with restraint, by Hoss and Sidikhin. The writer and director, Max Faerberboeck, employs a level gaze and avoids for the most part artificial sentimentality. The physical production is convincing. The movie is just enough too long that we realize we've already seen everything it has to observe.

The Women ★ ★ ★
PG-13, 114 m., 2008

Meg Ryan (Mary Haines), Annette Bening (Sylvie Fowler), Eva Mendes (Crystal Allen), Debra Messing (Edie Cohen), Jada Pinkett Smith (Alex Fisher), Carrie Fisher (Bailey Smith), Cloris Leachman (Maggie), Debi Mazar (Tanya), Bette Midler (Leah Miller), Candice Bergen (Catherine Frazier), India Ennenga (Molly Haines). Directed by Diane English and produced by English, Victoria Pearman, Mick Jagger, and Bill Johnson. Screenplay by English, based on the play by Clare Booth Luce.

What a pleasure this movie is, showcasing actresses I've admired for a long time, all at the top of their form. Yes, they're older now, as are we all, but they look great and know what they're doing. *The Women* is not, as it claims, "based on the play by Clare Booth Luce." The credits should read "inspired by." Nor does it draw from the screenplay of the 1939 film, although it also has no males on the screen.

The film revolves around four close friends, one married with four kids, one married with one kid but being cheated on, one a high-profile professional woman, one a lesbian. Sound a little familiar? But these woman are wiser, funnier, and more articulate than the *SATC* team, and their lives are not as shallow. Maybe it helps that there aren't a lot of men hanging around and chewing up screen time. There are two husbands and a boss, but we only hear this end of the telephone conversations.

The movie is a comedy, after all, and we're not looking for deep insights, but writer-director Diane English (one of the creative forces behind *Murphy Brown*) focuses on story and character, and even in a movie that sometimes plays like an infomercial for Saks Fifth Avenue, we find ourselves intrigued by these women.

Meg Ryan and Annette Bening get top billing as Mary, the wife of a Wall Street millionaire, and Sylvie, editor of a fashion magazine. They've long been best friends, but complications involving Mary's husband and Sylvie's job drive them apart. Then Sylvie, who has never been a mother, finds herself acting as one for Mary's precocious daughter Molly (India Ennenga). A scene where she gives the young girl direct, honest advice about sex is one of the best in the movie. And there's another striking scene when Mary's own mother (Candice Bergen) gives her brutally frank advice about how to deal with a cheating husband.

SPOILER WARNING: Debra Messing, from *Will & Grace,* plays Edie, the mother of four. And I will have to reveal that she gives birth to a fifth, in order to observe that she finds a way to distinguish the obligatory childbirth scene. She does some screaming that, in its own way, equals Meg Ryan's famous restaurant scene in *When Harry Met Sally.* As for the fourth friend, Alex Fisher (Jada Pinkett Smith), she's a lesbian and, well, that's about it. She does what she can with the role, but

there's not much to do. Her current lover, a supermodel, is introduced for a few pouts and hustled off-screen. In one scene with peculiar staging, Alex walks down a sidewalk *behind* Mary and Sylvie and never has one word of dialogue. What's with that?

There's strong comedic acting in some of the supporting roles, including Cloris Leachman as Mary's housekeeper, Eva Mendes as the bombshell "spritzer girl" at the Saks perfume counter, Bette Midler as a jolly Hollywood agent, and Debi Mazar as a talkative manicure girl from Long Island. Carrie Fisher gets points for playing her entire scene while furiously pumping a workout machine.

George Cukor's 1939 version of *The Women* remains a classic. It played like a convention of Hollywood's top female stars (Norma Shearer, Joan Crawford, Rosalind Russell, Paulette Goddard, Joan Fontaine). This 2008 version also brings together stars, but in a way that illuminates a shift in the Hollywood sensibility. Is there an actress today of the mythical stature of those five?

Meryl Streep, you say? A better actress than any of them, but does she sell tickets in a market dominated by action pictures and comic book superheroes? Angelina Jolie? Big star, but too old for the perfume girl and too young for the others. Nicole Kidman? She gets a nod in the dialogue. The novelty in 1939 was seeing so much star power in a single movie (also true of *Grand Hotel*). Here what we're seeing is an opportunity to regret that we didn't see more of these actresses in roles deserving of them. The old MGM would have kept them busy.

The Women isn't a great movie, but how could it be? Too many characters and too much melodrama for that, and the comedy has to be somewhat muted to make the characters semi-believable. But as a well-crafted, well-written, and well-acted entertainment, it drew me in and got its job done. Did I say that there are no males at all in the movie? True, except for one shot.

World's Greatest Dad ★★★
R, 99 m., 2009

Robin Williams (Lance Clayton), Alexie Gilmore (Claire), Daryl Sabara (Kyle Clayton), Evan Martin (Andrew), Geoff Pierson (Principal

Anderson), Henry Simmons (Mike Lane), Mitzi McCall (Bonnie). Directed by Bobcat Goldthwait and produced by Tim Perell, Howard Gertler, Sean McKittrick, and Richard Kelly. Screenplay by Goldthwait.

Bobcat Goldthwait makes a daring assault in *World's Greatest Dad* against our yearning to mythologize the dead. But he loses his nerve just before the earth is completely scorched. I have a notion his first-draft screenplay might have been unremittingly dark and cynical. It might not have been "commercial." This version may have a better chance. Audiences think they like bleak pessimism, but they expect the plane to pull put of its dive and land safely.

Robin Williams is the star, demonstrating once again that he's sometimes better in drama than comedy. He has that manic side he indulges, and he works better (for me, anyway) when he's grounded. Here he plays Lance, a high school teacher, the divorced father of a loathsome teenager. His son dies by hanging and becomes the object of a cult of veneration and mourning at the school where he was a student and his dad still teaches.

This premise is well established because of a disturbingly good performance by Daryl Sabara as Kyle, the disgusting son. Kyle is a compulsive masturbator who makes no effort to conceal his pastime from his father. At school, he's a vulgar sexist, insulting girls in the corridors. At all times he is as angry and hostile as he can possibly be, and is genuinely disliked by the student body—with the sad exception of Andrew (Evan Martin), his "friend" and victim.

Lance comes home to find his son has strangled himself. He has loved the boy despite everything, and now he attempts to rewrite the story of his death. He manufactures misleading evidence for the police to find—and although he is a failed author with five rejected novels in the drawer, he now finds his perfect genre by forging a diary allegedly left behind by Kyle at his death.

This diary he posts on the Internet, it goes viral at the high school, and the student body is overtaken with remorse about the way Kyle was treated. Soon he becomes the deity of a death cult, led no doubt by *Twilight* fans, and

students start wearing his photo. Lance is now seen as a heroic father.

The way this becomes an obsession is possibly the real point of Goldthwait's film. There's nothing like death to stir the herd instinct. For example, yes, Michael Jackson was a creative and talented artist. But was he as venerated a week before his death as much as a week after? Would anyone have foreseen the state funeral? What, exactly, did it mean when fans staged an all-night vigil at Neverland? Some were motivated by grief, more perhaps by a desire to participate vicariously in fame. Like fanatic sports fans, they seek identities through the objects of their adulation.

The Kyle cult becomes a tiger that Lance, the hero's father, has to ride. As he passes through the corridors, the path clears before him and a hush falls. He becomes much more interesting to his girlfriend, Claire (Alexie Gilmore), a fellow teacher, who had shown alarming signs of growing sweet on Mike (Henry Simmons), a handsome younger faculty member.

The only character who doubts the story about Kyle's death and his diary is Andrew—the only one who knew him, and his onanism, at all well. Lance otherwise triumphs as he creates a fake son in place of his real son, and all leads up to Kyle Clayton Day at the school. It is quite true, as the critic Stephen Holden points out, that the phony death story has brought out the better natures of the survivors. My question is whether Goldthwait, the creator, after all, of *Shakes the Clown*, started out with that intention. There is an inexorably black satire somewhere inside *World's Greatest Dad*, signaling to be saved.

The Wrestler ★ ★ ★ ★
R, 109 m., 2008

Mickey Rourke (Randy "The Ram" Robinson), Marisa Tomei (Cassidy), Evan Rachel Wood (Stephanie Robinson). Directed by Darren Aronofsky and produced by Aronofsky and Scott Franklin. Screenplay by Robert Siegel.

The Wrestler is about a man who can do one thing well, and keeps on doing it because of need, weary skill, and pride. He wrestles for a living. Pro wrestling is a fake sport, right? Yes, but as an *activity*, it's pretty real. I watch it on TV with fascination. It's scripted that the villain sneaks up on the hero, who pretends not to see him, and pushes the hero over the ropes and out of the ring. Fake. But when the hero hits the floor, how fake is that? "Those guys learn how to fall," people tell me. Want to sign up for the lessons?

Mickey Rourke plays the battered, broke, lonely hero, Randy "The Ram" Robinson. This is the performance of his lifetime, will win him a nomination, may win him the Oscar. Like many great performances, there is an element of truth in it. Rourke himself was once young and glorious and made the big bucks. He did professional boxing just for the hell of it. He alienated a lot of people. He fell from grace and stardom, but kept working because he was an actor and that was what he did. Now here is his comeback role, playing Randy the Ram's comeback.

This is Rourke doing astonishing physical acting. He has the physique of a body builder, perhaps thanks to some steroid use, which would also be true of Randy. He gets into the ring and does the work. Rourke may not be physically performing every single thing we see, including the leaps off ropes and ladders and the nasty falls. Special effects have robbed movies of their believability. But I've seen a lot of F/X, and I have to say it looked to me like he was really doing these things.

Not that it matters. It appears that he is, and his ring performances and the punishment he takes supply the bedrock for the story, which involves his damaged relationship with his daughter, Stephanie (Evan Rachel Wood), and what he hopes will become a relationship with the stripper Cassidy (Marisa Tomei). Except for his backstage camaraderie with other wrestling old-timers, Randy has burned all his bridges in life. Stephanie is far, far from happy to see him at her door again. And he doesn't quite believe Cassidy, whose real name is Pam, when she carefully explains that she is not available.

Here is the irony, which he won't accept. Cassidy is as much a performer as Randy. He is a ring worker. She is a sex worker. They put on a show and give the customers what they want. It pays the rent. There is always a chasm between pros and their audiences. That's why so many showbiz people marry one another. Magicians say, "The trick is told when the trick is sold." Think about that.

But Randy has grown a little wiser with the years, less blinded by stardom, more able to admit emotional need. Maybe, too, he was using more drugs in those days, and they always take first place before relationships. (He gets a sales pitch from a fellow wrestler who seems to stock more drugs than Walgreen's.) Randy has a residual charm and sentimentality, which helps him and also deceives him. He makes some small progress with his daughter. And as for Cassidy—have you ever seen Marisa Tomei play a bitch? I haven't. I don't know if she can. She seems to have something good at the heart of her that endows this stripper with warmth and sympathy. Not that Randy should get his hopes up.

The most fascinating elements in Darren Aronofsky's film is the backstage detail about wrestling. He does this so well yet has never made a film even remotely like this before. In the snow and slush of New Jersey, Randy and his opponents make the rounds of shabby union halls, school gyms, community centers, and Legion halls, using whatever they can find for dressing rooms, taping their damaged parts, psyching themselves up and agreeing beforehand on the script. We learn beforehand how they make themselves bleed, prepare for violent "surprises," talk through each match. And then they go out and do it. As nearly as I can tell, their planning only means that they get hurt in the ways they expect and not in unforeseen ways.

I cared as deeply about Randy the Ram as any movie character I've seen this year. I cared about Mickey Rourke, too. The way this role and this film unfold, that almost amounts to the same thing. Rourke may not win the Oscar for best actor. But it would make me feel good to see him up there. It really would.

Note: This is one of the year's best films. It wasn't on my "best films" list for complicated and boring reasons.

X

The X-Files: I Want to Believe ★ ★ ★ ½
PG-13, 104 m., 2008

David Duchovny (Fox Mulder), Gillian Anderson (Dana Scully), Amanda Peet (Dakota Whitney), Billy Connolly (Father Joe), Alvin "Xzibit" Joiner (Agent Drummy). Directed by Chris Carter and produced by Carter and Frank Spotnitz. Screenplay by Carter and Spotnitz.

The X-Files: I Want to Believe arrives billed as a "stand-alone" film that requires no familiarity with the famous television series. So it is, leaving us to piece together the plot on our own. And when I say "piece together," trust me, that's exactly what I mean.

In an early scene, a human arm turns up, missing its body, and other spare parts are later discovered. The arm is found in a virtuoso scene showing dozens of FBI agents lined up and marching across a field of frozen snow. They are led by a white-haired, entranced old man who suddenly drops to his knees and cries out that this is the place! And it is.

Now allow me to jump ahead and drag in the former agents Mulder and Scully. Mulder (David Duchovny) has left the FBI under a cloud because of his belief in the paranormal. Scully (Gillian Anderson) is a top-level surgeon, recruited to bring Mulder in from the cold, all his sins forgiven, to help on an urgent case. An agent is missing, and the white-haired man, we learn, is Father Joe (Billy Connolly), a convicted pedophile who is said to be a psychic.

Scully brings in Mulder but detests the old priest's crimes and thinks he is a fraud. Mulder, of course, wants to believe Father Joe could help on the case. But hold on one second. Even assuming that Father Joe planted the severed arm himself, you'll have to admit it's astonishing that he can lead agents to its exact resting place in a snow-covered terrain the size of several football fields with no landmarks. Even before he started weeping blood instead of tears, I believed him. Scully keeps right on insulting him right to his face. She wants *not* to believe.

Scully is emotionally involved in the case of a young boy who will certainly die if he doesn't have a risky experimental bone marrow treatment. This case, interesting in itself, is irrelevant to the rest of the plot except that it inspires a Google search that offers a fateful clue. Apart from that, what we're faced with is a series of victims, including Agent Dakota Whitney (Amanda Peet) and eventually Mulder himself, who are run off the road by a weirdo with a snowplow.

Who is doing this? And why does Father Joe keep getting psychic signals of barking dogs? And is the missing agent still alive, as he thinks she is? And won't anyone listen to Mulder, who eventually finds himself all alone in the middle of a blizzard, being run off the road, and then approaching a suspicious building complex after losing his cell phone? And how does he deal with a barking dog?

I make it sound a little silly. Well, it is a little silly, but it's also a skillful thriller, giving us just enough cutaways to a sinister laboratory to keep us fascinated. What happens in this laboratory you will have to find out for yourself, but the solution may be more complex than you think if you watch only casually. Hint: Pay close attention to the hands.

What I appreciated about *The X-Files: I Want to Believe* was that it involved actual questions of morality, just as *The Dark Knight* does. It's not simply about good and evil, but about choices. Come to think of it, Scully's dying child may be connected to the plot in another way, since it poses the question: Are any means justified to keep a dying person alive?

The movie lacks a single explosion. It has firearms, but nobody is shot. The special effects would have been possible in the era of *Frankenstein*. Lots of stunt people were used. I had the sensation of looking at real people in real spaces, not motion-capture in CGI spaces. There was a tangible quality to the film that made the suspense more effective because it involved the physical world.

Of course, it involves a psychic world, too. And the veteran Scottish actor Billy Connolly creates a quiet, understated performance as a man who hates himself for his sins, makes no great claims, does not understand his psychic powers, is only trying to help. He wants to believe he can be forgiven. As for Duchovny and

Anderson, these roles are their own. It's like they're in repertory. They still love each other and still believe they would never work as a couple. Or should I say they want to believe?

The movie is insidious. It involves evil on not one level but two. The evildoers, it must be said, are singularly inept; they receive bills for medical supplies under their own names, and surely there must be more efficient ways to abduct victims and purchase animal tranquilizers. But what they're up to is so creepy, and the snow-covered Virginia landscapes so haunting, and the wrongheadedness of Scully so frustrating, and the FBI bureaucracy so stupid, and Mulder so brave, that the movie works like thrillers used to work, before they were required to contain villains the size of buildings.

X Games 3D: The Movie ★ ½
PG, 92 m., 2009

Featuring Shaun White, Danny Way, Bob Burnquist, Ricky Carmichael, Travis Pastrana, and Kyle Loza. Narrated by Emile Hirsch. A documentary directed by Steve Lawrence and produced by Phil Orlins. Screenplay by Lawrence and Greg Jennings.

Well, it's awesome all right, what these X Games stars achieve. It's also awesome how little there is to be said about it. If you're a fan of extreme skateboarding, motorcycling, and motocross, this is the movie for you. If not, not. And even if you are, what's in the film other than what you might have seen on TV? Yes, it's in 3-D, which adds nothing and dims the picture.

Although *X Games 3D: The Movie* is billed as a documentary, let me mention two things that struck me as peculiar. During the final Mega Ramp extreme skateboarding competition in the Staples Center in Los Angeles, we learn almost accidentally that this is a sport that is scored on a point system, like diving or gymnastics. This is referred to only indirectly by the narrator, Emile Hirsch, who lavishes time on such inanities as "He treats gravity like some people do evolution, as only a theory," and "The present is past; only the future has currency." The flaw in this time theory is that when the future becomes the present it is the past. And gravity is more than a theory when you fall fifty feet onto a hard surface, as one X Gamer does.

We start to notice the competitors glancing up at what must be a scoreboard, but we're never shown it or informed of anybody's score. Why not? The film also has an annoying way of frequently not showing the beginning, middle, and end of a shot in one unbroken take. What's the point? During a two-car motocross "race," it's peculiar that the two cars are only seen together in one brief shot, as one flies off a dirt ramp and over the other, crossing below. Are they on different tracks? The narrator doesn't ever say.

What the athletes do is dangerous and risky. For example, hurtling down an almost perpendicular incline on a skateboard, using your speed to climb another terrifying ramp, and then launching into midair to perform "360s" and even "540s" before landing again on another ramp. Or, flying straight up from a ramp, doing a flip and/or a rotation, and landing again on the same ramp.

On motorcycles, they fly off earthen ramps, twist in the air, and land on another ramp. Or they do a high jump—flying almost straight up in the air to clear a bar at thirty-two or thirty-three feet. Often they fail, fall hard, and there's a tense silence while medics rush to the rescue. One competitor, Danny Way, apparently breaks something at Staples and returns to jump two more times. Earlier, he breaks his ankle in a practice jump and returns the next day to attempt to go over the Great Wall of China on a skateboard.

Athletes are asked why they take such risks and play with such pains (all of them have had broken bones and concussions). Their answers are the usual sports clichés about challenges and "taking the sport to a new level." Their cars and clothing are plastered with commercial endorsements, and at the X Games there are big ads for Pizza Hut, the navy, and so on. I guess they get paid. A lot, I hope.

"Who wants an A in history when you can get an X?" we're asked. Here's my theory about time. Yesterday is history, tomorrow's a mystery—so why get killed today?

X-Men Origins: Wolverine ★ ★
PG-13, 107 m., 2009

Hugh Jackman (Wolverine), Liev Schreiber (Sabretooth), Taylor Kitsch (Gambit), Daniel

Henney (Agent Zero), Danny Huston (General William Stryker), Kevin Durand (The Blob), will.i.am (Wraith). Directed by Gavin Hood and produced by John Palermo, Lauren Shuler Donner, Ralph Winter, and Hugh Jackman. Screenplay by David Benioff and Skip Woods.

X-Men Origins: Wolverine finally answers the burning question, left hanging after all three previous *Wolverine* movies, of the origins of Logan, whose knuckles conceal long and wicked blades. He is about 175 years old, he apparently stopped changing when he reached Hugh Jackman's age, and neither he, nor we, find out how he developed such an interesting mutation.

His half brother was Victor (Liev Schreiber). Their story starts in "1840—the Northwest Territories of Canada," a neat trick, since Canada was formed in 1867, and its Northwest Territories in 1870. But you didn't come here for a history lesson. Or maybe you did, if you need to know that Logan and Victor became Americans (still before they could be Canadians) and fought side by side in the Civil War, World War I, World War II, and Vietnam. Why they did this, I have no idea. Maybe they just enjoyed themselves.

Booted out of the army in Vietnam, Logan/Wolverine joined a secret black ops unit under General Stryker (Danny Huston), until finally, in Nigeria, he got fed up with atrocities. Nevertheless, he was recruited by Stryker for a *super* secret plan to create a mutant of mutants, who would incorporate all available mutant powers, including those of the kid whose eyes are like laser beams. He wears sunglasses. Lotta good they'll do him.

Am I being disrespectful to this material? You bet. It is Hugh Jackman's misfortune that when they were handing around superheroes, he got Wolverine, who is, for my money, low on the charisma list. He never says anything witty, insightful, or very intelligent; his utterances are limited to the vocalization of primitive forces: anger, hurt, vengeance, love, hate, determination. There isn't a speck of ambiguity. That Wolverine has been voted the number one comic book hero of all time must be the result of a stuffed ballot box.

At least, you hope, he has an interesting vulnerability? I'm sure X-Men scholars can tell you what it is, although since he has the gift of instant healing, it's hard to pinpoint. When a man can leap from an exploding truck in midair, cling to an attacking helicopter, slice the rotor blades, ride it to the ground, leap free, and walk away (in that ancient cliché where there's a fiery explosion behind him but he doesn't seem to notice it), here's what I think: Why should I care about this guy? He feels no pain, and nothing can kill him, so therefore he's essentially a story device for action sequences.

Oh, the film is well made. Gavin Hood, the director, made the great film *Tsotsi* (2005) and the damned good film *Rendition* (2007) before signing on here. Fat chance *Wolverine* fans will seek out those two. Why does a gifted director make a film none of his earlier admirers would much want to see? That's how you get to be a success in Hollywood. When you make a big box-office hit for mostly fanboys, you've hit the big time. Look at Justin Lin with *The Fast and the Furious.*

Such films are assemblies of events. There is little dialogue, except for the snarling of threats, vows, and laments, and the recitation of essential plot points. Nothing here about human nature. No personalities beyond those hauled in via typecasting. No lessons to learn. No joy to be experienced. Just mayhem, noise, and pretty pictures. I have been powerfully impressed by film versions of Batman, Spider-Man, Superman, Iron Man, and the Iron Giant. I wouldn't walk across the street to meet Wolverine.

But wait! you say. Doesn't the film at least provide a learning experience for Logan about his origins for Wolverine? Hollow laugh. Because we know that the modern Wolverine has a form of amnesia, it cannot be a spoiler for me to reveal that at the end of *X-Men Origins: Wolverine,* he forgets everything that has happened in the film. Lucky man.

XXY ★ ★ ★ ½
NO MPAA RATING, 91 m., 2008

Ines Efron (Alex), Martin Piroyanski (Alvaro), Ricardo Darin (Kraken), Valeria Bertuccelli (Suli), German Palacios (Ramiro), Carolina Peleritti (Erika). Directed by Lucia Puenzo and produced by Luis Puenzo and Jose Maria

Morales. Screenplay by Lucia Puenzo, based on a short story by Sergio Bizzio.

Alex was born with both male and female sex organs. Although "reassignment" surgery was considered after birth, she has lived as a woman until the age of fifteen, when *XXY* takes up the story. She uses hormones to subdue her male characteristics, but now she has become unsure how she really feels. Alex is neither a man in a woman's body nor a woman in a man's body, but both, in the body of a high-spirited tomboy who broods privately in uncertainty and confusion.

"Hermaphrodite" is no longer the PC term for such people, who prefer "intersex," although it seems to me that they are not so much between the sexes as encompassing them. Their stories are often exploited in lurid, sensationalistic accounts. Lucia Puenzo's *XXY* is the first film I've seen on the subject that is honest and sensitive—indeed, the only one. It is not a message picture, never lectures, contains partial nudity but avoids explicit images, and grows into a touching human drama. It will be described in terms of Alex's sexual ambiguity, but that would simplify it, and this is not a simple film but a subtle and observant one.

Alex (Ines Efron) is the child of a Marine biologist named Kraken (Ricardo Darin) and his wife, Suli (Valeria Bertuccelli). They have moved their family from Argentina to an island off the shore of Uruguay, where Kraken can study specimens and Alex can grow up more privately. That has not been easy. "I'm sick of doctors and changing schools," she tells her mother. Since other kids somehow sense something strange about her, she cannot easily keep her secret. Recently she has stopped taking the hormones. Perhaps (Alex never says) it will be easier to account for a penis if she does not live as a girl.

Guests arrive on the island: a plastic surgeon named Ramiro (German Palacios), his wife, Erika (Carolina Peleritti), and their son, Alvaro (Martin Piroyanski), about Alex's age. Suli has invited them so the doctor can "get to know Alex" and tells her husband she has not told them about their child's secret. Alex and Alvaro are attracted to each other, and together have what is possibly the first sexual experience for either. This is shown with great dramatic impact, but not with graphic intimacy; the point is not what they do, but how they feel about it.

The film gives full weight to all of the characters. When Kraken first saw his newborn infant, "I thought she was perfect." He wants to give Alex the right to make her own decision about having surgery. His wife thinks Alex's penis should be removed, but is not shrill or insistent. Both in their different ways love and care for their child.

In contrast, the surgeon is brutally cruel in a conversation with his own son, who may possibly be starting to realize he is gay and may be attracted to the androgynous Alex for that reason. Alex and Alvaro sense some sort of unstated, even unconscious, common bond. There are problems on the island. Alex has broken the nose of her boyfriend, possibly (I'm not sure) because he wanted to explore her body. And local teenagers chase Alex on the beach and pin her down to settle the mystery of her physiology.

I am making the film sound too melodramatic. The shots are beautifully composed, the editing paces the process of self-discovery, the dialogue is spare and heartfelt, the performances are deeply human—especially by Efron, who I learn was twenty-two when the film was made, but never looks it.

Nor does she look too distractingly male or female, and so is convincing as both. The film accumulates its force through many small moments and some larger ones. It assembles its story as a careful novelist might, out of many precise, significant brush strokes. And Efron finds a sure line through the pitfalls of her role, succeeding in playing not girl or boy, but—Alex. We understand that Alex is in despair, and we see it reflected in a sketchbook she has drawn. She is weary of being poked and prodded by the unhealthy curiosity of society, weary of being considered a freak. She wants to be accepted as herself, but isn't sure who that is. In wanting her to find happiness, her parents provide a refuge, even though they hardly even discuss her intersexuality with her in so many words. And finally that's why this film can avoid a "solution" and yet end with a bittersweet glow.

Note: XXY won the top prize in Critics' Week at Cannes 2007.

Y

Year One ★
PG-13, 100 m., 2009

Jack Black (Zed), Michael Cera (Oh), Oliver Platt (High Priest), David Cross (Cain), Hank Azaria (Abraham), Juno Temple (Eema). Directed by Harold Ramis and produced by Judd Apatow, Clayton Townsend, and Nicholas Weinstock. Screenplay by Ramis, Gene Stupnitsky, and Lee Eisenberg.

Harold Ramis is one of the nicest people I've met in the movie business, and I'm so sorry *Year One* happened to him. I'm sure he had the best intentions. In trying to explain why the movie was produced, I have a theory. Ramis is the top-billed of three writers, and he is so funny that when he read some of these lines, they sounded hilarious. Pity he didn't play one of the leads in his own film.

As always, I carefully avoided any of the movie's trailers, but I couldn't avoid the posters or the ads. "Meet Your Ancestors," they said, with big photos of Jack Black and Michael Cera. I assumed it was about Adam and Eve. Cera has smooth, delicate features, and with curly locks falling to below his shoulders, I thought: "Michael Cera in drag. I wonder where Harold will take that?"

But no, even though Cera is sometimes mistaken for a woman, he's all primitive man, banging women on the head. Then he and Black eat of the forbidden apple and make a leap from tribal "hunter-gatherers" (a term they enjoy) to royal security guards. Everyone throughout the film talks like anyone else in a Judd Apatow comedy, somewhere between stoned and crafty.

It must be said that Jack Black and Michael Cera were not born to be costars. Black was fresh and funny once, a reason then to welcome him in a movie, but here he forgets to act and simply announces his lines. Cera plays shy and uncertain, but then he always does, and responds to Black as if Jack were Juno and a source of intimidating wit.

Another leading role is taken by Oliver Platt, as an extremely hairy high priest, who orders Cera to massage his chest with oil. The close-up of Cera kneading his matted chest foliage is singularly unappetizing. There are several good-looking babes in the city (did I mention it is Sodom?), who, as required in such films, all find the heroes inexplicably attractive. Cera and Juno Temple have a good exchange. She plays a slave. "When do you get off?" he asks. "Never."

That and several other of the film's better moments are in the trailer, of which it can be said, if they were removed from the film, it would be nearly bereft of better moments. The movie takes place in the land now known as Israel (then too, I think), although no one does much with that. The Sodomites include in their number Abraham, Cain, and Abel; it's surprising to find them still in action in the Year One, since Genesis places them—well, before the time of the Year One. Sodomy is not very evident in Sodom, perhaps as a result of the movie being shaved down from an R to a PG-13.

The film has shaggy crowds that mill about like outtakes from *Monty Python and the Holy Grail*, and human sacrifice in which virgins are pitched into the blazing mouth of a stone ox, and a cheerful turn when the gods more appreciate a high priest than a virgin. But *Year One* is a dreary experience, and all the ending accomplishes is to bring it to a close. Even in the credit cookies, you don't sense the actors having much fun.

Yella ★ ★ ★ ½
NO MPAA RATING, 89 m., 2008

Nina Hoss (Yella), Devid Striesow (Philipp), Hinnerk Schoenemann (Ben), Christian Redl (Yella's Father). Directed by Christian Petzold and produced by Florian Koerner von Gustorf. Screenplay by Simone Baer and Petzold.

Yella is a reserved young woman with unrevealed depths of intelligence, larceny, and passion. Their gradual revelation makes this more than an ordinary thriller, in great part because of the performance of Nina Hoss in the title role. Soon after we meet her, she's followed down the street by her former husband, Ben (Hinnerk Schoenemann), who will stalk her throughout the film. Partly to escape him, she leaves her small town in the former East Germany and goes to Hanover to take a job.

Her mistake is to accept a ride to the train station from him. He declares his love, accuses her of betrayal, moans about his business losses. "What time is your train?" he asks. When she says "8:22," he knows her destination. Shortly after, he drives his SUV off a bridge and into a river. Miraculously, they escape. Soaking wet, she runs to the train station and catches the 8:22. Yella has pluck.

That the man who hired her in Hanover has been fired and locked out of his office is the first of her discoveries about the world of business. That night in her hotel lobby, she meets Philipp (Devid Striesow), who sees her looking at his laptop and asks, "You like spreadsheets?" She does. She trained as an accountant.

He asks her to go along with him to a business meeting, carefully coaching her about when to gaze at the spreadsheet, when to gaze at the would-be client, and when to lean over and whisper in his ear—a lawyer's strategy he learned from Grisham movies. She does more than that. She actually reads the spreadsheet and boldly points out deceptions and false assets. She controls the meeting.

Philipp, who now respects her, brings her along to more meetings during which she figures out for herself what he eventually confesses to her: "I cheat." She doesn't mind. And then the film enters more deeply into one particular deal involving shaky patent rights and potential fortunes. Her career seems on an upswing, if it were not that Ben has followed her to Hanover.

All of this time, there are eerie episodes when her ears ring, she hears the harsh cry of a bird, and she seems able to intuitively understand things about people. These episodes remain unexplained until the last minute of the film. And just as well. Nina Hoss is an actress who rewards close observation; she is often seen in profile as a passenger in Philipp's car, her eyes observing him carefully, her expression neutral, then sometimes smiling at what he says, and sometimes only to herself. One of the pleasures of the film is trying to read her mind.

The writer-director, Christian Petzold, uses a spare, straightforward visual style for the most part, except for those cutaways to trees blowing in the wind whenever we heard the harsh bird cry. He trusts his story and characters. And he trusts us to follow the business deals and become engrossed in the intrigue. I did. I could see this being remade as one of those business thrillers with Michael Douglas looking cruel and expensive and finding his female equal. I'm not recommending that, just imagining it.

The male leads have an unsettling similarity in physical presence. You can't say she's attracted to the type, since she's fleeing from Ben and meets Philipp by accident. But they're both ruthless in their way, and Philipp is uncannily effective at imagining things about her that turn out to be pretty accurate. Maybe one thing he senses is that she would be a willing partner in crime. He sets a trap for her, to see if she will return an extra 25,000 euros he entrusted to her. That she would have kept the money angers him at first, but later he apparently decides that by being willing to steal it, she actually passed his test.

There are surprises along the way. One involves the key executive of a company they're dealing with, and is handled with a creepy beginning and a poignant ending. Another surprise in the film I will not even hint at, except to say that I could happily have done without it. It has all the value of the prize in a box of Cracker Jack: worthless, but working your way down to it is a lot of fun.

The Yellow Handkerchief ★★★
PG-13, 102 m., 2010

William Hurt (Brett), Maria Bello (May), Kristen Stewart (Martine), Eddie Redmayne (Gordy). Directed by Udayan Prasad and produced by Arthur Cohn and Terence Rosemore. Screenplay by Erin Dignam, based on the story by Pete Hamill.

The action in *The Yellow Handkerchief* takes place within the characters, who don't much talk about it, so the faces of the actors replace dialogue. That's more interesting than movies that lay it all out. This is the story of three insecure drifters who improbably find themselves sharing a big convertible and driving to New Orleans not long after Hurricane Katrina.

The car's driver is a painfully insecure teenager named Gordy (Eddie Redmayne), who doubts most of what he does and seems to apologize just by standing there. At a rural convenience store he encounters Martine (Kristen Stewart), running away from her life. He says he's driving to New Orleans. No reason. She decides to come along. No reason. They meet a quiet, reserved man named Brett (William Hurt), and she thinks he should come along. No particular reason.

We now have the makings of a classic road picture. Three outsiders, a fabled destination, Louisiana back roads. and a big old convertible. It must be old because modern cars have no style; three strangers can't go On the Road in a Corolla. It must be a convertible because it makes it easier to light and see the characters and the landscape they pass through. They must be back roads because what kind of a movie is it when they drive at a steady seventy on the interstate?

The formula is obvious, but the story, curiously, turns out to be based on fact. It began as journalism by Pete Hamill, published in the early 1970s. In the movie's rendition, Brett fell in love with a woman named May (Maria Bello), then spent six years in prison for manslaughter, although his guilt is left in doubt. Martine slowly coaxes his story out of the secretive man.

You don't need an original story for a movie. You need original characters and living dialogue. *The Yellow Handkerchief,* written by Erin Dignam, directed by Udayan Prasad, has those, and evocative performances. William Hurt occupies the silent center of the film. In many movies we interpret his reticence as masking intelligence. Here we realize it's a blank slate and could be masking anything. Although his situation is an open temptation for an actor to signal his emotions, Hurt knows that the best movie emotions are intuited by the audience, not read from emotional billboards.

Kristen Stewart is, quite simply, a wonderful actress. I must not hold *Twilight* against her. She played the idiotic fall-girl written for her as well as that silly girl could be played, and now that the movie has passed a $200 million gross, she has her choice of screenplays for her next three films, as long as one of them is *The Twilight Saga: Eclipse.* In recent film after film, she shows a sure hand and an intrinsic power. I last saw her in *Welcome to the Rileys,* where she played a runaway working as a hooker in New Orleans. In both films she had many scenes with experienced older actors (Hurt, James Gandolfini). In both she was rock solid. Playing insecure and neurotic, yes, but rock solid.

The story of Eddie Redmayne, who plays Gordy, is unexpected. He fits effortlessly into the role of the scrawny, uncertain fifteen-year-old Louisiana kid. Yet I learn he is twenty-seven, a Brit who went to Eton, a veteran of Shakespeare and Edward Albee. Michael Caine explained to me long ago why it's easier for British actors to do American accents than the other way around. Whatever. You can't find a crack in his performance here.

These three embark on a road odyssey that feels like it takes longer than it might in real life. Their secrets are very slowly confided. They go through emotional relationships expected and not expected. They learn lessons about themselves, which is required in such films, but are so slowly and convincingly arrived at here that we forgive them. There is rarely a film where the characters are exactly the same at the end as they were at the beginning. (Note: Being triumphant is not a character change.)

The filmmaker, Udayan Prasad, made a wonderful British film in 1997, *My Son the Fanatic.* I've seen none of his work since. Now this redneck slice of life. Since the characters are so far from the lives of the actors and the director, this is a creation of the imagination. As it must be. The ending is a shade melodramatic, but what the heck. In for one yellow handkerchief, in for a hundred.

Yes Man ★ ★
PG-13, 104 m., 2008

Jim Carrey (Carl Allen), Zooey Deschanel (Allison), Bradley Cooper (Peter), John Michael Higgins (Nick), Rhys Darby (Norman), Terence Stamp (Terrence Bundley). Directed by Peyton Reed and produced by Richard D. Zanuck, David Heyman, and Jim Carrey. Screenplay by Nicholas Stoller, Jarrad Paul, and Andrew Mogel.

Jim Carrey made a movie in 1997 titled *Liar Liar* in which his character is a lawyer who suddenly finds he cannot tell a lie. Now here is *Yes Man*, with Carrey playing a bank loan executive who cannot say no. If the movie had been made just a little later to take advantage of the mortgage crisis, it could have been a docudrama.

Carrey begins as a recluse mired in depression, a man named Carl who has been avoiding his friends and not returning his messages for three years, all because his great love walked out on him. His negative stance makes it easy to do his job, which amounts to denying loan applications. He's so indifferent to this work that he isn't even nice to his boss, who desperately wants to make friends. For Carl, it's just up in the morning and no, no, no all day.

Saying no all the way, he's dragged to a meeting of Say Yes!, which is one of those con games that convince large numbers of people to fill hotel convention centers and enrich those who have reduced the secrets of life to a PowerPoint presentation. The Guru of Yes is named Terrence Bundley, and is played by Terence Stamp, whose agent didn't wonder about the extra R. Stamp's message is: Turn your life around by saying yes to everything. This could be dangerous. Anyone who could word the questions cleverly could get you to do anything. For example, "Will you give me all of your money?"—an example used in the film.

The problem with the premise is that the results are clearly telegraphed by the plot. When Carl meets a beautiful girl named Allison (Zooey Deschanel), for example, he is clearly destined to fall in love with her. And when he encounters his sex-mad, toothless, elderly neighbor (Fionnula Flanagan), he is fated to—I wish the movie hadn't gone there. I get uncomfortable seeing reenactments of the dirty jokes we told when we were twelve.

Carrey performs some zany physical humor in the movie, including a drunken bar fight with a fearsome jealous boyfriend who, like all fearsome jealous boyfriends in the movies, stands tall and has a shaved skull. Remember when baldness was a sign of the milquetoast and not the bruiser? I like that phrase "stands tall." Makes me think of John Wayne,

who was bald enough, but came along before Mr. Clean.

Every time there's a setup in *Yes Man* we know what must happen. If a homeless guy comes along and asks for a midnight ride to a forest preserve, of course Carl must say yes. We can also foresee what will happen when Allison doubts his love because maybe he only said yes because of his vow. Allison's doubts come perfectly timed to supply the movie's third act crisis. In fact, the whole story plays as if written by a devout student of the screenplay guru Robert McKee, who also fills rented ballrooms but has the advantage of being smarter and more entertaining than the Guru of Yes. Also, I think you will make more money by saying yes to *Casablanca* than to everything else.

Jim Carrey works the premise for all it's worth, but it doesn't allow him to bust loose and fly. When a lawyer *must* tell the truth and wants desperately not to (even pounding himself over the head with a toilet seat to stop himself), it's funny. When a loan officer must say yes and *wants* to, where is the tension? The premise removes all opportunity for frustration, at which Carrey is a master, and reduces Carl to a programmed creature who, as long as he follows instructions, lacks free will.

As I watched *Yes Man*, I observed two things: (1) Jim Carrey is heroic at trying to keep the movie alive, and succeeds when he is free to be goofy and not locked into yes-and-consequences. (2) It is no news that Zooey Deschanel is a splendid actress and a great beauty, but this is her first movie after which two of my fellow critics proposed marriage to the screen. And I thought they only sat in the front row to better appreciate the film stock.

The Yes Men Fix the World ★★★
NO MPAA RATING, 96 m., 2009

A documentary directed by Andy Bichlbaum and Mike Bonanno and produced by Doro Bachrach, Ruth Charny, Laura Nix, Jess Search, and Juliette Timsit. Screenplay by Bichlbaum and Bonanno.

The Yes Men are a New York political action cooperative specializing in hoaxes that embarrass corporations by dramatizing their evils and excesses. They put up phony Web sites, print fake business cards, and pose as representatives from the companies that are their targets.

It's amazing what they get away with. Maybe not so amazing if you study the faces of some of their audiences. These are people so accustomed to sitting through corporate twaddle that they fail to question the most preposterous presentations.

Consider the "SurvivaBall." This is a fake survival suit, built by the Yes Men but presented as a new product from Halliburton. It's an inflated padded globe completely containing a human body and round as a beach ball. Obviously, if you fell over, you'd have no way to stop yourself from rolling, or be able to stand up on your own. There's a closable face opening, air filters, little extendable gloves, and a port, which, unless I miss my guess, is intended for extra-suit urination. It comes with the big red Halliburton trademark.

The Yes Men seriously pitch this invention at a conference for the security industry. Study the faces in the audience. No one is laughing. People look bored or perhaps mildly curious. There isn't a look of incredulity in the room. The few questions are desultory. Not a single security "expert" seems to suspect a hoax.

Experts in the news business are no more suspicious. The Yes Men faked a BBC interview during which a "spokesman for Dow Chemical" announced a multibillion-dollar payment to the victims of a notorious 1985 explosion at a Union Carbide insecticide factory in Bhopal, India, that killed eight thousand, injured many more, and spread poisons that cause birth defects to this day.

Think of that. Twice as many dead as on 9/11, we know exactly who did it, and Dow (which absorbed Union Carbide) has never paid a dime of reparation. At the news it was finally settling the suit, Dow Chemical's stock price plunged on Wall Street: Things like this could cost money. The Yes Men were unmasked as the hoaxers.

They were also behind a stunt that made the news recently: staging a phony press conference at the National Press Club in Washington, announcing the U.S. Chamber of Commerce was reversing its stand on global warming. Some news organizations double-checked this, but not Fox News, which repeated the story all day.

Another hoax, inspiring the question Why does the U.S. Chamber of Commerce resist the theory of global warming? What is the USCC, anyway? Is it supported by the dues of countless merchants on Main Street, or is it a front financed by energy companies? Only a month ago, Exelon, the largest U.S. electric utility, announced it would no longer pay dues to support the USCC right-wing agenda.

The Yes Men are represented in this documentary by Andy Bichlbaum and Mike Bonanno. You may have seen them on TV—as themselves or as "corporate spokesmen." It's remarkable no one recognizes them. They don't wear beards or dark glasses. They are disguised, in fact, in a way that makes them above suspicion: Why, they look and talk exactly like middle-aged white men in conservative business suits.

The film is entertaining in its own right, and thought-provoking. Why don't more people quickly see through their hoaxes? Would you believe in a product such as the SurvivaBall? As head of security for your corporation, would you invest in it? It's surprising we don't look outside and see, marching down the street, a parade of emperors without any clothes.

You, the Living ★★★★
NO MPAA RATING, 95 m., 2009

Jessica Lundberg (Anna), Elisabet Helander (Mia), Bjorn Englund (Tuba Player), Leif Larsson (Carpenter), Ollie Olson (Consultant), Birgitta Persson (Tuba Player's Wife), Kemal Sener (Barber), Hakan Angses (Psychiatrist), Gunnar Ivarsson (Businessman). Directed by Roy Andersson and produced by Pernilla Sandstrom. Screenplay by Andersson.

In a sad world and a sad city, sad people lead sad lives and complain that they hate their jobs and nobody understands them. The result is in some ways a comedy with a twist of the knife, and in other ways a film like nobody else has ever made—except for its director, Roy Andersson of Sweden.

Andersson's *You, the Living* is hypnotic. Drab, weary people slog through another depressing day in a world without any bright colors. A bitter, alcoholic woman sits on a park bench hatefully insulting a fat, meek man, screams that she will never see him again, finds out there's veal roast for dinner, and says she may drop by later. A tuba player complains that the bank has lost 34 percent of his retirement fund. He says this while a naked Brunhilda with a Viking helmet has loud sex with him. A carpet salesman loses a sale because someone sold the end off a ten-foot runner.

So it goes. There are fifty vignettes in this film, almost all shot with a static camera, in medium and long shot. Sometimes the characters look directly at us and complain. A psychiatrist says he has spent twenty-seven years trying to help mean and selfish people be happy and asks, what's the point? A girl imagines her marriage with the rock guitarist she has a crush on. The tuba player is hated by his wife and his downstairs neighbor. A bass drum player is also unpopular when he rehearses.

This is the kind of comedy where you don't laugh aloud, I think, although I've not seen it with an audience. You laugh to yourself, silently, although you're never quite sure why. Andersson choreographs the movements of actors who enter and leave rooms, call off-screen or interact with other people we see in other rooms beyond them. He films in bedrooms, living rooms, kitchens, a bar, restaurants, offices, a courtyard, a barber shop, a bus stop in the rain.

Or it looks like he does. I learn that every space in this movie was constructed on a set. It took three years to shoot, was financed from six countries and eighteen sources, and used mostly plain-looking nonactors. It is meticulous, perfectionist in its detail. Andersson's tone has been compared to Jacques Tati's, and certainly they're similar in constructing large, realistic sets that allow them to control every detail of the decor, sound, and lighting.

There's joy in watching a movie like *You, the Living*. It is flawless in what it does, and we have no idea what that is. It's in sympathy with its characters. It shares their sorrow, and yet is amused that each thinks his suffering is unique. The alcoholic woman, who complains over and over that no one understands her, is all too understandable. She calls her mother a sadist for serving nonalcoholic beer with dinner: "What's the point of living if you can't get drunk?"

There are elaborate set pieces that are masterful. One involves long banquet tables lined with joyous people in evening wear who enact a peculiar, traditional ritual involving them standing on their chairs. Another involves a man who proposes to yank a tablecloth out from under all the dishes on a table. And then there's the scene of the young woman imagining her honeymoon with the rock guitarist. This one I won't say a word about: You have to watch it as it plays. Keep in mind that the film was all shot on sound stages. I believe the publicity that says 26,200 screws were used in this production.

Roy Andersson, now sixty-six, has been one of Europe's most successful directors of TV commercials but has made only four features in thirty years. I showed his *Songs from the Second Floor*, winner of the Jury Prize at Cannes 2000, at my Ebertfest. I can only imagine what he must be like. After the failure of his second film, he waited twenty-five years to make the third one. We invited him to Ebertfest, and he sent two of his actors—one who never spoke in the movie and never spoke on-stage, either.

You, the Living is a title that perhaps refers to his characters: Them, the Dead. Yet this isn't a depressing film. His characters are angry and bitter, but stoic and resigned, and the musicians (there are also a banjo player and a cornetist) seem happy enough as they play Dixieland. In their world, it never seems to get very dark out, but in the bar it's always closing time.

You Don't Mess with the Zohan ★ ★ ★
PG-13, 113 m., 2008

Adam Sandler (Zohan), John Turturro (The Phantom), Emmanuelle Chriqui (Dalia), Nick Swardson (Michael), Lainie Kazan (Gail), Rob Schneider (Salim), Michael Buffer (Walbridge). Directed by Dennis Dugan and produced by Adam Sandler and Jack Giarraputo. Screenplay by Sandler, Robert Smigel, and Judd Apatow.

The crowd I joined for *You Don't Mess with the Zohan* roared with laughter, and I understand why. Adam Sandler's new comedy is shameless in its eagerness to extract laughs from every possible breach of taste or decorum, and why am I even mentioning taste and decorum in this context? This is a mighty hymn of and to vulgarity, and either you enjoy it or you don't. I found myself enjoying it a surprising amount of the time, even though I was thoroughly ashamed of myself. There is a tiny part of me that still applauds the great minds who invented the whoopee cushion.

Sandler plays an ace agent for the Mossad, the Israeli secret police, who has no interest in counterterrorism and spends as much time as possible hanging out with babes on the beach. Known as The Zohan, he has remarkable physical skills—and equipment, as his bikini briefs and the crotches of all his costumes make abundantly clear. The laws of gravity do not limit him; he can travel through cities like Spider-Man, but without the web strings. He can simply jump for hundreds of feet.

The Zohan harbors one secret desire. He wants to be a hairdresser. His equivalent of pornography is an old Paul Mitchell catalog, and one day he simply cuts his ties with Israel and smuggles himself into the United States in a crate carrying two dogs whose hair he does en route. In America, he poses as an Australian with a very peculiar accent and, asked for his name, combines the names of his airborne flight buddies: Scrappy Coco-man. His auditions in various hair salons are unsuccessful (in a black salon, he attacks a dreads wig as if it were a hostile animal), until finally he is hired by the beautiful Dalia (Emmanuelle Chriqui), a Palestinian.

This plot is simply the skeleton for sight gags. Early on, we saw how much pain he could endure when he dropped a sharp-toothed fish into the crotch of his bikini swimming trunks. Now we see such sights as his sexual adventures with old ladies in the salon. In my notes, I scribbled in the dark: "An angel with the flexibility of a circus freak," adding, "he tells old lady," although maybe the old lady told him. At home with his new friend Michael (Nick Swardson), he effortlessly seduces the friend's mother (the zaftig Lainie Kazan).

His archenemy, the Palestinian agent known as The Phantom (John Turturro), is also in New York, and they make war. The Phantom's training regime is severe. He takes eggs, cracks them, and live chicks emerge. These he puts in a glass and chugs. He punches not only sides of beef but a living cow. Like The Zohan, he is filled with confidence in his own abilities, and with reason (he can cling to ceilings). Their confrontation will be a battle of the Middle Eastern superheroes.

Now creeps in a belated plot, involving a shady developer (Michael Buffer, of "Let's get ready to rumble!" fame). He wants to tear down a street of Arab and Israeli electronics stores and falafel and hummus shops to put up a mall. This would be a terrible thing, particularly given the prominent role that hummus plays in the film. Opposition to the mall unites the Israelis and Arabs, unconvincingly, on the way to peace and brotherhood at the end.

There are scenes here that make you wince. One involves a savage game of hacky-sack using not a hacky-sack bag but a living cat. Only the consolation that it's done with special effects allows us to endure the cries of the cat. Mariah Carey appears, starts to sing "The Star-Spangled Banner," and somehow survives a cameo with the mall builder. (Maybe his contract says Buffer appears in all movies involving the national anthem.) And something must be said about The Zohan's speech, which in addition to the broad comic accent involves the word "no" in a series that can run from two ("no-no!") to his usual five ("no-no-no-no-no!") to the infinite.

Sandler works so hard at this, and so shamelessly, that he battered down my resistance. Like a Jerry Lewis out of control, he will do, and does, anything to get a laugh. No thinking adult should get within a mile of this film. I must not have been thinking. For my sins, I laughed. Sorry. I'll try to do better next time.

The Young Victoria ★★★
PG, 100 m., 2009

Emily Blunt (Queen Victoria), Rupert Friend (Prince Albert), Paul Bettany (Lord Melbourne), Miranda Richardson (Duchess of Kent), Jim Broadbent (King William), Thomas Kretschmann (King Leopold), Mark Strong (Sir John Conroy). Directed by Jean-Marc Vallee and produced by Sarah Ferguson, Tim

Headington, Graham King, and Martin Scorsese. Screenplay by Julian Fellowes.

Orson Welles allegedly said a movie studio was the best toy train set a child could ever desire. He should have been Queen Victoria. She was crowned in 1837 and ruled until 1901, queen of the greatest empire the world has ever known. She was married to Albert, her great love, from 1840 to 1861, and though she was a widow for the next forty years, at least unlike many monarchs, she wed the man of her choice.

We think of her as the formidable matron of official portraits. She was a girl once. She had teenage crushes. She resented authority. She hated being ordered about. She fell in love with a pen pal, the Victorian equivalent of an online romance. *The Young Victoria* is about those years.

Emily Blunt makes Victoria as irresistible a young woman as Dame Judi Dench made her an older one in *Mrs. Brown* (1997). In seeking fascinating women from that century of the repression of women, we often find them among courtesans or royalty—two classes that need answer to no man. Come to think of it, that answers a question I wrote about twenty-five years ago: Why do so many actresses get their Oscar nominations by playing whores or queens?

The director is Jean-Marc Vallee, and the screenplay is by Julian Fellowes, who in his script for *Vanity Fair* showed a feeling for the same period, and in Altman's *Gosford Park,* a genius for understanding the power struggle within a great household. Their engaging approach is to show Victoria at the center of a mighty struggle that also involved her adolescent emotions.

She is next in line after her uncle, King William (Jim Broadbent), who is gormless. As he approaches death, her mother, the Duchess of Kent (Miranda Richardson), falls under the control of the ambitious Sir John Conroy (Mark Strong). His hope: William will die before Victoria is eighteen, and the duchess will appoint him as regent to rule in her place. Whether William cooperates with this scheme you already know.

Victoria lives in a hermetically sealed world. She meets no one not vetted by the palace hierarchy, has no meaningful independence, is having her life mapped for reasons of state, not the heart. King Leopold of Belgium (Thomas Kretschmann) hopes to marry her to his son, Albert (Rupert Friend). Albert has no enthusiasm for being used as a pawn but is drilled in her likes and dislikes and sent to meet her. Whether deliberately or by misadventure, he reveals he's been coached on her tastes. When she calls him on it, he admits it and begins to win her heart.

But not quite. There are still the attractions of handsome Lord Melbourne (Paul Bettany), the sort of cad most mothers, but not hers, would warn her about. This plays like a Jane Austen story moved from the dollar to the twenty-five-dollar table: We're talking about the heart of the empress of India here.

I'm a pushover for British historical dramas, partly because I'm an Anglophile, partly because it's alarmingly easy for me to identify with these vivid and beautiful characters. The British have a leg up in sets and locations because they often use real ones; nine stately castles and homes get a workout here, and Westminster Abbey, of course.

The *Empire* magazine reviewer Kim Newman writes: "If you're collecting British royal history by installments in the cinema, you'll know exactly how to place this on a shelf with *Elizabeth, Restoration, The Madness of King George* and *The Queen.*" Wouldn't that make a great weekend of videos? Yes, *The Young Victoria* belongs on the same shelf but at the lower end, I'm afraid. It's a charmer but lacks the passion of the others, perhaps because it's so, well, Victorian.

Youssou N'Dour: I Bring What I Love ★★★
PG, 102 m., 2009

With Youssou N'Dour, Peter Gabriel, Moustapha Mbaye, Kabou Gueye, Bono, and Fathi Salama. A documentary directed, written, and produced by Elizabeth Chai Vasarhelyi.

The Grammy Award–winning Youssou N'Dour is a superstar of world music from Senegal in West Africa, famous in Africa and Europe, now winning a North American following. He also seems to be a nice man, with his heart in the right place. The documentary *Youssou N'Dour: I Bring What I Love* opens with his anthem to Africa, *Wake Up (It's Africa Calling)*, in which he calls on the continent to unify itself, insist on honest leaders, and realize its potential. It follows him on tour at home and abroad, showing him as a charismatic stage presence whose music is powerful, joyous, and danceable; many of his fans may have no understanding of his French, Wolof, and Arabic lyrics, and he also sings in English, which must leave other fans behind. But the music translates itself.

N'Dour, born into a family that encouraged serious study, wanted to be a musician from an early age, hanging out in the music clubs of Dakar and eventually running away from home to perform in the Ivory Coast. His father brought the runaway home and relented to his musical ambitions, and he quickly became a star.

He is one of the creators of the world music genre fusing African, traditional Muslim, Caribbean, and Cuban traditions, and even a flavoring of American jazz and soul. He considers himself a griot singer, and through his grandmother is a member of that West African caste of singers of praise and celebration. We see him at his grandmother's bedside and sense the love flowing between them.

He is popular not only because of his persuasive music, but also because of his unaffected, natural presence, and his closeness with audiences, and his lack of big-star affectations. It also has something to do with his message. N'Dour is Sunni Muslim, reflecting that faith's mystical orientation in contrast with more worldly Muslim traditions. He sings of an African-Arab connection, and that led him into trouble.

In 2004, he made a new album named *Egypt,* which mixed secular and religious music and, worse, was released during the holy month of Ramadan. He was sharply criticized by Sunni leaders for this breach of observance, and although the album sold well abroad, it was his first failure at home. This documentary regards the fallout, as a beloved man fell from local favor despite his intention to bring together religious and musical material.

Then an unexpected thing happened. The album won a Grammy Award. All was for-

given. He was a heroic figure again, paraded through the streets of Dakar, his Grammy held aloft, and invited to a reception at the presidential palace. It's characteristic that N'Dour, a wealthy man, learned the news not at the Beverly Hills ceremony but at home with family and close friends.

This documentary by Elizabeth Chai Vasarhelyi could have used more music for my taste, and fewer talking heads. But it's absorbing all the same. N'Dour is the sort of humanitarian bridge we need in a world so sharply divided.

Youth in Revolt ★★★
R, 90 m., 2010

Michael Cera (Nick Twisp/Francois), Portia Doubleday (Sheeni Saunders), Zach Galifianakis (Jerry), Ray Liotta (Lance Wescott), Justin Long (Paul Saunders), Jean Smart (Estelle Twisp), Adhir Kalyan (Vijay Joshi), Fred Willard (Mr. Ferguson), Steve Buscemi (George Twisp). Directed by Miguel Arteta and produced by David Permut. Screenplay by Gustin Nash, based on the novel by C. D. Payne.

Michael Cera is not a sissy. It's more like he's unusually diffident. Laid back to a point approaching the horizontal. Yet he yearns. He's so filled with desire it slops over. I speak not of the real Cera, unknown to me, but of the persona he has perfected in such movies as *Superbad, Juno, Nick and Norah's Infinite Playlist,* and *Paper Heart.*

That was the comedy that pretended to be a documentary about his romance with Charlyne Yi, which was also going on in real life. That made for some ambivalent scenes, particularly since Ms. Yi herself is laid back so far the two could star in a movie based on *Flatland.*

Youth in Revolt gives Cera the twee name Nick Twisp, surrounds his aging virgin act with divorced parents who are both shacked up with lustful vulgarians, and then provides him with a dream come true in the person of Sheeni Saunders. She's played by Portia Doubleday, a new actress whose name will always be more melodious than those of her characters. They meet during family vacations at the sublimely named Restless Axles trailer park. For Sheeni, who speaks as if influenced by Juno, virginity is a once-touching affectation, and Nick Twisp is oh-so-eager to join her in this opinion. But there are many obstacles to their bliss, worst of all his family's tragic return home.

His family. His mother, Estelle (Jean Smart), lives with Jerry (Zach Galifianakis), a beer-swilling, belching lout who makes Nick's skin crawl. His father, George Twisp (Steve Buscemi), recently laid off, has robbed the cradle for his live-in, Lacey (Ari Graynor). Both parents all but flaunt their lovers before poor Nick; at Restless Axles, his mom asks Nick to clean up after dinner while she and Jerry (after his post-prandial burp) retire to the bedroom a few feet away for noisy rumpy-pumpy.

Sheeni's parents have much less screen time, so they're cast to make an immediate impression. Try to image M. Emmet Walsh and Mary Kay Place as your parents. OK. Nick is desperate to be reunited with Sheeni, tries to float reasons he needs to take a trip right away, and really inadvertently (honest) sets in motion an explosive, fiery chain of events.

Cera's style lends itself to one note, and the movie wisely gives him another character to play, an imaginary alter ego named Francois Dillinger, inspired by Jean-Paul Belmondo. Of course Nick would know who Belmondo is. I'd believe him if he were inspired by Jean Gabin. In this role, he has a mustache and smokes, but true to character, his mustache is wispy and he always smokes like it's his first cigarette.

It's often observed that comedy never works if an actor signals that he's just said something funny. I don't know if Michael Cera *can* do that. It requires such bold assertion. You'd get suicidal trying to get him to laugh at a joke. This passiveness is why he's funnier than Jack Black, for example, in their movie *Year One*. One of the secrets of *Youth in Revolt* is that Nick Twisp seems bewildered by his own desires and strategies. He knows how he feels, he knows what he wants, but he'd need a map to get from A to B. It's Nick's self-abashing modesty that makes the movie work. Here, you feel, is a movie character who would find more peace on the radio.

Z

Zack and Miri Make a Porno ★ ★ ★
R, 101 m., 2008

Seth Rogen (Zack), Elizabeth Banks (Miri Linky), Craig Robinson (Delaney), Jason Mewes (Lester), Jeff Anderson (Deacon), Traci Lords (Bubbles), Katie Morgan (Stacey), Ricky Mabe (Barry). Directed by Kevin Smith and produced by Scott Mosier. Screenplay by Smith.

Kevin Smith begins with the advantage of being raised with deeply embedded senses of sin and guilt. He's thirty-eight, and he still believes sex is dirty and that it's funny to shock people with four-letter words and enough additional vulgarisms to fill out a crossword puzzle. This is sort of endearing. It gives his potty-mouth routines a certain freshness; we've heard these words over and over again, but never so many of them so closely jammed together. If you bleeped this movie for broadcast TV, it would sound like a conga line of Iron Men going through a metal detector.

Zack and Miri Make a Porno, as the title hints, is about Zack (Seth Rogen) and Miri (Elizabeth Banks) making a porno. "I don't know bleep about directing," Smith once confided to me. "But I'm a bleeping good writer." He is. Since he likes to eat, I will describe him in food terms. He isn't a gourmet chef, supplying little nuggets of armadillo surrounded by microscopic carrots and curlicues of raspberry-avocado-mint juice. He's the kind of chef I've valued for a lifetime, the kind you see behind the ledge in a Formica diner, pulling down new orders from revolving clips. The kind of diner where the waitresses wear paper Legionnaire hats, pop their gum, and say, "What ya havin' today, hon?"

In Kevin Smith's fantasy diner, the waitresses at this joint strip naked and have noisy lesbian sex, and then Jose the busboy joins in the fun. They all scream loudly: "Bleep, you bleeping bleep! I bleep your bleep! Bleep! Bleep! I'm bleeping bleeping!" *Variety*, the showbiz bible, trains its critics as keen observers of detail, and their alert senior critic Todd McCarthy observes: "There's scarcely a line of dialogue that doesn't feature the F-word, A-word, one of the C- or P-words or some variant of them."

Zack and Miri are poverty-row roommates who have lived together for years, I guess, but never have sex because you might feel funny around a good friend if you bleeped them, and a good friend is so much harder to come by than a bleep. Now they face eviction and ruin, and might have to become bleeping sidewalk-mates. After some little jerk videotapes them—not bleeping but looking like (B)ILFs—they become superstars of the nether lands of YouTube, and have a brilliant idea: They'll cash in on their fame by making a porn film.

Of course, this will require them to bleep on camera, a sacrifice they are willing to make, as long as what happens in the porno, stays in the porno. They enlist aid from a kid (Jeff Anderson) who videos football games, the abundantly tumescent Jason Mewes (Silent Bob's friend Jay), and the well-known Traci Lords, who at last is the only grown-up in a movie.

As they edge uneasily toward their big scene, Miri and Zack pull off the complex feat of being unfaithful to each other with themselves, who they meet on the set. This does not happen easily, and is accompanied by a flood of scatological humor. Their producer is Delaney (Craig Robinson), a guy Zack works with at a Starbucks wannabe, and who is funny as he tries to responsibly perform duties he knows only in theory.

And, of course, awwww, Zack and Miri admit they've been in love all along, and achieve something you *never* see in a porn film, lovemaking with barely visible sex and very genuine romance. Seth Rogen and Elizabeth Banks make a lovable couple; she's pretty and goes one-for-one on the bleep language, and Rogen, how can I say this, is growing on me, the big lug.

Will this movie offend you? Somehow Kevin Smith's very excesses defuse the material. He's like the guy at a party who tells dirty jokes so fast, Dangerfield-style, that you laugh more at the performance than the material. He's always coming back for more. Once during a speech at the Indie Spirits, he actually sounded like he was offering his wife as a door prize. Anything for a laugh. Nobody laughed. They all looked at one another sort of stunned. You can't say he didn't try.

Zombieland ★★★

R, 81 m., 2009

Jesse Eisenberg (Columbus), Woody Harrelson (Tallahassee), Emma Stone (Wichita), Abigail Breslin (Little Rock), Amber Heard (Maggie), Bill Murray (Himself). Directed by Ruben Fleischer and produced by Gavin Polone. Screenplay by Rhett Reese and Paul Wernick.

There's no getting around it: Zombies are funny. I think they stopped being scary for me along toward the end of *Night of the Living Dead*. OK, maybe in a few others, like *28 Days Later*. They're the Energizer bunnies of corpses, existing primarily to be splattered. But who would have guessed such a funny movie as *Zombieland* could be made around zombies? No thanks to the zombies.

The movie is narrated by a guy played by Jesse Eisenberg, named after his hometown of Columbus, Ohio, who is making his way back home again across a zombie-infested America. The landscape is strewn with burned-out cars and dead bodies. He encounters another nonzombie survivor, Tallahassee (Woody Harrelson). The two team up, not without many disagreements, and eventually find two healthy women: the sexy Wichita (Emma Stone) and her little sister, Little Rock (Abigail Breslin).

The plot comes down to a road movie threatened by the undead, as countless zombies are shot, mashed, sledge-hammered, and otherwise inconvenienced. Wichita and Little Rock turn out to be con women, dashing the hopes of the love-struck Columbus. Yet eventually they all join in an odyssey to a Los Angeles amusement park, for no better reason than that there's no location like a carnival for

a horror movie. Yes, even with a haunted house, the usual ominous calliope music, and a zombie clown. Columbus, like so many others, is phobic about clowns, making Eisenberg an ingrate, since his mother put him through grade school by playing clowns at children's parties.

All of this could have been dreary, but not here. The filmmakers show invention and well-tuned comic timing, and above all there's a cameo by Bill Murray that gets the single biggest laugh I've heard this year. The foursome hauls up at Murray's vast Beverly Hills mansion, so palatial it is surely a grand hotel, and finds him still in residence. More than that I will not say, except that not many zombie comedies can make me think simultaneously about *Psycho* and *Garfield*.

Eisenberg, a good actor, here plays a pleasant nerd who has compiled a seemingly endless survival list for the United States of Zombies. These items are displayed in on-screen graphics that pop up for laughs, and include a tribute to the Back Seat Rule of my Little Movie Glossary, which instructs us—but I'm sure you remember.

Woody Harrelson takes a great deal of relish in killing zombies, often declining to use a gun because he prefers killing them with car doors, tire irons, and whatever else comes to hand. As usual, the zombies are witless, lumbering oafs who dutifully line up to be slaughtered.

Vampires make a certain amount of sense to me, but zombies not so much. What's their purpose? Why do they always look so bad? Can there be a zombie with good skin? How can they be smart enough to determine that you're food, and so dumb they don't perceive you're about to blast them? I ask these questions only because I need a few more words in this review. I will close by observing that Bill Murray is the first comedian since Jack Benny who can get a laugh simply by standing there. ☞

The Best Films of the Decade

1. *Synecdoche, New York* (2008)

January 1, 2010—*Synecdoche, New York* is the best film of the decade. It intends no less than to evoke the strategies we use to live our lives. After beginning my first viewing of it in confusion, I began to glimpse its purpose and by the end was eager to see it again, then once again, and I am not finished. Charlie Kaufman understands how I live my life, and I suppose his own, and I suspect most of us. Faced with the bewildering demands of time, space, emotion, morality, lust, greed, hope, dreams, dreads, and faiths, we build compartments in our minds. It is a way of seeming sane.

The workings of the mind are a concern in all his screenplays, but in *Synecdoche* (2008), his first film as a director, he makes it his subject, and what huge ambition that demonstrates. He's like a novelist who wants to get it all in the first book in case he never publishes another. Those who felt the film was disorganized or incoherent would benefit from seeing it again. It isn't about a narrative, although it pretends to be. It's about a *method,* the method by which we organize our lives and define our realities.

Very few people live their lives on one stage, in one persona, wearing one costume. We play different characters. We know this and accept it. In childhood we begin as always the same person, but quickly we develop strategies for our families, our friends, our schools. In adolescence these strategies are not well controlled. Sexually, teenagers behave one way toward some dates and a different way toward others. We find those whose personas match one of our own, and that defines how we interact with that person. If you are not an aggressor and are sober, there are girls (or boys) you do it with and others you don't, and you don't desire those people to discover what goes on away from them.

But already *Synecdoche* has me thinking in terms of the film's insight. That is its power. Let me stand back and consider it as a movie. It's about a theater director named Caden Cotard (Philip Seymour Hoffman), who begins with a successful regional production, is given a MacArthur genius grant, and moves with a troupe of actors into a New York warehouse. Here they develop a play that grows and grows, and he devises a set representing their various rooms and lives. The film begins as apparently realistic, but it shades off into—fantasy? chaos? complexity?

In those earlier scenes, he was married to Adele (Catherine Keener). She leaves, and he marries Claire (Michelle Williams), who to some degree is intended to literally replace the first wife, as many second spouses are. Why do some people marry those who resemble their exes? They're casting for the same role. Caden has hired an actor named Sammy Barnathan (Tom Noonan) to star in the play, as a character somewhat like himself. Many writers and directors create fiction from themselves, and are often advised to.

What happens in the film isn't supposed to happen in life. The membrane between fact and fiction becomes permeable, and the separate lives intermingle. Caden hardly seems to know whose life he's living; his characters develop minds of their own. How many authors have you heard say their dialogue involves "just writing down what the characters would say"?

Living within different personas is something many people do. How can a governor think to have a mistress in Argentina? An investment counselor think to steal all the money he's entrusted with? A famous athlete be revealed as a sybarite? A family man be discovered to have two families? I suspect such people, and to a smaller degree many of us, find no more difficulty in occupying those different scenarios than we might in eating meat some days and on others calling ourselves vegetarian.

Synecdoche is accomplished in all the technical areas, including its astonishing set. The acting requires great talent to create characters who are always in their own reality, however much it shifts. Philip Seymour Hoffman's character experiences a deterioration of body, as we all do, finds it more difficult to see outside himself, as we all do, and becomes less sure of who "himself" is, as sooner or later we all do.

Kaufman has made the most perceptive film I can recall about how we live in the world. This is his debut as a director, but his most important contribution is the screenplay. Make no mistake that he sweated blood over this screenplay. Somebody had to know what was happening on all those levels, and that had to be the writer. Of course he directed it. Who else could have comprehended it?

The other top films of the decade follow, with a nod to the fact that the decade still has one year to go. If it doesn't, you were two on your first birthday.

2. *The Hurt Locker* (2009)

A film that concerns not the war but the warrior. It's set in Iraq, and by nature we identify with the hero, James (Jeremy Renner). But it focuses not on the enemy but on the bomb disposal expert himself, who risks his life hundreds of times when the slightest mistake would mean maiming or death. "War is a drug," the opening titles tell us. The man's fellow soldiers are angry with him for the chances he takes. He considers bomb disposal a battle of the wits between himself and the designer. Yes, but the designer is not there if a bomb explodes. He is. Yet he volunteers.

Apart from this psychological puzzle, Kathryn Bigelow's film has a masterful command of editing, tempo, character, and photography. Using no stunts and CGI, she creates a convincing portrayal of the conditions a man like James faces. She builds with classical tools. She evokes suspense, dread, identification. She asks if a man like James *requires* such a fearsome job. The film is a triumph of theme and execution, and very nearly flawless.

3. *Monster* (2004)

An Egyptian film critic told me in disbelief that this film made him sympathize with a serial killer. I knew what he meant. We are enjoined to love not the sin but the sinner. Patty Jenkins's film is based on the life of Aileen Wuornos, a damaged woman who committed seven murders. It doesn't excuse the murders. It asks that we witness the woman's final desperate attempt to be a better person than her fate intended.

Charlize Theron's performance in the role is one of the greatest performances in the history of the cinema. She transforms herself into a character with an uncanny resemblance to the real Aileen Wuornos—but mere impersonation isn't as difficult as *embodying* another person. Aileen, abused all of her life, knows she is doing evil but is driven to it by her deep need to provide for another person, her lover Selby (Christina Ricci), as she was never provided for herself. This doesn't make murder right in her mind, but she believes it's necessary. We disagree. But we're asked to empathize with her ruined soul, and because of Theron and Jenkins, we find that possible.

4. *Juno* (2007)

One of a kind, a film that delighted me from beginning to end, never stepping wrong with its saucy young heroine who faces an unexpected pregnancy with forthright boldness. To be sure, life doesn't always provide parents and an adoptive mother for the baby as comforting as Juno's. But Jason Reitman's second feature doesn't set out to be realistic; it's a fable about how the sad realities of teen pregnancy might be transformed in a good-hearted world. Ellen Page creates a character to be long cherished, a smart, articulate sixteen-year-old who keeps a brave front and yet deeply feels what she's going through.

Juno's dialogue is so nimble and funny that some said no real person thinks that fast and talks like that. Real people may not. Juno does. The original screenplay by Diablo Cody is pitch-perfect comedy writing, assuming the audience is as intelligent as Juno. Have you noticed how many stupid people are presented as normal, especially in mainstream comedies? I was surprised how much I laughed during *Juno,* and then surprised how much I cared, especially during a luminous scene when the woman who will adopt her baby (Jennifer Garner) solemnly places her hand on Juno's pregnant belly and the two exchange a look so beautiful that if I'd known it was coming I don't know if I could have looked.

5. *Me and You and Everyone We Know* (2005)

Another extraordinary film centered on a woman. Is it possible that women in the movies more readily embody emotion, and men tend more toward external action? But women as wildly different as Aileen Wuornos, Juno, and Miranda July's Christine are tuned to inner channels that drive them with feeling, not plots. This first feature shows a certainty about the tone it wants to strike, which is of fragile magic. We don't learn a lot about Christine—more, actually, about Richard (John Hawkes), the awkward shoe salesman she likes—but the story's not about her life; it's about how, for her, love requires someone who speaks her rare emotional language, a language of whimsy and daring, of playful mind games and bold challenges.

Imagine Christine and Richard as they walk down the street. Still strangers, she suggests that the block they are walking down is their lives. And now, she says, they're halfway down the street and halfway through their lives. Before long they will be at the end. It's impossible to suggest how poetic this scene is; when it's over, you think, that was a perfect scene, and no other scene can ever be like it. And we are all on the sidewalk. July's film fits no genre, fulfills no expectations, creates its own rules, and seeks only to share a strange and lovable mind with us.

6. *Chop Shop* (2008)

Here is the third world, thriving under the flight path to LaGuardia. Ale (Alejandro Polanco), a twelve-year-old boy, works for the owner of an auto repair shop in an area few New Yorkers know about: Willets Point, square blocks of auto and tire shops that hustle for business. He's an orphan, dreaming of being reunited with his sixteen-year-old sister. He steals a little, cons a little, sells pirated DVDs, and mostly works hard. He lives in a room knocked together in the crawl space of the shop. He's not educated, but is bright, resourceful, and happy.

Poised on the edge of adolescence, he senses changes coming. As his sister (Isamar Gonzales) moves in with him, he proudly tries to support her—to be the man in the family he lost. Ramin Bahrani observed Willets Point for a year and worked with two nonactors to achieve remarkably fluent and convincing performances. His film is a vibrant modern equivalent of the Italian Neorealist classics like *Shoeshine*. It stays resolutely within its story, never making the mistake of drawing conclusions. It's riveting, entertaining, unforgettable,

with a meticulous visual strategy. Bahrani, an Iranian-American born in Winston-Salem, North Carolina, has made three films (including *Man Push Cart* and *Goodbye Solo*), and all three have made my Best 10 lists. In my opinion, he's the new director of the decade.

7. *The Son* (2002)

In a career filled with great films, *Le Fils* by Jean-Pierre and Luc Dardenne is stunning. It focuses intensely on two characters: Olivier (Olivier Gourmet), a Belgian carpenter, and Francis (Morgan Marinne), a young apprentice that a social worker wants to place with him. Olivier refuses. The moment they leave, Olivier scurries after them like a feral animal, spies on them through a door opening, and leaps onto a metal cabinet to look through a high window. Then he says he will take the boy.

That's all I choose to say. What connects them is revealed so carefully and deliberately that any hint would diminish the experience. Once again, as with all the films on this list, writing and acting are crucial. Yes, they're well directed, but you know, there are a lot of fine directors. There's a scene here where Francis and Olivier are working in a lumber warehouse, shifting and loading heavy planks. We know enough by then to invest the scene with meaning. The Dardennes achieve their effect primarily through sound: the raw, harsh sound of one plank upon another. I can think of many ways to film such a scene, none better.

8. *25th Hour* (2003)

A film about the last twenty-four hours of freedom for Monty Brogan (Edward Norton), a convicted drug dealer. He lives in a heightened state. He focuses on the remaining important things: his lover, his father, his best friends. Spike Lee, working with David Benioff's adaptation of his own novel, gives adequate screen time to all the people in Monty's life; their lives will continue but, his friends agree, they will never see Monty again. Not the Monty they know.

The film avoids crime-movie clichés. It's about the time remaining. Lee reflects Monty's acute awareness of this with scenes of startling inventiveness, one an angry monolog delivered to a mirror, another a shared fantasy as his father (Brian Cox) drives him to prison. Too many movies now require their expensive stars to be onscreen in almost every frame. *25th Hour* is enriched by supporting performances, notably by Philip Seymour Hoffman as a pudgy English teacher, not accustomed to drinking, who makes a devastating mistake involving appearance and reality. Spike Lee writes eloquently with his camera in strategies that are anything but conventional.

9. *Almost Famous* (2000)

The story of a fifteen-year-old kid (Patrick Fugit), smart and terrifyingly earnest, who through luck and pluck gets assigned by *Rolling Stone* magazine to do a profile of a rising rock band. The magazine has no idea he's fifteen. Clutching his pencil and his notebook like talismans, phoning a veteran critic for advice, he plunges into the experience that will make and shape him. It's as if Huckleberry Finn came back to life in the 1970s, and instead of taking a raft down the Mississippi, got on the bus with the band. I was hugging myself as I watched it: This is my story. Well, except in the details.

Cameron Crowe, the writer-director, was inspired by his own experiences, here transformed by an ability to step outside the first person and clearly see the hero's mother (Frances McDormand), a band groupie (Kate Hudson), the lead singer (Jason Lee), and the veteran journalist (Philip Seymour Hoffman, again). This is a coming-of-age story with the feel of plausible experience, because when you're fifteen even the most implausible things seem likely if they're happening to you.

10. *My Winnipeg* (2008)

If I said *Almost Famous* was my life, would you believe *My Winnipeg* tells the history of my hometown? All except for the details—which, for that matter, don't particularly pertain to Winnipeg, either. Guy Maddin's films are like silent movies dreaming they can speak. No frame of his work could be mistaken for anyone else's. He combines documentary, lurid melodrama, newsreels, feverish fantasies, and tortured typography into a form that appears to contain urgent information. His sound tracks are sometimes clear narration, sometimes soap opera, sometimes snatches that seem heard over a radio from long ago and far away. The effect is hypnotic.

The city fathers of Winnipeg asked Maddin, their famous local filmmaker, to direct a documentary on their city. God knows what they thought of it. Now they can reassure the taxpayers it's one of the best films of the decade. There are perhaps sights, sounds, and even facts in *My Winnipeg* that are accurate, but how can you be sure when some of the most sensible elements are false and the most incredible are true? This is the story of everyone's hometown; we piece it together in childhood and in some sense continue to regard it as true even when it isn't. His beliefs about secret parallel taxi companies operating along invisible alleys are as reasonable as my own beliefs about the Bone Yard in Urbana-Champaign—which is, after all, only a drainage ditch, but you can't tell me that.

* * *

Those 10, and these 10, alphabetically, because all twenty titles are magnificent:

Adaptation, The Bad Lieutenant, City of God, Crash, Kill Bill Vols. 1 and 2, Minority Report, No Country for Old Men, Pan's Labyrinth, Silent Light, Waking Life.

The Best Films of 2009

December 18, 2009—Since Moses brought the tablets down from the mountain, lists have come in tens, not that we couldn't have done with several more commandments. Who says a year has ten best films, anyway? Nobody but readers, editors, and most other movie critics. There was hell to pay last year when I published my list of twenty best. You'd have thought I belched at a funeral. So on this list I have devoutly limited myself to exactly ten films. On each of two lists. (Animated features and documentaries get their own lists at the end.)

The lists are divided into mainstream films and independent films. This neatly sidesteps two frequent complaints: (1) "You name all these little films most people have never heard of," and (2) "You pick all blockbusters and ignore the indie pictures." Which is my official Top Ten? They both are equal, and every film here is entitled to name itself "One of the Year's Ten Best!" Alphabetically:

The Top Ten Mainstream Films

1. *Bad Lieutenant*

Werner Herzog's edgy noir fed off Nicolas Cage's flywheel intensity in a portrait of a cokehead cop out of control in post-Katrina New Orleans. He starts out bad and, driven by a painful back and pain meds, goes crazy and gets away with it because of the badge. Herzog paints the storied city in dark shadows and a notable lack of glamour, and when he involves Cage in a stare-down with an iguana, it somehow needs no explanation. I predict they'll work together again. They probably got along as well as Herzog and Klaus Kinski.

2. *Crazy Heart*

This year's late-opening sleeper, built on a probable Oscar-winning performance by Jeff Bridges. He plays a nearly forgotten country-and-western singer, touring nasty dives and smoky honky-tonks for a few dollars and change. He had hits, but alcoholism eroded him. Maggie Gyllenhaal is inspired as the woman who cares for him but doubts his newfound sobriety—and no, this isn't a cornball story about romantic redemption. After the screening a critic said: "This year's *Wrestler*." That sounded about right. Astonishing debut direction by Scott Cooper.

3. *An Education*

A star is born with Carey Mulligan's performance as a sixteen-year-old schoolgirl who is flattered and romanced, along with her protective parents, by an attractive, mysterious man in his mid-thirties (Peter Sarsgaard). He's sophisticated, she's not; she sees him as a way out of London suburbia and into the circles she dreams of entering. He's not a molester but an opportunist and role-player, and Lone Scherfig's film is wise about what people want in a relationship and what they get. Faithfully adapted by Nick Hornby from the memoirs of the well-known British journalist Lynn Barber.

4. *The Hurt Locker*

"War is a drug," the opening title informs us, and in one of the best war movies ever, Jeremy Renner plays an expert member of an elite bomb disposal unit in Iraq. Somewhat guarded by a protective suit, he handles delicate mechanisms designed to outwit him. It's like chess. He's very good at his job, but is that what drives him to put his life on the line hundreds of times? Not pro-war, not antiwar, not about the war in Iraq, but about the minds of dedicated combat soldiers. Directed flawlessly by Kathryn Bigelow; as one critic's group after another honored it in their year-end awards, it became a sure thing for picture, actor, and director nominations.

5. *Inglourious Basterds*

Quentin Tarantino is a natural and joyous filmmaker who feeds off genres. Here he takes the richness of World War II films and molds it into a flamboyant, melodramatic story that fearlessly rewrites history. It finally comes down to a conflict between a fatuous Nazi monster (Christoph Waltz) and a fearless French Jewish heroine (Melanie Laurent), with Brad Pitt as a knife-wielding American commando leader. Waltz won best actor at Cannes 2009, has swept the critic's awards, and is a shoo-in as best supporting actor.

6. *Knowing*

Among the best of science fiction films— frightening, suspenseful, intelligent, and, when it needs to be, rather awesome. In its very different way it's comparable to the great *Dark City*, by the same director, Alex Proyas. That film was about the hidden nature of the world men think they inhabit, and so is this one. I loved the film's extravagance of energy and the hard-charging Nicolas Cage performance (so different from *Bad Lieutenant*). My praise stirred up a fierce pro and con debate among readers: http://j.mp/4MmMss.

7. *Precious*

The heartrending story of an overweight, abused young teenager and the support she finds from a teacher and a social worker, who both glimpse her potential. Harrowing, depressing, and yet uplifting, as director Lee Daniels uses her fantasies to show the dreams inside. What a sure and brave lead performance by newcomer Gabourey Sidibe, and what a powerful one by Mo'Nique, as her heartless mother. She, Mariah Carey, Paula Patton, and Sherri Shepherd are all but unrecognizable as they disappear into key supporting roles.

8. *A Serious Man*

Another great film by the Coen brothers, returning to their homeland of the Minneapolis suburbs to tell the story of a modern-day Job who strives to be a good man, a "serious man," and finds everything—but everything—going wrong. Michael Stuhlbarg gives a virtuoso lead performance as the suffering man, who earnestly tries to do the right thing. Fred Melamed is brilliant as his best friend, who, he discovers, is having an affair with his wife. The friend tries to console him; he is grief and grief counselor at once.

9. *Up in the Air*

George Clooney plays a man for the first decade of this uncertain century. "Where do you live?" he's asked while seated in a first-class airplane seat. "Here." He wants no home, no wife, no family, and says he is happy. His job is depriving others of theirs; he's a termination facilitator. He fires people for a living. Vera Farmiga plays his friendly fellow road warrior who sleeps with him on the road. Anna Kendrick is the sincere young college grad whose first job is terminating others. The third wonderful film by Jason Reitman, after *Thank You for Smoking* and *Juno*.

10. *White Ribbon*

The subterranean and labyrinthine secret history of a German village in the years before World War I. A mysterious series of deaths descends like a vengeance. Michael Haneke's elegant black-and-white photography etches the rural community in striking portraits of sinister normality. We become familiar with the important villagers, we follow their stories, we comprehend everything that happens— but something else is happening, something unspoken, kept secret from them, among them, and from us. Infinitely tantalizing.

* * *

Now you are thinking, hey, what about *Avatar*? Faithful readers know of my annual Special Jury Prize. This year it goes to James Cameron's ground-breaking epic. No, that doesn't mean it's the best film of the year. It means it won the Special Jury Prize.

The Top Ten Independent Films

1. *Departures*

In Japan, a young man apprentices to the trade of "encoffinment," the preparation of corpses before their cremation. It is the only employment he can find, after he loses his job as a cellist in an orchestra that goes broke. The company owner approaches the job as a sacred vocation, and although the hero and his wife find the task unsettling, he slowly learns a new respect for himself through respect for the dead. A visually beautiful and poetic film by Yojiro Takita.

2. *Disgrace*

A masterful performance by John Malkovich as a disgraced Cape Town English professor forced to resign during the first years of Mandela's administration. He goes to live with his daughter (Jessica Haines) on her remote farm, where the manager (Eriq Ebouaney) seems to be establishing an independence of his own. The hard, ambiguous issues of the new South African world are squarely engaged in Steve Jacobs's film, based on the novel by Nobel winner J. M. Coetzee.

3. *Everlasting Moments*

The great Swedish filmmaker Jan Troell (*The Emigrants* and *The New Land*) tells the story of the wife of an alcoholic dock worker in Malmo in 1911. He's not a bad man, except when he drinks. She wins a camera in a lottery and tries to pawn it, but the camera store owner tells her to keep taking pictures. Her inner life is transformed by discovering that she has an artistic talent. A luminous performance by Maria Heiskanen.

4. *Goodbye Solo*

The third remarkable film by Ramin Bahrani, after *Man Push Cart* and *Chop Shop*. In Winston-Salem, North Carolina, a white man around seventy (onetime Elvis bodyguard Red West) gets into the taxi of an African immigrant (Souleymane Sy Savane, from the Ivory Coast). For $1,000, paid immediately, he wants to be driven in ten days to the top of a mountain in Blowing Rock National Park, to a place so windy that the snow falls up. He says nothing about a return trip. As a friendship develops between them, the days tick inexorably away.

5. *Julia*

The most striking performance in Tilda Swinton's exciting career. Only poor marketing prevented this from succeeding as the thriller of the year. Swinton plays an alcoholic slut who agrees to help kidnap a child and ends up with him on an odyssey in Mexico through a thorn thicket of people you do not want to meet. If there's one thing consistent about her behavior, it's how she lies to all of them. Directed by Erick Zonca.

6. *Silent Light*

A story of romance and conscience set among the Mennonites of Mexico. A happily married man falls in love with a single woman, and she with him, and they are both haunted by guilt. Their gravitas is a stark contrast to the casual attitude toward sex in most films; they are violating rules they respect,

hurting people they love. Carlos Reygadas tells his story with a clarity and attention worthy of a Bresson.

7. *Sin Nombre*

Up through Mexico, those hopeful of entering the United States ride the top of a freight train. We meet a girl from Honduras with her father and uncle, and a young gang member fleeing for his life. The journey is difficult and dangerous, but also oddly lovely and epic. A parallel story involves a gang set up to rob the would-be immigrants, who often carry all their wealth. Written and directed by Cary Fukunaga, another of this year's remarkable debut filmmakers.

8. *Skin*

The Sandra Laing story obsessed South Africans in 1965. She was the daughter of white Afrikaners. She didn't look white. Her father fights to the Supreme Court to have her reclassified as white, and then when she falls in love with a black man, she tries to have her classification changed. A wrenching dilemma, starring Sophie Okonedo (*Dirty Pretty Things*) in a tricky and compelling role, and Sam Neill as her deeply conflicted father.

9. *Trucker*

Michelle Monaghan is remarkable as a truck driver who has just paid off her own rig. She's thirtyish, hard-drinking, promiscuous, estranged from the father (Benjamin Bratt) of her twelve-year-old son. In an emergency she has to take the boy back, and that leads from an arm's-length relationship to difficult personal discoveries. A powerful debut by writer-director James Mottern.

10. *You, the Living*

In a sad world and a sad city, sad people lead sad lives and complain that they hate their jobs and nobody understands them. The result is in some ways a comedy with a twist of the knife, and in other ways a film like nobody else has ever made—except for its director, Roy Andersson of Sweden. Fifty vignettes, almost all shot with a static camera, in medium and long shot. You laugh to yourself, silently, although you're never quite sure why. Flawless in what it does, and we have no idea what that is.

Interviews

Judd Apatow

July 26, 2009—If there is a King of Comedy right now in Hollywood, that would be Judd Apatow. I have a list here of a dozen comedies he has produced and/or directed just in the last five years, and I left out the titles I didn't like. He has been writing since he was a kid, producing since he was twenty-three, and then he directed *The 40-Year-Old Virgin* (2005) and *Knocked Up* (2007) himself. He is only forty-one. I think he's hitting his stride.

Now he has directed Adam Sandler, arguably the top comic star in town, in a film about a stand-up comic who gets a death sentence from his doctors. And no, *Funny People* isn't about how this is a wake-up call for the comic, making him into a better human being.

"I thought an interesting story would be about someone who goes the other way and learns almost nothing from their near-death experience," Apatow informed me.

It's that kind of inversion of stereotypes that he did so well in his first two directorial credits. A forty-year-old man isn't expected to be a virgin. A woman with a big TV job shouldn't become pregnant with some basically nice guy she meets in a club. She shouldn't be basically nice, either.

Apatow has written hundreds of thousands of words for some of the best comedians in America, including Roseanne, Garry Shandling, and Jim Carrey. Most producers don't write much of anything, and some even pay people to read for them. He worked outside the formulas in producing sixty-five episodes of *The Larry Sanders Show,* on which timing and nuance were everything. You have the feeling *Funny People* grows directly out of his experiences and observations.

"Because I was a comedy fan first and foremost," he said in an e-mail interview, "I had a good ear for writing in the voice of the comics I was writing jokes for, but it took me decades to believe my own point of view would be interesting to people. I could never believe that comics would allow me into their world. The hard part about writing this movie was the fact that the comedians I wrote for were very nice to me. Nothing dramatic ever happened."

George Simmons, the Sandler character, is not a very nice man. He's not an evil creep or a drugged zombie or anything like that, but he's closed off, cool to people, very rich, successful, with his own TV series, imperious, with no friends. Think Jerry Seinfeld if all of those things were true of him, which they certainly are not. Then show your hero hearing his doctor informing him he has a limited time remaining on Earth.

"Sadly," Apatow said, "I have known quite a few people who have been seriously ill in the last few years. I've watched them struggle with the ups and downs of their situations. There are many important lessons that people learn when they are fighting an illness. Aspects of it can be very positive, and their connections with their friends and family often become much closer and richer.

"George Simmons's ego is so out of control that he interprets all the wrong lessons from his situation, and that's where the comedy comes from. In movies on this subject the lead character usually changes dramatically and becomes a perfect person. I thought it would be more fun and more truthful to show someone resist the change."

There are a lot of laughs in *Funny People,* even though much of it is about funny people when they are not being funny. Stand-ups frequently make a living being funny about their miseries, and the habit is not easily broken. Remember Richard Pryor being hilarious about his conversations with cocaine.

"My goal was to make a film that was just as funny as my other two films, but which also dug a lot deeper and was not afraid to be more emotional," Apatow said. "We didn't put anything in the film just to be funny—also had to get at the truth of this type of situation. It was very scary because I am so used to letting the laugh count guide me as to whether or not the movie is working well. Sometimes this movie is working really well when there are no laughs. That's new for me. I prefer to hear noises from the crowd wall-to-wall to make me sleep better at night."

I have not been the biggest fan of Adam Sandler's films. Yet he has surprised me whenever he moves outside his basic childish persona and works for a director with other ideas. He is a good actor, and he can go there. Consider Paul Thomas Anderson's *Punch-Drunk Love* (2002). Or his work in Mike Binder's *Reign Over Me* (2007). Or Peter Segal's *50 First Dates* (2004). Now consider *Funny People,* and his performance built from nuance, timing, and a lot of insight into a famous comic who is a lot more than famous or comic.

Apatow and Sandler have long known each other, although amazingly they've never worked together. Apatow's wife, the actress Leslie Mann, costarred with Sandler in *Big Daddy* ten years ago, became a close friend, and in *Funny People* she plays a person he can trust.

"I think Adam hesitates to take on more serious work because he looks for directors he trusts. We've known each other for twenty years, so he was willing to completely put himself in my hands. There was never a moment when he said, 'I don't want to do this because it might make me look bad,' or because 'it cuts too close to the bone.' He was very brave. And I must say, it was very painful to watch him perform the more intense scenes when his character was sick because I knew that he had experienced moments like that with his family in real life, as had I."

Apatow as a teenager hung out in comedy clubs on Long Island, "used to highlight the *TV Guide* so I would know who was going to be on which show that week," got a job as a comedy club dishwasher, idolized the stand-up guys. It's not hard to figure who the autobiographical character is in *Funny People.* That would be the newly thin Seth Rogen, as a rookie comic who becomes George Simmons's assistant, flunky, and even opening act.

His admirable weight loss makes Rogen look younger, which suits the role, and also provides dialogue. "I always try to acknowledge what the audience might be thinking," Apatow said. "I knew people would notice Seth's new skinny physique, and it made sense

that his friend in the movie, played by Jonah Hill, would mock him for it. He tells him that nobody wants to laugh at a physically fit man. I must say there's an argument that that's true. My friend Kevin Rooney used to say, 'If you have time to work out, you don't have time to work on your act.'"

Funny. I was thinking that the same is true about film criticism. But I'll keep that to myself. Rim shot. Thank you very much. You've been a great audience.

Jeff Bridges

December 22, 2009—After a career as a leading actor that began with *The Last Picture Show* in 1971 and has included four Academy Award nominations, Jeff Bridges seems poised to be nominated again for his pitch-perfect performance as Bad Blake, a broken-down country singer in *Crazy Heart.* He has been the leader in the best actor category of many year-end awards by critics' groups.

RE: This performance seems fueled by a lot of inner passion. It is about redemption and inner reclamation. You must have known people like Bad Blake. You show a lot of empathy.

JB: Well, I know myself pretty well. I guess empathy starts there.

RE: Along comes a first-time director named Scott Cooper and makes one of your very best films. You knew him as an actor? He had this screenplay?

JB: I didn't know him as an actor. I originally turned down the script, not because I had any trouble working with a first-time director; some of my most gratifying and successful experiences have been with first-time directors. The screenplay was fine, but it was missing an essential ingredient; there was no music or music supervisor attached to this material. It was finding out that my old buddy T-Bone Burnett was interested that got me to the party.

RE: Maggie Gyllenhaal. Her character arrives at the correct note at the end but not the expected one. That required subtle modulation from both of you.

JB: It was a joy working with Maggie. Each take was fresh, with unexpected results.

RE: I heard there was a time when *Crazy Heart* was headed for cable.

JB: I'm not sure if that's true, but I do see Fox Searchlight as our hero. Getting distribution

637

these days is tough. I don't think we could have had a better distributor.

RE: Actually, three of your five Oscar nominations (I include this one) were directed by first-time filmmakers. You believe . . .?

JB: I think first-time directors bring something wonderful to a movie. After all, we haven't done much better than *Citizen Kane*, Orson Welles's first movie.

RE: There was an excellent article about you some years back in the *New York Times Magazine*, at the time of *Starman*, calling you something like the best American "effortless" actor. It's true you never chew the scenery, or never even nibble. Innate or learned?

JB: I'd say it's a combination of both. A lot has to do with the bed I was born in. Lloyd and Dorothy Bridges were wonderful parents and teachers.

RE: Your first meaningful lead was in *The Last Picture Show*. You get nominated. That was one of those seminal films like *Bonnie and Clyde* that made new stars. But at the time, while you were shooting it . . . ?

JB: Even though most of the actors were green at the time, we knew we were involved in something very special. I think it stands by itself. It's like nothing else, and nothing else is like it.

RE: *The Big Lebowski* has inspired the Church of the Latter Day Dude, which our *Sun-Times* religion editor has written about in a book. Are you devout?

JB: I tend to be Buddhistly bent.

RE: *The Contender*. A political film really about something. And an illustration of the sharklike devouring of all celebrities, including political celebrities, that was unknown when we both started out.

JB: *The Contender* was a wonderful experience. Again, directed by a first-time director, Rod Lurie. He, like Scott Cooper, the director of *Crazy Heart*, was steeped in his subject. Rod knew all of the ins and outs of Washington, D.C.

RE: *The Iceman Cometh*. I was able to get it on DVD and be reminded of its greatness. What a cast. One of Frankenheimer's finest hours, as he himself thought. Lee Marvin, Robert Ryan, Fredric March: three giants. You'd made some films by then, but it must have been a heady experience, and a taste of Frankenheimer's experience with TV drama.

JB: Yes, it was. It was a turning point in my life. That was the film where I decided that I could make acting the focus of my career and bring my other interests, like music, art, photography, et cetera, to it.

Willem Dafoe

October 20, 2009—Has there been a more harrowing and courageous performance this year? Willem Dafoe plays a wholly evil man occupying a wholly evil world in Lars von Trier's *Antichrist*, a new film that challenges its viewers so boldly that some have fled from the theater. Von Trier's films often stir up heated discussion, but never has he made a film quite this formidable.

Dafoe, known for his risk-taking, plays He opposite Charlotte Gainsbourg's She, in a film without other characters except for their baby, who dies in the opening sequence. Although the film never says so, their relationship is founded on the reality of a universe without goodness. It seems to me this is necessary if you introduce an antichrist figure, just as matter is impossible in an antimatter universe.

Whatever the interpretation, there's no questioning the extremes von Trier demands from his actors. Dafoe has repeatedly played difficult characters for great but demanding directors. Indulge me in making a list: Paul Schrader, Werner Herzog, Abel Ferrara, Theodoros Angelopoulos, Oliver Stone, Spike Lee, Martin Scorsese, Sam Raimi, Wes Anderson.

Even in this company, von Trier has a reputation of being the most difficult; after *Dogville*, Nicole Kidman was quoted as saying she not only didn't want to act for him again, but to ever speak with him again. Yet *Antichrist* is Dafoe's second film with von Trier, after *Manderlay*.

It's not a love affair. "His impulses are often perverse," Dafoe informed me, adding the mixed compliment: "He's one of the most bitterly funny people I know." We shared an exchange via e-mail:

RE: What did von Trier say was the meaning of the story?

WD: Lars spoke nothing of the meaning of the story. He did share the origins of the screenplay, which grew out of a collection of personal images, dreams, and anxieties that haunted him in his depression, that were organized around the idea of these two people confronting a Nature created by Satan, not God.

RE: Did you agree, or did you use your own inner interpretation?

WD: I didn't feel the need to interpret the story. In a film where there are basically only two actors, you become the story. I felt like I could best serve the film by looking no further than each scene and having no particular design outside the character's objective in each scene. I had no real interest to craft an arc of a performance. If you have an interpretation of the story, as an actor, it makes you more self-conscious and you measure your impulses. In this case I felt it would inhibit me.

RE: What sorts of discussions did you have with Charlotte Gainsbourg about the nature of your performances?

WD: Our communication was an unspoken trust in each other, which was formed by mutual fear, confusion, respect, and a desire to give Lars what he needed. We discussed very little.

RE: In your experience, how do actors feel about performance intimacy that violates their personal space?

WD: Many actors have a not-so-secret desire to expose themselves emotionally—and in some cases, literally! If you really are committed to playing, to *becoming*, a character, you don't really have personal space. Vulnerability becomes strength. Some people feel stronger with their clothes off, or doing private things publicly. I think sometimes people want to "play house" when they have intimate scenes in order to assure they become practiced at intimacy or to encourage chemistry for the camera. With Charlotte and I, we had great intimacy on the set but the truth is we barely knew each other. We kissed in front of the camera the first time; we got naked for the first time with the camera rolling. This is pure pretending. Since our intimacy only exists before the camera it makes it more potent for us.

RE: You've been fearless in your choice of roles. Yet from all I know and have observed, you're far from a wild man—instead, a thoughtful, kind, private person. What resources do you summon to take on such challenges?

WD: I suppose I am a fearful, average man in life and cling to social conventions like most people so as not to be vulnerable. Grace, manners, and form in behavior are very important to me. My upbringing has instilled in me the importance of self-reliance and "don't burden anybody"—for better and for worse. In film, in telling stories, in inhabiting characters, I have an opportunity to play out fantasies, test limits, empathize with people unlike me, think the unthinkable in an environment, a form. I feel free to play with my darker nature and test it in a constructive way. Challenges that engage you in a full way become so seductive and consuming that you don't think about consequence or failure; you only think about the quality of being there—which can become totally intoxicating and transforming.

RE: The antichrist, of course, represents in Christian terms the antithesis of all that is right and good. My theory is that the film suggests a world lacking all joy and virtue. Your character is not evil by choice, but is acting out his nature. What's your theory, from this sort of theological POV?

WD: I don't know about the theological . . . my character's well-meaning, but arrogant. But he comes to accept a kind of darkness, an utter futility. Admitting helplessness, acknowledging unpleasant truth. Far more than we could possibly imagine. We cannot save ourselves. Imagined knowledge blinds us. This kind of journey puts us in touch with our humanness and awakens compassion for ourselves and others.

RE: You've worked with an astonishing variety of great directors, including von Trier before. What distinguishes von Trier?

WD: Lars's impulses are often perverse. He has an incredible knack for considering the taboo, the unthinkable, the suppressed thoughts and actions that reside inside of us. He has incredible technical facility as a filmmaker, but he subverts it—almost as his duty as an artist. He is also one of the most bitterly funny people I know.

RE: I have a film festival that honors overlooked films that deserve more attention. I've long felt *Shadow of the Vampire* falls in that category. Agree? Other films you wish more people had seen?

WD: *Shadow of the Vampire* was important to me because I had found a character that somehow really presented me with a mask that my imagination responded to—so I felt very free in performing that character. I have a hard time judging the film because I had too much fun playing that role. Do you mean films I've done? I get self-conscious about judging film that I've done because, of course, I can't separate my involvement with the result. I will say, I feel very bad that Abel Ferrara's imperfect but beautifully personal film *Go Go Tales* hasn't been distributed in the U.S. It's a beautiful portrait of a dreamer, and almost a metaphor for scrappy independent filmmakers like Abel. It is also a role that actually makes me laugh and one of the few times I did a lot of improvising in a movie with I think good results.

RE: *John Carter of Mars*. Will it lose anything by being pitched for a PG-13?

WD: I don't think so. But I am just starting to prepare, so I can't say anything with authority, except I'm excited to work with Andrew Stanton, and the drawings and designs I've seen so far look incredible.

Leonardo DiCaprio

February 16, 2010—*Shutter Island* is the fourth film Leonardo DiCaprio and Martin Scorsese have made together, and the most unexpected. It's not a biopic (*The Aviator*) or a modern gangster movie (*The Departed*) or a historical gangster movie (*Gangs of New York*). It securely occupies that most American of genres, the film noir—the dark film, the film that takes place in the shadows of human nature.

DiCaprio plays Teddy Daniels, a United States marshal. The time is 1954, toward the end of the original film noir era. His assignment: Help find a woman killer who has disappeared from a prison for the criminally insane on a remote and craggy island. It's a Locked Room mystery, because there seems to be no way to leave the island alive.

Daniels and his partner, Chuck (Mark Ruffalo), arrive seen with those two invaluable props of the film noir hero, fedora hats and cigarettes. They talk like film noir heroes—tough and aggressive. On Shutter Island they encounter a man, however, who seems to come more from the horror genre than film noir. This is Dr. Cawley (Ben Kingsley), the precise and remote man in charge. Reading the original novel by Dennis Lehane, Scorsese was reminded of the hero, if that is the word, of the silent film icon *The Cabinet of Dr. Caligari*.

I sent DiCaprio some questions. His replies, as I might have expected, were thoughtful and perceptive. He is and always has been (ever since *This Boy's Life* and *What's Eating Gilbert Grape* in 1993) an intelligent actor, never content to be only a star, although that certainly happened after *Titanic* in 1997. *This Boy's Life* was his first major feature, and it's interesting that he costarred with Scorsese's muse, Robert De Niro.

RE: I hear that Marty showed you some classic film noir before you began shooting. Which actors did you respond to? Was there a particular film that struck you?

LD: Certainly Dana Andrews and Jimmy Stewart. And you know on my own, Travis Bickle in *Taxi Driver*. The films that we saw ranged from *Steel Helmet* to *Laura* to *Out of the Past* to *Vertigo* to a documentary about a mental asylum called *Titicut Follies*. All of which are great points of reference when you're on the set working with Mr. Scorsese.

Because like a great painter you're a part of the pre-production process while you're working with the actors and the cinematographer and the set director, who decorated to really give us a deep understanding of the movie he was trying to create through cinema's past. So with Scorsese it's always a unique, enjoyable experience that gets you excited about making movies.

RE: The viewer gradually realizes you play a very complex and layered character in *Shutter Island*. How did you deal with that in performance? By prefiguring it or ignoring it?

LD: We very much were conscious of the different ways to portray Teddy. Oftentimes we would take him to different emotional extremes. This was something that not only I was aware of but all other actors were aware of on set.

There's a lot of ambiguity in this film. And there were a lot of different directions to go, character-wise. So we left all those options open for Marty and Thelma Schoonmaker in the editing room to decide at what point they would want to push the character emotionally.

But I think that the screenplay was almost deceiving at first. There are these very complex descriptions of Teddy's past and his memory and things that were, in fact, you know, a dream. And the lines become blurred. But in every situation we deal with highly emotional, highly intense pursuits of the truth. And to do that we needed to, you know, keep pushing the boundaries of Teddy's emotional reactions.

RE: Thrillers based on atmosphere, character, and plot grab me more than those based on action. You?

LD: Well, I do feel the same way. And as much as technology's going to take a place in cinema's future, the most important thing to me is story. If I'm not emotionally engaged with the character, if I have to go to the set as an actor and know that the lines that I say mean exactly what they mean, that's a boring day at work for me.

I love the challenge of being able to take on characters that aren't always what they seem. Be part of story lines that on second and third viewing of the film can take on a different meaning for me as an audience member. I think *Shutter Island* is very much indicative of those types of films.

Although there's a lot of ambiguity in this film, on second- and third-time viewing, things become more specific and they could be a completely unique experience watching them on the next go-around.

RE: You and De Niro are Marty's signature actors, yet your styles are quite distinct. Do you think that's influenced some of Marty's story choices?

LD: Well, I still don't know what my style is. But look. I'm as big of a fan as anyone of their collaborations together. Artistically, they've forged maybe the greatest director-actor relationship in cinematic history and made some of the biggest masterpieces. So I have to look at my relationship with Marty in a very unique way. Never do I try to compare that relationship—it's too high a mantle to try to surpass.

So what I basically do is commit myself fully to whatever the story lends itself to, and give Marty everything he needs, and try to push myself to the extremes that I can go to. Ultimately, I know he has the best intentions and has such unique, distinct tastes that I trust that any journey he wants to go on will be one that's the right one.

RE: I thought *Revolutionary Road* (2008) was spectacularly good, as was your performance. There again you reach back to the 1950s, yet the characters could hardly be more different. I think also of your Howard Hughes

in *The Aviator,* going back further. What interests you about characters of that vintage?

LD: There are different aspects. Certainly you know what was prevalent in *Aviator, Revolutionary Road,* and certainly *Shutter Island* was war—and the forming of what our country ultimately became after World War II. How all these characters reacted in different ways to that war. It was a theme that was constant throughout this movie. It's just fascinating to see through these different characters' eyes, and historically, the formation of what our country ultimately is today in response to war.

Obviously, Frank Wheeler of *Revolutionary Road* and Teddy from this film go to much different extremes and have completely different reactions to the post-traumatic stress, you might say, of warfare. It's a definitive moment in American history and it results in a lot of great story lines and interesting characters.

RE: And soon it's said you and Scorsese will make *Sinatra,* who came up in the 1940s and '50s. What do you think about that?

LD: Well, there are no set plans to do *Sinatra* as of yet. I know Marty's been developing it. Like with any experience working with a director of that caliber, you know you'd only take on a subject matter like that with a director like that—because, you know, Sinatra led a very complex life. He was obviously such a force of nature. And such an icon that you have to handle with kid gloves. But until that challenge presents itself to me, I haven't really deeply delved into how to solve it.

RE: Scorsese is known as a meticulous camera stylist. Are you aware of that when you're working?

LD: Oftentimes people ask me if I would ever want to direct, as a result of working with a master filmmaker like Marty. But the truth is, I'm so completely and truly focused on what I do as an actor that it's hard to watch his mastery at work. I almost feel that's unfortunate at times. I want to maybe come to the set at some point to just watch him do his thing without me having any specific job.

But I do know that what has been forged from my relationship in working with him that might translate itself to directing is the way he works with actors. He empowers the actors to completely embody the roles that he puts up on the screen. And you feel not only a great responsibility for bringing truth to the character, but it empowers you. I can only wish that if I am ever to direct, I would give the actors the same feeling.

RE: Much is made of *Avatar* passing *Titanic* at the box office. I think this is silliness. Ticket prices and attendance records make such comparisons impossible. Are you tiring of the so-called box office race?

LD: The truth of the matter is that *Avatar* has won financially, and I absolutely enjoyed my experience watching *Avatar*. I don't think about those types of numbers until, you know, until it's actually over with.

So now, in reaction to it, Godspeed to them. I hope they keep going and going. Because James Cameron has been able to tap into something that audiences want to see worldwide. And he's intrigued them in such a unique way that he may do it again with whatever his next movie is. He is that type of filmmaker.

RE: IMDb says you have no less than twenty-seven projects "in development." Does this become dizzying?

LD: It's the grand search to try to find good material. As I'm sure you know, as a critic, finding films that have a great story line are few and far between. So I formed my production company, Appian Way, to try to create movies that are challenging, complex roles for me. And hopefully they will have good enough narrative and story lines for directors to want to attach themselves to.

It's the development process that really takes forever. And I'm not a story teller, per se. So I'm still in this grand search to find those projects. That's the reason I formed my production company in the first place. And so far *Aviator* has been the one, and hopefully there are going to be more.

Michael Douglas and Oliver Stone

Cannes, France, May 18, 2010—The way Michael Douglas and Oliver Stone explained it to me, modern Hollywood is doing the same thing modern Wall Street is: trading for its own benefit and not for the good of its customers.

"Let's put it this way," Stone said. "If you look at the figures at Goldman Sachs, 67 percent of their profit in 2008 came to their own house. They made most of their money for themselves

and 11 percent for their customers. That's a huge difference from my father's era when all these houses were essentially agent houses; they were agents. It's like our business; the agents took over."

His father was a stockbroker. Michael Douglas's father was a movie star. They grew up at about the same time in two company towns.

"For an analogy," Douglas said, picking up, "traditionally, your agent worked his ass off for you and got a 10 percent commission. Then the agents said, wait a minute, we'll put our clients together, we'd get a package in commission, and we'll do this and we'll do that, and—the next thing you know, *you're* working for the agency."

Stone said: ". . . then they're buying real estate, they're buying television. Now they're expanding into other things. Like they have sports people. Ron Meyer was Michael's agent, and now he's still the longest-running head of a studio because he always got somebody else to take the fall."

This was on the day their new movie, *Wall Street: Money Never Sleeps,* premiered at Cannes. It picks up Gordon Gekko's story after he's released from prison, and involves his relationship with his daughter, Winnie (Carey Mulligan), her fiancé, Jacob (Shia LaBoeuf), the man who brought Gekko's firm down (Josh Brolin), and Jacob's father figure (Frank Langella). There's also a reprise of Charlie Sheen's character from the earlier picture.

LaBoeuf shares the lead in this story with Douglas, and we enter a Wall Street populated by traders who work single-mindedly in their own interests, and start baseless rumors for the sole purpose of driving down stocks they've shorted.

The movie opened here to decidedly negative reviews from French critics, but the buzz I hear suggests the American reviews may be more positive. Some critics said the romance between LaBoeuf and Mulligan isn't a good fit with the financial stuff, but (a) how could it be? and (b) it turns out to be a better fit than you think.

My hypothesis is that the English language might have been a barrier. The French critics are generally strong in English, but the English of *Wall Street* includes such impenetrables as "derivatives," a word it turns out few people in

America understand. I remember Spike Lee telling me why *Do the Right Thing* didn't win a major prize here: "There is no way subtitles could capture the language in the film." Imagine subtitles or non-native speakers trying to deal with dialogue that sounds sometimes like a Jim Cramer rant.

Douglas and Stone had a huge hit with their original *Wall Street* (1987), in which Douglas's character, Gordon Gekko, famously decreed, "Greed is good." The film was intended as a warning about a culture of greed in American finance, but anecdotal evidence suggests it became an inspiration. Young men saw it and wanted to grow up to be just like Gordon Gekko.

"I remember how kinda stunned and surprised we were with how strongly they embraced this insider trader image," Douglas said. "You know, the company wreckers, destroying companies, and all they saw was the exterior, not the value. I can imagine all those MBAs twenty-two years ago are probably the heads of investment banking companies now. Because nothing seems to have changed. There is no sense of, you know, looking into the mirror."

"No morality," I said.

"No morality whatsoever."

"It's a casino with insiders," Stone said. "When you go to a real casino, you know the odds are against you. In Wall Street you don't even know the odds; you don't know what you're doing."

"Unless you're inside, you're outside, and nobody's really got a chance," Douglas said.

This was in a hotel on the Croisette, overlooking the beach and the festival and lots of people who no doubt felt their ideas for films didn't have a chance. Not that it's a perfect parallel, but American movie distribution does seem increasingly to be a system run for the house, which hammers huge grosses out of audiences before they find out that the game is stacked against them.

"I love the line that Gordon says," Stone said. "'You never got it, kid, it's just a game. It's not about the money, it's just a game.' They lose sight of the actual worth of the money. It's about beating the other guy. I was with Rupert Murdoch the other night and it was very warm and he was, like, saying money is fungible. It's not about the money, it's about what you do

with the money. He'd rather run a media empire. Other people would take their money and they'd wanna transfer it to something else, like take over a bank or swap mortgage home loans. It doesn't matter; it has no social purpose.

"I think Rupert has a social purpose, but I'm talking about what the banks are doing. They bundled off the loans to every other bank, and they started countertrading each other. The most dangerous moment was when the money markets closed on that horrible week in September. That was the crush point."

He talked about Greece, and J. P. Morgan in World War I, and other things, and it boiled down to this: The financial system is gambling with people's assets in order to maximize paper profits, and the figures are stacked so high you can't find the underlying value, and the bankers claim the structure has grown too large to fail. Oh, and nobody on Wall Street cares because, as the movie makes a point of demonstrating, many investment decisions are inspired only by the size of the bonuses they will generate.

"Oliver," I asked, "tell me one thing. What do you think is a safe investment today?"

"I carry around my gold piece. I think that's pretty safe. That's a lucky charm. Actually, that was worth thirty-six dollars when I was a kid; it's now worth twelve hundred dollars. That's a good mark-up."

"Gold is good as long as you carry it," Douglas said. "I would diversify, you know, keep diversifying. Buy art, buy real estate, buy a little bit of everything."

"Don't you think Michael is looking more and more like Kirk?" Stone asked.

"Kirk," Michael said, "told me one day he was watching television when one of his old movies came on. He's looking at the movie and he can't remember it, and he says, 'Wait a minute, that's not me, it's Michael.'"

Atom Egoyan

March 26, 2010—Atom Egoyan often makes erotic melodramas. There was a time when audiences perked up at the prospect of, oh, you know, sex and nudity and stuff, but these days moviegoers seem strangely neutered. They'd rather look at fighting machines or 3-D animals. They like their porn the way it's presented on the Net, wham-bam, thank you, man. The notion of erotic tension uncoiling within the minds of characters and unfolding languidly in sensuous photography is, I dunno, too artistic.

Egoyan is the Canadian filmmaker who is attracted to the riskier edges of characters. His best-known film is *The Sweet Hereafter* (1997), about the hidden meaning of a small-town bus accident. His best film may be *Exotica* (1994), about a man and a table dancer who meet for motives that are nothing at all as they seem. His plots are rarely linear, but double back to question our, and their own, assumptions.

Egoyan's remarkable new film *Chloe,* now opening around the country, is erotic, melodramatic, and even reveals itself as a concealed thriller. I found it fascinating; it involved deep issues within the characters. I found the casting uncanny: the smooth self-assurance of Amanda Seyfried as a call girl, the brittle insecurity of Julianne Moore as a gynecologist, the apparent innocence of Liam Neeson as her husband. Since we can't be sure exactly what any of them are doing, how can we not be drawn in?

Seyfried is the revelation. "I auditioned her before she made *Mamma Mia,*" Egoyan told me not long ago in Chicago. "In all honesty, I'm not sure if I'd seen her in that film, she would have had the same impression on me. We all have preconceptions of what an actor's range is and that's unfortunate.

"Chloe is a sex worker and she says her job is to read what her clients are looking for. But she's never been asked to do anything like this before, being hired by a wife to check whether her husband is open to an affair. And when she starts telling these stories to Catherine (Julianne Moore), she's overwhelmed because she's being listened to with such intensity by a woman who is outside her world. An older woman who's so respectable that she can't help but fall in love with her. That's asking a lot for a young actress and she got it. She was able to understand and to negotiate all of this. And also, handle the major shift in the film."

The film puts Julianne Moore in a surprising and deceptive position, pure melodrama, and Egoyan said, "She understands the nature of melodrama. I mean that only in the best sense of the word. You have an unfiltered access to the emotional life of these characters. They can speak what's on their mind, even though they may not know exactly why it's on their mind."

When Chloe was speaking and Catherine was sexually stirred, he said, "there's an interesting parallel to Bergman's *Persona.* In the relationship between the two women and the storytelling. I'm thinking of the scene where Bibi Andersson delivers the monologue of the orgy on the beach to Liv Ullmann. That was one of the most powerful things, most erotic things, I've ever heard. When someone is listening so intently and you can't help but feel it's because they're connected to you. That may not be the case. This is the tragedy of Chloe, I think, is that she totally misreads Catherine, and yet you understand why."

The films he loves, Egoyan said, were made in a time when filmmakers were more free to explore sexual feelings. When he made the perplexing thriller *Where the Truth Lies* (2005), he was slapped with an NC-17 rating by the MPAA, primarily for a sex scene involving Kevin Bacon and Colin Firth.

"I think if that film had been made with actors that were not as well known, that scene may have not provoked the same degree of panic. And yet, that's a dramatic scene. Arsinee (Khanjian, his wife) worked with Catherine Breillat, a French filmmaker, and did a film called *Fat Girl,* and that was really groundbreaking, amazing, where she goes. But again, they weren't famous actors. That's what I really admire with some of these European films. Who can forget *Don't Look Now,* with Donald Sutherland and Julie Christie? That just seemed so honest and raw. I don't know if two actors of that stature would play that scene today. People right now are flipped out about seeing well-known actors go to certain places."

He met Liam Neeson when he directed him in London in Samuel Beckett's *Eh Joe.* Originally a film for television, it involves the camera very slowly approaching an actor's face during an extended single shot, as an unseen woman delivers a monologue. "It's the most extended reaction shot in history," he observed. "Through that experience I realized what an astonishing actor he is and how generous he is in being able to take this role of a listener. In this film, with that monologue that Julianne Moore has under the awning where she's just really pouring out her heart, he's just listening."

In the films he loved by Bergman and Fassbinder, he said, "The viewer is watching a mysterious process of investigating the close-up as this almost quintessential cinematic gesture. But that's becoming more and more rare as an experience, to see a human face just projected on that scale."

In *Chloe,* the whole point is the faces, and what the characters are thinking, and what they're thinking about each other, and what we're thinking about them.

Videos from my interview with Atom Egoyan are here: http://j.mp/a51040.

Michael Moore

September 20, 2009—Whether or not you agree with Michael Moore, he has one piece of invaluable advice in his new film, *Capitalism: A Love Story.* If a bank forecloses on your home, ask them to prove their ownership by producing a copy of the mortgage.

In the film, Marcy Kaptur, the congresswoman from Toledo, says, "Don't leave your house if they try to throw you out." Why not? "In many cases, they can't," Moore explains, "because it's already been cut up, chopped up, and bundled and rebundled and a piece of this mortgage is sitting in China."

Capitalism is Moore's latest populist rabble-rouser, not his funniest but probably his angriest. The strange thing is, there's not much in it to offend his usual critics. It comes at a time when the U.S. economy essentially serves him as a footnote.

His study of the meltdown leads him to the puzzling matter of "derivatives," the mysterious financial instruments involved in the bank collapses. In the film, Moore asks three "experts" to explain a derivative to him. They can't.

"Nobody wants to look stupid," he told me, "so everybody sort of nods their heads and goes, 'Oh yeah, yeah, I understand that.' You're not supposed to understand it. It's like a snipe hunt on Wall Street.

"I gotta tell you this story. I talked to a guy who used to sit on one of the nine Federal Reserve Boards. They brought somebody in to explain these credit default loans, and everyone sat around the table going, 'Ah hum, ah hum.' He told me he didn't have a clue what the guy was saying but was afraid to look stupid.

"After the crash, he calls up some of the guys on the board and admits he didn't understand half of what he was hearing. He got the sense that nobody in the room understood it. But a weird thing happens amongst smart people. They won't admit it. Like I don't wanna admit to you that I've never read *Moby-Dick* because I think I'm a fairly smart guy."

So OK, I told him. You made the film. I want *you* to explain derivatives to me.

Moore, who didn't go to college, is happy to.

"Imagine you've got this crazy brother-in-law and he likes to gamble but doesn't wanna go to the normal casino. He wants to go to the virtual casino, where you never really actually touch any of the money. He wants to place bets with money that isn't his and he starts to win some of it and he starts to think it's his money.

"But he's actually not touching that money either. He starts to get a little nervous about all this betting because he never really actually sees any money. So he says, 'You know, I need to take out an insurance policy just in case this isn't real.' So these derivatives are essentially bets on bets.

"They've been betting against whether people are going to be able to pay their mortgage. They've been betting against the economy. If the economy gets worse, jobs are gonna have to be cut. That should help Wall Street because as unemployment goes up, the Dow Jones goes up. Wall Street likes it when you get rid of people because it's good for the bottom line. Employees are your No. 1 expense.

"Before the derivative action starts, they've taken people's mortgages and split them up and sold off the pieces. Let's say they've taken one hundred people in your neighborhood and taken 10 percent of each of their mortgages, put them into a brand-new document, and sold it to somebody. That's why they can't find your mortgage."

Moore is rolling now. It's an inspiration to see him under a head of steam, his red baseball cap bobbing and his hands waving.

"You hear commentators blaming the shiftless people who took out the mortgages: 'They're living beyond their means!' They really pushed that after the crash—that these low-income people and their subprime mortgages did this to us. It had a racial overtone in it and was really a little creepy. What they never say is, the number-one reason people go bankrupt in this country is medical bills.

"I carefully picked my foreclosed people for this film. One, his farm was in the family for four decades. The family down in Miami, twenty-two years in the house. These are people who got snookered.

"Elizabeth Warren, the law professor from Harvard, she has taken, like, those refinancing contracts into her law class, and she hands them out she says, 'OK, tell me what the interest rate is.' You read the fifty pages; you can't figure it out. A law student or professor can't figure out how it's gonna balloon. It's deliberately confusing."

Moore argues the current crisis was caused by a capitalist love of money that transcends all other motivations: "It's about how the wealthiest 1 percent, who have more financial wealth than the combined lower 95 percent, not only love their money, they love our money. They love everybody's money and they want as much of it as possible, and their love is so blind that they recklessly go about taking our money and spending it any way they see fit; usually in making bets on bets—derivatives.

"One guy comes to the table and takes nine slices of the pie and everybody else at the table has to split the last slice. That's not democracy; that's not what Jesus said. All the great religions actually say the same thing. They all have the same basic beliefs about how to treat the poor and how the rich are not to suck everything up and make life miserable for everybody else."

But even now, I said, we hear about executives paying themselves multimillion-dollar bonuses.

"They do it because they can get away with it. It's been a year since the crash and not one single regulation has been put back in place. Why hasn't there been more outrage? I'm doing my part. In Pittsburgh I showed the movie to a bunch of steelworkers, and during that scene where the judge is putting kids in the privatized juvenile homes so he can get a little kickback money, this guy like rises half out of his seat and he starts shouting at the screen, 'Shame, shame, shaaaaame!' People are ready to rumble."

Jason Reitman

February 16, 2010—Talking with Jason Reitman is uncannily like talking to a real person

and not the director of an Oscar contender. He's not on autopilot. He's not using sound bites. He's just talking.

When he went on a PR tour to promote *Up in the Air* last year, he counted the questions he was asked over and over again, and produced a pie chart. Question No. 1: "What was it like working with George Clooney?" Reitman should have simply answered differently every time: "Like working with Lady Gaga." "Like working with Glenn Beck."

Now *Up in the Air* is tied with *Avatar* at nine Academy Award nominations, and Reitman and his wife, Michelle, have flown to Chicago to do the *Oprah* show, the most valuable TV exposure in existence. I said his life has become like the Clooney character's. The director of an Oscar nominee lives in airports and on planes. Then I realized that observation no doubt gets a giant slice of his new pie chart.

"No, I'm finished with pie charts. I'm working on my new screenplay. I started on Monday and I'm on page forty. I'm just having an amazing week."

On the advice of his wife, he's also stopped reading what bloggers say about him on the Internet. Jason Reitman is a blameless man, you understand, who is happily married and has a much-loved daughter and gets along fine with his parents and has made three movies that were all extremely good. What's for a blogger not to like?

"I was at the Broadcast Film Critics Awards," he said, "and we won for screenplay. I accepted the award and then I took a step back for Sheldon, the cowriter, to talk and they turned the music on. So some bloggers blamed this on me as if I'd slighted him, when really I just kinda took a step back. In that moment I realized how much it's like running for political office. Everyone is watching your every move. Every little gesture can be interpreted incorrectly.

"When I was a kid there was one night, and it was the Oscars. Now, I realize, it's three months of award shows and you get to know everyone. I see Kathryn Bigelow every other day, I see James Cameron every other day, I see Lee Daniels every other day. They're all lovely. But there's this strange line between being proud of your film and feeling as though you're running for political office."

So he's cut way back on Google. "There are a

few bloggers I think are thoughtful in their approach. But some of them are really snarky. If the Internet is supposed to show humanity for what it is, it's a little scary. Because given a chance to say anything you want and given anonymity, we can become really dark and scary people."

He said it's frightening that Twitter now renders an instant verdict on a movie while the credits are still playing. "I remember when I went to Sundance in 1998. I was nineteen years old, I brought a short film and someone said, 'We're putting short films on the Internet.' And I remember looking at him like he was crazy. By the time I played *Up in the Air* for the first time, it was assumed it would have been decided on whether my film was good or not within five minutes of the film ending at Telluride.

"I remember running into [respected veteran film writer] Anne Thompson at Telluride. She said, 'I'm exhausted. I used to have the weekend. On the flight back I'd start writing my round-up. These kids, they don't sleep. After the first showing they walk out already writing, they're up all night, they're gonna see a movie at seven in the morning, they're gonna see a movie at midnight.'"

Reitman said it was true. "It's a strange thing to have your film decided on that quickly. It'll be scary the day I make the film that just doesn't work. It'll be dead on arrival. They're gonna be tweeting in the middle of a movie."

The blogosphere outdid itself with *Avatar*, I noted. It declared the film dead months before anyone had even seen it. Then there were all these articles saying, "Gee, it's good, once you see it."

I asked Michelle what it was like being the candidate's wife.

She smiled. "Well, I've tried to smile and be supportive. But I'm crying a lot because I'm just so proud when he wins an award."

Jason said, "It's tricky, though. You also told me not to read press, particularly the online stuff."

Michelle said, "It gets into your head and it's just one person's opinion and you don't know whether it comes from malice or envy or what. I'm just looking out for Jason. That's what I kinda think my role is right now. I want to make sure he doesn't read a review that's just

nasty or malicious. I want him to be enjoying this right now."

But Jason still tweets, I said.

"Yeah, I gotta admit," he said. "What'd you think of the iPad? I'm a sucker. Michelle's come along with me a couple of times to wait in line for things coming out and she thinks it's ridiculous."

Michelle laughed. "I have a business degree and I'm loyal to the Dells and the PCs. It's a battle in our house. I'm BlackBerry, Jason's iPhone. I'm PC, he's Mac . . ."

"This is what keeps it spicy," Jason said.

"OK," she said, "I admit. I just asked for an iTouch so we can download little cartoons and show our daughter."

"Next I'll be making films with an iPhone," Jason said. "Canon has a new camera called the 5Dmark2 and it shoots twenty-four frames 1080 HD on it. It looks beautiful. I shot some footage on *Up in the Air* with it."

So after *Oprah*, he said, he would fly back home and go back to work on the new screenplay. He's adapting *Labor Day*, a 2009 novel by Joyce Maynard about a thirteen-year-old boy, his unhappy mother, and his growing pains. Maynard was in the news after the death of J. D. Salinger; she had a now-famous affair with the reclusive author. I asked Reitman how, as the director of *Juno*, he might approach filming Salinger's *The Catcher in the Rye*.

"Oddly," he said, "the trick to *The Catcher in the Rye* is not making it. It is the perfect experience within itself. I don't know how you make that experience any different or any better."

Holden Caulfield might have thought, well, he might be an adult, but at least he isn't a phony.

Gabourey Sidibe

October 27, 2009—In her next film, Gabby Sidibe will play Miss Popularity. This is a fair distance from the abused, fearful victim she plays in the title role of *Precious*. People half-convinced the actress must be like the character will need a readjustment.

Gabourey Sidibe, whom you may be seeing at the Oscars, is older, funnier, and much more confident than Precious.

"I'm excited *anyone* could take a look at this film and think I could play Miss Popularity," she was telling me. "Well, I kind of *was* Miss

Popularity back in junior high, except Hollywood would never peg me as Miss Popularity, so I guess I'm playing against type."

The film, named *Yelling to the Sky*, comes out of the Sundance indie workshop.

"She's the queen of the school, she's a bad girl, she makes out with her boyfriend, and she drinks," Gabby told me cheerfully.

Her popularity in junior high is connected to how she got the nickname Gabby.

"My name is Gabourey, which is Senegalese," she said. "People tortured my name my whole life and so around junior high I let people call me Gabby. My mom wanted to call me Gabby, and I hit her in the face, as a baby. I didn't mean to, I promise.

"I was ornery, like a little gremlin child, but when I changed my name to Gabby, I got a personality, which is weird, but it came along and it's a happier name. It's sunshiny; it means 'my trust is in God.' Is that weird?"

Gabby, *Precious*, and its director, Lee Daniels, have been riding a whirlwind since the film won the important Audience Award at Sundance 2009. Since then it added the Audience Awards at Sundance and just last week at Chicago. Backed by the cheerleading of Oprah Winfrey, it seems poised as a come-from-nowhere contender like last year's *Slumdog Millionaire*.

For Gabourey Sidibe, twenty-six, it's meant a dramatic life change. She was a college student when she went to an enormous open audition for the lead in the film of Sapphire's novel *Push*. She was called back the next day to the office of Daniels, whose Hollywood start came as producer of *Monster's Ball*.

"He talked to me for, like, forty-five minutes about nothing of importance, about sunglasses and Lenny Kravitz and cake from Brooklyn," Gabby remembered. "And then he asked, 'If you get this film, what happens to your college classes?' And I said, 'Whoa, something would have to give. It's not every day you're up for a movie role.' And he said, 'I want you to be in my film,' without making me read again. So that's how that happened."

On the first day of shooting, she said, she was working with Paula Patton, who plays Ms. Rain, the teacher who determines to help her.

"I say, 'Oh cool, a real actress is here!' And she gets so mad at me: 'You're a real actress. Don't ever say that you're not because you are in this role—and this is who you are, an actress.'

"But I think that nervousness kind of worked. It worked especially with Mo'Nique (who plays her abusive mother, Mary). I was afraid of her because I idolized her. And Precious is afraid of Mary. For those scenes it worked that I was scared. Eventually it fades away because at the end of the day I had to do a job, no matter what, nervousness aside."

The camera sees the truth, I said.

"I've seen actors and actresses who have been to all these different acting technique courses. I've never taken one. I think sometimes you can have too much information. I feel weird saying it came natural to me, but I mean, I know this girl. I know her in my family, I know her in my friends, I've seen her, I've lived beside this girl. And there's no class I could have taken to help me to learn more about her because I knew her already." A pause. "I didn't want to be friends with those girls because they had too much drama going on in their lives. I feel guilty for having ignored them."

This was at the Wit Hotel on the afternoon before the movie's red carpet premiere at the Chicago festival. I mentioned the movie's fantasy scenes, which provide a respite for Precious's grim daily reality. She imagines herself as a fashion model and movie star.

"Oh, they were the best scenes because on some days I was bleeding and had dirt on me. So when I got to have makeup on and really pretty hair and a pretty dress, those were just the best days. Because on other days I sometimes had a pregnancy pad on and it just made it worse. Yeah, not only did I have to wear tight, unflattering clothes, sometimes I'd have to be on the ground in leaves or underneath a bridge or a cold gutter or someplace and so it was all hell as a fat girl."

And the scenes of her being assaulted and abused at home . . .

"While Precious loves her mother, and I think later on it becomes evident that Mary loves Precious, they're enemies. But Mo'Nique and I love each other; we do. And I think with the gravity of those scenes we had to love each other twice as hard during the filming. So on 'action' we were enemies. But at 'cut,' we hugged each other. We sang, we danced, we joked around. We had to do it in order to survive it."

Lee Daniels said: "I mean, take 4 of the hallway scene? All three of us, we were hysterical. Mo'Nique's saying, 'You no-good bitch; you ain't never been nothin', you ain't ever gonna be nothin', and da, da, da, da, da.' I said, 'Keep going, Mo'Nique.' She's, 'Lee, there's nothing else I can call her.' And we just started laughing."

Daniels said he made the film first of all for his family. "My mother and family members don't really get *Monster's Ball*. They saw *Monster's Ball*, *The Woodsman*, *Shadowboxer*, and they were like, 'Why can't you make movies like Tyler Perry? Miss Maybelle from the church said somethin' happened to you, because why you makin' a movie 'bout a pedophile?'" (Kevin Bacon's character in *The Woodsman*).

"So I really made this movie for African-Americans. For my family. One night I was outside a 7-Eleven at Sundance and this Chinese-American lady broke down crying in my arms. And I realized that it was a universal story; that just by telling my truth that it was universal."

Quentin Tarantino

August 18, 2009—It is fairly widely known, three months after the film's premiere at Cannes, that Quentin Tarantino's *Inglourious Basterds* has, shall we say, a surprise ending. How did Tarantino feel about rewriting history? He uses admirable logic in arguing that he did not:

"At no time during the start, the middle, or ever, did I have the intention of rewriting history. It was only when I was smack dab up against it that I decided to go my own way. It just came to me as I was doing what I do, which is follow my characters as opposed to lead."

So he told me in the course of an e-mail interview.

"My characters don't know that they are part of history. They have no pre-recorded future, and they are not aware of anything they can or cannot do. I have never predestined my characters, ever. And I felt now wasn't the time to start. So basically, where I'm coming from on this issue is: (1) My characters changed the course of the war. (2) Now that didn't happen because in real life my characters didn't exist. (3) But if they had've existed, from Frederick

Zoller on down, everything that happens is quite plausible."

This argument is, to me, refreshing and actually almost logical. Every World War II movie in history is made with audience knowledge of how the war ended. Many of them take place at a point in the war where the characters could not know, but films approaching or arriving at the end of the war do not presume to revise it. It's a dilemma faced by Bryan Singer's *Valkyrie*, where Tom Cruise plays a member of a secret plot to assassinate Hitler. He doesn't know he will fail, but we do.

In putting history up for grabs, Tarantino is audacious, but then audacity has long been his calling card. In the process, this director, who is so much in love with movie genres, blows up all of our generic expectations. It's quite an explosion.

Inglourious Basterds' German actor Christoph Waltz won the Best Actor Award at Cannes. He is probably also destined for an Academy Award nomination as Colonel Hans Landa, the mannered, arch–Nazi villain. He has an opening scene with Denis Menochet that is masterful. Not often does a big-scale war movie open with so much dialogue, so carefully crafted, so lovingly performed.

"It was one of the very first scenes I wrote in 1998," Tarantino said. "How I wrote it is how I write all my big dialogue scenes. I basically start the characters talking to each other, and they take it from there. I will add that one of the reasons I never gave up on the script during the years was I knew how good that scene was."

During the film's press conference after its first Cannes screening, Tarantino said he had auditioned countless actors before Waltz walked into the room, but he sensed immediately he'd found his Hans Landa.

"Except for the opening farmhouse scene, I didn't let Christoph rehearse with anybody else," he told me. "All through the production, Landa was this unseen presence hanging over the characters and the actors. I wanted to keep them nervous and anxious about Landa. So I didn't want them to know what Landa would do until we were doing the later scenes. Christoph understood that, but he still wanted his rehearsal time with me, so he and I rehearsed the other scenes alone. And we had many many discussions about Landa, especially about the ways and wherefores of his interrogation techniques."

Those are mannered, I said, but not declawed. Landa toys with his foils as a cat does with a helpless mouse. There are moments when he pretends to be letting them escape, for example, when he plays along with the German actress Bridget von Hammersmark (Diana Kruger), a double agent for the Allies. Observe how he compliments her and leads her on—before, so to speak, dropping the other shoe.

Tarantino's photography of both Kruger and Melanie Laurent, who plays the heroic cinema owner Shosanna, is striking. Von Sternberg could not have lavished more attention on Dietrich. On Shosanna's big night in the theater, Tarantino studies her lips, shoes, facial veil, slinky dress, cigarettes, in a fetishistic way.

"I have to admit to coming to Von Sternberg very late in life," he said. "First, by reading a book about him, which made me seek out his films for study. Then his autobiography, which is I think one of the finest critical books of cinema art and its limitations ever written. Now I consider that of the cinema geniuses like Kubrick and Welles . . . my favorite genius is Von Sternberg. I thought I gave Kruger the Von Sternberg treatment more than Laurent."

Laurent creates a virtuoso performance, from the frightened young girl in the opening scene to the ingenue on the ladder to the femme fatale in the projection booth.

"Ingenue, yes. But you have to believe she would kill that poor innocent film lab guy if he didn't do what they said. Also, I like the idea that maybe this isn't the first time [her lover] Marcel and her have had to resort to these tactics during her years of survival."

Tarantino has always been distinctive in his dialogue. It often works to create imaginary frightening scenarios in the minds of the viewer, an effective way to create suspense. Consider in *Pulp Fiction*, for example, how lovingly the dangerous Marsellus Wallace is set up. I asked Tarantino about that stylistic strategy.

"A director I never really thought much about before," he said, "was Joseph Mankiewicz. I always lumped him in with the Fred Zimmermans, Mervyn LeRoys, Robert Wises, and William Wylers. However, I discovered him two years ago and, especially when he directs his own scripts, found a lot in common with

him. And I believe, as much as me, if Mankiewicz were to take on a Western, a war film, or a Hercules muscle-man movie, it would be a dialogue-driven 'talky' version. The use of the word 'talky' like it's a bad thing really irks me. His *All About Eve* is most definitely 'talky.' It's also most definitely brilliant."

As with all of his films, Tarantino somehow seems to avoid a single tone, freely moving among drama, melodrama, parody, satire, action, suspense, romance, and intrigue. So I observed to him.

"All of the above. Except I think parody and satire go hand in hand. The only scene of actual parody, to me, would be the Mike Myers scene, which is a parody of a WWII bunch of guys on a mission movie, with the big map, the big room, the opening exposition scenes. I would add comedy to that lineup, losing either parody or satire."

I had a few more questions:

—Brad Pitt speaking Italian. Fun to work on? Temptation for him to break up? I enjoyed how studious he liked to seem. You found a fine line just below over the top.

"I have to say it was Brad's idea to go so big with the hillbilly *buon giorno*. And as soon as he did it, even though we talked about it, it was obvious it was right."

—With your eyes closed during the Morricone opening, you'd assume you were watching a Western. Yes?

"For the first two chapters I wanted it to be like a spaghetti Western with World War II iconography."

—Did you shoot on celluloid, or has video actually gotten that good? My opinion is celluloid.

"No f——ing way would I ever shoot on video! Celluloid all the way!"

Note: Here is the video I took of Tarantino's Cannes press conference with Pitt, Waltz, Kruger, Laurent, and Eli Roth: www.youtube.com/ watch?v = gqhHmEoQnj4&feature = channel_ page. And this is part two: http://www.youtube. com/watch?v=rifDy_ejNoA&feature=channel_ page.

Anna Thomas

April 13, 2010—I met Anna Thomas at the 1975 Chicago Film Festival. She was not yet thirty, and already the world's most famous vegetarian cookbook author because of *The Vegetarian Epicure*, published by Knopf when she was twenty-four. It sold well over a million copies.

Anna was at Chicago with her husband, Gregory Nava, and their film *The Confessions of Amans*, which won the Golden Hugo as best first feature. She also wrote and directed *The Haunting of M*, which I thought was a wonderful film but is unhappily not available on DVD. Together, they made the great film *El Norte*, Gregory directing, Anna producing. Their cowritten screenplay was nominated for an Academy Award. She also cowrote and produced their movie *My Family*.

Greg and Anna have become lifelong friends of Chaz's and mine, despite my rule of rarely growing close to movie professionals. It had something to do with a bowl of soup.

Anna is a senior lecturer at the American Film Institute, lives in Ojai, California, and has continued to create cookbooks. Her newest one is *Love Soup* (W. W. Norton). You cannot open it without wanting to get out a pot. It was just nominated for the James Beard Award for the year's best cookbook. It's not a movie, but I want only the best for my readers, so I asked her to do an e-mail interview.

RE: I still recall my first bowl of mushroom soup at your table in Los Angeles, prepared from wild mushrooms Greg picked and vouched for. Do you remember that soup?

AT: Wow, what a memory! But I do remember it. . . . I had taken Greg to Poland, and my relatives there took us for a long walk in the forest to show us their favorite boletus areas. When we got back to California, he joined the mycological society and became a complete enthusiast.

One early spring day, foraging in Nojoqui, near the coast up north of Santa Barbara, he found an incredible amount of chanterelles— we had a pile of chanterelles on the patio table that came up shoulder high to me! And they were immense. Chanterelles are one of the most sought-after wild mushrooms, so this was like having a bucket of truffles or a sinful of caviar.

I started cooking chanterelles in every possible way, sautéed, in omelets, in risotto, with pasta, and of course—in soup. So I think we had a lovely chanterelle soup that night, and a good time was had by all. But you must have

had many bowls of mushroom soup before that—and I am horrified to imagine that some of them were from cans. Could it be that that one was your first mushroom soup from scratch? No wonder it was memorable! Maybe you lost your mushroom soup virginity that night!

RE: I approached that vegetarian meal with such wariness, although after all I'd had many meatless meals. Why are people so standoffish?

AT: I think we're just creatures of habit. People tend to be afraid of change. Now things are much different—vegetarian food is mainstream in most places I know (perhaps not Texas).

But there's also the fact that at that time— back when dinosaurs roamed Wilshire Boulevard—trying to get a good meatless meal was like trying to get a good coffee in England. Damn hard! (Thankfully, both areas have improved dramatically.) And the people who were making noise about being vegetarian at that time weren't talking about delicious chanterelle risotto or arugula salad—they were nattering about mock meatloaf and nutritious tofu shakes and generally feeling saintly for saying no to meat, and letting the meat eaters know just how they felt about them. They were being self-righteous.

Well—in my experience, self-righteousness and deliciousness rarely arrive together. So I can understand why many people were put off by the whole idea and called it a weird, fringe diet. There was a vegetarian restaurant in London for many years that was called Cranks—maybe you ate there?—because they decided to embrace the name calling and make a joke of it.

I don't believe in the us-and-them thing. I look forward to the day when there is no distinction made, when the porcini pasta is not a "vegetarian meal" and Kathryn Bigelow is not a "female director"—when good is good, and that's it. But these things take time. Habits only fade when they are replaced by new habits. . . . That's why I'm always working on delicious new recipes, new ways of making healthy eating a constant pleasure. I don't think you get anywhere telling people not to do something that they like. I believe that any success I've had in the food world has come from offering people delicious, attractive options—and then leaving it alone.

RE: How did you get started on vegetarian cooking when it was far from widespread?

AT: I wasn't following any trends, that's for sure!

Actually, I never decided to be a vegetarian—it just happened. I grew up in a Polish immigrant household, surrounded by kielbasa, but once I went off to college I found myself eating less and less meat, and then—whaddayaknow?—I wasn't eating much at all. Guess I was a vegetarian. But the label definitely followed the action.

Now the cooking—that was just a matter of survival. I was so poor when I went to UCLA! I had to figure out how to get jobs, stay in school, support myself somehow . . . and eating out was not in the budget. So I had to learn to cook. And since I wasn't eating meat, I developed my own cooking style. It was fun. I used to buy *Gourmet* magazine (RIP—can you believe they shut that down?) and read it cover to cover, and then I'd figure out how to adapt ideas to meatless meals. Or I'd just experiment with whatever I had from the market—or dip into Julia or James or Elizabeth David and then apply my own ideas. . . .

Later, when I traveled in Italy and France and Greece, I saw that there was so much wonderful meatless food that was a traditional part of these cuisines—that it wasn't relegated to some special section of the menu, the vegetarian ghetto, but was simply part of what people always ate. That was a marvelous experience for me, and inspired me so much for the second book.

RE: Wasn't your first book, *The Vegetarian Epicure*, essentially the first vegetarian cookbook devoted to gourmet or fine cooking?

AT: I think that might be true. And guess what—everyone likes good food!

Not that I thought of it as gourmet when I was writing it. I was just writing about the food I liked to cook and eat. Remember—I was a kid. A college student. I was cooking for myself, and for my friends at school, and they'd all say, "Wow, Anna, your food is so good, you should really write a cookbook!" Of course, now I look back and realize that we were all hungry students—my friends were just so happy to get a home-cooked meal—

they probably would have said that to anyone who fed them!

But it is absolutely true that I was after delicious food. I liked to have a good time—you know that! I was a hedonist. Food was so beautiful, so tasty, such a pleasure when it was good . . . and I just didn't see any reason why it shouldn't always be good. I had stopped eating meat, but I hadn't stopped eating. So my primary goal with everything I cooked was to make it delicious, make it a wonderful experience, whether it was simple or fancy. I wanted everyone to have a good time. I still feel the same way.

And I was completely uninterested in dictating to people about their diets, or criticizing them. I was just inviting people to sample some new, tasty options. I think that made my first book attractive for a lot of people who would otherwise not have touched anything called "vegetarian." I'm sure I didn't sell a million copies only to vegetarians.

RE: You got off the plane in New York and your editor at Knopf was startled to discover how young you were.

AT: I think it was probably a shock to Judith Jones, although she must have known I was a student. I was so naive! I knew nothing about the book world, the food world, publishing—I don't think I had ever been to New York before that trip. That was probably the worst of all, in the eyes of the New Yorkers. But Judith was great to me, a very good editor. She taught me a lot, but she didn't over-edit. She believed that I was the new "voice" that was needed at that moment. Imagine hearing such a thing when you're twenty-one.

RE: The saga of you living in a dorm closet . . .

AT: Hahahahahahaha! Oh, that was really something. I guess I really, really wanted to go to school, because I wasn't going to be deterred by the fact that I couldn't afford to live anywhere.

After a month in L.A., I was totally broke—I couldn't even rent a room. But I had some friends from high school who were living in the new coed dorm. There were separate floors for boys and for girls, and my friends were all guys. A couple of them took me in—they actually thought it was so completely exciting to do this illicit, dangerous thing—to have a girl staying in the room. They cleared the top shelf of the long closet and we put some bedding up there. At night, I'd get in my PJs and stand stiff as a board, and two of them would grab me by the ankles and the shoulders and just sort of vault me up into that shelf. That's where I slept. And various other people on that floor started sharing their meal cards with me whenever they weren't going to be using them, so I had plenty of opportunity to taste the dorm food. I was adopted by the sixth floor at Weyburn Hall!

I loved those guys, they were like my brothers, but I was so glad when my student loan came through, and I could share an apartment with a bunch of girls—and have a bed. That's when I started to cook.

RE: The new book is for soups. People seem more receptive to vegetarian soups than main courses.

AT: People are used to having vegetable soups, it's not a shocking idea to them. And as a rule, the appetizer course of a formal meal, which is where we have generally encountered soup, is wide open—and that's exactly why so often the most inventive and interesting food on a restaurant menu is found in that category!

But my new book, *Love Soup*, is about more than soup—and much more than soup as an appetizer. It's about what I call living the soup life—a way of eating that is simpler, but still based on fresh food, homemade food. When you're living alone, or in the middle of a big remodel and don't have much of a kitchen, or you're just busy with a million other things, there's still a way to eat wholesome, delicious, home-cooked meals—*soup*. That's what I discovered when I was camped out in the eighty-one-inch kitchen while my house was being ripped down. I turned to soup again and again, and found I could have lovely, satisfying meals with a great, hearty soup at the center of the meal. And that's why a third of the book is devoted to recipes for breads, salads, hummus, a few easy desserts—all my favorite go-with things that make soup a satisfying, casual meal.

It's a return to a simpler way of doing things. When I learned to build those casual meals around soup, I started entertaining that way, too, and the soup suppers we had in the studio were phenomenal fun. Then I did the soup-tasting party with Alanis Morissette—a blast! Now a friend of mine has started a soup club in

Ojai—the Gang of Soup. We get together once a month and someone cooks one or two or three soups, whatever they feel like doing, and other people bring other things in free-form potluck style. . . . I honestly feel sometimes that it's like a movement. Hmmm . . . is soup a lifestyle choice, or was I born that way?

Seriously, though—what could be nicer on a blustery day than a big bowl of minestrone with those wonderful, creamy cannellini beans and a big chunk of whole grain bread? Or a Green Soup with Mushrooms sprinkled with feta cheese, and a sourdough roll. I don't think people need a lot of persuading to think that sounds good.

RE: Why can't they all be made in a rice cooker? (heh, heh)

AT: Well, I'm so glad you asked, Roger. Yes, many soups do adapt to your favorite kitchen item. Soup is the easiest food in the world to make, that's why it's such an egalitarian thing—good food can be for anybody, home-cooking can be for anybody, healthy food can be for anybody—and there are soups that can be made just by putting everything together in one pot and simmering till done. However—there are a few more things to know about cooking, things that can elevate your soups from good to great.

As I endlessly repeat, the most important thing is to start with good, fresh ingredients. But then—there are a few techniques I use to develop maximum flavor in those good ingredients.

Many of my soups start with a well-caramelized onion or two. The slow cooking of that onion in a bit of olive oil, that's magic. The onion turns to marmalade, and the flavor is deep and rich. Same onion, but a whole different world of flavor.

Sometimes I toast spices for a moment or two, then grind them. Freshly toasted cumin, ground and tossed into a black bean soup or a lentil soup—wow.

And here's a great one: Take a basket full of homely root vegetables, those stalwarts of the winter season like potatoes, carrots, turnips, parsnips. . . . Add a few onions . . . cut them all up in pieces, toss with some good olive oil and some sea salt—and roast in a hot oven for an hour or more. You will be amazed at the flavor that those plain-Jane vegetables develop! Then use them in soup, in risotto, in salad, or just eat them by the bowlful as they are.

And while the oven is on, why not cut up some day-old bread and make those excellent homemade croutons?

And what about that great thing, the homemade broth? It's dead easy to do, but you need a big mother of a stockpot. These are techniques that require a sauté pan or an oven or a mortar—sometimes you do need something besides the faithful rice cooker.

RE: What has really changed in the vegetarian world since you were starting out? Farmers' markets?

AT: The farmers' markets have changed everything, not just vegetarian cooking. What a transformation they have made in our day-to-day food culture! Even the many people who have never shopped at a farmers' market benefit from them because every supermarket and grocery store has had to step up its game as a result. People have much higher expectations now, and know more about lots of interesting produce.

Just the other night I was sitting around with some friends and we were talking about farro—actually we were chowing down a delicious farro salad—and someone wanted to know what was farro and why was it suddenly turning up everywhere? Well, farro is actually an ancient variety of wheat, making its comeback. Then someone reminisced about when nobody had heard of arugula, and it was the big new thing. Yes, there was such a time.

The point is—everything has changed. There is an abundance of great, interesting produce available, there is ever greater consciousness about the importance of fresh food, and of eating seasonally and as locally as possible. People everywhere are more sophisticated. And the vegetarian world is now part of the mainstream food culture where I live. I think that's probably true in many parts of the country. I know that in California I can go to pretty much any restaurant and find something to eat on the menu. Probably something good, and without making a fuss. Hey—I even managed in a steakhouse in Chicago with Chaz!

When I was invited to do a vegetarian Thanksgiving menu for *Gourmet* magazine about ten years ago, I knew that things were really, really different.

Now, it's the vegans who are the cutting edge, and they talk to each other all the time on the Internet, blog like crazy, exchange recipes over the big backyard e-fence.

RE: Will I live longer if I'm a vegetarian?

AT: Well, Roger, that depends what else you're doing.

You know as well as I do that the main thing about longevity is to get lucky with your genetic starter kit—and then don't do too much to screw it up. But I think I can fairly say that other things being equal, yes, it's a healthier diet.

RE: One review said your book would charm even carnivores. Why are we so obsessed with meat?

AT: Hey, can we all just get along?

I think that reviewer meant that this is good food, it's delicious and easy and accessible, so why would anyone not like it? It's for anyone who likes to eat. But I'm not telling anyone they have to stop eating meat. I'm just giving them a hundred fabulous soup recipes. (And those good "go-withs.")

RE: What is the most delicious soup in your book? Come on, now. The one you would serve to the Obamas?

AT: Aah. The big question. Which soup wins? And the answer is . . . Roger, how can I choose a favorite from among these soups? They are all my favorites, they are all delicious!

There's a whole section in my introduction about this. It's called, "What Is the Greatest Soup?" And it's really about how many things can make this particular soup the best one for this particular moment. What is the season, what is the weather, what is the occasion, what is your mood? Who made that soup? Can you imagine how I feel when one of my sons makes a soup for me? Right there—that's my favorite soup! It has to be.

OK, OK. The Obamas are coming for dinner. Christmas Eve Porcini Soup—utterly simple, yet utterly fabulous. Or maybe Green Soup with Mushrooms, favorite of rock stars—and a favorite of mine, as well. (I actually have a whole chapter on the green soups, it's become a cult.) And for dessert we would have Cold Cherry and Lemon Soup. Eat it and fall in love.

RE: How did Teddy and Christopher relate to vegetarian meals as kids? What did they tell their friends?

AT: They were fine with everything because I didn't force them into any particular diet. They were carnivores, then they went through periods of not eating meat, then they went back to being carnivores, and then . . . You get it. I just kept offering them tasty, fresh food. They liked it, and so did their friends. In fact, at one point Teddy was going through a phase when he refused to eat anything I cooked, politely but consistently. (He now admits this was tedious rebellion.) But his friends would come over and eat up all the Green Soup—they'd ask for it! He was mortified. But what to tell their friends? This did not ever come up as a problem.

RE: What is the most common weakness of people who alter a vegetarian soup recipe (apart from sneaking in animal protein?).

AT: I think leaning on things like bad packaged vegetable broth, or (horror!) bouillon cubes or powders—that can really ruin a soup. (I use a canned broth sometimes—but only one brand. And yes, I name it in the book—Swanson's, the inexpensive one at the supermarket.) But other than that, I think the same ideas apply to soup that apply to all cooking: start with good ingredients, cook mindfully, use your taste buds. And use common sense. If you are making, for instance, Potato and Roasted Garlic Soup, and you find that you don't have any garlic on hand—for Pete's sake, make another soup. Soup is very flexible and adaptable, and you can make all sorts of substitutions, but don't try to get around a main flavor component.

And by the way, sneaking in an animal protein won't ruin a soup at all—it will just make it into something different, but if that's what you want—go for it. I am not here to make rules, except this one: When you think your onion is caramelized, keep cooking it slowly for another half hour. You will thank me.

RE: Where do you stand in the great tofu debate?

AT: Hmmm. What is the great tofu debate?

I like tofu when it's good, and well prepared. I've had wonderful tofu dishes in certain Japanese and Chinese restaurants. I don't use tofu as a substitute for other things, if that's what you mean—I don't *hide* it in casseroles, and so on. But you know my style—I like things to be what they are, not imitation versions of anything else.

In fact, I don't cook with tofu much, although I enjoy it when I'm eating out, because I don't do a lot of Asian-style cooking. It's just not my corner. But now Teddy makes delicious tofu scrambles sometimes, and I always have some and they rock!

So—what is the great debate?

Essays

The Aging of Harry Potter

July 22, 2009—*Harry Potter and the Half-Blood Prince* is in certain ways one of the best of the Harry Potter series, and in other ways a comedown. I received mail from readers noticing that my positive review seemed less enthusiastic than many other critics—and so it was, contrasted to eight important writers who rated it ninety or above on Metacritic. I suppose my three stars seemed a little reluctant.

Not really. I admired the film, I thought the sequence involving the underground cave was masterful, and I am anticipating *Harry Potter and the Deathly Hallows: Part I* in 2010 and *Part II* in 2011. But didn't it seem to you this sixth film was not as light, magical, and fun as the earlier ones? In fantasy, the term "sense of wonder" is often used. Remember how much wonder we felt in 2001, when *Harry Potter and the Sorcerer's Stone* was released? Delivery owls! Quidditch! King's Cross Platform No. 9¾!

Harry's universe has grown familiar. Of course it has. There are some owls perched about in *Harry Potter and the Half-Blood Prince,* but the Quidditch match is really unnecessary except that it is expected. CGI has become so commonplace it's almost pro forma.

Harry was eleven at the time of the first movie. Since J. K. Rowling's novels each cover one year of his life, that would make him sixteen in the new movie, and I guess he'll be seventeen at the end of *Harry Potter and the Deathly Hallows,* which is one book being made into two films. Whether he ages at the same pace in the films is unclear, and there was an extra year between *Chamber of Secrets* (2002) and *Prisoner of Azkaban* (2004).

In any event, Harry is now older than the heroine of *Twilight.* Daniel Radcliffe is now nineteen and will be twenty-one by the end, a little old for school days. He is a man, and needs to be about, can we say, his father's business? If Hogwarts and the world of magic seemed like a jolly lark at the outset, life for Harry has taken on darker tones and more urgent responsibilities. Even the hallowed halls of Hogwarts, once so charming, have grown grim and gothic. Remember that Harry's mission is to prevent Voldemort from exercising rule over the Muggles (i.e., the human race).

The two halves of *Deathly Hallows* therefore involve an apocalyptic struggle between Harry and Lord Voldemort. The book is long since a best-seller and we know that it ends, as it really must, with Harry's hard-fought victory after the deaths of some beloved characters.

The problem is that Harry in the process must become an adult, leave behind his childish ways, and deal with such possibilities as defeat and death. And there is a sense in which the Rowling world is challenged to contain such possibilities. At first the whole magical world seemed invented almost just for Harry's delight. Now it has grown larger than he is. A wand and a spell may not be adequate weapons. Recall the Death-Eaters.

What this means is that as it ages, the Harry Potter series is hard-pressed to maintain its spectacular level of pure entertainment. There is still much to be revealed but little to be discovered. The extended passages involving stores of memories in *Prince* are an example of the labyrinths now opening before Harry. And speaking of labyrinths, in *Hallows* Harry will marry Ginny. There is no way round it, unless he asks out that cute girl he met in the café on the London Underground.

These will not be unwelcome developments. It's in the nature of things that we grow older and life grows more serious. I am simply observing that the Potter series can't easily remain as magical as its beginnings. And in purely movie terms, these concluding films must be less enchanting. Some of the praise bestowed on *Harry Potter and the Half-Blood Prince* came because of its "increased maturity." As if that's what we were hoping for.

The Toys That Ate Hollywood

July 9, 2009—Will any child's toy escape being blockbustered?

With *Transformers* passing the $300 million mark at the U.S. box office, Hollywood studios are lathering to snatch up the rights to anything that a child might once have loved.

The same screenwriters who were paid $8 million to write *Transformers* have now been signed by DreamWorks for an undisclosed sum to produce a movie version of Asteroids, an old video arcade game that features triangles trying to shoot at circular objects. DreamWorks promises it will be family friendly.

The *Hollywood Reporter* also says Dream-Works is in talks with Mattel for the rights to Fisher-Price's View-Master, the 3-D viewer kids used for 3-D still shots of superheroes. Their fathers were rumored to have found 3-D shots of alternative subjects. The studio is hoping to get the $8 million men on board for this project.

The possibilities are endless:

—*Slap Yo Paddle!* Two races of space aliens, the Yo-Yos and Paddle Balls, engage in a thrilling 3-D battle over the heads of the audience. Shia LeBeouf and John Turturro use their mastery of the extraterrestrial skills to fight for the attention of Megan Fox.

—*Li'l Orphan Annie!* An interactive film. Audience members are issued headsets and Secret Decoder Rings. Daddy Warbucks has kidnapped the heroine, and audience members use secret messages received from Annie to try to save her. Annie has sent them all the same message, and the orphan is in danger of exploding from drinking too much Ovaltine. After her plight is revealed, it is up to each audience member to decide whether to continue feeding her.

—*Pac-Man the Predator!* Pac-Man, a voracious mutant microbe, nibbles at the screen. When it is all ate up, the movie is over. With deleted scenes of the microbe getting sick to its stomach.

—*Gotcha!* At a suburban high school, Britney Spears and Paris Hilton fight each other in the lunchroom using water balloons. Both are wearing thin T-shirts and get drenched. No nudity.

—*Explode Me Elmo!* Elmo (Seth Rogen) is a bright red space alien. Humans discover that when they tickle him once, he chortles. Twice, and he laughs aloud. Three times, and he explodes and destroys Earth.

—*Spud Guns from Space!* Aliens from space land and find Earth potatoes are unsatisfactory. They fire helpless humans at one another.

—*Marbles! Secret of the Universe!* Nicolas Cage plays an astrophysicist at MIT who intercepts the feed from the Hubble Space Telescope and determines that the stars in the sky are, in fact, giant, brilliantly glowing marbles. Enhancing the digital information, he discovers a giant thumb and forefinger in the abyss beyond space. They hold an aggie.

—*Pounders!* Giant tool-using aliens from outer space enslave humans, cruelly force them into square, circular, and triangular shapes, and pound them into an intergalactic workbench.

—*Sandbox! The Movie!* Giant red, yellow, and green plastic buckets, shovels, and scoops attack from outer space, dig up the earth's topsoil, and throw it all over the place.

—*Toy Story.* The neglected toys of a fickle child come to life and—sorry, only kidding.

The Plague of Movie Trivia

September 1, 2009—When people cheerfully tell me, "I have a trivia question" for you, I have a cheerful answer for them, but I rarely express it: "I'm a professional. Ask an amateur." Why in the name of Buster would I want to clutter my memory with useless facts? During long, hard years of being asked trivia questions, I have learned one thing for sure. The person asking me is in the possession of one fact and is pretty confident I don't know it. Therefore, my admission of defeat will demonstrate their superiority.

I know something about the movies, and here is how I really should reply: "Before I even attempt to answer your question, let me ask you five questions to see if you are qualified to even take up the time of a busy, busy man such as myself. (1) What is the name of the film that codified the language of the cinema? (2) Who was the third great silent clown? (3) Is color intrinsically better than black-and-white? (4) What movie set key scenes on board a train going from Chicago to Urbana, Illinois? (5) Name at least five directors of the French New Wave."

I know the answers. Not everybody can be expected to. Therefore, am I smarter than you? No, we just know different things. I would argue that the answers to all but Question No. 4

are part of the armory of a well-informed cineaste. No. 4, of course, is gold-plated trivia.

The reason game shows like *The Price Is Right* are popular is that most viewers think they know the approximate answer. The reason *Wheel of Fortune* is one of the longest-running shows on TV is that anybody but a dunderhead can sit at home, observe the letters as they fill in the blanks, and usually provide the answer more quickly than the contestants can.

From 1959 to 1970, there was a TV game titled *College Bowl*, on which teams from various universities competed to see which could more quickly supply the answers to questions testing general, but not trivial, information. The University of Minnesota traditionally fielded winning teams. The show's popularity faded as audiences gradually lost their interest in smart people. This was years before the term "the elites" came into favor.

The reason a quiz show based on movie trivia has never been successful is that no viewer can be expected to know any of the answers. If they do, the answers are too easy. Example: "Who played the first Tarzan in the movies?" Answer: "Elmo Lincoln." A surprising number of people know this. Never mind that they are wrong. The correct answer would be the child actor who portrayed the son of Lord and Lady Greystoke, the infant who grew up to become Tarzan. "Tarzan" was the first name he knew.

My friend McHugh posed this question to the distinguished film director Gregory Nava, who lost a ten-dollar bet that to this very day he has refused to make good on. Nava fumed that McHugh had pulled a low trick based on a technicality. He had reason to be annoyed. Nava is scholarly on the subject of film, and McHugh claims he has seen only one film in his entire life, *How Green Was My Valley*. In his memory this was always playing in his hometown of Sligo. Every time he was told to take his younger brothers to the movies, he brought them back home and nine months later there was another brother. Eventually there were ten McHugh brothers, so you can understand how he came to resent the movies.

The younger Greystoke was played by Gordon Griffith, who was ten. You must admit that from a standpoint of pure logic, McHugh was right. Nava's refusal to pay off the bet is based on labyrinthine reasoning that boils down to "That's no fair!" No one ever asks you a trivia question they have the slightest reason to believe you will know the answer to. There are few sights in the course of conversation more gratifying than the deflated face of a trivia "expert" whose question has been correctly answered.

To be sure, trivia sometimes serves a useful purpose. During a boozy office Christmas party at *Newsday*, my friend Bill Nack once leaped upon the city desk and correctly recited the names of every single one of the winners of the Kentucky Derby. As a result, he won the job of the newspaper's turf reporter, a position that eventually led him to *Sports Illustrated*, made him the biographer of Secretariat, and had Frank Whaley portraying him in *Ruffian* (2007).

The very sight of the words "*Ruffian* (2007)" leads me into another area of trivia. For some reason we film critics like to follow the titles of films with their year, in parentheses. We all walk around with hundreds of release years in our memories. This is not the convenience it might seem, because the year always has to be checked on IMDb anyway.

The fatal flaw in the concept of trivia is that it mistakes information for knowledge. There is no end to information. Some say the entire universe is made from it, when you get right down to the bottom, under the turtles. There is, alas, quite a shortage of knowledge. I think I will recite this paragraph the next time I'm asked a trivia question.

A Torch for Derrion Albert

October 2, 2009—Need we mourn that Chicago has lost its bid to host the Olympics? Yes, but not for too long. We are still Chicago, and that is a mighty consolation.

Watching the Beijing Olympics on TV, I hoped that my city would win the opportunity to show off to the world like that. My conceptions about China were fundamentally altered. I know that for too many people Chicago is known for gangsters and "machine politics." There is truth in every cliché, but as I drive or walk around this glorious city, it strikes me every day how beautiful, flower-filled, towering, and happy a place it is.

Yes, we have our share of heartbreak. The death of Derrion Albert inspires a cry of

"Shame!" that every student in Chicago cannot be certain of returning home safely. His beating is the Chicago image that has gone around the world, and not beauty shots of our skyline and lakefront.

We have lost the Olympics bid. Perhaps this is our opportunity to win Derrion Albert's bid. He was an honor student, not a gang member, not a dropout. He was murdered by a crowd of thugs. More generally, he was murdered by a system that has failed our neighborhoods, our schools, and our children.

We were prepared to raise millions to prepare the city for the Olympics. Without missing a beat, we should devote our money and energy to preparing the city for a new generation of Derrion Alberts.

This will not require new "infrastructure" and all the delay and bureaucracy and waste that often implies. It will require immediate investment in a resource we have in abundant supply: human beings.

We need to *enforce* safety, order, and civility in our streets and schools, and I hope we act quickly. We need more police and more crossing guards armed with cell phones. We need more teachers and smaller classes. We need higher teacher salaries. In this time of economic desperation, that will draw strong new candidates to join our overworked teachers and reward those who fight in the trenches.

We need separate schools for congenital troublemakers. I agree with the teachers' union that such students should be transferred quickly, not after months of delay. I trust school administrators and staffs to be fair in choosing students deserving a transfer. The Second Chance Academies they are transferred to must be well-staffed, high-security, and no-nonsense. They should also be real schools, not holding pens.

In neighborhoods plagued by gangs or feuding cliques of teenagers, we need to enlist adults to monitor the sidewalks their windows overlook, and call a special number immediately when they see trouble.

Where will we find the money to make the city safe for Derrion Albert? We will make that our top priority. Other funding will have to be put on hold. It will hurt. It must be done. Mayor Daley can do it.

By 2016, when the Olympic torch burns in Rio de Janeiro, can our torch for Derrion Albert also burn? It will be brighter, and cast its light longer, and it will also, as the Olympics were said to, provide benefits for all Chicagoans.

Hoop Dreams: The Great American Documentary

November 6, 2009—Today, fifteen years after I first saw it, I believe *Hoop Dreams* is the great American documentary. No other documentary has ever touched me more deeply. It was relevant then, and today, as inner-city neighborhoods sink deeper into the despair of children murdering children, it is more relevant. It tells the stories of two fourteen-year-olds, Arthur Agee and William Gates, how they dreamed of stardom in the NBA, and how basketball changed their lives. Basketball, and this film.

Hoop Dreams observed its fifteenth anniversary Wednesday, November 4, 2009, at the Gene Siskel Film Center in Chicago. Agee and Gates were both there. Gates, now a minister, observed that in one period of time he buried twenty victims of gang violence, sixteen of them under sixteen. Agee said when he looks at his friends in the film today, "Ten of them are no longer with us." Yet there they sat, men of around forty now, articulate, thoughtful. They spoke about how their lives began to change on a Chicago playground twenty-two years ago when a movie camera showed up.

"We started out to make a little thirty-minute documentary about a kid who had basketball dreams," Steve James, the director of the film, said Wednesday night. It was a benefit for Kartemquin Films, the forty-year-old Chicago documentary group that produced the film. "We ended up five years later with 250 hours of film. We edited it down to just under three hours. We only had enough money to shoot a half-hour film. We never did get much more, but we kept on filming."

How could they stop? *Hoop Dreams* unfolds as a human drama so powerful it seems crafted from fiction and arrives at a climax more exciting than any other sports film. And it's about so much more than that. It's about two young men whom we follow from grade school to college. About the poor neighborhoods they grow up in, and about the wider society they hope to enter. About their families. About life and death. About the elusive dream of stardom in professional sports. And about the indomitable human spirit.

"Do you all wonder sometimes how I am living?" Arthur's mother, Sheila, asks the filmmakers at one point, turning directly to the camera. "How my children survive, and how they're living? It's enough to really make people want to go out there and just lash out and hurt somebody."

During the course of the film, Sheila's husband leaves and gets into trouble, she suffers chronic back pain, she loses a job and goes on welfare, and Arthur can't meet the tuition and is dropped by St. Joseph's, the suburban high school that recruited him. After the school actually refuses him a copy of his transcript for not paying bills his family wouldn't have if St. Joseph's hadn't foraged in his neighborhood for a winning team, he transfers to the public Marshall High School and leads them to the state finals. Take that, St. Joe's.

Gates and Agee reflected on the twenty-two years since they first saw Steve James and his Kartemquin collaborators, Peter Gilbert and Frederick Marx, and the fifteen years since the Sundance premiere. Today they're university graduates with satisfying jobs (William a minister, Arthur running the Arthur Agee Role Model Foundation, funded by his line of Hoop Dreams sporting wear).

When they were fourteen, things weren't headed that way. "You see my father one time in the film," William Gates said. "That's probably how many times I saw him."

When Arthur was being courted with scholarship offers, his parents told him, "Do what *you* want to do." His father said, "We'll support you. If I have to steal paint to do it, I'll do it."

William's girlfriend, Catherine, got pregnant. He was offered a scholarship to Marquette and felt he had to accept it, but his decision caused them troubled times—even though he made the list of Marquette's all-time basketball letter winners.

On Wednesday night, he introduced Catherine in the audience: "My wife of seventeen years. She was determined to get a college degree, but we couldn't both be in school at once. We made an agreement: I promised when I got mine, I would work to help put her through

school. Today we have two college graduates in the house."

"What did we know then about what we wanted when we were fourteen?" Arthur asked. "I plan to study communications." He was mocking how serious he sounded at fourteen. "Yeah, communications. What is that? It's easy, that's what. All the athletes study it."

"Hey, I have a degree in communications!" William said.

"Me too," Arthur said. "Don't mean I *wanted* to!"

"Hey, so do I!" said Steve James.

"I'm the same person inside as that confident fourteen-year-old," William said. "I was so gifted. Basketball came naturally to me. It was like walking. But I've had a better life than if I'd gone into the NBA. As a pastor, I can talk to the young people. They see the film and know I came from where they're coming from. If I'd been an NBA star, they'd need an appointment to see me."

Avatar Revisited

December 18, 2009—The thing about James Cameron is, he can get his mind around a project the size of *Avatar* and keep his cool. If it requires the development of untested technology, he takes the time to work on it. If he wants to create aliens human enough to be sexy and yet keep them out of the Uncanny Valley, he test-drives them. If it costs $250 million, as reported, or $350 million, as rumored, you reflect: That's a lot of money, but after seeing the movie, I guess I saw most of it up there on the screen.

It has become a favorite sport in some Hollywood circles, and even among critics not a million miles distant from myself, to publicly doubt Cameron's claims. He takes ten years, starting with a story he began writing ten years before *that*? He was determined to film in 3-D, but no 3-D was good enough, so he had to perfect the next generation of that contentious process. The film needed 163 minutes to be told, causing anxiety among exhibitors eager to usher in a new audience every 120 minutes? If that's what it took, that's what it took.

After the epic success of his *Titanic*, the highest-grossing movie ever made, no one was prepared to say no to him. That is a risky business

to be in, and Hollywood is littered with the corpses of films that followed big hits by their makers. There's even a joke abut that:
"Now that you've set box office records, what are you going to do next?"
"I've got this script in my desk drawer that I've been working on since the 1980s, but before now no one has ever wanted to back it."

Doubt descended upon Cameron's fans after he previewed eighteen minutes of *Avatar* in the autumn. Audiences were underwhelmed. Did the alien race of Na'vi look a little creepy? Or not creepy enough? The term Uncanny Valley is used by robot theorists and special effects technicians to describe artificial humanoids who look *too* human, so that their artificiality becomes unsettling. Better Robby the Robot as your housecleaner than a Stepford Wife.

In the days before the first press screenings of *Avatar,* a sort of frenzy gripped certain Web fan sites. Then the great day arrived, 20th Century-Fox issued individuals invitations and posted guards at the door, the chosen people filed in, the movie began, silence descended, interest grew, and doubts were dispelled. Cameron had done it.

Fox made much of a press embargo: No critics were to review the film until Friday, December 18, 2009, its opening day. A flaw in this theory was that the movie opened a week sooner in England, and American fans, not witless, were instantly devouring the London reviews.

Kirk Honeycutt of the *Hollywood Reporter* broke the U.S. embargo and referred to Cameron's infamous speech when *Titanic* won as best picture: "A dozen years later, James Cameron has proven his point: He is king of the world." Todd McCarthy of *Variety* was also an embargo breaker: "Cameron delivers again with a film of universal appeal that just about everyone who ever goes to the movies will need to see."

You could call those the kinds of reviews Hollywood likes to read, and it's unlikely Honeycutt or McCarthy will be denied entry to Fox screenings anytime soon. What was the point of an embargo, anyway? Was Fox afraid the reviews would be negative? By last Friday afternoon editors at the *Sun-Times* and *Tribune* were growing restless as the good news leaked

out, and both papers published reviews. Soon a movie that wasn't supposed to be reviewed was sporting high numbers in the Tomatometer (86 percent as I write).

More sincere praise came from a woman seated not far from me (no, not Chaz), who felt the call of nature, raced out to the facilities, hurried back in, sat down, and twenty minutes later realized she'd forgotten to put her 3-D glasses back on.

Avatar creates a new world from scratch, and as Lucas did in *Star Wars,* fills it with such countless minute details that it doesn't seem artificial. Well, it does, but as real as a movie can seem, if you see what I mean. The creatures of this planetary forest are many-toothed and fantastical, but not the grotesque artifices of so many monster movies. Their battles seem sincere and earnest, and not the banging of pots and pans as in *Transformers 2.*

The special effects pioneer Ray Harryhausen, who made horses fly and sent skeletons into battle, is still alive at eighty-nine. If he sees *Avatar,* he may feel the kind of pride Wernher von Braun might have felt the day men walked on the moon.

Cameron has told a story with comprehensible emotional motivation, physical events that make sense at least within the realities of his imaginary world, and an alien race that exists not as foils for ray guns but as indigenous people living in harmony with their environment. His movie has a Green message and an antiwar message, both effective and part of the plot.

Those towering blue Na'vi with their long tails look peculiar at first, but it's strange how quickly they grow on us. You don't whip up aliens like that with a sketch pad. It takes trial runs and countless hours. And Cameron was equal to the test. He also overcame the bane of 3-D, which is dimness. His Dolby 3-D seems noticeably brighter. And his use of 3-D is restrained; he doesn't poke his picture in our eyes, and his editing makes sense of things, unlike Michael Bay's Mixmaster approach.

James Cameron set out to do a lot of very difficult things and to do them all correctly. It took him and his many collaborators a long time and a lot of money, but how many filmmakers could have done it at all? As I said in my review, the king of the world has been re-elected.

See You at the Movies

March 25, 2010—Yes, Chaz and I are still going ahead with our plans for a new movie review program on television. No, the recent cancellation of *At the Movies* hasn't discouraged us. We believe a market still exists for a weekly show where a couple of critics review new movies.

I can't prove it, but I have the feeling that more different people are seeing more different movies than ever before. With the explosion of DVD, Netflix, Redbox, and many forms of video on demand, virtually all movies are easily available to virtually all North American moviegoers. This has created a huge potential audience. When people tell me how many titles they have in their Netflix queues, I reflect that until recent years they'd be telling me how many movies never even played in their town.

I can't reveal details about the talks we're deeply involved in. I can say that the working title was *Roger Ebert Presents Fill in Words Here*, and that it has now become *Roger Ebert Presents At the Movies*. Gene Siskel and I started using that title way back in 1980, when we left PBS for Tribune Broadcasting. I can also say the thumbs will return.

I can also say that we held video tests with several potential hosts two weeks ago in Los Angeles, and know who we will use. We also know we will have a strong Web presence. We will go full-tilt New Media: television, Net streaming, cell phone apps, Facebook, Twitter, iPad, the whole enchilada. The disintegration of the old model creates an opening for us. I'm more excited than I would be if we were trying to do the same old same old. I've grown up with the Internet. I came aboard back when MCI Mail was the e-mail of choice. I had a forum on CompuServe when it ruled the Web. My Web site and blog at the *Sun-Times* site have changed the way I work, and even the way I think. When I lost my speech, I speeded up instead of slowing down.

We'll also go New Cinema. Not just the One Weekend Wonders, although you gotta have 'em, but indie films, foreign films, documentaries, restored classics, the new Herzog, the new Bahrani, the new Almodóvar. What's new on Instant Streaming? What great movies should everyone see? Hey, Paramount just announced $1 million for ten $100,000 movies.

Those kinds of films. What kind of a real movie lover cares who has the *exclusive* first trailer in the newest extrusion of the *Transformers* franchise? It's time to smarten up.

It isn't only *At the Movies* that died Wednesday. It was a whole genre of television. We thought of it as a movie review program. The television industry thought of it as a half-hour weekly syndicated show. Those are shows sold market by market and usually placed in a weekend time slot. The first time Siskel and I attended NATPE, the annual trade show of syndication, there were so many shows they jammed the floor of the Convention Center in New Orleans. Wolfgang Puck flew in to cater private dinners. We were approached by *Fishin' Fever* and asked if we wanted to be Celebrity Guest Anglers.

At the Movies was one of the last survivors of half-hour syndication. It didn't fail so much as have its format shot out from beneath it. Don't blame Disney. Don't blame Tony Scott and Michael Phillips, the final cohosts, critics I admire who still have five months left on the air. Don't blame Ben Mankiewicz. Don't blame my pal Richard Roeper, who didn't fancy following the show in a "new direction." Don't blame the cancer that forced me off the show. Don't even blame Ben Lyons. He was the victim of a mistaken hiring decision.

Blame the fact that five-day-a-week syndicated shows like *Wheel of Fortune* went to six days. Blame the fact that cable TV and the Internet have fragmented the audience so much that stations are losing market share no matter what they do. Blame the economy, because many stations would rather sell a crappy half-hour infomercial than program a show they respect. Blame the fact that everything seems to be going to hell in a handbasket.

Chaz and I will produce the show. Yes, I'd like to make occasional appearances on the air. I'm not foolish enough to believe any form of back-and-forth debate is possible, but I could do Great Movies segments, or a wrap-up from Cannes or Toronto. With all the publicity about me "getting my voice back," some people have the idea that a computer program has magically allowed me to speak again. That will never happen. I type, and the words come out. No one can type fast enough for conversational repartee. With the new software from Edinburgh the words will come out sounding like me. That's huge. It will work well on the new show in voice-over narration of TV packages.

There has been a fragmentation of movie watching. Theatrical distribution is now dominated by the big-budget, heavily marketed 3-D of the Week. Such films have a success utterly independent of critics. Like junk food, they're consumed by habit and may be filling but are high in cinematic sugar and fat. The consumers of that product don't think of a movie as an investment of two hours of their lives.

When the *New York Times* put an interactive Netflix map online, allowing me to search by zip code and see what my neighbors were renting, the top title was *Milk,* followed by such films as *The Wrestler, Slumdog Millionaire, Doubt,* and *Rachel Getting Married.* Think about that. Good movies. *Transformers 2* was nowhere to be seen. (*Milk,* in case you're wondering, was first or second in most Chicago zip codes, not just mine.)

Those are the kinds of people who might want to watch a movie review program. Our show will try to reach people who think before they watch a movie, and value their time, and their minds. Does that sound like a pitch? Probably. I think it's also a business plan.

I've written before about my adventures as a movie critic on TV. I've said what I have to say. Was I sad when *At the Movies* was canceled? You bet I was. I received a nice phone call from two of the Disney executives in charge, who had been aboard since day one, and that was a kindness. Week in and week out since 1980, Disney produced a weekly movie review program, and to my certain knowledge never once tried to influence the reviews of any of its movies. When Rich Frank was president of the Disney Studios, at speeches he'd even show video clips of Siskel and I trashing some of his films. I think he felt a certain pride in our independence.

All those years under Michael Eisner and Bob Iger, that never changed. We got support. We made friends. It was a long, strange trip for Gene and myself, Richard, Michael, Tony, Ben, and Ben and all of our cohosts. One of the show's guest cohosts, Kim Morgan, tweeted Wednesday night that it was an "honor" to sit in the chair. I replied, "It was the chair that was honored." Doing that show is harder than it

may seem. But I can tell you this: It's every bit as much fun as it looks like.

For years we closed with, "The balcony is closed." Before that it was, "See you at the movies." That's the right note to end on.

Hey! Don't Call Me a Dirty Commie!

May 10, 2010—The impression is spreading that I have drawn an equation between the American flag and the hammer and the sickle. I'm currently serving for target practice on some right-wing Web sites, and a group of tweeters are having jolly fun portraying me as an America hater and worse.

This is the result of one single tweet of mine, and those who were eager to misunderstand it. Tweets are limited to 140 characters, and here is what I tweeted:

@ebertchicago: *Kids who wear American Flag t-shirts on 5 May should have to share a lunchroom table with those who wear a hammer and sickle on 4 July.*

Now what do you suppose I meant by that? It was tweeted at the height of the discussion over five white California kids who wore matching T-shirts to school on Cinco de Mayo, and were sent home by their school. This inspired predictable outrage in the usual circles.

Tweeted from lonestarag05: *Its the USA not Mexico. They are allowed to be proud of their country. I wonder sometimes why you even stay here.*

Many others informed me that Americans have the right to be proud of our flag and wear it on T-shirts. Of course they do. That isn't the question. It's not what my tweet said. What I suggested, in its 108 letters, is that we could all use a little empathy. I wish I had worded it better.

Let's begin with a fact few Americans know: Celebrating Cinco de Mayo is an American custom. The first such celebration was held in California in 1863, and they have continued without interruption. In Mexico itself it is not observed, except in the state of Puebla—the site of Mexico's underdog victory over the French on May 5, 1862.

Cinco de Mayo's purpose is to celebrate Mexican-American culture in the United States. We are a nation of immigrants and have many such observances, for example, St. Patrick's Day parades, which began in Boston in 1737 and not in Ireland until 1931. Or Pulaski Day, officially established in Illinois in 1977, and not observed in Poland. The first Chinese New Year's parade was held in San Francisco in the 1860s, and such parades began only later in China. In Chicago this August we will have the eighty-first annual Bud Billiken Parade, one of the largest parades in America celebrating the African-American heritage.

I invite you to perform four easy thought experiments:

1. You and four friends are in Boston and attend the St. Patrick's Day parade wearing matching Union Jack T-shirts, which of course you have every right to do.

2. You and your pals are in Chicago on Pulaski Day, and wear a T-shirt with a photograph of Joseph Stalin, which is your right.

3. In San Francisco's Chinatown for the parade, your crowd wears T-shirts saying, "My granddad was at the Rape of Nanking and all I got was this lousy T-shirt."

4. In Chicago for the Bud Billiken Parade, you and your crowd, back in shape after three hospitalizations, turn up with matching T-shirts sporting the Confederate flag.

The question is obviously not whether Americans, or anyone else, has the right to wear our flag on their T-shirts. But empathetic people realize much depends on context. If, on Cinco de Mayo, you turn up at your school with a large Mexican-American student population wearing such shirts, are you (1) joining in the spirit of the holiday, or (2) looking for trouble?

I suggest you intend to insult your fellow students. Not because they do not respect *their* flag, but because you do not respect their heritage. That there are five of you in matching shirts demonstrates you want to be deliberately provocative.

Therefore, you and your buddies should try wearing the hammer and sickle on the Fourth of July. You could try it at a NASCAR race, for example.

In Memoriam

Dennis Hopper

June 1, 2010—Dennis Hopper's career began as an actor of alienation in movies like *Rebel Without a Cause*. His career as a director began with *Easy Rider*. His career as an art collector began when he bought one of Andy Warhol's soup can paintings for seventy-five dollars. His career as a drug abuser began at around the same time, and he told me, simply and factually, "I spent some time in a rubber room."

Then he got clean and sober, and his careers started all over again, as an actor, as a director, as a photographer much in demand, as a painter, as an icon. Hopper's death came on May 29, 2010, at age seventy-four, surrounded by family and friends in the modernist house he built on Venice Beach in Los Angeles and filled with modern art.

For Hopper, life was an art form. His acting took such shape because he was able to reinvent himself as a character. More than many actors, he created characters we remember vividly for themselves: James Dean's sidekick in *Rebel*, Marlon Brando's drug-crazed acolyte in *Apocalypse Now*, the terrifying gas-sniffing pervert of *Blue Velvet*, the town drunk in *Hoosiers*, a hit man in *Red Rock West*, the villain in *Waterworld*.

He was also an intellectual, although that side was masked by his somewhat notorious drug abuse, gradually escalating from the 1960s until about 1983. Some of those years were lost. "I was thinking I had no life or any memory really until now," he told me one day in 1990. "There's always this fear of not being able to make the films, not being able to do the work. I don't think anybody, no matter how successful they get, ever loses that fear. If you've ever had a period of time where you weren't allowed to work—maybe because you were doing drugs and alcohol, but you didn't know that was their reason—then the fear is always with you."

He was an honor student in school, he developed an early love of Shakespeare, he studied under Thomas Hart Benton as a child, he studied Method acting with Lee Strasberg, his photographs commanded gallery prices, and as an art collector he was early onto Pop Art and his collection became famous and influential.

As a director, he practiced a classic style. "I'm back with John Ford and Huston and Hawks— and Hathaway," he told me. "I learned a lot from Henry Hathaway when I was acting in *The Sons of Katie Elder*." That would have been gratifying for Hathaway to hear; Wikipedia reports that on *From Hell to Texas*, Hopper refused Hathaway's instructions for eighty different takes over a few days.

The turning point of his professional career came when he directed *Easy Rider* (1969) and starred in it with Peter Fonda and Jack Nicholson; it was the movie that lifted his close friend Nicholson from obscure B movies into a stardom that lasts to this day.

"We left America with a little motorcycle picture," he recalled, "we took it to the Cannes Film Festival, and we came back with a hit in our hands." The picture won the festival's Camera d'Or award for best first film. "All of a sudden I was an auteur," he said.

The film cost $400,000 and grossed $60 million (in 1970s dollars) in its first three years in release. When I was writing a screenplay at 20th Century–Fox at the time, a producer moaned to me: "We're making these war movies and Westerns, and every producer in town has his nephew out in the desert shooting a motorcycle picture."

Dennis Hopper had no affectations. He was friendly, accessible, easy to talk with. He'd had great success without the affliction of great stardom. He was only eighteen when he was signed by Warner Bros., nineteen when he made *Rebel Without a Cause* (1955), and in those days when Hollywood was a studio town, he made friends and found work quickly, especially in countless episodes of TV dramas. Among his pals as a young man was John Wayne; they had their Republican politics in common.

At the end it was widely reported that he was broke, but in part that was because of a deathbed dispute with his wife, Victoria Duffy, about the disposition of his art collection. Visibly ill, he made one of his last appearances on March 26, 2010, at the dedication of his star on the Hollywood Walk of Fame. Describing himself as a "farm boy from Dodge City, Kansas," as he accepted his star, he said, "Hollywood was my college."

John Hughes

August 6, 2009—Few directors have left a more distinctive or influential body of work than John Hughes. The creator of the modern American teenager film, who died August 6, 2009, in New York, made a group of films that is still watched and quoted today.

Hughes, who was fifty-nine, died of a heart attack during an early morning walk while visiting family in New York City, his publicist said. He lived all his life in the northern suburbs of Chicago, southern Wisconsin, and on a farm he operated in northern Illinois.

Refusing to move to Los Angeles, he once told me why he preferred to bring his young acting discoveries to Chicago to film: "I like to check them into a motel far away from their friends, keep them out of trouble, and have them focus on the work."

The list of films Hughes directed, produced, or wrote includes such enduring hits as *Sixteen Candles; The Breakfast Club; Ferris Bueller's Day Off; Planes, Trains and Automobiles; Some Kind of Wonderful; Curly Sue; Mr. Mom; Home Alone; Pretty in Pink; Weird Science; She's Having a Baby; National Lampoon's Christmas Vacation; Beethoven; 101 Dalmatians; Uncle Buck;* and *Baby's Day Out.*

His films helped establish an international notion of ordinary American teenagers, and he was as popular abroad as at home. Once when I was visiting the largest movie theater in Calcutta, I asked if *Star Wars* had been their most successful American film. No, I was told, it was *Baby's Day Out,* a Hughes comedy about a baby wandering through a big city, which played for more than a year.

Hughes, who graduated in 1968 from Glenbrook High School in Northbrook, Illinois, used the northern suburbs as the setting for many of his films, notably *Ferris Bueller* and *The Breakfast Club.* He converted the gymnasium of the former Maine North High School in Des Plaines for use as a sound stage, assigning his

actors schoolrooms as dressing rooms and corridor lockers with their own combinations.

Hughes was a star maker for a generation. Among the actors he introduced or popularized were Matthew Broderick, Molly Ringwald, Emilio Estevez, Anthony Michael Hall, Ally Sheedy, Judd Nelson, Macaulay Culkin, and John Candy, who worked in eight Hughes films. Some of those actors, freed from their confinement under Hughes, later became famous as the Brat Pack.

He took teenagers seriously, and his films are distinctive for showing them as individuals with real hopes, ambitions, problems, and behavior.

"Kids are smart enough to know that most teenage movies are just exploiting them," he told me on the set of *The Breakfast Club.* "They'll respond to a film about teenagers as people. (My) movies are about the beauty of just growing up. I think teenage girls are especially ready for this kind of movie, after being grossed out by all the sex and violence in most teenage movies. People forget that when you're sixteen, you're probably more serious than you'll ever be again. You think seriously about the big questions.

"I'm going to do all my movies here in Chicago," he told me. "The *Tribune* referred to me as a 'former Chicagoan.' As if, to do anything, I had to leave Chicago. I never left. I worked until I was twenty-nine at the Leo Burnett advertising agency, and then I quit to do this. This is a working city, where people go to their jobs and raise their kids and live their lives. In Hollywood, I'd be hanging around with a lot of people who don't have to pay when they go to the movies."

After Hughes died, some reports referred to him as "a recluse who disappeared somewhere in Illinois." A few years ago, a friend of mine ran into him and kidded him about having disappeared from the Hollywood radar.

"I haven't disappeared," he said. "I'm standing right here. I'm just not in Los Angeles."

Hughes was incredibly productive as a screenwriter. He personally directed eight films, produced twenty-three, and wrote thirty-seven, most recently *Drillbit Taylor* (2008). Such filmmakers as Judd Apatow and Kevin Smith cite him as an influence, Smith once saying, "Basically everything I do is just a raunchy John Hughes movie."

Hughes is survived by his wife of thirty-nine years, Nancy, two sons, and four grandchildren.

Lou Jacobi

October 27, 2009—"These two newlyweds are driving down to Florida on their honeymoon," Lou Jacobi was telling me. "The guy puts his hand on his wife's leg. 'We're married now,' she tells him. 'Why don't you go a little farther?' So, he goes to Fort Lauderdale."

This was in a restaurant in Toronto in 1999, where we were having lunch before Lou was scheduled to dedicate his star on Canada's Walk of Fame. Lou died Friday, October 23, 2009, at ninety-five.

Every time I saw Lou, he told me new jokes. I called him on the phone, he told me jokes. We went to dinner, he did ten minutes of stand-up for the people at the next table. Lou Jacobi was not happy unless everyone around him was smiling.

Lou was the only man I know who can be introduced just like Jack Benny: star of stage, screen, radio, TV, records, and the violin. He made his stage debut at the age of twelve, playing a violin prodigy in *The Priest and the Rabbi*, a Toronto stage play where it turned out (I'm not entirely clear about this) that he was the son of the priest, or of the rabbi, or they were brothers. "I was off after the first act," he said, so maybe he never got to stay around for the end of the play.

You may remember him from Woody Allen's *Everything You Ever Wanted to Know About Sex,* where he played a dinner guest who excused himself, went upstairs, raided the hostesses' closet, put on a dress, was almost caught, escaped out a window, and was arrested by a cop who wanted to know why a man was wearing a dress and a mustache.

He was also in Barry Levinson's *Avalon,* as the Jewish uncle who drove out to the suburbs from the old city neighborhood, arrived late, stood in the doorway, and said disbelievingly, "You cut the turkey without me?" And he was the bartender in Billy Wilder's *Irma la Douce,* and a lot of other films, and did a lot of TV (he was a regular on the Dean Martin program). On Broadway, he starred in Neil Simon's first play, *Come Blow Your Horn,* in *The Diary of Anne Frank,* in Simon's *Sunshine Boys,* and in *Don't Drink the Water,* a play Woody Allen wrote for him.

I am writing down these credits partly because it was Lou Jacobi's day. But mostly I am writing them because I love Lou and his wife, Ruth, whom he didn't marry until he was forty-three, his sister told me, "because finally he knew he'd found the right girl."

I met Lou at Dusty and Joan Cohl's annual Chinese dinner at the Toronto Film Festival twenty years ago. He offered the toast at my wedding. "Thank you for your warm welcome," he told our guests. "I don't deserve it. Of course, I've got arthritis, and I don't deserve that, either."

I reviewed a few of his film performances, but at eighty-five, Lou was just about retired. What inspired me was the way Lou and Ruth preserved their zest for living. They attacked every moment like a thrilling opportunity.

That day, halfway through that year's film festival, Lou and Ruth were at lunch with their friends Dusty and Joan. Bill Marshall, who founded the festival with Dusty, was also at the table, along with film critic Kathleen Carroll and man about town Billy Ballard.

"On our first date in 1947, Dusty took me to a benefit at a club, and Lou was the entertainment," Joan told me. "He was wearing a dress and a blond wig and was sprawled on a piano, singing about a naughty lady named Sadie."

In those days, Lou played the Canadian borscht belt, nightclubs, weddings, and stag parties. ("Oooooh, I told the dirtiest jokes!" he twinkled.) Only later did he become a stage star, first in London, then on Broadway. Even after he became admired as a serious actor, he still went for laughs; his record albums have titles like *Tijuana Al and His Jewish Brass* and *The Yiddish Are Coming! The Yiddish Are Coming!*

As you make your way through life, sometimes you happen upon people who know how to be happy. I remember Lou, and I'm not afraid to be old like Lou is, if I can get there in Lou's style.

At lunch that day, Lou had a new joke. He had to stand up to tell it.

"An old guy is walking down the street with two big watermelons in his hands," Lou said. "A guy asks him, 'How do I get to CBS?'"

Lou pantomimed an old man with arthritis.

"First he leans over and puts down one watermelon.

"Then he leans over and puts down the other watermelon.

"Then he puts up his hands and shrugs."

Film Festival

Cannes Film Festival
On a Darkling Plain

Cannes, France, May 12, 2010—Fifty years ago, the Palme d'Or winner at Cannes was Fellini's *La Dolce Vita.* More every year I realize that it was the film of my lifetime. But indulge me while I list some more titles.

The other entries in the official competition included *Ballad of a Soldier* by Grigori Chukhrai, *Lady with a Dog* by Iosif Kheifits, *Home from the Hill* by Vincente Minnelli, *The Virgin Spring* by Ingmar Bergman, *Kagi* by Kon Ichikawa, *L'Avventura* by Michelangelo Antonioni, *Le Trou* by Jacques Becker, *Never on Sunday* by Jules Dassin, *Sons and Lovers* by Jack Cardiff, *The Savage Innocents* by Nicholas Ray, and *The Young One* by Luis Bunuel.

And many more. But I am not here at the 2010 Cannes Film Festival to mourn the present and praise the past.

Cannes is still the most important annual event in the world of what some of us consider good cinema. The Official Competition here is so much better, as a group, than all the nominees for the Academy Award that it makes you want to cry. My friend Richard Corliss thought the 2009 Cannes festival was the best in its history. I fully expect this year's Cannes to show me great movies.

But we are here at the end of something and not the beginning. The traditional model we grew up with is dying. We expected to hear about new films through news from festivals, Hollywood premieres, and reviews from New York and Los Angeles, to begin with. Then the films and the reviews would fan out across the country. In my Illinois hometown, I was able to see all twelve of the films listed above in 35 mm, on a big screen.

Some few of you may be able to see several of this year's Cannes successes if you live in big cities. Others will play via Video on Demand, or stream online. They'll be on DVD. The one you will surely be able to see is the opening night film, Ridley Scott's *Robin Hood,* starring Russell Crowe. That film has no business here. But remember that Cannes is an attraction as well as a festival, and all the world will goggle at photos and TV of Crowe and Cate Blanchett on the red carpet. And for a moment, this will seem once again to be the center of the world of film. We of the critical corps will begin every day at the 8:30 a.m. press screening and see one another again three or four movies later. We will jam the press conferences. You will be able to read hundreds of thousands of Cannes reports, all with the subtext, "Man, am I happy to be here." It will be a fabulous ten days.

But at home, the studios have won an important victory, and will now be able to premiere their new releases on television on the *same day* they open in theaters. There is nothing to compel them to prescreen them for the critics. If they don't, the result will be a mainstream cinema based *entirely* on advertising and marketing.

Some of those video premieres will be on ad-free cable. Some will be on cable and network outlets with advertising. Imagine seeing *Precious* the first time with commercial interruptions.

It may not get that bad. It may. In my nightmares, I imagine first-run Hollywood cinema becoming the Movie of the Week, pitched at the broadest possible audience. If box office grosses are a sad way to rate a movie's success, how much worse are opening night Nielsen ratings? I see stories pitched to safe genres: horror, romcom, sci-fi. I see quirky pictures, what we amusingly call Art Films, disregarded.

Disney has already announced it will make no more ordinary first-run movies, and will focus on 3-D, animation, superheroes, and franchises. The studio that gave us *Down and Out in Beverly Hills, Pretty Woman,* and *Good Morning, Vietnam* wants to do so no more. The new, well-financed CBS Films says it will focus on "midstream" movies. Their second: the appalling *The Back-Up Plan.* Think what that could gross in one night on TV with a good ad campaign. The stinkero word of mouth would arrive the morning after.

Cannes has just added one more film to this

year's lineup, Ken Loach's *Route Irish*. It's the story of an employee of a private contractor in Iraq, such as Blackwater, whose friend is killed. Conventional wisdom is that Iraq war films die at the box office. I guess they do. Vietnam films didn't. That's an idea for another piece. Most of the people reading this will know very well who Ken Loach is. Most other people don't know and don't care. Loach, who cares more about his films than his bank account, has just opened a YouTube channel and posted several of his movies for free. You want to start somewhere, start with *Kes*.

Other directors with new films here this year include Alejandro Gonzalez Inarritu, Abbas Kiarostami, Takeshi Kitano, Chang-dong Lee, Mike Leigh, Doug Liman, Nikita Mikhalkov, and Bertrand Tavernier. I've had a problem with Kiarostami, but I eagerly await his next one, just as I awaited David Lynch's work in years when I wasn't responding to it. There's no doubt in my mind Kiarostami is a serious artist with a fierce dedication, and whether he connects with me is not his problem, it's mine. A director who creates outside crass, dumbed-down channels is a human resource.

The best film here this year will quite likely be by a director I'm unfamiliar with. That'll be all the better. I'll be there every morning to join my fellow acolytes in worship at the Temple of Cinema, also known as the Palais des Festivals. And we'll be hurrying down the rue d'Antibes for a small indie film showing in the Marketplace. This world may be dying, but not yet.

A Magical Curtain for Jacques Tati

May 14, 2010—I walked into Cinema Arcades, behind our hotel, for a Cannes market screening of *The Illusionist* and saw the magically melancholy final act of Jacques Tati's career.

Tati, of course, was the tall Frenchman, bowing from the waist, pipe in mouth, often wearing a trench coat, pants too short, always the center of befuddlements.

If you've seen *Mr. Hulot's Holiday,* you know who he was, and if you haven't, it belongs in your holding pattern.

Tati, who died in 1982, wrote the screenplay for this film, but never made it. He intended it for live action. His daughter Sophie Tatischeff still had the script, and handed it to Sylvain Chomet, who made the miraculously funny animated film *The Triplets of Belleville* (2003). He has drawn it with a lightness and beauty worthy of a older, sadder Miyazaki story. Animation suits it. Live action would overwhelm its fancy with realism.

The story involves a magician named Tatischeff who fails in one music hall after another, and ends up in Scotland, where at last he finds one fan: a young woman who idealizes him, moves in with him, tends to him, cooks and cleans, and would probably offer sex if he didn't abstemiously sleep on the couch. He's a good magician on a small scale, flawless at every trick except producing a rabbit from a hat. His problem there involves his frisky rabbit, which likes to sleep on Tatischeff's stomach at night. The rabbit makes it a practice during the act to pop up and peep around at inopportune moments.

Tatischeff finally ends up in Edinburgh, a city I think has never looked more bleak and beautiful in a film. Time has passed him by. Audiences prefer pop groups to aging magicians. He reaches the lowest stage in his career, performing in a shop window. He remains quiet, reflective, almost indifferent to the girl (although he buys her a pretty frock).

If you recall the opening scenes of *Up*, you know that animation is sometimes more effective than live action for conveying the arc of a life. This man does what he does very well, but there's no longer a purpose for him. Did Tati feel the same when he wrote this in the 1950s, before *Hulot* was a worldwide success?

Important to the charm of *Illusionist* is the grace with which the character of Tatischeff has been drawn. He looks like Tati, but much more important, he has the inimitable body language. The polite formality, the deliberate movement, the hesitation, the diffidence. His world is an illusion, which he produces nightly from a hat.

"Definite Palme d'Or possibility," Toby Talbot told me. *Definite,* Dan Talbot agreed. We'd all just come from the screening of the Official Competition selection *The Housemaid,* by Sang-soo Im of South Korea. You hear predictions like that three times a day at Cannes. When it comes from the Talbots it means something. Dan Talbot founded New Yorker Films in 1965; starting even earlier the Talbots ran the beloved New Yorker theater in New

York, and if you've seen classics by Herzog, Fassbinder, Godard, Wadja, and Bergman, chances are they came from New Yorker. They're been coming to Cannes longer than I have, and they have a feel for these things.

The Housemaid is extraordinary, further evidence that right now South Korea is producing many of the best films in the world. It takes place almost entirely within the huge modern house of a very rich man, and centers on the young woman he has hired as a nanny. It involves the man, his wife, his daughter, the older woman who runs his household, and the mothers of the wife and the nanny.

This is a house where living is an expensive form of art. The couple are smooth, calm, sophisticated. They value themselves very highly. The nanny forms a bond with their seven-year-old daughter and assists the wife during a pregnancy with twins. More than that I choose not to specify.

But look at the mastery of the film's construction. The nuanced performances. The implacable deliberation of the plot. The way the house acts as a hothouse to force the growth of anger. And the film's unforgiving portrait of people damaged by great wealth. This is a thriller about the ideas people have of themselves.

Chatroom, an official selection in the Un Certain Regard section, is a virtual thriller, so to speak, by Hideo Nakata. Set in the United Kingdom, by the director of *Ring* (1998), it's about a group that gathers in a chat room where the dynamics could lead to a suicide. The Internet is suggested with an evocative set: A corridor crowded with people who may or may not enter various rooms (Web sites) along the way. In these rooms, their virtual relationships form. Then Nakata cuts to real life to observe where they lead. The film is rather frightening in the way it portrays some of the possible consequences of the online life.

Here it is Friday and Cannes is still relatively quiet. Maybe the usual weekend crowds will appear, but they'll be tourists. What I notice is that some of the screenings have more empty seats than you'd expect, and the after-screening crowd at the press mailboxes doesn't seem as big as usual. It's probably too early to draw any conclusions, just as it's early to predict the Palme winner. But not too early to speculate.

A Good Film, a Bad Film, and a Friend

May 16, 2010—Mike Leigh has long been a great director, but now he is surely at the top of his form. *Another Year* has premiered here and is the film everyone I talk with loves the most. It is so beautifully sure and perceptive in its record of one year in the life of a couple happily married, and their relatives and friends, not so happy. After *Vera Drake* (2004) and *Happy-Go-Lucky* (2008), Leigh cannot seem to step wrong.

A woman at the press conference asked Leigh, "Did you have to make Mary so sad?" She might as well have asked, "Did you have to make Tom and Gerri so happy?"

They're a long-married couple, played by Jim Broadbent and Ruth Sheen, and they seem in complete accord about their life together. They garden, they work, they welcome their friends, they hope their son will find the right girl, they are in love.

Their steadfast joy in each other's company is essential, I believe, to provide the film with a center around which the characters revolve. Remarkably, these days, their thirty-year-old son loves them and is happy, and they have no issues. Theirs is the home poor Sally comes to when she realizes she has made no home of her own.

As Leigh's film grows through spring, summer, autumn, and winter, it involves the lives touched by Tom and Gerri (yes, they smile about their names). In particular they observe Mary (Lesley Manville), who is single, lonely, getting older, and alcoholic. "It's a shame," Tom says at one point after she's ended yet another sad visit, and that's all he has to say.

These people are not us, and yet we know them. They attend the funeral of Tom's sister-in-law, and we have never been to a funeral quite like it, and yet it is like many funerals. The uninvolved clergyman, the efficient undertakers, the remote father, the angry son, the handful of neighbors who didn't know the deceased all that well, the family skeletons. In particular, notes of social embarrassment that Leigh specializes in—the ways people display their anguish without meaning to.

It will have to be quite a film to snare the Palme d'Or away from this one, but there is a week to go. If *Another Year* isn't the Palme winner, then Lesley Manville is a good choice for Best Actress. When the film opens I'll have to find words to describe her work, but for now all I can say is, it is astonishing.

Outrage by Takeshi Kitano, on the other hand, is as bad as *Another Year* is good. People left the theater joining in that ancient query, "Why in the hell did they select this film?" Kitano is a gifted Japanese director who has made many films I admire, but this must be his worst. It involves two warring factions in the Yakuza, or Japanese mafia, and by the end of the film just about everyone on both sides is dead.

That's what happens. No characterization. Minimal plot. Many murders, nicely stylized. Kitano makes it a point to set everything in a sterile environment. No Japanese tradition here, except for an eating-house. Only steel, aluminum, glass, plastic, and shiny black limos. Black, white, silver, and blood red used as an artist's signature after every killing.

He has one idea in this film: The Yakuza code is being used to eradicate the Yakuza. Unfortunately, he doesn't take the entire 109 minutes to tell it. It only takes him a minute to tell, and he tells it 109 times.

Paul Cox is here. That is a blessing to be shouted. The great Australian director has returned after receiving a liver transplant in December. Over the years I've admired his films (*A Woman's Tale* and *Innocence* were at Ebertfest), and his spirit. He's one of the warriors, an independent director who does nothing for hire, who makes only films close to his heart, whose humanism you could call spiritual.

I first saw his work through the Chicago Film Festival, and then we found ourselves meeting at least annually, at Toronto, Cannes, Chicago, Sundance, Telluride, and once at Calcutta where a projectionist succeeded in the theoretically impossible feat of showing his film upside-down.

Last year at Cannes we met for what we both feared could be the last time. I was in my current condition, and Paul had been told he had serious liver disease. He'd been a friend to Chaz and me during our troubles, and now it was our turn, as he embarked on a difficult search for a liver that matched his blood type.

We exchanged a lot of e-mails. He was always Paul, amused, philosophical, keenly aware of life. He didn't drink much, but he loved to smoke his pipe, and reported almost in triumph that the doctors told him his liver problems seemed linked to no vice.

No liver appeared. His hopes faded. On Christmas Day 2009, joined by his loved ones, he believed he had days to live. On that day, the phone rang, and he learned a suitable liver had been found. He had the transplant operation, it seems to have been successful, and at one point he warned me not to e-mail any jokes good enough to burst his stitches. Few people have ever suggested any of my e-mail jokes were that good.

Paul visited us for dinner in the company of Nate Kohn, his daughters Sophie and Lily, and his friend Christie. Paul and Nate have been close for years. Nate, director of Ebertfest, is teaching a University of Georgia class here, and Sophie is blogging on my site this year. We sat in the little lobby of the Hotel Splendid and shared the sense that, by God, it is Cannes and we are here again, and who can deny it?

Waiting for Godard

May 17, 2010—When I began as a film critic, Jean-Luc Godard was widely thought to have reinvented the cinema with *Breathless* (1960). Now he is almost eighty and has made what is said to be his last film, and he's still at the job, reinventing. If only he had stopped while he was ahead. That would have been sometime in the 1970s. Maybe the 1980s. For sure, the 1990s. Without a doubt, before he made his Cannes entry, *Film: Socialisme.*

The thousands of seats in the Auditorium Debussy were jammed, and many were turned away. We lucky ones sat in devout attention to this film, such is the spell Godard still casts. There is an abiding belief that he has something radical and new to tell us. It is doubtful that anyone else could have made this film and found an audience for it.

He shows us a series of shots from a cruise ship traveling the Mediterranean, and also shots that travel through human history, which for the film's purposes involve Egypt, Greece, Palestine, Odessa (notably its steps), Naples, Barcelona, Tunisia, and other ports. Then we see fragments of a story involving two women (one a TV cameraman) and a family living at a roadside garage. A mule and a llama also live at the garage. There are shots of kittens, obscurely linked to the Egyptians, as well as parrots. The cruise ship is perhaps a metaphor for our human voyage through time. The garage is anybody's guess.

There is also much topical footage, both moving and still. Words are spoken, some of them bits of language from eminent authors. These words appear in widely spaced all-uppercase subtitles, and are mostly nouns. My impression, with imperfect French, is that some of the spoken wordage might be comprehensible. The subtitles, Godard has explained, are deliberately in what he calls Navajo English, which is a good deal like American French ("You . . . give . . . food?")

The words and images add up to an incoherent mosaic involving socialism, gambling, nationalism, Hitler, Stalin, art, Islam, women, Jews, Hollywood, war, and other large topics. I confess I have no idea what meaning they're intended to convey. I have not the slightest doubt it will all be explained by some of his defenders, or should I say disciples. Although a commenter on my blog recently made sarcastic remarks about such a shameless liberal as me basking on the Riviera and drinking in Godard's socialism, there is nothing in the film to offend the most rabid Tea Party communicant, who would be hard-pressed to say what, if anything, the film has to say about socialism.

As I was watching it, my mind wrote down a possible opening sentence for this notice: "Jean-Luc Godard's new film is about what you think about when you watch it." All films fit that definition, but some fit it better than others, and Film: Socialisme fits it best of all. Godard depends on us to do the heavy lifting. Some people are fond of saying, "Let me just put an idea into your head." Godard has sent my mind scurrying between ancient history and the modern entertainment industries, via Marxism and Nazism, to ponder—well, everything.

I think it's probable that a French speaker would obtain more from the film (which also contains several other languages), but I must console myself that the titles will be in English everywhere and for all audiences. Godard has provided an excellent jumping-off point for whatever you want to conclude about anything, so long as you connect it somehow with the words "Godard" and "Godardian."

Film: Socialisme is very good-looking. Apparently, in addition to standard digital video, Godard used a state-of-the-art iteration of high-def video; some shots, especially aboard the cruise ship, are so beautiful and glossy they could be an advertisement for something, perhaps a cruise ship.

The film closes with large block letters: "NO COMMENT." It ended, and I looked forward to attending Godard's press conference. I have seen him before at Cannes, after more explicable films, and once at Montreal I sat next to him at a little dinner for film critics, at which he arranged his garden peas into geometric forms on his plate and told us, "Cinema is the train. It is not the station." Or perhaps my memory is tricking me, and he said, "Cinema is the station. It is not the train." Both are equally true.

Todd McCarthy was standing in the row behind us, still scrutinizing the credits, and said he'd heard that Godard had canceled his press conference. Todd often receives such intelligence, perhaps by telepathy, during screenings. But he didn't believe it. We agreed to go check it out, just on the odd chance. One would feel such a fool for having missed Godard's last press conference at Cannes.

Peter Howell, the film critic of the Toronto Star, tall as an NBA forward, was already in a crowd of perhaps one hundred outside the press conference room. These hopefuls had turned up on the off chance of Godard changing his mind. With Godard, you never know. Word went around that Godard would hold the press conference after all, and had canceled it only in order to make a statement. A helpful festival guard said he knew nothing. From no other director is such behavior expected, or accepted. Then another guard told us that Godard would definitely not be holding a press conference.

So perhaps that was consistent with "NO COMMENT," and by turning up for the canceled conference anyway, we had learned/observed/refuted/proven the point. That Godard, what a card. Still cute at eighty.

Of Emotion and Its Absence

May 18, 2010—Of the twelve films I've seen at Cannes, the most warmly cheered has been the South African Life, Above All. That's possibly more significant than in other years.

The audiences at Cannes this year have been oddly restrained, and there's less clapping at the names of directors; even Jean-Luc Godard received only perfunctory applause. Is this becoming less a directors' festival and more a trade fair?

Perhaps I leap unfairly to conclusions. Some traditions remain. Before every screening at the Auditorium Debussy, for example, someone in the dark is sure to call out "Raoul!" There's laughter and a little buzz as old-timers explain to their neighbors that once in dim antiquity a moviegoer entered after the lights went down, was unable to find his friend, and shouted out "Raoul!" The search continues.

Oliver Schmitz's *Life, Above All* has been the best heart-warmer and tearjerker so far—and when I write from Cannes I use the term "tearjerker?" as a compliment, because this is a hardened crowd and when you hear snuffling in the dark you know it has been honestly earned. The film is about deep human emotions, evoked with sympathy and love.

Life, Above All takes place entirely within a South African township, one with moderate prosperity and well-tended homes. It centers on the twelve-year-old Chanda, who takes on the responsibility of holding her family together after her baby sister dies. Her mother is immobilized by grief, her father by drink, and a neighbor woman helps her care for two younger siblings.

Suspicion spreads in the neighborhood that the real cause of the family's problems is AIDS, although the word itself isn't said aloud until well into the film. More plot details can await my review, but let me particularly praise the performances of young Khomotso Manyaka, in her first role as Chanda; Keaobaka Makanyane as her mother; and Tinah Mnumzana as the neighbor. The film's ending frightens the audience with a dire threat, and then finds an uplift that's unlikely enough in its details to qualify as magic realism.

Life, Above All must be particularly effective in South Africa, where former president Thabo Mbeki persisted in puzzling denial about the causes and treatment of AIDS. This contributed to a climate of ignorance and mystery surrounding the disease, which in fact increased its spread. By directly dealing with the poisonous climate of rumor and gossip, the film takes a stand. But in nations where AIDS has been demystified, *Love, Above All* will play strongly as pure human drama, and of two women, one promptly and one belatedly, rising courageously to a challenge.

I saw *Life, Above All* not long after posting a few comments critical of my previous blog entry about Jean-Luc Godard's new *Film: Socialisme*. His film failed to impress or engage me, and seemed an obscure exercise in stylistic arrogance, with disdain for the audience. A critical comment by Jeremy Fassler was affectionate about his sometime hero, but Ezra Scalzo informed me: "There was a time when the critic had a duty to propel artists into new territory, which Godard has gone to despite your libel, and if we should be so lucky, he will continue to stimulate cinematic discussion in every way that your petty lifetime anecdotes, tawdry punk scripts and political ramblings do not."

As I read this, I recalled writing similar things myself in the 1960s about the philistines who did not embrace Godard. I felt that way about his films made then, and I still do, but I believe he has grown needlessly obscure and difficult, and I ask: Who does he make movies for? Those who will extrapolate meanings from them? Those who will helpfully explain what we missed? Or people who go to a movie and would appreciate a fair chance of figuring out what the damned thing is about?

I assume anyone who goes to a Godard film is unlikely to be stupid—is likely, indeed, to know a great deal about film. But this hypothetical person, however well-meaning, is unlikely to extract anything comprehensible, moving, or useful from *Film: Socialisme*. It is a sterile exercise.

Returning to the hotel three movies later (one of them was *Life, Above All*), I found Todd McCarthy's review of the Godard. He had a response similar to mine: "This is a film to which I had absolutely no reaction—it didn't provoke, amuse, stimulate, intrigue, infuriate or challenge me. What we have here is failure to communicate." McCarthy concludes: "Whereas Godard's one-time comrade-in-art-and-arms and subsequent favorite whipping boy Truffaut adhered to Jean Renoir's generosity of spirit, Godard has long since become the mean-minded anti-Renoir, someone who can say nothing good about anyone except himself. Like his film, it's not a worldview that says anything to me at this point."

I feel much the same. Because Godard meant something years ago, because he had a towering presence and a considerable influence, we continue to see his films, for smaller and smaller rewards. I believe he has contempt for the mass of moviegoers. Truffaut once described the beautiful sight of walking to the front of a cinema and seeing all those eyes uplifted to the screen, sharing the director's dream. What are Godard's dreams? We cannot know, because he chooses not to share them.

I don't have a problem with difficult films, those that are about themselves, those that challenge the audience. Consider a film like Charlie Kaufman's *Synecdoche, New York,* which is as Brechtian as Godard could possibly desire. Kaufman has something he desperately wants to say about the nature of life, and he says it in a complex way suited to his message. He wants to communicate, not to withhold.

Thinking of these films, my choice is clear: I prefer those that want to tell me something, to feel empathy with its characters. I reject those that are sealed off and sadistically enigmatic. I'm sure Godardians will be able to provide an explanation of his film—indeed, many explanations, all different. But we will be reading what they bring to the film, not from it.

A Campaign for Real Movies

May 19, 2010—There's something in the United Kingdom called the Campaign for Real Ale. It was started in the *Guardian* in the 1970s by Richard Boston, a journalist (naturally) who was alarmed by traditional British pubs being taken over by mass-produced, heavily marketed, rapidly brewed beer.

The real thing, he said, was not carbonated, was brewed in its own time, and had a distinctive flavor. It was drawn up by gravity from a cooled cellar, not forced through hoses under pressure. It wasn't tweaked to make it taste like all other beers, matching some international formula like Budweiser or Heineken's. I've tasted it. It went down smoothly, and you didn't belch.

We should start a Campaign for Real Movies. These also would not be carbonated by CGI or 3-D. They would be carefully created by

artists, from original recipes, that is, screenplays. Each movie would be different. There would be no effort to force them into conformity with commercial formulas.

These notions took shape while I was viewing some well-made Real Movies I've seen this year at Cannes: Bertrand Tavernier's *La Princesse de Montpensier,* Sang-soo Im's *The Housemaid,* Mike Leigh's *Another Year,* Mahamet-Saleh Haroun's *Un Homme Qui Crie,* Alejandro Gonzalez Inarritu's *Biutiful,* Oliver Schmitz's *Life, Above All,* and Chang-dong Lee's *Poetry.*

These aren't all masterpieces, although some are, but they're all Real Movies. None follows a familiar story arc. All involve intense involvement with their characters. All do something that is perhaps the most important thing a movie can do: They take us outside our personal box of time and space, and invite us to empathize with those of other times, places, races, creeds, classes, and prospects. I believe empathy is the most essential quality of civilization.

Consider the Tavernier. Here is a great filmmaker who has never made two similar films. He starts all over again every time. *La Princesse de Montpensier,* based on a well-known short story by Madame de La Fayette, is about a beautiful young woman who is forced by her father to marry one man although she loves another. The story is set circa 1570, when the land is aflame with religious wars between Catholics and Huguenots, and she is lodged for safety in the castle of her new husband, where a tutor is engaged to feed her obvious intelligence.

She encourages the man she loves. She deceives her husband. Her tutor, a man who deserted an army because he became disenchanted with all wars, falls in love with her. It's the kind of film where at a masked ball a confidence is shared with precisely the wrong man. But why do I say "the kind of film"? Tavernier is precise about how and why the mistake is made, and unblinking in considering its results.

Real movies are permitted to have movie stars, just like the fizzy ones. This one stars Melanie Thierry, who brings her fresh beauty to the role of a young woman playing with fire. She creates a great deal of unhappiness, not least for herself and her tutor. Tavernier makes the tutor's love truly romantic, and not a matter of conquest or persuasion, and by avoiding all the clichés of a "love triangle," he makes a Real Movie.

Un Homme Qui Crie (*The Man Who Screamed*), said to be the first feature from the African nation of Chad, is about a proud man who loses his job. Adam, tall and handsome, resplendent in his white uniform, is in charge of the pool at an upscale business hotel. Everyone calls him "Champ," because years ago he won the Central African swimming championship. A rebel group is having success in attacking government forces, stability and prosperity are affected, and he is demoted to a post as guard at the hotel's front gate and given another uniform. "The pool is my life," he despairs.

This is, of course, the same story as F. W. Murnau's silent classic *The Last Laugh,* yet not the same at all. What Mahamet-Saleh Haroun does is original: He considers an African war not in terms of bloodshed and politics, but in the ways it overturns the lives of ordinary people, whose status and security hang by a thread. The film gives us a remarkable idea of Chad, like all African nations more complex than most of us realize. Adam could be my father, or yours, out of work after years of what looked like a lifetime job.

Alejandro Gonzalez Inarritu's *Biutiful* stars Javier Bardem in a virtuoso performance as a low-level criminal in Barcelona who is told by his doctor he has very little time to live. He works as a middleman in an industry that makes fake luxury items in sweatshops and sells them to tourists via sidewalk vendors. You've seen the Gucci bags lined up on pavements.

Uxbal's life is a mess. He is separated from his bipolar wife. He tries to care for the sons he loves. He is under urgent pressure from his criminal associates; he helps supply illegal Asian immigrants for the sweatshops. There is blood in his pee. He works in crime but is not a bad man, and indeed under sentence of death he is moved, like the hero of Kurosawa's *Ikiru,* to try to do something good.

One gesture he makes ends in tragic consequences. Uxbal made the gesture but also tried to make some money on it. He's devastated. Inarritu follows his last days with great intimacy, burying his camera in the seamy street life Uxbal lives, introducing many characters in sharp and colorful relief. He grants his characters the dignity of having feelings and reasons, and not simply behaving as mechanical inhabitants of a crime plot. Bardem is a possibility for the festival's Best Actor award.

Poetry, by Chang-dong Lee, tells the story of a South Korean woman (Jeong-hee Yoon) who learns that her son was involved in a rape with five classmates. The girl committed suicide. Shortly before discovering this, with great shyness, she signs up for a poetry class, and makes some new friends who encourage her to find beauty everywhere; has she ever *really* looked at an apple?

She works a few days a week as a caregiver for a rich man whose right side has been paralyzed by a stroke. She begins to meet with the fathers of the other five students. They talk about raising funds to buy off the mother of the dead girl. And she writes some poems. All of these strands come together and illuminate one another, in a film that never takes its eyes off her for long. The film contains certainly the most poignant badminton match I can imagine.

Among other Real Movies at Cannes this year, I wrote about *Another Year* and *The Housemaid* earlier. *Robin Hood,* which opened the festival was, sadly, carbonated, and pumped into theaters under pressure.

Of Lies and Ghosts and Fathers

The days dwindle down to a precious few. At 6 p.m. on Friday, Cannes is oddly silent. The tumult on the streets a week ago today is forgotten. There are empty seats at some screenings. The locals of Cannes know this is the time to stand in the ticket lines. The daily editions of *Varsity* and *Hollywood Reporter* ceased Thursday. Friends are in Paris, or London, or home. Some few diehards stay for the award ceremony Sunday night.

As we walked over to the Palais Friday morning, there were crowds in the streets, to be sure: crowds of uniformed officers of the national gendarmerie. Their ominous black buses, the windows covered with grates, were lined up along the curbs. Hundreds of cops.

One of the day's official entries was *Hors-la-Loi* (*Outside the Law*), a film by Rachid Bouchareb about the Algerian War. It included footage of massacres in Algeria by the French, circa 1945. The authorities feared riots between

French of Algerian descent and French right-wingers. There were no riots, maybe because of the gendarmes, maybe not. For some people at Cannes, a film is important enough to get your head bloodied for.

One of the festival's most solid films has been *Fair Game,* by Doug Liman, based on books by Valerie Plame and Joseph Wilson, and starring Sean Penn and Naomi Watts. They were the husband and wife involved in the early controversy about whether Saddam was building a nuclear bomb.

This movie doesn't pull punches. Using real names and a good many facts, it argues: (1) Saddam had no WMD; (2) the CIA knew it; (3) the White House knew it; (4) the agenda of Cheney and his White House neocons required an invasion of Iraq no matter what; and (5) therefore, the evidence was ignored and we went to war because of phony claims.

The last thing I want to do is start a flame war about whether this version of events is true. Let's just agree that the film agrees with Plame and Wilson that it is, and that it fits all the facts known to me. *Fair Game* deals with events after Wilson, a former American ambassador, went to Niger seeking evidence of uranium sales to Iraq. The Bush administration says there had been. Wilson found there'd not been. After his report was rejected, Wilson wrote about his findings in an op-ed in the *New York Times,* and then someone in the administration leaked the information to Robert Novak that Wilson's wife, Plame, was a CIA agent.

Cheney's aide, Scooter Libby, was tried and convicted of obstruction of justice and perjury, sentenced to prison, and his sentence was quickly commuted by Bush. Cheney was angry he wasn't pardoned. In the film, we see that Plame, under a variety of aliases, ran secret networks of informants in Baghdad and other Middle Eastern cities. When the administration blew her cover, several of her informants were killed; some reports say seventy. Then the Bush spin doctors leaked the story that she was only a CIA "secretary."

Well. That's what the film says. There will no doubt be dissent. Few people are happy to be portrayed as liars and betrayers. What amazes me is that *Fair Game* doesn't play the game of using fictional names. They're all right there,

including Cheney essentially ordering the intelligence to be falsified.

Naomi Watts looks uncannily like the real-life Plame, but that's beside the point; what I related to was the serious, workmanlike tone of her Plame, who doesn't see herself as a heroine but as a skilled operative. She has scenes where she devastates other characters with what she knows about them, and how she can use that information. Sean Penn plays Ambassador Wilson, more combative than his wife, outraged by the way administration leakers try to destroy them. The film is realistic about the ways the Plame-Wilson marriage almost failed.

What's effective is how matter-of-fact *Fair Game* is. This isn't a lathering, angry attack picture. Wilson and Plame are both seen as good, loyal government employees, not particularly political until they discover the wrong information. The unstated implication is that if the Bush administration hadn't suppressed their information and smeared them, there might have been no Iraq war, and untold thousands of lives would have been saved.

Although India has the world's second most active film industry, *Udaan,* by Vikramaditya Motwane, is its first competition entry in seven years. It's well made and involving, but (to my eyes at least) not particularly Indian. This story could have been set anywhere; it doesn't depend on location, but on personalities.

The hero, Rohan (Rajat Barmecha), is the son of a manufacturer, sent into storage for eight years at one of India's best boarding schools. He and his high-spirited friends get caught after hours in a cinema, he's expelled and sent home, and discovers only at that point that his father remarried, the marriage "didn't work out," and he has a young half-brother.

The father is a tyrant with no gift for parenthood. The son is determined to be a writer. The father won't hear of this. I hear the same thing over and again from Korean, Chinese, Japanese, and Indian friends: If you want to do something artistic with your life instead of being a doctor or scientist, etc., you risk being disowned.

The story is told with force and conviction, and the Indian TV actor Ronit Roy is scary and effective as the father. The character isn't a sadist and martinet because he enjoys it, he conveys, but because he considers it his duty.

Apparently he was shaped that way in childhood, and his son is lucky that boarding school spared him the same fate.

Perhaps when I say the film isn't especially "Indian" I am expecting something more exotic. But India has one of the world's largest middle classes, and its members spend very little time riding around on elephants. They are, I suppose, something like those we see here, with problems we can identify with.

A film that is exotic is the dreamy, mystical story from Thailand, *Uncle Boonmee Who Can Recall His Past Lives.* The director is Apichatpong Weerasethakul, who studied at the Art Institute of Chicago.

This is a movie that includes ghosts and reincarnations made present and visible, but it is not a ghost story in any sense, more of an exploration of various levels of existence. Uncle Boonmee, who is dying of kidney failure, is cared for in a jungle house by family members and a male nurse from Laos—an illegal immigrant, although national borders have no meaning in this world. At dinner one night Boonmee is joined by his wife, who is dead, and then by his son, who appears very much like a character from *Planet of the Apes.* The wife's apparition is one of the more effective spectral presences I've seen in a movie; the son's easily the least, including his glowing red eyes.

There is a long, magical interlude in a vast cave, containing sparkling lights and blind fish, and Boonmee decides that it is the womb that brought him into the world, not necessarily in human form. All of this is told in gentle images, calmly photographed. It isn't the kind of film I respond strongly to, but to the extent I understand what Weerasethakul intends, I can respect it. Barbara Scharres praises it on her blog, and Jim Hoberman at the *Village Voice* thinks it may have a chance at prizes.

I've seen and admired all the films by Lodge Kerrigan, a somber poet of mental illness. If you've seen *Clean, Shaven; Keane;* and the devastating *Claire Dolan,* you understand his world. I'm not sure what parts of that world his strange new film represents.

Rebecca H. (Return to the Dogs) is an appropriately fractured title for a fractured narrative. This is a film within a film about a film, and if that makes three films, none of them work. It

stars Geraldine Pailhas as both herself and an actress portraying Grace Slick of Jefferson Airplane, and Kerrigan himself appears onscreen directing her, as we watch several takes of one scene. She talks a lot in first person about her admiration in younger years for Slick, and for the French director Maurice Pialat, and about how she met the great man and even worked for him.

Then there are scenes with Pascal Greggory, who plays both an actor in the film within the film, and her real-life brother. And apparently she is raped and murdered, because we know that didn't happen to Slick. And she seems bipolar at some times and not at others.

And that's about it. I watched it with the greatest admiration for Lodge Kerrigan, but with a falling heart. Some of the film works a scene at a time and Geraldine Pailhas is very good, but at the end of the day it doesn't come together.

Cannes Postmortem: Is That the Wrong Word?

May 24, 2010—Everyone seems to believe that Tim Burton and his festival jury did the best they could with slim pickings. The 2010 winners at Cannes were for the most part fair, well-distributed, uncontroversial, and safe. You could say the same about the films in the festival.

Last year I left Cannes having seen *Up, Precious, Antichrist, Inglourious Basterds, Broken Embraces, A Prophet, The White Ribbon, Police, Adjective, Thirst,* and many other good films. Of the first *Antichrist* screening, I wrote: "There's electricity in the air. Every seat is filled, even the little fold-down seats at the end of every row."

This year, I saw some good films but felt little electricity. The opening night fun of *Up* was replaced by the drudgery of *Robin Hood.* I was in awe of Mike Leigh's *Another Year* and the South African *Life, Above All,* but not much else. I didn't see some of the winners, including *Of Gods and Men* and Kiarostami's *Certified Copy,* for boring reasons having nothing to do with my desire to see them. Of the other films I saw, the only real enthusiasm I felt was for Inarritu's *Biutiful,* Bertrand Tavernier's *La Princesse de Montpensier,* the first Chad feature *A Screaming Man,* the South Korean *Poetry,* and the out-of competition documentary *Inside Job.*

I await a second viewing of Apichatpong Weerasethakul's winner of the Palme d'Or, *Uncle Boonmee Who Can Recall His Past Lives.* I felt affection and respect for it, but no passion. But reflect that when you see a subdued and challenging film late in the festival, you come to it dazed with movie overload. I know myself well enough to suspect it will play much better first thing on a Monday morning at a press screening here in Chicago.

Weerasethakul, who says we can call him Joe, has made a film about a man who moves through planes of existence that involve humans, animals, spirits, memories, dreams, and fantasies. The man is in the last stages of kidney failure, being cared for by a male nurse in an unexplained house that seems to be surrounded by jungle. His dead wife and son come to visit. Mystical characters materialize and interact with nature. The voices are mostly muted. The forest is enveloping.

There are many theories about the film. I have one that may be completely off the wall. If the dying man is on pain medication, this may be a literal transcription of his hallucinatory dreams. At stages of my own surgeries, I was on a good deal of pain meds, and had dreams or fantasies that remain, to this moment, more vivid than many of my actual memories. Even without drugs, he could be moving toward a mental reconciliation of death and nature. Then nothing needs to be explained, not even when his son appears as an ape with glowing red eyes. It is all his mind sorting through available images. The key, I think, is to declare the film to be entirely from his point of view, and not an objective one.

Of other winners, all are honorable except one, which is inexplicable. The jury awarded the Best Director award to Mathieu Amalric for *Tournée* (*On Tour*), the story of a failed TV producer touring France with a troupe of American burlesque performers not in the first bloom of youth.

I like the situation. The women are road warriors, experienced performers who work hard, party a little, laugh a lot, and like one another most of the time. They look like the real thing because they are; they've performed in revivals of old-time burlesque. They're deliberate parodies of the bump-and-grind artistes who used to parade at houses such as the old Follies on South State Street. They trowel on so much makeup they would make drag queens look fresh-scrubbed.

They're natural and convincing, and the footage involving them feels like it belongs in a documentary. Nothing feels very scripted, and there's a lot of spontaneity. The problem is with the surrounding plot involving the tour manager, played by Amalric himself. The development and resolution of issues in his own life makes an awkward fit with the strippers, who are so defiantly real they resist standing in for any needs or deprivations of his own. The two threads of the film never come together, and that's why it's strange that the jury should have chosen it for Best Direction.

* * *

The jury prize went to *A Screaming Man,* a film from Chad by Mahamat-Saleh Haroun that I greatly admired. In a way, it was Murnau's *The Last Laugh* transplanted to an African nation in recent times, torn by civil war. I respond warmly to films that closely observe a few people and how they work and live, and this one supplied a human context for year after year of news about war and unease in remote places.

Adam was the swimming champ of central Africa years ago and now rules in his handsome uniform over the swimming pool of a luxury hotel. As perilous times come, he is demoted to the post of guarding the hotel gate. "But the pool is my life," he cries. The unique quality of the movie is to look at Adam's life, the way he values his job almost more than his son, and the way status conferred by a Western hotel has bewitched him. The film is well made, but that isn't the point: It has a world to tell us about, it opens our lives, and for some it will be the first experience of Chad they have ever had.

Apart from the films themselves, a general cloud of gloom and doubt seemed to hang over the Croisette. The films that Cannes favors are hard to finance this year. Serious directors find themselves frustrated. Everything is falling apart. Manohla Dargis wrote of her complex feelings upon discovering that Cannes, even Cannes, seems ready to abandon film for video.

While the festivals was under way, the announcement came that some studios want to release their big first-run films to On Demand TV within a month of their theatrical openings. This is bad news for theaters, bad news for what seeing a movie has traditionally meant, and bad news for adults, because that distribution pattern will lend itself to easily promoted "high concept" trivia.

I've been to thirty-five festivals in Cannes. I'll tell you the truth. I doubt if there will even be a Cannes Film Festival in another thirty-five years. If there is, it will have little to do with the kinds of films and audiences we grew up treasuring. More and more, I'm feeling it's goodbye to all that.

Ebert's Journal

The Ten Best Documentaries of 2009

December 22, 2009—Some of the best documentaries of 2009 hardly seemed to exist. *What's the Matter with Kansas*, based on a best-seller, is still awaiting its fifth vote at IMDb. *The Beaches of Agnes*, a luminous film by the New Wave pioneer Agnes Varda, grossed $127,605. *Of Time and the City*, by a great British director, grossed $32,000. *Anvil! The Story of Anvil*, a hit in terms of buzz and critical reception, brought in $666,659. *Tyson*, $827,046.

Such figures come from IMDb, which may be wrong, but if it's $1 million off, we're still not talking big numbers. What we're really talking about is eyeballs, or, as old Jewish exhibitors used to ask, "How many *toochis* on the seats?" The audiences for these films were found first at film festivals and will now be found on DVD and video on demand. None of them played more than one theater in Chicago—five of them at Facets. Yet I take heart from the comments after my earlier list of the year's best feature films.

Many said they used critics' year-end lists as a guide for DVD watching. I was told four of my films were already available for instant viewing on Netflix. The future of video on demand is here, and I hardly noticed. Whether this will be a future in which a filmmaker can make any money is yet to be decided. We may be headed for a time when we can choose between mass-market blockbusters and a permanent series of personal classic viewings. More than a century of movies are in existence, enough to last us for a while.

Am I being ludicrously pessimistic? I hope so. I really do. I'll be going to Sundance 2010. Last year there certainly wasn't a feeding frenzy. Have you heard about *We Live in Public*? It won the Grand Jury Prize for docs at Sundance 2009. I wonder what the mood will be like this year. I expect the usual mob scenes. But are the mobs there to see, sell, and buy good films—small ones in particular? It's my impression more actual business was done at

Sundance when it was half the size. But it sure makes a great business expense.

I know the comments in my blog don't represent an enormous horde of eager film consumers. But they give me optimism. I hear from moviegoers in India, South Korea, and Uruguay who have seen the new movies we're discussing right now. Sometimes they go to theaters, especially if they live in large cities. Sometimes they obtain DVDs, or watch streaming video, which is easier for them because their Internet infrastructure is often faster than ours. Sometimes they—well, you know what they do. That's a fact of life, and sooner or later the industry will have to figure out how to deal with it. Piracy represents theft to the studios, and rightly so. For a marginal indie filmmaker, it represents their audience.

Well. On that cheerful note, here are my ten favorite documentaries from 2009. Look on the sunny side: You have some good films to look forward to.

Anvil! The Story of Anvil. A story of hope, dogged perseverance, and rock and roll, with rock and roll only the occasion for the first two. In 1973, two friends in Toronto started a band and vowed to make rock and roll until they were old. Now they are old, at least for heavy metal rockers. The band endured a moderate rise and a long, long fall, but they refused to give up, and loyal fans around the world kept the faith and treasure the T-shirts. The founders scrape by with telephone sales, demolition, and school meal delivery, but keep on rocking. This is the sound of optimism: "Everything on the tour went drastically wrong. But at least there was a tour for it to go wrong on."

Beaches of Agnes. Made in her eightieth year by Agnes Varda, one of the founders of the French New Wave, who brims with joy and energy as she dances on the beach with her family and revisits the places of her life and such locations as the street outside her door, which she once turned into a beach. Of regrets she has few, apart from the untimely death of her beloved Jacques Demy. Includes the most poetic shot about the cinema I have ever seen: Two old fishermen, who were young when she filmed them, watch themselves years later as they push a movie projector and screen on a cart through the night streets of their village.

Collapse. Terrifying. Michael Ruppert, a controversial blogger from way back, transcends opinion about himself by flatly and concisely laying out facts: We have passed the halfway mark in world oil consumption, and it is rising as China and India come online. We will run out in about forty years. Alternative energy sources use oil. You do the math. We are finished by about 2050, and there's not much we can do. A mesmerizing use of images, music, and Ruppert's implacable voice. By Chris Smith, of the classic *American Movie.*

Food, Inc. A handful of giant corporations control the growth, processing, and sale of food in this country and don't want you to realize the extent of their power. They enforce their policies and threaten reprisals against those raising crops and animals by organic and green methods. They dictate cruel and unhealthy living conditions for animals and place our health second to their profits. And they back it all with multimillion-dollar ad campaigns portraying themselves as benefactors. By Robert Kenner.

Must Read After My Death. A cry from the grave. A woman who died at eighty-nine left behind fifty hours of audiotapes, two hundred home movies, and three hundred pages of documents, ending thirty years earlier on the death of her husband. It tells a story of a marriage from hell. Now assembled by one of her sons, it portrays a toxic marriage, an overwhelmed mother, and a monstrous road warrior father named Charley who was a Good-Time Charley, but not at home. After his death, the woman never mentioned him again. But she kept these records. I've never seen anything like it.

Of Time and the City. The British filmmaker Terence Davies, whose subject has often been his own life, now turns to his city, Liverpool, and regrets not the joys of his youth but those he didn't have, especially the sexual experiences forbidden by the Catholic Church to which he was devoted. He was born into a

modest home, shaped by the church, tortured by his forbidden homosexual feelings, and "prayed until my knees bled." His memories, mixed with those of the city, use remarkable archival footage collated from a century. Includes classical and pop music, and Davies's deep voice, sometimes quoting poems that match the images. A film of a reverie.

The September Issue. What a piece of work is Anna Wintour, the editor of *Vogue,* the most ad-heavy magazine in history. Arguably the most powerful woman in fashion, she rules from behind dark glasses and a detached expression. Every word is law. Her staff is on tiptoes, all except for Grace Coddington, a Julia Childian former model who has been on the staff as long as Wintour and is as earthy as Wintour is aloof. Filmed behind the scenes during the ramp-up for *Vogue*'s all-time record September 2007 issue. *The Devil Wears Prada* didn't tell the half of it. By R. J. Cutler.

Tyson. James Tobak's surprising documentary discovers a Mike Tyson we didn't know existed, a bullied little boy who grew up determined to protect himself and often fought out of fear. It's as if the victim of big kids is still speaking to us from within the intimidating form of perhaps the most punishing heavyweight champion of them all. Working with an unlikely friendship going back many years, Toback asks the right questions and Tyson opens up in ways he may never have before. What emerges is a nuanced and revealing portrait of a heavyweight champion who is anything but the "animal" many people thought they saw.

We Live in Public. Josh Harris is billed in this film as "the greatest Internet pioneer you've never heard of." He was a myopic visionary, a man who saw the future more vividly than his own life. His Pseudo.com, sold for $80 million circa 1990, financed a project named Quiet: About one hundred of the best and brightest he could find agreed to live twenty-four hours a day in a cavernous space below street level. They would be under video surveillance every moment. How this worked in practice makes a doc all the more fascinating because filmmaker Ondi Timoner was on the scene from the start. Winner of the Grand Jury Prize for best doc at Sundance 2009.

What's the Matter with Kansas? Portraits of

Kansans, right and left, in a state that seems to be letting them down. We meet a likable Christian mother and farmer named Angel Dillard, and a populist farmer named Donn Teske, both struggling to keep their family farms afloat after two drought years. The doc argues that voters in the heartland vote against their own economic and social well-being, because they consider hot-button issues more important. An evangelical con game is excused as the will of God.

The Ten Best Animated Films of 2009

December 24, 2009—True, the once-neglected art of animation has undergone a rebirth in both artistry and popularity. Yet having escaped one blind alley, it seems headed into another one: the dumbing-down of stories out of preference for meaningless nonstop action. Classic animated features were models of three-act stories: Recall *Snow White and the Seven Dwarfs* or *The Lion King*. The characters were embedded in stories that made sense and involved making decisions based on values. Now too many stories end in brain-numbing battles, often starring heroes the age of the younger audience members. Here is no food for growth or for the imagination, just brainless kinetic behavior.

This year saw more animated films intended for adults, and *Waltz with Bashir* used the freedom of the form to show matters unthinkable in a live-action feature. Several of these films were true crossovers, truly freed from the demographic vise. Audiences, having grown up with animation, no longer make the mistake of thinking of it as a medium for children.

The other problem came for me with the widely heard prediction that all animated features in the future would be in 3-D. I hope not. The illusion of dimension in 2-D is usually *more* convincing than in 3-D, because that's how our eyes read information. Artificial focal lengths throw us off. Above all, films that project images toward the audience are disturbing. Few directors show discipline in using dimensions; at year's end, James Cameron indeed demonstrated an understanding of the medium with *Avatar*, which in a majority of its CGI scenes was as much an animated film as *Snow White*.

The year's ten best were all good films, but not in all cases deserving four or even three and a half stars. Still, tradition enforces a list of ten, and these were the ten:

A Christmas Carol. Robert Zemeckis, whose *Polar Express* and *Who Framed Roger Rabbit* were delightful, creates a fantastical vision of the familiar Dickens tale. The Ghosts of Christmas have never seemed more haunting, and Ebenezer Scrooge never thinner, more stooped, more bitter. Zemeckis places these characters in a London that twists and stretches its setting to reflect the macabre mood. The visual imagination involved is remarkable.

Coraline. By Henry Selick, who made *The Nightmare Before Christmas* and again combines his mastery of stop-motion and other animation with 3-D. Coraline is not a nice little girl and is rude to her parents, but once she enters that mysterious little door in the wall, she finds herself in a world that teaches her to envy her own. A distinctive visual style and great imagination combine with the deliberate oddness of the animation to create an eerie effect. The story is unusually pointed: You see what can happen to rude little children.

The Fantastic Mr. Fox. In an age of limitless computer-generated images, the next of the year's best animated features also uses the stop-action method that reaches back to *King Kong* and before. Wes Anderson's landscapes and structures are picture-booky. Yet the extraordinary faces of his animals are almost disturbingly human (for animals, of course), and you feel as if Mr. Fox's fur is strokeable. The film tells a fable about a reformed chicken thief leading a war with the farmers.

Sita Sings the Blues. Animated features are an expensive, high-stakes medium, but a visionary named Nina Paley staged an end run around the big guys with this enchanting feature made at home on her own computer. She combines the epic Indian tale of Ramayana with the 1920s jazz vocals of Annette Hanshaw, and this not only works, but seems inevitable. Failing to obtain the rights to the long-unavailable recordings, she outsmarted the system by giving the film away—and made money doing it!

9. A devastating war is survived by humanoid little rag dolls with binocular eyes. Led by the brave number 9, the others venture

out into a frightening postapocalyptic world and do battle with the fearsome Beast, left behind by the horror. It features an intriguing beginning, too many pure action scenes toward the end for my taste, but delicate artistry by filmmaker Shane Acker, who first imagined this world in a student film that won an Oscar in 2006.

Ice Age 3: Dawn of the Dinosaurs. The best of the three films about the interspecies herd of plucky prehistoric heroes uses a masterstroke that essentially allows the series to take place anywhere: There is this land beneath the surface of the earth, you see. Scratt the saber-toothed squirrel pairs with the comely Scratte, and Sid the Sloth adopts three dinosaur eggs and plans to raise the babies, which is asking for trouble. Carlos Saldanha, writer of the 2002 film, is the director, and some of his sequences are in the spirit of the brilliant Scratt-and-acorn scene that opened the first *Ice Age.*

Ponyo. The word to describe *Ponyo* is magical. This poetic, visually breathtaking work by the greatest of all animators, Hayao Miyazaki, has deep charm. It involves a friendship between a five-year-old living at the seaside and a goldfish who magically turns into a playmate. But the fish's crossing from sea to land triggers a tsunami. The two make a dreamlike journey among flooded treetops in a small boat—one of Miyazaki's most beautiful scenes; the opening is another.

The Princess and the Frog. The opening scenes are like a cool shower after a long and sweaty day. This is what classic animation once was like! No 3-D! No glasses! No extra ticket charge! No frantic frenzies of meaningless action! And . . . good gravy! A story! And one starring the first African-American heroine in the genre. A young New Orleans girl named Tiana is cherished by her parents, but her father goes off to the First World War and doesn't return. The brave and resourceful Tiana holds fast to her dream of opening a restaurant and serving up her dad's gumbo. Real substance.

Up. Pixar's latest success began with a grumpy old man who tied balloons to his house and is astonished to float away to South America, where he encounters a reclusive old air explorer. A young boy is a stowaway, and they have exciting adventures and meet strange creatures, but the film also has a meaningful undertone, and opens with an extraordinary sequence summarizing the youth and early romance of the crabby old Carl.

Waltz with Bashir. A devastating Israeli animated film that tries to reconstruct how and why thousands of innocent civilians were massacred because those with the power to stop them took no action. The event took place during the 1982 invasion of Lebanon. The victims were in Palestinian refugee camps. They were killed by a Christian militia. Israelis were in nominal control of the militia but did not stop the massacre. Ari Folman's film uses flashbacks as witnesses try to assemble their fragmented memories of the day.

The Best Foreign Films of 2009

December 27, 2009—Look at it this way: We have the chance to see virtually every American film that's released and many of the English-language films in general. But with the crisis in U.S. distribution, the only foreign-language films available are those someone paid hard cash for and risked opening here. "You always like those foreign films," I'm told, often by someone making it sound like a failing. Not always, but often. They tend to involve characters of intelligence and complexity. If they're about people of subnormal intelligence, they're *about* that, or acknowledge it. In most of the world, people want to hurry into adulthood, not cling to adolescence.

Have you noticed how many American mainstream films are about stupid people who are presented as normal? One opened recently: *Did You Hear About the Morgans?* No one in that film has an interesting thought as they stumble from one plot point to the next. I prefer characters who are articulate. Foreign films tend to be about people like that. Many American films are, too; in release now, for example, *Up in the Air, A Single Man, Crazy Heart, Me and Orson Welles, Mammoth, Invictus.*

My list of the year's best foreign films contains fifteen titles. Why? Because that's how many I put on the list. Five others were on my earlier lists. Altogether now, adding my lists of documentaries and animated films, I have fifty-six "best films." Does that mean I'm getting soft? No, it means I reviewed 284 films in 2009, and these 20 percent were the best. Why do people insist that critics stick to a magic number? Manohla Dargis listed her top ten films. Including ties, her list came to nineteen movies. That's the spirit. These were very good:

Broken Embraces. Pedro Almodovar's *Broken Embraces* is a voluptuary of a film, drunk on primary colors, caressing Penelope Cruz, using the devices of a Hitchcock to distract us with surfaces while the sinister uncoils beneath. It involves a blind man who lost his great love in a car crash and years later learns the truth of her death and how another man destroyed his last film. Penelope Cruz, Almodovar's constant muse for more than a decade, plays a prostitute who was with the blind man's producer when she fell in love with him—true love, and doomed. Dripping with primary colors, especially red, this is the year's most sumptuous film.

The Class is about the power struggle between a teacher who wants to do good and students who disagree about what "good" is. In a lower-income melting pot neighborhood in Paris, a school year begins with high hopes. The students' intelligence may be one of their problems: They can see clearly that the purpose of the class is to make them model citizens in a society that has little use for them. The director, Laurent Cantet, worked for a year with Francois Begaudeau, as the teacher, and the young actors who play students to achieve an uncanny spontaneity and realism. Winner of the Palme d'Or at Cannes 2008.

Coco Before Chanel begins with an abandoned orphan girl (Audrey Tautou) and watches her grow into a music hall chanteuse who sidesteps prostitution by becoming a mistress. From behind the clouds of her cigarettes she regards the world with realism and stubborn ambition. She becomes the most influential fashion icon of the twentieth century. An unsentimental approach to Chanel's life—less of a biopic, more of a drama. It's not about rags to riches but about survival of the fittest. Coco likes a rich playboy, but signed aboard for money, status, and entrée, not merely romance. She isn't a brazen temptress but a capitalist who collects on her investment. Directed by Anne Fontaine.

Gomorrah. Remorseless drama about the foot soldiers of the Camorra, the crime syndicate based in Naples, which is larger than the Mafia but less known. The recruits know De Palma's *Scarface* by heart. Living a life surrounded by drugs and women is a bargain they're willing to make even if it means death. It almost always does. An implacable algebra tightens the noose on day laborers, who kill one another for peanuts while invisible millionaires grow richer. Grimy and pitiless; the Grand Prize winner at Cannes 2008. Directed by Matteo Garrone.

Lorna's Silence. The story by the Dardenne brothers, among the best living filmmakers, involves a young woman from Albania, now living in Belgium thanks to a marriage-for-sale deal with a pathetic drug addict. The vermin who has arranged the marriage now plans to kill the addict to benefit a Russian who will pay her to marry him so he can obtain a passport and she will be free to marry her lover. Sounds like it may be about plot, but it's about personalities, as intensely observed as always with the Dardennes. In a way, everyone knows what has to happen.

Munyurangabo considers the genocide in Rwanda through the lives of two teenagers. They aren't symbols—simply boys who have been surviving on their own in a big city but are not toughened, and essentially good. They embark on a cross-country journey for purposes that eventually become sadly clear. Directed by Lee Isaac Chung, thirty, a first-generation Korean-American who grew up on a small farm in rural Arkansas, it was shot on location in Rwanda in two weeks, involved only local actors, and is in every frame a beautiful and powerful film—a masterpiece. Invited to Ebertfest 2010.

O'Horton. Bittersweet deadpan whimsy about a retiring Norwegian railroad engineer named Odd Horten. He sets his life by the railroad timetable and is baffled by retirement. Left on his own, he finds himself being driven by a blind man, sitting through a farewell party thrown by his fellow engineers (who sing him the *choo-choo-choo woo-woo-woo* song), and climbing a scaffold into the wrong apartment. Like Monsieur Hulot, he can always count on the consolation of his pipe. Directed by Bent Hamer.

Paris is about a group of Parisians. Their lives are not interlocking but parallel. Cedric

Klapisch, the writer-director, creates a symphonic tribute to the city he loves, with each character a movement: a dying dancer, his sister (Juliette Binoche), a historian of the city with a creepy romantic obsession, an architect, a street vendor, a prejudiced bakery owner. At the end, one of the characters happens to glimpse some of the others through a taxi window: anonymous Parisians, getting on with their lives.

Police, Adjective. A young Romanian cop is assigned to tail a suspected sixteen-year-old pot smoker. The kid is guilty, but the cop, having just witnessed the freedom in Prague on his honeymoon, doesn't want to arrest him and ruin his life with eight to fifteen years in prison. This leads, not to the routine action ending of many American pictures, but to a curiously suspenseful argument with his captain over the dictionary definitions of the words *conscience* and *justice*. A good example of the emerging Romanian cinema. Won both the Un Certain Regard jury prize and the Critics' Prize at Cannes 2009.

Revanche. Tamara is a prostitute from Ukraine; Alex is an ex-con who works as a bouncer in her Vienna brothel. They're having a secret affair and lack the nerve to challenge the reprehensible pimp who rules their world. Alex plots an "easy" bank robbery and brings her along in the getaway car. It goes wrong. He hides on the farm of his proud old grandfather, who lives alone, mourns his wife, and feeds his friends, the cows. Alex meets Susanne, a friendly neighbor's wife, and loneliness confronts with tragic coincidence. A 2009 Oscar nominee.

Seraphine is built upon one of the year's most acclaimed performances, by Yolande Moreau. She is a bulky, work-worn house cleaner who fiercely scrubs the floor, then slips away from work to steal turpentine from the church votive candles, blood from the butcher, and clay from the fields. These she combines with other elements to mix the paints she uses at night, covering panels with fruits and flowers that seem to regard us in alarm. Inspired by the true story of a woman whose work is now in many museums, the movie came from France as the year's most honored film, winner of seven Cesars from the French Academy, including Best Film and Best Actress.

Still Walking. Twelve years ago, the eldest son, doted on by his parents, drowned while saving a life. Every year the family gathers in his memory; the second son hates this because his father blames him for not being the one who died. The guest of honor is the pudgy, squirmy loser whose life was saved. This annual rite, we realize, is an ordeal for everyone except the bitter father, and probably for him, too. Written and directed by the great Hirokazu Koreeda, in some ways the heir to Ozu. Winner for Best Director, 2009 Asian Film Awards.

Summer Hours begins on Helene's seventy-fifth birthday. She's joined in the French countryside by her three children and their families. Much of the talk is about how far two of them had to travel, and they're eager to be going home. Helene understands this. She understands a great deal. The film builds its emotional power by stealth, indirectly, refusing to be a tearjerker, always realistic, and yet respectful of how sad it is to see your life disappear. Written and directed by Olivier Assayas, with Juliette Binoche and Charles Berling.

Tokyo Sonata is about a family so locked into their lives they scarcely know one another. The autocratic father is fired and says nothing. He leaves "for the office" every day and lingers with other jobless men. His son secretly takes piano lessons his father has forbidden. His wife observes much and is silent. Then the director, Kiyoshi Kurosawa, derails our expectations with two totally unexpected scenes, the second of spellbinding beauty, which somehow resolve this story with masterful indirection.

Tulpan shows such an unfamiliar world it might as well be Mars. The horizon is a straight line against the sky in every direction. There are no landmarks, no signs, no roads. We are among the modern yurt dwellers of Kazakhstan. A young sailor has come home to live with his sister and her family. They negotiate with a poker-faced man and his hostile wife for the hand of their daughter. There is humor involving a veterinarian on a motorcycle and a fresh-cucumber salesman, and a great silence and desolation, which we sense they love. Doesn't there have to come a time in everyone's life when they should see a deadpan comedy about the yurt dwellers of Kazakhstan? Won the Un Certain Regard award at Cannes 2008.

Note: In addition to these films, on my earlier best films lists for 2009 I named Departures; Everlasting Moments; Silent Light; You, the Living; *and* The White Ribbon.

Caché: A Riddle, Wrapped in a Mystery, Inside an Enigma

January 18, 2010—What if there's not an answer? What if Michael Haneke's *Caché* is a puzzle with only flawed solutions? What if life is like that? What if that makes it a better film? I imagine many viewers will be asking such questions in a few years, now that Martin Scorsese has optioned it for an American version. We can ask them now.

There's only one way to discuss such matters, and that's by going into detail about the film itself. I hesitate to employ the hackneyed word *spoiler* here, because no one in his right mind should read this without experiencing the film. I won't even bother with a plot synopsis. You've seen it.

The mystery, of course, involves the identity of the person or persons sending the videos that disrupt the bourgeois routine of a Parisian family. The interim solution by many viewers seems to be that Pierrot, the evasive and distant son, is their source. This despite the fact that the movie also places suspicion on Majid, the childhood victim of Georges, and on Majid's own son.

They would all have a motive. As Majid tells Georges, his life and his education were forever changed by Georges's actions as a five-year-old boy. Georges felt threatened by his parent's decision to adopt the Algerian orphan and lied in telling them the boy was spitting up blood—an alarming signal of tuberculosis. In a wretched scene, observed in long shot from (presumably) Georges's POV, social workers drag Majid away from the only home he's known.

Only Majid would know that happened— and Georges, who isn't talking. Therefore, only Majid's knowledge could have informed the childish drawings of the cartoon figure with blood spurting from its mouth and neck. The three people who could have drawn them are Pierrot, Majid, and Majid's son. This son is not given a name in the film, so let's refer to him by the actor's name, Walid.

That's clear enough. What muddies the water is the film's last shot, showing Pierrot leaving his school and meeting Majid's son, several years older, on the steps. These two people should not know each other. Many viewers, seeing them meet, come to the conclusion that the two sons did it together. Yet we have no idea whether this is the latest of several meetings or a first meeting, sought by Walid after the death of his father. It's true they shouldn't know each other. But what does it prove that they do?

Haneke, in an interview, is amused that about half the audience fails to even notice the two sons on the steps. His doctor friend, the first person he showed the movie to, missed it. He can't be blamed. Given basic rules of composition, our attention is focused on a point in foreground just to the right of center—a woman with her back turned, waiting for school to be let out, dressed in slightly lighter colors. Walid enters from right and moves diagonally up the stairs to join Pierrot in left background. The composition is a subtle achievement: Most of us notice them, but Haneke does nothing obvious to draw attention to them.

Why and how do these two know each other? Pierrot at the end of the film should not know anything at all about Majid and Walid. Walid had to have learned about Georges from his father. So he would have been the one to seek out the younger boy. But when? Recently, after the suicide of his father? Some time ago? If back then, to what purpose? To plan the scheme, presumably. Walid would have found a disturbed adolescent alienated from his parents. Georges in particular is shown as critical and cool toward his son. Pierrot might have been open to a suggested collaboration.

How did they hit upon the notion of sending anonymous videos, if they did? We will never know. But Walid must have sent them, with or without Pierrot. His access to Majid's apartment proves that. On the school stairs, Majid and Walid have a conversation with body language that is suggestive—but of what? I believe but can't prove it indicates this is not their first meeting. What is important in Haneke's use of the shot is that these two know each other. That's what we can say for sure.

All right, now. We have two characters with motives, and together they would have the means to make the videos. It is likely that Walid physically placed the cameras(s). Pierrot is under closer supervision. We cannot be sure of his whereabouts at every time in the movie (even his parents are not). My guess is that Haneke deliberately kept some uncertainty. In any event, Walid is free at any time to drop packages, ring doorbells, and make anonymous telephone calls. Pierrot is free much of the time to help. Pierrot is not, however, strictly speaking, necessary.

Other questions arise. Where is the first camera hidden? Georges appears in one video to be looking directly at it. Haneke elsewhere in the film gives us a good look at where it must have been. Somewhere on the side of that building, perhaps hidden in some plantings. That would imply access to the building, but let's not even go there. The point is, we can clearly see that a camera could apparently not be hidden there. It couldn't? Well, a camera was. Case closed. And it must have required an electrical outlet, since it had to run for long periods. We can eliminate the possibility that it's motion sensitive, because it runs when there's no motion.

The point, I think, is not how the family was watched, but that it was watched. Our difficulty in figuring out how is not Haneke's problem.

The childish drawings. Who made them? Could be Walid, Pierrot, or, not to rule him out, Majid. Their style is deliberately that of a child of five. Their subject is designed to evoke a traumatic event at that age, which could be linked, too, to Georges's memory of Majid chopping off the rooster's head. I saw chickens beheaded in my grandmother's garage at that age and can vividly remember it now. In the 1940s you might bring home a live chicken from a cousin's farm and kill it for dinner, especially with postwar rationing.

Now, then. Certainly Walid. Probably Pierrot working with him. Probably not Majid; his protestation of innocence completely convinced me. How did you feel? We come to the smoking gun I referred to in my review at around the 20:39 point in the DVD. I was thinking specifically of the boy with blood in his mouth, and the shots on either side are also crucial. As the critic Michael Mirasol writes in his discussion of the film, a preceding shot "refers to the spot where Georges' house is being recorded (the film's opening shot). It has to be a POV, but from whose?

"The film tricks us (as it did me) with the next brief shot of a boy with a bleeding mouth. If you watch carefully, the camera pans across the room to the bleeding boy by the window. This is not Georges' adult home, it's from his childhood home. The living room in this sequence is the same as the same sequence later in the film where Georges is leaving his mother's house. The boy I believe is Majid, from Georges' childhood memories."

He continues: "Think about it. Shot #3 I believe is from Pierrot's POV, looking at the spot where he can record his videos. The shot involving the bleeding boy reveals why Georges must have wanted Majid to be taken away. As a boy, he must have discovered Majid bleeding, and being young, did not understand what his condition meant, leading to the film's disturbing revelations."

Well, yes and no. To begin with, there is no evidence of whom the POV shot belongs to, although Mirasol and many other viewers assume it is Pierrot's. In my mind it's very unlikely that Pierrot took the videos, although I'm convinced he knew about them. But the shots around 20:39 establish a connection between the tapes and the childhood experience of Majid. What is the origin of the shot of the bleeding boy? Majid's memory? George's memory? Pierrot's visualization of something told him by Walid? We cannot be sure. Haneke specifically avoids making us sure.

So. We have a good idea of what happened on the farm in the childhoods of Majid and Georges. We know the videos exist. We know making them must have involved Walid and probably Pierrot. We cannot be sure of the method, but the method is beside the point. Does the "smoking gun" at 20:39 establish a connection between Majid's childhood and the present story? Yes, but we cannot be exactly sure whose memories are involved. How, in fact, do we know it's not Majid's own, and has nothing to do with the POV shot immediately before?

It functions, in any event, as apparent proof that Georges didn't make up the TB story from thin air. Majid did cough blood. But wait. How do we know that? The shot is of a past event, and all past events in the film are seen only from Georges's POV. Therefore, it must be Georges's memory, or his memory of a visualization inspired by his story—because how likely is it that Majid and he were in the same bathroom in the middle of the night? We have no objective evidence that Majid ever had TB. And the POV from the window could also be Georges's, trying to discover where a camera was concealed so he didn't see it.

Let's pull back to consider the whole film. Much of it involves the relationship between Georges (Daniel Auteuil) and his wife, Anne (Juliette Binoche). The tapes breed discord in their marriage. Anne suspects Georges, rightly, of concealing things from her. He cannot trust her with her his childhood memories. He doesn't want them himself. The film recalls an incident during the Algerian War when the bodies of hundreds of Algerian immigrants were found floating in the Seine. Among them may have been Majid's parents, who went to Paris to join a demonstration and were never seen again. This tragedy has been all but erased from the French public's memory. It doesn't want them.

But those things happened. The past is always with us, just as it is always with Majid and Georges, whose lives have been so certainly shaped by the past. And the message of the tapes is not so much that someone is watching, but that someone sees. Who this is, and how and why it is, will change with the generations. But the sight will remain.

In his interview on the DVD, Haneke seems almost jovial as he mentions various theories about his film and how the film seems to deflate them. You can never be sure, he says— in life, as well. Bad things happen and have bad consequences. It is impossible to sift back through history to account for them. The laying of blame may be clear, but the evidence trail is not. *Caché* resists a simple solution. There are still other possibilities. One, however bizarre it may seem, is that Georges himself is somehow responsible for the tapes. I think that's hardly possible, but it can't entirely be ruled out.

An unwritten code of film is that when it is important to know who did something, it

must be a character in the film, unless that character can be clearly eliminated. I'll rule out Georges. That leaves almost certainly Walid, probably Pierrot, and to a very uncertain degree Majid. The only other possibility is—none of the above, but someone none of the characters is aware of. In the real world, that would be possible. The film itself would necessarily be unaware of this observer and could see only the consequences. The chances of that are vanishingly slight, but with Michael ("You can never know") Haneke, it can't be completely ruled out. Consider his current success with *The White Ribbon.* "The children did it," I hear. How can anyone be sure of that?

What was Haneke's purpose with *Caché*? I suspect it was to inspire just such questions as we're having. We saw the film. It has no fancy footwork. The shots and editing are clear. With all of our training from other movies, we assume they will add up and yield to our analysis. They add up all too well but produce no certain solution. If I told you "Walid" (Majid's son) is the only person I know for sure was involved, you will no doubt inform me why I am wrong. Majid's son has not been fingered as the guilty one in any reviews I know about. Most people assume it was Pierrot, or the two working together. I believe I've ruled out Pierrot as a solo act.

Once I read your comments I'll know for sure, but right now I fear I've made an error in my reasoning, and that the film has no provable solution at all. As Haneke says, no matter what you come up with, there's a flaw. And yet nothing in this film is impossible. These are the people; it happened to them. These are the events; they took place. No explanation is satisfactory.

In life, there are situations like that. For me, the murder of John F. Kennedy is one. All of the explanations of that assassination are excellent at one thing: pointing out the errors in all the other explanations. The brilliance of Oliver Stone's *JFK* is how it caters to our conviction that the true story has never been told—no, not even by Stone. What Haneke has done, here and in other films, is demolish our faith in rational analysis. It would be fascinating to see him take on Sherlock Holmes. Scorsese has his work cut out for him in making his film. It will not be a "remake" any more than Werner Herzog's *Bad Lieutenant* is. It will be a Scorsese film. Assuming he retains the broad outline, he can (a) solve the mystery, or (b) leave the mystery hanging, as I believe Haneke does. Can you get away with that in a Hollywood film, with Leonardo DiCaprio already attached as Georges? Will the mass American moviegoing public let him get away with it? If anyone can, maybe Scorsese can. He'll try to be clever enough to conceal that he got away with it.

Smash His Camera, but Not Immediately

January 25, 2010—He is a viper, a parasite, a stalker, a vermin. He is also, I have decided, a national treasure. Ron Galella, the best known of all paparazzi, lost a lawsuit to Jackie Kennedy Onassis and five teeth to Marlon Brando, but he also captured many of the iconic photographs of his era. At seventy-seven, he is still active, making the drive from his New Jersey home and his pet bunny rabbits through the Lincoln Tunnel to Manhattan, the prime grazing land of his prey.

I had an idea, as many of us do, about Galella and the species of paparazzi. It was a hypocritical idea. I disapproved of him and enjoyed his work. Yes, he comes close to violating the rights of public people, and sometimes crosses the line. He certainly crossed the line with Jackie's children.

But he sold his photographs to publications that we bought, we looked at them with enjoyment and curiosity, and his career was made possible by our human nature. These are conclusions I've arrived at after seeing Leon Gast's *Smash His Camera*, a new documentary shown here at Sundance. It shows Galella triumphant, installed with his devoted Betty in his Jersey mini-mansion with a large Italian garden for the bunnies. A friend says, "You look at his house, and you think—Sopranos!"

In his basement archives are the prints and negatives of more than three million of his photographs. He has published coffee table books filled with them. He's had several gallery shows. Collectors pay premium prices for signed prints of his work. He is the go-to man if you want shots of Sinatra, Michael Jackson, Capote, Liz and Dick, Nicholson, Mick Jagger, Elvis. You know that shot of the startled Duke of Windsor in the back of a limo, and the shapely legs of the Duchess? Galella.

"A great photograph," Andy Warhol said, "shows the famous doing something unfamous. Ron Galella is my favorite photographer." He hid in bushes and behind trees. Driving like a madman, he outraced celebrities to their destinations. He bribed doormen, chauffeurs, headwaiters, security guards. He lurked in parking garages. He knew the back ways into ballrooms. He forged credentials. He chased his prey for blocks on foot. Year after year, he outworked, outran, and outsmarted his competition, and he ran with a ferocious pack. Even now when he is wealthy, he hasn't stopped standing in the cold to get his shot.

That's what I respond to. His life force. In his passion for his work, he is a genuine man. Consider his obsession with Jackie, his favorite subject. His favorite out of three million photographs is the one of Jackie striding across a Manhattan street, smiling, her hair tossed around her face by the wind. It may indeed be the best photograph of her ever taken, because it is not posed, not self-aware. It reflects her spirit. "Look at that smile," Galella says. "That's my *Mona Lisa*."

"I think at the time Jackie became my girl-friend," Galella muses. "I wasn't married, I didn't have a girlfriend...." Galella is a big and burly man, and I suspect if he had seen someone endangering Jackie, he would have hurled himself forward in disregard of his own life. In the famous court case, Jackie testified she "didn't know" if she could be considered famous. For Galella, her celebrity was catnip: Galella's attorneys presented evidence that the two most famous women in the world were Jackie and the queen.

You couldn't keep this guy down. The court ordered him to keep seventy-five yards from Jackie. The distance was later lowered to twenty-five feet. He tipped a pal to be outside the Beverly Hills Hotel when he knew Jackie would be there. The pal took a photo of him holding a tape measure. I know. I expect lots of readers to tell me he is deranged and I am deluded. But you gotta hand it to the guy.

Look how he handled the famous incident with Marlon Brando. Sure, he was stalking him, as is a paparazzo's nature. Brando socked him in the jaw so hard he lost five teeth. He went to an emergency room to be treated and turned up later with his jaw wired, still shooting. On the next occasion he wanted to photograph Brando, he wore a football helmet. And made sure they were photographed together.

I think he loves celebrities. First, they earn his living for him. I am unaware of a single Galella photograph taken as pure art, and the film and a Web search reveal none. For Ron, the subject *was* the photograph. I can't speak as a stalked celebrity, but is there something a little touching about a guy who will travel halfway around the world and stand all night in the rain to take your picture? Or lock himself into a warehouse overlooking the Thames for a weekend, with food and toilet paper, to shoot Liz and Dick's yacht when they arrived on board?

At his Sundance press conference, Robert Redford was asked about *Smash His Camera*. Redford, of course, had a long-running feud with the relentless Galella. He said he hadn't seen the film, but he would tell a Galella story, "because it's one where I win." He began a tale of shooting *Three Days of the Condor* on location outside the *New York Times* building, and how to elude Galella he entered one end of the building, raced through its second floor to the other end, slipped into his trailer, disguised his stand-in as a double, and had him run to his car and be driven away. He was able to enjoy the sight of Galella hurling himself onto the trunk of the limo to shoot through its back window. Touché! Still, you gotta hand it to the guy.

I said he captured the icons of an era. That era is over. The film has a curiously touching scene of an apparently bright young woman looking at the enlargements on Galella's photos at a New York art gallery. She wonders who Sophia Loren is. Doesn't recognize Bianca Jagger. Thinks maybe that might be . . . Robert Kennedy? We are spared the possibility she wouldn't recognize Sinatra, Katharine Hepburn, Warren Beatty, Steve McQueen, Truman Capote.

Hey, those people are *famous*! They were to us, anyway. What Galella shares in common with his celebrities is that they inhabited the same moment in time, and he took it very seriously indeed. I hesitate to suggest this, but I suspect Jackie would be pleased by that photo of her in full stride. What's not to love?

Smash His Camera won the Best Documentary award at Sundance 2010.

The Ecstasy of the Filmmaker Herzog

April 5, 2010—I saw *Aguirre, the Wrath of God* for the first time in a defrocked Lutheran church in the Lincoln Park neighborhood, which Milos Stehlik had taken over for his newly born Facets Multimedia. "It is a film you must see," he told me. "Bring a pillow. The pews can get hard."

I saw a great film, one of the greatest ever made. An essential film. In 1999, I made it one of the first titles in my Great Movies Collection. Now I wonder if I really saw it at all.

Werner Herzog is in Boulder this week, to join another great director, Ramin Bahrani, in viewing *Aguirre* a shot at a time. It is a lifetime experience for a film lover. We're at the 62nd Annual Conference on World Affairs. Maybe one thousand people crowded into Macky Auditorium, where Bahrani and Herzog sat side by side in the dark, Jim Emerson froze the DVD frames when required, people shouted out questions, and Herzog spoke about the making of the film.

This program was born in 2009. Last year, Bahrani joined us for a "Cinema Interruptus" of his *Chop Shop*. He spoke of film with such respect and love. He is a meticulous director; not a frame is filmed with inattention. He mentioned how much he would love to meet Herzog. An idea was born. This year Ramin and I invited Herzog to join us. Herzog came, and was mesmerizing. I could listen to him all night. His imagination is not beaten dead by popular culture. He seeks new visions—literally, at the poles, in the deserts, in the sea, on mountaintops, and in the human mind. Here he was discussing his experiences in filming the first seventeen minutes of *Aguirre*, for that's as far as we got on the first day of the week.

The film opens with a shot of perhaps two hundred Spanish Conquistadores and Indian slaves, making their way down a narrow path with a two-thousand-meter drop on either side. They drag cannons and supplies. It is muddy and slippery. Only half a dozen were professional actors. The others were native Indians or hippies and street people recruited in the nearest small city. He sent them up the path in the reverse order that he wanted them to descend. Were they happy to wait up there? The path was too narrow for two to pass. If he held up the line at the bottom, they had no choice.

They descend at first in a very long shot, indistinct in the mist, dwarfed by the Peruvian rain forest. Then, in the same unbroken shot, the camera adjusting, we see them appear in the foreground, moving from left to right, Right, the positive direction, because they believe they are approaching El Dorado. Not professional faces. Weathered, tired, lived-in faces. The Indians wear the clothes they were wearing when they arrived at the shoot.

Herzog had only one take. He would never be able to persuade his actors to climb again for a second one. As we watched them descend, he froze the DVD frame to discuss several of the actors. A fat man who ate all the mangos. A close friend, semiliterate, who had bicycled thirty-five thousand miles around North America and later became a great photographer. Above all, his star Klaus Kinski, about whom some years later he made a film: *My Best Fiend.*

Kinski, in constant rage. Describing himself as a "natural man" who could live in the forest like an animal. Then complaining that his tent leaked. Then complaining that the thatch shelter built over the tent leaked. Then moving at great inconvenience to the production into a shabby hotel where he beat his wife nightly, the crew discreetly removing the blood stains.

"A coward," Herzog says.

"Is it true," a voice from the dark asks, "that the Indians asked your permission to murder him?"

"No. That was on *Fitzcarraldo.*"

Bahrani freezes a frame showing a small covered carrier like a tent, borne through the jungle on poles by bearers. It contains one of the women in the party. This detail, and most of the film, has no real basis in fact. Everything comes from Herzog's imagination.

"Is that your hand?" Bahrani asks. We see a bare hand shoot out to steady the carrier, and then disappear.

"Yes, that is my appearance in the film,"

Herzog says. "I was afraid they would lose their footing."

"When I show this film to my students at Columbia," Bahrani says, "I always tell them, I'll bet that's Herzog's hand."

The party arrives at the Urubamba River, with its famous rapids. It is January 2, 1971—flood season. They construct rafts so that an advance party, led by Aguirre, can go on ahead. They can film the river scenes only once, because the jungle makes it impossible to walk back along its banks. One of the rafts is deliberately steered into an eddy. This was very dangerous, Herzog says; they had men above them on a cliff with ropes to lower if the raft capsized. Only the toughest of the actors were on this raft, "with a very substantial increase in pay."

A quarter mile upstream from this shot, Herzog says, he returned only a year ago to the Urubamba to shoot a scene for his latest film, *My Son, My Son, What Have Ye Done.* Nobody asked him why, and indeed it is hard to pinpoint a reason why footage from a Peruvian rapids was required for a crime drama set in San Diego. Somehow, with Herzog, you don't ask such a question.

There were other problems. Herzog grabbed a tree that was a highway for fire ants, then hit the tree with his machete and dislodged hundreds more that fell upon him. A thieving transportation company bribed customs officials to stamp its documents, and then dumped the cans of negatives in a field, where Herzog's brother later discovered and rescued them. Herzog shot the second half of the film not knowing if he had the negatives of the first half.

He said he doesn't give a great deal of thought to composition. "I focus entirely on the subject of the shot." One shot shows the fat man straddling a cannon and eating a mango. A voice asks, "Is that a phallic symbol?" Herzog replies, "It honestly never occurred to me until you pointed it out. I wanted to have a shot showing the man who consumed all our mangos."

There is audience discussion of the "painterly composition" of a shot of a camp the Spanish party makes in a clearing.

"I am a filmmaker, not a painter," Herzog says. "I have a gift for arranging men and horses. It comes easy for me."

It is 6 p.m., and we have been through only seventeen minutes of the film. Herzog can spare only one more day away from his current film. Then Bahrani will take over, and after him, Jim Emerson and the actress Julia Sweeney. Many of those in the audience are old hands at this process. They are amazingly well-informed.

Herzog must return to work. He has been granted three hours to film inside the Cave of Chauvet-Pont-d'Arc in southern France, where the wall paintings have been dated to thirty-two thousand years ago. There is no documentarian better suited than Herzog to make this film of a sacred place unseen for centuries. He will bring to it awe and poetry.

I said earlier I wondered if I had ever truly seen *Aguirre, the Wrath of God*. I've seen it many times, and analyzed it a shot at a time. But I realize that to some degree I saw it through eyes conditioned by commercial movies.

Herzog has spoken of the Voodoo of Location. By that I think he means the ways in which an actual location, where actual events take place, carries a psychic, or emotional, or sensory, charge to the screen. There are no special effects at all in *Aguirre*. What you see is what was actually there. Many of the shots were done in one take. Some two. Only a few dialogue passages in three or four. In some cases, the events shown could take place only one time.

The film documents a daring and inspirational enterprise, and a reckless one. It shows Europeans invading a new land, tragically unsuited to survive in it and ruinous to the existing culture. They searched for gold—which, in some way, explains all colonialism. But Herzog said, "I give no thought to symbols or messages." He also has only contempt for story arc, "the Hollywood hero going through a pleasing series of events." Nor does he care about time; he is willing to let a shot extend beyond its conventional length if the duration creates a feeling within us.

It is all the experience itself, the immediate experience. During some of the scenes on the river rafts, he said, "we were all joined together—actors and crew members—and we knew we could only do this one time." What they did put their lives at risk, although no one died. They did it for many reasons. Then it was done. Now we see the film—the film, and the record of the creation of a vision.

McLaren and Meyer and Rotten and Vicious and Me

April 11, 2010—"I need you out here," Russ Meyer told me on the phone in 1977. It was 6 a.m. He could not conceive that I might still be asleep. "Have you ever heard of the Sex Pistols?"

"No," I said.

"They're a rock band from England. They got a lot of publicity for saying 'f—k' on TV. Now they have some money and want me to direct their movie."

"The Sex Pistols?" I said.

"Their manager is a guy named Malcolm McLaren. He called me from London. He said their singers were big fans of *Beyond the Valley of the Dolls*. They go to see it every weekend they're in London. It's playing at the Electric Cinema on Portobello Road."

No director except possibly for Stanley Kubrick was better informed than Russ about where his movies were playing. Kubrick used to call specific theaters to complain about light intensity. Russ used to call to complain about theft.

"Their lead singers are named Johnny Rotten and Sid Vicious. They demanded the same team that made *Beyond the Valley of the Dolls*. We can go wild on this. I've got a couple of big-titted London girls already in mind."

"They liked it that much?"

"Rotten says it's true to life."

Malcolm McLaren announced his imminent arrival from London, and I flew out to Los Angeles for a briefing. I stayed as always at the Sunset Marquis, half a block down from Sunset on Alta Loma, a semi-residential hotel that had provided homes over the years for such as Tiny Tim, Van Heflin, Elaine May, Roy Scheider, and Jim Belushi. It is now an A-list hotel. In those days, you dialed room service and a voice answered, "Greenblatt's Deli."

Malcolm McLaren appeared with Russ in my room at the Marquis. He was a ginger-haired, wiry man in his thirties, who wore a "Destroy" T-shirt and leather pants equipped with buckles and straps. These were, I learned, the infamous Bondage Pants he introduced at SEX, the celebrated King's Road boutique he ran with his romantic partner Vivienne Westwood. The T-shirt was also hers. The pants offered the ultimate in bondage convenience.

When the mood struck, you didn't have to rummage about for belts and braces; all your needs were built in. On his feet he wore what Russ approvingly noted were brothel creepers.

After pleasantries ("We're going to make a f——g great movie," McLaren told us), we got into Russ's bright red Cadillac to visit a house a few blocks uphill from Sunset. This was, as I recall, the office of a record producer somehow associated with McLaren, and typical of the area, where many houses look like homes but few are. This one contained a large videotape machine, uncommon in the days before home video, and McLaren showed us videotapes of the notorious BBC appearance during which, the *Daily Mirror* reported, they used "the filthiest language ever heard on British television." Then he played us Sex Pistols albums at full blast.

Meyer, dressed as frequently in military khaki slacks, an open-neck dress shirt, a blazer, and sturdy penny loafers, sat next to McLaren on a black leather sofa and listened studiously to "God Save the Queen," "Anarchy in the UK," "Pretty Vacant," and other songs. Occasionally he would nod his head attentively. When the album had played, he said, "So these records are big in England?"

"F——g huge," said McLaren. He told us what sort of a film he had in mind. His ideas didn't involve a plot or a story line. As I recall, his only concern was that it star the Sex Pistols. Russ proposed *Beyond the Valley of the Dolls* meets *A Hard Day's Night.*

Meyer said we would headquarter in my room at the Sunset Marquis. I don't remember why we didn't use his house up on Arrowhead over the hill behind the Hollywood sign. It was another apparent residence that contained office furniture, editing equipment, prints and souvenirs, plus one king-size bed and what he referred to as "an industrial-strength kitchen." The only other time I heard him use this term was in "industrial-strength bra." Perhaps, I learn from a Meyer bio by Jimmy McDonough, we met at the Marquis because McLaren and Meyer could not be left alone in the same room for long without fierce arguments. McLaren thought of Meyer as a fascist. Meyer thought of McLaren as a source for money to make an RM film. In any event, we drove up to the house on Arrowhead

and brought down an office chair and a card table, which Meyer planted with satisfaction in front of the TV, explaining, "You won't be watching TV."

I've mentioned before that, for Russ, typing was synonymous with writing. If he didn't hear the typewriter, no writing was being done. When I was writing *Beneath the Valley of the Ultra Vixens* for him, he located me in his living room (all office furniture) and listened from his upstairs office. When my typewriter fell silent, he'd call down, "What's the matter?"

A meeting was set the next day involving McLaren, Meyer, and a Dutch director named Rene Daalder, who had enjoyed a hit with *Massacre at Central High* (1976). Daalder has since had great success in the areas of virtual reality and special effects and directed several films. In those days he considered Meyer a mentor, and had flown at his behest to England to work on screenplay ideas with McLaren. Apparently he had been pulled out of Meyer's orbit into McLaren's and had returned with a screenplay that Meyer tossed into his big kitchen wastebasket. That's when Russ called me.

We began with the title *Anarchy in the UK*. Daalder contributed to some earlier scenes in the story. In England, long unemployment lines represent an economic collapse, and there is resentment against the upper classes. The Sex Pistols represent the voice of rebellion and conceive of a scheme to bring down Britain with anarchy. The details of their scheme I will leave to future scholars of the screenplay. I wrote one scene that I particularly liked, involving Johnny Rotten encountering a storefront Church of Scientography and being persuaded to be "clocked" on something called an H-Meter. This was a device hooked to a steering wheel and an accelerator, which somehow . . .

EXT. SOHO STORE FRONT

This is the London headquarters of the Church of Scientography. JOHNNY ROTTEN *looks in. A sign on the window reads:* "HAVE YOU BEEN CLOCKED?"

A young, fresh-faced GIRL, *with the light of true zeal burning in her eyes, comes out onto the sidewalk as* JOHNNY ROTTEN *looks in a lackluster way at the window.*

GIRL
Are you coming in, then?

JOHNNY ROTTEN
No, I'm not.

GIRL
Why not then? Are you afraid?

JOHNNY ROTTEN
Afraid? Not bloody likely.

GIRL
The H-Meter doesn't lie.

JOHNNY ROTTEN
The what?

He scowls at her, unable to make out her game.

GIRL
The H-Meter. Haven't you ever
been clocked?

JOHNNY ROTTEN
I had a bloody hard time of it last
night.

GIRL
I can just look at you and see you're
living over the limit.

JOHNNY ROTTEN
That's the f——g truth.

GIRL
Come in, then.

*Baffled, he follows her. In the gloom, he makes
out a gigantic poster, upon which a man wearing a racing helmet, goggles, a white gown, and
long, wavy hair, is surrounded by beams of light
projected from the top of a pyramid.*

JOHNNY ROTTEN
What's all this, then?

GIRL
Just sit down here.

*He sees an automobile seat facing a steering
wheel, a gas pedal, and a speedometer.*

JOHNNY ROTTEN
I've got my provisional license—
and I haven't got a car anyway.

GIRL
The H-Meter has nothing to do
with driving.

JOHNNY ROTTEN
What the f—— is it then?

GIRL
This is the Church of Scientography.
And this is the H-Meter, named after
our leader, the Holy Man from Italy,
Guru Vaser-Rati.

JOHNNY ROTTEN
I've heard of him somewhere.

GIRL
Just grasp the steering wheel, which
picks up the electrical vibrations
from your hands, and when I ask
you questions, push down hard on
the accelerator for "yes" and on the
brake for "no."

JOHNNY ROTTEN
What if I don't know the answer?

GIRL
That's about thirty-six miles per
hour.

* * *

McLaren fed us with ideas. He particularly
specified a scene showing Sid Vicious in bed
with his mother as they shot heroin. Russ was
dubious.

"Do you think Sid will go for that?"

"Why wouldn't he? It's all based on fact."

"It should be obvious why it would piss
him off."

"Nah. The more shocking, the better. That's
what the boys stand for. Just put it in, and we'll
run it past Sid in London, see what he says."

Day after day, I pounded at the typewriter
as Meyer and McLaren went out on business
meetings at Twentieth Century–Fox and then
returned, Meyer expecting many more pages,
McLaren unconcerned, as if screenplays wrote
themselves. In the evenings, Russ and I dined
in restaurants serving large forms of meat,
while we outlined the next day's material on
yellow legal pads. This had also been our
method on *Beyond the Valley of the Dolls*. We
rarely knew more than a day ahead what
would happen next.

Finally I arrived at the end:

AN OVERHEAD SHOT *shows his prone body
on the floor in the spotlight. The first and only*

person to move is JOHNNY ROTTEN. *He walks slowly forward to the dead body. Looks down at it. Turns it over with the toe of his boot, so that the dead face gazes sightlessly skyward. Speaks so softly not everyone can hear.*

> JOHNNY ROTTEN
> (*down at the body*)
> Will success spoil Johnny Rotten?
> (*pause*)
> No. He will waste, spoil, smash,
> blow up, and destroy success!

Another pause. The room is hushed. JOHNNY ROTTEN *looks slowly up and directly into the camera.*

> JOHNNY ROTTEN
> Did yer ever have the feeling yer
> being watched?
>   FADE TO BLACK

* * *

This was in July 1977. Shortly after, Meyer and McLaren flew to London. Meyer insisted on the aisle seat: "If we go down, McLaren will get his bondage straps tangled up with the chair and I'll be trapped."

I flew to London for screenplay meetings. Russ had rented lodgings on Cheyne Walk in Chelsea, close by the scenes of McLaren's triumphs on King's Road. I stayed not far away on Sloane Street, at the Cadogan Hotel, scene of Oscar Wilde's downfall.

Casting was already under way. Marianne Faithful had been signed for the tricky role of Sid Vicious's mother. For the role of P. J. Proby, a British rock star, we had P. J. Proby himself, who was from Texas but was better known in England, and who had played Elvis on stage. For another key role, one afternoon Russ held an audition for Jon Finch, a respected actor who had played the title role in Polanski's *Macbeth* (1971). I reflected that day on the actor's life, auditioning for roles clearly unsuited for him simply because to be out of a job is the actor's nightmare.

We had meetings with both Vicious and Rotten. I don't remember ever meeting the other two Sex Pistols, Paul Cook and Steve Jones. McLaren implied that their roles in the band were limited to actually performing the music, since Sid and Johnny had their hands full insulting the audience and inspiring erup-

tions of manic hostility. I actually met Jones years later at a party at our house in Michigan, of all places, and liked him.

The meeting with Vicious was fraught. McLaren had come around for it in person. Sid seemed a nice enough bloke, decorated with safety pins and so on, but calm and interested. No acting out. McLaren handed him the script.

"Here's the scene we want you to read, Sid."

INT. NIGHT. BEDROOM

The shades are drawn. Propped up against the pillows of the bed, Sid's MOTHER *is just in the act of shooting up. As* SID VICIOUS *appears in the doorway, she pulls the needle from her arm. He leans against the door, regarding her. She releases the rubber tube from around her arm.*

> SID VICIOUS
> (*not unkindly*)
> Still on the shit, Mum?

She looks up and sees him. We sense this is not the first time he's seen her shooting up.

> MOTHER
> (*a surprised greeting*)
> Sid!
> (*pause*)
> How are you, then?

> SID VICIOUS
> All right. . . . I came for my
> things, Mum.

> MOTHER
> Your things?
> (*brightens*)
> You got a job, then?

> SID VICIOUS
> Not a chance!

His MOTHER *nods to confirm that of course there was not a chance. She sits upright on the side of the bed.*

> MOTHER
> I thought Tony told you not to
> come 'round here anymore.

> SID VICIOUS
> Bugger Tony. It's your house too—
> isn't it?

MOTHER
He pays the rent. . . . Come on then, sit down.

She pats the bed next to her. He sits.

SID VICIOUS
I didn't come 'round because I wanted to. I need money, Mum. I'm starving.

His mother isn't giving him her total attention.

SID VICIOUS
(continuing)
I'm starving, Mum. . . .

He puts an arm around her. She looks at the hand on her arm, lets it stay. Her dialogue implies more than it says.

MOTHER
What if Tony walks in?

SID VICIOUS
He won't come walking in here. He's down at the pub with his mates.

MOTHER
I don't want you to get hurt, Sid. You'd better get out in case Tony comes.

He pulls her closer to him, and kisses her on the cheek.

SID VICIOUS
What's the matter, Mum?

She is deep into the rush of the heroin.

MOTHER
He could come walking in here any time now. . . .

Effortlessly, SID VICIOUS *pushes his mother back on the bed and moves to cover her with half his body. He kisses her on the neck and lips.*

SID VICIOUS
I told you—he's at the pub with his mates, getting sloshed.

MOTHER
But he doesn't have the money to get sloshed, Sid. He'll be back.

SID VICIOUS
Come on, Mum. Give us a kiss.

She does. And then she puts her free arm around him, and they begin the preliminaries of love-making.

* * *

The scene continues in some detail before Tony does indeed burst in. It was a scene owning something to the scene in *Beyond the Valley of the Dolls* when Randy Black, the heavyweight champion, bursts in on sweet Petronella Danforth in the arms of clean-cut Emerson Thorne.

Sid Vicious studied it. Russ, Malcolm, and I studied him. He read carefully, smoking. Finally he closed the screenplay.

"I don't think me mum will like the part about the heroin."

On another night, Russ and I took Johnny Rotten out to dinner. "Ebert," he said, because he often began sentences with the name of the person he was addressing, "we're going to the mountaintop again." This was always understood between us as referring to the triumph of *Beyond the Valley of the Dolls*.

He said the Sex Pistols would be the occasion of "a real RM film," and he had agents scouting the land for beautiful actresses with improbable bosoms. He had never been concerned before about plausibility in a screenplay, and he wasn't going to start now. If the Sex Pistols never encountered a woman requiring less than a DD cup, even in their audiences, that was fine with him. He appreciated the fact that the Sex Pistols songs would provide the occasion of another sex, drugs, and rock and roll picture like *BVD*.

For dinner, I suggested Beauchamp Place, then not as trendy as now, a street not far from Harrods that was chockablock with restaurants. In the black cab Meyer informed Rotten: "You look like you haven't eaten in a week."

"That f——r McLaren doesn't pay us anything. He gives us an allowance of five quid a week. I'm living in a doss-house."

We alighted in front of a selection of Thai, Italian, Persian, Chinese, Moroccan, and French restaurants.

"Ebert, what have you gotten us into?" Meyer asked with alarm. "John needs a big piece of meat."

We found a grill house in a basement supplied with dark, cavelike booths. To my surprise, no one recognized Johnny Rotten except our waitress, who confided, "I'll keep it quiet." She offered to recite the daily chef's selections. Russ firmly cut her off: "We'll have three of the Trencherman's Specials." Russ entertained a fancy that the Trencherman's Special was as standard in every decent restaurant as a glass of water and a basket of bread.

"I don't think we have that on the menu," the waitress said, looking to Johnny for support. He looked as if he stayed above such details. We compromised with the three largest steaks the chef could find in his kitchen.

"Will you be having jacket potatoes with those?"

"Baked will be fine, my dear."

Meyer opened up by informing Johnny Rotten that with his stovepipe arms he wouldn't have survived one day in the army.

"What do I want with the f——g army?" Rotten said.

"You listen to me, you little shit. We won the Battle of Britain for you!"

I reflected that America had not been involved in the Battle of Britain, and that John Lydon (his real name) was Irish, and therefore from a nonparticipant nation. I kept these details to myself.

After dinner, we drove Johnny in a cab to where he lived, on an anonymous street in Notting Hill. "F——g McLaren," he said. "That was the first decent meal I've had in a month." Meyer gave him five pounds and we waited outside a convenience store for him to buy lager and canned pork and beans. "F——g great," Johnny said.

In all the years I knew him, I never heard Russ Meyer say the word "f——g." Perhaps he had too devout a respect for the concept. He preferred such synonyms as "wail," "pound," "pummel," "belabor," and "conjoin," always pronounced with enthusiasm.

I flew home. Russ called to say they had a budget from Fox. I had suggested the title be improved to *Who Killed Bambi*, and this was embraced. The first day of filming involved the shooting of a deer by a singer P. J. Proby managed—"the greatest rock star in the world," referred to only as "M.J."

EXT. THE QUEEN'S GAME PRESERVE—DAY

A Rolls Royce careens through the narrow lanes, narrowly missing trees on either side before it skids to a halt near a clearing. On its doors, gilt initials are carefully lettered: M.J.

CAMERA ESTABLISHES M.J., *surrounded by his luxurious automobile.*

A CHAUFFEUR, *seven feet tall, leaps out and opens the door for M.J., the world's greatest rock star, who emerges expensively dressed in youthful-looking but very expensive hunting clothing, cut as a cross between hunting gear and contemporary fashion. Over his shoulder there's a quiver filled with steel-tipped hunting arrows. He carries a hunting bow as he moves stealthily into the woods.*

CUT TO:
EXT. FOREST PRESERVE—M.J.'S POV

A deer flashes through a clearing.

SMASH CUT TO:
M.J.

One of M.J.'s arrows stops it cold in its tracks. He nods with quiet satisfaction. It's important here that we see him as youthful, strong, and virile—and not yet aware that he is a member of the previous generation.

* * *

This was, as nearly as I know, the only scene ever filmed for *Who Killed Bambi*. There is more than one account of what went wrong. McLaren claimed Twentieth Century–Fox read the screenplay and pulled the plug. This seems unlikely because the studio would not have green-lighted the film without reading the script. Meyer called me to say McLaren had made false promises of financing and was broke. Electricians and others had walked off after not being paid. Meyer himself demanded each week's salary be deposited every Monday morning.

On Wikipedia, I find: "This is however challenged as being incorrect according to Julian Bray, who supplied location services to Malcolm McLaren's Matrixbest company. . . . Bray recalls that respected production manager Joyce Heirley asked if Julian's location catering crew and film location services unit would provide a range of location services on a special train consisting of vintage carriages hired from Lord McAlpine's Carnforth railway collection including a LMS 1930s dining car and a Southern Railway."

It may be true that Heirley asked Bray about this, but to my knowledge no train scenes were ever shot. Russ's own footage can be briefly glimpsed in *The Great Rock 'n' Roll Swindle* (1980), directed by Julien Temple. This film essentially starred McLaren. Vicious, Cook, and Jones, but Rotten had bailed out of the band after a tumultuous American tour. *Swindle* has been described as a "continuation" of the Meyer project, but the two are completely different, except for the few seconds of Russ's footage.

The best account of the debacle appears in Jimmy McDonough's unauthorized biography, *Big Bosoms and Square Jaws: The Biography of Russ Meyer, King of the Sex Films.* He writes nothing about any train scenes and believes the film's fate was sealed when Princess Grace, a member of the Fox board, said, "We don't want to make another Meyer x film." This was harsh because, as Fox has never acknowledged, *Beyond the Valley of the Dolls* returned enormous profits at a crucial low point in Fox's fortunes and is to this day one of the two or three most-often-revived films of 1970.

Temple was so unwise as to tell the British press that Meyer had personally shot a deer with a pistol on that first day. Meyer sued for libel in England, the last country where you ever want to be sued for libel. "I don't give a shit about damages," he told me. "I want to clear my name. I don't go around shooting deer with pistols." Temple purchased a full-page ad in *Screen International* to apologize.

All parties seem to agree that the Sex Pistols grew to despise McLaren, even more so after he depicted them in *The Great Rock 'n' Roll Swindle* as no-talent frauds elevated to stardom by his own promotional genius. That was cruel, because Rotten and Vicious were authentic originals who struck an enormously influential note that continues to reverberate today. They may not have been gifted guitar soloists, but as performers they were phenomena. In less than two years, they fought constantly, insulted the press, spit on their fans, were banned from TV, were fired by one record company twenty-four hours after being signed, released only one album, pushed safety pins through their noses and ear lobes to more or less invent the modern style of body piercing, broke up during a tour

of the United States, and saw Sid Vicious accused of murdering his girlfriend and dying of a drug overdose.

In 2000, Julien Temple returned with another film, *The Filth and the Fury*, this time telling the Sex Pistols story from their own point of view and trashing McLaren. The surviving members appear backlit, perhaps to spare us the sight of their middle-aged faces. Incredibly, McLaren agreed to appear in his own defense, speaking from within a rubber bondage mask.

I wrote from the film's Sundance premiere: "The Sex Pistols never had a period that could be described as actual success. Even touring England at the height of their fame, they had to be booked into clubs under false names. They were hated by the establishment, shut down by the police, and pilloried by the press (*The Filth and the Fury* takes its title from a banner headline that once occupied a full front page of the *Daily Mirror*). That was bad enough. Worse was that their own fans sometimes attacked them, lashed into a frenzy by the front line of Rotten and Vicious, who were sometimes performers, sometimes bear-baiters.

"Rotten was the victim of a razor attack while walking the streets of London; McLaren not only failed to provide security; he wouldn't pay taxi fares. Vicious was his own worst enemy, and if there was one thing that united the other three band members and McLaren, it was hatred for Sid's girlfriend, Nancy Spungen, who they felt was instrumental in his drug addiction. 'Poor sod,' John Lydon says of his dead bandmate.

"To see this film's footage from the '70s is to see the beginning of much of pop and fashion iconography for the next two decades. After the premiere of *The Filth and the Fury* at Sundance, I ran into Temple, who observed, 'In the scenes where they're being interviewed on television, they look normal. It's the interviewers who look like freaks.' Normal, no. But in torn black T-shirts and punk haircuts, they look contemporary, unlike the dated, polyestered, wide-lapelled and blow-dried creatures interviewing them.

"England survived the Sex Pistols, and they mostly survived England, although Lydon still feels it is unsafe for him to return there. [He and the other survivors did concerts and tours as recently as 2008.] Cook and Jones lead settled lives. McLaren still has bright ideas. Vivienne Westwood has emerged as one of Britain's most successful designers and poses for photographs in which she bears a perfect resemblance to Mrs. Thatcher. [She is now Dame Vivien Westwood.] And as for Sid, my notes from the movie say that while the Pistols were signing a record deal in front of Buckingham Palace and insulting the queen, Sid's father was a Grenadier Guard on duty in front of the palace. Surely I heard that wrong?"

Malcolm McLaren died of cancer on April 8, 2010, in a Swiss clinic. He will be buried in London's fabled Highgate Cemetery, resting with Karl Marx, George Eliot, Christina Rossetti, Radclyffe Hall, Douglas Adams, Sir Ralph Richardson, and other congenial companions. He is survived by the son he had with Westwood, Joseph Corre. The apple fell close to the tree. Corre is cofounder of Agent Provocateur, which began as a small Soho shop selling provocative lingerie and now has thirty stores in fourteen countries.

The Golden Age of Movie Critics

April 30, 2010—This is a golden age for film criticism. Never before have more critics written more or better words for more readers about more films. But already you are ahead of me and know this is because of the Internet.

Twenty years ago a good-sized city might have contained a dozen people making a living from writing about films, and for half of them the salary might have been adequate to raise a family. Today that city might contain hundreds, although (the catch-22) not more than one or two are making a living.

Film criticism is still a profession, but it's no longer an occupation. You can't make any money at it. This provides an opportunity for those who care about movies and enjoy expressing themselves. Anyone with access to a computer need only to use free blogware and set up in business.

Countless others write long and often expert posts on such sites as IMDb, Amazon, Rotten Tomatoes, and in the comment threads of blogs such as this one.

Sean P. Means, my friend at the *Salt Lake Tribune*, has been compiling a dreary list of movie critics who have lost their jobs. Does anyone compile a list of first-rank critics now active on the Internet? I suspect there are twenty or thirty for every name on Sean's list; some of them are, in fact, on Sean's list. I'm discovering new ones every week. The World Wide Web is an enormous bushel, and you can hide a lot of lights under it.

Long ago, when this transition was first taking shape, I came across a young man named James Berardinelli, who had started reviewing films online from somewhere in New Jersey. We corresponded, and I found he was in his twenties, had a job as an engineer, a passion for film, and long evenings to fill because of a loss in his life. He said he traveled to New York or Philadelphia to see screenings or attend theaters. He was extraordinarily self-disciplined and wrote more reviews than most "full-time" critics. He began to attract attention.

Today, by some measures, Berardinelli is among the half dozen most-read critics in the world. He still works as an engineer. His site doesn't support him. The studios and other industry advertisers don't give a damn about film criticism, preferring to direct most of their online ad budgets to celebrity and gossip sites. Well, Jim has never made a living from his site, so he's used to that. He told me once his Amazon resale commissions helped to offset his out-of-pocket costs.

I knew from finding links on IMDb, the Movie Review Query Engine, Metacritic, RT, and other conglomerators that there were many good critics in the world. They were only the tip of the iceberg. When I started this blog two years ago, I decided to personally approve the comments because I didn't want my site to enable the subliterate goon squads infesting so many comment threads. I've received more than six hundred thousand comments so far, and not even four hundred of them have been worthless. Goons don't bother, but intelligent posts abhor a vacuum.

I savored some of the comments. I looked forward to the next posts of their authors. I began to realize they were from all over—not just America, but dozens of nations. They linked to their blogs, and I discovered a world of film criticism that thrived below the radar.

These writers are never linked by the conglomerators, but one of their reviews might be better than anything linked on IMDb—and I include my own work. The conglomerators have little curiosity and limited quality control. I've gone to linked "reviews" on IMDb that consisted of a one-paragraph synopsis written from a trailer.

The sites link mostly to North American sources, with a few reviews from the United Kingdom, Australia, Ireland, and so on. IMDb to its credit has a few links to France, Italy, Germany, and Scandinavia, but in the local languages. Well, of course, they're in the local languages. But English is a de facto international language, and the writers I found through my blog write not only in English but in elegant English.

Last fall I finally surrendered and joined Twitter. Ah, that's a story in itself. Sifting and following and unfollowing, I compiled an assortment of other tweeters who met only one criterion: I considered them worth my time. If I clicked on their avatars, often they linked to blogs. Now I was truly astonished. I found them writing on all possible topics, and they were often more evocative and gripping than the usual mainstream sources. Most of these bloggers wrote for the joy of writing, because they wanted to and had something to say. What more do you want?

Eventually I recruited some of my foreign critics to contribute guest reviews to my site. They became the Far-Flung Correspondents. At Ebertfest 2010, every single one of them attended (one was delayed by a volcano, but not defeated). They became the defining element of the twelfth annual festival, appearing on panels, joining in Q&As, mixing at parties, simply sitting in the audience and chatting with those around them. They were from Egypt, Turkey, the Philippines, Mexico, South Korea. There were Americans of Pakistani and British origins. A Chinese-Canadian. I knew how well they wrote. That's how I found them.

Here's an interesting footnote. They paid for their own transportation. In other words, they had income that didn't depend on movie criticism. I had two lawyers, a city administrator, an IT expert, two students, an international marketing consultant, a university

teacher. I enjoy Ebertfest beyond all measure, but they made this year's very special. Their transforming presence was possible because of the Internet and discoveries I made through my blog.

I am obviously approaching the end of my own career. April 1, 2010, was my forty-second anniversary at the *Chicago Sun-Times*. I wouldn't bet on either one of us making it to fifty. But the Internet has transformed me and is transforming the *Sun-Times*. In the vast sea of the Internet, readers need brands to help them navigate. The *Chicago Sun-Times* is a successful brand. I prefer the word "title," or, hey, even "newspaper," but "brand" has replaced "name," just as "market" has replaced "city." When TV people tell me, "I came here from the Atlanta market," I keep my thoughts to myself.

Yes, I'm sad that traditional newspapers have come upon hard times and that traditional print venues for film criticism are disappearing. I thank God I got into journalism at sixteen, that I edited pages over turtles in the print shops of hot lead operations, that I felt the rumble of the building when the presses started to roar, that I worked beside reporters who had hats on their heads, cigars in their teeth, and bottles in their desk drawers, and shouted "BOY!" when they needed a copy kid. All that belongs to the past in the same way as horse-mounted cavalry and India clipper ships.

But I'm feeling good these days. I love movies, and I love writing about them and reading about them. I feel like part of a truly World Wide Web (and what a magical term that is—worthy of science fiction). I know good movies are valued everywhere, and good writing. Michael Caine loves to say, "Not many people know that." I know secrets not everybody knows, one of which is that a large part of the future of literary English centers on the Indian subcontinent.

Another thing not everybody knows is that some of the best critical writing on the Web can be found in seemingly specialist sites, devoted to science fiction, film noir, animation, horror, silent films, anime, and so on—and video games, whether or not they're art. I haven't even mentioned drama, classical music, architecture, dance, photography, painting, and on and on. Great critics have been and are being developed. They mostly aren't making money, but now they have limitless outlets, and not long ago there were a handful.

Recently a friend of mine sent an e-mail to several movie critics. He was Jeff Shannon of Seattle, a good critic who has been in a wheelchair since an accident in youth.

"Guys," he said, "I've been asked to provide career advice to a young disabled college student who wants to pursue a career as a film critic. I'm not one to sugarcoat reality, so my immediate advice for him would be to enjoy film criticism/appreciation through blogging and possibly attempting to write books about films, etc. In all sincerity I can't advise the kid to pursue this career under present circumstances. From my perspective as someone who had various highs and lows in the job since 1984, I'd feel like I was doing the kid a disservice if I told him he could make a decent living at it. I just don't see that happening for anyone apart from the upper-echelon critics who've been established for years or decades (and recent cutbacks at *Variety* prove that even the 'A-list' critics are under siege).

"So, in all sincerity and honesty, do you think I should encourage the kid to follow his passion (which is what I would normally do), or give him a hard dose of reality? Maybe he could consider other work in the film-biz that holds more potential?"

The best response to this question came from my hero David Bordwell, who is the most knowledgeable film critic in America. I won't even get an argument about that. David and his wife, Kristin Thompson, herself on the topmost shelf, have published many invaluable books, including textbooks few film students fail to use. These textbooks are extraordinary above all because they are books, written in classical English prose and a great pleasure to read. Now David and Kristin have transformed their own careers with the best single movie blog on the Web. After distinguished careers as much-published writers, it's as if the Internet allowed them to unleash their real energy.

Here's what David wrote back: "Last year I moderated an Ebertfest panel consisting of a dozen or so critics. A student from the audience said he wanted to be a critic, too. Instead of advising him to get into a more financially rewarding form of endeavor, like selling consumer electronics off the back of a truck, the panelists encouraged him. This form of altruism, in which you help people to become your competitor, is alarmingly common in the arts.

"A moderator doesn't get to talk much, so I couldn't respond. What I wanted to say was: Forget about becoming a film critic. Become an intellectual, a person to whom ideas matter. Read in history, science, politics, and the arts generally. Develop your own ideas, and see what sparks they strike in relation to films."

Yes! This is the best possible advice. I tell young students: Take film courses, certainly. But cover the liberal arts. Take English literature, drama, art, music, and the areas Bordwell lists. Learn something about science and math. A physical anthropology course was my introduction to the theory of evolution, which is an opening to all of modern science. Don't train for a career—train for a life. The career will take care of itself, and give you more satisfaction than a surrender to corporate or professional bureaucracy. If you make careers in that world, you will be more successful because your education was not narrow.

What the Internet is creating is a class of literate, gifted amateur writers, in an old tradition. Like Trollope, who was a British Post official all his working life, they write for love and because they must. Like Rohinton Mistry, a banking executive, or Wallace Stevens, an insurance executive, or Edmund Wilson, who spent his most productive years sitting in his big stone house in upstate New York and writing about what he damned well pleased. Samuel Pepys, who wrote the greatest diary in the language, was a high official in the British Admiralty. Many people can write well and yearn to, but they are not content, like Pepys, for their work to go unread. A blog on the Internet gives them a place to publish. Maybe they don't get a lot of visits, but it's out there. As a young woman in San Francisco, Pauline Kael wrote the notes for screenings of great films, and did a little freelancing. If she'd had a blog, no telling what she might have written during those years.

At this year's Ebertfest, Chaz and I hosted a "meet and greet" for the Correspondents and Ebert Club members. One man in his early twenties looked somehow familiar. I discovered this was Homer, whom I met as a kid on an Ebert & Roeper Film Festival at Sea a decade ago. He said he'd just graduated college. We asked him what he had studied.

"English literature," he said, "because that's what you told me to take, instead of locking into a career path."

What are you doing now?

"I'm in law school."

Then Homer said words of the greatest significance: "I'm trying to figure out what I can do with that."

That's what an education is for. That's what life is for. That's the discovery made by these extraordinary writers I've found on the World Wide Web. Find out all you can, and see what you can do with it.

Whole Lotta Cantin' Going On

July 18, 2010—Can a film be great without question? Is it demented to find fault with *Inception*? Or *Citizen Kane*? Not at all. Scolds have emerged in recent days to smack at those critics who disapproved of *Inception*, but as a fervent admirer of the film I can understand why others might not agree. In fact, the reasons cited by David Edelstein in his much-attacked negative review seem reasonable. I don't agree with him, but that's another matter.

I've been trying to think of one film that *everyone* reading this entry might agree is unquestionably great. You might think I'd name *Citizen Kane* or *The Rules of the Game*, the two films that in recent decades have consistently been at the top of *Sight & Sound* magazine's poll of the world's directors and cineastes. But no. I've taught both shot by shot and had many students who confessed they didn't feel the greatness. There are people Bergman doesn't reach. And Ozu. I've never met anyone who doesn't like Hitchcock, but I promise you I will in the comments under this entry. Many Hitchcock fans don't admire *Vertigo*, which I think is his best film.

The Godfather, I think, comes closest to being a film everyone agrees about. It's currently number 2 on the (debatable) IMDb list of the 250 greatest films of all time. *The Shawshank Redemption* is number 1, and in the number 3 position is . . . *Inception*. It will drop. The first two have nine hundred thousand votes between them, and *Inception* only twenty thousand.

All the same, if you say you dislike *The Godfather* or *Shawshank*, I can't say you're wrong. The one thing you can never be wrong about is your own opinion. It's when you start giving your *reasons* that you lay yourself open. Many years ago there was a critic in Chicago who said *The Valachi Papers* was a better film than *The Godfather*. "Phil," I told him, "film criticism is a matter of subjective opinion. Only rarely does it stray into objective fact. When you said *The Valachi Papers* was better than *The Godfather*, that was an error of objective fact."

Edelstein wrote: "*Inception* is full of brontosaurean effects, like the city that folds over on top of itself, but the tone is so solemn I felt out of line even cracking a smile. It lacks the nimbleness of Spielberg's *Minority Report* or the Jungian-carnival bravado of Joseph Ruben's *Dreamscape* or the eerily clean lines and stylized black-suited baddies of *The Matrix*—or, for that matter, the off-kilter intensity of Nolan's own *Insomnia*. The attackers in *Inception* are anonymous, the tone flat and impersonal. Nolan is too literal-minded, too caught up in ticktock logistics, to make a great, untethered dream movie."

Edelstein is correct in his comparisons with the other films. *Inception* does lack those qualities. I love his phrase "ticktock logistics," and plan to steal it. In my case, I didn't crack a smile while watching the film because Nolan didn't call for one, nor was I looking for the qualities David found in the other films. I found it refreshing that Nolan's villains didn't wear matching uniforms (do the bad guys in *The Matrix* and the Bond movies all share locker rooms?). It's true that Nolan is literal-minded and logistical, but I believe the film depends on the conceit that you can *think* your way into someone else's dream with your own intelligence. The last thing he wanted was an untethered dream movie. Nolan successfully made the film he had in mind and shouldn't be faulted for failing to make someone else's film.

Edelstein concludes: "The movie is a metaphor for the power of delusional hype—a metaphor for itself." This is a statement with a certain appeal. The notorious thing about metaphors, as everyone who has ever graded student papers knows, is that almost anything can be read as a metaphor of whatever you want it to be. (The *New Yorker* used to have fillers headed, "Block that metaphor!") But Edelstein is right that *Inception* was preceded by enormous hype on the Internet. Only once you had seen it, of course, could you decide if it was delusional hype.

It's unlikely Nolan anticipated the "delusional hype" and made *Inception* as a preemptive metaphor, but you never know. Still, I understand where Edelstein is coming from. I can understand how a critic could react to the film in his way. His review is justified and valuable, more stimulating to a lover of the film than still more praise. It helps you to see it. If you don't agree with his litany of faults, you have to ask yourself, why not?

Compare Edelstein with Armond White, whose review joins David's in the dock at the current online heresy trial. White calls *Inception* a "con game," and explains: "Its essential con is that, as in *Memento*, Nolan ignores the morality of his characters' actions; he accepts that they will do anything—which is the cynicism critics admired in *Memento*, the con-man's motivating nihilism."

White is correct to say Nolan ignores morality, but is he correct to think that's a fault? Does White admire other films that ignore morality? What about *Transformers: Revenge of the Fallen*, which he found superior to *Toy Story 3*? White doesn't say *why* a film shouldn't ignore morality. Where does Bunuel fit into his view? Actually, we learn, Nolan lacks not only morality, but basic craftsmanship: "Nolan doesn't have a born filmmaker's natural gift for detail, composition and movement." Then what is White's idea of great composition? Of *Transformers: Revenge of the Fallen*, he writes: "In the history of motion pictures, Bay has created the best canted angles—ever."

Ever? Many would argue that *The Third Man* makes a better use of canted angles. You could also make a case for *Night and the City*, and indeed *Citizen Kane*. If pressed, I might be able to make a case for every noir ever made.

But never mind. White never illustrates *how* Nolan's compositions are lacking. He cites no shots that are badly canted. He assumes artistic gifts are "natural," implying filmmakers are born, not made, thus coming down on the side of genetics against environment. Maybe he's right, but it would take an essay to defend that sentence.

Edelstein's review describes the film I saw, and deals with it. White dismisses the film with preemptive contempt for anyone caught enjoying it. Edelstein's review is about the film. White's review is about charlatans defrauding the ignorant with snake oil. There are, of course, other dissenting reviews of *Inception*. Matthew Zoller Seitz didn't like the film, and tweeted this about Steven Boone's review on the new site Capital: "The most original and insightful pan of *Inception*. And moving. Damn. How often does criticism *move* you?"

Boone's review fits my definition of usefulness. It doesn't matter whether I agree with him. He helps me see things. So, always, does Stanley Kauffmann. That Seitz praised the Boone review, and was even moved by it, implies something good to know about him as a critic. He wasn't doing it simply because he agreed.

There's a human tendency to resent anyone who disagrees with our pleasures. The less mature interpret that as a personal attack on themselves. They're looking for support and vindication. In the area of movies, no phenomenon has dramatized this more than the rise of Rotten Tomatoes. When a movie is running at 100 percent on the Tomatometer, an inevitable death watch occurs, as readers await the first negative vote. Recently the perfect ratings for *Toy Story 3* and *Inception* were "spoiled" by Armond White. There was outrage. The Twitterverse was in flames. A. O. Scott and twenty-two others also disliked the film, but it was White who got the attention, because he has been cast as the spoiler. As many actors will tell you, it's more fun to be the villain than the hero. Actually, the Meter on *Inception* is holding at around 84 percent, but that's small consolation for some of its fans. They require perfection.

It's possible that if the Tomatometer didn't exist Armond White would attract attention only from those readers who actually wanted to read what he wrote. There would be a lot; he's not boring and is capable of wicked insights. It's also possible that there's a method in the manner he uses to assiduously vote against the grain—which is why the Tomatometer can be mischievous.

In the "open marketplace of ideas," it is believed, the better ones will eventually rise to the top. Sites like Rotten Tomatoes are where critics bring their ideas to market, but some readers come only to window-shop. It is a melancholy fact that for some, ideas have been replaced by the *meter reading itself*. It doesn't matter nearly so much what anyone actually said, as whether "everyone" agrees with you.

This is not a hypothetical conversation:

"What did the critics say?"

"Seventy-three."

I've seen it claimed on the Web that Armond White said Grand Theft Auto (the video game, I assume, not the movie) was better than *Inception*. He did no such thing. He *compared* them. He wrote: "Like Grand Theft Auto's quasi-cinematic extension of noir and action-flick plots, *Inception* manipulates the digital audience's delectation for relentless subterfuge." This is true. He assumes such a parallel would be bad. The point is that some of White's attackers never actually read his review. That wasn't necessary.

For some fans, what was necessary was to find validation for their opinions. The Tomatometer, Metacritic, MRQE, Movie Review Intelligence, and the IMDb User Score are easy places to do that. What it comes down to is that you "liked" it and so you require everyone else to "like" it too. When I attacked *Transformers: Revenge of the Fallen*, I got 874 comments. About 600 of them were outraged, and most of those were offended that I disagreed with them.

So what? I thought *Dark City* was the best film of its year and *Synecdoche, New York*, the best film of its decade. I was in the minority both times. Long years ago, I was also in the minority in my love for *Bonnie and Clyde* and *2001*. Lots of people, right at the first, disagreed. That's the way it goes. I was outraged, but not about some goofy meter reading.

Questions for the Movie Answer Man

Academy Award Categories

Q. In reading your review of *The Hurt Locker*, in which you laud Jeremy Renner's performance and predict an Oscar nomination, I got to thinking about those very categories of Best Actor/Actress. For this role, Renner has taken an original character and crafted his own unique persona. It has occurred to me that this type of performance is, if not more difficult, at least quite different from, say, Sean Penn as Harvey Milk, because Harvey Milk was a real person with a preexisting persona. I'm not saying there isn't great skill involved in carrying out that type of role; I'm merely wondering if the distinction is significant enough to warrant consideration when the merits of various performances are discussed—or, even crazier, to warrant two different categories (that is, something akin to the two separate screenplay awards—one for original, one for adapted).

In fact, the more I think about it, the more it seems like there may be an inherent advantage in portraying a nonfictional character, because the actor/actress is likely being judged on the accuracy of his/her impression of that character as much as anything else ("Wow, Sean Penn does a really convincing Harvey Milk"). Meanwhile, Renner has no accuracy to strive for, no pictures or videos of the real William James to study. The role is his to mold, for better or worse.

A look back at how these awards have played out in recent years seems to lend credence to my point: Penn's performance as Milk, Whitaker as Idi Amin, Hoffman as Capote, Foxx as Ray Charles, and so forth. And on the women's side, Cotillard as Piaf, Mirren as Queen Elizabeth, Witherspoon as June Carter Cash, Theron as Aileen Wuornos, and so on. Again, not trying to take anything away from these performances, but I just feel like there is something worth talking about here.

—Roey Gilberg, Berkeley, California

A. Points do seem to be awarded for impersonation. On the other hand, Sean Penn won for his completely original character in *Mystic River*, and look at Daniel Day-Lewis in *There Will Be Blood*. And look at Meryl Streep. Although she is known for her accurate evocations of such real people as Julia Child, all sixteen of her Oscar nominations came for either original characters or those with whom few audiences were familiar.

Q. In your recent journal you noted that the Israeli film *The Band's Visit* was not considered for Best Foreign Language Film because more than half the film was in English. But the film was produced and made in another country. Why does the Academy consider the language spoken to be the only factor in determining whether it's a foreign film or not? They should solely look at where the film was produced and made. The category of Best Foreign Language Film is ridiculous. Who made the picture, that's what matters.

—Alex Lovering, Los Angeles, California

A. I completely agree. It's time for the Academy to wake up and smell the coffee. English is a common universal language. It was the only one the Israelis and Egyptians both spoke. I once complimented an Indian reader for his command of English and he wrote back: "In India we have been speaking it longer than you have."

Action Thriller Romantic Comedy Genre

Q. Right now, we seem to be having an explosion in the heretofore uncommon "Action Thriller Romantic Comedy" genre. We've got *The Bounty Hunter* currently in cinemas, then there's *Date Night* with Steve Carrell and Tina Fey, then in June there'll be both *Killers* with Katherine Heigl and Ashton Kutcher, and James Mangold's *Knight and Day* with Tom Cruise and Cameron Diaz. Do you have any idea what exactly about the current Hollywood scene or socioeconomic climate provokes such an interest in nutty romantic couples getting shot at whilst their speeding car drives through explosions, and so on?

—Craig Sheehan, Hazelbrook, New South Wales, Australia

A. Other than a grievous lack of imagination and ambition to excel, perhaps Hollywood is driven to prove it can make a better movie than *The Bounty Hunter*?

All About Steve

Q. I haven't seen Sandra Bullock's *All About Steve*, but judging from your description it sounds a little like someone was trying to synthesize, for a female lead, the Adam Sandler formula for highly profitable movies. She sounds like a borderline crazy person with a *gold heart*, who means well but proceeds to wreak havoc on the lives of normal people around her while having *cute* eccentric affectations of some sort.

—Kevin McLoughlin, Albany, New York

A. Yeah, you could say that—but Adam Sandler movies are better. After I wrote that review, it occurred to me that a great many movies are about people who are actually insane. If I started pointing that out with any consistency, there'd be no end to it.

Robert Altman

Q. Roger, you have written some of the most interesting things on Altman over the years. I am still moved when I think of the way you closed your piece on Altman directing the opera version of *A Wedding*: "'Where the years have gone, I don't know,' Altman mused at the end of the afternoon. 'But they're gone. I used to look for a decade—now I look for a couple more years.' I advise him to keep on telling time by making films and he will never die, because it won't be in the production schedule."

The *LA Times* published Richard Schickel's nasty and dismissive piece on Altman in his review of *Robert Altman: The Oral Biography* by Mitchell Zuckoff. Despite his lofty perch as critic for *Time* magazine, I never took him seriously as a writer, filmmaker, or historian. What's your take?

—David Ortega, East Chicago, Indiana

A. I take him seriously as a writer, filmmaker, and historian. I find his opinion of

Robert Altman deplorable, baffling, and just plain mean. What did Altman ever do to deserve such contempt?

Amelia

Q. You mentioned a continuing interest in the story of the trail-breaking aviator Amelia Earhart. You may be interested in a radio program that aired on WBEZ this morning about the search for Amelia Earhart. It talks about the part that a young girl at the time played in recording a transcript that she discovered, to her horror, were Earhart's distress calls being broadcast on shortwave radio.

—Raymond G. Riesterer, Chicago, Illinois

A. NPR's *The Story* Web site pointed me to this page, which reproduces the incredibly touching notes written by young Betty Brown: http://j.mp/4lhtcs.

Avatar

Q. In *Avatar*, how does the good-guy hero mate with the female wookie (or whatever the hell they're called)? This is important stuff, Rog, like all those questions from readers in the back of old *Superman* comics, where they want to know how Superman's X-ray vision knows when to stop X-raying.

—Jeff Greenfield, New York, New York

A. Superman's X-ray vision saw only the specific things it needed to see. Like, he could see hostages locked in a bank vault by looking straight through three city blocks and still see the hostages with all their clothes on. I shouldn't have to be telling you, of all people, that this is easily explained on a quantum level.

As for sexual relations between humans and Na'vi, I have no idea, in the words of the old limerick, who would do what, and with which, and to whom. Since Na'vi are not mammals, they have no apparent need of mammary glands, but Cameron insisted that their females wear bras—and require them, if you follow me. I have speculated this was because the sight of Jake Scully smooching with a breastless Neytiri would inflame antigay crusaders.

Begging Naked

Q. I'm still thinking about *Begging Naked*, a documentary you showed at Ebertfest 2010.

How is Elise Hill doing? You said her paintings sold out at the festival. Is she still painting?

—Susan Lake, Urbana, Illinois

A. Elise Hill is the subject of the film, a former stripper and prostitute and drug addict and dedicated artist who sometimes painted even from the stage of Show World, where she worked near 42nd Street. She now lives in Central Park. Karen Gehry, the director of the film, tells me: "Elise's paintings continued to sell like hotcakes even weeks after Ebertfest. Powerful stuff your festival mixing with Elise's work plus that audience!"

The Big Lebowski

Q. I read your Great Movies entry on *The Big Lebowski* with pleasure but was a bit disappointed that you only alluded to the element that always gives me the greatest pleasure in watching the movie: namely, that it serves as a wonderful parody of the detective story that is so ingrained in us. The Dude and Walter make no wilder assumptions about the clues they find than the Philip Marlowes and Sam Spades (and Thomas Magnums and Patrick Kenzies) do, but in this movie they are completely, totally wrong about each and every one of them. The case, such as it is, just solves itself.

—O. J. Hanau, Hamburg, Germany

A. Quite true. If it were left to Walter and the Dude, the movie still wouldn't be over.

Blood Dust

Q. This is a ridiculous question, but one I would like an answer to nonetheless. What was the first movie with "blood dust"? That's what I call it when someone gets shot and a cloud of red dust bursts out of the wound. I can't imagine that happens when someone really gets shot, but it's a neat little Hollywood invention that I was wondering the origins of. The first time I remember seeing it was in *Red Dawn*, but it may go back further than that. Like I said, ridiculous.

—Joe Campbell, Philadelphia, Pennsylvania

A. The only *first time* I'm sure about is when Clark Gable said *damn* in a movie for the first time.

Q. Recently an Answer Man question re-marked that the "blood dust" that jumps from a shooting victim's chest seems implausible. It is not. This is actually vaporized blood and body tissue, and this "geyser" can occur when someone is shot at close range with a heavy caliber weapon. On a related point, in *Wyatt Earp*, the marshal's shirt catching on fire after he's shot is also very real. It was common with older smoky gunpowders and happens less frequently with modern propellants, but it's still possible. This was the only time I've seen this in a movie.

We rarely see authentic effects of a shooting on screen. Either it's overdone, like someone getting yanked off his feet from taking a bullet (doesn't happen—if anything, he simply crumples), or it's *humanely rendered*, like the old TV Westerns, where you don't even see where the bullet goes in. I do get a kick about the incessant and unnecessary clicking sound that weapons make, apparently on their own—and how the bad guy can threaten someone with an uncocked pistol. Oh well, I'm watching a movie, fer Pete's sake, not a documentary. At least they don't show silencers on revolvers much anymore.

—Sam Waas, Houston, Texas

A. And as you know, blades always make a snicker-snack sound as they move through the air.

Blood: The Last Vampire

Q. In regards to why Saya wears a sailor suit in *Blood: The Last Vampire*, those are standard uniforms for Japanese high schools. The only reason she's out of place at the school in the movie is that it's part of an American base situated in Japan.

—Daniel Zelter, Los Angeles, California

A. The American students mock her, so they must not get off.

Body Heat Sequel

Q. Remember at the beginning of *The Player*, Buck Henry is pitching a sequel to *The Graduate*, because all the principals are still alive, and so on? Here's one that makes sense: a sequel to *Body Heat*. Again, all the principals are alive. The movie came out twenty-nine years ago, and when we last left Ned Racine (William Hurt), he was facing double murder

707

charges. And Matty Walker (Kathleen Turner) was enjoying her millions on a beach somewhere. So, now he is being released, and, I'm imagining, he's pissed.

—Mike Spearns, St. John's, Newfoundland, Canada

A. Promising, but simple. There needs to be a twist. Like, Matty joined Mother Teresa's order and has devoted her life to good works. Ned still hates her, but when he sees those helpless little kids who depend on her, he sees a way to steal their endowment and pin it on her.

The Book of Eli

Q. In your review of *The Book of Eli*, you say it takes the hero thirty years to walk across America, and add, "I'm pretty sure it doesn't take that long." OK, I'll bite. How long does it take?

—Greg Larson, Chicago, Illinois

A. It's my theory that no human being has ever seen more of the earth's surface at ground level with his own eyes than the great travel writer and novelist Paul Theroux. So naturally I put the question to him. He replies:

"Thanks for your interesting query. In my novel *O-Zone*, set in the future, a group of people walk from the Ozarks to NYC. No time specified. They witness desolation and abomination. Many stunt travelers must have walked across the USA. One was the young (at the time) English woman Ffyona Campbell, who claims she has walked around the world and has written three books about it. But after she walked across the USA it was revealed that she had gotten pregnant en route and was given lifts for 1,000 of the miles.

"My take: A healthy person ought to be able to walk 15–25 miles a day. I did this when I walked a lot of the British coast in *The Kingdom by the Sea*. Say 19 miles/day as an average. Divide the distance from NY to LA by 17, and add at least one day a week as a rest day. And make some allowance for the fact that it's not a straight line and that the weather might not be perfect. That would be a pretty good figure."

Me again. So in other words, less than thirty years, but Eli has an alibi.

708

Q. Regarding the Answer Man question inspired by *The Book of Eli* about how long it would take to walk from New York to Los Angeles, Google actually maps out the most direct route here: http://j.mp/9xHv5g. It requires 680 directions, and Google suggests it will take 37 days, 18 hours. But I think we might want to stop and sleep once in a while. So, using Mr. Theroux's numbers: 2,777 miles divided by 19 miles a day is about 146 days. Divide it by 7 to find the number of rest days you'll need and we get 21 days. Add the rest days in and it would take about 167 days or five and a half months. Now my question is, how many pairs of shoes would you need?

—Mike Kory

A. I think these old Hush Puppies should hold out that long. It's amazing that Google has "walking directions." My favorites are "555. Turn left at Jackrabbit Dr. 556. Slight left toward Coal Slurry Pipeline." They prudently note: "Use caution—this route may be missing sidewalks or pedestrian paths."

Q. You did not comment in your review of *The Book of Eli* on the relation of the villain's name, "Carnegie," and the character's quest for a book. Andrew Carnegie established almost half the libraries in America by the time of his death. Many of these libraries were in small towns. Do you believe your readers are generally aware of the actual connection to the name used in the film and the character's quest? Do you consider a comment inappropriate, and, if so, why?

In contrast to the Carnegie character's looking to obtain a single book by force, Andrew Carnegie was giving away books by the millions. Andrew Carnegie wanted to spread knowledge while the film's Carnegie character wants to control knowledge and the book.

—Joseph Jacobson, Dallas, Texas

A. In fact, the Urbana Free Library, which had a big impact on my life, benefitted from Andrew Carnegie. Not incidentally, he was also responsible for the most inspiring buildings in some of those towns. Yes, it's an irony that the Gary Oldman character has the same name. I hope he's not a descendant.

Box-Office Records

Q. Does the fanfare made over *Avatar* dethroning *Titanic* as all-time box-office champ make any sense to you considering no inflation adjustment was done and there is a ten-year period between the release of both movies? Then again, the *Titanic* record stands only if you consider the box-office receipts from other movies such as *Gone with the Wind* in nonadjusted dollars. And *Avatar* and *Titanic* were released at a time when we knew the DVD was coming in a few months, thus lowering any urgency to see it repeatedly in a theater.

—Gerardo Valero, Mexico City, Mexico

A. This question comes up every time a box-office record is challenged, inspiring debates that usually dribble off with, "But there are no reliable box office figures for *Birth of a Nation*." It is impossible to find authoritative figures accounting for box-office prices, inflation, and reporting accuracy. All we know is that if a movie was *really* successful, it's always mentioned in stories like these.

Brand Upon the Brain!

Q. I showed Guy Maddin's *Brand Upon the Brain!* to my philosophy class last night. Their homework for next week was to apply Platonic and Aristotelian views on art and figure out what the hell it's about. Did you ever see the film performed live? That would have been something. I asked Guy if he wanted me to tell the students anything before I showed his movie, thinking he might just say, "Tell them to have fun" or something, but instead he wrote me a frickin novel-length e-mail, ha ha. His remarks took so long to get through that the class ran overtime!

—Jeff McLaughlin, Thompson Rivers University, Kamloops, British Columbia, Canada

A. Having studied my own review of the film, I regret I cannot help you with your question. Please ask Mr. Maddin to give his permission to run the letter here, and my readers will help. All of them are philosophers. Only yesterday one informed me that I am Nothingness.

Bruno

Q. In your review for *Bruno*, you mentioned that Sacha Baron Cohen's stereotyped gay character is flamboyant, but you didn't comment on just how offensive this stereotype is. I can imagine many people seeing this film and walking away thinking that Mr. Cohen accurately portrayed the average gay man. As I'm sure you know, stereotypes can be extremely harmful and I believe there is a link between stereotypes and violence against whatever group is being stereotyped.

I don't think Sacha Baron Cohen's portrayal of a gay man is any different from the racist portrayals of black people in films from the earlier part of the twentieth century.

I wonder what your review would be like if the film were about a white person who puts on blackface and puts himself in various situations in which he acts no differently than the way white people acted in blackface in films from the silent era and early talkies.

—Warren Jones, San Francisco, California

A. I didn't use the word *stereotype* in my review, and Bruno in my opinion is not a stereotype of any human being living or dead. Anyone who thinks he is an "average gay man" is three cards short of a full house.

Q. I disagree with your negative characterization of Representative Ron Paul in your review of *Bruno*. I supported him in his presidential campaign, and I found Sacha Baron Cohen's treatment of Dr. Paul deplorable and disrespectful. Dr. Paul was right to walk out, and his reactionary attitude reflects a defensive mechanism inherent in heterosexuals. You allowed your politically correct bias to impose "decidedly liberal" values on the reader, and for that you should be ashamed. Keep political bias on the sideline when reviewing the film except when the topic of the film is political.

—Aaron Heineman, Provo, Utah

A. In all fairness, I wrote, "It is no doubt unfair of Cohen to victimize an innocent like Ron Paul. Watching Paul trying to deal with this weirdo made me reflect that as a fringe candidate, he has probably been subjected to a lot of strange questions on strange TV shows, and is prepared to sit through almost anything for TV exposure."

Q. In replying to a question about your review of *Bruno* in July you said that "in all fairness" you wrote: "It is no doubt unfair of Cohen to victimize an innocent like Ron Paul. Watching Paul trying to deal with this weirdo made me reflect that as a fringe candidate, he has probably been subjected to a lot of strange questions on strange TV shows and is prepared to sit through almost anything for TV exposure."

I note how you believe you were responding "in all fairness." I suppose that in your expressed mainstream liberal view you believe you were fair. But consider this: Ron Paul as a "fringe candidate"? He is a Republican United States congressman from the Fourteenth District of Texas, my district. How is it that makes him fringe? OK, I know the answer. He is not a Republican or Democratic member of the mainstream war party. He seriously supports the Constitution of the United States. Presidents give an oath to support the Constitution. Neither Obama nor Bush showed anything but contempt for that oath.

I believe you probably watched many of last year's presidential debates. Did you notice how the mainstream media hosts treated Representative Paul with contempt while fawning over every mainstream candidate, including the likes of Giuliani and Huckabee? Ron Paul showed equanimity and calm under the sarcasm of the "pundits."

—Bruce Niebuhr

A. As a presidential candidate, Ron Paul is "fringe." That's a fact, not an opinion. I often find him refreshing and forthright. He often cuts straight through the clichés and boilerplate of politics. It is perhaps only *as* a fringe candidate that he feels the freedom to be direct and blunt, since he isn't seriously expecting to be nominated. The Democrat Dennis Kucinch is also, I would argue, a fringe candidate, and likewise empowered. The MSM treats both with disregard. However, if a mainstream candidate dared to say some of the things they say, the MSM would smack him back into line.

Let me speculate, however, that if Ron Paul were to announce in the Fourteenth District of Texas that he thought there might be some validity to the theory of evolution, he could not win reelection. I guess you pick your fights.

Casablanca

Q. I was reading a review of the recent release of the *Casablanca* Ultimate Collector's Edition on DVD, and the reviewer states that your commentary is amazing because you are so knowledgeable about everything surrounding this movie. A few days ago I was reading something interesting about this movie and was wondering if you would be able to confirm or deny this rumor.

The International Jack Benny Fan Club claims on their Web site that, according to the *Casablanca* press book, Jack Benny has an uncredited cameo in *Casablanca*. My understanding from what they say on their site is that Jack was visiting the studio one day and Bogart invited him to be an extra in one of the scenes. Jack made a film at Warner Bros. in 1942, so it's entirely possible that he could have been there.

Most of the people who've posted on the Web site for the Jack Benny fan club seem to think he's a man in the background starting at seven minutes into the film. Sam is singing, and behind him is a table with several people sitting at it. The man most visible is wearing a uniform and smoking a cigarette. I agree that he resembles Jack, but I don't think it's him. Are you familiar with this rumor? And if the rumor is true, would you happen to know where in the film he's hiding?

—Ethan J. Muse, Keene, Texas

A. It looks something like him. That's all I can say. On this thread on a Benny fan site, it's pointed out that the press book indeed makes such a claim, and Bogart appeared on Benny's radio show at roughly the same time: http://j.mp/8NHSHQ.

Q. After reading your *Answer Man* column in the *Sun-Times* yesterday, I pulled out my DVD of *Casablanca* to see what I could see. My DVD player has the capability to zoom in on the picture, as well as slow the film down.

There is no doubt in my mind that it is indeed Jack Benny of Waukegan sitting at the table behind Sam.

We have a local station that replays many old TV shows (*Terry and the Pirates, Dragnet, Ozzie and Harriet, Love That Bob*) from the 1950s and *The Jack Benny Program* is on twice a week. Just from watching the few moments of the film, you can see the traits and distinct idiosyncrasies that made him who he was.

So as not to "ham it up," Jack turns away from the camera several times to have a conversation with another actor. Interestingly, later in the same scene, when Bogart hides the "letters of transit" in Sam's piano, Jack has been replaced with another extra. I can only assume that Mr. Benny had a dispute with the waiter over the bill and got the boot.

—Dave Bahnsen, Coralville, Iowa

A. I think you're right. The International Jack Benny Fan Club can feel vindicated.

Charlie Kaufman Movies

Q. In most of Charlie Kaufman's films (*Being John Malkovich, Synecdoche, New York,* and *Eternal Sunshine of the Spotless Mind,* at least), a character smokes marijuana, which I thought was an interesting similarity. In each of these films, the plot is full of delightful but completely bizarre moments. It seems to reflect the state of someone's mind while pot smoking (that is, misheard words, distorted reality). What is your opinion?

—Nick Duval, Wallingford, Connecticut

A. My theory is that it's entirely plausible.

Chicago Movie Theatres

Q. Well, sure, agreed. The Music Box probably is the best place to see a movie in Chicago (I read your tweet). It's the best place where I've seen a movie in Chicago, but I'm a twenty-three-year-old suburbanite, wishing toward urbanism in my recession-plagued nothingness. I love the Music Box; it truly is a classic venue. But twenty-something miles west is the Tivoli Theater of Downers Grove! It's literally a spit away from the train tracks that offer a twenty-three-minute ride into the Loop, and it is so much better. It's a one-screen landmark. Sure, you've probably heard of it by now. It is a beautiful historical landmark—and the world's second sound theater. Point is, I think you should give the Tivoli some publicity.

—John Wilmes, Downers Grove, Illinois

A. The Tivoli is indeed a jewel box, superbly programmed. I was limiting myself to Chicago, but you are right that we must cher-

ish these treasures wherever they can be found. Such structures will never again be constructed, so they're part of our heritage and can continue as great venues into the future. Aw, I'm getting worked up.

Look how the Chicago Loop has benefitted by saving the Chicago, Oriental, Palace, Michael Todd, and Cinestage and recycling them into a theater district showcasing the Goodman Theater.

Children's Movies

Q. My eight-year-old son, Andrew, has taken an interest in my movie collection. We've been watching movies atypical for someone that young: *Rushmore, Spellbound* (the spelling bee documentary), *The Right Stuff, Tell No One* (with subtitles, no less!), and this past Friday, a movie near and dear to you: *Dark City.*

It appears that kids can handle complex characters and story lines better than we think. Very rarely do I have to explain what is going on, and his comments indicate that he is getting it (during *Rushmore*: "Sometimes Max is not nice, but I like him"; *Dark City*'s ending: "He knows all about her, but she doesn't know about him!").

But what strikes me the most is how *natural* cinematic grammar is understood by children. No one has to sit down and explain things like cutaways, flashbacks, dream sequences, POV shots, and the passage of time in films. How do they learn this stuff? Do you think the thematic material in the movies I listed is too much for eight-year-olds, or can I continue to brag and bore my friends?

—Mike Spearns, St. John's, Newfoundland, Canada

A. Start bragging. IMHO, kids up until about the age of eleven are more open to good movies than they will be again for some years. Any kid knows, as any adult does, that *Twilight* is a crashing bore. I suspect many teenagers like it because they have been ordered to by their peers.

Younger children instinctively love a Miyazaki animated film more than the meaningless action of films such as *Monsters vs. Aliens* or *Kung Fu Panda.* They're open to the magic. Later, some seem to need to be battered by noise and chaos. I've never met a

711

preschooler who didn't respond well to silent comedy. A film critic friend of mine and his novelist wife raised their daughter on nothing but good films, and she developed such good taste that she never has been able to stomach visual junk food.

As for understanding the language, the grammar of film seems to have evolved directly from the instincts of the first filmmakers. It requires no theory to understand the difference between a close-up and a long shot, or that a dream sequence is a dream sequence. A good movie contains all the instructions you need about how to watch it. This is true of the greatest films. Only junk like *Transformers 2* requires an instruction manual.

Q. I enjoyed your recent Answer Man response to the parent whose child loves watching great movies. I have a three-year-old daughter who is getting interested in cartoons and movies, but the dreck available on regular television is appalling. We have started with the Looney Toons collections, which she loves, but I sense she is ready for more variety. Do you have a list of recommended movies for children?

—Jim Martin, St. Louis, Missouri

A. Of course the Looney Tunes are great fun and involve a lot of artistry. And the Disney classics such as *Pinocchio* and *Dumbo* are terrific. Some modern Disney is a little advanced for three-year-olds. The best of all animated films are by Hayao Miyazaki. My favorite of those is *My Neighbor Totoro*, and children seem fascinated by it. It's dubbed in English, but then all animated films are dubbed.

City Lights

Q. I just viewed Charlie Chaplin's classic *City Lights* for the first time, in a film class. After letting the film's spell settle on us, my professor asked us to consider the final scene: Specifically, what does the girl really see? Most of our answers felt pretty obvious—she sees the truth that the man she had loved is the tramp, and not a millionaire; she sees that he is still the same person she loved and she accepts him, and so on. I thought most of this was made fairly clear. That last look in her face, particularly when she puts the tramp's hand to her heart and seems to gasp to hold back tears (which I took to be tears of overwhelmed joy), followed by his anxious, almost rapturous, smile, seemed to indicate that she clearly accepts him and even loves him.

My professor, however, seemed to think there was more ambiguity in the scene. She certainly has no problem with the fact that he's a tramp, and doesn't mind that he's not at all like the tall handsome man she'd imagined . . . but my prof suggested we cannot be sure how much she knows and thus to what extent she really accepts and loves him. Aside from the fact that she can't know for sure that he wasn't rich when he was still with her, and thus doesn't know how he struggled to help her or how he was deceiving her, she could be so overwhelmed by the revelation of his identity that she just doesn't have enough time to think through everything in that scene, not enough to really know if she returns his love completely.

In your Great Movie essay, you said, "She sees, and yet still smiles at him, and accepts him. The tramp guessed correctly: She has a good heart and is able to accept him as himself." I definitely thought this much, at least. Do you think there is much ambiguity about her feelings in that scene? Is it too much for me to assume she returns his love, more than merely accepting him as a good man who happens to be the tramp?

—David Michael, Milpitas, California

A. I think the power of the scene resides in the fact that she now knows who he really is, and her love is not only unchanged, but even enhanced.

The Coen Brothers

Q. I noted your four-star review of *A Serious Man*, the new Coen brothers film, and was thinking of the new book by your *Sun-Times* colleague, Cathleen Falsani, *The Dude Abides: The Gospel According to the Coen Brothers*. Cathleen calls *A Serious Man* easily the most overtly religious of all their films. She is also the "Dudey Satva" of Dudeism (the tongue-in-cheek—but sixty-thousand-strong—"religion" based on the theology and ethics of the Coens' movie *The Big Lebowski*).

—Kelly Hughes, Chicago, Illinois

A. I knew of Cathleen's wonderful book but didn't register that she's so instrumental in Dudeism. I discover on Wikipedia: "Dudeism encourages the practice of 'going with the flow' and 'taking it easy,' believing this is the only way to live in harmony with our inner nature. It aims to assuage feelings of inadequacy in societies which place a heavy emphasis on achievement and personal fortune. Consequently, simple pleasures like bathing and bowling are seen as preferable to the spending of money as a means to achieve happiness and spiritual fulfillment."

Comcast Holiday Movies

Q. I don't know if you use Comcast, but if you go to its "Movie Collections" on-demand section and then to the new "Holiday Movies" section, you will find such titles as *The Godfather*, *Die Hard*, and *Three Days of the Condor*. True, at least parts of these movies occur at the holiday season. And, come to think of it, is there anything like the CIA postman delivery scene to make a person feel Christmassy? I dunno. Maybe it will help if I take another look at *Lethal Weapon*, another Comcast holiday movie.

—Zay N. Smith, Chicago, Illinois

A. How did they overlook *Antichrist*?

Couples Retreat

Q. Without hesitation, *Couples Retreat* is one of the worst movies I've seen in years, so unpleasant that I felt compelled to write. I hope others heed your review (I ended up in the theater after my first two choices were sold out). It's our Thanksgiving Day weekend here in Canada and I was planning on going to a couple of movies, but after sitting through *Couples Retreat* I just can't contemplate a return to the theater any time soon.

—Wendy Myshak, Edmonton, Alberta, Canada

A. Wendy! Wendy! It's not *all* movies! It's just that one!

The Cove

Q. What's your reaction to the Tokyo Film Festival rejecting *The Cove*? The film won't hit my small town until next month, but I have been following it with interest. I didn't realize that Japan was restricting artistic expression as much as the Chinese these days. Can anything be done to shame the organizers of the Tokyo Film Festival into changing their mind?

—K. V. Anderson, Fort Collins, Colorado

A. The documentary is strongly critical of a Japanese practice of luring dolphins to a trap by using sonar, then selling some to theme parks and labeling the (mercury-tainted) flesh of the rest as whale meat. The film has been widely acclaimed (94 percent on the Tomatometer). The motive of the festival seems all too transparent.

Crazy Heart

Q. I figure you must get this type of question frequently, so please be patient with me. I am interested in knowing why a film that is critically acclaimed like *Crazy Heart* is arriving in south Florida for the first time today and the arrival is limited to only four theaters in all of south Florida. And those four theaters are not what one would consider main or popular theaters and locations.

—Steve Bloom, Florida

A. You're lucky you got it that soon. The film was heavily previewed for movie critics in December, and because it was indeed so good, it cleaned up most of the year-end prizes by critics' groups, and Jeff Bridges won the Golden Globe and now got the Oscar nomination. That was all precisely according to the Twentieth Century–Fox plans and/or hopes. Now it goes into wide release the Friday after the nominations, along with such other Oscar beneficiaries as *An Education* and *The Last Station*.

Credits

Q. Do you have any idea as to why movies from a certain era—let's say before the mid-1960s—don't have an extensive list of end credits the way that today's films do? This has bothered me for years, but I haven't been able to find a concrete reason for this, save for this being a union-influenced action.

—Pete Croatto, East Brunswick, New Jersey

A. Two reasons: unions, and sometimes to add a few songs that can be included on the sound track album. What really annoys me is that films no longer routinely open with the names of the actors, and at the end they usually make you wait through countless other credits before getting around to the actors. Doesn't the Screen Actors Guild have any clout?

Q. When did studios get so coy about revealing the name of actors? In several recent movies, the house lights were on and half the audience had left before the actors' names finally appeared on the screen.

—Greg Nelson, Chicago, Illinois

A. I know exactly what you mean. A movie opens with the animated credits of half a dozen producing companies, which are there for bragging rights, and then plunges directly into the action. After it's over, we often get countless technical credits before it finally divulges the names of the actors. In the classic tradition, the actors were named right at the top, after the title.

Q. Did you catch the closing credits of *Harry Potter and the Half-Blood Prince*? (I'm referring to the initial casting credits, not the crawling credits that list cast members in order of appearance.) Timothy Spall's name appeared prominently and by itself about halfway through. He appeared in two scenes for no more than three seconds each, one in which he answered a door, and the other when one is slammed in his face. Listed last and sharing screen space with two other names? Bonnie Wright, who played Harry's love interest Ginny (and who has also been in more Harry Potter films than Spall). I know credit order is usually determined by a mix of screen time and star power, but this is beyond crazy. I'd like to think perhaps several of Spall's scenes were cut long after the credits were designed, but the character he plays is in the book for just as long!

—Erik Dresner, Elmhurst, New York

A. Credits are a matter of delicate negotiation involving agents. My guess is that Spall personally doesn't much care. But his agent might have argued he is a true star and deserves a good billing. Conversely, some actors like Bill Murray often take no billing at all, which is a form of reverse status.

Critics Buying Tickets

Q. Kevin Smith, the director, says movie critics should be made to buy tickets to the movies they review. My question to you is, would you pay to see a movie like his *Cop Out*?

—Andy Tate, Regina, Saskatchewan, Canada

A. Gladly. But I'd want to attend before 2 p.m. on a Tuesday.

The Dark Knight

Q. I heard that Warner Bros. and Christopher Nolan are going to make an announcement of the next Batman film in January 2010. Do you think any other director will ever do such a good job on the Batman franchise like Mr. Nolan? Do you think that *The Dark Knight* deserved more Oscar nominations, including Best Picture, Best Director, Best Adapted Screenplay, and Best Original Score? Will *The Dark Knight* be included in the Great Movies section?

—Ben McCarthy, Cambridge, United Kingdom

A. He certainly made the only one that's a GM candidate, so he's out in the lead.

Die Hard with a Vengeance/Dick Cheney

Q. I have seen *Die Hard with a Vengeance* an embarrassing amount of times (not as many as *Die Hard*, though), and I have never been able to spot Dick Cheney. He's listed in the movie's credits and it's on his IMDb page.

—Cory B. Wingerter

A. It is said he "plays a cameo as an NYPD police official." You know what? I seriously doubt it. My best guesses: (1) It was another Dick Cheney; or (2) somebody hacked IMDb.

Directors

Q. Why is it that many directors seem to lock in on a certain type of genre and never let go? I mean, you pretty much know what you're going to get when you see a film by Michael Bay, Kevin Smith, or even Quentin Tarantino. But look at a career like Billy Wilder's. He did film noir, drama, and comedy (and did it very well). Why won't other directors get out of their comfort zones and try something new? Is it for commercial reasons?

Or am I naive to think they *want* to try different things? At least Scorsese didn't stick to just making gangster films.

—Paul Santa Cruz, Phoenix, Arizona

A. A lot of it may have to do with the studio desire to assemble a "package" of known elements. The great directors who make a variety of films always have trouble getting them financed, Scorsese included. But the best directors work outside boundaries: Sidney Lumet, Atom Egoyan, Robert Altman. That's difficult for packagers because they have to evaluate each project on its intrinsic merit. To put it in simpler terms, the executives in the golden age had better seats on their pants.

Q. What is your opinion of film directors such as Clint Eastwood, Woody Allen, Steven Spielberg, Brian De Palma, and John Landis, who refuse to provide audio commentaries on their DVDs, instead opting for their films to "speak for themselves"? Would someone such as yourself, who has, indeed, provided commentaries on various films, tend to agree that these directors are cheating fans and scholars by withholding their own personal insights?

Those directors who have, such as William Friedkin, Martin Scorsese, John Woo, John Boorman, Francis Ford Coppola, Billy Bob Thornton, George Miller, and Oliver Stone, have aided our ability to enjoy their work on a higher, more detailed, and enjoyable level. And speaking of Stone, he had so much to say regarding the making of his film *Nixon* that he generously provides not one but two separate audio tracks, something that I have never seen (or, perhaps, heard) on any other DVD.

—Kevin Fellman, Arizona

A. It's their film and they can do what they like. I once tried to enlist Orson Welles in talking through *Citizen Kane*, and his response was, "I'm tired of talking about that film."

Douglas Pratt

Q. I wonder if you know what Douglas Pratt, the writer of *DVD Laser* newsletter, is up to lately. I was a big fan of his *Laserdisc Newsletter* in the '90s and thought he was, without question, one of the best reviewers of films and home video I have ever seen. But after the '90s, he seems to have vanished. His Web site is now filled with broken links, and e-mail sent to him is bounced.

—Kevin Yip, New York, New York

A. I agree with your high opinion. He is especially strong on the technical details of DVDs. You'll find him writing at MovieCityNews.com.

Dubbed Movies

Q. I've heard most foreign films playing in French, German, Spanish, and Italian-speaking countries are dubbed into the local language rather than subtitled. Is this true? I'm thinking about moving to Spain. Dubbing is such a crude, destructive practice, it's hard to believe it's routinely employed in supposedly sophisticated Europe. Are great performances in great films being obliterated by second-rate local actors? Can it be that the distinctive voices of Katharine Hepburn, John Wayne, Sean Connery, Rosie Perez, and Steve Buscemi are unknown to European audiences who think these iconic actors sound just like the grocery clerk down the street?

—Rich Gruber, New York, New York

A. Quite so. In cities such as Paris, the original version ("VO") will play, but elsewhere in a country, it's dubbed all the way. I think it might have been Peter Bogdanovich who told me his John Wayne impression fell flat at a dinner party in Rome because no one at the table knew what John Wayne sounded like.

An Education

Q. Just caught the movie *An Education* and really loved it. I noticed something I haven't noticed before: "Rated PG-13 for smoking." It's a great movie and I'm thrilled that kids under seventeen can see this—but smoking? Of all things, smoking?

After knowing a few friends who were involved with older men (not at sixteen, more around twenty), I thought Peter Sarsgaard nailed how his character looked and facially reacted to this much younger girl. I met only one of my best friend's older involvements at a holiday event, but he looked and reacted to her in exactly the same way: a combination of excitement over someone new (read: young), nervousness, guilt, and lust. Sometimes all in

715

the scope of five minutes. After seeing movies like *Lolita* (both versions) and some of the few other movies that somewhat deal with this topic, Sarsgaard was the only actor I've seen utterly nail the facial expressions. Far and above the rich character he played, he brought a lot of subtlety to that part.

—Jennifer Grandy, Chicago, Illinois

A. Actually, the MPAA rating specifies "for historical smoking." You might confuse that as meaning "few smokers in history have smoked this much," but actually it means, "Kids, your stupid grandparents did this in the olden days."

Film Buff Choices

Q. You're a lonely single film buff and it's Saturday night. Hitchcock or Kurosawa?

—Matrcus Burciaga

A. What are my choices?

Food, Inc.

Q. I just read your review of *Food, Inc.* and I have to say I am disappointed in how easily you put aside your critical thinking skills and fell for a scare tactic. This film exaggerates, stages, or just plain lies about a number of issues. This film scared you because that's what they wanted to do to you—facts be damned. There are certainly some legitimate problems in the food industry, but scare tactics, like those used in this film, are the same as those used by the Bush administration to justify all sorts of questionable activities such as the Patriot Act, NSA wiretapping, and the war in Iraq. These scare tactics effectively prevent any constructive and rational dialogue from taking place between the food industry and its critics, and it's time to get past that so that real progress can be made.

—Bryan Hughes, Texas Tech, Lubbock, Texas

A. You steered me to the Web site www.safefoodinc.org, which has a rebuttal of the film. The issues are complex, and I concede I should not have taken it entirely at face value, but neither should we believe we are not eating factory food.

Francois Truffaut

Q. I just watched Truffaut's whole Antoine Doinel cycle (*The 400 Blows*, *Bed and Board*,

716

and *Love on the Run*) yet again. More than any other film, I wish there would be a continuation to these. I picture a movie where Christine has passed away, Antoine becomes a grandfather, and his son moves into his home due to marital problems, and then the son's wife moves in, too, and Antoine becomes the mediator to get them back together. Comedic Antoine babysitting scenes with his grandchild . . . I don't know, I'm making this up as I go, because the possibilities are endless.

I contacted Truffaut's daughter and she responded negatively. But I know that people say things and feel things at times in their life, and later change their minds.

"It means a lot that my father's films still touch some people in such a personal manner. About the Doinel series, my father was absolutely determined that *Love on the Run* had to mark the end of the series. To him it felt wrong to portray the character becoming middle-aged. For one thing, a main trait of Antoine D is that he can't quite accept to grow up and to be an adult. Seeing Antoine as a middle-aged man still fumbling through life would have been somewhat bitter, my father thought. Also, the movies started with a strong biographical bend, but as my father succeeded in his line of work while his character tried his hands at many different jobs with mixed results, they were really parting ways, and he felt he couldn't really go much further in that vein. It didn't ring true to him, I guess, in the way the earlier films did. Even *Love on the Run* felt like a stretch for my father.

"Both my father and Jean-Pierre Leaud were determined to end the series with *Love on the Run*. I don't believe my father would have liked the idea of a continuation by another director, and honestly my sisters and I would never approve it as we are certain of his wishes on the matter. I hope you enjoy your first trip to France too—Paris still looks pretty much the way it did in *Stolen Kisses* if you avoid all the McDonald's and Starbucks! Laura Truffaut."

One test might be to ask Jean-Pierre Leaud if he would consider doing it all these years later, if Truffaut had been OK with it.

—Peter Fawthrop

A. Francois Truffaut died at fifty-two. His New Wave contemporary Claude Chabrol, two years older, has a new film in this year's Chicago International Film Festival. Think of all the wonderful films that were claimed by his death.

Future of Horror Movies

Q. I am concerned with the future of horror movies. I recently saw two fantastic yet different films: Orphan and Let the Right One In. In Orphan, the film was filled with countless horror movie clichés. Why do so many movies, and more specifically horror movies, continue to use "the formula" and get away with it? I'm thirty-two and I know I'm outside of the demographic, but I know teenagers still cannot be truly happy with the same scenarios and gimmicks as you suggest in your review. I've been tired of these for years, yet I still find myself drawn to watch the movies even though I haven't been scared since I was a teenager. In the film Let the Right One In, "formula" wasn't used as directly as in Orphan, but I think that's because it was a foreign film. Now, I'm frustrated to hear that there will be a U.S. remake of this one! Here we go again! So sad.

—Samuel Mills, Woodstock, Georgia

A. Of course you picked two good movies, one very good. In Let the Right One In Lina Leandersson was unforgettable as Eli, the vampire. The role is played in the remake (called Let Me In) by Chloe Moretz, who certainly displayed a lot of confidence in Kick Ass and was good in 500 Days of Summer. It will be a test of the Hollywood remake to be as effective and chilling as the original. Will it dilute the truly disturbing implications of the story?

Gates of Heaven

Q. I read your Great Movies review of Errol Morris's Gates of Heaven today. It ended with: "Cal Harberts promises in the film that his park will still be in existence in 30, 50 or 100 years. Twenty years have passed. I searched for the Bubbling Well Pet Memorial Park on the World Wide Web, and found it (www.bubbling-well.com). There is information about its 'Garden of Companionship,' 'Kitty Curve,' and 'Pre-Need Plans,' but no mention of this film. Or of the Harberts."

I found an article in my local free paper saying that as of that date, Dan Harberts was running the place. I loved Gates of Heaven and it makes me feel better to know that a Harberts is in charge. Several of my childhood pets are there.

—Chuck Kubota, Campbell, California

A. Yes, I actually heard from Dan not long ago. Seemed like a nice man. Many readers can't believe I selected a documentary about a pet cemetery as one of the best films of all time. But that film remains a fascination to me. Is it satire, or serious? Does it honor, or mock? Should we bury our pets in a pet cemetery, or in a Dumpster? A woman in the film says, "There's your dog, your dog's dead. But there has to be something to make it move. Well, hasn't there?" The more you think, the more profound her question grows.

The Girl with the Dragon Tattoo

Q. After seeing The Girl with the Dragon Tattoo, on the car ride home, we couldn't help but discuss how different an American version of the film would be. Besides the obvious sexual situations and probably the villains' background, we came upon an obvious difference. An American film would have to explain to the audience the titular tattoo. It was great to see a movie leave so many plot threads unanswered.

—Mark Coale, editor/publisher, OdessaSteps.com

A. The name of the movie is The Girl with the Dragon Tattoo. The heroine of the movie is a girl with a dragon tattoo. Yes, a lot of viewers would have to puzzle that out. Don't get me started on The Man with No Name.

Good Acting

Q. I'm deaf and consider myself eloquently mute. Here's my question: How do you recognize good acting these days, and is it at all different compared to the '60s, '70s, or '80s?

—Julie Tibbitt

A. Bergman said the great subject of film is the human face. I imagine that may be doubly true when one is deaf. A great actor is one whose face (and body) is an instrument for

717

the effective but not obvious conveyance of emotion. That isn't easy. For example, Pierce Brosnan may not be your idea of a great actor. But I've recently seen him in two quite unrelated roles, both ripe for overacting, and his choices were unerringly good. This is even more of an accomplishment because he labors under the burden of being improbably handsome.

Green Zone

Q. Regarding *Green Zone*: Did you ever think it was inane, or at least fake, how Damon always emerges from a death match in a kitchen or tiny bathroom leaving a dead guy and suffering only a paper cut? I am former USAF, but why should I tell you that; you were probably a ninja.

—Frank Shaffer

A. Yes, I did. I've given up on complaining about that phenomenon in thrillers. It's a variation of the fact that bad guys with machine guns never hit the hero, who fires back with a handgun and kills them all. I know this, and I wasn't even a ninja turtle.

Q. In your *Green Zone* review, where do you get your information on your "no WMD" statements regarding Iraq? If you are going down that path, why then do you not mention that our satellites showed considerable tractor-trailer activity at each suspected WMD site several days before Hans Blix's UN inspection teams show up to "inspect" each site? Our satellites traced many tractor-trailer envoys into Syria with cargo loaded from these sites. The TV newscasts were showing them live on the air. What exactly do you think those envoys were moving into Syria? Saddam's moonshine stash?

We also found several live bioweapon labs, we found four hundred nuclear scientists enriching uranium (against UN sanctions and policy), and we found three thousand military-grade chemical weapons suits. Saddam also chemical bombed one of his own cities in 1989, killing tens of thousands of his own citizens. Do nuclear weapons, chemical weapons, and bioweapons meet your definition of WMDs? Whew. Never mind the ten thousand citizens per year dying in torture chambers—does that meet WMD criteria? If you are going to get political in your reviews, how about "manning up" and presenting both sides?

—Adam D. Porter, Pittsburgh, Pennsylvania

A. In October 2004, President Bush said at his press conference: "Iraq did not have the weapons that our intelligence believed were there." In August 2006: "The main reason we went into Iraq at the time was we thought he had weapons of mass destruction. It turns out he didn't, but he had the capacity to make weapons of mass destruction."

Hello, Dolly!

Q. Having heard a lot about the movie *Hello, Dolly!*, and having listened to the songs from the *Wall-E* soundtrack, I liked it so much I saw it twice (and a half) on the same day. I loved Barbra Streisand, I loved Walter Matthau, Michael Crawford, and so on, the costumes, the art direction, and the cinematography, but what I can't understand is how a lot of people hated the movie, based on a pile of reviews in IMDb and Rotten Tomatoes. Maybe there's something I'm missing, so that's why I am writing to you, to know if I have to like this movie or not, for I usually agree with your reviews, which have always assisted me in times of great confusion and indecision. Please help this fifteen-year-old movie-lover to realize what's wrong with this masterpiece that makes lots of people hate it.

—Juan Manuel, Cafferata, Argentina

A. Not much, according to me. I gave it a four-star review, but my review seems to be missing online. I'm looking for it. I see the IMDb rating is 6.8, not bad. The comment boards on IMDb and Rotten Tomatoes are often interesting and useful, sometimes appalling.

Hitoshi Matsumoto

Q. I just read your review of *Big Man Japan*, where at the end you write that Hitoshi Matsumoto's name is misspelled *Hitosi Matumoto*, and that this is a "little joke." Actually, I'm not sure it is a joke. There are various ways of transcribing Japanese characters into English, and the different spellings of Matsumoto's name simply reflect that difference. In other words, *si* and *shi* are exactly the same thing, as are *tu* and *tsu*. We only tend to romanize using *shi* and *tsu* because it helps us English speakers effect a pronunciation that is closer to the original. On the other hand, if this really was meant to be a joke, then I'm afraid I'm missing something.

—Timothy Martin, Princeton, New Jersey

A. In *Variety*'s review from Cannes by Russell Edwards, I read: "A popular standup comedian in Japan, Matumoto is a notorious prankster. In this spirit, his name both onscreen, in press materials and in the Quinzaine catalog is a deliberate misspelling of his actual name, Hitoshi Matsumoto." Edwards, based in Australia, specializes in the films of Japan and Korea.

Hot Tub Time Machine

Q. You gave three stars to *Hot Tub Time Machine*. Really? This might be the worst movie my wife and I have ever seen. And the use of the F word . . . can you say *overdone*! We chose this movie on the basis of your comments in the movie ad: "It succeeds beyond any expectations." Are you serious? Have your "expectations" diminished to this level? People at our show were walking out. This was truly a stupid movie. John Cusack should be embarrassed to be associated with this work. I guess we will research other critics next time.

—Bob Racette, Orland Park, Illinois

A. If you research them on the basis of their comments quoted in movie ads, you might not find too many negatives. What I wrote was: "succeeds beyond any expectations suggested by the title."

Q. I presume your *Hot Tub Time Machine* review has sent thousands to IMDb to review the John Cusack catalog. I am certain I'm not the only one to suggest that perhaps *Tapeheads* is not good. This from a girl who adores both John Cusack and Tim Robbins. Or at least I adored Tim Robbins until that whole thing about him donating to Michele Bachmann came to light.

—Elise Christenson, Minneapolis, Minneapolis

A. He *did*? Now I understand the divorce. Yeah, my Cusack-o-meter was malfunctioning when I wrote that review. He makes

an extraordinarily high percentage of good movies, but their number doesn't include, for example, *Class*, *America's Sweethearts*, and *Must Love Dogs*. Oh, and *Tapeheads*.

How to Train Your Dragon

Q. Regarding the animated film *How to Tame Your Dragon*. Take a look at the photo recently used as their media promo shot, with graphic phallic imagery so blatantly used. Am I the only adult on the planet who may be wondering how and why the cute dragon illustrated in the original book suddenly takes on a highly suggestive shape?

—Sally Davis, Irvine, California

A. I guess it all depends on how you look at it.

I Love You, Beth Cooper

Q. I just read your review of *I Love You, Beth Cooper*. I am curious about what you meant when you wrote: "They may not become the most popular girl in school, but they don't care. That honor carries with it a terrible lifetime price tag." I have read many of your reviews and know that you carefully construct your writing; therefore, I believe that your choice of words was intentionally strong, or alludes to something. For whatever reason, I have been thinking about this for a little while and am puzzled. What is the terrible lifetime price tag? I have ideas as to what you meant and possibly as to why you wrote it, but in general, feel like I might be reading too much into a few words or am missing something entirely.

—Steven Robinson, Montrose, British Columbia, Canada

A. Perhaps those words were not very carefully chosen. You can *be* popular and live a wonderful life. But I fear that if you tailor your behavior *in order to be* popular, your prospects are not as bright.

"Imma Star (Everywhere We Are)"

Q. Do you have any reaction to your shout-out in "Imma Star (Everywhere We Are)," the pop song by Chicago R&B singer Jeremih? In bragging about his fame, he sings, "Don't need Roger Ebert or the paparazzi / Take on and already the country stop me." It's sort of

719

cryptic, as Jeremih doesn't seem to have done any film work outside of music videos. But the song has a local following and has been showing up for weeks in B-96's "Nine Most Wanted."

—Earl Hofert, Chicago, Illinois

A. I am most honored, and know how he feels. The country stop me all the time too, especially during the previous administration.

Indiana Jones/Shia LaBeouf

Q. Didn't Shia LaBeouf break some sort of unwritten rule by criticizing Spielberg over the last Indiana Jones movie? He indeed put him down by stating he had long discussions with Harrison Ford about the poor job they both thought he was doing, all this while making the film. For starters, if I were Oliver Stone, I might be a little apprehensive about Shia's opinion on my work in the coming *Wall Street* sequel. I know people do this all the time in everyday life but with the exception of Marlon Brando with *The Freshmen* (someone known as a bit of an eccentric) you don't see this every day, especially concerning one of the most powerful men in Hollywood.

—Gerardo Valero, Mexico City, Mexico

A. I imagine LaBeouf's agent smacked his forehead with his palm when he read that— not because of Spielberg's possible reaction, but because his client comes off looking negative. Other directors might consider that. Spielberg, I think, is beyond caring about LaBeouf's opinion. I certainly don't think Shia should have betrayed a private conversation with Harrison Ford.

The Informant!

Q. I guess I saw a different movie from you, but *The Informant!* movie offended in the worst way—it was boring! Matt Damon was boring, the dialogue was boring, the direction was boring. You need to curb your crushes on movie stars and start critiquing movies again based on their merits, not on how much your heart throbs. After giving this piece of crap four stars, you have lost all credibility. I wrote my newspaper, suggesting they drop you and rehire the local movie reviewer who recently lost his job. You aren't worth the money they pay.

—Doris Jewett

A. According to Rotten Tomatoes, 76 percent of the nation's critics approved of the movie. That doesn't make me right. But what with the economy the way it is, do you think we can afford for that many people to be fired?

Inglourious Basterds

Q. Is it just me or is Quentin Tarantino's *Inglourious Basterds* very similar to a Massive Attack video called "Eternal Feedback"? Did Tarantino direct the video? Or does he like Massive Attack?

—Anton Kainer, Toronto, Ontario, Canada

A. I checked it out and don't see a similarity, but it's a good video.

Q. Am I the only one that's noticed that the AMPAS has somehow managed to nominate Quentin Tarantino in the wrong category for Writing (Original Screenplay) for *Inglourious Basterds*? It was obviously based on Enzo G. Castellari's original 1978 Italian war film *Quel maledetto treno blindato* (translated as *That Damned Armored Train* yet released in the United States as *The Inglorious Bastards*), and since he's never been shy about admitting his influences, shouldn't Tarantino technically have been nominated in the Writing (Adapted Screenplay) category? Tarantino even appears with Castellari on the original *Bastards*' three-disc DVD extras as part of an interview, discussing his admiration of Castellari and his original film.

— Kevin Fellman, Phoenix, Arizona

A. Tarantino quotes, borrows from, or pays homage to so many different films that the Academy could hardly list whom he has "adapted." That said, his screenplay is an original, not least with the Tarantinian dialogue. It draws inspiration from earlier works, but sets out anew. Sort of the same relationship that the New Testament has with the Old Testament.

Invictus

Q. You point out that Clint Eastwood's *Invictus* is certainly not the Nelson Mandela biopic you, or indeed anyone, would have expected. You also point out one very likely reason Mr. Eastwood chose it: He was able to get it made. May I posit another potential reason?

I had to disappoint my son by explaining that I did not think it was an appropriate film for me to take him to. He has seen the previews and is desperate to see the movie. He is a big rugby fan, and there is a local team here in Dallas, the Dallas Harlequins, that we watch regularly. I explained this was not simply a movie about rugby. This led to a long and detailed conversation about apartheid, Mandela, De Klerk, the ANC, and the history of South Africa. We spent time looking at photos of District Six. He found it very difficult to believe that people could treat one another that way because of a difference in skin color. My son is six years old and is a white child at a majority-minority public school.

I suspect that conversations happening between fathers and sons just like that may be the reason this is the movie that was made, rather than a more traditional biopic. If not for the sight of a rugby scrum on the TV I doubt he would have glanced up. It's maybe not a big "grabber" in the USA, but rugby is an international sport, and God knows racism is an international problem.

I look forward to seeing *Invictus* this weekend with my wife—after I take my son to the Dallas 'Quins game, of course.

—Jason M. Fitzmaurice, Dallas, Texas

A. You make me suspect my review was written from an insufficient perspective.

It's a Wonderful Life

Q. Upon recently asking my twenty-five-year-old sister what she would like for Christmas, she responded with the following: "*It's a Wonderful Life* on DVD—but make sure it's in color!" Disgusted, I asked her why she would ever want to watch the colorized version over the original black-and-white release. Her response made me laugh. "Well, how am I supposed to tell what color Zuzu's petals are?"

My family did grow up watching the colorized version of the Capra classic, but I have since returned to watching it in black-and-white, and find it less nauseating on the whole. The colorized version seems hardly

colorized at all; it's merely a mix of hodge-podge faux "colors" that clash when they appear together on screen. I kind of like not knowing what color Zuzu's petals really are. But then again, when one watches the distorted colorized version (Shame on you, Ted Turner), is it even possible to tell then?

—Jordan C. Wellin, South Bend, Indiana

A. About colorization, Bette Davis said, "Nobody had to be told that Jezebel's dress was red." But as to your question, Zuzu's petals were a lovely pink in the center, surrounded by a deeper hue, and does your sister have small feet? See http://j.mp/594k8l.

Q. In the Answer Man, you got into a discussion of what color Zuzu's petals were in *It's a Wonderful Life*. Why don't you ask Zuzu? Karolyn Grimes, the actress who played her, now lives in Carnation, Washington. She travels the country and makes appearances at Christmas shows and always includes her most famous movie line ("Every time a bell rings, another angel gets his wings") in her autograph.

—R. S. Lindsay

A. I did indeed ask Zuzu herself, and Karolyn Grimes replied: "I guess it is time to tell all. :-) My rose was a burgundy color. Not a fancy rose at all but to a little girl in the dead of winter I guess it was very beautiful, especially if you won it. Wonder what I did to win that rose?

"The film is timeless. . . . It applies to yesterday, today, and tomorrow. . . . We can all identify with the fellow whose dreams never quite work out the way he envisioned for himself. But in the end we reflect on our own lives and realize that we have touched others and truly made a difference. We also are reminded, once again, what really are the most important things in our lives . . . faith, family, and friends.

"There is a needlepoint sampler on the wall of the Bailey Building and Loan. It is in George's office. When there is a run on the bank, before he goes out to address the people, he pauses a moment and looks at the portrait of his father and under it is a needlepoint sampler that says 'All you can take with you, is that which you've given away.' Too bad our bankers of today can't learn something from that."

Japanese Filmmaking

Q. I read your review of Yojiro Takita's *Departures*, which sounds very intriguing. I've been a big fan of Koreeda's since I saw *After Life*, and I'm a huge fan of the Japanese masters, so hearing that Takita-san has given us another fine Japanese film that isn't exploitative animation or another (often fun, of course) blood-soaked gun- and sword-play action film is good news. Miyamoto-san and Takahata-san (and everyone at Ghibli) seem to be the only animators in Japan still interested in making meaningful and whimsical films.

I say this because I've been on a mission to find the modern Japanese masters, and I'm having a tough time. Do you think they are simply having a hard time getting their movies made or that it's just an overall lull in live-action, dramatic filmmaking in general? We could no doubt level the same criticism at American directors. I've recently watched some "Beat" Takeshi (Takeshi Kitano) films and enjoyed them (although *Kikujiro* was very uncomfortable); Miyazaki is eternal. But I am getting ever closer to having seen all of Kurosawa's and Ozu's films from an entirely different era, and as I watch these incredibly moving and astonishing movies, I wonder more and more what happened to the industry.

—Sean Campbell, Kingston, Tennessee

A. The three great world cinemas are American, French, and Japanese. The rise of the brain-numbing Hollywood blockbuster and the global virus of U.S. fanboy tastes have made it harder for creative directors to work in all three countries. The French remain productive, but the Japanese are challenged. Yet just recently we've seen such amazing films as *Departures*, Koreeda's *Still Walking*, Miyazaki's *Ponyo*, and Kiyoshi Kurosawa's *Tokyo Sonata*. Beat/Takeshi Kitano has a new film arriving.

Q. In a recent Answer Man response you stated, "The three great world cinemas are American, French, and Japanese." Wouldn't a certain Oscar-winning director, about whom you wrote a recent book, strongly disagree with that statement?

—Keith Nelson, Arlington, Virginia

A. Scorsese might revise it: "The four great world cinemas are American, French, Japanese, and Italian." And Scorsese might be right.

John Carter Movies

Q. I agree with your reader Todd A. Kennard, who questioned making Edgar Rice Burroughs's John Carter novels into PG-13 movies. As I'm sure you know, those novels were originally written for adult readers. The last I heard, *Princess of Mars* was going to be made by Disney. Their treatment of Tarzan may have been OK in the same sense that most of the previous Tarzan movies were. However, I believe that given treatment like Disney's *20,000 Leagues Under the Sea* or Lucas's *Star Wars*, Burroughs's novels would be financially and critically successful.

—Tom Muelleman, West Chicago, Illinois

A. In an attempt to maximize opening weekends pitched at the teenage audience base, many "naturally" R-rated movies, even horror films, are being scaled back to PG-13. This movie would possibly not be made if it had to be an R. That said, it could be the launch of a colorful new franchise like *Indiana Jones*. The director is Pixar's Andrew Stanton, who is temporarily leaving animation for live action. He directed *Finding Nemo* and *WALL-E*, and those good films were not handicapped by their ratings.

John Wayne

Q. Regarding your memories of John Wayne in Durango. Did the Duke, the icon of macho America, really play 1. P-Q4 as White? He preferred the closed, positional game to the more enterprising, aggressive style of 1. P-K4? Say it ain't so!

—Eric Isaacson, Bloomington, Indiana

A. That'll be the day. Hey, I play Queen's Gambit, too. Me, Capablanca, and Alekhine. Us guys.

Julie and Julia

Q. I was taken by your comment about the male roles in *Julie and Julia*. You wrote, "Both husbands are, frankly, a little boring: They've been assigned their supporting roles in their marriages and are reluctant to question the single-mindedness of their wives." I disagree only to the degree that Stanley Tucci is such a wonderful actor that he can take the underwritten role of Paul Child and imbue it with a lifetime of experience and character.

What struck me about your comment is that it made me reflect on how often women moviegoers must have the exact same experience. The women in *Julie and Julia*—even Julie's friend, even Simone Beck and Louisette Bertholle—are fairly well-rounded, while the men remain flat. In hundreds of movies released each year, the male characters feature prominently, while the women are little more than sidekicks. Even in films in which the female characters play a larger supporting role, they are often little more than clever cipher or aggressive cipher or sexy cipher. And if you're the second female character, good luck getting that much. Obviously, the solution is to "smarten up" the writing for women, rather than dumb down the writing for men, and this observation doesn't excuse the weak characterization in *Julie and Julia*. It's just an observation.

—John Bliss, Chicago, Illinois

A. This started becoming true after World War II, when women were returned to supporting roles on the screen and in life. Unless it's a biopic "relationship picture," the women will rarely be given more importance than the men. In action movies the women are treated as more equal in this sense: They're made honorary men, born with the ability to handle automatic weapons and engage in hand-to-hand combat.

Q. My wife and I went to (and loved) *Julie and Julia*. The audience was audibly shocked by the number of scenes (I counted fifteen!) in which a boom microphone appeared. To be honest, I've never noticed such apparent sloppiness in a big-budget film. It wasn't just our print; I've found many references to this on the Internet (Google "*Julie and Julia* boom mic"). This seems easily fixed postproduction by just cropping the frame, so why wasn't this done?

—Dr. Eric Kujawsky, music director,
Redwood Symphony, Redwood City, California

A. Nine times out of ten, when you see a boom mike, the reason is an improperly framed picture in the projector of your theater. If it happens several times, the odds go up to 100 percent. If you complain to management, they'll explain, "It was made that way."

Q. You ended your movie review of *Julie and Julia* by mentioning that you are writing a cookbook for the rice cooker. I am very curious to know whether this is true or a joke. (If a joke, I'm sorry to be so dense.) If it is true, I am incredibly interested. My husband and I received not one but two rice cookers as anniversary presents that we were unable to exchange or return, and I have no immediate need for even one. I love to cook, and I'd love to be able to use it for something else. Would you mind letting me know? If this is a real project, I'd also like to know how/when to obtain a copy.

—Lynn Frassetti

A. Very true indeed. *The Pot and How to Use It* was published in fall 2010 by Andrews McMeel Publishing. In a pinch, a rice cooker is almost the only cooking implement you need, for every meal all day long, starting with flawless oatmeal for breakfast, cooked with fruits. Oatmeal with bananas and peaches! Yes!

The Last Airbender

Q. Regarding the M. Night Shyamalan vehicle *The Last Airbender*—what do you think about the whitewashing of the production so that all of the original Asian cultural landmarks, architecture, philosophy, and costume design are being retained while they cast white kids to play the main characters?

—Arlene C. Harris

A. Wrong. The original series *Avatar: The Last Airbender* was highly regarded and popular for three seasons on Nickelodeon, and its fans take it for granted that its heroes are Asian. Why would Paramount and Shyamalan go out of their way to offend these fans? There are a lot of capable young actors with Asian ethnicity.

Lee Marvin

Q. I have recently been rediscovering Lee Marvin. Coming across your review of *Point*

Blank, I found you awarded it three stars and seemed not too impressed. I, frankly, was rather floored, by Marvin and by John Boorman's direction. What a striking crime film! Your review of *Point Blank* was written around 1967. Have you seen it recently enough for your opinion of it to have changed?

—Thom Rhodes

A. Yes, I have, and yes, it has. Marvin was a great original.

The Lovely Bones

Q. In your review of *The Lovely Bones* you make some strange assertions. I think what you are describing is actually some kind of nirvana-like state. I would not fault you except that you use the word *heaven,* which is by and large a concept that belongs to Christianity (though this is doubtless because Christianity is so deeply tied to the development of the English language). I cannot help but point out that in that idea of heaven, while it is true that the blessed are outside of time and space, this does not mean that they lack sensations or intellect, nor that they simply *are.* Perhaps it would be more appropriate to say that, according to this schema, the state of blessed can only be grasped by the living in the final stages of contemplative prayer, and even then it cannot be perfectly expressed with language or imagery, which is perhaps what makes the film somewhat unsatisfactory. I would also point out that, while you may have some theologians on your side (perhaps of the Paul Tillich school), I again think that referring to the thoughts that such thinkers might have had concerning the hereafter as corresponding to the idea of *heaven* is a little misleading.

—Kevin Corbett, Perrysburg, Ohio

A. I'll let the professionals off the hook and take full responsibility for the theology in that review. It alarms me that one might remain with sensations and intellect *forever.* Forever. Without end. That, for me, would be a better definition of hell. I would prefer nirvana. Of course, I don't get to choose.

Low-Budget Indies?

Q. I gobbled up your "Now on DVD" review of *Matinee* today, having seen the movie

when it came out in 1993. It brought back fond memories of Mants (as if there are any other kind of Mant-related memories). But afterward, I got sentimental. Is there still room for a guy "with a few bucks and a big imagination" to make a movie nowadays? Has your opinion changed since 1993?

—Geoff Hayward, Wakefield, Rhode Island

A. Ah, yes. Mants: men-ant mutants. They were featured in the horror film that hustling producer John Goodman was self-distributing in that very funny comedy. Can something like that happen now? An indie director with a few bucks and an imagination can still sometimes hit the jackpot, as in *Blair Witch* or *Paranormal Activity.* But a genuine sci-fi monster movie like *Mant* wouldn't be low-budget anymore, because the major studios have grabbed that market; their summer releases are often essentially circa-1965 American-International exploitation movies with big stars and $200 million budgets.

Malls R Us

Q. Regarding your review of *Malls R Us:* Though I can understand how some may criticize malls as the bane of consumerism, there is a reason why people love them, too. I love going to them not for the shopping, but for the climate. In Asia and especially the Middle East, people can't wait to get to the malls just to be comfortable and do something. You just won't see a lot of Westerners going for outdoor sports or taking leisurely strolls in temperatures ranging from the mid-30s to upper 40s (Celsius) or 95 to 118 (Fahrenheit).

—Michael Mirasol, Manila, Philippines

A. The film has a love-hate relationship with malls, as do a lot of us.

The Men Who Stare at Goats

Q. *The Men Who Stare at Goats* was the worst movie we have seen since *Hangover.* Has Ebert lost his mind by giving it a good review?

—Stuart Berson, Mahwah, New Jersey

A: Oh, come on. It wasn't anywhere near as bad as *Francis the Talking Mule.* In the version I saw, the man doesn't speak with goats but only sits there and stares at them.

Q. In *The Men Who Stare at Goats*, my friend says they used special effects to make the ghosts keel over, but I say they used those special Fainting Goats.

—R. Z. Barzell, Los Angeles, California

A. Fainting Goats are a protected species. They only employed them to train the regular goats.

Metropolis

Q. I just learned that Fritz Lang's *Metropolis* (1927) with the newly rediscovered scenes added already has been shown in Buenos Aires. Now, to sit and wait until it gets to San Diego, I guess (I doubt it will ever play in any towns in Mexico, other than Mexico City).

—Joel Meza, film critic, Mexicali, Baja California, Mexico

A. I think those long-lost scenes were found in the first place in Buenos Aires, so that's appropriate. The longest version seen in the United States has been 123 minutes. The restored version is 210 minutes long! *Metropolis* is already number 87 in the IMDb top films voting. Now the sky's the limit.

MILF

Q. In your review of *Gentleman Broncos* you state, "Hard as it is to believe, 'MILF' was not used until Stifler's mom appeared on the scene." As a college student in the early '90s I can assure you that the term *MILF* was in wide use among young men my age. *American Pie* only let the cat out of the bag. Although I will say that to this day she played the iconic MILF.

—Rich Bennett, Baltimore, Maryland

A. Still unresolved: the origin of ROFL.

Mississippi Burning

Q. You picked *Mississippi Burning* as your top film in 1988. What do you think about the movie in retrospect? Does it still hold up? It drew quite a bit of criticism at the time from some civil rights movement veterans as well as journalists. It may fascinate you to know that the movie played a role in the reopening of the real case, ending in the 2005 conviction of Edgar Ray Killen. Is this a movie we should show high school and college students?

—Jerry Mitchell

A. It was said, accurately, that the movie made the FBI look more proactive in civil rights investigations at that time than it really was under J. Edgar Hoover, whose enthusiasm for civil rights was limited. True. But the film itself remains a powerful *story*, a parable if you want. Its facts may not be accurate but its feelings are powerful and sound. And Gene Hackman and Frances McDormand have a scene together that is one of the best in either of their careers.

Moon

Q. SPOILER WARNING: In the case of the movie *Moon*, starring Sam Rockwell, I have a thought about the plot: When Sam 1 (the first one we meet, and who we assume is human or the original human) manages to make a phone call directly to his home number, he discovers that fifteen years have elapsed, not merely three. However, what I notice and am pretty sure about is that the father in that home, who speaks in the background to ask his daughter who's calling, is voiced by Sam Rockwell. I think Sam 1 as well as Sam 2, 3, 4, and so on are *all* clones. I think the point might be that the original Sam spent his three years in space, during which time clones were made of him (whether he was unwittingly part of that or not I have no idea).

It is the clones who have been operating the business for the past twelve years. When Sam 2, at the very end, makes it back to Earth and is reported to have announced himself to Congress as a clone, nobody believes him! But I think that is the point. I'm basing this on the sound of the father's voice, but I like the way it wraps up the plot. It explains, also, some of my confusion about what happens to Sam 1 and Sam 2 on the ship. In fact, every clone might be rigged to have an accident and die in the lunar module, for all we know.

—Beth Solomon

A. Given the premise of the clones, your theory seems to solve some of the film's apparent contradictions.

Movie Choices

Q. Where are all the summer movies? We have about thirty screens locally, and the only thing new that's opening this Friday is *Bruno*.

—Teresa Ash, Rock Island, Illinois

725

A. Many American moviegoers never get a chance to sample the range of new movies because the multiplexes are mass-booked with a handful of the same pictures.

Movie Franchises

Q. As an eighteen-year-old I have watched countless comic book adaptations: from *Superman* to *Spider-Man*. These movies are franchises. Their plots are constructed in ways to keep me busy for two hours. For example, In *The Dark Knight* nothing horrendous happens to the Joker or Batman; they both live. To me this is not for the sake of the story, but just to keep the characters alive for the next film in two or three years. These are not films; they are just ways to escape reality for a few hours. Similar to McDonald's in which you're eating some sort of food, here you are watching some sort of movie; but if quality is in mind, both these movies and fast food pale in the eye of the keen observer.

—Bobby Hamidifard

A. *The Dark Knight* was a good film. So were *Spider-Man 2* and *Iron Man*. Yes, they're franchises, but the original comic books were franchises. Batman, Superman, Spider-Man, and the rest have been through hundreds or thousands of stories and they *haven't died*. They must be exhausted by now. Well, not Superman.

Even in his case, it's astonishing that a substance from outer space, Kryptonite, has arrived on Earth in sufficient quantities that after some seventy years of comic books his enemies are still able to find some when they need it. Why doesn't he just hurl it into orbit beyond Jupiter? Oh, wait: He can't touch it.

Movie Posters

Q. Would you agree that movie posters of yesteryear are a lost art form? When I was a young boy growing up in the '70s, I always admired (and coveted) the never-ending amount of promotional movie memorabilia that studios happily provided movie theaters with to decorate their lobby walls. I'm speaking fondly of 8 x 10 glossy black-and-white stills, colored lobby cards, inserts, and, of course, the folded one-sheet posters, that, to me, were nothing less than absolute works of art. Posters for films such as *The Poseidon Adventure*, *Jaws*, *The Sting*, *Star Wars*, and *Apocalypse Now* (which were actually reproduced from paintings) were so striking, so vibrant, so exciting in their composition that today's movie posters literally pale in comparison.

Studios now issue multiple "teaser" one-sheets, featuring enormous glamour-style head shots of various cast members, eventually leading up to the one-sheet that is meant to advertise the film. Of course, today's movie theater lobbies more resemble airports, and beside the bland advertising material, we're now treated to enormous twenty-foot cardboard stand-ups advertising either the latest Disney/DreamWorks/Pixar animated feature or Julia Roberts's new romantic comedy. And though Steven Soderbergh's 2006 film *The Good German*'s one-sheet was still technically a composite of photos, I was deeply impressed by its obvious nod to *Casablanca*'s original poster. Now that's art!

—Kevin Fellman, Phoenix, Arizona

A. I couldn't agree with you more. I'd guess maybe a third of recent movie posters involve the male lead in the foreground looking out of the poster, with the female lead in the background looking at him. Or the two equal leads looking at each other. Photographic head shots. No imagination, no artistry, no reason to collect.

Movie Projectors

Q. I read in one of your articles about the fact that movies are filmed with certain projector-light requirements in order to correctly show the movie. You also suggested that some movie theaters might show the movies at a reduced lighting setting to save money on their electric bill. I suspect my local theater is doing this on a regular basis. Some movies are so dark, you can barely tell what's going on. My question is how can you know (a) what the setting is; and (b) what setting is being projected? Is a light meter relevant to this matter?

—Jim "Catfish" Chapman

A. Of course there can be dark scenes. If the whole movie looks noticeably dim, it's probably not being projected at the correct level. As the AM has tirelessly explained: Some theater owners believe that if they turn down the power of the expensive projector bulb, the bulb's life span will be lengthened. This is not true. Steve Kraus of Chicago's Lake Street Screening Room tells me: "A technician with a light meter can read the reflected brightness of the screen with the projector running without film. It should be sixteen foot-lamberts." Ask your theater if they've checked lately.

Q. I recently went and saw *The Wizard of Oz* projected at the AMC Mazza Gallerie, in Chevy Chase, Maryland. They began to show it in a 1.85:1 stretched widescreen format. I complained, and they reluctantly switched the film back to its proper academy ratio. Apparently a regional manager told them to zoom the film because "it looked small . . . like it was on TV." You would think someone in management in a theater chain would know better. So after fighting for years to get widescreen films shown in letterbox on TV, do we now have to worry about seeing *Gone with the Wind* or *Casablanca* incorrectly shown in widescreen for fear people will complain about the black bars on the side of the screen (or have a projectionist who doesn't know better)?

—Jeff Swearingen, Arlington, Virginia

A. If that is true, then the manager should not be employed in the movie business. Such ignorance is discouraging. All titles should be projected in the aspect ratio they were filmed in. How did this man become an adult and not learn that virtually *all* movies filmed before 1952, and a great many of them afterward, were filmed in the "academy ratio," which is 4:3, or four parts wide for every three parts high? When widescreen first came in, the legendary German director Fritz Lang said, "It is only good for filming snakes."

My Sister's Keeper

Q. In your review of *My Sister's Keeper*, you make this assertion: "If you're pro-life, you would require Anna to donate her kidney, although there is a chance she could die, and her sister doesn't have a good prognosis. If you're pro-choice, you would support Anna's lawsuit." I am pro-life and you are wrong. Being pro-life means you do not destroy one life (Anna) for the convenience or comfort of another (Kate). It is the *pro-choice* position

that results in a life sacrificed, often horribly, for the convenience and comfort of another.

—Kris French, Orlando, Florida

A. I may have been using faulty logic. Does the principle that she must act to save another life apply equally in both cases?

NASCAR

Q. If NASCAR put a small parachute in the front end where the nameplate is, and when the car hit a negative G force, it opened, slowing the car down, therefore stopping the rear-end-over-end flip, would that work?

—William King

A. Yes, if the driver is played by Justin Timberlake. No, if it is Amy Winehouse.

New Best Picture Nomination Rules

Q. Are you personally "buying" the AMPAS's supposed reasoning behind their new rule in now nominating ten films for Best Picture? Why don't they just admit that they couldn't handle all of last year's negative criticism from the media over *The Dark Knight* failing to get a Best Picture nomination? Just because it didn't make the final five doesn't necessarily mean it wasn't nominated. Perhaps it was number six in the nomination process, yet failed to make the cut by a mere one or two votes (and since the Academy will never release their voting results only they will know for sure). And what's the Academy going to do next year when the media start slamming them for failing to nominate film number eleven?

—Kevin Fellman, Phoenix, Arizona

A. Whatever the Academy's reasoning, the change strikes me as absurd. Ten nominees is guaranteed to produce an unwieldy and bloated Oscar ceremony. I think there's a fair chance that the vote totals will tail off fairly rapidly, so the final ten will include all the films most people could reasonably expect to be nominated. So we'll never know if *Avatar* didn't make the top five.

Night Stalks the Mansion

Q. One of my favorite haunted house stories, *Night Stalks the Mansion*, was supposed to be made into a movie and released to the public in fall of 2009. There's a Web site for the movie and I have sent e-mails to the producer and the production company and have received no replies. Is this movie going to be released?

—Steve Wheeler, Wyoming, Michigan

A. The original book has many fans, and the Web site is atmospheric, but as a general rule if a movie has no listing in IMDb, there are no production plans. In fact, this is the first title I've ever encountered with a Web site but no IMDb listing.

Old Dogs

Q. In general I don't like activities done with irony, because it drips of hipsterness. I listen to the music I listen to because I like it—same with TV and film. I made an exception recently when I was compelled to go see *Old Dogs*. Is it as bad as I've heard? It seems hysterically bad, so I just had to see it. I have to say it was worth making the exception. The movie's physics alone are worth the price of admission (at a discount theater, mind you). Do you ever enjoy a film on that level, the so-bad-it's-good level?

—Jim Bruce

A. "Stupefyingly dimwitted" was one of the descriptions I used in my review. Its physics? Are you referring to the strap-on rocket mount that drops Robin Williams in that pond in a shot repeated from four different angles? I believe in the concept of "so bad it's good," but *Old Dogs* was so bad it fell below that, to "so bad it's bad."

Q. Regarding Jim Bruce's contention to the Answer Man that *Old Dogs* is "so bad it's good": I have not seen it, but I suggest applying these rules:

Rule 1: The only way that bad can be good is that it has to literally be "laughably" bad. It must make you laugh *at* it, not with it.

Rule 2: Comedies cannot be so bad they are good, because of Rule 1. If you laugh, it works. If its lack of comedy becomes funny, you are working at a rarefied level of irony that few can attain.

Rule 3: A movie cannot strive to be so bad it's good. It has to be unwitting.

Rule 4: Lazy movies are never so bad they are good. The ineptitude has to be coupled with earnestness and a true (albeit misguided) belief in the material. "Phoning in" a movie is never funny; it's an insult to the audience.

Rule 5: The badness can exist side by side with an empathy or affection for the artist. (I feel for Ed Wood.)

It sounds like Jim's reaction is more of the "shocked that a movie could be so bad" category, which does not make it good, but instead makes one question the ability of mankind to work together to create something so horrible.

—Mike Spearns, St. John's, Newfoundland, Canada

A. Thanks for the handy guidelines. I will henceforward exercise strictest control over my use of the phrase "so bad it's good."

Paranormal Activity

Q. Have you been following the enormous buzz over director Oren Peli's independent horror film *Paranormal Activity*? The film, rumored to have cost a mere $11,000 and shot in the director's own home over a period of one week, is being hailed by many reputable critics as perhaps the most frightening film since *The Exorcist*. Shot in *Blair Witch*–camera style, the film features an unmarried couple who attempt to videotape the allegedly paranormal entity that is haunting their bedroom. It first premiered at the 2008 Slamdance Film festival, where the word of mouth spread like wildfire. Just days ago it had a showing (in the pouring rain) at the Abel Gance Open Air Cinema at Telluride. The great news is that after DreamWorks allegedly passed on the distribution rights, Paramount has now stepped in and agreed to market it. Just curious if you were aware of all the hype, if you planned on commenting on it at some point, and if you've spoken with any of your colleagues who may have been lucky enough to have actually seen the film.

—Kevin Fellman, Phoenix, Arizona

A. So far, no distributor. Those critics who've seen it praise it. It had one press screening in Chicago, at midnight for Fantastic Fest, and I took a pass. Presumably if it gets distribution I'll have a chance to see it. Its user rating in IMDb is a phenomenal 8.7, but pre-release you can never be sure what that means.

Q. I read that *Paranormal Activity*, which reportedly cost between $11,000 and $18,000 to make, blew out the opposition pictures with multimillion-dollar budgets. Some of my friends have liked it, but I'm wondering. . . .
—Greg Nelson, Chicago, Illinois

A. The movie proves once again that horror is the only genre that transcends budgets and the star system. The horror itself is the star, and if you're scared, you don't ask what the budget was. But its box-office performance inspired me to ask its producer, Steven Schneider, about his philosophy. After all, he has a degree in philosophy from the University of London. Why, I asked, did Paramount make its decision to bet real money on his little sleeper? He told me:

"Credit for Paramount's decision to release the movie goes to a number of individuals who saw it for what it was and believed in what it could be. From the acumen of producer Jason Blum to the vision of Paramount topper Adam Goodman and his VP Ashley Brucks, to the salesmanship of IM Global's Stuart Ford and the deal making of Linda Lichter and CAA agents Martin Spencer and Brian Kavanaugh-Jones. And of course the incredible marketing team at Paramount, headed by Josh Greenstein and Megan Colligan, and others such as Amy Powell and Amy Mastriona. Not the typical true Hollywood story, but because Oren Peli made such an incredible little movie, everyone rallied around it and . . . here we are!"

Note to Steven: You might want to shorten that list a little for your Oscar acceptance speech.

Payoffs

Q. You might get this question all the time but I was thinking about this as I was driving home last night. It occurred to me that you have considerable "pull" in the film industry and I'm guessing that a positive review from you might add millions of dollars to a movie's gross. I'm sure this isn't lost on movie executives, and I was just wondering if anyone's ever approached you with any kind of cash offer or a payoff for giving their crappy film a good review?
—Minder Singh, New Brunswick, New Jersey

A. They're lining up for appointments. I only see the indie directors with their little Sundance films. They pay the big bucks.

Pink Floyd: The Wall

Q. I've read enough of your writing to gather that you admire, or did admire at one time, the film *Pink Floyd: The Wall*. This is one of my all-time favorite films, and you are my all-time favorite film writer. I've read enough of your reviews and commentary to pick up on multiple references to this film, always positive, but have never read your actual full-length review of the film. I assume there must be one. Maybe there isn't. I can't find it on IMDb or your own Web site.
—Paul Apel

A. I did and do love it. I have no idea why I didn't review it at the time. It has been chosen for opening night of Ebertfest 2010, and between now and then I plan to write a Great Movie piece about it.

Pirate Radio

Q. Your review of *Pirate Radio* stated that Radio Caroline didn't play the Beatles. Wrong. From mid-'63 to '64 I was stationed at a tiny U.S. Navy base on the southeastern coast of Spain at a town called Cartagena. From midnight to 4 or 5 a.m. we were able to get Radio Caroline and we heard all the British bands, definitely including the Beatles; in fact, we may have heard them there before folks back in the United States did. It was great. I don't remember being aware of any high jinks on the air or anything special about the DJs; as I recall it was pretty much wall-to-wall music. And to quote Kristofferson, "Buddy, that was good enough for me!" Caroline helped us pass many a miserable hour on midnight-to-4-a.m. watch. Bless 'em.
—Rich Coleman, Potomac, Maryland

A. I worded that badly. The review incorporates a running commentary on Caroline's streaming audio over iTunes, and while I was listening it didn't play any Beatles.

729

Pirate Sites

Q. Pirate sites give me better access to the history of cinema than I'd get if I lived in NYC or Paris and went to art houses all the time. Some pirate sites even sponsor custom subtitles for movies they feel are important. Corporate moviemaking is pretty narrow and dull now, but there's a lot of stuff going on in the edges.

I know it's stealing, and I'm not proud of it. But a lot of the best stuff isn't available any other way; the market isn't big enough for someone to package and sell a DVD. And the pirate sites tend to have boards where people talk about movies and put you on to titles you might not see otherwise. I think these sites are where people who love cinema hang out now. Do you think that on balance piracy is a good or bad thing for the movies?

—Name Withheld

A. If it involves films available to you through legal means, it is theft. If the makers of a film have departed this life, or will not make it available in a legal format, I choose not to cast the first stone.

Pixelvision

Q. If I am not mistaken, when I was a kid, I saw a movie you made with a Fisher-Price Pixelvision camera. I believe you screened it on your show. My parents would not buy me one of those cameras, so I spent the next ten years of my life trying to find one (more complicated in those days before eBay). I am happy to say that today I still have a working Pixelvision camera I picked up in high school for twenty dollars and have recently earned an MFA in film production. You made a difference in my life! I would really like to see the movie you made again. I remember almost nothing about it except a shot of your lips filling the screen. Do you still have that movie? Is it available online anywhere? Have you made any others?

—David R. Witzling

A. Damn! You're remembering *Siskel's* movie! He used that gimmick from the Conan O'Brien show where you saw lips moving in a photograph, and filmed his own lips behind a photo of me. Of my own Pixelvision film, I will say only that it ended with a

close-up of a license plate saying *ROZEBUD*. We were having a contest for one of our holiday gift guides, which may still be online somewhere.

Porn Movie Titles

Q. Are porno filmmakers breaking the law when they "borrow" their titles from legitimate, mainstream productions and produce such works as *Breast Side Story*; *Chitty, Chitty, Gang Bang*; *The Sexorcist*; *On Golden Blonde*; *Load Warrior*; and *Saturday Night Beaver*? Steven Spielberg allegedly made no secret of his disapproval over *Shaving Ryan's Privates*, but where is the legal line drawn? Obviously, no one is going to confuse these XXX films with their original inspirations, so why can't everyone just laugh? Alan Ball, the Oscar-winning screenwriter of *American Beauty*, once admitted that he was honored when he discovered *American Booty*. In fact, he appreciated the gag so much that he bought a bunch to give out as gifts. No word yet on what David Fincher thought of *The Curious Case of Benjamin's Butt*.

—Kevin Fellman, Phoenix, Arizona

A. I've requested a ruling from the Motion Picture Academy of Farts and Appliances.

Postapocalyptic Films

Q. Can you think of any postapocalyptic film where a better America arises from the rubble? True, that war, virus, flood, earthquake, or asteroid was a very bad thing, but these films are typically set decades afterward. Why can screenwriters only imagine Americans behaving badly? Bad teeth, I can understand, in a postdental world.

—Bill Stamets, Chicago, Illinois

A. Surely there must be. Memory fails me. Readers may help. I checked the Wikipedia entry on apocalyptic fiction, and all I can say is, it was depressing: http://twitpic.com/ylcfd.

Q. Regarding the reader who asked if there was ever a positive movie about postapocalyptic America, the people seemed to behave fairly decently toward one another in *Testament*. I am pretty certain that there are others along these lines but none are coming to mind. I'd have said *The Bed Sitting Room* but that was England.

—Peter Sobcynski, Chicago, Illinois

A. *Testament* remains one of the best American independent films. It blew me away at Telluride. America after the Bomb.

Q. Bill Stamets asked if there were any postapocalyptic films that showed America as a better place. The *Star Trek* universe is set after the worldwide Eugenics Wars, which is what caused Khan (Ricardo Montalban) to flee Earth in the original series episode "Space Seed." That episode was the genesis for what became *Star Trek II: The Wrath of Khan.* The character of Commander Riker (Jonathan Frakes) also alluded to the wars in the film *Star Trek: First Contact.* The scenes on Earth are all set in the postwar years but before the human renaissance that gave birth to the Federation. The *Star Trek* series is not marketed as a postapocalyptic series per se, but it is a hopeful future after a devastating world war.

—Harry Thomas, *San Antonio Express-News*

A. Given the Black Plague, I guess we're living in a postapocalyptic world now.

Public Enemies

Q. I recently saw Michael Mann's new movie *Public Enemies,* and I was disappointed by the fact that I could barely watch the movie without feeling that my eyes were playing tricks on me. In only a handful of shots did my eye actually relax and drink in the beautiful cinematography. The rest of the time the picture looked dark and blurry, but if you asked me to pinpoint an exact spot on the screen that was one of the above, I couldn't do it. My eye just couldn't focus on a single object in the frame without being distracted by the entire shot's resolution. I'm asking if you have any ideas on this. I understand it might just be due to my local theater and a shoddy projectionist, or perhaps my contact lenses, but I think it might be more. Mann shot this in a digital format, right? And I know he intended to use the shaky cam, which disoriented me even further, but even in static shots, I had a tendency to itch my eyes just by looking at the picture.

—Kyle Warnke, West Palm Beach, Florida

A. Mann is a perfectionist. My guess is it involved problems at your theater. The film was shot in HD digital, so everyone saw the "same" print.

Q. In *Public Enemies,* in the scene showing the escape from the prison in Indiana, it is a little strange that the soldiers guarding the prison were wearing the shoulder insignia of the Thirty-third Infantry Division of the Illinois National Guard.

—Frank Fabbri

A. General Blagojevich was in the mood for an invasion.

Q. Regarding your review of *Public Enemies,* I would quarrel with you regarding the movie not having closure. I have been a fan of Jay Robert Nash for thirty-five years. I still have a hardbound copy of *Bloodletters and Badmen,* purchased in 1974, and I still use it as a reference. However, in that book and the later *Dillinger Dossier,* he puts forth the theory that the man shot at the Biograph Theater was not Dillinger. The theory has been discredited by historians and forensic pathologists. I would like to know if he has changed his mind or if he still adheres to his theory.

—Martin Gaspar

A. Nash sticks to his theory. He even claims the most famous Dillinger exhibit in the FBI's museum could not have belonged to Dillinger.

Race in Casting

Q. A friend and I got in a discussion over whether it is racist to have race be a criterion while casting a role. My friend was of the opinion that the best actor should get the role. I felt that if the part was written for, say, a young African-American male, the audition pool should be limited to young African-American males. This discussion specifically focused on the movie *The Last Airbender,* which is based on an American-made animated show called *Avatar: The Last Airbender.*

Two of the characters in the show were not white, yet their movie counterparts will be white. I felt that the movie-casting choice was not true to the source material while my friend thought the casting choice (from a racial perspective) was irrelevant. Is casting white actors into nonwhite roles a form of racism/whitewashing? Would the opposite also be racist? Or should the best actor, regardless of race or any other physical consideration, be chosen?

—Colleen Stone, Woodbury, Minnesota

A. It was racist in the days when minority actors just plain couldn't get work in anything but stereotyped roles. The situation has improved. If I'd been making *The Last Airbender*, I would probably have decided the story was so well known to my core audience that it would be a distraction to cast those roles with white actors. I'm guessing, but I suspect the American group most underrepresented in modern Hollywood is young Asian-American males.

Rambo IV

Q. Is *Rambo IV* mistakenly titled? This might be nitpicking, but first movie was *First Blood* and the second was *Rambo: First Blood Part II*. Technically, this is *Rambo III: First Blood Part IV*, right?

—Steve Forstneger, Chicago, Illinois

A. Yeah, and it's titled simply *Rambo*, which makes it sound like the first in the series. *Rambo V* is said to be in production for a 2011 release. Me, I'm still arguing that *The Other Side of the Mountain, Part 2* should have been titled *This Side of the Mountain*.

Reel Bad Arabs

Q. I was wondering if you have viewed Jack Shaheen's documentary *Reel Bad Arabs*, and how you feel about the overwhelmingly negative Arab and Muslim stereotypes in Hollywood films—such as *Rules of Engagement*, if you need a reference.

—Haney Noureldin, Gilberts, Illinois

A. Arabs seem to have become the Nazis du jour in certain filmmaking circles, and that is particularly unfortunate because most are peaceful people who want only to get on with their lives as we all do. By demonizing a group on the basis of a few members, we are pushing them away with the same kind of prejudice that is such a regrettable part of the American tradition. It is time for good people to meet in the middle.

Review Writing

Q. I'm a writer for an online movie Web site. Over the past couple of years, I've heard folks talk about "print vs. online" with the former as a dying model. While I believe this is true from a business perspective, I've also heard it used in regards to the legitimacy of the writers. I recently participated in a panel where I had to keep grimacing every time the "legitimacy of print" was mentioned, because I feel that talented writing isn't beholden to the medium. I am just curious as to your thoughts.

—Matt Goldberg, managing editor, Collider.com

A. In the mind of the reader, a review either usefully discusses a movie or it does not. That's true no matter where it appears.

Q. For two years now I have managed an eight-screen movie theater. For about six months I have been writing movie reviews for our local paper. My question is: How do we not become repetitive after seeing so many common themes repeated ad nauseam at the cineplex? Today with so many movies being derivative of prior material, sequels, remakes, and reboots, how do we express to our readers the wonder of really finding something new?

It's obvious to anyone who has seen more than a dozen movies that the romantic comedic female lead is not going to marry the guy she is engaged to at the beginning of the film. She is going to wind up with the awkward but charming stranger she can't stand to be around at first. We know the girl in the sex scene is going to get murdered first. They're going to manage to kill the shark. How do we write as to keep our material from being as derivative and repetitive as the movies?

—Aaron Lane Morris, Glasgow, Kentucky

A. The hard part is expressing "the wonder of finding something really new." Many moviegoers actually want to see movies that are already familiar. That's why genres are popular. If a critic informs them of a "masterpiece," their first reaction is, "That doesn't sound like anything I'd like to see." Your challenge is to evoke for them the experience you had.

As for the deadly predictability of some movies: In a way, that's why I started the Little Movie Glossary—to have fun with clichés, archetypes, stereotypes, and automatic plotting. But remember your readers haven't seen everything you have. The new *Karate Kid* faithfully follows the original plot, but that doesn't mean it isn't entertaining.

Robin Hood

Q. Just saw *Robin Hood*. Sat through the whole movie thinking, "Which century are we in?" and not really getting involved in the movie. In the introductory plot setup it was written that the action in the movie was taking place "at the turn of the twelfth century." However, the place/time setting on a scene a few minutes later indicated the action was taking place in "1199." Isn't 1199 the turn of the thirteenth century? My trying to justify this possible error, due to my advanced age, took me the rest of the movie, and indeed to this very moment (and perhaps beyond), to worry about—is it me or them having a memory/reasoning lapse? It's not nice to do this to old people.

—Pdgmobil2

A. It's them. Hollywood sometimes has problems counting centuries. Give a moment's thought to Twentieth Century–Fox.

Q. I couldn't agree more with your assessment of *Robin Hood*, except I refuse to see the new remake on principle. My "Robin Hood" is Errol Flynn and his costume has green sparkles. Why mess with perfection? What will be next? A remake of *Gone with the Wind* or *The Wizard of Oz*? Oh, the horror.

—Stefanie Rehbein

A. Political correctness might make a modern remake of *Gone with the Wind* impossible. I can imagine Prissy saying, "Lawzy, we don't need a doctor. I'm a skilled obstetrician."

Q. I'm so glad you reviewed *Robin Hood* as a "loss of innocence." I couldn't agree with you more. I would much rather see people laugh, love, and be absurd in movies, rather than hate, fight, and disembowel. I'm so glad you felt this way, because most of what Russell Crowe does falls into the latter. Modern guys feel they have to have a certain level of intensity about them or else they are wimps, I guess. I for one am glad I retain something of the dreamer, the wanderer, and the lazy laugh of my childhood. I rarely go to the movies anymore because I don't want images of violence or gore impressed upon my subconscious, regardless of whether they are "real" or not.

—Stephen Sian, North Vancouver, British Columbia, Canada

A. Robin Hood always used to have fun in the movies. Now even his Merry Men are pissed off. Do you sometimes think Russell Crowe acts as if he has a hangover?

Roman Polanksi

Q. I want to voice my disappointment to find a review of Roman Polanski's latest film on your site. The director's artistic brilliance does not excuse the heinous crime of which he was convicted, nor his cowardly and unrepentant stance. I believe he should be ignored.

—Nadine Menard, Montreal, Quebec, Canada

A. A film is a film. It is good or bad. If I began making moral judgments of directors—or actors, or writers—where would it end?

Salo, or the 120 Days of Sodom

Q. I recently watched Pasolini's *Salo, or the 120 Days of Sodom*. I got tired of people telling me it was "the most disturbing movie ever made" and that I'd regret ever watching it and gouge my own eyes out to try and take away the memory, but I'm sorry to say that none of that happened. Simply put, I don't think it's *that* bad. Sure, some of it is pretty hardcore (the nails in cake scene springs to mind) but nothing to "mess you up" as my friend said it would. If you've seen it, what are your thoughts?

—Qasim Hussain, Staffordshire, United Kingdom

A. I've owned that movie since it came out on laser disc and still haven't viewed it, because time and time again I was told it was unbelievably revolting. Not "horror movie revolting" but *really* revolting. Your question leads me to realize the time is now. Or one of these days soon, for sure. . . .

The Searchers

Q. Good calls on *The Searchers*, but there's also this: It's the grave marker—her grandmother's— that Debbie is sent out to hide behind when the Comanches attack, where Scar finds her. It allows us to raise the question of Ethan being a man who hates Comanches because of what they are or because of what some of them did. The inscription on the marker itself is virtually invisible in the movie. It says, "Here lies Mary Jane Edwards. Killed by Commanches May 12, 1852. A good wife and mother in her 41st year." I obtained it through a computer screen capture—technology unavailable to anyone in a movie audience in 1956. I think the question of who was meant to see it is pretty obvious; it was there for Wayne to see.

—Steve Paradis, Davison, Michigan

A. Yes, although if the audience can't read it, does it serve a purpose? Your computer skills raise the question: What else is hidden onscreen waiting for us to discover?

See It/Rent It

Q. I love the new *At the Movies* with Michael Phillips and A. O. Scott (good riddance to you know who), but I must say that I still don't get the "See It/Rent It" distinction. Either a movie is worth seeing, or it's not, right? I mean, I think it does work on the show as a sort of "thumbs sideways" to deal with the two-and-a-half-star movies that can't quite be recommended but still have some value that deserves to be recognized.

What I really don't understand is why our standards are supposed to be lower for rentals rather than theatrical releases. When you go out to see a current release you have to make compromises. Maybe the movie you really wanted to see is sold out or just finished its run, so now you have to pick the second-best thing at that theater. Or you're with a large group that doesn't want to see a foreign film, so you have to settle on the most tolerable current blockbuster.

When you rent a movie, however, you have nearly the entirety of cinematic history at your disposal. That makes the competition for rentals much more fierce. Looking at *Time Out New York*, I see that there are fifty-one

movies out here right now. That's a lot, but compare that to the thousands of choices available on Netflix. Why would I rent a marginal film such as *New York, I Love You* when I still need to see *Killer of Sheep, Au Hasard Balthazar, Mishima,* and *The Grey Zone*?

—Rhys Southan, New York, New York

A. Amen. I've been against "rent it" from the first time I was exposed to the concept. It makes no sense. Either a film is good enough to see or not good enough to see. Here's my theory about the invention of this ersatz category: It's an attempt to pander to those who would rather die than rent a great film like, say, Hitchcock's *North by Northwest* rather than a rent it–style dim bulb like *Couples Retreat*. I think some editors—not mine—are terrified that readers might get the idea a critic is stuck up. If you'd rather rent *Couples Retreat* than the newly restored *North by Northwest, Bonnie and Clyde,* or *Cool Hand Luke*, that's what I am: stuck up and happy to be.

Sex and the City 2

Q. Is there the slightest possibility that *SATC2* is actually satirizing the shallow absurdity of its protagonists, but a large fraction of its audience has not realized that they are the target of its mockery? I suspect that the cast is also not in on the joke. If not, I may have to abandon my last shred of hope for the multiplex-going public.

—Carl Zetie, Waterford, Virginia

A. Whatever else it is, it's not a satire. I suspect some of its box-office appeal can be explained because it's like a social occasion: Women enjoy dressing up and wearing great shoes to attend it. A lot of that is a tribute to their fondness for the characters as they were seen on the original HBO series. The women of *SATC2* are apples who have fallen far, far from the tree.

Q. I respect Ebert's opinion most of the time on movies; everyone has one, so it's great. But when will the time come that he admits a generational change has occurred when it comes to cinema or even "art," for that matter? I understand that *Sex and the City 2* is going to be a terrible movie, but it's a show that many women love. Good for them that they get to pay twelve dollars to see a two-hour-long episode. It makes them happy. But to read him discussing the ratings on thrusting and saying he knows about taste makes me heartily laugh. I'm sure he does. In his old codgery way I'm sure he does know what taste means to him. I'm not going to be taking serious movie advice from my grandmother. God love her, she still thinks Obama's the antichrist. It's a generational thing. This guy is reviewing poppy, bubble-gum movies and acting surprised that they are terrible.

—David W., Edmond, Oklahoma

A. I wasn't complaining about thrusting and pumping. I was complaining about the hypocrisy of the MPAA ratings board. It has long been informally understood that graphic thrusting and pumping, so to speak, should be limited to two (2) thrusts and/or pumps per one (1) R-rated movie. Why wasn't that enforced here when it has been applied to many better films?

Now about my age: I was the youngest daily newspaper film critic in America, and now I may be the oldest. Live with it. Years of reviewing movies may possibly have been useful to me. There are countless movie critics your age, which I am guessing is between eight and eighteen. They will see things as people of your age do. You already know those things. Consider me a change of pace. And don't despair: As you grow older, you learn stuff. You really do.

Q. Would you please refer me to a review you have written where you refer to a man as a "sexaholic slut" because he has engaged in the same sexual behavior as Samantha's? No doubt you cannot refer me to any such review. I assume you get my point.

—Kathleen Dunham, Costa Mesa, California

A. Damn! I received this too late to describe the Michael Douglas character in *Solitary Man* as a "sexaholic slut." Of course, the dictionary says *slut* is a word referring to a woman, but I am willing to bend the rules. Amazingly, according to the global word search on my computer, *SATC2* is the first time I have ever used the word *sexaholic*.

Sherlock Holmes

Q. Heavens! I understand that Sherlock Holmes, in the new *Sherlock Holmes*, doesn't smoke his Sherlock Holmes pipe! The fact that he doesn't wear his deerstalker hat is one thing: I always thought it would make him too visible. But to not smoke his pipe? Surely a pipe smoker is deeply attached to his favorite pipe!

—Ron Barzell, Los Angeles, California

A. We may think of Holmes as smoking a Meerschaum Calabash, but that was associated with him largely because of the many Basil Rathbone films. The famous Sidney Paget illustrations appearing with the original Arthur Conan Doyle stories showed him with a much more conventional pipe.

Q. In response to your recent Q&A concerning Sherlock Holmes's iconic Meerschaum pipe: Although the great Basil Rathbone made great use of the prop, he certainly wasn't the man who made it the familiar image in the public mind. The Meerschaum pipe was first used by the well-known nineteenth-century American actor William Gillette, who made his fame and fortune playing Holmes on the stage. Gillette originally used a conventional pipe as shown in the Paget drawings, but found it awkward to deliver his lines with the small straight pipe. I imagine it rather waggled in the air like FDR's cigarette holder. Gillette switched to the curved pipe as it was easier to handle on stage. By Rathbone's time, it was a convention of the stage.

—Mark S. Chenail, Champaign, Illinois

A. I'm gathering the Holmes of Arthur Conan Doyle never used such a smoking implement. Sidney Paget's famous drawings make him look too sleek. The Meerschaum fits better with a certain shaggy quality, don't you think?

And here's another image challenged: Wikipedia reports: "Holmes is never actually described as wearing a deerstalker, although in *The Adventure of Silver Blaze*, the narrator of the bulk of the stories, Dr. John Watson, describes him at one point as wearing a similar-in-design ear-flapped travelling cap." The entry points out that Holmes in any event was too fashionable to wear such a hat in the city; it is properly worn only in rural settings.

Q. When you mentioned the twenty-two actors who have played Sherlock Holmes, you forgot to mention Ronald Howard, son of Leslie Howard, who played Sherlock Holmes in thirty-nine episodes of the 1954–55 British television series. He was one of the best Sherlock Holmeses ever.

—Ted Hazen, Carlisle, Pennsylvania

A. Make that twenty-three.

Shutter Island

Q. In *Shutter Island*, I noticed something odd. About midway through the movie, the Leo DiCaprio character is interviewing a female patient. His partner, Chuck, gives her a glass of water. At first she only pantomimes drinking the water, then in the next shot you see her putting down an empty glass. When at last she leaves the table, the glass is shown half full. I assume that Scorsese did this intentionally and that it isn't a blooper, but my movie/symbolism vocabulary is not such that I could interpret the meaning.

—Mike

A. It may mean that all perceived reality is deceptive. On the other hand, I think it's more likely it's a continuity error.

Q. Need help settling a debate: Is *Shutter Island* considered "noir"? My friend's boyfriend says it is not due to the lack of dim lighting and shadow techniques; I say it is because of its detective story and feel. Who is right? Why?

—Roberto Fuentes, Manchester, New Hampshire

A. You are right. There are some stylistic conventions that are often found in noir, and shadows are certainly one of them, but *Shutter Island* is filled with shadows and dark corners. More important, its hero has in common with most noir heroes a flaw in his past that returns to haunt him. A noir hero by definition, I think, cannot be entirely a good guy.

Q. When I saw that *Shutter Island*, Scorsese's follow-up to *The Departed*, was moved out of "awards season," I assumed it meant one thing: When the studio saw it, they knew it was crap and didn't want to put it forward

for Oscars. Now that it has opened and is apparently not crap, I have to wonder if this means that having ten Best Picture slots means that studios are no longer as worried about losing out on nominations for their films because they came out too early in the year, and will start scheduling good movies all year.

—Greg Packnett, Madison, Wisconsin

A. *Shutter Island* was set to open October 3, but Paramount moved it to February. The *Los Angeles Times* reported the studio thought its *Up in the Air* and *The Lovely Bones* were Oscar contenders, and in these hard times didn't want to spend too much on Oscar advertising.

Fair enough, although who in his right mind would have considered a stinker like *The Lovely Bones* an Oscar contender? Because the studio postponed the Scorsese picture, the tinfoil cap–wearing buzz blogs bleated that it had to be bad. Turned out they were wrong, didn't it?

Sid and Nancy

Q. I recently watched *Sid and Nancy* for the first time, and was amazed to find out afterward that Gary Oldman wasn't nominated for an Oscar for his balls-out portrayal of Sid Vicious. I feel that if a performance like that were given today it would be the talk of the award season. Do you think the Academy praises different kinds of performances today than they have in the past?

—Peter Kane, Bronx, New York

A. The nominees for that year were Paul Newman, who won for *The Color of Money*, Dexter Gordon for *'Round Midnight*, Bob Hoskins for *Mona Lisa*, William Hurt for *Children of a Lesser God*, and James Woods for *Salvador*. Was Oldman's performance on a level with theirs? I suspect they would all say it was.

However, it is suspected that the members of the Academy are sometimes reluctant to nominate a film that would be an awkward fit on the Oscarcast. Can you think of a scene from *Sid and Nancy* that would feel at home?

The Silence

Q. After watching the Criterion edition of Bergman's *The Silence*, I read your Great

Movies review and was puzzled by one sentence: "The doorway between their rooms is the portal through which they stage their rivalry, and only Johan passes back and forth thoughtlessly."

Considering that the sisters did, indeed, pass through the doorway several times—literally and figuratively—are we to read *thoughtlessly* as "without portent" or "innocently"? Although an innocent, Johan did wonder what was happening within the closed doors of Anna's—and, by extension, his—bedroom, most significantly when he happened upon "the lover" while retrieving a book.

Forty years later, the movie's bedroom and bathtub scene couldn't even have been filmed in the United States, let alone shown here. Time marches backward.

—Gary Dretzka, Chicago, Illinois

Q. I think the key word is indeed *thoughtlessly*, in the sense that Johan simply moves back and forth, and when each sister enters the other's room, it is with premeditated purpose. That is one masterpiece.

South Korean Thrillers

Q. I saw the South Korean thriller *The Chaser* on IFC two weeks ago. It brought so many emotions out in me. The most potent was anger. The South Koreans like killing off people in their movies that you don't want to die. They seem to revel in it. I was angry at *The Host* for that, among others.

At one point I yelled "*Noooooooooo!*" loudly enough to wake my downstairs neighbor at two in the morning. I've never done that before—screamed in complete outrage at a movie. I'm willing to bet that if I do it again it will probably be while watching a South Korean film. I fully understand that not all films will have or must have a happy ending. I've seen plenty, but why do the South Koreans have such a hard-on for killing people they make you care about? And they are masters at it.

—Andrew P. Malik, West Haven, Connecticut

A. I have a feeling you haven't watched your last South Korean thriller. They are consistently violent and remorseless, and consistently well-made. Which is better? A thriller where characters we care about get killed, or a thriller where characters we don't care about get to live?

Strange Days

Q. I just watched *Strange Days* for the first time and didn't know until the closing credits it was written, produced, edited, and so forth, by James Cameron (though directed by Kathryn Bigelow). Naturally, I was struck by the strong virtual reality concept it had in common with *Avatar*. You gave *Strange Days* four stars back in the day. Any comment?

—David Zimmerman, Oklahoma City, Oklahoma

A. Cameron seems fascinated by the general theme of characters who control— or are controlled by forces or methods outside their control. I frankly don't think he'd be interested in a straightforward human story. *Strange Days* is certainly a great film, and I don't understand why it didn't do better.

Surrogates

Q. I just read your review on *Surrogates*, about people who experience life through the bodies of humanoid robots. You mentioned how it would be awkward for the hosts themselves to have sex with each other as they really look; you said something about them masturbating at home. I think you may have overlooked a key phrase given in the trailer: "Feel what they feel."

—Mike Magnotti

A. So in other words, when two robots have sex, their hosts experience what it would feel like for two cars to be in a fender bender? If they were totaled, would that mean the best sex they've ever had?

The Third Man

Q. I recently saw *The Third Man*. It's completely mesmerizing from start to finish. As usual you were spot-on about its qualities. Wartime Vienna cannot be duplicated. Anna is hopelessly lost in her obsession with Harry. And that score. God, that score. It'll be a while before I can hum something else.

—Michael Mirasol, Philippines

A. The score is entirely performed by Anton Karas on the zither. He was discovered in a Vienna coffeehouse. "The Third Man Theme" was number one on the Hit Parade longer than any other movie theme song. Reed, Graham Greene, and Orson Welles had to fight the producer, David O. Selznick, to keep it in. Selznick fumed that he hated "that damned zither."

Q. I need to share this blasphemous rumor with you: It is said Leonardo DiCaprio and Tobey Maguire will costar in a remake of *The Third Man*. Can't we just all agree that some movies are sacred?
—Hisham Teymour, Mount Prospect, Illinois

A. My instinctive reaction was to throw up. On second thought, I'll reserve judgment until I see this shameless project. Some remakes are good enough to stand beside their originals: Herzog's *Nosferatu*, for example. The screenplay is allegedly being written by Steven Knight, who wrote *Dirty Pretty Things* and *Eastern Promises*, two splendid films. The original film was written by (cough) Graham Greene. A director isn't set.

But it's not the story, is it, so much as the look and feel and sound of that supreme masterpiece? Can a remake even be contemplated without zither music and the immortal *Third Man* theme? Will the tilt shots and oblique POV angles be preserved? Will the classic chase through the sewers of Vienna, with one offscreen gunshot, be preserved? Will it be shot in color, when *The Third Man* is one of the *most* black-and-white films of all time? And what actor dares to invoke Orson Welles as Harry Lime? The undertaking seems foolhardy.

The Time Traveler's Wife

Q. In your review of *The Time Traveler's Wife*, you wrote: "One thing's for sure: It's hard to explain how a gene for time travel could develop in the Darwinian model, since it's hard to see how an organism could ever find out that was an advantage."

Not so hard at all. Mutations occur; those that are not advantageous are less likely to be passed on. Advantageous mutations are more likely to become prevalent in the general population, but a mutation does not have to be advantageous to be passed on—the organism merely needs to survive long enough to re-

produce. Whether precursor mutations are needed for the time travel gene is not clear.
—Scott Rothstein, Massapequa, New York

A. And how could you be sure they were precursors, given the nature of time travel? The film argues that such genes could not be successfully passed down, as demonstrated in the case of the couple's first child. Time travel is fortunately impossible, but if it were, I wonder how the Darwinian selection process would take place.

Toy Story 3

Q. I was a little surprised by how your review of *Toy Story 3* was largely dismissive of the film as a derivative sequel, stating it is "happier with action and jokes than with characters and emotions." You say the first two films were about a boy and his toys, whereas this one leaves the toys to fend for themselves. On this point, I'd argue that there's more Andy in this film than any before. The earlier films were all about getting back to the house and facing the dangers of highways, a deranged kid, and worse in the process. Andy was rarely seen in his entirety save a few moments at the beginning and the end. Here the film follows the usual formula, yes (toys get lost, toys get into trouble, toys find their way back home), but there is a heartbreaking coda that allows Andy to have the spotlight for the first time in the series. These ending scenes were, for me, the most emotionally involving of the series and an excellent example of a franchise that works hard to make the sequel enrich and enhance what came before it. On the topic of 3-D, however, I heartily agree.
—Steven Avigliano, Rockaway, New Jersey

A. I have to be honest with you. I fully believe if I could see the film in 2-D, my opinion would deepen and improve. I realize I'm in danger of sounding like an obsessive on this topic, but I find 3-D an annoyance and a distraction, and the light in the screen invariably dimmer than it should be. The so-called third dimension is getting between me and the heart of the story.

Trailers

Q. You make a good point in your review of *A Perfect Getaway* that many filmmakers can't seem to resist giving away the entire plot or best jokes in their trailers. The trailer for *Valkyrie*, for instance, practically showed the entire film, saving me the time and expense of going to see it. As a history buff, I would have loved to have seen *Valkyrie*, but the endless trailer spoiled it for me. Why do you think so many filmmakers are hell-bent on spoiling their work by giving away the story in the previews?

—Bob Downes

A. My long-standing theory: Trailers use exactly the same principle as supermarket demonstrations that supply a sample of cheese on a toothpick. Once you eat it, you know *exactly* how the cheese will taste. All you lack is having eaten the whole cheese.

Transformers: Revenge of the Fallen

Q. I want you to seriously *stop* bashing *Transformers*, a movie that was not meant for the Academy Awards or for people who are over the hill. I'm sorry if you don't enjoy cool cars, giant fighting robots, gorgeous women in their early twenties, or big explosions, but it seems a whole lot more people around the world do. And just for your info, the two "black" characters in the new movie are not black; they learned how to talk through the World Wide Web, which is why different Transformers talk differently. That's why one has a British accent. I don't see all the Brits freaking out because one said "bollocks."

—Matt Boswick, Halifax, Nova Scotia

A. You mean the two robots from an alien world are, in fact, not actual black people? Glad I didn't mention them in my review. Whew. I do enjoy "cool cars, giant fighting robots, gorgeous women in their early twenties, or big explosions," but only when I find them in a better movie than this one. I guess that's why I gave the first *Transformers* movie three stars.

Q. I read your original review of *The Hurt Locker* and was amused to see another dig at Michael Bay and *Transformers*. Having not seen *Transformers* (and not planning to until DVD), I have no opinion about your opinion. I was surprised to see that, hours later, the review is missing the section where you called

Michael Bay "pathetic." Why did the review change?

—Jeremy Schultz, Carlisle, Pennsylvania

A. I decided it was bad writing to do anything to distract from the greatness of *The Hurt Locker*. It makes the use of explosions in *Transformers* look—well, I was about to say "pathetic."

Q. I am a junior in high school. I would have walked out on *Transformers* had I not gone with a group who was willing to drive me home. As we exited the cinema, my friends were describing their favorite scenes, like "the car rammed into the building" or "that big-ass explosion." As I tried to figure out why I was hanging around with these people, the words "that movie sucked" unfortunately slipped out of my mouth. My friends stopped discussing *Transformers* (the only positive outcome of my comment) and looked at me the same way that Quayle looked at Bentsen. And after a heated one-on-six debate, I walked home. In conclusion, my father is driving me down to Chicago so I can see a very anticipated *The Hurt Locker*. I just wanted to let you know that while most of the youth out there probably think that *Gone with the Wind* is about farts and that *Transformers* is a masterpiece, there is at least one teenager who still knows a horrible piece of rotten robotic garbage when he sees one.

—Alex, Madison, Wisconsin

A. You have a great dad.

Q. I own and write for the movie-based Web site RopeofSilicon.com. After I posted the satirical *Transformers 3* video you linked to from your Twitter account, some of my readers were steamed. You once wrote, "Those who think *Transformers* is a great or even a good film are, may I tactfully suggest, not sufficiently evolved. Film by film, I hope they climb a personal ladder into the realm of better films, until their standards improve." I plan to address this issue in an editorial asking how far is too far when painting the picture of a film's intended or eventual audience?

—Brad Brevet, RopeofSilicon.com

A. Yeah, I heard plenty about that comment of mine. I believe it. If you think, as some of its fans have actually stated, that

Transformers: Revenge of the Fallen is better than *Citizen Kane*, then there's no getting around it. In terms of your taste in movies, you have a heap of evolving still ahead of you. Sorry, but that's just the way it is.

2012

Q. I am a journalist with *Mirror Evening* newspaper, Beijing, China. I've seen your review on the movie *2012*, which is well written, and I would like to ask you to make some comments on the Chinese elements in the movie *2012*.

The movie and its stunning special effects have raised heated discussions among Chinese filmgoers, mostly because of its Chinese elements. For example, Chinese people appear in the film's opening ten minutes, when an officer tells survivors of an earthquake that the government will help them rebuild their homes. When the protagonist and his family land in Tibet, a Chinese officer says in fluent English: "Welcome to the People's Republic of China." This is where the modern Noah's Arks by which the human race escapes from being destroyed are built. Could you comment on the Chinese elements used in the film?

—Shelby Liu, journalist, Beijing, China

A. It's bad enough that you hold a trillion dollars of our debt. Can't you at least respect the tradition that the world is always saved by an American, preferably a vice president?

Q. Has *2012* finally put an end to the advancement of special effects? Ever since the early days of black-and-white monster movies and stop-motion, each year our holiday seasons have been accompanied by an effects movie more impressive than the last. Over the years it's been great fun watching filmmakers competing to outdo one another in the wake of improving technology, creativity (and budgets), and a big part of the fun for me was the anticipation of what they'd pull out next. I am now genuinely worried that this long-running tradition has finally come to an end. There no longer seems to be anything considered "unfilmable" with today's resources—as proved so hilariously by Roland Emmerich last weekend. Has the special effects subgenre finally hit a dead end? Is *2012* as far as we are likely to go, in a visual sense? Perhaps now

Hollywood will be forced to redirect their attention to the writers' room.

—Simon Gray, London, England

A. Too soon. Earth was destroyed, but the universe was untouched.

Q. I want to correct part of your *2012* review. You write, "Also on board are the humans chosen to survive, including all the characters who have not already been crushed, drowned, or fallen into great crevices opening up in the earth. These include the heroic Jackson Curtis (John Cusack) and his estranged wife, Kate (Amanda Peet); President Wilson (Danny Glover); his chief science adviser, Adrian Helmsley (Chiwetel Ejiofor); and his chief of staff, Carl Anheuser (Oliver Platt)."

However, one of the emotionally impacting scenes is the phone call where President Wilson calls his daughter to tell her that he is *not* going to be getting on the plane that is heading to the Arks. Just thought he might want to revise that, since he clearly does not get on the Ark.

—Joli M. McCarthy, West Chester, Pennsylvania

A. Quite true. However, although my chronology may be off, I'm under the impression that by that point in the film he had already been crushed, drowned, or otherwise inconvenienced by a giant tsunami that dropped the aircraft carrier *John F. Kennedy* on the White House.

The Twilight Saga: New Moon

Q. I saw your review for the new movie *The Twilight Saga: New Moon*. You have a lot of nerve! I remember when you and Siskel reviewed the movie *The Accidental Tourist* and gave it four stars and with that recommendation, I went and saw it and you know what? It was the *biggest piece of* **** known to man! I decided from that day that I would not listen to you or Gene and save my money. So, for the next year or so, I did not go to the movies and today, I use my formula, wait two months after a movie comes out, and spend the $1 at Redbox to rent it if I dare. Thanks, Roger. Thanks for making people not want to go to the movies.

—Joe Flambe

A. Hey, in the case of *New Moon*, that was the least I could do.

Tyler Perry Movies

Q. Why do you seem to categorically refuse to review Tyler Perry movies? *I Can Do Bad All by Myself* is now the number-one movie in America, as were a few of his previous films, but there is rarely a review on your site. Am I missing it or are you avoiding reviewing them?

—Letitia N. Patterson, Detroit, Michigan

A. The Tyler Perry movies are never pre-screened for critics, preventing opening-weekend reviews. I've been intending to see one in a theater but was covering the Toronto Film Festival when the latest one opened (Perry was there, too, as executive producer of *Precious*). I reviewed *Diary of a Mad Black Woman* (2005), and confess I had never heard of Perry or his character Madea before going to see it.

After my negative review, I was branded as a racist on two Chicago radio stations, apparently by people unfamiliar with my reviews over the years. I was relieved that many others came to my defense. I suspect Perry's films may be critic-proof.

The Ugly Truth

Q. In your review of *The Ugly Truth*, your main argument is that there is, essentially, too much out-of-context "blue" material and that the film drags down the cast. Fair enough. But I'm confused about the line in your final graf: "Amazing that this raunchy screenplay was written by three women." So what? Women are not allowed to write raunchy screenplays, when they are the gold standard for successful men's comedies these days? As formulaic and standard as *The Ugly Truth* was, I would have to say I embraced the curse words and innuendos, versus the inane *Austin Powers*–like innuendo a PG-13 rating requires. No matter the rating, they still get their sex jokes in, one way or another. Typically, these standard rom-coms also force the female character to completely change her personality before she gets the man; while here, Abby realizes that she need not change anything. She's still a control freak at the end, and Mike's still a thug. Do

you think this vulgarity for vulgarity's sake drags all of these comedies down, or just that women writers and/or stars should be held to a higher standard?

—Kim Brown, writer, *Tulsa World*

A. Women screenwriters should certainly have all the latitude of men. It's just that *The Ugly Truth* is so outspokenly vulgar it surprised me, and I don't usually associate that sort of screenplay with women.

Video Games

Q. Given your admiration of *Antichrist* and your distaste for video games, do you have any thoughts on the reported video game sequel, called Eden? When you asked me, I said my shot-in-the-dark guess is that it would be a dark, moody, horror-themed game wherein you played some random character trapped in the forest, attempting to survive or escape through solving puzzles and finding the correct "passageways." And then, of course, there's the possibility that the article was just a hoax to start with.

—Steven Koczak, Rensselaer, New York

A. First off, I do *not* dislike video games. But I'm in hot water for not believing they are likely to evolve into an art form.

Wikipedia reports: "According to the Danish newspaper *Politiken*, a video game called 'Eden,' which is based on the film, is in the works. It will start where the film ends. 'It will be a self-therapeutic journey into your own darkest fears, and will break the boundaries of what you can and can't do in video games,' says video game director Morten Iversen."

I'm thinking, "self-therapeutic"?

Wet Streets

Q. Why does it seem like all the streets are wet even when it's sunny in the movies?

—Tom Armbruster, East Peoria, Illinois

A. They wet them down. They look better that way, especially at night.

What Makes a Bad Movie

Q. What makes a movie a bad movie? Do you ever like a movie that the critics just dislike? In the era of "we've seen it all," is it more difficult to make a movie that pleases both critics and audience? How about foreign movies? Are they likable because they're foreign?

—Alex Tho, Jakarta, Indonesia

A. Yeah, I've been in the minority. There's no checklist of what makes a movie bad, but one thing that bothers me is when it seems content to grab some quick profits from a marketing campaign and not really care about word of mouth. *The A-Team* was a "hit," for example, before the word got around. It dropped off quickly, but not quickly enough to spare its victims.

What Makes a Great Movie

Q. I am an admirer of film. What do you think makes a great movie? I know this seems like a redundant question to ask, but I'm a film major and I really want to take this with all seriousness. Right now, I'm in a creative writing class trying to set forth all these ideas and eventually work my way into screenwriting. To make it a little less general and broad, what's one important aspect that makes a great movie? There, I narrowed it down! I made it easier for the both of us.

—Giovanni Martinez

A. One aspect? Just one? I always quote Derek Malcolm, the London film critic, who said, "A great film is a film you cannot bear the thought of never being able to see again."

Winter's Bone

Q. In your review of *Winter's Bone,* you wrote: "Ree's travels in search of her father lead her to his brother, Teardrop (John Hawkes), whose existence inflicts a wound on the gift of being alive." That last phrase, what the heck is that supposed to mean?

—Mark Pool, Crown Point, Indiana

A. Just some fancy writing. Roughly, "who is an insult to the human race."

Zombieland

Q. Last night I visited the Rotten Tomatoes site, and four reviews of *Zombieland* mentioned a surprise star cameo. This morning, my son noticed you gave the movie three

stars, then asked, "Did you know Bill Murray was in it?" He hadn't even started reading the review—you listed him in the cast! In the future, could you please refrain from giving away something like that?

—D. Massi, Ontario, Canada

A. Ouch! I goofed. However, the fact of Murray's cameo isn't funny by itself. The line that he says gets the biggest laugh I've heard all year. I guess I'd better not quote it here.

Q. You ask questions about zombies at the end of your *Zombieland* review. If we set aside the George Romero playbook, which states that "they're us" and which makes associations between zombies and American consumer culture, the military complex, and technological addictions, the general purpose of zombies is simply to give audiences a glimpse of what happens to the body after death.

In the United States particularly, natural processes of death and decay are hidden away as taboo, or at best are sanitized to the point where, for the average person, there is a pretty large and troubling knowledge gap when it comes to the subject. Zombies let us see "what happens" behind the scenes of the ultimate disappearing act. They naturally look bad because they are in the process of rotting, which is the whole idea. I suppose if they could come back after being embalmed, it might make them appear a bit more up to code, but I'm unclear as to whether that's allowed or not.

As for obtaining food versus avoiding being blasted, well, zombies are nothing more than instinctual eating machines. Did Bruce the shark try to avoid gulping down the oxygen tank as it was attempting to eat Roy Scheider? Same principle. Some creatures simply don't care as long as there are munchies in the vicinity. But this only raises the question: *Why* do zombies only want to eat living human flesh? I think it might be a status issue among monsters.

—Kenton Sem, Bethlehem, Pennsylvania

A. You make good sense, Pennsylvania zombieologist. Since the living eat the dead, why shouldn't the dead turn the tables?

Ebert's Little Movie Glossary

These are the year's new contributions to my glossary project. Hundreds of entries were collected in *Ebert's Bigger Little Movie Glossary,* published in 1999. Contributions are always welcome.

* * *

The About-Face Traffic Rule. When the driver of a car receives a phone call requiring him or her to be somewhere urgently (such as a cop contacted by a dispatcher or a husband learning his wife is in labor), the driver always turns the car around 180 degrees. There is no exception to this rule.

—Alberto Diamante, Toronto, Ontario, Canada

The Discerning Wind of Whimsy. Whenever some sort of magical character swap happens (like an old person becoming a young person or parents becoming their children), there is always an outdoor scene where a wind gently blows (usually accompanied by wind chimes), blowing in this magic. Oddly, the magical wind is discerning enough to deposit the magic only on those upon whom the movie is based.

—Ricardo Dittmer, Streator, Illinois

Dreamworld Mortality Rule. Characters that psychically enter simulated worlds (*The Matrix, The Thirteenth Floor*) or dreams (*Dreamscape, A Nightmare on Elm Street*) will die in real life if they die in the simulation. Although this would seem a severe design shortcoming in simulations and against the normal rules of dreaming, there will not be any reasonable explanation given for why this is so.

—Andy Hutton, Fremont, California

Ex-Husbands Are Losers. When an ex-husband goes to pick up his kid from his ex-wife, it is nearly always raining, snowing, or freezing cold. That gives the poor sop an opportunity to stand bedraggled on the doorstep. Meanwhile, we get to see the warm, glowing interior, the expensive 4 x 4 on the driveway, and so on. The new husband always looks like a Greek god as he stands there smirking in the doorway, arm draped over the shoulder of the sullen-looking ex-missus.

—Kate Dyson-McIlroy, Ringwood, United Kingdom

The Foreign Anguish Rule. When a character is troubled and is watching a foreign film (usually in black and white), there will be a scene where they imagine they are inside of it. Examples include *Precious* and *500 Days of Summer.*

—Nick Duval, Wallingford, Connecticut

Front-Page News. Shots of newspaper articles always show the front page. Articles important to the plot never run on an inside page.

—Alberto Diamante, Toronto, Ontario, Canada

The Glossary Entry Rule. Whenever a rule appears in Ebert's Little Movie Glossary, that rule will rarely, if ever, appear in a movie again. In fact, the reverse effect might even appear; for example, when a close-up of a hand is shown with a finger tightening on the trigger, it will most likely be fired, surprising audiences who have grown accustomed to it not being fired. ELMG thus serves as a barometer of rules having become clichés.

—Mike Buesseler, Great Falls, Montana

How About Friday? When dates are made in movies, the guy will say, "How about Friday night?" Girl: "OK." Then they part. But when are they going to meet? Does he know where she lives? What should she wear? Do they have each other's phone numbers?

—Geoff Stacks, Aurora, Colorado

Inevitable Vehicle Mishap. In every road movie, something bad will happen to the car. The vehicle always undergoes some kind of damage (*About Schmidt, Little Miss Sunshine, The Good Life,* and *Sideways*). Getting it repaired usually involves dealing with local people, who may be helpful, unhelpful, or sinister.

—Alberto Diamante, Toronto, Ontario, Canada

Kung Fu Wake-Up. To prove how aware/crazy/focused a movie character is, a friend will wake the sleeping character. The character will instantly, ferociously, leap up from a deep sleep and pull a knife, gun, or kung fu choke hold on his friend, before apologizing for almost killing him. As seen in *Lethal Weapon* and *Gladiator*.

—Joe Coulter, Manchester, New Hampshire

Let's Pick Up Where We Left Off. Two people can start a discussion in one location, and then the scene will change and the audience will find them continuing their conversation elsewhere. One is forced to assume that time has elapsed, yet their dialogue flows so naturally that one must also assume they walked in silence to another spot before casually resuming their chat.

—Simon Holloway, Sydney, Australia

Lonely Answering Machine. If you need to demonstrate that your character is lonely or has no social life, merely have them check their answering machine. Its automated voice will always say "You have . . . *no* new messages." This can be done even in films set in contemporary times where few if any people still use answering machines.

—Tadd Van Cleve, Dallas, Texas

The Lunesta Challenge. No actor is allowed to be awake at the moment Oscar nominations are announced. All performers must be sleeping and be awakened by phone calls from their publicists. This includes performers who live on the East Coast, who therefore must remain unconscious until well after 9 a.m. The only exception to this rule is when a performer is overseas on a location shoot. In this case, the news must come to the performer just prior to filming an important scene. More research is required to determine whether actors who are *not* nominated are awakened with the bad news or are allowed to continue sleeping.

—Mark Woodward, Chicago, Illinois

The No Windows Rule. No film uses either the Windows or Mac operating systems that the rest of the world use on a daily basis. All movie computers have their own OS that pops up in windows that make aesthetically pleasing sounds and respond to everything with busy little noises. Even if the computer is a recognizable brand (such as Tom Cruise's Apple laptop in *Mission: Impossible*), the OS does not resemble what is sold off the shelf.

—Harry Thomas, *San Antonio Express-News*

Raindrops Keep Fallin' on My Mail. A character will read a letter in the rain and make no effort to keep it from getting wet, no matter how precious the letter itself is. Similarly, someone wearing normal shoes, socks, and pants will not hesitate to walk in thigh-deep water, even though in reality they'd be wet, cold, and miserable for the rest of the day.

—Rob Carney, Reading, Massachusetts

Red Man Walking. Anybody walking away from an explosion, particularly if the explosion frames the walker in a slightly tinged, chiseled-god sort of way as he saunters in slow motion, is the guy who set off the bomb! Duh! This is the first person all the others on the scene should be looking for, but no! They just run right by him, oblivious. Don't movie characters ever actually, you know, watch movies?

—Mark Still, Philadelphia, Pennsylvania

Rule of Confessional Time Lapses. When a character goes to a priest for confession, the first thing we learn is that he/she hasn't done so in (a) an extremely long amount of time (see Michael Corleone in *Godfather III*) or (b) in an extremely short amount of time (Clint Eastwood in *Million Dollar Baby*, Catherine Zeta-Jones in *Mask of Zorro*). It is never in a relatively normal period, as the filmmakers will use this fact to make a point to the audience about just how screwed up the character is.

—Gerardo Valero, Mexico City, Mexico

Silence the Gun as Well as the Gunshots. Anytime guns are shown in a movie, they invariably make endless "clicky" noises as they are handed out or moved from character to character. Anyone with gun experience knows guns are just like rocks: Unless you do something to them, they are silent.

—Joe Coulter, Manchester, New Hampshire

Skylight of Doom Rule. Whenever a skylight is shown in a movie, sooner or later somebody will fall through it.

—Brian Holly, Pittsburgh, Pennsylvania

Tragedy of the Bridesmaid Dresses. In films, bridesmaids' dresses will invariably harbor fatal and tragic fashion flaws that render them impossible to wear in real life by any real person with any taste. Such flaw can be in shape (puffy shoulders, prom skirts, bows), fabric (metallic, sequins, velvet), color (pastels, brights, neon), or any combination of the above. This rule survives no matter how tasteful the bride's dress may be.

—Grace Wang, Toronto, Ontario, Canada

The Vin Scully Rule. Many movies that include a sporting event will have an announcer doing play-by-play over the stadium's PR system, which doesn't happen anywhere. This ignores the fact that (a) the people in the stands don't need the description, because they're already at the game, and (b) most people watching the movie really do understand the basics of the sport.

—Jason Lindquist, Cincinnati, Ohio

Index

A

Aattou, Fu'ad Ait: *Last Mistress, The*, 312

Abbass, Hiam: *Amreeka*, 15; *Limits of Control, The*, 322; *Visitor, The*, 582

Abbott, Michael, Jr.: *Shotgun Stories*, 483

Abdalla, Khalid: *Green Zone*, 223

Abdul, Paula: *Bruno*, 77

Abe, Hiroshi: *Still Walking*, 511

Abeckaser, Danny A.: *Holy Rollers*, 240

Abel, Dominique: *Rumba*, 458; dir., *Rumba*, 458

Abel, Jake: *Tru Loved*, 557

Abercrombie, Ian: *Star Wars: The Clone Wars*, 507

Abkarian, Simon: *Persepolis*, 408

Aboutboul, Alon: *Body of Lies*, 56

Abraham, Marc: dir., *Flash of Genius*, 179

Abrahams, Jon: *Who Do You Love?*, 604

Abrams, Floyd: *Nothing but the Truth*, 387

Abrams, J.J.: dir., *Star Trek*, 506

Abrham, Josef: *I Served the King of England*, 281

Abruzzese, Salvatore: *Gomorrah*, 211

Abtahi, Omid: *Space Chimps*, 499

Accomplices, 1

Accorsi, Stefano: *Shall We Kiss?*, 479

Acker, Amy: *21 and a Wakeup*, 559

Acker, Shane: dir., *9*, 383

Acosta, Carlos: *New York, I Love You*, 377

Adabashian, Alexander: *12*, 559

Adam, 2

Adams, Amy: *Doubt*, 139; *Julie and Julia*, 295; *Leap Year*, 317; *Night at the Museum: Battle of the Smithsonian*, 380; *Sunshine Cleaning*, 516

Adams, Joey Lauren: *Trucker*, 555

Adams, Paul III: *Providence Effect, The*, 425

Addy, Mark: *Red Riding Trilogy*, 440; *Robin Hood*, 451

Adebimpe, Tunde: *Rachel Getting Married*, 433

Adler, Sarah: *Jellyfish*, 286

Adoration, 3

Advani, Nikhil: dir., *Chandi Chowk to China*, 86

Adventureland, 4

Affleck, Ben: *Extract*, 162; *He's Just Not That Into You*, 239; *State of Play*, 508

Affleck, Casey: *Killer Inside Me, The*, 301

After.Life, 4

Aghdashloo, Shohreh: *Stoning of Soraya M., The*, 512

Aguilera, Christina: *Shine a Light*, 481

Ajami, 5

Akerman, Malin: *Couples Retreat*, 111; *Proposal, The*, 424; *Watchmen*, 593

Akin, Faith: dir., *Edge of Heaven, The*, 148; *New York, I Love You*, 377

Akinnuoye-Agbaje, Adewale: *G.I. Joe: The Rise of Cobra*, 205

Aktouche, Abdelhamid: *Secret of the Grain, The*, 467

Alba, Jessica: *Killer Inside Me, The*, 301; *Love Guru, The*, 329; *Valentine's Day*, 576

Alda, Alan: *Diminished Capacity*, 135; *Flash of Genius*, 179; *Nothing but the Truth*, 387

Alesi, Fausto Russo: *Vincere*, 581

Alessandrin, Patrick: dir., *District 13: Ultimatum*, 138

Alexander, Jane: *Gigantic*, 204; *Terminator: Salvation*, 529

Alexander, Lexi: dir., *Punisher: War Zone, The*, 427

Alexandra, 6

Alexandre, Manuel: *Elsa & Fred*, 153

Alexandrov, Constantin: *OSS 117: Cairo, Nest of Spies*, 394

Alfi, Guri: *Secrets, The*, 468

Alfredson, Tomas: dir., *Let the Right One In*, 320

Ali, Mahmoud Hamid: *Brothers at War*, 75

Alice in Wonderland, 7

Alien Trespass, 9

All About Steve, 10

Allen, Debbie: *Fame*, 166; *Next Day Air*, 378

Allen, Joan: *Death Race*, 130; *Rape of Europa, The*, 436

Allen, Karen: *Indiana Jones and the Kingdom of the Crystal Skull*, 266

Allen, Norman: *Enlighten Up!*, 156

Allen, Tim: *Redbelt*, 439; *Toy Story 3*, 548

Allen, Woody: dir., *Cassandra's Dream*, 85; *Vicky Cristina Barcelona*, 579; *Whatever Works*, 596

Allier, Edward: *Brothers at War*, 75

Allix, Annie: *Man on Wire*, 340

Almodovar, Pedro: dir., *Broken Embraces*, 71

Alonso, Laz: *Avatar*, 28; *Fast and Furious*, 169; *Miracle at St. Anna*, 353

Alter, Jeremy: dir., *Perfect Sleep, The*, 407

Alter, Joseph: *Enlighten Up!*, 156

Alterman, Eric: *Boogie Man: The Lee Atwater Story*, 57

Altman, Scott D.: *IMAX: Hubble 3-D*, 262

Alvaro, Dan: *Serbis*, 471

Amalric, Mathieu: *Christmas Tale, A*, 95; *Quantum of Solace*, 431; *Secret, A*, 463

Ambrose, Lauren: *Cold Souls*, 105; *Where the Wild Things Are*, 601

Amelia, 10

Amendola, Tony: *Perfect Sleep, The*, 407

American Teen, 12

American Violet, 12

America the Beautiful, 14

Amiel, Jon: dir., *Creation*, 115

Amreeka, 15

Anaya, Elena: *Savage Grace*, 462

Anders, Sean: dir., *Sex Drive*, 477

N